THE

LIFE AND EPISTLES

OF

ST. PAUL

THE

LIFE AND EPISTLES

OF

ST. PAUL

BY

THE REV. W. J. CONYBEARE, M.A.

LATE FELLOW OF TRINITY COLLEGE, CAMBRIDGE

and

THE VERY REV. J. S. HOWSON, D.D.

DEAN OF CHESTER

WM. B. EERDMANS PUBLISHING COMPANY

GRAND RAPIDS   MICHIGAN

Reprinted, June 1983

PHOTOLITHOPRINTED BY EERDMANS PRINTING COMPANY
GRAND RAPIDS, MICHIGAN, UNITED STATES OF AMERICA

CONTENTS

---◦◦◦---

CHAPTER I

CHAPTER II.

CHAPTER III.

CHAPTER IV.

CHAPTER V.

CHAPTER VI.

CHAPTER VII.

CHAPTER VIII.

CHAPTER IX.

CHAPTER XXIV.

CHAPTER XXV.

CHAPTER XXVI.

CHAPTER XXVII.

CHAPTER XXVIII.

APPENDICES.

LIST OF ILLUSTRATIONS

INTRODUCTION [1]

THE PURPOSE of this work is to give a living picture of St. Paul himself, and of the circumstances by which he was surrounded.

The biography of the Apostle must be compiled from two sources; first, his own letters, and secondly, the narrative in the Acts of the Apostles. The latter, after a slight sketch of his early history, supplies us with fuller details of his middle life ; and his Epistles afford much subsidiary information concerning his missionary labours during the same period. The light concentrated upon this portion of his course, makes darker by contrast the obscurity which rests upon the remainder ; for we are left to gain what knowledge we can of his later years, from scattered hints in a few short letters of his own, and from a single sentence of his disciple Clement.

But in order to present anything like a living picture of St. Paul's career, much more is necessary than a mere transcript of the Scriptural narrative, even where it is fullest. Every step of his course brings us into contact with some new phase of ancient life, unfamiliar to our modern experience, and upon which we must throw light from other sources, if we wish it to form a distinct image in the mind. For example, to comprehend the influences under which he grew to manhood, we must realise the position of a Jewish family in Tarsus ; we must understand the kind of education which the son of such a family would receive as a boy in his Hebrew home, or in the schools of his native city, and in his riper youth ' at the feet of Gamaliel' in Jerusalem ; we must be acquainted with the profession for which he was to be prepared by this training, and appreciate the station and duties of an expounder of the Law. And that we may be fully qualified to do all this, we should have a clear view of the state of the Roman Empire at the time, and especially of its system in the provinces ; we should also understand the political position of the

---

[1] [It has been thought better to leave this Introduction quite untouched, though the passages relating to views and illustrations are not strictly applicable to the present edition. H.]

Jews of the 'dispersion:' we should be (so to speak) hearers in their synagogues, we should be students of their Rabbinical theology. And in like manner, as we follow the Apostle in the different stages of his varied and adventurous career, we must strive continually to bring out in their true brightness the half-effaced forms and colouring of the scene in which he acts; and while he 'becomes all things to all men, that he might by all means save some,' we must form to ourselves a living likeness of the *things* and of the *men* among which he moved, if we would rightly estimate his work. Thus we must study Christianity rising in the midst of Judaism; we must realise the position of its early churches with their mixed society, to which Jews, Proselytes, and Heathens had each contributed a characteristic element; we must qualify ourselves to be umpires (if we may so speak) in their violent internal divisions; we must listen to the strife of their schismatic parties, when one said, 'I am of Paul, and another, I am of Apollos;' we must study the true character of those early heresies which even denied the resurrection, and advocated impurity and lawlessness, claiming the right ' to sin that grace might abound,'[1] ' defiling the mind and conscience '[2] of their followers, and making them ' abominable and disobedient, and to every good work reprobate; '[3] we must trace the extent to which Greek philosophy, Judaising formalism, and Eastern superstition blended their tainting influence with the pure fermentation of that new leaven which was at last to leaven the whole mass of civilised society.

Again, to understand St. Paul's personal history as a missionary to the Heathen, we must know the state of the different populations which he visited; the character of the Greek and Roman civilisation at the epoch; the points of intersection between the political history of the world and the scriptural narrative; the social organisation and gradation of ranks, for which he enjoins respect; the position of women, to which he specially refers in many of his letters; the relations between parents and children, slaves and masters, which he not vainly sought to imbue with the loving spirit of the Gospel; the quality and influence, under the early Empire, of the Greek and Roman religions, whose effete corruptness he denounces with such indignant scorn; the public amusements of the people, whence he draws topics of warning or illustration; the operation of the Roman law, under which he was so frequently arraigned; the courts in which he was tried, and the magistrates by whose sentence he suffered; the legionary soldiers who acted as his guards; the roads by which he travelled, whether through the mountains of Lycaonia, or

---

[1] Rom. vi. 1.   [2] Tit. i. 15.   [3] Tit. i. 16.

the marshes of Latium; the course of commerce by which his journeys were so often regulated ; and the character of that imperfect navigation by which his life was so many times[1] endangered.

While thus trying to live in the life of a bygone age, and to call up the figure of the past from its tomb, duly robed in all its former raiment, every help is welcome which enables us to fill up the dim outline in any part of its reality. Especially we delight to look upon the only one of the manifold features of that past existence, which still is living. We remember with pleasure that the earth, the sea, and the sky still combine for us in the same landscapes which passed before the eyes of the wayfaring Apostle. The plain of Cilicia, the snowy distances of Taurus, the cold and rapid stream of the Cydnus, the broad Orontes under the shadow of its steep banks with their thickets of jasmine and oleander ; the hills which ' stand about Jerusalem,'[2] the ' arched fountains cold ' in the ravines below, and those ' flowery brooks beneath, that wash their hallowed feet ;' the capes and islands of the Grecian Sea, the craggy summit of Areopagus, the land-locked harbour of Syracuse, the towering cone of Etna, the voluptuous loveliness of the Campanian shore ; all these remain to us, the imperishable handiwork of nature. We can still look upon the same trees and flowers which he saw clothing the mountains, giving colour to the plains, or reflected in the rivers ; we may think of him among the palms of Syria, the cedars of Lebanon, the olives of Attica, the green Isthmian pines of Corinth, whose leaves wove those ' fading garlands,' which he contrasts[3] with the ' incorruptible crown,' the prize for which he fought. Nay, we can even still look upon some of the works of man which filled him with wonder, or moved him to indignation. The ' temples made with hands '[4] which rose before him—the very apotheosis of idolatry—on the Acropolis, still stand in almost undiminished majesty and beauty. The mole on which he landed at Puteoli still stretches its ruins into the blue waters of the bay. The remains of the Baian Villas whose marble porticoes he then beheld glittering in the sunset—his first specimen of Italian luxury—still are seen along the shore. We may still enter Rome as he did by the same Appian Road, through the same Capenian Gate, and wander among the ruins of ' Cæsar's palace '[5] on the Palatine, while our eye rests upon the same aqueducts radiating over the Campagna to the unchanging hills. Those who have visited these spots must often have felt a thrill of recollection as they trod in the footsteps of the Apostle ; they must have been conscious

---

[1] 'Thrice have I suffered shipwreck,' 2 Cor. xi. 25; and this was before he was wrecked upon Melita.
[2] ' The hills stand about Jerusalem ;'

even so ' standeth the Lord round about his people.' Ps. cxxv. 2.
[3] 1 Cor. ix. 25.   [4] Acts xvii. 24.
[5] Phil. i. 13.

how much the identity of the outward scene brought them into communion with him, while they tried to image to themselves the feelings with which he must have looked upon the objects before them. They who have experienced this will feel how imperfect a biography of St. Paul must be, without faithful representations of the places which he visited. It is hoped that the views[1] which are contained in the present work (which have been diligently collected from various sources) will supply this desideratum. And it is evident that, for the purposes of such a biography, nothing but true and faithful representations of the real scenes will be valuable ; these are what is wanted, and not ideal representations, even though copied from the works of the greatest masters ; for, as it has been well said, ' nature and reality painted at the time, and on the spot, a nobler cartoon of St. Paul's preaching at Athens than the immortal Rafaelle afterwards has done.'[2]

For a similar reason Maps have been given (in addition to careful Geographical descriptions), exhibiting with as much accuracy as can at present be attained the physical features of the countries visited, and some of the ancient routes through them, together with plans of the most important cities, and maritime Charts of the coasts and harbours where they were required.

While thus endeavouring to represent faithfully the natural objects and architectural remains connected with the narrative, it has likewise been attempted to give such illustrations as were needful of the minor productions of human art as they existed in the first century. For this purpose engravings of Coins have been given in all cases where they seemed to throw light on the circumstances mentioned in the history ; and recourse has been had to the stores of Pompeii and Herculaneum, to the columns of Trajan and Antoninus, and to the collections of the Vatican, the Louvre, and especially of the British Museum.

But after all this is done,—after we have endeavoured, with every help we can command, to reproduce the picture of St. Paul's deeds and times,—how small would our knowledge of himself remain, if we had no other record of him left us but the story of his adventures. If his letters had never come down to us, we should have known indeed what he did and suffered, but we should have had very little idea of what he was.[3] Even if we could

---

[1] [See note on p. xi. The sentence in the text applies in strictness only to the quarto edition. In the intermediate edition it was remarked in a note, that even there 'most of the larger engravings were necessarily omitted, on account of their size.' H.]

[2] Wordsworth's *Athens and Attica*, p. 76.

[3] For his speeches recorded in the Acts, characteristic as they are, would by themselves have been too few and too short to add much to our knowledge of St. Paul ; but illustrated as they now are by his Epistles. they become

perfectly succeed in restoring the image of the scenes and circumstances in which he moved,—even if we could, as in a magic mirror, behold him speaking in the school of Tyrannus, with his Ephesian hearers in their national costume around him,—we should still see very little of Paul of Tarsus. We must listen to his words, if we would learn to know him. If fancy did her utmost, she could give us only his outward, not his inward life. 'His bodily presence' (so his enemies declared) 'was weak and contemptible ;' but 'his letters' (even they allowed) ' were weighty and powerful.'[1] Moreover an effort of imagination and memory is needed to recall the past, but in his Epistles St. Paul is present with us. 'His words are not dead words, they are living creatures with hands and feet,'[2] touching in a thousand hearts at this very hour the same chord of feeling which vibrated to their first utterance. We, the Christians of the nineteenth century, can bear witness now, as fully as could a Byzantine audience fourteen hundred years ago, to the saying of Chrysostom, that 'Paul by his letters still lives in the mouths of men throughout the whole world ; by them not only his own converts, but all the faithful even unto this day, yea, and all the saints who are yet to be born, until Christ's coming again, both have been and shall be blessed.' His Epistles are to his inward life what the mountains and rivers of Asia and Greece and Italy are to his outward life,—the imperishable part which still remains to us, when all that time can ruin has passed away.

It is in these letters then that we must study the true life of St. Paul, from its inmost depths and springs of action, which were 'hidden with Christ in God,' down to its most minute developments, and peculiar individual manifestations. In them we learn (to use the language of Gregory Nazianzene) ' what is told of Paul by Paul himself.' Their most sacred contents indeed rise above all that is peculiar to the individual writer ; for they are the communications of God to man concerning the faith and life of Christians ; which St. Paul declared (as he often asserts) by the immediate revelation of Christ Himself. But his manner of teaching these eternal truths is coloured by his human character, and peculiar to himself. And such individual features are naturally impressed much more upon epistles than upon any other kind of composition. For here we have not treatises, or sermons, which may dwell in the general and abstract, but genuine letters, written to meet the actual wants of living men ; giving immediate

an important part of his personal biography.
[1] 2 Cor. x. 10.

[2] Luther, as quoted in Archdeacon Hare's *Mission of the Comforter*, p. 449.

answers to real questions, and warnings against pressing dangers; full of the interests of the passing hour. And this, which must be more or less the case with all epistles addressed to particular Churches, is especially so with those of St. Paul. In his case it is not too much to say that his letters are himself—a portrait painted by his own hand, of which every feature may be 'known and read of all men.'

It is not merely that in them we see the proof of his powerful intellect, his insight into the foundations of natural theology,[1] and of moral philosophy ;[2] for in such points, though the philosophical expression might belong to himself, the truths expressed were taught him of God. It is not only that we there find models of the sublimest eloquence, when he is kindled by the vision of the glories to come, the perfect triumph of good over evil, the manifestation of the sons of God, and their transformation into God's likeness, when they shall see Him no longer[3] 'in a glass darkly, but face to face,'—for in such strains as these it was not so much he that spake, as the Spirit of God speaking in Him ;[4]—but in his letters, besides all this which is divine, we trace every shade, even to the faintest, of his human character also. Here we see that fearless independence with which he 'withstood Peter to the face ;'[5]—that impetuosity which breaks out in his apostrophe to the 'foolish Galatians ;'[6]—that earnest indignation which bids his converts 'beware of dogs, beware of the concision,'[7] and pours itself forth in the emphatic 'God forbid,'[8] which meets every Antinomian suggestion ;—that fervid patriotism which makes him 'wish that he were himself accursed from Christ for his brethren, his kinsmen according to the flesh, who are Israelites ;'[9]—that generosity which looked for no other reward than 'to preach the Glad-tidings of Christ without charge,'[10] and made him feel that he would rather 'die than that any man should make this glorying void ;'—that dread of officious interference which led him to shrink from 'building on another man's foundation ;'[11]—that delicacy which shows itself in his appeal to Philemon, whom he might have commanded, 'yet for love's sake rather beseeching him, being such an one as Paul the aged, and now also a prisoner of Jesus Christ,'[12] and which is even more striking in some of his farewell greetings, as (for instance) when he bids the Romans

---

[1] Rom. i. 20.
[2] Rom. ii. 14, 15.
[3] 1 Cor. xiii. 12.
[4] Mat. x. 20.
[5] Gal. ii. 11.
[6] Gal. iii. 1.
[7] Phil. iii. 2.

[8] Rom. vi. 2 ; 1 Cor. vi. 15, &c. It is difficult to express the force of the original by any other English phrase.
[9] Rom. ix. 3.
[10] 1 Cor. ix. 15 and 18.
[11] Rom. xv. 20.
[12] Philemon 9.

salute Rufus, and *his mother, who is also mine*; '[1]—that scrupulous fear of evil appearance which ' would not eat any man's bread for nought, but wrought with labour and travail night and day, that he might not be chargeable to any of them ; '[2]—that refined courtesy which cannot bring itself to blame till it has first praised,[3] and which makes him deem it needful almost to apologise for the freedom of giving advice to those who were not personally known to him ;[4]—that self-denying love which 'will eat no flesh while the world standeth, lest he make his brother to offend ; '[5]—that impatience of exclusive formalism with which he overwhelms the Judaisers of Galatia, joined with a forbearance so gentle for the innocent weakness of scrupulous consciences ;[6]—that grief for the sins of others, which moved him to tears when he spoke of the enemies of the cross of Christ, 'of whom I tell you even weeping ; '[7]—that noble freedom from jealousy with which he speaks of those who, out of rivalry to himself, preach Christ even of envy and strife, supposing to add affliction to his bonds ; 'What then ? notwithstanding, every way, whether in pretence or in truth, Christ is preached ; and I therein do rejoice, yea, and will rejoice ; '[8]—that tender friendship which watches over the health of Timothy, even with a mother's care ;[9]—that intense sympathy in the joys and sorrows of his converts, which could say, even to the rebellious Corinthians, 'ye are in our hearts, to die and live with you '[10]—that longing desire for the intercourse of affection, and that sense of loneliness when it was withheld, which perhaps is the most touching feature of all, because it approaches most nearly to a weakness, ' When I had come to Troas to preach the Glad-tidings of Christ, and a door was opened to me in the Lord, I had no rest in my spirit, because I found not Titus my brother ; but I parted from them, and came from thence into Macedonia.' And 'when I was come into Macedonia, my flesh had no rest, but I was troubled on every side ; without were fightings, within were fears. But God, who comforts them that are cast down, comforted me by the coming of Titus.'[11] 'Do thy utmost to come to me speedily ; for Demas hath forsaken me, having loved this present world, and is departed to Thessalonica ; Crescens to Galatia, Titus to Dalmatia ; only Luke is with me.[12]

[1] Rom. xvi. 13.
[2] 1 Thess. ii. 9.
[3] Compare the laudatory expressions in 1 Cor. i. 5–7, and 2 Cor. i. 6, 7, with the heavy and almost unmingled censure conveyed in the whole subsequent part of these Epistles.
[4] Rom. xv. 14, 15.
[5] 1 Cor. viii. 13.
[6] 1 Cor. viii. 12, and Rom. xiv. 21.
[7] Phil. iii. 18.
[8] Phil. i. 15.
[9] 1 Tim. v. 23.
[10] 2 Cor. vii. 3.
[11] 2 Cor. ii. 13, and vii. 5.
[12] 2 Tim. iv. 9.

Nor is it only in the substance, but even in the style of these writings that we recognise the man Paul of Tarsus. In the parenthetical constructions and broken sentences, we see the rapidity with which the thoughts crowded upon him, almost too fast for utterance ; we see him animated rather than weighed down by ' the crowd that presses on him daily, and the care of all the churches,' [1] as he pours forth his warnings or his arguments in a stream of eager and impetuous dictation, with which the pen of the faithful Tertius can hardly keep pace. [2] And above all, we trace his presence in the postscript to every letter, which he adds as an authentication, in his own characteristic handwriting, [3] ' which is a token in every epistle : Thus I write.' [4] Sometimes, as he takes up the pen he is moved with indignation when he thinks of the false brethren among those whom he addresses ; ' the salutation of me Paul with my own hand,—if any man love not the Lord Jesus Christ, let him be accursed.' [5] Sometimes, as he raises his hand to write, he feels it cramped by the fetters which bind him to the soldier who guards him, [6] ' I, Paul salute you with my own hand,— remember my chains.' Yet he always ends with the same blessing, ' The grace of our Lord Jesus Christ be with you,' to which he sometimes adds still further a few last words of affectionate remembrance, ' My love be with you all in Christ Jesus.' [7]

But although the letters of St. Paul are so essentially a part of his personal biography, it is a difficult question to decide upon the form in which they should be given in a work like this. The object to be sought is, that they may really represent in English what they were to their Greek readers when first written. Now this object would not be attained if the Authorised Version were adhered to : and yet a departure from that whereof so much is interwoven with the memory and deepest feelings of every religious mind should be grounded on strong and sufficient cause. It is hoped that the following reasons may be held such.

1st. The Authorised Version was meant to be a standard of authority and ultimate appeal in controversy ; hence it could not venture to depart, as an ordinary translation would do, from the exact words of the original, even where some amplification was absolutely required to complete the sense. It was to be the version unanimously accepted by all parties, and therefore must simply represent the Greek text word for word. This it does most faithfully

---

[1] 2 Cor. xi. 28.

[2] Rom. xvi. 22. ' I, Tertius, who wrote this Epistle, salute you in the Lord.'

[3] Gal. vi. 11. ' See *the size of the characters* in which I write to you

with my own hand.'

[4] 2 Thess. iii. 17.

[5] 1 Cor. xvi. 22.

[6] Col. iv. 18.

[7] 1 Cor. xvi. 24.

so far as the critical knowledge of the sixteenth [1] century permitted. But the result of this method is sometimes to produce a translation unintelligible to the English reader. [2] Also if the text admit of two interpretations, our version endeavours, if possible, to preserve the same ambiguity, and effects this often with admirable skill; but such indecision, although a merit in an authoritative version, would be a fault in a translation which had a different object.

2nd. The imperfect knowledge existing at the time when our Bible was translated, made it inevitable that the translators should occasionally render the original incorrectly; and the same cause has made their version of many of the argumentative portions of the Epistles perplexed and obscure.

3rd. Such passages as are affected by the above-mentioned objections, might, it is true, have been recast, and the authorised translation retained in all cases where it is correct and clear; but if this had been done, a patchwork effect would have been produced like that of new cloth upon old garments; moreover the devotional associations of the reader would have been offended, and it would have been a rash experiment to provoke such a contrast between the matchless style of the Authorised Version and that of the modern translator, thus placed side by side.

4th. The style adopted for the present purpose should not be antiquated; for St. Paul was writing in the language used by his Hellenistic readers in every-day life.

5th. In order to give the true meaning of the original, something more than a mere verbal rendering is often absolutely required. St. Paul's style is extremely elliptical, and the gaps must be filled up. And moreover the great difficulty in understanding his argument is to trace clearly the transitions [3] by which he passes from one step to another. For this purpose something must occasionally be supplied beyond the mere literal rendering of the words.

In fact, the meaning of an ancient writer may be rendered into a modern language in three ways : either, first, by a *literal version*; or, secondly, by a *free translation*; or, thirdly, by a *para-*

---

[1] Being executed at the very beginning of the seventeenth.

[2] Yet had any other course been adopted, every sect would have had its own Bible; as it is, this one translation has been all but unanimously received for three centuries.

[3] In the translation of the Epistles given in the present work, it has been the especial aim of the translator to represent these transitions correctly.

They very often depend upon a word which suggests a new thought, and are quite lost by a want of attention to the verbal coincidence. Thus, for instance, in Rom. x. 16, 17. 'Who hath given faith to our *teaching*? So then faith cometh by *teaching*;' how completely is the connection destroyed by such inattention in the Authorised Version: 'Who hath believed our *report*? So then faith cometh by *hearing*.'

phrase. A recent specimen of the first method may be found in the corrected edition of the Authorised Version of the Corinthians by Prof. Stanley, of the Galatians and Ephesians, by Prof. Ellicott, and of the Thessalonians, Galatians, and Romans, by Prof. Jowett, all of which have appeared since the first edition of the present work. The experiment of these translations (ably executed as they are) has confirmed the view above expressed of the unsatisfactory nature of such a literal rendering ; for it cannot be doubted that though they correct the mistakes of the Authorised Version, yet they leave an English reader in more hopeless bewilderment as to St. Paul's meaning than that version itself. Of the third course (that of *paraphrase*) an excellent specimen is to be found in Prof. Stanley's paraphrases of the Corinthian Epistles. There is perhaps no better way than this of conveying the general meaning of the Epistles to an English reader ; but it would not be suitable for the biography of St. Paul, in which not only his general meaning, but his every sentence and every clause should, so far as possible, be given. There remains the intermediate course of a *free translation*, which is that adopted in the present work ; nor does there seem any reason why a translation of St. Paul should be rendered inaccurate by a method which would generally be adopted in a translation of Thucydides.

It has not been thought necessary to interrupt the reader by a note,[1] in every instance where the translation varies from the Authorised Version. It has been assumed that the readers of the notes will have sufficient knowledge to understand the reason of such variations in the more obvious cases. But it is hoped that no variation which presents any real difficulty has been passed over without explanation.

It should further be observed, that the translation given in this work does not adhere to the Textus Receptus, but follows the text authorised by the best MSS. Yet, though the Textus Receptus has no authority in itself, it seems undesirable to depart from it without necessity, because it is the text familiar to English readers. Hence the translator has adhered to it in passages where the MSS. of highest authority are equally divided between its reading and some other; and also in some cases where the difference between it and the true text is merely verbal.

The authorities consulted upon the chronology of St. Paul's life, the reasons for the views taken of disputed points in it, and for the dates of the Epistles, are stated (so far as seems needful) in the body

---

[1] [See again note on p. xi. In this edition no note appended to the translations has been altered in meaning. Only such changes are made as is required by the omission of Greek words. H.]

of the work or in the Appendices, and need not be further referred to here.

In conclusion, the authors would express their hope that this biography may, in its measure, be useful in strengthening the hearts of some against the peculiar form of unbelief most current at the present day. The more faithfully we can represent to ourselves the life, outward and inward, of St. Paul, in all its fulness, the more unreasonable must appear the theory that Christianity had a mythical origin ; and the stronger must be our ground for believing his testimony to the divine nature and miraculous history of our Redeemer. No reasonable man can learn to know and love the Apostle of the Gentiles without asking himself the question, ' What was the principle by which through such a life he was animated ? What was the strength in which he laboured with such immense results ? ' Nor can the most sceptical inquirer doubt for one moment the full sincerity of St. Paul's belief that ' the life which he lived in the flesh he lived by the faith of the Son of God, who died and gave Himself for him.' [1] ' To believe in Christ crucified and risen, to serve Him on earth, to be with Him hereafter ;—these, if we may trust the account of his own motives by any human writer whatever, were the chief if not the only thoughts which sustained Paul of Tarsus through all the troubles and sorrows of his twenty years' conflict. His sagacity, his cheerfulness, his forethought, his impartial and clear-judging reason, all the natural elements of his strong character are not indeed to be overlooked : but the more highly we exalt these in our estimate of his work, the larger share we attribute to them in the performance of his mission, the more are we compelled to believe that he spoke the words of truth and soberness when he told the Corinthians that " last of all Christ was seen of him also," [2] that " by the grace of God he was what he was," that " whilst he laboured more abundantly than all, it was not he, but the grace of God that was in him." [3]

---

[1] Gal. ii. 20
[2] 1 Cor. xv. 8.

[3] Stanley's *Sermons on the Apostolic Age*, p. 186.

POSTSCRIPT

It may be well to add, that while Mr. Conybeare and Dr. Howson have undertaken the joint revision of the whole work, the translation of the Epistles and Speeches of St. Paul is contributed by the former; the Historical portion of the work principally, and the Geographical portion entirely, by the latter; Dr. Howson having written Chapters I., II., III., IV., V., VI., VII., VIII., IX., X., XI., XII., XIV., XVI., XX., XXI. (except the earlier portion), XXII. (except some of the later part), XXIII., XXIV., the latter pages of XVII., and the earlier pages of XXVI.; with the exception of the Epistles and Speeches therein contained; and Mr. Conybeare having written the Introduction and Appendices, and Chapters XIII., XV., XVII. (except the conclusion), XVIII., XIX., XXV., XXVI. (except the introductory and topographical portions), XXVII., XXVIII., the earlier pages of XXI., and some of the later pages of XXII.[1]

[1] This seems the proper place for explaining the few abbreviations used. T. R. stands for *Textus Receptus*; O. T. for *Old Testament*; N. T. for *New Testament*; A. V. for *Authorised Version*; and LXX. (after a quotation from the Old Testament) means that the quotation is cited by St. Paul, according to the *Septuagint* translation. In such references, however, the numbering of verses and chapters according to the Authorised Version (not according to the Septuagint) has been retained, to avoid the causing of perplexity to English readers who may attempt to verify the references.

THE

LIFE AND EPISTLES

OF

ST. PAUL

———◦◦◦———

CHAPTER I.

Great Men of Great Periods.—Period of Christ's Apostles.—Jews, Greeks,
and Romans.—Religious Civilisation of the Jews.—Their History and its
Relation to that of the World.—Heathen Preparation for the Gospel.—
Character and Language of the Greeks.—Alexander.—Antioch and Alexandria.—Growth and Government of the Roman Empire.—Misery of Italy
and the Provinces.—Preparation in the Empire for Christianity.—Dispersion
of the Jews in Asia, Africa, and Europe.—Proselytes.—Provinces of Cilicia
and Judæa.—Their Geography and History.—Cilicia under the Romans.—
Tarsus.—Cicero.—Political Changes in Judæa.—Herod and his Family.—The
Roman Governors.—Conclusion.

THE LIFE of a great man, in a great period of the world's history,
is a subject to command the attention of every thoughtful mind.
Alexander on his Eastern expedition, spreading the civilisation of
Greece over the Asiatic and African shores of the Mediterranean
Sea,—Julius Cæsar contending against the Gauls, and subduing
the barbarism of Western Europe to the order and discipline of
Roman government,—Charlemagne compressing the separating
atoms of the feudal world, and reviving for a time the image of
imperial unity,—Columbus sailing westward over the Atlantic to
discover a new world which might receive the arts and religion of
the old,—Napoleon on his rapid campaigns, shattering the ancient
system of European States, and leaving a chasm between our present
and the past :—these are the colossal figures of history, which
stamp with the impress of their personal greatness the centuries in
which they lived.

The interest with which we look upon such men is natural and
inevitable, even when we are deeply conscious that, in their character and their work, evil was mixed up in large proportions with
the good, and when we find it difficult to discover the providential
design which drew the features of their respective epochs. But this

natural feeling rises into something higher, if we can be assured
that the period we contemplate was designedly prepared for great
results, that the work we admire was a work of unmixed good, and
the man whose actions we follow was an instrument specially
prepared by the hands of GOD.   Such a period was that in which
the civilised word was united under the first Roman emperors : such
a work was the first preaching of the Gospel : and such a man was
Paul of Tarsus.

Before we enter upon the particulars of his life and the history
of his work, it is desirable to say something, in this introductory
chapter, concerning the general features of the age which was prepared for him.   We shall not attempt any minute delineation of
the institutions and social habits of the period.   Many of these
will be brought before us in detail in the course of the present
work.   We shall only notice here those circumstances in the state
of the world, which seem to bear the traces of a providential pre-
arrangement.

Casting this general view on the age of the first Roman emperors,
which was also the age of JESUS CHRIST and His Apostles, we find
our attention arrested by three great varieties of national life. The
Jew, the Greek, and the Roman appear to divide the world between
them.   The outward condition of Jerusalem itself, at this epoch,
might be taken as a type of the civilised world.   Herod the Great,
who rebuilt the Temple, had erected, for Greek and Roman enter-
tainments, a theatre within the same walls, and an amphitheatre in
the neighbouring plain.[1]   His coins, and those of his grandson
Agrippa, bore Greek inscriptions : that piece of money, which was
brought to our Saviour (Matt. xxii., Mark xii., Luke xx.), was the
silver *Denarius*, the ' image ' was that of the emperor, the ' superscription ' was in Latin : and at the same time when the common
currency consisted of such pieces as these,—since coins with the
images of men or with Heathen symbols would have been a pro-
fanation to the ' Treasury,'—there might be found on the tables of
the money-changers in the Temple, shekels and half-shekels with
Samaritan letters, minted under the Maccabees. Greek and Roman
names were borne by multitudes of those Jews who came up to
worship at the festivals.   Greek and Latin words were current in
the popular ' Hebrew ' of the day : and while this Syro-Chaldaic
dialect was spoken by the mass of the people with the tenacious affection of old custom, Greek had long been well known among the
upper classes in the larger towns, and Latin was used in the courts
of law, and in the official correspondence of magistrates.   On a
critical occasion of St. Paul's life,[2] when he was standing on the
stair between the Temple and the fortress, he first spoke to the
commander of the garrison in Greek, and then turned round and
addressed his countrymen in Hebrew ; while the letter[3] of Claudius

[1] JOSEPH. *Ant.* xv. 8, 1.   *War,* i.
21, 8.   Our reference to the two great
works of Josephus, the *Jewish Antiquities* and the *Jewish War,* will be
very frequent.   Occasionally also we
shall refer to his *Life* and his discourse

against Apion.
[2] Acts xxi. xxii.
[3] Acts xxiii.   A document of this
kind, sent with a prisoner by a subordinate to a superior officer, would
almost certainly be in Latin.

Lysias was written, and the oration [1] of Tertullus spoken, in Latin. We are told by the historian Josephus, [2] that on a parapet of stone in the Temple area, where a flight of fourteen steps led up from the outer to the inner court, pillars were placed at equal distances, with notices, some in Greek and some in Latin, that no alien should enter the sacred enclosure of the Hebrews. And we are told by two of the Evangelists, [3] that when our blessed Saviour was crucified, 'the superscription of His accusation' was written above His cross 'in letters of Hebrew, and Greek, and Latin.'

The condition of the world in general at that period wears a similar appearance to a Christian's eye. He sees the Greek and Roman elements brought into remarkable union with the older and more sacred elements of Judaism. He sees in the Hebrew people a divinely-laid foundation for the superstructure of the Church, and in the dispersion of the Jews a soil made ready in fitting places for the seed of the Gospel. He sees in the spread of the language and commerce of the Greeks, and in the high perfection of their poetry and philosophy, appropriate means for the rapid communication of Christian ideas, and for bringing them into close connection with the best thoughts of unassisted humanity. And he sees in the union of so many incoherent provinces under the law and government of Rome, a strong framework which might keep together for a sufficient period those masses of social life which the Gospel was intended to pervade. The City of God is built at the confluence of three civilisations. We recognise with gratitude the hand of God in the history of His world : and we turn with devout feelings to trace the course of these three streams of civilised life, from their early source to the time of their meeting in the Apostolic age.

We need not linger about the fountains of the national life of the Jews. We know that they gushed forth at first, and flowed in their appointed channels, at the command of God. The call of Abraham, when one family was chosen to keep and hand down the deposit of divine truth,—the series of providences which brought the ancestors of the Jews into Egypt,—the long captivity on the banks of the Nile,—the works of Moses, whereby the bondsmen were made into a nation,—all these things are represented in the Old Testament as occurring under the immediate direction of Almighty power. The people of Israel were taken out of the midst of an idolatrous world, to become the depositories of a purer knowledge of the one true God than was given to any other people. At a time when (humanly speaking) the world could hardly have preserved a spiritual religion in its highest purity, they received a divine revelation enshrined in symbols and ceremonies, whereby it might be safely kept till the time of its development in a purer and more heavenly form.

The peculiarity of the Hebrew civilisation did not consist in the culture of the imagination and intellect, like that of the Greeks, nor in the organisation of government, like that of Rome,—but its distinguishing feature was *Religion*. To say nothing of the

---

[1] Acts xxiv. Dean Milman (*Bampton Lectures*, p. 185) has remarked on the peculiarly Latin character of Ter-tullus's address.

[2] *War*, v. 5, 2. Compare vi. 2, 4.
[3] Luke xxiii. 38; John xix. 20.

Scriptures, the prophets, the miracles of the Jews,—their frequent festivals, their constant sacrifices,—everything in their collective and private life was connected with a revealed religion : their wars, their heroes, their poetry, had a sacred character,—their national code was full of the details of public worship,—their ordinary employments were touched at every point by divinely-appointed and significant ceremonies. Nor was this religion, as were the religions of the Heathen world, a creed which could not be the common property of the instructed and the ignorant. It was neither a recondite philosophy which might not be communicated to the masses of the people, nor a weak superstition, controlling the conduct of the lower classes, and ridiculed by the higher. The religion of Moses was for the use of all and the benefit of all. The poorest peasant of Galilee had the same part in it as the wisest Rabbi of Jerusalem. The children of all families were taught to claim their share in the privileges of the chosen people.

And how different was the nature of this religion from that of the cotemporary Gentiles ! The pious feelings of the Jew were not dissipated and distracted by a fantastic mythology, where a thousand different objects of worship, with contradictory attributes, might claim the attention of the devout mind. ' One God,' the Creator and Judge of the world, and the Author of all good, was the only object of adoration. And there was nothing of that wide separation between religion and morality, which among other nations was the road to all impurity. The will and approbation of Jehovah was the motive and support of all holiness : faith in His word was the power which raised men above their natural weakness : while even the divinities of Greece and Rome were often the personifications of human passions, and the example and sanction of vice. And still farther :—the devotional scriptures of the Jews express that heartfelt sense of infirmity and sin, that peculiar spirit of prayer, that real communion with God, with which the Christian, in his best moments, has the truest sympathy.[1] So that, while the best hymns of Greece[2] are only mythological pictures, and the literature of Heathen Rome hardly produces anything which can be called a prayer, the Hebrew psalms have passed into the devotions of the Christian church. There is a light on all the mountains of Judæa which never shone on Olympus or Parnassus: and the ' Hill of Zion,' in which ' it pleased God to dwell,' is the type of ' the joy of the whole earth,'[3] while the seven hills of Rome are the symbol of tyranny and idolatry. ' He showed His word unto Jacob, His statutes and ordinances unto Israel. He dealt not so with any nation ; neither had the Heathen knowledge of His laws.'[4]

But not only was a holy religion the characteristic of the civili-

---

[1] Neander observes that it has been justly remarked that the distinctive peculiarity of the Hebrew nation from the very first, was, that *conscience* was more alive among them than any other people.

[2] There are some exceptions, as in the hymn of the Stoic Cleanthes, who was born at Assos 350 years before St. Paul was there; yet it breathes the sentiment rather of acquiescence in the determinations of Fate, than of resignation to the goodness of Providence. See on Acts xvii. 28.

[3] Ps. xlviii. 2, lxviii. 16.

[4] Ps. cxlvii. 19, 20.

sation of the Jews, but their religious feelings were directed to something in the future, and all the circumstances of their national life tended to fix their thoughts on One that was to come. By types and by promises, their eyes were continually turned towards a Messiah. Their history was a continued prophecy. All the great stages of their national existence were accompanied by effusions of prophetic light. Abraham was called from his father's house, and it was revealed that in him ' all families of the earth should be blessed.' Moses formed Abraham's descendants into a people, by giving them a law and national institutions ; but while so doing he spake before of Him who was hereafter to be raised up a ' Prophet like unto himself.' David reigned, and during that reign, which made so deep and lasting an impression on the Jewish mind, psalms were written which spoke of the future King. And with the approach of that captivity, the pathetic recollection of which became perpetual, the prophecies took a bolder range, and embraced within their widening circle the redemption both of Jews and Gentiles. Thus the pious Hebrew was always, as it were, in the attitude of *expectation*: and it has been well remarked that, while the golden age of the Greeks and Romans was the past, that of the Jews was the future. While other nations were growing weary of their gods,—without anything in their mythology or philosophy to satisfy the deep cravings of their nature,—with religion operating rather as a barrier than a link between the educated and the ignorant,— with morality divorced from theology,—the whole Jewish people were united in a feeling of attachment to their sacred institutions, and found in the facts of their past history a pledge of the fulfilment of their national hopes.

It is true that the Jewish nation, again and again, during several centuries, fell into idolatry. It is true that their superiority to other nations consisted in the light which they possessed, and not in the use which they made of it ; and that a carnal life continually dragged them down from the spiritual eminence on which they might have stood. But the Divine purposes were not frustrated. The chosen people was subjected to the chastisement and discipline of severe sufferings: and they were fitted by a long training for the accomplishment of that work, to the conscious performance of which they did not willingly rise. They were hard pressed in their own country by the incursions of their idolatrous neighbours, and in the end they were carried into a distant captivity. From the time of their return from Babylon they were no longer idolaters. They presented to the world the example of a pure Monotheism. And in the active times which preceded and followed the birth of Christ, those Greeks or Romans who visited the Jews in their own land where they still lingered at the portals of the East, and those vast numbers of proselytes whom the dispersed Jews had gathered round them in various countries, were made familiar with the worship of one God and Father of all.[1]

[1] Humboldt has remarked, in the chapter on Poetic Descriptions of Nature (*Kosmos*, Sabine's Eng. trans., vol. ii. p. 44), that the descriptive poetry of the Hebrews is a reflex of Monotheism, and portrays nature, not as self-subsisting, but ever in relation to a Higher Power.

The influence of the Jews upon the Heathen world was exercised mainly through their *dispersion*: but this subject must be deferred for a few pages, till we have examined some of the developments of the Greek and Roman nationalities. A few words, however, may be allowed in passing, upon the consequences of the *geographical position* of Judæa.

The situation of this little but eventful country is such, that its inhabitants were brought into contact successively with all the civilised nations of antiquity. Not to dwell upon its proximity to Egypt on the one hand, and to Assyria on the other, and the influences which those ancient kingdoms may thereby have exercised or received, Palestine lay in the road of Alexander's Eastern expedition. The Greek conqueror was there before he founded his mercantile metropolis in Egypt, and thence went to India, to return and die at Babylon. And again, when his empire was divided, and Greek kingdoms were erected in Europe, Asia, and Africa, Palestine lay between the rival monarchies of the Ptolemies at Alexandria and the Seleucids at Antioch,—too near to both to be safe from the invasion of their arms or the influence of their customs and their language. And finally, when the time came for the Romans to embrace the whole of the Mediterranean within the circle of their power, the coast-line of Judæa was the last remote portion which was needed to complete the fated circumference.[1]

The full effect of this geographical position of Judæa can only be seen by following the course of Greek and Roman life, till they were brought so remarkably into contact with each other, and with that of the Jews : and we turn to those other two nations of antiquity, the steps of whose progress were successive stages in what is called in the Epistle to the Ephesians (i. 10) 'the dispensation of the fulness of time.'

If we think of the civilisation of the Greeks, we have no difficulty in fixing on its chief characteristics. High perfection of the intellect and imagination, displaying itself in all the various forms of art, poetry, literature, and philosophy—restless activity of mind and body, finding its exercise in athletic games or in subtle disputations—love of the beautiful—quick perception—indefatigable inquiry—all these enter into the very idea of the Greek race. This is not the place to inquire how far these qualities were due to an innate peculiarity, or how far they grew up, by gradual development, amidst the natural influences of their native country,—the variety of their hills and plains, the clear lights and warm shadows of their climate, the mingled land and water of their coasts. We have only to do with this national character so far as, under divine Providence, it was made subservient to the spread of the Gospel.

We shall see how remarkably it subserved this' purpose, if we consider the tendency of the Greeks to trade and colonisation.

[1] For reflections on the geographical position of Palestine in relation to its history, see Stanley's *Sinai and Palestine,* Kurtz's *History of the Old Covenant* (in Clark's ' Foreign Theological Library'), and the *Quarterly Review* for October, 1859.

Their mental activity was accompanied with a great physical restlessness. This clever people always exhibited a disposition to
spread themselves. Without aiming at universal conquest, they
displayed (if we may use the word) a remarkable catholicity of
character, and a singular power of adaptation to those whom they
called Barbarians.[1]   In this respect they were strongly contrasted
with the Egyptians, whose immemorial civilisation was confined to
the long valley which extends from the cataracts to the mouths of
the Nile.   The Hellenic[2] tribes, on the other hand, though they
despised foreigners, were never unwilling to visit them and to
cultivate their acquaintance. At the earliest period at which
history enables us to discover them, we see them moving about in
their ships on the shores and among the islands of their native
seas ; and, three or four centuries before the Christian era, Asia
Minor, beyond which the Persians had not been permitted to
advance, was bordered by a fringe of Greek colonies ; and Lower
Italy, when the Roman republic was just beginning to be conscious of its strength, had received the name of Greece itself.[3]   To
all these places they carried their arts and literature, their philosophy, their mythology, and their amusements. They carried also
their arms and their trade. The heroic age had passed away, and
fabulous voyages had given place to real expeditions against Sicily
and constant traffic with the Black Sea. They were gradually
taking the place of the Phœnicians in the empire of the Mediterranean. They were, indeed, less exclusively mercantile than those
old discoverers. Their voyages were not so long. But their influence on general civilisation was greater and more permanent.
The earliest ideas of scientific navigation and geography are due to
the Greeks. The later Greek travellers, Strabo and Pausanias,
will be our best sources of information on the topography of St.
Paul's journeys.

With this view of the Hellenic character before us, we are prepared to appreciate the vast results of Alexander's conquests. He
took up the meshes of the net of Greek civilisation, which were
lying in disorder on the edges of the Asiatic shore, and spread them
over all the countries which he traversed in his wonderful campaigns. The East and the West were suddenly brought together.
Separated tribes were united under a common government. New
cities were built, as the centres of political life. New lines of
communication were opened, as the channels of commercial activity.
The new culture penetrated the mountain ranges of Pisidia and
Lycaonia. The Tigris and Euphrates became Greek rivers. The
language of Athens was heard among the Jewish colonies of
Babylonia ; and a Grecian Babylon[4] was built by the conqueror in
Egypt, and called by his name.

The empire of Alexander was divided, but the effects of his cam-

---

[1] In the N. T. the word 'barbarian'
is used in its strict classical sense, *i.e.*
for a man who does not speak Greek.
See Acts xxviii. 2, 4; Rom. i. 14;
1 Cor. xiv. 11; Col. iii. 11.

[2] 'Hellenic' and 'Hellenistic,' corresponding respectively to the 'Greek'
and 'Grecian' of the Authorised Version, are words which we must often
use. See below, p. 9, n. 3.

[3] Magna Græcia.

[4] Alexandria.

paigns and policy did not cease. The influence of the fresh elements of social life was rather increased by being brought into independent action within the spheres of distinct kingdoms. Our attention is particularly called to two of the monarchical lines which descended from Alexander's generals,—the Ptolemies, or the Greek kings of Egypt,—and the Seleucids, or the Greek kings of Syria. Their respective capitals, *Alexandria* and *Antioch*, became the metropolitan centres of commercial and civilised life in the East. They rose suddenly; and their very appearance marked them as the cities of a new epoch. Like Berlin and St. Petersburg, they were modern cities built by great kings at a definite time and for a definite purpose. Their histories are no unimportant chapters in the history of the world. Both of them were connected with St. Paul: one indirectly, as the birthplace of Apollos ; the other directly, as the scene of some of the most important passages of the Apostle's own life. Both abounded in Jews from their first foundation. Both became the residences of Roman governors, and both afterwards were patriarchates of the primitive Church. But before they had received either the Roman discipline or the Christian doctrine, they had served their appointed purpose of spreading the Greek language and habits, of creating new lines of commercial intercourse by land and sea, and of centralising in themselves the mercantile life of the Levant. Even the Acts of the Apostles remind us of the traffic of Antioch with Cyprus and the neighbouring coasts, and of the sailing of Alexandrian corn-ships to the more distant harbours of Malta and Puteoli.

Of all the Greek elements which the cities of Antioch and Alexandria were the means of circulating, the spread of the language is the most important. Its connection with the whole system of Christian doctrine—with many of the controversies and divisions of the Church—is very momentous. That language, which is the richest and most delicate that the world has seen, became the language of theology. The Greek tongue became to the Christian more than it had been to the Roman or the Jew. The mother-tongue of Ignatius at Antioch, was that in which Philo [1] composed his treatises at Alexandria, and which Cicero spoke at Athens. It is difficult to state in a few words the important relation which *Alexandria* more especially was destined to bear to the whole Christian Church. In that city, the representative of the Greeks of the East, where the most remarkable fusion took place of the peculiarities of Greek, Jewish, and Oriental life, and at the time when all these had been brought in contact with the mind of educated Romans,—a *theological language* was formed, rich in the phrases of various schools, and suited to convey Christian ideas to all the world. It was not an accident that the New Testament was written in Greek, the language which can best express the highest thoughts and worthiest feelings of the intellect and heart, and which is adapted to be the instrument of education for all nations : nor was it an accident that the composition of these books and the promulgation of the Gospel

---

[1] We shall frequently have occasion to mention this learned Alexandrian Jew. He was a cotemporary of St. Paul. See p. 30.

were delayed, till the instruction of our Lord, and the writings of His Apostles, could be expressed in the dialect of Alexandria. This also must be ascribed to the foreknowledge of Him, who 'winked at the times of ignorance,' but who 'made of one blood all nations of men for to dwell on all the face of the earth, and determined the times before appointed, and the bounds of their habitation.'[1]

We do not forget that the social condition of the Greeks had been falling, during this period, into the lowest corruption. The disastrous quarrels of Alexander's generals had been continued among their successors. Political integrity was lost. The Greeks spent their life in worthless and frivolous amusements. Their religion, though beautiful beyond expression as giving subjects for art and poetry, was utterly powerless, and worse than powerless, in checking their bad propensities. Their philosophers were sophists ; their women might be briefly divided into two classes,—those who were highly educated and openly profligate on the one side, and those who lived in domestic and ignorant seclusion on the other. And it cannot be denied that all these causes of degradation spread with the diffusion of the race and the language. Like Sybaris and Syracuse, Antioch and Alexandria became almost worse than Athens and Corinth. But the very diffusion and development of this corruption was preparing the way, because it showed the necessity, for the interposition of a Gospel. The disease itself seemed to call for a *Healer.* And if the prevailing evils of the Greek population presented obstacles, on a large scale, to the progress of Christianity,—yet they showed to all future time the weakness of man's highest powers, if unassisted from above ; and there must have been many who groaned under the burden of a corruption which they could not shake off, and who were ready to welcome the voice of Him, who 'took our infirmities and bare our sicknesses.'[2] The 'Greeks,'[3] who are mentioned by St. John as coming to see JESUS at the feast, were, we trust, the types of a large class ; and we may conceive His answer to Andrew and Philip as expressing the fulfilment of the appointed times in the widest sense—'The hour is come, that the Son of Man should be glorified.'

Such was the civilisation and corruption connected with the spread of the Greek language when the Roman power approached to the eastern parts of the Mediterranean Sea. For some centuries this irresistible force had been gathering strength on the western side of the Apennines. Gradually, but surely, and with ever-increasing rapidity, it made to itself a wider space—northward into Etruria, southward into Campania. It passed beyond its Italian boundaries. And six hundred years after the building of the City, the Roman eagle had seized on Africa at the point of Carthage, and Greece at the Isthmus of Corinth, and had turned its eye towards the East.

---

[1] Acts xvii. 30, 26.
[2] Matt. viii. 17.
[3] John xii. 20. It ought to be observed here, that the word '*Grecian*' in the Authorised Version of the New Testament is used for a Hellenist, or Grecising Jew—as in Acts vi. 1, ix. 29—while the word '*Greek*' is used for one who was by birth a Gentile, and who might, or might not, be a proselyte to Judaism, or a convert to Christianity.

The defenceless prey was made secure, by craft or by war ; and before
the birth of our Saviour, all those coasts, from Ephesus to Tarsus
and Antioch, and round by the Holy Land to Alexandria and
Cyrene, were tributary to the city of the Tiber. We have to
describe in a few words the characteristics of this new dominion,
and to point out its providential connection with the spread and
consolidation of the Church.

In the first place, this dominion was not a pervading influence
exerted by a restless and intellectual people, but it was the grasp-
ing power of an external government. The idea of law had grown
up with the growth of the Romans ; and wherever they went they
carried it with them. Wherever their armies were marching or
encamping, there always attended them, like a mysterious presence,
the spirit of the City of Rome. Universal conquest and permanent occupation were the ends at which they aimed. Strength and
organisation were the characteristics of their sway. We have seen
how the Greek science and commerce were wafted, by irregular
winds, from coast to coast : and now we follow the advance of
legions, governors, and judges along the Roman Roads, which
pursued their undeviating course over plains and mountains, and
bound the City to the furthest extremities of the provinces.

There is no better way of obtaining a clear view of the features
and a correct idea of the spirit of the Roman age, than by considering the material works which still remain as its imperishable
monuments. Whether undertaken by the hands of the government, or for the ostentation of private luxury, they were marked
by vast extent and accomplished at an enormous expenditure. The
gigantic roads of the Empire have been unrivalled till the present
century. Solid structures of all kinds, for utility, amusement, and
worship, were erected in Italy and the provinces,—amphitheatres
of stone, magnificent harbours, bridges, sepulchres, and temples.
The decoration of wealthy houses was celebrated by the poets of
the day. The pomp of buildings in the cities was rivalled by
astonishing villas in the country. The enormous baths, by which
travellers are surprised, belong to a period somewhat later than
that of St. Paul ; but the aqueducts, which still remain in the Campagna, were some of them new when he visited Rome. Of the
metropolis itself it may be enough to say, that his life is exactly
embraced between its two great times of renovation, that of
Augustus on the one hand, who (to use his own expression) having
found it a city of brick left it a city of marble, and that of Nero on
the other, when the great conflagration afforded an opportunity for
a new arrangement of its streets and buildings.

These great works may be safely taken as emblems of the magnitude, strength, grandeur, and solidity of the Empire ; but they
are emblems, no less, of the tyranny and cruelty which had presided over its formation, and of the general suffering which pervaded it. The statues, with which the metropolis and the Roman
houses were profusely decorated, had been brought from plundered
provinces, and many of them had swelled the triumphs of conquerors on the Capitol. The amphitheatres were built for shows
of gladiators, and were the scenes of a bloody cruelty, which had

been quite unknown in the licentious exhibitions of the Greek theatre. The roads, baths, harbours, aqueducts, had been constructed by slave-labour. And the country villas, which the Italian traveller lingered to admire, were themselves vast establishments of slaves.

It is easy to see how much misery followed in the train of Rome's advancing greatness. Cruel suffering was a characteristic feature of the close of the Republic. Slave wars, civil wars, wars of conquest, had left their disastrous results behind them. No country recovers rapidly from the effects of a war which has been conducted within its frontier; and there was no district of the Empire which had not been the scene of some recent campaign. None had suffered more than Italy itself. Its old stock of freemen, who had cultivated its fair plains and terraced vineyards, was utterly worn out. The general depopulation was badly compensated by the establishment of military colonies. Inordinate wealth and slave factories were the prominent features of the desolate prospect. The words of the great historian may fill up the picture. ' As regards the manners and mode of life of the Romans, their great object at this time was the acquisition and possession of money. Their moral conduct, which had been corrupt enough before the Social war, became still more so by their systematic plunder and rapine. Immense riches were accumulated and squandered upon brutal pleasures. The simplicity of the old manners and mode of living had been abandoned for Greek luxuries and frivolities, and the whole household arrangements had become altered. The Roman houses had formerly been quite simple, and were built either of bricks or peperino, but in most cases of the former material; now, on the other hand, every one would live in a splendid house and be surrounded by luxuries. The condition of Italy after the Social and Civil wars was indescribably wretched. Samnium had become almost a desert; and as late as the time of Strabo there was scarcely any town in that country which was not in ruins. But worse things were yet to come.' [1]

This disastrous condition was not confined to Italy. In some respects the provinces had their own peculiar sufferings. To take the case of Asia Minor. It had been plundered and ravaged by successive generals,—by Scipio in the war against Antiochus of Syria,—by Manlius in his Galatian campaign,—by Pompey in the struggle with Mithridates. The rapacity of governors and their officials followed that of generals and their armies. We know what Cilicia suffered under Dolabella and his agent Verres: and Cicero reveals to us the oppression of his predecessor Appius in the same province, contrasted with his own boasted clemency. Some portions of this beautiful and inexhaustible country revived under the emperors.[2] But it was only an outward prosperity. Whatever may have been the improvement in the external details of provincial government, we cannot believe that governors were gentle and forbearing, when Caligula was on the throne, and when Nero was

[1] Niebuhr's *Lectures on the History of Rome*, vol. i. pp. 421, 422.			[2] Niebuhr's *Lect. on Hist. of Rome*, vol. i. p. 406, and the note.

seeking statues for his golden house. The contempt in which the Greek provincials themselves were held by the Romans may be learnt from the later correspondence of the Emperor Trajan with Pliny the governor of Bithynia. We need not hesitate to take it for granted, that those who were sent from Rome to dispense justice at Ephesus or Tarsus, were more frequently like Appius and Verres, than Cicero[1] and Flaccus,—more like Pilate and Felix, than Gallio and Sergius Paulus.

It would be a delusion to imagine that, when the world was reduced under one sceptre, any real principle of unity held its different parts together. The emperor was deified,[2] because men were enslaved. There was no true peace when Augustus closed the Temple of Janus. The Empire was only the order of external government, with a chaos both of opinions and morals within. The writings of Tacitus and Juvenal remain to attest the corruption which festered in all ranks, alike in the senate and the family. The old severity of manners, and the old faith in the better part of the Roman religion, were gone. The licentious creeds and practices of Greece and the East had inundated Italy and the West : and the Pantheon was only the monument of a compromise among a multitude of effete superstitions. It is true that a remarkable religious toleration was produced by this state of things : and it is probable that for some short time Christianity itself shared the advantage of it. But still the temper of the times was essentially both cruel and profane ; and the Apostles were soon exposed to its bitter persecution. The Roman Empire was destitute of that unity which the Gospel gives to mankind. It was a kingdom of this world ; and the human race were groaning for the better peace of 'a kingdom not of this world.'

Thus, in the very condition of the Roman Empire, and the miserable state of its mixed population, we can recognise a negative preparation for the Gospel of Christ. This tyranny and oppression called for a *Consoler*,[3] as much as the moral sickness of the Greeks called for a Healer; a Messiah was needed by the whole Empire as much as by the Jews, though not looked for with the same conscious

---

[1] Much of our best information concerning the state of the provinces is derived from Cicero's celebrated 'Speeches against Verres,' and his own Cilician Correspondence, to which we shall again have occasion to refer. His 'Speech in Defence of Flaccus' throws much light on the condition of the Jews under the Romans. We must not place too much confidence in the picture there given of this Ephesian governor.

[2] The image of the emperor was at that time the object of religious reverence : he was a deity on earth (Dis æqua potestas, Juv. iv. 71) ; and the worship paid to him was a real worship. It is a striking thought, that in those times (setting aside effete forms of re-

ligion), the only two genuine worships in the civilised world were the worship of a Tiberius or a Nero on the one hand, and the worship of CHRIST on the other.

[3] We may refer here to the apotheosis of Augustus with Tiberius at his side, as represented on the 'Vienna Cameo' in the midst of figures indicative of the misery and enslavement of the world. An engraving of this Cameo is given in the quarto edition. Its best contrast will be found in Scheffer's modern picture—'Christus Consolator,'—where the Saviour is seated in the midst of those who are miserable, and the eyes of all are turned to Him for relief.

expectation. But we have no difficulty in going much farther than this, and we cannot hesitate to discover in the circumstances of the world at this period, significant traces of a positive preparation for the Gospel.

It should be remembered, in the first place, that the Romans had already become Greek to some considerable extent, before they were the political masters of those eastern countries, where the language, mythology, and literature of Greece had become more or less familiar. How early, how widely, and how permanently this Greek influence prevailed, and how deeply it entered into the mind of educated Romans, we know from their surviving writings, and from the biography of eminent men. Cicero, who was governor of Cilicia about half a century before the birth of St. Paul, speaks in strong terms of the universal spread of the Greek tongue among the instructed classes ; and about the time of the Apostle's martyrdom, Agricola, the conqueror of Britain, was receiving a Greek education at Marseilles. Is it too much to say, that the general Latin conquest was providentially delayed till the Romans had been sufficiently imbued with the language and ideas of their predecessors, and had incorporated many parts of that civilisation with their own ?

And if the wisdom of the divine pre-arrangements is illustrated by the period of the spread of the Greek language, it is illustrated no less by that of the completion and maturity of the Roman government. When all parts of the civilised world were bound together in one empire,—when one common organisation pervaded the whole—when channels of communication were everywhere opened—when new facilities of travelling were provided,—then was 'the fulness of time' (Gal. iv. 4), then the Messiah came. The Greek language had already been prepared as a medium for preserving and transmitting the doctrine ; the Roman government was now prepared to help the progress even of that religion which it persecuted. The manner in which it spread through the provinces is well exemplified in the life of St. Paul; his right of citizenship rescued him in Macedonia[1] and in Judæa ;[2] he converted one governor in Cyprus,[3] was protected by another in Achaia,[4] and was sent from Jerusalem to Rome by a third.[5] The time was indeed approaching, when all the complicated weight of the central tyranny, and of the provincial governments, was to fall on the new and irresistible religion. But before this took place, it had begun to grow up in close connection with all departments of the Empire. When the supreme government itself became Christian, the ecclesiastical polity was permanently regulated in conformity with the actual constitution of the state. Nor was the Empire broken up, till the separate fragments, which have become the nations of modern Europe, were themselves portions of the Catholic Church.

But in all that we have said of the condition of the Roman world, one important and widely diffused element of its population has not been mentioned. We have lost sight for some time of the Jews,

---

[1] Acts xvi. 37—39.   [2] Acts xxii. 25.   [3] Acts xiii. 12.
[4] Acts xviii. 14—17.   [5] Acts xxv. 12, xxvii. 1

and we must return to the subject of their dispersion, which was purposely deferred till we had shown how the intellectual civilisation of the Greeks, and the organising civilisation of the Romans, had, through a long series of remarkable events, been brought in contact with the religious civilisation of the Hebrews. It remains that we point out that one peculiarity of the Jewish people which made this contact almost universal in every part of the Empire.

Their dispersion began early ; though, early and late, their attachment to Judæa has always been the same. Like the Highlanders of Switzerland and Scotland, they seem to have combined a tendency to foreign settlements with the most passionate love of their native land. The first scattering of the Jews was compulsory, and began with the Assyrian exile, when, about the time of the building of Rome, natives of Galilee and Samaria were carried away by the Eastern monarchs ; and this was followed by the Babylonian exile, when the tribes of Judah and Benjamin were removed at different epochs,—when Daniel was brought to Babylon, and Ezekiel to the river Chebar. That this earliest dispersion was not without influential results may be inferred from these facts ;—that, about the time of the battles of Salamis and Marathon, a Jew was the minister, another Jew the cupbearer, and a Jewess the consort, of a Persian monarch. That they enjoyed many privileges in this foreign country, and that their condition was not always oppressive, may be gathered from this,—that when Cyrus gave them permission to return, the majority remained in their new home, in preference to their native land. Thus that great Jewish colony began in Babylonia, the existence of which may be traced in Apostolic times,[1] and which retained its influence long after in the Talmudical schools. These Hebrew settlements may be followed through various parts of the continental East, to the borders of the Caspian, and even to China. We, however, are more concerned with the coasts and islands of Western Asia. Jews had settled in Syria and Phœnicia before the time of Alexander the Great. But in treating of this subject, the great stress is to be laid on the policy of Seleucus, who, in founding Antioch, raised them to the same political position with the other citizens. One of his successors on the throne, Antiochus the Great, established two thousand Jewish families in Lydia and Phrygia. From hence they would spread into Pamphylia and Galatia, and along the western coasts from Ephesus to Troas. And the ordinary channels of communication, in conjunction with that tendency to trade which already began to characterise this wonderful people, would easily bring them to the islands, such as Cyprus[2] and Rhodes.

Their oldest settlement in *Africa* was that which took place after the murder of the Babylonian governor of Judæa, and which is connected with the name of the prophet Jeremiah.[3] But, as in the case of Antioch, our chief attention is called to the great metropolis of the period of the Greek kings. The Jewish quarter of Alex-

---

[1] See 1 Pet. v. 13.

[2] The farming of the copper mines in Cyprus by Herod (Jos. *Ant.* xvi. 4, 5) may have attracted many Jews.

There is a Cyprian inscription which seems to refer to one of the Herods.

[3] See 2 Kings xxv. 22—26, Jer. xliii. xliv.

andria is well known in history ; and the colony of Hellenistic Jews in Lower Egypt is of greater importance than that of their Aramaic[1] brethren in Babylonia. Alexander himself brought Jews and Samaritans to his famous city ; the first Ptolemy brought many more ; and many betook themselves hither of their free will, that they might escape from the incessant troubles which disturbed the peace of their fatherland. Nor was their influence confined to Egypt, but they became known on one side in Æthiopia, the country of Queen Candace,[2] and spread on the other in great numbers to the ' parts of Libya about Cyrene.' [3]

Under what circumstances the Jews made their first appearance in *Europe* is unknown ; but it is natural to suppose that those islands of the Archipelago which, as Humboldt has said, were like a bridge for the passage of civilisation, became the means of the advance of Judaism. The journey of the proselyte Lydia from Thyatira to Philippi (Acts xvi. 14), and the voyage of Aquila and Priscilla from Corinth to Ephesus (Ibid. xviii. 18), are only specimens of mercantile excursions which must have begun at a far earlier period. Philo[4] mentions Jews in Thessaly, Bœotia, Macedonia, Ætolia, and Attica, in Argos and Corinth, in the other parts of Peloponnesus, and in the islands of Eubœa and Crete : and St. Luke, in the Acts of the Apostles, speaks of them in Philippi, Thessalonica, and Berœa, in Athens, in Corinth, and in Rome. The first Jews came to Rome to decorate a triumph ; but they were soon set free from captivity, and gave the name to the 'Synagogue of the Libertines' [5] in Jerusalem. They owed to Julius Cæsar those privileges in the Western Capital which they had obtained from Alexander in the Eastern. They became influential, and made proselytes. They spread into other towns of Italy ; and in the time of St. Paul's boyhood we find them in large numbers in the island of Sardinia, just as we have previously seen them established in that of Cyprus.[6] With regard to Gaul, we know at least that two sons of Herod were banished, about this same period, to the banks of the Rhone ; and if (as seems most probable) St. Paul accomplished that journey to Spain of which he speaks in his letters, there is little doubt that he found there some of the scattered children of his own people. We do not seek to pursue them further ; but, after a few words on the proselytes, we must return to the earliest scenes of the Apostle's career.

The subject of the proselytes is sufficiently important to demand a separate notice. Under this term we include at present all who were attracted in various degrees of intensity towards Judaism,— from those who by circumcision had obtained full access to all the privileges of the temple-worship, to those who only professed a

[1] This term is explained in the next chapter, see p. 29, note 6.

[2] Acts viii. 27.

[3] Acts ii. 10. The second book of Maccabees is the abridgment of a work written by a Hellenistic Jew of Cyrene. A Jew or proselyte of Cyrene bore our Saviour's cross. And the mention of this city occurs more than once in the Acts of the Apostles.

[4] See note, p. 8.

[5] This body doubtless consisted of manumitted Jewish slaves. The synagogue or synagogues mentioned in Acts vi. 9 are discussed in the next chapter.

[6] In the case of Sardinia, however, they were forcibly sent to the island, to die of the bad climate.

general respect for the Mosaic religion, and attended as hearers in the synagogues. Many proselytes were attached to the Jewish communities wherever they were dispersed.[1] Even in their own country and its vicinity, the number, both in early and later times, was not inconsiderable. The Queen of Sheba, in the Old Testament ; Candace, Queen of Æthiopia, in the New ; and King Izates, with his mother Helena, mentioned by Josephus, are only royal representatives of a large class. During the time of the Maccabees, some alien tribes were forcibly incorporated with the Jews. This was the case with the Ituræans, and probably with the Moabites, and, above all, with the Edomites, with whose name that of the Herodian family is historically connected. How far Judaism extended among the vague collection of tribes called Arabians, we can only conjecture from the curious history of the Homerites, and from the actions of such chieftains as Aretas (2 Cor. xi. 32). But as we travel towards the West and North, into countries better known, we find no lack of evidence of the moral effect of the synagogues, with their worship of JEHOVAH, and their prophecies of the Messiah. ' Nicolas of Antioch ' (Acts vi. 5) is only one of that ' vast multitude of Greeks ' who, according to Josephus,[2] were attracted in that city to the Jewish doctrine and ritual. In Damascus, we are even told by the same authority that the great majority of the women were proselytes ; a fact which receives a remarkable illustration from what happened to Paul at Iconium (Acts xiii. 50). But all further details may be postponed till we follow Paul himself into the synagogues, where he so often addressed a mingled audience of ' Jews of the dispersion ' and ' devout ' strangers.

This chapter may be suitably concluded by some notice of the provinces of *Cilicia* and *Judæa*. This will serve as an illustration of what has been said above, concerning the state of the Roman provinces generally ; it will exemplify the mixture of Jews, Greeks, and Romans in the east of the Mediterranean, and it will be a fit introduction to what must immediately succeed. For these are the two provinces which require our attention in the early life of the Apostle Paul.

Both these provinces were once under the sceptre of the line of the Seleucids, or Greek kings of Syria ; and both of them, though originally inhabited by a ' barbarous '[3] population, received more or less of the influence of Greek civilisation. If the map is consulted, it will be seen that Antioch, the capital of the Græco-Syrian kings, is situated nearly in the angle where the coast-line of Cilicia, running eastwards, and that of Judæa, extended northwards, are brought to an abrupt meeting. It will be seen also, that, more or less parallel to each of these coasts, there is a line of mountains, not far from the sea, which are brought into contact with each other in heavy and confused forms, near the same angle ; the principal break in the continuity of either of them being the valley of the Orontes, which passes by Antioch. One of these mountain lines is the range of *Mount Taurus*, which is so often mentioned as a great

---

[1] In illustration of this fact, it is easy to adduce abundance of Heathen testimony.

[2] *War,* vii. 3, 3.

[3] See p. 7, note 1.

geographical boundary by the writers of Greece and Rome ; and *Cilicia* extends partly over the Taurus itself, and partly between it and the sea.   The other range is that of *Lebanon*—a name made sacred by the scriptures and poetry of the Jews ; and where its towering eminences subside towards the south into a land of hills and valleys and level plains, there is *Judæa*, once the country of promise and possession to the chosen people, but a Roman province in the time of the Apostles.

Cilicia, in the sense in which the word was used under the early Roman emperors, comprehended two districts, of nearly equal extent, but of very different character.   The Western portion, or *Rough Cilicia*, as it was called, was a collection of the branches of Mount Taurus, which come down in large masses to the sea, and form that projection of the coast which divides the Bay of Issus from that of Pamphylia.   The inhabitants of the whole of this district were notorious for their robberies : the northern portion, under the name of Isauria, providing innumerable strongholds for marauders by land ; and the southern, with its excellent timber, its cliffs, and small harbours, being a natural home for pirates. The Isaurians maintained their independence with such determined obstinacy, that in a later period of the Empire, the Romans were willing to resign all appearance of subduing them, and were content to surround them with a *cordon* of forts.   The natives of the coast of Rough Cilicia began to extend their piracies as the strength of the kings of Syria and Egypt declined.   They found in the progress of the Roman power, for some time, an encouragement rather than a hindrance ; for they were actively engaged in an extensive and abominable slave trade, of which the island of Delos was the great market ; and the opulent families of Rome were in need of slaves, and were not more scrupulous than some Christian nations of modern times about the means of obtaining them.   But the expeditions of these buccaneers of the Mediterranean became at last quite intolerable ; their fleets seemed innumerable ; their connections were extended far beyond their own coasts ; all commerce was paralysed ; and they began to arouse that attention at Rome which the more distant pirates of the Eastern Archipelago not long ago excited in England.   A vast expedition was fitted out under the command of Pompey the Great ; thousands of piratic vessels were burnt on the coast of Cilicia, and the inhabitants dispersed.   A perpetual service was thus done to the cause of civilisation, and the Mediterranean was made safe for the voyages of merchants and Apostles.   The town of Soli, on the borders of the two divisions of Cilicia, received the name of Pompeiopolis,[1] in honour of the great conqueror, and the splendid remains of a colonnade which led from

---

[1] A similar case. on a small scale, is that of Philippeville in Algeria; and the progress of the French power, since the accession of Louis Philippe, in Northern Africa, is perhaps the nearest parallel in modern times to the history of a Roman province. As far as regards the pirates, Lord Ex- mouth, in 1816, really did the work of Pompey the Great.   It may be doubted whether Marshal Bugeaud was more lenient to the Arabs than Cicero to the Eleuthero-Cilicians.

Chrysippus the Stoic, whose father was a native of Tarsus, and Aratus, whom St. Paul quotes, lived at Soli.

the harbour to the city may be considered a monument of this signal destruction of the enemies of order and peace.

The Eastern, or *Flat Cilicia*, was a rich and extensive plain. Its prolific vegetation is praised both by the earlier and later classical writers, and, even under the neglectful government of the Turks, is still noticed by modern travellers.[1] From this circumstance, and still more from its peculiar physical configuration, it was a possession of great political importance. Walled off from the neighbouring countries by a high barrier of mountains, which sweep irregularly round it from Pompeipolis and Rough Cilicia to the Syrian coast on the North of Antioch,—with one pass leading up into the interior of Asia Minor, and another giving access to the valley of the Orontes, —it was naturally the high road both of trading caravans and of military expeditions. Through this country Cyrus marched, to depose his brother from the Persian throne. It was here that the decisive victory was obtained by Alexander over Darius. This plain has since seen the hosts of Western Crusaders; and, in our own day, has been the field of operations of hostile Mahommedan armies, Turkish and Egyptian. The Greek kings of Egypt endeavoured, long ago, to tear it from the Greek kings of Syria. The Romans left it at first in the possession of Antiochus: but the line of Mount Taurus could not permanently arrest them: and the letters of Cicero remain to us among the most interesting, as they are among the earliest, monuments of Roman Cilicia.

Situated near the western border of the Cilician plain, where the river Cydnus flows in a cold and rapid stream, from the snows of Taurus to the sea, was the city of Tarsus, the capital of the whole province, and 'no mean city' (Acts xxi. 39) in the history of the ancient world. Its coins reveal to us its greatness through a long series of years:—alike in the period which intervened between Xerxes and Alexander,—and under the Roman sway, when it exulted in the name of *Metropolis*,—and long after Hadrian had rebuilt it, and issued his new coinage with the old mythological types.[2] In the intermediate period, which is that of St. Paul, we have the testimony of a native of this part of Asia Minor, from which we may infer that Tarsus was in the Eastern basin of the Mediterranean almost what Marseilles was in the Western. Strabo says that, in all that relates to philosophy and general education, it was even more illustrious than Athens and Alexandria. From his description it is evident that its main character was that of a Greek city, where the Greek language was spoken, and Greek literature studiously cultivated. But we should be wrong in supposing that the general population of the province was of Greek origin, or spoke the Greek tongue. When Cyrus came with his army from the Western Coast,

[1] Laborde's illustrated work on Syria and Asia Minor contains some luxuriant specimens of the modern vegetation of Tarsus; but the banana and the prickly pear were introduced into the Mediterranean long after St. Paul's day.

[2] The coin at the end of the chapter was struck under Hadrian, and is preserved in the British Museum. The word *Metropolis* is conspicuous on it. The same figures of the Lion and the Bull appear in a fine series of silver coins of Tarsus, assigned by the Duc de Luynes to the period between Xerxes and Alexander.

and still later, when Alexander penetrated into Cilicia, they found the inhabitants 'Barbarians.' Nor is it likely that the old race would be destroyed, or the old language obliterated, especially in the mountain districts, during the reign of the Seleucid kings. We must rather conceive of Tarsus as like Brest, in Brittany, or like Toulon, in Provence,—a city where the language of refinement is spoken and written, in the midst of a ruder population, who use a different language, and possess no literature of their own.

If we turn now to consider the position of this province and city under the Romans, we are led to notice two different systems of policy which they adopted in their subject dominions. The purpose of Rome was to make the world subservient to herself : but this might be accomplished directly or indirectly. A governor might be sent from Rome to take the absolute command of a province : or some native chief might have a kingdom, an ethnarchy,[1] or a tetrarchy assigned to him, in which he was nominally independent, but really subservient, and often tributary. Some provinces were rich and productive, or essentially important in the military sense, and these were committed to Romans under the Senate or the Emperor. Others might be worthless or troublesome, and fit only to reward the services of an useful instrument, or to occupy the energies of a dangerous ally. Both these systems were adopted in the East and in the West. We have examples of both—in Spain and in Gaul—in Cilicia and in Judæa. In Asia Minor they were so irregularly combined, and the territories of the independent sovereigns were so capriciously granted or removed, extended or curtailed, that it is often difficult to ascertain what the actual boundaries of the provinces were at a given epoch. Not to enter into any minute history in the case of Cilicia, it will be enough to say, that its rich and level plain in the east was made a Roman province by Pompey, and so remained, while certain districts in the western portion were assigned, at different periods, to various native chieftains. Thus the territories of Amyntas, King of Galatia, were extended in this direction by Antony, when he was preparing for his great struggle with Augustus : just as a modern Rajah may be strengthened on the banks of the Indus, in connection with wars against Scinde and the Sikhs. For some time the whole of Cilicia was a consolidated province under the first emperors : but again, in the reign of Claudius, we find a portion of the same Western district assigned to a king called Polemo II. It is needless to pursue the history further. In St. Paul's early life the political state of the inhabitants of Cilicia would be that of subjects of a Roman governor : and Roman officials, if not Roman soldiers, would be a familiar sight to the Jews who were settled in Tarsus.[2]

We shall have many opportunities of describing the condition of provinces under the dominion of Rome ; but it may be interesting here to allude to the information which may be gathered from the writings of that distinguished man, who was governor of Cilicia a few years after its first reduction by Pompey. He was entrusted

---

[1] See note at the end of Ch. III.

[2] Tarsus, as a 'Free City' (*Urbs Libera*), would have the privilege of being garrisoned by its own soldiers. See next chapter.

with the civil and military superintendence of a large district in this corner of the Mediterranean, comprehending not only Cilicia, but Pamphylia, Pisidia, Lycaonia, and the island of Cyprus ; and he has left a record of all the details of his policy in a long series of letters, which are a curious monument of the Roman procedure in the management of conquered provinces, and which possess a double interest to us, from their frequent allusions to the same places which St. Paul refers to in his Epistles. This correspondence represents to us the governor as surrounded by the adulation of obsequious Asiatic Greeks. He travels with an interpreter, for Latin is the official language ; he puts down banditti, and is saluted by the title of Imperator ; letters are written, on various subjects, to the governors of neighbouring provinces,—for instance, Syria, Asia, and Bithynia ; ceremonious communications take place with the independent chieftains. The friendly relations of Cicero with Deiotarus, King of Galatia, and his son, remind us of the interview of Pilate and Herod in the Gospel, or of Festus and Agrippa in the Acts. Cicero's letters are rather too full of a boastful commendation of his own integrity ; but from what he says that he did, we may infer by contrast what was done by others who were less scrupulous in the discharge of the same responsibilities. He allowed free access to his person ; he refused expensive monuments in his honour ; he declined the proffered present of the pauper King of Cappadocia ; [1] he abstained from exacting the customary expenses from the states which he traversed on his march ; he remitted to the treasury the moneys which were not expended on his province ; he would not place in official situations those who were engaged in trade ; he treated the local Greek magistrates with due consideration, and contrived at the same time to give satisfaction to the Publicans. From all this it may be easily inferred with how much corruption, cruelty, and pride, the Romans usually governed ; and how miserable must have been the condition of a province under a Verres or an Appius, a Pilate or a Felix. So far as we remember, the Jews are not mentioned in any of Cicero's Cilician letters ; but if we may draw conclusions from a speech which he made at Rome in defence of a cotemporary governor of Asia,[2] he regarded them with much contempt, and would be likely to treat them with harshness and injustice.[3]

That Polemo II., who has lately been mentioned as a king in Cilicia, was one of those curious links which the history of those times exhibits between Heathenism, Judaism, and Christianity. He became a Jew to marry Berenice,[4] who afterwards forsook him, and whose name, after once appearing in Sacred History (Acts xxv., xxvi.), is lastly associated with that of Titus, the destroyer of Je-

---

[1] See Hor. 1 *Ep.* vi. 39.
[2] This was L. Valerius Flaccus, who had served in Cilicia, and was afterwards made Governor of *Asia*,—that district with which, and its capital Ephesus, we are so familiar in the Acts of the Apostles.
[3] See especially Cic. *Flacc.* 28 ; and

for the opinion which educated Romans had of the Jews, see Hor. 1 *Sat.* iv. 143, v. 100, v. 69.
[4] He was the last King of Pontus. By Caligula he was made King of Bosphorus ; but Claudius gave him part of Cilicia instead of it. Joseph. *Ant.* xx. 7, 3.

rusalem. The name of Berenice will at once suggest the family of the Herods, and transport our thoughts to Judæa.

The same general features may be traced in this province as in that which we have been attempting to describe. In some respects, indeed, the details of its history are different. When Cilicia was a province, it formed a separate jurisdiction, with a governor of its own, immediately responsible to Rome : but Judæa, in its provincial period, was only an appendage to Syria. It has been said[1] that the position of the ruler resident at Cæsarea in connection with the supreme authority at Antioch may be best understood by comparing it with that of the governor of Madras or Bombay under the governor-general who resides at Calcutta. The comparison is in some respects just : and British India might supply a further parallel. We might say that when Judæa was not strictly a province, but a monarchy under the protectorate of Rome, it bore the same relation to the contiguous province of Syria which, before the recent war, the territories of the king of Oude[2] bore to the presidency of Bengal. Judæa was twice a monarchy : and thus its history furnishes illustrations of the two systems pursued by the Romans, of direct and indirect government.

Another important contrast must be noticed in the histories of these two provinces. In the Greek period of Judæa, there was a time of noble and vigorous independence. Antiochus Epiphanes, the eighth of the line of the Seleucids, in pursuance of a general system of policy, by which he sought to unite all his different territories through the Greek religion, endeavoured to introduce the worship of Jupiter into Jerusalem.[3] Such an attempt might have been very successful in Syria or Cilicia : but in Judæa it kindled a flame of religious indignation, which did not cease to burn till the yoke of the Seleucidæ was entirely thrown off : the name of Antiochus Epiphanes was ever afterwards held in abhorrence by the Jews, and a special fast was kept up in memory of the time when the 'abomination of desolation' stood in the holy place. The champions of the independence of the Jewish nation and the purity of the Jewish religion were the family of the Maccabees or Asmonæans : and a hundred years before the birth of Christ the first Hyrcanus was reigning over a prosperous and independent kingdom. But in the time of the second Hyrcanus and his brother, the family of the Maccabees was not what it had been, and Judæa was ripening for the dominion of Rome. Pompey the Great, the same conqueror who had already subjected Cilicia, appeared in Damascus, and there judged the cause of the two brothers. All the country was full of his fame. In the spring of the year 63 he came

---

[1] See the introduction to Dr. Traill's Josephus, a work which was interrupted by the death of the translator during the Irish famine, and was continued by Mr. Isaac Taylor.

[2] Another coincidence is, that we made the Nabob of Oude a king. He had previously been hereditary Vizier of the Mogul.

[3] Here we may observe that there are extant coins of Antiochus Epiphanes, where the head of Jupiter appears on the obverse, in place of the portrait usual in the Alexandrian, Seleucid, and Macedonian series. Since such emblems on ancient coins have always sacred meanings, it is very probable that this arose from the religious movement alluded to in the text.

down by the valley of the Jordan, his Roman soldiers occupied the ford where Joshua had crossed over, and from the Mount of Olives he looked down upon Jerusalem.[1] From that day Judæa was virtually under the government of Rome. It is true that, after a brief support given to the reigning family, a new native dynasty was raised to the throne. Antipater, a man of Idumean birth, had been minister of the Maccabean kings ; but they were the *Rois Fainéants* of Palestine, and he was the *Maire du Palais*. In the midst of the confusion of the great civil wars, the Herodian family succeeded to the Asmonæan, as the Carlovingian line in France succeeded that of Clovis. As Pepin was followed by Charlemagne, so Antipater prepared a crown for his son Herod.

At first Herod the Great espoused the cause of Antony ; but he contrived to remedy his mistake by paying a prompt visit, after the battle of Actium, to Augustus in the island of Rhodes. This singular interview of the Jewish prince with the Roman conqueror in a Greek island was the beginning of an important period for the Hebrew nation. An exotic civilisation was systematically introduced and extended. Those Greek influences, which had been begun under the Seleucids, and not discontinued under the Asmonæans, were now more widely diffused: and the Roman customs,[2] which had hitherto been comparatively unknown, were now made familiar. Herod was indeed too wise, and knew the Jews too well, to attempt, like Antiochus, to introduce foreign institutions without any regard to their religious feelings. He endeavoured to ingratiate himself with them by rebuilding and decorating their national temple ; and a part of that magnificent bridge which was connected with the great southern colonnade is still believed to exist,—remaining, in its vast proportions and Roman form, an appropriate monument of the Herodian period of Judæa.[3] The period when Herod was reigning at Jerusalem under the protectorate of Augustus was chiefly remarkable for great architectural works, for the promotion of commerce, the influx of strangers, and the increased diffusion of the two great languages of the heathen world. The names of places are themselves a monument of the spirit of the times. As Tarsus was called Juliopolis from Julius Cæsar, and Soli Pompeiopolis from his great rival, so Samaria was called Sebaste after the Greek name of Augustus, and the new metropolis, which was built by Herod on the sea-shore, was called Cæsarea in honour of the same Latin emperor: while Antipatris, on the road (Acts xxiii. 31) between the old capital and the new,[4] still

---

[1] Pompey heard of the death of Mithridates at Jericho. His army crossed at Scythopolis, by the ford immediately below the lake of Tiberias.

[2] Antiochus Epiphanes (who was called Epimanes from his mad conduct) is said to have made himself ridiculous by adopting Roman fashions, and walking about the streets of Antioch in a toga.

[3] See the woodcut opposite. The arch extends about fifty feet along the wall,

and its radius must have been about twenty feet. It is right to say that there is much controversy about its origin. Dr. Robinson assigns it to the age of Solomon: Mr. Fergusson to that of Herod : Mr. Williams holds it to be a fragment of the great Christian works constructed in this southern part of the Temple area in the age of Justinian.

[4] The tracing of the road by which St. Paul travelled on this occasion is

REMAINS OF ANCIENT BRIDGE AT JERUSALEM.

commemorated the name of the king's Idumæan father. We must not suppose that the internal change in the minds of the people was proportional to the magnitude of these outward improvements. They suffered much; and their hatred grew towards Rome and towards the Herods. A parallel might be drawn between the state of Judæa under Herod the Great, and that of Egypt under Mahomet Ali,[1] where great works have been successfully accomplished, where the spread of ideas has been promoted, traffic made busy and prosperous, and communication with the civilised world wonderfully increased,—but where the mass of the people has continued to be miserable and degraded.

After Herod's death, the same influences still continued to operate in Judæa. Archelaus persevered in his father's policy, though destitute of his father's energy. The same may be said of the other sons, Antipas and Philip, in their contiguous principalities. All the Herods were great builders, and eager partizans of the Roman emperors: and we are familiar in the Gospels with that *Cæsarea* (Cæsarea Philippi), which one of them built in the upper part of the valley of the Jordan, and named in honour of Augustus,—and with that *Tiberias* on the banks of the lake of Gennesareth, which bore the name of his wicked successor. But while Antipas and Philip still retained their dominions under the protectorate of the emperor, Archelaus had been banished, and the weight of the Roman power had descended still more heavily on Judæa. It was placed under the direct jurisdiction of a governor, residing at Cæsarea by the Sea, and depending, as we have seen above, on the governor of Syria at Antioch. And now we are made familiar with those features which might be adduced as characterising any other province at the same epoch,—the prætorium,[2]—the publicans,[3]—the tribute-money,[4]—soldiers and centurions recruited in Italy,[5]—Cæsar the only king,[6] and the ultimate appeal against the injustice of the governor.[7] In this period the ministry, death, and resurrection of JESUS CHRIST took place, the first preaching of His Apostles, and the conversion of St. Paul. But once more a change came over the political fortunes of Judæa. Herod Agrippa was the friend of Caligula, as Herod the Great had been the friend of Augustus; and when Tiberius died, he received the grant of an independent principality in the north of Palestine.[8] He was able to ingratiate himself with Claudius, the succeeding

one of the most interesting geographical questions which will come before us.

[1] There are many points of resemblance between the character and fortunes of Herod and those of Mahomet Ali; the chief differences are those of the times. Herod secured his position by the influence of Augustus; Mahomet Ali secured his by the agreement of the European powers.

[2] John xviii. 28.

[3] Luke iii. 12, xix. 2.

[4] Matt. xxii. 19.

[5] Most of the soldiers quartered in Syria were recruited in the province: but the Cohort, to which Cornelius belonged, probably consisted of Italian volunteers. The ' *Italian Band*' (Acts x. 1) will come under our notice in Chap. IV., and the '*Augustan Band*' (Ibid. xxvii. 1) in Chap. XXII.

[6] John xix. 15.

[7] Acts xxv. 11.

[8] He obtained under Caligula, first, the tetrarchy of his uncle Philip, who died; and then that of his uncle Antipas, who followed his brother Archelaus into banishment.

emperor. Judæa was added to his dominion, which now embraced the whole circle of the territory ruled by his grandfather. By this time St. Paul was actively pursuing his apostolic career. We need not, therefore, advance beyond this point, in a chapter which is only intended to be a general introduction to the Apostle's history.

Our desire has been to give a picture of the condition of the world at this particular epoch ; and we have thought that no grouping would be so successful as that which should consist of Jews, Greeks, and Romans. Nor is this an artificial or unnatural arrangement, for these three nations were the divisions of the civilised world. And in the view of a religious mind they were more than this. They were 'the three peoples of God's election ; two for things temporal, and one for things eternal. Yet even in the things eternal they were allowed to minister. Greek cultivation and Roman polity prepared men for Christianity.'[1] These three peoples stand in the closest relation to the whole human race. The Christian, when he imagines himself among those spectators who stood round the cross, and gazes in spirit upon that 'superscription,' which the Jewish scribe, the Greek proselyte, and the Roman soldier could read, each in his own tongue, feels that he is among those who are the representatives of all humanity.[2] In the ages which precede the crucifixion, these three languages were like threads which guided us through the labyrinth of history. And they are still among the best guides of our thought, as we travel through the ages which succeed it. How great has been the honour of the Greek and Latin tongues ! They followed the fortunes of a triumphant church. Instead of Heathen languages, they gradually became Christian. As before they had been employed to express the best thoughts of unassisted humanity, so afterwards they became the exponents of Christian doctrine and the channels of Christian devotion. The words of Plato and Cicero fell from the lips and pen of Chrysostom and Augustine. And still those two languages are associated together in the work of Christian education, and made the instruments for training the minds of the young in the greatest nations of the earth. And how deep and pathetic is the interest which attaches to the Hebrew ! Here the thread seems to be broken. 'Jesus, King of the Jews,' in Hebrew characters. It is like the last word of the Jewish Scriptures,—the last warning of the chosen people. A cloud henceforth is upon the people and the language of Israel. 'Blindness in part is happened unto Israel, till the fulness of the Gentiles be come in.' Once again Jesus, after

---

[1] Dr. Arnold, in the journal of his Tour in 1840 (*Life*, ii. 413, 2nd edit.). The passage continues thus :—' As Mahometanism can bear witness; for the East, when it abandoned Greece and Rome, could only reproduce Judaism. Mahometanism, six hundred years after Christ, proving that the Eastern man could bear nothing perfect, justifies the wisdom of God in Judaism.

[2] This is true in another, and perhaps a higher sense. The *Roman*, powerful but not happy—the *Greek*, distracted with the inquiries of an unsatisfying philosophy—the *Jew*, bound hand and foot with the chain of a ceremonial law, all are together round the cross. Christ is crucified in the midst of them—crucified for all. The 'superscription' of His accusation' speaks to all the same language of peace, pardon, and love.

His ascension, spake openly from Heaven 'in the Hebrew tongue' (Acts xxvi. 14): but the words were addressed to that Apostle who was called to preach the Gospel to the philosophers of Greece, and in the emperor's palace at Rome.[1]

[1] See inscription in the three languages on a Christian tomb in the Roman Catacombs, at the end of the work.

Coin of Tarsus.   Hadrian.   (See p. 18, n. 2.)

CHAPTER II.

Jewish Origin of the Church.—Sects and Parties of the Jews.—Pharisees and Sadducees.—St. Paul a Pharisee.—Hellenists and Aramæans.—St. Paul's Family Hellenistic but not Hellenising.—His Infancy at Tarsus.—The Tribe of Benjamin. — His Father's Citizenship. — Scenery of the Place. — His Childhood.—He is sent to Jerusalem.—State of Judæa and Jerusalem.—Rabbinical Schools.—Gamaliel.—Mode of Teaching.—Synagogues.—Student-Life of St. Paul.—His early Manhood.—First Aspect of the Church.—St. Stephen.—The Sanhedrin.—St. Stephen the Forerunner of St. Paul.—His Martyrdom and Prayer.

CHRISTIANITY has been represented by some of the modern Jews as a mere school of Judaism. Instead of opposing it as a system antagonistic and subversive of the Mosaic religion, they speak of it as a phase or development of that religion itself,—as simply one of the rich outgrowths from the fertile Jewish soil. They point out the causes which combined in the first century to produce this Christian development of Judaism. It has even been hinted that Christianity has done a good work in preparing the world for receiving the pure Mosaic principles which will, at length, be universal.[1]

We are not unwilling to accept some of these phrases as expressing a great and important truth. Christianity *is* a school of Judaism : but it is the school which absorbs and interprets the teaching of all others. It *is* a development; but it is that development which was divinely foreknown and predetermined. It is the grain of which mere Judaism is now the worthless husk. It is the image of Truth in its full proportions ; and the Jewish remnants are now as the shapeless fragments which remain of the block of marble when the statue is completed. When we look back at the Apostolic age, we see that growth proceeding which separated the husk from the grain. We see the image of Truth coming out in clear expressiveness, and the useless fragments falling off like scales, under the careful work of divinely-guided hands. If we are to realise the earliest appearance of the Church, such as it was when Paul first saw it, we must view it as arising in the midst of Judaism ; and if we are to comprehend all the feelings and principles of this Apostle, we must consider first the Jewish preparation of his own younger days. To these two subjects the present chapter will be devoted.

[1] This notion, that the doctrine of Christ will be re-absorbed in that of Moses, is a curious phase of the recent Jewish philosophy. ' We are sure,' it has been well said, ' that Christianity can never disown its source in Judaism : but a more powerful spell than this philosophy is needed to charm back the stately river into the narrow, rugged, picturesque ravine, out of which centuries ago it found its way.'

We are very familiar with one division which ran through the Jewish nation in the first century. The Sadducees and Pharisees are frequently mentioned in the New Testament, and we are there informed of the tenets of these two prevailing parties. The belief in a future state may be said to have been an open question among the Jews, when our Lord appeared and 'brought life and immortality to light.' We find the Sadducees established in the highest office of the priesthood, and possessed of the greatest powers in the Sanhedrin : and yet they did not believe in any future state, nor in any spiritual existence independent of the body. The Sadducees said that there was 'no resurrection, neither Angel nor Spirit.'[1] They do not appear to have held doctrines which are commonly called licentious or immoral. On the contrary, they adhered strictly to the moral tenets of the Law, as opposed to its mere formal technicalities. They did not overload the Sacred Books with traditions, or encumber the duties of life with a multitude of minute observances. They were the disciples of reason without enthusiasm,—they made few proselytes,—their numbers were not great, and they were confined principally to the richer members of the nation.[2] The Pharisees, on the other hand, were the enthusiasts of the later Judaism. They 'compassed sea and land to make one proselyte.' Their power and influence with the mass of the people was immense. The loss of the national independence of the Jews,—the gradual extinction of their political life, directly by the Romans, and indirectly by the family of Herod,—caused their feelings to rally round their Law and their Religion, as the only centre of unity which now remained to them. Those, therefore, who gave their energies to the interpretation and exposition of the Law, not curtailing any of the doctrines which were virtually contained in it and which had been revealed with more or less clearness, but rather accumulating articles of faith, and multiplying the requirements of devotion;—who themselves practised a severe and ostentatious religion, being liberal in almsgiving, fasting frequently, making long prayers, and carrying casuistical distinctions into the smallest details of conduct;—who consecrated, moreover, their best zeal and exertions to the spread of the fame of Judaism, and to the increase of the nation's power in the only way which now was practicable,—could not fail to command the reverence of great numbers of the people. It was no longer possible to fortify Jerusalem against the Heathen : but the Law could be fortified like an impregnable city. The place of the brave is on the walls and in the front of the battle : and the hopes of the nation rested on those who defended the sacred outworks, and made successful inroads on the territories of the Gentiles.

Such were the Pharisees. And now, before proceeding to other features of Judaism and their relation to the Church, we can hardly help glancing at St. Paul. He was 'a Pharisee, the son of a Pharisee,'[3] and he was educated by Gamaliel,[4] 'a Pharisee.'[5]

---

[1] Acts xxiii. 8. See Matt. xxii. 23–34.
[2] See what Josephus says of the Sadducees : *Ant.* xiii. 10, 6 ; xviii. 1, 4, comparing the question asked, John vii. 48.
[3] Acts xxiii. 6.
[4] Acts xxii. 3.
[5] Acts v. 34.

Both his father and his teacher belonged to this sect. And on three distinct occasions he tells us that he himself was a member of it. Once when at his trial, before a mixed assembly of Pharisees and Sadducees, the words just quoted were spoken, and his connection with the Pharisees asserted with such effect, that the feelings of this popular party were immediately enlisted on his side. 'And when he had so said, there arose a dissension between the Pharisees and the Sadducees ; and the multitude was divided. . . . And there arose a great cry ; and the Scribes that were of the Pharisees' part arose, and strove, saying, We find no evil in this man.'[1] The second time was, when, on a calmer occasion, he was pleading before Agrippa, and said to the king in the presence of Festus : 'The Jews knew me from the beginning, if they would testify, that after the most straitest sect of our religion I lived a Pharisee.'[2] And once more, when writing from Rome to the Philippians, he gives force to his argument against the Judaizers, by telling them that if any other man thought he had whereof he might trust in the flesh, he himself had more :—' circumcised the eighth day, of the stock of Israel, of the tribe of Benjamin, a Hebrew of the Hebrews ; as touching the Law, a Pharisee.'[3] And not only was he himself a Pharisee, but his father also. He was 'a Pharisee, the son of a Pharisee.' This short sentence sums up nearly all we know of St. Paul's parents. If we think of his earliest life, we are to conceive of him as born in a Pharisaic family, and as brought up from his infancy in the 'straitest sect of the Jews' religion.' His childhood was nurtured in the strictest belief. The stories of the Old Testament,—the angelic appearances,—the prophetic visions,—to him were literally true. They needed no Sadducean explanation. The world of spirits was a reality to him. The resurrection of the dead was an article of his faith. And to exhort him to the practices of religion, he had before him the example of his father, praying and walking with broad phylacteries, scrupulous and exact in his legal observances. He had, moreover, as it seems, the memory and tradition of ancestral piety ; for he tells us in one of his latest letters,[4] that he served God 'from his forefathers.' All influences combined to make him 'more exceedingly zealous of the traditions of his fathers,'[5] and 'touching the righteousness which is in the Law, blameless.'[6] Everything tended to prepare him to be an eminent member of that theological party, to which so many of the Jews were looking for the preservation of their national life, and the extension of their national creed.

But in this mention of the Pharisees and Sadducees, we are far from exhausting the subject of Jewish divisions, and far from enumerating all those phases of opinion which must have had some connection with the growth of rising Christianity, and all those elements which may have contributed to form the character of the Apostle of the Heathen. There was a sect in Judæa which is not mentioned in the Scriptures, but which must have acquired considerable influence in the time of the Apostles, as may be inferred

---

[1] Acts xxiii.   [2] Acts xxvi.   [3] Phil. iii. 4.
[4] 2 Tim. i. 3.   [5] Gal. i. 14.   [6] Phil. iii. 6.

from the space devoted to it by Josephus [1] and Philo. These were the *Essenes*, who retired from the theological and political distractions of Jerusalem and the larger towns, and founded peaceful communities in the desert or in villages, where their life was spent in contemplation, and in the practices of ascetic piety. It has been suggested that John the Baptist was one of them. There is no proof that this was the case; but we need not doubt that they did represent religious cravings which Christianity satisfied. Another party was that of the *Zealots*,[2] who were as politically fanatical as the Essenes were religiously contemplative, and whose zeal was kindled with the burning desire to throw off the Roman yoke from the neck of Israel. Very different from them were the *Herodians*, twice mentioned in the Gospels,[3] who held that the hopes of Judaism rested on the Herods, and who almost looked to that family for the fulfilment of the prophecies of the Messiah. And if we were simply enumerating the divisions and describing the sects of the Jews, it would be necessary to mention the *Therapeutæ*,[4] a widely-spread community in Egypt, who lived even in greater seclusion than the Essenes in Judæa. The *Samaritans* also would require our attention. But we must turn from these sects and parties to a wider division, which arose from the dispersion of the Hebrew people, to which some space has been devoted in the preceding chapter.

We have seen that early colonies of the Jews were settled in Babylonia and Mesopotamia. Their connection with their brethren in Judæa was continually maintained; and they were bound to them by the link of a common language. The Jews of Palestine and Syria, with those who lived on the Tigris and Euphrates, interpreted the Scriptures through the Targums [5] or Chaldee paraphrases, and spoke kindred dialects of the language of Aram; [6] and hence they were called *Aramæan* Jews. We have also had occasion to notice that other dispersion of the nation through those countries where Greek was spoken. Their settlements began with Alexander's conquests, and were continued under the successors of those who partitioned his empire. Alexandria was their capital. They used the Septuagint translation of the Bible; [7] and they were commonly called *Hellenists*, or Jews of the Grecian speech.

The mere difference of language would account in some degree

---

[1] *War*, ii. 8.

[2] We have the *word* in the 'Simon Zelotes' of the Gospel (Luke vi. 15) though the *party* was hardly then matured.

[3] Mark iii. 6; Matt. xxii. 16: see Mark xii. 13.

[4] Described in great detail by Philo.

[5] It is uncertain when the written Targums came into use, but the practice of paraphrasing orally in Chaldee must have begun soon after the Captivity.

[6] Aram — the 'Highlands' of the Semitic tribes—comprehended the tract of country which extended from Taurus and Lebanon to Mesopotamia and Arabia. There were two main dialects of

the Aramæan stock, the eastern or Babylonian, commonly called *Chaldee* (the 'Syrian tongue' of 2 Kings xviii. 26; Isai. xxxvi. 11; Ezra iv. 7; Dan. ii. 4); and the western, which is the parent of the *Syriac*, now, like the former, almost a dead language. The first of these dialects began to supplant the older *Hebrew* of Judæa from the time of the captivity, and was the 'Hebrew' of the New Testament, Luke xxiii. 38; John xix. 20; Acts xxi. 40, xxii. 2, xxvi. 14. *Arabic*, the most perfect of the Semitic languages, has now generally overspread those regions.

[7] See p. 31, n. 2.

for the mutual dislike with which we know that these two sections
of the Jewish race regarded one another. We were all aware how
closely the use of a hereditary dialect is bound up with the warmest
feelings of the heart. And in this case the Aramæan language was
the sacred tongue of Palestine. It is true that the tradition of the
language of the Jews had been broken, as the continuity of their
political life had been rudely interrupted. The Hebrew of the time
of Christ was not the oldest Hebrew of the Israelites ; but it was a
kindred dialect; and old enough to command a reverent affection.
Though not the language of Moses and David, it was that of Ezra
and Nehemiah. And it is not unnatural that the Aramæans should
have revolted from the speech of the Greek idolaters and the tyrant
Antiochus,[1]—a speech which they associated moreover with innovating doctrines and dangerous speculations.

For the division went deeper than a mere superficial diversity of
speech. It was not only a division, like the modern one of German
and Spanish Jews, where those who hold substantially the same
doctrines have accidentally been led to speak different languages.
But there was a diversity of religious views and opinions. This is
not the place for examining that system of mystic interpretation
called the Cabbala,[2] and for determining how far its origin might be
due to Alexandria or to Babylon. It is enough to say, generally,
that in the Aramæan theology, Oriental elements prevailed rather
than Greek, and that the subject of Babylonian influences has more
connection with the life of St. Peter than that of St. Paul. The
Hellenists, on the other hand, or Jews who spoke Greek, who lived
in Greek countries, and were influenced by Greek civilisation, are
associated in the closest manner with the Apostle of the Gentiles.
They are more than once mentioned in the Acts, where our English
translation names them 'Grecians,' to distinguish them from the
Heathen or proselyte 'Greeks.'[3] Alexandria was the metropolis
of their theology. Philo was their great representative. He was
an old man when St. Paul was in his maturity : his writings were
probably known to the Apostles ; and they have descended with the
inspired Epistles to our own day. The work of the learned Hellenists may be briefly described as this,—to accommodate Jewish
doctrines to the mind of the Greeks, and to make the Greek
language express the mind of the Jews. The Hebrew principles
were 'disengaged as much as possible from local and national
conditions, and presented in a form adapted to the Hellenic world.'
All this was hateful to the zealous Aramæans. The men of the
East rose up against those of the West. The Greek learning was
not more repugnant to the Roman Cato, than it was to the strict
Hebrews. They had a saying, 'Cursed be he who teacheth his son
the learning of the Greeks.'[4] We could imagine them using the

---

[1] See pp. 21, 22, and notes.
[2] See Ch. XIII.
[3] See Chap. I. p. 9, note 3.
[4] This repugnance is illustrated by
many passages in the Talmudic writings. Rabbi Levi Ben Chajathah,
going down to Cæsarea, heard them

reciting their phylacteries in Greek,
and would have forbidden them ; which
when Rabbi Jose heard, he was very
angry, and said, 'If a man doth not
know how to recite in the holy tongue,
must he not recite them at all ? Let
him perform his duty in what lan-

words of the prophet Joel (iii. 6), 'The children of Judah and the children of Jerusalem have ye sold unto the Grecians, that ye might remove them from their border :' and we cannot be surprised that, even in the deep peace and charity of the Church's earliest days, this inveterate division re-appeared, and that, 'when the number of the disciples was multiplied, there arose a murmuring of the Grecians against the Hebrews.'[1]

It would be an interesting subject of inquiry to ascertain in what proportions these two parties were distributed in the different countries where the Jews were dispersed, in what places they came into the strongest collision, and how far they were fused and united together. In the city of Alexandria, the emporium of Greek commerce from the time of its foundation, where, since the earliest Ptolemies, literature, philosophy, and criticism had never ceased to excite the utmost intellectual activity, where the Septuagint translation of the Scripture had been made,[2] and where a Jewish temple and ceremonial worship had been established in rivalry to that in Jerusalem,[3]—there is no doubt that the Hellenistic element largely prevailed. But although (strictly speaking) the Alexandrian Jews were nearly all Hellenites, it does not follow that they were all Hellenizers. In other words, although their speech and their Scriptures were Greek, the theological views of many among them undoubtedly remained Hebrew. There must have been many who were attached to the traditions of Palestine, and who looked suspiciously on their more speculative brethren : and we have no difficulty in recognising the picture presented in a pleasing German fiction,[4] which describes the debates and struggles of the two tendencies in this city, to be very correct. In Palestine itself, we have every reason to believe that the native population was entirely Aramæan, though there was no lack of Hellenistic synagogues [5] in Jerusalem, which at the seasons of the festivals would be crowded with foreign pilgrims, and become the scene of animated discussions. Syria was connected by the link of language with Palestine and Babylonia ; but Antioch, its metropolis, commercially and politically, resembled Alexandria : and it is probable that, when Barnabas and Saul were establishing the great Christian community in that city,[6]

guage he can.' The following saying is attributed to Rabban Simeon, the son of Gamaliel : ' There were a thousand boys in my father's school, of whom five hundred learned the law, and five hundred the wisdom of the Greeks ; and there is not one of the latter now alive, excepting myself here, and my uncle's son in Asia.' We learn also from Josephus that a knowledge of Greek was lightly regarded by the Jews of Palestine.

[1] Acts vi. 1.

[2] It is useless here to enter into any of the legends connected with the number 'seventy.' This translation came into existence from 300 to 150 B.C. Its theological importance cannot be exaggerated. The quotations in the N. T. from the O. T. are generally made from it. See p. 33.

[3] This temple was not in the city of Alexandria, but at Leontopolis. It was built (or rather it was an old Heathen temple repaired) by Onias, from whose family the high-priesthood had been transferred to the family of the Maccabees, and who had fled into Egypt in the time of Ptolemy Philopator. It remained in existence till destroyed by Vespasian. See Josephus, *War*, i. 1, 1, vii. 10, 3; *Ant.* xiii. 3.

[4] Helon's *Pilgrimage to Jerusalem*, published in German in 1820, translated into English in 1824.

[5] See Acts vi. 9.

[6] Acts xi. 25, &c.

the majority of the Jews were 'Grecians' rather than 'Hebrews.' In Asia Minor we should at first sight be tempted to imagine that the Grecian tendency would predominate : but when we find that Antiochus brought Babylonian Jews into Lydia and Phrygia, we must not make too confident a conclusion in this direction ; and we have grounds for imagining that many Israelitish families in the remote districts (possibly that of Timotheus at Lystra)[1] may have cherished the forms of the traditionary faith of the Eastern Jews, and lived uninfluenced by Hellenistic novelties. The residents in maritime and commercial towns would not be strangers to the Western developments of religious doctrines : and when Apollos came from Alexandria to Ephesus,[2] he would find himself in a theological atmosphere not very different from that of his native city. Tarsus in Cilicia will naturally be included under the same class of cities of the West, by those who remember Strabo's assertion that, in literature and philosophy, its fame exceeded that of Athens and Alexandria. At the same time, we cannot be sure that the very celebrity of its Heathen schools might not induce the families of Jewish residents to retire all the more strictly into a religious Hebrew seclusion.

That such a seclusion of their family from Gentile influences was maintained by the parents of St. Paul, is highly probable. We have no means of knowing how long they themselves, or their ancestors, had been Jews of the dispersion. A tradition is mentioned by Jerome that they came originally from Giscala, a town in Galilee, when it was stormed by the Romans. The story involves an anachronism, and contradicts the Acts of the Apostles.[3] Yet it need not be entirely disregarded ; especially when we find St. Paul speaking of himself as 'a Hebrew of the Hebrews,'[4] and when we remember that the word 'Hebrew' is used for an Aramaic Jew, as opposed to a 'Grecian' or 'Hellenist.'[5] Nor is it unlikely in itself that before they settled in Tarsus, the family had belonged to the Eastern dispersion, or to the Jews of Palestine. But, however this may be, St. Paul himself must be called a Hellenist ; because the language of his infancy was that idiom of the Grecian Jews in which all his letters were written. Though, in conformity with the strong feeling of the Jews of all times, he might learn his earliest sentences from the Scripture in Hebrew, yet he was familiar

---

[1] Acts xvi. 1 ; 2 Tim. i. 5, iii. 15.

[2] Acts xviii. 24.

[3] Acts xxii. 3.

[4] Phil. iii. 5. Cave sees nothing more in this phrase than that 'his parents were Jews, and that of the ancient stock, not entering in by the gate of proselytism, but originally descended from the nation.— *Life of St. Paul*, i. 2. Benson, on the other hand, argues, from this passage and from 2 Cor. xi. 22, that there was a difference between a 'Hebrew' and an 'Israelite.'—'A person might be descended from Israel, and yet not be a Hebrew but a Hellenist... St. Paul appeareth to me to have plainly intimated, that a man might be of the stock of Israel and of the tribe of Benjamin, and yet not be a Hebrew of the Hebrews ; but that, as to himself, he was, both by father and mother, a Hebrew ; or of the race of that sort of Jews which were generally most esteemed by their nation.'—*History of the First Planting of the Christian Religion*, vol. i. p. 117.

[5] Acts vi. 1. For the absurd Ebionite story that St. Paul was by birth not a Jew at all, but a Greek, see the next Chapter.

with the Septuagint translation at an early age. For it is observed that, when he quotes from the Old Testament, his quotations are from that version; and that, not only when he cites its very words, but when (as is often the case) he quotes it from memory.[1] Considering the accurate knowledge of the original Hebrew which he must have acquired under Gamaliel at Jerusalem, it has been inferred that this can only arise from his having been thoroughly imbued at an earlier period with the Hellenistic Scriptures. The readiness, too, with which he expressed himself in Greek, even before such an audience as that upon the Areopagus at Athens, shows a command of the language which a Jew would not, in all probability, have attained, had not Greek been the familiar speech of his childhood.[2]

But still the vernacular Hebrew of Palestine would not have been a foreign tongue to the infant Saul; on the contrary, he may have heard it spoken almost as often as the Greek. For no doubt his parents, proud of their Jewish origin, and living comparatively near to Palestine, would retain the power of conversing with their friends from thence in the ancient speech. Mercantile connections from the Syrian coast would be frequently arriving, whose discourse would be in Aramaic; and in all probability there were kinsfolk still settled in Judæa, as we afterwards find the nephew of St. Paul in Jerusalem.[3] We may compare the situation of such a family (so far as concerns their language) to that of the French Huguenots who settled in London after the revocation of the Edict of Nantes. These French families, though they soon learned to use the English as the medium of their common intercourse and the language of their household, yet, for several generations, spoke French with equal familiarity and greater affection.[4]

Moreover, it may be considered as certain that the family of St. Paul, though Hellenistic in speech, were no *Hellenizers* in theology; they were not at all inclined to adopt Greek habits or Greek opinions. The manner in which St. Paul speaks of himself, his father, and his ancestors, implies the most uncontaminated

[1] See Tholuck's *Essay on the early life of St. Paul*, Eng. Trans. p. 9. Out of eighty-eight quotations from the Old Testament, Koppe gives grounds for thinking that forty-nine were cited from memory. And Bleek thinks that every one of his citations without exception is from memory. He adds, however, that the Apostle's memory reverts occasionally to the Hebrew text, as well as to that of the Septuagint. See an article in the Christian Remembrancer for April, 1848, on Grinfield's *Hellenistic Ed. of the N. T.*

[2] We must not, however, press these considerations too far, especially when we take Phil. iii. 5 into consideration. Dr. Schaff presents the subject under a different view, as follows: 'Certain it is that the groundwork of Paul's intellectual and moral training was Jewish:

yet he had at least some knowledge of Greek literature, whether he acquired it in Tarsus, or in Jerusalem under Gamaliel, who himself was not altogether averse to the Hellenistic philosophy, or afterwards in his missionary journeyings and his continual intercourse with Hellenists.'—*Hist. of the Christian Church.*

[3] Acts xxiii. 16.

[4] St. Paul's ready use of the spoken Aramaic appears in his speech upon the stairs of the Castle of Antonia at Jerusalem, 'in the Hebrew tongue.' This familiarity, however, he would necessarily have acquired during his student-life at Jerusalem, if he had not possessed it before. The difficult question of the 'Gift of Tongues' will be discussed in Chap. XIII.

hereditary Judaism. 'Are they Hebrews? so am I. Are they Israelites? so am I.   Are they the seed of Abraham? so am I.'[1]—'A
Pharisee' and 'the son of a Pharisee.'[2]—'Circumcised the eighth
day, of the stock of Israel, of the tribe of Benjamin, *a Hebrew of
the Hebrews.*'[3]

There is therefore little doubt that, though the native of a city
filled with a Greek population and incorporated with the Roman
Empire, yet Saul was born and spent his earliest days in the shelter
of a home which was Hebrew, not in name only but in spirit.   The
Roman power did not press upon his infancy : the Greek ideas did
not haunt his childhood : but he grew up an Israelitish boy, nurtured
in those histories of the chosen people which he was destined so often
to repeat in the synagogues,[4] with the new and wonderful commentary supplied by the life and resurrection of a crucified Messiah.
'From a child he knew the Scriptures,' which ultimately made him
'wise unto salvation through faith which is 'in Christ Jesus,' as he
says of Timothy in the second Epistle (iii. 15).   And the groups
around his childhood were such as that which he beautifully describes in another part of the same letter to that disciple, where he
speaks of 'his grandmother Lois, and his mother Eunice.' (i. 5.)

We should be glad to know something of the mother of St. Paul.
But though he alludes to his father, he does not mention her.   He
speaks of himself as set apart by God 'from his mother's womb,'
that the Son of God should in due time be revealed in him, and by
him preached to the Heathen.[5]   But this is all.   We find notices of
his sister and his sister's son,[6] and of some more distant relatives :[7]
but we know nothing of her who was nearer to him than all of them.
He tells us of his instructor Gamaliel ; but of her, who, if she lived,
was his earliest and best teacher, he tells us nothing.   Did she die
like Rachel, the mother of Benjamin, the great ancestor of his tribe ;
leaving his father to mourn and set a monument on her grave, like
Jacob, by the way of Bethlehem?[8]   Or did she live to grieve over
her son's apostasy from the faith of the Pharisees, and die herself
unreconciled to the obedience of Christ?   Or did she believe and
obey the Saviour of her son?   These are questions which we cannot
answer.   If we wish to realise the earliest infancy of the Apostle,
we must be content with a simple picture of a Jewish mother and
her child.   Such a picture is presented to us in the short history of
Elizabeth and John the Baptist, and what is wanting in one of the
inspired Books of St. Luke may be supplied, in some degree, by the
other.

The same feelings which welcomed the birth and celebrated the
naming of a son in the 'hill country' of Judæa,[9] prevailed also
among the Jews of the dispersion.   As the 'neighbours and cousins'
of Elizabeth 'heard how the Lord had showed great mercy upon her,
and rejoiced with her,'—so it would be in the household at Tarsus,
when Saul was born.   In a nation to which the birth of a Messiah

[1] 2 Cor. xi. 22.   [5] Gal. i. 15.
[2] Acts xxiii. 6.   [6] Acts xxiii. 16.
[3] Phil. iii. 5.   [7] Rom. xvi. 7, 11, 21.
[4] Acts xiii. 16–41 ; see xvii. 2, 3, 10,   [8] Gen. xxxv. 16–20, xlviii. 7.
11, xxviii. 23.   [9] Luke i. 39.

was promised, and at a period when the aspirations after the fulfilment of the promise were continually becoming more conscious and
more urgent, the birth of a son was the fulfilment of a mother's
highest happiness : and to the father also (if we may thus invert the
words of Jeremiah) 'blessed was the man who brought tidings,
saying, A man child is born unto thee ; making him glad.'[1]   On
the eighth day the child was circumcised and named.   In the case
of John the Baptist, 'they sought to call him Zacharias, after the
name of his father.   But his mother answered, and said, Not so ;
but he shall be called John.'   And when the appeal was made to
his father, he signified his assent, in obedience to the vision.   It
was not unusual, on the one hand, to call a Jewish child after the
name of his father ; and, on the other hand, it was a common
practice, in all ages of Jewish history, even without a prophetic
intimation, to adopt a name expressive of religious feelings.   When
the infant at Tarsus received the name of Saul, it might be 'after
the name of his father ;' and it was a name of traditional celebrity
in the tribe of Benjamin, for it was that of the first king anointed
by Samuel.[2]   Or, when his father said 'his name is Saul,' it may
have been intended to denote (in conformity with the Hebrew derivation of the word) that he was a son who had long been desired,
the first born of his parents, the child of prayer, who was thenceforth, like Samuel, to be consecrated to God.[3]   'For this child I
prayed,' said the wife of Elkanah ; 'and the Lord hath given me
my petition which I asked of Him : therefore also I have lent him
to the Lord ; as long as he liveth he shall be lent unto the Lord.'[4]

Admitted into covenant with God by circumcision, the Jewish
child had thenceforward a full claim to all the privileges of the chosen
people.   His was the benediction of the 128th Psalm :—'The Lord
shall bless thee out of Zion : thou shalt see the good of Jerusalem
all the days of thy life.'   From that time, whoever it might be
who watched over Saul's infancy, whether, like king Lemuel,[5] he
learnt 'the prophecy that his mother taught him,' or whether he
was under the care of others, like those who were with the sons of
king David and king Ahab [6]—we are at no loss to learn what the
first ideas were, with which his early thought was made familiar.
The rules respecting the diligent education of children, which were
laid down by Moses in the 6th and 11th chapters of Deuteronomy,
were doubtless carefully observed : and he was trained in that
peculiarly *historical* instruction, spoken of in the 78th Psalm, which
implies the continuance of a chosen people, with glorious recollections
of the past, and great anticipations for the future : 'The Lord made
a covenant with Jacob, and gave Israel a law, which He commanded
our forefathers to teach their children ; that their posterity might

---

[1] Jer. xx. 15.

[2] 'A name frequent and common in
the tribe of Benjamin ever since the
first King of Israel, who was of that
name, was chosen out of that tribe ;
in memory whereof they were wont to
give their children this name at their
circumcision.' — Cave, i. 3 ; but he

gives no proof.

[3] This is suggested by Neander.

[4] 1 Sam. i. 27, 28.

[5] Prov. xxxi. 1.   Cf. Susanna, 3.
2 Tim. iii. 15, with 1 Tim. i. 5.

[6] 1 Chron. xxvii. 32 ; 2 Kings x. 1,
5.   Cf. Joseph. *Life,* 76 ; *Ant.* xvi.
8, 3.

know it, and the children which were yet unborn; to the intent
that when they came up, they might show their children the same:
that they might put their trust in God, and not to forget the works
of the Lord, but to keep his commandments' (ver. 5-7). The
histories of Abraham and Isaac, of Jacob and his twelve sons, of
Moses among the bulrushes, of Joshua and Samuel, Elijah, Daniel,
and the Maccabees, were the stories of his childhood. The destruction of Pharaoh in the Red Sea, the thunders of Mount Sinai, the
dreary journeys in the wilderness, the land that flowed with milk and
honey,—this was the earliest imagery presented to his opening
mind. The triumphant hymns of Zion, the lamentations by the
waters of Babylon, the prophetic praises of the Messiah, were the
songs around his cradle.

Above all, he would be familiar with the destinies of his own
illustrious tribe.[1] The life of the timid Patriarch, the father of the
twelve ; the sad death of Rachel near the city where the Messiah
was to be born ; the loneliness of Jacob, who sought to comfort
himself in Benoni 'the son of her sorrow,' by calling him Benjamin[2]
'the son of his right hand ;' and then the youthful days of this
youngest of the twelve brethren, the famine, and the journeys into
Egypt, the severity of Joseph, and the wonderful story of the silver
cup in the mouth of the sack ;—these are the narratives to which he
listened with intense and eager interest. How little was it imagined
that, as Benjamin was the youngest and most honoured of the Patriarchs, so this listening child of Benjamin should be associated with
the twelve servants of the Messiah of God, the last and most illustrious of the Apostles ! But many years of ignorance were yet to
pass away, before that mysterious Providence, which brought Benjamin to Joseph in Egypt, should bring his descendant to the knowledge and love of Jesus, the Son of Mary. Some of the early
Christian writers[3] see in the dying benediction of Jacob, when he said
that 'Benjamin should ravin as a wolf, in the morning devour the
prey, and at night divide the spoil,' a prophetic intimation of him
who, in the morning of his life, should tear the sheep of God, and
in its evening feed them, as the teacher of the nations.[4] When St.
Paul was a child and learnt the words of this saying, no Christian
thoughts were associated with it, or with that other more peaceful
prophecy of Moses, when he said of Benjamin, 'The beloved of
the Lord shall dwell in safety by Him : and the Lord shall cover him
all the day long, and he shall dwell between His shoulders.'[5] But

---

[1] It may be thought that here, and
below, p. 45, too much prominence has
been given to the attachment of a Jew
in the Apostolic age to his own particular tribe. It is difficult to ascertain
how far the tribe-feeling of early times
lingered on in combination with the
national feeling, which grew up after
the Captivity. But when we consider
the care with which the genealogies
were kept, and when we find the tribe
of Barnabas specified (Acts iv. 36),
and also of Anna the prophetess (Luke
ii. 36), and when we find St. Paul

alluding in a pointed manner to his
tribe (see Rom. xi. 1, Phil. iii. 5, and
compare Acts xiii. 21, and also xxvi.
7), it does not seem unnatural to believe that pious families of so famous
a stock as that of Benjamin should
retain the hereditary enthusiasm of
their sacred clanship. See, moreover,
Matt. xix. 28; Rev. v. 5, vii. 4-8.

[2] Gen. xxxv. 18.
[3] Gen. xlix. 27.
[4] e.g. Tertullian.
[5] Deut. xxxiii. 12.

he was familiar with the prophetical words, and could follow in imagination the fortunes of the sons of Benjamin, and knew how they went through the wilderness with Rachel's other children, the tribes of Ephraim and Manasseh, forming with them the third of the four companies on the march, and reposing with them at night on the west of the encampment.[1] He heard how their lands were assigned to them in the promised country along the borders of Judah:[2] and how Saul, whose name he bore, was chosen from the tribe which was the smallest,[3] when 'little Benjamin'[4] became the 'ruler' of Israel. He knew that when the ten tribes revolted, Benjamin was faithful:[5] and he learnt to follow its honourable history even into the dismal years of the Babylonian Captivity, when Mordecai, 'a Benjamite who had been carried away,'[6] saved the nation: and when, instead of destruction, 'the Jews,' through him, 'had light, and gladness, and joy, and honour : and in every province, and in every city, whithersoever the king's commandment and his decree came, the Jews had joy and gladness, a feast and a good day. And many of the people of the land became Jews ; for the fear of the Jews fell upon them.'[7]

Such were the influences which cradled the infancy of St. Paul ; and such was the early teaching under which his mind gradually rose to the realisation of his position as a Hebrew child in a city of Gentiles. Of the exact period of his birth we possess no authentic information.[8] From a passage in a sermon attributed to St. Chrysostom, it has been inferred[9] that he was born in the year 2 B.C. of our era. The date is not improbable ; but the genuineness of the sermon is suspected ; and if it was the undoubted work of the eloquent Father, we have no reason to believe that he possessed any certain means of ascertaining the fact. Nor need we be anxious to possess the information. We have a better chronology than that which reckons by years and months. We know that St. Paul was a young man at the time of St. Stephen's martyrdom,[10] and therefore we know what were the features of the period, and what the circumstances of the world, at the beginning of his eventful life. He must have been born in the later years of Herod, or the earlier of his son Archelaus. It was the strongest and most flourishing time of the reign of Augustus. The world was at peace ; the pirates of the Levant were dispersed ; and Cilicia was lying at rest, or in stupor, with other provinces, under the wide shadow of the Roman power. Many governors had ruled there since the days of Cicero. Athenodorus, the emperor's tutor, had been one of them. It was about the time when Horace and Mæcenas died, with others whose names will never be forgotten; and it was about the time when Caligula was born, with others who were destined to make the world miserable. Thus is the epoch fixed in the manner in which

---

[1] Numb. ii. 18–24 ; x. 22–24.
[2] Josh. xviii. 11.
[3] 1 Sam. ix. 21.
[4] Ps. lxviii. 27.
[5] 2 Chron. xi. : see 1 Kings xii.
[6] Esther ii. 5, 6.
[7] Esther viii. 16, 17.
[8] As regards the chronology of St.

Paul's life, it is enough to refer to Ch. IV. and especially to the appendix at the end of the work
[9] This is on the supposition that he died A.D. 66, at the age of 68.
[10] Acts vii. 58. It must be remembered, however, that the term νεανίας was applied to all men under 40.

the imagination most easily apprehends it. During this pause in the world's history St. Paul was born.

It was a pause, too, in the history of the sufferings of the Jews. That lenient treatment which had been begun by Julius Cæsar was continued by Augustus ;[1] and the days of severity were not yet come, when Tiberius and Claudius drove them into banishment, and Caligula oppressed them with every mark of contumely and scorn. We have good reason to believe that at the period of the Apostle's birth the Jews were unmolested at Tarsus, where his father lived and enjoyed the rights of a Roman citizen. It is a mistake to suppose that this citizenship was a privilege which belonged to the members of the family, as being natives of this city.[2] Tarsus was not a *municipium*, nor was it a *colonia*, like Philippi in Macedonia,[3] or Antioch in Pisidia ; but it was a ' free city '[4] (*urbs libera*), like the Syrian Antioch and its neighbour-city, Seleucia on the sea. Such a city had the privilege of being governed by its own magistrates, and was exempted from the occupation of a Roman garrison, but its citizens did not necessarily possess the *civitas* of Rome. Tarsus had received great benefits both from Julius Cæsar and from Augustus, but the father of St. Paul was not on that account a Roman citizen. This privilege had been granted to him, or had descended to him, as an individual right ; he might have purchased it for a ' large sum ' of money ;[5] but it is more probable that it came to him as a reward of services rendered, during the civil wars, to some influential Roman.[6] We should not be in serious error, if we were to say, in language suggested by the narrative of St. Stephen's martyrdom (Acts vi. 9), that St. Paul's father was a *Cilician Libertinus.*[7] That Jews were not unfrequently Roman citizens, we learn from Josephus, who mentions in the ' Jewish War '[8] some even of the equestrian order who were illegally scourged and crucified by Florus at Jerusalem ; and (what is more to our present point) enumerates certain of his countrymen who possessed the Roman franchise at Ephesus, in that important series of decrees relating to the Jews, which were issued in the time of Julius Cæsar, and are preserved in the fourteenth book of the 'Antiquities.'[9] The

---

[1] Cæsar, like Alexander, treated the Jews with much consideration. Suetonius speaks in strong terms of their grief at his death. Augustus permitted the largess, when it fell on a Sabbath, to be put off till the next day.

[2] Some of the older biographers of St. Paul assume this without any hesitation : and the mistake is very frequent still. It is enough to notice that the Tribune (Acts xxi. 39, xxii. 24) knew that St. Paul was a Tarsian, without being aware that he was a citizen.

[3] Acts xvi. 12.

[4] It appears that Antony gave Tarsus the privileges of an *Urbs libera*, though it had previously taken the side of Augustus, and been named Juliopolis.   [5] Acts xxii. 28.

[6] Great numbers of Jews were made slaves in the Civil Wars, and then manumitted. A slave manumitted with due formalities became a Roman citizen. Thus it is natural to suppose that the Apostle, with other Cilician Jews, may have been, like Horace, *libertino patre natus.* (Sat. I. vi. 45.)

[7] This suggestion is due to Wieseler, who translates the verse which describes Stephen's great opponents, so as to mean ' Libertines' from ' Cyrene, Alexandria, Cilicia, and Asia.' We think, as is observed below (p. 50, note 6), that another view is more natural : but at least we should observe that we find Saul, a *Roman citizen*, actively cooperating in persecution with those who are called *Libertini.*

[8] *War*, ii. 14, 9.   [9] *Ant.* xiv. 10, 3.

family of St. Paul were in the same position at Tarsus as those who
were Jews of Asia Minor and yet citizens of Rome at Ephesus; and
thus it came to pass, that, while many of his cotemporaries were
willing to expend ' a large sum ' in the purchase of ' this freedom,'
the Apostle himself was ' free-born.'

The question of the double name of ' Saul ' and ' Paul ' will
require our attention hereafter, when we come in the course of our
narrative to that interview with Sergius Paulus in Cyprus, coinci-
dently with which the appellation in the Acts of the Apostles is
suddenly changed.   Many opinions have been held on this subject,
both by ancient and modern theologians.[1]   At present it will be
enough to say, that, though we cannot overlook the coincidence, or
believe it accidental, yet it is most probable that both names were
borne by him in his childhood, that ' Saul ' was the name of his
Hebrew home, and ' Paul ' that by which he was known among the
Gentiles.   It will be observed that ' *Paulus,*' the name by which
he is always mentioned after his departure from Cyprus, and by
which he always designates himself in his Epistles, is a Roman, not
a Greek, word.   And it will be remembered, that, among those
whom he calls his 'kinsmen' in the Epistle to the Romans, two
of the number, *Junia* and *Lucius,* have Roman names, while the
others are Greek.[2]   All this may point to a strong Roman connection.   These names may have something to do with that honourable
citizenship which was an heirloom in the household ; and the appellation ' Paulus' may be due to some such feelings as those which
induced the historian Josephus to call himself ' Flavius,' in honour
of Vespasian and the Flavian family.

If we turn now to consider the social position of the Apostle's
father and family, we cannot on the one hand confidently argue,
from the possession of the citizenship, that they were in the enjoyment of affluence and outward distinction.   The *civitas* of Rome,
though at that time it could not be purchased without heavy expense, did not depend upon any conditions of wealth, where it was
bestowed by authority.   On the other hand, it is certain that the
manual trade, which we know that St. Paul exercised, cannot be
adduced as an argument to prove that his circumstances were
narrow and mean ; still less, as some have imagined, that he lived
in absolute poverty.   It was a custom among the Jews that all boys
should learn a trade.   ' What is commanded of a father towards his
son ?' asks a Talmudic writer.   ' To circumcise him, to teach him
the law, to teach him a trade.'   Rabbi Judah saith, ' He that
teacheth not his son a trade, doth the same as if he taught him to
be a thief ;' and Rabban Gamaliel saith, ' He that hath a trade in
his hand, to what is he like ? he is like a vineyard that is fenced.'
And if, in compliance with this good and useful custom of the
Jews, the father of the young Cilician sought to make choice of a

[1] Origen says that he had both
names from the first ; that he used one
among the Jews, and the other afterwards.   Augustine, that he took the
name when he began to preach.   Chrysostom, that he received a new title,
like Peter, at his ordination in Antioch.
Bede, that he did not receive it till the
Proconsul was converted; and Jerome,
that it was meant to commemorate that
victory.

[2] Rom. xvi. 7, 11, 21.

trade, • which might fortify his son against idleness, or against adversity, none would occur to him more naturally than the profitable occupation of the making of tents, the material of which was hair-cloth, supplied by the goats of his native province, and sold in the markets of the Levant by the well-known name of *cilicium*.[1] The most reasonable conjecture is that his father's business was concerned with these markets, and that, like many of his scattered countrymen, he was actively occupied in the traffic of the Mediterranean coasts: and the remote dispersion of those relations, whom he mentions in his letter from Corinth to Rome, is favourable to this opinion.   But whatever might be the station and employment of his father or his kinsmen, whether they were elevated by wealth above, or depressed by poverty below, the average of the Jews of Asia Minor and Italy, we are disposed to believe that this family were possessed of that highest respectability which is worthy of deliberate esteem.   The words of Scripture seem to claim for them the tradition of a good and religious reputation.   The strict piety of St. Paul's ancestors has already been remarked ; some of his kinsmen embraced Christianity before the Apostle himself,[2] and the excellent discretion of his nephew will be the subject of our admiration, when we come to consider the dangerous circumstances which led to the nocturnal journey from Jerusalem to Cæsarea.[3]

But, though a cloud rests on the actual year of St. Paul's birth, and the circumstances of his father's household must be left to imagination, we have the great satisfaction of knowing the exact features of the scenery in the midst of which his childhood was spent. The plain, the mountains, the river, and the sea still remain to us. The rich harvests of corn still grow luxuriantly after the rains in spring.   The same tents of goat's hair are still seen covering the plains in the busy harvest.[4]   There is the same solitude and silence in the intolerable heat and dust of the summer.   Then, as now, the mothers and children of Tarsus went out in the cool evenings, and looked from the gardens round the city, or from their terraced roofs, upon the heights of Taurus.   The same sunset lingered on the pointed summits.   The same shadows gathered in the deep ravines. The river Cydnus has suffered some changes in the course of 1800 years.   Instead of rushing, as in the time of Xenophon, like the Rhone at Geneva, in a stream of two hundred feet broad through the city, it now flows idly past it on the east.   The Channel, which floated the ships of Antony and Cleopatra, is now filled up ; and wide unhealthy lagoons occupy the place of the ancient docks.[5]   But

---

[1] Hair-cloth of this kind is manufactured at the present day in Asia Minor, and the word is still retained in French, Spanish, and Italian.

[2] 'Salute Andronicus and Junia, my kinsmen, and my fellow-prisoners, who are of note among the Apostles, who also were in Christ before me.'—Rom. xvi. 7.

[3] Acts xxiii.

[4] 'The plain presented the appearance of an immense sheet of corn-stubble, dotted with small camps of tents : these tents are made of hair-cloth, and the peasantry reside in them at this season, while the harvest is reaping and the corn treading out.'— Beaufort's *Karamania*, p. 273.

[5] In Strabo's day there was an inconvenient 'bar' at the mouth of the Cydnus.   Here (as in the case of the Pyramus and other rivers on that coast) the land has since that time encroached on the sea.   The unhealthi-

its upper waters still flow, as formerly, cold and clear from the snows of Taurus : and its waterfalls still break over the same rocks, when the snows are melting, like the Rhine at Schaffhausen. We find a pleasure in thinking that the footsteps of the young Apostle often wandered by the side of this stream, and that his eyes often looked on these falls. We can hardly believe that he who spoke to the Lystrians of the ' rain from heaven,' and the ' fruitful seasons,' and of the ' living God who made heaven and earth and the sea,'[1] could have looked with indifference on beautiful and impressive scenery. Gamaliel was celebrated for his love of nature : and the young Jew, who was destined to be his most famous pupil, spent his early days in the close neighbourhood of much that was well adapted to foster such a taste. Or if it be thought that in attributing such feelings to him we are writing in the spirit of modern times; and if it be contended that he would be more influenced by the realities of human life than by the impressions of nature,—then let the youthful Saul be imagined on the banks of the Cydnus, where it flowed through the city in a stream less clear and fresh, where the wharves were covered with merchandise, in the midst of groups of men in various costumes, speaking various dialects. St. Basil says, that in his day Tarsus was a point of union for Syrians, Cilicians, Isaurians, and Cappadocians. To these we must add the Greek merchant, and the agent of Roman luxury. And one more must be added—the Jew, —even then the pilgrim of Commerce, trading with every nation, and blending with none. In this mixed company Saul, at an early age, might become familiar with the activities of life and the diversities of human character, and even in his childhood make some acquaintance with those various races, which in his manhood he was destined to influence.

We have seen what his infancy was ; we must now glance at his boyhood. It is usually the case that the features of a strong character display themselves early. His impetuous fiery disposition would sometimes need control. Flashes of indignation would reveal his impatience and his honesty.[2] The affectionate tenderness of his nature would not be without an object of attachment, if that sister, who was afterwards married,[3] was his playmate at Tarsus. The work of tent-making, rather an amusement than a trade, might sometimes occupy those young hands, which were marked with the toil of years when he held them to the view of the Elders at Miletus.[4] His education was conducted at home rather than at school : for, though Tarsus was celebrated for its learning, the Hebrew boy would not lightly be exposed to the influence of Gentile teaching. Or, if he went to a school, it was not a Greek school, but rather to some room connected with the synagogue,

ness of the sea-coast near the Gulf of Scanderoon is notorious, as can be testified by more than one of those who contributed drawings to the quarto edition of this book, which contains views of Tarsus and of the falls of the Cydnus.

[1] Acts xiv. 17, 15.

[2] See Acts ix. 1, 2, xxiii. 1—5 : and

compare Acts xiii. 13; xv. 38, with 2 Tim. iv. 11.

[3] Acts xxiii. 16.

[4] Acts xx. 34. ' Ye yourselves know that *these hands* have ministered to my necessities, and to them that were with me.' Compare xviii. 3; 1 Cor. iv. 12; 1 Thess. ii. 9; 2 Thess. iii. 8.

where a noisy class of Jewish children received the rudiments of instruction, seated on the ground with their teacher, after the manner of Mahomedan children in the East, who may be seen or heard at their lessons near the mosque.[1] At such a school, it may be, he learnt to read and to write, going and returning under the care of some attendant, according to that custom which he afterwards used as an illustration in the Epistle to the Galatians[2] (and perhaps he remembered his own early days while he wrote the passage) when he spoke of the Law as the Slave who conducts us to the School of Christ. His religious knowledge, as his years advanced, was obtained from hearing the Law read in the synagogue, from listening to the arguments and discussions of learned doctors, and from that habit of questioning and answering, which was permitted even to the children among the Jews. Familiar with the pathetic history of the Jewish sufferings, he would feel his heart filled with that love to his own people which breaks out in the Epistle to the Romans (ix. 4, 5)—to that people ' whose were the adoption and the glory and the covenants, and of whom, as concerning the flesh, Christ was to come '—a love not then, as it was afterwards, blended with love towards all mankind, ' to the Jew first, and also to the Gentile,'—but rather united with a bitter hatred to the Gentile children whom he saw around him. His idea of the Messiah, so far as it was distinct, would be the carnal notion of a temporal prince—a ' Christ known after the flesh '[3]—and he looked forward with the hope of a Hebrew to the restoration of ' the kingdom of Israel.'[4] He would be known at Tarsus as a child of promise, and as one likely to uphold the honour of the Law against the half-infidel teaching of the day. But the time was drawing near when his training was to become more exact and systematic. He was destined for the school of Jerusalem. The educational maxim of the Jews, at a later period, was as follows :—' At five years of age, let children begin the Scripture; at ten, the Mischna; at thirteen, let them be subjects of the Law.'[5] There is no reason to suppose that the general practice was very different before the

---

[1] This is written from the recollection of a Mahomedan school at Bildah in Algeria, where the mosques can now be entered with impunity. The children, with the teacher, were on a kind of upper story like a shelf, within the mosque. All were seated on this floor, in the way described by Maimonides below (p. 51). The children wrote on boards, and recited what they wrote; the master addressed them in rapid succession; and the confused sound of voices was unceasing. For pictures of an Egyptian and a Turkish school, see the *Bible Cyclopædia*, 1841; and the *Cyclopædia of Biblical Literature*, 1847.

[2] Gal. iii. 24, where the word inaccurately rendered ' Schoolmaster' denotes the attendant slave who accom-

panied the child to the school. A Jewish illustration of a custom well known among the Greeks and Romans is given by Buxtorf. He describes the child as taken to the preceptor under the skirt of a Rabbi's cloak, and as provided with honey and honey-cakes, symbolising such passages as Deut. xxxii. 13, Cant. iv. 11, Ps. xix. 10.

[3] 2 Cor. v. 16.

[4] Acts i. 6.

[5] We learn from Buxtorf that at 13 there was a ceremony something like Christian confirmation. The boy was then called a ' Child of the Law;' and the father declared in the presence of the Jews that his son fully understood the Law, and was fully responsible for his sins.

floating maxims of the great doctors were brought together in the Mischna. It may therefore be concluded, with a strong degree of probability, that Saul was sent to the Holy City[1] between the ages of ten and thirteen. Had it been later than the age of thirteen, he could hardly have said that he had been ' brought up ' in Jerusalem.

The first time anyone leaves the land of his birth to visit a foreign and distant country, is an important epoch in his life. In the case of one who has taken this first journey at an early age, and whose character is enthusiastic and susceptible of lively impressions from without, this epoch is usually remembered with peculiar distinctness. But when the country which is thus visited has furnished the imagery for the dreams of childhood, and is felt to be more truly the young traveller's home than the land he is leaving, then the journey assumes the sacred character of a pilgrimage. The nearest parallel which can be found to the visits of the scattered Jews to Jerusalem, is in the periodical expedition of the Mahomedan pilgrims to the sanctuary at Mecca. Nor is there anything which ought to shock the mind in such a comparison ; for that localising spirit was the same thing to the Jews under the highest sanction, which it is to the Mahomedans through the memory of a prophet who was the enemy and not the forerunner of Christ. As the disciples of Islam may be seen, at stated seasons, flocking towards Cairo or Damascus, the meeting-places of the African and Asiatic caravans,—so Saul had often seen the Hebrew pilgrims from the interior of Asia Minor come down through the passes of the mountains, and join others at Tarsus who were bound for Jerusalem. They returned when the festivals were over ; and he heard them talk of the Holy City, of Herod, and the New Temple, and of the great teachers and doctors of the Law. And at length Saul himself was to go,—to see the land of promise and the City of David, and grow up a learned Rabbi ' at the feet of Gamaliel.'

With his father, or under the care of some other friend older than himself, he left Tarsus and went to Jerusalem. It is not probable that they travelled by the long and laborious land-journey which leads from the Cilician plain through the defiles of Mount Amanus to Antioch, and thence along the rugged Phœnician shore through Tyre and Sidon to Judæa. The Jews, when they went to the festivals, or to carry contributions, like the Mahomedans of modern days, would follow the lines of natural traffic :[1] and now that the Eastern Sea had been cleared of its pirates, the obvious course would be to travel by water. The Jews, though merchants, were not seamen. We may imagine Saul, therefore, setting sail from the Cydnus on his first voyage, in a Phœnician trader, under the patronage of the gods of Tyre ; or in company with Greek mariners in a vessel adorned with some mythological emblem, like that Alexandrian corn-ship which subsequently brought him to Italy,

---

[1] That he came from Tarsus at an early age is implied in Acts xxvi. 4.— ' My manner of life *from my youth,* which was *at the first* among mine own nation at Jerusalem, know all the Jews,

which knew me from the beginning.'

[2] In 1820, Abd-el-Kader went with his father on board a French brig to Alexandria, on their way to Mecca.

'whose sign was Castor and Pollux."[1] Gradually they lost sight of
Taurus, and the heights of Lebanon came into view. The one had
sheltered his early home, but the other had been a familiar form
to his Jewish forefathers. How histories would crowd into his
mind as the vessel moved on over the waves, and he gazed upon
the furrowed flanks of the great Hebrew mountain ! Had the
voyage been taken fifty years earlier, the vessel would probably
have been bound for Ptolemais, which still bore the name of the
Greek kings of Egypt ;[2] but in the reign of Augustus or Tiberius,
it is more likely that she sailed round the headland of Carmel, and
came to anchor in the new harbour of Cæsarea,—the handsome
city which Herod had rebuilt, and named in honour of the
Emperor.

To imagine incidents when none are recorded, and confidently to
lay down a route without any authority, would be inexcusable in
writing on this subject. But to imagine the feelings of a Hebrew
boy on his first visit to the Holy Land, is neither difficult nor
blamable. During this journey Saul had around him a different
scenery and different cultivation from what he had been accustomed
to,—not a river and a wide plain covered with harvests of corn, but
a succession of hills and valleys, with terraced vineyards watered
by artificial irrigation. If it was the time of a festival, many
pilgrims were moving in the same direction, with music and the
songs of Zion. The ordinary road would probably be that mentioned in the Acts, which led from Cæsarea through the town of
Antipatris[3] (Acts xxiii. 31). But neither of these places would
possess much interest for a 'Hebrew of the Hebrews.' The one
was associated with the thoughts of the Romans and of modern
times ; the other had been built by Herod in memory of Antipater,
his Idumean father. But objects were not wanting of the deepest
interest to a child of Benjamin. Those far hill-tops on the left
were close upon Mount Gilboa, even if the very place could not be
seen where 'the Philistines fought against Israel . . . and the
battle went sore against Saul . . . and he fell on his sword
. . . and died, and his three sons, and his armour-bearer, and
all his men, that same day together.'[4] After passing through the
lots of the tribes of Manasseh and Ephraim, the traveller from
Cæsarea came to the borders of Benjamin. The children of Rachel
were together in Canaan as they had been in the desert. The lot
of Benjamin was entered near Bethel, memorable for the piety of
Jacob, the songs of Deborah, the sin of Jeroboam, and the zeal
of Josiah.[5] Onward a short distance was Gibeah, the home of
Saul when he was anointed King[6], and the scene of the crime
and desolation of the tribe, which made it the smallest of the
tribes of Israel.[7] Might it not be too truly said concerning the

---

[1] Acts xxviii. 11.

[2] See, for instance, 1 Maccab. v. 15,
x. 1. Ptolemais was still a busy sea-
port in St. Paul's day, though Cæsarea
had become the most important harbour,
and indeed (politically) the most important city, in Palestine. See Acts
xxi. 7.

[3] See p. 22, n. 4.

[4] 1 Sam. xxxi. 1—6.

[5] Gen. xxviii. 19; Judg. iv. 5; 1
Kings xii. 29; 2 Kings xxiii. 15.

[6] 1 Sam. x. 26, xv. 34.

[7] Judges xx. 43, &c.

Israelites even of that period : 'They have deeply corrupted themselves, as in the days of Gibeah : therefore the Lord will remember
their iniquity, He will visit their sins'?[1]   At a later stage of his
life, such thoughts of the unbelief and iniquity of Israel accompanied St. Paul wherever he went.   At the early age of twelve
years, all his enthusiasm could find an adequate object in the
earthly Jerusalem ; the first view of which would be descried about
this part of the journey.   From the time when the line of the
city wall was seen, all else was forgotten.   The further border of
Benjamin was almost reached.   The Rabbis said that the boundary
line of Benjamin and Judah, the two faithful tribes, passed through
the Temple.   And this City and Temple was the common sanctuary
of all Israelites.   'Thither the tribes go up, even the tribes of the
Lord : to testify unto Israel, to give thanks unto the name of the
Lord.   There is little Benjamin their ruler, and the princes of
Judah their council, the princes of Zebulon and the princes of
Nephthali : for there is the seat of judgment, even the seat of the
house of David.'   And now the Temple's glittering roof was seen,
with the buildings of Zion crowning the eminence above it, and
the ridge of the Mount of Olives rising high over all.   And now
the city gate was passed, with that thrill of the heart which none
but a Jew could know.   'Our feet stand within thy gates, O
Jerusalem.   O pray for the peace of Jerusalem : they shall prosper
that love thee.   Peace be within thy walls : and plenteousness
within thy palaces.   O God, wonderful art thou in thy holy places :
even the God of Israel.   He will give strength and power unto
His people.   Blessed be God.'[2]

And now that this young enthusiastic Jew is come into the land
of his forefathers, and is about to receive his education in the schools
of the Holy City, we may pause to give some description of the state
of Judæa and Jerusalem.   We have seen that it is impossible to fix
the exact date of his arrival, but we know the general features of
the period ; and we can easily form to ourselves some idea of the
political and religious condition of Palestine.

Herod was now dead.   The tyrant had been called to his last
account ; and that eventful reign, which had destroyed the nationality of the Jews, while it maintained their apparent independence,
was over.   It is most likely that Archelaus also had ceased to
govern, and was already in exile.   His accession to power had been
attended with dreadful fighting in the streets, with bloodshed at
sacred festivals, and with wholesale crucifixions ; his reign of ten
years was one continued season of disorder and discontent ; and, at
last, he was banished to Vienna on the Rhone, that Judæa might
be formally constituted into a Roman province.[3]   We suppose Saul

---

[1] Hosea ix. 9.
[2] See Ps. lxviii. and cxxii.
[3] While the question of succession
was pending, the Roman soldiers under
Sabinus had a desperate conflict with
the Jews.   Fighting and sacrificing
went on together.   Varus, the governor
of Syria, marched from Antioch to
Jerusalem, and 2,000 Jews were crucified.   The Herodian family, after their
father's death, had gone to Rome,
where Augustus received them in the
Temple of Apollo.   Archelaus had
never the title of king, though his
father had desired it.

to have come from Tarsus to Jerusalem when one of the four governors, who preceded Pontius Pilate, was in power,—either Coponius or Marcus Ambivius, or Annius Rufus, or Valerius Gratus. The governor resided in the town of Cæsarea. Soldiers were quartered there and at Jerusalem, and throughout Judæa, wherever the turbulence of the people made garrisons necessary. Centurions were in the country towns :[1] soldiers on the banks of the Jordan.[2] There was no longer even the show of independence. The revolution, of which Herod had sown the seeds, now came to maturity. The only change since his death in the appearance of the country was that everything became more Roman than before. Roman money was current in the markets. Roman words were incorporated in the popular language. Roman buildings were conspicuous in all the towns. Even those two independent principalities which two sons of Herod governed, between the provinces of Judæa and Syria, exhibited all the general character of the epoch. Philip, the tetrarch of Gaulonitis, called Bethsaida, on the north of the lake of Gennesareth, by the name of Julias, in honour of the family who reigned at Rome. Antipas, the tetrarch of Galilee, built Tiberias on the south of the same lake, in honour of the emperor who about this time (A. D. 14) succeeded his illustrious step-father.

These political changes had been attended with a gradual alteration in the national feelings of the Jews with regard to their religion. That the sentiment of political nationality was not extinguished was proved too well by all the horrors of Vespasian's and Hadrian's reigns ; but there was a growing tendency to cling rather to their Law and Religion as the centre of their unity. The great conquests of the Heathen powers may have been intended by Divine Providence to prepare this change in the Jewish mind. Even under the Maccabees, the idea of the state began to give place, in some degree, to the idea of religious life. Under Herod, the old unity was utterly broken to pieces. The high priests were set up and put down at his caprice ; and the jurisdiction of the Sanhedrin was invaded by the most arbitrary interference. Under the governors, the power of the Sanhedrin was still more abridged ; and high priests were raised and deposed, as the Christian patriarchs of Constantinople have for some ages been raised and deposed by the Sultan: so that it is often a matter of great difficulty to ascertain who was high priest of Jerusalem in any given year at this period.[3] Thus the hearts of the Jews turned more and more towards the fulfilment of Prophecy,—to the practice of Religion,—to the interpretation of the Law. All else was now hopeless. The Pharisees, the Scribes, and the Lawyers were growing into a more important body even than the Priests and the Levites ;[4] and that system of 'Rabbinism' was beginning, 'which, supplanting the original religion of the Jews, became, after the ruin of the Temple

---

[1] Luke vii. 1—10.
[2] Luke iii. 14.
[3] See Acts xxiii. 5.
[4] In earlier periods of Jewish history, the prophets seem often to have been a more influential body than the priests. It is remarkable that we do not read of 'Schools of the Prophets' in any of the Levitical cities. In these schools, some were Levites, as Samuel; some belonged to the other tribes, as Saul and David.

and the extinction of the public worship, a new bond of national union, the great distinctive feature in the character of modern Judaism.'[1]

The Apostolic age was remarkable for the growth of learned Rabbinical schools ; but of these the most eminent were the rival schools of Hillel and Schammai.   These sages of the law were spoken of by the Jews, and their proverbs quoted, as the seven wise men were quoted by the Greeks.   Their traditional systems run through all the Talmudical writings, as the doctrines of the Scotists and Thomists run through the Middle Ages.[2]   Both were Pharisaic schools : but the former upheld the honour of tradition as even superior to the law ; the latter despised the traditionists when they clashed with Moses.   The antagonism between them was so great, that it was said that even 'Elijah the Tishbite would never be able to reconcile the disciples of Hillel and Schammai.'

Of these two schools, that of Hillel was by far the most influential in its own day, and its decisions have been held authoritative by the greater number of later Rabbis.   The most eminent ornament of this school was Gamaliel, whose fame is celebrated in the Talmud.   Hillel was the father of Simeon, and Simeon the father of Gamaliel.   It has been imagined by some that Simeon was the same old man who took the infant Saviour in his arms, and pronounced the *Nunc Dimittis*.[3]   It is difficult to give a conclusive proof of this; but there is no doubt that this Gamaliel was the same who wisely pleaded the cause of St. Peter and the other Apostles,[4] and who had previously educated the future Apostle St. Paul.[5]   His learning was so eminent, and his character so revered, that he is one of the seven who alone among Jewish doctors have been honoured with the title of 'Rabban.'[6]   As Aquinas, among the schoolmen, was called *Doctor Angelicus*, and Bonaventura *Doctor Seraphicus*, so Gamaliel was called the 'Beauty of the Law;' and it is a saying of the Talmud, that 'since Rabban Gamaliel died, the glory of the Law has ceased.'   He was a Pharisee ; but anecdotes[7] are told of him, which show that he was not trammelled by the narrow bigotry of the sect.   He had no antipathy to the Greek learning.   He rose above the prejudices of his party.   Our impulse is to class him with the best of the Pharisees, like Nicodemus and Joseph of Arimathæa.   Candour and wisdom seem to have been features of his character ; and this agrees with what we read of him in the Acts of the Apostles,[8] that he was 'had in reputation of all the people,' and

[1] Milman's *History of the Jews*, vol. iii. p. 100.

[2] See Prideaux's *Connection*, part II. pref. p. 12, and beginning of book viii.

[3] Luke ii. 25—35.

[4] Acts v. 34—40.   [5] Acts xxii. 3.

[6] This title is the same as 'Rabboni' addressed to our Lord by Mary Magdalene.

[7] He bathed once at Ptolemais in an apartment where a statue was erected to a Heathen goddess; and being asked how he could reconcile this with the Jewish law, he replied, that the bath was there before the statue; that the bath was not made for the goddess, but the statue for the bath. Tholuck, Eng. transl. p. 17.

[8] Acts v. 34.   Yet Nicodemus and Joseph declared themselves the friends of Christ, which Gamaliel never did. And we should hardly expect to find a violent persecutor among the pupils of a really candid and unprejudiced man.

with his honest and intelligent argument when Peter was brought before the Council. It has been imagined by some that he became a Christian : and why he did not become so is known only to Him who understands the secrets of the human heart. But he lived and died a Jew ; and a well-known prayer against Christian heretics was composed or sanctioned by him.[1] He died eighteen years before the destruction of Jerusalem,[2] about the time of St. Paul's shipwreck at Malta, and was buried with great honour. Another of his pupils, Onkelos, the author of the celebrated Targum, raised to him such a funeral-pile of rich materials as had never before been known, except at the burial of a king.

If we were briefly to specify the three effects which the teaching and example of Gamaliel may be supposed to have produced on the mind of St. Paul, they would be as follows :—candour and honesty of judgment,—a willingness to study and make use of Greek authors,—and a keen and watchful enthusiasm for the Jewish law. We shall see these traits of character soon exemplified in his life. But it is time that we should inquire into the manner of communicating instruction, and learn something concerning the place where instruction was communicated, in the schools of Jerusalem.

Until the formation of the later Rabbinical colleges, which flourished after the Jews were driven from Jerusalem, the instruction in the divinity schools seems to have been chiefly oral. There was a prejudice against the use of any book except the Sacred Writings. The system was one of Scriptural Exegesis. Josephus remarks, at the close of his 'Antiquities,'[3] that the one thing most prized by his countrymen was power in the exposition of Scripture. 'They give to that man,' he says, 'the testimony of being a wise man, who is fully acquainted with our laws, and is able to interpret their meaning.' So far as we are able to learn from our sources of information, the method of instruction was something of this kind.[4] At the meetings of learned men, some passage of the Old Testament was taken as a text, or some topic for discussion propounded in Hebrew, translated into the vernacular tongue by means of a Chaldee paraphrase, and made the subject of commentary : various interpretations were given : aphorisms were propounded : allegories suggested: and the opinions of ancient doctors quoted and discussed. At these discussions the younger students were present, to listen or to inquire,—or, in the sacred words of St. Luke, 'both hearing them and asking them questions :' for it was a peculiarity of the Jewish schools, that the pupil was encouraged to catechise the teacher. Contradictory opinions were expressed with the utmost freedom. This is evident from a cursory examination of the Talmud, which

---

[1] The prayer is given in Mr. Horne's *Introduction to the Scriptures*, 8th ed. vol. iii. p. 261, as follows : ' Let there be no hope to them who apostatise from the true religion; and let heretics, how many soever they be, all perish as in a moment. And let the kingdom of pride be speedily rooted out and broken in our days. Blessed art thou, O Lord our God, who destroyest the wicked, and bringest down the proud.'

[2] His son Simeon, who succeeded him as president of the Council, perished in the ruins of the city.

[3] *Ant.* xx. 11, 2.

[4] See Dr. Kitto's *Cyclopædia of Biblical Literature*, article ' Schools and Synagogues.'

gives us the best notions of the scholastic disputes of the Jews. This remarkable body of Rabbinical jurisprudence has been compared to the Roman body of civil law : but in one respect it might suggest a better comparison with our own English common law, in that it is a vast accumulation of various and often inconsistent precedents. The arguments and opinions which it contains, show very plainly that the Jewish doctors must often have been occupied with the most frivolous questions ;—that the ' mint, anise, and cummin ' were eagerly discussed, while the ' weightier matters of the law ' were neglected :—but we should not be justified in passing a hasty judgment on ancient volumes, which are full of acknowledged difficulties. What we read of the system of the Cabbala has often the appearance of an unintelligible jargon : but in all ages it has been true that ' the words of the wise are as goads, and as nails fastened by the masters of assemblies.'[1] If we could look back upon the assemblies of the Rabbis of Jerusalem, with Gamaliel in the midst, and Saul among the younger speakers, it is possible that the scene would be as strange and as different from a place of modern education as the schools now seen by travellers in the East differ from cotemporary schools in England. But the same might be said of the walks of Plato in the Academy, or the lectures of Aristotle in the Lyceum. It is certain that these free and public discussions of the Jews tended to create a high degree of general intelligence among the people ; that the students were trained there in a system of excellent dialectics ; that they learnt to express themselves in a rapid and sententious style, often with much poetic feeling ; and acquired an admirable acquaintance with the words of the ancient Scriptures.[2]

These ' Assemblies of the Wise ' were possibly a continuation of the ' Schools of the Prophets,' which are mentioned in the historical books of the Old Testament.[3] Wherever the earlier meetings were held, whether at the gate of the city, or in some more secluded place, we read of no buildings for purposes of worship or instruction before the Captivity. During that melancholy period, when the Jews mourned over their separation from the Temple, the necessity of assemblies must have been deeply felt, for united prayer and mutual exhortation, for the singing of the ' Songs of Zion,' and for remembering the ' Word of the Lord.' When they returned, the public reading of the law became a practice of universal interest : and from this period we must date the erection of *Synagogues*[4] in the different towns of Palestine. So that St. James could say, in the council at Jerusalem : ' Moses of old time hath in every city them that preach him, being read in the synagogues every Sabbath

---

[1] Eccles. xii. 11.

[2] It seems that half-yearly examinations were held on four sabbaths of the months Adar and Elul (February and August), when the scholars made recitations and were promoted : the punishments were, confinement, flogging, and excommunication.

[3] 1 Sam. x. 5, 6, xix. 20 ; 2 Kings ii. 3, 5, iv. 38.

[4] Basnage assigns the erection of *synagogues* to the time of the Maccabees. Meuschen says that *schools* were established by Ezra ; but he gives no proof. It is probable that they were nearly cotemporaneous.

day.'[1] To this later period the 74th Psalm may be referred, which
laments over 'the burning of all the synagogues of God in the
land.'[2] These buildings are not mentioned by Josephus in any of
the earlier passages of his history. But in the time of the Apostles
we have the fullest evidence that they existed in all the small towns
in Judæa, and in all the principal cities where the Jews were dispersed
abroad. It seems that the synagogues often consisted of two apart-
ments, one for prayer, preaching, and the offices of public worship;
the other for the meetings of learned men, for discussions concerning
questions of religion and discipline, and for purposes of education.[3]
Thus the *Synagogues* and the *Schools* cannot be considered as two
separate subjects. No doubt a distinction must be drawn between
the smaller schools of the country villages, and the great divinity
schools of Jerusalem. The synagogue which was built by the Centurion at Capernaum[4] was unquestionably a far less important place
than those synagogues in the Holy City, where 'the Libertines, and
Cyrenians,[5] and Alexandrians, with those of Asia and Cilicia,' rose
up as one man, and disputed against St. Stephen.[6] We have here
five groups of foreign Jews,—two from Africa, two from Western
Asia, and one from Europe ; and there is no doubt that the Israelites
of Syria, Babylonia, and the East were similarly represented. The
Rabbinical writers say that there were 480 synagogues in Jerusalem ;
and though this must be an exaggeration, yet no doubt all shades
of Hellenistic and Aramaic opinions found a home in the common
metropolis. It is easy to see that an eager and enthusiastic student
could have had no lack of excitements to stimulate his religious and
intellectual activity, if he spent the years of his youth in that city
' at the feet of Gamaliel.'

It has been contended, that when St. Paul said he was ' brought
up' in Jerusalem ' at the feet of Gamaliel,' he meant that he had
lived at the Rabban's house, and eaten at his table. But the words
evidently point to the customary posture of Jewish students at a
school. There is a curious passage in the Talmud, where it is said,
that ' from the days of Moses to Rabban Gamaliel, they stood up
to learn the Law ; but when Rabban Gamaliel died, sickness came
into the world, and they sat down to learn the Law.' We need not

[1] Acts xv. 21.
[2] Ps. lxxiv. 8.
[3] The place where the Jews met for worship was called Bet-ha-Cneset, as opposed to the Bet-ha-Midrash, where lectures were given. The latter term is still said to be used in Poland and Germany for the place where Jewish lectures are given on the Law.
[4] Luke vii. 5.
[5] The beautiful coins of Cyrene show how entirely it was a Greek city, and therefore imply that its Jews were Hellenistic, like those of Alexandria. See above, p. 15, note 3.
[6] Acts vi. 9. It is difficult to classify with confidence the synagogues mentioned in this passage. According to

Wieseler's view, mentioned above, only one synagogue is intended, belonging to *libertini* of certain districts in North-ern Africa and Western Asia. Others conceive that five synagogues are in-tended, viz. the *Asian, Cilician, Alex-andrian, Cyrenian,* and that of *Jewish freedmen from Italy.* We think the most natural view is to resolve the five groups into three, and to suppose three synagogues, one *Asiatic,* one *African,* and one *European.* An ' Alexandrian synagogue,' built by Alexandrian ar-tisans who were employed about the Temple, is mentioned in the Talmud. We have ventured below to use the phrase ' Cilician Synagogue,' which cannot involve any serious inaccuracy.

stop to criticise this sentence, and it is not easy to reconcile it with other authorities on the same subject. 'To sit at the feet of a teacher' was a proverbial expression ; as when Mary is said to have 'sat at Jesus' feet and heard His word.'[1] But the proverbial expression must have arisen from a well-known custom. The teacher was seated on an elevated platform, or on the ground, and the pupils around him on low seats or on the floor. Maimonides says :—'How do the masters teach ? The doctor sits at the head, and the disciples surround him like a crown, that they may all see the doctor and hear his words. Nor is the doctor seated on a seat, and the disciples on the ground ; but all are on seats, or all on the floor.' St. Ambrose says, in his Commentary on the 1st Epistle to the Corinthians (xiv.), that 'it is the tradition of the synagogue that they sit while they dispute ; the elders in dignity on high chairs, those beneath them on low seats, and the last of all on mats upon the pavement.' And again Philo says, that the children of the Essenes sat at the feet of the masters who interpreted the Law, and explained its figurative sense. And the same thing is expressed in that maxim of the Jews—'Place thyself in the dust at the feet of the wise.'

In this posture the Apostle of the Gentiles spent his schoolboy days, an eager and indefatigable student. 'He that giveth his mind to the law of the Most High, and is occupied in the meditation thereof, will seek out the wisdom of all the ancient, and be occupied in prophecies. He will keep the sayings of the renowned men ; and where subtle parables are, he will be there also. He will seek out the secrets of grave sentences, and be conversant in dark parables. He shall serve among great men, and appear among princes : he will travel through strange countries ; for he hath tried the good and the evil among men.'[2] Such was the pattern proposed to himself by an ardent follower of the Rabbis ; and we cannot wonder that Saul, with such a standard before him, and with so ardent a temperament, 'outran in Judaism many of his own age and nation, being more exceedingly zealous of the traditions of his Fathers.'[3] Intellectually his mind was trained to logical acuteness, his memory became well stored with 'hard sentences of old,' and he acquired the facility of quick and apt quotation of Scripture. Morally, he was a strict observer of the requirements of the Law ; and, while he led a careful conscientious life, after the example of his ancestors,[4] he gradually imbibed the spirit of a fervent persecuting zeal. Among his fellow-students, who flocked to Jerusalem from Egypt and Babylonia, from the coasts of Greece and his native Cilicia, he was known and held in high estimation as a rising light in Israel. And if we may draw a natural inference from another sentence of the letter which has just been quoted, he was far from indifferent to the praise of men.[5] Students of the Law were called 'the holy people ;' and we know one occasion when it was said,

[1] Luke x. 39 : see viii. 35.
[2] Ecclus. xxxix. 1–4.
[3] Gal. i. 14.
[4] 2 Tim. i. 3.
[5] Gal. i. 10. 'Am I *now* seeking to conciliate men ? . . . . Nay, if I still strove (as once I did) to please men, I should not be the servant of Christ.'

' This people who knoweth not the Law are cursed.'.[1]   And we can imagine him saying to himself, with all the rising pride of a successful Pharisee, in the language of the Book of Wisdom : ' I shall have estimation among the multitude, and honour with the elders, though I be young.   I shall be found of a quick conceit in judgment, and shall be admired in the sight of great men.   When I hold my tongue, they shall bide my leisure ; and when I speak, they shall give good ear unto me.'[2]

While thus he was passing through the busy years of his student-life, nursing his religious enthusiasm and growing in self-righteousness, others were advancing towards their manhood, not far from Jerusalem, of whom then he knew nothing, but for whose cause he was destined to count that loss which now was his highest gain.[3] There was one at Hebron, the son of a priest ' of the course of Abia,' who was soon to make his voice heard throughout Israel as the preacher of repentance ; there were boys by the Lake of Galilee, mending their fathers' nets, who were hereafter to be the teachers of the world ; and there was ONE, at Nazareth, for the sake of whose love—they, and Saul himself, and thousands of faithful hearts throughout all future ages, should unite in saying :—' He must increase, but I must decrease.'   It is possible that Gamaliel may have been one of those doctors with whom JESUS was found conversing in the Temple.   It is probable that Saul may have been within the precincts of the Temple at some festival, when Mary and Joseph came up from Galilee.   It is certain that the eyes of the Saviour and of His future disciple must often have rested on the same objects,—the same crowd of pilgrims and worshippers,—the same walls of the Holy City,—the same olives on the other side of the valley of Jehoshaphat.   But at present they were strangers. The mysterious human life of JESUS was silently advancing towards its great consummation.   Saul was growing more and more familiar with the outward observances of the Law, and gaining that experience of the ' spirit of bondage ' which should enable him to understand himself, and to teach to others, the blessings of the ' spirit of adoption.'   He was feeling the pressure of that yoke, which, in the words of St. Peter, ' neither his fathers nor he were able to bear.' He was learning (in proportion as his conscientiousness increased) to tremble at the slightest deviation from the Law as jeopardising salvation : ' whence arose that tormenting scrupulosity which invented a number of limitations, in order (by such self-imposed restraint) to guard against every possible transgression of the Law.'[4]   The struggles of this period of his life he has himself described in the seventh chapter of Romans.   Meanwhile, year after year passed away.   John the Baptist appeared by the waters of the Jordan.   The greatest event of the world's history was finished on Calvary.   The sacrifice for sin was offered at a time when sin appeared to be the most triumphant.   At the period of the Crucifixion, three of the principal persons who demand the historian's attention are—the Emperor Tiberius, spending his life of shameless lust on the island of Capreæ,—his vile minister,

[1] John vii. 49.   [2] Wisdom viii. 10-12.   [3] See Phil. iii. 5-7.   [4] Neander.

Sejanus, revelling in cruelty at Rome,—and Pontius Pilate, at Jerusalem, mingling with the sacrifices the blood of the Galilæans.[1] How refreshing is it to turn from these characters to such scenes as that where St. John receives his Lord's dying words from the cross, or where St. Thomas meets Him after the resurrection, to have his doubts turned into faith, or where St. Stephen sheds the first blood of martyrdom, praying for his murderers !

This first martyrdom has the deepest interest for us ; since it is the first occasion when Saul comes before us in his early manhood. Where had he been during these years which we have rapidly passed over in a few lines,—the years in which the foundations of Christianity were laid ? We cannot assume that he had remained continuously in Jerusalem. Many years had elapsed since he came, a boy, from his home at Tarsus. He must have attained the age of twenty-five or thirty years when our Lord's public ministry began. His education was completed ; and we may conjecture, with much probability, that he returned to Tarsus. When he says, in the first letter to the Corinthians (ix. 1),—' Have I not seen the Lord ? ' and when he speaks in the second (v. 16) of having ' known Christ after the flesh,' he seems only to allude, in the first case, to his vision on the road to Damascus ; and, in the second, to his carnal opinions concerning the Messiah. It is hardly conceivable, that if he had been at Jerusalem during our Lord's public ministration there, he should never allude to the fact.[2] In this case, he would surely have been among the persecutors of Jesus, and have referred to this as the ground of his remorse, instead of expressing his repentance for his opposition merely to the Saviour's followers.[3]

If he returned to the banks of the Cydnus, he would find that many changes had taken place among his friends in the interval which had brought him from boyhood to manhood. But the only change in himself was that he brought back with him, to gratify the pride of his parents, if they still were living, a mature knowledge of the Law, a stricter life, a more fervent zeal. And here, in the schools of Tarsus, he had abundant opportunity for becoming acquainted with that Greek literature, the taste for which he had caught from Gamaliel, and for studying the writings of Philo and the Hellenistic Jews. Supposing him to be thus employed, we will describe in a few words the first beginnings of the Apostolic Church, and the appearance presented by it to that Judaism in the midst of which it rose, and follow its short history to the point where the 'young man, whose name was Saul,' reappears at Jerusalem, in connection with his friends of the Cilician Synagogue, ' disputing with Stephen.'

Before our Saviour ascended into heaven, He said to His disciples : ' Ye shall be witnesses unto me both in Jerusalem, and in all Judæa,

---

[1] Luke xiii. 1.

[2] In the absence of more information, it is difficult to write with confidence concerning this part of St. Paul's life. Benson thinks he was a young student during our Lord's ministry, and places a considerable interval between the Ascension of Christ and the persecution of Stephen. Lardner thinks that the restraint and retirement of a student might have kept him in ignorance of what was going on in the world.

[3] 1 Cor. xv. 9 ; Acts xxii. 20.

and in Samaria, and unto the uttermost parts of the earth.'[1] And when Matthias had been chosen, and the promised blessing had been received on the day of Pentecost, this order was strictly followed. First the Gospel was proclaimed in the City of Jerusalem, and the numbers of those who believed gradually rose from 120 to 5000.[2] Until the disciples were 'scattered,'[3] 'upon the persecution that arose about Stephen,'[4] Jerusalem was the scene of all that took place in the Church of Christ. We read as yet of no communication of the truth to the Gentiles, nor to the Samaritans ; no hint even of any Apostolic preaching in the country parts of Judæa. It providentially happened, indeed, that the first outburst of the new doctrine, with all its miraculous evidence, was witnessed by ' Jews and proselytes ' from all parts of the world.[5] They had come up to the Festival of Pentecost from the banks of the Tigris and Euphrates, of the Nile and of the Tiber, from the provinces of Asia Minor, from the desert of Arabia, and from the islands of the Greek Sea ; and when they returned to their homes, they carried with them news which prepared the way for the Glad Tidings about to issue from Mount Zion to ' the uttermost parts of the earth.' But as yet the Gospel lingered on the Holy Hill. The first acts of the Apostles were ' prayer and supplication ' in the ' upper room ;' breaking of bread ' from house to house ;'[6] miracles in the Temple : gatherings of the people in Solomon's cloister ; and the bearing of testimony in the council chamber of the Sanhedrin.

One of the chief characteristics of the Apostolic Church was the bountiful charity of its members one towards another. Many of the Jews of Palestine, and therefore many of the earliest Christian converts, were extremely poor. The odium incurred by adopting the new doctrine might undermine the livelihood of some who depended on their trade for support, and this would make almsgiving necessary. But the Jews of Palestine were relatively poor, compared with those of the dispersion. We see this exemplified on later occasions, in the contributions which St. Paul more than once anxiously promoted.[7] And in the very first days of the Church, we find its wealthier members placing their entire possessions at the disposal of the Apostles. Not that there was any abolition of the rights of property, as the words of St. Peter to Ananias very well show.[8] But those who were rich gave up what God had given them, in the spirit of generous self-sacrifice, and according to the true principles of Christian communism, which regards property as entrusted to the possessor, not for himself, but for the good of the whole community,—to be distributed according to such methods as his charitable feeling and conscientious judgment may approve. The Apostolic Church was, in this respect, in a healthier condition than the Church of modern days. But even then we find un-

---

[1] Acts i. 8.
[2] Acts i. 15, ii. 41, iv. 4.
[3] Acts viii. 1.
[4] Acts xi. 19.
[5] Acts ii. 9–11.
[6] Or rather ' at home,' Acts ii. 46,
—i. e. in their meetings at the private houses of Christians, as opposed to the public devotions in the Temple.
[7] Acts xi. 29, 30; and again Rom. xv. 25, 26, compared with Acts xxiv. 17; 1 Cor. xvi. 1-4; 2 Cor. viii. 1-4.
[8] Acts v. 4.

generous and suspicious sentiments growing up in the midst of the general benevolence. That old jealousy between the Aramaic and Hellenistic Jews reappeared. Their party feeling was excited by some real or apparent unfairness in the distribution of the fund set apart for the poor. 'A murmuring of the Grecians against the Hebrews,'[1] or of the Hebrews against the Grecians, had been a common occurrence for at least two centuries ; and, notwithstanding the power of the Divine Spirit, none will wonder that it broke out again even among those who had become obedient to the doctrine of Christ. That the widows' fund might be carefully distributed, seven almoners or deacons[2] were appointed, of whom the most eminent was St. Stephen, described as a man 'full of faith, and of the Holy Ghost,' and as one who, 'full of faith and power, did great wonders and miracles among the people.' It will be observed that these seven men have Greek names, and that one was a proselyte from the Greco-Syrian city of Antioch. It was natural, from the peculiar character of the quarrel, that Hellenistic Jews should have been appointed to this office. And this circumstance must be looked on as divinely arranged. For the introduction of that party, which was most free from local and national prejudices, into the very ministry of the Church, must have had an important influence in preparing the way for the admission of the Gentiles.

Looking back, from our point of view, upon the community at Jerusalem, we see in it the beginning of that great society, the Church, which has continued to our own time, distinct both from Jews and Heathens, and which will continue till it absorbs both the Heathen and the Jews. But to the cotemporary Jews themselves it wore a very different appearance. From the Hebrew point of view, the disciples of Christ would be regarded as a Jewish sect or synagogue. The synagogues, as we have seen, were very numerous at Jerusalem.[3] There were already the Cilician Synagogue, the Alexandrian Synagogue, the Synagogue of the Libertines,[4]—and to these was now added (if we may use so bold an expression) the Nazarene Synagogue, or the Synagogue of the Galilæans. Not that any separate building was erected for the devotions of the Christians ; for they met from house to house for prayer and the breaking of bread. But they were by no means separated from the nation :[5] they attended the festivals ; they worshipped in the Temple. They were a new and singular party in the nation, holding peculiar opinions, and interpreting the Scriptures in a peculiar way. This is the aspect under which the Church would first present itself to the Jews, and among others to Saul himself. Many different opinions were expressed in the syna-

[1] Acts vi. 1.

[2] The general question of the Diaconate in the primitive Church is considered in Chap. XIII.

[3] See p. 50.

[4] See pp. 15, 38, 50.

[5] 'The worship of the Temple and the synagogue still went side by side with the prayers, and the breaking of bread from house to house. . . . The Jewish family life was the highest expression of Christian unity. . . . The fulfilment of the ancient law was the aspect of Christianity to which the attention of the Church was most directed.'—Prof. Stanley's *Sermon on St. Peter*, p. 92 ; see James ii. 2, where the word 'synagogue' is applied to Christian assemblies.

gogues concerning the nature and office of the Messiah. These Galilæans would be distinguished as holding the strange opinion that the true Messiah was that notorious 'malefactor,' who had been crucified at the last Passover. All parties in the nation united to oppose, and if possible to crush, the monstrous heresy.

The first attempts to put down the new faith came from the Sadducees. The high priest and his immediate adherents[1] belonged to this party. They hated the doctrine of the resurrection ; and the resurrection of Jesus Christ was the corner-stone of all St. Peter's teaching. He and the other Apostles were brought before the Sanhedrin, who in the first instance were content to enjoin silence on them. The order was disobeyed, and they were summoned again. The consequences might have been fatal : but that the jealousy between the Sadducees and Pharisees was overruled, and the instrumentality of one man's wisdom was used, by Almighty God, for the protection of His servants. Gamaliel, the eminent Pharisee, argued, that if this cause were not of God, it would come to nothing, like the work of other impostors ; but, if it were of God, they could not safely resist what must certainly prevail ; and the Apostles of Jesus Christ were scourged, and allowed to ' depart from the presence of the council, rejoicing that they were counted worthy to suffer shame for His name.'[2] But it was impossible that those Pharisees, whom Christ had always rebuked, should long continue to be protectors of the Christians. On this occasion we find the teacher, Gamaliel, taking St. Peter's part : at the next persecution, Saul, the pupil, is actively concerned in the murder of St. Stephen. It was the same alternation of the two prevailing parties, first opposing each other, and then uniting to oppose the Gospel, of which Saul himself had such intimate experience when he became St. Paul.[3]

In many particulars St. Stephen was the forerunner of St. Paul. Up to this time the conflict had been chiefly maintained with the Aramaic Jews ; but Stephen carried the war of the Gospel into the territory of the Hellenists. The learned members of the foreign synagogues endeavoured to refute him by argument or by clamour. The *Cilician* Synagogue is particularly mentioned (Acts vi. 9, 10) as having furnished some conspicuous opponents to Stephen, who ' were not able to resist the wisdom and the spirit with which he spake.' We cannot doubt, from what follows, that Saul of Tarsus, already distinguished by his zeal and talents among the younger champions of Pharisaism, bore a leading part in the discussions which here took place. He was now, though still ' a young man ' (Acts vii. 58), yet no longer in the first opening of youth. This is evident from the fact that he was appointed to an important ecclesiastical and political office immediately afterwards. Such an appointment he could hardly have received from the Sanhedrin before the age of thirty, and probably not so early ; for we must remember that a peculiar respect for seniority distinguished the Rabbinical authorities. We can imagine Saul, then, the foremost in the Cilician Synagogue, ' disputing ' against the new doctrines

---

[1] Acts iv. 1, v. 17.   [2] Acts v. 41.   [3] See Acts xxiii. 6, 9, 14, 20.

of the Hellenistic Deacon, in all the energy of vigorous manhood, and with all the vehement logic of the Rabbis. How often must these scenes have been recalled to his mind, when he himself took the place of Stephen in many a Synagogue, and bore the brunt of the like furious assault; surrounded by 'Jews filled with envy, who spake against those things which were spoken by Paul, contradicting and blaspheming.'[1] But this clamour and these arguments were not sufficient to convince or intimidate St. Stephen. False witnesses were then suborned to accuse him of blasphemy against Moses and against God,—who asserted, when he was dragged before the Sanhedrin, that they had heard him say that Jesus of Nazareth should destroy the Temple, and change the Mosaic customs. It is evident, from the nature of this accusation, how remarkably his doctrine was an anticipation of St. Paul's. As a Hellenistic Jew, he was less entangled in the prejudices of Hebrew nationality than his Aramaic brethren; and he seems to have had a fuller understanding of the final intention of the Gospel than St. Peter and the Apostles had yet attained to. Not doubting the divinity of the Mosaic economy, and not faithless to the God of Abraham, Isaac, and Jacob, he yet saw that the time was coming, yea, then was, when the 'true worshippers' should worship Him, not in the Temple only or in any one sacred spot, but everywhere throughout the earth, 'in spirit and in truth:' and for this doctrine he was doomed to die.

When we speak of the *Sanhedrin*, we are brought into contact with an important controversy. It is much disputed whether it had at this period the power of inflicting death.[2] On the one hand, we apparently find the existence of this power denied by the Jews themselves at the trial of our Lord;[3] and, on the other, we apparently find it assumed and acted on in the case of St. Stephen. The Sanhedrin at Jerusalem, like the Areopagus at Athens, was the highest and most awful court of judicature, especially in matters that pertained to religion; but, like that Athenian tribunal, its real power gradually shrunk, though the reverence attached to its decisions remained. It probably assumed its systematic form under the second Hyrcanus;[4] and it became a fixed institution in the Commonwealth under his sons, who would be glad to have their authority nominally limited, but really supported, by such a council.[5] Under the Herods, and under the Romans, its jurisdiction was curtailed;[6] and we are informed, on Talmudical

[1] Acts xiii. 45.

[2] Most of the modern German critics are of opinion that they had not at this time the power of life and death. A very careful and elaborate argument for the opposite view will be found in Biscoe's *History of the Acts confirmed*, ch. vi. Dean Milman says that in his 'opinion, formed upon the study of the contemporary Jewish history, the power of the Sanhedrin, at this period of political change and confusion, on this, as well as on other points, was altogether undefined.' — *History of*

Christianity, vol. i. p. 340. Compare the narrative of the death of St. James. Joseph. *Ant.* xx. 9.

[3] John xviii. 31, xix. 6.

[4] See p. 21.

[5] The word from which 'Sanhedrin' is derived being Greek, makes it probable that its systematic organisation dates from the Græco-Macedonian (i.e. the Maccabæan) period.

[6] We see the beginning of this in the first passage where the council is mentioned by Josephus, *Antiq.* xiv. 9.

authority, that, forty years before the destruction of Jerusalem, it was formally deprived of the power of inflicting death. If this is true, we must consider the proceedings at the death of St. Stephen as tumultuous and irregular. And nothing is more probable than that Pontius Pilate (if indeed he was not absent at that time) would willingly connive, in the spirit of Gallio at Corinth, at an act of unauthorised cruelty in ' a question of words and names and of the Jewish law,'[1] and that the Jews would willingly assume as much power as they dared, when the honour of Moses and the Temple was in jeopardy.

The council assembled in solemn and formal state to try the blasphemer. There was great and general excitement in Jerusalem. 'The people, the scribes, and the elders' had been 'stirred up' by the members of the Hellenistic Synagogues.[2] It is evident, from that vivid expression which is quoted from the accusers' mouths,—' *this place* '—' *this holy place*,'—that the meeting of the Sanhedrin took place in the close neighbourhood of the Temple. Their ancient and solemn room of assembly was the hall Gazith,[3] or the ' Stone-Chamber,' partly within the Temple Court and partly without it. The president sat in the less sacred portion, and around him, in a semicircle, were the rest of the seventy judges.[4]

Before these judges Stephen was made to stand, confronted by his accusers. The eyes of all were fixed upon his countenance, which grew bright, as they gazed on it, with a supernatural radiance and serenity. In the beautiful Jewish expression of the Scripture, ' They saw his face as it had been that of an angel.' The judges, when they saw his glorified countenance, might have remembered the shining on the face of Moses,[5] and trembled lest Stephen's voice should be about to speak the will of Jehovah, like that of the great lawgiver. Instead of being occupied with the faded glories of the Second Temple, they might have recognised in the spectacle before them the Shechinah of the Christian soul, which is the living Sanctuary of God. But the trial proceeded. The judicial question, to which the accused was required to plead, was put by the president : ' Are these things so ? ' And then Stephen answered ; and his clear voice was heard in the silent council-hall, as he went through the history of the chosen people, proving his own deep faith in the sacredness of the Jewish economy, but suggesting, here and there, that spiritual interpretation of it which had always been the true one, and the truth of which was now to be made manifest to all. He began, with a wise discretion, from

---

[1] Acts xviii. 15.

[2] Acts vi. 12.

[3] It appears that the Talmudical authorities differ as to whether it was on the south or north side of the Temple. But they agree in placing it to the east of the most Holy Place.

[4] Selden describes the form in which the Sanhedrin sat, and gives a diagram with the ' President of the Council '

in the middle, the 'Father of the Council' by his side, and ' Scribes ' at the extremities of the semicircle.

[5] Exodus xxxiv. 29–35 ; see 2 Cor. iii. 7, 13. Chrysostom imagines that the angelic brightness on Stephen's face might be intended to alarm the judges; for, as he says, it is possible for a countenance full of spiritual grace to be awful and terrible to those who are full of hate.

the call of Abraham, and travelled historically in his argument through all the great stages of their national existence,— from Abraham to Joseph,—from Joseph to Moses,—from Moses to David and Solomon. And as he went on he selected and glanced at those points which made for his own cause. He showed that God's blessing rested on the faith of Abraham, though he had 'not so much as to set his foot on' in the land of promise (v. 5), on the piety of Joseph, though he was an exile in Egypt (v. 9), and on the holiness of the Burning Bush, though in the desert of Sinai (v. 30). He dwelt in detail on the Lawgiver, in such a way as to show his own unquestionable orthodoxy; but he quoted the promise concerning 'the prophet like unto Moses' (v. 37), and reminded his hearers that the Law, in which they trusted, had not kept their forefathers from idolatry (v. 39, &c.). And so he passed on to the Temple, which had so prominent a reference to the charge against him : and while he spoke of it, he alluded to the words of Solomon himself,[1] and of the prophet Isaiah,[2] who denied that any temple 'made with hands' could be the place of God's highest worship. And thus far they listened to him. It was the story of the chosen people, to which every Jew listened with interest and pride.

It is remarkable, as we have said before, how completely St. Stephen is the forerunner of St. Paul, both in the form and the matter of this defence. His securing the attention of the Jews by adopting the historical method, is exactly what the Apostle did in the synagogue at Antioch in Pisidia.[3] His assertion of his attachment to the true principles of the Mosaic religion is exactly what was said to Agrippa : 'I continue unto this day, witnessing both to small and great, saying none other things than those which the prophets and Moses did say should come.'[4] It is deeply interesting to think of Saul as listening to the martyr's voice, as he anticipated those very arguments which he himself was destined to reiterate in synagogues and before kings. There is no reason to doubt that he was present,[5] although he may not have been qualified to vote [6] in the Sanhedrin. And it is evident, from the thoughts which occurred to him in his subsequent vision within the precincts of the Temple,[7] how deep an impression St. Stephen's death had left on his

---

[1] 1 Kings viii. 27; 2 Chron. ii. 6, vi. 18.

[2] Is. lxvi. 1, 2.

[3] Acts xiii. 16–22.

[4] Acts xxvi. 22.

[5] Mr. Humphry, in his accurate and useful *Commentary on the Acts*, remarks that it is not improbable we owe to him the defence of St. Stephen as given in the Acts. Besides the resemblances mentioned in the text, he points out the similarity between Acts vii. 44, and Heb. viii. 5, between Acts vii. 5–8, and Rom. iv. 10–19, and between Acts vii. 60, and 2 Tim. iv. 16. And if the Epistle to the Hebrews was written by St. Paul, may we not suppose that this scene was present to

his mind when he wrote, ' Jesus suffered without the gate : let us go forth therefore unto Him without the camp, bearing His reproach?' (xiii. 12, 13.)

[6] One of the necessary qualifications of members of the Sanhedrin was, that they should be the fathers of children, because such were supposed more likely to lean towards mercy. If this was the rule when Stephen was tried, and if Saul was one of the judges, he must have been married at the time. See p. 64, n. 2.

[7] He said in his trance, 'Lord, they know that I imprisoned and beat in every synagogue them that believed on thee; and when the blood of thy martyr Stephen was shed, I also was

memory. And there are even verbal coincidences which may be traced between this address and St. Paul's speeches or writings. The words used by Stephen of the Temple call to mind those which were used at Athens.[1] When he speaks of the Law as received 'by the disposition of angels,' he anticipates a phrase in the Epistle to the Galatians (iii. 19). His exclamation at the end, 'Ye stiffnecked and uncircumcised in heart . . . who have received the law . . . and have not kept it,' is only an indignant condensation of the argument in the Epistle to the Romans : 'Behold, thou callest thyself a Jew, and restest in the law, and makest thy boast in God, and knowest His will . . . Thou, therefore, that makest thy boast of the law, through breaking the law dishonourest thou God ? . . . He is not a Jew which is one outwardly ; neither is that circumcision which is outward in the flesh : but he is a Jew which is one inwardly ; and circumcision is that of the heart, in the spirit, and not in the letter ; whose praise is not of man, but of God.' (ii. 17—29.)

The rebuke which Stephen, full of the Divine Spirit, suddenly broke away from the course of his narrative to pronounce, was the signal for a general outburst of furious rage on the part of his judges.[2] They 'gnashed on him with their teeth' in the same spirit in which they had said, not long before, to the blind man who was healed— 'Thou wast altogether born in sins, and dost thou teach us ?'[3] But, in contrast with the malignant hatred which had blinded their eyes, Stephen's serene faith was supernaturally exalted into a direct vision of the blessedness of the Redeemed. He, whose face had been like that of an angel on earth, was made like one of those angels themselves, 'who do always behold the face of our Father which is in Heaven.'[4] 'He being full of the Holy Ghost, looked up stedfastly into Heaven, and saw the glory of God, and Jesus standing on the right hand of God.' The scene before his eyes was no longer the council-hall at Jerusalem and the circle of his infuriated judges ; but he gazed up into the endless courts of the celestial Jerusalem, with its 'innumerable company of angels,' and saw Jesus, in whose righteous cause he was about to die. In other places, where our Saviour is spoken of in His glorified state, He is said to be, not standing, but seated, at the right hand of the Father.[5] Here alone He is said to be standing. It is as if (according to Chrysostom's beautiful thought) He had risen from His throne to succour His persecuted servant, and to receive him to Himself. And when Stephen saw his Lord—perhaps with the memories of what he had seen on earth crowding into his mind,—he suddenly exclaimed, in the ecstacy of his vision : 'Behold ! I see the Heavens opened and the Son of Man standing on the right hand of God !'

This was too much for the Jews to bear. The blasphemy of Jesus

standing by, and consenting unto his death, and kept the raiment of them that slew him.' Acts xxii. 19, 20.

[1] Acts xvii. 24.

[2] It is evident that the speech was interrupted. We may infer what the conclusion would have been from the analogy of St. Paul's speech at Antioch in Pisidia, Acts xiii.

[3] John ix. 34.

[4] Matt. xviii. 10.

[5] As in Eph. i. 20; Col. iii. 1; Heb. i. 3, viii. 1, x. 12, xii. 2; compare Rom. viii. 34, and 1 Pet. iii. 22.

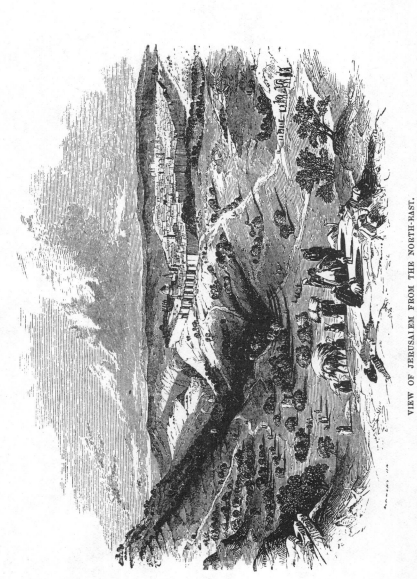

VIEW OF JERUSALEM FROM THE NORTH-EAST.

(From a Sketch by Mr. Bartlett.)

had been repeated. The follower of Jesus was hurried to destruction. 'They cried out with a loud voice, and stopped their ears, and ran upon him with one accord.' It is evident that it was a savage and disorderly condemnation.[1] They dragged him out of the council-hall, and, making a sudden rush and tumult through the streets, hurried him to one of the gates of the city,—and somewhere about the rocky edges of the ravine of Jehoshaphat, where the Mount of Olives looks down upon Gethsemane and Siloam, or on the open ground to the north, which travellers cross when they go towards Samaria or Damascus,—with stones that lay without the walls of the Holy City, this heavenly-minded martyr was murdered. The exact place of his death is not known. There are two traditions,[2]—an ancient one, which places it on the north, beyond the Damascus gate ; and a modern one, which leads travellers through what is now called the gate of St. Stephen, to a spot near the brook Kedron, over against the garden of Gethsemane. But those who look upon Jerusalem from an elevated point on the north-east, have both these positions in view ; and anyone who stood there on that day might have seen the crowd rush forth from the gate, and the witnesses (who according to the law were required to throw the first stones[3]) cast off their outer garments, and lay them down at the feet of Saul.

The contrast is striking between the indignant zeal which the martyr[4] had just expressed against the sin of his judges, and the forgiving love which he showed to themselves, when they became his murderers. He first uttered a prayer for himself in the words of Jesus Christ, which he knew were spoken from the cross, and which he may himself have heard from those holy lips. And then, deliberately kneeling down, in that posture of humility in which the body most naturally expresses the supplication of the mind, and which has been consecrated as the attitude of Christian devotion by Stephen and by Paul himself,[5]—he gave the last few moments of his consciousness to a prayer for the forgiveness of his enemies ; and the words were scarcely spoken when death seized upon him, or rather, in the words of Scripture, 'he fell asleep.'

'And Saul was consenting[6] to his death.' A Spanish painter,[7]

[1] As to whether it was a judicial sentence at all, see above, p. 57, n. 2.

[2] It is well known that the tradition which identifies St. Stephen's gate with the Damascus gate, and places the scene of martyrdom on the *North*, can be traced from an early period to the fifteenth century ; and that the modern tradition, which places both the gate and the martyrdom on the *East*, can be traced back to the same century. It is probable that the popular opinion regarding these sacred sites was suddenly changed by some monks from interested motives.

[3] See Deut. xvii. 5–7. The stoning was always outside the city. Levit. xxiv. 14 ; 1 Kings xxi. 10, 13.

[4] The Christian use of the word *martyr* begins with St. Stephen. See Mr. Humphry's note on Acts xxii. 20. See also what he says on the Christian use of the word *cemetery*, in allusion to Acts vii. 60.

[5] At Miletus (Acts xx. 36) and at Tyre (Acts xxi. 5). See Acts ix. 40.

[6] The word in Acts viii. 1, expresses far more than mere passive consent. St. Paul himself uses the same expression (Ibid. xxii. 20) when referring to the occurrence. Compare ix. 1 and xxvi. 11. We have said above (p. 59), that this scene made a deep impression on St. Paul's mind ; but the power of the impression was unfelt or resisted till after his conversion.

[7] Vicente Joannes, the founder of the Valencian school, one of the most

in a picture of Stephen conducted to the place of execution, has represented Saul as walking by the martyr's side with melancholy calmness.   He consents to his death from a sincere, though mistaken conviction of duty ; and the expression of his countenance is strongly contrasted with the rage of the baffled Jewish doctors and the ferocity of the crowd who flock to the scene of bloodshed.   Literally considered, such a representation is scarcely consistent either with Saul's conduct immediately afterwards, or with his own expressions concerning himself at the later periods of his life.[1]   But the picture, though historically incorrect, is poetically true.   The painter has worked according to the true idea of his art in throwing upon the persecutor's countenance the shadow of his coming repentance.   We cannot dissociate the martyrdom of Stephen from the conversion of Paul.   The spectacle of so much constancy, so much faith, so much love, could not be lost.   It is hardly too much to say with Augustine, that ' the church owes Paul to the prayer of Stephen.'

SI STEPHANUS NON ORASSET
ECCLESIA PAULUM NON HABERET.

austere of the grave and serious painters of Spain.   The picture is one of a series on St. Stephen ; it was once in the church of St. Stephen at Valencia, and is now in the Royal Gallery at Madrid.

See Stirling's *Annals of the Artists of Spain,* i. 363.
[1] See Acts xxii. 4, xxvi. 10 ; Phil. iii. 6 ; 1 Tim. i. 13.

CHAPTER III.

THE death of St. Stephen is a bright passage in the earliest history
of the Church.   Where, in the annals of the world, can we find so
perfect an image of a pure and blessed saint as that which is drawn
in the concluding verses of the seventh chapter of the Acts of the
Apostles ?   And the brightness which invests the scene of the
martyr's last moments is the more impressive from its contrast with
all that has preceded it since the Crucifixion of Christ.   The first
Apostle who died was a traitor.   The first disciples of the Christian
Apostles whose deaths are recorded were liars and hypocrites.   The
kingdom of the Son of Man was founded in darkness and gloom.
But a heavenly light reappeared with the martyrdom of St. Stephen.
The revelation of such a character at the moment of death was the
strongest of all evidences, and the highest of all encouragements.
Nothing could more confidently assert the Divine power of the new
religion ; nothing could prophesy more surely the certainty of its
final victory.

To us who have the experience of many centuries of Christian
history, and who can look back, through a long series of martyrdoms,
to this, which was the beginning and example of the rest, these
thoughts are easy and obvious ; but to the friends and associates of
the murdered Saint, such feelings of cheerful and confident assurance
were perhaps more difficult.   Though Christ was indeed risen from
the dead, His disciples could hardly yet be able to realise the full
triumph of the Cross over death.   Even many years afterwards,
Paul the Apostle wrote to the Thessalonians, concerning those who
had 'fallen asleep'[1] more peaceably than Stephen, that they ought
not to sorrow for them as those without hope ; and now, at the very
beginning of the Gospel, the grief of the Christians must have been
great indeed, when the corpse of their champion and their brother
lay at the feet of Saul the murderer.   Yet, amidst the consternation
of some and the fury of others, friends of the martyr were found,[2]

---

[1] 1 Thess. iv. 13. See Acts vii. 60.
[2] Acts viii. 2. Probably they were
Hellenistic Jews impressed in favour
of Christianity. It seems hardly likely

who gave him all the melancholy honours of a Jewish funeral, and carefully buried him, as Joseph buried his father, ' with great and sore lamentation.' [1]

After the death and burial of Stephen the persecution still raged in Jerusalem. That temporary protection which had been extended to the rising sect by such men as Gamaliel was now at an end. Pharisees and Sadducees—priests and people—alike indulged the most violent and ungovernable fury. It does not seem that any check was laid upon them by the Roman authorities. Either the procurator was absent from the city, or he was willing to connive at what seemed to him an ordinary religious quarrel.

The eminent and active agent in this persecution was Saul. There are strong grounds for believing that, if he was not a member of the Sanhedrin at the time of St. Stephen's death, he was elected into that powerful senate soon after ; possibly as a reward for the zeal he had shown against the heretic. He himself says that in Jerusalem he not only exercised the power of imprisonment by commission from the High Priests, but also, when the Christians were put to death, *gave his vote* against them. [2] From this expression it is natural to infer that he was a member of that supreme court of judicature. However this might be, his zeal in conducting the persecution was unbounded. We cannot help observing how frequently strong expressions concerning his share in the injustice and cruelty now perpetrated are multiplied in the Scriptures. In St. Luke's narrative, in St. Paul's own speeches, in his earlier and later epistles, the subject recurs again and again. He 'made havoc of the Church,' invading the sanctuaries of domestic life, 'entering into every house ;' [3] and those whom he thus tore from their homes he 'committed to prison ;' or, in his own words at a later period, when he had recognised as God's people those whom he now imagined to be His enemies, 'thinking that he ought to do many things contrary to the name of Jesus of Nazareth. . . . in Jerusalem . . . he shut up many of the saints in prison.' [4] And not only did men thus suffer at his hands, but women also,—a fact three times repeated as a great aggravation of his cruelty. [5] These persecuted people were scourged—'often' scourged,—'in many synagogues.' [6] Nor was Stephen the only one who suffered death, as we may infer from the Apostle's own confession. [7] And, what was worse than scourging

---

that they were avowed Christians. There is nothing in the expression itself to determine the point.

[1] See Gen. l. 10.

[2] The word 'voice' in the Auth. Vers. should be 'vote.' Acts xxvi. 10. If this inference is well founded, and if the qualification for a member of the Sanhedrin mentioned in the last chapter (p. 59, n. 6) was a necessary qualification, Saul must have been a married man, and the father of a family. If so, it is probable that his wife and children did not long survive; for otherwise, some notice of them would have occurred in the subsequent narrative, or

some allusion to them in the Epistles. And we know that, if ever he had a wife, she was not living when he wrote his first letter to the Corinthians. (1 Cor. vii.) It was customary among the Jews to marry at a very early age. Baron Bunsen has expressed his belief in the tradition that St. Paul was a widower. *Hippol.* ii. 344.

[3] Acts viii. 3. See ix. 2.

[4] Acts xxvi. 9, 10. See xxii. 3.

[5] Acts viii. 3, ix. 2, xxii. 4.

[6] Acts xxvi. 10.

[7] 'I persecuted this way unto the death, binding and delivering into prisons both men and women ' (xxii. 4) ;

or than death itself, he used every effort to make them 'blaspheme' that Holy Name whereby they were called.[1] His fame as an inquisitor was notorious far and wide. Even at Damascus Ananias had heard [2] 'how much evil he had done to Christ's saints at Jerusalem.' He was known there [3] as 'he that destroyed them which call on this Name in Jerusalem.' It was not without reason that in the deep repentance of his later years, he remembered how he had 'persecuted the Church of God and wasted it,' [4]—how he had been 'a blasphemer, a persecutor, and injurious;' [5]—and that he felt he was 'not meet to be called an Apostle,' because he 'had persecuted the Church of God.' [6]

From such cruelty, and such efforts to make them deny that Name which they honoured above all names, the disciples naturally fled. In consequence of 'the persecution against the Church at Jerusalem, they were all scattered abroad throughout the regions of Judæa and Samaria.' The Apostles only remained.[7] But this dispersion led to great results. The moment of lowest depression was the very time of the Church's first missionary triumph. 'They that were scattered abroad went everywhere preaching the Word.' [8] First the Samaritans, and then the Gentiles, received that Gospel which the Jews attempted to destroy. Thus did the providence of God begin to accomplish, by unconscious instruments, the prophecy and command which had been given :—'Ye shall be witnesses unto Me, both in Jerusalem and in all Judæa, and in Samaria, and unto the uttermost part of the earth.' [9]

The Jew looked upon the Samaritan as he looked upon the Gentile. His hostility to the Samaritan was probably the greater, in proportion as he was nearer. In conformity with the economy which was observed before the resurrection, Jesus Christ had said to His disciples, 'Go not into the way of the Gentiles, and into any city of the Samaritans enter ye not : but go rather to the lost sheep of the house of Israel.' [10] Yet did the Saviour give anticipative hints of His favour to Gentiles and Samaritans, in His mercy to the Syrophenician woman, and His interview with the woman at the well of Sychar. And now the time was come for both the 'middle walls of partition' to be destroyed. The dispersion brought Philip, the companion of Stephen, the second of the seven, to a city of Samaria.[11] He came with the power of miracles and with the message of salvation. The Samaritans were convinced by what they saw ; they listened to what he said ; and there was great joy in

'and when they were put to death; I gave my vote against them' (xxvi. 10).

[1] (Acts xxvi. 11.) It is not said that he succeeded in causing any to blaspheme. It may be necessary to explain to some readers that the Greek imperfect merely denotes that the attempt was made; so in Gal. i. 23, alluded to at the end of this chapter.

[2] Acts ix. 13.

[3] Acts ix. 21.

[4] Gal. i. 13; see also Phil. iii. 6.

[5] 1 Tim. i. 13.

[6] 1 Cor. xv. 9. It should be observed that in all these passages from the Epistles the same word for 'persecution' is used.

[7] Acts viii. 1.

[8] Acts viii. 4.   See xi. 19–21.

[9] Acts i. 8.

[10] Matt. x. 5, 6.

[11] (Acts viii. 5.) This was probably the ancient capital, at that time called 'Sebaste.' The city of Sychar (John iv. 5) had also received a Greek name. It was then 'Neapolis,' and is still 'Nablous.'

that city.' When the news came to Jerusalem, Peter and John were sent by the Apostles, and the same miraculous testimony attended their presence, which had been given on the day of Pentecost. The Divine Power in Peter rebuked the powers of evil, which were working[1] among the Samaritans in the person of Simon Magus, as Paul afterwards, on his first preaching to the Gentiles, rebuked in Cyprus Elymas the Sorcerer. The two Apostles returned to Jerusalem, preaching as they went 'in many villages of the Samaritans' the Gospel which had been welcomed in the city.

Once more we are permitted to see Philip on his labour of love. We obtain a glimpse of him on the road which leads down by Gaza[2] to Egypt. The chamberlain of Queen Candace [3] is passing southwards on his return from Jerusalem, and reading in his chariot the prophecies of Isaiah. Æthiopia is 'stretching out her hands unto God,' [4] and the suppliant is not unheard. A teacher is provided at the moment of anxious inquiry. The stranger goes 'on his way rejoicing;' a proselyte who had found the Messiah ; a Christian baptized 'with water and the Holy Ghost.' The Evangelist, having finished the work for which he had been sent, is called elsewhere by the Spirit of God. He proceeds to Cæsarea, and we hear of him no more, till, after the lapse of more than twenty years, he received under his roof in that city one who, like himself, had travelled in obedience to the Divine command 'preaching in all the cities.' [5]

Our attention is now called to that other traveller. We turn from the 'desert road' on the south of Palestine to the desert road on the north ; from the border of Arabia near Gaza, to its border near Damascus. 'From Dan to Beersheba' the Gospel is rapidly spreading. The dispersion of the Christians had not been confined to Judæa and Samaria. 'On the persecution that arose about Stephen' they had 'travelled as far as Phœnicia and Syria.' [6] 'Saul, yet breathing out threatenings and slaughter against the disciples of the Lord,'[7] determined to follow them. 'Being exceedingly mad against them, he persecuted them even to strange cities.'[8] He went of his own accord to the high priest, and desired of him letters to the synagogues in Damascus, where he had reason to believe that Christians were to be found. And armed with this

---

[1] The original word shows that Simon was in Samaria before Philip came, as Elymas was with Sergius Paulus before the arrival of St. Paul. Compare viii. 9–24 with xiii. 6–12. There is good reason for believing that Simon Magus is the person mentioned by Josephus (*Ant.* xx. 7, 2), as connected with Felix and Drusilla. See Acts xxiv. 24.

[2] For Gaza and the phrase 'which is desert' we may refer to the article in Smith's *Dict. of the Bible.*

[3] Candace is the name, not of an individual, but of a dynasty, like Aretas in Arabia, or like Pharaoh and Ptolemy. By Æthiopia is meant Meroë on the Upper Nile. Queens of Meroë with the title of Candace are mentioned by Greek and Roman writers. Probably this chamberlain was a Jew.

[4] Ps. lxviii. 31.

[5] 'But Philip was found at Azotus; and, passing through, he preached in all the cities, till he came to Cæsarea.' (Acts viii. 40.) 'And the next day we that were of Paul's company departed, and came to Cæsarea; and we entered into the house of Philip the Evangelist, which was one of the seven, and abode with him.' (Ibid. xxi. 8.)

[6] Acts xi. 19.   [7] Acts ix. 1.

[8] Acts xxvi. 11.

'authority and commission,'[1] intending 'if he found any of this way, whether they were men or women,'[2] to bring them bound unto Jerusalem to be punished,'[3] he journeyed to Damascus.

The great Sanhedrin claimed over the Jews in foreign cities the same power, in religious questions, which they exercised at Jerusalem. The Jews in Damascus were very numerous; and there were peculiar circumstances in the political condition of Damascus at this time, which may have given facilities to conspiracies or deeds of violence conducted by the Jews. There was war between Aretas, who reigned at Petra, the desert-metropolis of Stony Arabia,[4] and Herod Antipas, his son-in-law, the Tetrarch of Galilee. A misunderstanding concerning the boundaries of the two principalities had been aggravated into an inveterate quarrel by Herod's unfaithfulness to the daughter of the Arabian king, and his shameful attachment to 'his brother Philip's wife.' The Jews generally sympathised with the cause of Aretas, rejoiced when Herod's army was cut off, and declared that this disaster was a judgment for the murder of John the Baptist. Herod wrote to Rome and obtained an order for assistance from Vitellius, the Governor of Syria. But when Vitellius was on his march through Judæa, from Antioch towards Petra, he suddenly heard of the death of Tiberius (A.D. 37); and the Roman army was withdrawn, before the war was brought to a conclusion. It is evident that the relations of the neighbouring powers must have been for some years in a very unsettled condition along the frontiers of Arabia, Judæa, and Syria; and the falling of a rich border-town like Damascus from the hands of the Romans into those of Aretas would be a natural occurrence of the war. If it could be proved that the city was placed in the power of the Arabian Ethnarch[5] under these particular circumstances, and at the time of St. Paul's journey, good reason would be assigned for believing it probable that the ends for which he went were assisted by the political relations of Damascus. And it would indeed be a singular coincidence, if his zeal in persecuting the Christians were promoted by the sympathy of the Jews for the fate of John the Baptist.

But there are grave objections to this view of the occupation of

[1] Acts xxvi. 12.
[2] Acts ix. 2. [3] Acts xxii. 5.
[4] In this mountainous district of Arabia, which had been the scene of the wanderings of the Israelites, and which contained the graves both of Moses and Aaron, the Nabathæan Arabs after the time of the Babylonian captivity (or, possibly, the Edomites before them. See Robinson *Bib. Res.* vol. ii. pp. 557, 573) grew into a civilised nation, built a great mercantile city at Petra, and were ruled by a line of kings, who bore the title of 'Aretas.' The Aretas dynasty ceased in the second century, when Arabia Petræa became a Roman province under Trajan. In the Roman period, a great road united Ailah on the Red Sea with Petra, and thence diverged to the left towards Jerusalem and the ports of the Mediterranean; and to the right towards Damascus, in a direction not very different from that of the modern caravan-road from Damascus to Mecca. This state of things did not last very long. The Arabs of this district fell back into their old nomadic state. Petra was long undiscovered. Burckhardt was the first to see it, and Laborde the first to visit it. Now it is well known to Oriental travellers. Its Rock-theatre and other remains still exist, to show its ancient character of a city of the Roman Empire.
[5] 2 Cor. xi. 32. On the title 'Ethnarch' see note at the end of this chapter.

Damascus by Aretas. Such a liberty taken by a petty chieftain with the Roman power would have been an act of great audacity ; and it is difficult to believe that Vitellius would have closed the campaign, if such a city were in the hands of an enemy. It is more likely that Caligula,—who in many ways contradicted the policy of his predecessor,—who banished Herod Antipas and patronised Herod Agrippa,—assigned the city of Damascus as a free gift to Aretas.[1] This supposition, as well as the former, will perfectly explain the remarkable passage in St. Paul's letter, where he distinctly says that it was garrisoned by the Ethnarch of Aretas, at the time of his escape. Many such changes of territorial occupation took place under the Emperors,[2] which would have been lost to history, were it not for the information derived from a coin,[3] an inscription, or the incidental remark of a writer who had different ends in view. Any attempt to make this escape from Damascus a fixed point of absolute chronology will be unsuccessful ; but, from what has been said, it may fairly be collected, that Saul's journey from Jerusalem to Damascus took place not far from that year which saw the death of Tiberius and the accession of Caligula.

No journey was ever taken, on· which so much interest is concentrated, as this of St. Paul from Jerusalem to Damascus. It is so critical a passage in the history of God's dealings with man, and we feel it to be so closely bound up with all our best knowledge and best happiness in this life, and with all our hopes for the world to come, that the mind is delighted to dwell upon it, and we are eager to learn or imagine all its details. The conversion of Saul was like the call of a second Abraham. But we know almost more of the Patriarch's journey through this same district, from the north to the south, than we do of the Apostle's in an opposite direction. It is easy to conceive of Abraham travelling with his flocks and herds and camels. The primitive features of the East continue still unaltered in the desert ; and the Arabian Sheikh still remains to us a living picture of the patriarch of Genesis. But before the first century of the Christian era, the patriarchal life in Palestine had been modified, not only by the invasions and settlements of Babylonia and Persia, but by large influxes of Greek and Roman civilisation. It is difficult to guess what was the appearance of Saul's company on that memorable occasion.[4] We neither know

---

[1] This is argued with great force by Wieseler, who, so far as we know, is the first to suggest this explanation. His argument is not quite conclusive ; because it is seldom easy to give a confident opinion on the details of a campaign, unless its history is minutely recorded. The strength of Wieseler's argument consists in this, that his different lines of reasoning converge to the same result.

[2] See, for instance, what is said by Josephus (*Ant.* xviii. 5, 4), of various arrangements in the East at this very crisis. Similar changes in Asia Minor have been alluded to before, Chap. I. p. 19.

[3] Wieseler justly lays some stress on the circumstance that there are coins of Augustus and Tiberius, and, again, of Nero and his successors, but none of Caligula and Claudius, which imply that Damascus was Roman.

[4] In pictures, St. Paul is represented as on horseback on this journey. Probably this is the reason why Lord Lyttelton, in his observations on St. Paul's conversion, uses the phrase— 'Those in company with him *fell down from their horses*, together with Saul,' p. 318. (*Works*, 1774.) There is no proof that this was the case, though it is very probable.

how he travelled, nor who his associates were, nor where he rested on his way, nor what road he followed from the Judæan to the Syrian capital.

His journey must have brought him somewhere into the vicinity of the Sea of Tiberias. But where he approached the nearest to the shores of this sacred lake,—whether he crossed the Jordan where, in its lower course, it flows southwards to the Dead Sea, or where its upper windings enrich the valley at the base of Mount Hermon,— we do not know. And there is one thought which makes us glad that it should be so. It is remarkable that Galilee, where Jesus worked so many of His miracles, is the scene of none of those transactions which are related in the Acts. The blue waters of Tiberias, with their fishing-boats and towns on the brink of the shore, are consecrated to the Gospels. A greater than Paul was here. When we come to the travels of the Apostles, the scenery is no longer limited and Jewish, but Catholic and widely-extended, like the Gospel which they preached : and the Sea, which will be so often spread before us in the life of St. Paul, is not the little Lake of Gennesareth, but the great Mediterranean, which washed the shores and carried the ships of the historical nations of antiquity.[1]

Two principal roads can be mentioned, one of which probably conducted the travellers from Jerusalem to Damascus. The track of the caravans, in ancient and modern times, from Egypt to the Syrian capital, has always led through Gaza and Ramleh, and then, turning eastwards about the borders of Galilee and Samaria, has descended near Mount Tabor towards the Sea of Tiberias ; and so, crossing the Jordan a little to the north of the Lake by Jacob's Bridge, proceeds through the desert country which stretches to the base of Antilibanus. A similar track from Jerusalem falls into this Egyptian road in the neighbourhood of Djenin, at the entrance of Galilee ; and Saul and his company may have travelled by this route, performing the journey of one hundred and thirty-six miles, like the modern caravans, in about six days. But at this period, that great work of Roman road-making, which was actively going on in all parts of the empire, must have extended, in some degree, to Syria and Judæa; and, if the Roman roads were already constructed here, there is little doubt that they followed the direction indicated by the later Itineraries. This direction is from Jerusalem to Neapolis (the ancient Shechem), and thence over the Jordan to the south of the Lake, near Scythopolis, where the soldiers of Pompey crossed the river, and where the Galilean pilgrims used to cross it, at the time of the festivals, to avoid Samaria. From Scythopolis it led to Gadara, a Roman city, the ruins of which are still remaining, and so to Damascus.[2]

[1] The next historical notice of the Sea of Tiberias or Lake of Gennesareth after that which occurs in the Gospels is in Josephus.

[2] It is very conceivable that he travelled by Cæsarea Philippi, the city which Herod Philip had built at the fountains of the Jordan, on the natural line of communication between Tyre and Damascus, and likely to have been one of the 'foreign cities' (Acts xxvi. 11) which harboured Christian fugitives. Here, too, he would be in the footsteps of St. Peter; for here the great confession (Matt. xvi. 16) seems to have been made ; and this road also would probably have brought him past Neapolis. It is hardly likely that he

Whatever road was followed in Saul's journey to Damascus, it is almost certain that the earlier portion of it brought him to Neapolis, the Shechem of the Old Testament, and the Nablous of the modern Samaritans. This city was one of the stages in the Itineraries. Dr. Robinson followed a Roman pavement for some considerable distance in the neighbourhood of Bethel.[1] This northern road went over the elevated ridges which intervene between the valley of the Jordan and the plain on the Mediterranean coast. As the travellers gained the high ground, the young Pharisee may have looked back,—and, when he saw the city in the midst of its hills, with the mountains of Moab in the distance,—confident in the righteousness of his cause,—he may have thought proudly of the 125th Psalm : ' The hills stand about Jerusalem : even so standeth the Lord round about His people, from this time forth for evermore.' His present enterprise was undertaken for the honour of Zion. He was blindly fulfilling the words of One who said : ' Whosoever killeth you, will think that he doeth God service.'[2] Passing through the hills of Samaria, from which he might occasionally obtain a glimpse of the Mediterranean on the left, he would come to Jacob's Well, at the opening of that beautiful valley which lies between Ebal and Gerizim. This, too, is the scene of a Gospel history. The same woman, with whom JESUS spoke, might be again at the well as the Inquisitor passed. But as yet he knew nothing of the breaking down of the ' middle wall of partition.'[3] He could, indeed, have said to the Samaritans : ' Ye worship ye know not what : we know what we worship : for salvation is of the Jews.'[4] But he could not have understood the meaning of those other words : ' The hour cometh, when ye shall neither in Jerusalem, nor yet in this mountain, worship the Father : the true worshippers shall worship Him in spirit and in truth.'[5] His was not yet the Spirit of CHRIST. The zeal which burnt in him was that of James and John, before their illumination, when they wished (in this same district) to call down fire from heaven, even as Elias did, on the inhospitable Samaritan village.[6] Philip had already been preaching to the poor Samaritans, and John had revisited them, in company with Peter, with feelings wonderfully changed.[7] But Saul knew nothing of the little Church of Samaritan Christians ; or, if he heard of them and delayed among them, he delayed only to injure and oppress. The Syrian city was still the great object before him. And now, when he had passed through Samaria and was entering Galilee, the snowy peak of Mount Hermon, the highest point of Antilibanus, almost as far to the north as Damascus, would come into view. This is that tower of ' Lebanon which looketh towards Damascus.'[8] It is already the great landmark of his journey, as he passes through Galilee towards the sea of Tiberias, and the valley of the Jordan.

---

would have taken the Petra road (above, p. 67, n. 4), for both the modern caravans and the ancient Itineraries cross the Jordan more to the north.

[1] *Bib. Res.* iii. 77. More will be said on this subject, when we come to Acts xxiii. 23–31. See p. 23.

[2] John xvi. 2.
[4] John iv. 22.
[5] John iv. 21, 23.
[6] Luke ix. 51–56.
[7] See above, p. 65.
[8] Song of Sol. vii. 4.

[3] Eph. ii. 14.

Leaving now the 'Sea of Galilee,' deep among its hills, as a sanctuary of the holiest thoughts, and imagining the Jordan to be passed, we follow the company of travellers over the barren uplands, which stretch in dreary succession along the base of Antilibanus. All around are stony hills and thirsty plains, through which the withered stems of the scanty vegetation hardly penetrate. Over this desert, under the burning sky, the impetuous Saul holds his course, full of the fiery zeal with which Elijah travelled of yore, on his mysterious errand, through the same ' wilderness of Damascus.'[1] 'The earth in its length and its breadth, and all the deep universe of sky, is steeped in light and heat.' When some eminence is gained, the vast horizon is seen stretching on all sides, like the ocean, without a boundary ; except where the steep sides of Lebanon interrupt it, as the promontories of a mountainous coast stretch out into a motionless sea. The fiery sun is overhead ; and that refreshing view is anxiously looked for,—Damascus seen from afar, within the desert circumference, resting, like an island of Paradise, in the green enclosure of its beautiful gardens.

This view is so celebrated, and the history of the place is so illustrious, that we may well be excused if we linger a moment, that we may describe them both. Damascus is the oldest city in the world.[2] Its fame begins with the earliest patriarchs, and continues to modern times. While other cities of the East have risen and decayed, Damascus is still what it was. It was founded before Baalbec and Palmyra, and it has outlived them both. While Babylon is a heap in the desert, and Tyre a ruin on the shore, it remains what it is called in the prophecies of Isaiah, ' the head of Syria.'[3] Abraham's steward was ' Eliezer of Damascus,'[4] and the limit of his warlike expedition in the rescue of Lot was ' Hobah, which is on the left hand of Damascus.'[5] How important a place it was in the flourishing period of the Jewish monarchy, we know from the garrisons which David placed there,[6] and from the opposition it presented to Solomon.[7] The history of Naaman and the Hebrew captive, Elisha and Gehazi, and of the proud preference of its fresh rivers to the thirsty waters of Israel, are familiar to everyone. And how close its relations continued to be with the Jews, we know from the chronicles of Jeroboam and Ahaz, and the prophecies of Isaiah and Amos.[8] Its mercantile greatness is indicated by Ezekiel in the remarkable words addressed to Tyre :[9]—' Syria was thy merchant by reason of the multitude of the wares of thy making : they occupied in thy fairs with emeralds, purple, and broidered work, and fine linen, and coral, and agate. Damascus was thy merchant in the multitude of the wares of thy making, for

---

[1] 1 Kings xix. 15.
[2] Josephus makes it even older than Abraham. (*Ant.* i. 6, 3.) For the traditions of the events in the infancy of the human race, which are supposed to have happened in its vicinity, see Pococke, ii. 115, 116. The story that the murder of Abel took place here is alluded to by Shakspere, 1 *K. Hen. VI.* i. 3.

[3] Isai. vii. 8.
[4] Gen. xv. 2.
[5] Gen. xiv. 15.
[6] 2 Sam. viii. 6 ; 1 Chron. xviii. 6.
[7] 1 Kings xi. 24.
[8] See 2 Kings xiv. 28, xvi. 9, 10 ; 2 Chron. xxiv. 23, xxviii. 5, 23 ; Isai. vii. 8 ; Amos i. 3, 5.
[9] The port of Beyroot is now to Damascus what Tyre was of old.

the multitude of all riches ; in the wine of Helbon, and white wool.'[1] Leaving the Jewish annals, we might follow its history through continuous centuries, from the time when Alexander sent Parmenio to take it, while the conqueror himself was marching from Tarsus to Tyre—to its occupation by Pompey,[2]—to the letters of Julian the Apostate, who describes it as 'the eye of the East,'— and onward through its golden days, when it was the residence of the Ommiad Caliphs, and the metropolis of the Mahommedan world, —and through the period when its fame was mingled with that of Saladin and Tamerlane,—to our own days, when the praise of its beauty is celebrated by every traveller from Europe. It is evident, to use the words of Lamartine, that, like Constantinople, it was a 'predestinated capital.' Nor is it difficult to explain why its freshness has never faded through all this series of vicissitudes and wars.

Among the rocks and brushwood at the base of Antilibanus are the fountains of a copious and perennial stream, which, after running a course of no great distance to the south-east, loses itself in a desert lake. But before it reaches this dreary boundary, it has distributed its channels over the intermediate space, and left a wide area behind it, rich with prolific vegetation. These are the 'streams from Lebanon,' which are known to us in the imagery of Scripture ;[3]—the 'rivers of Damascus,' which Naaman not unnaturally preferred to all the 'waters of Israel.'[4] By Greek writers the stream is called Chrysorrhoas,[5] or 'the river of gold.' And this stream is the inestimable unexhausted treasure of Damascus. The habitations of men must always have been gathered round it, as the Nile has inevitably attracted an immemorial population to its banks. The desert is a fortification round Damascus. The river is its life. It is drawn out into watercourses, and spread in all directions. For miles around it is a wilderness of gardens,— gardens with roses among the tangled shrubberies, and with fruit on the branches overhead. Everywhere among the trees the murmur of unseen rivulets is heard. Even in the city, which is in the midst of the garden, the clear rushing of the current is a perpetual refreshment. Every dwelling has its fountain : and at night, when the sun has set behind Mount Lebanon, the lights of the city are seen flashing on the waters.

It is not to be wondered at that the view of Damascus, when the dim outline of the gardens has become distinct, and the city is seen gleaming white in the midst of them, should be universally famous. All travellers in all ages have paused to feast their eyes with the prospect : and the prospect has been always the same. It is true that in the Apostle's day there were no cupolas and no minarets : Justinian had not built St. Sophia, and the caliphs had erected no

---

[1] Ezek. xxvii. 16, 18.
[2] See above, Chap. I. p. 21. Its relative importance was not so great when it was under a Western power like that of the Seleucids or the Romans ; hence we find it less frequently mentioned than we might expect in Greek and

Roman writers. This arose from the building of Antioch and other cities in Northern Syria.
[3] Song of Sol. iv. 15.
[4] 2 Kings v. 12.
[5] Strabo and Ptolemy.

mosques. But the white buildings of the city gleamed then, as they do now, in the centre of a verdant inexhaustible paradise. The Syrian gardens, with their low walls and waterwheels, and careless mixture of fruits and flowers, were the same then as they are now.   The same figures would be seen in the green approaches to the town, camels and mules, horses and asses, with Syrian peasants, and Arabs from beyond Palmyra.   We know the very time of the day when Saul was entering these shady avenues.   It was at mid-day.[1] The birds were silent in the trees. The hush of noon was in the city. The sun was burning fiercely in the sky. The persecutor's companions were enjoying the cool refreshment of the shade after their journey : and his eyes rested with satisfaction on those walls which were the end of his mission, and contained the victims of his righteous zeal.

We have been tempted into some prolixity in describing Damascus.   But, in describing the solemn and miraculous event which took place in its neighbourhood, we hesitate to enlarge upon the words of Scripture.   And Scripture relates its circumstances in minute detail.   If the importance we are intended to attach to particular events in early Christianity is to be measured by the prominence assigned to them in the Sacred Records, we must confess that, next after the Passion of our blessed Lord, the event to which our serious attention is especially called is the Conversion of St. Paul.   Besides various allusions to it in his own Epistles, three detailed narratives of the occurrence are found in the Acts.   Once it is related by St. Luke (ix.),—twice by the Apostle himself,—in his address to his countrymen at Jerusalem (xxii.),—in his defence before Agrippa at Cæsarea (xxvi.).   And as, when the same thing is told in more than one of the Holy Gospels, the accounts do not verbally agree, so it is here.   St. Luke is more brief than St. Paul. And each of St. Paul's statements supplies something not found in the other.   The peculiar difference of these two statements, in their relation to the circumstances under which they were given, and as they illustrate the Apostle's wisdom in pleading the cause of the Gospel and reasoning with his opponents, will be made the subject of some remarks in the later chapters of this book.   At present it is our natural course simply to gather the facts from the Apostle's own words, with a careful reference to the shorter narrative given by St. Luke.

In the twenty-second and twenty-sixth chapters of the Acts we are told that it was, ' about noon '—' at mid-day '—when the ' great

---

[1] Acts xxii. 6, xxvi. 13. Notices of the traditional place where the vision was seen are variously given both by earlier and later travellers. The old writer, Quaresmius, mentions four theoretical sites : (1) twelve miles south of Damascus, where there is a stream on the right of the road, with the ruins of a church on a rising ground : (2) six miles south on the left of the road, where there are traces of a church and stones marked with crosses ; (3) two miles south on the same road; (4) half a mile from the city : and this he prefers on the strength of earlier authorities, and because it harmonises best with what is said of the Apostle being led in by the hand.   In one of these cases there is an evident blending of the scene of the *Conversion* and the *Escape* : and it would appear from Mr. Stanley's letter (quoted below, p. 83), that this spot is on the east and not the south of the city.

light' shone 'suddenly' from heaven (xxii. 6, xxvi. 13). And those who have had experience of the glare of a mid-day sun in the East will best understand the description of that light, which is said to have been 'a light above the brightness of the sun, shining round about Paul and them that journeyed with him.' All fell to the ground in terror (xxvi. 14), or stood dumb with amazement (ix. 7). Suddenly surrounded by a light so terrible and incomprehensible, ' they were afraid.' ' They heard not the voice of Him that spake to Paul ' (xxii. 9), or, if they heard a voice, 'they saw no man ' (ix. 7).[1] The whole scene was evidently one of the utmost confusion : and the accounts are such as to express, in the most striking manner, the bewilderment and alarm of the travellers.

But while the others were stunned, stupified and confused, a clear light broke in terribly on the soul of one of those who were prostrated on the ground.[2] A voice spoke articulately to him, which to the rest was a sound mysterious and indistinct. He heard what they did not hear. He saw what they did not see. To them the awful sound was without a meaning : he heard the voice of the Son of God. To them it was a bright light which suddenly surrounded them: he saw JESUS, whom he was persecuting. The awful dialogue can only be given in the language of Scripture. Yet we may reverentially observe that the words which Jesus spoke were 'in the Hebrew tongue.' The same language,[3] in which, during His earthly life, He spoke to Peter and to John, to the blind man by the walls of Jericho, to the woman who washed His feet with her tears—the same sacred language was used when He spoke from heaven to His persecutor on earth. And as on earth He had always spoken in parables, so it was now. That voice which had drawn lessons from the lilies that grew in Galilee, and from the birds that flew over the mountain slopes near the Sea of Tiberias, was now pleased to call His last Apostle with a figure of the like significance : ' Saul, Saul, why persecutest thou me ? It is hard for thee to kick against the goad.' As the ox rebels in vain against the goad[4] of its master, and as all its struggles do

[1] It has been thought both more prudent and more honest to leave these well-known discrepancies exactly as they are found in the Bible. They will be differently explained by different readers, according to their views of the inspiration of Scripture. Those who do not receive the doctrine of Verbal Inspiration will find in these discrepancies a confirmation of the general truth of the narrative. Those who lay stress on this doctrine may fairly be permitted to suppose that the stupified companions of Saul fell to the ground and then rose, and that they heard the voice but did not understand it. Dr. Wordsworth and Prof. Hackett point out that the word 'stood' in ix. 7, need only mean that their progress was arrested.

[2] It is evident from Acts ix. 6, 8,

xxvi. 16, that Saul was prostrate on the ground when Jesus spoke to him.

[3] It is only said in one account (xxvi. 14) that Jesus Christ spoke in Hebrew. But this appears incidentally in the other accounts from the Hebrew form of the name 'Saul' being used where *our Lord's own words* are given (ix. 4, xxii. 8). In the *narrative* portion (ix. 1, 8, &c.) it is the Greek, a difference which is not noticed in the Authorised Version. So Ananias (whose name is Aramaic) seems to have addressed Saul in Hebrew, not in Greek (ix. 17, xxii. 13).

[4] The 'prick' of Acts xxvi. 14 is the goad or sharp-pointed pole, which in southern Europe and in the Levant is seen in the hands of those who are ploughing or driving cattle.

nought but increase its distress—so is thy rebellion vain against
the power of my grace.   I have admonished thee by the word of
my truth, by the death of my saints, by the voice of thy conscience.   Struggle no more against conviction, 'lest a worse thing
come unto thee.'

It is evident that this revelation was not merely an inward impression made on the mind of Saul during a trance or ecstasy.   It
was the direct perception of the visible presence of Jesus Christ.
This is asserted in various passages, both positively and incidentally.   In St. Paul's first letter to the Corinthians, when he
contends for the validity of his own apostleship, his argument is,
' Am I not an Apostle ?   Have I not seen Jesus Christ, the Lord ?'
(1 Cor. ix. 1.)   And when he adduces the evidence for the truth of
the Resurrection, his argument is again, 'He was seen . . . . by
Cephas . . . . by James . . . . by all the Apostles . . . . last of
all by me . . . . as one born out of due time ' (xv. 8).   By Cephas
and by James at Jerusalem the reality of Saul's conversion was
doubted (Acts ix. 27); but ' Barnabas brought him to the Apostles,
and related to them how he had seen the Lord in the way, and had
spoken with Him.'   And similarly Ananias had said to him at their
first meeting in Damascus: ' The Lord hath sent me, even Jesus
who appeared to thee in the way as thou camest' (ix. 17).   ' The
God of our fathers hath chosen thee that thou shouldest see that
Just One, and shouldest hear the voice of His mouth ' (xxii. 14).
The very words which were spoken by the Saviour, imply the same
important truth.   He does not say,[1] ' I am the Son of God—the
Eternal Word—the Lord of men and of angels :'—but, ' I am
Jesus ' (ix. 5, xxvi. 15), ' Jesus of Nazareth ' (xxii. 8).   ' I am
that man, whom not having seen thou hatest, the despised prophet
of Nazareth, who was mocked and crucified at Jerusalem, who died
and was buried.   But now I appear to thee, that thou mayest know
the truth of my Resurrection, that I may convince thee of thy sin,
and call thee to be my Apostle.'

The direct and immediate character of this call, without the intervention of any human agency, is another point on which St. Paul
himself, in the course of his apostolic life, laid the utmost stress ;
and one, therefore, which it is incumbent on us to notice here.   ' A
called Apostle,' ' an Apostle by the will of God,'[2] ' an Apostle
sent not from men, nor by man, but by Jesus Christ, and God the
Father, who raised Him from the dead ; '[3]—these are the phrases
under which he describes himself, in the cases where his authority
was in danger of being questioned.   No human instrumentality intervened, to throw the slightest doubt upon the reality of the communication between Christ Himself and the Apostle of the Heathen.

---

[1] Chrysostom.

[2] See Rom. i. 1; 1 Cor. i. 1 ; 2 Cor. i.
1; Eph. i. 1 ; Col. i. 1.   These expressions are not used by St. Peter, St.
James, St. Jude, or St. John.   And it
is remarkable that they are not used
by St. Paul himself in the Epistles addressed to those who were most firmly
attached to him.   They are found in

the letters to the Christians of Achaia,
but not in those to the Christians of
Macedonia.   (See 1 Thess. i. 1 ; 2
Thess. i. 1 ; Phil. i. 1.)   And though
in the letters to the Ephesians and
Colossians, not in that to Philemon,
which is known to have been sent at
the same time.   See Philemon 1.

[3] Gal. i. 1.

And, as he was directly and miraculously called, so was the work immediately indicated, to which he was set apart, and in which in after years he always gloried,—the work of 'preaching among the Gentiles the unsearchable riches of Christ.' [1]　Unless indeed we are to consider the words which he used before Agrippa [2] as a condensed statement [3] of all that was revealed to him, both in his vision on the way, and afterwards by Ananias in the city : ' I am Jesus, whom thou persecutest : but rise, and stand upon thy feet ; for to this end I have appeared unto thee, to ordain thee a minister and a witness both of these things which thou hast seen, and of those things wherein I will appear unto thee.　And thee have I chosen from the House of Israel, and from among the Gentiles, unto whom now I send thee, to open their eyes, that they may turn from darkness to light, and from the power of Satan unto God ; that they may receive forgiveness of sins, and inheritance among the sanctified, by faith in Me.' [4]

But the full intimation of all the labours and sufferings that were before him was still reserved.　He was told to arise and go into the city, and there it should be told him what it had been ordained [5] that he should do.　He arose humbled and subdued, and ready to obey whatever might be the will of Him who had spoken to him from heaven.　But when he opened his eyes, all was dark around him.　The brilliancy of the vision had made him blind.　Those who were with him saw, as before, the trees and the sky, and the road leading into Damascus.　But he was in darkness, and they led him by the hand into the city.　Thus came Saul into Damascus ;—not as he had expected, to triumph in an enterprise on which his soul was set, to brave all difficulties and dangers, to enter into houses and carry off prisoners to Jerusalem ;—but he passed himself like a prisoner beneath the gateway : and through the colonnades [6] of the street called 'Straight,' where he saw not the crowd of those who gazed on him, he was led by the hands of others, trembling and helpless, to the house of Judas, [7] his dark and solitary lodging.

Three days the blindness continued.　Only one other space of three days' duration can be mentioned of equal importance in the history of the world.　The conflict of Saul's feelings was so great, and his remorse so piercing and so deep, that during this time he neither ate nor drank. [8]　He could have no communion with the Christians, for they had been terrified by the news of his approach.

---

[1] Eph. iii. 8.　See Rom. xi. 13, xv. 16 ; Gal. ii. 8 ; 1 Tim. ii. 7 ; 2 Tim. i. 11, &c.

[2] Acts xxvi. 15–18.

[3] It did not fall in with Paul's plan in his speech before Agrippa (xxvi.) to mention Ananias, as, in his speech to the Jews at Jerusalem (xxii.), he avoided any explicit mention of the Gentiles, while giving the narrative of his conversion.

[4] See notes on the passage in Chap. XXII.

[5] This is the expression in his own speech (xxii. 10).　See ix. 6, and compare xxvi. 16.

[6] See Mr. Porter's *Five Years in Damascus* (1856).　Recent excavations show that a magnificent street with a threefold colonnade extended from the Western gate to the Eastern (where a triple Roman archway remains).　Mr. Porter observes that this arrangement of the street is a counterpart of those of Palmyra and Jerash.　We may perhaps add Antioch.　See below, pp. 102, 103.

[7] Acts ix. 11,

[8] Acts ix. 9,

And the unconverted Jews could have no true sympathy with his present state of mind. He fasted and prayed in silence. The recollections of his early years,—the passages of the ancient Scriptures which he had never understood,—the thoughts of his own cruelty and violence,—the memory of the last looks of Stephen,—all these crowded into his mind, and made the three days equal to long years of repentance. And if we may imagine one feeling above all others to have kept possession of his heart, it would be the feeling suggested by Christ's expostulation : ' Why persecutest thou ME ? ' [1] This feeling would be attended with thoughts of peace, with hope, and with faith. He waited on God : and in his blindness a vision was granted to him. He seemed to behold one who came in to him,— and he knew by revelation that his name was Ananias,—and it appeared to him that the stranger laid his hand on him, that he might receive his sight. [2]

The economy of visions, by which God revealed and accomplished His will, is remarkably similar in the case of Ananias and Saul at Damascus, and in that of Peter and Cornelius at Joppa and Cæsarea. The simultaneous preparation of the hearts of Ananias and Saul, and the simultaneous preparation of those of Peter and Cornelius,— the questioning and hesitation of Peter, and the questioning and hesitation of Ananias,—the one doubting whether he might make friendship with the Gentiles, the other doubting whether he might approach the enemy of the Church,—the unhesitating obedience of each, when the Divine will was made clearly known,—the state of mind in which both the Pharisee and the Centurion were found,— each waiting to see what the Lord would say unto him,—this close analogy will not be forgotten by those who reverently read the two consecutive chapters, in which the baptism of Saul and the baptism of Cornelius are narrated in the Acts of the Apostles. [3]

And in another respect there is a close parallelism between the two histories. The same exact topography characterises them both. In the one case we have the lodging with ' Simon the Tanner,' and the house ' by the sea-side ' (x. 6),—in the other we have ' the house of Judas,' and ' the street called Straight' (ix. 11). And as the shore, where ' the saint beside the ocean prayed,' is an unchanging feature of Joppa, which will ever be dear to the Christian heart ; [4] so are we allowed to bear in mind that the thoroughfares of Eastern cities do not change, [5] and to believe that the ' Straight Street,' which still extends through Damascus in long perspective from the Eastern

[1] See Matt. xxv. 40, 45.

[2] Acts ix. 12.

[3] Acts ix. and x. Compare also xi. 5–18 with xxii. 12–16.

[4] See *The Christian Year*; Monday in Easter week.

[5] See Lord Nugent's remarks on the Jerusalem Bazaar, in his *Sacred and Classical Lands*, vol. ii. pp. 40, 41. Quaresmius says that the *Straight Street* at Damascus is the bazaar, which he describes as a street darkened and covered over, a mile long and as straight as an arrow. He adds that there the *house of Judas* is shown, a commodious dwelling, with traces of having been once a church, and then a mosque. The *place of Baptism*, he says, is a fountain not far off, near the beginning of the street, where a handsome church has been turned into a mosque. He enters also very fully into the description of the traditionary *house of Ananias*, and gives a ground plan of it.

Gate, is the street where Ananias spoke to Saul. More than this we do not venture to say. In the first days of the Church, and for some time afterwards, the local knowledge of the Christians at Damascus might be cherished and vividly retained. But now that through long ages Christianity in the East has been weak and degraded, and Mahommedanism strong and tyrannical, we can only say that the spots still shown to travellers as the sites of the house of Ananias, and the house of Judas, and the place of baptism, may possibly be true.[1]

We know nothing concerning Ananias, except what we learn from St. Luke or from St. Paul. He was a Jew who had become a ' disciple ' of Christ (ix. 10), and he was well reputed and held to be ' devout according to the Law,' among ' all the Jews who dwelt at Damascus ' (xxii. 12). He is never mentioned by St. Paul in his Epistles ; and the later stories respecting his history are unsupported by proof.[2] Though he was not ignorant of the new convert's previous character, it seems evident that he had no personal acquaintance with him ; or he would hardly have been described as ' one called Saul, of Tarsus,' lodging in the house of Judas. He was not an Apostle, nor one of the conspicuous members of the Church. And it was not without a deep significance,[3] that he, who was called to be an Apostle, should be baptized by one of whom the Church knows nothing, except that he was a Christian ' disciple,' and had been a ' devout ' Jew.

Ananias came into the house where Saul, faint, and exhausted[4] with three days' abstinence, still remained in darkness. When he laid his hands on his head, as the vision had foretold, immediately he would be recognised as the messenger of God, even before the words were spoken, ' Brother Saul, the Lord, even Jesus, that appeared unto thee in the way as thou camest, hath sent me, that thou mightest receive thy sight, and be filled with the Holy Ghost.' These words were followed, as were the words of Jesus Himself when He spoke to the blind, with an instantaneous dissipation of darkness : ' There fell from his eyes as it had been scales :[5] and he

[1] Compare, among the older travellers, Thevenot, parts i. and ii.; Maundrell (1714), p. 36; Pococke, ii. 119. Mr. Stanley says, in a letter to the writer, that there is no street now called *Straight* except by the Christians, and that the street so called by them does not contain the traditional house of Judas or of Ananias, which are both shown elsewhere. See below, p. 83, n. 6.

[2] Tradition says that he was one of the seventy disciples, that he was afterwards Bishop of Damascus, and stoned after many tortures under Licinius (or Lucianus) the Governor.

[3] Ananias, as Chrysostom says, was not one of the leading Apostles, because Paul was not to be taught of men. On the other hand, this very circumstance shows the importance attached by God

to baptism. Olshausen, after remarking that Paul was made a member of the Church, not by his Divine Call, but by simple baptism, adds that this baptism of Paul by Ananias did not imply any inferiority or dependence, more than in the case of our Lord and John the Baptist. Observe the strong expression in Acts xxii. 16.

[4] See Acts ix. 19.

[5] It is difficult to see why the words ' there fell from his eyes as it had been scales,' should be considered merely descriptive by Olshausen and others. One of the arguments for taking them literally is the peculiar exactness of St. Luke in speaking on such subjects. See a paper on the medical style of St. Luke in the *Gentleman's Magazine* for June 1841.

received sight forthwith' (ix. 18) : or, in his own more vivid expression, ' the same hour he looked up on the face of Ananias ' (xxii. 13). It was a face he had never seen before. But the expression of Christian love assured him of reconciliation with God. He learnt that ' the God of his fathers ' had chosen him ' to know His will,' —' to see that Just One,'—' to hear the voice of His mouth,'—to be ' His witness unto all men.' [1] He was baptized, and ' the rivers of Damascus ' became more to him than ' all the waters of Judah ' [2] had been. His body was strengthened with food ; and his soul was made strong to ' suffer great things ' for the name of Jesus, and to bear that name ' before the Gentiles, and kings, and the children of Israel.' [3]

He began by proclaiming the honour of that name to the children of Israel in Damascus. He was ' not disobedient to the heavenly vision ' (xxvi. 19), but ' straightway preached in the synagogues that Jesus was the Son of God,' [4]—and ' showed unto them that they should repent and turn to God, and do works meet for repentance.' His Rabbinical and Pharisaic learning was now used to uphold the cause which he came to destroy. The Jews were astounded. They knew what he had been at Jerusalem. They knew why he had come to Damascus. And now they saw him contradicting the whole previous course of his life, and utterly discarding that ' commission of the high-priests,' which had been the authority of his journey. Yet it was evident that his conduct was not the result of a wayward and irregular impulse. His convictions never hesitated ; his energy grew continually stronger, as he strove in the synagogues, maintaining the truth against the Jews, and ' arguing and proving that Jesus was indeed the Messiah.' [5]

The period of his first teaching at Damascus does not seem to have lasted long. Indeed it is evident that his life could not have been safe, had he remained. The fury of the Jews when they had recovered from their first surprise must have been excited to the utmost pitch; and they would soon have received a new commissioner from Jerusalem armed with full powers to supersede and punish one whom they must have regarded as the most faithless of apostates. Saul left the city, but not to return to Jerusalem. Conscious of his Divine mission, he never felt that it was necessary to consult ' those who were Apostles before him, but he went into Arabia, and returned again into Damascus.' [6]

Many questions have been raised concerning this journey into Arabia. The first question relates to the meaning of the word. From the time when the word ' Arabia ' was first used by any of the writers of Greece or Rome, it has always been a term of vague and uncertain import. Sometimes it includes Damascus ; sometimes it ranges over the Lebanon itself, and extends even to the borders of Cilicia. The native geographers usually reckon that stony district, of which Petra was the capital, as belonging to Egypt,—and

[1] Acts xxii. 14, 15.
[2] See 2 Kings v. 12.
[3] See Acts ix. 15, 16.
[4] Acts ix. 20. Where ' Jesus ' and not ' Christ ' is the true reading. Verse

22 would make this probable, if the authority of the MSS. were not decisive.
[5] Acts ix. 22.
[6] Gal. i. 17.

that wide desert toward the Euphrates, where the Bedouins of all ages have lived in tents, as belonging to Syria,—and have limited the name to the Peninsula between the Red Sea and the Persian Gulf, where Jemen, or 'Araby the Blest,' is secluded on the south. In the three-fold division of Ptolemy, which remains in our popular language when we speak of this still untravelled region, both the first and second of these districts were included under the name of the third. And we must suppose St. Paul to have gone into one of the former, either that which touched Syria and Mesopotamia, or that which touched Palestine and Egypt. If he went into the first, we need not suppose him to have travelled far from Damascus. For though the strong powers of Syria and Mesopotamia might check the Arabian tribes, and retrench the Arabian name in this direction, yet the Gardens of Damascus were on the verge of the desert, and Damascus was almost as much an Arabian as a Syrian town.

And if he went into Petræan Arabia, there still remains the question of his motive for the journey, and his employment when there. Either retiring before the opposition at Damascus, he went to preach the Gospel; and then, in the synagogues of that singular capital, which was built amidst the rocks of Edom,[1] whence 'Arabians' came to the festivals at Jerusalem,[2] he testified of Jesus :—or he went for the purpose of contemplation and solitary communion with God, to deepen his repentance and fortify his soul with prayer; and then perhaps his steps were turned to those mountain heights by the Red Sea, which Moses and Elijah had trodden before him. We cannot attempt to decide the question. The views which different inquirers take of it will probably depend on their own tendency to the practical or the ascetic life. On the one hand, it may be argued that such zeal could not be restrained, that Saul could not be silent, but that he would rejoice in carrying into the metropolis of King Aretas the Gospel which his Ethnarch could afterwards hinder at Damascus.[3] On the other hand, it may be said that, with such convictions recently worked in his mind, he would yearn for solitude,—that a time of austere meditation before the beginning of a great work is in conformity with the economy of God,—that we find it quite natural, if Paul followed the example of the Great Lawgiver and the Great Prophet, and of ONE greater than Moses and Elijah, who, after His baptism and before His ministry, 'returned from Jordan and was led by the Spirit into the wilderness.'[4]

While Saul is in Arabia, preaching the Gospel in obscurity, or preparing for his varied work by the intuition of Sacred Truth,—it seems the natural place for some reflections on the reality and the momentous significance of his conversion. It has already been remarked, in what we have drawn from the statements of Scripture,

---

[1] Strabo, in his description of Petra, says that his friend Athenodorus found great numbers of strangers there. In the same paragraph, after describing its cliffs and peculiar situation, he says that it was distant three or four days' journey from Jericho. See above, p. 67, n. 4.

[2] Acts ii. 11.
[3] See 2 Cor. xi. 32.
[4] Luke iv. 1.

that he was called directly by Christ without the intervention of any other Apostle, and that the purpose of his call was clearly indicated, when Ananias baptized him.   He was an Apostle 'not of men, neither by man,'[1] and the Divine will was 'to work among the Gentiles by his ministry.'[2]   But the unbeliever may still say that there are other questions of primary importance.   He may suggest that this apparent change in the current of Saul's thoughts, and this actual revolution in the manner of his life, was either the contrivance of deep and deliberate imposture, or the result of wild and extravagant fanaticism.   Both in ancient and modern times, some have been found who have resolved this great occurrence into the promptings of self-interest, or have ventured to call it the offspring of delusion.   There is an old story mentioned by Epiphanius, from which it appears that the Ebionites were content to find a motive for the change, in an idle story that he first became a Jew that he might marry the High Priest's daughter, and then became the antagonist of Judaism because the High Priest deceived him.[3]   And there are modern Jews, who are satisfied with saying that he changed rapidly from one passion to another, like those impetuous souls who cannot hate or love by halves.   Can we then say that St. Paul was simply a *fanatic* or an *impostor*?   The question has been so well answered in a celebrated English book,[4] that we are content to refer to it.   It will never be possible for anyone to believe St. Paul to have been a mere fanatic, who duly considers his calmness, his wisdom, his prudence, and, above all, his humility, a virtue which is not less inconsistent with fanaticism than with imposture.   And how can we suppose that he was an impostor who changed his religion for selfish purposes?   Was he influenced by the ostentation of learning?   He suddenly cast aside all that he had been taught by Gamaliel, or acquired through long years of study, and took up the opinions of fishermen of Galilee, whom he had scarcely ever seen, and who had never been educated in the schools.   Was it the love of power which prompted the change?   He abdicated in a moment the authority which he possessed, for power 'over a flock of sheep driven to the slaughter, whose Shepherd himself had been murdered a little before;' and 'all he could hope from that power was to be marked out in a particular manner for the same knife, which he had seen so bloodily drawn against them.'   Was it the love of wealth?   Whatever might be his own worldly possessions at the time, he joined himself to those who were certainly poor, and the prospect before him was that which was actually realised, of ministering to his necessities with the labour of his hands.[5]   Was it the love of fame? His prophetic power must have been miraculous, if he could look

[1] Gal. i. 1. This retirement into Arabia is itself an indication of his independent call. See Prof. Ellicott on Gal. i. 17.

[2] Acts xxi. 19.

[3] Epiphanius, after telling the story, argues its impossibility from its contradiction to Phil. iii. and 2 Cor. xi. Barnabas, though a Cyprian, was a Levite, and why not Paul a Jew though a Tarsian? And are we to believe, he adds, what Ebion says of Paul, or what Peter says of him (2 Pet. iii.)?

[4] Lord Lyttelton's *Observations on the Conversion and Apostleship of St. Paul.*

[5] Acts xx. 33, 34; 1 Cor. iv. 12; 1 Thess. ii. 9, &c.

beyond the shame and scorn which then rested on the servants of a crucified Master, to that glory with which Christendom now surrounds the memory of St. Paul.

And if the conversion of St. Paul was not the act of a fanatic or an impostor, then it ought to be considered how much this wonderful occurrence involves.   As Lord Lyttelton observes, 'the conversion and apostleship of St. Paul alone, duly considered, is of itself a demonstration sufficient to prove Christianity to be a Divine revelation.'   Saul was arrested at the height of his zeal, and in the midst of his fury.   In the words of Chrysostom, 'Christ, like a skilful physician, healed him when his fever was at the worst :' and he proceeds to remark, in the same eloquent sermon, that the truth of Christ's resurrection, and the present power of Him who had been crucified, were shown far more forcibly, than they could have been if Paul had been otherwise called.   Nor ought we to forget the great religious lessons we are taught to gather from this event. We see the value set by God upon honesty and integrity, when we find that he, 'who was before a blasphemer and a persecutor and injurious, obtained mercy because he did it ignorantly in unbelief.'[1] And we learn the encouragement given to all sinners who repent, when we are told that 'for this cause he obtained mercy, that in him first Jesus Christ might show forth all long-suffering, for a pattern to them which should hereafter believe on Him to life everlasting.'[2]

We return to the narrative.   Saul's time of retirement in Arabia was not of long continuance.   He was not destined to be the Evangelist of the East.   In the Epistle to the Galatians (i. 18),[3] the time, from his conversion to his final departure from Damascus, is said to have been 'three years,' which, according to the Jewish way of reckoning, may have been three entire years, or only one year with parts of two others.   Meantime Saul had 'returned to Damascus, preaching boldly in the name of Jesus.'   (Acts ix. 27.) The Jews, being no longer able to meet him in controversy, resorted to that which is the last argument of a desperate cause :[4] they resolved to assassinate him.   Saul became acquainted with the conspiracy : and all due precautions were taken to evade the danger. But the political circumstances of Damascus at the time made escape very difficult.   Either in the course of the hostilities which pre-

---

[1] 1 Tim. i. 13.   See Luke xii. 48, xxiii. 34; Acts iii. 17; 1 Cor. ii. 8. On the other hand, 'unbelieving ignorance' is often mentioned in Scripture, as an aggravation of sin : e. g. Eph. iv. 18, 19 ; 2 Thess. i. 7, 8.   A man is deeply wretched who sins through ignorance; and, as Augustine says, Paul in his unconverted state was like a sick man who through madness tries to kill his physician.

[2] A. Monod's *'Cinq Discours'* on St. Paul (Paris, 1852) were published shortly before the completion of the first edition of this work.   We have much pleasure here in referring to the

third of these eloquent and instructive sermons, on the character and results of St. Paul's conversion.

[3] In Acts ix. 23, the time is said to have been 'many days.'   Dr. Paley has observed in a note on the *Horæ Paulinæ* a similar instance in the Old Testament (1 Kings ii. 38, 39), where 'many days' is used to denote a space of 'three years :'—'And Shimei dwelt at Jerusalem *many days;* and it came to pass, at the end of *three years*, that two of the servants of Shimei ran away.'

[4] Chrysostom.

vailed along the Syrian frontiers between Herod Antipas and the Romans, on one side, and Aretas, King of Petra, on the other,—and possibly in consequence of that absence of Vitellius,[1] which was caused by the Emperor's death,—the Arabian monarch had made himself master of Damascus, and the Jews, who sympathised with Aretas, were high in the favour of his officer, the Ethnarch.[2] Or Tiberius had ceased to reign, and his successor had assigned Damascus to the King of Petra, and the Jews had gained over his officer and his soldiers, as Pilate's soldiers had once been gained over at Jerusalem. St. Paul at least expressly informs us,[3] that 'the Ethnarch kept watch over the city, with a garrison, purposing to apprehend him.' St. Luke says,[4] that the Jews 'watched the city-gates day and night, with the intention of killing him.' The Jews furnished the motive, the Ethnarch the military force. The anxiety of the 'disciples' was doubtless great, as when Peter was imprisoned by Herod, 'and prayer was made without ceasing of the Church unto God for him.'[5] Their anxiety became the instrument of his safety. From an unguarded part of the wall,[6] in the darkness of the night, probably where some overhanging houses, as is usual in Eastern cities, opened upon the outer country, they let him down from a window[7] in a basket. There was something of humiliation

---

[1] See above, p. 67.

[2] Some have supposed that this Ethnarch was merely an officer who regulated the affairs of the Jews themselves, such as we know to have existed under this title in cities with many Jewish residents (p. 89). See Joseph. *Ant.* xix. 7, 2, and 8, 5; *War*, ii. 6, 3. Anger imagines that he was an officer of Areta, accidentally residing in Damascus, who induced the Roman government to aid in the conspiracy of the Jews. Neither hypothesis seems very probable. Schrader suggests that the Ethnarch's wife might, perhaps, be a Jewish proselyte, as we know was the case with a vast number of the women of Damascus.

[3] 2 Cor. xi. 32.

[4] Acts ix. 24.

[5] Acts xii. 5.

[6] Quaresmius leaves the place in doubt. We conclude our notices of these traditional sites, by an extract from a letter received from the Rev. A. P. Stanley, shortly before the publication of his *Sinai and Palestine.* 'The only spot now pointed out is a few hundred yards from the town walls, on the eastern side of the city, near the traditional scene of the *Escape* over the wall. 'It is only marked by a mass of cement in the ground, with a hollow underneath, which the Damascus guides represent as a hole in which after his escape the Apostle concealed himself—

and this is the only tradition which in the popular mind attaches to the place. All knowledge or imagination of the *Conversion* or of its locality has entirely passed away. But the French monks in the Latin convent maintain (and no doubt truly) that this was the spot in earlier times believed to be the scene of that event, and that the remains of cement and masonry round about are the ruins of a Christian church or chapel built in memorial. It is, if I remember right, the fourth of the four places mentioned by Quaresmius. It is highly improbable that it can be the true place [of the *Conversion*,] because there is no reason to believe that the road from Jerusalem should have fetched such a compass as to enter Damascus on the east, instead of (as at present) on the west or south.' Mr. Porter (p. 43) says that it is only within the last century that the scene of the Conversion has been transferred, from interested motives, to the east from the west side of the city. His plan of Damascus now gives the means of seeing the traditionary localities very clearly.

[7] 2 Cor. xi. 33. So Rahab let down the spies; and so David escaped from Saul. St. Paul's word is used in the LXX. in both instances. The preposition 'through' being used both in Acts and 1 Cor., it is possible that the most exact explanation is that suggested by

in this mode of escape; and this, perhaps, is the reason why, in a letter written 'fourteen years' afterwards, he specifies the details, 'glorying in his infirmities,' when he is about to speak of 'his visions and revelations of the Lord.'[1]

Thus already the Apostle had experience of 'perils by his own countrymen, and perils in the city.' Already 'in journeyings often, in weariness and painfulness,'[2] he began to learn 'how great things he was to suffer' for the name of Christ.[3] Preserved from destruction at Damascus, he turned his steps towards Jerusalem. His motive for the journey, as he tells us in the Epistle to the Galatians, was a desire to become acquainted with Peter.[4] Not that he was ignorant of the true principles of the Gospel. He expressly tells us that he neither needed nor received any instruction in Christianity from those who were 'Apostles before him.' But he must have heard much from the Christians at Damascus of the Galilæan fisherman. Can we wonder that he should desire to see the Chief of the Twelve,—the brother with whom now he was consciously united in the bonds of a common apostleship,—and who had long on earth been the constant companion of his LORD?

How changed was everything since he had last travelled this road between Damascus and Jerusalem. If, when the day broke, he looked back upon that city from which he had escaped under the shelter of night, as his eye ranged over the fresh gardens and the wide desert, how the remembrance of that first terrible vision would call forth a deep thanksgiving to Him, who had called him to be a 'partaker of His sufferings.'[5] And what feelings must have attended his approach to Jerusalem. 'He was returning to it from a spiritual, as Ezra had from a bodily, captivity, and to his renewed mind all things appeared new. What an emotion smote his heart at the first distant view of the Temple, that house of sacrifice, that edifice of prophecy. Its sacrifices had been realised, the Lamb of God had been offered: its prophecies had been fulfilled, the Lord had come unto it. As he approached the gates, he might have trodden the very spot where he had so exultingly assisted in the death of Stephen, and he entered them perfectly content, were it God's will, to be dragged out through them to the same fate. He would feel a peculiar tie of brotherhood to that martyr, for he could not be now ignorant that the same Jesus who in such glory had called him, had but a little while before appeared in the same glory to assure the expiring Stephen. The ecstatic look and words of the dying saint now came fresh upon his memory with their real meaning. When he entered into the city, what deep thoughts were suggested by the haunts of his youth, and by the sight of the spots

---

Prof. Hackett. He observed at Damascus 'windows in the external face of the wall, opening into houses on the inside of the city.' (*Comm. on Acts.*) In the larger editions is a view of a portion of the wall of modern Damascus, supporting houses which project and face the open country.

[1] 2 Cor. xi. 30, xii. 1–5. Both Schrader and Wieseler are of opinion that the vision mentioned here is that which he saw at Jerusalem on his return from Damascus (Acts xxii. 17; see below, p. 86), and which was naturally associated in his mind with the recollection of his escape.

[2] 2 Cor. xi. 26, 27.

[3] Acts ix. 16.

[4] Gal. i. 18.

[5] 1 Pet. iv. 13.

where he had so eagerly sought that knowledge which he had now
so eagerly abandoned. What an intolerable burden had he cast off.
He felt as a glorified spirit may be supposed to feel on revisiting
the scenes of its fleshly sojourn.'[1]

Yet not without grief and awe could he look upon that city of his
forefathers, over which he now knew that the judgment of God was
impending. And not without sad emotions could one of so tender
a nature think of the alienation of those who had once been his
warmest associates. The grief of Gamaliel, the indignation of the
Pharisees, the fury of the Hellenistic Synagogues, all this, he knew,
was before him. The sanguine hopes, however, springing from his
own honest convictions, and his fervent zeal to communicate the
truth to others, predominated in his mind. He thought that they
would believe as he had believed. He argued thus with himself,—
that they well knew that he had 'imprisoned and beaten in every
synagogue them that believed in Jesus Christ,'—and that 'when
the blood of His martyr Stephen was shed, he also was standing by
and consenting unto his death, and kept the raiment of them that
slew him,'[2]—and that when they saw the change which had been
produced in him, and heard the miraculous history he could tell
them, they would not refuse to 'receive his testimony.'

Thus, with fervent zeal, and sanguine expectations, 'he attempted
to join himself to the disciples' of Christ.[3] But, as the Jews hated
him, so the Christians suspected him. His escape had been too
hurried to allow of his bringing 'letters of commendation.' Whatever distant rumour might have reached them of an apparition on
his journey, of his conduct at Damascus, of his retirement in Arabia,
they could not believe that he was really a disciple. And then it
was that Barnabas, already known to us as a generous contributor
of his wealth to the poor,[4] came forward again as the 'Son of
Consolation,'—'took him by the hand,' and brought him to the
Apostles.[5] It is probable that Barnabas and Saul were acquainted
with each other before. Cyprus is within a few hours' sail from
Cilicia. The schools of Tarsus may naturally have attracted one
who, though a Levite, was a Hellenist : and there the friendship
may have begun, which lasted through many vicissitudes, till it was
rudely interrupted in the dispute at Antioch.[6] When Barnabas
related how 'the Lord' Jesus Christ had personally appeared to
Saul, and had even spoken to him, and how he had boldly maintained the Christian cause in the synagogues of Damascus, then the
Apostles laid aside their hesitation. Peter's argument must have
been what it was on another occasion : 'Forasmuch as God hath
given unto him the like gift as He did unto me, who am I that I
should withstand God?'[7] He and James, the Lord's brother, the
only other Apostle[8] who was in Jerusalem at the time, gave to him

---

[1] *Scripture Biography*, by Archdeacon Evans, second series, p. 337.

[2] The argument used in his ecstasy
in the Temple (Acts xxii. 17-21),
when it was revealed to him that those
in Jerusalem would not receive his
testimony.

[3] Acts ix. 26.
[4] Acts iv. 36.
[5] Acts ix. 27.
[6] Acts xv. 39.
[7] Acts xi. 17.
[8] 'When Saul was come to Jerusalem . . . Barnabas took him and

' the right hands of fellowship.' And he was with them, 'coming in and going out,' more than forgiven for Christ's sake, welcomed and beloved as a friend and a brother.

This first meeting of the fisherman of Bethsaida and the tentmaker of Tarsus, the chosen companion of Jesus on earth and the chosen Pharisee who saw Jesus in the heavens, the Apostle of the circumcision and the Apostle of the Gentiles, is passed over in Scripture in a few words. The Divine record does not linger in dramatic description on those passages which a mere human writing would labour to embellish. What took place in the intercourse of these two Saints,—what was said of Jesus of Nazareth who suffered, died, and was buried,—and of Jesus, the glorified Lord, who had risen and ascended, and become 'head over all things to the Church,'— what was felt of Christian love and devotion,—what was learnt, under the Spirit's teaching, of Christian truth, has not been revealed, and cannot be known. The intercourse was full of present comfort, and full of great consequences. But it did not last long. Fifteen days passed away, and the Apostles were compelled to part. The same zeal which had caused his voice to be heard in the Hellenistic Synagogues in the persecution against Stephen, now led Saul in the same Synagogues to declare fearlessly his adherence to Stephen's cause. The same fury which had caused the murder of Stephen, now brought the murderer of Stephen to the verge of assassination. Once more, as at Damascus, the Jews made a conspiracy to put Saul to death : and once more he was rescued by the anxiety of the brethren.[1]

Reluctantly, and not without a direct intimation from on high, he retired from the work of preaching the Gospel in Jerusalem. As he was praying one day in the Temple, it came to pass that he fell into a trance,[2] and in his ecstasy he saw Jesus, who spoke to him, and said, 'Make haste and get thee quickly out of Jerusalem; for they will not receive thy testimony concerning me.' He hesitated to obey the command, his desire to do God's will leading him to struggle against the hindrances of God's providence—and the memory of Stephen, which haunted him even in his trance, furnishing him with an argument.[3] But the command was more peremptory than before : 'Depart; for I will send thee far hence unto the Gentiles.' The scene of his apostolic victories was not to be Jerusalem. For the third time it was declared to him that the field of his labours was among the Gentiles. This secret revelation to his soul conspired with the outward difficulties of his situation. The care of God gave the highest sanction to the anxiety of the

brought him to the Apostles . . . and he was with them coming in and going out at Jerusalem.' (Acts ix. 26–28.) 'After three years I went up to Jerusalem to see Peter, and abode with him fifteen days. But other of the Apostles saw I none, save James the Lord's brother.' (Gal. i. 18, 19.)

[1] Acts ix. 29, 30.

[2] See Acts xxii. 17–21. Though Schrader is sometimes laboriously un-

successful in explaining the miraculous, yet we need not entirely disregard what he says concerning the oppression of spirit, under the sense of being mistrusted and opposed, with which Saul came to pray in the Temple. And we may compare the preparation for St. Peter's vision, before the conversion of Cornelius.

[3] Compare the similar expostulations of Ananias, ix. 13, and of Peter, x. 14.

brethren.   And he suffered himself to be withdrawn from the Holy City.

They brought him down to Cæsarea by the sea,[1] and from Cæsarea they sent him to Tarsus.[2]   His own expression in the Epistle to the Galatians (i. 21) is that he went 'into the regions of Syria and Cilicia.'   From this it has been inferred that he went first from Cæsarea to Antioch, and then from Antioch to Tarsus.   And such a course would have been perfectly natural; for the communication of the city of Cæsar and the Herods with the metropolis of Syria, either by sea and the harbour of Seleucia, or by the great coast-road through Tyre and Sidon, was easy and frequent.   But the supposition is unnecessary.   In consequence of the range of Mount Taurus (p. 17), Cilicia has a greater geographical affinity with Syria than with Asia Minor.   Hence it has existed in frequent political combination with it from the time of the old Persian satrapies to the modern pachalics of the Sultan : and '*Syria and Cilicia*' appears in history almost as a generic geographical term, the more important district being mentioned first.[3]   Within the limits of this region Saul's activities were now exercised in studying and in teaching at Tarsus,—or in founding those Churches[4] which were afterwards greeted in the Apostolic letter from Jerusalem, as the brethren 'in Antioch, and Syria, and Cilicia,' and which Paul himself confirmed after his separation from Barnabas, travelling through 'Syria and Cilicia.'

Whatever might be the extent of his journeys within these limits, we know at least that he was at Tarsus.   Once more we find him in the home of his childhood.   It is the last time we are distinctly told that he was there.   Now at least, if not before, we may be sure that he would come into active intercourse with the Heathen philosophers of the place.[5]   In his last residence at Tarsus, a few years before,

---

[1] Olshausen is certainly mistaken in supposing that Cæsarea Philippi is meant. Whenever 'Cæsarea' is spoken of absolutely, it always means Cæsarea Stratonis. And even if it is assumed that Saul travelled by land through Syria to Tarsus, this would not have been the natural course.   It is true enough that this Cæsarea is nearer the Syrian frontier than the other; but the physical character of the country is such that the Apostle would naturally go by the other Cæsarea, unless indeed he travelled by Damascus to Antioch, which is highly improbable.

[2] Acts ix. 30.

[3] This is well illustrated by the hopeless feeling of the Greek soldiers in the Anabasis, when Cyrus had drawn them into Cilicia; by various passages in the history of the Seleucids; by the arrangements of the Romans with Antiochus; by the division of provinces in the Later Empire; and by the course of the Mahommedan conquests.

[4] Acts xv. 23, 41. When we find the existence of Cilician Churches mentioned, the obvious inference is that St. Paul founded them during this period.

[5] The passage in Strabo, referred to above, Chap. I. p. 15, is so important that we give a free translation of it here. 'The men of this place are so zealous in the study of philosophy and the whole circle of education, that they surpass both Athens and Alexandria, and every place that could be mentioned, where schools of philosophers are found. And the difference amounts to this. Here, those who are fond of learning are all natives, and strangers do not willingly reside here: and they themselves do not remain, but finish their education abroad, and gladly take up their residence elsewhere, and few return. Whereas, in the other cities which I have just mentioned, except Alexandria, the contrary takes place: for many come to them and live there willingly; but you will see few of the

he was a Jew, and not only a Jew but a Pharisee, and he looked on the Gentiles around him as outcasts from the favour of God. Now he was a Christian, and not only a Christian, but conscious of his mission as the Apostle of the Gentiles. Therefore he would surely meet the philosophers, and prepare to argue with them on their own ground, as afterwards in the 'market' at Athens with 'the Epicureans and the Stoics.'[1] Many Stoics of Tarsus were men of celebrity in the Roman Empire. Athenodorus, the tutor of Augustus, has already been mentioned.[2] He was probably by this time deceased, and receiving those divine honours, which, as Lucian informs us, were paid to him after his death. The tutor of Tiberius also was a Tarsian and a Stoic. His name was Nestor. He was probably at this time alive : for he lingered to the age of ninety-two, and, in all likelihood, survived his wicked pupil, whose death we have recently noticed. Now among these eminent sages and instructors of Heathen Emperors was one whose teaching was destined to survive, when the Stoic philosophy should have perished, and whose words still instruct the rulers of every civilised nation. How far Saul's arguments had any success in this quarter we cannot even guess ; and we must not anticipate the conversion of Cornelius. At least, he was preparing for the future. In the Synagogue we cannot believe that he was silent or unsuccessful. In his own family, we may well imagine that some of those Christian 'kinsmen,'[3] whose names are handed down to us,—possibly his sister, the playmate of his childhood, and his sister's son,[4] who afterwards saved his life,— were at this time by his exertions gathered into the fold of Christ.

Here this chapter must close, while Saul is in exile from the earthly Jerusalem, but diligently occupied in building up the walls of the 'Jerusalem which is above.' And it was not without one great and important consequence that that short fortnight had been spent in Jerusalem. He was now known to Peter and to James. His vocation was fully ascertained and recognised by the heads of the Judæan Christians. It is true that he was yet 'unknown by face' to the scattered Churches of Judæa.[5] But they honoured him of whom they had heard so much. And when the news came to them at intervals of all that he was doing for the cause of Christ, they praised God and said, 'Behold ! he who was once our perse-

---

natives either going abroad for the sake of philosophy, or caring to study it at home. The Alexandrians have both characters ; for they receive many strangers, and send out of their own people not a few.'

[1] Acts xvii. 17, 18.
[2] See p. 37.
[3] Rom. xvi. See p. 39.
[4] About twenty years after this time (Acts xxiii. 17, 23) he is called 'a young man,' the very word which is used of Saul himself (Acts vii. 58) at the stoning of Stephen. It is justly remarked by Hemsen that the young man's anxiety for his uncle (xxiii. 16-23) seems to imply a closer affec-

tion than that resulting from relationship alone.

[5] See Gal. i. 21-24. The form of the Greek words seems to imply a continued preaching of the Gospel, the intelligence of which came now and then to Judæa. From what follows, however ('Then fourteen years afterwards'), St. Paul appears to describe in i. 23, 24, the effect produced by the tidings not only of his labours in Tarsus, but of his subsequent and more extensive labours as a missionary to the Heathen. It should be added, that Wieseler thinks he stayed only half a year at Tarsus.

cutor is now bearing the glad tidings of that faith which formerly he laboured to root out ; ' 'and they glorified God in him.'

Coin of Aretas, King of Damascus.[1]

[1] Three members of this dynasty come prominently before us in history. The first is mentioned in the annals of the Maccabees. The second was cotemporary with the last of the Seleucids. Damascus was once in his power (Joseph. *Ant.* xiii. 13, 3; *War*, i. 6, 2), and it is his submission to the Roman Scaurus which is represented in the coin. The third is that of St. Paul.

As to the Aretas, who is mentioned in 2 Macc. v. 8, the words used there of the innovating high-priest Jason are so curiously applicable to the case of St. Paul, that we cannot forbear quoting them. ' In the end, therefore, he had an unhappy return, being accused before Aretas the king of the Arabians, fleeing from city to city, pursued of all men, hated as a forsaker of the laws, and being had in abomination as an open enemy of his country.'

A few words concerning the meaning of the word *Ethnarch* may fitly conclude this note. It properly denoted the governor of a dependent district, like Simon the high-priest under Syria (1 Macc. xiv. 47), or Herod's son Archelaus under Rome (Joseph. *Ant.* xvii. 11, 4). But it was also used as the designation of a magistrate or consul allowed to Jewish residents living under their own laws in Alexandria and other cities. (See Strabo, as quoted by Josephus, *Ant.* xiv. 7, 2.) Some writers (and among them Mr. Lewin, *Life and Epistles of St. Paul*, vol. i. p. 70) think that the word is used in that sense here. But such a magistrate would hardly have been called 'the Ethnarch of Aretas,' and (as Dean Alford observes on 2 Cor. xi. 32) he would not have had the power of guarding the city.

CHAPTER IV.

Wider Diffusion of Christianity.—Antioch.—Chronology of the Acts.—Reign of Caligula.—Claudius and Herod Agrippa I.—The Year 44.—Conversion of the Gentiles.—St. Peter and Cornelius.—Joppa and Cæsarea.—St. Peter's Vision.— Baptism of Cornelius.— Intelligence from Antioch.— Mission of Barnabas. — Saul with Barnabas at Antioch.— The Name 'Christian.' — Description and History of Antioch.—Character of its Inhabitants.—Earthquakes.—Famine.—Barnabas and Saul at Jerusalem.—Death of St. James and of Herod Agrippa.—Return with Mark to Antioch.—Providential Preparation of St. Paul.—Results of his Mission to Jerusalem.

HITHERTO the history of the Christian Church has been confined within Jewish limits. We have followed its progress beyond the walls of Jerusalem, but hardly yet beyond the boundaries of Palestine. If any traveller from a distant country has been admitted into the community of believers, the place of his baptism has not been more remote than the 'desert' of Gaza. If any 'aliens from the commonwealth of Israel' have been admitted to the citizenship of the spiritual Israelites, they have been 'strangers' who dwell among the hills of Samaria. But the time is rapidly approaching when the knowledge of Christ must spread more rapidly,—when those who possess not that Book, which caused perplexity on the road to Ethiopia, will hear and adore His name,—and greater strangers than those who drew water from the well of Sychar will come nigh to the Fountain of Life. The same dispersion which gathered in the Samaritans, will gather in the Gentiles also. The 'middle wall of partition' being utterly broken down, all will be called by the new and glorious name of ' Christian.'

And as we follow the progress of events, and find that all movements in the Church begin to have more and more reference to the Heathen, we observe that these movements begin to circulate more and more round a new centre of activity. Not Jerusalem, but Antioch,—not the Holy City of God's ancient people, but the profane city of the Greeks and Romans,—is the place to which the student of sacred history is now directed. During the remainder of the Acts of the Apostles our attention is at least divided between Jerusalem and Antioch, until at last, after following St. Paul's many journeys, we come with him to Rome. For some time Constantinople must remain a city of the future ; but we are more than once reminded of the greatness of Alexandria :[1] and thus even in the life of the Apostle we find prophetic intimations of four of the five great centres of the early Catholic Church.[2]

---

[1] See Acts vi. 9 (with ii. 10), xxvii. 6, xxviii. 11 ; and compare Acts xviii. 24, xix. 1, with 1 Cor. i. 12, iii. 4–6, and Tit. iii. 13.

[2] The allusion is to the Patriarchates of Jerusalem, Alexandria, Antioch, Rome, and Constantinople.

At present we are occupied with Antioch, and the point before us is that particular moment in the Church's history, when it was first called 'Christian.' Both the *place* and the *event* are remarkable : and the *time*, if we are able to determine it, is worthy of our attention. Though we are following the course of an individual biography, it is necessary to pause, on critical occasions, to look around on what is passing in the Empire at large. And, happily, we are now arrived at a point where we are able distinctly to see the path of the Apostle's life intersecting the general history of the period. This, therefore, is the right place for a few chronological remarks. A few such remarks, made once for all, may justify what has gone before, and prepare the way for subsequent chapters.

Some readers may be surprised that up to this point we have made no attempts to ascertain or to state exact chronological details.[1] But theologians are well aware of the difficulties with which such inquiries are attended, in the beginnings of St. Paul's biography. The early chapters in the Acts are like the narratives in the Gospels. It is often hardly possible to learn how far the events related were cotemporary or consecutive. We should endeavour in vain to determine the relations of time, which subsist between Paul's retirement into Arabia and Peter's visit to the converted Samaritans,[2] or between the journey of one Apostle from Joppa to Cæsarea and the journey of the other from Jerusalem to Tarsus.[3] Still less have we sufficient data for pronouncing upon the absolute chronology of the earliest transactions in the Church. No one can tell what particular folly or crime was engaging Caligula's attention, when Paul was first made a Christian at Damascus. No one can tell on what work of love the Christians were occupied when the Emperor was inaugurating his bridge at Puteoli,[4] or exhibiting his fantastic pride on the shores of the British Sea.[5] In a work of this kind it is better to place the events of the Apostle's life in the broad light cast by the leading features of the period, than to attempt to illustrate them by the help of dates, which, after all, can be only conjectural. Thus we have been content to say, that he was born in the strongest and most flourishing period of the reign of Augustus ; and that he was converted from the religion of the Pharisees about the time when Caligula succeeded Tiberius. But soon after we enter on the reign of Claudius we encounter a coincidence which arrests our attention. We must first take a rapid glance at the reign of his predecessor. Though the cruelty of that reign stung the Jews in every part of the empire, and produced an indignation which never subsided, one short paragraph will be enough for all that need be said concerning the abominable tyrant.[6]

In the early part of the year 37 Tiberius died, and at the close of the same year Nero was born. Between the reigns of these two

---

[1] See above, pp. 37, 68, 69, and 83.

[2] Acts viii. and Acts ix. (with Gal. i.).

[3] Acts ix. and Acts x.

[4] Where St. Paul afterwards landed, Acts xxviii. 13.

[5] Herod was with Caligula in this progress. This emperor's triumph had

no more meaning than Napoleon's column at Boulogne ; but in the next reign Britain was really conquered. See below.

[6] The reader is here requested to refer to pp. 23, 24, 37, 38, 45, 46, 53, 57, and the notes.

emperors are those of Caligula and Claudius. The four years during which Caligula sat on the throne of the world were miserable for all the provinces, both in the west and in the east.[1] In Gaul his insults were aggravated by his personal presence. In Syria his caprices were felt more remotely, but not less keenly. The changes of administration were rapid and various. In the year 36, the two great actors in the crime of the crucifixion had disappeared from the public places of Judæa. Pontius Pilate[2] had been dismissed by Vitellius to Rome, and Marcellus sent to govern in his stead. Caiaphas had been deposed by the same secular authority, and succeeded by Jonathan. Now, in the year 37, Vitellius was recalled from Syria, and Petronius came to occupy the governor's residence at Antioch. Marcellus at Cæsarea made way for Marullus : and Theophilus was appointed high-priest at Jerusalem in place of his brother Jonathan. Agrippa, the grandson of Herod the Great, was brought out of the prison where Tiberius had confined him, and Caligula gave a royal crown,[3] with the tetrarchies of two of his uncles, to the frivolous friend of his youth. And as this reign began with restless change, so it ended in cruelty and impiety. The emperor, in the career of his blasphemous arrogance, attempted to force the Jews to worship him as God.[4] One universal feeling of horror pervaded the scattered Israelites, who, though they had scorned the Messiah promised to their fathers, were unable to degrade themselves by a return to idolatry. Petronius, who foresaw what the struggle must be, wrote letters of expostulation to his master : Agrippa, who was then in Italy, implored his patron to pause in what he did : an embassy was sent from Alexandria, and the venerable and learned Philo[5] was himself commissioned to state the inexorable requirements of the Jewish religion. Everything appeared to be hopeless, when the murder of Caligula, on the 24th of January, in the year 41, gave a sudden relief to the persecuted people.

With the accession of Claudius (A.D. 41) the Holy Land had a king once more. Judæa was added to the tetrarchies of Philip and Antipas, and Herod Agrippa I. ruled over the wide territory which had been governed by his grandfather. With the alleviation of the distress of the Jews, proportionate suffering came upon the Christians. The 'rest' which, in the distractions of Caligula's reign, the

[1] The best portraits of this emperor are on the large copper imperial coins.

[2] He did not arrive at Rome till after the death of Tiberius. Like his predecessor, he had governed Judæa during ten or eleven years, the emperor having a great dislike to frequent changes in the provinces.

[3] Tiberius had imprisoned him, because of a conversation overheard by a slave, when Caligula and Herod Agrippa were together in a carriage. Agrippa was much at Rome both at the beginning and end of Caligula's reign. See p. 23, n. 8.

[4] It appears from Dio Cassius and Suetonius that this was part of a general system for extending the worship of himself through the empire.

[5] See above, pp. 8, 30, and 53. Philo's account of this embassy is, next after Josephus, the most important writing of the period for throwing light on the condition of the Jews in Caligula's reign. The Jewish envoys had their interview with the emperor at Puteoli, in the autumn of the same year (40 A.D.) in which he had made his progress through Gaul to the shore of the ocean.

Churches had enjoyed 'throughout all Judea, and Galilee, and Samaria,' was now at an end. 'About this time Herod the king stretched forth his hands to vex certain of the Church.' He slew one Apostle, and 'because he saw it pleased the Jews,' he proceeded to imprison another. But he was not long spared to seek popularity among the Jews, or to murder and oppress the Christians. In the year 44 he perished by that sudden and dreadful death which is recorded in detail by Josephus and St. Luke.[1] In close coincidence with this event we have the mention of a certain journey of St. Paul to Jerusalem. Here, then, we have one of those lines of intersection between the sacred history and the general history of the world, on which the attention of intelligent Christians ought to be fixed. This year, 44 A.D., and another year, the year 60 A.D. (in which Felix ceased to be governor of Judæa, and, leaving St. Paul bound at Cæsarea, was succeeded by Festus), are the two chronological pivots of the apostolic history.[2] By help of them we find its exact place in the wider history of the world. Between these two limits the greater part of what we are told of St. Paul is situated and included.

Using the year 44 as a starting-point for the future, we gain a new light for tracing the Apostle's steps. It is evident that we have only to ascertain the successive intervals of his life, in order to see him at every point, in his connection with the transactions of the Empire. We shall observe this often as we proceed. At present it is more important to remark that the same date throws some light on that earlier part of the Apostle's path which is confessedly obscure. Reckoning backwards, we remember that 'three years' intervened between his conversion and return to Jerusalem.[3] Those who assign the former event to 39 or 40, and those who fix on 37 or some earlier year, differ as to the length of time he spent at Tarsus, or in 'Syria and Cilicia.'[4] All that we can say with certainty is, that St. Paul was converted more than three years before the year 44.[5]

[1] *Ant.* xix. 8. Acts xii. The proof that his death took place in 44 may be seen in Anger and Wieseler ; and, indeed, it is hardly doubted by any. A coincident and corroborative proof of the time of St. Paul's journey to Jerusalem, is afforded by the mention of the *Famine*, which is doubtless that recorded by Josephus (see below, p. 104). Anger has shown that this famine must be assigned to the interval between 44 and 47 ; and Wieseler has fixed it more closely to the year 45. See the Chronological Table at the end of the work.

[2] It ought to be stated that the latter date cannot be established by the same exact proof as the former; but, as a *political fact*, it must always be a cardinal point of reference in any system of Scripture chronology. Anger and Wieseler, by a careful induction of particulars, have made it highly probable that Festus succeeded Felix in the year 60. More will be said on this subject when we come to Acts xxiv. 27.

[3] Gal. i. 18.

[4] Acts ix. 30 ; Gal. i. 21. Wieseler, with Schrader, thinks that he stayed at Tarsus only half a year or a year ; Anger, that he was there two years, between 41 and 43 : Hemsen, that he spent there the years 40, 41, and 42. Among the English writers, Bp. Pearson imagines that great part of the interval after 39 was passed in Syria ; Burton, who places the conversion very early, is forced to allow nine or ten years for the time spent in Syria and Cilicia.

[5] Wieseler places the Conversion in the year 39 or 40.

The date thus important for all students of Bible chronology is worthy of special regard by the Christians of Britain. For in that year the Emperor Claudius returned from the shores of this island to the metropolis of his empire. He came here in command of a military expedition, to complete the work which the landing of Cæsar, a century before, had begun, or at least predicted.[1] When Claudius was in Britain, its inhabitants were not Christian. They could hardly in any sense be said to have been civilised. He came, as he thought, to add a barbarous province to his already gigantic empire; but he really came to prepare the way for the silent progress of the Christian Church. His troops were the instruments of bringing among our barbarous ancestors those charities which were just then beginning to display themselves[2] in Antioch and Jerusalem. A 'new name' was faintly rising on the Syrian shore, which was destined to spread like the cloud seen by the Prophet's servant from the brow of Mount Carmel. A better civilisation, a better citizenship, than that of the Roman Empire, was preparing for us and for many. One Apostle at Tarsus was waiting for his call to proclaim the Gospel of Christ to the Gentiles. Another Apostle at Joppa was receiving a divine intimation that 'God is no respecter of persons, but that in every nation he that feareth Him and worketh righteousness, is accepted with Him.'[3]

If we could ascertain the exact chronological arrangement of these passages of Apostolical history, great light would be thrown on the circumstantial details of the admission of Gentiles to the Church, and on the growth of the Church's conviction on this momentous subject. We should then be able to form some idea of the meaning and results of the fortnight spent by Paul and Peter together at Jerusalem (p. 86). But it is not permitted to us to know the manner and degree in which the different Apostles were illuminated. We have not been informed whether Paul ever felt the difficulty of Peter,—whether he knew from the first the full significance of his call,—whether he learnt the truth by visions, or by the gradual workings of his mind under the teaching of the Holy Spirit.[4] All we can confidently assert is, that he did not learn from St. Peter the mystery 'which in other ages was not made known unto the sons of men, as it was now revealed unto God's holy Apostles by the Spirit; that the Gentiles should be fellow-heirs, and of the same body, and partakers of His promise in Christ by the Gospel.'[5]

If St. Paul was converted in 39 or 40, and if the above-mentioned rest of the Churches was in the last years of Caligula (A.D. 39–41), and if this rest was the occasion of that journey to Lydda and Joppa which ultimately brought St. Peter to Cæsarea, then it is evident that St. Paul was at Damascus or in Arabia when Cornelius was

---

[1] It may be gathered from Dio Cassius, that the Emperor left Rome in July 43, and returned in January 45.

[2] See Acts xi. 22–24, and 27–30.

[3] Acts x. 34, 35.

[4] The question touched on here, viz. *when* the complete truth of Christ was communicated to St. Paul, evidently opens a wide field for speculation. It is well treated by Dr. Davidson (*Introd.* vol. ii. pp. 75–80), who believes that the full disclosures of the Gospel were made to him in Arabia.

[5] Eph. iii. 4–6. See Col. i. 26, 27.

baptized.[1] Paul was summoned to evangelise the Heathen, and Peter began the work, almost simultaneously. The great transaction of admitting the Gentiles to the Church was already accomplished when the two Apostles met at Jerusalem. St. Paul would thus learn that the door had been opened for him by the hand of another ; and when he went to Tarsus, the later agreement[2] might then have been partially adopted, that he should 'go to the Heathen,' while Peter remained as the Apostle of 'the Circumcision.'

If we are to bring down the conversion of Cornelius nearer to the year 44, and to place it in that interval of time which St. Paul spent at Tarsus,[3] then it is natural to suppose that his conversations prepared Peter's mind for the change which was at hand, and sowed the seeds of that revolution of opinion, of which the vision at Joppa was the crisis and completion. Paul might learn from Peter (as possibly also from Barnabas) many of the details of our blessed Saviour's life. And Peter, meanwhile, might gather from Paul some of those higher views concerning the Gospel which prepared him for the miracles which he afterwards saw in the household of the Roman centurion. Whatever might be the obscurity of St. Paul's early knowledge, whether it was revealed to him or not that the Gentile converts would be called to overleap the ceremonies of Judaism on their entrance into the Church of Christ,—he could not fail to have a clear understanding that his own work was to lie among the Gentiles. This had been announced to him at his first conversion (Acts xxvi. 17, 18), in the words of Ananias (Acts ix. 15) : and in the vision preceding his retirement to Tarsus (Acts xxii. 21), the words which commanded him to go were, 'Depart, for I will send thee far hence to the Gentiles.'

In considering, then, the conversion of Cornelius to have happened after this journey from Jerusalem to Tarsus, and before the mission of Barnabas to Antioch, we are adopting the opinion most in accordance with the independent standing-point occupied by St. Paul. And this, moreover, is the view which harmonises best with the narrative of Scripture, where the *order* ought to be reverently regarded as well as the *words*. In the order of Scripture narration, if it cannot be proved that the preaching of Peter at Cæsarea was chronologically earlier than the preaching of Paul at Antioch, it is at least brought before us theologically, as the beginning of the Gospel made known to the Heathen. When an important change is at hand, God usually causes a silent preparation in the minds of men, and some great fact occurs, which may be taken as a type and symbol of the general movement. Such a fact was the conversion of Cornelius, and so we must consider it.

The whole transaction is related and reiterated with so much minuteness,[4] that, if we were writing a history of the Church, we should be required to dwell upon it at length. But here we have only to do with it as the point of union between Jews and Gentiles,

---

[1] This is Wieseler's view; but his arguments are not conclusive. By some (as by Schrader) it is hastily taken for granted that St. Paul preached the Gospel to Gentiles at Damascus.

[2] Gal. ii. 9.

[3] On the duration of this interval, see above, p. 93, n. 4.

[4] See the whole narrative, Acts x. 1 –xi. 19.

and as the bright starting-point of St. Paul's career. A few words may be allowed, which are suggested by this view of the transaction as a typical fact in the progress of God's dispensations. The two men to whom the revelations were made, and even the places where the Divine interferences occurred, were characteristic of the event. Cornelius was in Cæsarea and St. Peter in Joppa;—the Roman soldier in the modern city, which was built and named in the Emperor's honour,—the Jewish Apostle in the ancient sea-port which associates its name with the early passages of Hebrew history,—with the voyage of Jonah, the building of the Temple, the wars of the Maccabees.[1] All the splendour of Cæsarea, its buildings and its ships, and the Temple of Rome and the Emperor, which the sailors saw far out at sea,[2] all has long since vanished. Herod's magnificent city is a wreck on the shore. A few ruins are all that remain of the harbour. Joppa lingers on, like the Jewish people, dejected but not destroyed. Cæsarea has perished, like the Roman Empire which called it into existence.

And no men could well be more contrasted with each other than those two men, in whom the Heathen and Jewish worlds met and were reconciled. We know what Peter was—a Galilæan fisherman, brought up in the rudest district of an obscure province, with no learning but such as he might have gathered in the synagogue of his native town. All his early days he had dragged his nets in the lake of Gennesareth. And now he was at Joppa, lodging in the house of Simon the Tanner, the Apostle of a religion that was to change the world. Cornelius was an officer in the Roman army. No name was more honourable at Rome than that of the *Cornelian House*. It was the name borne by the Scipios, and by Sulla, and the mother of the Gracchi. In the Roman army, as in the army of modern Austria, the soldiers were drawn from different countries and spoke different languages. Along the coast of which we are speaking, many of them were recruited from Syria and Judæa.[3] But the corps to which Cornelius belonged seems to have been a cohort of Italians separate from the legionary soldiers,[4] and hence called the 'Italian cohort.' He was no doubt a true-born Italian. Educated in Rome, or some provincial town, he had entered upon a soldier's life, dreaming perhaps of military glory, but dreaming as little of that better glory which now surrounds the Cornelian name, —as Peter dreamt at the lake of Gennesareth of becoming the chosen companion of the Messiah of Israel, and of throwing open the doors of the Catholic Church to the dwellers in Asia and Africa, to the barbarians on the remote and unvisited shores of Europe, and to the undiscovered countries of the West.

But to return to our proper narrative   When intelligence came

---

[1] Jonah i. 3; 2 Chr. ii. 16. See Josh. xix. 46; Ezra iii. 7, and various passages in the Apocrypha, 1 Esd. v. 55; 1 Macc. x. 75, xiv. 5; 2 Macc. xii. 3, &c.

[2] A full account of Cæsarea will be given when we come to the period of St. Paul's imprisonment there.

[3] Joseph. *Ant.* xiv. 15, 10; *War*, i.

17, 1.

[4] Not a cohort of the '*Legio Italica*,' and which was raised by Nero. See above, p. 23, n. 5. Possibly the corps of Cornelius might be certain 'Italian volunteers,' mentioned in an inscription as serving in Syria. Akermann's *Numismatic Ill. of the New Test.* p. 34.

to Jerusalem that Peter had broken through the restraints of the Jewish Law, and had even ' eaten ' at the table of the Gentiles,[1] there was general surprise and displeasure among ' those of the circumcision.' But when he explained to them all the transaction, they approved his conduct, and praised God for His mercy to the Heathen.[2] And soon news came from a greater distance, which showed that the same unexpected change was operating more widely. We have seen that the persecution, in which Stephen was killed, resulted in a general dispersion of the Christians. Wherever they went, they spoke to their Jewish brethren of their faith that the promises had been fulfilled in the life and resurrection of Jesus Christ. This dispersion and preaching of the Gospel extended even to the island of Cyprus, and along the Phœnician coast as far as Antioch. For some time the glad tidings were made known only to the scattered children of Israel.[3] But at length some of the Hellenistic Jews, natives of Cyprus and Cyrene, spoke to the Greeks[4] themselves at Antioch, and the Divine Spirit gave such power to the Word, that a vast number ' believed and turned to the Lord.' The news was not long in travelling to Jerusalem. Perhaps some message was sent in haste to the Apostles of the Church. The Jewish Christians in Antioch might be perplexed how to deal with their new Gentile converts : and it is not unnatural to suppose that the presence of Barnabas might be anxiously desired by the fellow missionaries of his native island.

We ought to observe the honourable place which the island of Cyprus was permitted to occupy in the first work of Christianity. We shall soon trace the footsteps of the Apostle of the Heathen in the beginning of his travels over the length of this island ; and see here the first earthly potentate converted, and linking his name for ever with that of St. Paul.[5] Now, while Saul is yet at Tarsus, men of Cyprus are made the instruments of awakening the Gentiles ; one of them might be that ' Mnason of Cyprus,' who afterwards (*then* ' a disciple of old standing') was his host at Jerusalem ;[6] and Joses the Levite of Cyprus,[7] whom the Apostles had long ago called ' the Son of Consolation,' and who had removed all the prejudice which looked suspiciously on Saul's conversion,[8] is the first teacher sent by the Mother-Church to the new disciples at Antioch. ' He was a good man, and full of the Holy Ghost and of faith.' He

---

[1] Acts xi. 3. See x. 48. No such freedom of intercourse took place in his own reception of his Gentile guests, x. 23.

[2] Acts xi. 18.

[3] See xi. 19, 20.

[4] Acts xi. 20. We are strongly of opinion that the correct reading here is not 'Grecians' (A.V.), but Greeks, probably in the sense of proselytes of the Gate. Thus they were in the same position as Cornelius. It has been doubted which case was prior in point of time. Some are of opinion that the

events at Antioch took place first. Others believe that those who spoke to the Greeks at Antioch had previously heard of the conversion of Cornelius. There seems no objection to supposing the two cases nearly simultaneous, that of Cornelius being the great typical transaction on which our attention is to be fixed.

[5] Acts xiii. 6–9.

[6] Acts xxi. 16.

[7] Acts iv. 36. See, however, the next note but one.

[8] Acts ix. 27.

rejoiced when he saw what God's grace was doing ; he exhorted [1] all to cling fast to the Saviour whom they had found ; and he laboured himself with abundant success. But feeling the greatness of the work, and remembering the zeal and strong character of his friend, whose vocation to this particular task of instructing the Heathen was doubtless well known to him, ' he departed to Tarsus to seek Saul.'

Whatever length of time had elapsed since Saul came from Jerusalem to Tarsus, and however that time had been employed by him,—whether he had already founded any of those churches in his native Cilicia, which we read of soon after (Acts xv. 41),—whether (as is highly probable) he had there undergone any of those manifold labours and sufferings recorded by himself (2 Cor. xi.) but omitted by St. Luke,—whether by active intercourse with the Gentiles, by study of their literature, by travelling, by discoursing with the philosophers, he had been making himself acquainted with their opinions and their prejudices, and so preparing his mind for the work that was before him,—or whether he had been waiting in silence for the call of God's providence, praying for guidance from above, reflecting on the condition of the Gentiles, and gazing more and more closely on the plan of the world's redemption,—however this may be, it must have been an eventful day when Barnabas, having come across the sea from Seleucia, or round by the defiles of Mount Amanus, suddenly appeared in the streets of Tarsus. The last time the two friends had met was in Jerusalem. All that they then hoped, and probably more than they then thought possible, had occurred. ' God had granted to the Gentiles repentance unto life ' (xi. 18). Barnabas had ' seen the grace of God ' (xi. 23) with his own eyes at Antioch ; and under his own teaching ' a great multitude ' (xi. 24) had been ' added to the Lord.' But he needed assistance. He needed the presence of one whose wisdom was higher than his own, whose zeal was an example to all, and whose peculiar mission had been miraculously declared. Saul recognised the voice of God in the words of Barnabas : and the two friends travelled in all haste to the Syrian metropolis.

There they continued ' a whole year,' actively prosecuting the sacred work, teaching and confirming those who joined themselves to the assemblies [2] of the ever-increasing Church. As new converts, in vast numbers, came in from the ranks of the Gentiles, the Church began to lose its ancient appearance of a Jewish sect, [3] and to stand out in relief, as a great self-existing community, in the face both of Jews and Gentiles. Hitherto it had been possible, and even natural, that the Christians should be considered, by the Jews themselves, and by the Heathen whose notice they attracted, as only one among the many theological parties, which prevailed in Jerusalem and in the Dispersion. But when Gentiles began to listen to what was preached concerning Christ,—when they were united as brethren on equal terms, and admitted to baptism without the

---

[1] Acts xi. 23. The ' Son of Consolation,' of iv. 36, ought rather to be translated ' Son of Exhortation' or

' Son of Prophecy.' See xiii. 1.
[2] See Acts xi. 26.
[3] See above, pp. 26 and 55.

necessity of previous circumcision,—when the Mosaic features of this society were lost in the wider character of the New Covenant,— then it became evident that these men were something more than the Pharisees or Sadducees, the Essenes[1] or Herodians, or any sect or party among the Jews. Thus a new term in the vocabulary of the human race came into existence at Antioch about the year 44. Thus Jews and Gentiles, who, under the teaching of St. Paul, believed that Jesus of Nazareth was the Saviour of the world, ' were first called *Christians.*'

It is not likely that they received this name from the Jews. The ' Children of Abraham '[2] employed a term much more expressive of hatred and contempt. They called them ' the sect of the Nazarenes.'[3] These disciples of Jesus traced their origin to Nazareth in Galilee : and it was a proverb, that nothing good could come from Nazareth.[4] Besides this, there was a further reason why the Jews would not have called the disciples of Jesus by the name of ' Christians.' The word ' Christ' has the same meaning with ' Messiah ; ' and the Jews, however blinded and prejudiced on this subject, would never have used so sacred a word to point an expression of mockery and derision ; and they could not have used it in grave and serious earnest to designate those whom they held to be the followers of a false Messiah, a fictitious Christ. Nor is it likely that the ' Christians ' gave this name to themselves. In the Acts of the Apostles, and in their own letters, we find them designating themselves as ' brethren,' ' disciples,' ' believers,' ' saints.'[5] Only in two places[6] do we find the term ' Christians ; ' and in both instances it is implied to be a term used by those who are without. There is little doubt that the name originated with the Gentiles, who began now to see that this new sect was so far distinct from the Jews, that they might naturally receive a new designation. And the form of the word implies that it came from the Romans,[7] not from the Greeks. The word ' Christ' was often in the conversation of the believers, as we know it to have been constantly in their letters. ' Christ' was the title of Him, whom they avowed as their leader and their chief. They confessed that this Christ had been crucified; but they asserted that He was risen from the dead, and that He guided them by His invisible power. Thus ' Christian ' was the name which naturally found its place in the reproachful language of their enemies.[8] In the first instance,

[1] See above, p. 29.

[2] Matt. iii. 9 ; Luke iii. 8 ; John viii. 39.

[3] Acts xxiv. 5.

[4] John i. 46. See John vii. 41, 52 ; Luke xiii. 2, &c.

[5] Acts xv. 23, ix. 26, v. 14, ix. 32 ; Rom. xv. 25 ; Col. i. 2, &c.

[6] Acts xxvi. 28, and 1 Pet. iv. 16.

[7] So we read, in the Civil Wars, of ' Marians' and ' Pompeians,' for the partizans of Marius and Pompey ; and, under the Empire, of ' Othonians' and ' Vitellians,' for the partizans of Otho and Vitellius. The word ' Herodians' (Matt. xxii. 16 ; Mark iii. 6, xii. 13) is formed exactly in the same way.

[8] It is a Latin derivative from the Greek term for the Messiah of the Jews. It is connected with the office, not the name, of our Saviour; which harmonises with the important fact, that in the Epistles He is usually called not ' Jesus' but ' Christ.' The word ' Jesuit' (which, by the way, is rather Greek than Latin) did not come into the vocabulary of the Church till after the lapse of 1,500 years. It is

we have every reason to believe that it was a term of ridicule and derision.[1] And it is remarkable that the people of Antioch were notorious for inventing names of derision, and for turning their wit into the channels of ridicule.[2] In every way there is something very significant in the place where we first received the name we bear. Not in Jerusalem, the city of the Old Covenant, the city of the people who were chosen to the exclusion of all others, but in a Heathen city, the Eastern centre of Greek fashion and Roman luxury : and not till it was shown that the New Covenant was inclusive of all others ; then and there we were first called Christians, and the Church received from the world its true and honourable name.

In narrating the journeys of St. Paul, it will now be our duty to speak of Antioch, not Jerusalem, as his point of departure and return. Let us look, more closely than has hitherto been necessary, at its character, its history, and its appearance. The position which it occupied near the abrupt angle formed by the coasts of Syria and Asia Minor, and in the opening where the Orontes passes between the ranges of Lebanon and Taurus, has already been noticed.[3] And we have mentioned the numerous colony of Jews which Seleucus introduced into his capital, and raised to an equality of civil rights with the Greeks.[4] There was everything in the situation and circumstances of this city, to make it a place of concourse for all classes and kinds of people. By its harbour of Seleucia it was in communication with all the trade of the Mediterranean ; and, through the open country behind the Lebanon, it was conveniently approached by the caravans from Mesopotamia and Arabia. It united the inland advantages of Aleppo with the maritime opportunities of Smyrna. It was almost an oriental Rome, in which all the forms of the civilised life of the Empire found some representative. Through the first two centuries of the Christian era, it was what Constantinople became afterwards, ' the Gate of the East.' And, indeed, the glory of the city of Ignatius was only gradually eclipsed by that of the city of Chrysostom. That great preacher and commentator himself, who knew them both by familiar residence, always speaks of Antioch with peculiar reverence,[5] as the patriarchal city of the Christian name.

There is something curiously prophetic in the stories which are told of the first founding of this city. Like Romulus on the Palatine, Seleucus is said to have watched the flight of birds from

---

not a little remarkable that the word 'Jesuit' is a proverbial term of reproach, even in Roman Catholic countries ; while the word 'Christian' is used so proverbially for all that is good, that it has been applied to benevolent actions in which Jews have participated.

[1] It is needless to remark that it soon became a title of glory. Julian tried to substitute the term 'Galilean' for 'Christian.'

[2] Apollonius of Tyana was driven

out of the city by their insults, and sailed away (like St. Paul) from Seleucia to Cyprus, where he visited Paphos. See Chap. X.

[3] P. 16.

[4] P. 14.

[5] In his homilies on St. Matthew he tells the people of Antioch, that though they boasted of their city's pre-eminence in having first enjoyed the Christian name, they were willing enough to be surpassed in Christian virtue by more homely cities.

the summit of Mount Casius. An eagle took a fragment of the flesh of his sacrifice, and carried it to a point on the seashore, a little to the north of the mouth of the Orontes. There he founded a city, and called it *Seleucia*,[1] after his own name. This was on the 23rd of April. Again, on the 1st of May, he sacrificed on the hill Silpius ; and then repeated the ceremony and watched the auguries at the city of Antigonia, which his vanquished rival, Antigonus, had begun and left unfinished. An eagle again decided that this was not to be his own metropolis, and carried the flesh to the hill Silpius, which is on the south side of the river, about the place where it turns from a northerly to a westerly direction. Five or six thousand Athenians and Macedonians were ordered to convey the stones and timber of Antigonia down the river ; and *Antioch* was founded by Seleucus, and called after his father's name.[2]

This fable, invented perhaps to give a mythological sanction to what was really an act of sagacious prudence and princely ambition, is well worth remembering. Seleucus was not slow to recognise the wisdom of Antigonus in choosing a site for his capital, which should place it in ready communication both with the shores of Greece and with his eastern territories on the Tigris and Euphrates ; and he followed the example promptly, and completed his work with sumptuous magnificence. Few princes have ever lived with so great a passion for the building of cities ; and this is a feature of his character which ought not to be unnoticed in this narrative. Two at least of his cities in Asia Minor have a close connection with the life of St. Paul. These are the Pisidian Antioch[3] and the Phrygian Laodicea,[4] one called by the name of his father, the other of his mother. He is said to have built in all nine Seleucias, sixteen Antiochs, and six Laodiceas. This love of commemorating the members of his family was conspicuous in his works by the Orontes. Besides Seleucia and Antioch, he built, in the immediate neighbourhood, a Laodicea in honour of his mother, and an Apamea in honour of his wife. But by far the most famous of these four cities was the Syrian Antioch.

We must allude to its edifices and ornaments only so far as they are due to the Greek kings of Syria and the first five Cæsars of Rome.[5] If we were to allow our description to wander to the times of Justinian or the Crusaders, though these are the times of Antioch's greatest glory, we should be trespassing on a period of history which does not belong to us. Strabo, in the time of Augustus, describes the city as a Tetrapolis, or union of four cities. The two first were erected by Seleucus Nicator himself, in the situation already described, between Mount Silpius and the river, on that wide space of level ground where a few poor habitations still remain by the banks of the Orontes. The river has gradually changed its course and appearance as the city has decayed. Once it flowed

---

[1] See Acts xiii. 4.
[2] Some say that Seleucus called the city after his son.
[3] Acts xiii. 14, xiv. 21 ; 2 Tim. iii. 11.
[4] Coloss. iv. 13, 15, 16. See Rev. i. 11, iii. 14.

[5] In our larger editions is a plan of the ancient city, adopted (with some modifications) from the plan in the work mentioned below, p. 102, n. 4. See a fuller account of Antioch in Dr. Smith's *Dict. of Geog.*

round an island which, like the island in the Seine,[1] by its thorough-fares and bridges, and its own noble buildings, became part of a magnificent whole.   But, in Paris, the Old City is on the island ; in Antioch, it was the New City, built by the second Seleucus and the third Antiochus.   Its chief features were a palace, and an arch like that of Napoleon.   The fourth and last part of the Tetrapolis was built by Antiochus Epiphanes, where Mount Silpius rises abruptly on the south.   On one of its craggy summits he placed, in the fervour of his Romanising mania,[2] a temple dedicated to Jupiter Capitolinus ; and on another, a strong citadel which dwindled to the Saracen Castle of the first Crusade.   At the rugged bases of the mountain, the ground was levelled for a glorious street, which extended for four miles across the length of the city, and where sheltered crowds could walk through continuous colon-nades from the eastern to the western suburb.[3]   The whole was surrounded by a wall, which ascending to the heights and return-ing to the river, does not deviate very widely in its course from the wall of the Middle Ages, which can still be traced by the fragments of ruined towers.   This wall is assigned by a Byzantine writer to Tiberius, but it seems more probable that the Emperor only re-paired what Antiochus Epiphanes had built.[4]   Turning now to the period of the Empire, we find that Antioch had memorials of all the great Romans whose names have been mentioned as yet in this biography.   When Pompey was defeated by Cæsar, the con-queror's name was perpetuated in this Eastern city by an aqueduct and by baths, and by a basilica called Cæsarium.   In the reign of Augustus, Agrippa[5] built in all cities of the Empire, and Herod of Judæa followed the example to the utmost of his power.   Both found employment for their munificence at Antioch.   A gay suburb rose under the patronage of the one, and the other contributed a road and a portico.   The reign of Tiberius was less remarkable for great architectural works ; but the Syrians by the Orontes had to thank him for many improvements and restorations in their city. Even the four years of his successor left behind them the aqueduct and the baths of Caligula.

The character of the inhabitants is easily inferred from the influ-ences which presided over the city's growth.   Its successive enlarge-ment by the Seleucids proves that their numbers rapidly increased from the first.   The population swelled still further, when, instead of the metropolis of the Greek kings of Syria, it became the re-sidence of Roman governors.   The mixed multitude received new and important additions in the officials who were connected with the details of provincial administration.   Luxurious Romans were

---

[1] Julian the Apostate suggests a parallel between Paris and Antioch. See Gibbon's 19th and 23rd chapters.

[2] See above, p. 22, n. 2.

[3] A comparison has been instituted above between Paris and Antioch: and it is hardly possible now (1860) to revise this paragraph for the press with-out alluding to the Rue de Rivoli.

[4] See Müller, *Antiq. Antioch.* pp.

54 and 81.

[5] This friend of Augustus and Mæcenas must be carefully distinguished from that grandson of Herod who bore the same name, and whose death is one of the subjects of this chapter. For the works of Herod the Great at Antioch, see Joseph. *Ant.* xvi. 5, 3 ; *War*, i. 21, 11.

ALLEGORICAL STATUE OF ANTIOCH.

(By Mr. G. Scharf, from Pistolesi's *Vaticano*.)

attracted by its beautiful climate. New wants continually multiplied the business of its commerce. Its gardens and houses grew
and extended on the north side of the river. Many are the allusions
to Antioch, in the history of those times, as a place of singular
pleasure and enjoyment. Here and there, an elevating thought is
associated with its name. Poets have spent their young days at
Antioch,[1] great generals have died there,[2] emperors have visited
and admired it.[3] But, for the most part, its population was a
worthless rabble of Greeks and Orientals. The frivolous amusements of the theatre were the occupation of their life. Their passion
for races, and the ridiculous party quarrels[4] connected with them,
were the patterns of those which afterwards became the disgrace of
Byzantium. The oriental element of superstition and imposture
was not less active. The Chaldæan astrologers found their most
credulous disciples in Antioch.[5] Jewish impostors,[6] sufficiently
common throughout the East, found their best opportunities here.
It is probable that no populations have ever been more abandoned
than those of oriental Greek cities under the Roman Empire, and
of these cities Antioch was the greatest and the worst.[7] If we wish
to realise the appearance and reality of the complicated Heathenism
of the first Christian century, we must endeavour to imagine the
scene of that suburb, the famous Daphne,[8] with its fountains and
groves of bay trees, its bright buildings, its crowds of licentious
votaries, its statue of Apollo,—where, under the climate of Syria
and the wealthy patronage of Rome, all that was beautiful in
nature and in art had created a sanctuary for a perpetual festival
of vice.

Thus, if any city, in the first century, was worthy to be called the
Heathen Queen and Metropolis of the East, that city was Antioch.
She was represented, in a famous allegorical statue, as a female
figure, seated on a rock and crowned, with the river Orontes at her
feet.[9] With this image, which art has made perpetual, we conclude
our description. There is no excuse for continuing it to the age of
Vespasian and Titus, when Judæa was taken, and the Western Gate,

---

[1] See Cic. *pro Archia Poeta.*

[2] All readers of Tacitus will recognise the allusion. (See *Ann.* ii. 72.)
It is not possible to write about Antioch without some allusion to Germanicus and his noble-minded wife.
And yet they were the parents of
Caligula.

[3] For all that long series of emperors
whose names are connected with Antioch, see Müller.

[4] The *Blue Faction* and the *Green
Faction* were notorious under the
reigns of Caligula and Claudius. Both
emperors patronised the latter.

[5] Chrysostom complains that even
Christians, in his day, were led away
by this passion for horoscopes. Juvenal traces the superstitions of Heathen Rome to Antioch. 'In Tiberim

defluxit Orontes.'

[6] Compare the cases of Simon Magus
(Acts viii.), Elymas the Sorcerer (Acts
xiii.), and the sons of Sceva (Acts
xix.). We shall have occasion to return
to this subject again.

[7] Ausonius hesitates between Antioch and Alexandria, as to the rank
they occupied in eminence and vice.

[8] Gibbon's description of Daphne
(ch. xxiii.) is well known. The sanctuary was on the high ground, four
or five miles to the S.W. of Antioch.
See Smith's *Dict. of the Bible.*

[9] For this celebrated statue of the
Τύχη 'Αντιοχείας, or Genius of Antioch,
so constantly represented on coins, see
Müller, *Antiq. Antioch.* pp. 35–41.
The engraving here given is from
Pistolesi's *Vaticano.*

decorated with the spoils, was called the 'Gate of the Cherubim,'[1] —or to the Saracen age, when, after many years of Christian history and Christian mythology, we find the 'Gate of St. Paul' placed opposite the 'Gate of St. George,' and when Duke Godfrey pitched his camp between the river and the city-wall. And there is reason to believe that earthquakes, the constant enemy of the people of Antioch, have so altered the very appearance of its site, that such description would be of little use. As the Vesuvius of Virgil or Pliny would hardly be recognised in the angry neighbour of modern Naples, so it is more than probable that the dislocated crags, which still rise above the Orontes, are greatly altered in form from the fort-crowned heights of Seleucus or Tiberius, Justinian or Tancred.

Earthquakes occurred in each of the reigns of Caligula and Claudius.[2] And it is likely that, when Saul and Barnabas were engaged in their apostolic work, parts of the city had something of that appearance which still makes Lisbon dreary, new and handsome buildings being raised in close proximity to the ruins left by the late calamity. It is remarkable how often great physical calamities are permitted by God to follow in close succession to each other. That age, which, as we have seen, had been visited by earthquakes, was presently visited by famine. The reign of Claudius, from bad harvests, or other causes, was a period of general distress and scarcity 'over the whole world.'[3] In the fourth year of his reign, we are told by Josephus that the famine was so severe, that the price of food became enormous, and great numbers perished.[4] At this time it happened that Helena, the mother of Izates, king of Adiabene, and a recent convert to Judaism, came to worship at Jerusalem. Moved with compassion for the misery she saw around her, she sent to purchase corn from Alexandria and figs from Cyprus, for distribution among the poor. Izates himself (who had also been converted by one who bore the same name[5] with him who baptized St. Paul) shared the charitable feelings of his mother, and sent large sums of money to Jerusalem.

While this relief came from Assyria, from Cyprus, and from Africa to the Jewish sufferers in Judæa, God did not suffer His own Christian people, probably the poorest and certainly the most disregarded in that country, to perish in the general distress. And their relief also came from nearly the same quarters. While Barnabas and Saul were evangelising the Syrian capital, and gathering in the harvest, the first seeds of which had been sown by 'men of Cyprus and Cyrene,' certain prophets came down from Jerusalem to Antioch, and one of them named Agabus announced that

---

[1] The Byzantine writer Malalas says, that Titus built a theatre at Antioch where a synagogue had been.

[2] One earthquake, according to Malalas, occurred on the morning of March 23, in the year 37, and another soon afterwards.

[3] Besides the famine in Judæa, we read of three others in the reign of Claudius ; one in Greece, mentioned by Eusebius, and two in Rome, the first mentioned by Dio Cassius, the second by Tacitus.

[4] *Ant.* iii. 15, 3, xx. 2, 5, and 5, 2.

[5] This Ananias was a Jewish merchant, who made proselytes among the women about the court of Adiabene, and thus obtained influence with the king. (Joseph. *Ant.* xx. 2, 3.) See what has been said above (pp. 16, and 83, n. 2) about the female proselytes at Damascus and Iconium.

a time of famine was at hand.[1] The Gentile disciples felt that they were bound by the closest link to those Jewish brethren whom though they had never seen they loved. 'For if the Gentiles had been made partakers of their spiritual things, their duty was also to minister unto them in carnal things.'[2] No time was lost in preparing for the coming distress. All the members of the Christian community, according to their means, 'determined to send relief,' Saul and Barnabas being chosen to take the contribution to the elders at Jerusalem.[3]

About the time when these messengers came to the Holy City on their errand of love, a worse calamity than that of famine had fallen upon the Church. One Apostle had been murdered, and another was in prison. There is something touching in the contrast between the two brothers, James and John. One died before the middle of the first Christian century; the other lived on to its close. One was removed just when his Master's kingdom, concerning which he had so eagerly inquired[4], was beginning to show its real character; he probably never heard the word 'Christian' pronounced. Zebedee's other son remained till the antichristian[5] enemies of the faith were 'already come,' and was labouring against them when his brother had been fifty years at rest in the Lord. He who had foretold the long service of St. John revealed to St. Peter that he should die by a violent death.[6] But the time was not yet come. Herod had bound him with two chains. Besides the soldiers who watched his sleep, guards were placed before the door of the prison.[7] And 'after the passover'[8] the king intended to bring him out and gratify the people with his death. But Herod's death was nearer than St. Peter's. For a moment we see the Apostle in captivity and the king in the plenitude of his power. But before the autumn a dreadful change had taken place. On the 1st of August (we follow a probable calculation,[9] and borrow some circumstances from the Jewish historian[10]) there was a great commemoration in Cæsarea. Some say it was in honour of the Emperor's safe return from the island of Britain. However this might be, the city was crowded, and Herod was there. On the second day of the festival he came into the theatre. That theatre had been erected by his grandfather,[11] who had murdered the Innocents; and now the grandson was there, who had murdered an Apostle. The stone seats, rising in a great semicircle, tier above

[1] Acts xi. 28.
[2] Rom. xv. 27.
[3] Acts xi. 29, 30.
[4] See Mark x. 35–45 ; Acts i. 6.
[5] 1 John ii. 18, iv. 3 ; 2 John 7.
[6] John xxi. 18–22. See 2 Pet. i. 14.
[7] For the question of the distribution of soldiers on this occasion, we may refer to Hackett's notes on v. 4, and v. 40.
[8] Inadvertently translated 'after Easter' in the A. V. Acts xii. 4.
[9] That of Wieseler.
[10] Compare Acts xii. 20–24, with

Josephus, *Ant.* xix. 8, 2.
[11] See Joseph. *Ant.* xv. 9, 6. It is from his narrative (xix. 8, 2) that we know the theatre to have been the scene of Agrippa's death-stroke. The 'throne' (Acts xii. 21) is the official 'tribunal,' as in Acts xviii. 12, 16, 17. Josephus says nothing of the quarrel with the Tyrians and Sidonians. Probably it arose simply from mercantile relations (see 1 Kings v. 11 ; Ezek. xxvii. 17),and their desire for reconciliation (Acts xii. 20) would naturally be increased by the existing famine.

tier, were covered with an excited multitude. The king came in, clothed in magnificent robes, of which silver was the costly and brilliant material. It was early in the day, and the sun's rays fell upon the king, so that the eyes of the beholders were dazzled with the brightness which surrounded him. Voices from the crowd, here and there, exclaimed that it was the apparition of something divine. And when he spoke and made an oration to the people, they gave a shout, saying, 'It is the voice of a God and not of a man.' But in the midst of this idolatrous ostentation the angel of God suddenly smote him. He was carried out of the theatre a dying man, and on the 6th of August he was dead.

This was that year 44,[1] on which we have already said so much. The country was placed again under Roman governors, and hard times were at hand for the Jews. Herod Agrippa had courted their favour. He had done much for them, and was preparing to do more. Josephus tells us, that 'he had begun to encompass Jerusalem with a wall, which, had it been brought to perfection, would have made it impracticable for the Romans to take the city by siege : but his death, which happened at Cæsarea, before he had raised the walls to their due height, prevented him.'[2] That part of the city, which this boundary was intended to inclose, was a suburb when St. Paul was converted. The work was not completed till the Jews were preparing for their final struggle with the Romans : and the Apostle, when he came from Antioch to Jerusalem, must have noticed the unfinished wall to the north and west of the old Damascus gate. We cannot determine the season of the year when he passed this way. We are not sure whether the year itself was 44 or 45. It is not probable that he was in Jerusalem at the passover, when St. Peter was in prison, or that he was praying with those anxious disciples at the 'house of Mary the mother of John, whose surname was Mark.'[3] But there is this link of interesting connection between that house and St. Paul, that it was the familiar home of one who was afterwards (not always[4] without cause for anxiety or reproof) a companion of his journeys. When Barnabas and Saul returned to Antioch, they were attended by 'John, whose surname was Mark.' With the affection of Abraham towards Lot, his kinsman[5] Barnabas withdrew him from the scene of persecution. We need not doubt that higher motives were added,—that at the first, as at the last,[6] St. Paul regarded him as 'profitable to him for the ministry.'

Thus attended, the Apostle willingly retraced his steps towards Antioch. A field of noble enterprise was before him. He could not doubt that God, who had so prepared him, would work by his means great conversions among the Heathen. At this point of his

---

[1] Roman Catholic writers here insert various passages of the traditionary life of St. Peter; his journey from Antioch through Asia Minor to Rome; his meeting with Simon Magus, &c.: and the other Apostles; their general separation to preach the Gospel to the Gentiles in all parts of the world; the formation of the Apostles' Creed, &c. St. Peter is alleged to have held the See of Antioch for seven years before that of Rome.

[2] *War*, ii. 11, 6.
[3] Acts xii. 12.
[4] See Acts xiii. 13, xv. 37–39.
[5] Not necessarily 'nephew.' See note on Col. iv. 10.
[6] 2 Tim. iv. 11. See below.

life, we cannot avoid noticing those circumstances of inward and outward preparation, which fitted him for his peculiar position of standing between the Jews and Gentiles. He was not a Sadducee, he had never Hellenised,—he had been educated at Jerusalem,—everything conspired to give him authority, when he addressed his countrymen as a ' Hebrew of the Hebrews.' At the same time, in his apostolical relation to Christ, he was quite disconnected with the other Apostles ; he had come in silence to a conviction of the truth at a distance from the Judaising Christians, and had early overcome those prejudices which impeded so many in their approaches to the Heathen. He had just been long enough at Jerusalem to be recognised and welcomed by the apostolic college,[1] but not long enough even to be known by face ' unto the churches in Judæa.'[2] He had been withdrawn into Cilicia till the baptism of Gentiles was a notorious and familiar fact to those very churches.[3] He could hardly be blamed for continuing what St. Peter had already begun.

And if the Spirit of God had prepared him for building up the United Church of Jews and Gentiles, and the Providence of God had directed all the steps of his life to this one result, we are called on to notice the singular fitness of this last employment, on which we have seen him engaged, for assuaging the suspicious feeling which separated the two great branches of the Church. In quitting for a time his Gentile converts at Antioch, and carrying a contribution of money to the Jewish Christians at Jerusalem, he was by no means leaving the higher work for the lower. He was building for aftertimes. The interchange of mutual benevolence was a safe foundation for future confidence. Temporal comfort was given in gratitude for spiritual good received. The Church's first days were christened with charity. No sooner was its new name received, in token of the union of Jews and Gentiles, than the sympathy of its members was asserted by the work of practical benevolence. We need not hesitate to apply to that work the words which St. Paul used, after many years, of another collection for the poor Christians in Judæa :—' The administration of this service not only supplies the need of the Saints, but overflows in many thanksgivings unto God ; while they praise God for this proof of your obedience to the Glad Tidings of Christ.[4]

Coin of Claudius and Agrippa I.[5]

[1] Acts ix. 27. [2] Gal. i. 22. [4] 2 Cor. ix. 12–14.
[3] These were the churches of Lydda, Saron, Joppa, &c., which Peter had been visiting when he was summoned to Cæsarea. Acts ix. 32–43. [5] From the British Museum. See p. 116. We may refer here to Dr. Wordsworth's useful note on Acts xii. 1.

CHAPTER V.

Second Part of the Acts of the Apostles.—Revelation at Antioch.—Public Devotions.—Departure of Barnabas and Saul.—The Orontes.—History and Description of Seleucia.—Voyage to Cyprus.—Salamis.—Roman Provincial System.—Proconsuls and Propraetors.—Sergius Paulus.—Oriental Impostors at Rome and in the Provinces.—Elymas Barjesus.—History of Jewish Names —Saul and Paul.

THE second part of the Acts of the Apostles is generally reckoned to begin with the thirteenth chapter. At this point St. Paul begins to appear as the principal character; and the narrative, gradually widening and expanding with his travels, seems intended to describe to us, in minute detail, the communication of the Gospel to the Gentiles. The thirteenth and fourteenth chapters embrace a definite and separate subject: and this subject is the first journey of the first Christian missionaries to the Heathen. These two chapters of the inspired record are the authorities for the present and the succeeding chapters of this work, in which we intend to follow the steps of Paul and Barnabas, in their circuit through Cyprus and the southern part of Lesser Asia.

The history opens suddenly and abruptly. We are told that there were, in the Church at Antioch,[1] 'prophets and teachers,' and among the rest 'Barnabas,' with whom we are already familiar. The others were 'Simeon, who was surnamed Niger,' and 'Lucius of Cyrene,' and 'Manaen, the foster brother of Herod the Tetrarch,' —and 'Saul,' who still appears under his Hebrew name. We observe, moreover, not only that he is mentioned after Barnabas, but that he occupies the lowest place in this enumeration of 'prophets and teachers.' The distinction between these two offices in the Apostolic Church will be discussed hereafter.[2] At present it is sufficient to remark that the 'prophecy' of the New Testament does not necessarily imply a knowledge of things to come, but rather a gift of exhorting with a peculiar force of inspiration. In the Church's early miraculous days the 'prophet' appears to have been ranked higher than the 'teacher.'[3] And we may perhaps infer that, up to this point of the history, Barnabas had belonged to the rank of 'prophets,' and Saul to that of 'teachers :' which would be in strict conformity with the inferiority of the latter to the former, which, as we have seen, has been hitherto observed.

Of the other three, who are grouped with these two chosen missionaries, we do not know enough to justify any long disquisition.

[1] Acts xiii. 1.
[2] See Chap. XIII.
[3] Compare Acts xiii. 1 with 1 Cor. xii. 28, 29 ; Eph. iv. 11.

But we may remark in passing that there is a certain interest attaching to each one of them. Simeon is one of those Jews who bore a Latin surname in addition to their Hebrew name, like 'John whose surname was Mark,' mentioned in the last verse of the preceding chapter, and like Saul himself, whose change of appellation will presently be brought under notice.[1] Lucius, probably the same who is referred to in the Epistle to the Romans,[2] is a native of Cyrene, that African city which has already been noticed as abounding in Jews, and which sent to Jerusalem our Saviour's cross-bearer.[3] Manaen is spoken of as the foster-brother of Herod the Tetrarch : this was Herod Antipas, the Tetrarch of Galilee; and since we learn from Josephus[4] that this Herod and his brother Archelaus were children of the same mother, and afterwards educated together at Rome, it is probable that this Christian prophet or teacher had spent his early childhood with those two princes, who were now both banished from Palestine to the banks of the Rhone.[5]

These were the most conspicuous persons in the Church of Antioch, when a revelation was received of the utmost importance. The occasion on which the revelation was made seems to have been a fit preparation for it. The Christians were engaged in religious services of peculiar solemnity. The Holy Ghost spoke to them 'as they ministered unto the Lord and fasted.' The word here translated 'ministered,' has been taken by opposite controversialists to denote the celebration of the 'sacrifice of the mass' on the one hand, or the exercise of the office of 'preaching' on the other. It will be safer if we say simply that the Christian community at Antioch was engaged in one united act of prayer and humiliation. That this solemnity would be accompanied by words of exhortation, and that it would be crowned and completed by the Holy Communion, is more than probable ; that it was accompanied with Fasting[6] we are expressly told. These religious services might have had a special reference to the means which were to be adopted for the spread of the Gospel now evidently intended for all ; and the words 'separate me *now*[7] Barnabas and Saul for the work whereunto I have called them,' may have been an answer to specific

---

[1] See Acts xiii. 9. Compare Col. iv. 11.

[2] Rom. xvi. 21. There is no reason whatever for supposing that St. Luke is meant. The Latin form of his name would be 'Lucanus,' not 'Lucius.'

[3] See above, p. 15, n. 3.

[4] Their mother's name was Malthace, a Samaritan. *War*, i. 28, 4. See *Ant.* xvii. 1, 3. One of the sect of the Essenes (see p. 29), who bore the name of Manaen or Manaem, is mentioned by Josephus (*Ant.* xv. 10, 5) as having foretold to Herod the Great, in the days of his obscurity, both his future power and future wickedness. The historian adds, that

Herod afterwards treated the Essenes with great kindness. Nothing is more likely than that this Manaen was the father of the companion of Herod's children. Another Jew of the same name is mentioned, at a later period (*War*, ii. 17, 8, 9 ; *Life*, 5), as having encouraged robberies, and come to a violent end. The name is the same with that of the King of Israel. 2 Kings xv. 14–22.

[5] See above, pp. 23 and 45.

[6] For the association of Fasting with Ordination, see Bingham's *Antiq.* of the *Christ. Ch.* IV. vi. 6, XXI. ii. 8.

[7] This little word is important, and should have been in the A. V.

prayers. How this revelation was made, whether by the mouth of some of the prophets who were present, or by the impulse of a simultaneous and general inspiration,—whether the route to be taken by Barnabas and Saul was at this time precisely indicated,[1]— and whether they had previously received a conscious personal call, of which this was the public ratification,[2]—it is useless to enquire. A definite work was pointed out, as now about to be begun under the counsel of God; two definite agents in this work were publicly singled out: and we soon see them sent forth to their arduous undertaking, with the sanction of the Church at Antioch.

Their final consecration and departure was the occasion of another religious solemnity. A fast was appointed, and prayers were offered up; and, with that simple ceremony of ordination[3] which we trace through the earlier periods of Jewish history, and which we here see adopted under the highest authority in the Christian Church, 'they laid their hands on them, and sent them away.' The words are wonderfully simple; but those who devoutly reflect on this great occasion, and on the position of the first Christians at Antioch, will not find it difficult to imagine the thoughts which occupied the hearts of the Disciples during these first 'Ember Days' of the Church[4]—their deep sense of the importance of the work which was now beginning,—their faith in God, on whom they could rely in the midst of such difficulties,—their suspense during the absence of those by whom their own faith had been fortified,— their anxiety for the intelligence they might bring on their return.

Their first point of destination was the island of Cyprus. It is not necessary, though quite allowable, to suppose that this particular course was divinely indicated in the original revelation at Antioch. Four reasons at least can be stated, which may have induced the Apostles, in the exercise of a wise discretion, to turn in the first instance to this island. It is separated by no great distance from the mainland of Syria; its high mountain-summits are easily seen[5] in clear weather from the coast near the mouth of the Orontes; and in the summer season many vessels must often have been passing and repassing between Salamis and Seleucia. Besides this, it was the native-place of Barnabas.[6] Since the time when 'Andrew found his brother Simon, and brought him to Jesus,'[7] and the Saviour was beloved in the house of 'Martha and her sister and Lazarus,'[8] the ties of family relationship had not been without effect on the progress of the Gospel.[9] It could not be unnatural to

---

[1] It is evident that the course of St. Paul's journeys was often indeterminate, and regulated either by convenient opportunities (as in Acts xxi. 2, xxviii. 11), or by compulsion (as in xiv. 6, xvii. 14), or by supernatural admonitions (xxii. 21, xvi. 6–10).

[2] St. Paul at least had long been conscious of his own vocation, and could only be waiting to be summoned to his work.

[3] It forms no part of the plan of this

work to enter into ecclesiastical controversies. It is sufficient to refer to Acts vi. 6; 1 Tim. iv. 14, v. 22; 2 Tim. i. 6; Heb. vi. 2.

[4] See Bingham, as above.

[5] Colonel Chesney speaks of 'the lofty island of Cyprus as seen to the S. W. in the distant horizon,' from the bay of Antioch.

[6] Acts iv. 36.

[7] John i. 41, 42.   [8] John xi. 5.

[9] See an instance of this in the life

suppose that the truth would be welcomed in Cyprus, when it was
brought by Barnabas and his kinsman Mark[1] to their own connections or friends.   Moreover, the Jews were numerous in Salamis.[2]
By sailing to that city they were following the track of the synagogues.   Their mission, it is true, was chiefly to the Gentiles ; but
their surest course for reaching them was through the medium of
the Proselytes and the Hellenistic Jews.   To these considerations
we must add, in the fourth place, that some of the Cypriotes were
already Christians.   No one place out of Palestine, with the exception of Antioch, had been so honourably associated with the work
of successful evangelisation.[3]

The palaces of Antioch were connected with the sea by the river
Orontes.   Strabo says that in his time they sailed up the stream in
one day; and Pausanias speaks of great Roman works which had
improved the navigation of the channel.   Probably it was navigable
by vessels of some considerable size, and goods and passengers were
conveyed by water between the city and the sea.   Even in our own
day, though there is now a bar at the mouth of the river, there has
been a serious project of uniting it by a canal with the Euphrates,
and so of re-establishing one of the old lines of commercial intercourse between the Mediterranean and the Indian Sea.   The Orontes
comes from the valley between Lebanon and Anti-Lebanon, and
does not, like many rivers, vary capriciously between a winter-
torrent and a thirsty watercourse, but flows on continually to the
sea.   Its waters are not clear, but they are deep and rapid.   Their
course has been compared to that of the Wye.   They wind round
the bases of high and precipitous cliffs, or by richly cultivated
banks, where the vegetation of the South,—the vine and the fig-
tree, the myrtle, the bay, the ilex, and the arbutus,—are mingled
with dwarf oak and English sycamore.[4]   If Barnabas and Saul came
down by water from Antioch, this was the course of the boat which
conveyed them.   If they travelled the five or six leagues[5] by land,
they crossed the river at the north side of Antioch, and came along
the base of the Pierian hills by a route which is now roughly
covered with fragrant and picturesque shrubs, but which then
doubtless was a track well worn by travellers, like the road from the
Piræus to Athens, or from Ostia to Rome.[6]

Seleucia united the two characters of a fortress and a seaport.
It was situated on a rocky eminence, which is the southern extremity
of an elevated range of hills projecting from Mount Amanus.   From
the south-east, where the ruins of the Antioch Gate are still conspicuous, the ground rose towards the north-east into high and craggy

---

of St. Paul himself.   Acts xxiii. 16–
33.   Compare 1 Cor. vii. 16.
   [1] Acts xiii. 5.   See xii. 25, and p.
107, n. 4, above.
   [2] Acts xiii. 5.   See below, p. 115.
   [3] See Acts iv. 36, xi. 19, 20, xxi.
16.
   [4] For views, with descriptions, see
Fisher's *Syria*, I. 5, 19, 77, II. 28.
   [5] Colonel Chesney says, ' The wind-

ings give a distance of about forty-one
miles, whilst the journey by land is
only sixteen miles and a half.'—*R. G.
J*. viii. p. 230.
   [6] Dr. Yates observed traces of Roman
pavement on the line of road between
Antioch and Seleucia.   See his comprehensive paper on Seleucia, in the
Museum of Classical Antiquities for
June 1852.

summits; and round the greater part of its circumference of four miles the city was protected by its natural position. The harbour and mercantile suburb were on level ground towards the west; but here, as on the only weak point at Gibraltar, strong artificial defences had made compensation for the deficiency of nature. Seleucus, who had named his metropolis in his father's honour (p. 101), gave his own name to this maritime fortress; and here, around his tomb,[1] his successors contended for the key of Syria.[2] 'Seleucia by the Sea' was a place of great importance under the Seleucids and the Ptolemies; and so it remained under the sway of the Romans. In consequence of its bold resistance to Tigranes, when he was in possession of all the neighbouring country, Pompey gave it the privileges of a 'Free City;'[3] and a cotemporary of St. Paul speaks of it as having those privileges still.[4]

The most remarkable work among the extant remains of Seleucia, is an immense excavation,—probably the same with that which is mentioned by Polybius,—leading from the upper part of the ancient city to the sea. It consists alternately of tunnels and deep open cuttings. It is difficult to give a confident opinion as to the uses for which it was intended. But the best conjecture seems to be that it was constructed for the purpose of drawing off the water, which might otherwise have done mischief to the houses and shipping in the lower part of the town; and so arranged at the same time, as, when needful, to supply a rush of water to clear out the port. The inner basin, or dock, is now a morass; but its dimensions can be measured, and the walls that surrounded it can be distinctly traced.[5] The position of the ancient flood-gates, and the passage through which the vessels were moved from the inner to the outer harbour, can be accurately marked. The very piers of the outer harbour are still to be seen under the water. The southern jetty takes the wider sweep, and overlaps the northern, forming a secure entrance and a well-protected basin. The stones are of great size, 'some of them twenty feet long, five feet deep, and six feet wide;'[6] and they were fastened to each other with iron cramps. The masonry of ancient Seleucia is still so good, that not long since a Turkish Pasha[7] conceived the idea of clearing out and repairing the harbour.

These piers[8] were unbroken when Saul and Barnabas came down to Seleucia, and the large stones fastened by their iron cramps protected the vessels in the harbour from the swell of the western sea. Here, in the midst of unsympathising sailors, the two missionary

---

[1] Seleucus was buried here.

[2] We may refer especially to the chapters in which Polybius gives an account of the siege of Seleucia in the war of Antiochus the Great with Ptolemy. In these chapters we find the clearest description both of its military importance and of its topography.

[3] Strabo. See p. 38. Compare p. 19, n. 2.

[4] Pliny.

[5] Pococke gives a rude plan of Seleucia, with the harbour, &c. A more exact and complete one will be found in the memoir of Dr. Yates.

[6] Pococke, p. 183.

[7] Ali Pasha, governor of Bagdad in 1835, once governor of Aleppo.

[8] It seems that the names of the piers still retain the memory of this occasion. Dr. Yates says that the southern pier is called after the Apostle Paul, in contradistinction to its fellow, the pier of St. Barnabas.

Apostles, with their younger companion, stepped on board the vessel which was to convey them to Salamis. As they cleared the port, the whole sweep of the bay of Antioch opened on their left,—the low ground by the mouth of the Orontes,—the wild and woody country beyond it,—and then the peak of Mount Casius, rising symmetrically from the very edge of the sea to a height of five thousand feet.[1] On the right, in the south-west horizon, if the day was clear, they saw the island of Cyprus from the first.[2] The current sets north-east and northerly between the island and the Syrian coast.[3] But with a fair wind, a few hours would enable them to run down from Seleucia to Salamis; and the land would rapidly rise in forms well-known and familiar to Barnabas and Mark.

The coast of nearly every island of the Mediterranean has been minutely surveyed and described by British naval officers. The two islands which were most intimately connected with St. Paul's voyages, have been among the latest to receive this kind of illustration. The soundings of the coast of Crete are now proved to furnish a valuable commentary on the twenty-seventh chapter of the Acts: and the chart of Cyprus should at least be consulted when we read the thirteenth chapter. From Cape St. Andrea, the north-eastern point of the island, the coast trends rapidly to the west, till it reaches Cape Grego,[4] the south-eastern extremity. The wretched modern town of Famagousta is nearer the latter point than the former, and the ancient Salamis was situated a short distance to the north of Famagousta. Near Cape St. Andrea are two or three small islands, anciently called 'The Keys.' These, if they were seen at all, would soon be lost to view. Cape Grego is distinguished by a singular promontory of table land, which is very familiar to the sailors of our merchantmen and ships of war: and there is little doubt that the woodcut given in one of their manuals of sailing directions[5] represents that very 'rough, lofty, table-shaped eminence' which

[1] 'The lofty Jebel-el-Akrab, rising 5,318 feet above the sea, with its abutments extending to Antioch.'—Chesney, p. 228. This mountain is, however, a conspicuous and beautiful feature of this bay. St. Paul must have seen it in all his voyages to and from Antioch.

[2] See above, p. 111, n. 5.

[3] 'In sailing from the southern shores of Cyprus, with the winds adverse, you should endeavour to obtain the advantage of the set of the current, which between Cyprus and the mouths of the Nile always runs to the eastward, changing its direction to the N. E. and N. as you near the coast of Syria.'—Norie, p. 149. 'The current, in general, continues easterly along the Libyan coast, and E. N. E. off Alexandria; thence advancing to the coast of Syria, it sets N. E. and more northerly; so that country vessels bound from Damietta to an eastern port of Cyprus, have been carried by the current past the island.'—Purdy, p. 276. After leaving the Gulf of Scanderoon, the current sets to the westward along the south coast of Asia Minor, as we shall have occasion to notice hereafter. A curious illustration of the difficulty sometimes experienced in making this passage will be found in Meursius, *Cyprus, &c.*, p. 158; where the decree of an early council is cited, directing the course to be adopted on the death of a bishop in Cyprus, if the vessel which conveyed the news could not cross to Antioch.

[4] The Pedalium of Strabo and Ptolemy.

[5] See the sketch of Cape Grego 'N. W. by W., six miles' in Purdy, Pt. ii. p. 253.

Strabo mentions in his description of the coast, and which has been identified with the Idalium of the classical poets.

The ground lies low in the neighbourhood of Salamis; and the town was situated on a bight of the coast to the north of the river Pediæus. This low land is the largest plain in Cyprus, and the Pediæus is the only true river in the island, the rest being merely winter-torrents, flowing in the wet season from the two mountain ranges which intersect it from east to west. This plain probably represents the kingdom of Teucer, which is familiar to us in the early stories of legendary Greece. It stretches inwards between the two mountain ranges to the very heart of the country, where the modern Turkish capital, Nicosia, is situated.[1] In the days of historical Greece, Salamis was the capital. Under the Roman Empire, if not the seat of government, it was at least the most important mercantile town. We have the best reasons for believing that the harbour was convenient and capacious.[2] Thus we can form to ourselves some idea of the appearance of the place in the reign of Claudius. A large city by the sea-shore, a wide-spread plain with corn-fields and orchards, and the blue distance of mountains beyond, composed the view on which the eyes of Barnabas and Saul rested when they came to anchor in the bay of Salamis.

The Jews, as we should have been prepared to expect, were numerous in Salamis. This fact is indicated to us in the sacred narrative; for we learn that this city had several synagogues, while other cities had often only one.[3] The Jews had doubtless been established here in considerable numbers in the active period which succeeded the death of Alexander.[4] The unparalleled productiveness of Cyprus, and its trade in fruit, wine, flax, and honey would naturally attract them to the mercantile port. The farming of the copper mines by Augustus to Herod may probably have swelled their numbers.[5] One of the most conspicuous passages in the history of Salamis was the insurrection of the Jews in the reign of Trajan, when great part of the city was destroyed.[6] Its demolition

---

[1] See Pococke's description, vol. ii. pp. 214–217. He gives a rude plan of ancient Salamis. The ruined aqueduct which he mentions appears to be subsequent to the time of St. Paul.

[2] See especially the account in Diodorus Siculus of the great naval victory off Salamis, won by Demetrius Poliorcetes over Ptolemy. Scylax also says that Salamis had a good harbour.

[3] Acts xiii. 5. Compare vi. 9, ix. 20, and contrast xvii. 1, xviii. 4.

[4] Philo speaks of the Jews of Cyprus.

[5] See above, p. 14, n. 2.

[6] 'The flame spread to Cyprus, where the Jews were numerous and wealthy. One Artemio placed himself at their head. They rose and massacred 240,000 of their fellow-citizens; the whole populous city of Salamis became

a desert. The revolt of Cyprus was first suppressed; Hadrian, afterwards emperor, landed on the island, and marched to the assistance of the few inhabitants who had been able to act on the defensive. He defeated the Jews, expelled them from the island, to whose beautiful coasts no Jew was ever after permitted to approach. If one were accidentally wrecked on the inhospitable shore, he was instantly put to death.'—Milman, iii. 111, 112. The author says above (p. 109), that the Rabbinical traditions are full of the sufferings of the Jews in this period. In this island there was a massacre before the time of the rebellion, 'and the sea that broke upon the shores of Cyprus was tinged with the red hue of carnage.'

was completed by an earthquake. It was rebuilt by a Christian emperor, from whom it received its medieval name of Constantia.[1]

It appears that the proclamation of the Gospel was confined by Barnabas and Saul to the Jews and the synagogues. We have no information of the length of their stay, or the success of their labours. Some stress seems to be laid on the fact that John (i.e. Mark) 'was their minister.' Perhaps we are to infer from this, that his hands baptized the Jews and Proselytes, who were convinced by the preaching of the Apostles.

From Salamis they travelled to Paphos, at the other extremity of the island. The two towns were probably connected together by a well-travelled and frequented road.[2] It is indeed likely that, even under the Empire, the islands of the Greek part of the Mediterranean, as Crete and Cyprus, were not so completely provided with lines of internal communication as those which were nearer the metropolis, and had been longer under Roman occupation, such as Corsica and Sardinia. But we cannot help believing that Roman roads were laid down in Cyprus and Crete, after the manner of the modern English roads in Corfu and the other Ionian islands, which islands, in their social and political condition, present many points of resemblance to those which were under the Roman sway in the time of St. Paul. On the whole, there is little doubt that his journey from Salamis to Paphos, a distance from east to west of not more than a hundred miles, was accomplished in a short time and without difficulty.

Paphos was the residence of the Roman governor. The appearance of the place (if due allowance is made for the differences of the nineteenth century and the first) may be compared with that of the town of Corfu in the present day, with its strong garrison of imperial soldiers in the midst of a Greek population, with its mixture of two languages, with its symbols of a strong and steady power side by side with frivolous amusements, and with something of the style of a court about the residence of its governor. All the occurrences, which are mentioned at Paphos as taking place on the arrival of Barnabas and Saul, are grouped so entirely round the governor's person, that our attention must be turned for a time to the condition of Cyprus, as a Roman province, and the position and character of Sergius Paulus.

From the time when Augustus united the world under his own power, the provinces were divided into two different classes. The business of the first Emperor's life was to consolidate the imperial system under the show of administering a republic. He retained the names and semblances of those liberties and rights which Rome had once enjoyed. He found two names in existence, the one of which was henceforth inseparably blended with the Imperial dignity and Military command, the other with the authority of the Senate and its Civil administration. The first of these names was 'Prætor,'

[1] Jerome speaks of it under this name.

[2] On the west of Salamis, in the direction of Paphos, Pococke saw a church and monastery dedicated to Barnabas, and a grotto where he is said to have been buried, after suffering martyrdom in the reign of Nero. A road is marked between Salamis and Paphos in the Peutingerian Table

the second was 'Consul.' Both of them were retained in Italy ;
and both were reproduced in the Provinces as 'Proprætor' and
'Proconsul.'[1] He told the Senate and people that he would relieve them of all the anxiety of military proceedings, and that he
would resign to them those provinces, where soldiers were unnecessary to secure the fruits of a peaceful administration.[2] He would
take upon himself all the care and risk of governing the other
provinces, where rebellion might be apprehended, and where the
proximity of warlike tribes made the presence of the legions perpetually needful. These were his professions to the Senate : but
the real purpose of this ingenious arrangement was the disarming
of the Republic, and the securing to himself the absolute control
of the whole standing army of the Empire.[3] The scheme was sufficiently transparent ; but there was no sturdy national life in
Italy to resist his despotic innovations, and no foreign civilised
powers to arrest the advance of imperial aggrandisement ; and
thus it came to pass that Augustus, though totally destitute of the
military genius either of Cromwell or Napoleon, transmitted to his
successors a throne guarded by an invincible army, and a system
of government destined to endure through several centuries.

Hence we find in the reign, not only of Augustus, but of each of
his successors, from Tiberius to Nero, the provinces divided into
these two classes. On the one side we have those which are supposed to be under the Senate and people. The governor is appointed by lot, as in the times of the old republic. He carries
with him the lictors and fasces, the insignia of a Consul ; but he is
destitute of military power. His office must be resigned at the
expiration of a year. He is styled 'Proconsul,' and the Greeks,
translating the term, call him Ἀνθύπατος.[4] On the other side are
the provinces of Cæsar. The Governor may be styled 'Proprætor,' or Ἀντιστράτηγος, but he is more properly 'Legatus,' or
Πρεσβευτής,—the representative or 'Commissioner' of the Emperor.
He goes out from Italy with all the pomp of a military commander,
and he does not return till the Emperor recalls him.[5] And to complete the symmetry and consistency of the system, the subordinate
districts of these imperial provinces are regulated by the Emperor's
'Procurator' (Ἐπίτροπος), or 'High Steward.' The New Testament, in the strictest conformity with the other historical autho-

---

[1] It is important, as we shall see
presently, to notice Dio Cassius's
further statement, that all governors
of the Senate's provinces were to be
called Proconsuls, whatever their previous office might have been, and all
governors of the Emperor's provinces
were to be styled Legati or Proprætors,
even if they had been Consuls.

[2] The 'unarmed provinces' of Tacitus, in his account of the state of the
Empire at the death of Nero. *Hist.*
i. 11.

[3] Suetonius and Dio Cassius.

[4] Which our English translators

have rendered by the ambiguous word
'deputy.' Acts xiii. 7. 'The *deputy* of
the country, Sergius Paulus.' 'Gallio
was the *deputy* of Achaia,' Ibid. xviii.
12. 'There are *deputies*,' Ibid. xix. 38.

[5] All these details are stated, and
the two kinds of governors very accurately distinguished in the 53rd
Book of Dio Cassius, ch. 13. It should
be remarked that ἐπαρχία (the word
still used for the subdivisions of the
modern Greek Kingdom) is applied
indiscriminately to both kinds of provinces.

rities of the period, gives us examples of both kinds of provincial administration. We are told by Strabo, and by Dio Cassius, that 'Asia' and 'Achaia' were assigned to the Senate; and the title, which in each case is given to the Governor in the Acts of the Apostles, is 'Proconsul.'[1] The same authorities inform us that Syria was an imperial province,[2] and no such title as 'Proconsul' is assigned by the sacred writers to 'Cyrenius Governor of Syria,'[3] or to Pilate, Festus, and Felix,[4] the Procurators of Judæa, which, as we have seen (p. 21), was a dependency of that great and unsettled province.

Dio Cassius informs us, in the same passage where he tells us that Asia and Achaia were provinces of the Senate, that Cyprus was retained by the Emperor for himself.[5] If we stop here, we naturally ask the question,—and some have asked the question rather hastily, —how it comes to pass that St. Luke speaks of Sergius Paulus by the style of 'Proconsul?' But any hesitation concerning the strict accuracy of the sacred historian's language is immediately set at rest by the very next sentence of the secular historian,[6]—in which he informs us that Augustus restored Cyprus to the Senate in exchange for another district of the Empire,—a statement which he again repeats in a later passage of his work.[7] It is evident, then, that the governor's style and title from this time forward would be 'Proconsul.' But this evidence, however satisfactory, is not all that we possess. The coin, which is engraved at the end of the chapter, distinctly presents to us a Cyprian Proconsul of the reign of Claudius. And inscriptions, which could easily be adduced,[8] supply us with the names of additional governors,[9] who were among the predecessors or successors of Sergius Paulus.

It is remarkable that two men called Sergius Paulus are described in very similar terms by two physicians who wrote in Greek, the one a Heathen, the other a Christian. The Heathen writer is Galen. He speaks of his cotemporary as a man interested and well versed in philosophy.[10] The Christian writer is St. Luke, who tells us here that the governor of Cyprus was a 'prudent' man, who 'desired to hear the Word of God.' This governor seems to have been of a candid and inquiring mind; nor will this philosophical disposition be thought inconsistent with his connection with the Jewish impostor, whom Saul and Barnabas found at the Paphian court, by those who are acquainted with the intellectual and religious tendencies of the age.

---

[1] Ἀνθύπατος, xviii. 12, xix. 38.
[2] Strabo and Dio.
[3] Luke ii. 2.
[4] The word invariably used in the New Testament is Ἡγεμών. This is a general term, like the Roman 'Præses' and the English 'Governor;' as may be seen by comparing Luke ii. 2 with iii. 1, and observing that the very same word is applied to the offices of the Procurator of Judæa, the Legatus of Syria, and the Emperor himself. Josephus generally uses Ἐπίτροπος for the Procurator of Judæa, and Ἡγεμών

for the Legatus of Syria.
[5] Along with Syria and Cilicia.
[6] Dio Cass. liii. 12.   [7] Ibid. liv. 4.
[8] One is given in the larger editions of this work.
[9] When we find, either on coins and inscriptions, or in Scripture, detached notices of provincial governors not mentioned elsewhere, we should bear in mind what has been said above (p. 116), that the Proconsul was appointed *annually.*
[10] The two were separated by an interval of a hundred years.

For many years before this time, and many years after, impostors from the East, pretending to magical powers, had great influence over the Roman mind. All the Greek and Latin literature of the empire, from Horace to Lucian, abounds in proof of the prevalent credulity of this sceptical period. Unbelief, when it has become conscious of its weakness, is often glad to give its hand to superstition. The faith of educated Romans was utterly gone. We can hardly wonder, when the East was thrown open,—the land of mystery,—the fountain of the earliest migrations,—the cradle of the earliest religions,—that the imagination both of the populace and the aristocracy of Rome became fanatically excited, and that they greedily welcomed the most absurd and degrading superstitions. Not only was the metropolis of the empire crowded with 'hungry Greeks,' but 'Syrian fortune-tellers' flocked into all the haunts of public amusement. Athens and Corinth did not now contribute the greatest or the worst part of the 'dregs' of Rome ; but (to adopt Juvenal's use of that river of Antioch we have lately been describing) 'the Orontes itself flowed into the Tiber.'

Every part of the East contributed its share to the general superstition. The gods of Egypt and Phrygia found unfailing votaries. Before the close of the republic, the temples of Isis and Serapis had been more than once erected, destroyed, and renewed. Josephus tells us that certain disgraceful priests of Isis[1] were crucified at Rome by the second Emperor ; but this punishment was only a momentary check to their sway over the Roman mind. The more remote districts of Asia Minor sent their itinerant soothsayers ; Syria sent her music and her medicines ; Chaldæa her 'Babylonian numbers' and 'mathematical calculations.'[2] To these corrupters of the people of Romulus we must add one more Asiatic nation,— the nation of the Israelites ;—and it is an instructive employment to observe that, while some members of the Jewish people were rising, by the Divine power, to the highest position ever occupied by men on earth, others were sinking themselves, and others along with them, to the lowest and most contemptible degradation. The treatment and influence of the Jews at Rome were often too similar to those of other Orientals. One year we find them banished ;[3] another year we see them quietly re-established.[4] The Jewish beggar-woman was the gipsy of the first century, shivering and crouching in the outskirts of the city, and telling fortunes,[5] as Ezekiel said of old, 'for handfuls of barley, and for pieces of bread.'[6] All this catalogue of Oriental impostors, whose influx into Rome was a characteristic of the period, we can gather from that revolting satire of Juvenal, in which he scourges the follies and vices of the Roman women. But not only were the women of

---

[1] *Ant.* xviii. 3, 4.

[2] Babylonii Numeri, Hor. i. *Od.* xi. 2. Chaldaïcæ rationes, Cic. *Div.* ii. 47. See the whole passage 42–47. The Chaldæan astrologers were called 'Mathematici' (Juv. vi. 562, xiv. 248). See the definition in Aulus Gellius, i. 9. 'Vulgus, quos gentilitio vocabulo Chal-

dæos dicere oportet, mathematicos dicit.' There is some account of their proceedings at the beginning of the fourteenth book of the *Noctes Atticæ*.

[3] Acts xviii. 2.

[4] Acts xxviii. 17.

[5] Juv. *Sat.* iii. 13–16, vi. 542–546.

[6] Ezek. xiii. 19.

Rome drawn aside into this varied and multiplied fanaticism ; but the eminent men of the declining republic, and the absolute sovereigns of the early Empire, were tainted and enslaved by the same superstitions. The great Marius had in his camp a Syrian, probably a Jewish [1] prophetess, by whose divinations he regulated the progress of his campaigns. As Brutus, at the beginning of the republic, had visited the oracle of Delphi, so Pompey, Crassus, and Cæsar, at the close of the republic, when the oracles were silent,[2] sought information from Oriental astrology. No picture in the great Latin satirist is more powerfully drawn than that in which he shows us the Emperor Tiberius 'sitting on the rock of Capri, with his flock of Chaldæans round him.'[3] No sentence in the great Latin historian is more bitterly emphatic than that in which he says that the astrologers and sorcerers are a class of men who 'will always be discarded and always cherished.'[4]

What we know, from the literature of the period, to have been the case in Rome and in the Empire at large, we see exemplified in a province in the case of Sergius Paulus. He had attached himself to 'a certain sorcerer, a false prophet, a Jew, whose name was Barjesus,' and who had given himself the Arabic name of 'Elymas,' or 'The Wise.' But the Proconsul was not so deluded by the false prophet,[5] as to be unable, or unwilling, to listen to the true. 'He sent for Barnabas and Saul,' of whose arrival he was informed, and whose free and public declaration of the 'Word of God' attracted his inquiring mind. Elymas used every exertion to resist them, and to hinder the Proconsul's mind from falling under the influence of their Divine doctrine. Truth and falsehood were brought into visible conflict with each other. It is evident, from the graphic character of the narrative,—the description of Paul 'setting his eyes'[6] on the sorcerer,—'the mist and the darkness' which fell on Barjesus, —the 'groping about for some one to lead him,'[7]—that the opposing wonder-workers stood face to face in the presence of the

---

[1] Niebuhr thinks she was a Jewess. Her name was Martha.

[2] Cic. *Div.* ii. 47.

[3] Juv. *Sat.* x. 93.

[4] Tac. *Hist.* i. 22.

[5] For the good and bad senses in which the word Μάγος was used, see Professor Trench's recent book on the Second Chapter of St. Matthew. It is worth observing, that Simon Magus was a Cyprian, if he is the person mentioned by Josephus. *Ant.* xx. 5, 2.

[6] The word in Acts xiii. 9 is the same which is used in xxiii. 1, for 'to look intently.' Our first impression is, that there was something searching and commanding in St. Paul's eye. But if the opinion is correct, that he suffered from an affection of the eyes, this word may express a peculiarity connected with his defective vision. See the Bishop of Win-

chester's note (*Ministerial Character of Christ*, p. 555), who compares the LXX. in Numb. xxxiii. 55; Josh. xxiii. 13, and applies this view to the explanation of the difficulty in Acts xxiii. 1–5. And it is remarkable that, in both the traditional accounts of Paul's personal appearance which we possess (viz. those of Malalas and Nicephorus), he is said to have had contracted eyebrows. Many have thought that 'the thorn in his flesh,' 2 Cor. xii. 7, was an affection of the eyes. Hence, perhaps, the statement in Gal. iv. 14–16, and the allusion to his large handwriting, Gal. vi. 11. (See our Preface.)

[7] It may be added that these phrases seem to imply that the person from whence they came was an eye-witness. Some have inferred that Luke himself was present.

Proconsul,—as Moses and Aaron withstood the magicians at the Egyptian court,—Sergius Paulus being in this respect different from Pharaoh, that he did not 'harden his heart.'

The miracles of the New Testament are generally distinguished from those of the Old, by being for the most part works of mercy and restoration, not of punishment and destruction. Two only of Our Lord's miracles were inflictions of severity, and these were attended with no harm to the bodies of men. The same law of mercy pervades most of those interruptions of the course of nature which He gave His servants, the Apostles, power to effect. One miracle of wrath is mentioned as worked in His name by each of the great Apostles, Peter and Paul; and we can see sufficient reasons why liars and hypocrites, like Ananias and Sapphira, and powerful impostors, like Elymas Barjesus, should be publicly punished in the face of the Jewish and Gentile worlds, and made the examples and warnings of every subsequent age of the Church.[1] A different passage in the life of St. Peter presents a parallel which is closer in some respects with this interview of St. Paul with the sorcerer in Cyprus. As Simon Magus,—who had 'long time bewitched the people of Samaria with his sorceries,'—was denounced by St. Peter 'as still in the gall of bitterness and bond of iniquity,' and solemnly told that 'his heart was not right in the sight of God;'[2]—so St. Paul, conscious of his apostolic power, and under the impulse of immediate inspiration, rebuked Barjesus, as a child of that Devil who is the father of lies,[3] as a worker of deceit and mischief,[4] and as one who sought to pervert and distort that which God saw and approved as right.[5] He proceeded to denounce an instantaneous judgment; and, according to his prophetic word, the 'hand of the Lord' struck the sorcerer, as it had once struck the Apostle himself on the way to Damascus; —the sight of Elymas began to waver,[6] and presently a darkness settled on it so thick, that he ceased to behold the sun's light. This blinding of the false prophet opened the eyes of Sergius Paulus. That which had been intended as an opposition to the Gospel, proved the means of its extension. We are ignorant of the degree of this extension in the island of Cyprus. But we cannot doubt that when the Proconsul was converted, his influence would make Christianity reputable; and that from this moment the Gentiles of the island, as well as the Jews, had the news of salvation brought home to them.

And now, from this point of the Apostolical history, PAUL appears as the great figure in every picture. Barnabas, henceforward, is always in the back-ground. The great Apostle now enters on his work as the preacher to the Gentiles; and simultaneously with his active occupation of the field in which he was called to labour, his name is suddenly changed. As 'Abram' was changed into 'Abra-

---

[1] It is not necessary to infer from these passages, or from 1 Cor. v. 3–5, 1 Tim. i. 20, that Peter and Paul had power to inflict these judgments at their will. Though, even if they had this power, they had also the spirit of love and supernatural knowledge to guide them in the use of it.

[2] Acts viii. 21–23.   [3] John viii. 44.

[4] The word in Acts xiii. 10 expresses the cleverness of a successful imposture.

[5] With Acts xiii. 10, compare viii. 21.

[6] Acts xiii. 11. This may be used, in Luke's medical manner, to express the stages of the blindness. Compare the account of the recovery of the lame man in iii. 8.

ham,' when God promised that he should be the 'father of many
nations;'—as 'Simon' was changed into 'Peter,' when it was said,
'On this· rock I will build my church;'—so 'Saul' is changed
into 'Paul,' at the moment of his first great victory among the
Heathen. What 'the plains of Mamre by Hebron' were to the
patriarch,—what 'Cæsarea Philippi,'[1] by the fountains of the
Jordan, was to the fisherman of Galilee,—that was the city of 'Paphos,' on the coast of Cyprus, tó the tent-maker of Tarsus. Are we
to suppose that the name was now really given him for the first time,
—that he adopted it himself as significant of his own feelings,—or
that Sergius Paulus conferred it on him in grateful commemoration
of the benefits he had received,—or that 'Paul,' having been a
Gentile form of the Apostle's name in early life conjointly with the
Hebrew 'Saul,' was now used to the exclusion of the other, to indicate that he had receded from his position as a Jewish Christian,
to become the friend and teacher of the Gentiles? All these
opinions have found their supporters both in ancient and modern
times. The question has been alluded to before in this work (p.
39). It will be well to devote some further space to it now, once
for all.

It cannot be denied that the words in Acts xiii. 9—'Saul who
is also Paul'—are the line of separation between two very distinct
portions of St. Luke's biography of the Apostle, in the former of
which he is uniformly called 'Saul,' while in the latter he receives,
with equal consistency, the name of 'Paul.' It must also be observed, that the Apostle always speaks of himself under the latter
designation in every one of his Epistles, without any exception; and
not only so, but the Apostle St. Peter, in the only passage where he
has occasion to allude to him,[2] speaks of him as 'our beloved brother
Paul.' We are, however, inclined to adopt the opinion that the Cilician Apostle had this Roman name, as well as his other Hebrew name,
in his earlier days, and even before he was a Christian. This adoption of a Gentile name is so far from being alien to the spirit of a
Jewish family, that a similar practice may be traced through all the
periods of Hebrew History. Beginning with the *Persian* epoch
(B.C. 550–350) we find such names as 'Nehemiah,' 'Schammai,'
'Belteshazzar,' which betray an Oriental origin, and show that
Jewish appellatives followed the growth of the living language. In
the *Greek* period we encounter the names of 'Philip,'[3] and his son
'Alexander,'[4] and of Alexander's successors, 'Antiochus,' 'Lysimachus,' 'Ptolemy,' 'Antipater;'[5] the names of Greek philosophers, such as 'Zeno,' and 'Epicurus;'[6] even Greek mythological
names, as 'Jason' and 'Menelaus.'[7] Some of these words will

---

[1] See Gen. xiii. 18, xvii. 5; Matt.
xvi. 13–18; and Prof. Stanley's *Sermon on St. Peter.*

[2] 2 Pet. iii. 15.

[3] Matt. x. 3; Acts vi. 5, xxi. 8;
Joseph. *Ant.* xiv. 10, 22.

[4] Acts xix. 33, 34. See 2 Tim. iv. 14.
Alexander was a common name
among the Asmonæans. It is said
that when the great conqueror passed
through Judæa, a promise was made

to him that all the Jewish children
born that year should be called Alexander.'

[5] 1 Macc. xii. 16, xvi. 11; 2 Macc.
iv. 29; Joseph. *Ant.* xiv. 10.

[6] These names are in the Mischna
and the Berenice Inscription.

[7] Jason, Joseph. *Ant.* xii. 10, 6;
perhaps Acts xvii. 5–9; Rom. xvi.
21; Menelaus, Joseph. *Ant.* xii. 5, 1.
See 2 Macc. iv. 5

have been recognised as occurring in the New Testament itself.
When we mention *Roman* names adopted by the Jews, the coincidence is still more striking. 'Crispus,'[1] 'Justus,'[2] 'Niger,'[3]
are found in Josephus[4] as well as in the Acts. 'Drusilla' and
'Priscilla' might have been Roman matrons. The 'Aquila' of St.
Paul is the counterpart of the 'Apella' of Horace.[5] Nor need we
end our survey of Jewish names with the early Roman Empire;
for, passing by the destruction of Jerusalem, we see Jews, in the
earlier part of the *Middle Ages,* calling themselves, 'Basil,' 'Leo,'
'Theodosius,' 'Sophia;' and, in the latter part, 'Albert,' 'Benedict,' 'Crispin,' 'Denys.' We might pursue our inquiry into the
nations of modern Europe; but enough has been said to show, that
as the Jews have successively learnt to speak Chaldee, Greek,
Latin, or German, so they have adopted into their families the
appellations of those Gentile families among whom they have lived.
It is indeed remarkable that the Separated Nation should bear, in
the very names recorded in its annals, the trace of every nation
with whom it has come in contact and never united.

It is important to our present purpose to remark that double
names often occur in combination, the one national, the other
foreign. The earliest instances are 'Belteshazzar-Daniel,' and
'Esther-Hadasa.'[6] Frequently there was no resemblance or natural connection between the two words, as in 'Herod-Agrippa,' 'Salome-Alexandra,' 'Juda-Aristobulus,' 'Simon-Peter.' Sometimes
the meaning was reproduced, as in 'Malich-Kleodemus.' At other
times an alliterating resemblance of sound seems to have dictated
the choice, as in 'Jose-Jason,' 'Hillel-Julus,' '*Saul-Paulus*'—
'*Saul, who is also Paul.*'

Thus it seems to us that satisfactory reasons can be adduced for
the double name borne by the Apostle,—without having recourse[7]
to the hypothesis of Jerome, who suggests that, as Scipio was called
Africanus from the conquest of Africa, and Metellus called Creticus
from the conquest of Crete, so Saul carried away his new name
as a trophy of his victory over the Heathenism of the Proconsul
Paulus—or to that notion, which Augustine applies with much
rhetorical effect in various parts of his writings, where he alludes
to the literal meaning of the word '*Paulus,*' and contrasts Saul,
the unbridled king, the proud self-confident persecutor of David,
with Paul, the lowly, the penitent,—who deliberately wished to
indicate by his very name, that he was 'the *least* of the Apostles,'[8]
and '*less than the least* of all Saints.'[9] Yet we must not neglect
the coincident occurrence of these two names in this narrative of
the events which happened in Cyprus. We need not hesitate to
dwell on the associations which are connected with the name of
'Paulus,'—or on the thoughts which are naturally called up, when

---

[1] Acts xviii. 8.　　　[2] Acts i. 23.
[3] Acts xiii. 1.
[4] Joseph. *Life,* 68, 65; *War,* iv. 6. 1.
Compare 1 Cor. i. 14; Acts xviii. 7;
Col. iv. 11.
[5] Hor. I. *Sat.* v. 100. Priscilla appears under the abbreviated form
'Prisca,' 2 Tim. iv. 19.

[6] Dan. x. 1; Esther ii. 7. So Zerubbabel was called Sheshbazzar. Compare Ezra v. 16, with Zech. iv. 9. The
Oriental practice of adopting names
which were significant must not be left
out of view.
[7] See p. 39, n. 1.　　[8] 1 Cor. xv. 9.
[9] Eph. iii. 8.

we notice the critical passage in the sacred history, where it is first given to Saul of Tarsus. It is surely not unworthy of notice that, as Peter's first Gentile convert was a member of the *Cornelian House* (p. 96), so the surname of the noblest family of the *Æmilian House*[1] was the link between the Apostle of the Gentiles and his convert at Paphos. Nor can we find a nobler Christian version of any line of a Heathen poet, than by comparing what Horace says of him who fell at Cannæ,—'*animæ magnæ prodigum Paulum,*'—with the words of him who said at Miletus, '*I count not my life dear unto myself,* so that I might finish my course with joy, and the ministry which I have received of the Lord Jesus.'[2]

And though we imagine, as we have said above, that Saul had the name of Paul at an earlier period of his life,—and should be inclined to conjecture that the appellation came from some connection of his ancestors (perhaps as manumitted slaves) with some member of the Roman family of the Æmilian Pauli;[3]—yet we cannot believe it accidental that the words,[4] which have led to this discussion, occur at this particular point of the inspired narrative. The Heathen name rises to the surface at the moment when St. Paul visibly enters on his office as the Apostle of the Heathen. The Roman name is stereotyped at the moment when he converts the Roman governor. And the place where this occurs is Paphos, the favourite sanctuary of a shameful idolatry. At the very spot which was notorious throughout the world for that which the Gospel forbids and destroys,—there, before he sailed for Perga, having achieved his victory, the Apostle erected his trophy,[5]—as Moses, when Amalek was discomfited, 'built an altar, and called the name of it Jehovah-Nissi,—the Lord my banner.'[6]

Proconsul of Cyprus.[7]

[1] Paulus was the cognomen of a family of the Gens Æmilia. The stemma is given in Smith's *Dictionary of Classical Biography,* under Paulus Æmilius. The name must of course have been given to the first individual who bore it from the smallness of his stature. It should be observed, that both Malalas and Nicephorus (quoted above) speak of St. Paul as short of stature.

[2] Hor. i. *Od.* xii. 37; Acts xx. 24. Compare Phil. iii. 8.

[3] Compare the case of Josephus, alluded to above, p. 38.

[4] Acts xiii. 9.

[5] The words of Jerome alluded to above are: 'Victoriæ suæ *tropæa* retulit, erexitque *vexillum.*'

[6] Exod. xvii. 15.

[7] The woodcut is from Akerman's *Numismatic Illustrations,* p. 41. Specimens of the coin are in the Imperial Cabinet at Vienna, and in the Bibliothèque du Roi. There are other Cyprian coins of the Imperial age, with PROCOS in Roman characters. Many Cyprian coins of the reign of Claudius are of the red copper of the island: a fact peculiarly interesting to us, if the notion, mentioned p. 14, n. 2, and p. 114, be correct.

CHAPTER VI.

Old and New Paphos.—Departure from Cyprus.—Coast of Pamphylia.—Perga.
—Mark's Return to Jerusalem.—Mountain Scenery of Pisidia.—Situation of
Antioch.—The Synagogue.—Address to the Jews.—Preaching to the Gentiles.
—Persecution by the Jews.—History and Description of Iconium.—Lycaonia.
—Derbe and Lystra.—Healing of the Cripple.—Idolatrous Worship offered to
Paul and Barnabas.—Address to the Gentiles.—St. Paul stoned.—Timotheus.
-The Apostles retrace their Journey.—Perga and Attaleia.—Return to Syria.

THE banner of the Gospel was now displayed on the coasts of the
Heathen.   The Glad Tidings had 'passed over to the isles of
Chittim,'[1] and had found a willing audience in that island, which,
in the vocabulary of the Jewish Prophets, is the representative of
the trade and civilisation of the Mediterranean Sea.   Cyprus was
the early meeting-place of the Oriental and Greek forms of social
life.   Originally colonised from Phœnicia, it was successively subject
to Egypt, to Assyria, and to Persia.   The settlements of the Greeks
on its shores had begun in a remote period, and their influence
gradually advanced, till the older links of connection were entirely
broken by Alexander and his successors.   But not only in political
and social relations, by the progress of conquest and commerce, was
Cyprus the meeting-place of Greece and the East.   Here also their
forms of idolatrous worship met and became blended together.
Paphos was, indeed, a sanctuary of Greek religion : on this shore
the fabled goddess first landed, when she rose from the sea : this
was the scene of a worship celebrated in the classical poets, from
the age of Homer, down to the time when Titus, the son of Vespasian, visited the spot in the spirit of a Heathen pilgrim, on his
way to subjugate Judæa.[2]   But the polluted worship was originally
introduced from Assyria or Phœnicia : the Oriental form under
which the goddess was worshipped, is represented on Greek coins :[3]
the Temple bore a curious resemblance to those of Astarte at Carthage or Tyre : and Tacitus pauses to describe the singularity of
the altar and the ceremonies, before he proceeds to narrate the
campaign of Titus.   And here it was that we have seen Christianity
firmly established by St. Paul,—in the very spot where the super-

---

[1] The general notion intended by
the phrases 'isles' and 'coasts' of
'Chittim,' seems to have been 'the
islands and coasts of the Mediterranean
to the west and north-west of Judæa.'
Numb. xxiv. 24; Jer. ii. 10; Ezek.
xxvii. 6. See Gen. x. 4, 5; Isai. xxiii.
1 ; Dan. xi. 30.   But primarily the
name is believed to have been connected with *Citium*, which was a Phœnician colony in Cyprus.

[2] Tac. *Hist.* ii. 2-4.   Compare Suet.
Tit. 5.   Tacitus speaks of magnificent
offerings presented by kings and others
to the Temple at Old Paphos.

[3] A specimen is given in the larger
editions,

stition of Syria had perverted man's natural veneration and love of mystery, and where the beautiful creations of Greek thought had administered to what Athanasius, when speaking of Paphos, well describes as the ' deification of lust.'

The Paphos of the poets, or *Old Paphos*, as it was afterwards called, was situated on an eminence at a distance of nearly two miles from the sea. *New Paphos* was on the sea-shore, about ten miles to the north.[1] But the old town still remained as the sanctuary which was visited by Heathen pilgrims ; profligate processions, at stated seasons, crowded the road between the two towns, as they crowded the road between Antioch and Daphne (p. 103) ; and small models of the mysterious image were sought as eagerly by strangers as the little ' silver shrines ' of Diana at Ephesus. (Acts xix. 24.) Doubtless the position of the old town was an illustration of the early custom, mentioned by Thucydides, of building at a safe distance from the shore, at a time when the sea was infested by pirates ; and the new town had been established in a place convenient for commerce, when navigation had become more secure. It was situated on the verge of a plain, smaller than that of Salamis, and watered by a scantier stream than the Pediæus.[2] Not long before the visit of Paul and Barnabas it had been destroyed by an earthquake. Augustus had rebuilt it ; and from him it had received the name of Augusta or Sebaste.[3] But the old name still retained its place in popular usage, and has descended to modern times. The ' Paphos ' of Strabo, Ptolemy, and St. Luke became the ' Papho ' of the Venetians and the ' Baffa ' of the Turks. A second series of *Latin* architecture has crumbled into decay. Mixed up with the ruins of palaces and churches are the poor dwellings of the Greek and Mahommedan inhabitants, partly on the beach, but chiefly on a low ridge of sandstone rock, about two miles[4] from the ancient port ; for the marsh, which once formed the limit of the port, makes the shore unhealthy during the heats of summer by its noxious exhalations. One of the most singular features of the neighbourhood consists of the curious caverns excavated in the

---

[1] Or rather the north-west. See the Admiralty Chart.

[2] See p. 114.

[3] The Greek form *Sebaste*, instead of *Augusta*, occurs in an inscription found on the spot, which is further interesting as containing the name of another *Paulus*.

[4] This is the distance between the Ktema and the Marina given by Captain Graves. In Purdy's *Sailing Directions* (p. 251) it is stated to be only half a mile. Captain Graves says : ' In the vicinity are numerous ruins and ancient remains ; but when so many towns have existed, and so many have severally been destroyed, all must be left to conjecture. A number of columns broken and much mutilated are lying about, and some

substantial and well-built vaults, or rather subterraneous communications, under a hill of slight elevation, are pointed out by the guides as the remains of a temple dedicated to Venus. Then there are numerous excavations in the sandstone hills, which probably served at various periods the double purpose of habitations and tombs. Several monasteries and churches now in ruins, of a low Gothic architecture, are more easily identified ; but the crumbling fragments of the sandstone with which they were constructed only add to the incongruous heap around, that now covers the palace of the Paphian Venus.'—MS. note by Captain Graves, R.N.

rocks, which have been used both for tombs and for dwellings. The harbour is now almost blocked up, and affords only shelter for boats. ' The Venetian stronghold, at the extremity of the Western mole, is fast crumbling into ruins. The mole itself is broken up, and every year the massive stones of which it was constructed are rolled over from their original position into the port.'¹ The approaches to the harbour can never have been very safe, in consequence of the ledge of rocks² which extends some distance into the sea. At present, the eastern entrance to the anchorage is said to be the safer of the two. The western, under ordinary circumstances, would be more convenient for a vessel clearing out of the port, and about to sail for the Gulf of Pamphylia.

We have remarked in the last chapter, that it is not difficult to imagine the reasons which induced Paul and Barnabas, on their departure from Seleucia, to visit first the island of Cyprus. It is not quite so easy to give an opinion upon the motives which directed their course to the coast of Pamphylia, when they had passed through the native island of Barnabas, from Salamis to Paphos. It might be one of those circumstances which we call accidents, and which, as they never influence the actions of ordinary men without the predetermining direction of Divine Providence, so were doubtless used by the same Providence to determine the course even of Apostles. As St. Paul, many years afterwards, joined at Myra that vessel in which he was shipwrecked,³ and then was conveyed to Puteoli in a ship which had accidentally wintered at Malta,⁴—so on this occasion there might be some small craft in the harbour at Paphos, bound for the opposite gulf of Attaleia, when Paul and Barnabas were thinking of their future progress. The distance is not great, and frequent communication, both political and commercial, must have taken place between the towns of Pamphylia and those of Cyprus.⁵ It is possible that St. Paul, having already preached the Gospel in Cilicia,⁶ might wish now to extend it among those districts which lay more immediately contiguous, and the population of which was, in some respects, similar to that of his native province.⁷ He might also reflect that the natives of a comparatively unsophisticated district might be more likely to receive the message of salvation than the inhabitants of those provinces which were more completely penetrated with the corrupt civilisation of Greece and Rome. Or his thoughts might be turning to those numerous families of Jews, whom he well knew to be settled in the great towns beyond Mount Taurus, such as Antioch in Pisidia, and Iconium in Lycaonia, with the hope that his Master's cause would be most successfully advanced

---

¹ Captain Graves. MS.

² 'A great ledge of rock lies in the entrance to Papho, exending about a league; you may sail in either to the eastward or westward of it, but the eastern passage is the widest and best.' —Purdy, p. 251. The soundings may be seen in the Admiralty Chart.

³ Acts xxvii. 5, 6.

⁴ Acts xxviii. 11–13.

⁵ And perhaps Paphos more especially, as the seat of government. At present Khalandri (Gulnar), to the south-east of Attaleia and Perga, is the port from which the Tatars from Constantinople, conveying government despatches, usually cross to Cyprus.

⁶ See pp. 87–89.

⁷ Strabo states this distinctly.

among those Gentiles who flocked there, as everywhere, to the worship of the Synagogue. Or, finally, he may have had a direct revelation from on high, and a vision, like that which had already appeared to him in the Temple,[1] or like that which he afterwards saw on the confines of Europe and Asia,[2] may have directed the course of his voyage. Whatever may have been the calculations of his own wisdom and prudence, or whatever supernatural intimations may have reached him, he sailed, with his companions Barnabas and John, in some vessel, of which the size, the cargo, and the crew, are unknown to us, past the promontories of Drepanum and Acamas, and then across the waters of the Pamphylian Sea, leaving on the right the cliffs[3] which are the western boundary of Cilicia, to the innermost bend of the bay of Attaleia.

This bay is a remarkable feature in the shore of Asia Minor ; and it is not without some important relations with the history of this part of the world. It forms a deep indentation in the general coast-line, and is bordered by a plain, which retreats itself like a bay into the mountains. From the shore to the mountains, across the widest part of the plain, the distance is a journey of eight or nine hours. Three principal rivers intersect this level space : the Catarrhactes, which falls over sea-cliffs near Attaleia, in the waterfalls which suggested its name; and farther to the east the Cestrus and Eury-medon, which flow by Perga and Aspendus, to a low and sandy shore. About the banks of these rivers, and on the open waters of the bay, whence the eye ranges freely over the ragged mountain summits which inclose the scene, armies and fleets had engaged in some of those battles of which the results were still felt in the day of St. Paul. From the base of that steep shore on the west, where a rugged knot of mountains is piled up into snowy heights above the rocks of Phaselis, the united squadron of the Romans and Rhodians sailed across the bay in the year 190 B.C. ; and it was in rounding that promontory near Side on the east, that they caught sight of the ships of Antiochus, as they came on by the shore with the dreadful Hannibal on board. And close to the same spot where the Latin power then defeated the Greek king of Syria, another battle had been fought at an earlier period, in which the Greeks gave one of their last blows to the retreating force of Persia, and the Athenian Cimon gained a victory both by land and sea; thus winning, according to the boast of Plutarch, in one day the laurels of Platæa and Salamis. On that occasion a large navy sailed up the river Eurymedon as far as Aspendus. Now, the bar at the mouth of the river would make this impossible. The same is the case with the river Cestrus, which, Strabo says, was navigable in his day, for sixty stadia, or seven miles, to the city of Perga. Ptolemy calls this city an inland town of Pamphylia ; but so he speaks of Tarsus in Cilicia. And we have seen that Tarsus, though truly called an inland town, as being some distance from the coast, was nevertheless a mercantile harbour. Its relation with the Cydnus was similar to that of Perga with the

[1] Acts xxii. 17–21. See p. 86.
[2] Acts xvi. 9.
[3] About C. Anamour (Anemurium, the southernmost point of Asia Minor),

and Alaya (the ancient Coracesium), there are cliffs of 500 and 600 feet high.

Cestrus : and the vessel which brought St. Paul to win more glorious victories than those of the Greek and Roman battles of the Eurymedon,—came up the course of the Cestrus to her moorings near the Temple of Diana.

All that Strabo tells us of this city is that the Temple of Diana was on an eminence at some short distance, and that an annual festival was held in honour of the goddess. The chief associations of Perga are with the Greek rather than the Roman period : and its existing remains are described as being ' purely Greek, there being no trace of any later inhabitants.' [1] Its prosperity was probably arrested by the building of Attaleia [2] after the death of Alexander, in a more favourable situation on the shore of the bay. Attaleia has never ceased to be an important town since the day of its foundation by Attalus Philadelphus. But when the traveller pitches his tent at Perga, he finds only the encampments of shepherds, who pasture their cattle amidst the ruins. These ruins are walls and towers, columns and cornices, a theatre and a stadium, a broken aqueduct encrusted with the calcareous deposit of the Pamphylian streams, and tombs scattered on both sides of the site of the town. Nothing else remains of Perga but the beauty of its natural situation, ' between and upon the sides of two hills, with an extensive valley in front, watered by the river Cestrus, and backed by the mountains of the Taurus.' [3]

The coins of Perga are a lively illustration of its character as a city of the Greeks. [4] We have no memorial of its condition as a city of the Romans ; nor does our narrative require us to delay any longer in describing it. The Apostles made no long stay in Perga. This seems evident, not only from the words used at this point of the history, [5] but from the marked manner in which we are told that they *did* stay, [6] on their return from the interior. One event, however, is mentioned as occurring at Perga, which, though noticed incidentally and in few words, was attended with painful feelings at the time, and involved the most serious consequences. It must have occasioned deep sorrow to Paul and Barnabas, and possibly even then some mutual estrangement : and afterwards it became the cause of their quarrel and separation. [7] Mark ' departed from them from Pamphylia, and went not with them to the work.' He came with them up the Cestrus as far as Perga ; but there he forsook them, and, taking advantage of some vessel which was sailing towards Palestine, he ' returned to Jerusalem,' [8] which had been his home in earlier years. [9] We are not to suppose that this implied an absolute rejection of Christianity. A soldier who has wavered in one battle may live to obtain a glorious victory. Mark was

[1] Perhaps some modification is requisite here. Mr. Falkener noticed that the architectural details of the theatre and stadium are Roman.

[2] Acts xiv. 25.

[3] This description is quoted or borrowed from Sir C. Fellows' *Asia Minor*, 1839, pp. 190–193.

[4] One of them, with Diana and the stag, is given in the larger edition.

[5] This will be seen by comparing the Greek of Acts xiii. 14, with xiv. 24. Similarly, a rapid journey is implied in xvii. 1.

[6] ' When they had preached the Word in Perga, they went down,' &c. —Acts xiv. 25.

[7] Acts xv. 37–39.

[8] Acts xiii. 13.

[9] Acts xii. 12, 25.

afterwards not unwilling to accompany the Apostles on a second
missionary journey ;[1] and actually did accompany Barnabas again
to Cyprus.[2] Nor did St. Paul always retain his unfavourable
judgment of him (Acts xv. 38), but long afterwards, in his Roman
imprisonment, commended him to the Colossians, as one who was
'a fellow-worker unto the Kingdom of God,' and 'a comfort' to
himself :[3] and in his latest letter, just before his death, he speaks
of him again as one 'profitable to him for the ministry.'[4] Yet if
we consider all the circumstances of his life, we shall not find it
difficult to blame his conduct in Pamphylia, and to see good reasons
why Paul should afterwards, at Antioch, distrust the steadiness of
his character. The child of a religious mother, who had sheltered
in her house the Christian Disciples in a fierce persecution, he had
joined himself to Barnabas and Saul, when they travelled from
Jerusalem to Antioch, on their return from a mission of charity.
He had been a close spectator of the wonderful power of the
religion of Christ,—he had seen the strength of faith under trial in
his mother's home,—he had attended his kinsman Barnabas in his
labours of zeal and love,—he had seen the word of Paul sanctioned
and fulfilled by miracles,—he had even been the 'minister' of
Apostles in their successful enterprise ;[5] and now he forsook them,
when they were about to proceed through greater difficulties to
more glorious success. We are not left in doubt as to the real character of his departure. He was drawn from the work of God by
the attraction of an earthly home.[6] As he looked up from Perga to
the Gentile mountains, his heart failed him, and he turned back
with desire towards Jerusalem. He could not resolve to continue
persevering, 'in journeyings often, in perils of rivers, in perils of
robbers.'[7]

'Perils of rivers' and 'perils of robbers'—these words express
the very dangers which St. Paul would be most likely to encounter
on his journey from Perga in Pamphylia to Antioch in Pisidia. The
lawless and marauding habits of the population of those mountains
which separate the table-land in the interior of Asia Minor from
the plains on the south coast, were notorious in all parts of ancient
history. Strabo uses the same strong language both of the Isaurians[8] who separated Cappadocia from Cilicia, and of their neighbours the Pisidians, whose native fortresses were the barrier
between Phrygia and Pamphylia. We have the same character of
the latter of these robber-tribes in Xenophon, who is the first to
mention them ; and in Zosimus, who relieves the history of the
later empire by telling us of the adventures of a robber-chief, who
defied the Romans, and died a desperate death in these mountains.[9]

---

[1] Acts xv. 37.
[2] Acts xv. 39.
[3] Col. iv. 10.
[4] Or rather, 'profitable to minister'
to him. 2 Tim. iv. 11.
[5] See Acts xiii. 5.
[6] Matthew Henry pithily remarks:
'Either he did not like the work, or
he wanted to go and see his mother.'

[7] 2 Cor. xi. 26.
[8] See p. 17.
[9] The beautiful story of St. John and
the robber (Euseb. *Eccl. Hist.* iii. 23)
will naturally occur to the reader. See
also the frequent mention of Isaurian
robbers in the latter part of the life of
Chrysostom, prefixed to the Benedictine
edition of his works.

Alexander the Great, when he heard that Memnon's fleet was in the Ægean, and marched from Perga to rejoin Parmenio in Phrygia, found some of the worst difficulties of his whole campaign in penetrating through this district. The scene of one of the roughest campaigns connected with the wars of Antiochus the Great was among the hill-forts near the upper waters of the Cestrus and Eurymedon. No population through the midst of which St. Paul ever travelled, abounded more in those 'perils of robbers,' of which he himself speaks, than the wild and lawless clans of the Pisidian Highlanders.

And if on this journey he was exposed to dangers from the attacks of men, there might be other dangers, not less imminent, arising from the natural character of the country itself. To travellers in the East there is a reality in 'perils of rivers,' which we in England are hardly able to understand. Unfamiliar with the sudden flooding of thirsty water-courses, we seldom comprehend the full force of some of the most striking images in the Old and New Testaments.[1] The rivers of Asia Minor, like all the rivers in the Levant, are liable to violent and sudden changes.[2] And no district in Asia Minor is more singularly characterised by its 'water floods' than the mountainous tract of Pisidia, where rivers burst out at the bases of huge cliffs, or dash down wildly through narrow ravines. The very notice of the *bridges* in Strabo, when he tells us how the Cestrus and Eurymedon tumble down from the heights and precipices of Selge to the Pamphylian Sea, is more expressive than any elaborate description. We cannot determine the position of any bridges which the Apostle may have crossed ; but his course was never far from the channels of these two rivers : and it is an interesting fact, that his name is still traditionally connected with one of them, as we learn from the information recently given to an English traveller by the Archbishop of Pisidia.[3]

Such considerations respecting the physical peculiarities of the country now traversed by St. Paul, naturally lead us into various trains of thought concerning the scenery, the climate, and the seasons.[4] And there are certain probabilities in relation to the time of the year when the Apostle may be supposed to have journeyed this way, which may well excuse some remarks on these

---

[1] Thus the true meaning of 2 Cor. xi. 26 is lost in the English translation. Similarly, in the Sermon on the Mount (Matt. vii. 25, 27), the word for 'rivers,' is translated 'floods,' and the image confused. See Ps. xxxii. 6.

[2] The crossing of the Halys by Crœsus, as told by Herodotus, is an illustration of the difficulties presented by the larger rivers of Asia Minor.

[3] 'About two hours and a half from Isbarta, towards the south-east is the village of Sav, where is the source of a river called the Sav-Sou. Five hours and a half beyond, and still towards the south-east, is the village of *Paoli*

(*St. Paul*) ; and here the river, which had continued its course so far, is lost in the mountains, &c.' — Arundell's *Asia Minor*, vol. ii. p. 31. The river is probably the Eurymedon.

[4] The descriptive passages which follow are chiefly borrowed from '*Asia Minor*, 1839,' and '*Lycia*, 1841,' by Sir C. Fellows, and '*Travels in Lycia*, 1847,' by Lieutenant Spratt, R.N. and Professor E. Forbes. The writer desires also to acknowledge his obligations to various travellers, especially to the lamented Professor Forbes, also to Mr. Falkener, and Dr. Wolff.

subjects. And this is all the more allowable, because we are absolutely without any data for determining the year in which this first
missionary expedition was undertaken. All that we can assert
with confidence is that it must have taken place somewhere in the
interval between the years 45 and 50.[1]   But this makes us all the
more desirous to determine, by any reasonable conjectures, the
movements of the Apostle in reference to a better chronology than
that which reckons by successive years,—the chronology which furnishes us with the real imagery round his path,—the chronology of
the seasons.

Now we may well suppose that he might sail from Seleucia to
Salamis at the beginning of spring. In that age and in those
waters, the commencement of a voyage was usually determined by
the advance of the season. The sea was technically said to be
' open' in the month of March. If St. Paul began his journey in
that month, the lapse of two months might easily bring him to
Perga, and allow sufficient time for all that we are told of his proceedings at Salamis and Paphos. If we suppose him to have been
at Perga in May, this would have been exactly the most natural
time for a journey to the mountains. Earlier in the spring, the
passes would have been filled with snow.[2] In the heat of summer
the weather would have been less favourable for the journey. In
the autumn the disadvantages would have been still greater, from
the approaching difficulties of winter. But again, if St. Paul was
at Perga in May, a further reason may be given why he did not
stay there, but seized all the advantages of the season for prosecuting his journey to the interior. The habits of a people are
alway determined or modified by the physical peculiarities of their
country ; and a custom prevails among the inhabitants of this part
of Asia Minor, which there is every reason to believe has been
unbroken for centuries. At the beginning of the hot season they
move up from the plains to the cool basin-like hollows on the
mountains. These *yailahs* or summer retreats are always spoken
of with pride and satisfaction, and the time of the journey anticipated with eager delight. When the time arrives, the people may
be seen ascending to the upper grounds, men, women, and children,
with flocks and herds, camels and asses, like the patriarchs of old.[3]
If then St. Paul was at Perga in May, he would find the inha-

[1] See the Chronological Table in the Appendix.

[2] ' *March* 4.—The passes to the Yailahs from the upper part of the valley being still shut up by snow, we have no alternative but to prosecute our researches amongst the low country and valleys which border the coast.'—Sp. and F. I. p. 48. The valley re-ferred to is that of the Xanthus, in Lycia.

[3] ' *April* 30.— We passed many families *en route* from Adalia to the mountain plains for the summer.'—Sp. and F. I. p. 242. Again, p. 248 (*May* 3). See p. 54. During a halt in the valley of the Xanthus (*May* 10), Sir C. Fellows says that an almost uninter-rupted train of cattle and people (nearly twenty families) passed by. ' What a picture would Landseer make of such a pilgrimage ! The snowy tops of the mountains were seen through the lofty and dark-green fir-trees, terminating in abrupt cliffs. . . . From clefts in these gushed out cascades . . . and the waters were carried away by the wind in spray over the green woods. . . . In a zigzag course up the wood lay the track leading to the cool places In advance of the pastoral groups were the straggling goats, browsing on the

bitants deserting its hot and silent streets.   They would be moving in the direction of his own intended journey.   He would be under no temptation to stay.   And if we imagine him as joining[1] some such company of Pamphylian families on his way to the Pisidian mountains, it gives much interest and animation to the thought of this part of his progress.

Perhaps it was in such company that the Apostle entered the first passes of the mountainous district, along some road formed partly by artificial pavement, and partly by the native marble, with high cliffs frowning on either hand, with tombs and inscriptions, even then ancient, on the projecting rocks around, and with copious fountains bursting out ' among thickets of pomegranates and oleanders.'[2] The oleander, 'the favourite flower of the Levantine midsummer,' abounds in the lower watercourses; and in the month of May it borders all the banks with a line of brilliant crimson.[3]   As the path ascends, the rocks begin to assume the wilder grandeur of mountains, the richer fruit-trees begin to disappear, and the pine and walnut succeed ; though the plane-tree still stretches its wide leaves over the stream which dashes wildly down the ravine, crossing and re-crossing the dangerous road.   The alteration of climate which attends on the traveller's progress is soon perceptible.   A few hours will make the difference of weeks or even months.   When the corn is in the ear on the lowlands, ploughing and sowing are hardly well begun upon the highlands.   Spring flowers may be seen in the mountains by the very edge of the snow,[4] when the anemone is

fresh blossoms of the wild almond as they passed.   In more steady courses followed the small black cattle . . . then came the flocks of sheep, and the camels . . . bearing piled loads of ploughs, tent-poles, kettles . . . and amidst this rustic load was always seen the rich Turkey carpet and damask cushions, the pride even of the tented Turk.'—*Lycia*, pp. 238, 239.

[1] It has always been customary for travellers in Asia Minor, as in the patriarchal East, to join caravans, if possible.

[2] In ascending from Limyra, a small plain on the coast not far from Phaselis, Spratt and Forbes mention ' a rock-tablet with a long Greek inscription . . . by the side of an ancient paved road, at a spot where numerous and copious springs gush out among thickets of pomegranates and ole-anders.'   (i. p. 160.)   Fellows, in coming to Attaleia from the north, 'suddenly entered a pass between the mountains, which diminished in width until cliffs almost perpendicular inclosed us on either side.   The descent became so abrupt that we were compelled to dismount and walk for two hours, during which time we continued rapidly

descending an ancient paved road, formed principally of the native marble rock, but which had been perfected with large stones at a very remote age ; the deep ruts of chariot wheels were apparent in many places.   The road is much worn by time ; and the people of a later age, diverging from the track, have formed a road with stones very inferior both in size and arrangement. About half an hour before I reached the plain . . . a view burst upon me through the cliffs . . . I looked down from the rocky steps of the throne of winter upon the rich and verdant plain of summer, with the blue sea in the distance . . . Nor was the foreground without its interest; on each projecting rock stood an ancient sarcophagus, and the trees half concealed the lids and broken sculptures of innumerable tombs.' —*A. M.* pp. 174, 175.   This may very probably have been the pass and road by which St. Paul ascended.

[3] See the excellent chapter on the 'Botany of Lycia' in Spratt and Forbes, vol. ii. ch. xiii.

[4] '*May* 9.—Ascending through a winterly climate, with snow by the side of our path, and only the crocus and anemones in bloom • • • we beheld a

withered in the plain, and the pink veins in the white asphodel flower are shrivelled by the heat. When the cottages are closed and the grass is parched, and everything is silent below in the purple haze and stillness of midsummer, clouds are seen drifting among the Pisidian precipices, and the cavern is often a welcome shelter from a cold and penetrating wind.[1] The upper part of this district is a wild region of cliffs, often isolated and bare, and separated from each other by valleys of sand, which the storm drives with blinding violence among the shivered points. The trees become fewer and smaller at every step. Three belts of vegetation are successively passed through in ascending from the coast: first the oak woods, then the forests of pine, and lastly the dark scattered patches of the cedar-juniper: and then we reach the treeless plains of the interior, which stretch in dreary extension to the north and the east.

After such a journey as this, separating, we know not where, from the companions they may have joined, and often thinking of that Christian companion who had withdrawn himself from their society when they needed him most, Paul and Barnabas emerged from the rugged mountain passes, and came upon the central table-land of Asia Minor. The whole interior region of the peninsula may be correctly described by this term; for, though intersected in various directions by mountain-ranges, it is, on the whole, a vast plateau, elevated higher than the summit of Ben Nevis above the level of the sea.[2] This is its general character, though a long journey across the district brings the traveller through many varieties of scenery. Sometimes he moves for hours along the dreary margin of an inland sea of salt,[3]—sometimes he rests in a cheerful hospitable town by the shore of a freshwater lake.[4] In some places the ground is burnt and volcanic, in others green and fruitful. Sometimes it is depressed into watery hollows, where wild swans visit the pools, and storks are seen fishing and feeding among the

new series of cultivated plains to the west, being in fact table-lands, nearly upon a level with the tops of the mountains which form the eastern boundary of the valley of the Xanthus . . . Descending to the plain, probably 1,000 feet, we pitched our tent, after a ride of 7½ hours. . . . Upon boiling the thermometer, I found that we were more than 4,000 feet above the sea, and, cutting down some dead trees, we provided against the coming cold of the evening by lighting three large fires around our encampment.' —Fell. *Lycia*, p. 234. This was in descending from Almalee, in the great Lycian yailah, to the south-east of Cibyra.

[1] For further illustrations of the change of season caused by difference of elevation, see Sp. and F. I. p. 242. Again, p. 293, 'Every step led us from spring into summer ;' and the follow-

ing pages. See also Fellows : ' Two months since at Syria the corn was beginning to show the ear, whilst here they have only in a few places now begun to plough and sow.'—*A. M.* 158. ' The corn, which we had the day before seen changing colour for the harvest, was here not an inch above the ground, and the buds of the bushes were not yet bursting.'—*Lycia*, p. 226.

[2] The yailah of Adalia is 3,500 feet above the sea: Sp. and F. I. p. 244. The vast plain, ' at least fifty miles long and twenty wide,' south of Kiutayah in Phrygia, is about 6,000 feet above the sea. Fell. *A. M.* p. 155. This may be overstated, but the plain of Erzeroum is quite as much.

[3] We shall have occasion to mention the salt lakes hereafter.

[4] The two lakes of Buldur and Eyerdir are mentioned below. Both are described as very beautiful.

weeds:[1] more frequently it is spread out into broad open downs, like Salisbury Plain, which afford an interminable pasture for flocks of sheep.[2] To the north of Pamphylia, the elevated plain stretches through Phrygia for a hundred miles from Mount Taurus to Mount Olympus.[3] The southern portion of these bleak uplands was crossed by St. Paul's track, immediately before his arrival at Antioch in Pisidia. The features of human life which he had around him are probably almost as unaltered as the scenery of the country,—dreary villages with flat-roofed huts and cattle-sheds in the day, and at night an encampment of tents of goats' hair,—tents of *cilicium* (see p. 40),—a blazing fire in the midst,—horses fastened around,—and in the distance the moon shining on the snowy summits of Taurus.[4]

The *Sultan Tareek*, or Turkish Royal Road from Adalia to Kiutayah and Constantinople, passes nearly due north by the beautiful lake of Buldur.[5] The direction of Antioch in Pisidia bears more to the east. After passing somewhere near Selge and Sagalassus, St. Paul approached by the margin of the much larger, though perhaps not less beautiful, lake of Eyerdir.[6] The position of the city is not far from the northern shore of this lake, at the base of a mountain-range which stretches through Phrygia in a south-easterly direction. It is, however, not many years since this statement could be confidently made. Strabo, indeed, describes its position with remarkable clearness and precision. His words are as follows:—' In the district of Phrygia called Paroreia, there is a certain mountain-ridge, stretching from east to west. On each side there is a large plain below this ridge: and it has two cities in its neighbourhood; Philomelium on the north, and on the other side Antioch, called Antioch near Pisidia. The former lies entirely in the plain, the latter (which has a Roman colony) is on a height.' With this description before him, and taking into account certain indications of distance furnished by ancient authorities, Colonel Leake, who has perhaps done more for the elucidation of Classical Topography than any other man, felt that Ak-Sher, the position assigned to Antioch by D'Anville and other geographers, could not be the true place: Ak-Sher is on the north of the ridge, and the position could not be made to harmonise with the Tables.[7] But he **was** not in possession of any information which could lead him to

---

[1] ' *March* 27 (*near Kiutayah*).—I counted 180 storks fishing or feeding in one small swampy place not an acre in extent. The land here is used principally for breeding and grazing cattle, which are to be seen in herds of many hundreds.'—Fell. *Asia Minor*, p. 155. ' *May* 8.—The shrubs are the rose, the barbary, and wild almond; but all are at present fully six weeks later than those in the country we have lately passed. I observed on the lake many stately wild swans (*near Almalee*, 3,000 feet above the sea).'—Fell. *Lycia*, p. 228.

[2] We shall have occasion to return

presently to this character of much of the interior of Asia Minor when we come to the mention of Lycaonia (Acts xiv. 6).

[3] Fellows' *Asia Minor*, p. 155, &c.

[4] See Fellows' *Asia Minor*, p. 177, and especially the mention of the goats' hair tents.

[5] See above, p. 133, n. 4.

[6] See the descriptions in Arundel's *Asia Minor*, ch. xiii., and especially ch. xv.

[7] See Leake's *Asia Minor*, p. 41. The same difficulties were perceived by Mannert.

the true position; and the problem remained unsolved till Mr. Arundell started from Smyrna, in 1833, with the deliberate purpose of discovering the scene of St. Paul's labours. He successfully proved that Ak-Sher is Philomelium, and that Antioch is at Ya-lobatch, on the other side of the ridge. The narrative of his successful journey is very interesting: and every Christian ought to sympathise in the pleasure with which, knowing that Antioch was seventy miles from Apamea, and forty-five miles from Apollonia, he first succeeded in identifying Apollonia; and then, exactly at the right distance, perceived, in the tombs near a fountain, and the vestiges of an ancient road, sure indications of his approach to a ruined city; and then saw, across the plain, the remains of an aqueduct at the base of the mountain; and, finally, arrived at Jalobatch, ascended to the elevation described by Strabo, and felt, as he looked on the superb ruins around, that he was 'really on the spot consecrated by the labours and persecution of the Apostles Paul and Barnabas.'[1]

The position of the Pisidian Antioch being thus determined by the convergence of ancient authority and modern research, we perceive that it lay on an important line of communication, westward by Apamea with the valley of the Mæander, and eastward by Iconium with the country behind the Taurus. In this general direction, between Smyrna and Ephesus on the one hand, and the Cilician Gates which lead down to Tarsus on the other, conquering armies and trading caravans, Persian satraps, Roman proconsuls, and Turkish pachas, have travelled for centuries.[2] The Pisidian Antioch was situated about halfway between these extreme points. It was built (as we have seen in an earlier chapter, IV. p. 101) by the founder of the Syrian Antioch: and in the age of the Greek kings of the line of Seleucus it was a town of considerable importance. But its appearance had been modified, since the campaigns of Scipio and Manlius, and the defeat of Mithridates,[3] by the introduction of Roman usages, and the Roman style of building. This was true to a certain extent, of all the larger towns of Asia Minor: but this change had probably taken place in the Pisidian Antioch more than in many cities of greater importance; for, like Philippi,[4] it was a Roman *Colonia*. Without delaying, at present, to explain the full meaning of this term, we may say that the character impressed on any town in the Empire which had been made subject to military colonisation was particularly *Roman*, and that all such towns were bound by a tie of peculiar closeness to the Mother City. The insignia of Roman power were displayed more

[1] See Arundell's *Asia Minor*, ch. xii. xiii. xiv., and the view as given in our quarto edition. There is also a view in Laborde. The opinion of Mr. Arundell is fully confirmed by Mr. Hamilton, *Researches in Asia Minor*, vol. i. ch. xxvii. The aqueduct conveyed water to the town from the Sultan Dagh (Strabo's 'mountain ridge').

[2] In illustration of this we may refer to the caravan routes and Persian military roads as indicated in Kiepert's *Hellas*, to Xenophon's *Anabasis*, to Alexander's campaign and Cicero's progress, to the invasion of Tamerlane. and the movements of the Turkish and Egyptian armies in 1832 and 1833.

[3] See p. 11.

[4] Acts xvi. 12. The constitution of a *Colonia* will be explained when we come to this passage.

conspicuously than in other towns in the same province. In the provinces where Greek was spoken, while other towns had Greek letters on their coins, the money of the colonies was distinguished by Latin superscriptions. Antioch must have had some eminence among the eastern colonies, for it was founded by Augustus, and called Cæsarea.[1] Such coins as that represented at the end of this chapter were in circulation here, though not at Perga or Iconium, when St. Paul visited these cities : and more than at any other city visited on this journey, he would hear Latin spoken side by side with the Greek and the ruder Pisidian dialect.[2]

Along with this population of Greeks, Romans, and native Pisidians, a greater or smaller number of Jews was intermixed. They may not have been a very numerous body, for only one synagogue[3] is mentioned in the narrative. But it is evident, from the events recorded, that they were an influential body, that they had made many proselytes, and that they had obtained some considerable dominion (as in the parallel cases of Damascus recorded by Josephus,[4] and Berœa and Thessalonica in the Acts of the Apostles[5]) over the minds of the Gentile women.

On the Sabbath days the Jews and the proselytes met in the synagogue. It is evident that at this time full liberty of public worship was permitted to the Jewish people in all parts of the Roman Empire, whatever limitations might have been enacted by law or compelled by local opposition, as relates to the form and situation of the synagogues. We infer from Epiphanius that the Jewish places of worship were often erected in open and conspicuous positions.[6] This natural wish may frequently have been checked by the influence of the Heathen priests, who would not willingly see the votaries of an ancient idolatry forsaking the temple for the synagogue : and feelings of the same kind may probably have hindered the Jews, even if they had the ability or desire, from erecting religious edifices of any remarkable grandeur and solidity. No ruins of the synagogues of imperial times have remained to us, like those of the temples in every province, from which we are able to convince ourselves of the very form and size of the sanctuaries of Jupiter, Apollo, and Diana. There is little doubt that the sacred edifices of the Jews have been modified by the architecture of the remote countries through which they have

---

[1] We should learn this from the inscription on the coins, COL. CÆS. ANTIOCHIÆ, if we did not learn it from Strabo and Pliny. Mr. Hamilton found an inscription at Yalobatch, with the letters ANTIOCH EAE CAESARE. Another coin of this colony, exhibiting the wolf with Romulus and Remus, is engraved in this volume. Others exhibit two oxen, which illustrate the Roman mode of marking out by a plough the colonial limits.

[2] We shall have to return to this subject of language again, in speaking of the ' speech of Lycaonia.' Acts xiv. 11.

[3] See remarks on Salamis, p. 114.

[4] The people of Damascus were obliged to use caution in their scheme of assassinating the Jews ;—'through fear of their women, all of whom, except a few, were attached to the Jewish worshippers.'—*War*, ii. 20, 2.

[5] Acts xvii. 4, 12.

[6] He is speaking of the synagogue at Nablous. Such buildings were frequently placed by the waterside for the sake of ablution. Compare Acts xvi. 13, with Joseph. *Ant.* xiv. 10, 23.

been dispersed, and the successive centuries through which they have continued a separated people. Under the Roman Empire it is natural to suppose that they must have varied, according to circumstances, through all gradations of magnitude and decoration, from the simple *proseucha* at Philippi [1] to the magnificent prayer-houses at Alexandria. [2] Yet there are certain traditional peculiarities which have doubtless united together by a common resemblance the Jewish synagogues of all ages and countries. [3] The arrangement for the women's places in a separate gallery, or behind a partition of lattice-work,—the desk in the centre, where the Reader, like Ezra in ancient days, from his ' pulpit of wood,' may ' open the Book in the sight of all the people . . . and read in the Book the Law of God distinctly, and give the sense, and cause them to understand the reading,' [4]—the carefully closed Ark on the side of the building nearest to Jerusalem, for the preservation of the rolls or manuscripts of the Law,—the seats all round the building, whence ' the eyes of all them that are in the synagogue ' may 'be fastened ' on him who speaks, [5]—the ' chief seats,' [6] which were appropriated to the ' ruler ' or ' rulers ' of the synagogue, according as its organisation might be more or less complete, [7] and which were so dear to the hearts of those who professed to be peculiarly learned or peculiarly devout,—these are some of the features of a synagogue, which agree at once with the notices of Scripture, the descriptions in the Talmud, and the practice of modern Judaism.

The meeting of the congregations in the ancient synagogues may be easily realised, if due allowance be made for the change of costume, by those who have seen the Jews at their worship in the large towns of Modern Europe. On their entrance into the building, the four-cornered Tallith [8] was first placed like a veil over the head, or like a scarf over the shoulders. [9] The prayers were then recited by an officer called the ' Angel,' or ' Apostle,' of the assembly. [10] These prayers were doubtless many of them identically

[1] Acts xvi. 13. The question of the identity or difference of the *proseucha* and *synagogue* will be considered hereafter. Probably the former is a general term.

[2] Mentioned by Philo.

[3] Besides the works referred to in the notes to Chap. II., Allen's *Modern Judaism* and Bernard's *Synagogue and Church* may be consulted with advantage on subjects connected with the synagogue.

[4] Nehem. viii. 4–8.

[5] See Luke iv. 20.

[6] These chief seats (Matt. xxiii. 6) seemed to have faced the rest of the congregation. See Jam. ii. 3.

[7] With Luke xiii. 14, Acts xviii. 8, 17, compare Luke vii. 3, Mark v. 22, and Acts xiii. 15. Some are of opinion that the smaller synagogues had one ' ruler,' the larger many. It is more probable that the ' chief ruler ' with the ' elders ' formed a congregational council, like the kirk-session in Scotland.

[8] The use of the Tallith is said to have arisen from the Mosaic commandment directing that fringes should be worn on the four corners of the garment.

[9] When we read 1 Cor. xi. 4, 7, we must feel some doubt concerning the wearing of the Tallith on the head during worship at that period. De Wette says that 'it is certain that in the Apostolic age the Jews did not veil their heads during their exhortations in the synagogues.' It is quite possible that the Tallith, though generally worn in the congregation, might be removed by anyone who rose to speak or who prayed aloud.

[10] Vitringa, who compares Rev. ii. 1.

the same with those which are found in the present service-books of the German and Spanish Jews, though their liturgies, in the course of ages, have undergone successive developments, the steps of which are not easily ascertained. It seems that the prayers were sometimes read in the vernacular language of the country where the synagogue was built; but the Law was always read in Hebrew. The sacred roll[1] of manuscript was handed from the Ark to the Reader by the Chazan, or 'Minister;'[2] and then certain portions were read according to a fixed cycle, first from the Law and then from the Prophets. It is impossible to determine the period when the sections from these two divisions of the Old Testament were arranged as in use at present;[3] but the same necessity for translation and explanation existed then as now. The Hebrew and English are now printed in parallel columns. Then, the reading of the Hebrew was elucidated by the Targum or the Septuagint, or followed by a paraphrase in the spoken language of the country.[4] The Reader stood[5] while thus employed, and all the congregation sat around. The manuscript was rolled up and returned to the Chazan.[6] Then followed a pause, during which strangers or learned men, who had 'any word of consolation' or exhortation, rose and addressed the meeting. And thus, after a pathetic enumeration of the sufferings of the chosen people[7] or an allegorical exposition[8] of some dark passage of Holy Writ, the worship was closed with a benediction and a solemn 'Amen.'[9]

To such a worship in such a building a congregation came together at Antioch in Pisidia, on the Sabbath which immediately succeeded the arrival of Paul and Barnabas. Proselytes came and seated themselves with the Jews: and among the Jewesses behind the lattice were 'honourable women'[10] of the colony. The two strangers entered the synagogue, and, wearing the Tallith, which was the badge of an Israelite,[11] 'sat down'[12] with the rest. The prayers were recited, the extracts from 'the Law and the Prophets' were read;[13] the 'Book' returned to the 'Minister,'[14] and then we are told that 'the rulers of the synagogue' sent to the new comers, on whom

---

[1] The words in Luke iv. 17, 20, imply the acts of rolling and unrolling. See 1 Macc. iii. 48.

[2] Luke iv. 17, 20.

[3] A full account both of the *Paraschioth* or Sections of the Law, and the *Haphtaroth* or Sections of the Prophets, as used both by the Portuguese and German Jews, may be seen in Horne's *Introduction*, vol. iii. pp. 254–258.

[4] See p. 29. In Palestine the Syro-Chaldaic language would be used; in the Dispersion, usually the Greek. Lightfoot seems to think that the Pisidian language was used here. Strabo speaks of a dialect as peculiar to this district.

[5] Acts xiii. 16. On the other hand, Our Lord was seated during solemn teaching, Luke iv. 20.

[6] See Luke iv. 20.

[7] The sermon in the synagogue in 'Helon's Pilgrimage' is conceived in the true Jewish feeling. Compare the address of St. Stephen.

[8] We see how an inspired Apostle uses allegory. Gal. iv. 21–31.

[9] See Neh. viii. 6; 1 Cor. xiv. 16.

[10] Acts xiii. 50.

[11] 'As I entered the synagogue [at Blidah in Algeria], they offered me a Tallith, saying in French, "Êtes-vous Israëlite?" I could not wear the Tallith, but I opened my English Bible and *sat down*, thinking of Paul and Barnabas at Antioch in Pisidia.'—*Extract from a Private Journal.*

[12] Acts xiii. 14.

[13] Acts xiii. 15.

[14] Luke iv. 20.

many eyes had already been fixed, and invited them to address the assembly, if they had words of comfort or instruction to speak to their fellow Israelites.[1]   The very attitude of St. Paul, as he answered the invitation, is described to us.   He 'rose' from his seat, and with the animated and emphatic gesture which he used on other occasions,[2] 'beckoned with his hand.'[3]

After thus graphically bringing the scene before our eyes, St. Luke gives us, if not the whole speech delivered by St. Paul, yet at least the substance of what he said.   For into however short a space he may have condensed the speeches which he reports, yet it is no mere outline, no dry analysis of them which he gives.   He has evidently preserved, if not *all* the words, yet the *very* words uttered by the Apostle ; nor can we fail to recognise in all these speeches a tone of thought, and even of expression, which stamps them with the individuality of the speaker.

On the present occasion we find St. Paul beginning his address by connecting the Messiah whom he preached, with the preparatory dispensation which ushered in His advent.   He dwells upon the previous history of the Jewish people, for the same reasons which had led St. Stephen to do the like in his defence before the Sanhedrin.   He endeavours to conciliate the minds of his Jewish audience by proving to them that the Messiah whom he proclaimed, was the same whereto their own prophets bare witness ; come, not to destroy the Law, but to fulfil ; and that His advent had been duly heralded by His predicted messenger.   He then proceeds to remove the prejudice which the rejection of Jesus by the authorities at Jerusalem (the metropolis of their faith) would naturally raise in the minds of the Pisidian Jews against his divine mission.   He shows that Christ's death and resurrection had accomplished the ancient prophecies, and declares this to be the 'Glad Tidings' which the Apostles were charged to proclaim.   Thus far the speech contains nothing which could offend the exclusive spirit of Jewish nationality. On the contrary, St. Paul has endeavoured to carry his hearers with him by the topics on which he has dwelt ; the Saviour whom he declares is 'a Saviour unto Israel;' the Messiah whom he announces is the fulfiller of the Law and the Prophets.   But having thus conciliated their feelings, and won their favourable attention, he proceeds in a bolder tone, to declare the Catholicity of Christ's salvation, and the antithesis between the Gospel and the Law.   His concluding words, as St. Luke relates them, might stand as a summary representing in outline the early chapters of the Epistle to the Romans ; and therefore, conversely, those chapters will enable us to realise the manner in which St. Paul would have expanded the heads of argument which his disciple here records.   The speech ends with a warning against that bigoted rejection of Christ's doctrine, which this latter portion of the address was so likely to call forth.

The following were the words (so far as they have been preserved to us) spoken by St. Paul on this memorable occasion :—

---

[1] Acts xiii. 15.   The word is the same as that which is used in the descriptive title of Barnabas, p. 97.

[2] Acts xxvi. 1, xxi. 40.   See xx. 34

[3] Acts xiii. 16.

' Men of Israel, and ye, proselytes of the Gentiles, who worship the God of Abraham, give audience.

God's choice
of Israel to be
His people,
and of David
to be the progenitor of the
Messiah.
' The God of this people Israel chose our fathers, and raised up His people, when they dwelt as strangers in the land of Egypt; and with an high arm brought He them out therefrom. And about 18 the time of forty years, even as a nurse beareth her child, so bare He them [1] through the wilderness. And He destroyed seven nations in the land of 19 Canaan, and gave their land as a portion unto His people. And after that He gave unto them Judges 20 about the space [2] of four hundred and fifty years, until Samuel the Prophet; then desired they a king, and He gave unto them Saul, the son of Cis, a man 21 of the tribe of Benjamin,[3] to rule them for forty years. And when He had removed Saul, He raised 22 up unto them David to be their king; to whom also He gave testimony, and said: 𝕴 𝔥𝔞𝔟𝔢 𝔣𝔬𝔲𝔫𝔡 𝔇𝔞𝔟𝔦𝔡, 𝔱𝔥𝔢 𝔰𝔬𝔫 𝔬𝔣 𝔍𝔢𝔰𝔰𝔢, 𝔞 𝔪𝔞𝔫 𝔞𝔣𝔱𝔢𝔯 𝔪𝔶 𝔬𝔴𝔫 𝔥𝔢𝔞𝔯𝔱, 𝔴𝔥𝔦𝔠𝔥 𝔰𝔥𝔞𝔩𝔩 𝔣𝔲𝔩𝔣𝔦𝔩 𝔞𝔩𝔩 𝔪𝔶 𝔴𝔦𝔩𝔩.[4] Of this man's seed 23 hath God, according to His promise, raised unto Israel a Saviour Jesus.

' And John was 𝔱𝔥𝔢 𝔪𝔢𝔰𝔰𝔢𝔫𝔤𝔢𝔯 𝔴𝔥𝔬 𝔴𝔢𝔫𝔱 𝔟𝔢𝔣𝔬𝔯𝔢 24 𝔋𝔦𝔰 𝔣𝔞𝔠𝔢 [5] 𝔱𝔬 𝔭𝔯𝔢𝔭𝔞𝔯𝔢 𝔋𝔦𝔰 𝔴𝔞𝔶 𝔟𝔢𝔣𝔬𝔯𝔢 𝔋𝔦𝔪, and he preached the baptism of repentance to all the people of Israel. And as John fulfilled his course [6] his saying was, "Whom think ye that I am? I 25 am not He. But behold there cometh one after me whose shoes' latchet I am not worthy to loose."[7]

---

[1] The beauty of this metaphor has been lost to the Authorised Version on account of the reading adopted in the Received Text. There is an evident allusion to Deut. i. 31.

[2] We need not trouble our readers with the difficulties which have been raised concerning the chronology of this passage. Supposing it could be proved that St. Paul's knowledge of ancient chronology was imperfect, this need not surprise us; for there seems no reason to suppose (and we have certainly no right to assume *à priori*) that Divine inspiration would instruct the Apostles in truth discoverable by uninspired research, and non-essential to their religious mission. See note on Galatians iii. 17.

[3] [For the speaker's own connection with the tribe of Benjamin, see pp. 36, 37, and 43.—H.]

[4] Compare Ps. lxxxix. 20, with 1 Sam. xiii. 14. The quotation is from the LXX., but not *verbatim*, being apparently made from memory.

[5] Mal. iii. 1, as quoted Matt. xi. 10, not exactly after the LXX., but rather according to the literal translation of the Hebrew.

[6] [Here, and in the speech at Miletus (xiii. 25), it is worthy of notice that St. Paul uses one of his favourite and characteristic metaphors drawn from the foot-race.—H.]

[7] The imperfect is used here.

26 'Men and Brethren,[1] whether ye be children of The rulers of Jerusalem fulfilled the Prophets by causing the death of Jesus.
the stock of Abraham, or proselytes of the Gen-
tiles, to you have been sent the tidings of this
27 salvation: for the inhabitants of Jerusalem, and
their rulers, because they knew Him not, nor yet
the voices of the prophets which are read in their
synagogues every Sabbath day, have fulfilled the
28 Scriptures in condemning Him. And though they
found in Him no cause of death, yet besought they
29 Pilate that He should be slain. And when they
had fulfilled all which was written of Him, they
took Him down from the tree, and laid Him in a
sepulchre.

30 'But God raised Him from the dead. HIS RESUR-RECTION.

31 'And He was seen for many days by them who Attested by many witnesses.
came up with Him from Galilee to Jerusalem, who
are now[2] His witnesses to the people of Israel.[3]

32 'And while they[4] proclaim it in Jerusalem, we The Glad Tidings of the Apostles is the Announcement that Christ's resurrection had fulfilled God's promises.
declare unto you the same Glad Tidings concerning
the promise which was made to our fathers; even
that God hath fulfilled the same unto us their
children, in that He hath raised up Jesus from the
33 dead;[5] as it is also written in the second psalm,
𝕿𝖍𝖔𝖚 𝖆𝖗𝖙 𝖒𝖞 𝕾𝖔𝖓, 𝖙𝖍𝖎𝖘 𝖉𝖆𝖞 𝖍𝖆𝖛𝖊 𝕴 𝖇𝖊𝖌𝖔𝖙𝖙𝖊𝖓 𝖙𝖍𝖊𝖊.[6]
34 And whereas He hath raised Him from the grave,
no more to return unto corruption, He hath said
on this wise, 𝕿𝖍𝖊 𝖇𝖑𝖊𝖘𝖘𝖎𝖓𝖌𝖘 𝖔𝖋 𝕯𝖆𝖛𝖎𝖉 𝖜𝖎𝖑𝖑 𝕴 𝖌𝖎𝖛𝖊
𝖞𝖔𝖚, 𝖊𝖛𝖊𝖓 𝖙𝖍𝖊 𝖇𝖑𝖊𝖘𝖘𝖎𝖓𝖌𝖘 𝖜𝖍𝖎𝖈𝖍 𝖘𝖙𝖆𝖓𝖉 𝖋𝖆𝖘𝖙 𝖎𝖓 𝖍𝖔𝖑𝖎=
35 𝖓𝖊𝖘𝖘.[7] Wherefore it is written also in another
psalm, 𝕿𝖍𝖔𝖚 𝖘𝖍𝖆𝖑𝖙 𝖓𝖔𝖙 𝖘𝖚𝖋𝖋𝖊𝖗 𝖙𝖍𝖎𝖓𝖊 𝕳𝖔𝖑𝖞 𝕺𝖓𝖊 𝖙𝖔
36 𝖘𝖊𝖊 𝖈𝖔𝖗𝖗𝖚𝖕𝖙𝖎𝖔𝖓.[8] Now David, after he had ministered in his own generation[9] to the will of God, fell
asleep, and was laid unto his fathers, and saw cor-

---

[1] Literally '*men that are my bre-thren.*' So in Acts xvii. 22,—'*men of Athens.*' It might be rendered simply '*Brethren.*'

[2] The word for 'now,' evidently very important here, is erroneously omitted by the Textus Receptus.

[3] 'The people,' always means the *Jewish* people.

[4] Observe 'we preach to you' emphatically contrasted with the preceding 'they to the Jewish nation'(Humphry).

[5] 'Raised up *from the dead.*' We cannot agree with Mr. Humphry that the word can here (consistently with the context) have the same meaning as in vii. 37.

[6] Ps. ii. 7, according to LXX. trans.

[7] Isaiah lv. 3 (LXX.). The verbal connection (*holy—Holy One*) between vv. 34 and 35 should be carefully noticed.

[8] Ps. xvi. 10 (LXX.).

[9] David's ministration was performed (like that of other men) *in his own generation*; but the ministration of Christ extended to all generations. The thought is similar to Heb. vii. 23, 24. We depart here from the Authorised Version, because the use of the Greek words for ' to serve one's own genera-tion,' does not accord with the analogy of the N. T.

ruption; but He whom God raised from the dead 37
saw no corruption.[1]

Catholicity of
Christ's salva-
tion. Anti-
thesis between
the Gospel
and the Law.
'Be it known unto you, therefore, men and 38
brethren, that through this Jesus is declared unto
you the forgiveness of sins. And in Him all who 39
have faith are justified from all transgressions,
wherefrom in the Law of Moses ye could not be
justified.

'Beware, therefore, lest that come upon you 40
which is spoken in the Prophets, 𝔅𝔢𝔥𝔬𝔩𝔡, 𝔶𝔢 𝔡𝔢=41
𝔰𝔭𝔦𝔰𝔢𝔯𝔰, 𝔞𝔫𝔡 𝔴𝔬𝔫𝔡𝔢𝔯, 𝔞𝔫𝔡 𝔭𝔢𝔯𝔦𝔰𝔥; 𝔣𝔬𝔯 𝔍 𝔴𝔬𝔯𝔨 𝔞 𝔴𝔬𝔯𝔨
𝔦𝔫 𝔶𝔬𝔲𝔯 𝔡𝔞𝔶𝔰, 𝔞 𝔴𝔬𝔯𝔨 𝔴𝔥𝔦𝔠𝔥 𝔶𝔢 𝔰𝔥𝔞𝔩𝔩 𝔦𝔫 𝔫𝔬 𝔴𝔦𝔰𝔢
𝔟𝔢𝔩𝔦𝔢𝔟𝔢, 𝔱𝔥𝔬𝔲𝔤𝔥 𝔞 𝔪𝔞𝔫 𝔡𝔢𝔠𝔩𝔞𝔯𝔢 𝔦𝔱 𝔲𝔫𝔱𝔬 𝔶𝔬𝔲.'[2]

This address made a deep and thrilling impression on the audience.
While the congregation were pouring out of the synagogue, many
of them[3] crowded round the speaker, begging that 'these words,'
which had moved their deepest feelings, might be repeated to them
on their next occasion of assembling together.[4] And when at length
the mass of the people had dispersed, singly or in groups, to their
homes, many of the Jews and proselytes still clung to Paul and Barnabas, who earnestly exhorted them (in the form of expression which
we could almost recognise as St. Paul's, from its resemblance to the
phraseology of his Epistles,) 'to abide in the grace of God.'[5]

'With what pleasure can we fancy the Apostles to have observed
these hearers of the Word, who seemed to have heard it in such
earnest. How gladly must they have talked with them,—entered
into various points more fully than was possible in any public address,
—appealed to them in various ways which no one can touch upon
who is speaking to a mixed multitude. Yet, with all their pleasure
and their hope, their knowledge of man's heart must have taught
them not to be over confident; and therefore they would earnestly
urge them to continue in the grace of God; to keep up the impression
which had already outlasted their stay within the synagogue;—to
feed it and keep it alive, and make it deeper and deeper, that it
should remain with them for ever. What the issue was we know
not,—nor does that concern us,—only we may be sure that here,
as in other instances, there were some in whom their hopes and
endeavours were disappointed; there were some in whom they were
to their fullest extent realised.'[6]

---

[1] We are here reminded of the arguments of St. Peter on the day of
Pentecost, just as the beginning of the
speech recalls that of St. Stephen
before the Sanhedrin. Possibly, St.
Paul himself had been an auditor of
the first, as he certainly was of the last.

[2] Habak. i. 5 (LXX.).

[3] The words rendered 'Gentiles'
(Auth. Vers.) in the Textus Receptus,
have caused a great confusion in this
passage. They are omitted in the best
MSS. See below, p. 146, n. 4.

[4] It is not quite certain whether we
are to understand the words in v. 42 to
mean 'the next Sabbath' or some *intermediate* days of meeting during the
week. The Jews were accustomed to
meet in the synagogues on Monday
and Thursday as well as on Saturday.

[5] Acts xiii. 43. Compare Acts xx.
24; 1 Cor. xv. 10; 2 Cor. vi. 1; Gal.
ii. 21.

[6] Dr. Arnold's Twenty-fourth Sermon *on the Interpretation of Scripture.*

The intervening week between this Sabbath and the next had not only its days of meeting in the synagogue,[1] but would give many opportunities for exhortation and instruction in private houses; the doctrine would be noised abroad, and, through the proselytes, would come to the hearing of the Gentiles. So that 'on the following Sabbath almost the whole city came together to hear the Word of God.' The synagogue was crowded.[2] Multitudes of Gentiles were there in addition to the Proselytes. This was more than the Jews could bear. Their spiritual pride and exclusive bigotry was immediately roused. They could not endure the notion of others being freely admitted to the same religious privileges with themselves. This was always the sin of the Jewish people. Instead of realising their position in the world as the prophetic nation for the good of the whole earth, they indulged the self-exalting opinion, that God's highest blessings were only for themselves. Their oppressions and their dispersions had not destroyed this deeply-rooted prejudice; but they rather found comfort under the yoke, in brooding over their religious isolation; and even in their remote and scattered settlements, they clung with the utmost tenacity to the feeling of their exclusive nationality. Thus, in the Pisidian Antioch, they who on one Sabbath had listened with breathless interest to the teachers who spoke to them of the promised Messiah, were on the next Sabbath filled with the most excited indignation, when they found that this Messiah was 'a light to lighten the Gentiles,' as well as 'the glory of His people Israel.' They made an uproar, and opposed the words of Paul[3] with all manner of calumnious expressions, 'contradicting and blaspheming.'

Then the Apostles, promptly recognising in the willingness of the Gentiles and the unbelief of the Jews the clear indications of the path of duty, followed that bold[4] course which was alien to all the prejudices of a Jewish education. They turned at once and without reserve to the Gentiles. St. Paul was not unprepared for the events which called for this decision. The prophetic intimations at his first conversion, his vision in the Temple at Jerusalem, his experience at the Syrian Antioch, his recent success in the island of Cyprus, must have led him to expect the Gentiles to listen to that message which the Jews were too ready to scorn. The words with which he turned from his unbelieving countrymen were these : 'It was needful that the Word of God should first be spoken unto you; but inasmuch as ye reject it, and deem yourselves unworthy of eternal life, lo! we turn to the Gentiles.' And then he quotes a prophetical passage from their own sacred writings. 'For thus hath the Lord commanded us, saying, I have set thee for a light to the Gentiles, that thou shouldst be for salvation to the ends of the earth.'[5] This is the first recorded instance of a scene which was often re-enacted. It is the course which St. Paul himself defines in his Epistle to the

[1] See n. 4 on the preceding page.
[2] Acts xiii. 44.
[3] The words in Acts xiii. 45, imply indirectly that Paul was the 'chief speaker,' as we are told, xiv. 12.
[4] Compare 1 Thess. ii. 2, where the circumstances appear to have been very similar.

[5] Isai. xlix. 6, quoted with a slight variation from the LXX. See Isai. xlii. 6; Luke ii. 32.

Romans, when he describes the Gospel as coming first to the Jew and then to the Gentile;[1] and it is the course which he followed himself on various occasions of his life, at Corinth,[2] at Ephesus,[3] and at Rome.[4]

That which was often obscurely foretold in the Old Testament,—that those should 'seek after God who knew Him not,' and that He should be honoured by 'those who were not a people;'[5]—that which had already seen its first fulfilment in isolated cases during Our Lord's life, as in the centurion and the Syrophœnician woman, whose faith had no parallel in all the people of 'Israel;'[6]—that which had received an express accomplishment through the agency of two of the chiefest of the Apostles, in Cornelius, the Roman officer at Cæsarea, and in Sergius Paulus, the Roman governor at Paphos,—began now to be realised on a large scale in a whole community. While the Jews blasphemed and rejected Christ, the Gentiles 'rejoiced and glorified the Word of God.' The counsels of God were not frustrated by the unbelief of His chosen people. A new 'Israel,' a new 'election,' succeeded to the former.[7] A Church was formed of united Jews and Gentiles; and all who were destined to enter the path of eternal life[8] were gathered into the Catholic brotherhood of the hitherto separated races. The synagogue had rejected the inspired missionaries, but the apostolic instruction went on in some private house or public building belonging to the Heathen. And gradually the knowledge of Christianity began to be disseminated through the whole vicinity.[9]

The enmity of the Jews, however, was not satisfied by the expulsion of the Apostles from their synagogue. What they could not accomplish by violence and calumny, they succeeded in effecting by a pious intrigue. That influence of women in religious questions, to which our attention will be repeatedly called hereafter, is here for the first time brought before our notice in the sacred narrative of St. Paul's life. Strabo, who was intimately acquainted with the social position of the female sex in the towns of Western Asia, speaks in strong terms of the power which they possessed and exercised in controlling and modifying the religious opinions of the men. This general fact received one of its most striking illustrations in the case of Judaism. We have already more than once alluded to the influence of the female proselytes at Damascus:[10] and the good service which women contributed towards the early progress of Christianity is abundantly known both from the Acts and the Epistles.[11] Here they appear in a position less honourable, but not less influential. The Jews contrived, through the female prose-

---

[1] Rom. i. 16, ii. 9. Compare xi. 12, 25.

[2] Acts xviii. 6.

[3] Acts xix. 9.

[4] Acts xxviii. 28.

[5] See Hosea i. 10, ii. 23, as quoted in Rom. ix. 25, 26.

[6] Matt. viii. 5–10, xv. 21–28.

[7] See Rom. xi. 7; and Gal. vi. 16.

[8] Acts xiii. 48. It is well known that this passage has been made the subject of much controversy with reference to the doctrine of predestination. Its bearing on the question is very doubtful. The same participle is used in Acts xx. 13, and also in Luke iii. 13, and Rom. xiii. 1.

[9] Acts xiii. 49.

[10] See above, p. 16, and p. 136, n. 4.

[11] See Acts xvi. 14, xviii. 2; Phil. iv. 3; 1 Cor. vii. 16.

lytes at Antioch, to win over to their cause some influential members of their sex, and through them to gain the ear of men who occupied a position of eminence in the city. Thus a systematic persecution was excited against Paul and Barnabas. Whether the supreme magistrates of the colony were induced by this unfair agitation to pass a sentence of formal banishment, we are not informed;[1] but for the present the Apostles were compelled to retire from the colonial limits.

In cases such as these, instructions had been given by our Lord himself how His Apostles were to act. During His life on earth, He had said to the Twelve, ' Whosoever shall not receive you, nor hear you, when ye depart thence, shake off the dust under your feet for a testimony against them. Verily, I say unto you, it shall be more tolerable for Sodom and Gomorrah in the day of judgment, than for that city.'[2] And while Paul and Barnabas thus fulfilled Our Lord's words, shaking off from their feet the dust of the dry and sunburnt road,[3] in token of God's judgment on wilful unbelievers, and turning their steps eastwards in the direction of Lycaonia, another of the sayings of Christ was fulfilled, in the midst of those who had been obedient to the faith : ' Blessed are ye, when men shall revile you and persecute you, and shall say all manner of evil against you falsely, for my sake. Rejoice and be exceeding glad : for great is your reward in heaven ; for so persecuted they the prophets which were before you.'[4] Even while their faithful teachers were removed from them, and travelling across the bare uplands[5] which separate Antioch from the plain of Iconium, the disciples of the former city received such manifest tokens of the love of God, and the power of the ' Holy Ghost,' that they were ' filled with joy' in the midst of persecution.

Iconium has obtained a place in history far more distinguished than that of the Pisidian Antioch. It is famous as the cradle of the rising power of the conquering Turks.[6] And the remains of its Mahommedan architecture still bear a conspicuous testimony to the victories and strong government of a tribe of Tatar invaders. But

---

[1] We should rather infer the contrary, since they revisited the place on their return from Derbe (xiv. 21).

[2] Mark vi. 11; Matt. x. 14, 15; Luke ix. 5. For other symbolical acts expressing the same thing, see Nehem. v. 13; Acts xviii. 6. It was taught in the schools of the Scribes that the dust of a Heathen land defiled by the touch. Hence the shaking of the dust off the feet implied that the city was regarded as profane.

[3] ' Literally may they have shaken off the dust of their feet, for even now (Nov. 9) the roads abound with it, and in the summer months it must be a plain of dust.'—Arundell's *Asia Minor*, vol. i. p. 319.

[4] Matt. v. 11, 12.

[5] Leake approached Iconium from the northern side of the mountains which separate Antioch from Philomelium (see p. 171). He says : ' On the descent from a ridge branching eastward from these mountains, we came in sight of the vast plain around Konieh, and of the lake which occupies the middle of it ; and we saw the city with its mosques and ancient walls, still at the distance of twelve or fourteen miles from us,' p. 45. Ainsworth travelled in the same direction, and says : ' We travelled three hours along the plain of Konieh, always in sight of the city of the Sultans of Roum, before we reached it.'—*Trav. in Asia Minor*, ii. p. 58.

[6] Iconium was the capital of the Seljukian Sultans, and had a great part in the growth of the Ottoman Empire.

there are other features in the view of modern *Konieh* which to us are far more interesting. To the traveller in the footsteps of St. Paul, it is not the armorial bearings of the Knights of St. John, carved over the gateways in the streets of Rhodes, which arrest the attention, but the ancient harbour and the view across the sea to the opposite coast. And at Konieh his interest is awakened, not by minarets and palaces and Saracenic gateways, but by the vast plain and the distant mountains.[1]

These features remain what they were in the first century, while the town has been repeatedly destroyed and rebuilt, and its architectural character entirely altered. Little, if anything, remains of Greek or Roman Iconium, if we except the ancient inscriptions and the fragments of sculptures which are built into the Turkish walls.[2] At a late period of the Empire it was made a *Colonia*, like its neighbour, Antioch : but it was not so in the time of St. Paul. There is no reason to suppose that its character was different from that of the other important towns on the principal lines of communication through Asia Minor. The elements of its population would be as follows :—a large number of trifling and frivolous Greeks, whose principal places of resort would be the theatre and the market-place ; some remains of a still older population, coming in occasionally from the country, or residing in a separate quarter of the town ; some few Roman officials, civil or military, holding themselves proudly aloof from the inhabitants of the subjugated province ; and an old established colony of Jews, who exercised their trade during the week, and met on the Sabbath to read the Law in the Synagogue.

The same kind of events took place here as in Antioch, and almost in the same order.[3] The Apostles went first to the Synagogue, and the effect of their discourses there was such, that great numbers both of the Jews and Greeks (i. e. Proselytes or Heathens, or both[4]) believed the Gospel. The unbelieving Jews raised up an indirect persecution by exciting the minds of the Gentile population against those who received the Christian doctrine. But the Apostles persevered and remained in the city some considerable time, having their confidence strengthened by the miracles which God worked through their instrumentality, in attestation of the truth of His Word. There is an apocryphal narrative of certain events assigned to this residence at Iconium :[5] and we may innocently adopt so

---

[1] 'Konieh extends to the east and south over the plain far beyond the walls, which are about two miles in circumference. . . . Mountains covered with snow rise on every side, excepting towards the east, where a plain, as flat as the desert of Arabia, extends far beyond the reach of the eye.'—Capt. Kinneir.

[2] 'The city wall is said to have been erected by the Seljukian Sultans : it seems to have been built from the ruins of more ancient buildings, as broken columns, capitals, pedestals, bas-reliefs,

and other pieces of sculpture, contribute towards its construction. It has eighty gates, of a square form, each known by a separate name, and, as well as most of the towers, embellished with Arabic inscriptions. . . . I observed a few Greek characters on the walls, but they were in so elevated a situation that I could not decipher them.'—Capt. Kinneir.

[3] See Acts xiv. 1–5.

[4] Perhaps 'Greeks' (v. 1) may mean 'proselytes,' as opposed to the 'Gentiles' of v. 2.

[5] The legend of Paul and Thecla.

much of the legendary story, as to imagine St. Paul preaching long and late to crowded congregations, as he did afterwards at Assos,[1] and his enemies bringing him before the civil authorities, with the cry that he was disturbing their households by his sorcery, or with complaints like those at Philippi and Ephesus, that he was ' exceedingly troubling their city,' and ' turning away much people.'[2] We learn from an inspired source[3] that the whole population of Iconium was ultimately divided into two great factions (a common occurrence, on far less important occasions, in these cities of Oriental Greeks), and that one party took the side of the Apostles, the other that of the Jews. But here, as at Antioch, the influential classes were on the side of the Jews. A determined attempt was at last made to crush the Apostles, by loading them with insult and actually stoning them. Learning this wicked conspiracy, in which the magistrates themselves were involved,[4] they fled to some of the neighbouring districts of Lycaonia, where they might be more secure, and have more liberty in preaching the Gospel.

It would be a very natural course for the Apostles, after the cruel treatment they had experienced in the great towns on a frequented route, to retire into a wilder region and among a ruder population. In any country, the political circumstances of which resemble those of Asia Minor under the early emperors, there must be many districts, into which the civilisation of the conquering and governing people has hardly penetrated. An obvious instance is furnished by our Eastern presidencies, in the Hindoo villages, which have retained their character without alteration, notwithstanding the successive occupations by Mahommedans and English. Thus, in the Eastern provinces of the Roman Empire there must have been many towns and villages where local customs were untouched, and where Greek, though certainly understood, was not commonly spoken. Such, perhaps, were the places which now come before our notice in the Acts of the Apostles,—small towns, with a rude dialect and primitive superstition[5]—' Lystra and Derbe, cities of Lycaonia.'[6]

The district of Lycaonia extends from the ridges of Mount Taurus and the borders of Cilicia, on the south, to the Cappadocian hills, on the north. It is a bare and dreary region, unwatered by streams, though in parts liable to occasional inundations. Strabo mentions one place where water was even sold for money. In this respect there must be a close resemblance between this country and large tracts of Australia. Nor is this the only particular in which the resemblance may be traced. Both regions afford excellent pasture for flocks of sheep, and give opportunities for obtaining large possessions by trade in wool. It was here, on the downs of Lycaonia, that Amyntas, while he yet led the life of a nomad chief, before the time of his political elevation,[7] fed his three hundred

The story will be found in Jones *on the Canon* (vol. ii. pp. 353–403).

[1] Acts xx. 7–11.
[2] Acts xvi. 20, xix. 26.
[3] Acts xiv. 4.
[4] It is impossible to determine ex-

actly the meaning of the word rendered ' rulers.'

[5] Acts xiv. 11, 12, &c.
[6] Acts xiv. 6.
[7] See above, Chap. I. p. 19.

flocks. Of the whole district Iconium[1] was properly the capital: and the plain round Iconium may be reckoned as its great central space, situated midway between Cilicia and Cappadocia. This plain is spoken of as the largest in Asia Minor.[2] It is almost like the steppes of Great Asia, of which the Turkish invaders must often have been reminded,[3] when they came to these level spaces in the west; and the camels which convey modern travellers to and from Konieh, find by the side of their path tufts of salt and prickly herbage, not very dissimilar to that which grows in their native deserts.[4]

Across some portion of this plain Paul and Barnabas travelled before as well as after their residence in Iconium. After leaving the high land to the north-west,[5] during a journey of several hours before arriving at the city, the eye ranges freely over a vast expanse of level ground to the south and the east. The two most eminent objects in the view are certain snowy summits,[6] which rise high above all the intervening hills in the direction of Armenia,— and, in the nearer horizon, the singular mountain mass called the 'Kara-Dagh,' or 'Black Mount,' south-eastwards in the direction of Cilicia.[7] And still these features continue to be conspicuous, after Iconium is left behind, and the traveller moves on over the plain towards Lystra and Derbe. Mount Argæus still rises far to the north-east, at the distance of one hundred and fifty miles. The Black Mountain is gradually approached, and discovered to be an isolated mass, with reaches of the plain extending round it like channels of the sea.[8] The cities of Lystra and Derbe were some-

---

[1] Xenophon, who is the first to mention Iconium, calls it 'the last city of Phrygia,' in the direction of 'Lycaonia.'

[2] See Leake, p. 93.

[3] The remark is made by Texier in his *'Asie Mineure.'*

[4] Ainsworth (ii. p. 68) describes the camels, as he crossed this plain, eagerly eating the tufts of Mesembryanthemum and Salicornia, 'reminding them of plains with which they were probably more familiar than those of Asia Minor.' The plain, however, is naturally rich.

[5] See above, p. 134.

[6] Leake supposed these summits to be those of Mount Argæus, but Hamilton thinks he was in error.

[7] See Leake, p. 45. 'To the south-east the same plains extend as far as the mountains of Karaman (Laranda). At the south-east extremity of the plains beyond Konieh, we are much struck with the appearance of a remarkable insulated mountain, called Kara-Dagh (Black Mountain), rising to a great height, covered at the top with snow [Jan. 31], and appearing like a lofty island in the midst of the sea. It is about sixty miles distant.' The lines marked on the Map are the Roman roads mentioned in the Itineraries.

A view of the Kara-Dagh is given in Chap. VIII.

[8] See Leake, pp. 93–97. '(*Feb. 1. From Konieh to Tshumra*).—Our road pursues a perfect level for upwards of twenty miles. (*Feb. 2. From Tshumra to Kassaba.*)—Nine hours over the same uninterrupted level of the finest soil, but quite uncultivated, except in the immediate neighbourhood of a few widely dispersed villages. It is painful to behold such desolation in the midst of a region so highly favoured by nature. Another characteristic of these Asiatic plains is the exactness of the level, and the peculiarity of their extending, without any previous slope, to the foot of the mountains, which rise from them like lofty islands out of the surface of the ocean. The Karamanian ridge seems to recede as we approach it, and the snowy summits of Argæus [?] are still to be seen to the north-east. . . . At three or four miles short of Kassaba, we are

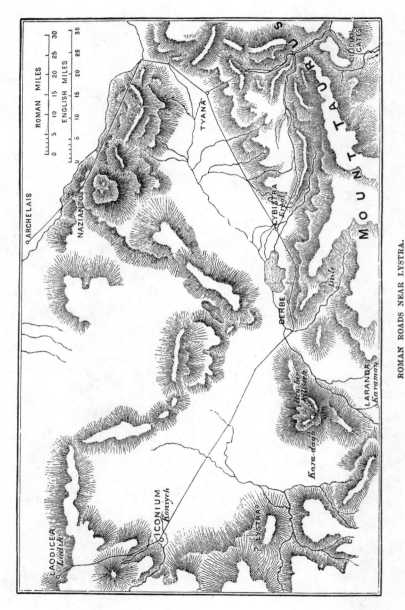

ROMAN ROADS NEAR LYSTRA.

(After Kiepert.)

where about the bases of the Black Mountain. We have dwelt thus minutely on the physical characteristics of this part of Lycaonia, because the positions of its ancient towns have not been determined. We are only acquainted with the general features of the scene. While the site of Iconium has never been forgotten, and that of Antioch in Pisidia has now been clearly identified, those of Lystra and Derbe remain unknown, or at best are extremely uncertain.[1] No conclusive coins or inscriptions have been discovered; nor has there been any such convergence of modern investigation and ancient authority as leads to an infallible result. Of the different hypotheses which have been proposed, we have been content in the accompanying map to indicate those [2] which appear the most probable.

abreast of the middle of the very lofty insulated mountain already mentioned, called Kara-Dagh. It is said to be chiefly inhabited by Greek Christians, and to contain 1001 churches; but we afterwards learnt that these 1001 churches (Bin-bir-Kilisseh) was a name given to the extensive ruins of an ancient city at the foot of the mountain. (*Feb. 3. From Kassaba to Karaman.*)—Four hours; the road still passing over a plain, which towards the mountains begins to be a little intersected with low ridges and ravines. . . . . Between these mountains and the Kara-Dagh there is a kind of strait, which forms the communication between the plain of Karaman and the great levels lying eastward of Konieh. . . . . Advancing towards Karaman, I perceive a passage into the plains to the north-west, round the northern end of Kara-Dagh, similar to that on the south, so that this mountain is completely insulated. We still see to the north-east the great snowy summit of Argæus, [?] which is probably the highest point of Asia Minor.' See a similar description of the isolation of the Kara-Dagh in Hamilton (II. 315, 320), who approached it from the east.

[1] Col. Leake wrote thus in 1824: 'Nothing can more strongly show the little progress that has hitherto been made in a knowledge of the ancient geography of Asia Minor, than that, of the cities which the journey of St. Paul has made so interesting to us, the site of one only (Iconium) is yet certainly known. Perga, Antioch of Pisidia, Lystra, and Derbe remain to be discovered,' p. 103. We have seen that two of these four towns have been fully identified,—Perga by Sir C. Fel-

lows, and Antioch by Mr. Arundell. It is to be hoped that the other two will yet be clearly ascertained.

[2] The general features of the map here given are copied from Kiepert's large map of Asia Minor, and his positions for Lystra and Derbe are adopted. Lystra is marked near the place where Leake conjectured that it might be, some twenty miles S. of Iconium. It does not appear, however, that he saw any ruins on the spot. There are very remarkable Christian ruins on the N. side of the Kara-Dagh, at Bin-bir-Kilisseh ('The 1001 churches'), and Leake thinks that they may mark the site of Derbe. We think Mr. Hamilton's conjecture much more probable, that they mark the site of Lystra, which has a more eminent ecclesiastical reputation than Derbe.

While this was passing through the press, the writer received an indirect communication from Mr. Hamilton, which will be the best commentary on the map. 'There are *ruins* (though slight) at the spot where Derbe is marked on Kiepert's map, and as this spot is *certainly on a line of Roman road*, it is not unlikely that it may represent Derbe. He did not actually visit Divlé, but the coincidence of name led him to think it might be Derbe. He does not know of any ruins at the place where Kiepert writes Lystra, but was not on that spot. There may be ruins there, but he thinks they cannot be of importance, as he did not hear of them, though in the neighbourhood; and he prefers Bin-bir-Kilisseh as the site of Lystra.'

The following description of the Bin-bir-Kilisseh is supplied by a letter from Mr. E. Falkener. ' The principal group of the Bin-bir-Kilisseh lies at the foot

We resume the thread of our narrative with the arrival of Paul and Barnabas at Lystra. One peculiar circumstance strikes us immediately in what we read of the events in this town ; that no mention occurs of any synagogue or of any Jews. It is natural to infer that there were few Israelites in the place, though (as we shall see hereafter) it would be a mistake to imagine that there were none. We are instantly brought in contact with a totally new subject,—with Heathen superstition and mythology ; yet not the superstition of an educated mind, as that of Sergius Paulus,—nor the mythology of a refined and cultivated taste, like that of the Athenians,—but the mythology and superstition of a rude and unsophisticated people. Thus does the Gospel, in the person of St. Paul, successively clash with opposing powers, with sorcerers and philosophers, cruel magistrates and false divinities. Now it is the rabbinical master of the Synagogue, now the listening proselyte from the Greeks, that is resisted or convinced,—now the honest inquiry of a Roman officer, now the wild fanaticism of a rustic credulity, that is addressed with bold and persuasive eloquence.

It was a common belief among the ancients that the gods occasionally visited the earth in the form of men. Such a belief with regard to Jupiter, ' the father of gods and men,' would be natural in any rural district : but nowhere should we be prepared to find the traces of it more than at Lystra ; for Lystra, as it appears from St. Luke's narrative,[1] was under the tutelage of Jupiter, and tutelary divinities were imagined to haunt the cities under their protection, though elsewhere invisible. The temple of Jupiter was a conspicuous object in front of the city-gates :[2] what wonder if the citizens should be prone to believe that their ' Jupiter, which was before the city,' would willingly visit his favourite people ? Again, the expeditions of Jupiter were usually represented as attended by Mercury. He was the companion, the messenger, the servant of the gods.[3] Thus the notion of these two divinities appearing together in Lycaonia is quite in conformity with what we know of the popular belief. But their appearance in that par-

---

of Kara-Dagh. . . . . Perceiving ruins on the slope of the mountain, I began to ascend, and on reaching these discovered they were churches; and, looking upwards, descried others yet above me, and climbing from one to the other I at length gained the summit, where I found two churches. On looking down, I perceived churches on all sides of the mountain, scattered about in various positions. The number ascribed to them by the Turks is of course metaphorical; but including those in the plain below, there are about two dozen in tolerable preservation, and the remains of perhaps forty may be traced altogether. . . . The mountain must have been considered sacred; all the ruins are of Christian epoch, and, with the exception of a huge palace, every building is a church.'

[1] It is more likely that a *temple* than a *statue* of Jupiter is alluded to. The temple of the tutelary divinity was outside the walls at Perga (see p. 127), and at Ephesus, as we learn from the story in Herodotus (i. 26), who tells us that in a time of danger the citizens put themselves under the protection of Diana, by attaching her temple by a rope to the city wall.

[2] Acts xiv. 13.

[3] See the references in Smith's *Dictionary of Classical Biography and Mythology*, under ' Hermes.' We may remark here, that we have always used the nearest Latin equivalents for the Greek divinities, i. e. Jupiter, Mercury, Diana, Minerva, for Zeus, Hermes, Artemis, Athene.

ticular district would be welcomed with more than usual credulity. Those who are acquainted with the literature of the Roman poets are familiar with a beautiful tradition of Jupiter and Mercury visiting in human form these very regions [1] in the interior of Asia Minor. And it is not without a singular interest that we find one of Ovid's stories reappearing in the sacred pages of the Acts of the Apostles. In this instance, as in so many others, the Scripture, in its incidental descriptions of the Heathen world, presents 'undesigned coincidences' with the facts ascertained from Heathen memorials.

These introductory remarks prepare us for considering the miracle recorded in the Acts. We must suppose that Paul gathered groups of the Lystrians about him, and addressed them in places of public resort, as a modern missionary might address the natives of a Hindoo village. [2] But it would not be necessary in his case, as in that of Schwartz or Martyn, to have learnt the primitive language of those to whom he spoke. He addressed them in Greek, for Greek was well understood in this border-country of the Lystrians, though their own dialect was either a barbarous corruption of that noble language, or the surviving remainder of some older tongue. He used the language of general civilisation, as English may be used now in a Welsh country-town like Dolgelly or Carmarthen. The subjects he brought before these illiterate idolaters of Lycaonia were doubtless such as would lead them, by the most natural steps, to the knowledge of the true God, and the belief in His Son's resurrection. He told them, as he told the educated Athenians,[3] of Him whose worship they had ignorantly corrupted; whose unity, power, and goodness they might have discerned through the operations of nature; whose displeasure against sin had been revealed to them by the admonitions of their natural conscience.

On one of these occasions [4] St. Paul observed a cripple, who was earnestly listening to his discourse. He was seated on the ground, for he had an infirmity in his feet, and had never walked from the hour of his birth. St. Paul looked at him attentively, with that remarkable expression of the eye which we have already noticed (p. 119). The same Greek word is used as when the Apostle is described as ' earnestly beholding the council,' and ' as setting his eyes on Elymas the sorcerer.' [5] On this occasion that penetrating glance saw, by the power of the Divine Spirit, into the very secrets of the cripple's soul. Paul perceived ' that he had faith to be saved.' [6] These words, implying so much of moral preparation in the heart of this poor Heathen, rise above all that is told

---

[1] See the story of Baucis and Philemon, Ovid. *Met.* viii. 611, &c. Even if the Lycaonians were a Semitic tribe, it is not unnatural to suppose them familiar with Greek mythology. An identification of classical and ' barbarian' divinities had taken place in innumerable instances, as in the case of the Tyrian Hercules and Paphian Venus.

[2] See, for instance, Fox's *Chapters on Missions*, p. 153, &c.

[3] It is very important to compare together the speeches at Lystra and Athens, and both with the first chapter of the Romans. See pp. 153, 154.

[4] Acts xiv. 8, &c.

[5] Acts xxiii. 1, xiii. 9.

[6] Acts xiv. 9. The word is the same as in xvi. 30.

us of the lame Jew, whom Peter, 'fastening his eyes upon him with John,' had once healed at the temple gate in Jerusalem.[1] In other respects the parallel between the two cases is complete. As Peter said in the presence of the Jews, 'In the name of Jesus Christ of Nazareth, rise up and walk,' so Paul said before his idolatrous audience at Lystra, 'Stand upright on thy feet.' And in this case, also, the word which had been suggested to the speaker by a supernatural intuition was followed by a supernatural result. The obedient alacrity in the spirit, and the new strength in the body, rushed together simultaneously. The lame man sprang up in the joyful consciousness of a power he had never felt before, and walked like those who had never had experience of infirmity.

And now arose a great tumult of voices from the crowd. Such a cure of a congenital disease, so sudden and so complete, would have confounded the most skilful and sceptical physicians. An illiterate people would be filled with astonishment, and rush immediately to the conclusion that supernatural powers were present among them. These Lycaonians thought at once of their native traditions, and crying out vociferously in their mother-tongue,[2]— and we all know how the strongest feelings of an excited people find vent in the language of childhood,—they exclaimed that the gods had again visited them in the likeness of men,—that Jupiter and Mercury were again in Lycaonia,—that the persuasive speaker was Mercury and his companion Jupiter. They identified Paul with Mercury, because his eloquence corresponded with one of that divinity's attributes. Paul was the 'chief speaker,' and Mercury was the god of eloquence. And if it be asked why they identified Barnabas with Jupiter, it is evidently a sufficient answer to say that these two divinities were always represented as companions[3] in their terrestrial expeditions, though we may well believe (with Chrysostom and others) that there was something majestically benignant in his appearance, while the personal aspect of St. Paul (and for this we can quote his own statements[4]) was comparatively insignificant.

How truthful and how vivid is the scene brought before us! and how many thoughts it suggests to those who are at once conversant with Heathen mythology and disciples of Christian theology! Barnabas, identified with the Father of Gods and Men, seems like a personification of mild beneficence and provident care;[5] while Paul appears invested with more active attributes, flying over the world on the wings of faith and love, with quick words of warning and persuasion, and ever carrying in his hand the purse of the 'unsearchable riches.'[6]

[1] Acts iii. Wetstein remarks on the greater faith manifested by the Heathen at Lystra than the Jew at Jerusalem.

[2] Some are of opinion that the 'speech of Lycaonia' was a Semitic language; others that it was a corrupt dialect of Greek. See the Dissertations of Jablonski and Gühling in Iken's *Thesaurus.*

[3] See, for instance, Ovid. *Fast.* v. 495.

[4] See 2 Cor. x. 1, 10, where, however, we must remember that he is quoting the statements of his adversaries.

[5] See Acts iv. 36, 37, ix. 27, xi. 22–25, 30. It is also very possible that Barnabas was *older*, and therefore more *venerable* in appearance than St. Paul.

[6] The winged heels and the purse are the well known insignia of Mercury.

The news of a wonderful occurrence is never long in spreading through a small country town. At Lystra the whole population was presently in an uproar. They would lose no time in paying due honour to their heavenly visitants. The priest attached to that temple of Jupiter before the city gates, to which we have before alluded,[1] was summoned to do sacrifice to the god whom he served. Bulls and garlands, and whatever else was requisite to the performance of the ceremony, were duly prepared, and the procession moved amidst crowds of people to the residence of the Apostles. They, hearing the approach of the multitude, and learning their idolatrous intention, were filled with the utmost horror. They 'rent their clothes,' and rushed out [2] of the house in which they lodged, and met the idolaters approaching the vestibule.[3] There, standing at the doorway, they opposed the entrance of the crowd ; and Paul expressed his abhorrence of their intention, and earnestly tried to prevent their fulfilling it, in a speech of which only the following short outline is recorded by St. Luke :—

'Sirs, why do ye these things? We also are men, of like passions with you; and we are come to preach to you the Glad Tidings, that you may turn from these vain idols to the living God, who made the heavens, and the earth, and the sea, and all things that are therein. For in the generations that are past, He suffered all the nations of the Gentiles to walk in their own ways. Nevertheless He left not Himself without witness, in that He blessed you, and gave you rain from heaven, and fruitful seasons, filling your hearts with food and gladness.'[4]

ACTS XIV. 15

This address held them listening, but they listened impatiently. Even with this energetic disavowal of his divinity and this strong appeal to their reason, St. Paul found it difficult to dissuade the Lycaonians from offering to him and Barnabas an idolatrous worship.[5] There is no doubt that St. Paul was the speaker, and, before we proceed further in the narrative, we cannot help pausing to observe the essentially Pauline character which this speech manifests, even

---

[1] P. 150.

[2] 'Ran out,' not 'ran in' is the reading sanctioned by the later critics on full manuscript authority. See Tischendorf.

[3] The word used here does not mean the gate of the city, but the vestibule or gate which gave admission from the public street into the court of the house. So it is used, Matt. xxvi. 71, for the vestibule of the high-priest's palace ; Luke xvi. 20, for that of Dives ; Acts x. 17, of the house where

Peter lodged at Joppa ; Acts xii. 13, of the house of Mary, the mother of John Mark. It is nowhere used for the gate of a city except in the Apocalypse. Moreover, it seems obvious that if the priest had only brought the victims to sacrifice them at the city gates, it would have been no offering to Paul and Barnabas.

[4] 'You' and 'your' are the correct readings, not 'us' and 'our.'

[5] Acts xiv. 18.

in so condensed a summary of its contents. It is full of undesigned coincidences in argument, and even in the expressions employed, with St. Paul's language in other parts of the Acts, and in his own Epistles. Thus, as here he declares the object of his preaching to be that the idolatrous Lystrians should 'turn from these vain idols to the living God,' so he reminds the Thessalonians how they, at his preaching, had 'turned from idols to serve the living and true God.' [1] Again, as he tells the Lystrians that 'God had in the generations that were past, suffered the nations of the Gentiles to walk in their own ways;' so he tells the Romans that 'God in His forbearance had passed over the former sins of men, in the times that were gone by;[2] and so he tells the Athenians,[3] that 'the past times of ignorance God had overlooked.' Lastly, how striking is the similarity between the natural theology with which the present speech concludes, and that in the Epistle to the Romans, where, speaking of the Heathen, he says that atheists are without excuse ; 'for that which can be known of God is manifested in their hearts, God himself having shown it to them. For His eternal power and Godhead, though they be invisible, yet are seen ever since the world was made, being understood by the works which He hath wrought.'

The crowd reluctantly retired, and led the victims away without offering them in sacrifice to the Apostles. It might be supposed that at least a command had been obtained over their gratitude and reverence, which would not easily be destroyed ; but we have to record here one of those sudden changes of feeling, which are humiliating proofs of the weakness of human nature and of the superficial character of religious excitement. The Lycaonians were proverbially fickle and faithless; but we may not too hastily decide that they were worse than many others might have been under the same circumstances. It would not be difficult to find a parallel to their conduct among the modern converts from idolatry to Christianity. And certainly no later missionaries have had more assiduous enemies than the Jews whom the Apostles had everywhere to oppose. Certain Jews from Iconium, and even from Antioch,[4] followed in the footsteps of Paul and Barnabas, and endeavoured to excite the hostility of the Lystrians against them. When they heard of the miracle worked on the lame man, and found how great an effect it had produced on the people of Lystra, they would be ready with a new interpretation of this occurrence They would say that it had been accomplished, not by Divine agency, but by some diabolical magic; as once they had said at Jerusalem, that He who came 'to destroy the works of the Devil,' cast out devils 'by Beelzebub the prince of the devils.'[5] And this is probably the true explanation of that sudden change of feeling among the Lystrians, which at first sight is very surprising. Their own interpretation of what they had witnessed having been disavowed by the authors of the miracle themselves, they would readily adopt a new interpretation, suggested

---

[1] 1 Thess. i. 9. The coincidence is more striking in the Greek, because the very same verb is used in each passage, and is intransitive in both.
[2] Rom. iii. 25 : the mistranslation of which in the Authorised Version entirely alters its meaning.
[3] Acts xvii. 30.
[4] Acts xiv. 19.
[5] Matt. xii. 24.

by those who appeared to be well acquainted with the strangers, and who had followed them from distant cities. Their feelings changed with a revulsion as violent as that which afterwards took place among the 'barbarous people' of Malta,[1] who first thought St. Paul was a murderer, and then a god. The Jews, taking advantage of the credulity of a rude tribe, were able to accomplish at Lystra the design they had meditated at Iconium.[2] St. Paul was stoned,—not hurried out of the city to execution like St. Stephen,[3] the memory of whose death must have come over St. Paul at this moment with impressive force,—but stoned somewhere in the streets of Lystra, and then dragged through the city gate, and cast outside the walls, under the belief that he was dead. This is that occasion to which the Apostle afterwards alluded in the words, 'once I was stoned,'[4] in that long catalogue of sufferings, to which we have already referred in this chapter.[5] Thus was he 'in perils by his own countrymen, in perils by the Heathen,'—'in deaths oft,'—'always bearing about in the body the dying of the Lord Jesus, that the life also of Jesus might be made manifest in his body. . . . Alway delivered unto death for Jesus' sake, that the life also of Jesus might be made manifest in his mortal flesh.'[6]

On the present occasion these last words were literally realised, for by the power and goodness of God he rose from a state of apparent death as if by a sudden resurrection.[7] Though 'persecuted,' he was not 'forsaken,'—though 'cast down,' he was 'not destroyed.' 'As the disciples stood about him, he rose up, and came into the city.'[8] We see from this expression that his labours in Lystra had not been in vain. He had found some willing listeners to the truth, some 'disciples' who did not hesitate to show their attachment to their teacher by remaining near his body, which the rest of their fellow-citizens had wounded and cast out. These courageous disciples were left for the present in the midst of the enemies of the truth. Jesus Christ had said,[9] 'when they persecute you in one city, flee to another;' and the very 'next day'[10] Paul 'departed with Barnabas to Derbe.'

---

[1] Acts xxviii. 4-6.   [2] Acts xiv. 5.

[3] See the end of Chap. II. At Jerusalem the law required that these executions should take place outside the city. It must be remembered that stoning was a Jewish punishment, and that it was proposed by Jews at Iconium, and instigated and begun by Jews at Lystra.

[4] See Paley's remark on the expression 'once I was stoned,' in reference to the previous *design* of stoning St. Paul at Iconium. 'Had the assault been completed, had the history related that a stone was thrown, as it relates that preparations were made both by Jews and Gentiles to stone Paul and his companions, or even had the account of this transaction stopped, without going on to inform us that Paul and his companions were "aware of the danger and fled," a contradiction between the history and the epistles would have ensued. Truth is necessarily consistent; but it is scarcely possible that independent accounts, not having truth to guide them, should thus advance to the very brink of contradiction without falling into it.'— *Horæ Paulinæ*, p. 69.

[5] See pp. 129, 130.

[6] Compare 2 Cor. iv. 8-12, and xi. 23-27.

[7] The natural inference from the narrative is, that the recovery was miraculous; and it is evident that such a recovery must have produced a strong effect on the minds of the Christians who witnessed it.   [8] Acts xiv. 20.

[9] Matt. x. 23.   [10] Acts xiv. 20.

But before we leave Lystra, we must say a few words on one spectator of St. Paul's sufferings, who is not yet mentioned by St. Luke, but who was destined to be the constant companion of his after years, the zealous follower of his doctrine, the faithful partner of his danger and distress. St. Paul came to Lystra again after the interval of one or two years, and on that occasion we are told[1] that he found a certain Christian there, 'whose name was Timotheus, whose mother was a Jewess, while his father was a Greek,' and whose excellent character was highly esteemed by his fellow-Christians of Lystra and Iconium. It is distinctly stated that at the time of this second visit Timothy was already a Christian ; and since we know from St. Paul's own expression,—'my own son in the faith,'[2] —that he was converted by St. Paul himself, we must suppose this change to have taken place at the time of the first visit. And the reader will remember that St. Paul in the second Epistle to Timothy (iii. 10, 11) reminds him of his own intimate and personal knowledge of the sufferings he had endured, ' *at Antioch, at Iconium, at Lystra,*'—the places (it will be observed) being mentioned in the exact order in which they were visited, and in which the successive persecutions took place. We have thus the strongest reasons for believing that Timothy was a witness of St. Paul's injurious treatment; and this too at a time of life when the mind receives its deepest impressions from the spectacle of innocent suffering and undaunted courage. And it is far from impossible that the generous and warm-hearted youth was standing in that group of disciples, who surrounded the apparently lifeless body of the Apostle at the outside of the walls of Lystra.

We are called on to observe at this point, with a thankful acknowledgment of God's providence, that the flight from Iconium, and the cruel persecution at Lystra, were events which involved the most important and beneficial consequences to universal Christianity. It was here, in the midst of barbarous idolaters, that the Apostle of the Gentiles found an associate, who became to him and the Church far more than Barnabas, the companion of his first mission. As we have observed above,[3] there appears to have been at Lystra no synagogue, no community of Jews and proselytes, among whom such an associate might naturally have been expected. Perhaps Timotheus and his relations may have been almost the only persons of Jewish origin in the town. And his 'grandmother Lois ' and ' mother Eunice '[4] may have been brought there originally by some accidental circumstance, as Lydia[5] was brought from Thyatira to Philippi.[6] And, though there was no synagogue at Lystra, this

---

[1] Acts xvi. 1.

[2] 1 Tim. i. 2. Compare i. 18 and 2 Tim. ii. 1. It is indeed possible that these expressions might be used, if Timothy became a Christian by his mother's influence, and through the recollection of St. Paul's sufferings; but the common view is the most natural. See what is said 1 Cor. iv. 14, 15: ' As my beloved sons I warn you; for though ye have ten thousand instructors in Christ, yet have ye not many fathers; for in Christ Jesus I have begotten you through the Gospel.'

[3] See p. 150.

[4] 2 Tim. i. 5.

[5] Acts xvi. 14.

[6] See also the remarks on the Jews settled in Asia Minor, Chap. I. p. 14; and on the Hellenistic and Aramæan Jews, Chap. II. pp. 31, 32.

family may have met with a few others in some *proseucha*, like that in which Lydia and her fellow-worshippers met 'by the river side.'[1] Whatever we conjecture concerning the congregational life to which Timotheus may have been accustomed, we are accurately informed of the nature of that domestic life which nurtured him for his future labours. The good soil of his heart was well prepared before Paul came, by the instructions[2] of Lois and Eunice, to receive the seed of Christian truth, sown at the Apostle's first visit, and to produce a rich harvest of faith and good works before the time of his second visit.

Derbe, as we have seen, is somewhere not far from the 'Black Mountain,' which rises like an island in the south-eastern part of the plain of Lycaonia. A few hours would suffice for the journey between Lystra and its neighbour-city. We may, perhaps, infer from the fact that Derbe is not mentioned in the list of places which St. Paul[3] brings to the recollection of Timothy as scenes of past suffering and distress, that in this town the Apostles were exposed to no persecution. It may have been a quiet resting-place after a journey full of toil and danger. It does not appear that they were hindered in 'evangelising' the city: and the fruit of their labours was the conversion of 'many disciples.'[4]

And now we have reached the limit of St. Paul's first missionary journey. About this part of the Lycaonian plain, where it approaches, through gradual undulations,[5] to the northern bases of Mount Taurus, he was not far from that well-known pass[6] which leads down from the central table-land to Cilicia and Tarsus. But his thoughts did not centre in an earthly home. He turned back upon his footsteps; and revisited the places, Lystra, Iconium, and Antioch,[7] where he himself had been reviled and persecuted, but where he had left, as sheep in the desert, the disciples whom his Master had enabled him to gather. They needed building up and strengthening in the faith,[8] comforting in the midst of their inevitable sufferings, and fencing round by permanent institutions. Therefore Paul and Barnabas revisited the scenes of their labours, undaunted by the dangers which awaited them, and using words of encouragement, which none but the founders of a true religion would have ventured to address to their earliest converts, that 'we can only enter the kingdom of God by passing through much tribulation.' But not only did they fortify their faith by passing words of encouragement; they ordained elders in every church after the pattern of the first Christian communities in Palestine,[9] and with that solemn observance which had attended their own consecration,[10]

---

[1] Acts xvi. 13. [2] 2 Tim. i. 5. [3] 2 Tim. iii. 11. [4] Acts xiv. 21.

[5] So Leake describes the neighbourhood of Karaman (Laranda), pp. 96, 97. Hamilton, speaking of the same district, mentions 'low ridges of cretaceous limestone, extending into the plain from the mountains.' II. 324.

[6] The 'Cilician Gates,' to which we shall return at the beginning of the second missionary journey (Acts xv.

41). See the Map.

[7] Mentioned (Acts xiv. 21) in the inverse order from that in which they had been visited before (xiii. 14, 51, xiv. 6).

[8] Acts xiv. 22.

[9] The first mention of presbyters in the Christian. opposed to the Jewish sense, occurs Acts xi. 30, in reference to the church at Jerusalem. See Chapter XIII.

[10] Chap. V. p. 110.

and which has been transmitted to later ages in connection with ordination,—' with fasting and prayer'—they 'made choice of fit persons to serve in the sacred ministry of the Church.'[1]

Thus, having consigned their disciples to Him 'in whom they had believed,' and who was 'able to keep that which was entrusted to Him,'[2] Paul and Barnabas descended through the Pisidian mountains to the plain of Pamphylia. If our conjecture is correct (see pp. 131, 132), that they went up from Perga in spring, and returned at the close of autumn,[3] and spent all the hotter months of the year in the elevated districts, they would again pass in a few days through a great change of seasons, and almost from winter to summer. The people of Pamphylia would have returned from their cold residences to the warm shelter of the plain by the sea-side; and Perga would be full of its inhabitants. The Gospel was preached within the walls of this city, through which the Apostles had merely passed[4] on their journey to the interior. But from St. Luke's silence it appears that the preaching was attended with no marked results. We read neither of conversions nor persecutions. The Jews, if any Jews resided there, were less inquisitive and less tyrannical than those at Antioch and Iconium; and the votaries of 'Diana before the city' at Perga (see p. 127) were less excitable than those who worshipped 'Jupiter before the city' at Lystra.[5] When the time came for returning to Syria, they did not sail down the Cestrus, up the channel of which river they had come on their arrival from Cyprus,[6] but travelled across the plain to Attaleia,[7] which was situated on the edge of the Pamphylian gulf.

Attaleia had something of the same relation to Perga, which Cadiz has to Seville. In each case the latter city is approached by a river-voyage, and the former is more conveniently placed on the open sea. Attalus Philadelphus, king of Pergamus, whose dominions extended from the north-western corner of Asia Minor to the Sea of Pamphylia, had built this city in a convenient position for commanding the trade of Syria or Egypt. When Alexander the Great passed this way, no such city was in existence: but since the days of the kings of Pergamus, who inherited a fragment of his vast empire, Attaleia has always existed and flourished, retaining the name of the monarch who built it.[8] Behind it is the plain through which the calcareous waters of the Catarrhactes flow, perpetually constructing and destroying and reconstructing their fantastic channels.[9] In front of it, and along the shore on each side, are long lines of cliffs,[10] over

---

[1] The First Collect for the Ember Weeks.

[2] Acts xiv. 23. Compare 2 Tim. i. 12.

[3] Wieseler thinks the events on this journey must have occupied more than one year. It is evident that the case does not admit of anything more than conjecture.

[4] See above, p. 127, and notes.

[5] Acts xiv. 13.   [6] Pp. 127, 128.

[7] A view may be seen in the work of Admiral Beaufort, who describes the city as 'beautifully situated round a

small harbour, the streets appearing to rise behind each other like the seats of a theatre . . . with a double wall and a series of square towers on the level summit of the hill.'

[8] Its modern name is *Satalia.*

[9] See Spratt and Forbes for a full account of the irregular deposits and variations of channel observable in this river.

[10] There are also ancient sea-cliffs at some distance behind the present coast line.

which the river finds its way in waterfalls to the sea, and which
conceal the plain from those who look toward the land from the
inner waters of the bay, and even encroach on the prospect of the
mountains themselves.

When this scene is before us, the mind reverts to another band of
Christian warriors, who once sailed from the bay of Satalia to the
Syrian Antioch.   Certain passages, in which the movements of the
Crusaders and Apostles may be compared with each other, are among
the striking contrasts of history.   Conrad and Louis, each with an
army consisting at first of 70,000 men, marched through part of the
same districts which were traversed by Paul and Barnabas alone and
unprotected.   The shattered remains of the French host had come
down to Attaleia through 'the abrupt mountain-passes and the deep
valleys' which are so well described by the cotemporary historian.[1]
They came to fight the battle of the Cross with a great multitude,
and with the armour of human power: their journey was encompassed with defeat and death; their arrival at Attaleia was disastrous
and disgraceful; and they sailed to Antioch a broken and dispirited
army.   But the Crusaders of the first century, the Apostles of Christ,
though they too passed 'through much tribulation,' advanced from
victory to victory.   Their return to the place 'whence they had
been recommended to the grace of God for the work which they
fulfilled,'[2] was triumphant and joyful, for the weapons of their warfare were 'not carnal.'[3]   The Lord himself was their tower and
their shield.

Coin of Antioch in Pisidia.[4]

[1] William of Tyre.
[2] Acts xiv. 26.

[3] See 2 Cor. x. 4.
[4] See note 1, p. 136.

CHAPTER VII.

Controversy in the Church.—Separation of Jews and Gentiles.—Difficulty in the Narrative.—Discontent at Jerusalem.—Intrigues of the Judaizers at Antioch.—Mission of Paul and Barnabas to Jerusalem.—Divine Revelation to St. Paul.—Titus.—Private Conferences.—Public Meeting.—Speech of St. Peter.—Narrative of Barnabas and Paul.—Speech of St. James.—The Decree.—Public Recognition of St. Paul's Mission to the Heathen.—St. John.—Return to Antioch with Judas, Silas, and Mark.—Reading of the Letter.—Weak Conduct of St. Peter at Antioch.—He is rebuked by St. Paul.—Personal Appearance of the two Apostles.—Their Reconciliation.

IF, when we contrast the voyage of Paul and Barnabas across the bay of Attaleia, with the voyage of those who sailed over the same waters in the same direction, eleven centuries later, our minds are powerfully drawn towards the pure age of early Christianity, when the power of faith made human weakness irresistibly strong ;—the same thoughts are not less forcibly presented to us, when we contrast the reception of the Crusaders at Antioch with the reception of the Apostles in the same city. We are told by the chroniclers, that Raymond, 'Prince of Antioch,' waited with much expectation for the arrival of the French king ; and that when he heard of his landing at Seleucia, he gathered together all the nobles and chief men of the people, and went out to meet him, and brought him into Antioch with much pomp and magnificence, showing him all reverence and homage, in the midst of a great assemblage of the clergy and people. All that St. Luke tells us of the reception of the Apostles after their victorious campaign, is, that they entered into the city and 'gathered together the Church, and told them how God had worked with them, and how He had opened a door of faith to the Gentiles.'[1] Thus the kingdom of God came at the first 'without observation,'[2]—with the humble acknowledgment that all power is given from above,—and with a thankful recognition of our Father's merciful love to all mankind.

No age, however, of Christianity, not even the earliest, has been without its difficulties, controversies, and corruptions. The presence of Judas among the Apostles, and of Ananias and Sapphira among the first disciples,[3] were proofs of the power which moral evil possesses to combine itself with the holiest works. The misunderstanding of 'the Grecians and Hebrews' in the days of Stephen,[4] the suspicion of the Apostles when Paul came from Damascus to Jerusalem,[5] the secession of Mark at the beginning of the first missionary journey,[6] were symptoms of the prejudice, ignorance, and infirmity, in the midst of which the Gospel was to win its way

---

[1] Acts xiv. 27.   [3] Acts v.   [5] P. 85.
[2] Luke xvii. 20.   [4] P. 55.   [6] P. 129.

in the hearts of men.   And the arrival of the Apostles at Antioch at the close of their journey was presently followed by a troubled controversy, which involved the most momentous consequences to all future ages of the Church ; and led to that visit to Jerusalem which, next after his conversion, is perhaps the most important passage in St. Paul's life.

We have seen (Chap. I.) that great numbers of Jews had long been dispersed beyond the limits of their own land, and were at this time distributed over every part of the Roman Empire.   'Moses had of old time, in every city, them that preached him, being read in the synagogues every Sabbath day.'[1]   In every considerable city, both of the East and West, were established some members of that mysterious people,—who had a written Law, which they read and re-read in the midst of the contempt of those who surrounded them, week by week, and year by year,—who were bound every-where by a secret link of affection to one City in the world, where alone their religious sacrifices could be offered,—whose whole life was utterly abhorrent from the temples and images which crowded the neighbourhood of their synagogues, and from the gay and licentious festivities of the Greek and Roman worship.

In the same way it might be said that Plato and Aristotle, Zeno and Epicurus,[2] 'had in every city those that preached them.'   Side by side with the doctrines of Judaism, the speculations of Greek philosophers were--not indeed read in connection with religious worship—but orally taught and publicly discussed in the schools. Hence the Jews, in their foreign settlements, were surrounded, not only by an idolatry which shocked all their deepest feelings, and by a shameless profligacy unforbidden by, and even associated with, that which the Gentiles called religion,—but also by a proud and contemptuous philosophy that alienated the more educated classes of society to as great a distance as the unthinking multitude.

Thus a strong line of demarcation between the Jews and Gentiles ran through the whole Roman Empire.   Though their dwellings were often contiguous, they were separated from each other by deep-rooted feelings of aversion and contempt.   The 'middle wall of partition'[3] was built up by diligent hands on both sides.   This mutual alienation existed, notwithstanding the vast number of pro-selytes, who were attracted to the Jewish doctrine and worship, and who, as we have already observed (Chap. I.), were silently preparing the way for the ultimate union of the two races.   The breach was even widened, in many cases, in consequence of this work of prose-lytism : for those who went over to the Jewish camp, or hesitated on the neutral ground, were looked on with some suspicion by the Jews themselves, and thoroughly hated and despised by the Gentiles.

It must be remembered that the separation of which we speak was both religious and social.   The Jews had a divine Law, which sanc-tioned the principle, and enforced the practice, of national isolation. They could not easily believe that this Law, with which all the glo-rious passages of their history were associated, was meant only to

[1] Acts xv. 21.   [2] See Acts xvii. 18.   [3] Eph. ii. 14.

endure for a limited period : and we cannot but sympathise in the difficulty they felt in accepting the notion of a cordial union with the uncircumcised, even after idolatry was abandoned and morality observed. And again, the peculiar character of the religion which isolated the Jews was such as to place insuperable obstacles in the way of social union with other men. Their ceremonial observances precluded the possibility of their eating with the Gentiles. The nearest parallel we can find to this barrier between the Jew and Gentile, is the institution of *caste* among the ancient populations of India, which presents itself to our politicians as a perplexing fact in the government of the presidencies, and to our missionaries as the great obstacle to the progress of Christianity in the East.[1] A Hindoo cannot eat with a Parsee, or a Mahommedan,—and among the Hindoos themselves the meals of a Brahmin are polluted by the presence of a Pariah,—though they meet and have free intercourse in the ordinary transaction of business. So it was in the patriarchal age. It was ' an abomination for the Egyptians to eat bread with the Hebrews.[2] The same principle was divinely sanctioned for a time in the Mosaic Institutions. The Israelites, who lived among the Gentiles, met them freely in the places of public resort, buying and selling, conversing and disputing : but their families were separate : in the relations of domestic life, it was ' unlawful,' as St. Peter said to Cornelius, ' for a man that was a Jew to keep company or come unto one of another nation.'[3] When St. Peter returned from the centurion at Cæsarea to his brother-christians at Jerusalem, their great charge against him was that he had 'gone in to men uncircumcised, and had eaten with them :'[4] and the weak compliance of which he was guilty, after the true principle of social unity had been publicly recognised, and which called forth the stern rebuke of his brother-apostle, was that, after eating with the Gentiles, he ' withdrew and separated himself, fearing them which were of the circumcision.'[5]

How these two difficulties, which seemed to forbid the formation of an united Church on earth, were ever to be overcome,—how the Jews and Gentiles were to be religiously united without the enforced obligation of the whole Mosaic Law,—how they were to be socially united as equal brethren in the family of a common Father,—the solution of this problem must in that day have appeared impossible. And without the direct intervention of Divine grace it would have been impossible. We now proceed to consider how that grace gave to the minds of the Apostles the wisdom, discretion, forbearance, and firmness which were required ; and how St. Paul was used as the great instrument in accomplishing a work necessary to the very existence of the Christian Church.

We encounter here a difficulty, well known to all who have examined this subject, in combining into one continuous narrative the

---

[1] See, for instance, the *Memoir of the Rev. H. W. Fox* (1850), pp. 123–125. A short statement of the strict regulations of the modern Jews, in their present dispersed state, concerning the slaughtering of animals for food and the sale of the meat, is given in Allen's *Modern Judaism*, chap. xxii.

[2] Gen. xliii. 32.
[3] Acts x. 28.
[4] Acts xi. 3.
[5] Gal. ii. 12.

statements in the Epistle to the Galatians and in the Acts of the Apostles. In the latter book we are informed of five distinct journeys made by the Apostle to Jerusalem after the time of his conversion; —first, when he escaped from Damascus, and spent a fortnight with Peter;[1] secondly, when he took the collection from Antioch with Barnabas in the time of the famine;[2] thirdly, on the occasion of the Council, which is now before us in the fifteenth chapter of the Acts; fourthly, in the interval between his second and third missionary journeys;[3] and, fifthly, when the uproar was made in the Temple, and he was taken into the custody of the Roman garrison.[4] In the Epistle to the Galatians, St. Paul speaks of two journeys to Jerusalem,—the first being 'three years' after his conversion,[5] the second 'fourteen years'[6] later, when his own Apostleship was asserted and recognised in a public meeting of the other Apostles.[7] Now, while we have no difficulty in stating, as we have done (p. 84), that the first journey of one account is the first journey of the other, theologians have been variously divided in opinion, as to whether the second journey of the Epistle must be identified with the second, third, or fourth of the Acts, or whether it is a separate journey, distinct from any of them. It is agreed by all that the fifth cannot possibly be intended.[8] The view we have adopted, that the second journey of the Epistle is the third of the Acts, is that of the majority of the best critics and commentators. For the arguments by which it is justified, and for a full discussion of the whole subject, we must refer the reader to the Appendix. Some of the arguments will be indirectly presented in the following narrative. So far as the circumstances combined together in the present chapter appear natural, consecutive, and coherent, so far some reason will be given for believing that we are not following an arbitrary assumption or a fanciful theory.

It is desirable to recur at the outset to the first instance of a Gentile's conversion to Christianity.[9] After the preceding remarks, we are prepared to recognise the full significance of the emblematical[10] vision which St. Peter saw at Joppa. The trance into which he fell at the moment of his hunger,—the vast sheet descending from heaven,—the promiscuous assemblage of clean and unclean animals,[11]—the voice from heaven which said, 'Arise, Peter, kill and *eat*,'—the whole of this imagery is invested with the deepest meaning, when we recollect all the details of religious and social life, which separated, up to that moment, the Gentile from the Jew. The words heard by St. Peter in his trance came like a shock on all

---

[1] P. 84.

[3] Acts xviii. 22.

[4] Acts xxi. &c.

[5] Gal. i. 18.

[6] We take the 'fourteen' (Gal. ii. 1) to refer to the preceding journey, and not to the conversion. This question, as well as that of the reading 'four,' is discussed in the Appendix. See also the Chronological Table in the Appendix.

[2] P. 105.

[7] Gal. ii. 1–10.

[8] Some writers, e.g. Paley and Schrader, have contended that an entirely different journey, not mentioned in the Acts, is alluded to. This also is discussed in the Appendix.

[9] Acts x. xi.

[10] The last emblematical visions (properly so called) were those seen by the prophet Zachariah.

[11] See Levit. xi.

the prejudices of his Jewish education.[1]   He had never so spoken
the Law of his forefathers as to eat anything it condemned as unclean.
And though the same voice spoke to him 'a second time,'[2] and
'answered him from heaven,'[3] —'What God has made clean that
call not thou common,'—it required a wonderful combination of
natural [4] and supernatural evidence to convince him that God is 'no
respecter of persons,' but ' in every nation' accepts him that
'feareth Him and worketh righteousness,'[5]—that all such distinctions as depend on 'meat and drink,' on 'holydays, new moons,
and sabbaths,' were to pass away,—that these things were only 'a
shadow of things to come,'—that 'the body is of Christ,'—and
that 'in Him we are complete . . . circumcised with a circumcision
not made with hands . . . buried with him in baptism,' and risen
with Him through faith.[6]

The Christians 'of the circumcision,'[7] who travelled with Peter
from Joppa to Cæsarea, were 'astonished' when they saw 'the gift
of the Holy Ghost poured out' on uncircumcised Gentiles : and
much dissatisfaction was created in the Church, when intelligence
of the whole transaction came to Jerusalem.   On Peter's arrival,
his having 'gone in to men uncircumcised, and eaten with them,'
was arraigned as a serious violation of religious duty.   When St.
Peter 'rehearsed the matter from the beginning, and expounded
it by order,' appealing to the evidence of the 'six brethren'
who had accompanied him, — his accusers were silent ; and so
much conviction was produced at the time, that they expressed
their gratitude to God, for His mercy in 'granting to the Gentiles
repentance unto life.'[8]   But subsequent events too surely proved
that the discontent at Jerusalem was only partially allayed.   Hesitation and perplexity began to arise in the minds of the Jewish
Christians, with scrupulous misgivings concerning the rectitude of
St. Peter's conduct, and an uncomfortable jealousy of the new converts.   And nothing could be more natural than all this jealousy
and perplexity.   To us, with our present knowledge, it seems that
the slightest relaxation of a ceremonial law should have been willingly and eagerly welcomed.   But the view from the Jewish standing-point was very different.   The religious difficulty in the mind
of a Jew was greater than we can easily imagine.   We can well

---

[1] The feeling of the Jews in all ages
is well illustrated by the following
extract from a modern Jewish work :
'If we disregard this precept, and say,
"What difference can it make to God
if I eat the meat of an ox or swine?"
we offend against His will, we pollute
ourselves by what goes into the mouth,
and can consequently lay no longer a
claim to holiness ; for the term "holiness," applied to mortals, means only
a framing of our desires by the will of
God. . . . . . Have we not enough to
eat without touching forbidden things ?
Let me beseech my dear fellow-believers
not to deceive themselves by saying,
"there is no sin in eating of aught that

lives ; " on the contrary, there is sin
and   contamination   too.' — Leeser's
Jews and the Mosaic Law; ch. on
'The forbidden Meats.' Philadelphia,
5594.

[2] Acts x. 15.

[3] Acts xi. 9.

[4] The coincidence of outward events
and inward admonitions was very similar to the circumstances connected with
St. Paul's baptism by Ananias at Damascus.   See above, p. 77.

[5] Acts x. 34, 35.

[6] See Col. ii. 8–23.

[7] Acts x. 45 with xi. 12.

[8] Acts xi. 1–18.

believe that the minds of many may have been perplexed by the
words and the conduct of our Lord Himself : for He had not
been sent 'save to the lost sheep of the house of Israel,' and He
had said that it was 'not meet to take the children's bread and cast
it to dogs.'[1]   Until St. Paul appeared before the Church in his
true character as the Apostle of the uncircumcision, few understood
that 'the law of the commandments contained in ordinances' had
been abolished by the cross of Christ ;[2] and that the 'other sheep,'
not of the Jewish fold, should be freely united to the 'one flock' by
the 'One Shepherd.'[3]

The smouldering feeling of discontent, which had existed from
the first, increased and became more evident as new Gentile converts
were admitted into the Church.   To pass over all the other events
of the interval which had elapsed since the baptism of Cornelius,
the results of the recent journey of Paul and Barnabas through
the cities of Asia Minor must have excited a great commotion
among the Jewish Christians.   'A door of faith' had been opened
'unto the Gentiles.'[4]   'He that wrought effectually in Peter to
the Apostleship of the circumcision, the same had been mighty in
Paul towards the Gentiles.'[5]   And we cannot well doubt that both
he and Barnabas had freely joined in social intercourse with the
Gentile Christians, at Antioch in Pisidia, at Iconium, Lystra, and
Derbe, as Peter 'at the first'[6] 'a good while ago'[7] had eaten with
Cornelius at Cæsarea.   At Antioch in Syria, it seems evident that
both parties lived together in amicable intercourse and in much
'freedom.'[8]   Nor, indeed, is this the city where we should have
expected the Jewish controversy to have come to a crisis : for it was
from Antioch that Paul and Barnabas had first been sent as missionaries to the Heathen :[9] and it was at Antioch that Greek proselytes
had first accepted the truth,[10] and that the united body of believers
had first been called 'Christians.'[11]

Jerusalem was the metropolis of the Jewish world.   The exclusive
feelings which the Jews carried with them wherever they were
diffused, were concentrated in Jerusalem in their most intense
degree.   It was there, in the sight of the Temple, and with all the
recollections of their ancestors surrounding their daily life, that the
impatience of the Jewish Christians kindled into burning indignation.   They saw that Christianity, instead of being the purest and
holiest form of Judaism, was rapidly becoming a universal and
indiscriminating religion, in which the Jewish element would be
absorbed and lost.   This revolution could not appear to them in
any other light than as a rebellion against all they had been taught
to hold inviolably sacred.   And since there was no doubt that
the great instigator of this change of opinion was that Saul of Tarsus
whom they had once known as a young Pharisee at the 'feet of
Gamaliel,' the contest took the form of an attack made by 'certain

[1] Matt. xv. 24, 26.
[2] Eph. ii. 15.
[3] Not literally 'one fold.' John x. 16.
[4] Acts xiv. 27.
[5] Gal. ii. 8.
[6] Acts xv. 14.

[7] Acts xv. 7.
[8] See Gal. ii. 4.
[9] Acts xiii. 1, &c
[10] Acts xi. 19–21.
[11] Acts xi. 26.

of the sect of the Pharisees' upon St. Paul. The battle which had been fought and lost in the 'Cilician synagogue' was now to be renewed within the Church itself.

Some of the 'false brethren' (for such is the name which St. Paul gives to the Judaisers [1]) went down ' from Judæa' to Antioch. [2] The course they adopted, in the first instance, was not that of open antagonism to St. Paul, but rather of clandestine intrigue. They came as 'spies' into an enemy's camp, creeping in 'unawares,' [3] that they might ascertain how far the Jewish Law had been relaxed by the Christians at Antioch ; their purpose being to bring the whole Church, if possible, under the 'bondage' of the Mosaic yoke. It appears that they remained some considerable time at Antioch, [4] gradually insinuating, or openly inculcating, their opinion that the observance of the Jewish Law was *necessary to salvation*. It is very important to observe the exact form which their teaching assumed. They did not merely recommend or enjoin, for prudential reasons, the continuance of certain ceremonies in themselves indifferent : but they said, ' Except ye be circumcised after the manner of Moses, *ye cannot be saved.*' Such a doctrine must have been instantly opposed by St. Paul with his utmost energy. He was always ready to go to the extreme verge of charitable concession, when the question was one of peace and mutual understanding : but when the very foundations of Christianity were in danger of being undermined, when the very continuance of 'the truth of the Gospel' [5] was in jeopardy, it was impossible that he should 'give place by subjection,' even ' for an hour.'

The 'dissension and disputation,' [6] which arose between Paul and Barnabas and the false brethren from Judæa, resulted in a general anxiety and perplexity among the Syrian Christians. The minds of ' those who from among the Gentiles were turned unto God' were 'troubled' and unsettled. [7] Those 'words' which 'perverted the Gospel of Christ' tended also to 'subvert the souls' of those who heard them. [8] It was determined, therefore, ' that Paul and Barnabas, with certain others, should go up to Jerusalem unto the Apostles and elders about this question.' It was well known that those who were disturbing the peace of the Church had their headquarters in Judæa. Such a theological party could only be successfully met in the stronghold of Jewish nationality. Moreover, the residence of the principal Apostles was at Jerusalem, and the community over which 'James' presided was still regarded as the Mother-Church of Christendom.

In addition to this mission with which St. Paul was entrusted by the Church at Antioch, he received an intimation of the Divine Will, communicated by direct revelation. Such a revelation at so momentous a crisis must appear perfectly natural to all who believe that Christianity was introduced into the world by the immediate power of God. If 'a man of Macedonia' appeared to Paul in the

---

[1] Gal. ii. 4.
[2] Acts xv. 1.
[3] Gal. ii. 4.
[4] This may be inferred from the im-

perfect in the Greek. Compare xiv. 28.
[5] Gal. ii. 5.   [6] Acts xv. 2.
[7] Acts xv. 19.
[8] Gal. i. 7. Acts xv. 24.

visions of the night, when he was about to carry the Gospel from Asia into Europe :[1] if ' the angel of God' stood by him in the night, when the ship that was conveying him to Rome was in danger of sinking ;[2] we cannot wonder when he tells us that, on this occasion, when he 'went up to Jerusalem with Barnabas,' he went 'by revelation.'[3] And we need not be surprised, if we find that St. Paul's path was determined by two different causes ; that he went to Jerusalem partly because the Church deputed him, and partly because he was divinely admonished. Such a combination and co-operation of the natural and the supernatural we have observed above,[4] in the case of that vision which induced St. Peter to go from Joppa to Cæsarea. Nor in adopting this view of St. Paul's journey from Antioch to Jerusalem, need we feel any great difficulty —from this circumstance, that the two motives which conspired to direct him are separately mentioned in different parts of Scripture. It is true that we are told in the Acts [5] simply that it was ' determined' at Antioch that Paul should go to Jerusalem ; and that in Galatians [6] we are informed by himself that he went ' by revelation.' But we have an exact parallel in an earlier journey, already related,[7] from Jerusalem to Tarsus. In St. Luke's narrative [8] it is stated that ' the brethren,' knowing the conspiracy against his life, ' brought him down to Cæsarea and sent him forth;' while in the speech of St. Paul himself,[9] we are told that in a trance he saw Jesus Christ, and received from Him a command to depart ' quickly out of Jerusalem.'

Similarly directed from without and from within, he travelled to Jerusalem on the occasion before us. It would seem that his companions were carefully chosen with reference to the question in dispute. On the one hand was Barnabas,[10] a Jew and 'a Levite' by birth,[11] a good representative of the church of the circumcision. On the other hand was Titus,[12] now first mentioned[13] in the course of our narrative, a convert from Heathenism, an uncircumcised ' Greek.' From the expression used of the departure of this company it seems evident that the majority of the Christians at Antioch were still faithful to the truth of the Gospel. Had the Judaisers triumphed, it would hardly have been said that Paul and his fellow-travellers were ' brought on their way by the Church.'[14] Their course was along the great Roman Road, which followed the Phœnician coast-line, and traces of which are still seen on the cliffs over-

---

[1] Acts xvi. 9.
[2] Acts xxvii. 23.
[3] Gal. ii. 2. Schrader (who does not however identify this journey with that in Acts xv.) translates thus—' to make a revelation,' which is a meaning the words can scarcely bear.
[4] Pp. 163, 164.
[5] Acts xv. 2.
[6] Gal. ii. 2.
[7] Chap. III. p. 87.
[8] Acts ix. 30.
[9] Acts xxii. 17, 18.
[10] Acts xv. 2.

[11] Acts iv. 36.
[12] Gal. ii. 1–5.
[13] Titus is not mentioned at all in the Acts of the Apostles, and besides the present Epistle and that to Titus himself, he is only mentioned in 2 Cor. and 2 Tim. In a later part of this work he will be noticed more particularly as St. Paul's 'fellow-labourer' (2 Cor. viii. 23).
[14] Acts xv. 3. So the phrase in xv. 40 may be reasonably adduced as a proof that the feeling of the majority was with Paul rather than Barnabas

hanging the sea :[1] and thence through the midland districts of Samaria and Judæa. When last we had occasion to mention Phœnice,[2] we were alluding to those who were dispersed on the death of Stephen, and preached the Gospel 'to Jews only' on this part of the Syrian coast. Now, it seems evident that many of the Heathen Syro-Phœnicians had been converted to Christianity : for, as Paul and Barnabas passed through, ' declaring the conversion of the Gentiles, they caused great joy unto all the brethren.' As regards the Samaritans,[3] we cannot be surprised that they who, when Philip first 'preached Christ unto them,' had received the Glad Tidings with 'great joy,' should be ready to express their sympathy in the happiness of those who, like themselves, had recently been 'aliens from the commonwealth of Israel.'

Fifteen years[4] had now elapsed since that memorable journey, when St. Paul left Jerusalem, with all the zeal of a Pharisee, to persecute and destroy the Christians in Damascus.[5] He had twice entered, as a Christian, the Holy City again. Both visits had been short and hurried, and surrounded with danger. The first was three years after his conversion, when he spent a fortnight with Peter, and escaped assassination by a precipitate flight to Tarsus.[6] The second was in the year 44, when Peter himself was in imminent danger, and when the messengers who brought the charitable contribution from Antioch were probably compelled to return immediately.[7] Now St. Paul came, at a more peaceful period of the Church's history, to be received as the successful champion of the Gospel, and as the leader of the greatest revolution which the world has seen. It was now undeniable that Christianity had spread to a wide extent in the Gentile world, and that he had been the great instrument in advancing its progress. He came to defend his own principles and practice against an increasing torrent of op-

[1] Dr. Robinson passed two Roman milestones between Tyre and Sidon (iii. 415), and observed traces of Roman road between Sidon and Beyrout. See also Fisher's *Syria* (i. 40) for a notice of the Via Antonina between Beyrout and Tripoli.

[2] P. 97. Acts xi. 19, 20. It may be interesting here to allude to the journey of a Jew in the Middle Ages from Antioch to Jerusalem. It is probable that the stations, the road, and the rate of travelling were the same, and the distribution of the Jews not very different. We find the following passage in the Itinerary of Benjamin of Tudela, who travelled in 1163 : 'Two days bring us from Antioch to Lega, which is Latachia, and contains about 200 Jews, the principal of whom are R. Chiia and R. Joseph. . . . . One day's journey to Gebal of the children of Ammon ; it contains about 150 Jews. . . . . Two days hence is Beyrut. The principal of its 50 Jewish inhabitants

are R. Solomon, R. Obadiah, and R. Joseph. It is hence one day's journey to Saida, which is Sidon of Scripture [Acts xxvii. 3], a large city, with about 20 Jewish families. . . . . One day's journey to New Sur [Tyre, Acts xxi. 3], a very beautiful city. . . . . The Jews of Sur are ship-owners and manufacturers of the celebrated Tyrian glass. . . . It is one day hence to Acre [Ptolemais, Acts xxi. 7]. It is the frontier town of Palestine ; and, in consequence of its situation on the shore of the Mediterranean, and of its large port, it is the principal place of disembarkation of all pilgrims who visit Jerusalem by sea.'—*Early Travels to Palestine*, pp. 78–81.

[3] See p. 65.

[4] Gal. ii. 1, where we ought probably to reckon inclusively. See Appendix.

[5] See Chap. III.

[6] P. 83. Compare p. 163.

[7] P. 105. Compare p. 163.

position, which had disturbed him in his distant ministrations at Antioch, but the fountain-head of which was among the Pharisees at Jerusalem.

The Pharisees had been the companions of St. Paul's younger days. Death had made many changes in the course of fifteen years ; but some must have been there who had studied with him ' at the feet of Gamaliel.' Their opposition was doubtless embittered by remembering what he had been before his conversion. Nor do we allude here to those Pharisees who opposed Christianity. These were not the enemies whom St. Paul came to resist. The time was past when the Jews, unassisted by the Roman power, could exercise a cruel tyranny over the Church. Its safety was no longer dependent on the wisdom or caution of Gamaliel. The great debates at Jerusalem are no longer between Jews and Christians in the Hellenistic synagogues, but between the Judaising and spiritual parties of the Christians themselves. Many of the Pharisees, after the example of St. Paul, had believed that Jesus was Christ.[1] But they had not followed the example of their school-companion in the surrender of Jewish bigotry. The battle, therefore, which had once been fought without was now to be renewed within, the Church. It seems that, at the very first reception of Paul and Barnabas at Jerusalem, some of these Pharisaic Christians ' rose up,' and insisted that the observance of Judaism was necessary to salvation. They said that it was absolutely ' needful to circumcise ' the new converts, and to ' command them to keep the Law of Moses.' The whole course of St. Paul's procedure among the Gentiles was here openly attacked. Barnabas was involved in the same suspicion and reproach ; and with regard to Titus, who was with them as the representative of the Gentile Church, it was asserted that, without circumcision, he could not hope to be partaker of the blessings of the Gospel.

But far more was involved than any mere opposition, however factious, to individual missionaries, or than the severity of any conditions imposed on individual converts. The question of liberty or bondage for all future ages was to be decided; and a convention of the whole Church at Jerusalem was evidently called for. In the meantime, before ' the Apostles and elders came together to consider of this matter,'[2] St. Paul had private conferences with the more influential members of the Christian community,[3] and especially with James, Peter, and John,[4] the great Apostles and ' Pillars ' of the Church. Extreme caution and management were required, in consequence of the intrigues of the 'false brethren,' both in Jerusalem and Antioch. He was, moreover, himself the great object of suspicion ; and it was his duty to use every effort to remove the growing prejudice. Thus, though conscious of his own inspiration, and tenaciously holding the truth which he knew to be essential, he yet acted with that prudence which was characteristic of his whole life,[5] and which he honestly avows in the Epistle to the Galatians.

If we may compare our own feeble imitations of Apostolic zeal and prudence with the proceedings of the first founders of the

[1] Acts xv. 5.
[2] Acts xv. 6.
[3] Gal. i. 2.

[4] Gal. ii. 9.
[5] See, for instance, the sixth and seventeenth verses of Acts xxiii.

Church of Christ, we may say that these preliminary conferences were like the private meetings which prepare the way for a great religious assembly in England. Paul and Barnabas had been deputed from Antioch ; Titus was with them as a sample of Gentile conversions, and a living proof of their reality ; and the great end in view was to produce full conviction in the Church at large. At length the great meeting was summoned,[1] which was to settle the principles of missionary action among the Gentiles. It was a scene of earnest debate, and perhaps in its earlier portion, of angry 'disputing:'[2] but the passages which the Holy Spirit has caused to be recorded for our instruction are those which relate to the Apostles themselves,—the address of St. Peter, the narrative of Barnabas and Paul, and the concluding speech of St. James. These three passages must be separately considered in the order of Scripture.

St. Peter was the first of the Apostles who rose to address the assembly.[3] He gave his decision against the Judaisers, and in favour of St. Paul. He reminded his hearers of the part which he himself had taken in admitting the Gentiles into the Christian Church. They were well aware, he said, that these recent converts in Syria and Cilicia were not the first Heathens who had believed the Gospel, and that he himself had been chosen by God to begin the work which St. Paul had only been continuing. The communication of the Holy Ghost was the true test of God's acceptance : and God had shown that He was no respecter of persons, by shedding abroad the same miraculous gifts on Jew and Gentile, and purifying by faith the hearts of both alike. And then St. Peter went on to speak, in touching language, of the yoke of the Jewish Law. Its weight had pressed heavily on many generations of Jews, and was well known to the Pharisees who were listening at that moment. They had been relieved from legal bondage by the salvation offered through faith ; and it would be tempting God, to impose on others a burden which neither they nor their fathers had ever been able to bear.

The next speakers were Paul and Barnabas. There was great silence through all the multitude,[4] and every eye was turned on the missionaries, while they gave the narrative of their journeys. Though Barnabas is mentioned here before Paul,[5] it is most likely

[1] This meeting is described (Acts xv. 6) as consisting of the 'Apostles and Elders;' but the decision afterwards given is said to be the decision of 'the Apostles and Elders with the whole Church' (ver. 22), and the decree was sent in the names of 'the Apostles, and Elders, and Brethren' (ver. 23). [The reading, however, in this verse is disputed. See note below, on the superscription of the decree, p. 176.] Hence we must suppose, either that the decision was made by the synod of the Apostles and Elders, and afterwards ratified by another larger meeting of the whole Church, or that

there was only one meeting, in which the whole Church took part, although only the 'Apostles and Elders' are mentioned.

[2] Acts xv. 7.

[3] Acts xv. 7–11.

[4] Acts xv. 12. The imperfect, which is here used, implies attention to a continued narrative.

[5] This order of the names in the narrative, xv. 12, and in the letter below, ver. 25 (not in ver. 22), is a remarkable exception to the phrase 'Paul and Barnabas,' which has been usual since Acts xiii. See below, p. 176, n. 4.

that the latter was 'the chief speaker.' But both of them appear to have addressed the audience.[1] They had much to relate of what they had done and seen together : and especially they made appeal to the miracles which God had worked among the Gentiles by them. Such an appeal must have been a persuasive argument to the Jew, who was familiar, in his ancient Scriptures, with many Divine interruptions of the course of nature. These interferences had signalised all the great passages of Jewish history. Jesus Christ had proved His Divine mission in the same manner. And the events at Paphos,[2] at Iconium,[3] and Lystra,[4] could not well be regarded in any other light than as a proof that the same Power had been with Paul and Barnabas, which accompanied the words of Peter and John in Jerusalem and Judæa.[5]

But the opinion of another speaker still remained to be given. This was James, the brother of the Lord,[6] who, from the austere sanctity of his character, was commonly called, both by Jews and Christians, 'James the Just.' No judgment could have such weight with the Judaising party as his. Not only in the vehement language in which he denounced the sins of the age, but even in garb and appearance, he resembled John the Baptist, or one of the older prophets, rather than the other Apostles of the new dispensation. 'Like the ancient saints, even in outward aspect, with the austere features, the linen ephod, the bare feet, the long locks and unshorn head of the Nazarite,'[7]—such, according to tradition, was the man who now came forward, and solemnly pronounced that Mosaic rites were not of eternal obligation. After alluding to the argument of Peter (whose name we find him characteristically quoting in its Jewish form[8]), he turns to the ancient prophets, and adduces a passage from Amos[9] to prove that Christianity is the fulfilment of Judaism. And then he passes to the historical aspect of the subject, contending that this fulfilment was predetermined by God himself, and that the Jewish Dispensation was in truth the preparation for the Christian.[10] Such a decision, pronounced by one who stood emphatically on the confines of the two dispensations, came with great force on all who heard it, and carried with it the general opinion of the assembly to the conclusion that those 'who from among the Gentiles had turned unto God' should not be 'troubled' with any Jewish obligations, except such as were

[1] See ver. 13, 'after *they* were silent.'
[2] Acts xiii. 11.
[3] Acts xiv. 3.
[4] Acts xiv. 8.
[5] Acts ii. v. ix.
[6] See Acts xv. 13–22. It is well known that there is much perplexity connected with those Apostles who bore the name of James. We are not required here to enter into the investigation, and are content to adopt the opinion which is most probable.
[7] Stanley's *Sermons and Essays*, &c., p. 295. We must refer here to the whole of the *Sermon on the Epistle of St. James*, and of the *Essay on the Tra-* ditions of James the Just, especially pp. 292, 302, 327.
[8] Acts xv. 14. So St. Peter names himself at the beginning of his Second Epistle.
[9] Amos ix. 11, 12. We are not required to express any opinion on the application of prophecy to the future destiny of the Jews; but we must observe, that the Apostles themselves apply such prophecies as this to the Christian Dispensation. See Acts ii. 17.
[10] 'Known from the beginning,' &c. 18. Compare Acts xvii. 26; Rom. i. 2; Eph. i. 10, iii. 9, 10; Col. i. 26.

necessary for peace and the mutual good understanding of the two parties.

The spirit of charity and mutual forbearance is very evident in the decree which was finally enacted. Its spirit was that expressed by St. Paul in his Epistles to the Romans and Corinthians. He knew, and was persuaded by the Lord Jesus, that nothing is unclean of itself : but to him that esteemeth anything to be unclean, to him it is unclean. He knew that an idol is nothing in the world, and that there is none other God but one. But all men have not this knowledge : some could not eat that which had been offered in sacrifice to an idol without defiling their conscience. It is good to abstain from everything whereby a weaker brother may be led to stumble. To sin thus against our brethren is to sin against Christ.[1] In accordance with these principles it was enacted that the Gentile converts should be required to abstain from that which had been polluted by being offered in sacrifice to idols, from the flesh of animals which had been strangled, and generally from the eating of blood. The reason for these conditions is stated in the verse to which particular allusion has been made at the beginning of the present chapter.[2] The Law of Moses was read every Sabbath in all the cities where the Jews were dispersed.[3] A due consideration for the prejudices of the Jews made it reasonable for the Gentile converts to comply with some of the restrictions which the Mosaic Law and ancient custom had imposed on every Jewish meal. In no other way could social intercourse be built up and cemented between the two parties. If some forbearance were requisite on the part of the Gentiles in complying with such conditions, not less forbearance was required from the Jews in exacting no more. And to the Gentiles themselves the restrictions were a merciful condition : for it helped them to disentangle themselves more easily from the pollutions connected with their idolatrous life. We are not merely concerned here with the question of social separation, the food which was a delicacy[4] to the Gentile being abominated by the Jew,—nor with the difficulties of weak and scrupulous consciences, who might fear too close a contact between 'the table of the Lord' and 'the table of Demons,'[5]— but this controversy had an intimate connection with the principles of universal morality. The most shameless violations of purity took place in connection with the sacrifices and feasts celebrated in

[1] Rom. xiv.; 1 Cor. viii.

[2] Above, p. 161. There is some difference of opinion as to the connection of this verse with the context. Some consider it to imply that, while it was necessary to urge these conditions on the Gentiles, it was needless to say anything to the Jews on the subject, since they had the Law of Moses, and knew its requirements. Dean Milman infers that the regulations were made because the Christians in general met in the same places of religious worship with the Jews. 'These provisions were necessary, because the Mosaic Law was universally read, and from immemorial usage, in the synagogue. The direct violation of its most vital principles by any of those who joined in the common worship would be incongruous, and of course highly offensive to the more zealous Mosaists.' — *Hist. of Christianity,* vol. i. p. 426, n.

[3] Acts xv. 21.

[4] We learn from Athenæus that the meat from 'things strangled' was regarded as a delicacy among the Greeks.

[5] 1 Cor. x. 21.

honour of heathen divinities.[1] Everything, therefore, which tended
to keep the Gentile converts even from accidental or apparent
association with these scenes of vice, made their own recovery from
pollution more easy, and enabled the Jewish converts to look on
their new Christian brethren with less suspicion and antipathy.
This seems to be the reason why we find an acknowledged sin
mentioned in the decree along with ceremonial observances which
were meant to be only temporary[2] and perhaps local.[3] We must
look on the whole subject from the Jewish point of view, and consider how violations of morality and contradictions of the ceremonial law were associated together in the Gentile world. It is
hardly necessary to remark that much additional emphasis is given
to the moral part of the decree, when we remember that it was
addressed to those who lived in close proximity to the profligate
sanctuaries of Antioch and Paphos.[4]

We have said that the ceremonial part of the decree was intended
for a temporary and perhaps only a local observance. It is not for
a moment implied that any Jewish ceremony is necessary to salvation. On the contrary, the great principle was asserted, once for all,
that man is justified, not by the Law, but by faith : one immediate
result was that Titus, the companion of Paul and Barnabas, 'was
not compelled to be circumcised.'[5] His case was not like that of
Timothy at a later period,[6] whose circumcision was a prudential
accommodation to circumstances, without endangering the truth of
the Gospel. To have circumcised Titus at the time of the meeting
in Jerusalem, would have been to have asserted that he was 'bound
to keep the whole Law.'[7] And when the alternative was between
' the liberty wherewith Christ has made us free,' and the reimposi-
tion of 'the yoke of bondage,' St. Paul's language always was,[8]
that if Gentile converts were circumcised, Christ could 'profit them
nothing.' By seeking to be justified in the Law, they fell from
grace.[9] In this firm refusal to comply with the demand of the
Judaisers, the case of all future converts from Heathenism was
virtually involved. It was asserted, once for all, that in the Christian Church there is 'neither Greek nor Jew, circumcision nor uncircumcision, barbarian, Scythian, bond, nor free ; but that Christ
is all and in all.'[10] And St. Paul obtained the victory for that
principle, which, we cannot doubt, will hereafter destroy the distinctions that are connected with the institution of slavery in
America and of caste in India.

Certain other points decided in this meeting had a more direct
personal reference to St. Paul himself. His own independent

---

[1] See Tholuck, in his *Nature and
Moral Influence of Heathenism*, part
iii.

[2] We cannot, however, be surprised
that one great branch of the Christian
Church takes a different view. The
doctrine of the Greek Church, both
Ancient and Modern, is in harmony
with the letter, as well as the spirit, of
the Apostolic council.

[3] At least the decree (Acts xv. 23)

is addressed only to the churches of
' Syria and Cilicia ; ' and we do not
see the subject alluded to again after
xvi. 4.

[4] See above, pp. 103 and 125.

[5] Gal. ii. 3.

[6] Acts xvi. 3.

[7] Gal. v. 3.

[8] Gal. v. 2.

[9] Gal. v. 4.

[10] Col. iii. 11.

mission had been called in question. Some, perhaps, said that he was antagonistic to the Apostles at Jerusalem, others that he was entirely dependent on them.[1]   All the Judaisers agreed in blaming his course of procedure among the Gentiles. This course was now entirely approved by the other Apostles. His independence was fully recognised. Those who were universally regarded as 'pillars of the truth,' James, Peter, and John,[2] gave to him and Barnabas the right hand of fellowship, and agreed that they should be to the Heathen what themselves were to the Jews. Thus was St. Paul publicly acknowledged as the Apostle of the Gentiles, and openly placed in that position from which 'he shall never more go out,' as a pillar of the Temple of the 'New Jerusalem,' inscribed with the 'New Name' which proclaims the union of all mankind in one Saviour.[3]

One of those who gave the right hand of fellowship to St. Paul, was the 'beloved disciple' of that Saviour.[4]   This is the only meeting of St. Paul and St. John recorded in Scripture. It is, moreover, the last notice which we find there of the life of St. John, until the time of the apocalyptic vision in the island of Patmos. For both these reasons the mind seizes eagerly on the incident, though it is only casually mentioned in the Epistle to the Galatians. Like other incidental notices contained in Scripture, it is very suggestive of religious thoughts. St. John had been silent during the discussion in the public assembly ; but at the close of it he expressed his cordial union with St. Paul in 'the truth of the Gospel.'[5]   That union has been made visible to all ages by the juxtaposition of their Epistles in the same Sacred Volume. They stand together among the pillars of the Holy Temple ; and the Church of God is thankful to learn how Contemplation may be united with Action, and Faith with Love, in the spiritual life.

To the decree with which Paul and Barnabas were charged, one condition was annexed, with which they gladly promised to comply. We have already had occasion to observe (p. 54) that the Hebrews of Judæa were relatively poor, compared with those of the dispersion, and that the Jewish Christians in Jerusalem were exposed to peculiar sufferings from poverty ; and we have seen Paul and Barnabas once before the bearers of a contribution from a foreign city for their relief (p. 105).   They were exhorted now to continue the same charitable work, and in their journeys among the Gentiles and the dispersed Jews, 'to remember the poor' at Jerusalem.[6]   In proof

---

[1] The charges brought against St. Paul by the Judaisers were very various at different times.

[2] It should be carefully observed here that James is mentioned first of these Apostles who were 'pillars,' and that Peter is mentioned by the name of Cephas, as in 1 Cor. i. 12.

[3] See Rev. iii. 12.   The same metaphor is found in 1 Tim. iii. 15, where Timothy is called (for this seems the natural interpretation), 'a pillar and support of the truth.'   In these passages it is important to bear in mind

the peculiarity of ancient architecture, which was characterised by vertical columns, supporting horizontal entablatures.   Inscriptions were often engraved on these columns.   Hence the words in the passage quoted from Revelations : 'I will write upon him . . . . my new name.'

[4] Gal. ii. 9.   [5] Gal. ii. 5.

[6] 'Only that we should remember the poor ; which also I was forward to do,' Gal. ii. 10, where the change from the plural to the singular should be noticed.   Is this because Barnabas

of St. Paul's faithful discharge of this promise, we need only allude to his zeal in making 'the contribution for the poor saints at Jerusalem' in Galatia, Macedonia, and Achaia,[1] and to that last journey to the Holy Land, when he went, ' after many years,' to take ' alms to his nation.'[2] It is more important here to consider (what indeed we have mentioned before) the effect which this charitable exertion would have in binding together the divided parties in the Church. There cannot be a doubt that the Apostles had this result in view. Their anxiety on this subject is the best commentary on the spirit in which they had met on this great occasion ; and we may rest assured that the union of the Gentile and Jewish Christians was largely promoted by the benevolent efforts which attended the diffusion of the Apostolic Decree.

Thus the controversy being settled, Paul's mission to the Gentiles being fully recognised, and his method of communicating the Gospel approved by the other Apostles, and the promise being given, that, in their journeys among the Heathen, they would remember the necessities of the Hebrew Christians in Judæa, the two missionaries returned from Jerusalem to Antioch. They carried with them the decree which was to give peace to the consciences that had been troubled by the Judaising agitators ; and the two companions, Judas and Silas,[3] who travelled with them, were empowered to accredit their commission and character. It seems also that Mark was another companion of Paul and Barnabas on this journey ; for the last time we had occasion to mention his name was when he withdrew from Pamphylia to Jerusalem (p. 128), and presently we see him once more with his kinsman at Antioch.[4]

The reception of the travellers at Antioch was full of joy and satisfaction.[5] The whole body of the Church was summoned together to hear the reading of the letter ; and we can well imagine the eagerness with which they crowded to listen, and the thankfulness and ' consolation ' with which such a communication was received, after so much anxiety and perplexity. The letter indeed is almost as interesting to us as to them, not only because of the principle asserted and the results secured, but also because it is the first document preserved to us from the acts of the Primitive Church. The words of the original document, literally translated, are as follows :—

was soon afterwards separated from St. Paul (Acts xv. 39), who had thenceforth to prosecute the charitable work alone ?

[1] 'As I have given order to the Churches of Galatia,' &c., 1 Cor. xvi.

1-4. ' It hath pleased them of Macedonia and Achaia,' &c. Rom. xv. 25, 26. See 2 Cor. viii. ix.

[2] Acts xxiv. 17.

[3] Acts xv. 22, 27, 32.

[4] Acts xv. 37.   [5] Acts xv. 31.

'THE APOSTLES, AND THE ELDERS, AND THE BRETHREN,[1] ACTS xv.
TO THE GENTILE BRETHREN IN ANTIOCH, AND SYRIA, 23
AND CILICIA, GREETING.[2]

'Whereas we have heard that certain men who 24
went out from us have troubled you with words,
and unsettled your souls[3] by telling you to circumcise yourselves and keep the Law although we
gave them no such commission:

'It has been determined by us, being assembled 25
with one accord, to choose some from amongst ourselves and send them to you with our beloved[4]
Barnabas and Saul, men that have offered up their 26
lives for the name of our Lord Jesus Christ. We 27
have sent therefore Judas and Silas, who themselves
also[5] will tell you by word the same which we tell
you by letter.

'For it has been determined by the Holy Spirit 28
and by us, to lay upon you no greater burden than
these necessary things: that ye abstain from meats 29
offered to idols, and from blood, and from things
strangled, and from fornication. Wherefrom if ye
keep yourselves it shall be well with you. FAREWELL.'

The encouragement inspired by this letter would be increased by
the sight of Judas and Silas, who were ready to confirm its contents
by word of mouth. These two disciples remained some short time
at Antioch. They were possessed of that power of 'prophecy'
which was one of the forms in which the Holy Spirit made His
presence known: and the Syrian Christians were 'exhorted and
confirmed' by the exercise of this miraculous gift.[6] The minds of
all were in great tranquillity when the time came for the return of
these messengers 'to the Apostles' at Jerusalem. Silas, however,

---

[1] We adhere to the Textus Receptus, although the '*and*' before 'Brethren' is omitted in many weighty
MSS. But it is supported by Chrysostom, by several of the uncial MSS.,
and by many of the most ancient versions. Its omission might have been
caused by hierarchical tendencies. It
should be observed that the phrase
without the conjunction is entirely unknown elsewhere, which is a strong
argument against its being the correct
reading here. Also the omission appears to render the superscription of
this document inconsistent with the
enumeration of the three distinct
parties to it in verse 22.

[2] 'Greeting.' The only other place
where this salutation occurs is James
i. 1; an undesigned coincidence, tending to prove the genuineness of this
document.

[3] Although the best MSS. omit the
words 'by telling . . . . Law,' yet we
think they cannot possibly be an interpolation.

[4] It is another undesigned coincidence, that the names of these two
Apostles are here in the reverse order
to that which, in St. Luke's *narrative*
(except when he speaks of Jerusalem),
they have assumed since chap. xiii.
In the view of the Church at Jerusalem,
Paul's name would naturally come after
that of Barnabas. See above, p. 170, n. 5.

[5] The present participle may be explained by the ancient idiom of letter-
writing, by which the writer transferred
himself into the time of the reader.

[6] Acts xv. 32. Compare xiii. 1.

either remained at Antioch or soon came back thither.[1] He was destined, as we shall see, to become the companion of St. Paul, and to be at the beginning of the second missionary journey what Barnabas had been at the beginning of the first.

Two painful scenes were witnessed at Antioch before the Apostle started on that second journey. We are informed[2] that Paul and Barnabas protracted their stay in this city, and were diligently occupied, with many others, in making the glad tidings of the Gospel known, and in the general work of Christian instruction. It is in this interval of time that we must place that visit of St. Peter to Antioch,[3] which St. Paul mentions in the Epistle to the Galatians,[4] immediately after his notice of the affairs of the Council. It appears that Peter, having come to Antioch for some reason which is unknown to us,[5] lived at first in free and unrestrained intercourse with the Gentile converts, meeting them in social friendship, and eating with them, in full consistency with the spirit of the recent Decree, and with his own conduct in the case of Cornelius. At this time certain Jewish brethren came 'from James,' who presided over the Church at Jerusalem. Whether they were really sent on some mission by the Apostle James, or we are merely to understand that they came from Jerusalem, they brought with them their old Hebrew repugnance against social intercourse with the uncircumcised ; and Peter in their society began to vacillate. In weak compliance with their prejudices, he 'withdrew and separated himself' from those whom he had lately treated as brethren and equals in Christ. Just as in an earlier part of his life he had first asserted his readiness to follow his Master to death, and then denied him through fear of a maid-servant,—so now, after publicly protesting against the notion of making any difference between the Jew and the Gentile, and against laying on the neck of the latter a yoke which the former had never been able to bear,[6] we find him contradicting his own principles, and 'through fear of those who were of the circumcision'[7] giving all the sanction of his example to the introduction of *caste* into the Church of Christ.

[1] Acts xv. 34. The reading here is doubtful. The question, however, is immaterial. If the verse is genuine, it modifies the phrase 'they were let go' in the preceding verse ; if not, we have merely to suppose that Silas went to Jerusalem and then returned.

[2] Acts xv. 35.

[3] Neander places this meeting of Peter and Paul later ; but his reasons are far from satisfactory. From the order of narration in the Epistle to the Galatians, it is most natural to infer that the meeting at Antioch took place soon after the Council at Jerusalem. Some writers wish to make it anterior to the Council, from an unwillingness to believe that St. Peter would have acted in this manner after the Decree. But it is a sufficient answer to this objection to say that his conduct here was equally inconsistent with his own previous conduct in the case of Cornelius.

Abp. Whately (in the work quoted below, p. 179, n. 6) assumes that Peter went to meet Paul at Jerusalem after the scene at Antioch, and sees a close resemblance between Peter's words (Acts xv. 11) and those of Paul (Gal. ii. 14–16).

[4] Gal. ii. 11, &c.

[5] The tradition which represents Peter as having held the See of Antioch before that of Rome has been mentioned before, p. 106, n. 1. Tillemont places the period of this episcopate about 36–42, A.D. He says it is 'une chose assez embarrassee ; ' and it is certainly difficult to reconcile it with Scripture.

[6] Acts xv. 9, 10.   [7] Gal. ii. 12.

Such conduct could not fail to excite in St. Paul the utmost indignation. St. Peter was not simply yielding a non-essential point, through a tender consideration for the consciences of others. This would have been quite in accordance with the principle so often asserted by his brother-Apostle, that 'it is good neither to eat flesh nor to drink wine, nor anything whereby thy brother stumbleth, or is made weak.' Nor was this proceeding a prudent and innocent accommodation to circumstances, for the sake of furthering the Gospel, like St. Paul's conduct in circumcising Timothy at Iconium ;[1] or, indeed, like the Apostolic Decree itself. St. Peter was acting under the influence of a contemptible and sinful motive, —the fear of man : and his behaviour was giving a strong sanction to the very heresy which was threatening the existence of the Church ; namely, the opinion that the observance of Jewish ceremonies was necessary to salvation. Nor was this all. Other Jewish Christians, as was naturally to be expected, were led away by his example : and even Barnabas, the chosen companion of the Apostle of the Gentiles, who had been a witness and an actor in all the great transactions in Cyprus, in Pisidia, and Lycaonia,—even Barnabas, the missionary, was 'carried away' with the dissimulation of the rest.[2] When St. Paul was a spectator of such inconsistency, and perceived both the motive in which it originated and the results to which it was leading, he would have been a traitor to his Master's cause, if he had hesitated (to use his own emphatic words) to rebuke Peter 'before all,' and to 'withstand him to the face.'[3]

It is evident from St. Paul's expression, that it was on some public occasion that this open rebuke took place. The scene, though slightly mentioned, is one of the most remarkable in Sacred History : and the mind naturally labours to picture to itself the appearance of the two men. It is, therefore, at least allowable to mention here that general notion of the forms and features of the two Apostles, which has been handed down in tradition, and was represented by the early artists.[4] St. Paul[5]

[1] Acts xvi. 3.   [2] Gal. ii. 13.
[3] Gal. ii. 14, 11.
We can only allude to the opinion of some early writers, that the whole scene was pre-arranged between Peter and Paul, and that there was no real misunderstanding. Even Chrysostom advocates this unchristian view.
[4] For the representations of St. Peter and St.Paul in early pictures and mosaics, see the first volume of Mrs. Jameson's *Sacred and Legendary Art*, especially pp. 145, 159, 161, 162, 201. They correspond with the traditionary descriptions referred to in the next note. 'St. Peter is a robust old man, with a broad forehead, and rather coarse features, an open undaunted countenance, short gray hair, and short thick beard, curled, and of a silvery white. Paul was a man of small and meagre stature, with an aquiline nose, and

sparkling eyes : in the Greek type the face is long and oval, the forehead high and bald ; the hair brown, the beard long, flowing, and pointed. . . . . These traditional characteristic types of the features and person of the two greatest Apostles were long adhered to. We find them most strictly followed in the old Greek mo aics, in the early Christian sculpture, and the early pictures, in all which the sturdy dignity and broad rustic features of St. Peter, and the elegant contemplative head of St. Paul, who looks like a Greek philosopher, form a most interesting and suggestive contrast.' The dispute at Antioch is the subject of a picture by Guido. See p. 167.
[5] The descriptions of St. Paul's appearance by Malalas and Nicephorus are given at length in the larger editions.

is set before us as having the strongly marked and prominent
features of a Jew, yet not without some of the finer lines indicative
of Greek thought. His stature was diminutive, and his body disfigured by some lameness or distortion, which may have provoked
the contemptuous expressions of his enemies.[1] His beard was long
and thin. His head was bald. The characteristics of his face
were, a transparent complexion, which visibly betrayed the quick
changes of his feelings, a bright gray eye under thickly overhanging
united eyebrows,[2] a cheerful and winning expression of countenance,
which invited the approach and inspired the confidence of strangers.
It would be natural to infer,[3] from his continual journeys and
manual labour, that he was possessed of great strength of constitution. But men of delicate health have often gone through the greatest
exertions:[4] and his own words on more than one occasion show
that he suffered much from bodily infirmity.[5] St. Peter is represented to us as a man of larger and stronger form, as his character
was harsher and more abrupt. The quick impulses of his soul revealed themselves in the flashes of a dark eye. The complexion
of his face was pale and sallow : and the short hair, which is described as entirely gray at the time of his death, curled black and
thick round his temples and his chin, when the two Apostles stood
together at Antioch, twenty years before their martyrdom.

Believing, as we do, that these traditionary pictures have probably some foundation in truth, we gladly take them as helps to
the imagination. And they certainly assist us in realising a remarkable scene, where Judaism and Christianity, in the persons of
two Apostles, are for a moment brought before us in strong antagonism. The words addressed by St. Paul to St. Peter before
the assembled Christians at Antioch, contain the full statement of
the Gospel as opposed to the Law. ' If thou, being born a Jew,
art wont to live [6] according to the customs of the Gentiles and not
of the Jews, why wouldest thou now constrain the Gentiles to keep
the ordinances of the Jews ? We are Jews by birth, and not unhallowed Gentiles ; yet, knowing that a man is not justified by the

[1] See above, p. 152.

[2] See above, p. 119, n. 6.

[3] See Acts xx. 7 ; 1 Thess. ii. 9 ;
2 Thess. iii. 8 ; 2 Cor. xi. 23–28. See
Tholuck's Essay on St. Paul's early
Life, for some speculations on the
Apostle's temperament.

[4] The instance of Alfred the Great
may be rightly alluded to. His biographer, Asser, says that from his
youth to his death he was always
either suffering pain or expecting it.

[5] See 2 Cor. xii. 7 ; Gal. iv. 13, 14.

[6] A spiritual sense is assigned to
the word ' live ' in this passage, by
Abp. Whately (*Lectures on the Characters of our Lord's Apostles*, 1853,
p. 193), and by Bp. Hinds (*Scripture
and the Authorised Version*, 1853, p.
18). The Archbishop says, rather

strongly, that he believes that ' any
competent judge, who carefully ex-
amines the original,' will acknowledge
the following to be the true sense of
the passage: ' If thou, though a Jew
by birth, yet hast life (i.e. *spiritual
life*) on the same terms as the Gentiles, and not by virtue of thy being a
Jew, why dost thou urge the Gentiles
to Judaise ?' It is, however, certain
that many competent persons have examined the passage carefully without
coming to this conclusion; and we cannot see that there is any real difficulty
in following the natural translation of
the words:—' If thou art in the habit
of living with the freedom of a Gentile
and not the strictness of a Jew, why
dost thou attempt to coerce the Gentiles into Judaism ?'

works of the law, but by the faith of Jesus Christ, we ourselves also have put our faith in Christ Jesus, that we might be justified by the faith of Christ, and not by the works of the law. For by the works of the law 𝖘𝖍𝖆𝖑𝖑 𝖓𝖔 𝖋𝖑𝖊𝖘𝖍 𝖇𝖊 𝖏𝖚𝖘𝖙𝖎𝖋𝖎𝖊𝖉.'[1] These sentences contain in a condensed form the whole argument of the Epistles to the Galatians and Romans.

Though the sternest indignation is expressed in this rebuke, we have no reason to suppose that any actual quarrel took place between the two Apostles. It is not improbable that St. Peter was immediately convinced of his fault, and melted at once into repentance. His mind was easily susceptible of quick and sudden changes; his disposition was loving and generous : and we should expect his contrition, as well as his weakness, at Antioch, to be what it was in the high-priest's house at Jerusalem. Yet, when we read the narrative of this rebuke in St. Paul's epistle, it is a relief to turn to that passage at the conclusion of one of St. Peter's letters, where, in speaking of the 'long-suffering of our Lord,' and of the prospect of sinless happiness in the world to come, he alludes, in touching words, to the Epistles of '*our beloved brother Paul.*'[2] We see how entirely all past differences are forgotten,—how all earthly misunderstandings are absorbed and lost in the contemplation of Christ and eternal life. Not only did the Holy Spirit overrule all contrarieties, so that the writings of both Apostles teach the Church the same doctrine : but the Apostle who was rebuked 'is not ashamed to call the attention of the Church to epistles in one page of which his own censure is recorded.'[3] It is an eminent triumph of Christian humility and love. We shall not again have occasion to mention St. Peter and St. Paul together, until we come to the last scene of all.[4] But, though they might seldom meet whilst labouring in their Master's cause, their lives were united, 'and in their deaths they were not divided.'

Coin of Antioch.[5]

[1] The quotation is from Psalm cxliii. 2, which is also quoted in the same connection, Rom. iii. 20. There is much difference of opinion among commentators on Gal. ii. as to the point where Paul's address to Peter terminates. Many writers think it continues to the end of the chapter. We are inclined to believe that it ends at ver. 16 ; and that the word which follow are intended to meet doctrinal objections (similar to those in Rom. iii. 3, 5, vi. 1, 15, vii. 7, 13) which the Galatians might naturally be supposed to make.

[2] 2 Pet. iii. 15, 16.

[3] Dr. Vaughan's *Harrow Sermons* (1846), p. 410.

[4] The martyrdom at Rome. See Mrs. Jameson's Work, especially pp. 180–183, 193–195.

[5] From the British Museum. See Mr. Scharf's drawing facing p. 103, and what is said there of the emblematical representation of Antioch. On this coin the seated figure bears a palm-branch, as the emblem of victory.

CHAPTER VIII.

Political Divisions of Asia Minor.—Difficulties of the Subject.—Provinces in the Reigns of Claudius and Nero.—I. ASIA.—II. BITHYNIA.—III. PAMPHYLIA.—IV. GALATIA.—V. PONTUS.—VI. CAPPADOCIA.—VII. CILICIA.—Visitation of the Churches proposed.—Quarrel and Separation of Paul and Barnabas.—Paul and Silas in Cilicia.—They cross the Taurus.—Lystra.—Timothy : his Circumcision.—Journey through Phrygia.—Sickness of St. Paul.—His Reception in Galatia.—Journey to the Ægean.—Alexandria Troas.—St. Paul's Vision.

THE life of St. Paul, being that of a traveller, and our purpose being to give a picture of the circumstances by which he was surrounded, it is often necessary to refer to the geography, both physical and political, of the countries through which he passed. This is the more needful in the case of Asia Minor, not only because it was the scene of a very great portion of his journeys, but because it is less known to ordinary readers than Palestine, Italy, or Greece. We have already described, at some length, the physical geography of those southern districts which are in the immediate neighbourhood of Mount Taurus.[1] And now that the Apostle's travels take a wider range, and cross the Asiatic peninsula from Syria to the frontiers of Europe, it is important to take a general view of the political geography of this part of the Roman Empire. Unless such a view is obtained in the first place, it is impossible to understand the topographical expressions employed in the narrative, or to conjecture the social relations into which St. Paul was brought in the course of his journeys[2] through Asia Minor.

It is, however, no easy task to ascertain the exact boundaries of the Roman provinces in this part of the world at any given date between Augustus and Constantine. In the first place, these boundaries were continually changing. The area of the different political districts was liable to sudden and arbitrary alterations. Such terms as 'Asia,'[3] 'Pamphylia,'[4] &c., though denoting the extent of a true political jurisdiction, implied a larger or smaller territory at one time than another. And again, we find the names of earlier and later periods of history mixed up together in inextricable confusion. Some of the oldest geographical terms, such as 'Æolis,' 'Ionia,' 'Caria,' 'Lydia,' were disappearing from ordinary use in the time of the Apostles :[5] but others, such as 'Mysia'[6] and 'Lycaonia,'[7]

---

[1] Chap. I. pp. 17–19. Chap. VI. pp. 126, 127.

[2] i.e. the journeys in Acts xvi. and Acts xviii.

[3] Acts ii. 9, vi. 9, xvi. 6, xix. 10, 27, 31, xx. 16, 18, xxvii. 2 ; 1 Cor. xvi. 19 ; 2 Cor. i. 8 ; 2 Tim. i. 15 ; 1 Pet. i. 1.

[4] Acts ii. 10, xiii. 13, xv. 38, xxvii. 5.

[5] Tacitus, Vitruvius, Justin, &c. speak of Pergamus, Ephesus, Cnidus, Thyatira, &c. as towns of *Asia*, not of Æolis, Ionia, Caria, Lydia, &c., respectively. See Acts xxvii. 2 ; Rev. i. 11.

[6] Acts xvi. 7, 8.

[7] Acts xiv. 6, 11.

still remained. Obsolete and existing divisions are presented to us
together : and the common maps of Asia Minor [1] are as unsatisfactory as if a map of France were set before us, distributed half into
provinces and half into departments. And in the third place, some
of the names have no political significance at all, but express rather
the ethnographical relations of ancient tribes. Thus, ' Pisidia,' [2]
denotes a district which might partly be in one province and partly
in another ; and ' Phrygia ' [3] reminds us of the diffusion of an
ancient people, the broken portions of whose territory were now
under the jurisdiction of three or four distinct governors. Cases of
this kind are, at first sight, more · embarrassing than the others.
They are not merely similar to the two-fold subdivision of Ireland,
where a province, like Ulster, may contain several definite counties :
but a nearer parallel is to be found in Scotland, where a geographical district, associated with many historical recollections,—
such as Galloway or Lothian,—may be partly in one county and
partly in another.

Our purpose is to elucidate the political subdivisions of Asia Minor
as they were in the reigns of Claudius and Nero,—or in other words,
to enumerate the provinces which existed, and to describe the boundaries which were assigned to them, in the middle of the first century
of the Christian era. The order we shall follow is from West to
East, and in so doing we shall not deviate widely from the order
in which the provinces were successively incorporated as substantive parts of the Roman Empire. We are not, indeed, to suppose
that St. Luke and St. Paul used all their topographical expressions in the strict political sense, even when such a sense was
more or less customary. There was an exact usage and a popular usage of all these terms. But the first step towards fixing
our geographical ideas of Asia Minor must be to trace the boundaries of the provinces. When this is done, we shall be better
able to distinguish those terms which, about the year 50 A.D.,
had ceased to have any true political significance, and to discriminate between the technical and the popular language of the sacred
writers.

I. ASIA.—There is sometimes a remarkable interest associated
with the history of a geographical term. One case of this kind is
suggested by the allusion which has just been made to the British
islands. Early writers speak of Ireland under the appellation of
' Scotia.' Certain of its inhabitants crossed over to the opposite
coast : [4] their name spread along with their influence : and at length
the title of Scotland was entirely transferred from one island to the
other. In classical history we have a similar instance in the name of
' Italy,' which at first only denoted the southernmost extremity of
the peninsula : then it was extended so as to include the whole with
the exception of Cisalpine Gaul : and finally, crossing the Rubicon,

[1] In the ordinary maps, ethnographical and political divisions of three
or four different periods are confused
together. In some of the more recent,
the Roman provincial divisions are in-

dicated, and the emperor's and senate's
provinces distinguished.
[2] Acts xiii. 14, xiv. 24.
[3] Acts ii. 10, xvi. 6, xviii. 23.
[4] See beginning of Bede's History.

it advanced to the Alps ; while the name of ' Gaul ' retreated beyond them. Another instance, on a larger scale, is presented to us on the south of the Mediterranean. The ' Africa ' of the Romans spread from a limited territory on the shore of that sea, till it embraced the whole continent which was circumnavigated by Vasco di Gama. And similarly the term, by which we are accustomed to designate the larger and more famous continent of the ancient world, traces its derivation to the ' Asian meadow by the streams of the Cayster,' [1] celebrated in the poems of Homer.

This is the earliest occurrence of the word ' Asia.' We find, however, even in the older poets,[2] the word used in its widest sense to denote all the countries in the far East. Either the Greeks, made familiar with the original Asia by the settlement of their kindred in its neighbourhood, applied it as a generic appellation to all the regions beyond it : [3] or the extension of the kingdom of Lydia from the banks of the Cayster to the Halys as its eastern boundary, diffused the name of Asia as far as that river, and thus suggested the division of Herodotus into ' Asia within the Halys' and ' Asia beyond the Halys.' [4] However this might be, the term retained, through the Greek and Roman periods, both a wider and a narrower sense ; of which senses we are concerned only with the latter. The Asia of the New Testament is not the continent which stretches into the remote East from the Black Sea and the Red Sea, but simply the western portion of that peninsula which, in modern times, has received the name of ' Asia Minor.' [5] What extent of country, and what political significance we are to assign to the term, will be shown by a statement of a few historical changes.

The fall of Crœsus reduced the Lydian kingdom to a Persian satrapy. With the rest of the Persian empire, this region west of the Halys fell before the armies of Alexander. In the confusion which followed the conqueror's death, an independant dynasty established itself at Pergamus, not far from the site of ancient Troy. At first their territory was narrow, and Attalus I. had to struggle with the Gauls who had invaded the peninsula, and with the neighbouring chieftains of Bithynia, who had invited them.[6] Antagonists still more formidable were the Greek kings of Syria, who claimed to be ' Kings of Asia,' and aimed at the possession of the

---

[1] Virgil adopts the phrase from Homer. It does not appear that the Roman prose writers ever used the word in its primitive and narrowest sense.

[2] As in Æschylus.

[3] Having the same general meaning as our phrase ' The East.' The words ' Levant ' and ' Anadoli ' (the modern name of Asia Minor) have come into use in the same way.

[4] We may compare the case of ' Palestine,' which at first meant only the country of the Philistines, and then was used by the Greeks and Romans to designate the whole of the land of Canaan.

[5] The peninsula which we call Asia Minor was never treated by the ancients as a geographical whole. The common divisions were, ' Asia within the Halys' and ' Asia beyond the Halys ' (as above); or, ' Asia within the Taurus ' and ' Asia beyond the Taurus.' It is very important to bear this in mind : for some interpreters of the New Testament imagine that the Asia there spoken of is the peninsula of Lesser Asia. The term ' Asia Minor ' is first found in Orosius, a writer of the fourth century, though ' Asia Major ' is used by Justin to denote the remote and eastern parts of the continent.

[6] See below, p. 185.

whole peninsula.[1] But the Romans appeared in the East, and ordered Antiochus to retire beyond the Taurus, and then conferred substantial rewards on their faithful allies. Rhodes became the mistress of Caria and Lycia, on the opposite coast ; and Eumenes, the son of Attalus, received, in the West and North-west, Lydia and Mysia, and a good portion of that vague region in the interior which was usually denominated 'Phrygia,'[2]—stretching in one direction over the district of Lycaonia.[3] Then it was that, as 150 years since the Margraves of Brandenburg became Kings of Prussia, so the Princes of Pergamus became 'Kings of Asia.' For a time they reigned over a highly-civilised territory, which extended from sea to sea. The library of Pergamus was the rival of that of Alexandria : and Attaleia, from whence we have lately seen the Apostle sailing to Syria[4] (Acts xiv. 25, 26) and Troas, from whence we shall presently see him sailing to Europe (Acts xvi. 11), were the southern and northern (or rather the eastern and western) harbours of King Attalus II. At length the debt of gratitude to the Romans was paid by King Attalus III., who died in the year 133 B.C., and left by testament the whole of his dominions to the benefactors of his house. And now the '*Province of Asia*' appears for the first time as a new and significant term in the history of the world. The newly acquired possession was placed under a prætor, and ultimately a pro-consul.[5] The letters and speeches of Cicero make us familiar with the names of more than one who enjoyed this distinction. One was the orator's brother, Quintus ; another was Flaccus, whose conduct as governor he defended before the Senate. Some slight changes in the extent of the province may be traced. Pamphylia was withdrawn from this jurisdiction. Rhodes lost her continental possessions, and Caria was added to Asia, while Lycia was declared independent. The boundary on the side of Phrygia is not easily determined, and was probably variable.[6] But enough has been said to give a general idea of what is meant in the New Testament by that '*Asia*,' which St. Paul attempted to enter (Acts xvi. 6), after passing through Phrygia and Galatia ; which St. Peter addressed in his First Epistle (1 Pet. i. 1), along with Pontus, Cappadocia, Galatia, and

[1] In the first book of Maccabees (viii. 6) we find Antiochus the Great called by this title. And even after his successors were driven beyond the Taurus by the Romans, we see it retained by them, as the title of 'King of France' was retained by our own monarchs until a very recent period. See 1 Macc. xi. 13, xii. 39, xiii. 32 ; 2 Macc. iii. 3.

[2] The case of Mysia, in consequence of the difficulties of Acts xvi. 7, 8, will be examined particularly, when we come to this part of St. Paul's journey.

[3] Thus Iconium, Lystra, and Derbe were probably once in 'Asia.' See below, under Galatia.

[4] Pp. 158, 159. Another Scripture city, the Philadelphia of Rev. i. 11, iii.

7, was also built by Attalus II. (Philadelphus).

[5] We learn from Acts xix. 38 — 'there are proconsuls (deputies)'— that it was a proconsular or senatorial province. The important distinction between the emperor's and the senate's provinces has been carefully stated in Chap. V. pp. 115–117. The incidental proof in the Acts is confirmed by Strabo and Dio, who tell us that Augustus made Asia a proconsular province.

[6] Hence we find both the sacred and heathen writers of the period sometimes including Phrygia in Asia and sometimes excluding it. In 1 Pet. i. 1 it seems to be included; in Acts ii. 9, 10, xvi. 6, it is expressly excluded.

Bithynia; and which embraced the 'seven churches' (Rev. i. 11) whose angels are mentioned in the Revelation of St. John.

II. BITHYNIA.—Next to Asia, both in proximity of situation and in the order of its establishment, was the province of Bithynia. Nor were the circumstances very different under which these two provinces passed under the Roman sceptre. As a new dynasty established itself after the death of Alexander on the north-eastern shores of the Ægean, so an older dynasty secured its independence at the western edge of the Black Sea. Nicomedes I. was the king who invited the Gauls with whom Attalus I. had to contend : and as Attalus III., the last of the House of Pergamus, paid his debt to the Romans by making them his heirs, so the last of the Bithynian House, Nicomedes III., left his kingdom as a legacy to the same power in the year 75. It received some accessions on the east after the defeat of Mithridates ; and in this condition we find it in the list given by Dio of the provinces of Augustus ; the debatable land between it and Asia being the district of Mysia, through which it is neither easy nor necessary to draw the exact frontier-line.[1] Stretching inland from the shores of the Propontis and Bosphorus, beyond the lakes near the cities of Nicæa and Nicomedia, to the upper ravines of the Sangarius, and the snowy range of Mount Olympus, it was a province rich in all the changes of beauty and grandeur. Its history is as varied as its scenery, if we trace it from the time when Hannibal was an exile at the court of Prusias,[2] to the establishment of Othman's Mahommedan capital in the city which still bears that monarch's name. It was Hadrian's favourite province, and many monuments remain of that emperor's partiality.[3] But we cannot say more of it without leaving our proper subject. We have no reason to believe that St. Paul ever entered it, though once he made the attempt.[4] Except the passing mention of Bithynia in this and one other place,[5] it has no connection with the apostolic writings. The first great passage of its ecclesiastical history is found in the correspondence of Trajan with its governor Pliny, concerning the persecution of the Christians. The second is the meeting of the first general Council, when the Nicene Creed was drawn up on the banks of the Lake Ascanius.

III. PAMPHYLIA.—This province has been already mentioned (Chap. VI.) as one of the regions traversed by St. Paul in his first missionary journey. But though its physical features have been described, its political limits have not been determined. The true

---

[1] See below, on Acts xvi. 7, 8.

[2] The town of *Broussa* reminds us of another illustrious African exile, Abd-el-Kader, who since the earthquake (after visiting Paris) has been permitted to withdraw to Damascus (1855).

[3] It was the birthplace of his favourite Antinous; and coins are extant which illustrate this feeling. Hadrian took it from the senate, and placed it under his own jurisdiction. But when St. Paul passed this way, it was under the senate, as may be proved by coins both of the reign of Claudius and subsequent dates.

[4] Acts xvi. 7.

[5] 1 Pet. i. 1.

Pamphylia of the earliest writers is simply the plain which borders the Bay of Attaleia, and which, as we have said (p. 127), retreats itself like a bay into the mountains. How small and insignificant this territory was, may be seen from the records of the Persian war, to which Herodotus says that it sent only thirty ships; while Lycia, on one side, contributed fifty, and Cilicia, on the other, a hundred. Nor do we find the name invested with any wider significance, till we approach the frontier of the Roman period. A singular dispute between Antiochus and the king of Pergamus, as to whether Pamphylia was really within or beyond Mount Taurus, was decided by the Romans in favour of their ally.[1] This could only be effected by a generous inclusion of a good portion of the mountainous country within the range of this geographical term. Henceforward, if not before, Pamphylia comprehended some considerable part of what was anciently called Pisidia. We have seen that the Romans united it to the kingdom of Asia. It was, therefore, part of the province of Asia at the death of Attalus. It is difficult to trace the steps by which it was detached from that province. We find it (along with certain districts of Asia) included in the military jurisdiction of Cicero, when he was governor of Cilicia.[2] It is spoken of as a separate province in the reign of Augustus.[3] Its boundary on the Pisidian side, or in the direction of Phrygia,[4] must be left indeterminate. Pisidia was included in this province : but, again, Pisidia is itself indeterminate : and we have good reasons for believing that Antioch in Pisidia was really under the governor of Galatia. Cilicia was contiguous to Pamphylia on the east. Lycia was a separate region on the west, first as an appendage to Rhodes[5] in the time of the republic, and then as a free state under the earliest emperors; but about the very time when Paul was travelling in these countries, Claudius brought it within the provincial system, and united it to Pamphylia :[6] and inscriptions make us acquainted with a public officer who bore the title of 'Proconsul of Lycia and Pamphylia.'[7]

IV. GALATIA. — We now come to a political division of Asia Minor, which demands a more careful attention. Its sacred interest is greater than that of all the others, and its history is more peculiar. The Christians of Galatia were they who received the Apostle 'as if he had been an angel,'—who, 'if it had been possible, would have plucked out their eyes and given them to him,'—and then were 'so soon removed' by new teachers 'from him that called them, to another Gospel,'—who began to 'run well,' and then

[1] See p. 184.
[2] *Ep. ad Att.* v. 21.
[3] Dio Cassius tells us that the Pamphylian districts bestowed on Amyntas were restored by Augustus to their own province. The same author is referred to below (n. 6) for a change in the reign of Claudius.
[4] Pisidia was often reckoned as a part of Phrygia, under the name of 'Pisidian Phrygia.'

[5] See above, p. 184.
[6] This we have on the authority of Dio Cassius and Suetonius. The latter writer says, that about the same time Claudius made over to the senate the provinces of Macedonia and Achaia. Hence we find a *proconsul* at Corinth. Acts xviii. 12.
[7] At a later period Lycia was a distinct province, with Myra as its capital. See Chap. XXIII.

were hindered,—who were 'bewitched' by that zeal which compassed sea and land to make one proselyte,—and who were as ready, in the fervour of their party spirit, to 'bite and devour one another,' as they were willing to change their teachers and their gospels.[1] It is no mere fancy which discovers, in these expressions of St. Paul's Epistle, indications of the character of that remarkable race of mankind, which all writers, from Cæsar to Thierry, have described as susceptible of quick impressions and sudden changes, with a fickleness equal to their courage and enthusiasm, and a constant liability to that disunion which is the fruit of excessive vanity,—that race, which has not only produced one of the greatest nations of modern times,[2] but which, long before the Christian era, wandering forth from their early European seats, burnt Rome and pillaged Delphi, founded an empire in northern Italy more than co-extensive with Austrian Lombardy,[3] and another in Asia Minor, equal in importance to one of the largest pachalics.

For the '*Galatia*' of the New Testament was really the '*Gaul*' of the East. The 'Epistle to the Galatians' would more literally and more correctly be called the 'Epistle to the Gauls.' When Livy, in his account of the Roman campaigns in Galatia, speaks of its inhabitants, he always calls them 'Gauls.'[4] When the Greek historians speak of the inhabitants of ancient France, the word they use is 'Galatians.'[5] The two terms are merely the Greek and Latin forms of the same 'barbarian' appellation.[6]

That emigration of the Gauls, which ended in the settlement in Asia Minor, is less famous than those which led to the disasters in Italy and Greece ; but it is, in fact, identical with the latter of these two emigrations, and its results were more permanent. The warriors who roamed over the Cevennes, or by the banks of the Garonne, reappear on the Halys and at the base of Mount Dindymus. They exchange the superstitions of Druidism for the ceremonies of the worship of Cybele. The very name of the chief Galatian tribe is one with which we are familiar in the earliest history of France ; and Jerome says that, in his own day, the language spoken at Ancyra was almost identical with that of Trêves.[7] The Galatians were a stream from that torrent of barbarians which poured into Greece in the third century before our era, and which recoiled in confusion from the cliffs of Delphi. Some tribes had previously separated from the main army, and penetrated into Thrace. There

---

[1] Gal. iv. 15, i. 6, v. 7, iii. 1, i. 7, v. 15.

[2] The French travellers (as Tournefort and Texier) seem to write with patriotic enthusiasm when they touch Galatia; and we have found our best materials in Thierry's history.

[3] This was written before 1859.

[4] The country of the Galatians was sometimes called Gallogræcia.

[5] Some have even thought that the word translated 'Galatia' in 2 Tim. iv. 10, means the country commonly called Gaul.

[6] And we may add that 'Galatæ' and 'Keltæ' are the same word. See Arnold's *Rome*, i. 522.

[7] It is very likely that there was some Teutonic element in these emigrating tribes, but it is hardly possible now to distinguish it from the Keltic. The converging lines of distinct nationalities become more faint as we ascend towards the point where they meet. Thierry considers the Tolistoboii, whose leader was Lutarius (Luther or Clothair?), to have been a Teutonic tribe.

they were joined by certain of the fugitives, and together they appeared on the coasts, which are separated by a narrow arm of the sea from the rich plains and valleys of Bithynia. The wars with which that kingdom was harassed, made their presence acceptable. Nicomedes was the Vortigern of Asia Minor : and the two Gaulish chieftains, Leonor and Lutar, may be fitly compared to the two legendary heroes of the Anglo-Saxon invasion. Some difficulties occurred in the passage of the Bosphorus, which curiously contrast with the easy voyages of our piratic ancestors. But once established in Asia Minor, the Gauls lost no time in spreading over the whole peninsula with their arms and devastation. In their first crossing over we have compared them to the Saxons. In their first occupation they may be more fitly compared to the Danes. For they were a movable army rather than a nation,—encamping, marching, and plundering at will. They stationed themselves on the site of ancient Troy, and drove their chariots in the plain of the Cayster. They divided nearly the whole peninsula among their three tribes. They levied tribute on cities, and even on kings. The wars of the East found them various occupation. They hired themselves out as mercenary soldiers. They were the royal guards of the kings of Syria, and the mamelukes of the Ptolemies in Egypt.[1]

The surrounding monarchs gradually curtailed their power, and repressed them within narrower limits. First Antiochus Soter drove the Tectosages,[2] and then Eumenes drove the Trocmi and Tolistobii, into the central district which afterwards became Galatia. Their territory was definitely marked out and surrounded by the other states of Asia Minor, and they retained a geographical position similar to that of Hungary in the midst of its German and Sclavonic neighbours. By degrees they coalesced into a number of small confederate states, and ultimately into one united kingdom.[3] Successive circumstances brought them into contact with the Romans in various ways ; first, by a religious embassy sent from Rome to obtain peaceful possession of the sacred image of Cybele ; secondly, by the campaign of Manlius, who reduced their power and left them a nominal independence ; and then through the period of hazardous alliance with the rival combatants in the Civil Wars. The first Deiotarus was made king by Pompey, fled before Cæsar at the battle of Pharsalia, and was defended before the conqueror by Cicero, in a speech which still remains to us. The second Deiotarus, like his father, was Cicero's friend, and took charge of his son and nephew during the Cilician campaign. Amyntas, who succeeded him, owed his power to Antony,[4] but prudently went over to Au-

---

[1] Even in the time of Julius Cæsar, we find four hundred Gauls (Galatians), who had previously been part of Cleopatra's body-guard, given for the same purpose to Herod. Joseph. *War*, xx. 3.

[2] His appellation of Soter or 'the Saviour' was derived from this victory.

[3] This does not seem to have been effectually the case till after the campaign of Manlius. The nation was for some time divided into four tetrarchies. Deiotarus was the first sole ruler ; first as tetrarch, then as king.

[4] He received some parts of Lycaonia and Pamphylia in addition to Galatia Proper. See above, Chap. I. p. 19.

gustus in the battle of Actium. At the death of Amyntas, Augustus made some modifications in the extent of Galatia, and placed it under a governor. It was now a province, reaching from the borders of Asia and Bithynia to the neighbourhood of Iconium, Lystra, and Derbe, 'cities of Lycaonia.' [1]

Henceforward, like the Western Gaul, this territory was a part of the Roman Empire, though retaining the traces of its history in the character and language of its principal inhabitants. There was this difference, however, between the Eastern and the Western Gaul, that the latter was more rapidly and more completely assimilated to Italy. It passed from its barbarian to its Roman state, without being subjected to any intermediate civilisation. [2] The Gauls of the East, on the other hand, had long been familiar with the Greek language and the Greek culture. St. Paul's Epistle was written in Greek. The cotemporary inscriptions of the province are usually in the same language. The Galatians themselves are frequently called Gallo-Græcians; [3] and many of the inhabitants of the province must have been of pure Grecian origin. Another section of the population, the early Phrygians, were probably numerous, but in a lower and more degraded position. The presence of great numbers of Jews [4] in the province, implies that it was, in some respects, favourable for traffic; and it is evident that the district must have been constantly intersected by the course of caravans from Armenia, the Hellespont, and the South. [5] The Roman Itineraries inform us of the lines of communication between the great towns near the Halys and the other parts of Asia Minor. These circumstances are closely connected with the spread of the Gospel, and we shall return to them again when we describe St. Paul's first reception in Galatia.

V. PONTUS.—The last independent dynasties in the north of the Peninsula have hitherto appeared as friendly or subservient to the Roman power. Asia and Bithynia were voluntarily ceded by Attalus and Nicomedes; and Galatia, on the death of Amyntas, quietly fell into the station of a province. But when we advance still further to the East, we are reminded of a monarch who presented a

[1] The Pamphylian portion was removed (see above), but the Lycaonian remained. Thus we find Pliny reckoning the Lystreni in Galatia, though he seems to imply elsewhere that the immediate neighbourhood of Iconium was in Asia. It is therefore quite possible, so far as geographical difficulties are concerned, that the Christian communities in the neighbourhood of Lystra might be called 'Churches of Galatia.' We think, however, as will be shown in the Appendix, that other difficulties are decisive against the view there mentioned.

[2] The immediate neighbourhood of Marseilles, which was thoroughly imbued with a knowledge of Greek, must of course be excepted.

[3] See above, p. 187, n. 4.

[4] See in Josephus (*Ant.* xvi. 6) the letter which Augustus wrote in favour of the Jews of Ancyra, and which was inscribed on a pillar in the temple of Cæsar. We shall have occasion hereafter to mention the 'Monumentum Ancyranum.'

[5] Gordium, one of the minor towns near the western frontier, was a considerable emporium. So was Tavium, the capital of the Eastern Galatians, the Trocmi, who dwelt beyond the Halys. The Tolistoboii were the western tribe, near the Sangarius, with Pessinus as their capital. The chief town of the Tectosages in the centre, and the metropolis of the nation, was Ancyra.

formidable and protracted opposition to Rome. The war with Mithridates was one of the most serious wars in which the Republic was
ever engaged; and it was not till after a long struggle that Pompey
brought the kingdom of Pontus under the Roman yoke.   In placing
Pontus among the provinces of Asia Minor at this exact point of
St. Paul's life, we are (strictly speaking) guilty of an anachronism.
For long after the western portion of the empire of Mithridates was
united partly with Bithynia and partly with Galatia,[1] the region
properly called Pontus[2] remained under the government of independent chieftains.   Before the Apostle's death, however, it was
really made a province by Nero.[3] Its last king was that Polemo II.
who was alluded to at the beginning of this work, as the contemptible husband of one of Herod's grand-daughters.[4] In himself he is
quite unworthy of such particular notice, but he demands our attention, not only because, as the last independent king in Asia Minor,
he stands at one of the turning points of history, but also because,
through his marriage with Berenice, he must have had some connection with the Jewish population of Pontus, and therefore probably with the spread of the Gospel on the shores of the Euxine.
We cannot forget that Jews of Pontus were at Jerusalem on the day
of Pentecost,[5] that the Jewish Christians of Pontus were addressed
by St. Peter in his first epistle,[6] and that ' a Jew born in Pontus '[7]
became one of the best and most useful associates of the Apostle of
the Gentiles.

VI. CAPPADOCIA.—Crossing the country southwards from the
birthplace of Aquila towards that of St. Paul, we traverse the wide
and varied region which formed the province of Cappadocia, intermediate between Pontus and Cilicia.   The period of its provincial
existence began in the reign of Tiberius.   Its last king was Archelaus,[8] the cotemporary of the Jewish tetrarch of the same name.[9]
Extending from the frontier of Galatia to the river Euphrates, and
bounded on the south by the chain of Taurus, it was the largest
province of Asia Minor.   Some of its cities are celebrated in eccle-

---

[1] See above, under Pamphylia, for
the addition to that province. A tract
of country, near the Halys, henceforward called Pontus Galaticus, was
added to the kingdom of Deiotarus.

[2] Originally, this district near the
Euxine was considered a part of Cappadocia, and called ' Cappadocia on
the sea (Pontus).' The name Pontus
gradually came into use, with the rising
power of the ancestors of Mithridates
the Great.

[3] It is probably impossible to determine the boundary which was ultimately arranged between the two contiguous provinces of Pontus and Cappadocia, when the last of the independent
monarchs had ceased to reign.   In the
division of Constantine, Pontus formed
two provinces, one called Helenopontus

in honour of his mother, the other still
retaining the name of Pontus Polemo-
niacus.

[4] P. 19, and p 20, n. 4. In or about
the year 60 A.D. we find Berenice again
with Agrippa in Judæa, on the occasion
of St. Paul's defence at Cæsarea. Acts
xxv., xxvi. It is probable that she
was with Polemo in Pontus about the
year 52, when St. Paul was travelling
in the neighbourhood.

[5] Acts ii. 9.   [6] 1 Pet. i. 1.

[7] Acts xviii. 2.

[8] He was made king by Antony, and
fifty years afterwards, was summoned
to Rome by Tiberius, who had been
offended by some disrespect shown to
himself in the island of Rhodes.

[9] Matt. ii. 22.

siastical history.[1] But in the New Testament it is only twice alluded to, once in the Acts,[2] and once in the Epistles.[3]

VII. CILICIA.—A single province yet remains, in one respect the most interesting of all, for its chief city was the Apostle's native town. For this reason the reader's attention was invited long ago to its geography and history.[4] It is therefore unnecessary to dwell upon them further. We need not go back to the time when Servilius destroyed the robbers in the mountains, and Pompey the pirates on the coast.[5] And enough has been said of the conspicuous period of its provincial condition, when Cicero came down from Cappadocia through the great pass of Mount Taurus,[6] and the letters of his correspondents in Rome were forwarded from Tarsus to his camp on the Pyramus. Nearly all the light we possess concerning the fortunes of Roman Cilicia is concentrated on that particular time. We know the names of hardly any of its later governors. One of the few allusions to its provincial condition about the time of Claudius and Nero, which we can adduce from any ancient writer, is that passage in the Acts, where Felix is described as inquiring 'of what province' St. Paul was. The use of the strict political term[7] informs us that it was a separate province ; but the term itself is not so explicit as to enable us to state whether the province was under the jurisdiction of the Senate or the Emperor.[8]

With this last division of the Heptarchy of Asia Minor we are brought to the starting-point of St. Paul's second missionary journey. Cilicia is contiguous to Syria, and indeed is more naturally connected with it than with the rest of Asia Minor.[9] We might illustrate this connection from the letters of Cicero ; but it is more to our purpose to remark that the Apostolic Decree, recently enacted at Jerusalem, was addressed to the Gentile Christians 'in Antioch, and Syria, and Cilicia,'[10] and that Paul and Silas travelled 'through Syria and Cilicia'[11] in the early part of their progress.

This second missionary journey originated in a desire expressed by Paul to Barnabas, that they should revisit all the cities where they had preached the Gospel and founded churches.[12] He felt that he was not called to spend a peaceful, though laborious, life at Antioch, but that his true work was ' far off among the Gentiles.'[13] He knew that his campaigns were not ended,—that, as the soldier of

[1] Especially Nyssa, Nazianzus, and Neocæsarea, the cities of the three Gregories, and Cæsarea, the city of Basil,—to say nothing of Tyana and Samosata.

[2] Acts ii. 9.

[3] 1 Pet. i. 1

[4] Pp. 17–21. See also 40, 41.

[5] P. 17.

[6] See below, pp. 198, 199.

[7] Ἐπαρχία. Acts xxiii. 34, the only passage where the word occurs in the New Testament. For the technical meaning of the term, see above, p. 116, n. 5.

[8] We should be disposed to infer, from a passage in Agrippa's speech to the Jews (Joseph. *War*, ii. 16, 4), where he says that Cilicia, as well as Bithynia, Pamphylia, &c., was ' kept tributary to the Romans without an army,' that it was one of the Senate's provinces. Other evidence, however, tends the other way, especially an inscription found at Caerleon in Monmouthshire. For fuller details we must refer to the larger editions.

[9] See p. 87, comparing Acts ix. 30 with Gal. i. 21.

[10] Acts xv. 23.

[11] Acts xv. 41.

[12] Acts xv. 36.

[13] Acts xxii. 21.

Jesus Christ, he must not rest from his warfare, but must 'endure hardness,' that he might please Him who had called him.[1] As a careful physician, he remembered that they, whose recovery from sin had been begun, might be in danger of relapse; or, to use another metaphor, and to adopt the poetical language of the Old Testament, he said,—' Come, let us get up early to the vineyards : let us see if the vine flourish.'[2] The words actually recorded as used by St. Paul on this occasion, are these :—' Come, let us turn back and visit our brethren in every city, where we have announced the word of the Lord, and let us see how they fare.'[3] We notice here, for the first time, a trace of that tender solicitude concerning his converts, that earnest longing to behold their faces, which appears in the letters which he wrote afterwards, as one of the most remarkable, and one of the most attractive, features of his character. Paul was the speaker, and not Barnabas. The feelings of Barnabas might not be so deep, nor his anxiety so urgent.[4] Paul thought doubtless of the Pisidians and Lycaonians, as he thought afterwards at Athens and Corinth of the Thessalonians, from whom he had been lately ' taken,—in presence not in heart,—endeavouring to see their face with great desire—night and day praying exceedingly that he might see their face, and might perfect that which was lacking in their faith.'[5] He was ' not ignorant of Satan's devices.'[6] He feared lest by any means the Tempter had tempted them, and his labour had been in vain.[7] He ' stood in doubt of them,' and desired to be 'present with them ' once more.[8] His wish was to revisit every city where converts had been made. We are reminded here of the importance of continuing a religious work when once begun. We have had the institution of presbyters,[9] and of councils,[10] brought before us in the sacred narrative ; and now we have an example of that system of church visitation, of the happy effects of which we have still some experience, when we see weak resolutions strengthened, and expiring faith rekindled, in confirmations at home, or in missionary settlements abroad.

This plan, however, of a combined visitation of the churches was marred by an outbreak of human infirmity. The two apostolic friends were separated from each other by a quarrel, which proved that they were indeed, as they had lately told the Lystrians, ' men of like passions ' with others.[11] Barnabas was unwilling to undertake the journey unless he were accompanied by his relation Mark. Paul could not consent to the companionship of one who ' departed

---

[1] 2 Tim. ii. 3, 4.

[2] Cant. vii. 12, quoted by Matthew Henry. See his excellent remarks on the whole passage.

[3] ' Let us go *now at last* ' would be a correct translation. The words seem to express something like impatience, especially when we compare it with the words ' after some days ' which precede. The tender feeling implied in the phrase rendered ' how they do ' fully justifies what we have said in the text.

[4] We might almost be inclined to suspect that Paul had previously urged the same proposal on Barnabas, and that he had hesitated to comply.

[5] 1 Thess. ii. 17, iii. 10.

[6] 2 Cor. ii. 11.

[7] 1 Thess. iii. 5.

[8] Gal. iv. 20.

[9] Acts xiv. 23. See pp. 157, 188, and Chap. XIII.

[10] Acts xv. See Chap. VII.

[11] Acts xiv. 15.

from them from Pamphylia, and went not with them to the work:'[1] and neither of them could yield his opinion to the other. This quarrel was much more closely connected with personal feelings than that which had recently occurred between St. Peter and St. Paul,[2] and it was proportionally more violent. There is little doubt that severe words were spoken on the occasion. It is unwise to be over-anxious to dilute the words of Scripture, and to exempt even Apostles from blame. By such criticism we lose much of the instruction which the honest record of their lives was intended to convey. We are taught by this scene at Antioch, that a good work may be blessed by God, though its agents are encompassed with infirmity, and that changes, which are violent in their beginnings, may be overruled for the best results. Without attempting to balance too nicely the faults on either side, our simplest course is to believe that, as in most quarrels, there was blame with both. Paul's natural disposition was impetuous and impatient, easily kindled to indignation, and (possibly) overbearing. Barnabas had shown his weakness when he yielded to the influence of Peter and the Judaisers.[3] The remembrance of the indirect censure he then received may have been perpetually irritated by the consciousness that his position was becoming daily more and more subordinate to that of the friend who rebuked him. Once he was spoken of as chief of those ' prophets at Antioch,'[4] among whom Saul was the last : now his name was scarcely heard, except when he was mentioned as the companion of Paul.[5] In short, this is one of those quarrels in which, by placing ourselves in imagination on the one side and the other, we can alternately justify both, and easily see that the purest Christian zeal, when combined with human weakness and partiality, may have led to the misunderstanding. How could Paul consent to take with him a companion who would really prove an embarrassment and a hindrance ? Such a task as that of spreading the Gospel of God in a hostile world needs a resolute will and an undaunted courage. And the work is too sacred to be put in jeopardy by any experiments.[6] Mark had been tried once and found wanting. ' No man, having put his hand to the plough, and looking back, is fit for the kingdom of God.'[7] And Barnabas would not be without strong arguments to defend the justice of his claims. It was hard to expect him to resign his interest in one who had cost him much anxiety and many prayers. His dearest wish was to see his young kinsman approving himself as a missionary of Christ. Now, too, he had been won back to a willing obedience,—he had come from his home at Jerusalem,—he was ready now to face all the difficulties

---

[1] Acts xv. 38, with xiii. 13. See pp. 128, 129.

[2] Pp. 177–179.

[3] Gal. ii. 13. P. 178.

[4] Acts xiii. Pp. 108, 109. Moreover, as a friend suggests, St. Paul was under personal obligations to Barnabas for introducing him to the Apostles (Acts ix. 27), and the feelings of Barnabas would be deeply hurt if he thought his friendship slighted.

[5] See p. 120.

[6] A timid companion in the hour of danger is one of the greatest evils. Matthew Henry quotes Prov. xxv. 19 : ' Confidence in an unfaithful man in time of trouble, is like a broken tooth and like a foot out of joint.'

[7] Luke ix. 62.

and dangers of the enterprise. To repel him in the moment of his repentance was surely 'to break a bruised reed' and to 'quench the smoking flax.'[1]

It is not difficult to understand the obstinacy with which each of the disputants, when his feelings were once excited, clung to his opinion as to a sacred truth. The only course which now remained was to choose two different paths and to labour independently; and the Church saw the humiliating spectacle of the separation of its two great missionaries to the Heathen. We cannot, however, suppose that Paul and Barnabas parted, like enemies, in anger and hatred. It is very likely that they made a deliberate and amicable arrangement to divide the region of their first mission between them, Paul taking the continental, and Barnabas the insular, part of the proposed visitation.[2] Of this at least we are certain, that the quarrel was overruled by Divine Providence to a good result. One stream of missionary labour had been divided, and the regions blessed by the waters of life were proportionally multiplied. St. Paul speaks of Barnabas afterwards[3] as of an Apostle actively engaged in his Master's service. We know nothing of the details of his life beyond the moment of his sailing for Cyprus; but we may reasonably attribute to him not only the confirming of the first converts,[4] but the full establishment of the Church in his native island. At Paphos the impure idolatry gradually retreated before the presence of Christianity; and Salamis, where the tomb of the Christian Levite[5] is shown,[6] has earned an eminent place in Christian history, through the writings of its bishop, Epiphanius.[7] Mark, too, who began his career as a 'minister' of the Gospel in this island,[8] justified the good opinion of his kinsman. Yet, the severity of Paul may have been of eventual service to his character, in leading him to feel more deeply the serious importance of the work he had undertaken. And the time came when Paul himself acknowledged, with affectionate tenderness, not only that he had again become his fellow-labourer,'[9] but that he was 'profitable to the ministry,'[10] and one of the causes of his own 'comfort.'[11]

It seems that Barnabas was the first to take his departure. The feeling of the majority of the Church was evidently with St. Paul, for when he had chosen Silas for his companion and was ready to begin his journey, he was specially 'commended by the brethren to

---

[1] Matt. xii. 20.

[2] If Barnabas visited Salamis and Paphos, and if Paul, after passing through Derbe, Lystra, and Iconium, went as far as Antioch in Pisidia (see below), the whole circuit of the proposed visitation was actually accomplished, for it does not appear that any converts had been made at Perga and Attaleia.

[3] 1 Cor. ix. 6.: whence also it appears that Barnabas, like St. Paul, supported himself by the labour of his hands.

[4] Paul took the copy of the Apostolic Decree into Cilicia. If the Judaising

tendency had shown itself in Cyprus, Barnabas would still be able to refer to the decision of the council, and Mark would stand in the same relation to him as a witness in which Silas did to Paul.

[5] Acts iv. 36.

[6] MS. note from Capt. Graves, R.N.

[7] The name of this celebrated father has been given to one of the promontories of the island, the ancient Acamas.

[8] Acts xiii. 5.

[9] Philemon 24.

[10] 2 Tim. iv. 11. See p. 129, n. 4

[11] Col. iv. 10, 11.

the grace of God.'¹ The visitation of Cyprus having now been undertaken by others, his obvious course was not to go by sea in the direction of Perga or Attaleia,² but to travel by the Eastern passes directly to the neighbourhood of Iconium. It appears, moreover, that he had an important work to accomplish in Cilicia. The early fortunes of Christianity in that province were closely bound up with the city of Antioch and the personal labours of St. Paul. When he withdrew from Jerusalem, 'three years' after his conversion, his residence for some time was in 'the regions of Syria and Cilicia.'³ He was at Tarsus in the course of that residence, when Barnabas first brought him to Antioch.⁴ The churches founded by the Apostle in his native province must often have been visited by him; for it is far easier to travel from Antioch to Tarsus, than from Antioch to Jerusalem, or even from Tarsus to Iconium. Thus the religious movements in the Syrian metropolis penetrated into Cilicia. The same great 'prophet' had been given to both, and the Christians in both were bound together by the same feelings and the same doctrines. When the Judaising agitators came to Antioch, the result was anxiety and perplexity, not only in Syria, but also in Cilicia. This is nowhere literally stated; but it can be legitimately inferred. We are, indeed, only told that certain men came down with false teaching from Judæa to Antioch.⁵ But the Apostolic Decree is addressed to 'the Gentiles of *Cilicia*'⁶ as well as those of Antioch, thus implying that the Judaising spirit, with its mischievous consequences, had been at work beyond the frontier of Syria. And, doubtless, the attacks on St. Paul's apostolic character had accompanied the attack on apostolic truth,⁷ and a new fulfilment of the proverb was nearly realised, that a prophet in his own country is without honour. He had, therefore, no ordinary work to accomplish as he went 'through Syria and Cilicia, confirming the churches;'⁸ and it must have been with much comfort and joy that he was able to carry with him a document, emanating from the Apostles at Jerusalem, which justified the doctrine he had taught, and accredited his personal character. Nor was he alone as the bearer of this letter, but Silas was with him also, ready 'to tell the same things by mouth.'⁹ It is a cause for thankfulness that God put it into the heart of Silas to 'abide still at Antioch'¹⁰ when Judas returned to Jerusalem, and to accompany St. Paul¹¹ on his northward journey. For when the Cilician Christians saw their countryman arrive without his companion Barnabas, whose name was coupled with his own

¹ Acts xv. 40.
² If no other causes had occurred to determine the direction of his journey, there might be no vessel at Antioch or Seleucia bound for Pamphylia; a circumstance not always sufficiently taken into account by those who have written on St. Paul's voyages.
³ Gal. i. 21; Acts ix. 30. See pp. 87, 88.
⁴ Acts xi. 25. See p. 98.
⁵ Acts xv. 1. ⁶ Acts xv. 23.
⁷ Pp. 166, 173.

⁸ Acts xv. 41. The work of allaying the Judaising spirit in Cilicia would require some time. Much might be accomplished during the residence at Antioch (xv. 36), which might very well include journeys to Tarsus. But we are distinctly told that the churches of Cilicia were 'confirmed' by St. Paul, when he was on his way to those of Lycaonia.
⁹ Acts xv. 27.
¹⁰ Or to return thither. See p. 177. n. 2.
¹¹ Acts xv. 40,

in the Apostolic letter,[1] their confidence might have been shaken,
occasion might have been given to the enemies of the truth to
slander St. Paul, had not Silas been present, as one of those who
were authorised to testify that both Paul and Barnabas were 'men
who had hazarded their lives for the name of our Lord Jesus
Christ.'[2]

Where 'the churches' were, which he 'confirmed' on his journey, — in what particular cities of 'Syria and Cilicia,' — we are
not informed. After leaving Antioch by the bridge over the Orontes,[3] he would cross Mount Amanus by the gorge which was anciently called the 'Syrian Gates,' and is now known as the Beilan
Pass.[4] Then he would come to Alexandria and Issus, two cities
that were monuments of the Macedonian conqueror; one as retaining his name, the other as the scene of his victory. After entering
the Cilician plain, he may have visited Adana, Ægæ, or Mopsuetia,
three of the conspicuous cities on the old Roman roads.[5] With all
these places St. Paul must have been more or less familiar: probably there were Christians in all of them, anxiously waiting for the
Decree, and ready to receive the consolation it was intended to
bring. And one other city must certainly have been visited. If
there were churches anywhere in Cilicia, there must have been one
at Tarsus. It was the metropolis of the province; Paul had resided
there, perhaps for some years, since the time of his conversion; and
if he loved his native place well enough to speak of it with something like pride to the Roman officer at Jerusalem,[6] he could not
be indifferent to its religious welfare. Among the 'Gentiles of
Cilicia,' to whom the letter which he carried was addressed, the
Gentiles of Tarsus had no mean place in his affections. And his
heart must have overflowed with thankfulness, if, as he passed
through the streets which had been familiar to him since his childhood, he knew that many households were around him where the
Gospel had come 'not in word only but in power,' and the relations between husband and wife, parent and child, master and slave,
had been purified and sanctified by Christian love. No doubt the
city still retained all the aspect of the cities of that day, where art
and amusement were consecrated to a false religion. The symbols
of idolatry remained in the public places,—statues, temples, and
altars,—and the various 'objects of devotion,' which in all Greek
towns, as well as in Athens (Acts xvii. 23), were conspicuous on

---

[1] Acts xv. 25.　　　[2] Acts xv. 26.

[3] See the description of ancient
Antioch above, Chap. IV. pp. 100, 101;
also p. 111.

[4] The 'Syrian Gates' are the entrance into Cilicia from Syria, as the
'Cilician Gates' are from Cappadocia.
The latter pass, however, is by far the
grander and more important of the two.
Intermediate between these two, in the
angle where Taurus and Amanus meet,
is the pass into Syria by which Darius
fled after the battle of Issus. Both
entrances fom Syria into Cilicia are

alluded to by Cicero, as well as the
great entrance from Cappadocia.

[5] If the Intineraries are examined and
compared together, the Roman roads
will be observed to diffuse themselves
among these different towns in the
Cilician plain, and then to come together again at the bend of the bay,
before they enter the Syrian Gates.
Mopsuetia and Adana were in the direct road from Issus to Tarsus; Ægæ
was on the coast-road to Soli. Baiæ
also was an important town, situated
to the S. of Issus.　　　[6] Acts xxi. 39.

every side. But the silent revolution was begun. Some families had already turned 'from idols to serve the living and true God.'[1] The 'dumb idols' to which, as Gentiles, they had been 'carried away even as they were led,'[2] had been recognised as 'nothing in the world,'[3] and been 'cast to the moles and to the bats.'[4] The homes which had once been decorated with the emblems of a vain mythology, were now bright with the better ornaments of faith, hope, and love. And the Apostle of the Gentiles rejoiced in looking forward to the time when the grace which had been triumphant in the household should prevail against principalities and powers,— when 'every knee should bow at the name of Jesus, and every tongue confess that He is Lord, to the glory of God the Father.'[5]

But it has pleased God that we should know more of the details of early Christianity in the wilder and remoter regions of Asia Minor. To these regions the footsteps of St. Paul were turned after he had accomplished the work of confirming the churches in Syria and Cilicia. The task now before him was the visitation of the churches he had formed in conjunction with Barnabas. We proceed to follow him in his second journey across Mount Taurus.

The vast mountain-barrier which separates the sunny plains of Cilicia and Pamphylia from the central table-land, has frequently been mentioned.[6] On the former journey[7] St. Paul travelled from the Pamphylian plain to Antioch in Pisidia, and thence by Iconium to Lystra and Derbe. His present course across the mountains was more to the eastward; and the last-mentioned cities were visited

---

[1] 1 Thess. i. 9.

[2] 1 Cor. xii. 2.

[3] 1 Cor. viii. 4.

[4] Isai. ii. 20. These remarks have been suggested by a recent discovery of much interest at Tarsus. In a mound which had formerly rested against a portion of the city wall, since removed, was discovered a large collection of terracotta figures and lamps. At first these were thought to be a sherd-wreck, or the refuse of some Ceramicus or pottery-work. But, on observing that the lamps had been used, and that the earthenware gods (*Di fictiles*) bore no trace of having been rejected because of defective workmanship, but, on the contrary, had evidently been used, it has been imagined that these terracottas must have been thrown away, as connected with idolatry, on the occasion of some conversion to Christianity. The figures are such as these,—a head of Pan, still showing the mortar by which it was set up in some garden or vineyard; the boy Mercury; Cybele, Jupiter, Ceres crowned with corn, Apollo with rays, a lion devouring a bull (precisely similar to that engraved, p. 25), with other symbols of general or local my-

thology. There are, moreover, some ears, legs, &c., which seem to have been votive offerings, and which, therefore, it would have been sacrilege to remove; and a great number of lamps or incense-burners, with a carbonaceous stain on them.

The date when these things were thrown 'to the moles and bats' seems to be ascertained by the dressing of the hair in one of the female figures, which is that of the period of the early emperors, as shown in busts of Domitia, or Julia, the wife of Titus, the same that is censured by the Roman satirist and by the Christian Apostle. Some of them are undoubtedly of an earlier period.

We owe the opportunity of seeing these remains, and the foregoing criticisms on them (by Mr. Abington, of Hanley, in Staffordshire), to the kindness of W. B. Barker, Esq., who was for many years a resident at Tarsus, and who has recently given much information on the history of Cilicia in his work entitled *Lares and Penates*.

[5] Phil. ii. 10, 11.

[6] Especially pp. 17, 40, 87, 129–134, 147, 157, 158.

[7] Acts xiii. 14.

first.   More passes than one lead up into Lycaonia and Cappadocia
through the chain of Taurus from Cilicia.[1] And it has been supposed[2] that the Apostle travelled through one of the minor passes,
which quits the lower plain at Pompeiopolis,[3] and enters the upland
plain of Iconium, not far from the conjectural site of Derbe.   But
there is no sufficient reason to suppose that he went by any other
than the ordinary road.   A traveller wishing to reach the Valais
conveniently from the banks of the Lago Maggiore would rather go
by the Simplon, than by the difficult path across the Monte Moro;
and there is one great pass in Asia Minor which may be called the
Simplon[4] of Mount Taurus, described as a rent or fissure in the
mountain-chain, extending from north to south through a distance
of eighty miles,[5] and known in ancient days by the name of the
' Cilician Gates,'—which has been, in all ages, the easiest and
most convenient entrance from the northern and central parts of the
peninsula to the level by the sea-shore, where the traveller pauses
before he enters Syria.   The securing of this pass was the greatest
cause of anxiety to Cyrus, when he marched into Babylonia to dethrone his brother.[6]   Through this gorge Alexander descended to
that Cilician plain, which has been finely described by a Greek historian as a theatre made by Nature's hand for the drama of great
battles.   Cicero followed in the steps of Alexander, as he tells his
friend Atticus in a letter written with characteristic vanity.   And
to turn to the centuries which have elapsed since the time of the
Apostles and the first Roman emperors: twice at least, this pass has
been the pivot on which the struggle for the throne of the East
seemed to turn,—once, in the war described by obscure historians,[7]
when a pretender at Antioch made the Taurus his defence against
the Emperor of Rome; and once in a war which we remember,
when a pretender at Alexandria fortified it and advanced beyond it
in his attempt to dethrone the Sultan.[8]   In the wars between the

---

[1] The principal passes are enumerated in the *Modern Traveller*.

[2] Wieseler thinks that this would be
the route adopted, because it leads
most directly to Derbe (Divlé). But,
in the first place, the site of this town
is very doubtful; and, secondly, the
shortest road across a mountain-chain
is not necessarily the best. The road
by the Cilician Gates was carefully
made and kept up, and enters the Lycaonian plain near where Derbe must
have been situated.

[3] For Pompeiopolis or Soli, see p.
17, and the note.

[4] Mr. Ainsworth points out some interesting particulars of resemblance
and contrast between the Alps and this
part of the Taurus.   *Travels and Researches in Asia Minor, &c.* (1842),
II. 80.

[5] Gen. Chesney in the *Euphrates Expedition*, i. 353.

[6] Mannert and Forbiger both think
that he went by a pass more to the
east; but the arguments of Mr. Ainsworth for the identity of Dana with
Tyana, and the coincidence of the route
of Cyrus with the ' Cilician Gates,'
appear to be conclusive.   *Travels in
the Track, &c.*, p. 40.

[7] The war between Severus and Pes-
cennius Niger.

[8] This was emphatically the case in
the first war between Mahomet Ali and
the Sultan, when Ibrahim Pasha crossed the Taurus and fought the battle
of Konieh, in December 1832.   In the
second war, the decisive battle was
fought at Nizib, in June 1839, further
to the East: but even then, while the
negotiations were pending, this pass
was the military boundary between the
opposing powers. See Mr. Ainsworth's
Travels and Researches, quoted below.
He was arrested in his journey by the

Crescent and the Cross, which have filled up much of the intervening period, this defile has decided the fate of many an army. The Greek historians of the first Saracen invasions describe it by a word, unknown to classical Greek, which denotes that when this passage (between Cappadocia and Cilicia) was secure, the frontier was closed. The Crusaders, shrinking from the remembrance of its precipices and dangers, called it by the more awful name of the ' Gates of Judas.'

Through this pass we conceive St. Paul to have travelled on his way from Cilicia to Lycaonia. And if we say that the journey was made in the spring of the year 51, we shall not deviate very far from the actual date.[1] By those who have never followed the Apostle's footsteps, the successive features of the scenery through which he passed may be compiled from the accounts of recent travellers, and arranged in the following order.[2]—After leaving Tarsus, the way ascends the valley of the Cydnus, which, for some distance, is nothing more than an ordinary mountain valley, with wooded eminences and tributary streams. Beyond the point where the road from Adana comes in from the right, the hills suddenly draw together and form a narrow pass, which has always been guarded by precipitous cliffs, and is now crowned by the ruins of a medieval castle. In some places the ravine contracts to a width of ten or twelve paces, leaving room for only one chariot to pass. It is an anxious place to any one in command of a military expedition. To one who is unburdened by such responsibility, the scene around is striking and impressive. A canopy of fir-trees is high overhead. Bare limestone cliffs rise above on either hand to an elevation of many hundred feet. The streams which descend towards the Cydnus are close by the wayside, and here and there undermine it or wash over it. When the higher and more distant of these streams are left behind, the road emerges upon an open and elevated region, 4,000 feet above the level of the sea. This space of high land may be considered as dividing the whole mountain journey into two parts. For when it is passed, the streams are seen to flow in a new direction. Not that we have attained the point where the highest land of Asia Minor[3] turns the waters north and south. The torrents which are seen descending to the right, are merely the tributaries of the Sarus, another river of Cilicia. The road is conducted northwards through this new ravine ;

battle of Nizib. For a slight notice of the two campaigns, see Yates' Egypt, I. xv. In the second volume (ch. v.) is a curious account of an interview with Ibrahim Pasha at Tarsus, in 1833, with notices of the surrounding country.

[1] We have no means of exactly determining either the year or the season. He left Corinth in the spring (Acts xviii. 21), 'after staying there a year and a half (Acts xviii. 11). He arrived, therefore, at Corinth in the autumn ; and probably, as we shall see, in the autumn of the year 52. Wieseler

calculates that a year might be occupied in the whole journey from Antioch through Asia Minor and Macedonia to Corinth. Perhaps it is better to allow a year and a half; and the spring is the more likely season to have been chosen for the commencement of the journey. See p. 131.

[2] Very full descriptions may be seen in Ainsworth and Kinneir.

[3] This is the Anti-Taurus, which, though far less striking in appearance than the Taurus, is really higher, as is proved by the course of the Sarus and other streams.

and again the rocks close in upon it, with steep naked cliffs, among cedars and pines, 'forming an intricate defile, which a handful of men might convert into another Thermopylæ.' When the highest peaks of Taurus are left behind, the road to Tyana is continued in the same northerly direction;[1] while that to Iconium takes a turn to the left, and passes among wooded slopes with rocky projections, and over ground comparatively level, to the great Lycaonian plain.

The whole journey from Tarsus to Konieh is enough, in modern times, to occupy four laborious days;[2] and, from the nature of the ground, the time required can never have been much less. The road, however, was doubtless more carefully maintained in the time of St. Paul than at the present day, when it is only needed for Tatar couriers and occasional traders. Antioch and Ephesus had a more systematic civilisation then, than Aleppo or Smyrna has now; and the governors of Cilicia, Cappadocia, and Galatia, were more concerned than a modern Pacha in keeping up the lines of internal communication.[3] At various parts of the journey from Tarsus to Iconium traces of the old military way are visible, marks of ancient chiselling, substructions, and pavement; stones that have fallen over into the rugged river-bed, and sepulchres hewn out in the cliffs, or erected on the level ground.[4] Some such traces still follow the ancient line of road where it enters the plain of Lycaonia, beyond Cybistra,[5] near the spot where we conceive the town of Derbe to have been formerly situated.[6]

As St. Paul emerged from the mountain-passes, and came among the lower heights through which the Taurus recedes to the Lycaonian levels, the heart which had been full of affection and

---

[1] The roads towards Syria from Cæsarea in Cappadocia, and Angora in Galatia, both meet at Tyana. The place is worthy of notice as the native city of Apollonius, the notorious philosopher and traveller. See the beginning of Chap. X.

[2] Mr. Ainsworth, in the month of November, was six days in travelling from Iconium to Adana. Major Rennell, who enters very fully into all questions relating to distances and rates of travelling, says that more than forty hours are occupied in crossing the Taurus from Eregli to Adana, though the distance is only 78 miles; and he adds, that fourteen more would be done on common ground in the same time. *Geog. of Western Asia.*

[3] Inscriptions in Asia Minor, relating to the repairing of roads by the governors of provinces and other officials, are not infrequent.

[4] See Ainsworth and Kinneir.

[5] See the Map with the line of Roman road, p. 149. Cybistra (Eregli) was one of Cicero's military stations. Its relation to the Taurus is very clearly

pointed out in his letters. Writing from this place, he was very near Derbe. He had come from Iconium, and afterwards went through the pass to Tarsus; so that his route must have nearly coincided with that of St. Paul. The bandit-chief, Antipater of Derbe, is one of the personages who play a considerable part in this passage of Cicero's life.

[6] See above, p. 149, n. 2, and p. 157. Mr. Hamilton gives a detailed account of his journey in this direction, and of the spots where he saw ruins, inscriptions, or tombs. He heard of Divlé when he was in a yailah on the mountains, but did not visit it in consequence of the want of water. There was none within eight hours. Compare what is said of the drought of Lycaonia by Strabo, as referred to above, p. 147.

Texier is of opinion that the true site of Derbe is Divlé, which he describes as a village in a wild valley among the mountains, with Byzantine remains. *Asie Mineure,* ii. 129, 130,

KARA-DAGH, NEAR LYSTRA.

The view of the mountain which forms so remarkable a feature in the scenery among which Timotheus passed his childhood is due to the kindness of the Rev. G. F. Weston, who crossed Lycaonia in 1845. It represents the appearance of the Kara-Dagh, as seen from the approach from Iconium.

anxiety all through the journey, would beat more quickly at the sight of the well-known objects before him.   The thought of his disciples would come with new force upon his mind, with a warm thanksgiving that he was at length allowed to revisit them, and to 'see how they fared.'[1]   The recollection of friends, from whom we have parted with emotion, is often strongly associated with natural scenery, especially when the scenery is remarkable.   And here the tender-hearted Apostle was approaching the home of his Lycaonian converts.   On his first visit, when he came as a stranger, he had travelled in the opposite direction:[2] but the same objects were again before his eyes, the same wide-spreading plain, the same black summit of the Kara-Dagh.   In the further reach of the plain, beyond the 'Black Mount,' was the city of Iconium; nearer to its base was Lystra; and nearer still to the traveller himself was Derbe,[3] the last point of his previous journey.   Here was his first meeting now with the disciples he had then been enabled to gather. The incidents of such a meeting,—the inquiries after Barnabas,— the welcome given to Silas,—the exhortations, instructions, encouragements, warnings, of St. Paul,—may be left to the imagination of those who have pleasure in picturing to themselves the features of the Apostolic age, when Christianity was new.

This is all we can say of Derbe, for we know no details either of the former or present visit to the place.   But when we come to Lystra, we are at once in the midst of all the interest of St. Paul's public ministry and private relations.   Here it was that Paul and Barnabas were regarded as Heathen divinities;[4] that the Jews, who had first cried 'Hosanna' and then crucified the Saviour, turned the barbarians from homage to insult;[5] and that the little Church of Christ had been fortified by the assurance that the kingdom of heaven can only be entered through 'much tribulation.'[6]   Here too it was that the child of Lois and Eunice, taught the Holy Scriptures from his earliest years, had been trained to a religious life, and prepared, through the Providence of God, by the sight of the Apostle's sufferings, to be his comfort, support, and companion.[7]

Spring and summer had passed over Lystra, since the Apostles had preached there.   God had continued to 'bless' them, and given them 'rain from heaven and fruitful seasons, filling their hearts with food and gladness.'[8]   But still 'the living God, who made the heavens, and the earth, and the sea, and all things that are therein,' was recognised only by a few.   The temple of the Lystrian Jupiter still stood before the gate, and the priest still offered the people's sacrifices to the imaginary protector of the city.[9]   Heathenism was

---

[1] See above, p. 192.

[2] Compare Acts xiv. with 2 Tim. iii. 10, 11.

[3] See the account of the topography of this district, Chap. VI. pp. 146, &c.

[4] Acts xiv. 12–18, pp. 152, &c.

[5] Acts xiv. 19, pp. 154, 155.

[6] Acts xiv. 22, p. 157.

[7] See pp. 156, 157.

[8] See the words used in St. Paul's address to the Lystrians, Acts xiv.,

and the remarks made, pp. 153, 154. New emphasis is given to the Apostle's words, if we remember what Strabo says of the absence of water in the pastures of Lycaonia.   Mr. Weston found that water was dearer than milk at Bin-bir-Kilisseh, and that there was only one spring, high up the Kara-Dagh.

[9] Some think that a *statue*, not a *temple* of Jupiter is meant.

invaded, but not yet destroyed. Some votaries had been withdrawn from that polytheistic religion, which wrote and sculptured in stone its dim ideas of 'present deities ;'[1] crowding its thoroughfares with statues and altars,[2] ascribing to the King of the gods the attributes of beneficent protection and the government of atmospheric changes,[3] and vaguely recognising Mercury as the dispenser of fruitful seasons and the patron of public happiness.[4] But many years of difficulty and persecution were yet to elapse before Greeks and Barbarians fully learnt, that the God whom St. Paul preached was a Father everywhere present to His children, and the One Author of every 'good and perfect gift.'

Lystra, however, contributed one of the principal agents in the accomplishment of this result. We have seen how the seeds of Gospel truth were sown in the heart of Timotheus.[5] The instruction received in childhood,—the sight of St. Paul's sufferings,—the hearing of his words,—the example of the 'unfeigned faith, which first dwelt in his grandmother Lois and his mother Eunice,'[6]—and whatever other influences the Holy Spirit had used for his soul's good,—had resulted in the full conviction that Jesus was the Messiah. And if we may draw an obvious inference from the various passages of Scripture, which describe the subsequent relation of Paul and Timothy, we may assert that natural qualities of an engaging character were combined with the Christian faith of this young disciple. The Apostle's heart seems to have been drawn towards him with peculiar tenderness. He singled him out from the other disciples. 'Him would Paul have to go forth with him.'[7] This feeling is in harmony with all that we read, in the Acts and the Epistles, of St. Paul's affectionate and confiding disposition. He had no relative ties which were of service in his apostolic work; his companions were few and changing; and though Silas may well be supposed to have supplied the place of Barnabas, it was no weakness to yearn for the society of one who might become, what Mark had once appeared to be, a *son* in the Gospel.[8] Yet how could he consistently take an untried youth on so difficult an enterprise? How could he receive Timothy into 'the glorious company of Apostles,' when he had rejected Mark? Such questions might be raised, if we were not distinctly told that the highest testimony was given to Timothy's Christian character, not only at Lystra, but at Iconium also.[9] We infer from this, that diligent inquiry was made concerning his fitness

---

[1] See note in the larger editions.

[2] See the remarks on Tarsus above, p. 196, and the note.

[3] Jupiter was often spoken of to this effect in poetry and inscriptions. Compare St. Paul's words, Acts xiv. 17.

[4] Such were the attributes of Mercury as represented in works of art.

[5] Pp. 156, 157. It is well known that commentators are not agreed whether Lystra or Derbe was the birthplace of Timothy. But the former opinion is by far the more probable. The latter rests on the view which

some critics take of Acts xx. 4. The whole aspect of Acts xvi. 1, 2, is in favour of Lystra.

[6] 2 Tim. i. 5.

[7] Acts xvi. 3. The wish was spontaneous, not suggested by others.

[8] This is literally what he afterwards said of Timothy: 'Ye know that, *as a son with the father*, he has served with me in the Gospel.' Phil. ii. 22. Compare also the phrases, 'my son,' 'my own son in the faith.' 1 Tim. i. 2, 18, and 2 Tim. ii. 1.

[9] Acts xvi. 2.

for the work to which he was willing to devote himself. To omit, at present, all notice of the prophetic intimations which sanctioned the appointment of Timothy,[1] we have the best proof that he united in himself those outward and inward qualifications which a careful prudence would require. One other point must be alluded to, which was of the utmost moment at that particular crisis of the Church. The meeting of the Council at Jerusalem had lately taken place. And, though it had been decided that the Gentiles were not to be forced into Judaism on embracing Christianity, and though St. Paul carried with him[2] the Decree, to be delivered 'to all the churches,' —yet still he was in a delicate and difficult position. The Jewish Christians had naturally a great jealousy on the subject of their ancient divine Law; and in dealing with the two parties the Apostle had need of the utmost caution and discretion. We see, then, that in choosing a fellow-worker, for his future labours, there was a peculiar fitness in selecting one, 'whose mother was a Jewess, while his father was a Greek.'[3]

We may be permitted here to take a short retrospect of the childhood and education of St. Paul's new associate. The hand of the Apostle himself has drawn for us the picture of his early years.[4] That picture represents to us a mother and a grandmother, full of tenderness and faith, piously instructing the young Timotheus in the ancient Scriptures, making his memory familiar with that 'cloud of witnesses' which encompassed all the history of the chosen people, and training his hopes to expect the Messiah of Israel.[5] It is not allowed to us to trace the previous history of these godly women of the dispersion. It is highly probable that they may have been connected with those Babylonian Jews whom Antiochus settled in Phrygia three centuries before:[6] or they may have been conducted into Lycaonia by some of those mercantile and other changes which affected the movements of so many families at the epoch we are writing of; such, for instance, as those which brought the household of the Corinthian Chloe into relations with Ephesus,[7] and caused the proselyte Lydia to remove from Thyatira to Philippi.[8] There is one difficulty which, at first sight, seems considerable; viz. the fact that a religious Jewess, like Eunice, should have been married to a Greek. Such a marriage was scarcely in harmony with the stricter spirit of early Judaism, and in Palestine itself it could hardly have taken place.[9] But among the Jews of the dispersion, and especially in remote districts, where but few of the scattered people were esta-

---

[1] 1 Tim. i. 18. See iv. 14. We ought to add, that 'the brethren' who gave testimony in praise of Timothy were the very converts of St. Paul himself, and, therefore, witnesses in whom he had good reason to place the utmost confidence.

[2] Acts xvi. 4.

[3] Acts xvi. 1.

[4] 2 Tim. i. 5, iii. 15, &c.

[5] If it is allowable to allude to an actual picture of a scene of this kind, we may mention the drawing of 'Jew-ish women reading the Scriptures,' in Wilkie's Oriental Sketches.

[6] See Chap. II. p. 32, also Chap. I. pp. 14, 15. The authority for the statement made there is Joseph. *Ant.* xii. 3, 4.

[7] 1 Cor. i. 11. [8] Acts xvi. 14.

[9] Learned men (Selden and Michaelis for instance) take different views of the lawfulness of such marriages. The cases of Esther and of various members of the Herodian family obviously occur to us.

blished, the case was rather different. Mixed marriages, under such circumstances, were doubtless very frequent. We are at liberty to suppose that in this case the husband was a proselyte. We hear of no objections raised to the circumcision of Timothy, and we may reasonably conclude that the father was himself inclined to Judaism :[1] if, indeed, he were not already deceased, and Eunice a widow. This very circumstance, however, of his mixed origin gave to Timothy an intimate connection with both the Jewish and Gentile worlds. Though far removed from the larger colonies of Israelitish families, he was brought up in a thoroughly Jewish atmosphere : his heart was at Jerusalem while his footsteps were in the level fields near Lystra, or on the volcanic crags of the Black Mount : and his mind was stored with the Hebrew or Greek[2] words of inspired men of old in the midst of the rude idolaters, whose language was 'the speech of Lycaonia.' And yet he could hardly be called a Jewish boy, for he had not been admitted within the pale of God's ancient covenant by the rite of circumcision. He was in the same position, with respect to the Jewish Church, as those, with respect to the Christian Church, who, in various ages, and for various reasons, have deferred their baptism to the period of mature life. And 'the Jews which were in those quarters,'[3] however much they may have respected him, yet, knowing 'that his father was a Greek,' and that he himself was uncircumcised, must have considered him all but an 'alien from the commonwealth of Israel.'

Now, for St. Paul to travel among the synagogues with a companion in this condition,—and to attempt to convince the Jews that Jesus was the Messiah, when his associate and assistant in the work was an uncircumcised Heathen,—would evidently have been to encumber his progress and embarrass his work. We see in the first aspect of the case a complete explanation of what to many has seemed inconsistent, and what some have ventured to pronounce as culpable, in the conduct of St. Paul. 'He took and circumcised Timotheus.' How could he do otherwise, if he acted with his usual far-sighted caution and deliberation ? Had Timothy not been circumcised, a storm would have gathered round the Apostle in his further progress. The Jews, who were ever ready to persecute him from city to city, would have denounced him still more violently in every synagogue, when they saw in his personal preferences, and in the co-operation he most valued, a visible revolt against the law of his forefathers. To imagine that they could have overlooked the absence of circumcision in Timothy's case, as a matter of no essential importance, is to suppose they had already become enlightened Christians. Even in the bosom of the Church we have seen[4] the

---

[1] The expression in the original (xvi. 3) means, 'he was a born Greek.' The most natural inference is, that his father was living, and most probably not a proselyte of righteousness, if a proselyte at all.

[2] We cannot tell how far this family is to be reckoned Hellenistic or Aramaic (see Chap. II.). But the Hellenistic element would be likely to predominate. In reference to this subject, Mr. Grinfield, in his recent work on the Septuagint, p. 53, notices the two quotations from that version in St. Paul's letters to Timothy. 1 Tim. v. 18 ; 2 Tim. ii. 19.

[3] Acts xvi. 3.

[4] Chap. VII.

difficulties which had recently been raised by scrupulousness and bigotry on this very subject.   And the difficulties would have been increased tenfold in the untrodden field before St. Paul by proclaiming everywhere on his very arrival that circumcision was abolished. His fixed line of procedure was to act on the cities through the synagogues, and to preach the Gospel first to the Jew and then to the Gentile.[1] He had no intention of abandoning this method, and we know that he continued it for many years.[2]   But such a course would have been impossible had not Timothy been circumcised. He must necessarily have been repelled by that people who endeavoured once (as we shall see hereafter) to murder St. Paul, because they imagined he had taken a Greek into the Temple.[3] The very intercourse of social life would have been hindered, and made almost impossible, by the presence of a half-heathen companion : for, however far the stricter practice may have been relaxed among the Hellenising Jews of the dispersion, the general principle of exclusiveness everywhere remained, and it was still ' an abomination ' for the circumcised to eat with the uncircumcised.[4]

It may be thought, however, that St. Paul's conduct in circumcising Timothy was inconsistent with the principle and practice he maintained at Jerusalem when he refused to circumcise Titus.[5] But the two cases were entirely different.   Then there was an attempt to enforce circumcision as necessary to salvation : now it was performed as a voluntary act, and simply on prudential grounds. Those who insisted on the ceremony in the case of Titus were Christians, who were endeavouring to burden the Gospel with the yoke of the Law : those for whose sakes Timothy became obedient to one provision of the Law, were Jews, whom it was desirable not to provoke, that they might more easily be delivered from bondage.   By conceding in the present case, prejudice was conciliated and the Gospel furthered : the results of yielding in the former case would have been disastrous, and perhaps ruinous, to the cause of pure Christianity.

If it be said that even in this case there was danger lest serious results should follow,—that doubt might be thrown on the freedom of the Gospel, and that colour might be given to the Judaising propensity ;—it is enough to answer, that indifferent actions become right or wrong according to our knowledge of their probable consequences,—and that St. Paul was a better judge of the consequences likely to follow from Timothy's circumcision than we can possibly be. Are we concerned about the effects likely to have been produced on the mind of Timotheus himself ?   There was no risk, at least, lest he should think that circumcision was necessary to salvation, for he had been publicly recognised as a Christian before he was circumcised :[6] and the companion, disciple, and minister of St. Paul was in no danger, we should suppose, of becoming a Judaiser. And as for the moral results which might be expected to follow in the minds of the other Lycaonian Christians,—it must be remembered

[1] Acts xiii. 5, 14, xiv. 1, xvii. 1, 2, 10, xviii. 4, 19, xix. 8, 9 ; and compare Rom. i. 16, ii. 9, 10.
[2] See Acts xxviii.
[3] Acts xxi. 29 with xxii. 22.
[4] See pp. 193, 194.
[5] Gal. ii. 3. See p. 173.
[6] Acts xvi. 1–3.

that at this very moment St. Paul was carrying with him and publishing the Decree which announced to all Gentiles that they were
not to be burdened with a yoke which the Jews had never been able
to bear. St. Luke notices this circumstance in the very next verse
after the mention of Timothy's circumcision, as if to call our attention to the contiguity of the two facts.[1] It would seem, indeed, that
the very best arrangements were adopted which a divinely enlightened
prudence could suggest. Paul carried with him the letter of the
Apostles and elders, that no Gentile Christian might be enslaved to
Judaism. He circumcised his minister and companion, that no
Jewish Christian might have his prejudices shocked. His language
was that which he always used,—'Circumcision is nothing, and
uncircumcision is nothing. The renovation of the heart in Christ
is everything.[2] Let every man be persuaded in his own mind.'[3]
No innocent prejudice was ever treated roughly by St. Paul. To
the Jew he became a Jew, to the Gentile a Gentile : ' he was all
things to all men, if by any means he might save some.'[4]

Iconium appears to have been the place where Timothy was circumcised. The opinion of the Christians at Iconium, as well as
those at Lystra, had been obtained before the Apostle took him as
his companion. These towns were separated only by the distance
of a few miles ;[5] and constant communication must have been going
on between the residents in the two places, whether Gentile, Jewish,
or Christian. Iconium was by far the more populous and important
city of the two,—and it was the point of intersection of all the great
roads in the neighbourhood.[6] For these reasons we conceive that
St. Paul's stay in Iconium was of greater moment than his visits to
the smaller towns, such as Lystra. Whether the ordination of
Timothy, as well as his circumcision, took place at this particular
place and time, is a point not easy to determine. But this view is
at least as probable as any other that can be suggested : and it gives
a new and solemn emphasis to this occasion, if we consider it as that
to which reference is made in the tender allusions of the pastoral
letters,—where St. Paul reminds Timothy of his good confession
before 'many witnesses,'[7] of the 'prophecies' which sanctioned
his dedication to God's service,[8] and of the 'gifts' received by the
laying on of 'the hands of the presbyters '[9] and the Apostle's ' own
hands.'[10] Such references to the day of ordination, with all its well-
remembered details, not only were full of serious admonition to

[1] See vv. 3, 4.
[2] Gal. v. 6, vi. 15. St. Paul's own conduct on the confines of Galatia is a commentary on the words he uses to the Galatians.
[3] Rom. xiv. 5.
[4] 1 Cor. ix. 20–22.
[5] To what has been said before (pp. 146, 148, &c.) add the following note from a MS. journal already quoted. ' Oct. 6.—Left Konieh at 12. Traversed the enormous plains for 5½ hours, when we reached a small Turcoman village.
Oct. 7.—At 11·30 we approached

the Kara-Dagh, and in about an hour began to ascend its slopes. We were thus about 11 hours crossing the plain from Konieh. This, with 2 on the other side, made in all 13 hours. We were heartily tired of the plain.'
[6] Roads from Iconium to Tarsus in Cilicia, Side in Pamphylia, Ephesus in Asia, Angora in Galatia, Cæsarea in Cappadocia, &c., are all mentioned in the ancient authorities.
[7] 1 Tim. vi. 12.
[8] 1 Tim. i. 18.
[9] 1 Tim. iv. 14.   [10] 2 Tim. i. 6.

Timothy, but possess the deepest interest for us.[1] And this interest becomes still greater if we bear in mind that the 'witnesses' who stood by were St. Paul's own converts, and the very 'brethren' who gave testimony to Timothy's high character at Lystra and Iconium;[2] —that the 'prophecy' which designated him to his office was the same spiritual gift which had attested the commission of Barnabas and Saul at Antioch,[3]—and that the College of Presbyters,[4] who, in conjunction with the Apostle, ordained the new minister of the Gospel, consisted of those who had been 'ordained in every Church'[5] at the close of that first journey.

On quitting Iconium St. Paul left the route of his previous expedition; unless indeed he went in the first place to Antioch in Pisidia, —a journey to which city was necessary in order to complete a full visitation of the churches founded on the continent in conjunction with Barnabas. It is certainly most in harmony with our first impressions, to believe that this city was not unvisited. No mention, however, is made of the place, and it is enough to remark that a residence of a few weeks at Iconium as his head-quarters would enable the Apostle to see more than once all the Christians at Antioch, Lystra, and Derbe.[6] It is highly probable that he did so: for the whole aspect of the departure from Iconium, as it is related to us in the Bible, is that of a new missionary enterprise, undertaken after the work of visitation was concluded. St. Paul leaves Iconium, as formerly he left the Syrian Antioch, to evangelise the Heathen in new countries. Silas is his companion in place of Barnabas, and Timothy is with him 'for his minister,' as Mark was with him then. Many roads were before him. By travelling westwards he would soon cross the frontier of the province of Asia,[7] and he might descend by the valley of the Mæander to Ephesus, its metropolis:[8] or the roads to the south[9] might have conducted him to Perga and Attaleia,

---

[1] This is equally true, if the ordination is to be considered coincident with the 'laying on of hands,' by which the miraculous gifts of the Holy Ghost were first communicated, as in the case of Cornelius (Acts x. 44), the Samaritans (viii. 17), the disciples at Ephesus (xix. 6), and St. Paul himself (ix. 17). See the Essay on the Apostolical Office in Stanley's *Sermons and Essays*, especially p. 71. These *gifts* doubtless pointed out the *offices* to which individuals were specially called. Compare together the three important passages: Rom. xii. 6–8; 1 Cor. xii. 28–30; Eph. iv. 11, 12; also 1 Pet. iv. 10, 11.

[2] Compare Acts xvi. 2 with Acts xiii. 51–xiv. 21.

[3] Compare 1 Tim. i. 18 with Acts xiii. 1–3.

[4] 1 Tim. iv. 14. See 2 Tim. i. 6.

[5] Acts xiv. 23.

[6] It would also be very easy for St. Paul to visit Antioch on his route from Iconium through Phrygia and Galatia. See below, p. 208.

[7] It is impossible, as we have seen (p. 184), to determine the exact frontier.

[8] The great road from Ephesus to the Euphrates ascended the valley of the Mæander to the neighbourhood of Laodicea, Hierapolis, and Colossæ [Col. iv. 13–16], and thence passed by Apamea to Iconium. This was Cicero's route, when he travelled from Ephesus to Cilicia.

[9] The Peutinger Table has a direct road from Iconium to Side, on the coast of Pamphylia. Thence another road follows the coast to Perga, and goes thence across Western Pisidia to the valley of the Mæander. None of the Itineraries mention any direct road from Antioch in Pisidia to Perga and Attaleia, corresponding to the journeys of Paul and Barnabas. Side was a harbour of considerable importance.

and the other cities on the coast of Pamphylia. But neither of these routes was chosen. Guided by the ordinary indications of Providence, or consciously taught by the Spirit of God, he advanced in a northerly direction, through what is called, in the general language of Scripture, 'Phrygia and the region of Galatia.'

We have seen[1] that the term 'Phrygia' had no political significance in the time of St. Paul. It was merely a geographical expression, denoting a debateable country of doubtful extent, diffused over the frontiers of the provinces of Asia and Galatia, but mainly belonging to the former. We believe that this part of the Apostle's journey might be described under various forms of expression, according as the narrator might speak politically or popularly. A traveller proceeding from Cologne to Hanover might be described as going through Westphalia or through Prussia. The course of the railroad would be the best indication of his real path. So we imagine that our best guide in conjecturing St. Paul's path through this part of Asia Minor is obtained by examining the direction of the ancient and modern roads. We have marked his route in our map along the general course of the Roman military way, and the track of Turkish caravans, which leads by Laodicea, Philomelium, and Synnada,—or, to use the existing terms, by Ladik, Ak-Sher, and Eski-Karahissar. This road follows the northern side of that ridge which Strabo describes as separating Philomelium and Antioch in Pisidia, and which, as we have seen,[2] materially assisted Mr. Arundell in discovering the latter city. If St. Paul revisited Antioch on his way,[3]—and we cannot be sure that he did not,—he would follow the course of his former journey,[4] and then regain the road to Synnada by crossing the ridge to Philomelium. We must again repeat, that the path marked down here is conjectural. We have nothing either in St. Luke's narrative or in St. Paul's own letters to lead us to any place in Phrygia, as certainly visited by him on this occasion, and as the home of the converts he then made. One city indeed, which is commonly reckoned among the Phrygian cities, has a great place in St. Paul's biography, and it lay on the line of an important Roman road.[5] But it was situated far within the province of Asia, and for several reasons we think it highly improbable that he visited Colossæ on this journey, if indeed he ever visited it at all. The most probable route is that which lies more to the northwards in the direction of the true Galatia.

The remarks which have been made on Phrygia, must be repeated, with some modification, concerning Galatia. It is true that Galatia was a province : but we can plainly see that the term is used here in its popular sense,—not as denoting the whole territory which was governed by the Galatian propraetor, but rather the primitive region of the tetrarchs and kings, without including those districts of Phrygia or Lycaonia, which were now politically

---

[1] Pp. 182–184, 186, &c., and the notes.
[2] See pp. 134, 135.
[3] See above, p. 207, n. 6.
[4] Acts xiv.
[5] Xenophon reckons Colossæ in Phrygia. So Strabo. It was on the great road mentioned above, from Iconium to Ephesus. We come here upon a question which we need not anticipate; viz. whether St. Paul was *ever* at Colossæ.

united with it.[1] There is absolutely no city in true Galatia which
is mentioned by the Sacred Writers in connection with the first
spread of Christianity. From the peculiar form of expression [2]
with which the Christians of this part of Asia Minor are addressed
by St. Paul in the Epistle which he wrote to them,[3] and alluded to
in another of his Epistles,[4]—we infer that ' the *churches* of Galatia,
were not confined to any one city, but distributed through various
parts of the country. If we were to mention two cities, which,
both from their intrinsic importance, and from their connection
with the leading roads,[5] are likely to have been visited and revisited by the Apostle, we should be inclined to select Pessinus
and Ancyra. The first of these cities retained some importance as
the former capital of one of the Galatian tribes,[6] and its trade was
considerable under the early Emperors. Moreover, it had an ancient and wide-spread renown, as the seat of the primitive worship
of Cybele, the Great Mother.[7] Though her oldest and most sacred
image (which, like that of Diana at Ephesus,[8] had ' fallen down
from heaven ') had been removed to Rome,—her worship continued to thrive in Galatia, under the superintendence of her
effeminate and fanatical priests or Galli,[9] and Pessinus was the
object of one of Julian's pilgrimages, when Heathenism was on
the decline.[10] Ancyra was a place of still greater moment : for it
was the capital of the province.[11] The time of its highest eminence
was not under the Gaulish but the Roman government. Augustus
built there a magnificent temple of marble,[12] and inscribed there a
history of his deeds, almost in the style of an Asiatic sovereign.[13]
This city was the meeting-place of all the great roads in the north
of the peninsula.[14] And, when we add that Jews had been estab-

---

[1] See pp. 188, 189, and the notes.

[2] ' The churches of Galatia,' in the
plural. The occurrence of this term
in the salutation gives the Epistle to
the Galatians the form of a circular
letter. The same phrase, in the Second Epistle to the Corinthians, conveys the impression that there was no
great central church in Galatia, like
that of Corinth in Achaia, or that of
Ephesus in Asia.

[3] Gal. i. 2.   [4] 1 Cor. xvi. 1.

[5] The route is conjecturally laid
down in the map from Synnada to
Pessinus and Ancyra. Mr. Hamilton
travelled exactly along this line, and
describes the bare and dreary country
at length. Near Pessinus he found an
inscription relating to the repairing of
the Roman road, on a column which
had probably been a milestone. Both
the Antonine and Jerusalem Itineraries give the road between Pessinus
and Ancyra, with the intermediate
stages.

[6] The Tolistoboii, or Western Galatians.

[7] See above, p. 188.

[8] Herodian's expression concerning
this image is identical with that in
Acts xix. 35.

[9] Jerome connects this term with
the name of the Galatians. See, however, Smith's *Dictionary of Antiquities*,
under the word. See also under ' Me-
galesia.'

[10] Ammian. Marc. xxii. 9.

[11] This appears from its coins at this
period. It was also called ' Sebaste,
from the favour of Augustus.

[12] This temple has been described by
a long series of travellers, from Lucas
and Tournefort to Hamilton and
Texier.

[13] Full comments on this inscription
will be found in Hamilton. We may
compare it with the recently deciphered
record of the victories of Darius Hy-
staspes on the rock at Behistoun. See
Vaux's *Nineveh and Persepolis*.

[14] Colonel Leake's map shows at one
glance what we learn from the Itineraries. We see there the roads radiating
from it in every direction.

lished there from the time of Augustus,[1] and probably earlier, we can hardly avoid the conclusion that the Temple and Inscription at Angora, which successive travellers have described and copied during the last three hundred years, were once seen by the Apostle of the Gentiles.

However this may have been, we have some information from his own pen, concerning his first journey through 'the region of Galatia.' We know that he was delayed there by sickness, and we know in what spirit the Galatians received him.

St. Paul affectionately reminds the Galatians [2] that it was '*bodily sickness* which caused him to preach the Glad Tidings to them at the first.' The allusion is to his first visit : and the obvious inference is, that he was passing through Galatia to some other district (possibly Pontus,[3] where we know that many Jews were established), when the state of his bodily health arrested his progress.[4] Thus he became, as it were, the Evangelist of Galatia against his will. But his zeal to discharge the duty that was laid on him did not allow him to be silent. He was instant 'in season and out of season.' 'Woe' was on him if he did not preach the Gospel. The same Providence detained him among the Gauls, which would not allow him to enter Asia or Bithynia :[5] and in the midst of his weakness he made the Glad Tidings known to all who would listen to him. We cannot say what this sickness was, or with absolute certainty identify it with that 'thorn in the flesh'[6] to which he feelingly alludes in his Epistles, as a discipline which God had laid on him. But the remembrance of what he suffered in Galatia seems so much to colour all the phrases in this part of the Epistle, that a deep personal interest is connected with the circumstance. Sickness in a foreign country has a peculiarly depressing effect on a sensitive mind. And though doubtless Timotheus watched over the Apostle's weakness with the most affectionate solicitude,—yet those who have experienced what fever is in a land of strangers will know how to sympathise, even with St. Paul, in this human trial. The climate and the prevailing maladies of Asia Minor may have been modified with the lapse of centuries : and we are without the guidance of St. Luke's medical language,[7] which sometimes throws a light on diseases alluded to in Scripture : but two Christian sufferers, in widely different ages of the Church, occur to the memory as we look on the map of Galatia. We could hardly mention any two men more thoroughly imbued with the spirit of St. Paul, than John Chrysostom and Henry Martyn.[8] And when

---

[1] See the reference to Josephus, p. 189, n. 4.

[2] Gal. iv. 13.

[3] See above p. 190.

[4] There can be no doubt that the *literal* translation is, '*on account of* bodily weakness.' And there seems no good reason why we should translate it differently, though most of the English commentators take a different view. Böttger, in harmony with his hypothesis that St. Luke's Galatia means the neighbourhood of Lystra and Derbe, thinks that the bodily weakness here alluded to was the result of the stoning at Lystra. Acts xiv.

[5] Acts xvi. 6, 7.

[6] 2 Cor. xii. 7-10. Paley (on Gal. iv. 11-16) assumes the identity, and he is probably right.

[7] See the paper alluded to, p. 78, n. 5.

[8] There was a great similarity in the last sufferings of these apostolic men ;

we read how these two saints suffered in their last hours from
fatigue, pain, rudeness, and cruelty, among the mountains of Asia
Minor which surround the place [1] where they rest,—we can well
enter into the meaning of St. Paul's expressions of gratitude to
those who received him kindly in the hour of his weakness.

The Apostle's reception among the frank and warm-hearted Gauls
was peculiarly kind and disinterested. No Church is reminded by
the Apostle so tenderly of the time of their first meeting.[2] The
recollection is used by him to strengthen his reproaches of their
mutability, and to enforce the pleading with which he urges them
to return to the true Gospel. That Gospel had been received in
the first place with the same affection which they extended to the
Apostle himself. And the subject, the manner, and the results of
his preaching are not obscurely indicated in the Epistle itself. The
great topic there, as at Corinth and everywhere, was ' *the cross of
Christ* ' — ' *Christ crucified* ' set forth among them.[3] The Divine
evidence of the Spirit followed the word, spoken by the mouth of
the Apostle, and received by 'the hearing of the ear.' [4] Many were
converted, both Greeks and Jews, men and women, free men and
slaves.[5] The worship of false divinities, whether connected with
the old superstition at Pessinus, or the Roman idolatry at Ancyra,
was forsaken for that of the true and living God.[6] And before St.
Paul left the ' region of Galatia ' on his onward progress, various
Christian communities [7] were added to those of Cilicia, Lycaonia,
and Phrygia.

In following St. Paul on his departure from Galatia, we come to
a passage of acknowledged difficulty in the Acts of the Apostles.[8]
Not that the words themselves are obscure. The difficulty relates,
not to grammatical construction, but to geographical details. The
statement contained in St. Luke's words is as follows :—After
preaching the Gospel in Phrygia and Galatia, they were hindered
from preaching it in Asia ; accordingly, when in Mysia or its neighbourhood, they attempted to penetrate into Bithynia ; and this also
being forbidden by the Divine Spirit, they passed by Mysia and
came down to Troas. Now everything depends here on the sense
we assign to the geographical terms. What is meant by the words
' Mysia,' ' Asia,' and ' Bithynia ? ' It will be remembered that all
these words had a wider and a more restricted sense.[9] They might
be used popularly and vaguely ; or they might be taken in their

---

—the same intolerable pain in the
head, the same inclement weather, and
the same cruelty on the part of those
who urged on the journey. In the
larger editions the details of Martyn's
last journal are compared with similar
passages in the Benedictine life of
Chrysostom.

[1] It is remarkable that Chrysostom
and Martyn are buried in the same
place. They both died on a journey,
at Tocat or Comana in Pontus.

[2] The references have been given
above in the account of Galatia, p. 186.

[3] Compare Gal. iii. 1 with 1 Cor. 1.
13, 17, ii. 2, &c.

[4] Gal. iii. 2. So at Thessalonica
1 Thess. ii. 13.

[5] Gal. iii. 27, 28.

[6] See the remarks above (pp. 196
197), in reference to Tarsus.

[7] The plural (Gal. i. 2, and 1 Cor.
xvi. 1) implies this. See pp. 248, 249.

[8] Acts xvi. 6, 7. For a similar accumulation of participles, see Acts xxv.
6–8.

[9] See above, p. 182

exacter political meaning. It seems to us that the whole difficulty disappears by understanding them in the former sense, and by believing (what is much the more probable, *à priori*) that St. Luke wrote in the usual popular language, without any precise reference to the provincial boundaries. We need hardly mention *Bithynia* ; for whether we speak of it traditionally or politically, it was exclusive both of Asia and Mysia.[1] In this place it is evident that *Mysia* is excluded also from Asia, just as Phrygia is above ;[2] not because these two districts were not parts of it in its political character of a province, but because they had a history and a traditional character of their own sufficiently independent to give them a name in popular usage. As regards *Asia*, it is simply viewed as the western portion of Asia Minor. Its relation to the peninsula has been very well described by saying that it occupied the same relative position which Portugal occupies with regard to Spain.[3] The comparison would be peculiarly just in the passage before us. For the Mysia of St. Luke is to Asia what Gallicia is to Portugal ; and the journey from Galatia and Phrygia to the city of Troas has its European parallel in a journey from Castile to Vigo.

We are evidently destitute of materials for laying down the route of St. Paul and his companions. All that relates to Phrygia and Galatia must be left vague and blank, like an unexplored country in a map (as in fact this region itself is in the maps of Asia Minor[4]), where we are at liberty to imagine mountains and plains, rivers and cities, but are unable to furnish any proofs. As the path of the Apostle, however, approaches the Ægean, it comes out into comparative light : the names of places are again mentioned, and the country and the coast have been explored and described. The early part of the route then must be left indistinct. Thus much, however, we may venture to say,—that since the Apostle usually turned his steps towards the large towns, where many Jews were established, it is most likely that Ephesus, Smyrna, or Pergamus was the point at which he aimed, when he sought ' to preach the Word in Asia.' There is nothing else to guide our conjectures, except the boundaries of the provinces and the lines of the principal roads. If he moved from Angora[5] in the general direction above pointed out,

[1] Mysia was at one time an apple of discord between the kings of Pergamus and Bithynia ; and the latter were for a certain period masters of a considerable tract on the shore of the Propontis. But this was at an end when the Romans began to interfere in the affairs of the East.

It may be well to add a few words on the history of Mysia, which was purposely deferred to this place. See p. 184, n. 2. Under the Persians this corner of Asia Minor formed the satrapy of *Little Phrygia* : under the Christian Emperors it was the province of *The Hellespont*. In the intermediate period we find it called ' Mysia,' and often divided into two parts : viz.

Little Mysia on the north, called also Mysia on the Hellespont, or Mysia Olympene, because it lay to the north of Mount Olympus ; and *Great Mysia*, or Mysia Pergamene, to the south and east, containing the three districts of Troas, Æolis, and Teuthrania.

[2] Acts xvi. 6.

[3] Paley's *Horæ Paulinæ*. (1 Cor. No. 2.)

[4] Kiepert's map, which is the best, shows this. Hardly any region in the peninsula has been less explored than Galatia and Northern Phrygia.

[5] Mr. Ainsworth mentions a hill near Angora in this direction, the Baulos-Dagh, which is named after the Apostle.

he would cross the river Sangarius near Kiutaya,[1] which is a great modern thoroughfare, and has been mentioned before (Chap. VI. p. 134) in connection with the route from Adalia to Constantinople; and a little further to the west, near Aizani, he would be about the place where the boundaries of Asia, Bithynia, and Mysia meet together, and on the watershed which separates the waters flowing northwards to the Propontis, and those which feed the rivers of the Ægean.

Here then we may imagine the Apostle and his three companions to pause,—uncertain of their future progress,—on the chalk downs which lie between the fountains of the Rhyndacus and those of the Hermus,—in the midst of scenery not very unlike what is familiar to us in England.[2] The long range of the Mysian Olympus to the north is the boundary of Bithynia. The summits of the Phrygian Dindymus on the south are on the frontier of Galatia and Asia. The Hermus flows through the province of Asia to the islands of the Ægean. The Rhyndacus flows to the Propontis, and separates Mysia from Bithynia. By following the road near the former river they would easily arrive at Smyrna or Pergamus. By descending the valley of the latter and then crossing Olympus,[3] they would be in the richest and most prosperous part of Bithynia. In which direction shall their footsteps be turned? Some Divine intimation, into the nature of which we do not presume to inquire, told the Apostle that the Gospel was not yet to be preached in the populous cities of Asia.[4] The time was not yet come for Christ to be made known to the Greeks and Jews of Ephesus,—and for the churches of Sardis, Pergamus, Philadelphia, Smyrna, Thyatira, and Laodicea, to be admitted to their period of privilege and trial, for the warning of future generations. Shall they turn, then, in the direction of Bithynia?[5] This also is forbidden. St. Paul (so far as we know)

---

[1] Kiutaya (the ancient Cotyæum) is now one of the most important towns in the peninsula. It lies too on the ordinary road between Broussa and Konieh.

[2] See Mr. Hamilton's account of the course of the Rhyndacus, his comparison of the district of Azanitis to the chalk scenery of England, and his notice of Dindymus, which seems to be part of the watershed that crosses the country from the Taurus towards Ida, and separates the waters of the Mediterranean and Ægean from those of the Euxine and Propontis. In the course of his progress up the Rhyndacus he frequently mentions the aspect of Olympus, the summit of which could not be reached at the end of March in consequence of the snow.

[3] The ordinary road from Broussa to Kiutayah crosses a part of the range of Olympus. The Peut. Table has a road joining Broussa with Pergamus.

[4] It will be observed that they were merely forbidden to *preach the Gospel* in Asia. We are not told that they did not *enter* Asia. Their road lay entirely through Asia (politically speaking) from the moment of leaving Galatia till their arrival at Troas. On the other hand, they were not allowed to *enter* Bithynia at all. Meyer's view of the word 'Asia' in this passage is surprising. He holds it to mean the eastern continent as opposed to 'Europe.' [See p. 182, &c.] He says that the travellers being uncertain whether Asia in the more limited sense were not intended, made a vain attempt to enter Bithynia, and finally learned at Troas that Europe was their destination.

[5] The route is drawn in the map past Aizani into the valley of the Hermus, and then northwards towards Hadriani on the Rhyndacus. This is merely an imaginary line, to express to the eye the changes of plan which occurred successively to St. Paul. The

never crossed the Mysian Olympus, or entered the cities of Nicæa and Chalcedon, illustrious places in the Christian history of a later age. By revelations, which were anticipative of the fuller and clearer communication at Troas, the destined path of the Apostolic Company was pointed out, through the intermediate country, directly to the West. Leaving the greater part of what was popularly called Mysia to the right,[1] they came to the shores of the Ægean, about the place where the deep gulf of Adramyttium, over against the island of Lesbos, washes the very base of Mount Ida.[2]

At Adramyttium, if not before, St. Paul is on the line of a great Roman road.[3] We recognise the place as one which is mentioned again in the description of the voyage to Rome. (Acts xxvii. 2.) It was a mercantile town, with important relations, both with foreign harbours and the cities of the interior of Asia Minor.[4] From this point the road follows the northern shore of the gulf,—crossing a succession of the streams which flow from Ida,[5]—and alternately descending to the pebbly beach and rising among the rocks and evergreen brushwood,—while Lesbos appears and reappears through the branches of the rich forest trees,[6]—till the sea is left behind at the city of Assos. This also is a city of St. Paul. The nineteen miles of road[7] which lie between it and Troas is the distance which he travelled by land before he rejoined the ship which had brought him from Philippi (Acts xx. 13); and the town across the strait, on the shore of Lesbos, is Mytilene,[8] whither the vessel proceeded when the Apostle and his companions met on board.

But to return to the present journey. Troas is the name either

scenery of the Rhyndacus, which is interesting as the frontier river, has been fully explored and described by Mr. Hamilton, who ascended the river to its source, and then crossed over to the fountains of the Hermus and Mæander, near which he saw an ancient road, probably connecting Smyrna and Philadelphia with Angora.

[1] The phrase in Acts xvi. 8, need not be pressed too closely. They passed along the frontier of Mysia, as it was popularly understood, and they *passed by* the whole district, without staying to evangelise it. Or, as a German writer puts it, they hurried through Mysia, because they knew that they were not to preach the Gospel in Asia.

[2] Hence it was sometimes called the Gulf of Ida.

[3] The characteristics of this bay, as seen from the water, will be mentioned hereafter when we come to the voyage from Assos to Mytilene (Acts xx. 14). At present we allude only to the *roads* along the coast. Two roads converge at Adramyttium : one which follows the shore from the south, mentioned in the Peutingerian Table; the other from Pergamus and the interior, men-

tioned also in the Antonine Itinerary. The united route then proceeds by Assos to Alexandria Troas, and so to the Hellespont.

[4] Fellows says that there are no traces of antiquities to be found there now, except a few coins. He travelled in the direction just mentioned, from Pergamus by Adramyttium and Assos to Alexandria Troas.

[5] Poets of all ages—Homer, Ovid, Tennyson, — have celebrated the streams which flow from the 'many-fountained' cliffs of Ida.

[6] See the description in Fellows. He was two days in travelling from Adramit to Assos. He says that the hills are clothed with evergreens to the top, and therefore vary little with the season; and he particularly mentions the flat stones of the shingle, and the woods of large trees, especially planes.

[7] This is the distance given in the Antonine Itinerary.

[8] The strait between Assos and Methymna is narrow. Strabo calls it 60 stadia; Pliny 7 miles. Mytilene is further to the south.

of a district or a town.   As a district it had a history of its own.
Though geographically a part of Mysia, and politically a part of the
province of Asia, it was yet usually spoken of as distinguished from
both.   This small region,[1] extending from Mount Ida to the plain
watered by the Simois and Scamander, was the scene of the Trojan
war; and it was due to the poetry of Homer that the ancient name
of Priam's kingdom should be retained.   This shore has been visited
on many memorable occasions by the great men of this world.
Xerxes passed this way when he undertook to conquer Greece.
Julias Cæsar was here after the battle of Pharsalia.   But, above
all, we associate the spot with a European conqueror of Asia, and
an Asiatic conqueror of Europe; with Alexander of Macedon and
Paul of Tarsus.   For here it was that the enthusiasm of Alexander
was kindled at the tomb of Achilles, by the memory of his heroic
ancestors; here he girded on their armour; and from this goal he
started to overthrow the august dynasties of the East.   And now
the great Apostle rests in his triumphal progress upon the same
poetic shore; here he is armed by heavenly visitants with the
weapons of a warfare that is not carnal; and hence he is sent forth
to subdue all the powers of the West, and bring the civilisation of
the world into captivity to the obedience of Christ.

Turning now from the district to the city of Troas, we must
remember that its full and correct name was Alexandria Troas.
Sometimes, as in the New Testament, it is simply called Troas;[2]
sometimes, as by Pliny and Strabo, simply Alexandria.   It was
not, however, one of those cities (amounting in number to nearly
twenty) which were built and named by the conqueror of Darius.
This Alexandria received its population and its name under the successors of Alexander.   It was an instance of that centralisation of
small scattered towns into one great mercantile city, which was
characteristic of the period.   Its history was as follows :—Antigonus, who wished to leave a monument of his name on this classical
ground, brought together the inhabitants of the neighbouring towns
to one point on the coast, where he erected a city, and called it
Antigonia Troas.   Lysimachus, who succeeded to his power on the
Dardanelles, increased and adorned the city, but altered its name,
calling it in honour of 'the man of Macedonia'[3] (if we may make
this application of a phrase which Holy Writ[4] has associated with
the place), Alexandria Troas.   This name was retained ever afterwards.   When the Romans began their eastern wars, the Greeks of
Troas espoused their cause, and were thenceforward regarded with
favour at Rome.   But this willingness to recompense useful service
was combined with other feelings, half-poetical, half-political, which
about this time took possession of the mind of the Romans.   They

[1] If we are not needlessly multiplying topographical illustrations, we may
compare the three principal districts
of the province of Asia, viz. Phrygia,
Lydia, and Mysia, to the three Ridings
of Yorkshire.   Troas will then be in
Mysia what Craven is in the West
Riding, a district which has retained a
distinctive name, and has found its

own historian.
[2] Acts xvi. 8, 11, xx. 5; 2 Cor. ii.
12 ; 2 Tim. iv. 13.
[3] Not the *Vir Macedo* of Horace
(*Od.* III. xvi. 14), the *Macedonian
Man* of Demosthenes (*Phil.* I.), but his
more eminent son.
[4] See Acts xvi. 9.

fancied they saw a primeval Rome on the Asiatic shore. The story of Æneas in Virgil, who relates in twelve books how the glory of Troy was transferred to Italy,[1]—the warning of Horace, who admonishes his fellow-citizens that their greatness was gone if they rebuilt the ancient walls,[2]—reveal to us the fancies of the past and the future, which were popular at Rome. Alexandria Troas was a recollection of the city of Priam, and a prophecy of the city of Constantine. The Romans regarded it in its best days as a 'New Troy:'[3] and the Turks even now call its ruins 'Old Constantinople.'[4] It is said that Julius Cæsar, in his dreams of a monarchy which should embrace the East and the West, turned his eyes to this city as his intended capital : and there is no doubt that Constantine, 'before he gave a just preference to the situation of Byzantium, had conceived the design of erecting the seat of empire on this celebrated spot, from whence the Romans derived their fabulous origin.'[5] Augustus brought the town into close and honourable connection with Rome by making it a *colonia* [6] and assimilated its land to that of Italy by giving it the *jus Italicum.* [7] When St. Paul was there, it had not attained its utmost growth as a city of the Romans. The great aqueduct was not yet built, by which Herodes Atticus brought water from the fountains of Ida, and the piers of which are still standing.[8] The enclosure of the walls, extending above a mile from east to west, and near a mile from north to south, may represent the limits of the city in the age of Claudius.[9] The ancient harbour, even yet distinctly traceable, and not without a certain desolate beauty, when it is the foreground of a picture with the hills of Imbros and the higher peak of Samothrace in the distance,[10] is an

---

[1] See especially Book VI.

[2] 'Ne nimium pii
Tecta velint reparare Trojæ.'
Od. III. iii.

[3] This name applies more strictly to *New Ilium*, which after many vicissitudes, was made a place of some importance by the Romans, and exempted from all imposts. The strong feeling of Julius Cæsar for the people of Ilium, his sympathy with Alexander, and the influence of the tradition which traced the origin of his nation, and especially his own family, to Troy, are described by Strabo. New Ilium, however, gradually sank into insignificance, and Alexandria Troas remained as the representative of the Roman partiality for the Troad.

[4] Eski-Stamboul.

[5] Gibbon, ch. XVII. He adds that, 'though the undertaking was soon relinquished, the stately remains of unfinished walls and towers attracted the notice of all who sailed through the Hellespont.'

[6] Its full name on coins of the Antonines is, ' Col. Alexandria Augusta Troas.'

[7] Deferring the consideration of *colo-*

nial privileges to its proper place, in connection with Philippi (Acts xvi. 12), we may state here the general notion of the *Jus Italicum*. It was a privilege entirely relating to the *land*. The maxim of the Roman law was ; 'Ager Italicus immunis est : ager provincialis vectigalis est.' ' Italian land is free : provincial land is taxed.' The Jus Italicum raised provincial land to the same state of immunity from taxation which belonged to land in Italy. But this privilege could only be enjoyed by those who were citizens. Therefore it would have been an idle gift to any community not possessing the *civitas* ; and we never find it given except to a *colonia*. Conversely, however, all colonies did not possess the Jus Italicum. Carthage was a colony for two centuries before it received it.

[8] See Clarke's *Travels*.

[9] See Pococke's *Travels*.

[10] The author of *Eöthen* was much struck by the appearance of Samothrace seen aloft over Imbros, when he recollected how Jupiter is described in the Iliad as watching from thence the scene of action before Troy. 'Now I knew,' he says, 'that Homer had

object of greater interest than the aqueduct and the walls. All further allusions to the topography of the place may be deferred till we describe the Apostle's subsequent and repeated visits.[1] At present he is hastening towards Europe. Everything in this part of our narrative turns our eyes to the West.

When St. Paul's eyes were turned towards the West, he saw that remarkable view of Samothrace over Imbros, which has just been mentioned. And what were the thoughts in his mind when he looked towards Europe across the Ægean? Though ignorant of the precise nature of the supernatural intimations which had guided his recent journey, we are led irresistibly to think that he associated his future work with the distant prospect of the Macedonian hills. We are reminded of another journey, when the Prophetic Spirit gave him partial revelations on his departure from Corinth, and on his way to Jerusalem. 'After I have been there I must also see Rome[2]—I have no more place in these parts[3]—I know not what shall befall me, save that the Holy Ghost witnesseth that bonds and afflictions abide me.'[4]

Such thoughts, it may be, had been in the Apostle's mind at Troas, when the sun set beyond Athos and Samothrace,[5] and the shadows fell on Ida and settled dark on Tenedos and the deep. With the view of the distant land of Macedonia imprinted on his memory, and the thought of Europe's miserable Heathenism deep in his heart, he was prepared, like Peter at Joppa,[6] to receive the full meaning of the voice which spoke to him in a dream. In the visions of the night, a form appeared to come and stand by him;[7] and he recognised in the supernatural visitant 'a man of Macedonia,'[8] who

passed along here,—that this vision of Samothrace over-towering the nearer island was common to him and to me.' —P. 64. The same train of thought may be extended to our present subject, and we may find a sacred pleasure in looking at any view which has been common to St. Paul and to us.

[1] Acts xvi. xx; 2 Cor. ii.; 2 Tim. iv.

[2] Acts xix. 21.

[3] Rom. xv. 23. It will be remembered that the Epistle to the Romans was written just before this departure from Corinth.

[4] Acts xx. 22, 23.

[5] Athos and Samothrace are the highest points in this part of the Ægean. They are the conspicuous points from the summit of Ida, along with Imbros, which is nearer. (Walpole's *Memoirs*, p. 122.) See the notes at the beginning of the next chapter. 'Mount Athos is plainly visible from the Asiatic coast at sunset, but not at other times. Its distance hence is about 80 miles. Reflecting the red rays of the sun, it appears from that coast like a huge mass of burnished gold. . . Mr. Turner being off the N.W. end of Mytilen (Lesbos) 22nd

June, 1814, says, "The evening being clear, we plainly saw the immense Mount Athos, which appeared in the form of an equilateral triangle." ' *Sailing Directory*, p. 150. In the same page a sketch is given of Mount Athos, N. by W. ¼ W., 45 miles. Compare Mr. Bowen's recent work, p. 26. 'At sunset we were halfway between Tenedos and the rugged Imbros. In the disc of the setting sun I distinguished the pyramidal form of Mount Athos.'

[6] See the remarks on St. Peter's vision, p. 77. See also p. 86, n. 2, and p. 163. [7] Acts xvi. 9.

[8] St. Paul may have known, by his dress, or by his words, or by an immediate intuition, that he was 'a man of Macedonia.' Grotius suggests the notion of a representative or guardian angel of Macedonia, as the 'prince of Persia,' &c., in Dan. x. The words 'help us' imply that the man who appeared to St. Paul was a representative of many. This is remarked by Baumgarten, whose observations on the significance of this vision are well worth considering. *Apostelgesch.*, ii. p. 199 (Eng. Trans. ii. 110.)

came to plead the spiritual wants of his country.   It was the voice of the sick inquiring for a physician,—of the ignorant seeking for wisdom,—the voice which ever since has been calling on the Church to extend the Gospel to Heathendom,—'Come over and help us.'

Virgil has described an evening[1] and a sunrise[2] on this coast, before and after an eventful night.   That night was indeed eventful in which St. Paul received his commission to proceed to Macedonia. The commission was promptly executed.[3]   The morning-star appeared over the cliffs of Ida.   The sun rose and spread the day over the sea and the islands as far as Athos and Samothrace.   The men of Troas awoke to their trade and their labour.   Among those who were busy about the shipping in the harbour were the newly arrived Christian travellers, seeking for a passage to Europe,   Paul, and Silas, and Timotheus,—and that new companion, 'Luke the beloved Physician,' who, whether by pre-arrangement, or by a providential meeting, or (it may be) even in consequence of the Apostle's delicate health,[5] now joined the mission, of which he afterwards wrote the history.   God provided a ship for the messengers He had chosen : and (to use the language of a more sacred poetry than that which has made these coasts illustrious)[6] 'He brought the wind out of His treasuries, and by His power He brought in the south wind,'[7] and prospered the voyage of His servants.

Coin of Tarsus.[8]

[4] We should notice here not only the change of *person* from the third to the first, but the simultaneous transition (as it has been well expressed) from the *historical* to the autoptical style, as shown by the fuller enumeration of details.   We shall return to this subject again, when we come to the point where St. Luke parts from St. Paul at Philippi : meantime we may remark, that it is highly probable that they had already met and laboured together at Antioch.

[5] We must remember the recent sickness in Galatia, p. 210.   See below, p. 241.

[6] The classical reader will remember that the throne of Neptune in Homer, whence he looks over Ida and the scene of the Trojan war, is on the peak of Samothrace (*Il.* XIII. 10–14), and his cave deep under the water between Imbros and Tenedos (*Il.* XIII. 32–35).

[7] Ps. cxxxv. 7, lxxviii. 26.   For arguments to prove that the wind was literally a *south wind* in this case, see the beginning of the next chapter.

[8] From the British Museum.   It may be observed that this coin illustrates the mode of strengthening sails by rope-bands, mentioned in Mr. Smith's important work on the *Voyage and Shipwreck of St. Paul*, 1848, p. 163.

CHAPTER IX.

Voyage by Samothrace to Neapolis.—Philippi.—Constitution of a Colony.—
Lydia.—The Demoniac Slave.—Paul and Silas arrested.—The Prison and the
Jailor.—The Magistrates.—Departure from Philippi.—St. Luke.—Macedonia
described.—Its Condition as a Province.—The Via Egnatia.—St. Paul's
Journey through Amphipolis and Apollonia.—Thessalonica.—The Synagogue.
—Subjects of St. Paul's Preaching.—Persecution, Tumult, and Flight.—The
Jews at Berœa.—St. Paul again persecuted.—Proceeds to Athens.

THE weather itself was propitious to the voyage from Asia to Europe.
It is evident that Paul and his companions sailed from Troas with
a fair wind. On a later occasion we are told that five days were
spent on the passage from Philippi to Troas.[1] On the present
occasion the same voyage, in the opposite direction, was made in
two. If we attend to St. Luke's technical expression,[2] which literally means that they 'sailed before the wind,' and take into
account that the passage to the west, between Tenedos and Lemnos,
is attended with some risk,[3] we may infer that the wind blew from
the southward.[4] The southerly winds in this part of the Archipelago
do not usually last long, but they often blow with considerable force.
Sometimes they are sufficiently strong to counteract the current
which sets to the southward from the mouth of the Dardanelles.[5]

[1] Compare Acts xvi. 11, 12 with xx.
6. For the expression, 'sailed from
Philippi' (xx. 6), and the relation of
Philippi with its harbour, Neapolis,
see below, p. 222, n. 1.

[2] It occurs again in Acts xxi. 1, evidently in the same sense.

[3] 'All ships should pass to the
eastward of Tenedos. . . . Ships that
go to the westward in calms may drift
on the shoals of Lemnos, and the S. E.
end of that island being very low is
not seen above nine miles off. . . . It
is also to be recollected, that very
dangerous shoals extend from the N.
W. and W. ends of Tenedos.'—Purdy's
Sailing Directory, pp. 158, 189. Captain Stewart says (p. 63): 'To work
up to the Dardanelles, I prefer going
inside of Tenedos . . . . you can go by
your lead, and, during light winds,
you may anchor anywhere. If you go
outside of Tenedos, and it falls calm,
the current sets you towards the shoal
off Lemnos.' [The writer has heard
this and what follows confirmed by

those who have had practical experience in the merchant service in the
Levant.]

[4] The same inference may be drawn
from the fact of their going to Samothrace at all. Had the wind blown
from the northward or the eastward,
they probably would not have done so.
Had it blown from the westward, they
could not have made the passage in
two days, especially as the currents are
contrary. This consistency in minute
details should be carefully noticed, as
tending to confirm the veracity of the
narrative.

[5] 'The current from the Dardanelles
begins to run strongly to the southward at Tenedos, but there is no difficulty in turning over it with a breeze.'
—Purdy, p. 159. 'The current in the
Archipelago sets almost continually to
the southward, and is increased or retarded according to the winds. In
lying at Tenedos, near the north of the
Dardanelles, I have observed a strong
south wind entirely stop it; but it

However this might be on the day when St. Paul passed over these waters, the vessel in which he sailed would soon cleave her way through the strait between Tenedos and the main, past the Dardanelles, and near the eastern shore of Imbros. On rounding the northern end of this island, they would open Samothrace, which had hitherto appeared as a higher and more distant summit over the lower mountains of Imbros.[1] The distance between the two islands is about twelve miles.[2] Leaving Imbros, and bearing now a little to the west, and having the wind still (as our sailors say) two or three points abaft the beam, the helmsman steered for Samothrace; and, under the shelter of its high shore, they anchored for the night.[3]

Samothrace is the highest land in the north of the Archipelago, with the exception of Mount Athos.[4] These two eminences have been in all ages the familiar landmarks of the Greek mariners of the Ægean. Even from the neighbourhood of Troas, Mount Athos is seen towering over Lemnos, like Samothrace over Imbros.[5] And what Mount Athos is, in another sense, to the superstitious Christian of the Levant,[6] the peak of Samothrace was, in the days of Heathenism, to his Greek ancestors in the same seas. It was the 'Monte Santo,' on which the Greek mariner looked with awe, as he gazed on it in the distant horizon, or came to anchor under the shelter of its coast. It was the sanctuary of an ancient superstition, which was widely spread over the neighbouring continents, and the history of which was vainly investigated by Greek and Roman writers. If St. Paul had staid here even a few days, we might be justified in saying something of the 'Cabiri;' but we have no reason to suppose that he even landed on the island. At present it possesses no good harbour, though many places of safe anchorage:[7] and if the wind was from the southward, there would be smooth water anywhere on the north shore. The island was, doubtless, better supplied with artificial advantages in an age not removed by many centuries from the flourishing period of that mercantile empire which the Phœnicians founded, and the Athenians inherited, in the Ægean Sea. The relations of Samothrace with the

---

came strong to the southward the moment the gale from that point ceased.' —Captain Stewart, ib. p. 62. For the winds, see pp. 63 and 163.

[1] 'The island Imbro is separated from Samothraki by a channel twelve miles in breadth. It is much longer and larger, but not so high, as that island.'—Purdy, p. 152.

[2] See the preceding note.

[3] Acts xvi. 11.

[4] 'Samothraki is the highest land in the Archipelago, except Candia and Mount Athos.'—Purdy, p. 152.

[5] An evening view has been quoted before (p. 217, n. 5). The following is a morning view. '*Nov.* 26, 1828, 8 A.M.— Morning beautifully clear. Lemnos just opening. Mount Athos was at first taken for an island about

five leagues distant, the outline and shades appearing so perfectly distinct, though nearly fifty miles off. The base of it was covered with haze, as was the summit soon afterwards; but toward sunset it became clear again. It is immensely high; and, as there is no other mountain like it to the northward of Negropont, it is an excellent guide for this part of the coast.'—Purdy, p. 150.

[6] See the account of Mount Athos (Monte Santo) in Curzon's *Monasteries of the Levant*, Pt. IV., and the view, p. 327. In his sail from the Dardanelles to the mountain,—the breeze, the shelter and smooth water on the shore of Lemnos, &c.,—there are points of resemblance with St. Paul's voyage.

[7] See Purdy, p. 152.

opposite coast were close and frequent, when the merchants of Tyre had their miners at work in Mount Pangæus,[1] and when Athens diffused her citizens as colonists or exiles on all the neighbouring shores.[2] Nor can those relations have been materially altered when both the Phœnician and Greek settlements on the sea were absorbed in the wider and continental dominion of Rome. Ever since the day when Perseus fled to Samothrace from the Roman conqueror,[3] frequent vessels had been passing and repassing between the island and the coasts of Macedonia and Thrace.

The Macedonian harbour at which St. Paul landed was Neapolis. Its direction from Samothrace is a little to the north of west. But a southerly breeze would still be a fair wind, though they could not literally ' run before it.' A run of seven or eight hours, notwithstanding the easterly current,[4] would bring the vessel under the lee of the island of Thasos, and within a few miles of the coast of Macedonia. The shore of the mainland in this part is low, but mountains rise to a considerable height behind.[5] To the westward of the channel which separates it from Thasos, the coast recedes and forms a bay, within which, on a promontory with a port on each side,[6] the ancient Neapolis was situated.

Some difference of opinion has existed concerning the true position of this harbour:[7] but the traces of paved military roads approaching the promontory we have described, in two directions corresponding with those indicated in the ancient Itineraries; the Latin inscriptions which have been found on the spot; the remains of a great aqueduct on two tiers of Roman arches, and of cisterns like those at Baiæ near the other Neapolis on the Campanian shore, seem to leave little doubt that the small Turkish village of Cavallo is the Naples of Macedonia, the ' Neapolis' at which St. Paul landed, and the seaport of Philippi,—the ' first city'[8] which the traveller reached on entering this 'part of Macedonia,' and a city of no little importance as a Roman military ' colony.'[9]

A ridge of elevated land, which connects the range of Pangæus with the higher mountains in the interior of Thrace, is crossed between Neapolis and Philippi. The whole distance is about ten

---

[1] Herod. vii. 112. Thasos was the head-quarters of the Phœnician mining operations in this part of the Ægean. Herodotus visited the island, and was much struck with the traces of their work. (vi. 47.)

[2] It is hardly necessary to refer to the formation of the commercial empire of Athens before the Peloponnesian war, to the mines of Scapte Hyle, and the exile of Thucydides. See Grote's *Greece*, ch. xxvi. xlvii. &c.

[3] Liv. xlv. 6.

[4] ' Inside of Thasso, and past Samothraki, the current sets to the eastward,' —Purdy, p. 62. ' The current at times turns by Monte Santo (Athos), from the S. W., strong toward the eastward, by Thasso.'—P. 152.

[5] See Purdy, p. 152, and the accurate delineation of the coast in the Admiralty charts.

[6] Clarke's *Travels*, chap. xii. and xiii. An important paper on Neapolis and Philippi has been written (after a recent visit to these places) by Prof. Hackett, in the *Bib. Sacra* for Oct. 1860.

[7] Cousinéry, in his *Voyage dans la Macédoine*, identifies Neapolis with Eski-Cavallo, a harbour more to the west; but his arguments are quite inconclusive. Colonel Leake, whose opinion is of great weight, though he did not personally visit Philippi and Neapolis, agrees with Dr. Clarke.

[8] Acts xvi. 12.

[9] For the meaning of these terms see p. 228, &c.

miles.[1] The ascent of the ridge is begun immediately from the town, through a defile formed by some precipices almost close upon the sea. When the higher ground is attained, an extensive and magnificent sea-view is opened towards the south. Samothrace is seen to the east; Thasos to the south-east; and, more distant and farther to the right, the towering summit of Athos.[2] When the descent on the opposite side begins and the sea is lost to view, another prospect succeeds, less extensive, but not less worthy of our notice. We look down on a plain, which is level as an inland sea, and which, if the eye could range over its remoter spaces, would be seen winding far within its mountain-enclosure, to the west and the north.[3] Its appearance is either exuberantly green,—for its fertility has been always famous,—or cold and dreary,—for the streams which water it are often diffused into marshes,—according to the season when we visit this corner of Macedonia; whether it be when the snows are white and chill on the summits of the Thracian Hæmus,[4] or when the roses, of which Theophrastus and Pliny speak, are displaying their bloom on the warmer slopes of the Pangæan hills.[5]

This plain, between Hæmus and Pangæus, is the plain of Philippi, where the last battle was lost by the republicans of Rome. The whole region around is eloquent of the history of this battle. Among the mountains on the right was the difficult path by which the republican army penetrated into Macedonia; on some part of the very ridge on which we stand were the camps of Brutus and Cassius;[6] the stream before us is the river which passed in front of them;[7] below us, 'upon the left hand of the even field,'[8] is the

---

[1] Hence it was unnecessary for Meyer to deride Olshausen's remark, that Philippi was the '*first city*' in Macedonia visited by the Apostle, because Neapolis was its harbour. Olshausen was quite right. The distance of Neapolis from Philippi is only twice as great as that from the Piræus to Athens, not much greater than that from Cenchreæ to Corinth, and less than that from Seleucia to Antioch, or from Ostia to Rome.

[2] We may quote here two passages from Dr. Clarke, one describing this approach to Neapolis from the neighbourhood, the other his departure in the direction of Constantinople. 'Ascending the mountainous boundary of the plain on its north-eastern side by a broad ancient paved way, we had not daylight enough to enjoy the fine prospect of the sea and the town of Cavallo upon a promontory. At some distance lies the isle of Thasos, now called Tasso. It was indistinctly discerned by us; but every other object, excepting the town, began to disappear as we descended towards Cavallo.'—Chap. xii. 'Upon quitting the town, we ascended a part of Mount Pangæus by a

paved road, and had a fine view of the bay of Neapolis. The top of the hill, towards the left, was covered with ruined walls, and with the ancient aqueduct, which here crosses the road. From hence we descended by a paved road as before . . . the isle of Thasos being in view towards the S. E. Looking to the E., we saw the high top of Samothrace, which makes such a conspicuous figure from the plains of Troy. To the S., towering above a region of clouds, appeared the loftier summit of Mount Athos.'—Chap. xiii.

[3] See the very full descriptions of the plain of Serrés, in the various parts of its extension, given by Leake and Cousinéry.

[4] Lucan's view is very winterly. *Phars.* i. 680.

[5] The 'Rosa centifolia,' which the latter mentions as cultivated in Campania and in Greece, near Philippi.

[6] The republicans were so placed as to be in communication with the sea. The triremes were at Neapolis.

[7] The Gangas or Gangites. Leake, p. 217.

[8] *Julius Cæsar*, act v. sc. i. The topography of Shakspere is perfectly

marsh[1] by which Antony crossed as he approached his antagonist; directly opposite is the hill of Philippi, where Cassius died; behind us is the narrow strait of the sea, across which Brutus sent his body to the island of Thasos, lest the army should be disheartened before the final struggle.[2] The city of Philippi was itself a monument of the termination of that struggle. It had been founded by the father of Alexander, in a place called, from its numerous streams, 'The Place of Fountains,' to commemorate the addition of a new province to his kingdom, and to protect the frontier against the Thracian mountaineers. For similar reasons the city of Philip was gifted by Augustus with the privileges of a *colonia*. It thus became at once a border-garrison of the province of Macedonia, and a perpetual memorial of his victory over Brutus.[3] And now a Jewish Apostle came to the same place, to win a greater victory than that of Philippi, and to found a more durable empire than that of Augustus. It is a fact of deep significance, that the 'first city' at which St. Paul arrived,[4] on his entrance into Europe, should be that 'colony,' which was more fit than any other in the empire to be considered the representative of Imperial Rome.

The characteristic of a *colonia* was, that it was a miniature resemblance of Rome. Philippi is not the first city of this kind to which we have traced the footsteps of St. Paul; Antioch in Pisidia (p. 135), and Alexandria Troas (p. 215), both possessed the same character: but this is the first place where Scripture calls our attention to the distinction; and the events which befell the Apostle at Philippi were directly connected with the privileges of the place as a Roman colony, and with his own privileges as a Roman citizen. It will be convenient to consider these two subjects together. A glance at some of the differences which subsisted among individuals and communities in the provincial system will enable us to see very clearly the position of the *citizen* and of the *colony*.

We have had occasion (Chap. I. p. 19) to speak of the combination of actual provinces and nominally independent states through which the power of the Roman Emperor was variously diffused; and again (Chap. V. p. 115), we have described the division of the provinces by Augustus into those of the Senate, and those of the Emperor. Descending now to examine the component population of any one province, and to inquire into the political condition of individuals and communities, we find here again a complicated system of rules

accurate. In this passage Octavius and Antony are looking at the field from the opposite side.

[1] The battle took place in autumn, when the plain would probably be inundated.

[2] Plutarch's *Life of Brutus*.

[3] The full and proper Roman name was *Colonia Augusta Julia Philippensis*. See the coin engraved at the end of Chap. XXVI. Cousinéry (ch. x.) enters fully into the present condition of Philippi, and gives coins and in-

scriptions.

[4] We regard the phrase in Acts xvi. 12 as meaning the first city in its geographical relation to St. Paul's journey; not the first politically ('chief city,' Auth. Vers.), either of Macedonia or a part of it. The chief city of the province was Thessalonica; and, even if we suppose the subdivisions of Macedonia Prima, Secunda, &c., to have subsisted at this time, the chief city of Macedonia Prima was not Philippi, but Amphipolis.

and exceptions. As regards individuals, the broad distinction we must notice is that between those who were citizens and those who were not citizens. When the Greeks spoke of the inhabitants of the world, they divided them into 'Greeks' and 'Barbarians,'[1] according as the language in which poets and philosophers had written was native to them or foreign. Among the Romans the phrase was different. The classes into which they divided mankind consisted of those who were politically 'Romans,'[2] and those who had no link (except that of subjection) with the city of Rome. The technical words were *Cives* and *Peregrini*,—'citizens' and 'strangers.' The inhabitants of Italy were 'citizens;' the inhabitants of all other parts of the Empire (until Caracalla extended to the provinces[3] the same privileges which Julius Cæsar had granted to the peninsula[4]) were naturally and essentially 'strangers.' Italy was the Holy Land of the kingdom of this world. We may carry the parallel further in order to illustrate the difference which existed among the citizens themselves. Those true-born Italians, who were diffused in vast numbers through the provinces, might be called Citizens of the Dispersion; while those strangers who, at various times, and for various reasons, had received the gift of citizenship, were in the condition of political Proselytes. Such were Paul and Silas,[5] in their relation to the empire, among their fellow-Romans in the colony of Philippi. Both these classes of citizens, however, were in full possession of the same privileges; the most important of which were exemption from scourging, and freedom from arrest, except in extreme cases; and in all cases the right of appeal from the magistrate to the Emperor.[6]

The remarks which have been made concerning individuals may be extended, in some degree, to *communities* in the provinces. The City of Rome might be transplanted, as it were, into various parts of the empire, and reproduced as a *colonia*; or an alien city might be adopted, under the title of a *municipium*,[7] into a close political com-

---

[1] Thus St. Paul, in writing his Greek epistles, uses this distinction. Rom. i. 14; Col. iii. 11. Hence also Acts xxviii. 2, 4; 1 Cor. xiv. 11.

[2] The word 'Roman' is always used *politically* in the New Testament. John xi. 48; Acts xvi. xxii. xxiii. xxviii.

[3] See Milman's *Gibbon*, i. p. 281 and the note.

[4] By the Julia Lex de Civitate (B.C. 90), supplemented by other laws.

[5] We can hardly help inferring, from the narrative of what happened at Philippi, that Silas was a Roman citizen as well as St. Paul. As to the mode in which he obtained the citizenship, we are more ignorant than in the case of St. Paul himself, whose father was a citizen (Acts xxii. 28). All that we are able to say on this subject has been given before, pp. 38–40.

[6] Two of these privileges will come

more particularly before us, when we reach the narrative of St. Paul's arrest at Jerusalem. It appears that Paul and Silas were treated with a cruelty which was only justifiable in the case of a slave, and was not usually allowed in the case of any freeman. It would seem, that an accused citizen could only be imprisoned before trial for a very heinous offence, or when evidently guilty. Bail was generally allowed, or retention in a magistrate's house was held sufficient.

[7] The privilege of a *colonia* was transplanted citizenship, that of a *municipium* was engrafted citizenship. We have nothing to do, however, with *municipia* in the history of St. Paul. We are more concerned with *liberæ civitates*, and we shall presently come to one of them in the case of Thessalonica.

munion with Rome. Leaving out of view all cities of the latter kind (and indeed they were limited entirely to the western provinces), we will confine ourselves to what was called a *colonia.* A Roman colony was very different from anything which we usually intend by the term. It was no mere mercantile factory, such as those which the Phœnicians established in Spain,[1] or on those very shores of Macedonia with which we are now engaged:[2] or such as modern nations have founded in the Hudson's Bay territory or on the coast of India. Still less was it like those incoherent aggregates of human beings which *we* have thrown, without care or system, on distant islands and continents. It did not even go forth, as a young Greek republic left its parent state, carrying with it, indeed, the respect of a daughter for a mother, but entering upon a new and independent existence. The Roman colonies were primarily intended as military safeguards of the frontiers, and as checks upon insurgent provincials. Like the military roads, they were part of the great system of fortification by which the Empire was made safe. They served also as convenient possessions for rewarding veterans who had served in the wars, and for establishing freedmen and other Italians whom it was desirable to remove to a distance. The colonists went out with all the pride of Roman citizens, to represent and reproduce the City in the midst of an alien population. They proceeded to their destination like an army with its standards;[3] and the limits of the new city were marked out by the plough. Their names were still enrolled in one of the Roman tribes. Every traveller who passed through a *colonia* saw there the insignia of Rome. He heard the Latin language, and was amenable, in the strictest sense, to the Roman law. The coinage of the city, even if it were in a Greek province, had Latin inscriptions.[4] Cyprian tells us that in his own episcopal city, which once had been Rome's greatest enemy, the Laws of the XII. Tables were inscribed on brazen tablets in the market-place.[5] Though the colonists, in addition to the poll-tax, which they paid as citizens, were compelled to pay a ground-tax (for the land on which their city stood was provincial land, and therefore tributary, unless it were assimilated to Italy by a special exemption);[6] yet they were entirely free from any intrusion by the governor of the province. Their affairs were regulated by their own magistrates. These officers were named Duumviri; and they took a pride in calling themselves by the Roman title of Prætors (στρατηγοι).[7] The primary settlers in the colony were, as we have seen, real Italians; but a state of things seems to have taken place, in many instances, very similar to what happened

---

[1] Especially in the mountains on the coast between Cartagena and Almeria.

[2] See above, p. 221, n. 1.

[3] See the standards on one of the coins of Antioch in Pisidia, p. 159. The wolf, with Romulus and Remus, which will be observed on the other coin, was common on colonial moneys. Philippi was in the strictest sense a military colony, formed by the establishment of a *cohors prætoria emerita.*

[4] This has been noticed before, p. 136. As a contrast with the coins of Philippi we may mention those of Thessalonica.

[5] *De Grat. Dei*, 10.

[6] Philippi had the *Jus Italicum*, like Alexandria Troas. This is explained above, p. 216.

[7] An instance of this is mentioned by Cicero in the case of Capua. See Hor. *Sat.* I. vi.

in the early history of Rome itself. A number of the native provincials grew up in the same city with the governing body; and thus two (or sometimes three) co-ordinate communities were formed, which ultimately coalesced into one, like the Patricians and Plebeians. Instances of this state of things might be given from Corinth and Carthage, and from the colonies of Spain and Gaul; and we have no reason to suppose that Philippi was different from the rest.

Whatever the relative proportion of Greeks and Romans at Philippi may have been, the number of Jews was small. This is sufficiently accounted for, when we remember that it was a military, and not a mercantile, city. There was no synagogue in Philippi, but only one of those buildings called *Proseuchæ*, which were distinguished from the regular places of Jewish worship by being of a more slight and temporary structure, and frequently open to the sky.[1] For the sake of greater quietness, and freedom from interruption, this place of prayer was ' outside the gate;' and, in consequence of the ablutions[2] which were connected with the worship, it was ' by the river side,' on the bank of the Gaggitas,[3] the fountains

---

[1] Extracts to this effect might be quoted from Epiphanius. A Proseucha may be considered as a *place of prayer*, as opposed to a synagogue, or a *house of prayer*. It appears, however, that the words were more or less convertible, and some consider them nearly equivalent. Josephus (*Life*, § 54) describes a Proseucha as ' a large building, capable of holding a considerable crowd:' and Philo mentions, under the same denomination, buildings at Alexandria, which were so strong that it was difficult to destroy them. Probably, it was the usual name of the meeting-place of Jewish congregations in Greek cities.

Other passages in ancient writers, which bear upon the subject, are alluded to in the following extract from Biscoe: ' The sea-shore was esteemed by the Jews a place most pure, and therefore proper to offer up their prayers and thanksgiving to Almighty God. Philo tells us that the Jews of Alexandria, when Flaccus the governor of Egypt, who had been their great enemy, was arrested by order of the Emperor Caius, not being able to assemble at their synagogues, which had been taken from them, crowded out at the gates of the city early in the morning, went to the neighbouring shores, and standing in a most pure place with one accord lifted up their voices in praising God. Tertullian says, that the Jews in his time, when they kept their great fast, left their synagogues, and on every shore sent forth their prayers to heaven : and in another place, among the ceremonies used by the Jews, mentions *orationes littorales*, the prayers they made upon the shores. And long before Tertullian's time there was a decree made at Halicarnassus in favour of the Jews, which, among other privileges, allows them to say their prayers near the shore, according to the custom of their country. (Joseph. *Ant.* xiv. 10, 23.) It is hence abundantly evident, that it was common with the Jews to choose the shore as a place highly fitting to offer up their prayers.'—P. 251. He adds that the words in Acts xvi. 13 ' may signify nothing more than that the Jews of Philippi were wont to go and offer up their prayers at a certain place by the river side, as other Jews who lived near the sea were accustomed to do upon the sea-shore.' See Acts xxi. 5.

[2] See the passage adduced by Biscoe from Josephus.

[3] Many eminent German commentators make a mistake here in saying that the river was the Strymon. The nearest point on the Strymon was many miles distant. This mistake is the more marked when we find that ' out of the gate' and not ' out of the city' is probably the right reading. No one would describe the Strymon as a stream outside the gate of Philippi. We may add, that the mention of the *gate* is an instance of St. Luke's autop-

of which gave the name to the city before the time of Philip of Macedon,[1] and which, in the great battle of the Romans, had been polluted by the footsteps and blood of the contending armies.

The congregation, which met here for worship on the Sabbath, consisted chiefly, if not entirely, of a few women ;[2] and these were not all of Jewish birth, and not all residents at Philippi. Lydia, who is mentioned by name, was a proselyte ;[3] and Thyatira, her native place, was a city of the province of Asia.[4] The business which brought her to Philippi was connected with the dyeing trade, which had flourished from a very early period, as we learn from Homer,[5] in the neighbourhood of Thyatira, and is permanently commemorated in inscriptions which relate to the 'guild of dyers' in that city, and incidentally give a singular confirmation of the veracity of St. Luke in his casual allusions.[6]

In this unpretending place, and to this congregation of pious women, the Gospel was first preached by an Apostle within the limits of Europe.[7] St. Paul and his companions seem to have arrived in the early part of the week ; for 'some days' elapsed before 'the Sabbath.' On that day the strangers went and joined the little company of worshippers at their prayer by the river side. Assuming at once the attitude of teachers, they 'sat down,'[8] and spoke to the women who were assembled together. The Lord, who had summoned His servants from Troas to preach the Gospel in Macedonia,[9] now vouchsafed to them the signs of His presence, by giving Divine energy to the words which they spoke in His name. Lydia 'was one of the listeners,'[10] and the Lord 'opened her heart, that she took heed to the things that were spoken of Paul.'[11]

Lydia, being convinced that Jesus was the Messiah, and having

---

tical style in this part of the narrative. It is possible that the Jews worshipped outside the gate at Philippi, because the people would not allow them to worship within. Compare what Juvenal says of the Jews by the fountain outside the Porta Capena at Rome (iii. 11).

[1] Crenides was the ancient name.

[2] Acts xvi. 13.

[3] Acts xvi. 14.

[4] See Rev. i. 11.

[5] *Il.* iv. 141.

[6] We may observe that the communication at this period between Thyatira and Philippi was very easy, either directly from the harbour of Pergamus, or by the road mentioned in the last chapter, which led through Adramyttium to Troas.

[7] At least this is the first historical account of the preaching of an Apostle in Europe. The traditions concerning St. Pete rest on no real proof. We do not here inquire into the knowledge of Christianity which may have spread, even to Rome, through those who returned from Pentecost (Acts ii.), or

those who were dispersed in Stephen's persecution (Acts viii.), or other travellers from Syria to the West.

[8] Acts xvi. 13. Compare Acts xiii. 14, and Luke iv. 20.

[9] Acts xvi. 10.

[10] The verb is in the imperfect. Acts xvi. 14. From the words used here we infer that Lydia was listening to *conversation* rather than *preaching.* The whole narrative gives us the impression of the utmost modesty and simplicity in Lydia's character.

Another point should be noticed, which exemplifies St. Luke's abnegation of self, and harmonises with the rest of the Acts ; viz. that, after saying '*we* spake' (ver. 13), he sinks his own person, and says that Lydia took heed 'to what was spoken by *Paul* (ver. 14). Paul was the chief speaker. The phrase and the inference are the same at Antioch in Pisidia (Acts xiii. 45), when Barnabas was with St. Paul. See p. 143, n. 3.

[11] ver. 14.

mad a profession of her faith, was forthwith baptized. The place of her baptism was doubtless the stream which flowed by the *pro-seucha.* The waters of Europe were 'sanctified to the mystical washing away of sin.' With the baptism of Lydia that of her 'household' was associated. Whether we are to understand by this term her children, her slaves, or the work-people engaged in the manual employment connected with her trade, or all these col-lectively, cannot easily be decided.[1] But we may observe that it is the first passage in the life of St. Paul where we have an example of that *family religion* to which he often alludes in his Epistles. The 'connections of Chloe,'[2] the 'household of Stephanas,'[3] the 'Church in the house' of Aquila and Priscilla,[4] are parallel cases, to which we shall come in the course of the narrative. It may also be rightly added, that we have here the first example of that Christian *hospitality* which was so emphatically enjoined,[5] and so lovingly practised, in the Apostolic Church. The frequent mention of the 'hosts' who gave shelter to the Apostles,[6] reminds us that they led a life of hardship and poverty, and were the followers of Him 'for whom there was *no room in the inn.*' The Lord had said to His Apostles, that, when they entered into a city, they were to seek out 'those who were worthy,' and with them to abide. The search at Philippi was not difficult. Lydia voluntarily presented herself to her spiritual benefactors, and said to them, earnestly and humbly,[7] that, 'since they had regarded her as a believer on the Lord,' her house should be their home. She admitted of no re-fusal to her request, and 'their peace was on that house.'[8]

Thus the Gospel had obtained a home in Europe. It is true that the family with whom the Apostles lodged was Asiatic rather than European: and the direct influence of Lydia may be supposed to have contributed more to the establishment of the church of Thyatira, addressed by St. John,[9] than to that of Philippi, which received the letter of St. Paul. But still the doctrine and practice of Christianity were established in Europe; and nothing could be more calm and tranquil than its first beginnings on the shore of that continent, which it has long overspread. The scenes by the river-side, and in the house of Lydia, are beautiful prophecies of the holy influence which women,[10] elevated by Christianity to their true position, and enabled by Divine grace to wear 'the ornament

[1] Meyer thinks they were female assistants in the business connected with her trade. It is well known that this is one of the passages often ad-duced in the controversy concerning infant baptism. We need not urge this view of it: for the belief that infant baptism is 'most agreeable with the institution of Christ' (Art. xxvii.) does not rest on this text.

[2] 1 Cor. i. 11.
[3] 1 Cor. i. 16, xvi. 15.
[4] Rom. xvi. 5. Compare Philem. 2.
[5] Heb. xiii. 2. 1 Tim. v. 10, &c.
[6] Rom. xvi. 23, &c.

[7] See above, p. 227, n. 10.
[8] Matt. x. 13.   [9] Rev. ii.
[10] Observe the frequent mention of women in the salutations in St. Paul's epistles, and more particularly in that to the Philippians. Rilliet, in his Com-mentary, makes a just remark on the peculiar importance of female agency in the then state of society:—'L'organ-isation de la société civile faisait des femmes un intermédiaire nécessaire pour que la prédication de l'Évangile parvînt jusqu'aux personnes de leur sexe.' See *Quarterly Review,* for Oct. 1860.

of a meek and quiet spirit,' have now for centuries exerted over
domestic happiness and the growth of piety and peace. If we wish
to see this in a forcible light, we may contrast the picture which is
drawn for us by St. Luke, with another representation of women in
the same neighbourhood given by the Heathen poets, who tell us
of the frantic excitement of the Edonian matrons, wandering,
under the name of religion, with dishevelled hair and violent cries,
on the banks of the Strymon.[1]

Thus far all was peaceful and hopeful in the work of preaching
the Gospel to Macedonia: the congregation met in the house or
by the river-side ; souls were converted and instructed ; and a
Church, consisting both of men and women,[2] was gradually built
up. This continued for 'many days.' It was difficult to foresee
the storm which was to overcast so fair a prospect. A bitter persecution, however, was unexpectedly provoked : and the Apostles
were brought into collision with heathen superstition in one of its
worst forms, and with the rough violence of the colonial authorities. As if to show that the work of Divine grace is advanced by
difficulties and discouragements, rather than by ease and prosperity, the Apostles, who had been supernaturally summoned to a
new field of labour, and who were patiently cultivating it with
good success, were suddenly called away from it, silenced, and imprisoned.

In tracing the life of St. Paul we have not as yet seen Christianity
directly brought into conflict with Heathenism. The sorcerer who
had obtained influence over Sergius Paulus in Cyprus was a Jew,
like the Apostle himself.[3] The first impulse of the idolaters of
Lystra was to worship Paul and Barnabas ; and it was only after
the Jews had perverted their minds, that they began to persecute
them.[4] But as we travel farther from the East, and especially
through countries where the Israelites were thinly scattered, we
must expect to find Pagan creeds in immediate antagonism with
the Gospel ; and not merely Pagan creeds, but the evil powers
themselves which give Paganism its supremacy over the minds of
men. The questions which relate to evil spirits, false divinities,
and demoniacal possession, are far too difficult and extensive to be
entered on here.[5] We are content to express our belief, that in the
demoniacs of the New Testament allusion is really made to personal
spirits who exercised power for evil purposes on the human will.

---

[1] Hor. *Od.* II. vii. 27, &c.

[2] This is almost necessarily implied
in ' the brethren' (ver. 40) whom Paul
and Silas visited and exhorted in the
house of Lydia, after their release from
prison.

[3] Chap. V. p. 119.

[4] Chap. VI. pp. 152, &c.

[5] The arguments on the two sides
of this question—one party contending
that the demoniacs of Scripture were
men afflicted with insanity, melancholy,
and epilepsy, and that the language
used of them is merely an accommodation to popular belief; the other
that these unhappy sufferers were
really possessed by evil spirits—may
be seen in a series of pamphlets (partly
anonymous) published in London in
1737 and 1738. For a candid statement of both views, see the article on
' Demoniacs' in Dr. Kitto's *Cyclo-
pedia of Biblical Literature.* Compare
that on the word 'Besessene,' in
Winer's *Real-Wörterbuch* ; and, above
all, Dean Trench's profound remarks
in his work on the *Miracles*, pp. 150,
&c.

The unregenerate world is represented to us in Scripture as a realm of darkness, in which the invisible agents of wickedness are permitted to hold sway under conditions and limitations which we are not able to define. The degrees and modes in which their presence is made visibly apparent may vary widely in different countries and in different ages.[1] In the time of JESUS CHRIST and His Apostles, we are justified in saying that their workings in one particular mode were made peculiarly manifest.[2] As it was in the life of our Great Master, so it was in that of His immediate followers. The dæmons recognised Jesus as 'the Holy One of God;' and they recognised His Apostles as the 'bondsmen of the Most High God, who preach the way of salvation.' Jesus 'cast out dæmons;' and, by virtue of the power which He gave, the Apostles were able to do in His name what he did in His own.

If in any region of Heathendom the evil spirits had pre-eminent sway, it was in the mythological system of Greece, which, with all its beautiful imagery and all its ministrations to poetry and art, left man powerless against his passions, and only amused him while it helped him to be unholy. In the lively imagination of the Greeks, the whole visible and invisible world was peopled with spiritual powers or *dæmons*. The same terms were often used on this subject by Pagans and by Christians. But in the language of the Pagan the dæmon might be either a beneficent or a malignant power; in the language of the Christian it always denoted what was evil.[3] When the Athenians said[4] that St. Paul was introducing 'new dæmons' among them, they did not necessarily mean that he was in league with evil spirits; but when St. Paul told the Corinthians[5] that though 'idols' in themselves were nothing, yet the sacrifices offered to them were, in reality, offered to 'dæmons,' he spoke of those false divinities which were the enemies of the True.[6]

Again, the language concerning physical changes, especially in the human frame, is very similar in the sacred and profane writers.

---

[1] For some suggestions as to the probable reasons why demoniacal possession is seldom witnessed now, see Trench, p. 162.

[2] Trench says, that 'if there was anything that marked the period of the Lord's coming in the flesh, and that immediately succeeding, it was the wreck and confusion of men's spiritual life . . . . the sense of utter disharmony . . . . . . The whole period was the hour and power of darkness; of a darkness which then, immediately before the dawn of a new day, was the thickest. It was exactly the crisis for such soul-maladies as these, in which the spiritual and bodily should be thus strangely interlinked; and it is nothing wonderful that they should have abounded at that time.'—P. 162. Neander and Trench, however, both refer to modern missionary accounts of something like the same possession among heathen nations, and of their cessation on conversion to Christianity.

[3] This is expressly stated by Origen and Augustine; and we find the same view in Josephus.

[4] Acts xvii. 18.

[5] 1 Cor. x. 20.

[6] It is very important to distinguish the word Διάβολος ('Devil'), which is only used in the singular, from δαίμων or δαιμόνιον ('dæmon'), which may be singular or plural. The former word is used, for instance, in Matt. xxv. 41; John viii. 44; Acts xiii. 10; 1 Pet. v. 8, &c.; the latter in John vii. 20; Luke x. 17; 1 Tim. iv. 1; Rev. ix. 20; also James iii. 15. For further remarks on this subject see below on Acts xvii. 18.

Sometimes it contents itself with stating merely the facts and symptoms of disease ; sometimes it refers the facts and symptoms to invisible personal agency.[1] One class of phenomena, affecting the mind as well as the body, was more particularly referred to preternatural agency. These were the prophetic conditions of mind, showing themselves in stated oracles or in more irregular manifestations, and accompanied with convulsions and violent excitement, which are described or alluded to by almost all Heathen authors. Here again we are brought to a subject which is surrounded with difficulties. How far, in such cases, imposture was combined with real possession ; how we may disentangle the one from the other ; how far the supreme will of God made use of these prophetic powers and overruled them to good ends ; such questions inevitably suggest themselves, but we are not concerned to answer them here. It is enough to say that we see no reason to blame the opinion of those writers, who believe that a wicked spiritual agency was really exerted in the prophetic sanctuaries and prophetic personages of the Heathen world. The Heathens themselves attributed these phenomena to the agency of Apollo,[2] the deity of Pythonic spirits ; and such phenomena were of very frequent occurrence, and displayed themselves under many varieties of place and circumstance. Sometimes those who were possessed were of the highest condition ; sometimes they went about the streets like insane impostors of the lowest rank. It was usual for the prophetic spirit to make itself known by an internal muttering or ventriloquism.[3] We read of persons in this miserable condition used by others for the purpose of gain. Frequently they were slaves ; and there were cases of joint proprietorship in these unhappy ministers of public superstition.

In the case before us it was a ' female slave '[4] who was possessed with ' a spirit of divination : '[5] and she was the property of more than one master, who kept her for the purpose of practising on the credulity of the Philippians, and realised ' much profit ' in this way. We all know the kind of sacredness with which the ravings of common insanity are apt to be invested by the ignorant ; and we can easily understand the notoriety which the gestures and words of this demoniac would obtain in Philippi. It was far from a matter of indifference, when she met the members of the Christian congregation on the road to the *proseucha*, and began to follow St. Paul, and to exclaim (either because the words she had overheard mingled with her diseased imaginations, or because the evil spirit in her was

---

[1] This will be observed in the Gospels, if we carefully compare the different accounts of Our Lord's miracles. Among heathen writers we may allude particularly to .Hippocrates, since he wrote against those who treated epilepsy as the result of supernatural possession. Some symptoms, he says, were popularly attributed to Apollo, some to the Mother of the Gods, some to Neptune, &c.

[2] Python is the name of Apollo in his oracular character.

[3] Such persons spoke with the mouth closed, and were called Pythons (the very word used here by St. Luke, Acts xvi. 16).

[4] Acts xvi. 16. The word is the same in xii. 13.

[5] Literally ' a spirit of Python' or ' a Pythonic spirit.'

compelled[1] to speak the truth) : ' These men are the bondsmen of the Most High God, who are come to announce unto you the way of salvation.' This was continued for ' several days,' and the whole city must soon have been familiar with her words. Paul was well aware of this; and he could not bear the thought that the credit even of the Gospel should be enhanced by such unholy means. Possibly one reason why our Blessed Lord Himself forbade the demoniacs to make Him known, was, that His holy cause would be polluted by resting on such evidence. And another of our Saviour's feelings must have found an imitation in St. Paul's breast,—that of deep compassion for the poor victim of demoniac power. At length he could bear this Satanic interruption no longer, and, ' being grieved, he commanded the evil spirit to come out of her.' It would be pro- faneness to suppose that the Apostle spoke in mere irritation, as it would be ridiculous to imagine that Divine help would have been vouchsafed to gratify such a feeling. No doubt there was grief and indignation, but the grief and indignation of an Apostle may be the impulses of Divine inspiration. He spoke, not in his own name, but in that of Jesus Christ, and power from above attended his words. The prophecy and command of Jesus concerning His Apostles were fulfilled : that ' in His name they should cast out dæmons.' It was as it had been at Jericho and by the Lake of Gennesareth. The demoniac at Philippi was restored ' to her right mind.' Her natural powers resumed their course; and the gains of her masters were gone.

Violent rage on the part of these men was the immediate result. They saw that their influence with the people, and with it ' all hope' of any future profit, was at end. They proceeded, therefore, to take a summary revenge. Laying violent hold of Paul and Silas (for Timotheus and Luke were not so evidently concerned in what had happened), they dragged them into the forum[2] before the city authorities. The case was brought before the Prætors (so we may venture to call them, since this was the title which colonial Duum- viri were fond of assuming);[3] but the complainants must have felt some difficulty in stating their grievance. The slave that had lately been a lucrative possession had suddenly become valueless; but the law had no remedy for property depreciated by exorcism. The true state of the case was therefore concealed, and an accusation was laid

[1] See what Trench says on the de- moniacs in the country of the Gada- renes. ' We find in the demoniac the sense of a misery in which he does not acquiesce, the deep feeling of inward discord, of the true life utterly shattered, of an alien power which has mastered him wholly, and now is cruelly lording over him, and ever drawing further away from Him in whom only any created intelligence' can find rest and peace. His state is, in the truest sense, " a possession ; " another is ruling in the high places of his soul, and has cast down the rightful lord from his seat;

and he knows this : and out of his con- sciousness of it there goes forth from him a cry for redemption, so soon as ever a glimpse of hope is afforded, an unlooked-for Redeemer draws near.'— P. 159.
[2] Acts xvi. 19.
[3] See above, p. 225, n. 7. The word στρατηγὸς is the usual Greek transla- tion of *prætor*. It is, however, often used generally for the supreme magis- trates of Greek towns. Wetstein tells us that the mayor in Messina was in his time still called *stradigo*.

before the Prætors in the following form. 'These men are throwing the whole city into confusion; moreover they are Jews;[1] and they are attempting to introduce new religious observances,[2] which we, being Roman citizens, cannot legally receive and adopt.' The accusation was partly true and partly false. It was quite false that Paul and Silas were disturbing the colony; for nothing could have been more calm and orderly than their worship and teaching at the house of Lydia, or in the *proseucha* by the water side. In the other part of the indictment there was a certain amount of truth. The letter of the Roman law, even under the Republic, was opposed to the introduction of foreign religions; and though exceptions were allowed, as in the case of the Jews themselves, yet the spirit of the law entirely condemned such changes in worship as were likely to unsettle the minds of the citizens, or to produce any tumultuous uproar; and the advice given to Augustus, which both he and his successors had studiously followed, was, to check religious innovations as promptly as possible, lest in the end they should undermine the Monarchy. Thus Paul and Silas had undoubtedly been doing what in some degree exposed them to legal penalties; and were beginning a change which tended to bring down, and which ultimately did bring down, the whole weight of the Roman law on the martyrs of Christianity.[3] The force of another part of the accusation, which was adroitly introduced, namely, that the men were 'Jews to begin with,' will be fully apprehended, if we remember, not only that the Jews were generally hated, suspected, and despised,[4] but that they had lately been driven out of Rome in consequence of an uproar,[5] and that it was incumbent on Philippi, as a colony, to copy the indignation of the mother city.

Thus we can enter into the feelings which caused the mob to rise against Paul and Silas,[6] and tempted the Prætors to dispense with legal formalities and consign the offenders to immediate punishment. The mere loss of the slave's prophetic powers, so far as it was generally known, was enough to cause a violent agitation: for mobs are always more fond of excitement and wonder than of truth and holiness. The Philippians had been willing to pay money for the demoniac's revelations, and now strangers had come and deprived them of that which gratified their superstitious curiosity. And when they learned, moreover, that these strangers were Jews, and were breaking the laws of Rome, their discontent became fanatical. It seems that the Prætors had no time to hesitate, if they would retain

---

[1] 'Being Jews to begin with,' is the most exact translation. The verb is the same as in Gal. ii. 14, being born a Jew,' p. 179.

[2] The word is similarly used Acts vi. 14, xxvi. 3, xxviii. 17.

[3] See the account of the martyrs of Gaul in Eusebius, v. 1. The governor, learning that Attalus was a Roman citizen, ordered him to be remanded to prison till he should learn the emperor's commands. Those who had the citizenship were beheaded. The rest were sent to the wild beasts.

[4] Cicero calls them 'suspiciosa ac-maledica civitas.'—*Flac.* 28. Other authors could be quoted to the same effect.

[5] Acts xviii. 2; which is probably the same occurrence as that which is alluded to by Suetonius, *Claud.* 25:— 'Judæos impulsore Christo assidue tumultuantes Roma expulit.' See pp. 256, 299.

[6] Acts xvi. 22.

their popularity. The rough words were spoken :[1] *Go, lictors: strip off their garments: let them be scourged.*'[2] The order was promptly obeyed, and the heavy blows descended. It is happy for us that few modern countries know, by the example of a similar punishment, what the severity of a Roman scourging was. The Apostles received 'many stripes ;' and when they were consigned to prison, bleeding and faint from the rod, the jailor received a strict injunction 'to keep them safe.' Well might St. Paul, when at Corinth, look back to this day of cruelty, and remind the Thessalonians how he and Silas had 'suffered before, and were shamefully treated at Philippi.'[3]

The jailor fulfilled the directions of the magistrates with rigorous and conscientious cruelty. Not content with placing the Apostles among such other offenders against the law as were in custody at Philippi, he 'thrust them into the inner prison,'[4] and then forced their limbs, lacerated as they were, and bleeding from the rod, into a painful and constrained posture, by means of an instrument employed to confine and torture the bodies of the worst malefactors.[5] Though we are ignorant of the exact relation of the outer and inner prisons,[6] and of the connection of the jailor's 'house' with both, we are not without very good notions of the misery endured in the Roman places of captivity. We must picture to ourselves something very different from the austere comfort of an English jail. It is only since that Christianity for which the Apostles bled has had influence on the hearts of men, that the treatment of felons has been a distinct subject of philanthropic inquiry, and that we have learnt to pray 'for all prisoners and captives.' The inner prisons of which we read in the ancient world were like that 'dungeon in the court of the prison,' into which Jeremiah was let down with cords, and where 'he sank in the mire.'[7] They were pestilential cells, damp and cold, from which the light was excluded, and where the chains rusted on the limbs of the prisoners. One such place may be seen

---

[1] The official order is given by Seneca. Some commentators suppose that the Duumviri tore off the garments of Paul and Silas with their own hands; but this supposition is unnecessary. It is quite a mistake to imagine that they rent *their own* garments, like the highpriest at Jerusalem.

[2] The original word strictly denotes 'to beat with rods,' as it is translated in 2 Cor. xi. 25.

[3] 1 Thess. ii. 2.   [4] Acts xvi. 24.

[5] The ξύλον was what the Romans called *nervus*. See the note in the *Pictorial Bible* on Job xiii. 27, and the woodcut of stocks used in India from Roberts's *Oriental Illustrations*.

[6] A writer on the subject (Walch) says that in a Roman prison there were usually three distinct parts: (1) the *communiora*, where the prisoners had light and fresh air; (2) the *inte-*

riora, shut off by iron gates with strong bars and locks; (3) the *Tullianum*, or dungeon. If this was the case at Philippi, Paul and Silas were perhaps in the second, and the other prisoners in the first part. The third was rather a place of execution than imprisonment. Walch says that in the provinces the prisons were not so systematically divided into three parts. He adds that the jailor or *commentariensis* had usually *optiones* to assist him. In Acts xvi. only one jailor is mentioned.

[7] 'Then took they Jeremiah and cast him into the dungeon of Malchiah, the son of Hammelech, *which was in the court of the prison ;* and they let down Jeremiah with cords. And in the dungeon there was no water, but mire; so Jeremiah sunk in the mire.' —*Jer.* xxxviii. 6. See the note in the *Pictorial Bible.*

to this day on the slope of the Capitol at Rome.[1] It is known to the readers of Cicero and Sallust as the place where certain notorious conspirators were executed. The *Tullianum* (for so it was called) is a type of the dungeons in the provinces; and we find the very name applied, in one instance, to a dungeon in the province of Macedonia.[2] What kind of torture was inflicted by the ' stocks,' in which the arms and legs, and even the necks, of offenders were confined and stretched, we are sufficiently informed by the allusions to the punishment of slaves in the Greek and Roman writers;[3] and to show how far the cruelty of Heathen persecution, which may be said to have begun at Philippi, was afterwards carried in this peculiar kind of torture, we may refer to the sufferings ' which Origen endured under an iron collar, and in the deepest recesses of the prison, when, for many days, he was extended and stretched *to the distance of four holes on the rack.*'[4]

A few hours had made a serious change from the quiet scene by the water side to the interior of a stifling dungeon. But Paul and Silas had learnt, ' in whatever state they were, therewith to be content.'[5] They were even able to ' rejoice' that they were ' counted worthy to suffer' for the name of Christ.[6] And if some thoughts of discouragement came over their minds, not for their own sufferings, but for the cause of their Master; and if it seemed 'a strange thing' that a work to which they had been beckoned by God should be arrested in its very beginning; yet they had faith to believe that His arm would be revealed at the appointed time. Joseph's feet, too, had been ' hurt in the stocks,'[7] and he became a prince in Egypt. Daniel had been cast into the lions' den, and he was made ruler of Babylon. Thus Paul and Silas remembered with joy the 'Lord our Maker, *who giveth songs in the night.*'[8] Racked as they were with pain, sleepless and weary, they were heard ' about midnight,' from the depth of their prison-house, ' praying and singing hymns to God.'[9] What it was that they sang, we know not; but the Psalms of David have ever been dear to those who suffer; they have instructed both Jew and Christian in the language of prayer and praise. And the Psalms abound in such sentences as these:—' The Lord looketh down from His sanctuary: out of heaven the Lord beholdeth the earth: that He might hear the mournings of such as are in captivity, and deliver the children appointed unto death.'—' O let the sorrowful sighing of the prisoners come before thee: according to the greatness of thy power, preserve thou those that are appointed to die.'—' The Lord helpeth

---

[1] For an account of it see Sir W. Gell's work on Rome, also Rich's *Dict. of Greek and Roman Antiquities,* from which the woodcut at the end of this chapter is taken.

[2] In Apuleius, where the allusion is to Thessaly.

[3] Especially in Plautus.

[4] Euseb. *Hist. Eccl.* vi. 39.

[5] Phil. iv. 11.   [6] Acts v. 41.

[7] Ps. cv. 18, Prayer-Book Version. Philo, writing on the history of Joseph

(Gen. xxxix. 21), has some striking remarks on the cruel character of jailors, who live among thieves, robbers, and murderers, and never see anything that is good.

[8] Job xxxv. 10.

[9] Acts xvi. 25. The tense is imperfect: for the word see Matt. xxvi. 30; Mark xiv. 26. The psalms sung on that occasion are believed to be Ps. cxiii.–cxviii. Compare Eph. v. 19; Col. iii. 16. Also Heb. ii. 12.

them to right that suffer wrong: the Lord looseth men out of prison: the Lord helpeth them that are fallen: the Lord careth for the righteous.'[1] Such sounds as these were new in a Roman dungeon. Whoever the other prisoners might be, whether they were the victims of oppression, or were suffering the punishment of guilt,— debtors, slaves, robbers, or murderers,—they listened with surprise to the voices of those who filled the midnight of the prison with sounds of cheerfulness and joy. Still the Apostles continued their praises, and the prisoners listened.[2] 'They that sit in darkness, and in the shadow of death: being fast bound in misery and iron; when they cried unto the Lord in their trouble, He delivered them out of their distress. For He brought them out of darkness, and out of the shadow of death; and brake their bonds in sunder. O that men would therefore praise the Lord for His goodness, and declare the wonders that He doeth for the children of men: for He hath broken the gates of brass, and smitten the bars of iron in sunder.'[3] When suddenly, as if in direct answer to the prayer of His servants, an earthquake shook the very foundations of the prison,[4] the gates were broken, the bars smitten asunder, and the bands of the prisoners loosed. Without striving to draw a line between the natural and supernatural in this occurrence, and still less endeavouring to resolve what was evidently miraculous into the results of ordinary causes, we turn again to the thought suggested by that single but expressive phrase of Scripture, '*the prisoners were listening.*'[5] When we reflect on their knowledge of the Apostles' sufferings (for they were doubtless aware of the manner in which they had been brought in and thrust into the dungeon[6]), and on the wonder they must have experienced on hearing sounds of joy from those who were in pain, and on the awe which must have overpowered them when they felt the prison shaken and the chains fall from their limbs; and when to all this we add the effect produced on their minds by all that happened on the following day, and especially the fact that the jailor himself became a Christian; we can hardly avoid the conclusion that the hearts of many of those unhappy bondsmen were prepared that night to receive the Gospel, that the tidings of spiritual liberty came to those whom, but for the captivity of the Apostles, it would never have reached, and that the jailor himself was their evangelist and teacher.

The effect produced by that night on the jailor's own mind has been fully related to us. Awakened in a moment by the earthquake, his first thought was of his prisoners:[7] and in the shock of surprise and alarm,—'seeing the doors of the prison open, and supposing that the prisoners were fled,'—aware that inevitable death awaited him,[8] with the stern and desperate resignation of a Roman official,

---

[1] Ps. cii. 19, 20, lxxix. 12, cxlvi. 6–8. See also Ps. cxlii. 8, 9, lxix. 34, cxvi. 14, lxviii. 6.

[2] The imperfects used in this passage imply continuance. The Apostles were singing, and the prisoners were listening, when the earthquake came.

[3] Ps. cvii. 10–16.

[4] Acts xvi. 26.

[5] See above.

[6] See above, on the form of ancient prisons.

[7] Acts xvi. 27.

[8] By the Roman law, the jailor was to undergo the same punishment which the malefactors who escaped by his negligence were to have suffered. Biscoe, p. 330.

he resolved that suicide was better than disgrace, and 'drew his sword.'

Philippi is famous in the annals of suicide. Here Cassius, unable to survive defeat, covered his face in the empty tent, and ordered his freedmen to strike the blow.[1] His messenger Titinius held it to be 'a Roman's part'[2] to follow the stern example. Here Brutus bade adieu to his friends, exclaiming, 'Certainly we must fly, yet not with the feet, but with the hands;'[3] and many, whose names have never reached us, ended their last struggle for the republic by self-inflicted death.[4] Here, too, another despairing man would have committed the same crime, had not his hand been arrested by an Apostle's voice. Instead of a sudden and hopeless death, the jailor received at the hands of his prisoner the gift both of temporal and spiritual life.

The loud exclamation[5] of St. Paul, 'Do thyself no harm: for we are all here,' gave immediate reassurance to the terrified jailor. He laid aside his sword, and called for lights, and rushed[6] to the 'inner prison,' where Paul and Silas were confined. But now a new fear of a higher kind took possession of his soul. The recollection of all he had heard before concerning these prisoners and all that he had observed of their demeanour when he brought them into the dungeon, the shuddering thought of the earthquake, the burst of his gratitude towards them as the preservers of his life, and the consciousness that even in the darkness of midnight they had seen his intention of suicide,—all these mingling and conflicting emotions made him feel that he was in the presence of a higher power. He fell down before them, and brought them out, as men whom he had deeply injured and insulted, to a place of greater freedom and comfort;[7] and then he asked them, with earnest anxiety, what he must do to be saved. We see the Apostle here self-possessed in the earthquake, as afterwards in the storm at sea,[8] able to overawe and control those who were placed over him, and calmly turning the occasion to a spiritual end. It is surely, however, a mistake to imagine that the jailor's inquiry had reference merely to temporal and immediate danger. The awakening of his conscience, the presence of the unseen world, the miraculous visitation, the nearness of death,—coupled perhaps with some confused recollection of the '*way of salvation*' which these strangers were said to have been proclaiming,—were enough to suggest that inquiry which is the most momentous that any human soul can make: '*What must I do to be saved?*'[9] Their answer was that of faithful Apostles. They preached 'not themselves, but

[1] Plut. *Brutus*, 43.

[2] *Julius Cæsar*, act v. sc. iii.

[3] Plut. *Brutus*, 52.

[4] 'The majority of the proscribed who survived the battles of Philippi put an end to their own lives, as they despaired of being pardoned,'—Niebuhr's *Lectures*, ii. 118.   [5] Acts xvi. 28.

[6] The whole phraseology seems to imply that the dungeon was subterraneous. Prof. Hackett, however, takes a different view.

[7] Either the outer prison or the space about the entrance to the jailor's dwelling, if indeed they were not identical.

[8] Acts xxvii. 20-25.

[9] We should compare ver. 30 with ver. 17. The words 'save' and 'salvation' must have been frequently in the mouth of St. Paul. It is probable that the demoniac, and possible that the jailor, might have heard them. See pp. 231, 232.

Christ Jesus the Lord.'[1] 'Believe, not in us, but *in the Lord Jesus, and thou shalt be saved;* and not only thou, but the like faith shall bring salvation to *all thy house.*' From this last expression, and from the words which follow, we infer that the members of the jailor's family had crowded round him and the Apostles.[2] No time was lost in making known to them 'the word of the Lord.' All thought of bodily comfort and repose was postponed to the work of saving the soul. The meaning of 'faith in Jesus' was explained, and the Gospel was preached to the jailor's family at midnight, while the prisoners were silent around, and the light was thrown on anxious faces and the dungeon-wall.

And now we have an instance of that sympathetic care, that interchange of temporal and spiritual service, which has ever attended the steps of true Christianity. As it was in the miracles of our Lord and Saviour, where the soul and the body were regarded together, so has it always been in His Church. 'In the same hour of the night'[3] the jailor took the Apostles to the well or fountain of water which was within or near the precincts of the prison, and there he washed their wounds, and there also he and his household were baptized. He did what he could to assuage the bodily pain of Paul and Silas, and they admitted him and his, by the 'laver of regeneration,'[4] to the spiritual citizenship of the kingdom of God. The prisoners of the jailor were now become his guests. His cruelty was changed into hospitality and love. 'He took them up[5] into his house,' and, placing them in a posture of repose, set food before them,[6] and refreshed their exhausted strength. It was a night of happiness for all. They praised God that His power had been made effectual in their weakness; and the jailor's family had their first experience of that joy which is the fruit of believing in God.

At length morning broke on the eventful night. In the course of that night the greatest of all changes had been wrought in the jailor's relations to this world and the next. From being the ignorant slave of a Heathen magistracy he had become the religious head of a Christian family. A change, also, in the same interval of time, had come over the minds of the magistrates themselves. Either from reflecting that they had acted more harshly than the case had warranted, or from hearing a more accurate statement of facts, or through alarm caused by the earthquake, or through that vague misgiving which sometimes, as in the case of Pilate and his wife,[7] haunts the minds of those who have no distinct religious

---

[1] 2 Cor. iv. 5.

[2] The preaching of the Gospel to the jailor *and his family* seems to have taken place immediately on coming out of the prison (vv. 30–32); then the baptism of the converts, and the washing of the Apostles' stripes (ver. 33); and finally the going up *into the house,* and the hospitable refreshment there afforded. It does not appear certain that they returned from the jailor's house into the dungeon before they were taken *out of custody* (ver. 40).

[3] Acts xvi. 33. Here and in ver. 34, a change of place is implied.

[4] Tit. iii. 5.

[5] Acts xvi. 34. The word implies at least that the house was higher than the prison. See p. 237, n. 6.

[6] The custom of Greek and Roman meals must be borne in mind. Guests were placed on couches, and tables, with the different courses of food, were brought and removed in succession.

[7] Matt. xxvii. 19.

convictions, they sent new orders in the morning to the jailor. The message conveyed by the lictors was expressed in a somewhat contemptuous form, ' *Let those men go.*' [1]   But the jailor received it with the utmost joy.   He felt his infinite debt of gratitude to the Apostles, not only for his preservation from a violent death, but for the tidings they had given him of eternal life.   He would willingly have seen them freed from their bondage ; but he was dependent on the will of the magistrates, and could do nothing without their sanction.   When, therefore, the lictors brought the order, he went with them [2] to announce the intelligence to the prisoners, and joyfully told them to leave their dungeon and ' go in peace.'

But Paul, not from any fanatical love of braving the authorities, but calmly looking to the ends of justice and the establishment of Christianity, refused to accept his liberty without some public acknowledgment of the wrong he had suffered.   He now proclaimed a fact which had hitherto been unknown,—that he and Silas were Roman citizens.   Two Roman laws had been violated by the magistrates of the colony in the scourging inflicted the day before. [3]   And this, too, with signal aggravations.   They were ' uncondemned.' There had been no form of trial, without which, in the case of a citizen, even a slighter punishment would have been illegal.   And it had been done ' publicly.'   In the face of the colonial population, an outrage had been committed on the majesty of the name in which they boasted, and Rome had been insulted in her citizens. ' No,' said St. Paul ; ' they have oppressed the innocent and violated the law.   Do they seek to satisfy justice by conniving at a secret escape ?   Let them come themselves and take us out of prison.   They have publicly treated us as guilty ; let them publicly declare that we are innocent.' [4]

' How often,' says Cicero, ' has this exclamation, *I am a Roman citizen,* brought aid and safety even among barbarians in the remotest parts of the earth !'—The lictors returned to the Prætors, and the Prætors were alarmed.   They felt that they had committed an act, which, if divulged at Rome, would place them in the utmost jeopardy.   They had good reason to fear even for their authority in the colony ; for the people of Philippi, ' being Romans,' might be expected to resent such a violation of the law.   They hastened, therefore, immediately to the prisoners, and became the suppliants of those whom they had persecuted.   They brought them at once out of the dungeon, and earnestly ' besought them to depart from the city.' [5]

The whole narrative of St. Paul's imprisonment at Philippi sets before us in striking colours his clear judgment and presence of mind.   He might have escaped by help of the earthquake and under the shelter of the darkness ; but this would have been to depart as a runaway slave.   He would not do secretly what he

---

[1] Or, as it might be translated, 'Let those fellows go.'

[2] It is evident from ver. 37, that they came into the prison with the jailor, or found the prisoners in the jailor's house (p. 238, n. 2), for St.

Paul spoke 'to *them*; on which they went and told the magistrates (ver. 38).

[3] The Lex Valeria (B.C. 508) and the Lex Porcia (B.C. 300).

[4] ver. 37.

[5] vv. 38, 39.

knew he ought to be allowed to do openly. By such a course his own character and that of the Gospel would have been disgraced, the jailor would have been cruelly left to destruction, and all religious influence over the other prisoners would have been gone. As regards these prisoners, his influence over them was like the sway he obtained over the crew in the sinking vessel.[1] It was so great, that not one of them attempted to escape. And not only in the prison, but in the whole town of Philippi, Christianity was placed on a high vantage-ground by the Apostle's conduct that night. It now appeared that these persecuted Jews were themselves sharers in the vaunted Roman privilege. Those very laws had been violated in their treatment which they themselves had been accused of violating. That no appeal was made against this treatment, might be set down to the generous forbearance of the Apostles. Their cause was now, for a time at least, under the protection of the law, and they themselves were felt to have a claim on general sympathy and respect.

They complied with the request of the magistrates. Yet, even in their departure, they were not unmindful of the dignity and self-possession which ought always to be maintained by innocent men in a righteous cause. They did not retire in any hasty or precipitate flight, but proceeded 'from the prison to the house of Lydia;'[2] and there they met the Christian brethren who were assembled to hear their farewell words of exhortation; and so they departed from the city. It was not, however, deemed sufficient that this infant church at Philippi should be left alone with the mere remembrance of words of exhortation. Two of the Apostolic company remained behind: Timotheus, of whom the Philippians 'learned the proof' that he honestly cared for their state, that he was truly like-minded with St. Paul, 'serving him in the Gospel as a son serves his father,'[3] and 'Luke the Evangelist, whose praise is in the Gospel,' though he never praises himself, or relates his own labours, and though we only trace his movements in connection with St. Paul by the change of a pronoun,[4] or the unconscious variation of his style.

Timotheus seems to have rejoined Paul and Silas, if not at Thessalonica, at least at Berœa.[5] But we do not see St. Luke again in the Apostle's company till the third missionary journey and the second visit to Macedonia.[6] At this exact point of separation, we observe that he drops the style of an eye-witness and resumes that of a historian, until the second time of meeting, after which he writes as an eye-witness till the arrival at Rome, and the very close of the Acts. To explain and justify the remark here made, we need only ask the reader to contrast the detailed narrative of events at Philippi with the more general account of what hap-

---

[1] Acts xxvii. [2] Acts xvi. 40.
[3] Phil. ii. 19–25.
[4] In chap. xvii. the narrative is again in the third person; and the pronoun is not changed again till we come to xx. 5. The modesty with which St. Luke leaves out all mention of his own labours need hardly be pointed out.
[5] Acts xvii. 14. He is not mentioned in the journey to Thessalonica, nor in the account of what happened there.
[6] Acts xx. 4–6.

pened at Thessalonica.[1] It might be inferred that the writer of the Acts was an eye-witness in the former city and not in the latter, even if the pronoun did not show us when he was present and when he was absent. We shall trace him a second time, in the same manner, when he rejoins St. Paul in the same neighbourhood. He appears again on a voyage from Philippi to Troas (Acts xx. 56), as now he has appeared on a voyage from Troas to Philippi. It is not an improbable conjecture that his vocation as a physician[2] may have brought him into connection with these contiguous coasts of Asia and Europe. It has even been imagined, on reasonable grounds,[3] that he may have been in the habit of exercising his professional skill as a surgeon at sea. However this may have been, we see no reason to question the ancient opinion, stated by Eusebius and Jerome, that St. Luke was a native of Antioch. Such a city was a likely place for the education of a physician.[4] It is also natural to suppose that he may have met with St. Paul there, and been converted at an earlier period of the history of the Church. His medical calling, or his zeal for Christianity, or both combined (and the combination has ever been beneficial to the cause of the Gospel), may account for his visits to the North of the Archipelago:[5] or St. Paul may himself have directed his movements, as he afterwards directed those of Timothy and Titus.[6] All these suggestions, though more or less conjectural, are worthy of our thoughts, when we remember the debt of gratitude which the Church owes to this Evangelist, not only as the historian of the Acts of the Apostles, but as an example of long-continued devotion to the truth, and of unshaken constancy to that one Apostle, who said with sorrow, in his latest trial, that others had forsaken him, and that ' only Luke ' was with him.[7]

Leaving their first Macedonian converts to the care of Timotheus and Luke, aided by the co-operation of godly men and women

---

[1] Observe, for instance, his mention of running before the wind, and staying for the night at Samothrace. Again, he says that Philippi was the first city they came to, and that it was a colony. He tells us that the place of prayer was outside the gate and near a river-side. There is no such particularity in the account of what took place at Thessalonica. See above, p. 119, n. 7. Similar remarks might be made on the other *autoptic* passages of the Acts, and we shall return to the subject again. A careful attention to this difference of style is enough to refute a theory lately advanced (Dr. Kitto's *Journal of Sacred Literature*, Sept. 1850) that Silas was the author of the Acts. Silas was at Thessalonica as well as Philippi. Why did he write so differently concerning the two places?

[2] See Tate's *Continuous History*, p. 41. Compare the end of the preceding chapter.

[3] This suggestion is made by Mr. Smith in his work on the *Shipwreck*, &c., p. 8. It is justly remarked, that the ancient ships were often so large that they may reasonably be supposed to have sometimes had surgeons on board. See p. 218.

[4] Alexandria was famous for the education of physicians, and Antioch was in many respects a second Alexandria.

[5] Compare the case of Democedes in Herodotus, who was established first in Ægina, then in Athens, and finally in Samos. At a period even later than St. Luke, Galen speaks of the medical schools of Cos and Cnidus, of Rhodes and of Asia.

[6] 1 Tim. i. 3; 2 Tim. iv. 9, 21; Tit. i. 5, iii. 12.

[7] 2 Tim. iv. 11. See the *Christian Year:* St. Luke's Day.

raised up among the Philippians themselves,[1] Paul and Silas set forth on their journey. Before we follow them to Thessalonica, we may pause to take a general survey of the condition and extent of Macedonia, in the sense in which the term was understood in the language of the day. It has been well said that the Acts of the Apostles have made Macedonia a kind of Holy Land;[2] and it is satisfactory that the places there visited and revisited by St. Paul and his companions are so well known, that we have no difficulty in representing to the mind their position and their relation to the surrounding country.

Macedonia, in its popular sense, may be described as a region bounded by a great semicircle of mountains, beyond which the streams flow westward to the Adriatic, or northward and eastward to the Danube and the Euxine.[3] This mountain barrier sends down branches to the sea on the eastern or Thracian frontier, over against Thasos and Samothrace;[4] and on the south shuts out the plain of Thessaly, and rises near the shore to the high summits of Pelion, Ossa, and the snowy Olympus.[5] The space thus enclosed is intersected by two great rivers. One of these is Homer's 'wide-flowing Axius,' which directs its course past Pella, the ancient metropolis of the Macedonian kings, and the birthplace of Alexander, to the low levels in the neighbourhood of Thessalonica, where other rivers[6] flow near it into the Thermaic gulf. The other is the Strymon, which brings the produce of the great inland level of Serres[7] by Lake Cercinus to the sea at Amphipolis, and beyond which was Philippi, the military outpost that commemorated the successful conquests of Alexander's father. Between the mouths of these two rivers a remarkable tract of country, which is insular

[1] The Christian *women* at Philippi have been alluded to before. P. 228. See especially Phil. iv. 2, 3. We cannot well doubt that *presbyters* also were appointed, as at Thessalonica. See below. Compare Phil. i. 1.

[2] 'The whole of Macedonia, and in particular the route from *Berœa* to *Thessalonica* and *Philippi*, being so remarkably distinguished by St. Paul's sufferings and adventures, becomes as a portion of *Holy Land*.'—Clarke's *Travels*, ch. xi.

[3] The mountains on the north, under the names of Scomius, Scordus, &c., are connected with the Hæmus or Balkan. Those on the west run in a southerly direction, and are continuous with the chain of Pindus.

[4] These are the mountains near the river Nestus, which, after the time of Philip, was considered the boundary of Macedonia and Thrace.

[5] The natural boundary between Macedonia and Thessaly is formed by the Cambunian hills, running in an easterly direction from the central chain of Pindus. The Cambunian range is vividly described in the following view from the 'giddy height' of Olympus, which rises near the coast. 'I seemed to stand perpendicularly over the sea, at the height of 10,000 feet. Salonica was quite distinguishable, lying north-east. Larissa [in Thessaly] appeared under my very feet. The whole horizon from north to south-west was occupied by mountains *hanging on, as it were, to Olympus*. This is the range that runs westward along the north of Thessaly, ending in Pindus.' —Urquhart's *Spirit of the East*, vol. i. p. 429.

[6] The Haliacmon, which flows near Berœa, is the most important of them.

[7] This is the great inland plain at one extremity of which Philippi was situated, and which has been mentioned above (p. 222). Its principal town at present is Serres, the residence of the governor of the whole district, and a place of considerable importance, often mentioned by Cousinéry, Leake, and other travellers.

rather than continental,[1] projects into the Archipelago, and divides itself into three points, on the furthest of which Mount Athos rises nearly into the region of perpetual snow.[2] Part of St. Paul's path between Philippi and Berœa lay across the neck of this peninsula. The whole of his route was over historical ground. At Philippi he was close to the confines of Thracian barbarism, and on the spot where the last battle was fought in defence of the Republic. At Berœa he came near the mountains, beyond which is the region of Classical Greece, and close to the spot where the battle was fought which reduced Macedonia to a province.[3]

If we wish to view Macedonia as a province, some modifications must be introduced into the preceding description. It applies, indeed, with sufficient exactness to the country on its first conquest by the Romans.[4] The rivers already alluded to, define the four districts into which it was divided. *Macedonia Prima* was the region east of the Strymon, of which Amphipolis was the capital ;[5] *Macedonia Secunda* lay between the Strymon and the Axius, and Thessalonica was its metropolis ; and the other two regions were situated to the south towards Thessaly, and on the mountains to the west.[6] This was the division adopted by Paulus Æmilius after the battle of Pydna. But the arrangement was only temporary. The whole of Macedonia, along with some adjacent territories, was made one province,[7] and centralised under the jurisdiction of a proconsul,[8] who resided at Thessalonica. This province included Thessaly,[9] and extended over the mountain chain which had been the western boundary of ancient Macedonia, so as to embrace a sea-board of considerable length on the shore of the Adriatic. The political limits, in this part of the Empire, are far more easily discriminated than those with which we have been lately occupied (Chap. VIII). Three provinces divided the whole surface which extends from the basin of the Danube to Cape Matapan. All of them are familiar to us in the writings of St. Paul. The extent of *Macedonia* has just been defined. Its relations with the other provinces were as follows. On the north-west it was contiguous to *Illyricum*,[10] which was spread down the shore of the Adriatic

---

[1] The peninsula anciently called Chalcidice.

[2] The elevation of Mount Athos is between 4,000 and 5 000 feet. The writer has heard English sailors say that there is almost always snow on Athos and Olympus, and that, though the land generally is high in this part of the Ægean, these mountains are by far the most conspicuous.

[3] Pydna is within a few miles of Berœa, on the other side of the Haliacmon.

[4] See Liv. xlv. 29.

[5] See above.

[6] *Macedonia Tertia* was between the Axius and Peneus, with Pella for its capital. Pelagonia was the capital of *Macedonia Quarta*. It is remark-able that no coins of the third division have been found, but only of the first, second, and fourth.

[7] By Metellus.

[8] At first it was one of the Emperor's provinces, but afterwards it was placed under the Senate.

[9] Thessaly was subject to Macedonia when the Roman wars began. At the close of the first war, under Flaminius, it was declared free; but ultimately it was incorporated with the province.

[10] At first the wars of Rome with the people of this coast merely led to mercantile treaties for the free navigation of the Adriatic. Julius Cæsar and Augustus concluded the series of wars which gradually reduced it to a province.

nearly to the same point to which the Austrian territory now extends, fringing the Mahommedan empire with a Christian border.[1] A hundred miles to the southward, at the Acroceraunian promontory, it touched *Achaia*, the boundary of which province ran thence in an irregular line to the bay of Thermopylæ and the north of Eubœa, including Epirus, and excluding Thessaly.[2] Achaia and Macedonia were traversed many times by the Apostle;[3] and he could say, when he was hoping to travel to Rome, that he had preached the Gospel 'round about unto Illyricum.'[4]

When we allude to Rome, and think of the relation of the City to the provinces, we are inevitably reminded of the military roads ; and here, across the breadth of Macedonia, was one of the greatest roads of the Empire. It is evident that, after Constantinople was founded, a line of communication between the Eastern and Western capitals was of the utmost moment ; but the *Via Egnatia* was constructed long before that period. Strabo, in the reign of Augustus, informs us that it was regularly made and marked out by milestones, from Dyrrhachium on the Adriatic, to Cypselus on the Hebrus in Thrace ; and, even before the close of the republic, we find Cicero speaking, in one of his orations, of 'that military way of ours, which connects us with the Hellespont.' Certain districts on the European side of the Hellespont had been part of the legacy of King Attalus,[5] and the simultaneous possession of Macedonia, Asia, and Bithynia, with the prospect of further conquests in the East, made this line of communication absolutely necessary. When St. Paul was on the Roman road at Troas[6] or Philippi, he was on a road which led to the gates of Rome. It was the same pavement which he afterwards trod at Appii Forum and the Three Taverns.[7] The nearest parallel which the world has seen of the imperial roads is the present European railway system. The Hellespont and the Bosphorus, in the reign of Claudius, were what the Straits of Dover and Holyhead are now ; and even the passage from Brundusium in Italy, to Dyrrhachium and Apollonia[8] in Mace-

---

[1] The border town was Lissus, the modern Alessio, not far from Scutari.

[2] Except in the western portion, the boundary nearly coincided with that of the modern kingdom of Greece. The provincial arrangements of Achaia will be alluded to more particularly hereafter.

[3] Observe how these provinces are mentioned together, Rom. xv. 26 ; 2 Cor. ix. 2, xi. 9, 10; also 1 Thess. i. 7, 8.

[4] Rom. xv. 19. Dalmatia (2 Tim. iv. 10) was a district in this province. See Chap. XVII. Nicopolis (Tit. iii. 12) was in Epirus, which, as we have seen, was a district in the province of Achaia, but it was connected by a branch road with the *Via Egnatia* from Dyrrhachium, which is mentioned below.

[5] See the preceding chapter, under 'Asia.'

[6] See what is said of the road between Troas and Pergamus, &c., p. 214.

[7] Acts xxviii. 15. For notices of the *Via Appia*, where it approaches the Adriatic, in the neighbourhood of *Egnatia* ('Gnatia lymphis iratis extructa'), whence, according to some writers, the Macedonian continuation received its name, see Horace's journey, Sat. I. v. Dean Milman's *Horace* contains an expressive representation of Brundusium, the harbour on the Italian side of the water.

[8] i.e. Apollonia on the Adriatic, which must be carefully distinguished from the other town of the same name, and on the same road, between Thessalonica and Amphipolis (Acts xvii. 1).

donia, was only a tempestuous ferry,—only one of those difficulties
of nature which the Romans would have overcome if they could,
and which the boldest of the Romans dared to defy.[1] From
Dyrrhachium and Apollonia, the Via Egnatia, strictly so called,
extended a distance of five hundred miles, to the Hebrus, in
Thrace.[2] Thessalonica was about half way between these remote
points, and Philippi was the last[3] important town in the province
of Macedonia. Our concern is only with that part of the Via
Egnatia which lay between the two last-mentioned cities.

The intermediate stages mentioned in the Acts of the Apostles are
Amphipolis and Apollonia. The distances laid down in the Itineraries are as follows:—*Philippi to Amphipolis, thirty-three miles;
Amphipolis to Apollonia, thirty miles; Apollonia to Thessalonica,
thirty-seven miles.* These distances are evidently such as might have
been traversed each in one day; and since nothing is said of any
delay on the road, but everything to imply that the journey was
rapid, we conclude (unless, indeed, their recent sufferings made
rapid travelling impossible) that Paul and Silas rested one night at
each of the intermediate places, and thus our notice of their journey
is divided into three parts.

From Philippi to Amphipolis, the Roman way passed across the
plain to the north of Mount Pangæus. A traveller, going direct
from Neapolis to the mouth of the Strymon, might make his way
through an opening in the mountains[4] nearer the coast. This is the
route by which Xerxes brought his army,[5] and by which modern
journeys are usually made.[6] But Philippi was not built in the time
of the Persian war, and now, under the Turks, it is a ruined village.
Under the Roman emperors, the position of this *colony* determined
the direction of the road. The very productiveness of the soil,[7] and
its liability to inundations,[8] must have caused this road to be care-

---

[1] See the anecdotes of Cæsar's bold
proceedings between Brundusium and
the opposite side of the sea in Plutarch.
The same writer tells us that Cicero,
when departing on his exile, was driven
back by a storm into Brundusium.
See below, p. 248, n. 3. The great
landing place on the Macedonian side
was Dyrrhachium, the ancient Epi-
damnus, called by Catullus 'Adriæ
Tabernæ.'

[2] The roads from Dyrrhachium and
Apollonia met together at a place called
Clodiana, and thence the Via Egnatia
passed over the mountains to Heraclea
in Macedonia. It entered the plain at
Edessa (see below), and thence passed
by Pella to Thessalonica. The stations, as given by the Antonine and
Jerusalem Itineraries and the Peutinger Table, will be found in Cramer's
Ancient Greece, v. i. pp. 81–84.

[3] See above, p. 222, n. 1, and p. 223,
n. 4.

[4] This opening is the Pieric valley.

See Leake, p. 180. 'Though the
modern route from Cavalla to Orphano
and Saloniki, leading by Pravista
through the Pieric valley along the
southern side of Mount Pangæum,
exactly in the line of that of Xerxes,
is the most direct, it does not coincide
with the Roman road or the Via Egnatia, which passed along the northern
base of that mountain, probably for
the sake of connecting both these important cities, the former of which was
a Roman colony.'

[5] Herod. vii. 112.

[6] Dr. Clarke and Cousinéry both
took this route.

[7] 'The plain is very fertile, and
besides yielding abundant harvests of
cotton, wheat, barley, and maize, contains extensive pastures peopled with
oxen, horses, and sheep. No part of
the land is neglected; and the district,
in its general appearance, is not inferior to any part of Europe.'—Leake,
p. 201.   [8] See Leake,

fully constructed. The surface of the plain, which is intersected by multitudes of streams, is covered now with plantations of cotton and fields of Indian corn,[1] and the villages are so numerous that, when seen from the summits of the neighbouring mountains, they appear to form one continued town.[2] Not far from the coast, the Strymon spreads out into a lake as large as Windermere;[3] and between the lower end of this lake and the inner reach of the Strymonic gulf, where the mountains leave a narrow opening, Amphipolis was situated on a bend of the river.

'The position of Amphipolis is one of the most important in Greece. It stands in a pass which traverses the mountains bordering the Strymonic gulf, and it commands the only easy communication from the coast of that gulf into the great Macedonian plains, which extend, for sixty miles, from beyond Meleniko to Philippi.'[4] The ancient name of the place was 'Nine Ways,' from the great number of Thracian and Macedonian roads which met at this point.[5] The Athenians saw the importance of the position, and established a colony there, which they called Amphipolis, because the river surrounded it. Some of the deepest interest in the history of Thucydides, not only as regards military and political movements,[6] but in reference to the personal experience of the historian himself,[7] is concentrated on this spot. And again, Amphipolis appears in the speeches of Demosthenes as a great stake in the later struggle between Philip of Macedon and the citizens of Athens.[8] It was also the scene of one striking passage in the history of Roman conquest: here Paulus Æmilius, after the battle of Pydna, publicly proclaimed that the Macedonians should be *free;*[9] and now another *Paulus* was here, whose message to the Macedonians was an honest proclamation of a better liberty, without conditions and without reserve.

St. Paul's next stage was to the city of Apollonia. After leaving Amphipolis, the road passes along the edge of the Strymonic gulf, first between cliffs and the sea, and then across a well-wooded maritime plain, whence the peak of Athos is seen far across the bay to the left.[10] We quit the sea-shore at the narrow gorge of Aulon, or

[1] 'Des plantes de coton, des rizières immenses, de grandes plantations de tabac, des vignes entrecoupées de terres à blé, formaient sous nos yeux le plus agréable spectacle. . . . . Les produits de cette plaine seraient immenses, si l'activité et l'industrie des habitans répondaient à la libéralité de la nature.' —Cousinéry, ii. 4, 5.

[2] Clarke, ch. xii. At the head of the chapter he gives a view of the plain as seen from the hills on the south.

[3] Anciently the lake *Cercinitis.*

[4] Leake. For other notices of the importance of this position, see Bp. Thirlwall's *Greece,* iii. 284, and especially Mr. Grote's *Greece,* vi. 554-562, and 625-647. A view of Amphipolis is given in our larger editions.

[5] See Herod. vii. 114. Here Xerxes crossed the Strymon, and offered a sacrifice of white horses to the river, and buried alive nine youths and maidens.

[6] See especially all that relates to Cleon and Brasidas in the fourth and fifth books.

[7] It was his failure in an expedition against Amphipolis that caused the exile of Thucydides.

[8] See the passages in the speeches which relate to Philip's encroachment on the Athenian power in the north of the Ægean.

[9] Livy's words (xlv. 30) show that the Romans fully appreciated the importance of the position.

[10] Dr. Clarke.

Arethusa,[1] and there enter the valley which crosses the neck of the Chalcidic peninsula. Up to this point we have frequent historical land-marks reminding us of Athens. Thucydides has just been mentioned in connection with Amphipolis and the Strymon. As we leave the sea, we have before us, on the opposite coast, Stagirus,[2] the birth-place of Aristotle; and in the pass, where the mountains close on the road, is the tomb of Euripides.[3] Thus the steps of our progress, as we leave the East and begin to draw near to Athens, are already among her historians, philosophers, and poets.

Apollonia is somewhere in the inland part of the journey, where the Via Egnatia crosses from the gulf of the Strymon to that of Thessalonica; but its exact position has not been ascertained. We will, therefore, merely allude to the scenery through which the traveller moves, in going from sea to sea. The pass of Arethusa is beautiful and picturesque. A river flows through it in a sinuous course, and abundant oaks and plane trees are on the rocks around.[4] Presently this stream is seen to emerge from an inland lake, whose promontories and villages, with the high mountains rising to the south-west, have reminded travellers of Switzerland.[5] As we journey towards the west, we come to a second lake. Between the two is the modern post-station of Klisali, which may possibly be Apollonia,[6] though it is generally believed to be on the mountain slope to the south of the easternmost lake. The whole region of these two lakes is a long valley, or rather a succession of plains, where the level spaces are richly wooded with forest trees, and the nearer hills are covered to their summits with olives.[7] Beyond the second lake, the road passes over some rising ground, and presently, after emerging from a narrow glen, we obtain a sight of the sea once more, the eye ranges freely over the plain of the Axius, and the city of Thessalonica is immediately before us.

Once arrived in this city, St. Paul no longer follows the course of the Via Egnatia. He may have done so at a later period, when he says that he had preached the Gospel 'round about unto Illyricum.'[8] But at present he had reached the point most favourable for the glad proclamation. The direction of the Roman road was of course determined by important geographical positions; and along the whole line from Dyrrhachium to the Hebrus, no city was so large and influential as Thessalonica.

The Apostolic city at which we are now arrived was known in

[1] Dr. Clarke, ch. xii., devotes several pages to this tomb. The Jerusalem Itinerary, besides another intermediate station at Pennana, mentions that *at the tomb of Euripides.*

[2] Leake identifies Stagirus with Stavros, a little to the south of Aulon, p. 167.

[3] See the last note but one.

[4] See Dr. Clarke. Cousinéry writes with great enthusiasm concerning this glen.

[5] See Dr. Clarke. Both he and Cousinéry make mention of the two villages, the Little Bechik and Great

Bechik, on its north bank, along which the modern road passes.

[6] This is Tafel's opinion; but Leake and Cousinéry both agree in placing it to the south of Lake Bolbe. We ought to add, that the Antonine and Jerusalem Itineraries appear to give two distinct roads between Apollonia and Thessalonica. See Leake, p. 46.

[7] See Clarke's *Travels.*

[8] See above, pp. 244, 245. This expression, however, might be used if nothing more were meant than a progress to the very frontier of Illyricum.

the earliest periods of its history under various names. Under that of Therma it is associated with some interesting recollections. It was the resting-place of Xerxes on his march; it is not unmentioned in the Peloponnesian war; and it was a frequent subject of debate in the last independent assemblies of Athens. When the Macedonian power began to overshadow all the countries where Greek was spoken, this city received its new name, and began a new and more distinguished period of its history. A sister of Alexander the Great was called Thessalonica, and her name was given to the city of Therma, when rebuilt and embellished by her husband, Cassander the son of Antipater.[1] This name, under a form slightly modified, has continued to the present day. The Salneck of the early German poets has become the Saloniki of the modern Levant. Its history can be followed as continuously as its name. When Macedonia was partitioned into four provincial divisions by Paulus Æmilius, Thessalonica was the capital of that which lay between the Axius and the Strymon.[2] When the four regions were united into one Roman province, this city was chosen as the metropolis of the whole. Its name appears more than once in the annals of the Civil Wars. It was the scene of the exile of Cicero;[3] and one of the stages of his journey between Rome and his province in the East.[4] Antony and Octavius were here after the battle of Philippi: and coins are still extant which allude to the ' freedom ' granted by the victorious leaders to the city of the Thermaic gulf. Strabo, in the first century, speaks of Thessalonica as the most populous town in Macedonia. Lucian, in the second century, uses similar language. Before the founding of Constantinople, it was virtually the capital of Greece and Illyricum, as well as of Macedonia, and shared the trade of the Ægean with Ephesus and Corinth. Even after the Eastern Rome was built and reigned over the Levant, we find both Pagan and Christian writers speaking of Thessalonica as the metropolis of Macedonia and a place of great magnitude. Through the Middle Ages it never ceased to be important: and it is, at the present day, the second city in European Turkey.[5] The reason of this continued pre-eminence is to be found in its geographical position. Situated on the inner bend of the Thermaic Gulf,—half-way between the Adriatic and the Hellespont,[6]—on the sea-margin of a vast plain watered by several rivers,[7]—and at the entrance of the pass[8] which commands

[1] The first author in which the new name occurs is Polybius. Some say that the name was given by Philip in honour of his daughter, and others that it directly commemorated a victory over the Thessalians. But the opinion stated above appears the most probable. Philip's daughter was called Thessalonica, in commemoration of a victory obtained by her father on the day when he heard of her birth. Cousinéry sees an allusion to this in the Victory on the coins of the city. See below.

[2] See above, pp. 243, 244.

[3] Both in going out and returning

he crossed the Adriatic, between Brundusium and Dyrrhachium. See p. 245, n. 1. In travelling through Macedonia he would follow the Via Egnatia.

[4] Several of his letters were written from Thessalonica on this journey.

[5] For a very full account of its modern condition see Dr. [Sir Henry] Holland's *Travels.*

[6] See above, p. 242.

[7] The chief of these are the Axius and Haliacmon. The whole region near the sea consists of low alluvial soil. See below, on the journey from Thessalonica to Berœa.

[8] This is the pass mentioned above,

the approach to the other great Macedonian level,—it was evidently destined for a mercantile emporium. Its relation with the inland trade of Macedonia was as close as that of Amphipolis; and its maritime advantages were perhaps even greater. Thus, while Amphipolis decayed under the Byzantine emperors, Thessalonica continued to prosper.[1] There probably never was a time, from the day when it first received its name, that this city has not had the aspect of a busy commercial town.[2] We see at once how appropriate a place it was for one of the starting-points of the Gospel in Europe; and we can appreciate the force of the expression used by St. Paul within a few months of his departure from the Thessalonians,[3] when he says, that 'from them the Word of the Lord had sounded forth like a trumpet,[4] not only in Macedonia and Achaia, but in every place.'

No city, which we have yet had occasion to describe, has had so distinguished a Christian history, with the single exception of the Syrian Antioch; and the Christian glory of the Patriarchal city gradually faded before that of the Macedonian metropolis. The heroic age of Thessalonica was the third century.[5] It was the bulwark of Constantinople in the shock of the barbarians; and it held up the torch of the truth to the successive tribes who overspread the country between the Danube and the Ægean,—the Goths and the Sclaves, the Bulgarians of the Greek Church, and the Wallachians,[6] whose language still seems to connect them with Philippi and the Roman colonies. Thus, in the medieval chroniclers, it has deserved the name of 'the Orthodox City.'[7] The remains of its Hippodrome, which is for ever associated with the history of Theodosius and Ambrose,[8] can yet be traced among the Turkish houses.

through which the road to Amphipolis passed, and in which Apollonia was situated.

[1] Notices of its mercantile relations in the Middle Ages are given by Tafel. For an account of its modern trade, and the way in which it was affected by the last war, see Holland's *Travels.*

[2] A view of the place, as seen from the sea, is given in the larger editions.

[3] 1 Thess. i. 8. The Epistle was written from Corinth very soon after the departure from Thessalonica. See Chap. XI.

[4] Chrysostom employs this image in commenting on 1 Cor. i.

[5] Tafel traces the history of Thessalonica, in great detail, through the Middle Ages; and shows how, after the invasion of the Goths, it was the means of converting the Sclaves, and through them the Bulgarians, to the Christian faith. The peasant population to the east of Thessalonica is Bulgarian, to the west it is Greek

(Cousinéry, p. 52). Both belong to the Greek Church.

[6] See what Cousinéry says (ch. i.) of the Wallachians, who are intermixed among the other tribes of modern Macedonia. They speak a corrupt Latin, and he thinks they are descended from the ancient colonies. They are a fierce and bold race, living chiefly in the mountains; and when trading caravans have to go through dangerous places they are posted in the front.

[7] One Byzantine writer who uses this phrase is Cameniata. His history is curious. He was crozier-bearer to the archbishop, and was carried off by the Arabs, and landed at Tarsus, where he wrote his book.

[8] Some accounts say that 15,000 persons were involved in the massacre, for which the archbishop of Milan exacted penance from the Emperor. See Gibbon, chap. xxvii. For some notice of the remains of the Hippodrome, which still retains its name, see Cousinéry, chap. ii.

Its bishops have sat in great councils.[1] The writings of its great preacher and scholar Eustathius[2] are still preserved to us. It is true that the Christianity of Thessalonica, both medieval and modern, has been debased by humiliating superstition. The glory of its patron saint, Demetrius, has eclipsed that of St. Paul, the founder of its Church. But the same Divine Providence, which causes us to be thankful for the past, commands us to be hopeful for the future; and we may look forward to the time when a new harvest of the 'work of faith, and labour of love, and patience of hope,'[3] shall spring up from the seeds of Divine Truth, which were first sown on the shore of the Thermaic Gulf by the Apostle of the Gentiles.

If Thessalonica can boast of a series of Christian annals, unbroken since the day of St. Paul's arrival, its relations with the Jewish people have continued for a still longer period. In our own day it contains a multitude of Jews[4] commanding an influential position, many of whom are occupied (not very differently from St. Paul himself) in the manufacture of cloth. A considerable number of them are refugees from Spain, and speak the Spanish language. There are materials for tracing similar settlements of the same scattered and persecuted people in this city, at intervals, during the Middle Ages;[5] and even before the destruction of Jerusalem we find them here, numerous and influential, as at Antioch and Iconium. Here, doubtless, was the chief colony of those Jews of Macedonia of whom Philo speaks;[6] for while there was only a *proseucha* at Philippi, and while Amphipolis and Apollonia had no Israelite communities to detain the Apostles, '*the synagogue*'[7] of the neighbourhood was at Thessalonica.

[1] We find the bishop of Thessalonica in the Council of Sardis, A.D. 347; and a decree of the Council relates to the place.

[2] Eustathius preached and wrote there in the twelfth century. He was highly esteemed by the Comneni, and is held to have been, 'beyond all dispute, the most learned man of his age.'

[3] 1 Thess. i. 3.

[4] Paul Lucas, in his later journey, says:—'Les Chrétiens y sont environ au nombre de 10,000. On y compte 30,000 Juifs, qui y ont 22 synagogues, et ce sont eux qui y font tout le commerce. Comme ils sont fort industrieux, deux grands-vizirs se sont mis successivement en tête de les faire travailler aux manufactures des draps de France, pour mettre la Turquie en état de se passer des étrangers; mais ils n'ont jamais pu réussir : cependant ils vendent assez bien leurs gros draps au grand seigneur, qui en fait habiller ses troupes.'—P. 37. In the 17th century a Turkish authority speaks of them as carpet and cloth makers, of

their liberality to the poor, and of their schools, with more than 1,000 children. Cousinéry reckons them at 20,000, many of them from Spain. He adds : 'Chaque synagogue à Salonique porte le nom de la province d'où sont originaires les familles qui la composent.'—P. 19. In the '*Jewish Intelligence*' for 1849, the Jews at Salonica are reckoned at 35,000, being half the whole population, and having the chief trade in their hands. They are said to have thirty-six synagogues, 'none of them remarkable for their neatness or elegance of style.'

[5] They are alluded to in the 7th century, and again in considerable numbers in the 12th. See Tafel.

[6] See Chap. I. p. 15.

[7] The best MSS. here have the definite article. If authority preponderated against it, still the phrase would imply that there was no synagogue in the towns recently passed through. There was another synagogue at Berœa. Acts xvii. 10.

The first scene to which we are introduced in this city is entirely Jewish. It is not a small meeting of proselyte women by the river side, but a crowded assembly of true-born Jews, intent on their religious worship, among whom Paul and Silas now make their appearance. If the traces of their recent hardships were manifest in their very aspect, and if they related to their Israelitish brethren how they had 'suffered before and been cruelly treated at Philippi' (1 Thess. ii. 2), their entrance in among them must have created a strong impression of indignation and sympathy, which explains the allusion in St. Paul's Epistle. He spoke, however, to the Thessalonian Jews with the earnestness of a man who has no time to lose and no thought to waste on his own sufferings. He preached not himself but Christ crucified. The Jewish Scriptures were the ground of his argument. He recurred to the same subject again and again. On three successive Sabbaths[1] he argued with them ; and the whole body of Jews resident in Thessalonica were interested and excited with the new doctrine, and were preparing either to adopt or oppose it.

The three points on which he insisted were these :—that He who was foretold in prophecy was to be a suffering Messiah,—that after death He was to rise again,—and that the crucified Jesus of Nazareth was indeed the Messiah who was to come. Such is the distinct and concise statement in the Acts of the Apostles (xvii. 3): and the same topics of teaching are implied in the first Epistle, where the Thessalonians are appealed to as men who had been taught to 'believe that Jesus had really died and risen again' (iv. 14), and who had turned to serve the true God, 'and to wait for His Son from heaven, whom He raised from the dead, even Jesus' (i. 10). Of the mode in which these subjects would be presented to his hearers we can form some idea from what was said at Antioch in Pisidia. The very aspect of the worshippers was the same ;[2] proselytes were equally attached to the congregations in Pisidia and Macedonia,[3] and the 'devout and honourable women' in one city found their parallel in the 'chief women' in the other.[4] The impression, too, produced by the address was not very different here from what it had been there. At first it was favourably received,[5] the interest of novelty having more influence than the seriousness of conviction. Even from the first some of the topics must have contained matter for perplexity or cavilling. Many would be indisposed to believe the fact of Christ's resurrection : and many more who, in their exile from Jerusalem, were looking intently for the restoration of an earthly kingdom,[6] must have heard incredulously and unwillingly of the humiliation of Messiah.

That St. Paul did speak of Messiah's glorious kingdom, the

---

[1] Acts xvii. 2.

[2] See the account of the synagogue-worship,—the desk, the ark, the manuscripts, the prayers, the Scripture-reading, the Tallith, &c.,—given in pp. 136–139.

[3] Compare Acts xiii. 16, 26 with xvii. 4. See Paley on 1 Thess.

[4] Compare Acts xiii. 50 with xvii. 4. It will be remembered that the women's place in the synagogues was in a separate gallery, or behind a lattice, p. 139.

[5] Acts xvii. 4 compared with xiii. 42–44.

[6] Acts i. 6.

kingdom foretold in the Prophetic Scriptures themselves, may be
gathered by comparing together the Acts and the Epistles to the
Thessalonians. The accusation brought against him (Acts xvii.
7) was, that he was proclaiming another *king,* and virtually rebelling
against the Emperor. And in strict conformity to this the Thessalonians are reminded of the exhortations and entreaties he gave
them, when among them, that they would 'walk worthily of the
God who had called them to His *kingdom* and glory' (1 Thess.
ii. 12), and they are addressed as those who had 'suffered affliction
for the sake of that *kingdom'* (2 Thess. i. 5). Indeed, the royal
state of Christ's second advent was one chief topic which was
urgently enforced, and deeply impressed, on the minds of the Thessalonian converts. This subject tinges the whole atmosphere through
which the aspect of this church is presented to us. It may be said
that in each of the primitive churches, which are depicted in the
Apostolic Epistles, there is some peculiar feature which gives it an
individual character. In Corinth it is the spirit of party,[1] in Galatia
the rapid declension into Judaism,[2] in Philippi it is a steady and
self-denying generosity.[3] And if we were asked for the distinguishing characteristic of the first Christians of Thessalonica, we should
point to their overwhelming sense of the nearness of the second
advent, accompanied with melancholy thoughts concerning those
who might die before it, and with gloomy and unpractical views of
the shortness of life and the vanity of the world. Each chapter in
the first Epistle to the Thessalonians ends with an allusion to this
subject; and it was evidently the topic of frequent conversations
when the Apostle was in Macedonia. But St. Paul never spoke
or wrote of the future as though the present was to be forgotten.
When the Thessalonians were admonished of Christ's advent, he
told them also of other coming events, full of practical warning to
all ages, though to our eyes still they are shrouded in mystery,—
of 'the falling away,' and of 'the man of sin.'[4] 'These awful revelations,' he said, 'must precede the revelation of the Son of God.
Do you not remember,' he adds with emphasis in his letter, '*that
when I was still with you I often*[5] *told you this? You know, therefore,* the hindrance why he is not revealed, as he will be in his own
season.' He told them, in the words of Christ himself, that 'the
times and the seasons' of the coming revelations were known only
to God :[6] and he warned them, as the first disciples had been
wârned in Judæa, that the great day would come suddenly on men
unprepared, ' as the pangs of travail on her whose time is full,' and
'as a thief in the night;' and he showed them, both by precept
and example, that, though it be true that life is short and the world
is vanity, yet God's work must be done diligently and to the last.

[1] 1 Cor. i. 10, &c.
[2] Gal. i. 6, &c.
[3] Phil. iv. 10-16.
[4] 2 Thess. ii.
[5] The verb is in the imperfect.
[6] 'But of the times and seasons,
brethren, when these things shall be,
you need no warning. For yourselves

know perfectly that the day of the Lord
will come as a thief in the night; and
while men say, Peace and safety, destruction shall come upon them in a
moment, as the pangs of travail on her
whose time is full.'—1 *Thess.* v. 1-3.
See Acts i. 7; Matt. xxiv. 43; Luke
xii. 39; 2 Pet. iii. 10.

The whole demeanour of St. Paul among the Thessalonians may be traced, by means of these Epistles, with singular minuteness. We see there, not only what success he had on his first entrance among them,[1] not only how the Gospel came 'with power and with full conviction of its truth,'[2] but also '*what manner of man* he was among them for their sakes.'[3] We see him proclaiming the truth with unflinching courage,[4] endeavouring to win no converts by flattering words,[5] but warning his hearers of all the danger of the sins and pollution to which they were tempted ;[6] manifestly showing that his work was not intended to gratify any desire of self-advancement,[7] but scrupulously maintaining an honourable and unblamable character.[8] We see him rebuking and admonishing his converts with all the faithfulness of a father to his children,[9] and cherishing them with all the affection of a mother for the infant of her bosom.[10] We see in this Apostle at Thessalonica all the devotion of a friend who is ready to devote his life for those whom he loves,[11] all the watchfulness of the faithful pastor, to whom 'each one' of his flock is the separate object of individual care.[12]

And from these Epistles we obtain further some information concerning what may be called the outward incidents of St. Paul's residence in this city. He might when there, consistently with the Lord's institution[13] and with the practice of the other Apostles,[14] have been 'burdensome' to those whom he taught, so as to receive from them the means of his temporal support. But that he might place his disinterestedness above all suspicion, and that he might set an example to those who were too much inclined to live by the labour of others, he declined to avail himself of that which was an

---

[1] '*You know yourselves*, brethren, that my coming amongst you was not fruitless.'—1 *Thess.* ii. 1.

[2] 1 Thess. i. 5.

[3] '*You know* the manner in which I behaved myself among you,' &c. 1 Thess. i. 5. ('What manner of men we were.'—*Auth. Vers.*) Though the words are in the plural, the allusion is to himself only. See the notes on the Epistle itself.

[4] 'After I had borne suffering and outrage, *as you know*, at Philippi, I *boldly* declared to you God's Glad Tidings, though its adversaries contended mightily against me.'—1 *Thess.* ii. 2.

[5] 'Neither did I use flattering words, *as you know*.'—1 *Thess.* ii. 5.

[6] 'This is the will of God, even your sanctification ; that you should keep yourselves from fornication. . . . not in lustful passions, like the heathen, who know not God. . . . All such the Lord will punish, *as I have forewarned you* by my testimony.'—1 *Thess.* iv. 4–6. It is needless to add that such temptations must have abounded in a city like

Thessalonica. We know from Lucian that the place had a bad character.

[7] 1 Thess. ii. 5.

[8] '*You are yourselves witnesses* how holy, and just, and unblamable, were my dealings towards you.'—1 *Thess.* ii. 10.

[9] '*You know* how earnestly, *as a father his own children*, I exhorted, and intreated, and adjured,' &c.—1 *Thess.* ii. 11.

[10] 'I behaved myself among you with mildness and forbearance ; and as a nurse cherishes *her own children*, so,' &c.—1 *Thess.* ii. 7. The Authorised Version is defective. St. Paul compares himself to a mother who is nursing her own child.

[11] 'It was my joy to give you, not only the Gospel of Christ, but my own life also, because ye were dear unto me.' —1 *Thess.* ii. 8.

[12] '*You know* how I exhorted *each one* among you to walk worthy of God.' —1 *Thess.* ii. 11.

[13] Matt. x. 10 ; Luke x. 7. See 1 Tim. v. 18.

[14] 1 Cor. ix. 4, &c.

undoubted right. He was enabled to maintain this independent
position partly by the liberality of his friends at Philippi, who once
and again, on this first visit to Macedonia, sent relief to his necessities (Phil. iv. 15, 16). And the journeys of those pious men who
followed the footsteps of the persecuted Apostles along the Via
Egnatia by Amphipolis and Apollonia, bringing the alms which had
been collected at Philippi, are among the most touching incidents
of the Apostolic history. And not less touching is that description
which St. Paul himself gives us of that other means of support—
'his own labour night and day, that he might not be burdensome
to any of them' (1 Thess. ii. 9). He did not merely 'rob other
churches,'[1] that he might do the Thessalonians service, but the
trade he had learnt when a boy in Cilicia[2] justified the old Jewish
maxim ;[3] 'he was like a vineyard that is fenced ;' and he was able
to show an example, not only to the 'disorderly busybodies' of
Thessalonica (1 Thess. iv. 11), but to all, in every age of the Church,
who are apt to neglect their proper business (2 Thess. iii. 11), and
ready to eat other men's bread for nought (2 Thess. iii. 8). Late at
night, when the sun had long set on the incessant spiritual labours
of the day, the Apostle might be seen by lamp-light labouring at
the rough hair-cloth,[4] 'that he might be chargeable to none.' It
was an emphatic enforcement of the 'commands'[5] which he found
it necessary to give when he was among them, that they should
'study to be quiet, and to work with their own hands' (1 Thess.
iv. 11), and the stern principle he laid down, that 'if a man will
not work, neither should he eat.' (2 Thess. iii. 10.)

In these same Epistles, St. Paul speaks of his work at Thessalonica as having been encompassed with afflictions,[6] and of the
Gospel as having advanced by a painful struggle.[7] What these
afflictions and struggles were, we can gather from the slight notices
of events which are contained in the Acts. The Apostle's success
among the Gentiles roused the enmity of his own countrymen.
Even in the synagogue the Proselytes attached themselves to him
more readily than the Jews.[8] But he did not merely obtain an influence over the Gentile mind by the indirect means of his disputations on the Sabbath in the synagogue, and through the medium
of the Proselytes ; but on the intermediate days[9] he was doubtless
in frequent and direct communication with the Heathen. We need
not be surprised at the results, even if his stay was limited to the
period corresponding to three Sabbaths. No one can say what
effects might follow from three weeks of an Apostle's teaching.
But we are by no means forced to adopt the supposition that the
time was limited to three weeks. It is highly probable that St.

---

[1] 2 Cor. xi. 8.

[2] Chap. II. pp. 39, 40.

[3] 'He that hath a trade in his hand,
to what is he like? He is like a vineyard that is fenced.'—P. 39.

[4] See p. 40, n. 1.

[5] Note the phrases,— 'as I commanded you,' and 'even when I was
with you I gave you this precept.'

[6] 1 Thess. i. 6.

[7] 1 Thess. ii. 2.

[8] ' Some of them [the Jews] believed
and consorted with Paul and Silas;
and of the devout Greeks a great multitude, and of the chief women not a few.'
—Acts xvii. 4.

[9] As at Athens. Acts xvii. 17.

Paul remained at Thessalonica for a longer period.[1] At other cities,[2] when he was repelled by the Jews, he became the evangelist of the Gentiles, and remained till he was compelled to depart. The Thessalonian Letters throw great light on the rupture which certainly took place with the Jews on this occasion, and which is implied in that one word in the Acts which speaks of their jealousy[3] against the Gentiles. The whole aspect of the Letters shows that the main body of the Thessalonian Church was not Jewish, but Gentile. The Jews are spoken of as an extraneous body, as the enemies of Christianity and of all men, not as the elements out of which the Church was composed.[4] The ancient Jewish Scriptures are not once quoted in either of these Epistles.[5] The converts are addressed as those who had turned, not from Hebrew fables and traditions, but from the practices of Heathen idolatry.[6] How new and how comforting to them must have been the doctrine of the resurrection from the dead. What a contrast must this revelation of 'life and immortality' have been to the hopeless lamentations of their own pagan funerals, and to the dismal teaching which we can still read in the sepulchral inscriptions[7] of Heathen Thessalonica,—such as told the bystander that after death there is no revival, after the grave no meeting of those who have loved each other on earth. How ought the truth taught by the Apostle to have comforted the new disciples at the thought of inevitable, though only temporary, separation from their Christian brethren. And yet how difficult was the truth to realise, when they saw those brethren sink into lifeless forms, and after they had committed them to the earth which had received all their heathen ancestors. How eagerly can we imagine them to have read the new assurances of comfort which came in the letter from Corinth, and which told them 'not to sorrow like other men who have no hope.'[8]

But we are anticipating the events which occurred between the Apostle's departure from Thessalonica and the time when he wrote the letter from Corinth. We must return to the persecution that led him to undertake that journey, which brought him from the capital of Macedonia to that of Achaia.

When the Jews saw Proselytes and Gentiles, and many of the leading women[9] of the city, convinced by St. Paul's teaching, they

---

[1] Paley, among others, argues for a longer residence than three weeks. *Horæ Paulinæ,* on 1 Thess. No. vi. Benson lays stress on the coming of repeated contributions from Philippi: to which it may be replied, on the other hand, that they might have come within three weeks, if they were sent by different contributors.

[2] Acts xiii. xviii. xix. &c.

[3] Acts xvii. 5.

[4] 'You have suffered the like persecution from your own countrymen which they [the churches in Judæa] endured from the Jews, who killed both the Lord Jesus and the prophets . . . a

people displeasing to God, and enemies to all mankind; who would hinder me from speaking to the Gentiles,' &c.— 1 *Thess.* ii. Contrast Rom. ix.

[5] The Epistles to Titus and Philemon, if we mistake not, are the only other instances.

[6] 1 Thess. i. 9.

[7] Here and there in such inscriptions is a hint of immortality; but the general feeling of the Greek world concerning the dead is that of utter hopelessness.

[8] 1 Thess. iv. 13.

[9] Acts xvii. 4. See above.

must have felt that his influence was silently undermining theirs. In proportion to his success in spreading Christianity, their power of spreading Judaism declined. Their sensitiveness would be increased in consequence of the peculiar dislike with which they were viewed at this time by the Roman power.[1] Thus they adopted the tactics which had been used with some success before at Iconium and Lystra,[2] and turned against St. Paul and his companions those weapons which are the readiest instruments of vulgar bigotry. They excited the mob of Thessalonica, gathering together a multitude of those worthless idlers about the markets and landing-places[3] which abound in every such city, and are always ready for any evil work. With this multitude they assaulted the house of Jason (perhaps some Hellenistic Jew,[4] whose name had been moulded into Gentile form, and possibly one of St. Paul's relations, who is mentioned in the Epistle to the Romans[5]), with whom Paul and Silas seem to have been lodging. Their wish was to bring Paul and Silas out to the *demus,* or assembly of the people. But they were absent from the house ; and Jason and some other Christians were dragged before the city magistrates. The accusation vociferously brought against them was to the following effect : ' These Christians, who are setting the whole world in confusion, are come hither at last ; and Jason has received them into his house ; and they are all acting in the face of the Emperor's decrees, for they assert that there is another king, whom they call Jesus.' We have seen[6] how some of the parts of St. Paul's teaching at Thessalonica may have given occasion to the latter phrase in this indictment ; and we obtain a deeper insight into the cause why the whole indictment was brought forward with so much vehemence, and why it was so likely to produce an effect on the magistrates, if we bear in mind the circumstance alluded to in reference to Philippi,[7] that the Jews were under the ban of the Roman authorities about this time, for having raised a tumult in the metropolis, at the instigation (as was alleged) of one Chrestus, or Christus ;[8] and that they must have been glad, in the provincial cities, to be able to show their loyalty and gratify their malice, by throwing the odium off themselves upon a sect whose very name might be interpreted to imply a rebellion against the Emperor.

Such were the circumstances under which Jason and his companions were brought before the *politarchs.* We use the Greek term advisedly ; for it illustrates the political constitution of Thessalonica, and its contrast with that of Philippi, which has lately

[1] See below.

[2] Acts xiv. See pp. 146, 154, &c. ; also pp. 144, 145.

[3] Like the Lazzaroni at Naples.

[4] Jason is the form which the name Joshua seem sometimes to have taken. See p. 122. It occurs 4 Macc. viii. 17, 2 Macc. ii. 23 ; also in Josephus, referred to p. 121, n. 7.

[5] Rom. xvi. 21. Tradition says that he became Bishop of Tarsus. For some remarks on St. Paul's kinsmen,

see pp. 39, 40.

[6] Above p. 252.

[7] Page 233.

[8] The words of Suetonius are quoted p. 233, n. 5. We shall return to them again when we come to Acts xviii. 2. At present we need only point out their probable connection with the word ' *Christian.*' See pp. 98, 99, and the notes. We should observe that St. Paul had proclaimed at Thessalonica that Jesus was the *Christ.* Acts xvii. 3.

been noticed. Thessalonica was not a colony, like Philippi, Troas, or the Pisidian Antioch, but a *free city* (*Urbs libera*), like the Syrian Antioch, or like Tarsus [1] and Athens. The privilege of what was technically called 'freedom' was given to certain cities of the Empire for good service in the Civil Wars, or as a tribute of respect to the old celebrity of the place, or for other reasons of convenient policy. There were few such cities in the western provinces,[2] as there were no *municipia* in the eastern. The free towns were most numerous in those parts of the Empire where the Greek language had long prevailed ; and we are generally able to trace the reasons why this privilege was bestowed upon them. At Athens it was the fame of its ancient eminence, and the evident policy of paying a compliment to the Greeks. At Thessalonica it was the part which its inhabitants had prudently taken in the great struggle of Augustus and Antony against Brutus and Cassius.[3] When the decisive battle had been fought, Philippi was made a military colony, and Thessalonica became *free.*

The privilege of such a city consisted in this, — that it was entirely self-governed in all its internal affairs, within the territory that might be assigned to it. The governor of the province had no right, under ordinary circumstances, to interfere with these affairs.[4] The local magistrates had the power of life and death over the citizens of the place. No stationary garrison of Roman soldiers was quartered within its territory.[5] No insignia of Roman office were displayed in its streets. An instance of the care with which this rule was observed is recorded by Tacitus, who tells us, that Germanicus, whose progress was usually distinguished by the presence of twelve lictors, declined to enter Athens attended with more than one. There is no doubt that the magistracies of such cities would be very careful to show their loyalty to the Emperor on all suitable occasions, and to avoid every disorder which might compromise their valued dignity, and cause it to be withdrawn. And on the other hand, the Roman State did wisely to rely on the Greek love of empty distinction ; and it secured its dominion as effectually in the East by means of these privileged towns, as by the stricter political annexation of the *municipia* in the West. The form of government in the free cities was very various.[6] In some

---

[1] See p. 38.

[2] There were a few in Gaul and Spain, none in Sardinia. On the other hand, they were very numerous in Greece, the Greek islands, and Asia Minor. Such complimentary privileges would have had little meaning if bestowed on a rude people, which had no ancient traditions.

[3] See the coins alluded to above, p. 248. Some have the word ΕΛΕΥΘΕΡΙΑΣ with the head of Octavia.

[4] He might, however, have his residence there, as at Antioch and Tarsus. We find, under the Republic, the governor of Asia directed to administer justice to free communities; but usu-

ally he did not interfere with the local magistrates. Even his financial officers did not enter the territory to collect the taxes, but the imposts were sent to Rome in some other way. We may add that a free city might have *libertas cum immunitate*, i.e. freedom from taxation, as a *Colonia* might have the *Jus Italicum.*

[5] Hence such cities were sometimes called 'ungarrisoned.'

[6] The degree of *libertas* was various also. It was settled by a distinct concordat (*fœdus*). The granting and withdrawing of this privilege, as well as its amount, was capricious and irregular under the Republic, and especi-

cases the old magistracies and customs were continued without any material modification. In others, a *senate,* or an *assembly,* was allowed to exist where none had existed before. Here, at Thessalonica, we find an assembly of the people (*Demus,*[1] Acts xvii. 5) and supreme magistrates, who are called *politarchs* (Acts xvii. 8). It becomes an interesting inquiry, whether the existence of this title of the Thessalonian magistracy can be traced in any other source of information. This question is immediately answered in the affirmative, by one of those passages of monumental history which we have made it our business to cite as often as possible in the course of this biography. An inscription which is still legible on an archway in Thessalonica gives this title to the magistrates of the place, informs us of their number, and mentions the very names of some who bore the office not long before the day of St. Paul.

A long street intersects the city from east to west.[2] This is doubtless the very direction which the ancient road took in its course from the Adriatic to the Hellespont ; for though the houses of ancient cities are destroyed and renewed, the lines of the great thoroughfares are usually unchanged.[3] If there were any doubt of the fact at Thessalonica, the question is set at rest by two triumphal arches which still, though disfigured by time and injury, and partly concealed by Turkish houses, span the breadth of this street, and define a space which must have been one of the public parts of the city in the apostolic age. One of these arches is at the western extremity, near the entrance from Rome, and is thought to have been built by the grateful Thessalonians to commemorate the victory of Augustus and Antony.[4] The other is further to the east, and records the triumph of some later emperor (most probably Constantine) over enemies subdued near the Danube or beyond. The second of these arches, with its sculptured camels,[5] has altogether an Asiatic aspect, and belongs to a period of the Empire much later than that of St. Paul. The first has the representation of consuls with the toga, and corresponds in appearance with that condition of the arts which marks the passing of the Republic into the Empire. If erected at that epoch, it was undoubtedly existing when the Apostle was in Macedonia. The inscription in Greek letters,[6] which is given on the opposite page, is engraved on this

---

ally during the Civil Wars. Under the Emperors it became more regulated, like all the other details of provincial administration.

[1] Tafel seems to think it had also a *senate.*

[2] See Cousinéry, ch. ii., and Leake, ch. xxvi.

[3] See a traveller's just remark, quoted in reference to Damascus, p. 77, n. 5.

[4] A view of the arch is given in Cousinéry, p. 26. See his description. He believes Octavius and Antony to have stayed here some time after the victory. The arch is also described by Sir H. Holland and Dr. Clarke, who

take the same view of its origin. The latter traveller says that its span is 12 feet, and its present height 18 feet, the lower part being buried to the depth of 27 feet more. It is now part of the modern walls, and is called the Vardar Gate, because it leads towards that river (the Axius).

[5] There is also a view of this arch in Cousinéry, p. 29. He refers its origin to one of Constantine's expeditions, mentioned by Zosimus. The whole structure formerly consisted of three arches; it is built of brick, and seems to have been faced with marble.

[6] From Boeckh, No. 1967. The inscription is given by Leake (p. 236),

ΠΟΛΕΙΤΑΡΧΟΥΝΤΩΝ ΣΩΣΙΠΑΤΡΟΥ ΤΟΥ ΚΛΕΟ

ΠΑΤΡΑΣ ΚΑΙ ΛΟΥΚΙΟΥ ΠΟΝΤΙΟΥ ΣΕΚΟΥΝΔΟΥ

ΠΟΥΒΛΙΟΥ ΦΛΑΟΥΙΟΥ ΣΑΒΕΙΝΟΥ ΔΗΜΗΤΡΙΟΥ

ΤΟΥ ΦΑΥΣΤΟΥ ΔΗΜΗΤΡΙΟΥ ΤΟΥ ΝΙΚΟΠΟΛΕΩΣ

ΖΩΙΛΟΥ ΤΟΥ ΠΑΡΜΕΝΙΩΝΟΣ ΤΟΥ ΚΑΙ ΜΕΝΙΣΚΟΥ

ΓΑΙΟΥ ΑΓΙΛΛΗΙΟΥ ΠΟΤΕΙΤΟΥ. . . . .

Inscription from Thessalonica.

(See p. 258, n. 6.)

arch of marble,[1] and informs us still of the magistracy which the
Romans recognised and allowed to subsist in the 'free city' of
Thessalonica. We learn from this source that the magistrates of
the city were called *politarchs*,[2] and that they were seven in number;
and it is perhaps worth observing (though it is only a curious coincidence) that three of the names are identical with three of St.
Paul's friends in this region,—*Sopater of Berœa*,[3] *Gaius the Macedonian*,[4] and *Secundus of Thessalonica*.[5]

It is at least well worth our while to notice, as a mere matter of
Christian evidence, how accurately St. Luke writes concerning the
political characteristics of the cities and provinces which he mentions. He takes notice in the most artless and incidental manner,
of minute details which a fraudulent composer would judiciously
avoid, and which in the mythical result of mere oral tradition
would surely be loose and inexact. Cyprus is a 'proconsular'
province.[6] Philippi is a 'colony.'[7] The magistrates of Thessalonica
have an unusual title, unmentioned in ancient literature ; but it
appears. from a monument of a different kind, that the title is
perfectly correct. And the whole aspect of what happened at
Thessalonica, as compared with the events at Philippi, is in perfect
harmony with the ascertained difference in the political condition
of the two places. There is no mention of the rights and privileges
of *Roman citizenship* ;[8] but we are presented with the spectacle of
a mixed mob of Greeks and Jews, who are anxious to show themselves to be '*Cæsar's friends*.'[9] No *lictors*,[10] with rods and fasces,
appear upon the scene ; but we hear something distinctly of a
demus,[11] or free assembly of the people. Nothing is said of *religious ceremonies*[12] which the citizens, 'being Romans,' may not
lawfully adopt ; all the anxiety, both of people and magistrates, is
turned to the one point of showing their loyalty to *the Emperor*.[13]
And those magistrates by whom the question at issue is ultimately
decided, are not Roman *prætors*[14] but Greek *politarchs*.[15]

It is evident that the magistrates were excited and unsettled[16] as
well as the multitude. No doubt they were anxious to stand well

with a slight difference in one of the
names. It goes on to mention the
ταμίας τῆς πόλεως and the γυμνασιάρχων.
The names being chiefly Roman, Leake
argues for a later date than that which
is suggested by Cousinéry. In either
case the confirmation of St. Luke's accuracy remains the same.

[1] The masonry consists of square
blocks of marble, six feet thick.

[2] Nor is this the only ancient inscription in Thessalonica, on which the
same technical term occurs.

[3] Acts xx. 4.
[4] Acts xix. 29.
[5] Acts xx. 4.
[6] See Chap. V. p. 117.
[7] See above, p. 223, &c.
[8] Compare Acts xvi. 21.
[9] The conduct and language of the

Jews in Acts xvii. 7, should, by all
means, be compared with what was
said to Pilate at Jerusalem : 'If thou
let this man go, thou art not *Cæsar's
friend* : whosoever maketh himself a
king speaketh against Cæsar.'—*John*
xix. 12.

[10] 'Ραβδοῦχοι. Acts xvi. 35, 38.
[11] Acts xvii. 5.
[12] Acts xvi. 21.
[13] Acts xvii. 7.
[14] Στρατηγοί. Acts xvi. 20, 22, 35,
&c. See p. 225, and p. 232.
[15] For a general account of Thessalonica, see the article in Smith's *Dictionary of Greek and Roman Geography*. A coin of the city is given at the
end of Chap. XI.
[16] The words imply some disturbance
of mind on the part of the magistrates.

with the Roman Government, and not to compromise themselves or the privileges of their city by a wrong decision in this dispute between the Christians and the Jews.[1] The course they adopted was to 'take security' from Jason and his companions. By this expression[2] it is most probably meant that a sum of money was deposited with the magistrates, and that the Christian community of the place made themselves responsible that no attempt should be made against the supremacy of Rome, and that peace should be maintained in Thessalonica itself. By these means the disturbance was allayed.

But though the magistrates had secured quiet in the city for the present, the position of Paul and Silas was very precarious. The lower classes were still excited. The Jews were in a state of fanatical displeasure. It is evident that the Apostles could not appear in public as before, without endangering their own safety, and compromising their fellow-Christians who were security for their good behaviour. The alternatives before them were, either silence in Thessalonica, or departure to some other place. The first was impossible to those who bore the divine commission to preach the Gospel everywhere. They could not hesitate to adopt the second course; and, under the watchful care of 'the brethren,' they departed the same evening from Thessalonica, their steps being turned in the direction of those mountains which are the western boundary of Macedonia.[3] We observe that nothing is said of the departure of Timotheus. If he was at Thessalonica at all, he stays there now, as Luke had stayed at Philippi.[4] We can trace in all these arrangements a deliberate care and policy for the well-being of the new Churches, even in the midst of the sudden movements caused by the outbreak of persecution. It is the same prudent and varied forethought which appears afterwards in the pastoral Epistles, where injunctions are given, according to circumstances,—to 'abide' while the Apostle goes to some other region,[5] 'hoping that he may come shortly' again,[6]—to 'set in order the things that are wanting, and ordain elders,'[7]—or 'to use all diligence' to follow[8] and co-operate again in the same work at some new place.

Passing under the Arch of Augustus and out of the Western Gate, the Via Egnatia crosses the plain and ascends the mountains which have just been mentioned,—forming a communication over a very rugged country between the Hellespont and the Adriatic.

---

[1] See above.

[2] Acts xvii. 9. It is very unlikely that this means, as has been imagined, that Jason and his friends gave bail for the appearance of Paul and Silas before the magistrates, for they sent them away the same night. Some think that Jason pledged himself not to receive them again into his house, or that he gave a promise of their immediate departure. Neither of these suppositions is improbable; but it is clear that it was impossible for Paul and Silas to stay, if the other Christians were security for the maintenance of the peace.

[3] Pp. 242, 243, and the notes.

[4] See p. 241.

[5] 1 Tim. i. 3.

[6] 1 Tim. iii. 14.

[7] Tit. i. 5.

[8] 2 Tim. iv. 9, 21, and especially Tit. iii. 12. The first injunction we read of, after this point, to Timotheus, in conjunction with Silas, is when St. Paul leaves Berœa, and they are told 'to come to him with all speed.' Acts xvii. 15.

Just where the road strikes the mountains, at the head of a bay of level ground, the city of Edessa is situated, described as commanding a glorious view of all the country, that stretches in an almost unbroken surface to Thessalonica and the sea.[1] This, however, was not the point to which St. Paul turned his steps. He travelled, by a less important road,[2] to the town of Berœa, which was farther to the south. The first part of the journey was undertaken at night, but day must have dawned on the travellers long before they reached their place of destination. If the journey was at all like what it is now,[3] it may be simply described as follows. After leaving the gardens which are in the immediate neighbourhood of Thessalonica, the travellers crossed a wide track of corn-fields, and came to the shifting bed of the 'wide-flowing Axius.' About this part of the journey, if not before, the day must have broken upon them. Between the Axius and the Haliacmon[4] there intervenes another wide extent of the same continuous plain. The banks of this second river are confined by artificial dykes to check its destructive inundations. All the country round is covered with a vast forest, with intervals of cultivated land, and villages concealed among the trees. The road extends for many miles through these woods, and at length reaches the base of the Western Mountains, where a short ascent leads up to the gate of Berœa.

Berœa, like Edessa, is on the eastern slope of the Olympian range, and commands an extensive view of the plain which is watered by the Haliacmon and Axius. It has many natural advantages, and is now considered one of the most agreeable towns in Rumili.[5] Plane-trees spread a grateful shade over its gardens. Streams of water are in every street. Its ancient name is said to have been derived from the abundance of its waters ; and the name still survives in the modern Verria, or Kara-Verria.[6] It is situated on the left of the Haliacmon, about five miles from the point where that river breaks through an immense rocky ravine from the mountains to the

---

[1] See p. 245, n. 2. For a description of Edessa (Vodhena) see Cousinéry. It seems to be on a plateau at the edge of the mountains, with waterfalls, like Tivoli.

[2] The Itineraries give two roads from Thessalonica to Berœa, one passing through Pella, the other more to the south. It is conceivable, but not likely, that St. Paul went by water from Thessalonica to the neighbourhood of Pydna. Colonel Leake, after visiting this city, took a boat from Eleftherokhori, and sailed across the gulf to Salonica. Vol. iii. pp. 436-438. So Dr. Clarke.

[3] The description of the journey is literally taken from Cousinéry, ch. iii. He was travelling from Salonica with a caravan to a place called Perlepe, on the mountains to the north-west. The usual road is up the Axius to Gradisca.

But one of the rivers higher up was said to be flooded and impassable; hence he went by Caraveria (Berœa), which is fourteen leagues from Salonica. Leake travelled from Salonica to Pella, crossing the Axius on his way. Chap. xxvii.

[4] The Haliacmon itself would not be crossed before arriving at Berœa (see below). But there are other large rivers which flow into it, and which are often flooded. Some of the 'perils of rivers' (p. 130) may very possibly have been in this district. See the preceding note. Compare Leake's remarks on the changing channels of these rivers, p. 437.

[5] See Leake, p. 290, &c.

[6] Leake uses the former term : Cousinéry calls the town 'Caraveria,' or 'Verria the Black.' In the eleventh century we find it called 'Verre.'

plain. A few insignificant ruins of the Greek and Roman periods may yet be noticed. The foundations of an ancient bridge are passed on the ascent to the city-gate ; and parts of the Greek fortifications may be seen above the rocky bed of a mountain stream. The traces of repairs in the walls, of Roman and Byzantine date,[1] are links between the early fortunes of Berœa and its present condition. It still boasts of eighteen or twenty thousand inhabitants, and is placed in the second rank of the cities of European Turkey.[2]

In the apostolic age Berœa was sufficiently populous to contain a colony of Jews.[3] When St. Paul arrived, he went, according to his custom, immediately to the synagogue. The Jews here were of a 'nobler' spirit than those of Thessalonica. Their minds were less narrowed by prejudice, and they were more willing to receive 'the truth in the love of it.' There was a contrast between two neighbouring communities apparently open to the same religious influences, like that between the 'village of the Samaritans,' which refused to receive Jesus Christ (Luke ix.), and that other 'city' in the same country where 'many believed' because of the word of one who witnessed of Him, and 'many more because of His own word' (John iv.). In a spirit very different from the ignoble violence of the Thessalonian Jews, the Berœans not only listened to the Apostle's arguments, but they examined the Scriptures themselves, to see if those arguments were justified by prophecy. And, feeling the importance of the subject presented to them, they made this scrutiny of their holy books their 'daily' occupation. This was the surest way to come to a strong conviction of the Gospel's divine origin. Truth sought in this spirit cannot long remain undiscovered. The promise that 'they who seek shall find' was fulfilled at Berœa ; and the Apostle's visit resulted in the conversion of 'many.' Nor was the blessing confined to the Hebrew community. The same Lord who is 'rich unto all that call upon Him,'[4] called many 'not of the Jews only, but also of the Gentiles.'[5] Both men and women,[6] and those of the highest rank, among the Greeks,[7] were added to the church founded by St. Paul in that provincial city of Macedonia, which was his temporary shelter from the storm of persecution.

The length of St. Paul's stay in the city is quite uncertain. From the fact that the Berœans were occupied '*daily*' in searching the Scriptures[8] for arguments to establish or confute the Apostle's doctrine, we conclude that he remained there several days at least. From his own assertion in his first letter to the Thessalonians,[9] that, at the time when he had been recently taken away from them, he was very anxious, and used every effort to revisit them, we cannot doubt that he lingered as long as possible in the neighbourhood of Thessalonica.[10] This desire would account for a residence of some

---

[1] It was a fortified city in the eleventh century.

[2] Cousinéry reckons the inhabitants at 15,000 or 20,000.

[3] Acts xvii. 10.

[4] Rom. x. 12.

[5] Acts ix. 24.

[6] Acts xvii. 12.

[7] The word 'Greek' (ver. 12) must be considered as belonging to 'men' as well as 'women.'

[8] Acts xvii. 11.

[9] 1 Thess. ii. 17.

[10] He says that he made more than

weeks; and there are other passages[1] in the same Epistle which
might induce us to suppose the time extended even to months.
But when we find, on the other hand, that the cause which led him
to leave Berœa was the hostility of the Jews of Thessalonica, and
when we remember that the two cities were separated only by a
distance of sixty miles,[2]—that the events which happened in the
synagogue of one city would soon be made known in the synagogue
of the other,—and that Jewish bigotry was never long in taking
active measures to crush its opponents,—we are led to the conclusion that the Apostle was forced to retreat from Berœa after no
long interval of time.   The Jews came like hunters upon their
prey, as they had done before from Iconium to Lystra.[3]   They
could not arrest the progress of the Gospel; but they 'stirred up
the people' there, as at Thessalonica before.[4]   They made his
friends feel that his continuance in the city was no longer safe.
He was withdrawn from Berœa and sent to Athens, as in the beginning of his ministry (Acts ix. 30) he had been withdrawn from
Jerusalem and sent to Tarsus.   And on this occasion, as on that,[5]
the dearest wishes of his heart were thwarted.   The providence of
God permitted 'Satan' to hinder him from seeing his dear Thessalonian converts, whom 'once and again' he had desired to revisit.[6]
The divine counsels were accomplished by means of the antagonism
of wicked men ; and the path of the Apostle was urged on, in the
midst of trial and sorrow, in the direction pointed out in the vision
at Jerusalem,[7] '*far hence unto the Gentiles.*'

An immediate departure was urged upon the Apostle ; and the
Church of Berœa suddenly [8] lost its teacher.   But Silas and Timotheus remained behind,[9] to build it up in its holy faith, to be a
comfort and support in its trials and persecutions, and to give it
such organisation as might be necessary.   Meanwhile some of the

one attempt to return ; and in this expression he may be referring to what
took place at Berœa, as probably as at
Athens.

[1] Those which relate to the widely-
extended rumour of the introduction
of Christianity into Thessalonica. See
below, on 1 Thess. The stay at Athens
was short, and the Epistle was written
soon after St. Paul's arrival at Corinth ; and, if a sufficient time had
elapsed for a general knowledge to be
spread abroad of what had happened
at Thessalonica, we should be inclined
to believe that the delay at Berœa was
considerable.

[2] Wieseler gives a different turn to
this consideration, and argues that, because the distance between Berœa and
Thessalonica was so great, therefore a
long time must have elapsed before the
news from the latter place could have
summoned the Jews from the former.
But we must take into account, not
merely the distance between the two

cities, but the peculiarly close commu-
nication which subsisted among the
Jewish synagogues. See, for instance,
Acts xxvi. 11.

[3] See pp. 154, 155.

[4] 'There also,' Acts xvii. 13.   Compare ver. 5.

[5] See the remarks on the vision at
Jerusalem, p. 86.

[6] See the preceding page.

[7] Acts xvii. 17–21.

[8] See ver. 14.

[9] Acts xvii. 14. The last mention
of Timothy was at Philippi, but it is
highly probable that he joined St. Paul
at Thessalonica. See above, p. 260.
Possibly he brought some of the contributions from Philippi, p. 254. We
shall consider hereafter the movements
of Silas and Timothy at this point of
St. Paul's journey. See note, p. 302.
Meantime, we may observe that Timotheus was very probably sent to Thessalonica (1 Thess. iii.) from *Berœa*,
and not from *Athens*.

new converts accompanied St. Paul on his flight ;[1] thus adding a new instance to those we have already seen of the love which grows up between those who have taught and those who have learnt the way of the soul's salvation.[2]

Without attempting to divine all the circumstances which may have concurred in determining the direction of this flight, we can mention some obvious reasons why it was the most natural course. To have returned in the direction of Thessalonica was manifestly impossible. To have pushed over the mountains, by the Via Egnatia, towards Illyricum and the western parts of Macedonia, would have taken the Apostle from those shores of the Archipelago to which his energies were primarily to be devoted. Mere concealment and inactivity were not to be thought of. Thus the Christian fugitives turned their steps towards the sea,[3] and from some point on the coast where a vessel was found, they embarked for Athens. In the ancient tables two roads[4] are marked which cross the Haliacmon and intersect the plain from Berœa, one passing by Pydna,[5] and the other leaving it to the left, and both coming to the coast at Dium near the base of Mount Olympus. The Pierian level (as this portion of the plain was called) extends about ten miles in breadth from the woody falls of the mountain to the sea-shore, forming a narrow passage from Macedonia into Greece.[6] Thus Dium was ' the great bulwark of Macedonia on the south ; ' and it was a Roman colony, like that other city which we have described on the eastern frontier.[7] No city is more likely than Dium to have been the last, as Philippi was ' the first,' through which St. Paul passed in his journey through the province.

Here then,—where Olympus, dark with woods, rises from the plain by the shore, to the broad summit, glittering with snow, which was the throne of the Homeric gods,[8]—at the natural termination of Macedonia,—and where the first scene of classical and poetic

---

[1] Acts xvii. 14, 15.

[2] See above, on the jailor's conversion, p. 238. Also p. 104.

[3] The words (Acts xvii. 14), translated ' as it were to the sea ' in the Authorised Version, do not imply that there was any stratagem, but simply denote the intention or the direction. It seems very likely that in the first instance they had no fixed plan of going to *Athens*, but merely to the *sea*. Their further course was determined by providential circumstances; and, when St. Paul was once arrived at Athens, he could send a message to Timothy and Silas to follow him (ver. 15). Those are surely mistaken who suppose that St. Paul travelled from Macedonia to Attica by land.

[4] The distance in the Antonine Itinerary is seventeen miles. A Byzantine writer says that Berœa is 160 stadia from the sea.

[5] Mr. Tate (*Continuous History, &c.*) suggests that St. Paul may have sailed from Pydna. But Pydna was not a seaport, and, for other reasons, Dium was more conveniently situated for the purpose.

[6] Leake describes the ruins of Dium, among which are probably some remains of the temple of Jupiter Olympius, who was honoured here in periodical games. Mount Olympus he describes as a conspicuous object for all the country round, as far as Saloniki, and as deriving from its steepness an increase of grandeur and apparent height.

[7] See above, on Philippi.

[8] The epithets given by Homer to this poetic mountain are as fully justified by the accounts of modern travellers, as the descriptions of the scenery alluded to at the close of the preceding chapter, p. 216, n. 10,

Greece opens on our view,—we take our leave, for the present, of the Apostle of the Gentiles. The shepherds from the heights [1] above the value of Tempe may have watched the sails of his ship that day, as it moved like a white speck over the outer waters of the Thermaic Gulf. The sailors, looking back from the deck, saw the great Olympus rising close above them in snowy majesty.[2] The more distant mountains beyond Thessalonica are already growing faint and indistinct. As the vessel approaches the Thessalian archipelago,[3] Mount Athos begins to detach itself from the isthmus that binds it to the main, and, with a few other heights of Northern Macedonia, appears like an island floating in the horizon.[4]

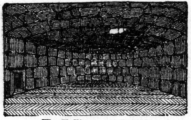

The Tullianum at Rome.[5]

[1] See Dr. Wordsworth's *Greece*, p. 197, and Mr. Urquhart's *Spirit of the East*, vol. i. p. 426.

[2] Compare p. 242, n. 5, and p. 243 n. 2. See also Purdy's *Sailing Directory*, p. 148: 'To the N.W. of the Thessalian Isles the extensive *Gulf of Salonica* extends thirty leagues to the north-westward, before it changes its direction to the north-eastward and forms the port. The country on the west, part of the ancient Thessaly, and now the province of Tricala, exhibits a magnificent range of mountains, which include *Pelion*, now Patras, *Ossa*, now Kissova, and *Olympus*, now Elymbo. The summit of the latter is six thousand feet above the level of the sea.

[3] The group of islands off the north end of Eubœa, consisting of Sciathos, Scopelos, Peparethos, &c. For an account of them, see Purdy, pp. 145–148.

[4] Cousinéry somewhere gives this description of the appearance of heights near Saloniki, as seen from the Thessalian islands. For an instance of a very unfavourable voyage in these seas, in the month of December, thirteen days being spent at sea between Salonica and Zeitun, the reader may consult Holland's *Travels*, chap. xvi.

[5] From Rich's *Dictionary of Greek and Roman Antiquities*.

CHAPTER X.

Arrival on the Coast of Attica.—Scenery round Athens.—The Piræus and the 'Long Walls.'—The Agora.—The Acropolis.—The 'Painted Porch' and the 'Garden.'—The Apostle alone in Athens.—Greek Religion.—The unknown God.—Greek Philosophy.—The Stoics and Epicureans.—Later Period of the Schools.—St. Paul in the Agora.—The Areopagus.—Speech of St. Paul.—Departure from Athens.

IN the life of Apollonius of Tyana,[1] there occurs a passage to the following effect :— ' Having come to anchor in the Piræus, he went up from the Harbour to the City. Advancing onward, he met several of the Philosophers. In his first conversation, finding the Athenians much devoted to Religion, he discoursed on sacred subjects. This was at Athens, where also altars of Unknown Divinities are set up.' To draw a parallel between a holy Apostle and an itinerant Magician would be unmeaning and profane : but this extract from the biography of Appollonius would be a suitable and comprehensive motto to that passage in St. Paul's biography on which we are now entering. The sailing into the Piræus,—the entrance into the city of Athens,—the interviews with philosophers, —the devotion of the Athenians to religious ceremonies,—the discourse concerning the worship of the Deity,—the ignorance implied by the altars to *unknown Gods*,[2]—these are exactly the subjects which are now before us. If a summary of the contents of the seventeenth chapter of the Acts had been required, it could not

---

[1] He has been alluded to before, p. 100, n. 2. 'His life by Philostratus is a mass of incongruities and fables;' but it is an important book as reflecting the opinions of the age in which it was written. Apollonius himself produced a great excitement in the Apostolic age. See Neander's *General Church History* (Eng. Trans.), pp. 40–48, and pp. 236–238. It was the fashion among the Antichristian writers of the third century to adduce him as a rival of our Blessed Lord; and the same profane comparison has been renewed by some of our English freethinkers. Without alluding to this any further, we may safely find some interest in putting his life by the side of that of St. Paul. They lived at the same time, and travelled through the same countries; and the life of the magician illustrates that peculiar state of phi-losophy and superstition which the Gospel preached by St. Paul had to encounter. Apollonius was partly educated at Tarsus; he travelled from city to city in Asia Minor; from Greece he went to Rome, in the reign of Nero, about the time when the magicians had lately been expelled; he visited Athens and Alexandria, where he had a singular meeting with Vespasian: on a second visit to Italy he vanished miraculously from Puteoli: the last scene of his life was Ephesus, or, possibly, Crete or Rhodes. See the Life in Smith's *Dictionary of Biography*. It is thought by many that St. Paul and Apollonius actually met in Ephesus and Rome. Burton's *Lectures on Ecclesiastical History*, pp. 157, 240.

[2] This subject is fully entered into below.

have been more conveniently expressed. The city visited by Apollonius was the Athens which was visited by St. Paul : the topics of discussion—the character of the people addressed—the aspect of everything around,—were identically the same. The difference was this, that the Apostle could give to his hearers what the philosopher could not give. The God whom Paul 'declared,' was worshipped by Apollonius himself as 'ignorantly' as by the Athenians.

We left St. Paul on that voyage which his friends induced him to undertake on the flight from Berœa. The vessel was last seen among the Thessalian islands.[1] About that point the highest land in Northern Macedonia began to be lost to view. Gradually the nearer heights of the snowy Olympus[2] itself receded into the distance as the vessel on her progress approached more and more near to the centre of all the interest of classical Greece. All the land and water in sight becomes more eloquent as we advance ; the lights and shadows, both of poetry and history, are on every side ; every rock is a monument ; every current is animated with some memory of the past. For a distance of ninety miles, from the confines of Thessaly to the middle part of the coast of Attica, the shore is protected, as it were, by the long island of Eubœa. Deep in the innermost gulf, where the waters of the Ægean retreat far within the land, over against the northern parts of this island, is the pass of Thermopylæ, where a handful of Greek warriors had defied all the hosts of Asia. In the crescent-like bay on the shore of Attica, near the s outhern extremity of the same island, is the maritime sanctuary of Marathon, where the battle was fought which decided that Greece was never to be a Persian Satrapy.[3] When the island of Eubœa is left behind, we soon reach the southern extremity of Attica—Cape Colonna,—Sunium's high promontory, still crowned with the white columns of that temple of Minerva, which was the landmark to Greek sailors, and which asserted the presence of Athens at the very vestibule of her country.[4]

After passing this headland, our course turns to the westward across the waters of the Saronic Gulf, with the mountains of the Morea on our left, and the islands of Ægina and Salamis in front. To one who travels in classical lands no moment is more full of interest and excitement than when he has left the Cape of Sunium behind and eagerly looks for the first glimpse of that city 'built nobly on the Ægean shore,' which was 'the eye of Greece, mother of arts and eloquence.'[5] To the traveller in classical times its position was often revealed by the flashing of the light on the armour of Minerva's colossal statue, which stood with shield and spear on the summit of the citadel.[6] At the very first sight of Athens, and even from the deck of the vessel, we obtain a vivid notion of the

[1] Above, p. 265.

[2] See the preceding chapter, p. 264, also 242.

[3] See *Quarterly Review* for Sept. 1846, and the first number of the *Classical Museum.*

[4] See Wordsworth's *Athens and*

Attica, chap. xxvii. A description of the promontory and ruins, will be found in Mure's *Journal of a Tour in Greece.* See Falconer's *Shipwreck,* iii. 526.

[5] *Paradise Regained,* iv. 240.

[6] This is stated by Pausanias.

characteristics of its position. And the place where it stands is so remarkable—its ancient inhabitants were so proud of its climate and its scenery—that we may pause on our approach to say a few words on Attica and Athens, and their relation to the rest of Greece.

Attica is a triangular tract of country, the southern and eastern sides of which meet in the point of Sunium ; its third side is defined by the high mountain ranges of Cithæron and Parnes, which separate it by a strong barrier from Bœotia and Northern Greece. Hills of inferior elevation connect these ranges with the mountainous surface of the south-east, which begins from Sunium itself, and rises on the south coast to the round summits of Hymettus, and the higher peak of Pentelicus near Marathon on the east. The rest of Attica is a plain, one reach of which comes down to the sea on the south, at the very base of Hymettus. Here, about five miles from the shore, an abrupt rock rises from the level, like the rock of Stirling Castle, bordered on the south by some lower eminences, and commanded by a high craggy peak on the north. This rock is the Acropolis of Athens. These lower eminences are the Areopagus, the Pnyx, and the Museum, which determined the rising and falling of the ground in the ancient city. That craggy peak is the hill of Lycabettus,[1] from the summit of which the spectator sees all Athens at his feet, and looks freely over the intermediate plain to the Piræus and the sea.

Athens and the Piræus must never be considered separately. One was the city, the other was its harbour. Once they were connected together by a continuous fortification. Those who looked down from Lycabettus in the time of Pericles, could follow with the eye all the long line of wall from the temples on the Acropolis to the shipping in the port. Thus we are brought back to the point from which we digressed. We were approaching the Piræus ; and, since we must land in maritime Athens before we can enter Athens itself, let us return once more to the vessel's deck, and look round on the land and the water. The island on our left, with steep cliffs at the water's edge, is Ægina. The distant heights beyond it are the mountains of the Morea. Before us is another island, the illustrious Salamis ; though in the view it is hardly disentangled from the coast of Attica, for the strait where the battle was fought is narrow and winding. The high ranges behind stretch beyond Eleusis and Megara, to the left towards Corinth, and to the right along the frontier of Bœotia. This last ridge is the mountain line of Parnes, of which we have spoken above. Clouds[2] are often seen to rest on it at all seasons of the year, and in winter it is usually white with snow. The dark heavy mountain rising close to us on the right immediately from the sea, is Hymettus. Between Parnes and

---

[1] The relation of Lycabettus to the crowded buildings below, and to the surrounding landscape, is so like that of Arthur's Seat to Edinburgh and its neighbourhood, and there is so much resemblance between Edinburgh Castle and the Acropolis, that a comparison between the city of the Saronic gulf and the city of the Forth has become justly proverbial.

[2] See the passage from the *Clouds* of Aristophanes quoted by Dr. Wordsworth. *Athens and Attica*, p. 58.

Hymettus is the plain ; and rising from the plain is the Acropolis ; distinctly visible, with Lycabettus behind, and seeming in the clear atmosphere to be nearer than it is.

The outward aspect of this scene is now what it ever was. The lights and shadows on the rocks of Ægina and Salamis, the gleams on the distant mountains, the clouds or the snow on Parnes, the gloom in the deep dells of Hymettus, the temple-crowned rock and the plain beneath it,—are natural features, which only vary with the alterations of morning and evening, and summer and winter.[1] Some changes indeed have taken place: but they are connected with the history of man. The vegetation is less abundant,[2] the population is more scanty. In Greek and Roman times, bright villages enlivened the promontories of Sunium and Ægina, and all the inner reaches of the bay. Some readers will indeed remember a dreary picture which Sulpicius gave his friend Atticus of the desolation of these coasts when Greece had ceased to be free ;[3] but we must make some allowances for the exaggerations of a poetical regret, and must recollect that the writer had been accustomed to the gay and busy life of the Campanian shore. After the renovation of Corinth,[4] and in the reign of Claudius, there is no doubt that all the signs of a far more numerous population than at present were evident around the Saronic Gulf, and that more white sails were to be seen in fine weather plying across its waters to the harbours of Cenchreæ[5] or Piræus.

Now there is indeed a certain desolation over this beautiful bay: Corinth is fallen, and Cenchreæ is an insignificant village. The *Piræus* is probably more like what it was than any other spot upon the coast. It remains what by nature it has ever been,—a safe basin of deep water, concealed by the surrounding rock; and now, as in St. Paul's time, the proximity of Athens causes it to be the resort of various shipping. We know that we are approaching it at the present day, if we see, rising above the rocks, the tall masts of an English line-of-battle ship, side by side with the light spars of a Russian corvette[6] or the black funnel of a French steamer. The details were different when the Mediterranean was a Roman lake. The heavy top-gear[7] of corn-ships from Alexandria or the Euxine might then be a conspicuous mark among the small coasting vessels and fishing boats ; and one bright spectacle was then pre-eminent, which the lapse of centuries has made cold and dim, the perfect buildings on the summit of the Acropolis, with the shield and spear of Minerva Promachus glittering in the sun.[8] But those who have coasted along beneath Hymettus,—and past the indentations in the shore,[9] which were sufficient harbours for Athens in the days of her early navigation,—and round by the ancient tomb, which

[1] This is written under the recollection of the aspect of the coast on a cloudy morning in winter. It is perhaps more usually seen under the glare of a hot sky.
[2] Athens was not always as bare as it is now. Plato complains that in his day the wood was diminishing.
[3] Cic. *Ep. Fam.* iv. 5.

[4] Corinth was in ruins in Cicero's time. For the results of its restoration, see the next chapter.
[5] See Acts xviii. 18. Rom. xvi. 1.
[6] This was written in 1850.
[7] See Smith's *Shipwreck, &c.*
[8] See above, p. 267.
[9] The harbours of Phalerum and Munychia.

tradition has assigned to Themistocles,[1] into the better and safer harbour of the Piræus,—require no great effort of the imagination to picture the Apostle's arrival. For a moment, as we near the entrance, the land rises and conceals all the plain. Idlers come down upon the rocks to watch the coming vessel. The sailors are all on the alert. Suddenly an opening is revealed ; and a sharp turn of the helm brings the ship in between two moles,[2] on which towers are erected. We are in smooth water ; and anchor is cast in seven fathoms in the basin of the Piræus.[3]

The Piræus, with its suburbs (for so, though it is not strictly accurate, we may designate the maritime city), was given to Athens as a natural advantage, to which much of her greatness must be traced. It consists of a projecting portion of rocky ground, which is elevated above the neighbouring shore, and probably was originally entirely insulated in the sea. The two rivers of Athens—the Cephisus and Ilissus—seem to have formed, in the course of ages, the low marshy ground which now connects Athens with its port. The port itself possesses all the advantages of shelter and good anchorage, deep water, and sufficient space.[4] Themistocles, seeing that the pre-eminence of his country could only be maintained by her maritime power, fortified the Piræus as the outpost of Athens, and enclosed the basin of the harbour as a dock within the walls. In the long period through which Athens had been losing its political power, these defences had been neglected, and suffered to fall into decay, or had been used as materials for other buildings : but there was still a fortress on the highest point ;[5] the harbour was still a place of some resort;[6] and a considerable number of seafaring people dwelt in the streets about the seashore. When the republic of Athens was flourishing, the sailors were a turbulent and worthless part of its population. And the Piræus under the Romans was not without some remains of the same disorderly class, as it doubtless retained many of the outward

[1] For the sepulchre by the edge of the water, popularly called the ' tomb of Themistocles,' see Leake's *Athens*, pp. 379, 380, and the notes.

[2] Some parts of the ancient moles are remaining. Leake, p. 272. See what is said of the colossal lions (now removed to Venice) which gave the harbour its modern name, p. 271.

[3] ' The entrance of the Piræus (Port Leoni) is known by a small obelisk, built on a low point by the company of H.M. ship "Cambria," in 1820, on the starboard hand going in. . . . The entrance lies E. by S. and W. by N., and has in it nine and ten fathoms. There are three moleheads, two of which you have on the starboard hand, and one on the larboard. When past these mole-heads, shorten all sail, luff up, and anchor in seven fathoms. The ground is clear and good. There is room enough for three frigates. As

the place is very narrow, great care is required. . . . During the summer months the sea-breezes blow, nearly all day, directly into the harbour. . . . The middle channel of the harbour, with a depth of 9 or 10 fathoms, is 110 feet in breadth ; the starboard channel, with 6 fathoms, 40 feet ; the larboard, with 2 fathoms, only 28 feet.' —Purdy's *Sailing Directions*, p. 83.

[4] See the preceding note.

[5] The height of Munychia.

[6] Strabo speaks of the population living in ' villages about the port.' One of them was probably near the theatre of Munychia, on the low ground on the east of the main harbour. Leake, p. 396. Even in the time of Alexander the Piræus had so much declined that a comic writer compared it to a great empty walnut. Leake, p. 402.

features of its earlier appearance :—the landing-places and covered porticoes [1] ; the warehouses where the corn from the Black Sea used to be laid up ; the stores of fish brought in daily from the Saronic Gulf and the Ægean ; the gardens in the watery ground at the edge of the plain ; the theatres [2] into which the sailors used to flock to hear the comedies of Menander ; and the temples [3] where they were spectators of a worship which had no beneficial effect on their characters.

Had St. Paul come to this spot four hundred years before, he would have been in Athens from the moment of his landing at the Piræus. At that time the two cities were united together by the double line of fortification, which is famous under the name of the 'Long Walls.' The space included between these two arms [4] of stone might be considered (as, indeed, it was sometimes called) a third city ; for the street of five miles in length thus formed across the plain, was crowded with people, whose habitations were shut out from all view of the country by the vast wall on either side. Some of the most pathetic passages of Athenian history are associated with this 'longomural' enclosure : as when, in the beginning of the Peloponnesian war, the plague broke out in the autumn weather among the miserable inhabitants, who were crowded here to suffocation ; [5] or, at the end of the same war, when the news came of the defeat on the Asiatic shore, and one long wail went up from the Piræus, 'and no one slept in Athens that night.' [6] The result of that victory was, that these long walls were rendered useless by being partially destroyed ; and though another Athenian admiral and statesman [7] restored what Pericles had first completed, this intermediate fortification remained effective only for a time. In the incessant changes which fell on Athens in the Macedonian period, they were injured and became unimportant [8] In the Roman siege under Sulla, the stones were used as materials for other military works. So that when Augustus was on the throne, and Athens had reached its ultimate position as a *free city* of the *province* of Achaia, Strabo, in his description of the place, speaks of the Long Walls as matters of past history ; and Pausanias, a century later, says simply that 'you see the ruins of the walls as you go up from the Piræus.' Thus we can easily imagine the aspect of these defences in the time of St. Paul, which is intermediate to these two writers. On each side of the road were the broken fragments of the rectangular masonry put together in the proudest days of Athens ; more conspicuous than they are at present (for now [9] only the foundations can be traced here and there

[1] We read especially of the 'long portico,' which was also used as a market.

[2] In one of the theatres near the harbour we have the mention of a great meeting during the Peloponnesian war. Leake, p. 394.

[3] See Pausanias. It is *here* that Pausanias mentions the altars to the *unknown gods*.

[4] 'Theseæ brachia longa viæ,' as they are called by Propertius (iii. 20, 24). But the name by which they were usually known at Athens, was 'the *Long legs*.'

[5] Thucyd. ii. 17.

[6] Xen. *Hell.* ii. 2, 3.

[7] Conon.

[8] Livy speaks of their ruins being objects of *admiration* in the time of Æm. Paulus.

[9] See Leake, Wordsworth, and other

across the plain), but still very different from what they were when two walls of sixty feet high, with a long succession of towers,[1] stood to bid defiance to every invader of Attica.

The consideration of the Long Walls leads us to that of the city walls themselves. Here many questions might be raised concerning the extent of the enclosure,[2] and the positions of the gates,[3] when Athens was under the Roman dominion. But all such inquiries must be entirely dismissed. We will assume that St. Paul entered the city by the gate which led from the Piræus, that this gate was identical with that by which Pausanias entered, and that its position was in the hollow between the outer slopes of the Pnyx and Museum.[4] It is no ordinary advantage that we possess a description of Athens under the Romans, by the traveller and antiquarian whose name has just been mentioned. The work of Pausanias[5] will be our best guide to the discovery of what St. Paul saw. By following his route through the city, we shall be treading in the steps of the Apostle himself, and shall behold those very objects which excited his indignation and compassion.

Taking, then, the position of the Peiraic gate as determined, or at least resigning the task of topographical inquiries, we enter the city, and with Pausanias as our guide, look round on the objects which were seen by the Apostle. At the very gateway we are met with proofs of the peculiar tendency of the Athenians to multiply their objects both of art and devotion.[6] Close by the building where the vestments were laid up which were used in the annual procession of their tutelary divinity Minerva, is an image of her rival Neptune, seated on horseback, and hurling his trident.[7] We pass by a temple of Ceres, on the walls of which an archaic inscrip-

modern travellers. It seems from what Spon and Wheler say, that in 1676, the remains were larger and more continuous than at present.

[1] 'There is no direct evidence of the height of the Long Walls; but, as Appian informs us that the walls of the Peiraic city were forty cubits high, we may presume those of the Long Walls were not less. Towers were absolutely necessary to such a work; and the inscription relating to the Long Walls leaves no question as to their having existed.'—Leake.

[2] Our plan of Athens is taken from that of Kiepert, which is based on Forchammer's arguments. It differs materially from that of Leake, especially in giving a larger area to the city on the east and south, and thus bringing the Acropolis into the centre. Forchammer thinks that the traces of ancient walls which are found on the Pnyx, &c., do not belong to the fortification of Themistocles, but to some later defences erected by Valerian.

[3] For various discussions on the gates, see Leake, Wordsworth, and Forchammer.

[4] Pausanias does not mention the Peiraic gate by that name. See Leake, Wordsworth, and Forchammer. The first of these authorities places it where the modern road from the Piræus enters Athens, beyond all the high ground to the north of the Pnyx; the second places it in the hollow between the Pnyx and the Museum; the third in the same direction, but more remote from the Acropolis, in conformity with his view concerning the larger circumference of the walls.

[5] Pausanias visited Athens about fifty years after St. Paul. It is probable that very few changes had taken place in the city, with the exception of the new buildings erected by Hadrian.

[6] Acts xvii. 23.

[7] We have used the terms 'Minerva, Neptune,' &c., instead of the more accurate terms 'Athene, Poseidon,' &c., in accommodation to popular language. So before (Chap. VI.), in the case of Jupiter and Mercury. See note p. 150 n. 3.

tion informs us that the statues it contains were the work of Praxiteles. We go through the gate: and immediately the eye is attracted by the sculptured forms of Minerva, Jupiter, and Apollo, of Mercury and the Muses standing near a sanctuary of Bacchus. We are already in the midst of an animated scene, where temples, statues, and altars are on every side, and where the Athenians, fond of publicity and the open air, fond of hearing and telling what is curious and strange,[1] are enjoying their climate, and inquiring for news. A long street is before us, with a colonnade or cloister on either hand, like the covered arcades of Bologna or Turin.[2] At the end of the street, by turning to the left, we might go through the whole Ceramicus,[3] which leads by the tombs of eminent Athenians to the open inland country and the groves of the Academy. But we turn to the right into the *Agora*, which *was* the centre of a glorious public life, when the orators and statesman, the poets and the artists of Greece, found there all the incentives of their noblest enthusiasm ; and still continued to be the meeting-place of philosophy, of idleness, of conversation, and of business, when Athens could only be proud of her recollections of the past. On the south side is the Pnyx,[4] a sloping hill partially levelled into an open area for political assemblies ; on the north side is the more craggy eminence of the Areopagus ;[5] before us, towards the east, is the Acropolis,[6] towering high above the scene of which it is the glory and the crown. In the valley enclosed by these heights is the Agora,[7] which must not be conceived of as a great 'market' (Acts xvii. 17), like the bare spaces in many modern towns, where little attention has been paid to artistic decoration,—but is rather to be compared to the beautiful squares of such Italian cities as Verona and Florence, where historical buildings have closed in the space within narrow limits, and sculpture has peopled it with impressive figures. Among the buildings of greatest interest are the porticoes or cloisters, which were decorated with paintings and statuary, like the Campo Santo at Pisa. We think we may be excused for multiplying these comparisons : for though they are avowedly imperfect, they are really more useful than any attempt at description could be, in enabling us to realise the aspect of ancient

---

[1] Acts xvii. 21.

[2] Forchammer makes this comparison. It is probable, however, that these covered walks were not formed with arches, but with pillars bearing horizontal entablatures. The position we have assigned to this street is in accordance with the plan of Forchammer, who places the wall and gate more remotely from the Agora than our English topographers.

[3] This term, in its full extent, included not only the road between the city wall and the Academy, but the Agora itself. See plan of Athens.

[4] It is remarkable that the Pynx, the famous meeting-place of the political assemblies of Athens, is not mentioned by Pausanias. This may be because there were no longer any such assemblies, and therefore his attention was not called to it ; or, perhaps, it is omitted because it was simply a level space, without any work of art to attract the notice of an antiquarian.

[5] See this more fully described below.

[6] See above, p. 268.

[7] We adopt the view of Forchammer, which is now generally received, that the position of the Agora was always the same. The hypothesis of a *new Agora* to the north of the Areopagus, was first advanced by Meursius and has been adopted by Leake.

Athens. Two of the most important of these were the Portico of the King, and the Portico of the Jupiter of Freedom.[1] On the roof of the former were statues of Theseus and the Day: in front of the latter was the divinity to whom it was dedicated, and within were allegorical paintings illustrating the rise of the Athenian democracy. One characteristic of the Agora was, that it was full of memorials of actual history. Among the plane-trees planted by the hand of Cimon, were the statues of the great men of Athens —such as Solon the lawgiver, Conon the admiral, Demosthenes the orator. But among her historical men were her deified heroes, the representatives of her mythology—Hercules and Theseus—and all the series of the Eponymi on their elevated platform, from whom the tribes were named, and whom an ancient custom connected with the passing of every successive law. And among the deified heroes were memorials of the older divinities,—Mercuries, which gave their name to the street in which they were placed,—statues dedicated to Apollo, as patron of the city,[2] and her deliverer from plague,[3]—and, in the centre of all, the Altar of the Twelve Gods, which was to Athens what the Golden Milestone was to Rome. If we look up to the Areopagus, we see the temple[4] of that deity from whom the eminence had received the name of 'Mars' Hill' (Acts xvii. 22) ; and we are aware that the sanctuary of the Furies[5] is only hidden by the projecting ridge beyond the stone steps and the seats of the judges. If we look forward to the Acropolis, we behold there, closing the long perspective, a series of little sanctuaries on the very ledges of the rock,—shrines of Bacchus and Æsculapius, Venus, Earth, and Ceres, ending with the lovely form of that Temple of Unwinged Victory[6] which glittered by the entrance of the Propylæa above the statues of Harmodius and Aristogeiton.[7] Thus, every god in Olympus found a place in the Agora. But the religiousness of the Athenians (Acts xvii. 22) went even further. For every public place and building was likewise a sanctuary. The Record-House was a temple of the Mother of the Gods. The Council-House held statues of Apollo and Jupiter, with an altar of Vesta.[8] The Theatre at the base of the

---

[1] In the plan, these two porticoes are placed side by side, after Kiepert.

[2] Apollo Patrous. His temple was called Pythium. In this building the naval car, used in the Panathenaic procession, was laid up after its festal voyages, to be exhibited to travellers ; ' as the Ducal barge of Venice, the Bucentoro, in which the Doge solemnised the annual marriage with the sea, is now preserved for the same purpose in the Venetian arsenal.' Wordsworth, p. 189.

[3] Apollo Alexicacus, who was believed to have made the plague to cease in the Peloponnesian war.

[4] See the plan.

[5] The sanctuary was in a deep cleft in the front of the Areopagus, facing the Acropolis. See below.

[6] The history of this temple is very curious. In 1676 it was found entire by Spon and Wheler. Subsequent travellers found that it had disappeared. In 1835 the various portions were discovered in an excavation, with the exception of two, which are in the British Museum. It is now entirely restored. The original structure belongs to the period of the close of the Persian wars.

[7] For their position, see Pausanias. These statues were removed by Xerxes ; and Alexander, when at Babylon, gave an order for their restoration. Images of Brutus and Cassius were at one time erected near them, but probably they were removed by Augustus.

[8] For these two buildings, the *Metroum* and *Bouleuterium*, see the plan.

Acropolis, into which the Athenians crowded to hear the words of their great tragedians, was consecrated to Bacchus.[1] The Pnyx, near which we entered, on whose elevated platform they listened in breathless attention to their orators, was dedicated to Jupiter on High,[2] with whose name those of the Nymphs of the Demus were gracefully associated. And, as if the imagination of the Attic mind knew no bounds in this direction, abstractions were deified and publicly honoured. Altars were erected to Fame, to Modesty, to Energy, to Persuasion, and to Pity.[3] This last altar is mentioned by Pausanias among 'those objects in the Agora which are not understood by all men: for,' he adds, 'the Athenians alone of all the Greeks give divine honour to Pity.'[4] It is needless to show how the enumeration which we have made (and which is no more than a selection from what is described by Pausanias) throws light on the words of St. Luke and St. Paul, and especially how the groping after the abstract and invisible, implied in the altars alluded to last, illustrates the inscription '*To the Unknown God,*' which was used by Apostolic wisdom (Acts xvii. 23) to point the way to the highest truth.

What is true of the Agora is still more emphatically true of the *Acropolis,* for the spirit which rested over Athens was concentrated here. The feeling of the Athenians with regard to the Acropolis was well, though fancifully, expressed by the rhetorician who said that it was the middle space of five concentric circles of a shield, whereof the outer four were Athens, Attica, Greece, and the world. The platform of the Acropolis was a museum of art, of history, and of religion. The whole was 'one vast composition of architecture and sculpture, dedicated to the national glory and to the worship of the gods.' By one approach only—through the Propylæa built by Pericles—could this sanctuary be entered. If St. Paul went up that steep ascent on the western front of the rock, past the Temple of Victory, and through that magnificent portal, we know nearly all the features of the idolatrous spectacle he saw before him. At the entrance, in conformity with his attributes, was the statue of Mercurius Propylæus. Further on, within the vestibule of the beautiful enclosure, were statues of Venus and the Graces. The recovery of one of those who had laboured among the edifices of the Acropolis was commemorated by a dedication to Minerva as the goddess of Health. There was a shrine of Diana, whose image had been wrought by Praxiteles. Intermixed with what had reference to divinities, were the memorials of eminent men and of great

Its position may be seen on the plan, on the south side of the Acropolis.

[2] This is attributed to the elevated position of the Pnyx as seen from the Agora. Wordsworth's *Athens and Attica,* p. 72.

[3] It is doubtful in what part of Athens the altars of Fame, Modesty, and Energy were placed. Æschines alludes to the altar of Fame. The altar of Persuasion was on the ascent of the Acropolis. There were many other memorials of the same kind in Athens. Cicero speaks of a temple or altar to Contumely. In the temple of Minerva Polias, in the Acropolis, Plutarch mentions an altar of Oblivion.

[4] He adds, that this altar was *not so much due to their human sympathy as to their peculiar piety towards the gods*; and he confirms this opinion by proceeding to mention the altars of Fame, Modesty, and Energy.

victories. The statue of Pericles, to whom the glory of the Acropolis was due, remained there for centuries. Among the sculptures on the south wall was one which recorded a victory we have alluded to,—that of Attalus over the Galatians.[1] Nor was the Roman power without its representatives on this proud pedestal of Athenian glory. Before the entrance were statues of Agrippa and Augustus ;[2] and at the eastern extremity of the esplanade a temple was erected in honour of Rome and the Emperor.[3] But the main characteristics of the place were mythological and religious, and truly Athenian. On the wide levelled area were such groups as the following :— Theseus contending with the Minotaur : Hercules strangling the serpents ; the Earth imploring showers from Jupiter ; Minerva causing the olive to sprout while Neptune raises the waves. The mention of this last group raises our thoughts to the *Parthenon*,— the Virgin's House,—the glorious temple which rose in the proudest period of Athenian history to the honour of Minerva, and which ages of war and decay have only partially defaced. The sculptures on one of its pediments represented the birth of the goddess : those on the other depicted her contest with Neptune.[4] Under the outer cornice were groups exhibiting the victories achieved by her champions. Round the inner frieze was the long series of the Panathenaic procession.[5] Within was the colossal statue of ivory and gold, the work of Phidias, unrivalled in the world, save only by the Jupiter Olympius of the same famous artist. This was not the only statue of the Virgin Goddess within the sacred precincts ; the Acropolis boasted of three Minervas.[6] The oldest and most venerated was in the small irregular temple called the Erectheium, which contained the mystic olive-tree of Minerva and the mark of Neptune's trident. This statue, like that of Diana at Ephesus (Acts xix. 35), was believed to have fallen from heaven.[7] The third, though less sacred than the Minerva Polias, was the most conspicuous of all.[8] Formed from the brazen spoils of the battle of Marathon, it rose in gigantic proportions above all the buildings of the Acropolis, and

[1] See p. 185. Several of the statues seen by Pausanias in Athens were those of the Greek kings who reigned over the fragments of Alexander's empire.

[2] One pedestal is still standing in this position, with the name of Agrippa inscribed on it. There is some reason to believe that some earlier Greek statues had been converted in this instance, as in so many others, into monuments of Augustus and Agrippa. Cicero, in one of his letters from Athens, speaks indignantly of this custom.

[3] Some fragments remain, and among them the inscription which records the dedication. Augustus did not allow the provinces to dedicate any temple to him except in conjunction with Rome. There was a temple of this kind at Cæsaræa. See p. 96.

[4] For descriptive papers on these pediments, see the *Classical Museum*, Nos. VI., XVIII., and XXII. With the remains themselves in the Elgin Room at the British Museum, the restoration of Mr. Lucas should be studied.

[5] For these sculptures, it is only necessary to refer to the Elgin Room in the British Museum.

[6] See here, especially, Dr. Wordsworth's chapter on the three Minervas.

[7] Its material was not marble nor metal, but olive-wood.

[8] For the position of this statue see coin at end of the chapter. The pedestal appears to have been twenty feet, and the statue fifty-five feet, in height. Leake, p. 351. The lower part of the pedestal has lately been discovered.

stood with spear and shield as the tutelary divinity of Athens and Attica. It was the statue which may have caught the eye of St. Paul himself, from the deck of the vessel in which he sailed round Sunium to the Piræus.[1] Now he had landed in Attica, and beheld all the wonders of that city which divides with one other city all the glory of Heathen antiquity. Here, by the statue of *Minerva Promachus*, he could reflect on the meaning of the objects he had seen in his progress. His path had been among the forms of great men and deified heroes, among the temples, the statues, the altars of the gods of Greece. He had seen the creations of mythology represented to the eye, in every form of beauty and grandeur, by the sculptor and the architect. And the one overpowering result was this :—' *His spirit was stirred within him, when he saw the city crowded with idols.*'

But we must associate St. Paul, not merely with the Religion, but with the Philosophy of Greece. And this, perhaps, is our best opportunity for doing so, if we wish to connect together, in this respect also, the appearance and the spirit of Athens. If the Apostle looked out from the pedestal of the Acropolis over the city and the open country, he would see the places which are inseparably connected with the names of those who have always been recognised as the great teachers of the pagan world. In opposite directions he would see the two memorable suburbs where Aristotle and Plato, the two pupils of Socrates, held their illustrious schools. Their positions are defined by the courses of the two rivers to which we have already alluded.[2] The streamless bed of the Ilissus passes between the Acropolis and Hymettus in a south-westerly direction, till it vanishes in the low ground which separates the city from the Piræus. Looking towards the upper part of this channel, we see (or we should have seen in the first century) gardens with plane-trees and thickets of agnus-castus, with ' others of the torrent-loving shrubs of Greece.'[3] At one spot, near the base of Lycabettus, was a sacred enclosure. Here was a statue of Apollo Lycius, represented in an attitude of repose, leaning against a column, with a bow in the left hand and the right hand resting on his head. The god gave the name to the Lyceum. Here among the groves, the philosopher of Stagirus,[4] the instructor of Alexander, used to walk. Here he founded the school of the Peripatetics. To this point an ancient dialogue represents Socrates as coming, outside the northern city-wall, from the grove of the Academy. Following, therefore, this line in an opposite direction, we come to the scene of Plato's school. Those dark olive groves have revived after all the disasters which have swept across the plain. The Cephisus has been more highly favoured than the Ilissus. Its waters still irrigate the suburban gardens of the Athenians.[5] Its nightingales are still vocal

---

[1] See above, pp. 267, 269.

[2] Above, p. 270.

[3] Leake, p. 275. See Plato's *Phædrus*. The Lyceum was remarkable for its plane-trees. Socrates used to discourse under them, and Aristotle and Theophrástus afterwards enjoyed

their shade. We cannot tell how far these groves were restored since the time of Sulla, who cut them down.

[4] See an allusion to his birthplace above, p. 247.

[5] The stream is now divided and distributed, in order to water the gar-

among the twinkling olive-branches.[1]   The gnarled trunks of the
ancient trees of our own day could not be distinguished from those
which were familiar with the presence of Plato, and are more
venerable than those which had grown up after Sulla's destruction
of the woods, before Cicero[2] visited the Academy in the spirit of a
pilgrim.   But the Academicians and Peripatetics are not the schools
to which our attention is called in considering the biography of
St. Paul.   We must turn our eye from the open country to the city
itself, if we wish to see the places which witnessed the rise of the
Stoics and *Epicureans.*   Lucian, in a playful passage, speaks of
Philosophy as coming up from the Academy, by the Ceramicus, to
the Agora : 'and there,' he says, 'we shall meet her by the Stoa
Pœcile.'   Let us follow this line in imagination, and, having
followed it, let us look down from the Acropolis into the Agora.
There we distinguish a cloister or colonnade, which was not mentioned before, because it is more justly described in connection with
the Stoics.   The *Stoa Pœcile,*[3] or the 'Painted Cloister,' gave its
name to one of those sects who encountered the Apostle in the
Agora.   It was decorated with pictures of the legendary wars of
the Athenians, of their victories over their fellow Greeks, and of the
more glorious struggle at Marathon.   Originally the meeting-place
of the poets, it became the school where Zeno met his pupils, and
founded the system of stern philosophy which found adherents both
among Greeks and Romans for many generations.   The system of
Epicurus was matured nearly at the same time and in the same
neighbourhood.   The site of the philosopher's *Garden*[4] is now unknown, but it was well known in the time of Cicero ;[5] and in the
time of St. Paul it could not have been forgotten, for a peculiarly
affectionate feeling subsisted among the Epicureans towards their
founder.   He left this garden as a legacy to the school, on condition that philosophy should always be taught there, and that he
himself should be annually commemorated.   The sect had dwindled

dens and olive-trees.   Plutarch calls
the Academy the best wooded of the
suburbs of Athens.

[1] See the well known chorus in So-
phocles. *Œd. Col.* 668.

[2] Cicero, at one time, contemplated
the erection of a monument to show
his attachment to the Academy. *Att.*
vi. 1.

[3] Στόα ποικίλη,—hence ' *Stoic.*'

[4] This garden was proverbially
known among the ancients.   See Juvenal, xiii. 172, xiv. 319.

[5] On his first visit to Athens, at the
age of twenty-eight, Cicero lodged
with an Epicurean.   On the occasion
of his second visit, the attachment of
the Epicureans to the garden of their
founder was brought before him in a
singular manner. 'There lived at this
time in exile at Athens C. Memmius.
. . . The figure which he had borne
in Rome gave him great authority in

Athens; and the council of Areopagus
had granted him a piece of ground to
build upon, where Epicurus formerly
lived, and where there still remained
the old ruins of his walls.   But this
grant had given great offence to the
whole body of the Epicureans, to see
the remains of their master in danger
of being destroyed.   They had written
to Cicero at Rome, to beg him to intercede with Memmius to consent to a
restoration of it; and now at Athens
they renewed their instances, and prevailed on him to write about it. . . . .
Cicero's letter is drawn with much art
and accuracy ; he laughs at the trifling zeal of these philosophers for the
old rubbish and paltry ruins of their
founder, yet earnestly presses Memmius to indulge them in a prejudice
contracted through weakness, not wickedness.'—Middleton's *Life of Cicero.*
Sect. VII.

into smaller numbers than their rivals, in the middle of the first century. But it is highly probable that, even then, those who looked down from the Acropolis over the roofs of the city, could distinguish the quiet garden, where Epicurus lived a life of philosophic contentment, and taught his disciples that the enjoyment of tranquil pleasure was the highest end of human existence.

The spirit in which Pausanias traversed these memorable places and scrutinised everything he saw, was that of a curious and rather superstitious antiquarian. The expressions used by Cicero, when describing the same objects, show that his taste was gratified, and that he looked with satisfaction on the haunts of those whom he regarded as his teachers. The thoughts and feelings in the mind of the Christian Apostle, who came to Athens about the middle of that interval of time which separates the visit of Pausanias from that of Cicero. were very different from those of criticism or admiration. He burned with zeal for that GOD whom, 'as he went through the city,' he saw dishonoured on every side. He was melted with pity for those who, notwithstanding their intellectual greatness, were ' wholly given to idolatry.' His eye was not blinded to the reality of things, by the appearances either of art or philosophy. Forms of earthly beauty and words of human wisdom were valueless in his judgment, and far worse than valueless, if they deified vice and made falsehood attractive. He saw and heard with an earnestness of conviction which no Epicurean could have understood, as his tenderness of affection was morally far above the highest point of the Stoic's impassive dignity.

It is this tenderness of affection which first strikes us, when we turn from the manifold wonders of Athens to look upon the Apostle himself. The existence of this feeling is revealed to us in a few words in the Epistle to the Thessalonians.[1] He was filled with anxious thoughts concerning those whom he had left in Macedonia, and the sense of solitude weighed upon his spirit. Silas and Timotheus were not arrived, and it was a burden and a grief to him to be ' *left in Athens alone.*' Modern travellers have often felt, when wandering alone through the streets of a foreign city, what it is to be out of sympathy with the place and the people. The heart is with friends who are far off ; and nothing that is merely beautiful or curious can effectually disperse the cloud of sadness. If, in addition to this instinctive melancholy, the thought of an irreligious world, of evil abounding in all parts of society, and of misery following everywhere in its train,—if this thought also presses heavily on the spirit,—a state of mind is realised which may be some feeble approximation to what was experienced by the Apostle Paul in his hour of dejection. But with us such feelings are often morbid and nearly allied to discontent. We travel for pleasure, for curiosity, for excitement. It is well if we can take such depressions

---

[1] Thess. iii. 1. It may be thought that too much is built here on this one expression. But we think the remarks in the text will be justified by those who consider the tone of the Epistles to the Thessalonians (see next chapter), and the depression and sense of isolation evidently experienced by St. Paul when he was without companions. See, especially, Acts xxviii. 15, and 2 Cor. ii. 13, vii. 6. Compare the Introduction.

thankfully, as the discipline of a wordly spirit. Paul travelled that he might give to others the knowledge of salvation. His sorrow was only the cloud that kindled up into the bright pillar of the divine presence. He ever forgot himself in his Master's cause. He gloried that God's strength was made perfect in his weakness. It is useful, however, to us, to be aware of the human weakness of that heart which God made strong. Paul was indeed one of us. He loved his friends, and knew the trials both of anxiety and loneliness. As we advance with the subject, this and similar traits of the *man* advance more into view,—and with them, and personified as it were in him, touching traits of the *religion* which he preached come before us,—and we see, as we contemplate the Apostle, that the Gospel has not only deliverance from the coarseness of vice and comfort for ruder sorrows, but sympathy and strength for the most sensitive and delicate minds.

No mere pensive melancholy, no vain regrets and desires, held sway over St. Paul, so as to hinder him in proceeding with the work appointed to him. He was 'in Athens alone,' but he was there as the Apostle of God. No time was lost ; and, according to his custom, he sought out his brethren of the scattered race of Israel. Though moved with grief and indignation when he saw the idolatry all around him, he deemed that his first thought should be given to his own people. They had a synagogue at Athens, as at Thessalonica ; and in this synagogue he first proclaimed his Master. Jewish topics, however, are not brought before us prominently here. They are casually alluded to ; and we are not informed whether the Apostle was welcomed or repulsed in the Athenian synagogue. The silence of Scripture is expressive ; and we are taught that the subjects to which our attention is to be turned, are connected, not with Judaism, but with Paganism. Before we can be prepared to consider the great speech, which was the crisis and consummation of this meeting of Christianity and Paganism, our thoughts must be given for a few moments to the characteristics of Athenian Religion and Athenian Philosophy.

The mere enumeration of the visible objects with which the city of the Athenians was crowded, bears witness (to use St. Paul's own words) to their 'carefulness in *Religion.*' [1] The judgment of the Christian Apostle agreed with that of his Jewish cotemporary Josephus,—with the proud boast of the Athenians themselves, exemplified in Isocrates and Plato,—and with the verdict of a multitude of foreigners, from Livy to Julian,—all of whom unite in declaring that Athens was peculiarly devoted to religion. Replete as the whole of Greece was with objects of devotion, the antiquarian traveller informs us that there were more gods in Athens than in all the rest of the country ; and the Roman satirist hardly exaggerates, when he says that it was easier to find a god there than a man. But the same enumeration which proves the existence of the religious sentiment in this people, shows also the valueless character of the religion which they cherished. It was a religion which ministered to art and amusement, and was entirely destitute of moral power.

[1] See below, on the Speech, p. 292.

Taste was gratified by the bright spectacle to which the Athenian awoke every morning of his life. Excitement was agreeably kept up by festal seasons, gay processions, and varied ceremonies. But all this religious dissipation had no tendency to make him holy. It gave him no victory over himself : it brought him no nearer to God. A religion which addresses itself only to the taste, is as weak as one that appeals only to the intellect. The Greek religion was a mere deification of human attributes and the powers of nature. It was doubtless better than other forms of idolatry which have deified the brutes : but it had no real power to raise him to a higher position than that which he occupied by nature. It could not even keep him from falling continually to a lower degradation. To the Greek this world was everything : he hardly even sought to rise above it. And thus all his life long, in the midst of everything to gratify his taste and exercise his intellect, he remained in ignorance of God. This fact was tacitly recognised by the monuments in his own religious city. The want of something deeper and truer was expressed on the very stones. As we are told by a Latin writer that the ancient Romans, when alarmed by an earthquake, were accustomed to pray, not to any specified divinity, but to a god expressed in vague language, as avowedly *Unknown* : so the Athenians acknowledged their ignorance of the True Deity by the altars ' with this inscription, TO THE UNKNOWN GOD,' which are mentioned by Heathen writers,[1] as well as by the inspired historian. Whatever the origin of these altars may have been,[2] the true significance of the inscription is that which is pointed out by the Apostle himself.[3] The Athenians were ignorant of the right object of worship. But if we are to give a true account of Athenian religion, we must go beyond the darkness of mere ignorance into the deeper darkness of corruption and sin. The most shameless profligacy was encouraged by the public works of art, by the popular belief concerning the character of the gods, and by the ceremonies of the established worship. Authorities might be crowded in proof of this statement, both from Heathen and Christian writings.[4] It is enough to say with Seneca, that ' no other effect could possibly be produced, but that all shame on account of sin must be taken away from men, if they believe in such gods ;' and with Augustine, that ' Plato himself, who saw well the depravity of the Grecian gods, and has seriously censured them,

[1] The two Heathen writers who mention these altars are Pausanias and Philostratus. See above, pp. 266 and 275.

[2] It is very probable that they originated from a desire to dedicate the altar to *the* god under whose censure the dedicator had fallen, whom he had unwittingly offended, or whom, in the particular case, he ought to propitiate. Eichhorn thinks that these altars belonged to a period when writing was unknown, and that the inscription was added afterwards by those who were ignorant of the deity to which they were consecrated. Jerome says that

the inscription was not as St. Paul quoted it, but in the form of a general dedication to all unknown gods. But unless St. Paul quoted the actual words, his application of the inscription would lose nearly all its point. Some have fancifully found in the inscription an allusion to the God of the Jews. For some of the notions of the older antiquarians concerning the 'temple' of the Unknown God, see Leake.

[3] Acts xvii. 23.

[4] A great number of passages are collected together by Tholuck, in his *Essay on the Nature and Moral Influence of Heathenism.*

better deserves to be called a god, than those ministers of sin.' It would be the worst delusion to infer any good of the Grecian religion from the virtue and wisdom of a few great ;Athenians whose memory we revere.   The true type of the character formed by the influences which surrounded the Athenian, was such a man as Alcibiades,—with a beauty of bodily form equal to that of one of the consecrated statues, — with an intelligence quick as that of Apollo or Mercury,—enthusiastic and fickle,—versatile and profligate,—able to admire the good, but hopelessly following the bad. And if we turn to the one great exception in Athenian history,— if we turn from Alcibiades to the friend who nobly and affectionately warned him,—who, conscious of his own ignorance, was yet aware that God was best known by listening to the voice within,—yet even of Socrates we cannot say more than has been said in the following words : ' His soul was certainly in some alliance with the Holy God ; he certainly felt, in his dæmon or guardian spirit, the inexplicable nearness of his Father in heaven ; but he was destitute of a view of the divine nature in the humble form of a servant, the Redeemer with the crown of thorns ; he had no ideal conception of that true holiness, which manifests itself in the most humble love and the most affectionate humility.   Hence, also, he was unable to become fully acquainted with his own heart, though he so greatly desired it.   Hence, too, he was destitute of any deep humiliation and grief on account of his sinful wretchedness, of that true humility which no longer allows itself a biting, sarcastic tone of instruction ; and destitute, likewise, of any filial, devoted love. These perfections can be shared only by the Christian, who beholds the Redeemer as a wanderer upon earth in the form of a servant ; and who receives in his own soul the sanctifying power of that Redeemer by intercourse with Him.' [1]

When we turn from the Religion of Athens to take a view of its *Philosophy*, the first name on which our eye rests is again that of Socrates. [2]   This is necessarily the case, not only because of his own singular and unapproached greatness ; but because he was, as it were, the point to which all the earlier schools converged, and from which the later rays of Greek philosophy diverged again.   The earlier philosophical systems, such as that of Thales in Asia Minor, and Pythagoras in Italy, were limited to physical inquiries : Socrates was the first to call man to the contemplation of himself, and became the founder of ethical science. [3]   A new direction was thus given to all the philosophical schools which succeeded ; and Socrates may be said to have prepared the way for the gospel, by leading the Greek mind to the investigation of moral truth.   He gave the impulse to the two schools, which were founded in the Lyceum and by the

[1] Tholuck's *Essay on Heathenism,* as above, p. 163.

[2] For Socrates, see especially the eighth volume of Grote's *History,* and the *Quarterly Review* for December 1850.

[3] ' La philosophie grecque avait été d'abord une philosophie de la nature :

arrivée à sa maturité, elle change de caractère et de direction, et elle devient une philosophie morale, sociale, humaine.   C'est Socrate qui ouvre cette nouvelle ère, et qui en représente le caractère en sa personne.'—Victor Cousin.

banks of the Cephisus,[1] and which have produced such vast results on human thought in every generation. We are not called here to discuss the doctrines of the Peripatetics and Academicians. Not that they are unconnected with the history of Christianity : Plato and Aristotle have had a great work appointed to them, not only as the Heathen pioneers of the Truth before it was revealed, but as the educators of Christian minds in every age: the former enriched human thought with appropriate ideas for the reception of the highest truth in the highest form; the latter mapped out all the provinces of human knowledge, that Christianity might visit them and bless them : and the historian of the Church would have to speak of direct influence exerted on the Gospel by the Platonic and Aristotelian systems, in recounting the conflicts of the parties of Alexandria, and tracing the formation of the theology of the Schoolmen. But the biographer of St. Paul has only to speak of the *Stoics* and *Epicureans.* They only, among the various philosophers of the day, are mentioned as having argued with the Apostle; and their systems had really more influence in the period in which the Gospel was established, though, in the Patristic and Medieval periods, the older systems, in modified forms, regained their sway. The Stoic and Epicurean, moreover, were more exclusively limited than other philosophers to moral investigations,[2]—a fact which is tacitly implied by the proverbial application of the two words to moral principles and tendencies, which we recognise as hostile to true Christianity.

Zeno, the founder of the *Stoic* school, was a native of the same part of the Levant with St. Paul himself.[3] He came from Cyprus to Athens at a time when patriotism was decayed and political liberty lost, and when a system, which promised the power of brave and self-sustaining endurance amid the general degradation, found a willing acceptance among the nobler minds. Thus in the Painted Porch, which, as we have said, had once been the meeting-place of the poets, those who, instead of yielding to the prevailing evil of the times, thought they were able to resist it, formed themselves into a school of philosophers. In the high tone of this school, and in some of its ethical language, Stoicism was an apparent approximation to Christianity ; but on the whole, it was a hostile system, in its physics, its morals, and its theology. The Stoics condemned the worship of images and the use of temples, regarding them as nothing better than the ornaments of art. But they justified the popular polytheism, and, in fact, considered the gods of mythology as minor developments of the Great World-God, which summed up their belief concerning the origin and existence of the world.

---

[1] See above, pp. 277, 278.

[2] 'Le caractère commun du Stoïcisme et de l'Épicurisme est de réduire presque entièrement la philosophie à la morale.'—Victor Cousin.

[3] He was born at Citium in Cyprus. See p. 124. His attention was turned to philosophy by the books brought from Athens by his father, who was a merchant. Somewhere between the ages of twenty and thirty he was shipwrecked near the Piræus, and settled in Athens. The exact dates of his birth and death are not known, but he lived through the greater part of the century between B.C. 350 and B.C. 250. A portrait-bust at Naples is assigned to him, but there is some doubt whether it is to be referred to him or to Zeno the Eleatic.

The Stoics were Pantheists ; and much of their language is a curious anticipation of the phraseology of modern Pantheism. In their view, God was merely the Spirit or Reason of the Universe. The world was itself a rational soul, producing all things out of itself, and resuming it all to itself again. Matter was inseparable from the Deity. He did not create: He only organised.[1] He merely impressed law and order on the substance, which was, in fact, Himself. The manifestation of the Universe was only a period in the development of God. In conformity with these notions of the world, which substitute a sublime destiny for the belief in a personal Creator and Preserver, were the notions which were held concerning the soul and its relation to the body. The soul was, in fact, corporeal. The Stoics said that at death it would be burnt, or return to be absorbed in God. Thus, a resurrection from the dead, in the sense in which the Gospel has revealed it, must have appeared to the Stoics irrational. Nor was their moral system less hostile to ' the truth as it is in Jesus.' The proud ideal which was set before the disciple of Zeno was, a magnanimous self-denial, an austere apathy, untouched by human passion, unmoved by change of circumstance. To the Wise man all outward things were alike. Pleasure was no good. Pain was no evil. All actions conformable to Reason were equally good ; all actions contrary to Reason were equally evil. The Wise man lives according to Reason : and living thus, he is perfect and self-sufficing. He reigns supreme as a king ;[2] he is justified in boasting as a god. Nothing can well be imagined more contrary to the spirit of Christianity. Nothing could be more repugnant to the Stoic than the news of a 'Saviour,' who has atoned for our sin, and is ready to aid our weakness. Christianity is the School of Humility ; Stoicism was the Education of Pride. Christianity is a discipline of life : Stoicism was nothing better than an apprenticeship for death.[3] And fearfully were the fruits of its principle illustrated both in its earlier and later disciples. Its first two leaders[4] died by their own hands ; like the two Romans[5] whose names first rise to the memory, when the school of the Stoics is mentioned. But Christianity turns the desperate resolution, that seeks to escape disgrace by death, into the anxious question, ' What must I do to be saved?'[6] It softens the pride of stern indifference into the consolation of mutual sympathy. How great is the con-

---

[1] ' Le Dieu des Stoïciens n'a pas créé la nature, il l'a formée et organisée.'—V. Cousin : who, however, will not allow the Stoical system to be Pantheistic.

[2] Hor. *Sat.* i. iii., *Ep.* i. i.

[3] ' Le Stoïcisme est essentiellement solitaire ; c'est le soin exclusif de son âme, sans regard à celle des autres ; et, comme la seule chose importante est la pureté de l'âme, quand cette pureté est trop en péril, quand on désespère d'être victorieux dans la lutte, on peut la terminer comme l'a terminée Caton. Ainsi la philosophie n'est plus qu'*un*

apprentissage de la mort et non de la vie ; elle tend à la mort par son image, l'apathie et l'ataraxie, et se résout définitivement en *un égoïsme sublime.*'—V. Cousin.

[4] Zeno and Cleanthes. And yet Cleanthes was the author of that hymn which is, perhaps, the noblest approximation to a Christian hymn that heathenism has produced. In the speech below (Acts xvii. 28) there is some doubt whether the Apostle quotes from Cleanthes or Aratus. See the note there.

[5] Cato and Seneca.

[6] See p. 237.

trast between the Stoic ideal and the character of Jesus Christ!
How different is the acquiescence in an iron destiny from the trust
in a merciful and watchful Providence! How infinitely inferior is
that sublime egotism, which looks down with contempt on human
weakness, to the religion which tells us that 'they who mourn are
blessed,' and which commands us to 'rejoice with them that rejoice,
and to weep with them that weep!'

If Stoicism, in its full development, was utterly opposed to
Christianity, the same may be said of the very primary principles of
the *Epicurean* [1] school. If the Stoics were Pantheists, the Epicureans were virtually Atheists. Their philosophy was a system of
materialism, in the strictest sense of the word. In their view, the
world was formed by an accidental concourse of atoms, and was not
in any sense created, or even modified, by the Divinity. They did
indeed profess a certain belief in what were called gods; but these
equivocal divinities were merely phantoms,—impressions on the
popular mind,—dreams, which had no objective reality, or at least
exercised no active influence on the physical world, or the business
of life. The Epicurean deity, if self-existent at all, dwelt apart, in
serene indifference to all the affairs of the universe. The universe
was a great accident, and sufficiently explained itself without any
reference to a higher power. The popular mythology was derided,
but the Epicureans had no positive faith in anything better. As
there was no creator, so there was no moral governor. All notions
of retribution and of judgment to come were of course forbidden
by such a creed. The principles of the atomic theory, when applied
to the constitution of man, must have caused the resurrection to
appear an absurdity. The soul was nothing without the body; or
rather, the soul was itself a body, composed of finer atoms, or at
best an unmeaning compromise between the material and the immaterial. Both body and soul were dissolved together and dissipated into the elements; and when this occurred, all the life of man
was ended. The moral result of such a creed was necessarily that
which the Apostle Paul described: [2]—'If the dead rise not, let us
eat and drink: for to-morrow we die.' The essential principle of the
Epicurean philosopher was that there was nothing to alarm him,
nothing to disturb him. His furthest reach was to do deliberately
what the animals do instinctively. His highest aim was to gratify
himself. With the coarser and more energetic minds, this principle
inevitably led to the grossest sensuality and crime; in the case of
others, whose temperament was more common-place, or whose taste
was more pure, the system took the form of a selfishness more
refined. As the Stoic sought to resist the evil which surrounded
him, the Epicurean endeavoured to console himself by a tranquil and
indifferent life. He avoided the more violent excitements of political
and social engagements, to enjoy the seclusion of a calm contentment. But pleasure was still the end at which he aimed; and if we

---

[1] Epicurus, who founded, and indeed
matured, this school (for its doctrines
were never further developed), was
born in Samos, b.c. 342, though his
parents were natives of Attica. He

died b.c. 270. An authentic bust has
been preserved of him, which is engraved in Milman's *Horace*, p. 391.
[2] 1 Cor. xv. 32.

remove this end to its remotest distance, and understand it to mean an enjoyment which involves the most manifold self-denial,—if we give Epicurus credit for taking the largest view of consequences,—and if we believe that the life of his first disciples was purer than there is reason to suppose,[1]—the end remains the same. Pleasure, not duty, is the motive of moral exertion ; expediency is the test to which actions are referred ; and the self-denial itself, which an enlarged view of expediency requires, will probably be found impracticable without the grace of God. Thus, the Gospel met in the Garden an opposition not less determined, and more insidious, than the antagonism of the Porch. The two enemies it has ever had to contend with are the two ruling principles of the Epicureans and Stoics—*Pleasure* and *Pride*.

Such, in their original and essential character, were the two schools of philosophy with which St. Paul was brought directly into contact. We ought, however, to consider how far these schools had been modified by the lapse of time, by the changes which succeeded Alexander and accompanied the formation of the Roman Empire, and by the natural tendencies of the Roman character. When Stoicism and Epicureanism were brought to Rome, they were such as we have described them. In as far as they were speculative systems, they found little favour : Greek philosophy was always regarded with some degree of distrust among the Romans. Their mind was alien from science and pure speculation. Philosophy, like art and literature, was of foreign introduction. The cultivation of such pursuits was followed by private persons of wealth and taste, but was little extended among the community at large. There was no public schools of philosophy at Rome. Where it was studied at all, it was studied, not for its own sake, but for the service of the state.[2] Thus, the peculiarly practical character of the Stoic and Epicurean systems recommended them to the notice of many. What was wanted in the prevailing misery of the Roman world was a philosophy of life. There were some who weakly yielded, and some who offered a courageous resistance, to the evil of the times. The former, under the name of Epicureans, either spent their time in a serene tranquillity, away from the distractions and disorders of political life, or indulged in the grossest sensualism, and justified it on principle. The Roman adherents of the school of Epicurus were never numerous, and few great names can be mentioned among them, though one monument remains, and will ever remain, of this phase of philosophy, in the poem of Lucretius. The Stoical school was more congenial to the endurance of the Roman character : and it educated the minds of some of the noblest men of the time, who scorned to be carried away by the stream of vice. Three great names can be mentioned, which divided the period between the preaching of St. Paul and the final establishment of Christianity,—Seneca, Epictetus, and Marcus Aurelius.[3]

[1] Ritter speaks strongly of scenes of sensuality witnessed in the Garden of Epicurus.

[2] Tennemann.

[3] The approximation of the latter Stoics, especially Epictetus, to Christianity is remarkable. Hence the emphasis laid by Milton on the Stoic's 'philosophick pride, by him called virtue.' *Paradise Regained,* iv. 300.

But such men were few in a time of general depravity and unbelief. And this was really the character of the time. It was a period in the history of the world, when conquest and discovery, facilities of travelling, and the mixture of races, had produced a general fusion of opinions, resulting in an indifference to moral distinctions, and at the same time encouraging the most abject credulity. The Romans had been carrying on the work which Alexander and his successors begun. A certain degree of culture was very generally diffused. The opening of new countries excited curiosity. New religions were eagerly welcomed. Immoral rites found willing votaries. Vice and superstition went hand in hand through all parts of society, and, as the natural consequence, a scornful scepticism held possession of all the higher intellects.

But though the period of which we are speaking was one of general scepticism, for the space of three centuries the old dogmatic schools still lingered on, more especially in Greece.[1] Athens was indeed no longer what she had once been, the centre from which scientific and poetic light radiated to the neighbouring shores of Asia and Europe. Philosophy had found new homes in other cities, more especially in Tarsus and Alexandria.[2] But Alexandria, though she was commercially great and possessed the trade of three continents, had not yet seen the rise of her greatest schools; and Tarsus could never be what Athens was, even in her decay, to those who travelled with cultivated tastes, and for the purposes of education. Thus Philosophy still maintained her seat in the city of Socrates. The four great schools, the Lyceum and the Academy, the Garden and the Porch, were never destitute of exponents of their doctrines. When Cicero came, not long after Sulla's siege, he found the philosophers in residence.[3] As the Empire grew, Athens assumed more and more the character of a university town. After Christianity was first preached there, this character was confirmed to the place by the embellishments and the benefactions of Hadrian.[4] And before the schools were closed by the orders of Justinian,[5] the city which had received Cicero and Atticus[6] as students together, became the scene of the college-friendship of St. Basil and St. Gregory[7], one of the most beautiful episodes of primitive Christianity.

Thus, St. Paul found philosophers at Athens, among those whom he addressed in the Agora. This, as we have seen, was the common meeting-place of a population always eager for fresh subjects of intellectual curiosity. Demosthenes had rebuked the Athenians for this idle tendency four centuries before, telling them that they were always craving after news and excitement, at the very moment when destruction was impending over their liberties. And they are

---

[1] Tennemann.

[2] For the schools of Tarsus, see pp. 18, 87, 88.

[3] See above, p. 278, and the note.

[4] Between the visits of St. Paul and Pausanias, Hadrian made vast additions to the buildings of Athens, and gave large endowments for the purposes of education.

[5] See Gibbon, xl.

[6] See Middleton's *Life of Cicero.*

[7] Basil and Gregory Nazianzene were students together at Athens from 351 to 355. Julian was there at the same time.

described in the same manner, on the occasion of St. Paul's visit, as giving their whole leisure to telling and hearing something newer than the latest news (Acts xvii. 21). Among those who sauntered among the plane-trees [1] of the Agora, and gathered in knots under the porticoes, eagerly discussing the questions of the day, were philosophers, in the garb of their several sects, ready for any new question, on which they might exercise their subtlety or display their rhetoric. Among the other philosophers, the Stoics and Epicureans would more especially be encountered ; for the 'Painted Porch' [2] of Zeno was in the Agora itself, and the 'Garden' [3] of the rival sect was not far distant. To both these classes of hearers and talkers—both the mere idlers and the professors of philosophy—any question connected with a new religion was peculiarly welcome ; for Athens gave a ready acceptance to all superstitions and ceremonies, and was glad to find food for credulity or scepticism, ridicule or debate. To this motley group of the Agora, St. Paul made known the two great subjects he had proclaimed from city to city. He spoke aloud of 'Jesus and the Resurrection,' [4]— of that Name which is above every name,—that consummation which awaits all the generations of men who have successively passed into the sleep of death. He was in the habit of conversing 'daily' on these subjects with those whom he met. His varied experience of men, and his familiarity with many modes of thought, enabled him to present these subjects in such a way as to arrest attention. As regards the philosophers, he was providentially prepared for his collision with them. It was not the first time he had encountered them. [5] His own native city was a city of philosophers, and was especially famous (as we have remarked before) for a long line of eminent Stoics, and he was doubtless familiar with their language and opinions.

Two different impressions were produced by St. Paul's words, according to the disposition of those who heard him. Some said that he was a mere 'babbler,' [6] and received him with contemptuous derision. Others took a more serious view, and, supposing that he was endeavouring to introduce new objects of worship, [7] had their curiosity excited, and were desirous to hear more. If we suppose a distinct allusion, in these two classes, to the two philosophical sects

---

[1] See above, p. 274. It is, of course, impossible to prove that Cimon's plane-trees were succeeded by others; but a boulevard is commonly renewed, when a city recovers from its disasters.

[2] For the '*Stoa Pœcile*,' see above, p. 278.

[3] See again above, p. 278.

[4] Acts xvii. 18.

[5] See Chap. III. p. 88. Two of the most influential of the second generation of Stoics were Antipater of Tarsus and Zeno of Tarsus. Chrysippus also is said by Strabo to have been a native of the same place.

[6] The Greek word here means properly a bird that picks up seeds from the ground, and it is so used in the *Birds* of Aristophanes. Hence, secondarily, it may mean a pauper who prowls about the market-place, or a parasite who lives by his wits, and hence 'a contemptible and worthless person.' Or, from the perpetual chattering or chirping of such birds, the word may denote an idle 'babbler.'

[7] Acts xvii. 18. These are the very words used in the accusation against Socrates. The term 'dæmon' is probably here used quite generally. This is the only place where it occurs in the Acts of the Apostles. See the remarks which have been made before on this subject, pp. 229-232.

which have just been mentioned, we have no difficulty in seeing that the Epicureans were those who, according to their habit, received the new doctrine with ridicule,—while the Stoics, ever tolerant of the popular mythology, were naturally willing to hear of the new ' dæmons ' which this foreign teacher was proposing to introduce among the multitude of Athenian gods and heroes.   Or we may imagine that the two classes denote the philosophers on the one hand, who heard with scorn the teaching of a Jewish stranger untrained in the language of the schools,—and the vulgar crowd on the other, who would easily entertain suspicion (as in the case of Socrates) against anyone seeking to cast dishonour on the national divinities, or would at least be curious to hear more of this foreign and new religion.   It is not, however, necessary to make any such definite distinction between those who derided and those who listened.   Two such classes are usually found among those to whom truth is presented.   When Paul came among the Athenians, he came ' not with enticing words of man's wisdom,' and to some of the ' Greeks ' who heard him, the Gospel was ' foolishness ;' [1] while in others there was at least that curiosity which is sometimes made the path whereby the highest truth enters the mind ; and they sought to have a fuller and more deliberate exposition of the mysterious subjects, which now for the first time had been brought before their attention.

The place to which they took him was the summit of the hill of Areopagus, where the most awful court of judicature had sat from time immemorial, to pass sentence on the greatest criminals, and to decide the most solemn questions connected with religion.   The judges sat in the open air, upon seats hewn out in the rock, on a platform which was ascended by a flight of stone steps immediately from the Agora. [2]   On this spot a long series of awful causes, connected with crime and religion, had been determined, beginning with the legendary trial of Mars, which gave to the place its name of ' Mars' Hill.'   A temple of the god, [3] as we have seen, was on the brow of the eminence ; and an additional solemnity was given to the place by the sanctuary of the Furies, [4] in a broken cleft of the

[1] See 1 Cor. i. 18—ii. 5.

[2] The number of steps is sixteen. See Wordsworth's *Athens and Attica*, p. 73. 'Sixteen stone steps cut in the rock, at its south-east angle, lead up to the hill of the Areopagus from the valley of the Agora, which lies between it and the Pnyx.   This angle seems to be the point of the hill on which the council of the Areopagus sat.   Immediately above the steps, on the level of the hill, is a bench of stone excavated in the limestone rock, forming three sides of a quadrangle, like a triclinium : it faces the south: on its east and west side is a raised block: the former may, perhaps, have been the tribunal, the two latter the rude stones which Pausanias saw here, and which are described by Euripides as assigned,

the one to the accuser, the other to the criminal, in the causes which were tried in this court.'   The stone seats are intermediate in position to the sites of the Temple of Mars and the Sanctuary of the Eumenides, mentioned below.

[3] This temple was on the southern slope of the Areopagus, immediately above the Agora, near the Eponymi and the statue of Demosthenes.

[4] In harmony with the euphemistic titles given by the Athenians to these dread goddesses, Pausanias says that their statues in this place had nothing ferocious in their aspect.   The proximity of this sanctuary to the Areopagite court must have tended to give additional solemnity to the place.

rock, immediately below the judges' seats. Even in the political decay of Athens, this spot and this court were regarded by the people with superstitious reverence.[1] It was a scene with which the dread recollections of centuries were associated. It was a place of silent awe in the midst of the gay and frivolous city. Those who withdrew to the Areopagus from the Agora, came, as it were, into the presence of a higher power. No place in Athens was so suitable for a discourse upon the mysteries of religion. We are not, however, to regard St. Paul's discourse on the Areopagus as a formal defence, in a trial before the court.[2] The whole aspect of the narrative in the Acts, and the whole tenor of the discourse itself, militate against this supposition. The words, half-derisive, half-courteous, addressed to the Apostle before he spoke to his audience, ' May we know what this new doctrine is ?' are not like the words which would have been addressed to a prisoner at the bar ; and still more unlike a judge's sentence are the words with which he was dismissed at the conclusion, ' We will hear thee again of this matter.'[3] Nor is there anything in the speech itself of a really apologetic character, as anyone may perceive, on comparing it with the defence of Socrates. Moreover, the verse[4] which speaks so strongly of the Athenian love of novelty and excitement is so introduced, as to imply that curiosity was the motive of the whole proceeding. We may, indeed, admit that there was something of a mock solemnity in this adjournment from the Agora to the Areopagus. The Athenians took the Apostle from the tumult of public discussion, to the place which was at once most convenient and most appropriate. There was everything in the place to incline the auditors, so far as they were seriously disposed at all, to a reverent and thoughtful attention. It is probable that Dionysius,[5] with other Areopagites, were on the judicial seats. And a vague recollection of the dread thoughts associated by poetry and tradition with the Hill of Mars, may have solemnised the minds of some of those who crowded up the stone steps with the Apostle, and clustered round the summit of the hill, to hear his announcement of the new divinities.

There is no point in the annals of the first planting of Christianity

[1] In some respects it seems that the influence of the court was increased under the Romans.

[2] Some are of opinion that he was forcibly apprehended and put on a formal trial. It may be argued that, if a public address was all that was required, the Pnyx would have been more suitable than the Areopagus. But we need not suppose the crowd about St. Paul to have been very great; and though the Pnyx might be equally accessible from the Agora, and more convenient for a general address, the Areopagus was more *appropriate* for a discourse upon religion. We are disposed, too, to lay great stress on the verse (21) which speaks of the curi-osity of the Athenians. Unless it were meant to be emphatic, it would almost have the appearance of an interpolation. The phrase in ver. 19 is a word of general import. See Acts ix. 27.

[3] There is indeed an apparent resemblance between Acts xvii. 32, and Acts xxiv. 25, but even in the latter passage, Felix is rather setting aside an irksome subject than giving a judicial decision.

[4] Acts xvii. 21.

[5] Tradition says that he was the first bishop of Athens. The writings attributed to him, which were once so famous, are now acknowledged to be spurious.

which seizes so powerfully on the imagination of those who are familiar with the history of the ancient world. Whether we contrast the intense earnestness of the man who spoke, with the frivolous character of those who surrounded him,—or compare the certain truth and awful meaning of the Gospel he revealed, with the worthless polytheism which had made Athens a proverb in the earth,—or even think of the mere words uttered that day in the clear atmosphere, on the summit of Mars' Hill, in connection with the objects of art, temples, statues, and altars, which stood round on every side,—we feel that the moment was, and was intended to be, full of the most impressive teaching for every age of the world. Close to the spot where he stood was the Temple of Mars. The sanctuary ' of the Eumenides was immediately below him ; the Parthenon of Minerva facing him above. Their presence seemed to challenge the assertion in which he declared here, that *in* TEMPLES *made with hands the Deity does not dwell.* In front of him, towering from its pedestal on the rock of the Acropolis,—as the Borromean Colossus, which at this day, with outstretched hand, gives its benediction to the low village of Arona ; or as the brazen statue of the armed angel, which from the summit of the Castel S. Angelo spreads its wings over the city of Rome,—was the bronze Colossus of Minerva, armed with spear, shield, and helmet, as the champion of Athens. Standing almost beneath its shade, he pronounced that the Deity was *not to be likened* either to that, the work of Phidias, or to other forms in *gold, silver, or stone, graven* by art, and *man's device,* which peopled the scene before him.' [1] Wherever his eye was turned, it saw a succession of such statues and buildings in every variety of form and situation. On the rocky ledges on the south side of the Acropolis, and in the midst of the hum of the Agora, were the 'objects of devotion' already described. And in the northern parts of the city, which are equally visible from the Areopagus, on the level spaces, and on every eminence, were similar objects, to which we have made no allusion,—and especially that Temple of Theseus, the national hero, which remains in unimpaired beauty, to enable us to imagine what Athens was when this temple was only one among the many ornaments of that city, which was ' crowded with idols.'

In this scene St. Paul spoke, probably in his wonted attitude, [2] ' stretching out his hand ;' his bodily aspect still showing what he had suffered from weakness, toil, and pain ; [3] and the traces of sadness and anxiety mingled on his countenance with the expression of unshaken faith. Whatever his personal appearance may have been, we know the words which he spoke. And we are struck with the more admiration, the more narrowly we scrutinise the characteristics of his address. To defer for the present all consideration of its manifold adaptations to the various characters of his auditors, we may notice how truly it was the outpouring of the emotions which, at the time, had possession of his soul. The mouth spoke out of the

---

[1] Wordsworth's *Athens and Attica,* p. 77. The word ' graven ' (Acts xvii. 29) should be noticed. The Apostle was surrounded by *sculpture* as well as by temples.

[2] See p. 139 and the note.

[3] See the account of what took place at Philippi, and compare p. 251.

fulness of the heart.   With an ardent and enthusiastic eloquence he
gave vent to the feelings which had been excited by all that he had
seen around him in Athens.   We observe, also, how the whole
course of the oration was regulated by his own peculiar prudence.
He was placed in a position, when he might easily have been
ensnared into the use of words which would have brought down
upon him the indignation of all the city.   Had he begun by
attacking the national gods in the midst of their sanctuaries and
with the Areopagites on the seats near him, he would have been in
almost as great danger as Socrates before him.   Yet he not only
avoids the snare, but uses the very difficulty of his position to make
a road to the convictions of those who heard him.   He becomes a
Heathen to the Heathen.   He does not say that he is introducing
new divinities.   He rather implies the contrary, and gently draws his
hearers away from polytheism by telling them that he was making
known the God whom they themselves were ignorantly endeavouring
to worship.   And if the speech is characterised by St. Paul's prudence, it is marked by that wisdom of his Divine Master, which is
the pattern of all Christian teaching.   As our Blessed Lord used the
tribute-money for the instruction of His disciples, and drew living
lessons from the water in the well of Samaria, so the Apostle of the
Gentiles employed the familiar objects of Athenian life to tell them
of what was close to them, and yet they knew not.   He had carefully observed the outward appearance of the city.   He had seen
an altar with an expressive, though humiliating, inscription.   And,
using this inscription as a text,[1] he spoke to them, as follows, the
Words of Eternal Wisdom.

Their altars to UNKNOWN GODS prove both their desire to worship and their ignorance in worshipping.   Ye men of Athens, all things which I behold bear witness to your carefulness in religion.[2]   For as I passed through your city, and beheld the objects of your worship, I found amongst them an altar with this inscription, TO THE[3] UNKNOWN GOD.   Whom, therefore, ye worship, though ye know Him not, Him declare I unto you. **ACTS xvii. 22 23**

God dwells not in the temples of the Acropolis, nor needs the   God, who made the world and all things therein, seeing that He is Lord of heaven and earth, dwelleth not in temples made with hands.[4]   Neither is He **24 25**

---

[1] The altar erected to Pity, above alluded to, was once used in a similar manner.   The Athenians were about to introduce gladiatorial shows, and Demonax the Cynic said : ' Do not do this till you have first thrown down the altar of Pity.'

[2] The mistranslation of this verse in the Authorised Version is much to be regretted, because it entirely destroys the graceful courtesy of St. Paul's opening address, and represents him as beginning his speech by offending his audience.

[3] Although there is no article before the adjective, yet we need not scruple

to retain the definite article of the Authorised Version ; for although, if we take the expression by itself, ' To *AN* Unknown God ' would be a more correct translation, yet if we consider the probable origin (see above) of these altars erected to unknown gods, it will be evident that ' To *THE* Unknown God ' would be quite as near the sense of the inscription upon any particular one of such altars.   Each particular altar was devoted to *the* unknown god to whom it properly belonged, though which of the gods it might be the dedicator knew not.

[4] Here again (as at Antioch in Pisi-

served by the hands of men, as though He needed service of His creatures. anything; for it is He that giveth unto all life, and
26 breath, and all things.   And He made of one blood [1] all the nations of mankind, to dwell upon the face of the whole earth; and ordained to each the appointed seasons of their existence, and the bounds of their
27 habitation.   That they should seek God,[2] if haply they might feel after Him and find Him, though He be not far from every one of us, for in Him we live
28 and move and have our being; as certain also of your own poets [3] have said

Man was created capable of knowing God, and ought not to have fallen into the follies of idolatry, even where it was adorned by the art of Phidias.

'For we are also His offspring.'

29   Forasmuch, then, as we are the offspring of God, we ought not to think that the Godhead is like unto gold, or silver, or stone, graven by the art and device of man.

30   Howbeit, those past times of ignorance God hath overlooked;[4] but now He commandeth all men
31 everywhere to repent, because He hath appointed a day wherein He will judge the world in right-eousness, by that Man whom He hath ordained; whereof He hath given assurance unto all,[5] in that He hath raised Him from the dead.

God had overlooked the past, but now calls the world to prepare for Christ's judgment.

Christ's mission is proved by his resurrection.

St. Paul was here suddenly interrupted, as was no doubt fre-quently the case with his speeches both to Jews and Gentiles. Some of those who listened broke out into laughter and derision. The doctrine of the 'resurrection' was to them ridiculous, as the notion of equal religious rights with the 'Gentiles' was offensive

dia) we find St. Paul employing the very words of St. Stephen. Acts vii. 48.

[1] '*Of one blood*;' excluding the boastful assumption of a different ori-gin claimed by the Greeks for them-selves over the barbarians. It is not necessary to take the words together so as to mean '*He caused to dwell*,' as some interpreters maintain.

[2] The reading of MSS. A. B. G. H. &c. ('God,' not 'Lord') is the best.

[3] The quotation is from Aratus, a Greek poet, who was a native of Cili-cia, a circumstance which would, per-

haps, account for St. Paul's familiarity with his writings. His astronomical poems were so celebrated, that Ovid declares his fame will live as long as the sun and moon endure. How little did the Athenian audience imagine that the poet's immortality would really be owing to the quotation made by the despised provincial who ad-dressed them. Nearly the same words occur also in the hymn of Cleanthes. [See p. 4, n. 2, and p. 284, n. 4. The opening lines of this hymn have been thus translated:—

'Thou, who amid the Immortals art thronèd the highest in glory,
Giver and Lord of life, who by law disposest of all things,
Known by many a name, yet One Almighty for ever,
Hail, O Zeus! for to Thee should each mortal voice be uplifted:
Offspring are we too of thine, we and all that is mortal around us.'   H.]

[4] See notes upon St. Paul's speech at Lystra. It should be observed that no such metaphor as 'winked at' is to

be found in the original.
[5] Observe the coincidence between this sentiment and that in Rom. i. 4.

and intolerable to the Hebrew audience at Jerusalem.[1] Others of
those who were present on the Areopagus said, with courteous indifference, that they would ' hear him again on the subject.' The
words were spoken in the spirit of Felix, who had no due sense of
the importance of the matter, and who waited for ' a convenient
season.' Thus, amidst the derision of some, and the indifference
of others,[2] St. Paul was dismissed, and the assembly dispersed.

But though the Apostle ' departed ' thus ' from among them,'
and though most of his hearers appeared to be unimpressed, yet
many of them may have carried away in their hearts the seeds of
truth, destined to grow up into the maturity of Christian faith and
practice. We cannot fail to notice how the sentences of this interrupted speech are constructed to meet the cases in succession of
every class of which the audience was composed. Each word in
the address is adapted at once to win and to rebuke. The Athenians
were proud of everything that related to the origin of their race and
the home where they dwelt. St. Paul tells them that he was struck
by the aspect of their city ; but he shows them that the place and
the time appointed for each nation's existence are parts of one great
scheme of Providence ; and that one God is the common Father of
all nations of the earth. For the general and more ignorant population, some of whom were doubtless listening, a word of approbation
is bestowed on the care they gave to the highest of all concerns ;
but they are admonished that idolatry degrades all worship, and
leads men away from true notions of the Deity. That more educated
and more imaginative class of hearers, who delighted in the diversified mythology which personified the operations of nature, and local-
ised the divine presence [3] in sanctuaries adorned by poetry and art,
are led from the thought of their favourite shrines and customary
sacrifices, to views of that awful Being who is the Lord of heaven
and earth, and the one Author of universal life. ' Up to a certain
point in this high view of the Supreme Being, the philosopher of the
Garden, as well as of the Porch, might listen with wonder and admiration. It soared, indeed, high above the vulgar religion; but in
the lofty and serene Deity, who disdained to dwell in the earthly
temple, and needed nothing from the hand of man, the Epicurean
might almost suppose that he heard the language of his own teacher.
But the next sentence, which asserted the providence of God as the
active, creative energy,—as the conservative, the ruling, the or-
daining principle,—annihilated at once the atomic theory, and the
government of blind chance, to which Epicurus ascribed the origin
and preservation of the universe.' [4] And when the Stoic heard the
Apostle say that we ought to rise to the contemplation of the Deity
without the intervention of earthly objects, and that we live and
move and have our being in Him—it might have seemed like an

[1] Acts xxii. 22.
[2] Some commentators find again in
these two classes the Stoics and Epicureans. It is not necessary to make
so precise a division.
[3] The sacred grottoes in the rocks
within view from the Areopagus should
be remembered, as well as the temples

&c. See Wordsworth.
[4] Milman's *History of Christianity*,
vol. ii. p. 18. See his observations on
the whole speech. He remarks, in a
note, the coincidence of St. Paul's
' needing nothing ' with the ' nihil
indiga nostri ' of the Epicurean Lucretius.

echo of his own thought [1]—until the proud philosopher learnt that it was no pantheistic diffusion of power and order of which the Apostle spoke, but a living centre of government and love—that the world was ruled, not by the iron necessity of Fate, but by the providence of a personal God—and that from the proudest philosopher repentance and meek submission were sternly exacted. Above all, we are called upon to notice how the attention of the whole audience is concentered at the last upon JESUS CHRIST, though His name is not mentioned in the whole speech. Before St. Paul was taken to the Areopagus, he had been preaching 'Jesus and the resurrection;'[2] and though his discourse was interrupted, this was the last impression he left on the minds of those who heard him. And the impression was such as not merely to excite or gratify an intellectual curiosity, but to startle and search the conscience. Not only had a revival from the dead been granted to that man whom God had ordained—but a day had been appointed on which by Him the world must be judged in righteousness.

Of the immediate results of this speech we have no further knowledge, than that Dionysius,[3] a member of the Court of Areopagus, and a woman whose name was Damaris,[4] with some others, were induced to join themselves to the Apostle, and became converts to Christianity. How long St. Paul stayed in Athens, and with what success, cannot possibly be determined. He does not appear to have been driven away by any tumult or persecution. We are distinctly told that he waited for some time at Athens, till Silas and Timotheus should join him; and there is some reason for believing that the latter of these companions did rejoin him in Athens, and was dispatched again forthwith to Macedonia.[5] The Apostle himself remained in the province of Achaia, and took up his abode at its capital on the Isthmus. He inferred, or it was revealed to him, that the Gospel would meet with a more cordial reception there than at Athens. And it is a serious and instructive fact that the mercantile populations of Thessalonica and Corinth received the message of God with greater readiness than the highly educated and polished Athenians. Two letters to the Thessalonians, and two to the Corinthians, remain to attest the flourishing state of those Churches. But we possess no letter written by St. Paul to the Athenians; and we do not read that he was ever in Athens again.[6]

Whatever may have been the immediate results of St. Paul's sojourn at Athens, its real fruits are those which remain to us still. That speech on the Areopagus is an imperishable monument of the first victory of Christianity over Paganism. To make a sacred

---

[1] This strikes us the more forcibly if the quotation is from the Stoic Cleanthes. See above.

[2] Acts xvii. 18.

[3] See above, p. 290, n. 5.

[4] Nothing is known of Damaris. But, considering the seclusion of the Greek women, the mention of her name, and apparently in connection with the crowd on the Areopagus, is remarkable.

[5] See 1 Thess. iii. 1. For the move-

ments of Silas and Timotheus about this time, see the note at p. 302.

[6] The church of Athens appears to have been long in a very weak state. In the time of the Antonines, Paganism was almost as flourishing there as ever. The Christian community seems at one time to have been entirely dispersed, and to have been collected again about A.D. 165. See Leake, p. 60.

application of the words used by the Athenian historian,[1] it was 'no mere effort for the moment,' but it is a 'perpetual possession,' wherein the Church finds ever fresh supplies of wisdom and guidance. It is in Athens we learn what is the highest point to which unassisted human nature can attain ; and here we learn also the language which the Gospel addresses to a man on his proudest eminence of unaided strength. God, in His providence, Has preserved to us, in fullest profusion, the literature which unfolds to us all the life of the Athenian people, in its glory and its shame ; and He has ordained that one conspicuous passage in the Holy Volume should be the speech, in which His servant addressed that people as ignorant idolaters, called them to repentance, and warned them of judgment. And it can hardly be deemed profane, if we trace to the same Divine Providence the preservation of the very imagery which surrounded the speaker—not only the sea, and the mountains, and the sky, which change not with the decay of nations—but even the very temples, which remain, after wars and revolutions, on their ancient pedestals in astonishing perfection. We are thus provided with a poetic and yet a truthful commentary on the words that were spoken once for all at Athens ; and Art and Nature have been commissioned from above to enframe the portrait of that Apostle, who stands for ever on the Areopagus as the teacher of the Gentiles.

Coin of Athens.[2]

---

[1] Thuc. i. 22.

[2] From the British Museum. This coin shows the position of the colossal statue of **Minerva Promachus**, facing the west.

CHAPTER XI.

Letters to Thessalonica written from Corinth.—Expulsion of the Jews from Rome.—Aquila and Priscilla.—St. Paul's Labours.—Arrival of Timothy and Silas.—*First Epistle to the Thessalonians.*—St. Paul is opposed by the Jews, and turns to the Gentiles.—His Vision.—*Second Epistle to the Thessalonians.* —Continued Residence in Corinth.

WHEN St. Paul went from Athens to Corinth, he entered on a scene very different from that which he had left. It is not merely that his residence was transferred from a free Greek city to a Roman colony; as would have been the case had he been moving from Thessalonica to Philippi.[1] His present journey took him from a quiet provincial town to the busy metropolis of a province, and from the seclusion of an ancient university to the seat of government and trade.[2] Once there had been a time, in the flourishing age of the Greek republics, when Athens had been politically greater than Corinth: but now that the little territories of the Levantine cities were fused into the larger political divisions of the empire, Athens had only the memory of its pre-eminence, while Corinth held the keys of commerce and swarmed with a crowded population. Both cities had recently experienced severe vicissitudes, but a spell was on the fortunes of the former, and its character remained more entirely Greek than that of any other place:[3] while the latter rose from its ruins, a new and splendid city, on the Isthmus between its two seas, where a multitude of Greeks and Jews gradually united themselves with the military colonists sent by Julius Cæsar from Italy,[4] and were kept in order by the presence of a Roman proconsul.[5]

The connection of Corinth with the life of St. Paul and the early progress of Christianity, is so close and eventful, that no student of Holy Writ ought to be satisfied without obtaining as correct and clear an idea as possible of its social condition, and its relation to other parts of the Empire. This subject will be considered in the

---

[1] See above, p. 257.

[2] A journey in the first century from Athens to Corinth might almost be compared to a journey, in the eighteenth, from Oxford to London. For the probabilities of St. Paul's actual route, see notes on p. 319.

[3] See the preceding chapter on Athens.

[4] At the close of the Republic Corinth was entirely destroyed. Thus we find Cicero travelling, not by Corinth, but

by Athens. But Julius Cæsar established the city on the Isthmus, in the form of a colony; and the mercantile population flocked back to their old place; so that Corinth rose with great rapidity, till it was a city of the second rank in the Empire. The historical details will be given in the next chapter.

[5] Acts xviii. 12 shows that the province of Achaia was proconsular. See, under Cyprus, pp. 115–117.

succeeding chapter. At present another topic demands our chief attention. We are now arrived at that point in the life of St. Paul when his first Epistles were written. This fact is ascertained, not by any direct statements either in the Acts or the Epistles themselves, but by circumstantial evidence derived from a comparison of these documents with one another.[1] Such a comparison enables us to perceive that the Apostle's mind, on his arrival at Corinth, was still turning with affection and anxiety towards his converts at Thessalonica. In the midst of all his labours at the Isthmus, his thoughts were continually with those whom he had left in Macedonia; and though the narrative[2] tells us only of his tent-making and preaching in the metropolis of Achaia, we discover, on a closer inquiry, that the Letters to the Thessalonians were written at this particular crisis. It would be interesting, in the case of any man whose biography has been thought worth preserving, to find that letters full of love and wisdom had been written at a time when no traces would have been discoverable, except in the letters themselves, of the thoughts which had been occupying the writer's mind. Such unexpected association of the actions done in one place with affection retained towards another, always seems to add to our personal knowledge of the man whose history we may be studying, and to our interest in the pursuits which were the occupation of his life. This is peculiarly true in the case of the *first Christian correspondence*, which has been preserved to the Church. Such has ever been the influence of letter-writing,—its power in bringing those who are distant near to one another, and reconciling those who are in danger of being estranged; —such especially has been the influence of Christian letters in developing the growth of faith and love, and binding together the dislocated members of the body of Our Lord, and in making each generation in succession the teacher of the next,—that we have good reason to take these Epistles to the Thessalonians as the one chief subject of the present chapter. The earliest occurrences which took place at Corinth must first be mentioned: but for this a few pages will suffice.

The reasons which determined St. Paul to come to Corinth (over and above the discouragement he seems to have met with in Athens) were, probably, twofold. In the first place, it was a large mercantile city, in immediate connection with Rome and the West of the Mediterranean, with Thessalonica and Ephesus in the Ægean, and with Antioch and Alexandria in the East.[3] The Gospel once established in Corinth, would rapidly spread everywhere. And, again, from the very nature of the city, the Jews established there were numerous. Communities of scattered Israelites were found in various parts of the province of Achaia,—in Athens, as we have recently seen,[4]—in Argos, as we learn from Philo,—in Bœotia and Eubœa. But their chief settlement must necessarily have been in that city, which not only gave opportunities of trade by land along the Isthmus between the Morea and the Continent, but received in its two har-

---

See the arguments below, p. 304, n. 2.

[2] Acts xviii. 1-4.

[3] For full details, see the next chapter.

[4] See the preceding chapter, p. 280.

bours the ships of the Eastern and Western seas. A religion which was first to be planted in the synagogue, and was thence intended to scatter its seeds over all parts of the earth, could nowhere find a more favourable soil than among the Hebrew families at Corinth.[1]

At this particular time there was a greater number of Jews in the city than usual ; for they had lately been banished from Rome by command of the Emperor Claudius.[2] The history of this edict is involved in some obscurity. But there are abundant passages in the cotemporary Heathen writers which show the suspicion and dislike with which the Jews were regarded.[3] Notwithstanding the general toleration, they were violently persecuted by three successive Emperors ;[4] and there is good reason for identifying the edict mentioned by St. Luke with that alluded to by Suetonius, who says that Claudius drove the Jews from Rome because they were incessantly raising tumults at the instigation of a certain *Chrestus.*[5] Much has been written concerning this sentence of the biographer of the Cæsars. Some have held that there was really a Jew called Chrestus, who had excited political disturbances, others that the name is used by mistake for Christus, and that the disturbances had arisen from the Jewish expectations concerning the Messiah, or Christ. It seems to us that the last opinion is partially true ; but that we must trace this movement not merely to the vague Messianic idea entertained by the Jews, but to the events which followed the actual appearance of *the Christ.* We have seen how the first progress of Christianity had been the occasion of tumult among the Jewish communities in the provinces[6] ; and there is no reason why the same might not have happened in the capital itself.[7] Nor need we be surprised at the inaccurate form in which the name occurs, when we remember how loosely more careful writers than Suetonius express themselves concerning the affairs of the Jews.[8] Chrestus was a common name ;[9] Christus was not : and we have a distinct statement by Tertullian and Lactantius[10] that in their day the former was often used for the latter.[11]

Among the Jews who had been banished from Rome by Claudius and had settled for a time at Corinth, were two natives of Pontus, whose names were Aquila and Priscilla.[12] We have seen before

---

[1] See what has been said above on Thessalonica.

[2] Acts xviii. 2.

[3] Tacitus, for instance, and Juvenal. See the quotation from Cicero, p. 233, n. 4.

[4] Four thousand Jews or Jewish proselytes were sent as convicts by *Tiberius* to the island of Sardinia. The more directly religious persecution of *Caligula* has been mentioned previously, Chap. IV. p. 92.

[5] The words are quoted p. 233, n. 5. Compare p. 256.

[6] In Asia Minor (Chap. VI.), and more especially in Thessalonica and Berœa (Chap. IX.)

[7] Christianity must have been more or less known in Rome since the return of the Italian Jews from Pentecost (Acts ii.).

[8] Even Tacitus.

[9] Moreover, *Christus* and *Chrestus* are pronounced alike in Romaic.

[10] See the passages quoted by Dean Milman (*Hist. of Christianity,* I. p. 430), who remarks that these tumults at Rome, excited by the mutual hostility of Jews and Christians, imply that Christianity must already have made considerable progress there.

[11] See pp. 99, 100, and Tac. *Ann.* xv. 44.

[12] Acts xviii. 2.

(Chap. VIII.) that Pontus denoted a province of Asia Minor on the shores of the Euxine, and we have noticed some political facts which tended to bring this province into relations with Judæa.[1] Though, indeed, it is hardly necessary to allude to this : for there were Jewish colonies over every part of Asia Minor, and we are expressly told that Jews from Pontus heard St. Peter's first sermon[2] and read his first Epistle.[3] Aquila and Priscilla were, perhaps, of that number. Their names have a Roman form ;[4] and we may conjecture that they were brought into some connection with a Roman family, similar to that which we have supposed to have existed in the case of St. Paul himself.[5] We find they were on the present occasion forced to leave Rome ; and we notice that they are afterwards addressed[6] as residing there again ; so that it is reasonable to suppose that the metropolis was their stated residence. Yet we observe that they frequently travelled ; and we trace them on the Asiatic coast on two distinct occasions, separated by a wide interval of time. First, before their return to Italy (Acts xviii. 18, 26 ; 1 Cor. xvi. 19), and again, shortly before the martyrdom of St. Paul (2 Tim. iv. 19), we find them at Ephesus. From the manner in which they are referred to as having Christian meetings in their houses, both at Ephesus and Rome,[7] we should be inclined to conclude that they were possessed of some considerable wealth. The trade at which they laboured, or which at least they superintended, was the manufacture of tents,[8] the demand for which must have been continual in that age of travelling,—while the *cilicium*,[9] or hair-cloth, of which they were made, could easily be procured at every large town in the Levant.

A question has been raised as to whether Aquila and Priscilla were already Christians, when they met with St. Paul.[10] Though it is certainly possible that they may have been converted at Rome, we think, on the whole, that this was probably not the case. They

---

[1] Especially the marriage of Polemo with Berenice, p. 20 and p. 190.

[2] Acts ii. 9.

[3] 1 Pet. i. 1.

[4] See p. 122, also p. 39. From the mention of Priscilla as St. Paul's 'fellow-labourer,' and as one of the instructors of Apollos, we might naturally infer that she was a woman of good education. Her name appears in 2 Tim. iv. 19 (also, according to the best MSS., in Rom. xvi. 3), under the form 'Prisca.' So, in Latin authors, 'Livia' and 'Livilla,' 'Drusa' and 'Drusilla,' are used of the same person. Prisca is well known as a Roman name. It is well worthy of notice that in both cases St. Paul mentions the name of Priscilla before that of Aquila. This conveys the impression that she was the more energetic character of the two. See the notice of these two Christians by the Archdeacon Evans (*Script.*

Biog.), and his remarks on the probable usefulness of Priscilla with reference to female converts, the training of Deaconesses, &c. Compare the note on Rom. xvi. 3.

[5] P. 38.

[6] Rom. xvi. 3.

[7] Rom. xvi. 3 ; 1 Cor. xvi. 19.

[8] Many meanings have been given by the commentators to the word,— weavers of tapestry, saddlers, mathematical instrument makers, ropemakers. But nothing is so probable as that they were simply makers of those hair-cloth tents, which are still in constant use in the Levant. That they were manufacturers of the cloth itself is less likely.

[9] An account of this cloth is given in Chap. II. p. 40. See p. 134, and p. 254.

[10] See the various commentators.

are simply classed with the other Jews who were expelled by Claudius ; and we are told that the reason why St. Paul ' camo and attached himself to them '[1] was not because they had a common religion, but because they had a common trade.   There is no doubt, however, that the connection soon resulted in their conversion to Christianity.[2]   The trade which St. Paul's father had taught him in his youth[3] was thus the means of procuring him invaluable associates in the noblest work in which man was ever engaged.   No higher example can be found of the possibility of combining diligent labour in the common things of life with the utmost spirituality of mind.   Those who might have visited Aquila at Corinth in the working-hours, would have found St. Paul quietly occupied with the same task as his fellow-labourers.   Though he knew the Gospel to be a matter of life and death to the soul, he gave himself to an ordinary trade with as much zeal as though he had no other occupation.   It is the duty of every man to maintain an honourable independence ; and this, he felt, was peculiarly incumbent on him, for the sake of the Gospel he came to proclaim.[4]   He knew the obloquy to which he was likely to be exposed, and he prudently prepared for it.   The highest motives instigated his diligence in the commonest manual toil.   And this toil was no hindrance to that communion with God, which was his greatest joy, and the source of all his peace.   While he ' laboured, working with his own hands,' among the Corinthians, as he afterwards reminded them,[5]—in his heart he was praying continually, with thanksgiving, on behalf of the Thessalonians, as he says to them himself[6] in the letters which he dictated in the intervals of his labour.

This was the first scene of St. Paul's life at Corinth.   For the second scene we must turn to the synagogue.   The Sabbath[7] was a day of rest.   On that day the Jews laid aside their tent-making and their other trades, and, amid the derision of their Gentile neighbours, assembled in the house of prayer to worship the God of their ancestors.   There St. Paul spoke to them of the ' mercy promised to their forefathers,' and of the ' oath sworn to Abraham,' being 'performed.'   There his countrymen listened with incredulity or conviction ; and the tent-maker of Tarsus ' reasoned' with them and ' endeavoured to persuade'[8] both the Jews and the Gentiles who were present, to believe in Jesus Christ as the promised Messiah and the Saviour of the World.

While these two employments were proceeding,—the daily labour in the workshop, and the weekly discussions in the synagogue,— Timotheus and Silas returned from Macedonia.[9]   The effect produced

---

[1] Acts xviii. 2.

[2] They were Christians, and able to instruct others, when St. Paul left them at Ephesus, on his voyage from Corinth to Syria.   See Acts xviii. 18, 26.

[3] See p. 40.

[4] See what is said above in reference to his labours at Thessalonica, pp. 253, 254.   We shall meet with the same

subject again in the Epistles to the Corinthians.   [5] 1 Cor. iv. 12.

[6] 1 Thess. i. 2,'ii. 13 ; 2 Thess. i. 11.

[7] See Acts xviii. 4.

[8] This is the sense of the imperfect.

[9] Acts xviii. 5.   We may remark here, that Silas and Timotheus were probably the ' brethren' who brought the collection mentioned, 2 Cor. xi. 9. Compare Phil. iv. 15.

by their arrival[1] seems to have been an instantaneous increase of the zeal and energy with which St. Paul resisted the opposition, which was even now beginning to hem in the progress of the truth. The

[1] There are some difficulties and differences of opinion, with regard to the movements of Silas and Timotheus, between the time when St. Paul left them in Macedonia and their rejoining him in Achaia.

The facts which are distinctly stated are as follows. (1.) Silas and Timotheus were left at Berœa (Acts xvii. 14) when St. Paul went to Athens. We are not told why they were left there, or what commissions they received; but the Apostle sent a message from Athens (Acts xvii. 15) that they should follow him with all speed, and (Acts xvii. 16) he waited for them there. (2.) The Apostle was rejoined by them when at Corinth (Acts xviii. 5). We are not informed how they had been employed in the interval, but they came 'from Macedonia.' It is not distinctly said that they came together, but the impression at first sight is that they did. (3.) St. Paul informs us (1 Thess. iii. 1), that he was 'left in Athens alone,' and that this solitude was in consequence of Timothy having been sent to Thessalonica (1 Thess. iii. 2). Though it is not expressly stated that Timothy was sent from Athens, the first impression is that he was.

Thus there is a seeming discrepancy between the Acts and Epistles; a journey of Timotheus to Athens, previous to his arrival with Silas at Corinth, appearing to be mentioned by St. Paul, and to be quite unnoticed by St. Luke.

Paley, in the *Horæ Paulinæ*, says that the Epistle 'virtually asserts that Timothy came to the Apostle at Athens,' and assumes that it is 'necessary' to suppose this, in order to reconcile the history with the Epistle. And he points out three intimations in the history, which make the arrival, though not expressly mentioned, extremely probable: first, the message that they should come with all speed; secondly, the fact of his waiting for them; thirdly, the absence of any appearance of haste in his departure from Athens to Corinth. 'Paul had ordered Timothy to follow him without delay: he waited at Athens on purpose that Timothy might come up with him, and he stayed

there as long as his own choice led him to continue.'

This explanation is satisfactory. But two others might be suggested, which would equally remove the difficulty. It is not expressly said that Timotheus was sent *from Athens* to Thessalonica. St. Paul was anxious, as we have seen, to revisit the Thessalonians; but since he was hindered from doing so, it is highly probable (as Hemsen and Wieseler suppose) that he may have sent Timotheus to them *from Berœa*. Silas might be sent on some similar commission, and this would explain why the two companions were left behind in Macedonia. This would necessarily cause St. Paul to be 'left alone in Athens.' Such solitude was doubtless painful to him; but the spiritual good of the new converts was at stake. The two companions, after finishing the work entrusted to them, finally rejoined the Apostle at Corinth. [We should observe that the phrase is 'from Macedonia,' not 'from Berœa.'] That he 'waited for them' at Athens need cause us no difficulty: for in those days the arrival of travellers could not confidently be known beforehand. When he left Athens and proceeded to Corinth, he knew that Silas and Timotheus could easily ascertain his movements, and follow his steps, by help of information obtained at the synagogue.

But, again, we may reasonably suppose, that in the course of St. Paul's stay at Corinth, he may have paid a second visit to Athens, after the first arrival of Timotheus and Silas from Macedonia; and that during some such visit he may have sent Timotheus to Thessalonica. This view may be taken without our supposing, with Böttger, that the First Epistle to the Thessalonians was written at Athens. Schrader and others imagine a visit to that city at a later period of his life; but this view cannot be admitted without deranging the arguments for the date of 1 Thess., which was evidently written soon after leaving Macedonia.

Two further remarks may be added. (1.) If Timothy did rejoin St. Paul at Athens, we need not infer that Silas was not with him, from the fact that the name of Silas is not mentioned.

remarkable word [1] which is used to describe the '*pressure*' which he experienced at this moment in the course of his teaching at Corinth, is the same which is employed of our Lord Himself in a solemn passage of the Gospels,[2] when He says, ' I have a baptism to be baptized with ; and how am I *straitened* till it be accomplished.' He who felt our human difficulties has given us human help to aid us in what He requires us to do.   When St. Paul's companions re-joined him, he was reinforced with new earnestness and vigour in combating the difficulties which met him.   He acknowledges himself that he was at Corinth ' in weakness, and in fear and much trem-bling ;'[3] but ' God, who comforteth those that are cast down, com-forted him by the arrival '[4] of his friends.   It was only one among many instances we shall be called to notice, in which, at a time of weakness, ' he saw the brethren and took courage.'[5]

But this was not the only result of the arrival of St. Paul's com-panions.   Timotheus[6] had been sent, while St. Paul was still at Athens, to revisit and establish the Church of Thessalonica.   The news he brought on his return to St. Paul caused the latter to write to these beloved converts ; and, as we have already observed, the letter which he sent them is the first of his Epistles which has been preserved to us.   It seems to have been occasioned partly by his wish to express his earnest affection for the Thessalonian Christians, and to encourage them under their persecutions ; but it was also called for by some errors into which they had fallen.   Many of the new converts were uneasy about the state of their relatives or friends, who had died since their conversion.   They feared that these de-parted Christians would lose the happiness of witnessing their Lord's second coming, which they expected soon to behold.   In this ex-pectation others had given themselves up to a religious excitement,

It is usually taken for granted that the second arrival of Timothy (1 Thess. iii. 6) is identical with the coming of Silas and Timotheus to Corinth (Acts xviii. 5); but here we see that only Timothy is mentioned, doubtless be-cause he was most recently and fami-liarly known at Thessalonica, and per-haps, also, because the mission of Silas was to some other place.   (2.) On the other hand, it is not necessary to as-sume, because Silas and Timotheus are mentioned together (Acts xviii. 5), that they came together.   All conditions are satisfied if they came about the same time.   If they were sent on missions to two different places, the times of their return would not necessarily coincide. [Something may be implied in the form of the Greek phrase, ' Silas *as well as* Timotheus.'] In considering all these journeys, it is very needful to take into account that they would be modified by the settled or unsettled state of the country with regard to banditti, and by the various opportunities of travel-ling, which depend on the season and the weather, and the sailing of vessels. Hindrances connected with some such considerations may be referred to in Phil. iv. 10.

[1] The state of mind, whatever it was. is clearly connected with the coming of Timothy and Silas, and seems to imply increasing zeal with increasing oppo-sition.   ' Instabat verbo.'   Compare ἀνάγκη, 1 Thess. iii. 7.   The A. V. rests on an incorrect reading, though the general result is the same.   Hackett's note is very much to the purpose. ' *He was engrossed with the word.*   The arrival of his associates relieved him from anxiety which had pressed heavily upon him ; and he could now devote himself with unabated energy to his work.

[2] Luke xii. 50.

[3] 1 Cor. ii. 3.

[4] 2 Cor. vii. 6.

[5] Acts xxviii. 15.   See above on his solitude in Athens, p. 279.

[6] See above, p. 295.

under the influence of which they persuaded themselves that they need not continue to work at the business of their callings, but might claim support from the richer members of the Church. Others, again, had yielded to the same temptations which afterwards influenced the Corinthian Church, and despised the gift of prophesying [1] in comparison with those other gifts which afforded more opportunity for display. These reasons, and others which will appear in the letter itself, led St. Paul to write to the Thessalonians as follows:—

FIRST EPISTLE TO THE THESSALONIANS.[2]

Salutation. PAUL, and Silvanus, and Timotheus, TO THE CHURCH OF THE THESSALONIANS, in God our Father, and our Lord Jesus Christ. Grace[3] be to you and peace.[4]　　i. 1

Thanksgiving for their conversion. I give[5] continual thanks to God for you all, and make mention of you in my prayers without ceasing;　　2

---

[1] 1 Thess. v. 20.

[2] The correctness of the date here assigned to this Epistle may be proved as follows:—(1.) It was written not long after the conversion of the Thessalonians (1 Thess. i. 8, 9), while the tidings of it were still spreading (the verb is in the present tense) through Macedonia and Achaia, and while St. Paul could speak of himself as only taken from them for a short season (1 Thess. ii. 17). (2.) St. Paul had been recently at Athens (iii. 1), and had already preached in Achaia (i. 7, 8). (3.) Timotheus and Silas were *just* returned (iii. 6) from Macedonia, which happened (Acts xviii. 5). soon after St. Paul's first arrival at Corinth.

We have already observed (Chap. IX. p. 255), that the character of these Epistles to the Thessalonians proves how predominant was the Gentile element in that church, and that they are among the very few letters of St. Paul in which not a single quotation from the Old Testament is to be found. The use, however, of the word ' Satan ' (1 Thess. ii. 18, and 2 Thess. ii. 9) might be adduced as implying some previous knowledge of Judaism in those to whom the letter was addressed. See also the note on 2 Thess. ii. 8.

[3] This salutation occurs in all St. Paul's Epistles, except the three Pastoral Epistles, where it is changed into ' Grace, mercy, and peace.'

[4] The remainder of this verse has been introduced into the Textus Receptus by mistake in this place, where it is not found in the best MSS. It properly belongs to 2 Thess. i. 2.

[5] It is important to observe in this place, once for all, that St. Paul uses ' we,' according to the idiom of many ancient writers, where a modern writer would use ' *I*.' Great confusion is caused in many passages by not translating, according to his true meaning, in the first person *singular*; for thus it often happens, that what he spoke of himself individually, appears to us as if it were meant for a general truth: instances will occur repeatedly of this in the Epistles to the Corinthians, especially the Second. It might have been supposed, that when St. Paul associated others with himself in the salutation at the beginning of an Epistle, he meant to indicate that the Epistle proceeded from them as well as from himself; but an examination of the body of the Epistle will always convince us that such was not the case, but that he was the sole author. For example, in the present Epistle, Silvanus and Timotheus are joined with him in the salutation; but yet we find .(ch. iii. 1, 2)—' *we* thought it good to be left in Athens *alone*. and sent Timothy *our* brother.' Now, *who* was it who thought fit to be left at Athens alone? Plainly St. Paul himself, and he only; neither Timo-

i. 3 remembering, in the presence of our God and Father,
the working of your faith, and the labours of your
love, and the stedfastness of your hope of our Lord
4 Jesus Christ.[1]	Brethren, beloved by God, I know
5 how God has chosen you ; for my Glad-tidings came
to you, not only in word, but also in power ; with the
might of the Holy Spirit, and with the full assur-
ance of belief.[2]	As you, likewise, know the manner
in which I behaved myself among you, for your
6 sakes.	Moreover, you followed in my steps, and in
the steps of the Lord ; and you received the word in
great tribulation,[3] with joy which came from the
7 Holy Spirit.	And thus you have become patterns to
8 all the believers in Macedonia and in Achaia.	For
from you the word of the Lord has been sounded
forth,[4] and not only has its sound been heard in Macedonia and Achaia, but also in every place the tidings
of your faith towards God have been spread abroad,
9 so that I have no need to speak of it at all.	For
others are telling of their own accord,[5] concerning
me, what welcome you gave me, and how you forsook your idols, and turned to serve God, the living
10 and the true ; and to wait for His Son from the
heavens, whom He raised from the dead, even Jesus
our deliverer from the coming wrath.

ii. 1	For, you know yourselves, brethren, that my *He reminds*
2 coming amongst you was not fruitless ; but after I *them of his own example.*
had borne suffering and outrage (as you know) at
Philippi, I trusted in my God, and boldly declared
to you God's Glad-tidings, in the midst of great
3 contention.	For my exhortations are not prompted
by imposture, nor by lasciviousness, nor do I speak in

theus (who is here expressly excluded)
nor Silvanus (who probably did not
rejoin St. Paul till afterwards at Corinth, Acts xviii. 5, and see the note,
p. 302) being included.	Ch. iii. 6 is
not less decisive—' but now that Timotheus is just come to *us* from you '—
when we remember that Silvanus came
with Timotheus.	Several other pas-
sages in the Epistle prove the same
thing, but these may suffice.

It is true, that sometimes the ancient
idiom in which a writer spoke of himself in the plural is more graceful, and
seems less egotistical, than the modern
usage; but yet (the modern usage
being what it is) a literal translation

of the ἡμεῖς very often conveys a confused idea of the meaning; and it appears better, therefore, to translate
according to the modern idiom.

[1] St. Paul is here referring to the
time when he first visited and converted the Thessalonians; the 'hope'
spoken of was the hope of our Lord's
coming.

[2] In illustration of the word here we
may refer to Rom. xiv. 5, and Heb. x.
22.

[3] This tribulation they brought on
themselves by receiving the Gospel.

[4] See p. 249, n. 4.

[5] ' Themselves,' emphatic.

guile.[1] But as God has proved my fitness for the ii. 4
charge of the Glad-tidings, so I speak, not seeking
to please men but God, who proves our hearts. For 5
never did I use flattering words, as you know; nor
hide covetousness under fair pretences (God is wit- 6
ness); nor did I seek honour from men, either from
you or others; although I might have been burdensome, as Christ's apostle.[2] But I behaved myself 7
among you with gentleness; and as a nurse cherishes
her own children,[3] so in my fond affection it was my 8
joy to give you not only the Glad-tidings of God,
but my own life also, because you were dear to me.
For you remember, brethren, my toilsome labours; 9
how I worked both night and day, that I might not
be burdensome to any of you, while I proclaimed to
you the message[4] which I bore, the Glad-tidings of
God. Ye are yourselves witnesses, and God also is 10
witness, how holy, and just, and unblamable, were
my dealings towards you that believe. You know 11
how earnestly, as a father his own children, I exhorted, and entreated, and adjured each one among
you to walk worthy of God, by whom you are called 12
into His own kingdom and glory.

Wherefore I also give continual thanks to God, be- 13
cause, when you heard from me the spoken word[5] of
God, you received it not as the word of man, but, as
it is in truth, the word of God; who Himself works
effectually in you that believe. For you, brethren, 14
followed in the steps of the churches of God in
Judæa, which are in Christ Jesus, inasmuch as
you suffered the like persecution from your own
countrymen, which they endured from the Jews;

---

[1] In this and the following verses, we have allusions to the accusations brought against St. Paul by his Jewish opponents. He would of course have been accused of *imposture*, as the preacher of a miraculous revelation; the charge of *impurity* might also have been suggested to impure minds, as connected with the conversion of female proselytes; the charge of *seeking to please men*, was repeated by the Judaisers in Galatia. See Gal. i. 10.

[2] One of the grounds upon which St. Paul's Judaising opponents denied his apostolic authority, was the fact that he (in general) refused to be maintained by his converts, whereas,

Our Lord had given to His apostles the right of being so maintained. St. Paul fully explains his reasons for not availing himself of that right in several passages, especially 1 Cor. ix.; and he here takes care to allude to his possession of the right, while mentioning his renunciation of it. Cf. 2 Thess. iii. 9.

[3] 'Her own children.' See p. 253, n. 10. It will be observed, also, that we adopt a different punctuation from that which has led to the received version.

[4] The original word involves the idea of *a herald proclaiming a message*.

[5] Literally *word received by hearing*, i.e. *spoken word*. Cf. Rom. x. 16.

i. 15 who killed both the Lord Jesus, and the prophets,
and who have driven me forth [from city to city[1]] ; a
16 people displeasing to God, and enemies to all mankind, who would hinder me from speaking to the
Gentiles for their salvation : continuing always to fill
up the measure of their sins; but the wrath [of God]
has overtaken them to destroy them.[2]

17   But I, brethren, having been torn from you for a   *Expresses his desire to see them.*
short season (in presence, not in heart), sought very
18 earnestly, to behold you [again] face to face.[3] Wherefore I, Paul (for my own part), desired to visit you
19 once and again ; but Satan hindered me.   For what
is my hope or joy ? what is the crown wherein I
glory ? what but your own selves, in the presence of
20 our Lord Jesus Christ at His appearing.[4]   Yea, you
are my glory and my joy.

iii. 1   Therefore, when I was no longer able to for-   *And his joy in hearing of their well-doing from Timotheus.*
bear, I determined willingly to be left at Athens
2 alone ; and I sent Timotheus, my brother, and
God's fellow-worker[5] in the Glad-tidings of Christ,
that he might strengthen your constancy, and
3 exhort you concerning your faith, that none of
you should waver in these afflictions ; since you
know yourselves that such is our appointed lot,
4 for when I was with you, I forewarned you that
affliction awaited us, as you know that it befel.
5 For this cause, I also, when I could no longer
forbear, sent to learn tidings of your faith ; fearing
lest perchance the tempter had tempted you, and
6 lest my labour should be in vain.   But now that
Timotheus has returned from you to me, and has
brought me the glad tidings of your faith and
love, and that you still keep an affectionate remembrance of me, longing to see me, as I to see
7 you—I have been comforted, brethren, on your
behalf, and all my own tribulation and distress[6]
8 has been lightened by your faith.   For now I
9 live,[7] if you be stedfast in the Lord.   What thanks-

---

[1] Referring to his recent expulsion from Thessalonica and Berœa.
[2] More literally, 'to make an end of them.'
[3] See what is said in the preceding chapter in connection with Berœa.
[4] The anticipative blending of the future with the present here is parallel with and explains Rom. ii. 15, 16.

[5] There is some doubt about the reading here. That which we adopt is analogous to 1 Cor. iii. 9.   The bold-ness of the expression probably led to the variation in the MSS. On the fact mentioned in these two verses, see the note at p. 302 above.
[6] See p. 303, and note.
[7] Compare Rom. vii. 9.

giving can I render to God for you, for all the
joy which you cause me in the presence of my
God? Night and day, I pray exceeding earnestly iii.
to see you face to face, and to complete what is
yet wanting in your faith. Now, may our God 11
and Father Himself, and our Lord Jesus,[1] direct
my path towards you. Meantime, may the Lord 12
cause you to increase and abound in love to one
another and to all men; even as I to you. And 13
so may He keep your hearts stedfast and unblamable in holiness, in the presence of our God and
Father, at the appearing of our Lord Jesus, with all
his saints.

Against sen-
suality.
Furthermore, brethren, I beseech and exhort iv.
you in the name of the Lord Jesus, that, as I
taught you how to walk that you might please
God, you would do so more and more. For you 2
know what commands I delivered to you by the
authority of the Lord Jesus. This, then, is the 3
will of God, even your sanctification; that you 4
should keep yourselves from fornication, that each
of you should learn to master his body,[2] in sanctification and honour; not in lustful passions, like 5
the Heathen who know not God; that no man 6
wrong his brother in this matter by transgression.[3]
All such the Lord will punish, as I forewarned
you by my testimony. For God called us not to 7
uncleanness, but His calling is a holy calling.[4]
Wherefore, he that despises these my words, de- 8
spises not man but God, who also has given unto
me [5] His Holy Spirit.

Exhortation
to love, peace,
and good
order.
Concerning brotherly love it is needless that I 9
should write to you; for ye yourselves are taught
by God to love one another; as you show by deeds 10
towards all the brethren through the whole of
Macedonia. But I exhort you, brethren, to abound 11

---

[1] The word for 'Christ' is omitted
by the best MSS. both here and in
verse 13.

[2] The original cannot mean *to possess*; it means, *to gain possession of*, to
acquire for one's own use. The use of
'vessel' for *body* is common, and
found 2 Cor. iv. 7. Now a man may
be said to *gain possession of his own
body* when he subdues those lusts
which tend to destroy his mastery
over it. Hence the interpretation

which we have adopted.

[3] The reading, adopted in the received Text, is allowed by all modern
critics to be wrong. The obvious
translation is, 'in the matter in question.'

[4] Literally 'in holiness,' not 'unto
holiness,' as in A.V.

[5] We have retained '*us*' with the
Received Text, on the ground of context; although the weight of MS.
authority is in favour of '*you*.'

still more; and be it your ambition to live quietly,
and to mind your own concerns;[1] and to work

12 with your own hands (as I commanded you); that
the seemly order of your lives may be manifest to
those without, and that you may need help from no
man.[2]

13 But I would not have you ignorant, brethren, Happiness of the Christian dead.
concerning those who are asleep, that you sorrow

14 not like other men who have no hope.[3] For if
we believe that Jesus died and rose again, so also
will God, through Jesus,[4] bring back those who

15 sleep, together with Him. This I declare to you,
in the word of the Lord, that we who are living,
who survive to the appearing of the Lord, shall

16 not come before those who sleep. For the Lord
himself shall descend from heaven with the shout
of war,[5] the Archangel's voice, and the trumpet
of God; and first the dead in Christ[6] shall rise;

17 then we the living, who remain, shall be caught up
with them among the clouds[7] to meet the Lord in
the air; and so we shall be for ever with the Lord.

18 Wherefore comfort[8] one another with these words.

r. 1 But of the times and seasons, brethren, you need The suddenness of Christ's coming a motive to watchfulness.

2 not that I should write to you. For yourselves
know perfectly that the day of the Lord will come

3 as a robber in the night; and while men say Peace
and Safety, destruction shall come upon them in a
moment, as the pangs of travail upon a woman

4 with child; and they shall find no escape. But
you, brethren, are not in darkness, that The Day
should come upon you as the robber on sleeping

5 men;[9] for you are all the children of the light and

---

[1] The original expression is almost equivalent to ' be ambitious to be un-ambitious.'

[2] It seems better to take this as masculine than as neuter. We may compare with these verses the similar directions in the speech at Miletus, Acts xx.

[3] This hopelessness in death is illustrated by the funeral inscriptions found at Thessalonica, referred to p. 255.

[4] This connection is more natural than that of the Authorised Version.

[5] The word denotes the shout used in battle.

[6] Equivalent to ' they that sleep in Christ.' (1 Cor. xv. 18.)

[7] [' Borne aloft from earth by up-bearing clouds,' as it is rendered by Professor Ellicott in his *Historical Lectures on the Life of our Lord*, p. 234. See his note there, and in his *Comm.* on 1 Thess. ii. H.]

[8] This verb, originally *to call to one's side*, thence sometimes *to comfort*, more usually to *exhort*, must be translated according to the context. [See on Barnabas, pp. 97, 98, 138, and notes. H.]

[9] There is some authority for the accusative plural,—' as the daylight surprises robbers;' and this sort of transition, where a word suggests a rapid change from one metaphor to another, is not unlike the style of St. Paul. We may add that the A. V. in

of the day. We are not of the night, nor of darkness; therefore let us not sleep as do others, but v. 6
let us watch and be sober; for they who slumber, 7
slumber in the night; and they who are drunken,
are drunken in the night; but let us, who are of 8
the day, be sober; putting on faith and love for a
breast-plate; and for a helmet, the hope of salvation. For not to abide His wrath, but to obtain 9
salvation, hath God ordained us, through our Lord
Jesus Christ, who died for us, that whether we 10
wake or sleep we should live together with Him.
Wherefore exhort one another, and build one another 11
up,[1] even as you already do.

The Presbyter to be duly regarded. I beseech you, brethren, to acknowledge those 12
who are labouring among you; who preside over
you in the Lord's name, and give you admonition.
I beseech you to esteem them very highly in love, 13
for their work's sake. And maintain peace among
yourselves.

POSTSCRIPT [ADDRESSED TO THE PRESBYTERS (?)].[2]

Duties of the Presbyters. But you, brethren, I exhort; admonish the dis- 14
orderly, encourage the timid, support the weak, be
patient with all. Take heed that none of you return 15
evil for evil, but strive to do good always, both to
one another and to all men. Rejoice evermore; 16
pray without ceasing; continue to give thanks 17,
whatever be your lot; for this is the will of God,
in Christ Jesus concerning you. Quench not [the 19
manifestation of] the Spirit; think not meanly of [3] 20

translating the word '*thief*,' both here
and elsewhere, gives an inadequate conception of the word. It is in fact the
modern Greek 'klepht,' and denotes
a *bandit*, who comes to murder as
well as to steal. For the meaning of
'The Day' (*the great day, the day of
Judgment*), compare 1 Cor. iii. 13.

[1] The full meaning is, 'build one
another up, that you may all together
grow into a temple of God.' The
word is frequently used by St. Paul
in this sense, which is fully explained
1 Cor. iii. 10–17. It is very difficult
to express the meaning by any single
word in English, and yet it would
weaken the expression too much if it
were diluted into a periphrasis fully
expressing its meaning.

[2] It appears probable, as Chrysostom

thought, that those who are here directed 'to admonish' are the same
who are described immediately before
(ver. 12) as 'giving admonition.' Also
they are very solemnly directed (ver.
27) to see that the letter be read to all
the Christians in Thessalonica; which
seems to imply that they presided over
the Christian assemblies. At the same
time it must be admitted that many of
the duties here enjoined are duties of
all Christians.

[3] We know, from the First Epistle
to Corinth, that this warning was not
unneeded in the early church. (See 1
Cor. xiv.) The gift of prophesying
(i.e. inspired preaching) had less the
appearance of a supernatural gift than
several of the other charisms; and
hence it was thought little of by those

21 prophesyings; try all [which the prophets utter];
22 reject [1] the false, but keep the good; hold yourselves aloof from every form of evil.[2]

23 Now may the God of peace Himself sanctify you Concluding prayers and salutations.
wholly; and may your spirit and soul and body all
together be preserved blameless, at the appearing
24 of our Lord Jesus Christ. Faithful is He who calls
you; He will fulfil my prayer.

26 Brethren, pray for me. Greet all the brethren
27 with the kiss of holiness.[3] I adjure you,[4] in the
name of the Lord, to see that this letter be read to
all the [5] brethren.

28 [6] The grace of our Lord Jesus Christ be with you.[7] Autograph benediction.

The strong expressions used in this letter concerning the malevo-
lence of the Jews, lead us to suppose that the Apostle was thinking
not only of their past opposition at Thessalonica,[8] but of the
difficulties with which they were beginning to surround him at
Corinth. At the very time of his writing, that same people who
had 'killed the Lord Jesus and their own prophets,' and had already
driven Paul 'from city to city,' were showing themselves 'a people
displeasing to God, and enemies to all mankind,' by endeavouring
to hinder him from speaking to the Gentiles for their salvation
(1 Thess. ii. 15, 16). Such expressions would naturally be used in

who sought more for display than edification.

[1] This word includes the notion of
rejecting that which does not abide the
test.

[2] Not 'appearance' (A. V.), but
species under a *genus*.

[3] This alludes to the same custom
which is referred to in Rom. xvi. 16;
1 Cor. xvi. 20; 2 Cor. xiii. 12. We
find a full account of it, as it was
practised in the early church, in the
Apostolic Constitutions (book ii. ch. 57).
The men and women were placed in
separate parts of the building where
they met for worship; and then, before receiving the Holy Communion,
the men kissed the men, and the women
the women: before the ceremony, a
proclamation was made by the principal deacon:—'Let none bear malice
against any; let none do it in hypocrisy.' 'Then,' it is added, 'let the
men salute one another, and the women
one another, with the kiss of the
Lord.' It should be remembered by
English readers, that a kiss was in

ancient times (as, indeed, it is now in
many foreign countries) the ordinary
mode of salutation between friends
when they met.

[4] *Whom* does he adjure here?
Plainly those to whom, in the first
instance, the letter was addressed, or
rather delivered. Now these must
probably have been the Presbyters.

[5] The word for 'holy' is omitted
in the best MSS.

[6] It should be remarked, that this
concluding benediction is used by St.
Paul at the end of the Epistles to the
Romans, Corinthians (under a longer
form in 2 Cor.), Galatians, Ephesians, Philippians, and Thessalonians.
And, in a shorter form, it is used also
at the end of all his other Epistles. It
seems (from what he says in 2 Thess.
iii. 17, 18) to have been always written
with his own hand.

[7] The 'Amen' of the Received Text
is a later addition, not found in the best
MSS.

[8] See above, Chap. IX.

a letter written under the circumstances described in the Acts (xviii. 6), when the Jews were assuming the attitude of an organised and systematic resistance,[1] and assailing the Apostle in the language of blasphemy,[2] like those who had accused our Saviour of casting out devils by Beelzebub.

Now, therefore, the Apostle left the Jews, and turned to the Gentiles. He withdrew from his own people with one of those symbolical actions, which, in the East, have all the expressiveness of language,[3] and which, having received the sanction of our Lord Himself,[4] are equivalent to the denunciation of woe. He shook the dust off his garments,[5] and proclaimed himself innocent of the blood[6] of those who refused to listen to the voice which offered them salvation. A proselyte, whose name was Justus,[7] opened his door to the rejected Apostle ; and that house became thenceforward the place of public teaching. While he continued doubtless to lodge with Aquila and Priscilla (for the Lord had said[8] that His Apostle should abide in the house where the ' Son of peace' was), he met his flock in the house of Justus. Some place convenient for general meeting was evidently necessary for the continuance of St. Paul's work in the cities where he resided. So long as possible, it was the synagogue. When he was exiled from the Jewish place of worship, or unable from other causes to attend it, it was such a place as providential circumstances might suggest. At Rome it was his own hired lodging (Acts xxviii. 30) ; at Ephesus it was the School of Tyrannus (Acts xix. 9). Here at Corinth it was a house ' contiguous to the synagogue,' offered on the emergency for the Apostle's use by one who had listened and believed. It may readily be supposed that no convenient place could be found in the manufactory of Aquila and Priscilla. There, too, in the society of Jews lately exiled from Rome, he could hardly have looked for a congregation of Gentiles ; whereas Justus, being a proselyte, was exactly in a position to receive under his roof indiscriminately, both Hebrews and Greeks.

Special mention is made of the fact, that the house of Justus was ' contiguous to the synagogue.' We are not necessarily to infer from this that St. Paul had any deliberate motive for choosing that locality. Though it might be that he would show the Jews, as in a visible symbol, that ' by their sin salvation had come to the Gentiles, to provoke them to jealousy,'[9]—while at the same time he remained as near to them as possible, to assure them of his readiness to return at the moment of their repentance. Whatever we may surmise concerning the motive of this choice, certain consequences must have followed from the contiguity of the house and the synagogue, and some incident resulting from it may have suggested the mention of the fact. The Jewish and Christian congregations would often

---

[1] St. Luke here uses a military term.
[2] Compare Matt. xii. 24–31.
[3] See Acts xiii. 51 [p. 145].
[4] Mark vi. 11.
[5] Acts xviii. 6.
[6] See Acts v. 28, xx. 26. Also Ezek. xxxiii. 8, 9, and Matt. xxvii. 24.

[7] Nothing more is known of him. The name is Latin.
[8] Luke x. 6, 7. St. Paul ' abode ' (imp.) in the house of Aquila and Priscilla (ver. 3), while it is merely said that he ' went to' (aor.) that of Justus (ver. 7).
[9] Rom. xi. 11.

meet face to face in the street ; and all the success of the Gospel would become more palpable and conspicuous.   And even if we leave out of view such considerations as these, there is a certain interest attaching to any phrase which tends to localise the scene of Apostolical labours.   When we think of events that we have witnessed, we always reproduce in the mind, however dimly, some image of the place where the events have occurred.   This condition of human thought is common to us and to the Apostles.   The house of John's mother at Jerusalem (Acts xii.), the *proseucha* by the water-side at Philippi (Acts xvi.), were associated with many recollections in the minds of the earliest Christians.   And when St. Paul thought, even many years afterwards, of what occurred on his first visit to Corinth, the images before the 'inward eye' would be not merely the general aspect of the houses and temples of Corinth, with the great citadel overtowering them, but the synagogue and the house of Justus, the incidents which happened in their neighbourhood, and the gestures and faces of those who encountered each other in the street.

If an interest is attached to the places, a still deeper interest is attached to the persons, referred to in the history of the planting of the Church.   In the case of Corinth, the names both of individuals and families are mentioned in abundance.   The family of Stephanas is the first that occurs to us ; for they seem to have been the earliest Corinthian converts.   St. Paul himself speaks of that household, in the first Epistle to the Corinthians (xvi. 15), as 'the first fruits of Achaia.'[1]   Another Christian of Corinth, well worthy of the recollection of the Church of after ages, was Caius (1 Cor. i. 14), with whom St. Paul found a home on his next visit (Rom. xvi. 23), as he found one now with Aquila and Priscilla.   We may conjecture, with reason, that his present host and hostess had now given their formal adherence to St. Paul, and that they left the synagogue with him.   After the open schism had taken place, we find the Church rapidly increasing.   'Many of the Corinthians began to believe, when they heard, and came to receive baptism.' (Acts xviii. 8.)   We derive some information from St. Paul's own writings concerning the character of those who became believers.   Not many of the philosophers,—not many of the noble and powerful (1 Cor. i. 26)— but many of those who had been profligate and degraded (1 Cor. vi. 11) were called.   The ignorant of this world were chosen to confound the wise ; and the weak to confound the strong.   From St. Paul's language we infer that the Gentile converts were more numerous than the Jewish.   Yet one signal victory of the Gospel over Judaism must be mentioned here,—the conversion of Crispus (Acts xviii. 8),—who, from his position as 'ruler of the synagogue,' may be presumed to have been a man of learning and high character, and who now, with all his family, joined himself to the new community.   His conversion was felt to be so important, that the Apostle deviated from his usual practice (1 Cor. i. 14–16), and

---

[1] In Rom. xvi. 5 we hold 'Asia' to be undoubtedly the right reading.   See note on the passage.   If, however, the reading 'Achaia' were retained, we should be at liberty to suppose that Epænetus was a member of the household of Stephanas, and thus we might reconcile 1 Cor. xvi. 15 with Rom. xvi. 5.

baptized him, as well as Caius and the household of Stephanas, with his own hand.

Such an event as the baptism of Crispus must have had a great effect in exasperating the Jews against St. Paul. Their opposition grew with his success. As we approach the time when the second letter to the Thessalonians was written, we find the difficulties of his position increasing. In the first Epistle the writer's mind is almost entirely occupied with the thought of what might be happening at Thessalonica: in the second, the remembrance of his own pressing trial seems to mingle more conspicuously with the exhortations and warnings addressed to those who are absent. He particularly asks for the prayers of the Thessalonians, that he may be delivered from the perverse and wicked men around him, who were destitute of faith.[1] It is evident that he was in a condition of fear and anxiety. This is further manifest from the words which were heard by him in a vision vouchsafed at this critical period.[2] We have already had occasion to observe, that such timely visitations were granted to the Apostle, when he was most in need of supernatural aid.[3] In the present instance, the Lord, who spoke to him in the night, gave him an assurance of His presence,[4] and a promise of safety, along with a prophecy of good success at Corinth, and a command to speak boldly without fear, and not to keep silence. From this we may infer that his faith in Christ's presence was failing,—that fear was beginning to produce hesitation,—and that the work of extending the Gospel was in danger of being arrested.[5] The servant of God received conscious strength in the moment of trial and conflict; and the divine words were fulfilled in the formation of a large and flourishing church at Corinth, and in a safe and continued residence in that city, through the space of a year and six months.

Not many months of this period had elapsed when St. Paul found it necessary to write again to the Thessalonians. The excitement which he had endeavoured to allay by his first Epistle was not arrested, and the fanatical portion of the church had availed themselves of the impression produced by St. Paul's personal teaching to increase it. It will be remembered that a subject on which he had especially dwelt while he was at Thessalonica,[6] and to which he had also alluded in his first Epistle,[7] was the second advent of Our Lord. We know that our Saviour Himself had warned His disciples that ' of that day and that hour knoweth no man, no, not the angels of heaven, but the Father only ; ' and we find these words remarkably fulfilled by the fact that the early Church, and even the Apostles themselves, expected[8] their Lord to come again in that very generation. St. Paul himself shared in that expectation, but being under the guidance

---

[1] See below, 2 Thess. iii. 2.
[2] Acts xviii. 9, 10.
[3] See p. 217.
[4] Compare Matt. xxviii. 20.
[5] Observe the strong expressions which St. Paul himself uses (1 Cor. ii. 3) of his own state of mind during this stay at Corinth.
[6] As he himself reminds his readers

(2 Thess. ii. 5), and as we find in the Acts (xvii. 7). See p. 252.
[7] 1 Thess. v. 1-11.
[8] [Professor Ellicott, in his note on 1 Thess. iv. 15, deprecates the inference that the Apostle definitely expected the second Advent to occur in his own lifetime. H.]

of the Spirit of Truth, he did not deduce therefrom any erroneous practical conclusions. Some of his disciples, on the other hand, inferred that, if indeed the present world were so soon to come to an end, it was useless to pursue their common earthly employments any longer. They forsook their work, and gave themselves up to dreamy expectations of the future ; so that the whole framework of society in the Thessalonian Church was in danger of dissolution. Those who encouraged this delusion, supported it by imaginary revelations of the Spirit :[1] and they even had recourse to forgery, and circulated a letter purporting to be written by St. Paul,[2] in confirmation of their views. To check this evil, St. Paul wrote his second Epistle. In this he endeavours to remove their present erroneous expectations of Christ's immediate coming, by reminding them of certain signs which must precede the second advent. He had already told them of these signs when he was with them; and this explains the extreme obscurity of his description of them in the present Epistle ; for he was not giving new information, but alluding to facts which he had already explained to them at an earlier period. It would have been well if this had been remembered by all those who have extracted such numerous and discordant prophecies and anathemas from certain passages in the following Epistle.

SECOND EPISTLE TO THE THESSALONIANS.[3]

1 PAUL, and Silvanus, and Timotheus, TO THE CHURCH OF THE THESSALONIANS, in God our Father, and our Lord Jesus Christ. — *Salutation.*

2 Grace be to you, and peace, from God our Father and our Lord Jesus Christ.

3   I[4] am bound to give thanks to God continually on your behalf, brethren, as is fitting, because of the abundant increase of your faith, and the overflowing love wherewith you are filled, every one of

4 you, towards each other. So that I myself boast of you among the churches of God, for your sted- — *Encouragement under their persecutions from the hope of Christ's coming.*

---

[1] 2 Thess. ii. 2.

[2] 2 Thess. ii. 2.   Compare iii. 17. Perhaps, however, these expressions may admit of being explained as referring to the rumour of a letter.

[3] It is evident that this Epistle was written at the time here assigned to it, soon after the first, from the following considerations :—

(1) The state of the Thessalonian Church described in both Epistles is almost exactly the same. (A.) The same excitement prevailed concerning the expected advent of Our Lord, only in a greater degree. (B.) The same party continued fanatically to neglect their ordinary employments. Compare 2 Thess. iii. 6–14 with 1 Thess. iv. 10–12, and 1 Thess. ii. 9.

(2) Silas and Timotheus were still with St. Paul. 2 Thess. i. 1. It should be observed that Timotheus was next with St. Paul at Ephesus ; and that, before then, Silas disappears from the history.

[4] See note on 1 Thess. i. 3.

fastness and faith, in all the persecutions and
afflictions which you are bearing. And these i. 5
things are a token that the righteous judgment of
God will count you worthy of His kingdom, for
which you are even now suffering. For doubtless 6
God's righteousness cannot but render back trouble
to those who trouble you, and give to you, who 7
now are troubled, rest with me,[1] when the Lord
Jesus shall be revealed from heaven with the angels
of His might, in flames of fire, taking vengeance 8
on those who know not God, and will not hearken
to the Glad-tidings of our Lord Jesus Christ.
And from [2] the presence of the Lord, and from the 9
brightness of His glorious majesty, they shall receive their righteous doom, even an everlasting
destruction; in that day, when He shall come to 10
be glorified in His saints, and to be admired in all
believers ; [and you are of that number], for you
believed my testimony. To this end I pray con- 11
tinually on your behalf, that our God may count
you worthy of the calling wherewith He has called
you, and mightily perfect within you all the content of goodness [3] and the work of faith. That 12
the name of our Lord Jesus may be glorified in
you, and that you may be glorified [4] in Him, according to the grace of our God, and of our Lord
Jesus Christ.

But concerning [5] the appearing of our Lord ii. 1
Jesus Christ, and our gathering together to meet
Him; I beseech you, brethren, not rashly to be 2
shaken from your soberness of mind, nor to be
agitated either by spirit,[6] or by rumour, or by
letter [7] attributed to me,[8] saying that the day of

---

[1] On the use of the plural pronoun,
see note on 1 Thess. i. 3.

[2] The preposition here has the sense
of ' proceeding from.'

[3] The same word is used in the sense
of *good will, good pleasure, satisfaction,*
in Luke ii. 14 and Rom. x. 1. The
A. V. here would require a word to be
supplied.

[4] The glory of our Lord at His coming will be manifested in His people
(see ver. 10) ; that is, they, by virtue
of their union with Him, will partake
of His glorious likeness. Cf. Rom.
viii. 17, 18, 19. And, even in this
world, this glorification takes place

partially, by their moral conformity to
His image. See Rom. viii. 30, and
2 Cor. iii. 18.

[5] *In respect of,* or perhaps (as Prof.
Jowett takes it) *on behalf of,* as though
St. Paul were pleading in honour of
that day ; it is wrongly translated in
A. V. as an adjuration.

[6] i.e. any pretended revelation of
those who claimed inspiration.

[7] See the preceding remarks upon
the occasion of this Epistle.

[8] Literally ' *as though originated by
me* ;' the words may include both
' spirit,' ' rumour,' and ' letter.'

the Lord is come.[1] Let no one deceive you, by
any means; for before that day, the falling away
must first have come, and the man of sin be re-
4 vealed, the son of perdition; who opposes himself
and exalts himself against all that is called God,
and against all worship; even to seat himself[2] in
the temple of God, and openly declare himself a
5 God. Do you not remember that when I was still
6 with you, I often[3] told you this? And now you
know the hindrance why he is not yet revealed, in
7 his own season. For the mystery of lawlessness[4]
is already working, only he, who now hinders, will
8 hinder till he be taken out of the way; and then
the lawless one will be revealed, whom the Lord
shall consume with the breath of His mouth,[5] and
shall destroy with the brightness of His appearing.
9 But the appearing of that lawless one shall be in
the strength of Satan's working, with all the might
and signs and wonders of falsehood, and all the
10 delusions of unrighteousness, for those who are in
the way of perdition; because they received not the
love of the truth, whereby they might be saved.
11 For this cause, God will send upon them an inward
working of delusion, making them believe in lies,
12 that all should be condemned who have not believed the truth, but have taken pleasure in unrighteousness.

13   But for you, brethren beloved of the Lord, I am
bound to thank God continually, because He chose
you from the first unto salvation, in sanctification
14 of the Spirit, and belief of the truth. And to this
He called you through my Glad-tidings, that you
might obtain the glory of our Lord Jesus Christ.
15 Therefore, brethren, be stedfast, and hold fast the
teaching which has been delivered to you, whether

Exhortation to stedfastness and obedience.

---

[1] Literally 'is present.' So the verb
is always used in the New Testament.
See Rom. viii. 38 ; 1 Cor. iii. 22 ; Gal.
i. 4 ; 2 Tim. iii. 1; Heb. ix. 9.
[2] The received text interpolates here
'*as God*,' but the MSS. do not confirm
this reading.
[3] The verb is in the imperfect.
[4] The proper meaning of ἄνομος is
one unrestrained by law; hence it is
often used as *a transgressor*, or, generally *a wicked man*, as ἀνομία is used
often simply for *iniquity* ; but in this

passage it seems best to keep to thy
original meaning of the word.
[5] This appears to be an allusion to
(although not an exact quotation of)
Isaiah xi. 4 ;— 'With the breath of
His lips He shall destroy the impious
man.' (LXX. version.) Some of the
Rabbinical commentators applied this
prophecy (which was probably in St.
Paul's thoughts) to the Messiah's coming, and interpreted 'the impious' to
mean an individual opponent of the
Messiah.

by my words or by my letters.   And may our Lord
Jesus Christ Himself, and our God and Father, who
has loved us, and has given us in His grace a consolation that is eternal, and a hope that cannot fail,
comfort your hearts, and establish you in all good- 17
ness both of word and deed.

He asks their prayers.

Finally, brethren, pray for me, that the word iii. 1
of the Lord Jesus may hold its onward course, and
that its glory may be shown forth towards others
as towards you ; and that I may be delivered from 2
the perverse and wicked ; for not all men have faith.
But the Lord is faithful, and He will keep you sted- 3
fast, and guard you from evil.   And I rely upon you 4
in the Lord, that you are following and will follow
my precepts.   And may the Lord guide your hearts 5
to the love of God, and to the stedfastness of Christ.

Exhorts to an orderly and diligent life, appealing to his own example.

I charge you, brethren, in the name of the Lord 6
Jesus Christ, to withdraw yourselves from every
brother who walks disorderly, and not according
to the rules which I delivered.   For you know 7
yourselves the way to follow my example ; you know
that my life among you was not disorderly, nor was
I fed by any man's bounty, but earned my bread 8
by my own labour, toiling night and day, that I
might not be burdensome to any of you.[1]   And this 9
I did, not because I am without the right[2] [of
being maintained by those to whom I minister], but
that I might make myself a pattern for you to
imitate.   For when I was with you I often[3] gave 10
you this rule : 'If any man will not work, neither
let him eat.'   Whereas I hear that some among you 11
are walking disorderly, neglecting their own work,
and meddling[4] with that of others.   Such, therefore, 12
I charge and exhort, by the authority of our Lord
Jesus Christ, to work in quietness, and eat their
own bread.   But you, brethren, notwithstanding,[5] 13

Mode of dealing with those who refuse obedience.

be not weary of doing good.   If any man be dis- 14
obedient to my written word,[6] mark that man, and

---

[1] Compare the speech at Miletus, Acts xx.

[2] See note on 1 Thess. ii. 6.

[3] Imperfect.

[4] The characteristic paronomasia here, is not exactly translatable into English.   '*Busy bodies* who do no *business*' would be an imitation.

[5] i.e. although your kindness may

have been abused by such idle tres-
passers on your bounty.

[6] Literally, *my word* [*sent*] *by the letter*, which probably refers to the directions sent in the former letter, 1 Thess. iv. 11, 12.   So a previous letter is referred to, 1 Cor. v. 9, and 2 Cor. vii. 8.

cease from intercourse with him, that he may be
i. 15 brought to shame.   Yet count him not as an enemy,
16 but admonish him as a brother. And may the Lord
of peace Himself give you peace in all ways and at
all seasons. The Lord be with you all.

17   The salutation of me Paul with my own hand, An autograph
which is my token in every letter. Thus I write.[1] sign of
18   The grace of our Lord Jesus Christ be with you Concluding
all.[2] benediction.

Such was the second of the two letters which St. Paul wrote to
Thessalonica during his residence at Corinth.   Such was the Christian correspondence now established, in addition to the political and
commercial correspondence existing before, between the two capitals of Achaia and Macedonia.   Along with the official documents
which passed between the governors of the contiguous provinces,[3]
and the communications between the merchants of the Northern
and Western Ægean, letters were now sent, which related to the
establishment of a 'kingdom not of this world,'[4] and to 'riches'
beyond the discovery of human enterprise.[5]
    The influence of great cities has always been important on the
wider movements of human life.   We see St. Paul diligently using
this influence, during a protracted residence at Corinth, for the
spreading and strengthening of the Gospel in Achaia and beyond.
As regards the province of Achaia, we have no reason to suppose
that he confined his activity to its metropolis.   The expression used
by St. Luke [6] need only denote that it was his head-quarters, or
general place of residence.   Communication was easy and frequent,
by land or by water,[7] with other parts of the province.   Two short
days' journey to the south were the Jews of Argos,[8] who might be
to those of Corinth what the Jews of Berœa had been to those of
Thessalonica.[9]   About the same distance to the east was the city
of Athens,[10] which had been imperfectly evangelised, and could be
visited without danger.   Within a walk of a few hours, along a
road busy with traffic, was the sea-port of Cenchreæ, known to us

---

[1] 'Thus.' With this we may compare Gal. vi. 11. We have before remarked that St. Paul's letters were
written by an amanuensis, with the
exception of an autograph postscript.
Compare Rom. xvi. 22.
    [2] 'Amen' here (as in the end of
1 Thess.) is a subsequent addition.
    [3] Cicero's Cilician Correspondence
furnishes many specimens of the letters
which passed between the governors of
neighbouring provinces.
    [4] John xviii. 36.
    [5] Eph. iii. 8.

[6] Acts xviii. 11.
    [7] Much of the intercourse in Greece
has always gone on by small coasters.
Pouqueville mentions traces of a paved
road between Corinth and Argos.
    [8] See pp. 15 and 299.
    [9] See above, p. 262.
    [10] We have not entered into the ques-
tion of St. Paul's journey from Athens
to Corinth. He may have travelled by
the coast road through Eleusis and
Megara; or a sail of a few hours, with
a fair wind, would take him from the
Piræus to Cenchreæ.

as the residence of a Christian community.[1] These were the 'Churches of God' (2 Thess. i. 4), among whom the Apostle boasted of the patience and the faith of the Thessalonians,[2]—the homes of 'the saints in all Achaia' (2 Cor. i. 1), saluted at a later period, with the Church of Corinth,[3] in a letter written from Macedonia. These Churches had alternately the blessings of the presence and the letters—the oral and the written teaching—of St. Paul. The former of these blessings is now no longer granted to us; but those long and wearisome journeys, which withdrew the teacher so often from his anxious converts, have resulted in our possession of inspired Epistles, in all their freshness and integrity, and with all their lessons of wisdom and love.

Coin of Thessalonica.[4]

---

[1] Rom. xvi. 1.
[2] Compare 1 Thess. i. 7, 8.
[3] It is possible that the phrase 'in every place' (1 Cor. i. 2) may have the same meaning.

[4] From the British Museum. For a long series of coins of this character, see Mionnet and the Supplement.

CHAPTER XII.

The Isthmus and Acrocorinthus.—Early History of Corinth.—Its Trade and Wealth. — Corinth under the Romans. — Province of Achaia.—Gallio the Governor.—Tumult at Corinth.—Cenchreæ.—Voyage by Ephesus to Cæsarea. —Visit to Jerusalem.—Antioch.

Now that we have entered upon the first part of the long series of St. Paul's letters, we seem to be arrived at a new stage of the Apostle's biography. The materials for a more intimate knowledge are before us. More life is given to the picture. We have advanced from the field of geographical description and general history to the higher interest of personal detail. Even such details as relate to the writing materials employed in the Epistles, and the mode in which these Epistles were transmitted from city to city,— all stages in the history of an Apostolic letter, from the hand of the amanuensis who wrote from the author's inspired dictation, to the opening and reading of the document in the public assembly of the church to which it was addressed,—have a sacred claim on the Christian's attention. For the present we must defer the examination of such particulars.[1] We remain with the Apostle himself, instead of following the journeys of his letters to Thessalonica, and tracing the effects which the last of them produced. We have before us a protracted residence in Corinth,[2] a voyage by sea to Syria,[3] and a journey by land from Antioch to Ephesus,[4] before we come to the next group of St. Paul's Epistles.

We must linger first for a time in Corinth, the great city where he stayed a longer time than at any point on his previous journeys, and from which, or to which, the most important of his letters were written.[5] And, according to the plan we have hitherto observed, we proceed to elucidate its geographical position, and the principal stages of its history.

The *Isthmus*[6] is the most remarkable feature in the Geography of Greece ; and the peculiar relation which it established between the land and the water—and between the Morea and the Continent— had the utmost effect on the whole course of the History of Greece. When we were considering the topography and aspect of Athens, all the associations which surrounded us were Athenian. Here at

[1] See a note on this subject in Chap. XXVI.
[2] Acts xviii. 11–18.
[3] Acts xviii. 18–22.
[4] Acts xviii. 23. See xix. 1.

[5] The Epistles to the Thessalonians, Corinthians, and Romans.
[6] It is from this Greek 'bridge of the sea' that the name *isthmus* has been given to every similar neck of land in the world.

the Isthmus, we are, as it were, at the centre of the activity of the Greek race in general. It has the closest connection with all their most important movements, both military and commercial.

In all the periods of Greek history, from the earliest to the latest, we see the military importance of the Isthmus. The phrase of Pindar is, that it was 'the bridge of the sea:' it formed the only line of march for an invading or retreating army. Xenophon speaks of it as 'the gate of the Peloponnesus,' the closing of which would make all ingress and egress impossible. And we find that it was closed at various times, by being fortified and re-fortified by a wall, some traces of which remain to the present day. In the Persian war, when consternation was spread amongst the Greeks by the death of Leonidas, the wall was first built. In the Peloponnesian war, when the Greeks turned fratricidal arms against each other, the Isthmus was often the point of the conflict between the Athenians and their enemies. In the time of the Theban supremacy, the wall again appears as a fortified line from sea to sea. When Greece became Roman, the provincial arrangements neutralised, for a time, the military importance of the Isthmus. But when the barbarians poured in from the North, like the Persians of old, its wall was repaired by Valerian. Again it was rebuilt by Justinian, who fortified it with a hundred and fifty towers. And we trace its history through the later period of the Venetian power in the Levant, from the vast works of 1463, to the peace of 1699, when it was made the boundary of the territories of the Republic.[1]

Conspicuous, both in connection with the military defences of the Isthmus, and in the prominent features of its scenery, is the *Acrocorinthus*, or citadel of Corinth, which rises in form and abruptness like the rock of Dumbarton. But this comparison is quite inadequate to express the magnitude of the Corinthian citadel. It is elevated two thousand feet[2] above the level of the sea; it throws a vast shadow across the plain at its base; the ascent is a journey involving some fatigue; and the space of ground on the summit is so extensive, that it contained a whole town,[3] which, under the Turkish dominion, had several mosques. Yet, notwithstanding its colossal dimensions, its sides are so precipitous, that a few soldiers are enough to guard it.[4] The possession of this fortress has been the object of repeated struggles in the latest wars between the Turks and the Greeks, and again between the Turks and the Venetians. It was said to Philip, when he wished to acquire possession of the Morea, that the Acrocorinthus was one of the *horns*

---

[1] The wall was not built in a straight line, but followed the sinuosities of the ground. The remains of square towers are visible in some places. The eastern portion abutted on the Sanctuary of Neptune, where the Isthmian games are held.

[2] Dodwell. The ascent is by a zigzag road, which Strabo says was thirty stadia in length. 'Looking down upon the Isthmus, *the shadow of the Acro-*

corinthus, of a conical shape, extended exactly half across its length, the point of the cone being central between the two seas.'—Dr. Clarke.

[3] Dodwell and Clarke. The city, according to Xenophon, was forty stadia in circumference without the Acropolis, and eighty-five with it.

[4] Plutarch says that it was guarded by 400 soldiers, 50 dogs, and as many keepers.

he must seize, in order to secure the heifer. Thus Corinth might well be called 'the eye of Greece' in a military sense, as Athens has often been so called in another sense. If the rock of Minerva was the Acropolis of the Athenian people, the mountain of the Isthmus was truly named 'the Acropolis of the Greeks.'

It will readily be imagined that the view from the summit is magnificent and extensive.[1] A sea is on either hand. Across that which lies on the east, a clear sight is obtained of the Acropolis of Athens, at a distance of forty-five miles.[2] The mountains of Attica and Bœotia, and the islands of the Archipelago, close the prospect in this direction. Beyond the western sea, which flows in from the Adriatic, are the large masses of the mountains of north-eastern Greece, with Parnassus towering above Delphi. Immediately beneath us is the narrow plain which separates the seas. The city itself is on a small table land[3] of no great elevation, connected with the northern base of the Acrocorinthus. At the edge of the lower level are the harbours which made Corinth the emporium of the richest trade of the East and the West.

We are thus brought to that which is really the characteristic both of Corinthian geography and Corinthian history, its close relation to the commerce of the Mediterranean. Plutarch says, that there was a want of good harbours in Achaia; and Strabo speaks of the circumnavigation of the Morea as dangerous.[4] Cape Malea was proverbially formidable, and held the same relation to the voyages of ancient days, which the Cape of Good Hope does to our own.[5] Thus, a narrow and level isthmus,[6] across which smaller vessels could be dragged from gulf to gulf[7] was of inestimable value to the early

---

[1] Wheler's description is as follows:—'We mounted to the top of the highest point, and had one of the most agreeable prospects in the world. On the right hand of us the Saronic Gulf, with all its little islands strewed up and down it, to Cape Colonne on the Promontory Sunium. Beyond that the islands of the Archipelago seemed to close up the mouth of the Gulf. On the left hand of us we had the Gulf of Lepanto or Corinth, as far as beyond Sicyon, bounded northward with all these famous mountains of old times, with the Isthmus, even to Athens, lying in a row, and presenting themselves orderly to our view. The plain of Corinth towards Sicyon or Basilico is well watered by two rivulets, well-tilled, well-planted with olive-yards and vine-yards, and, having many little villages scattered up and down it, is none of the least of the ornaments of this prospect. The town also that lieth north of the castle, in little knots of houses, surrounded with orchards and gardens of oranges, lemons, citrons, and cypress-trees, and mixed with cornfields between, is a sight not less delightful. So that it is hard to judge whether this plain is more beautiful to the beholders or profitable to the inhabitants.' This was in 1675, before the last conflicts of the Turks and Venetians.

[2] 'As from the Parthenon at Athens we had seen the citadel of Corinth, so now we had a commanding view, across the Saronic Gulf, of Salamis and the Athenian Acropolis.'—Dr. Clarke. See above, under Athens.

[3] Leake's description entirely corresponds with Strabo's.

[4] He adds that the Sicilian sea was avoided by mariners as much as possible.

[5] A proverb said of this south-eastern point of the Morea: 'When you are round Cape Malea, forget all you have at home.'

[6] See above, note on the word 'Isthmus.'

[7] Hence the narrowest part of the Isthmus was called by a word which in meaning and in piratic associations corresponds with the *Tarbert* of Scotch

traders of the Levant. And the two harbours which received the ships of a more maturely developed trade,—Cenchreæ[1] on the Eastern Sea, and Lechæum[2] on the Western, with a third and smaller port, called Schœnus,[3] where the isthmus was narrowest,—form an essential part of our idea of Corinth. Its common title in the poets is ' the city of the two seas.'[4] It is allegorically represented in art as a female figure on a rock, between two other figures, each of whom bears a rudder, the symbol of navigation and trade.[5] It is the same image which appears under another form in the words of the rhetorician, who said that it was ' the prow and the stern of Greece.'[6]

As we noticed above a continuous fortress which was carried across the Isthmus, in connection with its military history, so here we have to mention another continuous work, which was attempted, in connection with its mercantile history. This was the ship canal;—which, after being often projected, was about to be begun again near the very time of St. Paul's visit.[7] Parallels often suggest themselves between the relation of the parts of the Mediterranean to each other, and those of the Atlantic and Pacific: for the basins of the ' Midland Sea ' were to the Greek and Roman trade, what the Oceanic spaces are to ours. And it is difficult, in speaking of a visit to the Isthmus of Corinth in the year 52,[8]—which only preceded by a short interval the work of Nero's engineers,—not to be reminded of the Isthmus of Panama in the year 1852, during which active progress was made in an undertaking often projected, but never yet carried into effect.[9]

There is this difference, however, between the Oceanic and the Mediterranean Isthmus, that one of the great cities of the ancient world always existed at the latter. What some future Darien may be destined to become, we cannot prophesy: but, at a very early date, we find Corinth celebrated by the poets for its wealth. This wealth must inevitably have grown up, from its mercantile relations,

geography. The distance across is about three miles ; nearer Corinth it is six miles, whence the name of the modern village of *Hexamili.*

[1] For Cenchreæ, see below, p. 330. It was seventy stadia distant from the city.

[2] Lechæum was united to Corinth by long walls. It was about twelve stadia distant from the city.

[3] Schœnus was at the point where the Isthmus was narrowest, close to the Sanctuary of Neptune and the eastern portion of the Isthmian wall. The ship is described as sailing to this port in the early times when Athens had the presidency of the games.

[4] One phrase which was used of it is that which we find in Acts xxvii. 41.

[5] See this on the coin at the end of Chap. XIII.

[6] The phrase seems to have been proverbial.

[7] Demetrius Poliorcetes, Julius Cæsar, and Caligula had all entertained the notion of cutting through the Isthmus. Nero really began the undertaking in the year 52, but soon desisted. See Leake (pp. 297–302), who quotes all the authorities. The portion of the trench which remains is at the narrowest part, near the shore of the Corinthian Gulf. Dodwell came upon it, after crossing Mount Geraneia from Attica.

[8] The arguments for this date may be seen in Wieseler. We shall return to the subject again.

[9] Our first edition was published in 1852. At that time the various plans for an inter-oceanic canal were very much before the public. Now at least the railway is open for traffic from ocean to ocean.

even without reference to its two seas,—if we attend to the fact on which Thucydides laid stress, that it was the place through which all ingress and egress took place between Northern and Southern Greece, before the development of commerce by water.   But it was its conspicuous position on the narrow neck of land between the Ægean and Ionian Seas, which was the main cause of its commercial greatness.   The construction of the ship Argo is assigned by mythology to Corinth.   The Samians obtained their shipbuilders from her. The first Greek triremes,—the first Greek sea-fights,—are connected with her history.   Neptune was her god.   Her colonies were spread over distant coasts in the East and West; and ships came from every sea to her harbours.   Thus she became the common resort and the universal market of the Greeks.[1]   Her population and wealth were further augmented by the manufactures in metallurgy, dyeing, and porcelain, which grew up in connection with the import and export of goods.   And at periodical intervals the crowding of her streets and the activity of her trade received a new impulse from the strangers who flocked to the Isthmian games;—a subject to which our attention will often be called hereafter, but which must be passed over here with a simple allusion.[2]   If we add all these particulars together, we see ample reason why the wealth, luxury, and profligacy of Corinth were proverbial[3] in the ancient world.

In passing from the fortunes of the earlier, or Greek Corinth, to its history under the Romans, the first scene that meets us is one of disaster and ruin.   The destruction of this city by Mummius, about the same time that Carthage[4] was destroyed by Scipio, was so complete, that, like its previous wealth, it passed into a proverb.   Its works of skill and luxury were destroyed or carried away.   Polybius, the historian, saw Roman soldiers playing at draughts on the pictures of famous artists; and the exhibition of vases and statues that decorated the triumph of the Capitol, introduced a new era in the habits of the Romans.   Meanwhile, the very place of the city from which these works were taken remained desolate for many years.[5]   The honour of presiding over the Isthmian games was given to Sicyon; and Corinth ceased even to be a resting-place of travellers between the East and the West.[6]   But a new Corinth rose from the ashes of the old.   Julius Cæsar, recognising the importance of the Isthmus as a military and mercantile position, sent thither a colony of Italians,

---

[1] One writer in another place compares Corinth to a ship loaded with merchandise, and says that a perpetual fair was held yearly and daily at the Isthmus.

[2] See the beginning of Chap. XX., and the plan of the Posidonium there given.

[3] 'Non cuivis homini contingit adire Corinthum.'—Hor. *Ep.* i. 17, 36. The word 'Corinthianise' was used proverbially for an immoral life.

[4] See Chap. I. p. 11.

[5] 'Nevertheless,' says Colonel Leake, 'the site, I conceive, cannot have

been quite uninhabited, as the Romans neither destroyed the public buildings nor persecuted the religion of the Corinthians.   And as many of those buildings were still perfect in the time of Pausanias, there must have been some persons who had the care of them during the century of desolation.'

[6] We have noticed above (p. 297, n. 4) that on Cicero's journey between the East and West, we find him resting, not at Corinth, but at Athens.   In the time of Ovid the city was rising again.

who were chiefly freedmen.[1] This new establishment rapidly increased by the mere force of its position. Within a few years it grew, as Sincapore[2] has grown in our days, from nothing to an enormous city. The Greek merchants, who had fled on the Roman conquest to Delos and the neighbouring coasts, returned to their former home. The Jews settled themselves in a place most convenient both for the business of commerce and for communication with Jerusalem.[3] Thus, when St. Paul arrived at Corinth after his sojourn at Athens, he found himself in the midst of a numerous population of Greeks and Jews. They were probably far more numerous than the Romans, though the city had the constitution of a *colony*,[4] and was the metropolis of a *province*.

It is commonly assumed that Greece was constituted as a province under the name of Achaia, when Corinth was destroyed by Mummius. But this appears to be a mistake. There seems to have been an intermediate period, during which the country had a nominal independence, as was the case with the contiguous province of Macedonia. The description which has been given of the political limits of Macedonia (Ch. IX.) defines equally the extent of Achaia. It was bounded on all other sides by the sea, and was nearly co-extensive with the kingdom of Modern Greece. The name of *Achaia* was given to it, in consequence of the part played by the Achæan league in the last independent struggles of ancient Greece; and Corinth, the head of that league, became the metropolis.[5] The province experienced changes of government, such as those which have been alluded to in the case of Cyprus.[6] At first it was proconsular. Afterwards it was placed by Tiberius under a procurator of his own. But in the reign of Claudius it was again reckoned among the 'unarmed provinces,'[7] and governed by a proconsul.

One of the proconsuls who were sent out to govern the province of Achaia in the course of St. Paul's second missionary journey was Gallio.[8] His original name was Annæus Novatus, and he was the brother of Annæus Seneca the philosopher. The name under which he is known to us in sacred and secular history was due to his adoption into the family of Junius Gallio the rhetorician. The time of his government at Corinth, as indicated by the sacred historian, must be placed between the years 52 and 54, if the dates we have assigned to St. Paul's movements be correct. We have no exact information on this subject from any secular source, nor is he mentioned by any Heathen writer as having been proconsul

[1] Professor Stanley notices the great number of names of Corinthian Christians (Caius, Quartus, Fortunatus, Achaicus, Crispus, Justus), which indicate 'either a Roman or a servile origin.' *Pref. to Corinthians.*

[2] See the Life of Sir Stamford Raffles and later notices of the place in Rajah Brooke's journals, &c.

[3] See the preceding chapter for the establishment of the Jews at Corinth.

[4] See the Latin letters on its coins.

Its full name was 'Colonia Laus Julia Corinthus.' See coin at the end of this chapter.

[5] Ritter says that this is the meaning of 'Corinthus Achaiæ *urbs*,' in Tac. *Hist.* ii. 1.

[6] See Chap. V.

[7] A phrase applied to those provinces which were proconsular and required the presence of no army. See p. 191. n. 8.

[8] Acts xviii. 12.

of Achaia. But there are some incidental notices of his life, which give rather a curious confirmation of what is advanced above. We are informed by Tacitus and Dio that he died in the year 65. Pliny says that *after his consulship* he had a serious illness, for the removal of which he tried a sea-voyage : and from his brother Seneca we learn that it was *in Achaia* that he went on shipboard for the benefit of his health. If we knew the year of Gallio's consulship, our chronological result would be brought within narrow limits. We do not possess this information ; but it has been reasonably conjectured that his promotion, if due to his brother's influence, would be subsequent to the year 49, in which the philosopher returned from his exile in Corsica, and had the youthful Nero placed under his tuition. The interval of time thus marked out between the restoration of Seneca and the death of Gallio, includes the narrower period assigned by St. Luke to the proconsulate in Achaia.

The coming of a new governor to a province was an event of great importance. The whole system of administration, the general prosperity, the state of political parties, the relative position of different sections of the population, were necessarily affected by his personal character. The provincials were miserable or happy, according as a Verres or a Cicero was sent from Rome. As regards the personal character of Gallio, the inference we should naturally draw from the words of St. Luke closely corresponds with what we are told by Seneca. His brother speaks of him with singular affection ; not only as a man of integrity and honesty, but as one who won universal regard by his amiable temper and popular manners.[1] His conduct on the occasion of the tumult at Corinth is quite in harmony with a character so described. He did not allow himself, like Pilate, to be led into injustice by the clamour of the Jews ;[2] and yet he overlooked, with easy indifference, an outbreak of violence which a sterner and more imperious governor would at once have arrested.[3]

The details of this transaction were as follows :—The Jews, anxious to profit by a change of administration, and perhaps encouraged by the well-known compliance of Gallio's character, took an early opportunity of accusing St. Paul before him. They had already set themselves in battle array[4] against him, and the coming of the new governor was the signal for a general attack.[5] It is quite evident that the act was preconcerted and the occasion chosen. Making use of the privileges they enjoyed as a separate community, and well aware that the exercise of their worship was protected by the Roman State,[6] they accused St. Paul of violating their own religious law. They seem to have thought, if this violation of Jewish law could be proved, that St. Paul would become amenable to the

[1] The same character is given of him by the poet Statius.
[2] Acts xviii. 14.
[3] Acts xviii. 17.
[4] See p. 312, n. 1.
[5] Acts xviii. 12.
[6] Compare Joseph. *War,* ii. 14, 4, on Cæsarea. In Alexandria, there were four distinct classes of population, among which the Jews were citizens under their Ethnarch, like the Romans under their Juridicus. We need not discuss here the later position of the Jews, after Caracalla had made all freemen citizens.

criminal law of the Empire; or, perhaps, they hoped, as afterwards at Jerusalem, that he would be given up into their hands for punishment. Had Gallio been like Festus or Felix, this might easily have happened ; and then St. Paul's natural resource would have been to appeal to the Emperor, on the ground of his citizenship. But the appointed time of his visit to Rome was not yet come, and the continuance of his missionary labours was secured by the character of the governor, who was providentially sent at this time to manage the affairs of Achaia.

The scene is set before us by St. Luke with some details which give us a vivid notion of what took place. Gallio is seated on that proconsular chair[1] from which judicial sentences were pronounced by the Roman magistrates. To this we must doubtless add the other insignia of Roman power, which were suitable to a colony and the metropolis of a province. Before this Heathen authority the Jews are preferring their accusation with eager clamour. Their chief speaker is Sosthenes, the successor of Crispus, or (it may be) the ruler of another synagogue.[2] The Greeks[3] are standing round, eager to hear the result, and to learn something of the new governor's character; and, at the same time, hating the Jews, and ready to be the partisans of St. Paul. At the moment when the Apostle is ' about to open his mouth,'[4] Gallio will not even hear his defence, but pronounces a decided and peremptory judgment.

His answer was that of a man who knew the limits of his office, and felt that he had no time to waste on the religious technicalities of the Jews. Had it been a case in which the Roman law had been violated by any breach of the peace or any act of dishonesty, then it would have been reasonable and right that the matter should have been fully investigated; but, since it was only a question of the Jewish law, relating to the disputes of Hebrew superstition,[5] and to names of no public interest, he utterly refused to attend to it. They might excommunicate the offender, or inflict on him any of their ecclesiastical punishments ; but he would not meddle with trifling quarrels, which were beyond his jurisdiction. And without further delay he drove the Jews away from before his judicial chair.[6]

The effect of this proceeding must have been to produce the utmost rage and disappointment among the Jews. With the Greeks and other bystanders[7] the result was very different. Their dislike of a

---

[1] This chair, or tribunal, 'the indispensable symbol of the Roman judgment-seat,' as it has been called, is mentioned three times in the course of this narrative. It was of two kinds: (1) fixed in some open and public place; (2) movable, and taken by the Roman magistrates to be placed wherever they might sit in a judicial character. Probably here and in the case of Pilate (John xix. 13) the former kind of seat is intended. See Smith's *Dictionary of Antiquities*, under ' Sella.'

[2] Whether Sosthenes had really been elected to fill the place of Crispus, or was only a co-ordinate officer in the

same or some other synagogue, must be left undetermined. On the organisation of the synagogues, see Chap. VI. pp. 137, 138. It should be added, that we cannot confidently identify this Sosthenes with the ' brother' whose name occurs 1 Cor. i. 1.

[3] See note 7, on this page.

[4] Acts xviii. 14.

[5] Acts xviii. 15. We recognise here that much had been made by the Jews of the *name* of 'Christ' being given to Jesus.

[6] Acts xviii. 16.

[7] The true reading here does not specify who the persons were who beat

superstitious and misanthropic nation was gratified. They held the forbearance of Gallio as a proof that their own religious liberties would be respected under the new administration; and, with the disorderly impulse of a mob which has been kept for some time in suspense, they rushed upon the ruler of the synagogue, and beat him in the very presence of the proconsular tribunal. Meanwhile, Gallio took no notice[1] of the injurious punishment thus inflicted on the Jews, and with characteristic indifference left Sosthenes to his fate.

Thus the accusers were themselves involved in disgrace; Gallio obtained a high popularity among the Greeks, and St. Paul was enabled to pursue his labours in safety. Had he been driven away from Corinth, the whole Christian community of the place might have been put in jeopardy. But the result of the storm was to give shelter to the infant Church, with opportunity of safe and continued growth. As regards the Apostle himself, his credit rose with the disgrace of his opponents. So far as he might afterwards be noticed by the Roman governor or the Greek inhabitants of the city, he would be regarded as an injured man. As his own discretion had given advantage to the holy cause at Philippi, by involving his opponents in blame,[2] so here the most imminent peril was providentially turned into safety and honour.

Thus the assurance communicated in the vision was abundantly fulfilled. Though bitter enemies had 'set on' Paul (Acts xviii. 10), no one had 'hurt' him. The Lord had been 'with him,' and 'much people' had been gathered into His Church. At length the time came when the Apostle deemed it right to leave Achaia and revisit Judæa, induced (as it would appear) by a motive which often guided his journeys, the desire to be present at the great gathering of the Jews at one of their festivals,[3] and possibly also influenced by the movements of Aquila and Priscilla, who were about to proceed from Corinth to Ephesus. Before his departure, he took a solemn farewell of the assembled Church.[4] How touching St. Paul's farewells must have been, especially after a protracted residence among his brethren and disciples, we may infer from the affectionate language of his letters; and one specimen is given to us of these parting addresses, in the Acts of the Apostles. From the words spoken at Miletus (Acts xx.), we may learn what was said and felt at Corinth. He could tell his disciples here, as he told them there, that he had taught them 'publicly and from house to house;'[5] that he was 'pure from the blood of all men;'[6] that by the space of a year and a half he had 'not ceased to warn every one night and day with tears.'[7] And doubtless he forewarned them of 'grievous wolves entering in among them, of men speaking perverse things arising[8]

Sosthenes. It cannot, however, be well doubted that they were *Greeks*. The reading 'Jews,' found in some MSS., is evidently wrong.

[1] Acts xviii. 17. See above on Gallio's character.

[2] See p. 240.

[3] See Acts xviii. 21. There is little doubt that the festival was Pentecost.

We should not, however, leave unnoticed that it is doubtful whether this allusion to the festival ought to be in the text.

[4] Acts xviii. 18.   [5] Acts xx. 20.

[6] ver. 26. Compare xviii. 6, and see p. 312.

[7] ver. 31. Compare what is said of his tears at Philippi. Phil. iii. 18,

[8] vv. 29, 30.

of themselves, to draw away disciples after them.' And he could appeal to them, with the emphatic gesture of ' *those hands*' which had laboured at Corinth, in proof that he had ' coveted no man's gold or silver,' and in confirmation of the Lord's words, that ' it is more blessed to give than to receive.'[1] Thus he departed, with prayers and tears, from those who ' accompanied him to the ship ' with many misgivings that they might ' see his face no more.'[2]

The three points on the coast to which our attention is called in the brief notice of this voyage contained in the Acts,[3] are Cenchreæ, the harbour of Corinth; Ephesus, on the western shore of Asia Minor; and Cæsarea Stratonis, in Palestine. More suitable occasions will be found hereafter for descriptions of Cæsarea and Ephesus. The present seems to require a few words to be said concerning Cenchreæ.

After descending from the low table-land on which Corinth was situated, the road which connected the city with its eastern harbour extended a distance of eight or nine miles across the Isthmian plain. Cenchreæ has fallen with Corinth; but the name[4] still remains to mark the place of the port, which once commanded a large trade with Alexandria and Antioch, with Ephesus and Thessalonica, and the other cities of the Ægean. That it was a town of some magnitude may be inferred from the attention which Pausanias devotes to it in the description of the environs of Corinth; and both its mercantile character, and the pains which had been taken in its embellishment, are well symbolised in the coin[5] which represents the port with a temple on each enclosing promontory, and a statue of Neptune on a rock between them.

From this port St. Paul began his voyage to Syria. But before the vessel sailed, one of his companions performed a religious ceremony which must not be unnoticed, since it is mentioned in Scripture. Aquila[6] had bound himself by one of those vows, which the Jews often voluntarily took, even when in foreign countries, in consequence of some mercy received, or some deliverance from danger, or other occurrence which had produced a deep religious impression on the mind. The obligations of these vows were similar to those in the case of Nazarites,—as regards abstinence from strong drinks and legal pollutions, and the wearing of the hair uncut till the close of a definite length of time. Aquila could not be literally a Nazarite; for, in the case of that greater vow, the cutting of the hair, which denoted that the legal time was expired, could only take place at the Temple in Jerusalem, or at least in Judæa. In this case the ceremony was performed at Cenchreæ. Here Aquila,—who had been for some time conspicuous, even among the Jews and Christians at Corinth,

---

[1] Compare Acts xx. 33–35 with xviii. 3, and with 1 Cor. iv. 12.

[2] vv. 36–38.   [3] Acts xviii. 18–22.

[4] The modern name is *Kichries*.

[5] An engraving of this coin will be given at the end of Chap. XIX.

[6] This is left as it stood in the earlier editions. It must be admitted that the arguments from the structure of the original are rather in favour of referring the vow, not to Aquila, but to St. Paul. The difficulty lies not so much in supposing that Paul took a Jewish vow (see Acts xxi. 26), as in supposing that he made himself conspicuous for Jewish peculiarities while he was forming a mixed church at Corinth. But we are ignorant of the circumstances of the case.

for the long hair which denoted that he was under a peculiar religious restriction—came to the close of the period of obligation; and, before accompanying the Apostle to Ephesus, laid aside the tokens of his vow.

From Corinth to Ephesus, the voyage was among the islands of the Greek Archipelago. The Isles of Greece, and the waters which break on their shores, or rest among them in spaces of calm repose, always present themselves to the mind as the scenes of interesting voyages,—whether we think of the stories of early Legend, or the stirring life of Classical times, of the Crusades in the middle ages, or of the movements of Modern travellers, some of whom seldom reflect that the land and water round them were hallowed by the presence and labours of St. Paul. One great purpose of this book will be gained, if it tends to associate the Apostle of the Gentiles with the coasts which are already touched by so many other historical recollections.

No voyage across the Ægean was more frequently made than that between Corinth and Ephesus. They were the capitals of the two flourishing and peaceful provinces of Achaia and Asia,[1] and the two great mercantile towns on opposite sides of the sea. If resemblances may again be suggested between the Ocean and the Mediterranean, and between ancient and modern times, we may say that the relations of these cities of the Eastern and Western Greeks to each other was like that between New York and Liverpool. Even the time taken up by the voyages constitutes a point of resemblance. Cicero says that, on his eastward passage, which was considered a long one, he spent fifteen days, and that his return was accomplished in thirteen.[2]

A fair wind, in much shorter time than either thirteen or fifteen days, would take the Apostle across, from Corinth to the city on the other side of the sea. It seems that the vessel was bound for Syria, and stayed only a short time in harbour at Ephesus. Aquila and Priscilla remained there while he proceeded.[3] But even during the short interval of his stay, Paul made a visit to his Jewish fellow-countrymen, and (the Sabbath being probably one of the days during which he remained) he held a discussion with them in the synagogue concerning Christianity.[4] Their curiosity was excited by what they heard, as it had been at Antioch in Pisidia; and perhaps that curiosity would speedily have been succeeded by opposition, if their visitor had stayed longer among them. But he was not able to grant the request which they urgently made. He was anxious to attend the approaching festival at Jerusalem;[5] and, had he not proceeded with the ship, this might have been impossible. He was so far, however, encouraged by the opening which he saw, that he left the Ephesian Jews with a promise of his return. This promise was limited by an expression of that dependence on the divine will which is characteristic of a Christian's life,[6] whether his vocation be

---

[1] See how Achaia and Asia are mentioned by Tacitus, *Hist.* ii. 8.

[2] The voyage was often accomplished in three or four days. See Thuc. iii. 3.

[3] Acts xviii. 19.

[4] The aorist (ver. 19) should be con-trasted with the imperfect used (ver. 4) of the continued discussions at Corinth.

[5] Acts xviii. 21. See above.

[6] 'If God will.' See James iv. 15. 'If the Lord will, we shall live,' &c.

to the labours of an Apostle, or to the routine of ordinary toil. We shall see that St. Paul's promise was literally fulfilled, when we come to pursue his progress on his third missionary circuit.

The voyage to Syria lay first by the coasts and islands of the Ægean to Cos and Cnidus, which are mentioned on subsequent voyages,[1] and then across the open sea by Rhodes and Cyprus to Cæsarea.[2] This city has the closest connection with some of the most memorable events of early Christianity. We have already had occasion to mention it, in alluding to St. Peter and the baptism of the first Gentile convert.[3] We shall afterwards be required to make it the subject of a more elaborate notice, when we arrive at the imprisonment which was suffered by St. Paul under two successive Roman governors.[4] The country was now no longer under native kings. Ten years had elapsed since the death of Herod Agrippa, the last event alluded to (Chap. IV.) in connection with Cæsarea. Felix had been for some years already procurator of Judæa.[5] If the aspect of the country had become in any degree more national under the reign of the Herods, it had now resumed all the appearance of a Roman province.[6] Cæsarea was its military capital, as well as the harbour by which it was approached by all travellers from the West. From this city roads[7] had been made to the Egyptian frontier on the south, and northwards along the coast by Ptolemais, Tyre, and Sidon, to Antioch, as well as across the interior by Neapolis or Antipatris to Jerusalem and the Jordan.

The journey from Cæsarea to Jerusalem is related by St. Luke in a single word.[8] No information is given concerning the incidents which occurred there :—no meetings with other Apostles,—no controversies on disputed points of doctrine,—are recorded or inferred. We are not even sure that St. Paul arrived in time for the festival at which he desired to be present.[9] The contrary seems rather to be implied; for he is said simply to have 'saluted the Church,' and then to have proceeded to Antioch. It is useless to attempt to draw aside the veil which conceals the particulars of this visit of Paul of Tarsus to the city of his forefathers. As if it were no longer intended that we should view the Church in connection with the centre of Judaism, our thoughts are turned immediately to that other city,[10] where the name 'Christian,' was first conferred on it.

From Jerusalem to Antioch it is likely that the journey was accomplished by land. It is the last time we shall have occasion to mention a road which was often traversed, at different seasons of the year, by St. Paul and his companions. Two of the journeys along this Phœnician coast have been long ago mentioned. Many

---

[1] Acts xxi. 1, xxvii. 7.
[2] See Acts xxi. 1-3.
[3] See p. 96. Compare pp. 43, 44.
[4] Acts xxi. &c.
[5] Tac. *Ann.* xiv. 54, and Josephus.
[6] See pp. 22, 23, and 45.
[7] See the remarks, pp. 69, 70.
[8] 'When he had gone up,' Acts xviii. 22. Some commentators think that St. Paul did not go to Jerusalem at all, but that this participle merely denotes his going up from the ship into the

town of Cæsarea: but, independently of his intention to visit Jerusalem, it is hardly likely that such a circumstance would have been specified in a narrative so briefly given.

[9] We shall see, in the case of the later voyage (Acts xx. xxi.), that he could not have arrived in time for the festival, had not the weather been peculiarly favourable.

[10] Acts xviii. 22.

years had intervened since the charitable mission which brought relief from Syria to the poor in Judæa (Chap. IV.), and since the meeting of the council at Jerusalem, and the joyful return at a time of anxious controversy (Chap. VII.). When we allude to these previous visits to the Holy City, we feel how widely the Church of Christ had been extended in the space of very few years. The course of our narrative is rapidly carrying us from the East towards the West. We are now for the last time on this part of the Asiatic shore. For a moment the associations which surround us are all of the primeval past. The monuments which still remain along this coast remind us of the ancient Phœnician power, and of Baal and Ashtaroth,[1]—or of the Assyrian conquerors, who came from the Euphrates to the West, and have left forms like those in the palaces of Nineveh sculptured on the rocks of the Mediterranean,[2] —rather than of anything connected with the history of Greece and Rome. The mountains which rise above our heads belong to the characteristic imagery of the Old Testament : the cedars are those of the forests which were hewn by the workmen of Hiram and Solomon ; the torrents which cross the roads are the waters from ' the sides of Lebanon.'[3] But we are taking our last view of this scenery ; and, as we leave it, we feel that we are passing from the Jewish infancy of the Christian Church to its wider expansion among the Heathen.

Once before we had occasion to remark that the Church had no longer now its central point in Jerusalem, but in Antioch, a city of the Gentiles.[4] The progress of events now carries us still more remotely from the land which was first visited by the tidings of salvation. The world through which our narrative takes us begins to be European rather than Asiatic. So far as we know, the present visit which St. Paul paid to Antioch was his last.[5] We have already seen how new centres of Christian life had been established by him in the Greek cities of the Ægean. The course of the Gospel is further and further towards the West ; and the inspired part of the Apostle's biography, after a short period of deep interest in Judæa, finally centres in Rome.

Coin of Corinth.[6]

---

[1] The ruins of Tortosa and Aradus.

[2] The sculptures of Assyrian figures on the coast road near Beyrout are noticed in the works of many travellers.

[3] These torrents are often flooded, so as to be extremely dangerous; so that St. Paul may have encountered 'perils of rivers' in this district. Maundrell says that the traveller Spor lost his life in one of these torrents.

[4] pp. 90, 91.

[5] Antioch is not mentioned in the Acts after xviii. 22.

[6] From the British Museum. The head is that of Julius Cæsar himself.

CHAPTER XIII.

The Spiritual Gifts, Constitution, Ordinances, Divisions, and Heresies of the
Primitive Church in the Lifetime of St. Paul.

WE are now arrived at a point in St. Paul's history when it seems
needful, for the full understanding of the remainder of his career,
and especially of his Epistles, to give some description of the internal condition of those churches which looked to him as their
father in the faith. Nearly all of these had now been founded, and
regarding the early development of several of them, we have considerable information from his letters and from other sources.
This information we shall now endeavour to bring into one general
view ; and in so doing (since the Pauline churches were only particular portions of the universal Church), we shall necessarily have
to consider the distinctive peculiarities and internal condition of
the primitive Church generally, as it existed in the time of the
Apostles.

The feature which most immediately forces itself upon our notice,
as distinctive of the Church in the Apostolic age, is its possession of
supernatural gifts. Concerning these, our whole information must
be derived from Scripture, because they appear to have vanished
with the disappearance of the Apostles themselves, and there is no
authentic account of their existence in the Church in any writings
of a later date than the books of the New Testament. This fact
gives a more remarkable and impressive character to the frequent
mention of them in the writings of the Apostles, where the exercise
of such gifts is spoken of as a matter of ordinary occurrence.
Indeed, this is so much the case, that these miraculous powers are
not even mentioned by the Apostolic writers as a class apart (as we
should now consider them), but are joined in the same classification
with other gifts, which we are wont to term natural endowments or
'talents.'[1] Thus St. Paul tells us (1 Cor. xii. 11) that all these

---

[1] The two great classifications of
them in St. Paul's writings are as follows :—

I. (1 Cor. xii. 8.)

Class 1. $\begin{cases}(a_1) \text{ } the \text{ } word \text{ } of \text{ } wisdom. \\ (a_2) \text{ } the \text{ } word \text{ } of \text{ } knowledge.\end{cases}$
to one.

Class 2. $\begin{cases}(\beta_1) \text{ } faith. \\ (\beta_2) \text{ } gifts \text{ } of \text{ } healing. \\ (\beta_3) \text{ } working \text{ } of \text{ } miracles. \\ (\beta_4) \text{ } prophecy. \\ (\beta_5) \text{ } discerning \text{ } of \text{ } spirits.\end{cases}$
to another.

Class 3. $\begin{cases}(\gamma_1) \text{ } kinds \text{ } of \text{ } tongues. \\ (\gamma_2) \text{ } interpretation \text{ } of \\ \quad tongues\end{cases}$
to another.

II. (1 Cor. xii. 28.)

1. *apostles.*
2. *prophets.* See (β_4).
3. *teachers* ; including (a_1) and (a_2)
   perhaps.
4. *miracles.* See (β_2)
5. $\begin{cases}(1) \text{ } gifts \text{ } of \text{ } healing. \text{ See } (\beta_3). \\ (2) \text{ } helps. \\ (3) \text{ } governments. \\ (4) \text{ } diversities \text{ } of \text{ } tongues. \text{ See } (\gamma_1).\end{cases}$

It may be remarked, that the following divisions are in I. and not in II. ;
viz. β_1, β_5, and γ_2 : a_1 and a_2, though

charisms, or spiritual gifts, were wrought by one and the same Spirit, who distributed them to each severally according to His own will; and among these he classes the gift of Healing, and the gift of Tongues, as falling under the same category with the talent for administrative usefulness, and the faculty of Government. But though we learn from this to refer the ordinary natural endowments of men, not less than the supernatural powers bestowed in the Apostolic age, to a divine source, yet, since we are treating of that which gave a distinctive character to the Apostolic Church, it is desirable that we should make a division between the two classes of gifts, the extraordinary and the ordinary ; although this division was not made by the Apostles at the time when both kinds of gifts were in ordinary exercise.

The most striking manifestation of divine interposition was the power of working what are commonly called Miracles, that is, changes in the usual operation of the laws of nature. This power was exercised by St. Paul himself very frequently (as we know from the narrative in the Acts), as well as by the other Apostles ; and in the Epistles we find repeated allusions to its exercise by ordinary Christians.[1] As examples of the operation of this power, we need only refer to St. Paul's raising Eutychus from the dead, his striking Elymas with blindness, his healing the sick at Ephesus,[2] and his curing the father of Publius at Melita.[3]

The last-mentioned examples are instances of the exercise of the *gift of healing*, which was a peculiar branch of the *gift of miracles*, and sometimes apparently possessed by those who had not the higher gift. The source of all these miraculous powers was the charism of *faith;* namely, that peculiar kind of wonder-working faith spoken of in Matt. xvii. 20 ; 1 Cor. xii. 9, and xiii. 2, which consisted in an intense belief that all obstacles would vanish before the power given. This must of course be distinguished from that *disposition* of faith which is essential to the Christian life.

We have remarked that the exercise of these miraculous powers is spoken of both in the Acts and Epistles as a matter of ordinary occurrence ; and in that tone of quiet (and often incidental) allusion, in which we mention the facts of our daily life. And this is the case, not in a narrative of events long past (where uninten-

---

not explicitly in II., yet are probably included in it as necessary gifts for ' apostles,' and perhaps also for ' teachers,' as Neander supposes.

It is difficult to observe any principle which runs through these classifications ; probably I. was not meant as a systematic classification at all ; II., however, certainly was in some measure, because St. Paul uses the words ' *first, second, third, &c.*'

It is very difficult to arrive at any certain conclusion on the subject, because of our imperfect understanding of the nature of the *charisms* them-

selves ; they are alluded to only as things well known to the Corinthians, and of course without any precise description of their nature.

In Rom. xii. 6-8, another unsystematic enumeration of four charisms is given ; viz. (1) *prophecy*, (2) *ministry*, (3) *teaching*, (4) *exhortation*.

[1] Gal. iii. 5 (where observe the present tense) is one of many examples.

[2] Acts xix. 11, 12.

[3] On this latter miracle, see the excellent remarks in Smith's *Voyage and Shipwreck of St. Paul*, p. 115.

tional exaggeration might be supposed to have crept in), but in the
narrative of a cotemporary, writing immediately after the occurrence of the events which he records, and of which he was an eye-
witness ; and yet further, this phenomenon occurs in letters which
speak of those miracles as wrought in the daily sight of the readers
addressed.   Now the question forced upon every intelligent mind
is, whether such a phenomenon can be explained except by the
assumption that the miracles did really happen.   Is this assumption more difficult than that of Hume (which has been revived with
an air of novelty by modern infidels), who cuts the knot by assuming that whenever we meet with an account of a miracle, it is
ipso facto to be rejected as incredible, no matter by what weight of
evidence it may be supported?

Besides the power of working miracles, other supernatural gifts
of a less extraordinary character were bestowed upon the early
Church.   The most important were the *gift of tongues*, and the *gift
of prophecy*.   With regard to the former there is much difficulty,
from the notices of it in Scripture, in fully comprehending its
nature.   But from the passages where it is mentioned,[1] we may
gather thus much concerning it : *first*, that it was not a *knowledge*
of foreign languages, as is often supposed ; we never read of its
being exercised for the conversion of foreign nations, nor (except
on the day of Pentecost alone) for that of individual foreigners ;
and even on that occasion the foreigners present were all Jewish
proselytes, and most of them understood the Hellenistic[2] dialect.
Secondly, we learn that this gift was the result of a sudden influx
of supernatural inspiration, which came upon the new believer immediately after his baptism, and recurred afterwards at uncertain
intervals.   *Thirdly*, we find that while under its influence the exercise of the *understanding* was suspended, while the *spirit* was rapt
into a state of ecstasy by the immediate communication of the Spirit
of God.   In this ecstatic trance the believer was constrained by an
irresistible[3] power to pour forth his feelings of thanksgiving and
rapture in words ; yet the words which issued from his mouth were
not his own ; he was even (usually) ignorant of their meaning.   St.
Paul desired that those who possessed this gift should not be suffered to exercise it in the congregation, unless some one present
possessed another gift (subsidiary to this), called the *interpretation
of tongues*, by which the ecstatic utterance of the former might be
rendered available for general edification.   Another gift, also, was
needful for the checking of false pretensions to this and some other
charisms, viz. the gift of *discerning of spirits*, the recipients of

---

[1] Viz. Mark xvi. 17 ; Acts ii. 4, &c.,
Acts x. 46, Acts xi. 15–17, Acts xix.
6; 1 Cor. xii., and 1 Cor. xiv. We
must refer to the notes on these two
last-named chapters for some further
discussion of the difficulties connected
with this gift.

[2] This must probably have been the
case with all the foreigners mentioned,
except the Parthians, Medes, Elamites,

and Arabians, and the Jews from these
latter countries would probably understand the Aramaic of Palestine. [For
a different view of the *gift of tongues*
we may refer to Dr. Wordsworth's note
on Acts ii. 4.   H.]

[3] His spirit was not subject to his
will. See 1 Cor. xiv. 32. [Some power
of self-control does appear distinctly
implied in this passage and ver. 28.   H.]

which could distinguish between the real and the imaginary possessors of spiritual gifts.[1]

From the *gift of tongues* we pass, by a natural transition, to the *gift of prophecy.*[2] It is needless to remark that, in the Scriptural sense of the term, a *prophet* does not mean a *foreteller of future events*, but *a revealer of God's will to man;* though the latter sense may (and sometimes does) include the former. So the gift of prophecy was that charism which enabled its possessors to utter, with the authority of inspiration, divine strains of warning, exhortation, encouragement, or rebuke ; and to teach and enforce the truths of Christianity with supernatural energy and effect. The wide diffusion among the members of the Church of this prophetical inspiration was a circumstance which is mentioned by St. Peter as distinctive of the Gospel dispensation ;[3] in fact, we find that in the family of Philip the Evangelist alone,[4] there were four daughters who exercised this gift ; and the general possession of it is in like manner implied by the directions of St. Paul to the Corinthians.[5] The latter Apostle describes the marvellous effect of the inspired addresses thus spoken.[6] He looks upon the gift of prophecy as one of the great instruments for the conversion of unbelievers ; and far more serviceable in this respect than the gift of tongues, although by some of the new converts it was not so highly esteemed, because it seemed less strange and wonderful.

Thus far we have mentioned the *extraordinary* gifts of the Spirit which were vouchsafed to the Church of that age alone ; yet (as we have before said) there was no strong line of division, no ' great gulf fixed' between these, and what we now should call the ordinary gifts, or natural endowments of the Christian converts. Thus the *gift of prophecy* cannot easily be separated by any accurate demarcation from another charism often mentioned in Scripture, which we should now consider an ordinary talent, namely, the *gift of teaching.* The distinction between them appears to have been that the latter was more habitually and constantly exercised by its possessors than the former : we are not to suppose, however, that it was necessarily given to different persons ; on the contrary, an excess of divine inspiration might at any moment cause the *teacher* to speak as a *prophet*; and this was constantly exemplified in the case of the Apostles, who exercised the gift of prophecy for the conversion of their unbelieving hearers, and the gift of teaching for the building up of their converts in the faith.

Other gifts specially mentioned as charisms are the *gift of government* and the *gift of ministration.*[7] By the former, certain persons were specially fitted to preside over the Church and regulate its internal order ; by the latter its possessors were enabled to minister to the wants of their brethren, to manage the distribution of relief

---

[1] This latter charism seems to have been requisite for the presbyters. See 1 Thess. v. 21.

[2] If it be asked why we class this as among the *supernatural* or *extraordinary* gifts, it will be sufficient to refer to such passages as Acts xi. 27, 28.

[3] Acts ii. 17, 18.

[4] Acts xxi. 9.

[5] 1 Cor. xi. 4, and 1 Cor. xiv. 24, 31, 34.

[6] 1 Cor. xiv. 25.

[7] The ' charism' of 'ministry' or of 'help.'

among the poorer members of the Church, to tend the sick, and carry out other practical works of piety.

The mention of these latter charisms leads us naturally to consider the *offices* which at that time existed in the Church, to which the possessors of these gifts were severally called, according as the endowment which they had received fitted them to discharge the duties of the respective functions. We will endeavour, therefore, to give an outline of the constitution and government of the primitive Christian churches, as it existed in the time of the Apostles, so far as we can ascertain it from the information supplied to us in the New Testament.

Amongst the several classifications which are there given of church officers, the most important (from its relation to subsequent ecclesiastical history) is that by which they are divided into Apostles,[1] Presbyters, and Deacons. The monarchical, or (as it would be now called) the episcopal element of church government was, in this first period, supplied by the authority of the Apostles. This title was probably at first confined to 'the Twelve,' who were immediately nominated to their office (with the exception of Matthias) by our Lord Himself. To this body the title was limited by the Judaising section of the Church; but St. Paul vindicated his own claim to the Apostolic name and authority as resting upon the same commission given him by the same Lord; and his companion, St. Luke, applies the name to Barnabas also. In a lower sense, the term was applied to all the more eminent Christian teachers; as, for example, to Andronicus and Junias.[2] And it was also sometimes used in its simple etymological sense of *emissary*, which had not yet been lost in its other and more technical meaning. Still those only were called emphatically *the* Apostles who had received their commission from Christ Himself, including the eleven who had been chosen by Him while on earth, with St. Matthias and St. Paul, who had been selected for the office by their Lord (though in different ways) after His ascension.

[1] 'Apostles and Presbyters' are mentioned Acts xv. 2, and elsewhere; and the two classes of 'Presbyters and Deacons' are mentioned Phil. i. 1. See p. 340, n. 1.

The following are the facts concerning the use of the word ἀπόστολος in the New Testament.

It occurs—
once in St. Matthew;—of the Twelve.
once in St. Mark;—of the Twelve.
6 times in St. Luke;—5 times of the Twelve, once in its general etymological sense.
once in St. John;—in its general etymological sense.
30 times in Acts;—(always in plural) 28 times of the Twelve, and twice of Paul and Barnabas.
3 times in Romans;—twice of St. Paul, once of Andronicus.
16 times in Corinthians;—14 times of St. Paul or the Twelve, twice in etymological sense, viz. 2 Cor. viii. 23, and xi. 13.
3 times in Gal.;—of St. Paul and the Twelve.
4 times in Ephes.; of St. Paul and the Twelve.
once in Philip.;—etymological sense.
once in Thess.; of St. Paul.
4 times in Timothy;—of St. Paul.
once in Titus;—of St. Paul.
once in Hebrews (iii. 1);—of Christ Himself.
3 times in Peter;—of the Twelve.
once in Jude;—of the Twelve.
3 times in Apocalypse;—either of 'false apostles' or of the Twelve.

Besides this, the word ἀποστολή is used to signify the Apostolic office, once in Acts and three times by St. Paul (who attributes it to himself).

[2] Rom. xvi. 7.

In saying that the Apostles embodied that element in church government, which has since been represented by episcopacy, we must not, however, be understood to mean that the power of the Apostles was subject to those limitations to which the authority of bishops has always been subjected.   The primitive bishop was surrounded by his council of presbyters, and took no important step without their sanction; but this was far from being the case with the Apostles.   They were appointed by Christ Himself, with absolute power to govern His Church; to them He had given the keys of the kingdom of Heaven, with authority to admit or to exclude; they were also guided by His perpetual inspiration, so that all their moral and religious teaching was absolutely and infallibly true; they were empowered by their solemn denunciations of evil, and their inspired judgments on all moral questions, to bind and to loose, to remit and to retain the sins of men.[1]   This was the essential peculiarity of their office, which can find no parallel in the after history of the Church.   But, so far as their function was to govern, they represented the monarchical element in the constitution of the early Church, and their power was a full counterpoise to that democratic tendency which has sometimes been attributed to the ecclesiastical arrangements of the Apostolic period.   Another peculiarity which distinguishes them from all subsequent rulers of the Church is, that they were not limited to a sphere of action defined by geographical boundaries : the whole world was their diocese, and they bore the Glad-tidings, east or west, north or south, as the Holy Spirit might direct their course at the time, and governed the churches which they founded wherever they might be placed. Moreover, those charisms which were possessed by other Christians singly and severally, were collectively given to the Apostles, because all were needed for their work.   The *gift of miracles* was bestowed upon them in abundant measure, that they might strike terror into the adversaries of the truth, and win, by outward wonders, the attention of thousands whose minds were closed by ignorance against the inward and the spiritual.   They had the *gift of prophecy* as the very characteristic of their office, for it was their especial commission to reveal the truth of God to man; they were consoled in the midst of their labours by heavenly visions, and rapt in supernatural ecstasies, in which they ' spake in *tongues* ' ' to God and not to man.'[2]   They had the '*gift of government*,' for that which came upon them daily was 'the care of all the Churches;' the '*gift of teaching*,' for they must build up their converts in the faith; even the '*gift of ministration*' was not unneeded by them, nor did they think it beneath them to undertake the humblest offices of a deacon for the good of the Church.   When needful, they could 'serve tables' and collect alms, and work with their

---

[1] No doubt, *in a certain sense*, this power is shared (according to the teaching of our Ordination Service) by Christian ministers now, but it is in quite a secondary sense; viz. only so far as it is exercised in exact accordance with the inspired teaching of the Apostles.

[2] See note on 1 Cor. xiv. 18.   Also see 2 Cor. xii.

own hands at mechanical trades, 'that so labouring they might
support the weak;' inasmuch as they were the servants of Him
who came not to be ministered unto, but to minister.

Of the offices concerned with Church government, the next in
rank to that of the Apostles was the office of Overseers or Elders,
more usually known (by their Greek designations) as Bishops or
Presbyters. These terms are used in the New Testament as equivalent,[1] the former (ἐπίσκοπος) denoting (as its meaning of *overseer*
implies) the duties, the latter (πρεσβύτερος) the rank, of the office.
The history of the Church leaves us no room for doubt that on the
death of the Apostles, or perhaps at an earlier period (and, in either
case, by their directions), one amongst the Presbyters of each
Church was selected to preside over the rest, and to him was
applied emphatically the title of *the* bishop or overseer, which
had previously belonged equally to all; thus he became in reality
(what he was sometimes called) the successor of the Apostles,
as exercising (though in a lower degree) that function of government which had formerly belonged to them.[2] But in speaking of
this change we are anticipating; for at the time of which we are
now writing, at the foundation of the Gentile Churches, the Apostles themselves were the chief governors of the Church, and the
Presbyters of each particular society were co-ordinate with one
another. We find that they existed at an early period in Jerusalem, and likewise that they were appointed by the Apostles
upon the first formation of a church in every city. The same
name 'Elder,' was attached to an office of a corresponding nature
in the Jewish synagogues, whence both title and office were probably derived. The name of Bishop was afterwards given to
this office in the Gentile churches, at a somewhat later period, as
expressive of its duties, and as more familiar than the other title
to Greek ears.[3]

The office of the Presbyters was to watch over the particular
church in which they ministered, in all that regarded its external
order and internal purity; they were to instruct the ignorant,[4] to
exhort the faithful, to confute the gainsayers,[5] to 'warn the unruly,
to comfort the feeble-minded, to support the weak, to be patient
towards all.'[6] They were 'to take heed to the flock over which the
Holy Ghost had made them overseers, to feed the Church of God
which He had purchased with His own blood.'[7] In one word, it
was their duty (as it has been the duty of all who have been called

[1] Thus, in the address at Miletus,
the same persons are called ἐπισκόπους
(Acts xx. 28) who had just before
been named πρεσβυτέρους (Acts xx.
17). See also the Pastoral Epistles,
passim.

[2] Baron Bunsen (whom no one can
suspect of hierarchal tendencies) expressed his concurrence in this view.
He says : ' St. John established or sanctioned the institution of single Rectors,
called Overseers (ἐπίσκοποι), as presidents of the Presbytery. This form of

government, as being the more perfect
and practical, particularly in such difficult times, soon spread over the Christian world.'—Bunsen's *Hippolytus*, 2nd
ed. ii. 360.

[3] Ἐπίσκοπος was the title of the
Athenian commissioners to their subject
allies.

[4] 1 Tim. iii. 2.

[5] Tit. i. 9.

[6] 1 Thess. v. 14.

[7] Acts xx. 28.

to the same office during the nineteen centuries which have succeeded) to promote to the utmost of their ability, and by every means within their reach, the spiritual good of all those committed to their care.[1]

The last of the three orders, that of Deacons, did not take its place in the ecclesiastical organisation till towards the close of St. Paul's life; or, at least, this name was not assigned to those who discharged the functions of the Diaconate till a late period; the Epistle to the Philippians being the earliest in which the term occurs[2] in its technical sense. In fact the word (διάκονος) occurs thirty times in the New Testament, and only three times (or at most four) is it used as an official designation; in all the other passages it is used in its simple etymological sense of *a ministering servant*. It is a remarkable fact, too, that it never once occurs in the Acts as the title of those seven Hellenistic Christians who are generally (though improperly) called the seven deacons, and who were only elected to supply a temporary emergency.[3] But although the title of the Diaconate does not occur till afterwards, the office seems to have existed from the first in the Church of Jerusalem (see Acts v. 6, 10); those who discharged its duties were then called the *young men*, in contradistinction to the presbyters or *elders*; and it was their duty to assist the latter by discharging the mechanical services requis te for the well-being of the Christian community. Gradually, however, as the Church increased, the natural division of labour would suggest a subdivision of the ministrations performed by them; those which only required bodily labour would be intrusted to a less educated class of servants, and those which required the work of the head as well as the hands (such, for example, as the distribution of alms), would form the duties of the deacons; for we may now speak of them by that name, which became appropriated to them before the close of the Apostolic epoch.

There is not much information given us, with regard to their functions, in the New Testament: but, from St. Paul's directions to Timothy concerning their qualifications, it is evident that their office was one of considerable importance. He requires that they should be men of grave character, and 'not greedy of filthy lucre;'

---

[1] Other titles, denoting their office, are applied to the presbyters in some passages, e.g. Rom. xii. 8; and 1 Thess. v. 12; Heb. xiii. 7; Eph. iv. 11; 1 Cor. xii. 28. It is, indeed, possible (as Neander thinks) that the 'teachers' may at first have been sometimes different from the 'presbyters,' as the 'charism of teaching' was distinct from the 'charism of governing;' but those who possessed both gifts would surely have been chosen presbyters from the first, if they were to be found; and, at all events, in the time of the Pastoral Epistles we find the offices united. (1 Tim. iii. 2.) See, however, the note on 1 Tim. v. 17.

[2] In Rom. xvi. 1, it is applied to a woman; and we cannot confidently assert that it is there used technically to denote an office, especially as the word διάκονος is so constantly used in its non-technical sense of one who ministers in any way to others. [See next note but one. H.]

[3] See Chap. II. p. 55. We observe, also, that when any of the seven are referred to, it is never by the title of deacon; thus Philip is called 'the evangelist' (Acts xxi. 8). In fact, the office of 'the seven' was one of much higher importance than that held by the subsequent deacons. [Still it can hardly be doubted that we have here the beginning of the official diaconate in the Church. H.]

the latter qualification relating to their duty in administering the charitable fund of the Church. He desires that they should not exercise the office till after their character had been first subjected to an examination, and had been found free from all imputation against it. If (as is reasonable) we explain these intimations by what we know of the Diaconate in the succeeding century, we may assume that its duties in the Apostolic Churches (when their organisation was complete), were to assist the presbyters in all that concerned the outward service of the Church, and in executing the details of those measures, the general plan of which was organised by the presbyters. And, doubtless, those only were selected for this office who had received the *gift of ministration* previously mentioned.

It is a disputed point whether there was an order of Deaconesses to minister among the women in the Apostolic Church; the only proof of their existence is the epithet attached to the name of Phœbe,[1] which may be otherwise understood. At the same time, it must be acknowledged that the almost Oriental seclusion in which the Greek women were kept, would render the institution of such an office not unnatural in the churches of Greece, as well as in those of the East.

Besides the three orders of Apostles, Presbyters, and Deacons, we find another classification of the ministry of the Church in the Epistle to the Ephesians,[2] where they are divided under four heads, viz.,[3] 1st, Apostles; 2ndly, Prophets; 3rdly, Evangelists; 4thly, Pastors and Teachers. By the fourth class we must understand[4] the Presbyters to be denoted, and we then have two other names interpolated between these and the Apostles; viz. *Prophets* and *Evangelists*. By the former we must understand those on whom the gift of prophecy was bestowed in such abundant measure as to constitute their peculiar characteristic; and whose work it was to impart constantly to their brethren the revelations which they received from the Holy Spirit. The term *Evangelist* is applied to those missionaries, who, like Philip,[5] and Timothy,[6] travelled from place to place, to bear the Glad-tidings of Christ to unbelieving nations or individuals. Hence it follows that the Apostles were all Evangelists, although there were also Evangelists who were not Apostles. It is needless to add that our modern use of the word Evangelist (as meaning *writer of a Gospel*) is of later date, and has no place here.

All these classes of Church-officers were maintained (so far as they required it) by the contributions of those in whose service they laboured. St. Paul lays down, in the strongest manner, their right to such maintenance;[7] yet, at the same time, we find that he

---

[1] Rom. xvi. 1. See p. 341, n. 2. It should be observed, however, that the 'widows' mentioned 1 Tim. v. 9 were practically Deaconesses, although they do not seem, at the time of the Pastoral Epistles, to have been called by that name. [For a general discussion of this subject, see the *Quarterly Review* for Oct. 1860, especially pp. 357, 358, where a different view is held of the Scriptural authority for a female diaconate. H.]

[2] Eph. iv. 11.

[3] A similar classification occurs 1 Cor. xii. 28; viz., 1st, Apostles; 2ndly, Prophets; 3rdly, Teachers.

[4] See above, p. 341, n. 1.

[5] Acts xxi. 8.

[6] 2 Tim. iv. 5.   [7] 1 Cor. ix. 7–14.

very rarely accepted the offerings, which, in the exercise of this
right, he might himself have claimed. He preferred to labour with
his own hands for his own support, that he might put his disinterested motives beyond the possibility of suspicion; and he advises
the presbyters of the Ephesian Church to follow his example in
this respect, that so they might be able to contribute, by their own
exertions, to the support of the helpless.

The mode of appointment to these different offices varied with
the nature of the office. The Apostles, as we have seen, received
their commission directly from Christ Himself; the Prophets were
appointed by that inspiration which they received from the Holy
Spirit, yet their claims would be subjected to the judgment of those
who had received the gift of *discernment of spirits.* The Evangelists were sent on particular missions from time to time, by the
Christians with whom they lived (but not without a special revelation of the Holy Spirit's will to that effect), as the Church of
Antioch sent away Paul and Barnabas to evangelise Cyprus. The
Presbyters and Deacons were appointed by the Apostles themselves
(as at Lystra, Iconium, and Antioch in Pisidia [1]), or by their deputies, as in the case of Timothy and Titus; yet, in all such instances,
it is not improbable that the concurrence of the whole body of the
Church was obtained; and it is possible that in other cases, as well
as in the appointment of the seven Hellenists, the officers of the
Church may have been elected by the Church which they were to
serve.

In all cases, so far as we may infer from the recorded instances
in the Acts, those who were selected for the performance of Church
offices were solemnly set apart for the duties to which they devoted
themselves. This *ordination* they received, whether the office to
which they were called was permanent or temporary. The Church,
of which they were members, devoted a preparatory season to
'fasting and prayer;' and then those who were to be set apart were
consecrated to their work by that solemn and touching symbolical
act, the laying on of hands, which has been ever since appropriated
to the same purpose and meaning. And thus, in answer to the
faith and prayers of the Church, the spiritual gifts necessary for
the performance of the office were bestowed [2] by Him who is 'the
Lord and Giver of Life.'

Having thus briefly attempted to describe the Offices of the
Apostolic Church, we pass to the consideration of its Ordinances.
Of these, the chief were, of course, those two sacraments ordained
by Christ Himself, which have been the heritage of the Universal
Church throughout all succeeding ages. The sacrament of Baptism was regarded as the door of entrance into the Christian Church,
and was held to be so indispensable that it could not be omitted
even in the case of St. Paul. We have seen that although he had
been called to the Apostleship by the direct intervention of Christ
Himself, yet he was commanded to receive baptism at the hands of
a simple disciple. In ordinary cases, the sole condition required

---

[1] Acts xiv. 21–23.
[2] Compare 2 Tim. i. 6. 'The gift of God which is in thee by the putting on of my hands.'

for baptism was, that the persons to be baptized should acknowledge Jesus as the Messiah,[1] 'declared to be the Son of God with power, by His resurrection from the dead.' In this acknowledgment was virtually involved the readiness of the new converts to submit to the guidance of those whom Christ had appointed as the Apostles and teachers of His Church; and we find[2] that they were subsequently instructed in the truths of Christianity, and were taught the true spiritual meaning of those ancient prophecies, which (if Jews) they had hitherto interpreted of a human conqueror and an earthly kingdom. This instruction, however, took place *after* baptism, not before it; and herein we remark a great and striking difference from the subsequent usage of the Church. For, not long after the time of the Apostles, the primitive practice in this respect was completely reversed; in all cases the convert was subjected to a long course of preliminary instruction before he was admitted to baptism, and in some instances the catechumen remained unbaptized till the hour of death; for thus he thought to escape the strictness of a Christian life, and fancied that a deathbed baptism would operate magically upon his spiritual condition, and ensure his salvation. The Apostolic practice of immediate baptism would, had it been retained, have guarded the Church from so baneful a superstition.

It has been questioned whether the Apostles baptized adults only, or whether they admitted infants also into the Church; yet we cannot but think it probable that infant baptism[3] was their practice. This appears, not merely because (had it been otherwise) we must

---

[1] This condition would (at first sight) appear as if only applicable to Jews or Jewish proselytes, who already were looking for a Messiah; yet, since the acknowledgment of Jesus as the Messiah involves in itself, when rightly understood, the whole of Christianity, it was a sufficient foundation for the faith of Gentiles also. In the case both of Jews and Gentiles, the thing required, in the first instance, was a belief in the testimony of the Apostles, that 'this Jesus had God raised up,' and thus had 'made that same Jesus, whom they had crucified, both Lord and Christ.' The most important passages, as bearing on this subject, are the baptism and confirmation of the Samaritan converts (Acts viii.), the account of the baptism of the Ethiopian eunuch (Acts viii.), of Cornelius (Acts x.), of the Philippian gaoler (Acts xvi.) (the only case where the baptism of a non-proselyted Heathen is recorded), of John's disciples at Ephesus (Acts xix.), and the statement in Rom. x. 9, 10.

[2] This appears from such passages as Gal. vi. 6; 1 Thess. v. 12; Acts xx.

20, 28, and many others.

[3] It is at first startling to find Neander, with his great learning and candour, taking an opposite view. Yet the arguments on which he grounds his opinion, both in the *Planting and Leading* and in the *Church History*, seem plainly inconclusive. He himself acknowledges that the principles laid down by St. Paul (1 Cor. vii. 14) contain a justification of infant baptism, and he admits that it was practised in the time of Irenæus. His chief reason against thinking it an Apostolical practice (*Church History*, sect. 3) is, that Tertullian opposed it; but Tertullian does not pretend to call it an innovation. It is needless here to do more than refer to the well-known passages of Origen which prove that infant baptism prevailed in the church of Alexandria as early as the close of the second century. Surely if infant baptism had not been sanctioned by the Apostles, we should have found some one at least among the many churches of primitive Christendom resisting its introduction.

have found some traces of the first introduction of infant baptism afterwards, but also because the very idea of the Apostolic baptism, as *the entrance into Christ's kingdom*, implies that it could not have been refused to infants without violating the command of Christ : ' Suffer little children to come unto me, and forbid them not, for of such is the kingdom of heaven.' Again, St. Paul expressly says that the children of a Christian parent were to be looked upon as consecrated to God (ἅγιοι) by virtue of their very birth ;[1] and it would have been most inconsistent with this view, as well as with the practice in the case of adults, to delay the reception of infants into the Church till they had been fully instructed in Christian doctrine.

We know from the Gospels[2] that the new converts were baptized ' in the name of the Father, and of the Son, and of the Holy Ghost.' And after the performance[3] of the sacrament, an outward sign was given that God was indeed present with His Church, through the mediation of The Son, in the person of The Spirit ; for the baptized converts, when the Apostles had laid their hands on them, received some spiritual gift, either the power of working miracles, or of speaking in tongues, bestowed upon each of them by Him who ' divideth to every man severally as He will.' It is needless to add that baptism was (unless in exceptional cases) administered by immersion, the convert being plunged beneath the surface of the water to represent his death to the life of sin, and then raised from this momentary burial to represent his resurrection to the life of righteousness. It must be a subject of regret that the general discontinuance of this original form of baptism (though perhaps necessary in our northern climates) has rendered obscure to popular apprehension some very important passages of Scripture.

With regard to the other sacrament, we know both from the Acts and the Epistles how constantly the Apostolic Church obeyed their Lord's command : ' Do this in remembrance of me.' Indeed it would seem that originally their common meals were ended, as that memorable feast at Emmaus had been, by its celebration ; so that, as at the first to those two disciples, their Lord's presence was daily ' made known unto them in the breaking of bread.'[4] Subsequently the Communion was administered at the close of the public feasts of love (*Agapæ*[5]) at which the Christians met to realise their fellowship one with another, and to partake together, rich and poor,

---

[1] 1 Cor. vii. 14.

[2] Matt. xxviii. 19. We cannot agree with Neander (*Planting and Leading*, I. 25, and 188) that the evidence of this positive command is at all impaired by our finding baptism described in the Acts and Epistles as baptism *into the name of Jesus ;* the latter seems a condensed expression which would naturally be employed, just as we now speak of *Christian* baptism. The answer of St. Paul to the disciples of John the Baptist at Ephesus (Acts xix. 3), is a strong argument that the name of the Holy Ghost occurred in the baptismal formula then employed.

[3] The case of Cornelius, in which the gifts of the Holy Spirit were bestowed *before* baptism, was an exception to the ordinary rule.

[4] Luke xxiv. 35.

[5] Jude 12. This is the custom to which Pliny alludes, when he describes the Christians meeting to partake of *cibus promiscuus et innoxius.*

masters and slaves, on equal terms, of the common meal. But this practice led to abuses, as we see in the case of the Corinthian Church, where the very idea of the ordinance was violated by the providing of different food for the rich and poor, and where some of the former were even guilty of intemperance. Consequently a change was made, and the communion administered before instead of after the meal, and finally separated from it altogether.

The *festivals* observed by the Apostolic Church were at first the same with those of the Jews ; and the observance of these was continued, especially by the Christians of Jewish birth, for a considerable time. A higher and more spiritual meaning, however, was attached to their celebration ; and particularly the Paschal feast was kept, no longer as a shadow of good things to come, but as the commemoration of blessings actually bestowed in the death and resurrection of Christ. Thus we already see the germ of our Easter festival in the exhortation which St. Paul gives to the Corinthians concerning the manner in which they should celebrate the Paschal feast. Nor was it only at this annual feast that they kept in memory the resurrection of their Lord ; every Sunday likewise was a festival in memory of the same event ; the Church never failed to meet for common prayer and praise on that day of the week ; and it very soon acquired the name of the ' Lord's Day,' which it has since retained.

But the meetings of the first converts for public worship were not confined to a single day of the week ; they were always frequent, often daily. The Jewish Christians met at first in Jerusalem in some of the courts of the temple, there to join in the prayers and hear the teaching of Peter and John. Afterwards the private houses[1] of the more opulent Christians were thrown open to furnish their brethren with a place of assembly ; and they met for prayer and praise in some ' upper chamber,'[2] with the ' door shut for fear of the Jews.' The outward form and order of their worship differed very materially from our own, as indeed was necessarily the case where so many of the worshippers were under the miraculous influence of the Holy Spirit. Some were filled with prophetic inspiration ; some constrained to pour forth their ecstatic feelings in the exercise of the gift of tongues, ' as the Spirit gave them utterance.' We see, from St. Paul's directions to the Corinthians, that there was danger even then lest their worship should degenerate into a scene of confusion, from the number who wished to take part in the public ministrations ; and he lays down rules which show that even the exercise of supernatural gifts was to be restrained, if it tended to violate the orderly celebration of public worship. He directs that not more than two or three should prophesy in the same assembly ; and that those who had the gift of tongues should not exercise it, unless some one present had the gift of interpretation, and could explain their utterances to the congregation. He also forbids women (even though some of them might be

---

[1] See Rom. xvi. 5, and 1 Cor. xvi. 19, and Acts xviii. 7.

[2] 'The upper chamber where they were gathered together.'—*Acts* xx. 8.

prophetesses)[1] to speak in the public assembly ; and desires that they should appear veiled, as became the modesty of their sex.

In the midst of so much diversity, however, the essential parts of public worship were the same then as now, for we find that prayer was made, and thanksgiving offered up, by those who officiated, and that the congregation signified their assent by a unanimous Amen.[2] Psalms also were chanted, doubtless to some of those ancient Hebrew melodies which have been handed down, not improbably, to our own times in the simplest form of ecclesiastical music ; and addresses of exhortation or instruction were given by those whom the gift of prophecy, or the gift of teaching, had fitted for the task.

But whatever were the other acts of devotion in which these assemblies were employed, it seems probable that the daily worship always concluded with the celebration of the Holy Communion.[3] And as in this the members of the Church expressed and realised the closest fellowship, not only with their risen Lord, but also with each other, so it was customary to symbolise this latter union by the interchange of the kiss of peace before the sacrament, a practice to which St. Paul frequently alludes.[4]

It would have been well if the inward love and harmony of the Church had really corresponded with the outward manifestation of it in this touching ceremony. But this was not the case, even while the Apostles themselves poured out the wine and broke the bread which symbolised the perfect union of the members of Christ's body. The kiss of peace sometimes only veiled the hatred of warring factions. So St. Paul expresses to the Corinthians his grief at hearing that there were ' divisions among them,' which showed themselves when they met together for public worship. The earliest division of the Christian Church into opposing parties was caused by the Judaising teachers, of whose factious efforts in Jerusalem and elsewhere we have already spoken. Their great object was to turn the newly converted Christians into Jewish proselytes, who should differ from other Jews only in the recognition of Jesus as the Messiah. In their view the natural posterity of Abraham were still as much as ever the theocratic nation, entitled to God's exclusive favour, to which the rest of mankind could only be admitted by becoming Jews. Those members of this party who were really sincere believers in Christianity, probably expected that the majority of their countrymen, finding their own national privileges thus acknowledged and maintained by the Christians, would on their

---

[1] Acts xxi. 9.

[2] 1 Cor. xiv. 16.

[3] This seems proved by 1 Cor. xi. 20, where St. Paul appears to assume that the very object of ' coming together in Church' was ' to eat the Lord's Supper.' As the Lord's Supper was originally the conclusion of the Agape, it was celebrated in the evening ; and probably, therefore, evening was the time, on ordinary occasions, for the meeting of the Church. This was certainly the case in Acts xx. 8; a passage which Neander must have overlooked when he says (*Church History*, sect. 3) that the church service in the time of the Apostles was held early in the morning. There are obvious reasons why the evening would have been the most proper time for a service which was to be attended by those whose day was spent in working with their hands.

[4] See note on 1 Thess. v. 26.

part more willingly acknowledge Jesus as their Messiah ; and thus they fancied that the Christian Church would gain a larger accession of members than could ever accrue to it from isolated Gentile converts : so that they probably justified their opposition to St. Paul on grounds not only of Jewish but of Christian policy ; for they imagined that by his admission of uncircumcised Gentiles into the full membership of the Church, he was repelling far more numerous converts of Israelitish birth, who would otherwise have accepted the doctrine of Jesus. This belief (which in itself, and seen from their point of view, in that age, was not unreasonable) might have enabled them to excuse to their consciences, as Christians, the bitterness of their opposition to the great Christian Apostle. But in considering them as a party, we must bear in mind that they felt themselves more Jews than Christians. They acknowledged Jesus of Nazareth as the promised Messiah, and so far they were distinguished from the rest of their countrymen ; but the Messiah himself, they thought, was only a ' Saviour of His people Israel ; ' and they ignored that true meaning of the ancient prophecies, which St. Paul was inspired to reveal to the Universal Church, teaching us that the ' excellent things ' which are spoken of the people of God, and the city of God, in the Old Testament, are to be by us interpreted of the ' household of faith,' and ' the heavenly Jerusalem.'

We have seen that the Judaisers at first insisted upon the observance of the law of Moses, and especially of circumcision, as an absolute requisite for admission into the Church, ' saying, Except ye be circumcised after the manner of Moses, ye cannot be saved.' But after the decision of the ' Council of Jerusalem ' it was impossible for them to require this condition ; they therefore altered their tactics, and as the decrees of the Council seemed to assume that the Jewish Christians would continue to observe the Mosaic Law, the Judaisers took advantage of this to insist on the necessity of a separation between those who kept the whole Law and all others ; they taught that the uncircumcised were in a lower condition as to spiritual privileges, and at a greater distance from God ; and that only the circumcised converts were in a state of full acceptance with Him : in short, they kept the Gentile converts who would not submit to circumcision on the same footing as the *proselytes of the gate*, and treated the circumcised alone as *proselytes of righteousness*. When we comprehend all that was involved in this, we can easily understand the energetic opposition with which their teaching was met by St. Paul. It was no mere question of outward observance, no matter of indifference (as it might at first sight appear), whether the Gentile converts were circumcised or not ; on the contrary, the question at stake was nothing less than this, whether Christians should be merely a Jewish sect under the bondage of a ceremonial law, and only distinguished from other Jews by believing that Jesus was the Messiah, or whether they should be the Catholic Church of Christ, owing no other allegiance but to Him, freed from the bondage of the letter, and bearing the seal of their inheritance no longer in their bodies, but in their hearts. We can understand now the full truth of his indignant remonstrance, 'If ye be circumcised, Christ shall profit you nothing.' And we can understand also the exasperation which his teaching must have produced in those who held the very antithesis of this, namely, that Christianity without circumcision was utterly worthless.   Hence their long and desperate struggle to destroy the influence of St. Paul in every church which he founded or visited; in Antioch, in Galatia, in Corinth, in Jerusalem, and in Rome.   For as he was in truth the great prophet divinely commissioned to reveal the catholicity of the Christian Church, so he appeared to them the great apostate, urged by the worst motives [1] to break down the fence and root up the hedge, which separated the heritage of the Lord from a godless world.

We shall not be surprised at their success in creating divisions in the Churches to which they came, when we remember that the nucleus of all those Churches was a body of converted Jews and proselytes.   The Judaising emissaries were ready to flatter the prejudices of this influential body ; nor did they abstain (as we know both from tradition and from his own letters) from insinuating the most scandalous charges against their great opponent. [2]   And thus, in every Christian church established by St. Paul, there sprang up, as we shall see, a schismatic party, opposed to his teaching and hostile to his person.

This great Judaising party was of course subdivided into various sections, united in their main object, but distinguished by minor shades of difference. Thus, we find at Corinth that it comprehended two factions, the one apparently distinguished from the other by a greater degree of violence.   The more moderate called themselves the followers of Peter, or rather of Cephas, for they preferred to use his Hebrew name. [3] These dwelt much upon Our Lord's special promises to Peter, and the necessary inferiority of St. Paul to him who was divinely ordained to be the rock whereon the Church should be built.   They insinuated that St. Paul felt doubts about his own Apostolic authority, and did not dare to claim the right of maintenance, [4] which Christ had expressly given to His true Apostles.   They also depreciated him as a maintainer of celibacy, and contrasted him in this respect with the great Pillars of the Church, 'the brethren of the Lord and Cephas,' who were married. [5]   And no doubt they declaimed against the audacity of a converted persecutor, 'born into the Church out of due time,' in 'withstanding to the face' the chief of the Apostles.   A still more violent section called themselves, by a strange misnomer, the party of Christ. [6]

[1] That curious apocryphal book, the *Clementine Recognitions*, contains, in a modified form, a record of the view taken by the Judaisers of St. Paul, from the pen of the Judaising party itself, in the pretended epistle of Peter to James. The English reader should consult the interesting remarks of Prof. Stanley on the Clementines (Stanley's *Sermons*, p. 374, &c.), and also Neander's *Church History* (American translation, vol. ii. p. 35, &c.).

[2] We learn from Epiphanius that the Ebionites accused St. Paul of renouncing Judaism because he was a rejected candidate for the hand of the High Priest's daughter. See p. 81.

[3] The MS. reading is *Cephas*, not *Peter*, in those passages where the language of the Judaisers is referred to. See note on Gal. i. 18.

[4] 1 Cor. ix. 4, 6 ; 2 Cor. xi. 9, 10.

[5] 1 Cor. ix. 5.

[6] Such appears the most natural ex-

These appear to have laid great stress upon the fact, that Paul had never seen or known Our Lord while on earth ; and they claimed for themselves a peculiar connection with Christ, as having either been among the number of His disciples, or at least as being in close connection with the 'brethren of the Lord,' and especially with James, the head of the Church at Jerusalem.   To this subdivision probably belonged the emissaries who professed to come 'from James,'[1] and who created a schism in the Church of Antioch.

Connected to a certain extent with the Judaising party, but yet to be carefully distinguished from it, were those Christians who are known in the New Testament as the 'weak brethren.'[2]   These were not a factious or schismatic party ; nay, they were not, properly speaking, a party at all.   They were individual converts of Jewish extraction, whose minds were not as yet sufficiently enlightened to comprehend the fulness of 'the liberty with which Christ had made them free.'   Their conscience was sensitive, and filled with scruples, resulting from early habit and old prejudices ; but they did not join in the violence of the Judaising bigots, and there was even a danger lest they should be led, by the example of their more enlightened brethren, to wound their own conscience, by joining in acts which they, in their secret hearts, thought wrong. Nothing is more beautiful than the tenderness and sympathy which St. Paul shows towards these weak Christians.   While he plainly sets before them their mistake, and shows that their prejudices result from ignorance, yet he has no sterner rebuke for them than to express his confidence in their further enlightenment : 'If in anything ye be otherwise minded, God shall reveal this also unto you.'[3]   So great is his anxiety lest the liberty which they witnessed in others should tempt them to blunt the delicacy of their moral feeling, that he warns his more enlightened converts to abstain from lawful indulgences, let they cause the weak to stumble.   'If meat make my brother to offend, I will eat no meat while the world standeth, lest I make my brother to offend.'[4]   'Brethren, ye have been called unto liberty, only use not liberty for an occasion to the flesh, but by love serve one another.'[5]   'Destroy not him with thy meat for whom Christ died.'[6]

These latter warnings were addressed by St. Paul to a party very different from those of whom we have previously spoken ; a party who called themselves (as we see from his epistle to Corinth) by his own name and professed to follow his teaching, yet were not always animated by his spirit.   There was an obvious danger lest the opponents of the Judaising section of the Church should themselves imitate one of the errors of their antagonists, by combining as partizans rather than as Christians ; St. Paul feels himself neces-

planation of the 'Christ' party (1 Cor. i. 12).   As to the views held by some eminent commentators on the passage, it is a question whether they are consistent with 2 Cor. x. 7.   Surely St. Paul would never have said, '*As* those who claim some *imaginary communion* with Christ belong to Christ,

so also do I belong to Christ.'
[1] Gal. ii. 12.
[2] Rom. xiv. 1, 2 ; Rom. xv. 1 ; 1 Cor. viii. 7, ix. 22.
[3] Phil. iii. 15.
[4] 1 Cor. viii. 13.
[5] Gal. v. 13.
[6] Rom. xiv. 15.

sitated to remind them that the very idea of the Catholic Church
excludes all party combinations from its pale, and that adverse
factions, ranging themselves under human leaders, involve a contradiction to the Christian name. ' Is Christ divided ? was Paul
crucified for you? or were you baptized into the name of Paul ?'
' Who then is Paul, and who is Apollos, but ministers by whom ye
believed ?' [1]

The Pauline party (as they called themselves) appear to have
ridiculed the scrupulosity of their less enlightened brethren, and to
have felt for them a contempt inconsistent with the spirit of
Christian love. [2] And in their opposition to the Judaisers, they
showed a bitterness of feeling and violence of action, [3] too like that
of their opponents. Some of them, also, were inclined to exult
over the fall of God's ancient people, and to glory in their own
position, as though it had been won by superior merit. These are
rebuked by St. Paul for their ' boasting,' and warned against its
consequences. ' Be not high-minded, but fear ; for if God spared
not the natural branches, take heed lest He also spare not thee.' [4]
One section of this party seems to have united these errors with
one still more dangerous to the simplicity of the Christian faith;
they received Christianity more in an intellectual than a moral
aspect ; not as a spiritual religion, so much as a new system of
philosophy. This was a phase of error most likely to occur among
the disputatious [5] reasoners who abounded in the great Greek
cities ; and, accordingly, we find the first trace of its existence at
Corinth. There it took a peculiar form, in consequence of the
arrival of Apollos as a Christian teacher, soon after the departure
of St. Paul. He was a Jew of Alexandria, and as such had received
that Grecian cultivation, and acquired that familiarity with Greek
philosophy, which distinguished the more learned Alexandrian
Jews. Thus he was able to adapt his teaching to the taste of his
philosophising hearers at Corinth far more than St. Paul could do ;
and, indeed, the latter had purposely abstained from even attempting this at Corinth. [6] Accordingly, the School which we have
mentioned called themselves the followers of Apollos, and extolled
his philosophic views, in opposition to the simple and unlearned
simplicity which they ascribed to the style of St. Paul. It is easy
to perceive in the temper of this portion of the Church the germ of
that rationalising tendency which afterwards developed itself into
the Greek element of Gnosticism. Already, indeed, although that
heresy was not yet invented, some of the worst opinions of the
worst Gnostics found advocates among those who called themselves
Christians : there was, even now, a party in the Church which
defended fornication [7] on theory, and which denied the resurrection of the dead. [8] These heresies probably originated with those

---

[1] 1 Cor. i. 13, and 1 Cor. iii. 5.
[2] Rom. xiv. 10. 'Why dost thou
despise thy brother ? ' is a question
addressed to this party.
[3] See the admonitions addressed to
the 'spiritual' in Gal. v. 13, 14, 26,
and Gal. vi. 1-5.

[4] Rom. xi. 17-22.
[5] The 'disputers of this world,' 1
Cor. i. 20.
[6] 1 Cor. ii. 1.
[7] See 1 Cor. vi. 9-20.
[8] See 1 Cor. xv. 12.

who (as we have observed) embraced Christianity as a new philosophy; some of whom attempted, with a perverted ingenuity, to extract from its doctrines a justification of the immoral life to which they were addicted.   Thus, St. Paul had taught that the law was dead to true Christians : meaning thereby, that those who were penetrated by the Holy Spirit, and made one with Christ, worked righteousness, not in consequence of a law of precepts and penalties, but through the necessary operation of the spiritual principle within them.   For, as the law against theft might be said to be dead to a rich man (because he would feel no temptation to break it), so the whole moral law would be dead to a perfect Christian ; [1] hence, to a real Christian, it might in one sense be truly said that *prohibitions were abolished.* [2]   But the heretics of whom we are speaking took this proposition in a sense the very opposite to that which it really conveyed ; and whereas St. Paul taught that prohibitions were abolished for the righteous, they maintained that all things were lawful to the wicked.   'The law is dead' [3] was their motto, and their practice was what the practice of Antinomians in all ages has been.   'Let us continue in sin, that grace may abound,' was their horrible perversion of the Evangelical revelation that God is love. 'In Christ Jesus, neither circumcision availeth anything, nor uncircumcising.' [4]   'The letter killeth, but the Spirit giveth life.' [5] 'Meat commendeth us not to God ; for neither if we eat are we the better, nor if we eat not are we the worse ; ' [6] 'the kingdom of God is not meat and drink.' [7]   Such were the words in which St. Paul expressed the great truth, that religion is not a matter of outward ceremonies, but of inward life.   But these heretics caught up the words, and inferred that all outward acts were indifferent, and none could be criminal.   They advocated the most unrestrained indulgence of the passions, and took for their maxim the worst precept of Epicurean atheism, 'let us eat and drink, for to-morrow we die.'   It is in the wealthy and vicious cities of Rome and Corinth that we find these errors first manifesting themselves ; and in the voluptuous atmosphere of the latter it was not unnatural that there should be some who would seek in a new religion an excuse for their old vices, and others who would easily be led astray by those 'evil communications' whose corrupting influence the Apostle himself mentions as the chief source of this mischief.

The Resurrection of the Dead was denied in the same city and by the same [8] party ; nor is it strange that as the sensual Felix trembled when Paul preached to him of the judgment to come, so these profligate cavillers shrank from the thought of that tribunal before which account must be given of the things done in the body. Perhaps, also (as some have inferred from St. Paul's refutation of

---

[1] This state would be perfectly realised if the renovation of heart were complete; and it is practically realised in proportion as the Christian's spiritual union with Christ approaches its theoretic standard.   Perhaps it was perfectly realised by St. Paul when he wrote Gal. ii. 20.

[2] Compare 1 Tim. i. 9—'the law is not made for a righteous man.'

[3] 'All things are lawful unto me,' 1 Cor. vi. 12.

[4] Gal. v. 6.   [5] 2 Cor. iii. 6.

[6] 1 Cor. viii. 8.

[7] Rom. xiv. 17.

[8] This is proved by 1 Cor. xv. 35.

these heretics), they had misunderstood the Christian doctrine, which teaches us to believe in the resurrection of a spiritual body, as though it had asserted the re-animation of 'this vile body' of 'flesh and blood,' which 'cannot inherit the kingdom of God;' or it is possible that a materialistic philosophy[1] led them to maintain that when the body had crumbled away in the grave, or been consumed on the funeral pyre, nothing of the man remained in being. In either case, they probably explained away the doctrine of the Resurrection as a metaphor, similar to that employed by St. Paul when he says that baptism is the resurrection of the new convert;[2] thus they would agree with those later heretics (of whom were Hymenæus and Philetus) who taught 'that the Resurrection was past already.'

Hitherto we have spoken of those divisions and heresies which appear to have sprung up in the several churches founded by St. Paul at the earliest period of their history, almost immediately after their conversion. Beyond this period we are not yet arrived in St. Paul's life; and from his conversion even to the time of his imprisonment, his conflict was mainly with Jews or Judaisers. But there were other forms of error which harassed his declining years; and these we will now endeavour (although anticipating the course of our biography) shortly to describe, so that it may not be necessary afterwards to revert to the subject, and at the same time that particular cases, which will meet us in the Epistles, may be understood in their relation to the general religious aspect of the time.

We have seen that, in the earliest epoch of the Church, there were two elements of error which had already shown themselves; namely, the bigoted, exclusive, and superstitious tendency, which was of Jewish origin; and the pseudo-philosophic, or rationalising tendency, which was of Grecian birth. In the early period of which we have hitherto spoken, and onwards till the time of St. Paul's imprisonment at Rome, the first of these tendencies was the principal source of danger; but after this, as the Church enlarged itself, and the number of Gentile converts more and more exceeded that of Jewish Christians, the case was altered. The catholicity of the Church became an established fact, and the Judaisers, properly so called, ceased to exist as an influential party anywhere except in Palestine. Yet still, though the Jews were forced to give up their exclusiveness, and to acknowledge the uncircumcised as 'fellow-heirs and of the same body,' their superstition remained, and became a fruitful source of mischief. On the other hand, those who sought for nothing more in Christianity than a new philosophy, were naturally increased in number, in proportion as the Church gained converts from the educated classes; the lecturers in the schools of Athens, the 'wisdom seekers' of Corinth, the Antinomian perverters of St. Paul's teaching, and the Platonising rabbis of Alexandria, all would share in this tendency. The latter, indeed, as represented by the learned Philo, had already attempted to

---

[1] If this were the case, we must suppose them to have been of Epicurean tendencies, and, so far, different from the later Platonising Gnostics, who denied the Resurrection.

[2] Col. ii. 12. Compare Rom. vi. 4.

construct a system of Judaic Platonism, which explained away almost all the peculiarities of the Mosaic theology into accordance with the doctrines of the Academy. And thus the way was already paved for the introduction of that most curious amalgam of Hellenic and Oriental speculation with Jewish superstition, which was afterwards called the Gnostic heresy. It is a disputed point at what time this heresy made its first appearance in the Church ; some [1] think that it had already commenced in the Church of Corinth when St. Paul warned them to beware of the knowledge (*Gnosis*) which puffeth up ; others maintain that it did not originate till the time of Basilides, long after the last Apostle had fallen asleep in Jesus. Perhaps, however, we may consider this as a difference rather about the definition of a term than the history of a sect. If we define Gnosticism to be that combination of Orientalism and Platonism held by the followers of Basilides or Valentinus, and refuse the title of Gnostic to any but those who adopted their systems, no doubt we must not place the Gnostics among the heretics of the Apostolic age. But if, on the other hand (as seems most natural), we define a Gnostic to be one who claims the possession of a peculiar 'Gnosis' (i.e. a deep and philosophic insight into the mysteries of theology, unattainable by the vulgar), then it is indisputable that Gnosticism had begun when St. Paul warned Timothy against those who laid claim to a 'knowledge (*Gnosis*)[2] falsely so called.' And, moreover, we find that, even in the Apostolic age, these arrogant speculators had begun to blend with their Hellenic philosophy certain fragments of Jewish superstition, which afterwards were incorporated into the Cabbala.[3] In spite, however, of the occurrence of such Jewish elements, those heresies which troubled the later years of St. Paul, and afterwards of St. John, were essentially rather of Gentile[4] than of Jewish origin. So far as they agreed with the later Gnosticism, this must certainly have

---

[1] This is the opinion of Dr. Burton, the great English authority on the Gnostic heresy. (*Lectures*, pp. 84, 85.) We cannot refer to this eminent theologian without expressing our obligation to his writings, and our admiration for that union of profound learning with clear good sense and candour which distinguishes him. His premature death robbed the Church of England of a writer who, had his life been spared, would have been inferior to none of its brightest ornaments.

[2] Neander well observes, that the essential feature in Gnosticism is its re-establishing an *aristocracy of knowledge* in religion, and rejecting the Christian principle which recognises no religious distinctions between rich and poor, learned and ignorant. (*Church History*, sect. 4.) So in Hippolytus's recently discovered 'Refutation of Heresies,' we find that some of the earlier Gnostics are represented as interpreting the 'good ground' in the parable of the Sower to mean the higher order of intellects.

[3] Thus the 'genealogies' mentioned in the Pastoral Epistles were probably those speculations about the emanations of spiritual beings found in the Cabbala, at least, such is Burton's opinion. (Pp. 114 and 413.) And the Angel worship at Colossæ belonged to the same class of superstitions. It has been shown by Dr. Burton (pp. 304–306), as well as by Neander and other writers, that the later Gnostic theories of æons and emanations were derived, in some measure, from Jewish sources, although the essential character of Gnosticism is entirely anti-Judaical.

[4] In the larger editions is an Appendix on the 'Heretics of the later Apostolic Age.'

been the case, for we know that it was a characteristic of all the Gnostic sects to despise the Jewish Scriptures.[1] Moreover, those who laid claims to 'Gnosis' at Corinth (as we have seen) were a Gentile party, who professed to adopt St. Paul's doctrine of the abolition of the law, and perverted it into Antinomianism : in short, they were the opposite extreme to the Judaising party. Nor need we be surprised to find that some of these philosophising heretics adopted some of the wildest superstitions of the Jews ; for these very superstitions were not so much the natural growth of Judaism as ingrafted upon it by its Rabbinical corrupters and derived from Oriental sources. And there was a strong affinity between the neo-Platonic philosophy of Alexandria and the Oriental theosophy which sprang from Buddhism and other kindred systems, and which degenerated into the practice of magic and incantations.

It is not necessary, however, that we should enter into any discussion of the subsequent development of these errors ; our subject only requires that we give an outline of the forms which they assumed during the lifetime of St. Paul ; and this we can only do very imperfectly, because the allusions in St. Paul's writings are so few and so brief, that they give us but little information. Still, they suffice to show the main features of the heresies which he condemns, especially when we compare them with notices in other parts of the New Testament, and with the history of the Church in the succeeding century.

We may consider these heresies, first, in their doctrinal, and, secondly, in their practical, aspect. With regard to the former, we find that their general characteristic was the claim to a deep philosophical insight into the mysteries of religion. Thus the Colossians are warned against the false teachers who would deceive them by a vain affectation of 'Philosophy,' and who were 'puffed up by a fleshly mind.' (Col. ii. 8, 18.)[2] So, in the Epistle to Timothy, St. Paul speaks of these heretics as falsely claiming 'knowledge' (*gnosis*). And in the Epistle to the Ephesians (so called) he seems to allude to the same boastful assumption, when he speaks of the love of Christ as surpassing 'knowledge,' in a passage which contains other apparent allusions[3] to Gnostic doctrine. Connected with this claim to a deeper insight into truth than that possessed by the uninitiated, was the manner in which some of these heretics explained away the facts of revelation by an allegorical interpretation. Thus we find that Hymenæus and Philetus maintained that 'the Resurrection was past already.' We have seen that a heresy apparently identical with this existed at a very early period in the Church of Corinth, among the free-thinking, or pseudo-philosophical, party there ; and all the Gnostic sects of the second century were united in denying the resurrection of the dead.[4] Again, we find the Colossian heretics introducing a worship of angels, 'intruding into those things which they have not seen :' and so, in the

---

[1] Dr. Burton says :—'We find all the Gnostics agreed in rejecting the Jewish Scriptures, or at least in treating them with contempt.'—p. 39.

[2]. Compare 1 Cor. viii. 1 : 'Know-ledge (*gnosis*) puffeth up.'

[3] Eph. iii. 19. See Dr. Burton's remarks, *Lectures*, pp. 83 and 125.

[4] Burton, p. 131.

Pastoral Epistles, the 'self-styled Gnostics' (1 Tim. vi. 20) are occupied with 'endless genealogies,' which were probably fanciful myths,
concerning the origin and emanation of spiritual beings.[1]   This
latter is one of the points in which Jewish superstition was blended
with Gentile speculation ; for we find in the Cabbala,[2] or collection
of Jewish traditional theology, many fabulous statements concerning such emanations.   It seems to be a similar superstition which
is stigmatised in the Pastoral Epistles as consisting of 'profane and
old wives' fables ;'[3] and, again, of 'Jewish fables and commandments of men.'[4]   The Gnostics of the second century adopted and
systematised this theory of emanations, and it became one of the
most peculiar and distinctive features of their heresy.   But this
was not the only Jewish element in the teaching of these Colossian
heretics ; we find also that they made a point of conscience of observing the Jewish Sabbaths[5] and festivals, and they are charged
with clinging to outward rites (Col. ii. 8, 20), and making distinctions between the lawfulness of different kinds of food.

In their practical results, these heresies which we are considering
had a twofold direction.   On one side was an ascetic tendency, such
as we find at Colossæ, showing itself by an arbitrarily invented
worship of God,[6] an affectation of self-humiliation and mortification
of the flesh.   So, in the Pastoral Epistles, we find the prohibition
of marriage,[7] the enforced abstinence from food, and other bodily
mortifications, mentioned as characteristics of heresy.[8]   If this
asceticism originated from the Jewish element which has been mentioned above, it may be compared with the practice of the Essenes,[9]
whose existence shows that such asceticism was not inconsistent
with Judaism, although it was contrary to the views of the Judaising party properly so called.   On the other hand, it may have

---

[1] See p. 354, n. 3.   According to the
Cabbala, there were ten *Sephiroth*, or
emanations proceeding from God,
which appear to have suggested the
Gnostic æons.   Upon this theory was
grafted a system of magic, consisting
mainly of the use of Scriptural words
to produce supernatural effects.

[2] St. Paul denounces 'the tradition
of men' (Col. ii. 8) as the source of
these errors; and the word Cabbala
means tradition.   Dr. Burton says, 'the
Cabbala had certainly grown into a
system at the time of the destruction of Jerusalem ; and there is also
evidence that it had been cultivated
by the Jewish doctors long before.'—
p. 298. [See above, Chap. II. p. 49. H.]

[3] 1 Tim. iv. 7.

[4] Tit. i. 14.

[5] This does not prove them, however, to have been Jews, for the superstitious Heathen were also in the habit
of adopting some of the rites of Judaism, under the idea of their producing
some magical effect upon them ; as we

find from the Roman satirists.   Compare Horace, *Sat.* I. 9. 71. ('Hodie
tricesima sabbata,' &c.), and Juv. VI.
542–547.   See also some remarks on
the Colossian heretics in our introductory remarks on the Epistle to the
Colossians.

[6] 'Will-worship.'   Col. ii. 23.

[7] Which certainly was the reverse
of the Judaising exaltation of marriage.

[8] St. Paul declares that these errors
shall come 'in the last days' (2 Tim.
iii. 1); but St. John says 'the last
days' were come in his time (1 John
ii. 18) ; and it is implied by St. Paul's
words that the evils he denounces
were already in action ; just as he had
said before to the Thessalonians, 'the
mystery of lawlessness is already working' (2 Thess. ii. 7), where the peculiar expressions 'lawlessness' and
'the lawless one' seem to point to
the Antinomian character of these
heresies.

[9] [See above, Chap. II. p. 29. H.]

arisen from that abhorrence of matter, and anxiety to free the soul from the dominion of the body, which distinguished the Alexandrian Platonists, and which (derived from them) became a characteristic of some of the Gnostic sects.

But this asceticism was a weak and comparatively innocent form, in which the practical results of this incipient Gnosticism exhibited themselves. Its really dangerous manifestation was derived, not from its Jewish, but from its Heathen element. We have seen how this showed itself from the first at Corinth ; how men sheltered their immoralities under the name of Christianity, and even justified them by a perversion of its doctrines. Such teaching could not fail to find a ready audience wherever there were found vicious lives and hardened consciences. Accordingly it was in the luxurious and corrupt population of Asia Minor,[1] that this early Gnosticism assumed its worst form of immoral practice defended by Antinomian doctrine. Thus, in the Epistle to the Ephesians, St. Paul warns his readers against the sophistical arguments by which certain false teachers strove to justify the sins of impurity, and to persuade them that the acts of the body could not contaminate the soul,—' Let no man deceive you with vain words ; for because of these things cometh the wrath of God upon the children of disobedience.'[2] Hymenæus and Philetus are the first leaders of this party mentioned by name : we have seen that they agreed with the Corinthian Antinomians in denying the Resurrection, and they agreed with them no less in practice than in theory. Of the first of them it is expressly said that he[3] had ' cast away a good conscience,' and of both we are told that they showed themselves not to belong to Christ, because they had not His seal : this seal being described as twofold—' The Lord knoweth them that are His,' and ' Let every one that nameth the name of Christ depart from iniquity.'[4] St. Paul appears to imply that though they boasted their ' knowledge of God,' yet the Lord had no knowledge of them ; as our Saviour had Himself declared that to the claims of such false disciples He would reply, ' I never *knew* you; depart from me, ye *workers of iniquity.*' But in the same Epistle where these heresiarchs are condemned, St. Paul intimates that their principles were not yet fully developed ; he warns Timothy[5] that an outburst of immorality and lawlessness must be shortly expected within the Church beyond anything which had yet been experienced. The same anticipation appears in his farewell address to the Ephesian presbyters, and even at the early period of his Epistle to the Thessalonians ; and we see from the Epistles

---

[1] Both at Colossæ and in Crete it seems to have been the Jewish form of these heresies which predominated : at Colossæ they took an ascetic direction ; in Crete, among a simpler and more provincial population, the false teachers seem to have been hypocrites, who encouraged the vices to which their followers were addicted, and inoculated them with foolish superstitions (Tit. i. 14, iii. 9) ; but we do not find in these Epistles any mention

of the theoretic Antinomianism which existed in some of the great cities.

[2] Eph. v. 6. See also the whole of the warnings in Eph. v. The Epistle, though not addressed (at any rate, not exclusively) to the Ephesians, was probably sent to several other cities in Asia Minor.

[3] 1 Tim. i. 19, 20.

[4] 2 Tim. ii. 19.

[5] 2 Tim. iii.

of St. Peter and St. Jude, and from the Apocalypse of St. John, all addressed (it should be remembered) to the Churches of Asia Minor, that this prophetic warning was soon fulfilled. We find that many Christians used their liberty as a cloak of maliciousness;[1] 'promising their hearers liberty, yet themselves the slaves of corruption;'[2] 'turning the grace of God into lasciviousness;'[3] that they were justly condemned by the surrounding Heathen for their crimes, and even suffered punishment as robbers and murderers.[4] They were also infamous for the practice of the pretended arts of magic and witchcraft,[5] which they may have borrowed either from the Jewish soothsayers[6] and exorcisers,[7] or from the Heathen professors of magical arts who so much abounded at the same epoch. Some of them, who are called the followers of Balaam in the Epistles of Peter and Jude, and the Nicolaitans (an equivalent name) in the Apocalypse, taught their followers to indulge in the sensual impurities, and even in the idol-feasts of the Heathen.[8] We find, moreover, that these false disciples, with their licentiousness in morals, united anarchy in politics, and resistance to law and government. They 'walked after the flesh in the lust of uncleanness, and despised governments.' And thus they gave rise to those charges against Christianity itself, which were made by the Heathen writers of the time, whose knowledge of the new religion was naturally taken from those amongst its professors who rendered themselves notorious by falling under the judgment of the Law.

When thus we contemplate the true character of these divisions and heresies which beset the Apostolic Church, we cannot but acknowledge that it needed all those miraculous gifts with which it

[1] 1 Pet. ii. 16.
[2] 2 Pet. ii. 19.
[3] Jude 4.
[4] 1 Pet. iv. 15.
[5] Rev. ii. 20. Compare Rev. ix. 21, Rev. xxi. 8, and Rev. xxii. 15.
[6] Compare Juv. VI. 546 : 'Qualiacunque voles Judæi somnia vendunt.' [See above, Chap. V. pp. 118, 119. H.]
[7] See Acts xix. 13.
[8] Such, at least, seems the natural explanation of the words in Rev. ii. 20; for we can scarcely suppose so strong a condemnation if the offence had been only eating meat which had once formed part of a sacrifice. It is remarkable how completely the Gnostics of the second century resembled these earlier heretics in all the points here mentioned. Their immorality is the subject of constant animadversion in the writings of the Fathers, who tell us that the calumnies which were cast upon the Christians by the Heathen were caused by the vices of the Gnostics. Irenæus asserts that they said, 'as gold deposited in mud does not lose its beauty, so they themselves, whatever may be their outward immorality, cannot be injured by it, nor lose their spiritual substance.' And so Justin Martyr speaks of heretics, who said 'that though they live sinful lives, yet, *if they know God*, the Lord will not impute to them sin.' And Epiphanius gives the most horrible details of the enormities which they practised. Again, their addiction to magical arts was notorious. And their leaders, Basilides and Valentinus, are accused of acting like the Nicolaitans of the Apocalypse, to avoid persecution. Such accusations may, no doubt, be slanders, as far as those leaders were individually concerned. The increased knowledge of them which we have lately derived from the publication of Hippolytus's 'Refutation of Heresies' leads us to think of them as bold speculators, but not as bad men. Yet we cannot doubt that their philosophical speculations degenerated into the most superstitious theosophy in the hands of their followers. And the details furnished by Hippolytus prove that many of the Gnostics fully deserved the charges of immorality commonly brought against them.

was endowed, and all that inspired wisdom which presided over its organisation, to ward off dangers which threatened to blight its growth and destroy its very existence.   In its earliest infancy, two powerful and venomous foes twined themselves round its very cradle; but its strength was according to its day; with a supernatural vigour it rent off the coils of Jewish bigotry and stifled the poisonous breath of Heathen licentiousness; but the peril was mortal, and the struggle was for life or death.   Had the Church's fate been subjected to the ordinary laws which regulate the history of earthly commonwealths, it could scarcely have escaped one of two opposite destinies, either of which must have equally defeated (if we may so speak) the world's salvation.   Either it must have been cramped into a Jewish sect, according to the wish of the majority of its earliest members, or (having escaped this immediate extinction) it must have added one more to the innumerable schools of Heathen philosophy, subdividing into a hundred branches, whose votaries would some of them have sunk into Oriental superstitions, others into Pagan voluptuousness.   If we need any proof how narrowly the Church escaped this latter peril, we have only to look at the fearful power of Gnosticism in the succeeding century.   And, indeed, the more we consider the elements of which every Christian community was originally composed, the more must we wonder how the little flock of the wise and good[1] could have successfully resisted the overwhelming contagion of folly and wickedness.   In every city the nucleus of the Church consisted of Jews and Jewish proselytes; on this foundation was superadded a miscellaneous mass of Heathen converts, almost exclusively from the lowest classes, baptized, indeed, into the name of Jesus, but still with all the habits of a life of idolatry and vice clinging to them.   How was it, then, that such a society could escape the two temptations which assailed it just at the time when they were most likely to be fatal?   While as yet the Jewish element preponderated, a fanatical party, commanding almost necessarily the sympathies of the Jewish portion of the society, made a zealous and combined effort to reduce Christianity to Judaism, and subordinate the Church to the synagogue.   Over their great opponent, the one Apostle of the Gentiles, they won a temporary triumph, and saw him consigned to prison and to death.   How was it that the very hour of their victory was the epoch from which we date their failure?   Again,—this stage is passed,—the Church is thrown open to the Gentiles, and crowds flock in, some attracted by wonder at the miracles they see, some by hatred of the government under which they live, and by hopes that they may turn the Church into an organised conspiracy against law and order; and even the best, as yet unsettled in their faith, and ready to exchange their new belief for a newer, 'carried about with every wind of doctrine.' At such an epoch, a systematic theory is devised, reconciling the profession of Christianity with the practice of immorality; its teachers proclaim that Christ has freed them from the law, and that the man who has attained true spiritual enlightenment is

---

[1] Whom St. Paul calls 'perfect' (Phil. iii. 15), i.e. mature in the knowledge of Christian truth.

above the obligations of outward morality ; and with this seducing philosophy for the Gentile they readily combine the Cabbalistic superstitions of Rabbinical tradition to captivate the Jew. Who could wonder if, when such incendiaries applied their torch to such materials, a flame burst forth which well nigh consumed the fabric ? Surely that day of trial was 'revealed in fire,' and the building which was able to abide the flame was nothing less than the temple of God.

It is painful to be compelled to acknowledge among the Christians of the Apostolic Age the existence of so many forms of error and sin. It was a pleasing dream which represented the primitive Church as a society of angels ; and it is not without a struggle that we bring ourselves to open our eyes and behold the reality. But yet it is a higher feeling which bids us thankfully recognise the truth that 'there is no partiality with God ;'[1] that He has never supernaturally coerced any generation of mankind into virtue, nor rendered schism and heresy impossible in any age of the Church. So St. Paul tells his converts[2] that there must needs be heresies among them, that the good may be tried and distinguished from the bad ; implying that, without the possibility of a choice, there would be no test of faith or holiness. And so Our Lord Himself compared His Church to a net cast into the sea, which gathered fish of all kinds, both good and bad ; nor was its purity to be attained by the exclusion of evil, till the end should come. Therefore, if we sigh, as well we may, for the realisation of an ideal which Scripture paints to us and imagination embodies, but which our eyes seek for and cannot find ; if we look vainly and with earnest longings for the appearance of that glorious Church, 'without spot or wrinkle or any such thing,' the fitting bride of a heavenly spouse ;—it may calm our impatience to recollect that no such Church has ever existed upon earth, while yet we do not forget that it has existed and does exist in heaven. In the very lifetime of the Apostles, no less than now, 'the earnest expectation of the creature waited for the manifestation of the sons of God ;' miracles did not convert ; inspiration did not sanctify ; then, as now, imperfection and evil clung to the members, and clogged the energies, of the kingdom of God ; now, as then, Christians are fellow heirs, and of the same body with the spirits of just men made perfect ; now, as then, the communion of saints unites into one family the Church militant with the Church triumphant.

Coin of Corinth.[3]

---

[1] Acts x. 34. [2] 1 Cor. xi. 19. [3] The figures on the right and left represent the eastern and western harbours of Corinth, which is symbolised by the female figure on a rock in the centre. See p. 324.

CHAPTER XIV.

Departure from Antioch.—St. Paul's Companions.—Journey through Phrygia and Galatia.—Apollos at Ephesus and Corinth.—Arrival of St. Paul at Ephesus.—Disciples of John the Baptist.—The Synagogue.—The School of Tyrannus.—Ephesian Magic.—Miracles.—The Exorcists.—Burning of the Books.

THE next period of St. Paul's life opens with a third journey through the interior of Asia Minor.[1] In the short stay which he had made at Ephesus on his return from his second journey, he had promised to come again to that city, if the providence of God should allow it.[2] This promise he was enabled to fulfil, after a hasty visit to the metropolis of the Jewish nation, and a longer sojourn in the first metropolis of the Gentile Church.[3]

It would lead us into long and useless discussions, if we were to speculate on the time spent at Antioch, and the details of the Apostle's occupation in the scene of his early labours. We have already stated our reasons for believing that the discussions which led to the Council at Jerusalem, took place at an earlier period,[4] as well as the quarrel between St. Peter and St. Paul concerning the propriety of concession to the Judaisers.[5] But without knowing the particular form of the controversies brought before him, or the names of those Christian teachers with whom he conferred, we have seen enough to make us aware that imminent dangers from the Judaising party surrounded the Church, and that Antioch was a favourable place for meeting the machinations of this party, as well as a convenient starting-point for a journey undertaken to strengthen those communities that were likely to be invaded by false teachers from Judæa.

It is evident that it was not St. Paul's only object to proceed with all haste to Ephesus : nor indeed is it credible that he could pass through the regions of Cilicia and Lycaonia, Phrygia and Galatia, without remaining to confirm those Churches which he had founded himself, and some of which he had visited twice. We are plainly told that his journey was occupied in this work, and the few words which refer to this subject imply a systematic visitation.[6] He would be the more anxious to establish them in the true principles of the Gospel, in proportion as he was aware of the widely spreading

---

[1] Acts xviii. 23.
[2] Ibid. 21. See pp. 331, 332.
[3] See the end of Chap. XII.
[4] See Appendix I. for the answers to Wieseler's arguments on this subject.
[5] Neander is inclined to assign the

misunderstanding of the two Apostles to this time. So Olshausen. See pp. 177, 178.
[6] Acts xviii. 23. Notice the phrase 'in order.'

influence of the Judaisers. Another specific object, not unconnected
with the healing of divisions, was before him during the whole of
this missionary journey,—a collection for the relief of the poor
Christians in Judæa.[1] It had been agreed, at the meeting of the
Apostolic Council (Gal. ii. 9, 10), that while some should go to the
Heathen, and others to the Circumcision, the former should carefully
' remember the poor ; ' and this we see St. Paul, on the present
journey among the Gentile Churches, 'forward to do.' We even
know the ' order which he gave to the Churches of Galatia ' (1 Cor.
xvi. 1, 2). He directed that each person should lay by in store, on
the first day of the week, according as God had prospered him, that
the collection should be deliberately made, and prepared for an
opportunity of being taken to Jerusalem.

We are not able to state either the exact route which St. Paul
followed, or the names of the companions by whom he was attended.
As regards the latter subject, however, two points may be taken for
granted, that Silas ceased to be, and that Timotheus continued to be,
an associate of the Apostle. It is most probable that Silas remained
behind in Jerusalem, whence he had first accompanied Barnabas with
the Apostolic letter,[2] and where, on the first mention of his name,
he is stated to have held a leading position in the Church.[3] He is
not again mentioned in connection with the Apostle of the Gentiles.[4]
The next place in Scripture where his name occurs, is in the letter
of the Apostle of the Circumcision (1 Pet. v. 12), which is addressed
to the strangers scattered throughout Pontus, Galatia, Cappadocia,
Asia, and Bithynia. There, ' Silvanus ' is spoken of as one not
unknown to the persons addressed, but as ' a faithful brother unto
them ; '—by him the letter was sent which ' exhorted ' the Christians in the north and west of Asia Minor, and ' testified that that
was the true grace of God wherein they stood ; '—and the same
disciple is seen, on the last mention of his name, as on the first, to
be co-operating for the welfare of the Church, both with St. Peter
and St. Paul.[5]

It may be considered, on the other hand, probable, if not certain,
that Timotheus was with the Apostle through the whole of this
journey. Abundant mention of him is made, both in the Acts and
the Epistles, in connection with St. Paul's stay at Ephesus, and his
subsequent movements.[6] Of the other companions who were
undoubtedly with him at Ephesus, we cannot say with confidence
whether they attended him from Antioch, or joined him afterwards
at some other point. But Erastus (Acts xix. 22) may have remained with him since the time of his first visit to Corinth, and
Caius and Aristarchus (Acts xix. 29) since the still earlier period of
his journey through Macedonia.[7] Perhaps we have stronger reasons

[1] The steady pursuance of this object
in the whole course of this journey
may be traced through the following
passages :—1 Cor. xvi. 1–4; 2 Cor. viii.
ix.; Rom. xv. 25, 26; Acts xxiv. 17.
[2] See pp. 176, 177.
[3] Acts xv. 22.
[4] His name is in the salutation in
the Epistles to the Thessalonians, but

not in any subsequent letters. Compare 2 Cor. i. 19.
[5] Compare again the account of the
Council of Jerusalem and the mission
of Silas and Barnabas.
[6] See Acts xix. 22; 1 Cor. iv. 17,
xvi. 10 ; 2 Cor. i. 1; Rom. xvi. 21;
Acts xx. 4.
[7] See Tate, pp. 52, 53.

for concluding that Titus, who, though not mentioned in the Acts,[1] was certainly of great service in the second missionary journey, travelled with Paul and Timotheus through the earlier part of it. In the frequent mention which is made of him in the Second Epistle to the Corinthians, he appears as the Apostle's laborious minister, and as a source of his consolation and support, hardly less strikingly, than the disciple whom he had taken on the previous journey from Lystra and Iconium.[2]

Whatever might be the exact route which the Apostle followed from Antioch to Ephesus, he would certainly, as we have said, revisit those Churches, which twice[3] before had known him as their teacher. He would pass over the Cilician plain on the warm southern shore,[4] and the high table-land of Lycaonia on the other side of the Pass of Taurus.[5] He would see once more his own early home on the banks of the Cydnus;[6] and Timothy would be once more in the scenes of his childhood at the base of the Kara-Dagh.[7] After leaving Tarsus, the cities of Derbe, Lystra, and Iconium, possibly also Antioch in Pisidia,[8] would be the primary objects in the Apostle's progress. Then we come to Phrygia and Galatia, both vague and indeterminate districts, which he had visited once,[9] and through which, as before, we cannot venture to lay down a route.[10] Though the visitation of the Churches was systematic, we need not conclude that the same exact course was followed. Since the order in which the two districts are mentioned is different from that in the former instance,[11] we are at liberty to suppose that he travelled first from Lycaonia through Cappadocia[12] into Galatia, and then by Western Phrygia to the coast of the Ægean. In this last part of his progress we are in still greater doubt as to the route, and one question of interest is involved in our opinion concerning it. The great road from Ephesus by Iconium to the Euphrates passed along the valley of the Mæander, and near the cities of Laodicea, Colossæ, and Hierapolis; and we should naturally suppose that the Apostle would approach the capital

---

[1] Wieseler, indeed, identifies him with Justus, who is mentioned xviii. 7. See, on this subject, p. 167, n. 13.

[2] If we compare 2 Cor. xii. 18 with 1 Cor. xvi. 11, 12, it is natural to infer that the bearers of the First Epistle (from Ephesus to Corinth) were Titus, and some *brother*, who is unnamed, but probably identical with one of the *two brethren* sent on the subsequent mission (2 Cor. viii. 16–24), and with the Second Epistle (from Macedonia to Corinth). See also 2 Cor. viii. 6. This view is advocated by Prof. Stanley in his recently published Commentary; but it has been put forth independently, and more fully elaborated by Mr. Lightfoot in the *Cambridge Journal of Classical and Sacred Philology* (June 1855).

[3] He had been in Lycaonia on the first and second missionary journeys, in Cilicia on the second; but he had

previously been there at least once since his conversion.

[4] See p. 18, and the allusions to the climate in Chap. VI. and Chap. VIII.

[5] See again Chap. VI. and Chap. VIII. for Lycaonia and Mount Taurus.

[6] See pp. 19, 40, and 41.

[7] See Chap. VI. and Chap. VIII., with the map facing p. 149 and the engraving facing p. 201.

[8] See p. 207.

[9] Acts xvi. 6.   [10] See Chap. VIII.

[11] Compare Acts xvi. 6 with xviii. 23. In both cases we should observe that the phrase '*region* (or *country*) of Galatia' is used. The Greek in each passage is the same. See what is said on the expression 'Churches of Galatia,' p. 209.

[12] This is Wieseler's view. For the province of Cappadocia, see p. 190. The district is mentioned Acts ii. 9, and 1 Pet. i. 1.

of Asia along this well-travelled line.[1] But the arguments are so
strong for believing that St. Paul was never personally at Colossæ,[2]
that it is safer to imagine him following some road further to the
north, such as that, for instance, which, after passing near Thyatira,
entered the valley of the Hermus at Sardis.[3]

Thus, then, we may conceive the Apostle arrived at that region,
where he was formerly in hesitation concerning his future progress,[4]
—the frontier district of Asia and Phrygia,[5] the mountains which
contain the upper waters[6] of the Hermus and Mæander. And now
our attention is suddenly called away to another preacher of the
Gospel whose name, next to that of the Apostles, is perhaps the
most important in the early history of the Church. There came at
this time to Ephesus, either directly from Egypt by sea, as Aquila
or Priscilla from Corinth, or by some route through the intermediate countries, like that of St. Paul himself, a ' disciple ' named
Apollos, a native of Alexandria. This visit occurred at a critical
time, and led to grave consequences in reference to the establishment of Christian truth, and the growth of parties in the Church ;
while the religious community (if so it may be called) to which he
belonged at the time of his arrival, furnishes us with one of the
most interesting links between the Gospels and the Acts.[7]

Apollos,[8] along with twelve others,[9] who are soon afterwards
mentioned at Ephesus, was acquainted with Christianity only so far
as it had been made known by John the Baptist. They 'knew only
the baptism of John.'[10] From the great part which was acted by
the forerunner of Christ in the first announcement of the Gospel,
and from the effect produced on the Jewish nation by his appearance, and the number of disciples who came to receive at his hands
the baptism of repentance, we should expect some traces of his
influence to appear in the subsequent period, during which the
Gospel was spreading beyond Judæa. Many Jews from other

---

[1] See pp. 207, 208.

[2] From Col. ii. 1 we should naturally infer that St. Paul had never
been personally among the Colossians.
Compare Col. i. 4, 7, 8, and our note
below on Col. ii. 1. A full discussion
of the subject will be found in Dr.
Davidson's *Introduction.*

[3] The characteristic scenery of the
Mæander and Hermus is described in
several parts of Hamilton's travels.
See especially chap. viii.–x., xxviii.–xl.;
also li., lii., and especially vol. i. pp. 135,
149. We may observe that, on one of
his journeys, nearly in the direction in
which St. Paul was moving, he crossed
the mountains from near Afium Kara
Hissar (Synnada) to visit Yalobatch
(Antioch in Pisidia). The Apostle
might easily do the same.

[4] Acts xvi. 6–8.

[5] See description of this district in
p. 213.

[6] This part of the table-land of the

interior is what is meant by ' the
higher districts,' Acts xix. 1. It is
needless to say that the word ' coasts'
in the Authorised Version has no reference to the sea. Herodotus uses a similar expression of this region, i. 177.
Even Paley makes a curious mistake
here, by taking ' upper ' in the sense of
' northern.' *Hor. Paul.* 1 Cor. No. 5.

[7] See the excellent remarks of Olshausen on the whole narrative concerning Apollos and the other disciples
of John the Baptist.

[8] Winer remarks that this abbreviated form of the name *Apollonius* is
found in Sozomen. It is, however, very
rare ; and it is worth observing that
among the terra-cottas discovered at
Tarsus (described p. 197, note 4) is a
circular disc which has the name
ΑΠΟΛΛΩC inscribed on it in cursive
Greek.

[9] See Acts xix. 1–7.

[10] Acts xviii. 25. Compare xix. 2.

countries received from the Baptist their knowledge of the Messiah, and carried with them this knowledge on their return from Palestine. We read of a heretical sect, at a much later period, who held John the Baptist to have been himself the Messiah.[1] But in a position intermediate between this deluded party, and those who were travelling as teachers of the full and perfect Gospel, there were doubtless many, among the floating Jewish population of the Empire, whose knowledge of Christ extended only to that which had been preached on the banks of the Jordan. That such persons should be found at Ephesus, the natural meeting-place of all religious sects and opinions, is what we might have supposed *à priori.* Their own connection with Judæa, or the connection of their teachers with Judæa, had been broken before the day of Pentecost. Thus their Christianity was at the same point at which it had stood at the commencement of our Lord's ministry. They were ignorant of the full meaning of the death of Christ ; possibly they did not even know the fact of His resurrection ; and they were certainly ignorant of the mission of the Comforter.[2] But they knew that the times of the Messiah were come, and that one had appeared[3] in whom the prophecies were fulfilled. That voice had reached them, which cried, 'Prepare ye the way of the Lord' (Isa. xl. 3). They felt that the axe was laid to the root of the tree, that 'the kingdom of Heaven was at hand,' that 'the knowledge of Salvation was come to those that sit in darkness' (Luke i. 77), and that the children of Israel were everywhere called to 'repent.' Such as were in this religious condition were evidently prepared for the full reception of Christianity, so soon as it was presented to them ; and we see that they were welcomed by St. Paul and the Christians at Ephesus as fellow-disciples[4] of the same Lord and Master.

In some respects Apollos was distinguished from the other disciples of John the Baptist, who are alluded to at the same place, and nearly at the same time. There is much significance in the first fact that is stated, that he was 'born at Alexandria.' Something has been said by us already concerning the Jews of Alexandria, and their theological influence in the age of the Apostles.[5] In the establishment of a religion which was intended to be the complete fulfilment of Judaism, and to be universally supreme in the Gentile world, we should expect Alexandria to bear her part, as well as Jerusalem. The Hellenistic learning fostered by the foundations of the Ptolemies might be made the handmaid of the truth, no less than the older learning of Judæa and the schools of the Hebrews. As regards Apollos, he was not only an Alexandrian Jew by birth, but he had a high reputation for an eloquent and forcible power of speaking, and had probably been well trained in the rhetorical schools on the banks of the Nile.[6]

---

[1] The Zabeans. So in the *Clementine Recognitions* are mentioned some 'of John's disciples, who preached their master as though he were Christ.'

[2] Acts xix. 2.

[3] Kuinoel thinks they were not even aware of Christ's appearance.

[4] Note the word 'disciples,' xix. 1.

[5] See pp. 30–32. Also pp. 8, 14, 15, and 87.

[6] The A. V. is probably correct in rendering the word 'eloquent' rather

But though he was endued with the eloquence of a Greek orator, the subject of his study and teaching were the Scriptures of his forefathers. The character which he bore in the synagogues was that of a man 'mighty in the Scriptures.' In addition to these advantages of birth and education, he seems to have had the most complete and systematic instruction in the Gospel which a disciple of John could possibly receive.[1] Whether from the Baptist himself, or from some of those who travelled into other lands with his teaching as their possession, Apollos had received full and accurate instruction in the 'way of the Lord.' We are further told that his character was marked by a fervent zeal[2] for spreading the truth. Thus we may conceive of him as travelling, like a second Baptist, beyond the frontiers of Judæa,—expounding the prophecies of the Old Testament, announcing that the times of the Messiah were come, and calling the Jews to repentance in the spirit of Elias.[3] Hence he was, like his great teacher, diligently 'preparing the way of the Lord.'[4] Though ignorant of the momentous facts which had succeeded the Resurrection and Ascension, he was turning the hearts of the 'disobedient to the wisdom of the just,' and 'making ready a people for the Lord,'[5] whom he was soon to know 'more perfectly.' Himself 'a burning and a shining light,' he bore witness to 'that Light which lighteth every man that cometh into the world,'[6] —as, on the other hand, he was a 'swift witness' against those Israelites whose lives were unholy, and came among them 'to purify the sons of Levi, that they might offer unto the Lord an offering in righteousness,'[7] and to proclaim that, if they were unfaithful, God was still able 'to raise up children unto Abraham.'[8]

Thus burning with zeal, and confident of the truth of what he had learnt, he spoke out boldly in the synagogue.[9] An intense interest must have been excited about this time concerning the Messiah in the synagogue at Ephesus. Paul had recently been there, and departed with the promise of return.[10] Aquila and Priscilla, though taking no forward part as public teachers, would diligently keep the subject of the Apostle's instruction before the mind of the Israelites. And now an Alexandrian Jew presented himself among them, bearing testimony to the same Messiah with singular eloquence, and with great power in the interpretation of Scripture. Thus an unconscious preparation was made for the arrival of the Apostle, who was even now travelling towards Ephesus through the uplands of Asia Minor.

than 'learned,' inasmuch as in the same verse he is called 'mighty in the Scriptures.'

[1] Literally, 'he was catechetically instructed in the way of the Lord.'

[2] Acts xviii. 25.

[3] He was probably able to go further in Christian teaching than John the Baptist could do, by giving an account of the life of Jesus Christ. So far his knowledge was *accurate*. Further instruction from Aquila and Priscilla made it *more accurate*.

[4] The phrase 'way of the Lord' should be carefully compared with the passages in the Gospels and Prophets, where it occurs in reference to John the Baptist. Matt. iii. 3; Mark i. 3; Luke iii. 4; John i. 23; Isa. xl. 3 (LXX.). Compare Mal. iii. 1 (LXX.).

[5] Luke i. 16, 17.

[6] John v. 35, i. 9.

[7] Mal. iii. 3–5.

[8] Matt. iii. 9.

[9] Acts xviii. 26.

[10] See p. 331.

The teaching of Apollos, though eloquent, learned, and zealous, was seriously defective. But God had provided among his listeners those who could instruct him more perfectly. Aquila and Priscilla felt that he was proclaiming the same truth in which they had been instructed at Corinth. They could inform him that they had met with one who had taught with authority far more concerning Christ than had been known even to John the Baptist; and they could recount to him the miraculous gifts, which attested the outpouring of the Holy Ghost. Thus they attached themselves closely to Apollos;[1] and gave him complete instruction in that 'way of the Lord,' which he had already taught accurately,[2] though imperfectly: and the learned Alexandrian obtained from the tentmakers a knowledge of that 'mystery' which the ancient Scriptures had only partially revealed.

This providential meeting with Aquila and Priscilla in Asia became the means of promoting the spread of the Gospel in Achaia. Now that Apollos was made fully acquainted with the Christian doctrine, his zeal urged him to go where it had been firmly established by an Apostle.[3] It is possible, too, that some news received from Corinth might lead him to suppose that he could be of active service there in the cause of truth. The Christians of Ephesus encouraged[4] him in this intention, and gave him 'letters of commendation'[5] to their brethren across the Ægean. On his arrival at Corinth, he threw himself at once among those Jews who had rejected St. Paul, and argued with them publicly and zealously on the ground of their Scriptures,[6] and thus[7] became 'a valuable support to those who had already believed through the grace of God;' for he proved with power that that Jesus who had been crucified at Jerusalem, and whom Paul was proclaiming throughout the world, was indeed the Christ.[8] Thus he watered where Paul had planted, and God gave an abundant increase. (1 Cor. iii. 6.) And yet evil grew up side by side with the good. For while he was a valuable aid to the Christians, and a formidable antagonist to the Jews, and while he was honestly co-operating in Paul's great work of evangelising the world, he became the occasion of fostering party-spirit among the Corinthians, and was unwillingly held up as a rival of the Apostle himself. In this city of rhetoricians and sophists, the erudition and eloquent speaking of Apollos were contrasted with the unlearned simplicity with which St. Paul had studiously presented

---

[1] 'They took him to themselves,' ver. 26.

[2] Compare ver. 25 and ver. 26.

[3] Acts xviii. 27.

[4] The exhortation (ver. 27) may refer to him. At all events he was encouraged in his plan.

[5] Compare what is said here in ver. 27 with 2 Cor. iii. 1, where the reference is to commendatory letters addressed to or from the very same Church of Corinth.

[6] Compare in detail the expressions in ver. 28 with those in vv. 24–26.

[7] The word 'for' should be noticed. His coming was a valuable assistance to the Christians against the Jews, in the controversies which had doubtless been going on since St. Paul's departure.

[8] 'Showing by the Scriptures that Jesus was Christ,' ver. 28. The phrase is much more definite than those which are used above ('the way of the Lord,' and 'the things of the Lord,' ver. 25) of the time when he was not fully instructed.

the Gospel to his Corinthian hearers.[1]　Thus many attached themselves to the new teacher, and called themselves by the name of Apollos, while others ranged themselves as the party of Paul (1 Cor. i. 12),—forgetting that Christ could not be ‘ divided,’ and that Paul and Apollos were merely ‘ ministers by whom they had believed.’ (1 Cor. iii. 5.)　We have no reason to imagine that Apollos himself encouraged or tolerated such unchristian divisions. A proof of his strong feeling to the contrary, and of his close attachment to St. Paul, is furnished by that letter to the Corinthians, which will soon be brought under our notice,[2] where, after vehement rebukes of the schismatic spirit prevailing among the Corinthians, it is said, ‘ touching our brother Apollos,’ that he was unwilling to return to them at that particular time, though St. Paul himself had ‘ greatly desired it.’

But now the Apostle himself is about to arrive in Ephesus.　His residence in this place, like his residence in Antioch and Corinth, is a subject to which our attention is particularly called.　Therefore, all the features of the city—its appearance, its history, the character of its population, its political and mercantile relations— possess the utmost interest for us.　We shall defer such description to a future chapter, and limit ourselves here to what may set before the reader the geographical position of Ephesus, as the point in which St. Paul’s journey from Antioch terminated for the present.

We imagined him[3] about the frontier of Asia and Phrygia, on his approach from the interior to the sea.　From this region of volcanic mountains, a tract of country extends to the Ægean, which is watered by two of the long western rivers, the Hermus and the Mæander, and which is celebrated through an extended period of classical history, and is sacred to us as the scene of the Churches of the Apocalypse.[4]　Near the mouth of one of these rivers is Smyrna ; near that of the other is Miletus.　The islands of Chios and Samos are respectively opposite the projecting portions of coast, where the rivers flow by these cities to the sea.[5]　Between the Hermus and the Mæander is a smaller river, named the Cayster, separated from the latter by the ridge of Messogis, and from the former by Mount Tmolus.[6]　Here, in the level valley of the Cayster, is the early cradle of the Asiatic name,—the district of primeval ‘ Asia,’—not as understood in its political or ecclesiastical sense, but the Asia of

---

[1] See the remarks on the Corinthian parties in p. 351.

[2] 1 Cor. xvi. 12.　We may just mention, that a very different view has been taken of the character of Apollos and his relation to St. Paul,—viz. that he was the chief promoter of the troubles at Corinth, and that he acted rebelliously in refusing to return thither when the Apostle desired him to do so.　We have no doubt, however, that the ordinary view is correct.

[3] Above, p. 364.

[4] Rev. i. ii. iii.　Laodicea is in the basin of the Mæander ; Smyrna, Thyatira, Sardis, and Philadelphia are in that of the Hermus ; Pergamus is further to the north on the Caicus. For a description of this district, see Arundell’s *Visit to the Seven Churches,* and Fellows’ *Asia Minor.*

[5] In the account of St. Paul’s return we shall have to take particular notice of this coast.　He sailed between these islands and the mainland, touching at Miletus.　Acts xx.

[6] See p. 419.

old poetic legend.[1] And here, in a situation pre-eminent among
the excellent positions which the Ionians chose for their cities,
Ephesus was built, on some hills near the sea. For some time after its
foundation by Androclus the Athenian, it was inferior to Miletus ;
but with the decay of the latter city, in the Macedonian and Roman
periods, it rose to greater eminence, and in the time of St. Paul
it was the greatest city of Asia Minor, as well as the metropolis of
the *province* of Asia. Though Greek in its origin, it was half-
oriental in the prevalent worship, and in the character of its
inhabitants ; and being constantly visited by ships from all parts of
the Mediterranean, and united by great roads with the markets of
the interior, it was the common meeting-place of various characters
and classes of men.

Among those whom St. Paul met on his arrival, was the small
company of Jews above alluded to,[2] who professed the imperfect
Christianity of John the Baptist. By this time Apollos had departed to Corinth. Those ' disciples' who were now at Ephesus
were in the same religious condition in which he had been, when
Aquila and Priscilla first spoke to him, though doubtless they were
inferior to him both in learning and in zeal.[3] St. Paul found on
inquiry, that they had only received John's baptism, and that they
were ignorant of the great outpouring of the Holy Ghost, in which
the life and energy of the Church consisted.[4] They were even perplexed by his question.[5] He then pointed out, in conformity with
what had been said by John the Baptist himself, that that prophet
only preached repentance to prepare men's minds for Christ, who is
the true object of faith. On this they received Christian baptism ; [6]
and after they were baptized, the laying on of the Apostle's hands
resulted, as in all other Churches, in the miraculous gifts of Tongues
and of Prophecy.[7]

After this occurrence has been mentioned as an isolated fact, our
attention is called to the great teacher's labours in the synagogue.
Doubtless, Aquila and Priscilla were there. Though they are not
mentioned here in connection with St. Paul, we have seen them so
lately instructing Apollos (Acts xviii.), and we shall find them so
soon again sending salutations to Corinth in the Apostle's letter
from Ephesus (1 Cor. xvi.), that we cannot but believe he met his
old associates, and again experienced the benefit of their aid. It is
even probable that he again worked with them at the same trade :
for in the address to the Ephesian elders at Miletus (Acts xx. 34)
he stated that ' his own hands had ministered to his necessities,

---

[1] For the early history of the word
Asia, see pp. 182-184.

[2] Above, p. 364. See Acts xix. 1-7.

[3] It is impossible to know whether
these men were connected with Apollos. The whole narrative seems to
imply that they were in a lower state
of religious knowledge than he was.

[4] See Chap. XIII.

[5] The chief difficulty here is created
by the inaccurate rendering of the
aorists in the A. V. The Apostle's

question is, ' Did ye, when ye were
baptized, receive the miraculous gifts
of the Holy Ghost ? ' The aorist is
used again in the answer. We should
compare John vii. 39.

[6] On the inference derivable from
this passage, that the name of the
Holy Ghost was used in the baptismal
formula, see p. 345.

[7] See again Chap. XIII., and the
notes below on 1 Cor.

and to those who were with him;' and in writing to the Corinthians
he says (1 Cor. iv. 11, 12), that such toil had continued 'even to
that hour.' There is no doubt that he 'reasoned' in the synagogue
at Ephesus with the same zeal and energy with which his spiritual
labours had been begun at Corinth.[1]   He had been anxiously
expected, and at first he was heartily welcomed. A preparation
for his teaching had been made by Apollos and those who instructed
him. 'For three months' Paul continued to speak boldly in the
synagogue, 'arguing and endeavouring to convince his hearers of
all that related to the kingdom of God.'[2] The hearts of some were
hardened, while others repented and believed ; and in the end the
Apostle's doctrine was publicly calumniated by the Jews before
the people.[3] On this he openly separated himself, and withdrew
the disciples from the synagogue ; and the Christian Church at
Ephesus became a distinct body, separated both from the Jews and
the Gentiles.

As the house of Justus at Corinth[4] had afforded St. Paul a refuge
from calumny, and an opportunity of continuing his public instruction, so here he had recourse to 'the school of Tyrannus,' who
was probably a teacher of philosophy or rhetoric, converted by the
Apostle to Christianity.[5] His labours in spreading the Gospel were
here continued for two whole years. For the incidents which
occurred during this residence, for the persons with whom the
Apostle became acquainted, and for the precise subjects of his
teaching, we have no letters to give us information supplementary
to the Acts, as in the cases of Thessalonica and Corinth :[6] inasmuch
as that which is called the 'Epistle to the Ephesians,' enters into
no personal or incidental details.[7] But we have, in the address to
the Ephesian elders at Miletus, an affecting picture of an Apostle's
labours for the salvation of those whom his Master came to redeem.
From that address we learn, that his voice had not been heard
within the school of Tyrannus alone, but that he had gone about
among his converts, instructing them 'from house to house,' and
warning 'each one' of them affectionately 'with tears.'[8] The
subject of his teaching was ever the same, both for Jews and Greeks,
'repentance towards God, and faith towards our Lord Jesus
Christ.'[9] Labours so incessant, so disinterested, and continued
through so long a time, could not fail to produce a great result at
Ephesus. A large Church was formed over which many presbyters
were called to preside.[10] Nor were the results confined to the city.
Throughout the province of 'Asia' the name of Christ became

---

[1] Acts xviii. 4.
[2] Acts xix. 8.
[3] 'Before the multitude,' ver. 9.
[4] Acts xviii. 7. See p. 312.
[5] Those who are apt to see a Jewish
or Talmudical reference almost everywhere, think that Tyrannus may have
been a Jew, and his 'school' a place
for theological teaching such as those
mentioned pp. 49, 50.
[6] See the chapter containing the

two Epistles to the Thessalonians, and
those which contain the two Epistles
to the Corinthians.
[7] The peculiarities of this Epistle
will be considered hereafter.
[8] Acts xx. 20, 31. Compare ver. 19.
[9] Acts xx. 21.
[10] Acts xx. 17, 'the elders of the
church,' below (ver. 28) called 'overseers.' See what is said on this subject ,p. 340.

generally known, both to the Jews and the Gentiles;[1] and doubt-less, many daughter-churches were founded, whether in the course of journeys undertaken by the Apostle himself,[2] or by means of those with whom he became acquainted,—as for instance by Epa-phras, Archippus, and Philemon, in connection with Colossæ, and its neighbour cities Hierapolis and Laodicea.[3]

It is during this interval, that one of the two characteristics of the people of Ephesus comes prominently into view. This city was renowned throughout the world for the worship of Diana, and the practice of magic. Though it was a Greek city, like Athens or Corinth, the manners of its inhabitants were half Oriental. The image of the tutelary goddess resembled an Indian idol[4] rather than the beautiful forms which crowded the Acropolis of Athens :[5] and the enemy which St. Paul had to oppose was not a vaunting philosophy, as at Corinth,[6] but a dark and Asiatic superstition. The worship of Diana and the practice of magic were closely connected together. Eustathius says, that the mysterious symbols, called 'Ephesian Letters,' were engraved on the crown, the girdle, and the feet of the goddess. These Ephesian letters or monograms have been compared by a Swedish writer to the Runic characters of the North. When pronounced, they were regarded as a charm; and were directed to be used, especially by those who were in the power of evil spirits. When written, they were carried about as amulets. Curious stories are told of their influence. Crœsus is related to have repeated the mystic syllables when on his funeral pile ; and an Ephesian wrestler is said to have always struggled successfully against an antagonist from Miletus until he lost the scroll, which before had been like a talisman. The study of these symbols was an elaborate science : and books, both numerous and costly, were compiled by its professors.[7]

This statement throws some light on the peculiar character of the miracles wrought by St. Paul at Ephesus. We are not to suppose that the Apostles were always able to work miracles at will. An influx of supernatural power was given to them, at the time, and according to the circumstances, that required it. And the character of the miracles was not always the same. They were accommodated to the peculiar forms of sin, superstition, and ignorance they were required to oppose.[8] Here, at Ephesus, St. Paul was in the face of

---

[1] 'So that all they which dwelt in Asia,' &c., Acts xix. 10. There must have been many Jews in various parts of the province.

[2] What is said of his continued residence at Ephesus by no means implies that he did not make journeys in the province.

[3] See above (p. 364, n. 2) for the arguments against supposing that St. Paul *travelled to Ephesus* by Colossæ and the valley of the Mæander. The same arguments tend to prove that he never *visited this district from Ephesus.* It is thought by many that

Epaphras was converted by St. Paul at Ephesus, and founded the church of Colossæ. See Col. i. 7, iv. 12–17; Philem. 23.

[4] See the Coin at the end of this chapter, and the description of Diana's worship in Chapter XVI.

[5] See p. 275, &c.

[6] See p. 351.

[7] The lives of Alexander of Tralles in Smith's *Dict. of Biography* and in the Biography of the U. K. Society, contain some important illustrations of Ephesian magic.

[8] The narrative of what was done

magicians, like Moses and Aaron before Pharaoh; and it is distinctly said that his miracles were 'not ordinary wonders;'[1] from which we may infer that they were different from those which he usually performed. We know, in the case of our Blessed Lord's miracles, that though the change was usually accomplished on the speaking of a word, intermediate agency was sometimes employed; as when the blind man was healed at the pool of Siloam.[2] A miracle which has a closer reference to our present subject, is that in which the hem of Christ's garment was made effectual to the healing of a poor sufferer, and the conviction of the bystanders.[3] So on this occasion garments[4] were made the means of communicating a healing power to those who were at a distance, whether they were possessed with evil spirits, or afflicted with ordinary diseases.[5] Such effects, thus publicly manifested, were a signal refutation of the charms and amulets and mystic letters of Ephesus. Yet was this no encouragement to blind superstition. When the suffering woman was healed by touching the hem of the garment, the Saviour turned round and said, 'Virtue is gone out of *me.*'[6] And here at Ephesus we are reminded that it was God who 'wrought miracles by the hands of Paul' (ver. 11), and that 'the name,' not of Paul, but 'of *the Lord Jesus,* was magnified' (ver. 17).

These miracles must have produced a great effect upon the minds of those who practised curious arts in Ephesus. Among the magicians who were then in this city, in the course of their wanderings through the East, were several Jewish exorcists.[7] This is a circumstance which need not surprise us. The stern severity with which sorcery was forbidden in the Old Testament[8] attests the early tendency of the Israelites to such practices : the Talmud bears witness to the continuance of these practices at a later period;[9] and we have already had occasion, in the course of this history, to notice the spread of Jewish magicians through various parts of the

---

by St. Paul at Ephesus should be compared with St. Peter's miracles at Jerusalem, when 'many signs and wonders were wrought among the people . . . insomuch that they brought forth the sick into the streets, and laid them on beds and couches, that at the least the shadow of Peter passing by might overshadow some of them.' —*Acts* v. 12–16.

[1] Acts xix. 11.

[2] 'He spat on the ground, and made clay of the spittle, and anointed the eyes of the blind man with the clay, and said unto him, Go, wash in the pool of Siloam.'—*John* ix. 6, 7.

[3] Matt. ix. 20. See Trench *on the Miracles*, p. 189, &c.

[4] Both the words used here are Latin. The former, *sudarium*, is that which occurs Luke xix. 20 ; John xi. 44, xx. 7, and is translated 'napkin.' The latter, *semicinctium*, denotes some such article of dress—shawl, hand-

kerchief, or apron—as is easily laid aside. Baumgarten's remarks on the significance of these miracles are well worthy of consideration. He connects the *sudaria* and *semicinctia* with St. Paul's daily labour in his own support.

[5] Acts xix. 12.

[6] Luke viii. 46. Compare vi. 19.

[7] Acts xix. 13.

[8] See Exod. xxii. 18 ; Lev. xx. 27 ; Deut. xviii. 10, 11 ; 1 Sam. xxviii. 3, 9.

[9] A knowledge of magic was a requisite qualification of a member of the Sanhedrin, that he might be able to try those who were accused of such practices. Josephus (*Ant.* xx. 7, 2) speaks of a Cyprian Jew, a sorcerer, who was a friend and companion of Felix, and who is identified by some with Simon Magus. Again (*Ant.* viii. 2, 5), he mentions certain forms of incantation used by Jewish magicians which they attributed to King Solomon.

Roman Empire.[1] It was an age of superstition and imposture—an age also in which the powers of evil manifested themselves with peculiar force. Hence we find St. Paul classing 'witchcraft' among the works of the flesh (Gal. v. 20), and solemnly warning the Galatians both in words[2] and by his letters, that they who practise it cannot inherit the kingdom of God ; and it is of such that he writes to Timothy (2 Tim. iii. 13),—that 'evil men and *seducers*[3] shall wax worse and worse, deceiving and being deceived.' This passage in St. Paul's latest letter had probably reference to that very city in which we see him now brought into opposition with Jewish sorcerers. These men, believing that the name of Jesus acted as a charm, and recognising the Apostle as a Jew like themselves, attempted his method of casting out evil spirits.[4] But He to whom the demons were subject, and who had given to His servant 'power and authority' over them (Luke ix. 1), had shame and terror in store for those who presumed thus to take His Holy Name in vain.

One specific instance is recorded, which produced disastrous consequences to those who made the attempt, and led to wide results among the general population. In the number of those who attempted to cast out evil spirits by the 'name of Jesus,' were seven brothers, sons of Sceva, who is called a high priest,[5] either because he had really held this office at Jerusalem, or because he was chief of one of the twenty-four courses of priests. But the demons, who were subject to Jesus, and by His will subject to those who preached His Gospel, treated with scorn those who used His Name without being converted to His truth. 'Jesus I recognise, and Paul I know ;[6] but who are ye ?' was the answer of the evil spirit. And straightway the man who was possessed sprang upon them, with frantic violence, so that they were utterly discomfited, and 'fled out of the house naked and wounded.'[7]

This fearful result of the profane use of that Holy Name which was proclaimed by the Apostles for the salvation of all men, soon became notorious, both among the Greeks and the Jews.[8] Consternation and alarm took possession of the minds of many ; and in proportion to this alarm the name of the Lord Jesus began to be reverenced and honoured.[9] Even among those who had given their faith to St. Paul's preaching,[10] some appear to have retained their attachment to the practice of magical arts. Their conscience was moved by what had recently occurred, and they came and made a full confession to the Apostle, and publicly acknowledged and forsook their deeds of darkness.[11]

---

[1] See p. 118, &c.

[2] Observe the phrase in ver. 21, '*as I told you in time past*,' perhaps on the very journey through Galatia which we have just had occasion to mention.

[3] The word here used is the customary term for these wandering magicians.

[4] See ver. 13.

[5] Olshausen's version, that he was merely the chief rabbi of the Ephe-

sian Jews, can hardly be a correct rendering of the term.

[6] The two verbs in the original are different.

[7] ver. 16.

[8] ver. 17.

[9] The verb is in the imperfect.

[10] It seems unnatural to take the perfect participle in any other sense than 'those who had previously believed.'

[11] 'Their deeds,' which must surely

The fear and conviction seem to have extended beyond those who made a profession of Christianity. A large number of the sorcerers themselves [1] openly renounced the practice which had been so signally condemned by a higher power; and they brought together the books [2] that contained the mystic formularies, and burnt them before all the people. When the volumes were consumed, [3] they proceeded to reckon up the price at which these manuals of enchantment would be valued. Such books, from their very nature, would be costly; and all books in that age bore a value which is far above any standard with which we are familiar. Hence we need not be surprised that the whole cost thus sacrificed and surrendered amounted to as much as two thousand pounds of English money. [4] This scene must have been long remembered at Ephesus. It was a strong proof of honest conviction on the part of the sorcerers, and a striking attestation of the triumph of Jesus Christ over the powers of darkness. The workers of evil were put to scorn, like the priests of Baal by Elijah on Mount Carmel; [5] and the teaching of the doctrine of Christ 'increased mightily and grew strong.' [6]

With this narrative of the burning of the books, we have nearly reached the term of St. Paul's three years' residence at Ephesus. [7] Before his departure, however, two important subjects demand our attention, each of which may be treated in a separate chapter :— the First Epistle to the Corinthians, with the circumstances in Achaia which led to the writing of it,—and the uproar in the Ephesian Theatre, which will be considered in connection with a description of the city, and some notice of the worship of Diana.

Coins of Ephesus. [8]

refer to the particular practices in question. The verb denotes 'to make a full confession,' as in Matt. iii. 6; Jam. v. 16.

[1] ver. 19.

[2] Literally '*their* books.'

[3] The imperfect should be noticed, as imparting a graphic character to the whole narrative. The burning and blazing of the books went on for some considerable time. Compare the instances of the burning of magical books recorded in Liv. xl. 29; Suet. *Aug.* 31; also Tac *Ann.* xiii. 50; *Agr.* 2.

[4] The 'piece of silver' mentioned here was doubtless the *drachma*, the current Greek coin of the Levant: the value was about tenpence. There can be no reason to suppose with Grotius that the *shekel* is meant.

[5] 1 Kings xviii.

[6] ver. 20.

[7] See ver. 21, which immediately follows.

[8] From Akerman's *Numismatic Illustrations*, p. 49. For the form under which Diana is represented, see below, pp. 423, 424.

CHAPTER XV.

St. Paul pays a short Visit to Corinth.—Returns to Ephesus.—Writes a Letter to the Corinthians, which is now lost.—They reply, desiring further Explanations.—State of the Corinthian Church.—St. Paul writes the *First Epistle to the Corinthians.*

WE have hitherto derived such information as we possess, concern ing the proceedings of St. Paul at Ephesus, from the narrative in the Acts ; but we must now record an occurrence which St. Luke has passed over in silence, and which we know only from a few incidental allusions in the letters of the Apostle himself. This occurrence, which probably took place not later than the beginning of the second year of St. Paul's residence at Ephesus, was a short visit which he paid to the Church at Corinth.[1]

[1] The occurrence of this visit is proved by the following passages :

(1.) 2 Cor. xii. 14. ' Now for the third time I am prepared to come to you.'

(2.) 2 Cor. xiii. 1. ' Now for the third time I am coming to you.'

If the visit after leaving Ephesus was the *third,* there must have been a *second* before it.

(3.) 2 Cor. xii. 21. ' Lest again, when I come, God should humble me, and I should grieve many of those who sinned before.' He fears lest he should *again* be humbled on visiting them, and *again* have to mourn their sins. Hence there must have been a former visit, in which he was thus humbled and made to mourn.

Paley in the *Horæ Paulinæ,* and other commentators since, have shown that these passages (though they acknowledge their most natural meaning to be in favour of an intermediate visit) may be explained away ; in the first two St. Paul *might* perhaps only have meant ' this is the third time I have *intended* to come to you ; ' and in the third passage we, may take *again* with *come* in the sense of ' on my return.' But we think that nothing but the hypothesis of an intermediate visit can explain the following passages :

(4.) 2 Cor. ii. 1. ' I decided not to come again in grief to you ' (which is the reading of every one of the Uncial manuscripts). Here it would be exceedingly unnatural to join *again* with *come*; and the feeling of this probably led to the error of the Textus Receptus.

(5.) 2 Cor. xiii. 2 (according to the reading of the best MSS.). *I have warned you formerly, and I now forewarn you, as when I was present the second time, so now while I am absent, saying to those who had sinned before that time, and to all the rest, ' If I come again, I will not spare.'*

Against these arguments Paley sets (1st) St. Luke's silence, which, however, is acknowledged by all to be inconclusive, considering that so very many of St. Paul's travels and adventures are left confessedly unrecorded in the Acts (see note on 2 Cor. xi. 23, &c.). (2ndly) The passage, 2 Cor. i. 15, 16, in which St. Paul tells the Corinthians he did not wish now to give them a '*second* benefit ; ' whence he argues that the visit then approaching would be his *second visit.* But a more careful examination of the passage shows that St. Paul is speaking of his original intention of paying them a *double visit,* on his way to Macedonia, and on his return from Macedonia.

If we had not possessed any direct information that such a visit had been made, yet in itself it would have seemed highly probable that St. Paul would not have remained three years at Ephesus without revisiting his Corinthian converts. We have already remarked[1] on the facility of communication existing between these two great cities, which were united by a continual reciprocity of commerce, and were the capitals of two peaceful provinces. And examples of the intercourse which actually took place between the Christians of the two Churches have occurred, both in the case of Aquila and Priscilla, who had migrated from the one to the other (Acts xviii. 18, 19), and in that of Apollos, concerning whom, 'when he was disposed to pass into Achaia,' 'the brethren [at Ephesus] wrote, exhorting the disciples [at Corinth] to receive him' (Acts xviii. 27). In the last chapter, some of the results of this visit of Apollos to Corinth have been noticed ; he was now probably returned to Ephesus, where we know[2] that he was remaining (and, it would seem, stationary) during the third year of St. Paul's residence in that capital. No doubt, on his return, he had much to tell of the Corinthian converts to their father in the faith,— much of joy and hope, but also much of pain, to communicate ; for there can be little doubt that those tares among the wheat, which we shall presently see in their maturer growth, had already begun to germinate, although neither Paul had planted, nor Apollos watered them. One evil at least, we know, prevailed extensively, and threatened to corrupt the whole Church of Corinth. This was nothing less than the addiction of many Corinthian Christians to those sins of impurity which they had practised in the days of their Heathenism, and which disgraced their native city, even among the Heathen. We have before mentioned the peculiar licentiousness of manners which prevailed at Corinth. So notorious was this, that it had actually passed into the vocabulary of the Greek tongue ; and the very word ' to Corinthianise,' meant ' to play the wanton ;'[3] nay, the bad reputation of the city had become proverbial, even in foreign languages, and is immortalised by the Latin poets.[4] Such being the habits in which many of the Corinthian converts had been educated, we cannot wonder if it proved most difficult to root out immorality from the rising Church. The offenders against Christian chastity were exceedingly numerous[5] at this period ; and it was especially with the object of attempting to reform them, and to check the growing mischief, that St. Paul now determined to visit Corinth.

He has himself described this visit as a painful one ;[6] he went in sorrow at the tidings he had received, and when he arrived, he found the state of things even worse than he had expected ; he tells us that it was a time of personal humiliation[7] to himself, occasioned by the flagrant sins of so many of his own converts ; he reminds the Corinthians, afterwards, how he had ' mourned '

---

[1] p. 336.
[2] 1 Cor. xvi. 12.
[3] It is so used by Aristophanes.
[4] Hor. *Ep.* i. 17.   See p. 325, n. 3.
[5] Only a part of them, who remained

unrepentant after rebuke and warning, are called 'many.'   2 Cor. xii. 21.
[6] 2 Cor. ii. 1.
[7] 2 Cor. xii. 21.

over those who had dishonoured the name of Christ by 'the uncleanness and fornication and wantonness which they had committed.'[1]

But in the midst of his grief he showed the greatest tenderness for the individual offenders ; he warned them of the heinous guilt which they were incurring ; he showed them its inconsistency with their Christian calling ;[2] he reminded them how, at their baptism, they had died to sin, and risen again unto righteousness ; but he did not at once exclude them from the Church which they had defiled. Yet he was compelled to threaten them with this penalty, if they persevered in the sins which had now called forth his rebuke. He has recorded the very words which he used. 'If I come again,' he said, ' I will not spare.'[3]

It appears probable that, on this occasion, St. Paul remained but a very short time at Corinth. When afterwards, in writing to them, he says that he does not wish ' *now* to pay them a passing visit,' he seems[4] to imply, that his last visit had deserved that epithet. Moreover, had it occupied a large portion of the ' space of three years,' which he describes himself to have spent at Ephesus (Acts xx. 31), he would probably have expressed himself differently in that part of his address to the Ephesian presbyters ;[5] and a long visit could scarcely have failed to furnish more allusions in the Epistles so soon after written to Corinth. The silence of St. Luke also, which is easily explained on the supposition of a short visit, would be less natural had St. Paul been long absent from Ephesus, where he appears, from the narrative in the Acts, to be stationary during all this period.

On these grounds, we suppose that the Apostle, availing himself of the constant maritime intercourse between the two cities, had gone by sea to Corinth ; and that he now returned to Ephesus by the same route (which was very much shorter than that by land), after spending a few days or weeks at Corinth.

But his censures and warnings had produced too little effect upon his converts ; his mildness had been mistaken for weakness ; his hesitation in punishing had been ascribed to a fear of the offenders ; and it was not long before he received new intelligence that the profligacy which had infected the community was still increasing. Then it was that he felt himself compelled to resort to harsher measures ; he wrote an Epistle (which has not been preserved to us)[6] in which, as we learn from himself, he ordered the

[1] 2 Cor. xii. 21.

[2] There can be no doubt that he urged upon them the same arguments which he was afterwards obliged to repeat at 1 Cor. vi. 15.

[3] 2 Cor. xiii. 2.

[4] 1 Cor. xvi. 7. Yet this admits of another explanation ; for perhaps he only meant to say, ' I will not *now* (at once) come to you (by the direct route) on my way to Macedonia for a passing visit,' &c.

[5] Wieseler, however, gets over this,

by supposing that when St. Paul mentions *three years* spent among his hearers, he means to address not only the Ephesian presbyters whom he had summoned, but also the companions of his voyage (Acts xx. 4) who had been with him in Macedonia and Achaia.

[6] In proof of this, see the note on 1 Cor. v. 9–12. This lost Epistle must have been written *after* his second visit ; otherwise he need not have explained it in the passage referred to.

Christians of Corinth, by virtue of his Apostolic authority, ' to cease from all intercourse with fornicators.' By this he meant, as he subsequently explained his injunctions, to direct the exclusion of all profligates from the Church. The Corinthians, however, either did not understand this, or (to excuse themselves) they affected not to do so, for they asked, how it was possible for them to abstain from all intercourse with the profligate, unless they entirely secluded themselves from all the business of life, which they had to transact with their Heathen neighbours. Whether the lost Epistle contained any other topics, we cannot know with certainty; but we may conclude with some probability that it was very short, and directed to this one subject; [1] otherwise it is not easy to understand why it should not have been preserved together with the two subsequent Epistles.

Soon after this short letter had been dispatched, Timotheus, accompanied by Erastus, [2] left Ephesus for Macedonia. St. Paul desired him, if possible, to continue his journey to Corinth; but did not feel certain that it would be possible for him to do so [3] consistently with the other objects of his journey, which probably had reference to the great collection now going on for the poor Hebrew Christians at Jerusalem.

Meantime, some members of the household of Chloe, a distinguished Christian family at Corinth, arrived at Ephesus; and from them St. Paul received fuller information than he before possessed of the condition of the Corinthian Church. The spirit of party had seized upon its members, and well nigh destroyed Christian love. We have already seen in our general view of the divisions of the Apostolic Church, that the great parties which then divided the Christian world had ranked themselves under the names of different Apostles, whom they attempted to set up against each other as rival leaders. At Corinth, as in other places, emissaries had arrived from the Judaisers of Palestine, who boasted of their ' letters of commendation' from the metropolis of the faith; they did not, however, attempt, as yet, to insist upon circumcision, as we shall find them doing successfully among the simpler population of Galatia. This would have been hopeless in a great and civilised community like that of Corinth, imbued with Greek feelings of contempt for what they would have deemed a barbarous superstition. Here, therefore, the Judaisers confined themselves, in the first instance, to personal attacks against St. Paul, whose apostleship they denied, whose motives they calumniated, and whose authority they persuaded the Corinthians to repudiate. Some of them declared themselves the followers of 'Cephas,' whom the Lord Himself had selected to be the chief Apostle; others (probably the more

---

[1] Probably it was in this lost letter that he gave them notice of his intention to visit them on his way to Macedonia; for altering which he was so much blamed by his opponents.

[2] Erastus was probably the ' treasurer' of the city of Corinth, mentioned Rom. xvi. 23, and 2 Tim. iv. 20; and therefore was most likely proceeding at any rate to Corinth.

[3] Timotheus apparently did not reach Corinth on this occasion, or the fact would have been mentioned 2 Cor. xii. 18.

extreme members of the party)[1] boasted of their own immediate
connection with Christ Himself, and their intimacy with 'the
brethren of the Lord,' and especially with James, the head of the
Church at Jerusalem. The endeavours of these agitators to undermine the influence of the Apostle of the Gentiles met with unde-
served success ; and they gained over a strong party to their side.
Meanwhile, those who were still stedfast to the doctrines of St. Paul,
yet were not all unshaken in their attachment to his person : a
portion of them preferred the Alexandrian learning with which
Apollos had enforced his preaching, to the simple style of their
first teacher, who had designedly abstained, at Corinth, from
anything like philosophical argumentation.[2] This party, then, who
sought to form for themselves a philosophical Christianity, called
themselves the followers of Apollos ; although the latter, for his
part, evidently disclaimed the rivalry with St. Paul which was thus
implied, and even refused to revisit Corinth,[3] lest he should seem
to countenance the factious spirit of his adherents.

It is not impossible that the Antinomian Free-thinkers, whom we
have already seen to form so dangerous a portion of the Primitive
Church, attached themselves to this last-named party; at any rate,
they were, at this time, one of the worst elements of evil at Corinth:
they put forward a theoretic defence of the practical immorality in
which they lived; and some of them had so lost the very foundation
of Christian faith as to deny the resurrection of the dead, and thus
to adopt the belief as well as the sensuality of their Epicurean
neighbours, whose motto was 'Let us eat and drink, for to-morrow
we die.'

A crime recently committed by one of these pretended Christians, was now reported to St. Paul, and excited his utmost abhorrence : a member of the Corinthian Church was openly living in
incestuous intercourse with his step-mother, and that, during his
father's life; yet this audacious offender was not excluded from the
Church.

Nor were these the only evils : some Christians were showing
their total want of brotherly love by bringing vexatious actions
against their brethren in the Heathen courts of law; others were
turning even the spiritual gifts which they had received from the
Holy Ghost into occasions of vanity and display, not unaccompanied
by fanatical delusion ; the decent order of Christian worship was
disturbed by the tumultuary claims of rival ministrations ; women
had forgotten the modesty of their sex, and came forward, unveiled
(contrary to the habit of their country), to address the public
assembly; and even the sanctity of the Holy Communion itself was
profaned by scenes of revelling and debauch.

About the same time that all this disastrous intelligence was
brought to St. Paul by the household of Chloe, other messengers
arrived from Corinth, bearing the answer of the Church to his
previous letter, of which (as we have mentioned above) they requested an explanation ; and at the same time referring to his
decision several questions which caused dispute and difficulty.

---

[1] See above, pp. 349, 350.   [2] 1 Cor. ii. 1–5.   [3] 1 Cor. xvi. 12.

These questions related—1st, To the controversies respecting meat which had been offered to idols ; 2ndly, To the disputes regarding celibacy and matrimony; the right of divorce ; and the perplexities which arose in the case of mixed marriages, where one of the parties was an unbeliever : 3rdly, To the exercise of spiritual gifts in the public assemblies of the Church.

St. Paul hastened to reply to these questions, and at the same time to denounce the sins which had polluted the Corinthian Church, and almost annulled its right to the name of Christian. The letter which he was thus led to write is addressed, not only to this metropolitan Church, but also to the Christian communities established in other places in the same province,[1] which might be regarded as dependencies of that in the capital city; hence we must infer that these Churches also had been infected by some of the errors or vices which had prevailed at Corinth. The letter is, in its contents, the most diversified of all St. Paul's Epistles ; and in proportion to the variety of its topics, is the depth of its interest for ourselves. For by it we are introduced, as it were, behind the scenes of the Apostolic Church, and its minutest features are revealed to us under the light of daily life. We see the picture of a Christian congregation as it met for worship in some upper chamber, such as the house of Aquila, or of Gaius, could furnish. We see that these seasons of pure devotion were not unalloyed by human vanity and excitement ; yet, on the other hand, we behold the Heathen auditor pierced to the heart by the inspired eloquence of the Christian prophets, the secrets of his conscience laid bare to him, and himself constrained to fall down on his face and worship God ; we hear the fervent thanksgiving echoed by the unanimous Amen ; we see the administration of the Holy Communion terminating the feast of love. Again we become familiar with the perplexities of domestic life, the corrupting proximity of Heathen immorality, the lingering superstition, the rash speculation, the lawless perversion of Christian liberty; we witness the strife of theological factions, the party names, the sectarian animosities. We perceive the difficulty of the task imposed upon the Apostle, who must guard from so many perils, and guide through so many difficulties, his children in the faith, whom else he had begotten in vain ; and we learn to appreciate more fully the magnitude of that laborious responsibility under which he describes himself as almost ready to sink, 'the care of all the Churches.'

But while we rejoice that so many details of the deepest historical interest have been preserved to us by this Epistle, let us not forget to thank God who so inspired His Apostle, that in his answers to questions of transitory interest he has laid down principles of eternal obligation.[2] Let us trace with gratitude the providence of Him,

---

[1] See the translation of 1 Cor. ii. 2, and the note. Also p. 319.

[2] The contrast between the short-lived interest of the questions referred to him for solution, and the eternal principles by which they must be solved, was brought prominently before the mind of the Apostle himself by the Holy Spirit, under whose guidance he wrote ; and he has expressed it in those sublime words which might serve as a motto for the whole Epistle (1 Cor. vii. 29–31).

who 'out of darkness calls up light;' by whose mercy it was provided that the unchastity of the Corinthians should occasion the sacred laws of moral purity to be established for ever through the Christian world;—that their denial of the resurrection should cause those words to be recorded whereon reposes, as upon a rock that cannot be shaken, our sure and certain hope of immortality.

The following is a translation of the Epistle, which was written at Easter, in the third year of St. Paul's residence at Ephesus:—

FIRST EPISTLE TO THE CORINTHIANS.[1]

i. 1 PAUL, a called Apostle of Jesus Christ by the will Salutation.
2   of God, and Sosthenes [2] the Brother, TO THE CHURCH OF GOD AT CORINTH, hallowed in Christ Jesus, called Saints; [3] together with all [4] who call upon the name of Jesus Christ our

---

[1] The date of this Epistle can be fixed with more precision than that of any other. It gives us the means of ascertaining, not merely the year, but even (with great probability) the month and week, in which it was written.

(1) Apollos had been working at Corinth, and was now with St. Paul at Ephesus (1 Cor. i. 12; iii. 4, 22; iv. 6; xvi. 12). This was the case during St. Paul's residence at Ephesus (Acts xix. 1).

(2) He wrote during *the days of unleavened bread*, i.e. at Easter (1 Cor. v. 7: see the note on that passage), and intended to remain at Ephesus till Pentecost (xvi. 8, cf. xv. 32). After leaving Ephesus, he purposed to come by Macedonia to Achaia (xvi. 5–7). This was the route he took (Acts xx. 1, 2) on leaving Ephesus after the tumult in the theatre.

(3) Aquila and Priscilla were with him at Ephesus (xvi. 19). They had taken up their residence at Ephesus before the visit of St. Paul (Acts xviii. 26).

(4) The Great Collection was going on in Achaia (xvi. 1–3). When he wrote to the Romans from Corinth during his three months' visit there (Acts xx. 3), the collection was completed in Macedonia and Achaia (Rom. xv. 26).

(5) He hopes to go by Corinth to Jerusalem, and thence to Rome (xvi,

4, and xv. 25–28.) Now the time when he entertained this very purpose was towards the conclusion of his long Ephesian residence (Acts xix. 21).

(6) He had sent Timothy towards Corinth (iv. 17), but not direct (xvi. 10). Now it was at the close of his Ephesian residence (Acts xix. 22) that he sent Timothy with Erastus (the Corinthian) from Ephesus to Macedonia, which was one way to Corinth, but not the shortest.

[2] Sosthenes is, perhaps, the same mentioned Acts xviii. 17.

[3] The sense of the word for 'Saints' in the New Testament is nearly equivalent to the modern 'Christians;' but it would be an anachronism so to translate it here, since (in the time of St. Paul) the word 'Christian' was only used as a term of reproach. The objection to translating it 'saints' is, that the idea now often conveyed by that term is different from the meaning of the Greek word as used by St. Paul. Yet as no other English word represents it better, either the old rendering must be retained, or an awkward periphrasis employed. The English reader should bear in mind that St. Paul applies the term to all members of the Church.

[4] This is added to comprehend those Christians of the Church of Achaia who were not resident at Corinth, but in the neighbouring places of the same province. Compare 2 Cor. i. 1.

Lord in every place which is their home—and our home also.[1]

Grace be unto you and peace, from God our i. 3 Father, and from our Lord Jesus Christ.

I[2] thank my God continually on your behalf, for 4 the grace of God given unto you in Christ Jesus. Because, in Him, you were[3] every-wise enriched 5 with all the gifts of speech and knowledge, (for thus 6 my testimony to Christ was confirmed among you), so that you come behind no other church in any 7 gift; looking earnestly for the time when our Lord Jesus Christ shall be revealed to sight.[4]

And He also will confirm[5] you unto the end, that 8 you may be without reproach at the day of our Lord Jesus Christ. For God is faithful, by whom you 9 were called into fellowship with His Son, Jesus Christ, our Lord.

I exhort you, brethren, by the name of our Lord 10 Jesus Christ, to shun disputes, and have no divisions among you, but to be knit together in the same mind, and the same judgment.[6] For I have been 11 informed concerning you, my brethren, by the members of Chloe's household, that there are contentions among you. I mean, that one of you says, ' I am a 12 follower of Paul;' another, ' I of Apollos;' another, ' I of Cephas;'[7] another, ' I of Christ.' Is Christ 13

---

[1] The Authorised Version here appears scarcely reconcilable with the order of the Greek, though it is defended by the opinions of Chrysostom, Billroth, Olshausen, &c. The translation of Meyer, '*in every place under their and our dominion,*' seems more like a Papal than an Apostolic rescript; and that of De Wette, '*in every place both of their and our abode,*' is frigid. and adds nothing to the idea of 'every place.' St. Paul means to say that *he feels the home of his converts to be also his own.* Both sentiment and expression are the same as in Rom. xvi. 13 : ' His mother and mine.'

[2] Observe how ' I thank' and ' my' follow immediately after ' Paul and Sosthenes,' showing that, though the salutation runs in the name of both, the author of the Epistle was St. Paul alone. Compare the remarks on 1 Thess. i. 2.

[3] In this passage the aorists are here translated as aorists. But as the distinction between the aorist and perfect is by no means constantly observed in St. Paul's Hellenistic Greek, it may be doubted whether the aorists here are not used for perfects.

[4] See note on Rom. ii. 5.

[5] i.e. *He will do His part* to confirm you unto the end. If you fall, it will not be for want of His help.

[6] ' Mind' refers to the view taken by the understanding; 'judgment' to the practical decision arrived at.

[7] *Cephas* is the name by which St. Peter is called throughout this Epistle. It was the actual word used by our Lord Himself, and remained the Apostle's usual appellation among the Jewish Christians up to this time. It is strange that it should afterwards have been so entirely supplanted by its Greek equivalent, ' Peter,' even among the Jewish Christians. See

divided ? Was Paul crucified for you ? or were you
i, 14 baptized unto the name of Paul ? I thank God that
I baptized none of you except Crispus and Gaius [1]
15 (lest any one should say that I baptized unto my
16 own name) ; and I baptized also the household of
Stephanas ; besides these I know not that I baptized
17 any other. For Christ sent me forth as His Apostle,[2]
not to baptize, but to publish the Glad-tidings ; and
that, not with wisdom of word, lest thereby the
18 cross of Christ should be made void.[3] For the word
of the cross,[4] to those in the way of perdition, is
folly ; but to us in the way of salvation,[5] it is the
19 power of God. And so it is written, '𝕴 𝖜𝖎𝖑𝖑 𝖉𝖊𝖘𝖙𝖗𝖔𝖞
𝖙𝖍𝖊 𝖜𝖎𝖘𝖉𝖔𝖒 𝖔𝖋 𝖙𝖍𝖊 𝖜𝖎𝖘𝖊, 𝖆𝖓𝖉 𝖇𝖗𝖎𝖓𝖌 𝖙𝖔 𝖓𝖔𝖙𝖍𝖎𝖓𝖌 𝖙𝖍𝖊 𝖚𝖓𝖉𝖊𝖗-
20 𝖘𝖙𝖆𝖓𝖉𝖎𝖓𝖌 𝖔𝖋 𝖙𝖍𝖊 𝖕𝖗𝖚𝖉𝖊𝖓𝖙.'[6] Where is the Philosopher ?
Where is the Rabbi ? Where is the reasoner of this
world ?[7] Has not God turned the world's wisdom
21 into folly ? for when the world had failed to gain by
its wisdom the knowledge of God in the wisdom of
God, it pleased God, by the folly of our preaching,[8]
22 to save those who believe.[9] For the Jews require a
sign [from heaven], and the Greeks demand philo-
23 sophy ; but we[10] proclaim a Messiah crucified, to the
Jews a stumbling-block, and to the Greeks a folly ;
24 but to the called[11] themselves, whether they be Jews
or Greeks, Christ the power of God, and the wisdom
25 of God. For the folly of God is wiser than man's
wisdom, and the weakness of God is stronger than
26 man's strength. For you see, brethren, how God
has called you ; how few of you are wise in earthly

note on Gal. i. 18. For an explanation of the parties here alluded to, see
pp. 348-353.

[1] Or Caius, if we use the Roman
spelling ; see p. 313.

[2] The verb involves this.

[3] Compare the use of the same verb
in Rom. iv. 14.

[4] i.e. the tidings of *a crucified Messiah.*

[5] For the present participle we may
refer to Acts ii. 47, and to ii. 6 below.
In rendering the participles here,
'already dead,' and 'already saved,'
Prof. Stanley neglects the force of the
tense. [This is corrected in the 2nd
edition. H.]

[6] Isa. xxix. 14 ; not quite literally
quoted from the LXX.

[7] There are two words in the N. T.
translated 'world' in the A. V. That
which is used here involves the notion
of *transitory duration.* So in English
we speak of 'the notions (or spirit) of
the age.' Also in this expression is
contained a reference to 'the future
age,' the period of the final triumph of
Christ's kingdom.

[8] [Or, more correctly, 'that which
we preach,' viz. the Gospel, which
men deem folly. H.]

[9] Observe that the participle here is
present, not past.

[10] *We,* including St. Paul and the
other preachers of Christianity.

[11] All who make an outward profession of Christianity are, in St. Paul's
language, 'the called.' They have
received a message from God, which
has called them to enter into His
church.

wisdom, how few are powerful, how few are noble.
But the world's folly, God has chosen, to confound i. 27
its wisdom; and the world's weakness God has
chosen, to confound its strength; and the world's base 28
things, and things despised, yea, things that have no
being, God has chosen, to bring to nought the things
that be; that no flesh should glory in His presence. 29
But you are His children[1] in Christ Jesus, whom 30
God sent unto us as our wisdom,[2] and righteousness,
and sanctification, and redemption; that it might be
according as it is written, ' 𝔥𝔢 𝔱𝔥𝔞𝔱 𝔟𝔬𝔞𝔰𝔱𝔢𝔱𝔥, 𝔩𝔢𝔱 𝔥𝔦𝔪 31
𝔟𝔬𝔞𝔰𝔱 𝔦𝔫 𝔱𝔥𝔢 𝔏𝔬𝔯𝔡.' [3]

In his own teaching he had not aimed at establishing reputation for philosophy or eloquence, but had relied on the supernatural power and wisdom which belongs to the Spirit of God.

So, brethren, when I myself came among you, and ii. 1
declared to you the testimony of God, I came not
with surpassing skill of speech, or wisdom.   For no 2
knowledge did I purpose to display among you, but
the knowledge of Jesus Christ alone, and Him[4]—
crucified.   And in my intercourse with you, I was 3
filled with weakness and fear and much trembling.[5]
And when I proclaimed my message, I used not per- 4
suasive words of human wisdom, but showed forth 5
the working of God's Spirit and power, that your
faith might have its foundation not in the wisdom of
men, but in the power of God.

Nevertheless, among those who are ripe in under- 6
standing,[6] I speak wisdom; albeit not the wisdom of
this world, nor of its rulers, who will soon be nought.[7]
But it is God's wisdom that I speak, whereof the 7
secret is made known to His people;[8] even the

---

[1] 'Of Him.'

[2] Literally, *who became wisdom to us from God,* the preposition implying ' *sent from.*'

[3] Jerem. ix. 23, 24, from the LXX., but not literally. Quoted also 2 Cor. x. 17; see note there.

[4] i.e. Him, not exalted on the earthly throne of David, but condemned to the death of the vilest malefactor.

[5] St. Paul appears, on his first coming to Corinth, to have been suffering under great depression, perhaps caused by the bodily malady to which he was subject (cf. 2 Cor. xii. 8; see p. 210), perhaps by the ill success of his efforts at Athens. See p. 298.
The expression 'fear and trembling' is peculiarly Pauline, being used in four of St. Paul's Epistles,

and by no other writer in the New Testament. It does not mean *fear of personal danger*, but *a trembling anxiety to perform a duty.* Thus in Eph. vi. 5, slaves are charged to obey their masters thus, and this *anxious conscientiousness* is opposed to ' eye-service.'

[6] 'The perfect' is St. Paul's expression for those who had attained the maturity of Christian wisdom. Compare 1 Cor. xiv. 20, and Phil. iii. 15. Such men could understand that his teaching was in truth the highest philosophy.

[7] Literally, 'passing away into nothingness.'

[8] ' Wisdom in a mystery,' is a wisdom revealed to the *initiated*, i.e. (in this case) to Christians; but hidden from the rest of the world.

hidden wisdom which God ordained before the ages,
ii. 8 that we might be glorified thereby. But the rulers
of this world knew it not; for had they known it,
they would not have crucified the Lord of Glory.
9 But as it is written, '𝕰𝖞𝖊 𝖍𝖆𝖙𝖍 𝖓𝖔𝖙 𝖘𝖊𝖊𝖓, 𝖓𝖔𝖗 𝖊𝖆𝖗
𝖍𝖊𝖆𝖗𝖉, 𝖓𝖊𝖎𝖙𝖍𝖊𝖗 𝖍𝖆𝖇𝖊 𝖊𝖓𝖙𝖊𝖗𝖊𝖉 𝖎𝖓𝖙𝖔 𝖙𝖍𝖊 𝖍𝖊𝖆𝖗𝖙 𝖔𝖋 𝖒𝖆𝖓, 𝖙𝖍𝖊
𝖙𝖍𝖎𝖓𝖌𝖘 𝖜𝖍𝖎𝖈𝖍 𝕲𝖔𝖉 𝖍𝖆𝖙𝖍 𝖕𝖗𝖊𝖕𝖆𝖗𝖊𝖉 𝖋𝖔𝖗 𝖙𝖍𝖊𝖒 𝖙𝖍𝖆𝖙 𝖑𝖔𝖇𝖊
10 𝕳𝖎𝖒.'[1] Yet to us[2] God has revealed them by His
Spirit. For the Spirit fathoms all things, even the
11 depths of God. For who can know what belongs to
man but the spirit of man which is within him?
even so none can know what belongs to God, but
12 the Spirit of God alone. Now we have received,
not the spirit of the world, but the Spirit which is of
God; that we might understand those things which
have been freely given us by God.
13 These are the things whereof we speak, in words
not taught by man's wisdom, but by the Spirit;
14 explaining spiritual things to spiritual[3] men. But
the natural[4] man rejects the teaching of God's Spirit,
for to him it is folly; and he cannot comprehend it,
15 because it is spiritually discerned. But the spiritual
man judges all things truly, yet cannot himself be
16 truly judged by others. For '𝖂𝖍𝖔 𝖍𝖆𝖙𝖍 𝖐𝖓𝖔𝖜𝖓 𝖙𝖍𝖊
𝖒𝖎𝖓𝖉 𝖔𝖋 𝖙𝖍𝖊 𝕷𝖔𝖗𝖉 𝖙𝖍𝖆𝖙 𝖍𝖊 𝖘𝖍𝖔𝖚𝖑𝖉 𝖎𝖓𝖘𝖙𝖗𝖚𝖈𝖙 𝕳𝖎𝖒?'[5] but
we have the mind of the Lord[6] [within us].

iii. 1 And I, brethren, could not speak to you as spiritual
2 men, but as carnal, yea, as babes in Christ. I fed
you with milk, and not with meat; for you were not
3 able to bear it; nay, you are not yet able, for you are
still carnal. For while you are divided amongst
yourselves by jealousy, and strife, and factious parties, is it not evident that you are carnal, and walking
4 in the ways of men? When one says, 'I follow

The party which claimed to be 'the spiritual' are proved to be carnal by their dissensions.

[1] Isaiah lxiv. 4 is the nearest passage to this in the Old Testament.
The quotation is not to be found anywhere exactly.

[2] *Us*, including all the inspired
Christian teachers, and the rest of the
'perfect.'

[3] Compare iii. 1. It should be observed that this verb is often used by
LXX. for *explain, interpret*, as at Gen.
xl. 8.

[4] Properly man considered as endowed with the *anima* (the living

principle), as distinguished from the
spiritual principle. See Juv. *Sat.* xv.
148. Etymologically speaking, *the
animal man* would be the best translation; but to English readers this
would convey a harsher meaning than
the original.

[5] Isaiah xl. 13 (LXX.), quoted also
Rom. xi. 34.

[6] The best MSS. are divided between the readings of 'Christ' and
'Lord' here.

Paul,' and another ' I follow Apollos,' can you deny that you are carnal?

It is a contradiction in terms to make Christian teachers the leaders of opposing parties. Nature of their work.

Who then is Paul, or who is Apollos? what are iii. 5 they but servants, by whose ministration you believed? and was it not the Lord who gave to each of 6 them the measure of his success? I planted, Apollos watered; but it was God who made the seed to grow. So that he who plants is nothing, nor he who waters, 7 but God alone who gives the growth. But the 8 planter and the waterer are one together;[1] and each will receive his own wages according to his work. For we are God's fellow-labourers,[2] and you are 9 God's husbandry. You are God's building; God 10 gave me the gift of grace whereby like a skilful architect I laid a foundation; and on this foundation another builds; but let each take heed what he builds thereon—[' thereon,' I say,] for other founda- 11 tion can no man lay, than that already laid, which is JESUS CHRIST.[3] But on this foundation one may 12 raise gold, and silver, and precious stones; another, wood, hay, and stubble.[4] But each man's work will 13 be made manifest; for The Day[5] will make it known; because that day will be revealed with fire, and the fire will test each builder's work. He whose build- 14 ing stands unharmed, shall receive payment for his labour; he whose work is burned down, shall forfeit 15 his reward: yet he shall not himself be destroyed; but shall be saved as it were through the flames.

The Church is God's temple.

Know[6] ye not that you are God's temple, and that 16 you form a shrine wherein God's Spirit dwells? If 17 any man ruin the temple of God, God shall ruin[7] him; for the temple of God is holy; and holy[8] therefore are ye.

---

[1] 'And therefore cannot be set against each other' is implied.

[2] This remarkable expression is used by St. Paul more than once. Compare 2 Cor. vi. 1, and the note on 1 Thess. iii. 2.

[3] The MSS. vary here, but the same sense is virtually involved in all three readings; viz. that the Messiahship of Jesus was the foundation of the teaching of the Apostles.

[4] [The image becomes much more vivid, if we remember the contrasted buildings of an ancient city,—the sumptuous edifices of granite and marble, with ornaments of gold and silver, on the one hand, and the hovels of the poor on the other, with walls of wood and roof of thatch, and interstices stuffed with straw. See the description of Rome below, Chap. XXIII. H.]

[5] ' *The Day of Christ's coming.*' Compare 1 Thess. v. 4.

[6] The connection with what precedes is ' In calling you God's building, I tell you no new thing; you know already that you are God's temple.'

[7] The verbal link is lost in the A. V.

[8] Not ' *which temple* ' (A. V.).

iii. 18 Let none deceive himself; if any man is held wise ^{Intellectual} among you in the wisdom of this world, let him ^{party spirit} make himself a fool [in the world's judgment], that ^{christian.}

19 so he may become wise. For the wisdom of this world is foolishness with God, as it is written, '𝔥𝔢 𝔱𝔞𝔨𝔢𝔱𝔥 𝔱𝔥𝔢 𝔴𝔦𝔰𝔢 𝔦𝔫 𝔱𝔥𝔢𝔦𝔯 𝔬𝔴𝔫 𝔠𝔯𝔞𝔣𝔱𝔦𝔫𝔢𝔰𝔰.'[1] And again,

20 '𝔗𝔥𝔢 𝔏𝔬𝔯𝔡 𝔨𝔫𝔬𝔴𝔢𝔱𝔥 𝔱𝔥𝔢 𝔱𝔥𝔬𝔲𝔤𝔥𝔱𝔰 𝔬𝔣 𝔱𝔥𝔢 𝔴𝔦𝔰𝔢 𝔱𝔥𝔞𝔱 𝔱𝔥𝔢𝔶

21 𝔞𝔯𝔢 𝔳𝔞𝔦𝔫.'[2] Therefore let none of you make his boast

22 in men;[3] for all things are yours; both Paul and Apollos, and Cephas, and the whole world itself; both life and death, things present and things to

23 come—all are yours—but[4] you are Christ's; and Christ is God's.

iv. 1 Let us be accounted as servants of Christ, and ^{Christ's}

2 stewards of the mysteries of God.[5] Moreover, it is ^{Apostles are only stewards;}

3 required in a steward to be found faithful.[6] Yet to ^{that which they adminis-} me it matters nothing that I be judged by you or by ^{ter is not their own.} the doom[7] of man; nay, I judge not even myself.

4 For although I know not that I am guilty of unfaith- fulness, yet this does not justify me; but I must be

5 tried by the judgment of the Lord. Therefore judge nothing hastily, until the coming of the Lord; for He shall bring to light the secrets of darkness, and make manifest the counsels of men's hearts; and then shall each receive his due[8] praise from God.

6 But these things, brethren, I have represented ^{Contrast be-} under the persons of myself and Apollos, for your ^{tween the self exalta-} sakes; that by considering us you might learn not ^{tion of the pseudo-philo-} to think of yourselves above that which has been ^{sophical party and the abase-} written,[9] and that you may cease to puff yourselves ^{ment of Christ's Apostles.}

---

[1] Job v. 13, from LXX., with an im- material variation.

[2] Ps. xciv. 11, from LXX., with a slight change.

[3] The meaning is, 'Boast not of having this man or that as your leader; for all the Apostles, nay, all things in the universe, are ordained by God to co-operate for your good.'

[4] All things work together for the good of Christians; all things con- spire to do them service: but their work is to do Christ's service, even as He Himself came to do the will of His Father.

[5] *Mysteries* are *secrets revealed* (i.e. the Glad-tidings of Christ) *to the initiated*, i.e. to all Christians. See note on ii. 7. The metaphor here is,

that as a steward dispensed his mas- ter's bread to his fellow-servants, so Paul, Peter, and Apollos dispensed the knowledge of Christ to their brethren.

[6] [Or rather, 'Inquiry is made into a steward's conduct, in order that he may be proved faithful.' H.]

[7] This use of 'day' is peculiar to St. Paul; so that Jerome calls it a *Cilicism.* It is connected with that above (iii. 18), and occurs 1 Thess. v. 4.

[8] '*His* praise.' The error in A. V. was caused by not observing the article.

[9] This is ambiguous; the phrase is commonly employed in reference to the Old Testament; but here it suits

up in the cause [1] of one against another. For who iv. 7
makes thee to differ from another? what hast thou
that thou didst not receive? and how then canst
thou boast, as if thou hadst won it for thyself? But 8
ye forsooth have already eaten to the full [of spiritual
food], ye are already rich, ye have seated yourselves
upon your throne, and have no need [2] of me. Would
that you were indeed enthroned, that I too might 9
reign with you.   For,[3] I think, God has set forth us
the Apostles last of all, like criminals condemned to
die, to be gazed at in a theatre [4] by the whole world,
both men and angels.   We for Christ's sake are 10
fools, while you are wise in Christ; we are weak,
while you are strong; you are honourable, while we
are outcasts; even to the present hour we bear 11
hunger and thirst, and nakedness and stripes, and
have no certain dwelling place, and toil with our 12
own hands; curses we meet with blessings, persecution with patience, railings with good words.   We 13
have been made as it were the refuse of the earth,
the off-scouring of all things, unto this day.   I write 14
not thus to reproach you, but as a father I chide the
children whom I love.   For though you may have 15
ten thousand guardians [5] to lead you towards the
school of Christ, you can have but one father; and it
was I who begat you in Christ Jesus, by the Glad-
tidings which I brought.   I beseech you, therefore, 16
become followers of me.

Mission of
Timotheus;
warning to
the disobe-
dient faction
at Corinth.

For this cause I have sent to you Timotheus, my 17
beloved son, a faithful servant of the Lord, who shall
put you in remembrance of my ways in Christ, as I
teach everywhere in all the churches.   Now some 18
have been filled with arrogance, supposing that I am
not coming to you.   But I shall be with you shortly, 19

better with the context to take it as
referring to the preceding remarks of
St. Paul himself.
   [1] St. Paul probably means 'in the
cause of your party-leaders;' but
speaks with intentional indistinctness.
   [2] 'Without us.'
   [3] The connection is, 'The lot of an
Apostle is no kingly lot.'
   [4] Literally, *because we have been
made a theatrical spectacle.* Compare
Heb. x. 33. The spectacle to which
St. Paul here alludes was common in
those times. Criminals condemned to
death were exhibited for the amusement of the populace on the arena of
the amphitheatre, and forced to fight
with wild beasts, or to slay one another as gladiators. These criminals
were exhibited at the end of the spectacle as an exciting termination to the
entertainment ('set forth last of all').
So Tertullian paraphrases the passage
'*Nos Deus Apostolos novissimos elegit
velut bestiarios.*'
   [5] *The guardian slave who led the
child to school.* The word is the
same as in Gal. iii. 24. See the note
there.

if the Lord will; and then I shall learn, not the word
iv. 20 of these boasters, but their might. For mighty deeds,
not empty words, are the tokens of God's kingdom.

21 What is your desire? Must I come to you with the
rod, or in love and the spirit of meekness?

v. 1   It is reported that there is fornication generally[1] Judgment on
among you, and such fornication, as is not known[2] the incestuous
even among the Heathen, so that one among you has
2 his father's wife. And you forsooth have been puffed
up when you should have mourned, that the doer of
this deed might be put away from the midst of you.
3 For me—being present with you in spirit, although
absent in body,—I have already passed sentence, as
though present, on him who has done this thing;
4 [and I decree] in the name of our Lord Jesus Christ,
that you convene an assembly, and when you, and
my spirit with you, are gathered together, with the
5 power of our Lord Jesus Christ, that you deliver
over to Satan[3] the man who has thus sinned, for the
destruction of his fleshly lusts, that his spirit may be
6 saved in the day of the Lord Jesus. Unseemly is
your boasting; know ye not that 'a little leaven
7 leaveneth the whole lump?'[4] Cast out therefore
the old leaven, that you may be an untainted mass,
even as now[5] you are without taint of leaven; for

[1] The adverb seems most naturally joined with 'among you,' but it may be taken with 'reported' in the sense of '*universally*;' so Prof. Stanley, 'There is nothing heard of except this.'

[2] The 'is named' of T. R. is omitted by the best MSS.; 'is heard of,' or something equivalent, must be supplied.

[3] This expression appears used as equivalent to *casting out of the Church:* cf. 1 Tim. i. 20. From the following words there seems also a reference to the doctrine that Satan is the author of bodily disease. Compare 2 Cor. xii. 7.

[4] The same proverb is quoted Gal. v. 9.

[5] In spite of the opinion of some eminent modern commentators, which is countenanced by Chrysostom, we must adhere to the interpretation which considers these words as written at the Paschal season, and suggested by it. The words *leaven, lump, Paschal Lamb,* and *feast* all agree most naturally with this view. It has been objected, that St. Paul would not address the Co-

rinthians as engaged in a feast which he, at Ephesus, was celebrating; because it would be over before his letter could reach them. Any one who has ever written a birthday letter to a friend in India will see the weakness of this objection. It has also been urged that he would not address a mixed church of Jews and Gentiles as engaged in the celebration of a Jewish feast. Those who urge this objection must have forgotten that St. Paul addresses the Galatians (undoubtedly a mixed church) as if they had all been formerly idolaters (Gal. iv. 8); and addresses the Romans, sometimes as if they were all Jews (Rom. vii. 1), sometimes as if they were Gentiles (Rom. xi. 18). If we take 'as ye are unleavened' in a metaphorical sense, it is scarcely consistent with the previous 'cast out the old leaven;' for the passage would then amount to saying, 'Be free from leaven (metaphorically) as you are free from leaven (metaphorically);' whereas, on the other view, St. Paul says, 'Be free from leaven (metaphorically) as you

our Paschal Lamb is Christ, who was slain for us; therefore let us keep the feast, not with the old **v. 8** leaven, nor the leaven of vice and wickedness, but with the unleavened bread of purity and truth.

Open and flagitious offenders must be excluded from the Church.

I enjoined you in my letter[1] to keep no company **9** with fornicators : not that you should utterly forego **10** all intercourse with the men of this world who may be fornicators, or lascivious, or extortioners, or idolaters ; for so you would need to go utterly out of the world. But[2] my meaning was, that you should keep **11** no company with any man who, bearing the name of a Brother, is either a fornicator, or a wanton,[3] or an idolater, or a railer, or a drunkard, or an extortioner; with such a man, I say, you must not so much as eat. For what need have I to judge those also that are **12**

---

are free from leaven (literally).' There seems no difficulty in supposing that the Gentile Christians joined with the Jewish Christians in celebrating the Paschal feast after the Jewish manner, at least to the extent of abstaining from leaven in the love-feasts. And we see that St. Paul still observed the 'days of unleavened bread' at this period of his life, from Acts xx. 6. Also, from what follows, we perceive how naturally this greatest of Jewish feasts changed into the greatest of Christian festivals.

[1] Literally, '*I wrote to you in the letter,*' viz. *the letter which I last wrote,* or *the letter to which you refer in your questions* ; for they had probably mentioned their perplexity about this direction in it. So in 2 Cor. vii. 8 the present letter (1 Cor.) is referred to in the same phrase (*I grieved you in the letter*). There are two decisive reasons why these words must refer to a *previous* letter, not to the letter St. Paul is actually writing. (1.) No such direction as 'Keep no company with fornicators' occurs in what has gone before. (2.) If St. Paul had meant to say '*I have just written,*' he could not have added the words 'in the letter,' which would have been then worse than superfluous. Prof. Stanley (who has recently supported the view here opposed) urges that the aorist might be used of the present epistle as at 1 Cor. ix. 15, which is obviously true. He also urges that 'the letter' may sometimes refer to *the present letter ;* which may also be admitted in cases where the letter is referred to *as a*

whole in its postscript; e.g. '*I Tertius, who wrote the letter*' (Rom. xvi. 22). '*I charge you that the letter be read*' (1 Thess. v. 27). '*When the letter has been read among you, cause it to be read at Laodicea*' (Col. iv. 16). But none of these instances gives any support to the view that a writer could refer to his own words, just uttered, by such a phrase as 'I wrote to you in the letter.' We are forced, therefore, to conclude that these words refer to a *preceding* letter, which has not been preserved. And this view receives a strong confirmation from the words of St. Paul's Corinthian opponents (spoken before 2 Cor. was written): '*His letters* are weighty,' &c. (2 Cor. x. 10).

[2] The conjunction here seems not to be a particle of time, but of connection.

[3] The Greek word has the meaning of *a concupiscent man* in some passages of St. Paul's writings. Compare Eph. v. 5 (where it is coupled with *unclean*). So the corresponding substantive, in St. Paul, almost invariably means *lasciviousness.* See Eph. iv. 19, v. 3 (and the note), and Col. iii. 5. The only places where the word is used by St. Paul in the sense *covetousness* are 2 Cor. ix. 5, and 1 Thess. ii. 5, in the latter of which passages the other meaning would not be inadmissible. How the word contracted its Pauline meaning may be inferred from the similar use of *concupiscence* in English. [Since the above was first published, Prof. Stanley and Prof. Jowett have both expressed their concurrence in this rendering of the word; see note on Eph. v. 3.]

without? Is it not your part to judge those that
v. 13 are within? But those without are for God's judgment. '𝔉rom amongst yourselbes ye shall cast out the
ebil one.'[1]

vi. 1   Can there be any of you who dare to bring their Litigation be-
tween Chris-
private differences into the courts of law, before the tians must
wicked, and not rather bring them before the saints?[2] not be brought
into Heathen
2 Know ye not that the saints shall judge the world? courts; and
its existence
and if the world is subjected to your judgment, are is a proof of
evil.
3 you unfit to decide the most trifling matters? Know
ye not that we shall judge angels? how much more
4 the affairs of this life? If, therefore, you have
disputes to settle which concern the affairs of this
life, give the arbitration of them to the very least
5 esteemed in your Church. I speak to your shame.
Can it be that amongst you there is not so much as
one man wise enough to arbitrate between his
6 brethren, but must brother go to law with brother,
7 and that in the courts of the unbelievers? Nay,
farther, you are in fault, throughout, in having such
disputes at all. Why do you not rather submit to
wrong? Why not rather suffer yourselves to be
8 defrauded? Nay, you are yourselves wronging and
9 defrauding, and that your brethren. Know ye not No immo-
rality can
that wrong-doers shall not inherit the kingdom of consist with
true Christi-
God? Be not deceived—neither fornicators, nor anity.
idolaters, nor adulterers, nor self-defilers, nor sodom-
10 ites, nor robbers, nor wantons,[3] nor drunkards, nor
railers, nor extortioners, shall inherit the kingdom of
11 God. And such were some of you; but you have
washed away your stains,[4]—you have been hallowed,
you have been justified, in the name of the Lord
Jesus, and in the Spirit of our God.[5]

---

[1] Deut. xxiv. 7 (LXX.).

[2] It should be remembered that the Greek and Roman law gave its sanction to the decision pronounced in a litigated case by arbitrators privately chosen; so that the Christians might obtain a just decision of their mutual differences without resorting to the Heathen tribunals. The Jews resident in foreign parts were accustomed to refer their disputes to Jewish arbitrators. Josephus (*Ant.* xiv. 10, 17) gives a decree by which the Jews at Sardis were permitted to establish a 'private court,' for the purpose of deciding 'their mis-

understandings with one another.'

[3] *Persons given to concupiscence.* See note on v. 11.

[4] Observe that the Greek verb is middle, not passive, as in A. V.: cf. Acts xxii. 16. If the aorist is here used in its proper sense (of which we can never be sure in St. Paul), the reference is to the time of their first conversion, or baptism.

[5] The words may be paraphrased thus, 'by your fellowship with the Lord Jesus, whose name you bear, and by the indwelling of the Spirit of our God.'

'All things are lawful for me.'[1]   But not all vi. 12
things are good for me.   Though all things are in
my power, they shall not bring me under *their* power.
'Meat is for the belly, and the belly for meat,' 13
though God will soon put an end to both; but the
body is not for fornication, but for the Lord; and
the Lord for the body;[2] and as God raised the Lord 14
from the grave, so He will raise us also by His
mighty power.[3]   Know ye not that your bodies are 15
members of Christ's body?   Shall I then take the
members of Christ, and make them the members of
an harlot?   God forbid.   Know ye not, that he who 16
joins himself to an harlot becomes one body with
her?   For it is said '𝔱𝔥𝔢𝔶 𝔱𝔴𝔞𝔦𝔫 𝔰𝔥𝔞𝔩𝔩 𝔟𝔢 𝔬𝔫𝔢 𝔣𝔩𝔢𝔰𝔥.'[4]
But he who joins himself to the Lord, becomes one 17
spirit with Him.   Flee fornication.   The root of 18
sin is not in the body,[5] [but in the soul]; yet the
fornicator sins against his own body.   Know ye not 19
that your bodies are temples of the Holy Spirit which
dwells within you, which ye have received from
God?   And you are not your own, for you were 20
bought with a price.[6]   Glorify God, therefore, not in
your spirit only, but in your body also, since both
are His.[7]

As to the questions which you have asked me in vii.

[1] See the explanation of this in
Chap. XIII.; and compare (for the
true side of the phrase) Gal. v. 23,
'Against such there is no law.' Probably St. Paul had used the very words
'All things are lawful for me' in this
true sense, and the immoral party at
Corinth had caught them up, and used
them as their watchword. It is also
probable that this fact was mentioned
in the letter which St. Paul had just
received from Corinth (1 Cor. vii. 1).
Also see chap. viii. 1 below. From
what follows it is evident that these
Corinthian freethinkers argued that *the
existence of bodily appetites proved the
lawfulness of their gratification.*

[2] The body is for the Lord Jesus, to
be consecrated by His indwelling to
His service; and the Lord Jesus is for
the body, to consecrate it by dwelling
therein in the person of His Spirit.

[3] St. Paul's argument here is, that
sins of unchastity, though bodily acts,
yet injure a part of our nature (compare the phrase 'spiritual body,' 1 Cor.
xv. 44) which will not be destroyed by

death, and which is closely connected
with our moral well-being. And it is
a fact no less certain than mysterious,
that moral and spiritual ruin is caused
by such sins, which human wisdom
(when untaught by Revelation) held to
be actions as blameless as eating and
drinking.

[4] Gen. ii. 24 (LXX.), quoted by our
Lord, Matt. xix. 5.

[5] Literally, '*every sin which a man
commits is without* (external to) *the
body*.' The Corinthian freethinkers
probably used this argument also; and
perhaps availed themselves of our
Lord's words, Mark vii. 18: '*Do ye
not perceive that whatsoever thing from
without entereth into the man, it cannot
defile him, because it entereth not into
his heart,*' &c. (See the whole passage.)

[6] The price is the blood of Christ.
Compare Acts xx. 28, and Col. i. 14.

[7] The latter part of this verse, though
not in the best MSS., yet is implied in
the sense,

vii. 2 your letter, this is my answer. It is good for a man cerning mar-
riage and
to remain unmarried. Nevertheless, to avoid forni- divorce, with
cation,[1] let every man have his own wife, and every special refer-
ence to cases
3 woman her own husband. Let the husband live in of mixed
marriages.
the intercourse of affection with his wife, and like-
4 wise the wife with her husband. The wife has not
dominion over her own body, but the husband ; and
so also the husband has not dominion over his own
5 body, but the wife. Do not separate one from the
other, unless it be with mutual consent for a time,
that you may give yourselves without disturbance[2]
to prayer, and then return to one another, lest,
through your fleshly passions, Satan should tempt
6 you to sin. Yet this I say by way of permission, not
7 of command. Nevertheless I would that all men
were as I myself am ; but men have different gifts
8 from God, one this, another that. But to the unmarried and to the widows, I say that it would be
good for them if they should remain in the state
9 wherein I myself also am ; yet if they are incontinent,
let them marry ; for it is better to marry than to
10 burn. To the married, not I, but the Lord gives
commandment,[3] that the wife part not from her
11 husband ; (but if she be already parted, let her
remain single, or else be reconciled with him ;) and
also that the husband put not away his wife.
12 But to the rest, speak I, not the Lord. If any
Brother be married to an unbelieving wife let him
not put her away, if she be content to live with him ;
13 neither let a believing wife put away an unbelieving
14 husband who is willing to live with her ; for the unbelieving husband is hallowed by union with his
believing wife, and the unbelieving wife by union
with her believing husband ; for otherwise your
children would be unclean,[4] but now they are holy.
15 But if the unbelieving husband or wife seeks for
separation, let them be separated : for in such cases

---

[1] The plural in the Greek perhaps
means (as Prof. Stanley takes it) ' *because of the general prevalence of fornication,*' with special reference to the
profligacy of Corinth, where every unmarried person would be liable to special temptation.

[2] ' Fasting' is an interpolation, not
found in the best MSS.

[3] This commandment is recorded
Mark x. 11, 12 : *Whosoever shall put
away his wife, and marry another, com-*

*mitteth adultery against her. And if
a woman shall put away her husband,
and be married to another, she com-
mitteth adultery.*

[4] The term means literally ' unclean,' and is used in its Jewish sense,
to denote that which is *beyond the
hallowed pale of God's people* ; the antithesis to ' holy,' which was applied
to all *within the consecrated limits.* On
the inferences from this verse, with respect to infant baptism, see Chap. XIII

the believing husband or wife is not bound to remain
under the yoke.   But the call whereby God has
called[1] us, is a call of peace.[2]   For thou who art the vii. 16
wife of an unbeliever, how knowest thou whether
thou mayest save thy husband ? or thou who art the
husband, whether thou mayest save thy wife ?

General rule, that the converts should not quit that state of life wherein they were at their conversion. Only[3] let each man walk in the same path which 17
God allotted to him, wherein the Lord has called
him.   This rule I give in all the churches.   Thus, 18
if any man, when he was called,[4] bore the mark of
circumcision, let him not efface it ; if any man was
uncircumcised at the time of his calling, let him not
receive circumcision.   Circumcision is nothing, and 19
uncircumcision is nothing ; but obedience to the
commands of God.   Let each abide in the condition 20
wherein he was called.   Wast thou in slavery at the 21
time of thy calling ?   Care not for it.   Nay, though
thou have power to gain thy freedom,[5] rather make
use of thy condition.   For the slave who has been 22
called in the Lord is the Lord's freedman ; and so
also, the freeman who has been called, is Christ's
slave.   He has bought you all ;[6] beware lest you 23
make yourselves the slaves of man.[7]   Brethren, in 24
the state wherein he was called, let each abide with
God.

Answer to   Concerning your virgin daughters[8] I have no 25

---

[1] This verb, in St. Paul's writings, means 'to call into fellowship with Christ;' 'to call from the unbelieving World into the Church.'

[2] The inference is, 'therefore the profession of Christianity ought not to lead the believer to quarrel with the unbelieving members of his family.'

[3] Literally, *only, as God allotted to each, as the Lord has called each, so let him walk.*

[4] The past tense is mistranslated 'is called' in A. V. throughout this chapter.

[5] The Greek here is ambiguous, and might be so rendered as to give directly opposite precepts ; but the version given in the text (which is that advocated by Chrysostom, Meyer, and De Wette) agrees best with the order of the Greek words, and also with the context.   We must remember, with regard to this and other precepts here given, that they were given under the immediate anticipation of our Lord's coming.

[6] There is a change here in the Greek from singular to plural.   For the ' price ' see chap. vi. 20.

[7] Alluding to their servile adherence to party leaders.   Compare 2 Cor. xi. 20.

[8] We cannot help remarking, that the manner in which a recent infidel writer has spoken of this passage, is one of the most striking proofs how far a candid and acute mind may be warped by a strong bias.   In this case the desire of the writer is to disparage the moral teaching of Christianity ; and he brings forward this passage to prove his case, and blames St. Paul because he assumes these Corinthian daughters to be disposable in marriage at the will of their father ; as if any other assumption had been possible, in the case of Greek or Jewish daughters in that age.   We must suppose that this writer would (on the same grounds) require a modern missionary to Persia to preach the absolute incompatibility of despotic government

command from the Lord, but I give my judgment, as one who has been moved by the Lord's mercy[1]

vii. 26 to be faithful. I think, then, that it is good, by reason of the present[2] necessity, for all to be un-

27 married.[3] Art thou bound to a wife? seek not

28 separation; art thou free? seek not marriage; yet if thou marry, thou sinnest not.[4] And if your virgin daughters marry, they sin not; but the married will have sorrows in the flesh, and these I would spare

29 you.[5] But this I say, brethren, the time is short;[6] that henceforth both they that have wives be as

30 though they had none; and they that weep as though they wept not, and they that rejoice as though they rejoiced not, and they that buy as

31 though they possessed not, and they that use this world as not abusing[7] it; for the outward show of

32 this world is passing away.[8] But I would have you free from earthly care. The cares of the unmarried man are fixed upon the Lord, and he strives to

33 please the Lord. But the cares of the husband are fixed upon worldly things, striving to please his

34 wife. The wife also has this difference[9] from the virgin; the cares of the virgin are fixed upon the Lord, that she may be holy both in body and in spirit; but the cares of the wife are fixed upon worldly things, striving to please her husband.

35 Now this I say for your own profit; not that I may

---

with sound morality. A similar *ig-noratio elenchi* runs through all his remarks upon this chapter.

[1] Compare 'I obtained mercy,' 1 Tim. i. 13.

[2] The participle here can only mean *present*. See the note on 2 Thess. ii. 2. The word was mistranslated in this passage in the first edition.

[3] 'So,' namely 'as virgins.'

[4] Literally, *though thou shalt have married, thou hast not sinned*; the aorist used for the perfect, as constantly by St. Paul.

[5] I is emphatic, *I, if you followed my advice*; also observe the *present*, '*I am sparing you* [by this advice],' or, in other words, '*I would spare you.*'

[6] We adopt Lachmann's reading. 'The object of this contraction of your earthly life is, that you may henceforth set your affections on things above.'

[7] Literally, the verb appears to

mean *to use up*, as distinguished from *to use*. Compare ix. 18. It thus acquired the sense of *to abuse*, in which it is sometimes employed by Demosthenes and by the grammarians.

[8] Literally, '*passing by*,' flitting past, like the shadows in Plato's Cavern (*Repub.* vii. 1), or the figures in some moving phantasmagoria.

[9] The reading of Lachmann makes a considerable difference in the translation, which would thus run: ' *The husband strives to please his wife, and is divided* [*in mind*]. Both the *unmarried wife* [i.e. *the widow*] and the *virgin care for the things of the Lord*,' &c. This reading gives a more natural sense to 'divided' (cf. i. 13, so Stanley); but on the other hand, the use of 'unmarried wife' for *widow* is unprecedented; and in this very chapter (verse 8) the word *widows* is opposed to *unmarried*.

entangle you in a snare; but that I may help you to
serve the Lord with a seemly and undivided service.
But if any man think that he is treating his virgin vii. 3
daughter in an unseemly manner, by leaving her unmarried beyond the flower of her age, and if need so
require, let him act according to his will; he may do
so without sin; let them[1] marry. But he who is firm 37
in his resolve, and is not constrained to marry his
daughter, but has the power of carrying out his will,
and has determined to keep her unmarried, does well.
Thus he who gives his daughter in marriage does well, 38
but he who gives her not in marriage does better.

Marriage of widows.   The wife is bound by the law of wedlock so long 39
as her husband lives; but after his death she is free
to marry whom she will, provided that she choose
one of the brethren[2] in the Lord.   Yet she is happier 40
if she remain a widow, in my judgment; and I think
that I, no less[3] than others, have the Spirit of God.

Answer to questions concerning meats offered to idols.   As to the meats which have been sacrificed to viii.
idols, we know—(for 'we all have knowledge;'[4]
but knowledge puffs up, while love builds. If any 2
man prides himself on his knowledge, he knows
nothing yet as he ought to know; but whosoever 3
loves God, of him God hath knowledge[5])—as to 4
eating the meats sacrificed to idols, we know (I say)
that an idol has no true being, and that there is no
other God but one.   For though there be some who 5
are called gods, either celestial or terrestrial, and
though men worship many gods and many lords, yet 6
to us there is but one God, the Father, from whom
are all things, and we for Him; and one Lord Jesus
Christ, by whom are all things, and we by Him.[6]
But 'all' have not this 'knowledge;' on the con- 7
trary, there are some who still have a conscientious

---

[1] 'Them,' viz. the daughter and the suitor.

[2] Literally, *provided it be in the Lord.*

[3] The 'also' in 'I also' has this meaning.

[4] It is necessary, for the under-standing of this Epistle, that we should remember that it is an answer to a letter received from the Corinthian Church (1 Cor. vii. 1), and therefore constantly alludes to topics in that letter. It seems probable, from the way in which they are introduced,

that these words 'We all have know-ledge,' are quoted from that letter.

[5] That is, *God acknowledges him*; compare Gal. iv. 9.

[6] That is, *by whom the life of all things, and our life also, is originated and sustained.* So Col. i. 16: 'By Him and for Him were all created, and in Him all things subsist;' where it should be remarked that the 'for Him' is predicated of the Son, as in the present passage of the Father. Both passages show how fully St. Paul taught the doctrine of the Λόγος,

fear of the idol, and think the meat an idolatrous sacrifice, so that, if they eat it, their conscience being
ii. 8 weak is defiled. Now our food cannot change our place in God's sight; with Him we gain nothing by
9 eating, nor lose by not eating. But beware lest, perchance, this exercise of your rights[1] should be-
10 come a stumbling-block to the weak. For if one of them see thee, who boastest of thy knowledge,[2] feast-ing in an idol's temple, will not he be encouraged to eat the meat offered in sacrifice, notwithstanding the
11 weakness of his conscience?[3] And thus, through thy knowledge, will thy weak brother perish, for whom
12 Christ died. Nay, when you sin thus against your brethren, and wound their weak conscience, you sin
13 against Christ. Wherefore, if my food cast a stum-bling-block in my brother's path, I will eat no flesh while the world stands, lest thereby I cause my bro-ther's fall.[4]

x. 1 Is it denied that I am an apostle? Is it denied that I am free from man's authority?[5] Is it denied that I have seen Jesus[6] our Lord? Is it denied that you are the fruits of my labour in the Lord?
2 If to others I am no apostle, yet at least I am such to you; for you are yourselves the seal which stamps
3 the reality of my apostleship, in the Lord; this is my answer to those who question my authority.
4 Do they deny my right to be maintained[7] [by my
5 converts]? Do they deny my right to carry a believing wife with me on my journeys, like the rest of the apostles, and the brothers of the Lord,[8] and

He vindicates his claim to the Apostolic office against his Judaising detractors; and explains his renuncia-tion of some of the Apos-tolic privi-leges.

[1] 'This liberty of yours.' Observe again the reference to the language of the self-styled Pauline party at Co-rinth. Compare 'all things are lawful for me' (vi. 12). The decrees of the 'Council of Jerusalem' might seem to have a direct bearing on the ques-tion discussed by St. Paul in this pas-sage; but he does not refer to them as deciding the points in dispute, either here or elsewhere. Probably the rea-son of this is, that the decrees were meant only to be of temporary ap-plication; and in their terms they applied originally only to the churches of Syria and Cilicia (see Acts xv. 23; also Chap. VII.).

[2] Literally, *the possessor of know-ledge*; in allusion to the previous 'We all have knowledge.'

[3] Literally, *will not the conscience of him, though he is weak, be*, &c.

[4] The whole of this eighth chapter is parallel to Rom. xiv.

[5] 'Free.' Compare verse 19 and Gal. i. 1, 'an Apostle not of men.'

[6] 'Christ' here is omitted by the best MSS.

[7] This was a point much insisted on by the Judaisers (see 2 Cor. xii. 13–16). They argued that St. Paul, by not availing himself of this undoubted apostolic right, betrayed his own con-sciousness that he was no true Apostle.

[8] 'The brothers of the Lord.' It is a very doubtful question whether these were the sons of our Lord's mother's sister, viz. the Apostles James and Judas, the sons of Alphæus (Luke vi. 15, 16) (for *cousins* were called

Cephas? Or do they think that I and Barnabas ix. alone have no right to be maintained, except by the labour of our own hands? What soldier[1] ever serves at his private cost? What husbandman plants a[7] vineyard without sharing in its fruit? What shepherd tends a flock without partaking of their milk? Say I this on Man's judgment only, or says not the[8] Law the same? Yea, in the Law of Moses it is written '𝕮𝖍𝖔𝖚 𝖘𝖍𝖆𝖑𝖙 𝖓𝖔𝖙 𝖒𝖚𝖟𝖟𝖑𝖊 𝖙𝖍𝖊 𝖔𝖝 𝖙𝖍𝖆𝖙 𝖙𝖗𝖊𝖆𝖉𝖊𝖙𝖍 𝖔𝖚𝖙[9] 𝖙𝖍𝖊 𝖈𝖔𝖗𝖓.'[2] Is it for oxen that God is caring, or[10] speaks he altogether for our sake? For our sake, doubtless, it was written; because the ploughman ought to plough, and the thresher to thresh, with hope to share in the produce of his toil. If I have[11] sown for you the seed of spiritual gifts, would it be much if I were to reap some harvest from your carnal gifts? If others share this right over you,[12] how much more should I? Yet I have not used my right, but forego every claim,[3] lest I should by any means hinder the course of Christ's Glad-tidings. Know ye not that they[4] who perform the[13] service of the temple, live upon the revenues of the temple, and they who minister at the altar share with it in the sacrifices? So also the Lord commanded[5][14] those who publish the Glad-tidings to be maintained thereby. But I have not exercised any of these[15] rights, nor do I write[6] this that it may be practised in my own case. For I had rather die than suffer any man to make void my boasting. For, although[16] I proclaim the Glad-tidings, yet this gives me no ground of boasting; for I am compelled to do so by order of my[7] master. Yea, woe is me if I proclaim it not. For were my service of my own free[17] choice, I might claim wages to reward my labour; but since I serve by compulsion, I am a slave en-

---

brothers), or whether they were sons of Joseph by a former marriage, or actually sons of the mother of our Lord.

[1] He means to say that, to have this right of maintenance, a man need be no Apostle.

[2] Deut. xxv. 4 (LXX.), quoted also 1 Tim. v. 18.

[3] The proper meaning of the verb used here is *to hold out against*, as a fortress against assault, or ice against superincumbent weight. Compare xiii. 7, and 1 Thess. iii. 1.

[4] Numbers vii. and Deut. xviii.

[5] (Matt. x. 9, 10.) *Provide neither gold nor silver nor brass in your purses, nor scrip for your journey, neither two coats, neither shoes, nor yet staves: for the workman is worthy of his meat.*

[6] The aorist is the epistolary tense. There is considerable difference of reading in this verse, but not materially affecting the sense.

[7] 'Necessity' here is the compulsion exercised by a master over a slave. In calling his service compulsory, St. Paul refers to the miraculous character of his conversion.

trusted with a stewardship.[1] What then is my
x. 18 wage? It is to make the Glad-tidings free of cost
where I carry it, that I may forego my right as an
19 Evangelist.[2] Therefore, although free from the
authority of all men, I made myself the slave of all
20 that I might gain[3] the most. To the Jews I became
as a Jew, that I might gain the Jews; to those
under the law as though I were under the law (not
that I was myself subject to the law),[4] that I might
21 gain those under the law; to those without the law[5]
as one without the law (not that I was without law
before God, but under the law of Christ), that I
22 might gain those who were without the law. To
the weak, I became weak, that I might gain the
weak. I am become all things to all men, that by
23 all means I might save some. And this I do for the
sake of the Glad-tidings, that I myself may share
24 therein with those who hear me. Know ye not that
in the races of the stadium, though all run, yet but
one can win the prize?—(so run that you may win)
25 —and every man who strives in the matches, trains
himself by all manner of self-restraint.[6] Yet they
do it to win a fading crown,[7]—we, a crown that
26 cannot fade. I, therefore, run not like the racer
who is uncertain of his goal; I fight, not as the
27 pugilist who strikes out against the air;[8] but I
bruise[9] my body and force it into bondage; lest,
perchance, having called others to the contest,[10] I
should myself fail shamefully of the prize.

[1] This 'stewardship' consisted in dispensing his master's goods to his fellow-slaves. See iv. 1, 2.

[2] Literally, *that I may not fully use*. See note on vii. 31. The perplexity which commentators have found in this passage is partly due to the construction of the Greek, but principally to the oxymoron; St. Paul virtually says that *his wage is the refusal of wages*. The passage may be literally rendered, '*It is, that I should, while Evangelising, make the Evangel free of cost, that I may not fully use my right as an Evangelist.*'

[3] 'Gain' alludes to 'wage.' The souls whom he gained were his wage.

[4] The best MSS. here insert a clause which is not in the Textus Receptus.

[5] For 'without law' in the sense of 'heathen,' compare Rom. ii. 12.

[6] For a description of the severe training required, see notes at the beginning of Chap. XX.

[7] This was the crown made of the leaves of the pine, groves of which surrounded the Isthmian Stadium: the same tree still grows plentifully on the Isthmus of Corinth. It was the prize of the great Isthmian games. Throughout the passage St. Paul alludes to these contests, which were so dear to the pride and patriotism of the Corinthians. Compare also 2 Tim. ii. 5. And see the beginning of Chap. XX. on the same subject.

[8] Literally, *I run as one not uncertain [of the goal]; I fight as one not striking the air*.

[9] This is the literal meaning of the pugilistic term which the Apostle here employs.

[10] 'As a herald.' See the second note on Chap. XX.

He again
warns the
Corinthians
against immo-
rality, by ex-
amples of the
punishment of
God's ancient
people.

For[1] I would not have you ignorant, brethren, x.
that our forefathers all were guarded by the cloud,
and all passed safely through the sea. And all, in 2
the cloud, and in the sea, were baptized unto Moses.
And all of them alike ate the same spiritual food; 3
and all drank of the same spiritual stream; for they 4
drank from the spiritual rock which followed them;[2]
but that rock was Christ. Yet most of them lost 5
God's favour, yea, they were struck down and
perished in the wilderness. Now, these things were 6
shadows of our own case, that we might learn not
to lust after evil, as they lusted.[3] Nor be ye idola- 7
ters, as were some of them; as it is written,—
'𝕿𝖍𝖊 𝖕𝖊𝖔𝖕𝖑𝖊 𝖘𝖆𝖙 𝖉𝖔𝖜𝖓 𝖙𝖔 𝖊𝖆𝖙 𝖆𝖓𝖉 𝖉𝖗𝖎𝖓𝖐, 𝖆𝖓𝖉 𝖗𝖔𝖘𝖊 𝖚𝖕 𝖙𝖔
𝖕𝖑𝖆𝖞.'[4] Neither let us commit fornication, as some 8
of them committed, and fell in one day three and
twenty thousand.[5] Neither let us try the long- 9
suffering of Christ, as did some of them, who were
destroyed by the serpents.[6] Nor murmur as some 10
of them murmured, and were slain by the destroyer.[7]
Now all these things befell them as shadows of 11
things to come; and they were written for our
warning, on whom the ends of the ages are come.[8]
Wherefore, let him who thinks that he stands firm, 12
beware lest he fall. No trial has come upon you 13
beyond man's power to bear; and God is faithful to
His promises, and will not suffer you to be tried
beyond your strength, but will with every trial provide the way of escape, that you may be able to
sustain it.

They must re-
nounce all fel-

Wherefore, my beloved, flee from idolatry. I 14
speak as to men of understanding;[9] use your own 15

---

[1] The reading of the best MSS. is
'for.' The connection with what precedes is the possibility of failure even
in those who had received the greatest
advantages.

[2] St. Paul's meaning is, that, under
the allegorical representation of the
Manna, the Water, and the Rock, are
shadowed forth spiritual realities: for
the *Rock* is Christ, the only source of
living *water* (John iv.), and the *Manna*
also is Christ, the true *bread from
Heaven* (John vi.). For the Rabbinical
traditions about the rock, see Schött-
gen; and on the whole verse, see Prof.
Stanley's excellent note.

[3] Viz. after the flesh-pots of Egypt.

[4] Exod. xxxii. 6 (LXX.).

[5] Numbers xxv. 9, where twenty-

four thousand is the number given. See
the remarks in p. 140, n. 2, on the
speech at Antioch, and also the note
on Gal. iii. 17.

[6] Numbers xxi. 6.

[7] See Numbers xvi. 41. The murmuring of the Corinthians against the
Apostle is compared to the murmuring
of Korah against Moses.

[8] The coming of Christ was 'the
end of the ages,' i.e. the commencement of a new period of the world's
existence. So nearly the same phrase
is used Heb. ix. 26. A similar expression occurs five times in St. Matthew,
signifying *the coming of Christ to
judgment.*

[9] 'Wise men,' the character peculiarly affected by the Corinthians. The

x. 16 judgment upon my words.   When we drink the cup of blessing, which we bless, are we not all partakers in the blood of Christ?   When we break the bread, are we not all partakers in the body of Christ? [1]

17 For as the bread is one, so we, the many, are one
18 body; for of that one bread we all partake.   If you look to the carnal Israel, do you not see that those who eat of the sacrifices are in partnership with the
19 altar?   What would I say then? that an idol has any real being? or that meat offered to an idol is
20 really changed thereby?   Not so; but I say, that when the heathen offer their sacrifices, '𝔱𝔥𝔢𝔶 𝔰𝔞𝔠𝔯𝔦𝔣𝔦𝔠𝔢 𝔱𝔬 𝔡𝔢𝔪𝔬𝔫𝔰, 𝔞𝔫𝔡 𝔫𝔬𝔱 𝔱𝔬 𝔊𝔬𝔡;' [2] and I would not have
21 you become partners [3] with the demons.   You cannot drink the cup of the Lord, and the cup of demons; you cannot eat at the table of the Lord, and at the
22 table of demons.   Would we provoke the Lord to jealousy?   Are we stronger than He?

23   'All things are lawful,' [4] but not all things are expedient; 'all things are lawful,' but not all things
24 build up the church.   Let no man seek his own, but
25 every man his neighbour's good.   Whatever is sold in the market, you may eat, nor need you ask for con-
26 science sake whence it came: '𝔉𝔬𝔯 𝔱𝔥𝔢 𝔢𝔞𝔯𝔱𝔥 𝔦𝔰 𝔱𝔥𝔢
27 𝔏𝔬𝔯𝔡'𝔰, 𝔞𝔫𝔡 𝔱𝔥𝔢 𝔣𝔲𝔩𝔫𝔢𝔰𝔰 𝔱𝔥𝔢𝔯𝔢𝔬𝔣.' [5] And if any unbeliever invites you to a feast, and you are disposed to go, eat of all that is set before you, asking no questions
28 for conscience sake; but if any one should say to you, 'This has been offered to an idol,' eat not of that dish, for the sake of him who pointed it out, and for the
29 sake of conscience. [6] Thy neighbour's conscience, I say, not thine own; for [thou mayest truly say] 'why is my freedom condemned by the conscience of another?
30 and if I thankfully partake, why am I called a sinner for that which I eat with thanksgiving?' [7]

word is perhaps used with a mixture of irony, as at 1 Cor. iv. 10, and 2 Cor. xi. 19.

[1] Literally, *The cup of blessing which we bless, is it not a common participation in the blood of Christ?   The bread which we break, is it not a common participation in the body of Christ?*

[2] Deut. xxxii. 17: 'They sacrificed to demons, not to God.' (LXX.)

[3] This is addressed to those who were in the habit of accepting invitations to feasts celebrated in the temples of the heathen gods, 'sitting in the idol's temple' (viii. 10).   These feasts were, in fact, acts of idolatrous worship; the wine was poured in libation to the gods ('the cup of demons,' ver. 21), and the feast was given in honour of the gods.

[4] See vi. 12 and note.

[5] Psalm xxiv. 1 (LXX.).

[6] The repeated quotation is omitted in the best MSS.

[7] Compare Rom. xiv. 16: 'Let not your good be evil spoken of.'   Here again the hypothesis that St. Paul is quoting from the letter of the Corinthians removes all difficulty.

Therefore, whether you eat or drink, or what- x. 31 soever you do, do all for the glory of God.[1] Give no 32 cause of stumbling, either to Jews or Gentiles, or to the Church of God. For so I also strive to please 33 all men in all things, not seeking my own good, but the good of all,[2] that they may be saved. I beseech you follow my example, as I follow the example of Christ.

Censure on the custom of women appearing unveiled in the assemblies for public worship.

I praise you, brethren, that[3] 'you are always 2 mindful of my teaching, and keep unchanged the rules which I delivered to you.' But I would have 3 you know that Christ is the head of every man, and the man is the head of the woman, as God is the head of Christ. If a man should pray or prophesy 4 in the congregation with a veil over his head, he would bring shame upon his head[4] [by wearing the token of subjection]. But if a woman prays or pro- 5 phesies with her head unveiled, she brings shame upon her head, as much as she that is shaven. I 6 say, if she cast off her veil, let her shave her head at once; but if it is shameful for a woman to be shorn or shaven, let her keep a veil upon her head.[5] For a 7 man ought not to veil his head, since he is the likeness of God, and the manifestation of God's glory. But the woman's part is to manifest her husband's glory. For the man was not made from the woman, but the 8 woman from the man. Nor was the man created 9 for the sake of the woman, but the woman for the sake of the man. Therefore, the woman ought to 10 wear a sign[6] of subjection upon her head, because of the angels.[7] Nevertheless, in their fellowship with 11

---

[1] i.e. *that the glory of God may be manifested to men.*

[2] The phrase denotes not *many*, but *the many, the whole mass of mankind.*

[3] This statement was probably made in the letter sent by the Corinthian Church to St. Paul.

[4] It appears from this passage, that the Tallith which the Jews put over their heads when they enter their synagogues (see p. 137) was in the apostolic age removed by them when they officiated in the public worship. Otherwise St. Paul could not, while writing to a church containing so many born Jews as the Corinthian, assume it as evidently disgraceful to a man to officiate in the congregation with veiled head. It is true that the Greek practice was to keep the head

uncovered at their religious rites (as Grotius and Wetstein have remarked), but this custom would not have affected the Corinthian synagogue, nor have influenced the feelings of its members.

[5] For the character of this veil (or hood), see Canon Stanley's note *in loco.*

[6] The word is often used for *the dominion exercised by those in lawful authority over their subordinates* (see Luke vii. 8). Here it is used to signify the *sign* of that dominion.

[7] The meaning of this very difficult expression seems to be as follows:— The angels are sent as ministering servants to attend upon Christians, and are especially present when the church assembles for public worship; and they would be offended by any violation of

the Lord, man and woman may not be separated the
xi. 12 one from the other.[1]   For as woman was made from
man, so is man also borne by woman ; and all things
13 spring from God.   Judge of this matter by your own
feeling.   Is it seemly for a woman to offer prayers
14 to God unveiled ?   Or does not even nature itself
15 teach you that long hair is a disgrace to a man, but
a glory to a woman? for her hair has been given
16 her for a veil.   But if any one thinks to be con-
tentious in defence of such a custom, let him know
that it is disallowed by me,[2] and by all the Churches
of God.

17   [I said that I praised you, for keeping the rules   Censure on
their profana-
which were delivered to you;] but while I give you   tion of the
Lord's Supper
this commandment I praise you not ;   your solemn
18 assemblies are for evil rather than for good.   For
first, I hear that there are divisions among you,
when your congregation assembles ; and this I partly
19 believe.   For there must needs be not divisions only,[3]
but also adverse sects among you, that so the good
20 may be tested and made known.   Moreover,[4] when
you assemble yourselves together, it is not to eat the
21 Lord's Supper ; for each begins to eat [what he has
brought for] his own supper, before anything has
been given to others ; and while some are hungry,
22 others are drunken.[5]   Have you then no houses to eat
and drink in ?   or do you come to show contempt for
the congregation of God's people, and to shame the
poor ?[6]   What can I say to you ?   Shall I praise
23 you in this ?   I praise you not.   For I myself[7] received from the Lord that which I delivered to you,
that the Lord Jesus, in the night when He was
24 betrayed, took bread, and when He had given thanks,
He brake it, and said—' *Take, eat; this is my body,*

decency or order.   For other explanations, and a full discussion of the subject,
the reader is referred to Prof. Stanley's
note.

[1] In their relation to Christ, man and
woman are not to be severed the one
from the other.   Compare Gal. iii. 28.
St. Paul means to say that the distinction between the sexes is one which
only belongs to this life.

[2] Literally, *that neither I, nor the
churches of God, admit of such a custom.*

[3] 'There must be *also*,' &c.

[4] The second subject of rebuke is introduced here.

[5] For the explanation of this, see
Chap. XIII.   It should be observed
that a common meal, to which each
of the guests contributed his own
share of the provisions, was a form of
entertainment of frequent occurrence
among the Greeks, and known by the
name of ἔρανος.

[6] Literally, *Those who have not
houses to eat in,* and who therefore
ought to have received their portion at
the love-feasts from their wealthier
brethren.

[7] The 'I' is emphatic.

which is broken for you: this do in remembrance of me.'
In the same manner also, He took the cup after xi. 25
supper, saying, ' *This cup is the new covenant in my
blood: this do ye, as often as ye drink it, in remembrance of me.'* For as often as you eat this bread, 26
and drink this cup, you openly show forth the Lord's
death until He shall come again. Therefore, who- 27
soever shall eat this bread, or drink this cup of the
Lord unworthily, shall be guilty of profaning the
body and blood of the Lord. But let a man examine 28
himself, and so let him eat of this bread and drink of
this cup. For he who eats and drinks of it un- 29
worthily, eats and drinks judgment against himself,
not duly judging of the Lord's body.[1] For this 30
cause many of you are weak and sickly, and many
sleep. For if we had duly judged ourselves, we 31
should not have been judged. But now that we are 32
judged, we are chastened by the Lord, that we may
not be condemned together with the world. There- 33
fore, my brethren, when you are assembling to eat,
wait for one another ; and if any one is hungry, let 34
him eat at home, lest your meetings should bring
judgment upon you. The other matters I will set in
order when I come.

On the Spirit-
ual Gifts.
Concerning those who exercise[2] Spiritual Gifts, xii. 1
brethren, I would not have you ignorant. You know 2
that in the days of your heathenism you were blindly[3]
led astray to worship dumb and senseless idols [by
those who pretended to gifts from heaven]. This 3
therefore I call to your remembrance ; that no man
who is inspired by the Spirit of God can say ' Jesus
is accursed ; ' and no man can say ' Jesus is the
Lord,' unless he be inspired by the Holy Spirit.[4] More- 4

---

[1] If in this verse we omit, with the
majority of MSS., the words ' unworthily ' and ' of the Lord,' it will stand
as follows : *He who eats and drinks of
it, not duly judging of* [or, *discerning*]
*the Body, eats and drinks judgment
against himself.* The ' not discerning '
is explained by Canon Stanley, ' if he
does not discern that the body of the
Lord is in himself and in the Christian
society ; ' but the more usual and perhaps more natural explanation is, ' if
he does not distinguish between the
Eucharistic elements and a common
meal.'

[2] The adjective is here taken as masculine, because this agrees best with
the context, and also because another
word is used in this chapter for *spiritual
gifts.*

[3] *As ye chanced to be led at the will
of your leaders,* i.e. *blindly.*

[4] i.e. the mere outward profession
of Christianity is (so far as it goes) a
proof of the Holy Spirit's guidance.
Therefore the extraordinary spiritual
gifts which followed Christian baptism
in that age proceeded in all cases from
the Spirit of God, and not from the
Spirit of Evil. This is St. Paul's
answer to a difficulty apparently felt
by the Corinthians (and mentioned in

over, there are varieties of Gifts, but the same Spirit
xii. 5 gives them all; and [they are given for] various
6 ministrations, but all to serve the same Lord; and the
working whereby they are wrought is various, but
all are wrought in all by the working of the same
7 God.[1] But the gift whereby the Spirit becomes
8 manifest, is given to each for the profit of all. To
one[2] is given by the Spirit the utterance of Wisdom,
to another the utterance of Knowledge[3] according to
9 the working of the same Spirit. To another Faith[4]
through the same Spirit. To another gifts of Healing
10 through the same Spirit. To another the powers
which work Miracles; to another Prophecy; to another the discernment of Spirits;[5] to another varieties
of Tongues;[6] to another the Interpretation of Tongues.
11 But all these gifts are wrought by the working of
that one and the same Spirit, who distributes them
12 to each according to His will. For as the body is
one, and has many members, and as all the members,
13 though many,[7] are one body; so also is Christ. For
in the communion of one Spirit we all were[8] baptized
into one body, whether we be Jews or Gentiles,[9]
whether slaves or freemen, and were all made to drink
14 of the same Spirit. For the body is not one member,
15 but many. If[10] the foot should say, ' I am not the
hand, therefore I belong not to the body,' does it
16 thereby sever itself from the body? Or if the ear
should say, ' I am not the eye, therefore I belong not
to the body,' does it thereby sever itself from the body?
17 If the whole body were an eye, where would be the

their letter to him), whether some of
these gifts might not be given by the
Author of Evil to confuse the Church.
Prof. Stanley observes that the words
Jesus is accursed and *Jesus is the Lord*
(according to the reading of some of
the best MSS., which produces a much
livelier sense) ' were probably well-
known forms of speech; the first for
renouncing Christianity (compare *ma-*
ledicere Christo, Plin. *Ep.* x. 97), the
second for professing allegiance to Christ
at baptism.'

[1] It should be observed that the 4th,
5th, and 6th verses imply the doctrine
of the Trinity.

[2] On this classification of spiritual
gifts, see p. 334, note.

[3] *Knowledge* (*gnosis*) is the term used
throughout this Epistle for *a deep in-*
sight into divine truth; Wisdom is a
more general term, but here (as being
opposed to *gnosis*) probably means
practical wisdom.

[4] That is, *Wonder-working Faith.*
See Chap. XIII.

[5] See Chap. XIII.

[6] See Chap. XIII. for remarks on this
and the other gifts mentioned in this
passage.

[7] Some words of the Received Text
are omitted here by the best MSS.

[8] The past tense is mistranslated in
A. V. as present.

[9] See note on Rom. i. 16.

[10] The resemblance between this passage and the well-known fable of Me-
nenius Agrippa (Liv. II. 32) can
scarcely be accidental; and may perhaps be considered another proof that
St. Paul was not unacquainted with
classical literature.

hearing? If the whole body were an ear, where
would be the smelling? But now God has placed xii.
the members severally in the body according to His
will. If all were one member, where would be the 19
body? But now, though the members are many, 20
yet the body is one. And the eye cannot say to the 21
hand, ' I have no need of thee; ' nor again the head
to the feet, 'I have no need of you.' Nay, those parts 22
of the body which are reckoned the feeblest are the
most necessary, and those parts which we hold the 23
least honourable, we clothe with the more abundant
honour, and the less beautiful parts are adorned with
the greater beauty; whereas the beautiful need no 24
adornment. But God has tempered the body together,
and given to the lowlier parts the higher honour,
that there should be no division in the body, but that 25
all its parts should feel, one for the other, a common
sympathy. And thus, if one member suffer, every 26
member suffers with it; or if one member be honoured,
every member rejoices with it. Now ye are together 27
the body of Christ, and each one of you a separate
member. And God has set the members in the 28
Church, some in one place, and some in another: [1]
first, [2] Apostles; secondly, Prophets; thirdly, Teachers;
afterwards Miracles; then gifts of Healing; Serviceable Ministrations; gifts of Government; varieties
of Tongues. Can all be Apostles? Can all be Pro- 29
phets? Can all be Teachers? Can all work Miracles? Have all the gifts of Healing? Do all speak 30
with Tongues? Can all interpret the Tongues?
But I would have you delight [3] in the best gifts; and 31
moreover, beyond them all, [4] I will show you a path
wherein to walk.

Superiority of
Love to all　　　Though I speak in all the tongues of men and xiii

---

[1] The omission of the answering
clause in the Greek renders it necessary to complete the sense by this interpolation.

[2] On this classification, see p. 334,
note 1; on the particular charisms and
offices mentioned in it, see pp. 334–
340.

[3] The verb means originally *to feel
intense eagerness about* a person or
thing : hence its different senses of
love, jealousy, &c., are derived. Here
the wish expressed is, that the Corinthians should take that delight in the

exercise of the more useful gifts, which
hitherto they had taken in the more
wonderful, not that individuals should
' covet earnestly ' for themselves gifts
which God had not given them. Compare xiv. 39, and observe that the verb
is a different one in xiv. 1.

[4] This seems the meaning here. The
phrase can scarcely be taken as an
adjective with ' path,' as in A.V. Such
an instance as Rom. vii. 13 is not
parallel. In English the use of the
words *exceedingly sinful*, would not explain the expression *an exceedingly path.*

angels, if I have not love, I am no better than
iii. 2 sounding brass, or a tinkling cymbal.   And though
I have the gift of prophecy, and understand all the
mysteries, and all the depths of knowledge ; and
though I have the fulness of faith,[1] so that I could
3 remove mountains; if I have not love, I am nothing.
And though I sell all my goods to feed the poor, and
4 though I give my body to be burned,[2] if I have not
love, it profits me nothing.   Love is long suffering ;
5 love is kind ; love envies not ; love speaks no vaunts;
love swells not with vanity ;   love offends not by
rudeness ; love seeks not her own ; is not easily pro-
6 voked ; bears no malice ;[3] rejoices not over[4] iniquity,
7 but rejoices in the victory of truth ;[5] foregoes all
things,[6] believes all things, hopes all things, endures
all things.   Love shall never pass away ; but Pro-
8 phecies shall vanish, and Tongues shall cease, and
Knowledge shall come to nought.   For our Know-
9 ledge is imperfect, and our prophesying is imperfect.
10 But when the perfect is come, the imperfect shall
11 pass away.   When I was a child, my words were
childish, my desires were childish, my judgments
were childish ; but being grown a man, I have done
12 with the things of childhood. So now we see darkly,[7]
by a mirror,[8] but then face to face ; now I know in
part, but then shall I know, even as I now am[9]
13 known.   Yet while other gifts shall pass away, these
three, Faith, Hope, and Love, abide ; and the greatest
of these is Love.

[1] i.e. the charism of wonder-working
faith. See Chap. XIII. The ' removal
of mountains' alludes to the words of
our Lord, recorded Matt. xvii. 20.

[2] Some MSS. have ' give my body
that I may boast,' which gives a satisfactory sense.

[3] Literally, *does not reckon the evil*
[*against the evil doer*]. Compare 2
Cor. v. 19 : ' not reckoning their sins.'
The Authorised Version here, 'thinketh
no evil,' is so beautiful that one cannot
but wish it had been a correct translation.   The same disposition, however,
is implied by the ' believes all things'
below.

[4] This verb sometimes means *to rejoice in the misfortune* of another, and
the characteristic of love here mentioned
may mean that it does not exult in the

punishment of iniquity ; or may simply
mean that it does not delight in the
contemplation of wickedness.

[5] Literally, *rejoices when the Truth
rejoices.*

[6] For the meaning, see note on ix.
12.

[7] Literally, *in an enigma* ; thus we
see God (e.g.) in nature, while even
revelation only shows us His reflected
likeness.   There is, no doubt, an allusion to Numbers xii. 8.

[8] Not ' *through a glass,*' but *by
means of a mirror.*

[9] Literally, ' I was known,' i. e.
when in this world, by God.   The
tense used retrospectively ;   unless it
may be better to take it as the aorist
used in a perfect sense, which is not
uncommon in St. Paul's style.

Directions for
the exercise of
the gift of
Prophecy, and
the gift of
Tongues.

Follow earnestly after Love ; yet delight in the xiv spiritual gifts, but especially in the gift of Prophecy. For he who speaks in a Tongue, speaks not to men 2 but to God ; for no man understands him, but with his spirit he utters mysteries.   But he who prophe- 3 sies speaks to men, and builds them up, with exhortation and with comfort.   He who speaks in a Tongue 4 builds up himself alone ; but he who prophesies builds up the Church.   I wish that you all had the 5 gift of Tongues, but rather that you had the gift of Prophecy ; for he who prophesies is above him who speaks in Tongues, unless he interpret, that the Church may be built up thereby.   Now, brethren, if 6 when I came to you I were to speak in Tongues, what should I profit you, unless I should [also] speak either in Revelation or in Knowledge, either in Prophesying or in Teaching ?   Even if the lifeless 7 instruments of sound, the flute or the harp, give no distinctness to their notes, how can we understand their music ? If the trumpet utter an uncertain note, 8 how shall the soldier prepare himself for the battle ? So also if you utter unintelligible words with your 9 tongue, how can your speech be understood ? you will but be speaking to the air.   Perhaps there may 10 be as many languages in the world [as the Tongues in which you speak], and none of them is unmeaning. If, then, I know not the meaning of the language, I 11 shall be as a foreigner to him that speaks it, and he will be accounted a foreigner by me.   Wherefore, in 12 your own case (since you delight in spiritual gifts) strive that your abundant possession of them may build up the Church.   Therefore, let him who speaks in a 13 Tongue, pray that he may be able to interpret [1] what he utters.   For if I utter prayers in a Tongue, my 14 spirit indeed prays, but my understanding bears no fruit.   What follows, then ?   I will pray indeed with 15 my spirit, but I will pray with my understanding also ; I will sing praises with my spirit, but I will sing with my understanding also.   For if thou, with 16 thy spirit, offerest thanks and praise, how shall the Amen be said to thy thanksgiving by those worshippers who take no part [2] in the ministrations, while

---

[1] This verse distinctly proves that the *gift of Tongues* was not a *know-ledge* of foreign languages, as is often supposed. See Chap. XIII.

[2] Not *the unlearned* (A. V.), but *him who takes no part in the particular matter in hand.*

17 they are ignorant of the meaning of thy words? Thou
indeed fitly offerest thanksgiving, but thy neighbours
18 are not built up. I offer thanksgiving to God in
private,[1] speaking in Tongues [to Him], more than
19 any of you. Yet in the congregation I would rather
speak five words with my understanding so as to instruct others, than ten thousand words in a Tongue.
20 Brethren, be not children in understanding; but in
21 malice be children, and in understanding be men. It
is written in the Law,[2] '𝔚𝔦𝔱𝔥 𝔪𝔢𝔫 𝔬𝔣 𝔬𝔱𝔥𝔢𝔯 𝔱𝔬𝔫𝔤𝔲𝔢𝔰
𝔞𝔫𝔡 𝔬𝔱𝔥𝔢𝔯 𝔩𝔦𝔭𝔰 𝔴𝔦𝔩𝔩 𝔍 𝔰𝔭𝔢𝔞𝔨 𝔲𝔫𝔱𝔬 𝔱𝔥𝔦𝔰 𝔭𝔢𝔬𝔭𝔩𝔢; 𝔞𝔫𝔡 𝔶𝔢𝔱 𝔣𝔬𝔯
22 𝔞𝔩𝔩 𝔱𝔥𝔞𝔱 𝔱𝔥𝔢𝔶 𝔴𝔦𝔩𝔩 𝔫𝔬𝔱 𝔥𝔢𝔞𝔯 𝔪𝔢, 𝔰𝔞𝔦𝔱𝔥 𝔱𝔥𝔢 𝔏𝔬𝔯𝔡.' So that
the gift of Tongues is a sign[3] given rather to unbelievers than to believers; whereas the gift of Pro-
23 phecy belongs to believers. When, therefore, the
whole congregation is assembled, if all the speakers
speak in Tongues, and if any who take no part in
your ministrations, or who are unbelievers, should
enter your assembly, will they not say that you are
24 mad?[4] But if all exercise the gift of Prophecy,
then if any man who is an unbeliever, or who takes
no part in your ministrations, should enter the place
of meeting, he is convicted in conscience by every
25 speaker, he feels himself judged by all, and[5] the
secret depths of his heart are laid open; and so he
will fall upon his face and worship God, and report
26 that God is in you of a truth. What follows then,
brethren? If, when you meet together, one is prepared to sing a hymn of praise, another to exercise
his gift of Teaching, another his gift of Tongues, another to deliver a Revelation,[6] another an Interpretation; let all be so done as to build up the Church.
27 If there be any who speak in Tongues, let not more

---

[1] This is evidently the meaning of the verse. Compare verse 2, ' He who speaks in a tongue speaks not to him-self but to God,' and verse 28, ' Let him speak in private to himself and God alone.'

[2] Isa. xxviii. 11. Not exactly according to the Hebrew or LXX.

[3] That is, a *condemnatory* sign.

[4] We must not be led, from any apparent analogy, to confound the exercise of the gift of Tongues in the primitive Church with modern exhibitions of fanaticism, which bear a superficial resemblance to it. We must remember that such modern pre-

tensions to this gift must of course resemble the manifestations of the original gift in external features, because these very features have been the objects of intentional imitation. If, however, the inarticulate utterances of ecstatic joy are followed (as they were in some of Wesley's converts) by a life of devoted holiness, we should hesitate to say that they might not bear some analogy to those of the Corinthian Christians.

[5] The word for 'so' is omitted in the best MSS.

[6] This would be an exercise of the gift of 'prophecy.'

than two, or at the most three, speak [in the same assembly] ; and let them speak in turn ; and let the same interpreter explain the words of all.   But xiv. if there be no interpreter, let him who speaks in Tongues keep silence in the congregation, and speak in private to himself and God alone.   Of those who 29 have the gift of Prophecy, let two or three speak [in each assembly], and let the rest [1] judge ; but if 30 another of them, while sitting as hearer, receives a revelation [calling him to prophesy], let the first cease to speak.   For so you can each prophesy in 31 turn, that all may receive teaching and exhortation ; and the gift of Prophecy does not take from the 32 prophets [2] the control over their own spirits.   For 33 God is not the author of confusion, but of peace.

The women must not officiate publicly in the congregation.   [3] In your congregation, as in all the congregations of the Saints, the women must keep silence ; 34 for they are not permitted to speak in public, but to show submission, as saith also the Law.[4]   And if 35 they wish to ask any question, let them ask it of their own husbands at home ; for it is disgraceful to women to speak in the congregation.   [Whence is your claim 36 to change the rules delivered to you ?][5]   Was it from you that the word of God went forth ; or, are you the only Church which it has reached ?   Nay, if any 37 think that he has the gift of Prophecy, or that he is a spiritual [6] man, let him acknowledge the words which I write for commands of the Lord.   But if any 38 man refuse this acknowledgment, let him refuse it at his peril.

Therefore, brethren, delight in the gift of Pro- 39 phecy, and hinder not the gift of Tongues.   And let 40 all be done with decency and order.

The doctrine of the Resurrection of the Dead estab-   Moreover, brethren, I call to your remembrance xv. the Glad-tidings which I brought you, which also

---

[1] i.e. let the rest of the prophets judge whether those who stand up to exercise the gift have really received it. This is parallel to the direction in 1 Thess. v. 21.

[2] Literally, ' *the spirits of the prophets are under the control of the prophets.*' This is a reason why the rule given above can easily be observed. [This seems to modify what is said in p. 337. H.]

[3] This translation places a full-stop in the middle of the 33rd verse, and a comma at the end of it.

[4] Gen. iii. 16 : ' Thy husband shall have the dominion over thee.'

[5] The sentence in brackets, or something equivalent, is implied in the ἤ which begins the next. ' OR *was it* from you,'—i.e. ' *Or, if you set up your judgment against that of other Churches, was it from you,*' &c.

[6] ' Spiritual,' the epithet on which the party of Apollos (the ultra-Pauline party) especially prided themselves. See chap. iii. 1–3 and Gal. vi. 1.

v. 2 you received, wherein also you stand firm, whereby
also you are saved,[1] if you still hold fast the words
wherein I declared it to you; unless indeed you be-
3 lieved in vain. For the first thing I taught you was
that which I had myself been taught, that Christ
4 died for our sins, according to the Scriptures; [2] and
that He was buried, and that He rose [3] the third day
5 from the dead, according to the Scriptures; [4] and
that he was seen by Cephas, and then by The Twelve;
6 after that He was seen by about five hundred brethren at once, of whom the greater part are living at
7 this present time, but some are fallen asleep.[5] Next
He was seen by James, and then by all the Apostles;
8 and last of all he was seen by me also, who am placed
9 among the rest as it were by an untimely birth; for
I am the least of the Apostles, and am not worthy to
be called an Apostle, because I persecuted the Church
10 of God. But by the grace of God, I am what I am;
and His grace which was bestowed upon me was not
fruitless; but I laboured more abundantly than all
the rest; yet not I, but the grace of God which was
11 with me. So then, whether preached by me, or
them, this is what we preached, and this is what you
believed.

12 If then this be our tidings, that Christ is risen
from the dead, how is it that some among you say,
13 there is no resurrection of the dead? But if there
be no resurrection of the dead, then Christ is not
14 risen; and if Christ be not risen, vain is the message
we proclaim, and vain the faith with which you heard
15 it. Moreover, we are found guilty of false witness
against God; because we bore witness of God that
He raised Christ from the dead, whom He did not

[1] Literally, *you are in the way of salvation.* The words which follow (*the words wherein,* &c.) were joined (in our first edition) with *preached* in the preceding verse, according to Billroth's view. But further consideration has led us to think that they may be more naturally made dependent on *hold fast,* as they are taken by De Wette, Alford, and others.

[2] So our Lord quotes Isa. liii. 12, in Luke xxii. 37.

[3] In the original it is the perfect, not the aorist: '*He is risen,*' not '*He was raised,*' or (more literally), *He is awakened,* not *He was awakened;* because Christ, being once risen, dieth

no more. But this present-perfect cannot here be retained in the English.

[4] Among the 'Scriptures' here referred to by St. Paul, one is the prophecy which he himself quoted in the speech at Antioch from Ps. xvi. 10.

[5] Can we imagine it possible that St. Paul should have said this without knowing it to be true? or without himself having seen some of these 'five hundred brethren,' of whom the 'greater part' were alive when he wrote these words? The sceptical (but candid and honest) De Wette acknowledges this testimony as conclusive.

raise, if indeed the dead rise not. For if there be no xv.
resurrection of the dead, Christ himself [1] is not risen.
And if Christ be not risen, your faith is vain, you 17
are still in [2] your sins. Moreover, if this be so, they 18
who have fallen asleep in Christ, perished when they
died. If in this life only we have hope in Christ, we 19
are of all men most miserable. But now, Christ is 20
risen from the dead ; the first-fruits [3] of all who sleep.
For since by man came death, by man came also the 21
resurrection of the dead. For as, in Adam, all men 22
die, so, in Christ, shall all be raised to life. But 23
each in his own order ; Christ, the first-fruits ; afterwards they who are Christ's at His appearing ; finally, 24
the end shall come, when He shall give up His kingdom to God His Father, having destroyed all other
dominion, and authority, and power.[4] For He must 25
reign '𝔱𝔦𝔩𝔩 𝔥𝔢 𝔥𝔞𝔱𝔥 𝔭𝔲𝔱 𝔞𝔩𝔩 𝔢𝔫𝔢𝔪𝔦𝔢𝔰 𝔲𝔫𝔡𝔢𝔯 𝔥𝔦𝔰 𝔣𝔢𝔢𝔱.' [5]
And last of His enemies, Death also shall be de- 26
stroyed. For '𝔥𝔢 𝔥𝔞𝔱𝔥 𝔭𝔲𝔱 𝔞𝔩𝔩 𝔱𝔥𝔦𝔫𝔤𝔰 𝔲𝔫𝔡𝔢𝔯 𝔥𝔦𝔰 𝔣𝔢𝔢𝔱.' [6] 27
But in that saying, '𝔄𝔩𝔩 𝔱𝔥𝔦𝔫𝔤𝔰 𝔞𝔯𝔢 𝔭𝔲𝔱 𝔲𝔫𝔡𝔢𝔯 𝔥𝔦𝔪,' it
is manifest that God is excepted, who put all things
under Him. And when all things are made subject 28
to Him, then shall the Son also subject Himself to
Him who made them subject, that God may be all in
all.

Again, what will become of those who cause them- 29
selves to be baptized for the Dead,[7] if the dead never

[1] This argument is founded on the
union between Christ and His members: they so share His life, that because He lives for ever, they must live
also; and conversely, if we deny their
immortality, we deny His.

[2] Because we 'are saved' from our
sins 'by His life.' (Rom. v. 10.)

[3] On the second day of the feast of
Passover a sheaf of ripe corn was offered
upon the altar as a consecration of the
whole harvest. Till this was done it
was considered unlawful to begin reaping. See Levit. xxiii. 10, 11, and
Joseph. *Antiq.* iii. 10. The metaphor
therefore is, 'As the single sheaf of
first fruits represents and consecrates
all the harvest, so Christ's resurrection
represents and involves that of all who
sleep in Him.' It should be observed
that the verb is not present as in A. V. ;
but past ; not *is become*, but *became* ;
and that the best MSS. omit it.

[4] Compare Col. ii. 15 ; also Eph. i.
21.

[5] Ps. cx. 1 (LXX.). Quoted, and
similarly applied, by our Lord Himself,
Matt. xxii. 44.

[6] Ps. viii. 6, nearly after LXX.
Quoted also as Messianic, Eph. i. 22,
and Heb. ii. 8. See the note on the
latter place.

[7] The only meaning which the Greek
seems to admit here is a reference to
the practice of submitting to baptism
instead of some person who had died
unbaptized. Yet this explanation is
liable to very great difficulties. (1) How
strange that St. Paul should refer to
such a superstition without rebuking
it ! Perhaps, however, he may have
censured it in a former letter, and now
only refers to it as an *argumentum ad
homines*. It has, indeed, been alleged
that the present mention of it implies
a censure; but this is far from evident.
(2) If such a practice did exist in the
Apostolic Church, how can we account
for its being discontinued in the period
which followed, when a magical efficacy

rise again? Why then do they submit to baptism for the dead?

v. 30 And I too, why do I put my life to hazard every
31 hour? I protest by my[1] boasting (which I have [not in myself, but] in Christ Jesus our Lord) I die
32 daily. If I have fought (so to speak) with beasts at Ephesus,[2] what am I profited if the dead rise not?
33 '𝕷𝖊𝖙 𝖚𝖘 𝖊𝖆𝖙 𝖆𝖓𝖉 𝖉𝖗𝖎𝖓𝖐, 𝖋𝖔𝖗 𝖙𝖔-𝖒𝖔𝖗𝖗𝖔𝖜 𝖜𝖊 𝖉𝖎𝖊.'[3] Beware lest you be led astray; '*Converse with evil men cor-*
34 *rupts good manners.*'[4] Change your drunken revell-ings[5] into the sobriety of righteousness, and live no more in sin; for some of you know not God; I speak this to your shame.

35 But some one will say, 'How are the dead raised
36 up? and with what body do they come?'[6] Thou fool, the seed thou sowest is not quickened into
37 life till it hath partaken of death. And that which thou sowest has not the same body with the plant which will spring from it, but it is mere grain, of

was more and more ascribed to the material act of baptism? Yet the prac-tice was never adopted except by some obscure sects of Gnostics, who seem to have founded their custom on this very passage.

The explanations which have been adopted to avoid the difficulty, such as 'over the graves of the dead,' or 'in the name of the dead (meaning Christ),' &c., are all inadmissible, as being con-trary to the analogy of the language. On the whole, therefore, the passage must be considered to admit of no satis-factory explanation. It alludes to some practice of the Corinthians, which has not been recorded elsewhere, and of which every other trace has perished. The reader who wishes to see all that can be said on the subject should con-sult Canon Stanley's note.

[1] We read 'our' with Griesbach, on the authority of the Codex Alexan-drinus. If 'your' be the true reading, it can scarcely be translated (as has been proposed) '*my boasting of you.*' For though instances may be adduced (as Rom. xi. 31) when a possessive pro-noun is thus used objectively, yet they never occur except where the context renders mistake impossible. Indeed it is obvious that no writer would go out of his way to use a possessive pronoun in an unusual sense, when by so doing he would create ambiguity which might be avoided by adopting a usual form of expression.

[2] This is metaphorical, as appears by the qualifying expression translated in A.V., 'after the manner of men.' It must refer to some very violent op-position which St. Paul had met with at Ephesus, the particulars of which are not recorded.

[3] Isa. xxii. 13 (LXX.).

[4] St. Paul here quotes a line from The Thais, a comedy of Menander's. The line had probably passed into a proverbial expression. We see, from this passage, that the free-thinking party at Corinth joined immoral prac-tice with their licentious doctrine; and that they were corrupted by the evil example of their heathen neigh-bours.

[5] Not *awake* (as in A. V.), but *cease to be drunken.* And below, *do not go on sinning* (present).

[6] The form of this objection is con-clusive against the hypothesis of those who suppose that these Corinthians only disbelieved the Resurrection *of the body*; and that they believed the Resur-rection *of the dead.* St. Paul asserts the Resurrection of the dead; to which they reply, 'How can the dead rise to life again, when their body has perished?' This objection he proceeds to answer, by showing that individual existence may continue, without the continuance of the material body.

wheat, or whatever else it may chance to be. But XV. 38
God gives it a body according to His will; and to
every seed the body of its own proper plant. For all 39
flesh is not the same flesh; [1] [but each body is fitted
to the place it fills]; the bodies of men, and of beasts,
of birds, and of fishes, differ the one from the other.
And there are bodies which belong to heaven, and 40
bodies which belong to earth; but in glory the
heavenly differ from the earthly. The sun is more 41
glorious than the moon, and the moon is more glorious than the stars, and one star excels another in
glory. So likewise is the resurrection of the dead; 42
[they will be clothed with a body fitted to their lot];
it is sown in corruption, it is raised in incorruption;
it is sown in dishonour, it is raised in glory; it is 43
sown in weakness, it is raised in power; it is sown a 44
natural [2] body, it is raised a spiritual body; for as
there are natural bodies, so there are also spiritual
bodies.[3] And so it is written, '𝕮𝖍𝖊 𝖋𝖎𝖗𝖘𝖙 𝖒𝖆𝖓 𝕬𝖉𝖆𝖒 45
𝖜𝖆𝖘 𝖒𝖆𝖉𝖊 𝖆 𝖑𝖎𝖛𝖎𝖓𝖌 𝖘𝖔𝖚𝖑,' [4] the last Adam was made a
life-giving spirit. But the spiritual comes not till 46
after the natural. The first man was made of earthly 47
clay, the second man was the Lord from heaven. As 48
is the earthly, such are they also that are earthly;
and as is the heavenly, such are they also that are
heavenly; and as we have borne the image of the 49
earthly, we shall also bear the image of the heavenly.
But this I say, brethren, that flesh and blood [5] cannot 50

[1] Prof. Stanley translates '*no flesh is the same flesh,*' which is surely an untenable proposition, and moreover inconsistent with the context; though the words of the Greek no doubt admit of such a rendering.

[2] For the translation here, see note on ii. 14. The reference to this of the following '*soul*' (in the quotation) should be observed, though it cannot be retained in English.

[3] The difference of reading does not materially affect the sense of this verse.

[4] Gen. ii. 7, slightly altered from LXX. The second member of the antithesis is not a part of the quotation.

[5] The importance of the subject justifies our quoting at some length the admirable remarks of Dr. Burton (formerly Regius Professor of Divinity at Oxford) on this passage, in the hope that his high reputation for learning and for unblemished orthodoxy may lead some persons to reconsider the loose and unscriptural language which they are in the habit of using. After regretting that some of the early Fathers have (when treating of the *Resurrection of the Body*) appeared to contradict these words of St. Paul, Dr. Burton continues as follows:—

'It is nowhere asserted in the New Testament that we shall rise again *with our bodies.* Unless a man will say that the stalk, the blade, and the ear of corn are actually the same thing with the single grain which is put into the ground, he cannot quote St. Paul as saying that we shall rise again with the same bodies; or at least he must allow that the future body may only be like to the present one, inasmuch as both come under the same genus; i.e. we speak of human *bodies,* and we speak of heavenly *bodies.* But St. Paul's words do not warrant us in saying that the resemblance between the present and future body will be greater than between

inherit the kingdom of God, neither can corruption
xv.51 inherit incorruption. Behold, I declare to you a
mystery; we shall not [1] all sleep, but we shall all be
52 changed, in a moment, in the twinkling of an eye, at
the sound of the last trumpet; for the trumpet shall
sound, and the dead shall be raised incorruptible,
53 and we shall be changed. For this corruptible
must put on incorruption, and this mortal must put
on immortality.

54 But when this corruptible is clothed with incorruption, and this mortal is clothed with immortality,
then shall be brought to pass the saying, which is
written, '𝕯𝖊𝖆𝖙𝖍 𝖎𝖘 𝖘𝖜𝖆𝖑𝖑𝖔𝖜𝖊𝖉 𝖚𝖕 𝖎𝖓 𝖛𝖎𝖈𝖙𝖔𝖗𝖞.' [2] '𝕺
55 𝖉𝖊𝖆𝖙𝖍, 𝖜𝖍𝖊𝖗𝖊 𝖎𝖘 𝖙𝖍𝖞 𝖘𝖙𝖎𝖓𝖌?' '𝕺 𝖌𝖗𝖆𝖛𝖊, 𝖜𝖍𝖊𝖗𝖊 𝖎𝖘 𝖙𝖍𝖞
56 𝖛𝖎𝖈𝖙𝖔𝖗𝖞?' [3] The sting of death is sin, and the strength
57 of sin is the law; [4] but thanks be to God, who giveth
us the victory, through Our Lord Jesus Christ.

58 Therefore, my beloved brethren, be ye stedfast,
immovable, always abounding in the work of the
Lord; knowing that your labour is not ·in vain, in
the Lord.

---

a man and a star, or between a bird and a fish. Nothing can be plainer than the expression which he uses in the first of these two analogies, *Thou sowest not that body that shall be* (xv. 37). He says also with equal plainness, of the body, *It is sown a natural body; it is raised a spiritual body; there is a natural body, and there is a spiritual body* (ver. 44). These words require to be examined closely, and involve remotely a deep metaphysical question. In common language, the terms *Body* and *Spirit* are accustomed to be opposed, and are used to represent two things which are totally distinct. But St. Paul here brings the two expressions together, and speaks of a *spiritual body*. St. Paul, therefore, did not oppose *Body* to *Spirit*; and though the looseness of modern language may allow us to do so, and yet to be correct in our ideas, it may save some confusion if we consider *Spirit* as opposed to *Matter*, and if we take *Body* to be a generic term, which comprises both. *A body*, therefore, in the language of St. Paul, is something which has a distinct individual existence.

. . . . .

'St. Paul tells us that every individual, when he rises again, will have a spiritual body: but the remarks which

I have made may show how different is the idea conveyed by these words from the notions which some persons entertain, that we shall rise again with *the same identical body.* St. Paul appears effectually to preclude this notion, when he says, *Flesh and blood cannot inherit the kingdom of God'* (ver. 50). —Burton's *Lectures*, pp. 429–431.

[1] The other reading (adopted by Lachmann) gives the opposite assertion, viz. ' *we shall all sleep, but we shall not all be changed.*' It is easy to understand the motive which might have led to the substitution of this reading for the other; a wish, namely, to escape the inference that St. Paul expected some of that generation to survive until the general resurrection.

[2] Isa. xxv. 8. Not quoted from the LXX., but apparently from the Hebrew, with some alteration.

[3] Hosea xiii. 14. Quoted, but not exactly, from LXX., which here differs from the Hebrew.

[4] Why is the law called 'the strength of sin'? Because the Law of Duty, being acknowledged, gives to sin its power to wound the conscience; in fact, a moral law of precepts and penalties announces the fatal consequences of sin, without giving us any power of conquering sin. Compare Rom. vii. 7–11.

Directions
concerning
the collection
for the Judean
Christians.

Concerning the collection for the saints [at Jeru- salem] I would have you do as I have enjoined upon the churches of Galatia.   Upon the first day of the 2 week, let each of you set apart whatever his gains may enable him to spare; that there may be no col- lections when I come.   And when I am with you, 3 whomsoever you shall judge to be fitted for the trust, I will furnish with letters, and send them to carry your benevolence to Jerusalem; or if there shall seem 4 sufficient reason for me also to go thither, they shall go with me.   But I will visit you after I have passed 5 through Macedonia (for through Macedonia I shall pass), and perhaps I shall remain with you, or even 6 winter with you, that you may forward me on my far- ther journey, whithersoever I go.   For I do not wish 7 to see you now for a passing [1] visit; since I hope to stay some time with you, if the Lord permit.   But I 8 shall remain at Ephesus until Pentecost, for a door is 9 opened to me both great and effectual; and there are many adversaries [against whom I must contend].   If 10 Timotheus come to you, be careful to give him no cause of fear [2] in your intercourse with him, for he is labouring, as I am, in the Lord's work.   Therefore, 11 let no man despise him, but forward him on his way in peace, that he may come hither to me; for I expect him, and the brethren with him.

St. Paul's
future plans.

Timotheus.

Apollos.

As regards the brother Apollos, I urged him 12 much to visit you with the brethren [who bear this letter]; [3] nevertheless, he was resolved not to come to you at this time, but he will visit you at a more convenient season.

Exhortations.

Be watchful, stand firm in faith, be manful and 13 stout-hearted.[4]   Let all you do be done in love.   14

Stephanas,
Fortunatus,
and Achaicus.

You know, brethren, that the house of Stephanas [5] 15 were the first-fruits of Achaia, and that they have taken on themselves the task of ministering to the saints.   I exhort you, therefore, on your part, to 16 show submission towards men like these, and towards

---

[1] i.e. St. Paul had altered his origi- nal intention, which was to go from Ephesus by sea to Corinth, and thence to Macedonia. For this change of pur- pose he was reproached by the Judais- ing party at Corinth, who insinuated that he was afraid to come, and that he dared not support the loftiness of his pretensions by corresponding deeds (see 2 Cor. i. 17, and x. 1-12). He explains

his reason for postponing his visit in 2 Cor. i. 23. It was an anxiety to give the Corinthians time for repentance, that he might not be forced to use severity with them.

[2] The youth of Timotheus accounts for this request. Compare 1 Tim. iv. 12
[3] See notes, p. 363 and p. 418.
[4] i.e. under persecution.
[5] See p. 313.

xvi.17 all who work laboriously with them. I rejoice in
the coming of Stephanas and Fortunatus, and Achaicus, because they[1] have supplied all which you
18 needed; for they have lightened my spirit and yours.[2]
To such render due acknowledgment.

The Churches of Asia salute you. Aquila and Salutations from the
19 Priscilla send their loving salutation in the Lord, Province of Asia.
together with the Church which assembles at their
20 house. All the brethren here salute you. Salute one
another with the kiss of holiness.[3]

21 The salutation of me, Paul, with my own hand. Autograph
22 Let him who loves not the Lord Jesus Christ be Conclusion.
accursed. 𝕮𝖍𝖊 𝕷𝖔𝖗𝖉 𝖈𝖔𝖒𝖊𝖙𝖍.[4]
23 The grace of our Lord Jesus Christ be with you.
24 My love be with you all in Christ Jesus.[5]

In the concluding part of this letter we have some indication of
the Apostle's plans for the future. He is looking forward to a
journey through Macedonia (xvi. 5), to be succeeded by a visit to
Corinth (ib. 2-7), and after this he thinks it probable he may
proceed to Jerusalem (ib. 3, 4). In the Acts of the Apostles the
same intentions[6] are expressed, with a stronger purpose of going to
Jerusalem (xvi. 21), and with the additional conviction that after
passing through Macedonia and Achaia, and visiting Palestine, he
'must also see Rome' (ib.). He had won many of the inhabitants
of Asia Minor and Ephesus to the faith: and now, after the
prospect of completing his charitable exertions for the poor Chris-

---

[1] Compare 2 Cor. xi. 9, and Phil. ii.
30. It cannot well be taken objectively,
as '*my want of you*;' not only because
'my' would have been added, but also
because the expression is used in eight
passages by St. Paul, and in one by St.
Luke, and the genitive connected with
the word for 'want' is subjectively
used in seven out of these nine cases
without question, and ought therefore
also to be so taken in the remaining
two cases, where the context is not
equally decisive.

[2] Viz. by supplying the means of our
intercourse.

[3] See note on 1 Thess. v. 25.

[4] Maran-Atha means 'The Lord
cometh,' and is used apparently by St.
Paul as a kind of motto: compare 'the
Lord is nigh' (Phil. iv. 5). Billroth
thinks that he wrote it in Hebrew characters, as a part of the autograph by
which he authenticated this letter. See

the Hebrew and Greek together at the
end of this Chapter. Buxtorf (*Lex.
Chald.* 827) says it was part of a Jewish
cursing formula, from the 'Prophecy of
Enoch' (Jud. 14); but this view appears to be without foundation. In
fact, it would have been most incongruous to blend together a Greek
word (ANATHEMA) with an Aramaic phrase (MARAN ATHA), and
to use the compound as a formula of
execration. This was not done till (in
later ages of the Church) the meaning
of the terms themselves was lost.

[5] The 'Amen' is not found in the
best MSS.

[6] The important application made in
the *Horæ Paulinæ* of these coincidences
between the Acts and Corinthians, and
again of those referred to below between
the Acts and Romans, need only be
alluded to.

tians of Judæa, his spirit turns towards the accomplishment of remoter conquests. Far from being content with his past achievements, or resting from his incessant labours, he felt that he was under a debt of perpetual obligation to all the Gentile world.[1] Thus he expresses himself, soon after this time, in the Epistle to the Roman Christians, whom he had long ago desired to see (Rom. i. 10-15), and whom he hopes at length to visit, now that he is on his way to Jerusalem, and is looking forward to a still more distant and hazardous journey to Spain (ib. xv. 22-29). The path thus dimly traced before him, as he thought of the future at Ephesus, and made more clearly visible, when he wrote the letter at Corinth, was made still more evident[2] as he proceeded on his course. Yet not without forebodings of evil,[3] and much discouragement,[4] and mysterious delays,[5] did the Apostle advance on his courageous career. But we are anticipating many subjects which will give a touching interest to subsequent passages of this history. Important events still detain us in Ephesus. Though St. Paul's companions[6] had been sent before in the direction of his contemplated journey (Acts xix. 22), he still resolved to stay till Pentecost (1 Cor. xvi. 8). A 'great door' was open to him, and there were 'many adversaries,' against whom he had yet to contend.

ANAΘEMA מרן אתא

Anathema   *Maran-Atha.*[7]

[1] 'I am a debtor both to Greeks and Barbarians.'—*Rom.* i. 14.

[2] By the vision at Jerusalem (Acts xxiii. 11), and on board the ship (xxvii. 23, 24).

[3] Compare what he wrote to the Romans (Rom. xv. 30, 31) with what he said at Miletus (Acts xx. 22, 23), and with the scene at Ptolemais (ib. xxi. 10-14).

[4] The arrest at Jerusalem.

[5] The two years' imprisonment at Cæsarea, and the shipwreck.

[6] See pp. 362, 363. We have mentioned there, in a note, the probability that Titus was one of those who went to Corinth with the First Epistle. See 1 Cor. xvi. 11, 12 ; 2 Cor. xii. 18. We find that this is the view of Macknight. *Transl. &c. of the Apost. Epistles*, vol. i. p. 451. If this view is correct, it is interesting to observe that Titus is at first simply spoken of as 'a brother,'—but that gradually he rises into note with the faithful discharge of responsible duties. He becomes eminently conspicuous in the circumstances detailed below, Chap. XVII., and in the end he shares with Timothy the honour of associating his name with the pastoral Epistles of St. Paul.

[7] See note 4, p. 417.

CHAPTER XVI.

Description of Ephesus.—Temple of Diana.—Her Image and Worship.—Political Constitution of Ephesus.—The Asiarchs.—Demetrius and the Silversmiths.—Tumult in the Theatre.—Speech of the Town-clerk.—St. Paul's Departure.

THE boundaries of the province of Asia,[1] and the position of its chief city Ephesus,[2] have already been placed before the reader. It is now time that we should give some description of the city itself, with a notice of its characteristic religious institutions, and its political arrangements under the Empire.

No cities were ever more favourably placed for prosperity and growth than those of the colonial Greeks in Asia Minor. They had the advantage of a coast-line full of convenient harbours and of a sea which was favourable to the navigation of that day; and, through the long approaches formed by the plains of the great western rivers, they had access to the inland trade of the East. Two of these rivers have been more than once alluded to,—the Hermus and the Mæander.[3] The valley of the first was bounded on the south by the ridge of Tmolus; that of the second was bounded on the north by Messogis. In the interval between these two mountain ranges was the shorter course of the river Cayster.[4] A few miles from the sea a narrow gorge is formed by Mount Pactyas on the south, which is the western termination of Messogis, and by the precipices of Gallesus on the north, the pine-clad summits[5] of which are more remotely connected with the heights of Tmolus. This gorge separates the Upper 'Caystrian meadows'[6] from a small alluvial plain[7] by the sea. Partly on the long ridge of Cores-

---

[1] p. 182.

[2] p. 368.

[3] See above, pp. 364, 368.

[4] See p. 368.

[5] 'Our road lay at the foot of Gallesus, beneath precipices of a stupendous height, abrupt and inaccessible. In the rock are many holes inhabited by eagles; of which several were soaring high in the air, with crows clamouring about them, so far above us as hardly to be discernible.'—Chandler, p. 111. Of another journey he says: 'We rode among the roots of Gallesus, or the Aleman, through pleasant thickets abounding with goldfinches. The aërial summits of this immense mountain towered above us, clad with pines. Steep succeeded steep, as we advanced,

and the path became more narrow slippery, and uneven . . . . the known sureness of foot of our horses being our confidence and security by fearful precipices and giddy heights.'—p. 103. For the Cayster and the site of Ephesus, see p. 107. The approach from Sardis, by which we suppose St. Paul to have come (see above, p. 364), was on this side: and part of the pavement of the road still remains.

[6] For the 'Asian meadow,' see above, p. 183.

[7] The plain is said by Mr. Arundell to be about five miles long; and the morass has advanced considerably into the sea since the flourishing times of Ephesus.

sus, which is the southern boundary of this plain,—partly on the detached circular eminence of Mount Prion,—and partly on the plain itself, near the windings of the Cayster, and about the edge of the harbour,—were the buildings of the city. Ephesus was not so distinguished in early times as several of her Ionian sisters;[1] and some of them outlived her glory. But, though Phocæa and Miletus sent out more colonies, and Smyrna has ever remained a flourishing city, yet Ephesus had great natural advantages, which were duly developed in the age of which we are writing. Having easy access through the defiles of Mount Tmolus to Sardis, and thence up the valley of the Hermus far into Phrygia,[2]—and again, by a similar pass through Messogis to the Mæander, being connected with the great road through Iconium to the Euphrates,[3]—it became the metropolis of the province of Asia under the Romans, and the chief emporium of trade on the nearer side of Taurus. The city built by Androclus and his Athenian followers was on the slope of Coressus; but gradually it descended into the plain, in the direction of the Temple of Diana. The Alexandrian age produced a marked alteration in Ephesus, as in most of the great towns in the East; and Lysimachus extended his new city over the summit of Prion as well as the heights of Coressus. The Roman age saw, doubtless, a still further increase both of the size and magnificence of the place. To attempt to reconstruct it from the materials which remain, would be a difficult task,[4]—far more difficult than in the case of Athens, or even Antioch; but some of the more interesting sites are easily identified. Those who walk over the desolate site of the Asiatic metropolis see piles of ruined edifices on the rocky sides and among the thickets of Mount Prion:[5] they look out from its summit over the confused morass which once was the harbour,[6] where Aquila and Priscilla landed; and they visit in its deep recesses the dripping marble-quarries, where the marks of the tools are visible still.[7] On the outer edge of the same hill they trace the

[1] The Ephesian Diana, however, was the patroness of the Phocean navigators, even when the city of Ephesus was unimportant.

[2] In this direction we imagine St. Paul to have travelled. See above, p. 363.

[3] We have frequently had occasion to mention this great road. See pp. 206–208, 363. It was the principal line of communication with the eastern provinces; but we have conjectured that St. Paul did not travel by it, because it seems probable that he never was at Colossæ. See p. 364. A description of the route by Colossæ and Laodicea will be found in Arundell's *Asia Minor*. The view he gives of the cliffs of Colossæ should be noticed. Though St. Paul may never have seen them, they are interesting as connected with Epaphras and his other converts.

[4] A plan of the entire city, with a descriptive memoir, has been prepared by E. Falkener, Esq., Architect, but remains unpublished.

[5] Hamilton's *Researches in Asia Minor*, vol. ii. p. 23. Compare Chandler.

[6] 'Even the sea has retired from the scene of desolation, and a pestilential morass, covered with mud and rushes, has succeeded to the waters which brought up the ships laden with merchandise from every country.'—Arundell's *Seven Churches*, p. 27. Another occasion will occur for mentioning the harbour which was very indifferent. Some attempts to improve it were made about this time.

[7] Chandler. A curious story is told of the discovery of this marble. A shepherd named Pixodorus was feeding his flock on the hill: two of his rams fighting, one of them missed his anta-

enclosure of the Stadium,[1] which may have suggested to St. Paul many of those images with which he enforces Christian duty, in the first letter written from Ephesus to Corinth.[2] Farther on, and nearer Coressus, the remains of the vast Theatre[3] (the outline of the enclosure is still distinct, though the marble seats are removed) show the place where the multitude, roused by Demetrius, shouted out, for two hours, in honour of Diana.[4] Below is the Agora,[5] through which the mob rushed up to the well-known place of meeting. And in the valley between Prion and Coressus is one of the Gymnasia,[6] where the athletes were trained for transient honours and a perishable garland. Surrounding and crowning the scene, are the long Hellenic walls of Lysimachus, following the ridge of Coressus.[7] On a spur of the hill, they descend to an ancient tower, which is still called the Prison of St. Paul.[8] The name is doubtless legendary: but St. Paul may have stood here, and looked over the city and the plain, and seen the Cayster winding towards him from the base of Gallesus.[9] Within his view was another eminence, detached from the city of that day, but which became the Mahomedan town when ancient Ephesus was destroyed, and nevertheless preserves in its name a record of another Apostle, the 'disciple' St. John.[10]

gonist, and with his horn broke a crust of the whitest marble. The Ephesians were at this time in search of stone for the building of their temple. The shepherd ran to his fellow-citizens with the specimen, and was received with joy. His name was changed into Evangelus (giver of glad-tidings), and divine honours were afterwards paid to him.

[1] See Chandler, who measured the area and found it 687 feet in length. The side next the plain is raised on vaults, and faced with a strong wall.

[2] 1 Cor. ix. 24–27.

[3] 'Of the site of the theatre, the scene of the tumult raised by Demetrius, there can be no doubt, its ruins being a wreck of immense grandeur. I think it must have been larger than the one at Miletus, and that exceeds any I have elsewhere seen in scale, although not in ornament. Its form alone can now be spoken of, for every seat is removed, and the proscenium is a hill of ruins.'—Fellows' *Asia Minor*, p. 274. The Theatre of Ephesus is said to be the largest known of any that have remained to us from antiquity.

[4] Acts xix. Our second edition contains a view (from Laborde), combining the steps of the theatre with a general prospect towards the sea. See also the art. *Ephesus* in the *Dict. of the Bible*.

[5] The Agora, with its public buildings, would naturally be between the hill-side on which the theatre and stadium stood, and the harbour. For the general notion of a Greek Agora, see the description of Athens.

[6] See an engraving of these ruins in the second volume of *Ionian Antiquities*, published by the Dilettanti Society.

[7] 'An interesting feature in these ruins is the Hellenic wall of Lysimachus, ranging along the heights of Coressus. It extends for nearly a mile and three quarters, in a S.E. and N.W. direction, from the heights immediately to the S. of the gymnasium to the tower called the Prison of St. Paul, but which is in fact one of the towers of the ancient wall. . . . It is defended and strengthened by numerous square towers of the same character at unequal distances.'—Hamilton's *Researches*, vol. ii. p. 26. An engraving of one of the gateways is given, p. 27.

[8] Hamilton, as above.

[9] 'This eminence (a root of Coressus running out towards the plain) commands a lovely prospect of the river Cayster, which there crosses the plain from near Gallesus, with a small but full stream, and with many luxuriant meanders.'—Chandler.

[10] Ayasaluk which is a round hill like Prion, but smaller. Its name is said to be a corruption of ὁ ἅγιος Θεόλογος, 'the holy Theologian.' See p. 433, n. 4.

But one building at Ephesus surpassed all the rest in magnificence and in fame. This was the Temple of Artemis or Diana, which glittered in brilliant beauty at the head of the harbour, and was reckoned by the ancients as one of the wonders of the world. The sun, it was said, saw nothing in his course more magnificent than Diana's Temple. Its honour dated from a remote antiquity. Leaving out of consideration the earliest temple, which was cotemporaneous with the Athenian colony under Androclus, or even yet more ancient, we find the great edifice, which was anterior to the Macedonian period, begun and continued in the midst of the attention and admiration both of Greeks and Asiatics. The foundations were carefully laid, with immense substructions, in the marshy ground.[1] Architects of the highest distinction were employed.[2] The quarries of Mount Prion supplied the marble.[3] All the Greek cities of Asia contributed to the structure ; and Crœsus, the king of Lydia, himself lent his aid. The work thus begun before the Persian war, was slowly continued even through the Peloponnesian war ; and its dedication was celebrated by a poet cotemporary with Euripides.[4] But the building, which had been thus rising through the space of many years, was not destined to remain long in the beauty of its perfection. The fanatic Herostratus set fire to it on the same night in which Alexander was born. This is one of the coincidences of history, on which the ancient world was fond of dwelling : and it enables us, with more distinctness, to pursue the annals of 'Diana of the Ephesians.' The temple was rebuilt with new and more sumptuous magnificence. The ladies of Ephesus contributed their jewellery to the expense of the restoration. The national pride in the sanctuary was so great, that, when Alexander offered the spoils of his eastern campaign if he might inscribe his name on the building, the honour was declined. The Ephesians never ceased to embellish the shrine of their goddess, continually adding new decorations and subsidiary buildings, with statues and pictures by the most famous artists. This was the temple that kindled the enthusiasm of St. Paul's opponents (Acts xix.), and was still the rallying-point of Heathenism in the days of St. John and Polycarp. In the second century we read that it was united to the city by a long colonnade. But soon afterwards it was plundered and laid waste by the Goths, who came from beyond the Danube in the reign of Gallienus.[5] It sank entirely into decay in the age when Christianity was overspreading the Empire ; and its remains are to be sought for in mediæval buildings, in the columns of green jasper which support the dome of St. Sophia, or even in the naves of Italian cathedrals.[6]

Thus the Temple of Diana of Ephesus saw all the changes of Asia Minor, from Crœsus to Constantine. Though nothing now remains on the spot to show us what or even where it was, there is enough

---

[1] Pliny says that it was built in marshy ground, lest it should be injured by earthquakes.

[2] The first architect was Theodorus of Samos. He was succeeded by Chersiphon of Gnossus, then by his son

Metagenes. The building was completed by Demetrius and Pæonius.

[3] See above, pp. 420, 421.

[4] Timotheus.

[5] Arundell's *Seven Churches*, p. 46.

[6] Ibid. p. 47.

in its written memorials to give us some notion of its appearance and splendour. The reader will bear in mind the characteristic style which was assumed by Greek architecture, and which has suggested many of the images of the New Testament.[1] It was quite different from the lofty and ascending form of those buildings which have since arisen in all parts of Christian Europe, and essentially consisted in horizontal entablatures resting on vertical columns. In another respect, also, the temples of the ancients may be contrasted with our churches and cathedrals. They were not roofed over for the reception of a large company of worshippers, but were in fact colonnades[2] erected as subsidiary decorations, round the cell which contained the idol, and were, through a great part of their space, open to the sky. The colonnades of the Ephesian Diana really constituted an epoch in the history of Art, for in them was first matured that graceful Ionic style, the feminine beauty of which was more suited to the genius of the Asiatic Greek than the sterner and plainer Doric, in which the Parthenon and Propylæa of Athens were built. The scale on which the Temple was erected was magnificently extensive. It was 425 feet in length and 220 in breadth, and the columns were 60 feet high. The number of columns was 127, each of them the gift of a king; and 36 of them were enriched with ornament and colour. The folding doors were of cypress-wood; the part which was not open to the sky was roofed over with cedar; and the staircase was formed of the wood of one single vine from the island of Cyprus. The value and fame of the Temple were enhanced by its being the treasury, where a large portion of the wealth of Western Asia was stored up.[3] It is probable that there was no religious building in the world in which was concentrated a greater amount of admiration, enthusiasm, and superstition.

If the Temple of Diana at Ephesus was magnificent, the image enshrined within the sumptuous enclosure was primitive and rude. We usually conceive of this goddess, when represented in art, as the tall huntress, eager in pursuit, like the statue in the Louvre. Such was not the form of the Ephesian Diana, though she was identified by the Greeks with their own mountain-goddess, whose figure we often see represented on the coins of this city.[4] What amount of fusion took place, in the case of this worship, between Greek and Oriental notions, we need not inquire. The image may have been intended to represent Diana in one of her customary characters, as the deity of fountains;[5] but it reminds us rather of the idols of the far East, and of the religions which love to represent the life of all

---

[1] See, for instance, Gal. ii. 9, Rev. iii. 12, also 1 Tim. iii. 15; comparing what has been said above, p. 174.

[2] A friend suggests one parallel in Christian architecture, viz. the Atrium, or western court of St. Ambrogio at Milan, which is a colonnade west of the Church, itself enclosing a large oblong space not roofed over.

[3] A German writer says that the temple of the Ephesian Diana was

what the Bank of England is in the modern world.

[4] Hence she is frequently represented as the Greek Diana on coins of Ephesus. Some of these are given in the larger editions.

[5] This is the opinion of Guhl, whose elaborate work on ancient Ephesus is referred to several times in our larger editions.

animated beings as fed and supported by the many breasts of nature.[1] The figure which assumed this emblematic form above, was terminated below in a shapeless block. The material was wood. A bar of metal was in each hand. The dress was covered with mystic devices, and the small shrine, where it stood within the temple, was concealed by a curtain in front. Yet, rude as the image was, it was the object of the utmost veneration. Like the Palladium of Troy,—like the most ancient Minerva of the Athenian Acropolis,[2]—like the Paphian Venus[3] or Cybele of Pessinus,[4] to which allusion has been made,—like the Ceres in Sicily mentioned by Cicero,[5]—it was believed to have 'fallen down from the sky' (Acts xix. 35). Thus it was the object of the greater veneration from the contrast of its primitive simplicity with the modern and earthly splendour which surrounded it; and it was the model on which the images of Diana were formed for worship in other cities.

One of the idolatrous customs of the ancient world was the use of portable images or shrines, which were little models of the more celebrated objects of devotion. They were carried in processions, on journeys and military expeditions,[6] and sometimes set up as household gods in private dwellings. Pliny says that this was the case with the Temple of the Cnidian Venus ; and other Heathen writers make allusion to the 'shrines' of the Ephesian Diana, which are mentioned in the Acts (xix. 24). The material might be wood, or gold, or 'silver.' The latter material was that which employed the hands of the workmen of Demetrius. From the expressions used by St. Luke, it is evident that an extensive and lucrative trade grew up at Ephesus, from the manufacture and sale of these shrines. Few of those who came to Ephesus would willingly go away without a memorial of the goddess, and a model of her temple;[7] and, from the wide circulation of these works of art over the shores of the Mediterranean, and far into the interior, it might be said, with little exaggeration, that her worship was recognised by the 'whole world'[8] (Acts xix. 27).

The ceremonies of the actual worship at Ephesus were conducted

---

[1] The form of the image is described by Jerome : 'Scribebat Paulus ad Ephesios Dianam colentes, non hanc venatricem, quæ arcum tenet atque succincta est, sed illam *multimammiam*, quam Græci πολυμαστήν vocant.'— *Prœm. ad Eph.* Representations in ancient sculpture are very frequent. The coin at the end of Chap. XIV. gives a general notion of the form of the image.

[2] See above in the description of Athens, pp. 275-277.

[3] See the description of Paphos above, p. 125.

[4] See Herodian, as referred to above, p. 209.

[5] Cic. *in Verr.* v. 187. To this list we may add, without any misrepresentation, the house of our Lady of Loretto. See the *Quarterly Review* for Sept. 1853, and the *Christian Remembrancer* for Ap. 1855.

[6] We may compare Cicero's words of the Roman legionary eagle, *Cat.* i. 9.

[7] We cannot be sure, in this case, whether by the word used here is meant the whole temple, or the small shrine which contained the image. Perhaps its form is that represented on the first coin engraved in Mr. Akerman's paper in the *Numismatic Chronicle.*

[8] We find the image of the Ephesian Diana on the coins of a great number of other cities and communities, e.g. Hierapolis, Mytilene, Perga, Samos, Marseilles, &c. Inscriptions might be quoted to the same effect.

Η ΦΙΛΟΣΕΒΑΣΤΟΣ ΕΦΕΣΙΩΝ ΒΟΥΛΗ ΚΑ!
Ο ΝΕΩΚΟΡΟΣ ΔΗΜΟΣ ΚΑΘΙΕΡΩΣΑΝ ΕΠΙ
ΑΝΘΥΠΑΤΟΥ ΠΕΔΟΥΚΑΙΟΥ ΠΡΕΙΣΚΕΙΝΟΥ
ΨΗΦΙΣΑΜΕΝΟΥ ΤΙΒ. ΚΛ. ΙΤΑΛΙΚΟΥ ΤΟΥ
ΓΡΑΜΜΑΤΕΩΣ ΤΟΥ ΔΗΜΟΥ.

Inscription from Ephesus.   See p. 425, n. 5.

M. I. ΑΥΡ. ΔΙΟΝΥΣΙΟΝ ΤΟΝ ΙΕΡΟΚΗΡΥΚΑ
ΚΑΙ Β ΑΣΙΑΡΧΟΝ ΕΚ ΤΩΝ ΙΔΙΩΝ Τ ΦΛ
ΜΟΥΝΑΤΙΟΣ ΦΙΛΟΣΕΒΑΣΤΟΣ Ο ΓΡΑΜ-
ΜΑΤΕΥΣ ΚΑΙ ΑΣΙΑΡΧΗΣΑΣ.

Inscription from Ephesus.   See p. 428, n. 3.

by the members of a twofold hierarchy. And here again we see the traces of Oriental, rather than Greek, influences. The Megabyzi, the priests of Diana, were eunuchs from the interior, under one at their head, who bore the title of high-priest, and ranked among the leading and most influential personages of the city. Along with these priests were associated a swarm of virgin priestesses consecrated, under the name of Melissæ, to the service[1] of the deity, and divided into three classes, and serving, like the priests, under one head. And with the priests and priestesses would be associated (as in all the great temples of antiquity) a great number of slaves, who attended to the various duties connected with the worship, down to the care of sweeping and cleaning the Temple. This last phrase leads us to notice an expression used in the Acts of the Apostles, concerning the connection of Ephesus with the Temple of Diana. The term '*Neocoros,*' or '*Temple-sweeper*' (νεώκορος, xix. 35), originally an expression of humility, and applied to the lowest menials engaged in the care of the sacred edifice,[2] became afterwards a title of the highest honour, and was eagerly appropriated by the most famous cities.[3] This was the case with Ephesus in reference to her national goddess. The city was personified as Diana's devotee. The title '*Neocoros*' was boastfully exhibited on the current coins.[4] Even the free people of Ephesus was sometimes named '*Neocoros.*'[5] Thus, the town-clerk could with good reason begin his speech by the question,—'What man is there that knows not that the city of the Ephesians is neocoros of the great goddess Diana, and of the image which came down from heaven?'

The Temple and the Temple-services remained under the Romans as they had been since the period of Alexander. If any change had taken place, greater honour was paid to the goddess, and richer magnificence added to her sanctuary, in proportion to the wider extent to which her fame had been spread. Asia was always a favoured province,[6] and Ephesus must be classed among those cities of the Greeks, to which the conquerors were willing to pay distinguished respect.[7] Her liberties and her municipal constitution were left untouched, when the province was governed by an officer

---

[1] These priestesses belonged to the class of 'sacred slaves.' This class of devotees was common in the great temples of the Greeks. Different opinions have been expressed on the character of those at Ephesus: but, knowing what we do of Heathenism, it is difficult to have a favourable view of them.

[2] The term properly denotes 'sweeper of the temple,' and is nearly synonymous with the Latin 'ædituus,' or the French 'sacristan.'

[3] Primarily the term was applicable to persons, but afterwards it was applied to communities, and more especially in the Roman period. A city might be *Neocoros* with respect to several divinities, and frequently the title had regard to the deified emperor.

[4] See, for instance, that engraved at the end of this chapter. A great number of these coins are described in Mr. Akerman's paper, in the *Num. Chr.*

[5] On the opposite page an inscription is given containing the words *Neocoros, Proconsul,* and *Town-clerk.* The Proconsul is Peducius Priscinus, the Town-clerk is Tiberius Claudius Italicus. The other inscription is that which is mentioned below, p. 428, n. 3. There the Town-clerk is called Munatius, and he is also Asiarch. It is worth while to observe that these are all Roman names.

[6] The circumstances under which this province came under the Roman power were such as to provoke no hostility. See pp. 183, 184.

[7] See p. 257.

from Rome. To the general remarks which have been made before in reference to Thessalonica,[1] concerning the position of *free* or *autonomous* cities under the Empire, something more may be added here, inasmuch as certain political characters of Ephesus appear on the scene which is described in the sacred narrative.

We have said, in the passage above alluded to, that free cities under the Empire had frequently their senate and assembly. There is abundant proof that this was the case at Ephesus. Its old constitution was democratic, as we should expect in a city of the Ionians, and as we are distinctly told by Xenophon : and this constitution continued to subsist under the Romans. The senate, of which Josephus speaks,[2] still met in the Senate-house, which is noticed by another writer,[3] and the position of which was probably in the Agora below the Theatre.[4] We have still more frequent notices of the *demus* or people, and its *assembly*.[5] Wherever its customary place of meeting might be when legally and regularly convoked (ἐννόμῳ ἐκκλησίᾳ, Acts xix. 39), the *theatre*[6] would be an obvious place of meeting, in the case of a tumultuary gathering like that which will presently be brought before our notice.

Again, like other free cities, Ephesus had its magistrates, as Thessalonica had its politarchs (pp. 258, 259), and Athens its archons. Among those which our sources of information bring before us, are several with the same titles and functions as in Athens.[7] One of these was that officer who is described as ' *town-clerk* ' in the authorised version of the Bible (γραμματεύς, Acts xix. 35). Without being able to determine his exact duties, or to decide whether another term, such as ' Chancellor,' or ' Recorder,' would better describe them to us,[8] we may assert, from the parallel case of Athens,[9] and from the Ephesian records themselves, that he was a magistrate of great authority, in a high and very public position. He had to do with state-papers ; he was keeper of the archives ; he read what was of public moment before the senate and assembly ; he was present when money was deposited in the Temple ; and when letters were sent to the people of Ephesus, they were officially addressed to him. Thus, we can readily account for his name appearing so often on the coins [10] of Ephesus. He seems sometimes to have given the name to the year, like the archons at Athens, or the consuls at Rome. Hence no magistrate was more before the public at Ephesus. His very aspect was familiar to all the citizens ;

---

[1] See pp. 257–259, and compare p. 225.

[2] *Ant.* xiv. 10, 12, also 2, 5, and xvi. 6, 4, 7.

[3] Ach. Tat. viii.

[4] See the allusion to the Agora above, p. 421.

[5] In Josephus xiv. xvi. (as above) the senate and assembly are combined. We find δῆμος in inscriptions, and on coins, also ἐκκλησία. The senate is sometimes called βουλή, sometimes γερουσία.

[6] For illustrations of the habit of

Greek assemblies to meet in theatres, we may refer to what Tacitus says of Vespasian at Antioch, *Hist.* ii. 80 ; also to Joseph. *War*, vii. 3.

[7] For instance, besides the archons, strategi, gymnasiarchs, &c.

[8] In Luther's Bible the term ' Canzler' is used.

[9] There were several γραμματεῖς at Athens. Some of them were state-officers of high importance.

[10] The first coin described in Mr. Akerman's paper exhibits to us the same man as ἀρχιερεὺς and γραμματεύς.

and no one was so likely to be able to calm and disperse an angry and excited multitude. (See Acts xix. 35-41).

If we turn now from the city to the province of which it was the metropolis, we are under no perplexity as to its relation to the imperial government. From coins and from inscriptions,[1] from secular writers and Scripture itself (Acts xix. 38), we learn that Asia was a *proconsular* province.[2] We shall not stay to consider the question which has been raised concerning the usage of the plural in this passage of the Acts ; for it is not necessarily implied that more than one proconsul was in Ephesus at the time.[3] But another subject connected with the provincial arrangements requires a few words of explanation. The Roman citizens in a province were, in all legal matters, under the jurisdiction of the proconsul ; and for the convenient administration of justice, the whole country was divided into districts, each of which had its own assize town (*forum* or *conventus*).[4] The proconsul, at stated seasons, made a circuit through these districts, attended by his interpreter (for all legal business in the Empire was conducted in Latin),[5] and those who had subjects of litigation, or other cases requiring the observance of legal forms, brought them before him or the judges whom he might appoint. Thus Pliny, after the true Roman spirit, in his geographical description of the Empire, is always in the habit of mentioning the assize-towns, and the extent of the shires which surrounded them. In the province of Asia he takes especial notice of Sardis, Smyrna, and Ephesus, and enumerates the various towns which brought their causes to be tried at these cities. The official visit of the proconsul to Ephesus was necessarily among the most important ; and the town-clerk, in referring to the presence of the proconsuls, could remind his fellow-citizens in the same breath that it was the very time of the *assizes* (ἀγοραῖοι ἄγονται, Acts xix. 38).[6]

We have no information as to the time of the year[7] at which the

[1] See, for instance, the coin, p. 433, and the inscription opposite p. 425.

[2] See the account of this province in Chap. VIII., pp. 182-185.

[3] 'There are deputies (proconsuls).' It is enough to suppose that we have here simply the generic plural, as in Matt. ii. 20. In the Syriac version the word is in the singular. Some suppose that this was the time when the proconsulship was (so to speak) in commission under Celer and Ælius, as mentioned by Tacitus (*Ann.* xiii. 1). A more probable conjecture is, that some of the governors of the neighbouring provinces, such as Achaia, Cilicia, Cyprus, Bithynia, Pamphylia, might be present at the public games. The governors of neighbouring provinces were in frequent communication with each other. See pp. 19, 20.

[4] *Conventus* was used both for the assize-town and the district to which its jurisdiction extended. It was also used to denote the actual meeting for the assizes.

[5] See pp. 2 and 20.

[6] We are not, however, absolutely forced to assume that the assizes were taking place at this particular time. See the note of Canon Wordsworth, who gives the substance of the whole passage thus : 'Assize-days or court-days come round, and Proconsuls attend, before whom the cause may be tried.' The phrase ἀγοραίους [ἡμέρας] ἄγειν is equivalent to Cæsar's *conventus agere*, and Cicero's *forum agere*. We find the same Greek phrase in Strabo.

[7] We find Cæsar in Gaul holding the *conventus* in winter; but this was probably because he was occupied with military proceedings in the summer, and need not be regarded as a precedent for other provinces.

Ephesian assizes were held. If the meeting took place in spring, they might then be coincident with the great gathering which took place at the celebration of the national games. It seems that the ancient festival of the United Ionians had merged into that which was held in honour of the Ephesian Diana.[1] The whole month of May was consecrated to the glory of the goddess ; and the month itself received from her the name of Artemision. The Artemisian festival was not simply an Ephesian ceremony, but was fostered by the sympathy and enthusiasm of all the surrounding neighbourhood. As the Temple of Diana was called 'the Temple of Asia,' so this gathering was called 'the common meeting of Asia.'[2] From the towns on the coast and in the interior, the Ionians came up with their wives and children to witness the gymnastic and musical contests, and to enjoy the various amusements, which made the days and nights of May one long scene of revelry. To preside over these games, to provide the necessary expenses, and to see that due order was maintained, annual officers were appointed by election from the whole province. About the time of the vernal equinox each of the principal towns within the district called Asia chose one of its wealthiest citizens, and, from the whole number thus returned, ten were finally selected to discharge the duty of *Asiarchs*.[3] We find similar titles in use in the neighbouring provinces, and read, in books or on inscriptions and coins, of *Bithyniarchs*, *Galatarchs*, *Lyciarchs*, and *Syriarchs*. But the games of Asia and Ephesus were pre-eminently famous ; and those who held there the office of 'Presidents of the Games' were men of high distinction and extensive influence. Receiving no emolument from their office, but being required rather to expend large sums for the amusement of the people and their own credit,[4] they were necessarily persons of wealth. Men of consular rank were often willing to receive the appointment, and it was held to enhance the honour of any other magistracies with which they might be invested. They held for the time a kind of sacerdotal position ; and, when robed in mantles of purple and crowned with garlands, they assumed the duty of regulating the great gymnastic contests, and controlling the tumultuary crowd in the theatre, they might literally be called the 'Chief of Asia' (Acts xix. 31).

[1] What the festival of Delos was for the islands, the Panionian festival was for the mainland. But Ephesus seems ultimately to have absorbed and concentrated this celebration. These games were called Artemisia, Ephesia, and Œcumenica.

[2] We find this expressed on coins. In inscriptions the temple appears as 'the temple of Asia.'

[3] 'Ασίαρχαι, Acts xix., translated 'Chief of Asia' in the A. V. From what is said in Eusebius (*H. E.* iv. 15) of one Asiarch presiding at the martyrdom of Polycarp, it has been needlessly supposed that in this passage of the Acts we are to consider all but one to

have been assessors of the chief Asiarch, or else those to be meant who had held the office in previous years and retained the title, like the High Priest at Jerusalem. Among the Ephesian incriptions one is given opposite p. 425, containing the words *Asiarch* and *Town-clerk.* 'Twice Asiarch' appears on a coin of Hypressa, represented in Ak. *Num. Ill.* p. 51.

[4] Compare the case of those who discharged the state-services or *liturgies* at Athens. Such was often the position of the Roman ædiles : and the same may be said of the county sheriffs in England.

These notices of the topography and history of Ephesus, of its religious institutions, and political condition under the Empire, may serve to clear the way for the narrative which we must now pursue. We resume the history at the twenty-second verse of the nineteenth chapter of the Acts, where we are told of a continued stay[1] in Asia after the burning of the books of the magicians.[2] St. Paul was indeed looking forward to a journey through Macedonia and Achaia, and ultimately to Jerusalem and Rome (ver. 21); and in anticipation of his departure he had sent two of his companions into Macedonia before him (ver. 22). The events which had previously occurred have already shown us the great effects which his preaching had produced both among the Jews and Gentiles.[3] And those which follow show us still more clearly how wide a ' door '[4] had been thrown open to the progress of the Gospel. The idolatrous practices of Ephesus were so far endangered, that the interests of one of the prevalent trades of the place were seriously affected; and meanwhile St. Paul's character had risen so high, as to obtain influence over some of the wealthiest and most powerful personages in the province. The scene which follows is entirely connected with the religious observances of the city of Diana. The Jews[5] fall into the background. Both the danger and safety of the Apostle originate with the Gentiles.

It seems to have been the season of spring when the occurrences took place which are related by St. Luke at the close of the nineteenth chapter.[6] We have already seen that he purposed to stay at Ephesus ' till Pentecost; '[7] and it has been stated that May was the ' month of Diana,' in which the great religious gathering took place to celebrate the games.[8] If this also was the season of the provincial assize (which, as we have seen, is by no means improbable), the city would be crowded with various classes of people. Doubtless those who employed themselves in making the portable shrines of Diana expected to drive a brisk trade at such a time; and when they found that the sale of these objects of superstition was seriously diminished, and that the preaching of St. Paul was the cause of their merchandise being depreciated, ' no small tumult arose concerning that way' in which the new teacher was leading his disciples (ver. 23). A certain Demetrius, a master-manufacturer in the craft, summoned together his workmen, along with other artisans who were occupied in trades of the same kind—(among whom we may perhaps reckon ' Alexander the coppersmith ' (2 Tim. iv. 14), against whom the Apostle warned Timothy at a later period),— and addressed to them an inflammatory speech. It is evident that St. Paul, though he had made no open and calumnious attack on the divinities of the place, as was admitted below (ver. 37), had said something like what he had said at Athens, that we ought not to

---

[1] ' He himself stayed in Asia for a season.'
[2] Related above. Acts xix. 18-20.
[3] See Chap. XIV.
[4] 1 Cor. xvi. 9.
[5] Yet it seems that the Jews never ceased from their secret machinations.

In the address at Miletus (xx. 19), S Paul speaks especially of the temptations which befell him by the ' *lying in wait of the Jews.*'
[6] vv. 21-41.
[7] See the end of the preceding chapter.
[8] See above.

suppose that the deity is 'like gold or silver carved with the art and device of man' (Acts xvii. 29), and that 'they are no gods that are made with hands' (ver. 26). Such expressions, added to the failure in the profits of those who were listening, gave sufficient materials for an adroit and persuasive speech. Demetrius appealed first to the interest of his hearers,[1] and then to their fanaticism.[2] He told them that their gains were in danger of being lost—and, besides this, that 'the temple of the great goddess Diana' (to which we can imagine him pointing as he spoke[3]) was in danger of being despised, and that the honour of their national divinity was in jeopardy, whom not only 'all Asia,'[4] but 'all the civilised world,'[5] had hitherto held in the highest veneration. Such a speech could not be lost, when thrown like fire on such inflammable materials. The infuriated feeling of the crowd of assembled artisans broke out at once into a cry in honour of the divine patron of their city and their craft,—'Great is Diana of the Ephesians.'[6]

The excitement among this important and influential class of operatives was not long in spreading through the whole city.[7] The infection seized upon the crowds of citizens and strangers; and a general rush was made to the theatre, the most obvious place of assembly.[8] On their way, they seem to have been foiled in the attempt to lay hold of the person of Paul,[9] though they hurried with them into the theatre two of the companions of his travels, Caius and Aristarchus, whose home was in Macedonia.[10] A sense of the danger of his companions, and a fearless zeal for the truth, urged St. Paul, so soon as this intelligence reached him, to hasten to the theatre and present himself before the people; but the Christian disciples used all their efforts to restrain him. Perhaps their anxious solicitude might have been unavailing[11] on this occasion, as it was on one occasion afterwards,[12] had not other influential friends interposed to preserve his safety. And now was seen the advantage which is secured to a righteous cause by the upright character and unflinching zeal of its leading champion. Some of the Asiarchs,[13]

---

[1] See vv. 25, 26.　　[2] See ver. 27.

[3] See what is said above on the position of the Temple. It would probably be visible from the neighbourhood of the Agora, where we may suppose Demetrius to have harangued the workmen.

[4] ver. 27. Compare vv. 10 and 26; also 1 Cor. xvi. 19. See pp. 370, 371.

[5] 'The world,' ver. 27. Compare the town-clerk's words below, ver. 35.

[6] In an inscription which contains the words γραμματεὺς and ἀνθύπατος, we find special mention of '*the great goddess Diana before the city*,' and extracts might be given from ancient authors to the same effect. In illustration of this latter phrase, compare what has been said of the Lystrian Jupiter, p. 150.

[7] ver. 29.　　[8] See above, p. 421.

[9] Something of the same kind seems

to have happened as at Thessalonica (Acts xvii. 5, 6), when the Jews sought in vain for Paul and Silas in the house of Jason, and therefore dragged the host and some of the other Christians before the magistrates. Perhaps the house of Aquila and Priscilla may have been a Christian home to the Apostle at Ephesus, like Jason's house at Thessalonica. See Acts xviii. 18, 26, with 1 Cor. xvi. 19; and compare Rom. xvi. 3, 4, where they are said to have '*laid down their necks*' for St. Paul's life.

[10] The Greek word is the same in Acts xix. 29, and 2 Cor. viii. 19. See what is said above of these companions of St. Paul, p. 362.

[11] The imperfect (ver. 30) simply expresses the attempt.

[12] See Acts xxi. 13.

[13] For the office of the Asiarchs, see above, p. 428.

whether converted to Christianity or not, had a friendly feeling towards the Apostle; and well knowing the passions of an Ephesian mob when excited at one of the festivals of Asia, they sent an urgent message to him to prevent him from venturing into the scene of disorder and danger.[1] Thus he reluctantly consented to remain in privacy, while the mob crowded violently into the theatre, filling the stone seats, tier above tier, and rending the air with their confused and fanatical cries.[2]

It was indeed a scene of confusion; and never perhaps was the character of a mob more simply and graphically expressed, than when it is said, that 'the majority knew not why they were come together' (ver. 32). At length an attempt was made to bring the expression of some articulate words before the assembly. This attempt came from the Jews, who seem to have been afraid lest they should be implicated in the odium which had fallen on the Christians. By no means unwilling to injure the Apostle's cause, they were yet anxious to clear themselves, and therefore they 'put Alexander forward' to make an apologetic speech[3] to the multitude. If this man was really, as we have suggested, 'Alexander the coppersmith,' he might naturally be expected to have influence with Demetrius and his fellow-craftsmen. But when he stood up and 'raised his hand'[4] to invite silence, he was recognised immediately by the multitude as a Jew. It was no time for making distinctions between Jews and Christians; and one simultaneous cry arose from every mouth, 'Great is Diana of the Ephesians; and this cry continued for two hours.

The excitement of an angry multitude wears out after a time, and a period of reaction comes, when they are disposed to listen to words of counsel and reproof. And, whether we consider the official position of the 'Town-clerk,' or the character of the man as indicated by his speech, we may confidently say that no one in the city was so

---

[1] ver. 31. The danger in which St. Paul was really placed, as well as other points in the sacred narrative, is illustrated by the account of Polycarp's martyrdom. 'The proconsul, observing Polycarp filled with confidence and joy, and his countenance brightened with grace, was astonished, and sent the herald to proclaim, in the middle of the stadium, " Polycarp confesses that he is a Christian." When this was declared by the herald, all the multitude, Gentiles and Jews, dwelling at Smyrna, cried out, " This is that teacher of Asia, the father of the Christians, the destroyer of our gods; he that teaches multitudes not to sacrifice, not to worship." Saying this, they cried out, and asked Philip the Asiarch to let a lion loose upon Polycarp.' Euseb. *H. E.* iv. 15.

[2] ' Some cried one thing and some another,' ver. 32. An allusion has been made (p. 105) to the peculiar form of Greek theatres, in the account of

Herod's death at Cæsarea. From the elevated position of the theatre at Ephesus, we may imagine that many of the seats must have commanded an extensive view of the city and the plain, including the Temple of Diana.

[3] Our view of the purpose for which Alexander was put forward will depend upon whether we consider him to have been a Jew, or a Christian, or a renegade from Christianity. It is most natural to suppose that he was a Jew, that the Jews were alarmed by the tumult and anxious to clear themselves from blame, and to show they had nothing to do with St. Paul. As a Jew, Alexander would be recognised as an enemy to idolatry, and naturally the crowd would not hear him.

[4] The phrase is not quite identical with that used of St. Paul (Acts xiii. 16, xxi. 40), and of St. Peter (Acts xii. 17). See the remarks already made on the former passage.

well suited to appease this Ephesian mob. The speech is a pattern
of candid argument and judicious tact. He first allays the fanatical
passions of his listeners by this simple appeal :[1] ' Is it not known
everywhere that this city of the Ephesians is Neocoros of the great
goddess Diana and of the image that came down from the sky ? '
The contradiction of a few insignificant strangers could not affect
what was notorious in all the world.   Then he bids them remember
that Paul and his companions had not been guilty of approaching or
profaning the temple,[2] or of outraging the feelings of the Ephesians
by calumnious expressions against the goddess.[3] And then he turns
from the general subject to the case of Demetrius, and points out
that the remedy for any injustice was amply provided by the assizes
which were then going on,—or by an appeal to the proconsul. And
reserving the most efficacious argument to the last, he reminded them
that such an uproar exposed the city of Ephesus to the displeasure
of the Romans : for, however great were the liberties allowed to an
ancient and loyal city, it was well known to the whole population,
that a tumultuous meeting which endangered the public peace would
never be tolerated.   So, having rapidly brought his arguments to
a climax, he tranquillised the whole multitude and pronounced the
technical words which declared the assembly dispersed. (Acts xix.
41.) The stone seats were gradually emptied. The uproar ceased
(ib. xx. 1), and the rioters separated to their various occupations and
amusements.

Thus God used the eloquence of a Greek magistrate to protect
His servant, as before He had used the right of Roman citizenship
(p. 240), and the calm justice of a Roman governor (p. 329).   And,
as in the cases of Philippi and Corinth,[4] the narrative of St.
Paul's sojourn at Ephesus concludes with the notice of a deliberate and affectionate farewell. The danger was now over. With
gratitude to that Heavenly Master who had watched over his life
and his works, and with a recognition of that love of his fellow-
Christians and that favour of the ' Chief of Asia,' which had been
the instruments of his safety, he gathered together the disciples
(Acts xx. 1), and in one last affectionate meeting—most probably
in the school of Tyrannus—he gave them his farewell salutations,
and commended them to the grace of God, and parted from them
with tears.

This is the last authentic account which we possess,—if we
except the meeting at Miletus (Acts xx.),—of any personal connection of St. Paul with Ephesus ; for although we think it may be
inferred from the Pastoral Epistles that he visited the metropolis of
Asia again at a later period, yet we know nothing of the circumstances of the visit, and even its occurrence has been disputed. The
other historical associations of Christianity with this city are connected with a different Apostle and a later period of the Church.
Legend has been busy on this scene of apostolic preaching and
suffering. Without attempting to unravel what is said concerning

---

[1] For the Neocorate of Ephesus and
its notoriety, see above, p. 425.

[2] The rendering in the Authorised
Version, ' robbers of churches,' is un-

fortunate. Wiclif has, more correctly,
' sacrilegious.'

[3] ' Blasphemers of your goddess.'

[4] Acts xvi. 40, xviii. 18.

others who have lived and died at Ephesus,[1] we are allowed to believe that the robber-haunts[2] in the mountains around have witnessed some passages in the life of St. John, that he spent the last year of the first century in this 'metropolis of the Asiatic Churches,'[3] and that his body rests among the sepulchres of Mount Prion.   Here we may believe that the Gospel and Epistles were written, which teach us that 'love' is greater than 'faith and hope' (1 Cor. xiii. 13) ; and here,—though the 'candlestick' is removed, according to the prophetic word (Rev. ii. 5),—a monument yet survives, in the hill strewn with the ruins of many centuries,[4] of him who was called 'John the Theologian,' because he emphatically wrote of the 'Divinity of our Lord.'

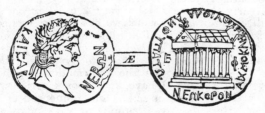

Coin of Ephesus.[5]

[1] It is said that Timothy died at Ephesus, and was buried, like St. John, on Mount Prion.   It has been thought better to leave in reverent silence all that has been traditionally said concerning the mother of our Blessed Lord.

[2] Euseb. *H. E.* iii. 23, which should be compared with 2 Cor. xi. 26.   See p. 129.

[3] Stanley's *Sermons, &c. on the Apostolic Age,* p. 250.   See the whole sermon, and the essay which follows it.

[4] Ayasaluk.   See above, p. 421, n. 10. For the meaning of the term 'Theologian,' or 'Divine,' as applied to St. John, see Stanley's *Sermons,* p. 271.

[5] From Ak. *Num. Ill.* p. 55.   This coin is peculiarly interesting for many reasons.   It has a representation of the temple, and the portrait and name of Nero, who was now reigning ; and it exhibits the words νεώκορος (Acts xix.) and ἀνθύπατος (ib.).   The name of the Proconsul is Aviola.   It is far from impossible that he might hold that office while St. Paul was at Ephesus (i.e. from the autumn of 54 to the spring of 57).   We learn from Seneca, Tacitus, and Suetonius, that a member of the same family was consul in the year 54, when Claudius died, and Nero became emperor.

CHAPTER XVII.

St. Paul at Troas.—He passes over to Macedonia.—Causes of his Dejection.—
He meets Titus at Philippi.—Writes the *Second Epistle to the Corinthians.*—
Collection for the poor Christians in Judæa.—Liberality of the Macedonians.
—Titus.—Journey by Illyricum to Greece.

AFTER his mention of the affectionate parting between St. Paul and
the Christians of Ephesus, St. Luke tells us very little of the
Apostle's proceedings during a period of nine or ten months ;—that
is, from the early summer of the year A.D. 57 to the spring of
A.D. 58.[1] All the information which we find in the Acts concerning
this period, is comprised in the following words :—' *He departed to
go into Macedonia, and when he had gone over those parts, and had
given them much exhortation, he came into Greece, and there abode
three months.*'[2] Were it not for the information supplied by the
Epistles, this is all we should have known of a period which was,
intellectually at least, the most active and influential of St. Paul's
career. These letters, however, supply us with many additional
incidents belonging to this epoch of his life ; and, what is more
important, they give us a picture drawn by his own hand of his
state of mind during an anxious and critical season ; they bring
him before us in his weakness and in his strength, in his sorrow
and in his joy ; they show the causes of his dejection and the source
of his consolation.

In the first place, we thus learn what we should, *à priori*, have
expected,—that he visited Alexandria Troas on his way from
Ephesus to Macedonia. In all probability he travelled from the one
city to the other by sea, as we know he did [3] on his return in the
following year. Indeed, in countries in such a stage of civilisation,
the safest and most expeditious route from one point of the coast to
another, is generally by water rather than by land ;[4] for the 'perils
in the sea,' though greater in those times than in ours, yet did not
so frequently impede the voyager, as the 'perils of rivers' and
'perils of robbers' which beset the traveller by land.

We are not informed who were St. Paul's companions in this

---

[1] The date of the year is according
to the calculations of Wieseler, of which
we shall say more when we come to the
period upon which they are founded.
The season at which he left Ephesus is
ascertained by St. Paul's own words
(1 Cor. xvi. 8) compared with Acts
xx. 1. The time of his leaving Corinth
on his return appears from Acts xx. 6.

[2] Acts xx. 1-3.

[3] Except the small space from Troas
to Assos by land, Acts xx. 13, 14.

[4] At the same time it should be remembered that this was the most populous part of one of the most peaceful
provinces, and that one of the great
roads passed by Smyrna and Pergamus
between Ephesus and Troas. A description of the country will be found
in Fellows' *Asia Minor*, chap. i. and ii.

journey; but as we find that Tychicus and Trophimus (both Ephesians) were with him at Corinth (Acts xx. 4) during the same apostolic progress, and returned thence in his company, it seems probable that they accompanied him at his departure. We find both of them remaining faithful to him through all the calamities which followed; both exerting themselves in his service, and executing his orders to the last; both mentioned as his friends and followers, almost with his dying breath.[1]

In such company, St. Paul came to Alexandria Troas. We have already described the position and character of this city, whence the Apostle of the Gentiles had set forth when first he left Asia to fulfil his mission,—the conversion of Europe. At that time, his visit seems to have been very short, and no results of it are recorded; but now he remained for a considerable time; he had meant to stay long enough to lay the foundation of a Church (see 2 Cor. ii. 12), and would have remained still longer than he did, had it not been for the non-arrival of Titus, whom he had sent to Corinth from Ephesus either with or soon after the First Epistle. The object of his mission[2] was connected with the great collection now going on for the Hebrew Christians at Jerusalem, but he was also enjoined to enforce the admonitions of St. Paul upon the Church of Corinth, and endeavour to defeat the efforts of their seducers; and then to return with a report of their conduct, and especially of the effect upon them of the recent Epistle. Titus was desired to come through Macedonia, and to rejoin St. Paul (probably) at Troas, where the latter had intended to arrive shortly after Pentecost; but now that he was forced to leave Ephesus prematurely, he had resolved to wait for Titus at Troas, expecting, however, his speedy arrival. In this expectation he was disappointed; week after week passed, but Titus came not. The tidings which St. Paul expected by him were of the deepest interest; it was to be hoped that he would bring news of the triumph of good over evil at Corinth: yet it might be otherwise; the Corinthians might have forsaken the faith of their first teacher, and rejected his messenger. While waiting in this uncertainty, St. Paul appears to have suffered all the sickness of hope deferred. 'My spirit had no rest, because I found not Titus my brother.'[3] Nevertheless, his personal anxiety did not prevent his labouring earnestly and successfully in his Master's service. He 'published the Glad-tidings of Christ'[4] there as in other places, probably preaching as usual, in the first instance, to the Jews in the synagogue. He met with a ready hearing; 'a door was opened to him in the Lord.'[5] And thus was laid the foundation of a Church which rapidly increased, and which we shall find him revisiting not long afterwards. At present, indeed, he was compelled to leave it prematurely; for the necessity of meeting

[1] In the 2nd Epistle to Timothy. For Tychicus, see Acts xx. 4; Eph. vi. 21; Col. iv. 7; 2 Tim. iv. 12; Tit. iii. 12. For Trophimus, see Acts xx. 4, Acts xxi. 29; 2 Tim. iv. 20.

[2] It is not impossible that Titus may have carried another letter to the Co-rinthians; if so, it may be referred to in 2 Cor. ii. 3, and 2 Cor. viii. 8; passages which some have thought too strong for the supposition that they only refer to the First Epistle.

[3] 2 Cor. ii. 13.

[4] 2 Cor. ii. 12.

[5] 2 Cor. ii. 12.

Titus, and learning the state of things at Corinth, urged him forward. He sailed, therefore, once more from Troas to Macedonia (a voyage already described [1] in our account of his former journey), and landing at Neapolis, proceeded immediately to Philippi. [2]

We might have supposed that the warmth of affection with which he was doubtless welcomed by his converts here, would have soothed the spirit of the Apostle, and restored his serenity. For, of all his converts, the Philippians seem to have been the most free from fault, and the most attached to himself. In the Epistle which he wrote to them, we find no censure, and much praise; and so zealous was their love for St. Paul, that they alone (of all the Churches which he founded) forced him from the very beginning to accept their contributions for his support. Twice, while he was at Thessalonica, [3] immediately after their own conversion, they had sent relief to him. Again they did the same while he was at Corinth, [4] working for his daily bread in the manufactory of Aquila. And we shall find them afterwards cheering his Roman prison, by similar proofs of their loving remembrance. [5] We might suppose from this that they were a wealthy Church; yet such a supposition is contradicted by the words of St. Paul, who tells us that 'in the heavy trial which had proved their stedfastness, the fulness of their joy had overflowed *out of the depth of their poverty*, in the richness of their liberality.' [6] In fact, they had been exposed to very severe persecution from the first. 'Unto them it was given,' so St. Paul reminds them afterwards,—'in the behalf of Christ, not only to believe on Him, but also to suffer for His sake.' [7] Perhaps, already their leading members had been prosecuted under the Roman law [8] upon the charge which proved so fatal in after times,—of propagating a 'new and illegal religion' (*religio nova et illicita*); or, if this had not yet occurred, still it is obvious how severe must have been the loss inflicted by the alienation of friends and connections; and this would be especially the case with the Jewish converts, such as Lydia, [9] who were probably the only wealthy members of the community, and whose sources of wealth were derived from the

---

[1] See Chap. IX.

[2] Philippi (of which Neapolis was the port) was the first city of Macedonia which he would reach from Troas. See pp. 221–223. The importance of the Philippian Church would, of course, cause St. Paul to halt there for some time, especially as his object was to make a general collection for the poor Christians of Jerusalem. Hence the scene of St. Paul's grief and anxiety (recorded, 2 Cor. vii. 5, as occurring *when he came into Macedonia*) must have been Philippi; and the same place seems (from the next verse) to have witnessed his consolation by the coming of Titus. So (2 Cor. xi. 9) we find '*Macedonia*' used as equivalent to *Philippi* (see note 4). We conclude, therefore, that the ancient tradition (embodied in the subscription of 2 Cor.),

according to which the Second Epistle to the Corinthians was written from Philippi, is correct.

[3] Phil. iv. 16. And see below, p. 468.

[4] 2 Cor. xi. 9. The Macedonian contributions there mentioned must have been from Philippi, because Philippi was the only Church which at that time contributed to St. Paul's support (Phil. iv. 15).

[5] Phil. iv. 16.

[6] 2 Cor. viii. 2.

[7] Phil. i. 29.

[8] It must be remembered that Philippi was a *Colonia*.

[9] Lydia had been a Jewish proselyte before her conversion. [We cannot assume that she was a permanent resident at Philippi. See Acts xvi. 14. H.]

commercial relations which bound together the scattered Jews throughout the Empire. What they gave, therefore, was not out of their abundance, but out of their penury; they did not grasp tenaciously at the wealth which was slipping from their hands, but they seemed eager to get rid of what still remained. They 're-membered the words of the Lord Jesus how He said, It is more blessed to give than to receive.' St. Paul might have addressed them in the words spoken to some who were likeminded with them: —'Ye had compassion of me in my[1] bonds, and took joyfully the spoiling of your goods, knowing that ye have in heaven a better and an enduring substance.'

Such were the zealous and loving friends who now embraced their father in the faith; yet the warmth of their welcome did not dispel the gloom which hung over his spirit; although amongst them[2] he found Timotheus also, his 'beloved son in the Lord,' the most endeared to him of all his converts and companions. The whole tone of the Second Epistle to Corinth shows the depression under which he was labouring; and he expressly tells the Corinthians that this state of feeling lasted, not only at Troas, but also after he reached Macedonia. 'When first I came into Macedonia,' he says, ' my flesh had no rest ; without were fightings, within were fears.' And this had continued until ' God, who comforts them that are cast down, comforted me by the coming of Titus.'

It has been sometimes supposed that this dejection was oc-casioned by an increase of the chronic malady under which St. Paul suffered;[3] and it seems not unlikely that this cause may have contributed to the result. He speaks much, in the Epistle written at this time from Macedonia, of the frailty of his bodily health (2 Cor. iv. 7 to 2 Cor. v. 10, and also 2 Cor. xii. 7–9, and see note on 2 Cor. i. 8); and, in a very affecting passage, he describes the earnestness with which he had besought his Lord to take from him this 'thorn in the flesh,'—this disease which continually impeded his efforts, and shackled his energy. We can imagine how severe a trial to a man of his ardent temper such a malady must have been. Yet this alone would scarcely account for his continued depression, especially after the assurance he had received, that the grace of

---

[1] Or 'on those in bonds,' if we adopt the reading of the best MSS. See note on Heb. x. 34.

[2] This we infer because Timotheus was with him when he began to write the Second Epistle to Corinth (2 Cor. i. 1), which (for the reasons mentioned in p. 436, n. 2) we believe to have been written at Philippi. Now Timotheus had been despatched on some commis-sion into Macedonia shortly before Easter, and St. Paul had then expected (but thought it doubtful) that he would reach Corinth and return thence to Ephesus; and that he would reach it *after* the reception at Corinth of the First Epistle to the Corinthians (1 Cor. xvi. 10, 11). This, however, Timotheus

seems not to have done ; for it was Titus, not Timotheus, who brought to St. Paul the first tidings of the recep-tion of the First Epistle at Corinth (2 Cor. vii. 6–11). Also, had Timo-theus reached Corinth, he would have been mentioned, 2 Cor. xii. 18. Hence it would appear that Timotheus must have been retained in Macedonia.

[3] We need not notice the hypothesis that St. Paul's long-continued dejection was caused by the danger which he in-curred on the day of the tumult in the theatre at Ephesus ; a supposition most unworthy of the character of him who sustained such innumerable perils of a more deadly character with unshrink-ing fortitude.

Christ was sufficient for him,—that the vessel of clay[1] was not too fragile for the Master's work,—that the weakness of his body would but the more manifest the strength of God's Spirit.[2] The real weight which pressed upon him was the 'care of all the Churches;' the real cause of his grief was the danger which now threatened tho souls of his converts, not in Corinth only, or in Galatia, but everywhere throughout the Empire. We have already described the nature of this danger, and seen its magnitude : we have seen how critical was the period through which the Christian Church was now passing.[3] The true question (which St. Paul was enlightened to comprehend) was no less than this ;—whether the Catholic Church should be dwarfed into a Jewish sect; whether the religion of spirit and of truth should be supplanted by the worship of letter and of form. The struggle at Corinth, the result of which he was now anxiously awaiting, was only one out of many similar struggles between Judaism[4] and Christianity. These were the 'fightings without' which filled him with 'fears within;' these were the agitations which 'gave his flesh no rest,' and 'troubled him on every side.'[5]

At length the long-expected Titus arrived at Philippi, and relieved the anxiety of his master by better tidings than he had hoped to hear.[6] The majority of the Corinthian Church had submitted to the injunctions of St. Paul, and testified the deepest repentance for the sins into which they had fallen. They had passed sentence of excommunication upon the incestuous person, and they had readily contributed towards the collection for the poor Christians of Palestine. But there was still a minority, whose opposition seems to have been rather embittered than humbled by the submission which the great body of the Church had thus yielded. They proclaimed, in a louder and more contemptuous tone than ever, their accusations against the Apostle. They charged him with craft in his designs, and with selfish and mercenary motives ;—a charge which they probably maintained by insinuating that he was personally interested in the great collection which he was raising. We have seen[7] what scrupulous care St. Paul took to

---

[1] See 2 Cor. iv. 7.

[2] 2 Cor. xii. 7–9.

[3] pp. 345–350.

[4] That the great opponents of St. Paul at Corinth were Judaising emissaries, we have endeavoured to prove below : at the same time a complication was given to the struggle at Corinth by the existence of another element of error in the free-thinking party, whose theoretic defence of their practical immorality we have already noticed.

[5] 2 Cor. vii. 5.

[6] Wieseler is of opinion that before the coming of Titus St. Paul had already resolved to send another letter to the Corinthians, perhaps by those two brethren who travelled with Titus soon after, bearing the Second Epistle ; and

that he wrote as far as the 2nd verse of the 7th chapter of the Second Epistle to the Corinthians before the appearance of Titus. He infers this from the change of tone which takes place at this point, and from St. Paul's returning to topics which, in the earlier portion of the Epistle, he appeared to have dismissed ; and from the manner in which the arrival of Titus is mentioned at 2 Cor. vii. 4–7. On this hypothesis some other person from Corinth must have brought intelligence of the first impression produced on the Corinthians by the Epistle which had just reached them ; and Titus conveyed the further tidings of their subsequent conduct.

[7] 1 Cor. xvi. 3.

keep his integrity in this matter above every shade of suspicion ; and we shall find still further proof of this as we proceed. Meanwhile it is obvious how singularly inconsistent this accusation was, in the mouths of those who eagerly maintained that Paul could be no true Apostle, because he did not demand support from the Churches which he founded. The same opponents accused him likewise of egregious vanity, and of cowardly weakness ; they declared that he was continually threatening without striking, and promising without performing ; always on his way to Corinth, but never venturing to come ; and that he was as vacillating in his teaching as in his practice ; refusing circumcision to Titus, yet circumcising Timothy ; a Jew among the Jews, and a Gentile among the Gentiles.

It is an important question, to which of the divisions of the Corinthian Church these obstinate opponents of St. Paul belonged. From the notices of them given by St. Paul himself, it seems certain that they were Judaisers (see 2 Cor. xi. 22) ; and still further, that they were of the Christine section of that party (see 2 Cor. xi. 7). It also appears that they were headed by an emissary from Palestine (2 Cor. xi. 4), who had brought letters of commendation from some members of the Church at Jerusalem,[1] and who boasted of his pure Hebrew descent, and his especial connection with Christ Himself.[2] St. Paul calls him a false apostle, a minister of Satan disguised as a minister of righteousness, and hints that he was actuated by corrupt motives. He seems to have behaved at Corinth with extreme arrogance, and to have succeeded, by his overbearing conduct, in impressing his partisans with a conviction of his importance, and of the truth of his pretensions.[3] They contrasted his confident bearing with the timidity and self-distrust which had been shown by St. Paul.[4] And they even extolled his personal advantages over those of their first teacher ; comparing his rhetoric with Paul's inartificial speech, his commanding appearance with the insignificance of Paul's 'bodily presence.'[5]

Titus, having delivered to St. Paul this mixed intelligence of the state of Corinth, was immediately directed to return thither (in company with two deputies specially elected to take charge of their contribution by the Macedonian Churches),[6] in order to continue the business of the collection. St. Paul made him the bearer of another letter, which is addressed (still more distinctly than the First Epistle), not to Corinth only, but to all the Churches in the whole province of Achaia, including Athens and Cenchreæ, and perhaps also Sicyon, Argos, Megara, Patræ, and other neighbouring towns ; all of which probably shared more or less in the agitation which so powerfully affected the Christian community at Corinth. The twofold character[7] of this Epistle is easily explained by the

---

[1] See 2 Cor. iii. 1. It may safely be assumed that Jerusalem was the head-quarters of the Judaising party, from whence their emissaries were despatched. Compare Gal. ii. 12 ; Acts xv. 1, and xxi. 20.

[2] See 2 Cor. xi. 22.

[3] See 2 Cor. xi. 18-20, and the note there.

[4] 1 Cor. ii. 3.

[5] 2 Cor. x. 10, 16.

[6] See notes on 2 Cor. viii. 18, 22.

[7] This twofold character pervades the *whole Epistle* ; it is incorrect to say

existence of the majority and minority which we have described in
the Corinthian Church.   Towards the former the Epistle overflows
with love; towards the latter it abounds with warning and menace.
The purpose of the Apostle was to encourage and tranquillise the
great body of the Church; but, at the same time, he was constrained
to maintain his authority against those who persisted in despising
the commands of Christ delivered by his mouth.   It was needful,
also, that he should notice their false accusations; and that (undeterred by the charge of vanity which they brought),[1] he should
vindicate his apostolic character by a statement of facts, and a
threat of punishment to be inflicted on the contumacious.   With
these objects, he wrote as follows :—

SECOND EPISTLE TO THE CORINTHIANS.[2]

Salutation.   PAUL, an Apostle of Jesus Christ by the will of God, i. 1
and Timotheus the Brother, TO THE CHURCH
OF GOD WHICH IS IN CORINTH, AND
TO ALL THE SAINTS THROUGHOUT
THE WHOLE PROVINCE OF ACHAIA.

Grace be unto you and peace, from God our 2
Father, and from our Lord Jesus Christ.

Thanksgiving
for his deliver-
ance from
great danger
in Procon-
sular Asia.   Thanks be to God the Father of our Lord Jesus 3
Christ, the father of compassion, and the God of all
comfort, who consoles me[3] in all my tribulation, 4

(as has been often said) that the portion before chap. x. is addressed to the
obedient section of the Church, and
that after chap. x. to the disobedient.
Polemical passages occur throughout
the earlier portion also; see i. 15–17,
ii. 17, iii. 1, v. 12, &c.

[1] It is a curious fact, and marks the
personal character of this Epistle, that
the verb for 'boast' and its derivatives
occur twenty-nine times in it, and only
twenty-six times in all the other Epistles of St. Paul put together.

[2] St. Paul has given us the following
particulars to determine the date of
this Epistle:—

(1.) He had been exposed to great
danger in Proconsular Asia, i.e. at
Ephesus (2 Cor. i. 8).   This had happened Acts xix. 23–41.

(2.) He had come thence to Troas,
and (after some stay there) had passed
over to Macedonia.   This was the
route he took, Acts xx. 1.

(3.) He was in Macedonia at the

time of writing (2 Cor. ix. 2, the verb
is in the present tense), and intended
(2 Cor. xiii. 1) shortly to visit Corinth.
This was the course of his journey,
Acts xx. 2.

(4.) The same collection is going on
which is mentioned in 1 Cor.   See 2
Cor. viii. 6, and 2 Cor. ix. 2; and
which was completed during his three
months' visit to Corinth (Rom. xv. 26),
and taken up to Jerusalem immediately
after, Acts xxiv. 17.

(5.) Some of the other topics mentioned in 1 Cor. are again referred to,
especially the punishment of the incestuous offender, in such a manner as to
show that no long interval had elapsed
since the first Epistle.

[3] For the translation here, see the
reasons given in the note on 1 Thess. i.
2.   It is evident here that St. Paul
considers himself alone the writer, since
Timotheus was not with him during
the danger in Asia; and, moreover, he
uses 'I' frequently, interchangeably

thereby enabling me to comfort those who are in any
affliction, with the same comfort wherewith I am
i. 5 myself comforted by God.   For as the sufferings of
Christ[1] have come upon me above measure, so by
Christ also my consolation is above measure multi-
6 plied.   But if, on the one hand, I am afflicted, it is
for your consolation and salvation, (which works in
you a firm endurance of the same sufferings which I
also suffer;[2] so that my hope is stedfast on your be-
7 half;) and if, on the other hand, I am comforted, it
is for your consolation,[3] because I know that as you
partake of my sufferings, so you partake also of my
8 comfort.   For I would have you know, brethren,
concerning the tribulation which befell me in the province of Asia,[4] that I was exceedingly pressed down
by it beyond my strength to bear, so as to despair
9 even of life.   Nay, by my own self I was already
doomed to death; that I might rely no more upon
myself, but upon God who raises the dead to life;
10 who delivered me from a death so grievous, and does
yet deliver me; in whom I have hope that He will
11 still deliver me for the time to come; you also helping
me by your supplications for me, that thanksgivings
may from many tongues be offered up on my behalf,
for the blessing gained to me by many prayers.[5]

12   For this is my boast, the testimony of my conscience, that I have dealt with the world, and above
all with you, in godly honesty and singleness of mind,[6]

Self-defence against accusation of double-dealing.

with 'we' (see verse 23); and when he
includes others in the 'we' he specifies
it, as in verse 19. See, also, other
proofs in the note on vi. 11.

[1] Compare Col. i. 24.
[2] This is the order given by the MS.
authorities.
[3] Here we follow Griesbach's text,
on the authority of the Alexandrian
and other MSS., and on grounds of
context.
[4] It has been questioned whether
St. Paul here refers to the Ephesian
tumult of Acts xix.; and it is urged
that he was *not* then in danger of his
life.   But had he been found by the
mob during the period of their excitement, there can be little doubt that he
would have been torn to pieces, or perhaps thrown to wild beasts in the
Arena; and it seems improbable that
within so short a period he should
again have been exposed to peril of his

life in the same place, and that nothing
should have been said of it in the Acts.
Some commentators have held (and
the view has been ably advocated by
Dean Alford) that St. Paul refers to a
dangerous attack of illness.   With this
opinion we so far agree that we believe
St. Paul to have been suffering from
bodily illness when he wrote this
Epistle.   See the preliminary remarks
above.   St. Paul's statement here that
he was 'self-doomed to death' certainly
looks very like a reference to a very
dangerous illness, in which he had despaired of recovery.
[5] Literally, *that from many persons
the gift given to me by means of many
may have thanks returned for it on my
behalf.*
[6] St. Paul here alludes to his opponents, who accused him of dishonesty
and inconsistency in his words and
deeds.   From what follows, it seems

not in the strength of carnal wisdom, but in the strength of God's grace. For I write nothing else to i. 1: you but what you read openly,[1] yea and what you acknowledge inwardly, and I hope that even to the end you will acknowledge,[2] as some of you[3] have 14 already acknowledged, that I am your boast, even as you are mine, in the day of the Lord Jesus.[4]

Reason for the postponement of his visit to Corinth.

And in this confidence it was my wish to come 15 first[5] to you, that [afterwards] you might have a second benefit; and to go by you into Macedonia, 16 and back again from Macedonia to you, and by you to be forwarded on my way to Judæa. Am I accused 17 then of forming this purpose in levity and caprice? or is my purpose carnal, to please all, by saying at once both yea and nay?[6] Yet as God is faithful, my 18 words to you are[7] no [deceitful] mixture of yea and nay. For when the Son of God, Jesus Christ, was 19 proclaimed among you by us, (by me, I say, and Silvanus, and Timotheus,) in Him was found no wavering between yea and nay, but in Him was yea alone; for all the promises of God have in Him the 20 yea [which seals their truth]; wherefore also through Him the Amen [which acknowledges their fulfilment,] is uttered to the praise of God by our voice.[8] But 21 God is He who keeps both us and you stedfast to His anointed, and we also are anointed[9] by Him. And He has set His seal upon us, and has given us 22

that he had been suspected of writing privately to some individuals in the Church, in a different strain from that of his public letters to them.

[1] The word properly means *you read aloud,* viz. when the Epistles of St. Paul were publicly read to the congregation. Compare 1 Thess. v. 27.

[2] There is a play upon the words here, which it is difficult in English to imitate.

[3] Compare chap. ii. 5, and Rom. xi. 25.

[4] i.e. the day when the Lord Jesus will come again.

[5] i.e. before visiting Macedonia. See p. 375, note.

[6] This translation (the literal English being, *do I purpose my purposes carnally, that both yea, yea, and nay, nay, may be [found] with me*) appears to give the full force, as much as that of Chrysostom: '*or must I hold to the purposes which I have formed from fleshly fear, lest I be accused of chang-*

ing my yea into nay ;' which is advocated by Winer, but which does not agree with the context.

[7] We follow here Lachmann, Tischendorf, and the best MSS.

[8] In the present edition we have adopted Lachmann's reading. The *Amen* was that in which the whole congregation joined at the close of the thanksgiving, as described in 1 Cor. xiv. 16. It should also be remembered (as Canon Stanley observes), that it is the Hebrew of 'yea.'

[9] The commentators do not seem to have remarked here the verbal connection. [This has been noticed by Prof. Stanley, since the above was first published.] The *anointing* spoken of as bestowed on the Apostles, was that grace by which they were qualified for their office. The 'we' and 'us' in verses 20, 21, and 22, include Silvanus and Timotheus, as is expressly stated verse 19.

the Spirit to dwell in our hearts, as the earnest [1] of

i . 23 His promises.   But for my [2] own part, I call God to witness, as my soul shall answer for it, that I gave up my purpose [3] of visiting Corinth because I wished

24 to spare you.   I speak not [4] as though your faith was enslaved to my authority, but because I desire to

ii. 1 help your joy ; [5] for your faith is stedfast.   But I de-

2 termined [6] not again [7] to visit you in grief ; for if I cause you grief, who is there to cause me joy, but

3 those whom I have grieved ?   And for this very reason I wrote [8] to you instead of coming, that I might not receive grief from those who ought to give me joy ; and I confide in you all that my joy is yours.

4 For I wrote to you out of much affliction and anguish of heart, with many tears ; not to pain you, but that you might know the abundance of my love.

5 As concerns him [9] who has caused the pain, it is not me that he has pained, but some of you ; [10] [some, I say,] that I may not press too harshly upon all. *Pardon of the incestuous person.*

6 For the offender [11] himself, this punishment, which has been inflicted on him by the sentence of the ma-

7 jority, [12] is sufficient without increasing it.   On the contrary, you ought rather to forgive and comfort him, lest he should be overwhelmed by the excess of

8 his sorrow.   Wherefore I beseech you fully to restore

---

[1] Literally, the *earnest money*, i.e. a small sum which was paid in advance, as the ratification of a bargain ; a custom which still prevails in many countries.   The gift of the Holy Spirit in this life is said by St. Paul to be the *earnest* of their future inheritance ; he repeats the expression 2 Cor. v. 5, and Eph. i. 14, and expresses the same thing under a different metaphor Rom. viii. 23.

[2] The 'I' here is emphatic.

[3] The A. V. 'not yet' is a mistake for 'no longer.'

[4] St. Paul adds this sentence to soften what might seem the magisterial tone of the preceding, in which he had implied his power to punish the Corinthians.

[5] i.e. I desire not to cause you sorrow, but to promote your joy.

[6] This can scarcely mean *for my own sake*, as Billroth and others propose to translate it.

[7] This alludes to the intermediate visit which St. Paul paid to Corinth. See p. 375, note.

[8] i.e. the First Ep. Cor.

[9] Literally, ' *if any man has caused pain* ;' a milder expression, which would not in English bear so definite a meaning as it does in the Greek.

[10] Such is the meaning according to the punctuation we adopt.   For the sense of one phrase, see chap. i. 14, and Rom. xi. 25.   With regard to the sentiment, St. Paul intends to say that not *all* the Corinthian Church had been included in his former censure, but only *that part of it* which had supported the offender ; and therefore the pain which the offender had drawn down on the Church was not inflicted on the whole Church, but only on that erring part of it.

[11] The expression is used elsewhere for a definite offending individual. Compare Acts xxii. 22, and 1 Cor. v. 5. It is not adequately represented by the English ' *such a man.*'

[12] Not '*many*' (A. V.) ; but *the majority*.   See, for the punishment, 1 Cor. v. 4.

him to your love.   For the very end which I sought i. 9
when I wrote before, was to test you in this matter,
and learn whether you would be obedient in all
things.   But whomsoever you forgive, I forgive also ; 10
for whatever[1] I have forgiven, I have forgiven on
your account in the sight[2] of Christ, that we[3] may 11
not be overreached by Satan ; for we are not ignorant
of his devices.

Cause of his leaving Troas.

When I had come to Troas to publish the Glad- 12
tidings of Christ, and a door was opened to me in the
Lord, I had no rest in my spirit because I found not 13
Titus my brother ; so that I parted from them,[4] and
came from thence into Macedonia.   But thanks be to 14
God who leads me on from place to place in the train
of his triumph, to celebrate his victory over the
enemies of Christ ;[5] and by me sends forth the knowledge of Him, a steam of fragrant incense, throughout
the world.   For Christ's is the fragrance[6] which I 15
offer up to God, whether among those in the way of
salvation,[7] or among those in the way of perdition ;
but to these it is an odour of death, to those of life.[8] 16

Defence of the manner in which he discharged his apostolic office, and its glory con-

And [if some among you deny my sufficiency],
who then is sufficient for these things ?   For I seek 17
not profit (like most[9]) by setting the word of God to
sale,[10] but I speak from a single heart, from the com-

---

[1] The best MSS. have the neuter not the masculine.

[2] Compare Proverbs viii. 30 (LXX). The expression is used somewhat differently in iv. 6.

[3] The *we* of this verse appears to include the readers, judging from the change of person before and after. They would all be 'overreached by Satan' if he robbed them of a brother.

[4] Namely, from *the Christians of Troas.*

[5] The verb here used (which is mistranslated in A. V.) means *to lead a man as a captive in a triumphal procession* ; the full phrase means, *to lead captive in a triumph over the enemies of Christ.* The metaphor is taken from the triumphal procession of a victorious general.   God is celebrating His triumph over His enemies ; St. Paul (who had been so great an opponent of the Gospel) is a captive following in the train of the triumphal procession, yet (at the same time, by a characteristic change of metaphor) an incense-bearer, scattering incense (which was

always done on these occasions) as the procession moves on.   Some of the conquered enemies were put to death when the procession reached the Capitol ; to them the smell of the incense was 'an odour of death unto death ;' to the rest who were spared, 'an odour of life unto life.'   The metaphor appears to have been a favourite one with St. Paul ; it occurs again Col. ii. 15.

[6] Literally, *Christ's fragrance am I, unto God.*

[7] Not '*who are saved*' (A. V.)   See note on 1 Cor. i. 18.

[8] Literally, *to these it is an odour of death, ending in death ; to those an odour of life, ending in life.*

[9] The mistranslation 'many' (A.V.), materially alters the sense.   He evidently alludes to his antagonists at Corinth ; see p. 439, and xi. 13.

[10] Literally, *to sell by retail,* including a notion of fraud in the selling.   Compare the similar imputations against his Judaising adversaries in 1 Thess. ii. 3.

mand of God, as in God's presence, and in fellowship iii. 1 with Christ. Will you say that I am again beginning to commend myself? Or think you that I need letters of commendation (like some other men) either 2 to you, or from you? Nay, ye are yourselves my letter of commendation, a letter written on[1] my heart, known and read[2] by all men; a letter[3] coming mani- 3 festly from Christ, and committed to my charge; written not with ink, but with the Spirit of the living God; not upon tablets of stone,[4] but upon the fleshly 4 tablets of the heart. But through Christ have I this 5 confidence[5] before God; not thinking myself sufficient to gain wisdom by my own reasonings,[6] as if it came from myself, but drawing my sufficiency from God. 6 For He it is who has made me suffice for the minis- tration of a new covenant, a covenant not of letter, but of spirit; for the letter kills,[7] but the spirit 7 makes the dead to live. Yet if a glory was shed upon the ministration of the law of death, (a law written in letters, and graven upon stones,)[8] so that the sons of Israel could not fix their eyes on the face of Moses, for the glory of his countenance, although its bright- 8 ness was soon to fade;[9] how far more glorious must 9 the ministration of the spirit be. For if the minis- tration of doom had glory, far more must the minis- 10 tration of righteousness abound in glory.[10] Yea, that which then was glorious has no glory now, because of[11] the surpassing glory wherewith it is 11 compared. For if a glory shone upon that which was doomed to pass away, much more doth glory rest[12] 12 upon that which remains for ever. Therefore, having

---

[1] It is possible that in using the plural here St. Paul meant to include Timotheus; yet as this supposition does not agree well with the context, it seems better to suppose it used merely to suit the plural form of the pronoun.

[2] The paronomasia cannot well be here imitated in English. Compare i. 14.

[3] Literally, *being manifestly shown to be a letter of Christ conveyed by my ministration.*

[4] Like the law of Moses.

[5] Viz. of his sufficiency. Compare ii. 16; iii. 5, 6.

[6] Literally, *to reach any conclusion by my own reason.*

[7] For the meaning, compare Rom.

vii. 9-11.

[8] Literally, *if the ministration of death in letters, graven upon stones, was born in glory.*

[9] See note on 1 Cor. ii. 6.

[10] The whole of this contrast be- tween the glory of the new and the old dispensations, appears to confirm the hypothesis that St. Paul's chief antagonists at Corinth were of the Judaising party.

[11] Literally, *For that which has been glorified in this particular, has not been glorified, because of the glory which sur- passes it.*

[12] 'Rest upon—Shine upon.' The prepositions in the original give this contrast.

this hope, I speak and act without disguise; and not iii. 13
like Moses, who spread a veil over his face, that[1] the
sons of Israel might not see the end of that fading
brightness. But their minds were blinded; yea to this 14
day, when they read in their synagogues[2] the ancient
covenant, the same veil rests thereon, nor[3] can they
see beyond it that the law is done away in Christ;
but even now, when Moses is read in their hearing, a 15
veil[4] lies upon their heart. But when their heart 16
turns to the Lord, the veil is rent away.[5] Now the 17
Lord is the Spirit; and where the Spirit of the Lord
abides, there bondage gives place to freedom; and we 18
all, while with face unveiled we behold in a mirror
the glory of the Lord, are ourselves transformed continually[6] into the same likeness; and the glory which
shines upon us[7] is reflected by us, even as it proceeds
from the Lord, the Spirit.

Therefore having this ministration,[8] I discharge iv. 1
it with no faint-hearted fears, remembering the
mercy which I[9] received. I have renounced the 2
secret dealings of shame, I walk not in the paths of
cunning, I[10] adulterate not the word of God; but
openly setting forth the truth, as in the sight of God,
I commend myself to the conscience of all men.
But if there be still a veil[11] which hides my Glad- 3
tidings from some who hear me, it is among those[12]
who are in the way of perdition; whose unbelieving 4

---

[1] See Exod. xxxiv. 35. St. Paul here (as usual) blends the allegorical with the historical view of the passage referred to in the Old Testament.

[2] *In their synagogues* is implied in the term used here. Compare Acts xv. 21.

[3] We take the phrase absolutely; literally, *it being not unveiled* [i.e. *not revealed to them*] *that it* [*the ancient covenant*] *is done away in Christ*. 'Done away' is predicated, not of the veil, but of the old covenant. Compare the preceding verse and verses 7 and 11.

[4] Perhaps there may be here an allusion to the Tallith, which (if we may assume this practice to be as old as the apostolic age) was worn in the synagogue by every worshipper, and was literally a veil hanging down over the breast. See p. 137, and compare the note on 1 Cor. xi. 4.

[5] Alluding to Exod. xxxiv. 34, where it is said, 'When Moses went

in before the Lord, he rent away the veil.' The most natural subject of the verb 'turn' is 'heart.'

[6] The tense is present.

[7] 'From glory' indicates the origin of this transformation, viz. *the glory shining on us*; 'To glory,' the effect; viz. *the reflection of that glory by us*. For the metaphor, compare 1 Cor. xiii. 12 and note. We observe in both passages that even the representation of divine truth given us by Christianity is only a *reflection* of the reality.

[8] Viz. 'the ministration of the Spirit.' (iii. 8.)

[9] Viz. in his conversion from a state of Jewish unbelief.

[10] St. Paul plainly intimates here (as he openly states xi. 17) that some other teachers were liable to these charges. See also ii. 17, and the note.

[11] In the participle used here, there is a reference to the preceding word 'veil.'

[12] Compare ii. 15, 16.

minds the God of this world[1] has blinded, and shut
out the glorious light of the Glad-tidings of Christ,
iv. 5 who is the image of God. For I proclaim not myself,
but Christ Jesus as Lord and Master,[2] and myself
6 your bondsman for the sake of Jesus. For God,
who called forth light out of darkness, has caused
His light to shine in my heart, that [upon others
also] might shine forth the knowledge of His glory
manifested in the face of Jesus Christ.[3]

7 But this treasure is lodged in a body of fragile
clay,[4] that so the surpassing might [which accom-
plishes the work] should be God's and not my own.
8 I am hard pressed, yet not crushed; perplexed, yet
9 not despairing; persecuted, yet not forsaken; struck
10 down, yet not destroyed.[5] In my body I bear about
continually the dying of Jesus,[6] that in my body the
11 life also of Jesus might be shown forth. For I, in
the midst of life, am daily given over to death for
the sake of Jesus, that in my dying flesh the life
whereby Jesus conquered death[7] might show forth
its power.

12 So then death working in me, works life[8] in you.
13 Yet having the same spirit of faith whereof it is
written ' 𝕴 𝖇𝖊𝖑𝖎𝖊𝖛𝖊𝖉, 𝖆𝖓𝖉 𝖙𝖍𝖊𝖗𝖊𝖋𝖔𝖗𝖊 𝖉𝖎𝖉 𝕴 𝖘𝖕𝖊𝖆𝖐,'[9] I also
14 believe, and therefore speak. For I know that He
who raised the Lord Jesus from the dead, shall raise
me also by Jesus, and shall call me into His presence
15 together with you; for all [my sufferings] are on
your behalf, that the mercy which has abounded
above them all, might call forth•your thankfulness;
that so the fulness of praise might be poured forth
to God, not by myself alone, but multiplied by many
16 voices.[10] Wherefore I faint not; but though my out-

In sickness and in danger his strength is from the power of Christ, and the hope of eternal life.

---

[1] See note on 1 Cor. i. 20.
[2] 'Lord' is the correlative of 'slave'
here; compare Eph. vi. 5.
[3] For the meaning of 'shine forth,'
compare verse 4.
[4] The whole of this passage, from
this point to chap. v. 10, shows (as we
have before observed) that St. Paul
was suffering from bodily illness when
he wrote. See also chap. xii. 7–9.
[5] Observe the force of the present
tense of all these participles, implying
that the state of things described was
constantly going on.
[6] 'Lord' is not found in the best
MSS. The word translated 'dying'
here (as Prof. Stanley observes) is

properly *the deadness of a corpse*; as
though St. Paul would say, '*my body
is no better than a corpse; yet a corpse
which shares the life-giving power of
Christ's resurrection.*
[7] Literally, ' *the life, as well as the
death,* of Jesus.'
[8] Literally, *while death works in me,
life works in you.* I.e. the mortal
peril to which St. Paul exposed himself was the instrument of bringing
spiritual life to his converts.
[9] Ps. cxvi. 10 (LXX.).
[10] The literal translation would be,
*that the favour which has abounded
might, through the thanksgiving of the
greater number, overflow to the praise*

ward man decays, yet my inward man is renewed
from day to day. For my light afflictions, which iv. 17
last but for a moment, work for me a weight of
glory, immeasurable and eternal. Meanwhile I look 18
not to things seen, but to things unseen : for the
things that are seen pass away ; but the things that
are unseen endure for ever. Yea, I know that if the v. 1
tent [1] which is my earthly house be destroyed, I
have a mansion built by God, a house not made with
hands, eternal in the heavens. And herein I groan 2
with earnest longings, desiring to cover [2] my earthly
raiment with the robes of my heavenly mansion. (If 3
indeed I shall be found [3] still clad in my fleshly
garment.) For we who are dwelling in the tent, 4
groan and are burdened ; not desiring to put off our
[earthly] clothing, but to put over it [our heavenly]
raiment, that this our dying nature might be swallowed up by life. And He who has prepared me for 5
this very end is God, who has given me the Spirit
as the earnest of my hope. Therefore, I am ever of 6
good courage, knowing that while my home is in the
body, I am in banishment from the Lord (for I 7
walk by faith, not by sight). Yea, my heart fails 8
me not, but I would gladly suffer banishment from
the body, and have my home with Christ.[4] There- 9

of God. This takes the preposition as governing ' thanksgiving ' and the verb as intransitive ; and it must be remembered that this verb is used twenty-six times by St. Paul, and only three times transitively. If, however, we make it transitive here, the sense will be, *might by means of the greater number cause the thanksgiving to overflow,* &c.; which does not materially alter the sense. Compare the similar sentiment at chap. i. 11.

[1] The *shifting tent* is here opposed to *enduring mansion*; the vile body of flesh and blood, to the spiritual body of the glorified saint.

[2] There is much force in 'clothe upon' as distinguished from 'clothe.'

[3] Literally, '*If indeed I shall be found clad, and not stripped of my clothing ;*' i.e. ' If, at the Lord's coming, I shall be found still living in the flesh.' We know from other passages, that it was a matter of uncertainty with St. Paul whether he should survive to behold the second coming of Christ or not. Compare 1 Thess. iv. 15, and 1

Cor. xv. 51. So, in the next verse, he expresses his desire that his fleshly body should be transformed into a spiritual body, without being ' unclad ' by death. The metaphor of ' nakedness ' as combined with ' tent ' seems suggested by the Oriental practice of striking the tent very early in the morning, often before the travellers are dressed. So we read in M'Cheyne's account of his journey through the desert, ' When morning began to dawn, our tents were taken down. Often we have found ourselves shelterless before being fully dressed.' (*Life of M'Cheyne*, p. 92.) It should be observed that the original denotes simply *dressed, clad,* the antithesis to *naked.* Prof. Stanley's translation, ' in the hope that after having put on our heavenly garment we shall be found not naked, but clothed,' involves a paralogism, being tantamount to saying, ' in the hope that after having clothed ourselves we shall be found to have clothed ourselves.'

[4] Literally, *the Lord.*

fore I strive earnestly that, whether in banishment
v. 10 or at home, I may be pleasing in His sight.   For we
must all be made manifest [1] without disguise before
the judgment seat of Christ, that each may receive
according to that which he has done in the body,
either good or evil.

11   Knowing therefore the fearfulness of the Lord's
judgment, though I seek to win men,[2] yet my
uprightness is manifest in the sight of God; and I
hope also that it is manifested by the witness of
12 your consciences.   I write not thus to repeat my
own commendation,[3] but that I may furnish you
with a ground of boasting on my behalf, that you
may have an answer for those whose boasting is in
the outward matters of sight, not in the inward
13 possessions of the heart.   For if I be mad,[4] it is for
14 God's cause; if sober, it is for yours.   For the love
of Christ constrains me, because I thus have judged,[5]
15 that if one died for all, then all died [in Him][6]; and
that He died for all, that the living might live no
longer to themselves, but to Him, who, for their
sakes, died and rose again.[7]
16   I[8] therefore, from henceforth, view no man
carnally; yea, though once my view of Christ was
17 carnal,[9] yet now it is no longer carnal.   Whosoever,
then, is in Christ, is a new creation; his old being
has passed away, and behold, all has become new.
18 But all comes from God, for He it is who reconciled
me to Himself by Jesus Christ, and charged me with
19 the ministry of reconciliation; for[10] God was in Christ

His earnest-ness springs from a sense of his respon-sibility to Christ, whose commission he bears, and by union with whom his whole nature has been changed.

---

[1] The translation in the Authorised
Version is incorrect.
[2] He was accused by the Judaisers
of 'trying to win men,' and 'trying to
please men.' See Gal. i. 10, and the note.
[3] This alludes to the accusation of
vanity brought against him by his antagonists; compare iii. 1.
[4] i.e. *if I exalt myself* (his opponents
called him beside himself with vanity),
*it is for God's cause; if I humble my-
self, it is for your sakes.*
[5] Or perhaps '*I thus judged*, viz. at
the time of my conversion;' if we
suppose the aorist used in its strict
sense.
[6] The original cannot mean *all were
dead* (A. V.), but *all died.* The death
of all for whom He died, was virtually
involved in His death.

[7] The best commentary on the 14th
and 15th verses is Gal. ii. 20.
[8] The pronoun is emphatic.
[9] We agree with Bilroth, Neander,
and De Wette, that this cannot refer to
any actual knowledge which St. Paul
had of our Lord when upon earth; it
would probably have been ' Jesus '
had that been meant; moreover, the
preceding phrase does not refer to
personal knowledge, but to *a carnal
estimate.* For other reasons against
such an interpretation, see p. 53.
St. Paul's *view of Christ was carnal*
when he looked (like other Jews) for a
Messiah who should be an earthly
conqueror.
[10] ' To wit that,' ' because that,'
pleonastic.

reconciling the world to Himself, reckoning their sins no more against them, and having ordained me to speak the word of reconciliation.   Therefore, I am v. 20 an ambassador for Christ, as though God exhorted you by my voice; in Christ's stead I beseech you be ye reconciled to God.   For Him who knew no sin, 21 God struck with the doom of sin [1] on our behalf; that we may be changed into the righteousness of God in Christ.   Moreover, as working [2] together with vi. 1 Him, I also exhort you, that the grace which you have received from God be not in vain.   For he 2 saith : '𝕴 𝔥𝔞𝔟𝔢 𝔥𝔢𝔞𝔯𝔡 𝔱𝔥𝔢𝔢 𝔦𝔫 𝔞𝔫 𝔞𝔠𝔠𝔢𝔭𝔱𝔞𝔟𝔩𝔢 𝔱𝔦𝔪𝔢, 𝔞𝔫𝔡 𝔦𝔫 𝔱𝔥𝔢 𝔡𝔞𝔶 𝔬𝔣 𝔰𝔞𝔩𝔳𝔞𝔱𝔦𝔬𝔫 𝔥𝔞𝔟𝔢 𝕴 𝔰𝔲𝔠𝔠𝔬𝔲𝔯𝔢𝔡 𝔱𝔥𝔢𝔢.' [3]   Behold, now is the acceptable time, behold, now is the day of salvation.

Vindication of the faithfulness with which he had discharged his duty, and appeal to the affection of his converts.

For I take heed to give no cause of stumbling, lest 3 blame should be cast on the ministration wherein I serve ; but in all things I commend myself [4] as one 4 who ministers to God's service; in stedfast endurance, in afflictions, in necessities, in straitness of distress, in stripes, in imprisonments, in tumults, in labours, 5 in sleepless watchings, in hunger and thirst; in 6 purity, in knowledge, in long-suffering, in kindness, in [the gifts of] the Holy Spirit, in love unfeigned ; speaking the word of truth, working with the power 7 of God, fighting with the weapons of righteousness, both for attack and for defence ; through good 8 report and evil, through honour and through infamy ; counted as a deceiver, yet being true ; as unknown 9 [by men], yet acknowledged [5] [by God]; as ever dying, yet behold I live ; as chastened by suffering, yet not destroyed ; as sorrowful, yet ever filled with 10 joy ; as poor, yet making many rich ; as having nothing, yet possessing all things.

Corinthians, my [6] mouth has opened itself to you 11 freely,—my heart is enlarged towards you.   You find 12 no narrowness in my love, but the narrowness is in

---

[1] The word 'sin' is used, for the sake of parallelism with the 'righteousness' which follows. God made Christ 'Sin,' that we might be made 'Righteousness.'

[2] See note on 1 Cor. iii. 9.   *I also exhort* refers to the preceding, *as though God exhorted you.*

[3] Isa. xlix. 8 (LXX.)

[4] An allusion apparently to the 'commend myself' and the 'commen-datory letters' of iii. 1 ; as though he said, *I commend myself, not by word, but by deed.* [The stress is not on 'myself' here, as in the former case. The order of the word shows this. H.]

[5] For the meaning, see 1 Cor. xiii. 12.

[6] Observe, as a confirmation of previous remarks as to St. Paul's use of the singular and plural pronouns, verses 11 13; also vii. 2, 3, 4.

vi. 13 your own.   I pray you therefore in return for my affection (I speak as to my children), let your hearts be opened in like manner.

14   Cease to yoke yourselves unequally in ill-matched intercourse with unbelievers; for what fellowship has righteousness with unrighteousness? what communion **15** has light with darkness? what concord has Christ with Belial? what partnership has a believer with an **16** unbeliever? what agreement has the temple of God with idols?   For ye are yourselves a temple of the living God, as God said: '𝔍 𝔴𝔦𝔩𝔩 𝔡𝔴𝔢𝔩𝔩 𝔦𝔫 𝔱𝔥𝔢𝔪, 𝔞𝔫𝔡 𝔴𝔞𝔩𝔨 𝔦𝔫 𝔱𝔥𝔢𝔪, 𝔞𝔫𝔡 𝔍 𝔴𝔦𝔩𝔩 𝔟𝔢 𝔱𝔥𝔢𝔦𝔯 𝔊𝔬𝔡, 𝔞𝔫𝔡 𝔱𝔥𝔢𝔶 𝔰𝔥𝔞𝔩𝔩 𝔟𝔢 **17** 𝔪𝔶 𝔭𝔢𝔬𝔭𝔩𝔢.' [1]   Wherefore, '𝔠𝔬𝔪𝔢 𝔬𝔲𝔱 𝔣𝔯𝔬𝔪 𝔞𝔪𝔬𝔫𝔤 𝔱𝔥𝔢𝔪 𝔞𝔫𝔡 𝔟𝔢 𝔶𝔢 𝔰𝔢𝔭𝔞𝔯𝔞𝔱𝔢, 𝔰𝔞𝔦𝔱𝔥 𝔱𝔥𝔢 𝔏𝔬𝔯𝔡, 𝔞𝔫𝔡 𝔱𝔬𝔲𝔠𝔥 𝔫𝔬𝔱 𝔱𝔥𝔢 **18** 𝔲𝔫𝔠𝔩𝔢𝔞𝔫 𝔱𝔥𝔦𝔫𝔤, 𝔞𝔫𝔡 𝔍 𝔴𝔦𝔩𝔩 𝔯𝔢𝔠𝔢𝔦𝔳𝔢 𝔶𝔬𝔲.' [2]   And '𝔍 𝔴𝔦𝔩𝔩 𝔟𝔢 𝔲𝔫𝔱𝔬 𝔶𝔬𝔲 𝔞 𝔣𝔞𝔱𝔥𝔢𝔯, 𝔞𝔫𝔡 𝔶𝔢 𝔰𝔥𝔞𝔩𝔩 𝔟𝔢 𝔪𝔶 𝔰𝔬𝔫𝔰 𝔞𝔫𝔡 **vii. 1** 𝔡𝔞𝔲𝔤𝔥𝔱𝔢𝔯𝔰, 𝔰𝔞𝔦𝔱𝔥 𝔱𝔥𝔢 𝔏𝔬𝔯𝔡 𝔄𝔩𝔪𝔦𝔤𝔥𝔱𝔶.' [3]   Having therefore these promises, my beloved, let us cleanse ourselves from every defilement, either of flesh or spirit, and perfect our holiness, in the fear of God.

2   [4] Give me a favourable hearing.   I have wronged no man, I have ruined [5] no man, I have defrauded no **3** man; I say not this to condemn you, [as though I had myself been wronged by you,] for I have said before that I have you in my heart, to live and die **4** with you.   Great is my freedom towards you, great

Side notes:
Exhortation to the Anti-Judaising party ('the spiritual') to shun all fellowship with heathen

Satisfaction at the tidings just brought by Titus from Corinth.

---

[1] Levit. xxvi. 11, 12 (according to LXX., with slight variations).

[2] Isaiah lii. 11 (according to LXX., with alterations); the words 'I will receive you' not being either in the LXX. or the Hebrew there, though found in Ezek. xx. 34.

[3] This passage is not to be found exactly in the Old Testament, although 2 Sam. vii. 14, and Jer. xxxi. 9, and xxxii. 38, contain the substance of it. St. Paul, as usual, quotes from memory.

[4] It is not impossible that the preceding part of the Epistle may have been written, as Wieseler supposes, before the coming of Titus. See above, p. 438, n. 6. But the opening words of this section are obviously connected with verses 12, 13, of the preceding chapter. The section from vi. 14 to vii. 1 is entirely unconnected with what precedes and follows it.

[5] St. Paul appears frequently to use the original word in this sense (compare 1 Cor. iii. 17), and not in the ordinary meaning of *corrupt*. We may remark here, that there is no need to suppose these aorists used aoristically (as they would be in classical Greek), since St. Paul constantly used the aorist for the perfect. Even those commentators who are most anxious to force upon the Hellenistic of the New Testament the nice observance of this classical distinction, are obliged sometimes to give up their consistency and translate the aorist as perfect. In fact, the aorist is continually joined with 'now' (e.g. Matt. xxvi. 65; John xiii. 31; Rom. xi. 31; Eph. iii. 5), which is of course decisive. It is not wonderful that there should be this ambiguity in the Hellenistic use of Greek tenses, considering that in Latin the same tense has to serve the purpose both of *aorist* and *perfect*. See note on Rom. v. 5. [See note on Gal. ii. 10. This grammatical question is discussed in the *Cambridge Journal of Classical and Sacred Philology*. H.]

is my boasting of you; I am filled with the comfort which you have caused me; I have more than an overweight of joy, for all the affliction which has befallen me. When first I came into Macedonia my vii. 5 flesh had no rest, but I was troubled on every side; without were fightings, within were fears. But God, 6 who comforts them that are cast down, comforted me by the coming of Titus; and not by his coming 7 only, but by the comfort which he felt on your account, and the tidings which he brought of your longing for my love, your mourning for my reproof, your zeal for my cause; so that my sorrow has been turned into joy. For though I grieved you in my 8 letter,[1] I do not regret it; but though I did regret it, (for I see that grief was caused you by that letter, though but for a season,) I now rejoice; not because 9 you were grieved, but because your grief led you to repentance;[2] for the grief I caused you was a godly sorrow; so that I might nowise harm you [even when I grieved you]. For the work of godly sorrow 10 is repentance not to be repented of, leading to salvation; but the work of worldly sorrow is death. Con- 11 sider what was wrought among yourselves when you were grieved with a godly sorrow; what earnestness it wrought in you, yea, what eagerness to clear yourselves from blame, what indignation,[3] what fear,[4] what longing,[5] what zeal,[6] what punishment of wrong. You have cleared yourselves altogether from every stain of guilt in this matter. Know, therefore, that 12 although I wrote to [rebuke] you, it was not so much to punish the wrong doer, nor to avenge him[7] who suffered the wrong, but that my earnest zeal for you in the sight of God might be manifest to yourselves.[8]

This, therefore, is the ground of my comfort; but[9] 13

[1] Viz. 1 Cor., unless we adopt the hypothesis that another letter had been written in the interval, according to the view mentioned p. 435, n. 2.

[2] The text of the whole passage, here adopted, is the same as that of Prof. Stanley, but punctuated differently.

[3] Indignation against the offender.

[4] Fear of the wrath of God.

[5] Longing for restoration to St. Paul's approval and love.

[6] Zeal on behalf of right, and against wrong.

[7] Viz. the father of the offender. We need not be perplexed at his wife's forming another connection during his lifetime, when we consider the great laxity of the law of divorce among the Greeks and Romans.

[8] If we adopt the other reading (which transposes 'you' and 'us'), it will give the sense *that your zeal for me might be manifested to yourselves*; which might be perhaps another (though an obscure) way of saying, *in order to bring out your zeal for me, so that you might all perceive how the majority felt for me*.

[9] The reading of the best MSS. gives this order.

besides my consolation on your account, I was beyond measure rejoiced by the joy of Titus, because his
vii. 14 spirit has been refreshed by you all. For whatever boast of you I may have made to him, I have not been ·put to shame. But as all I ever said to you was spoken in truth, so also my boasting of you to
15 Titus has been proved a truth. And his heart is more than ever drawn towards you, while he calls to mind the obedience of you all, and the fear and
16 trembling [1] wherewith you received him. I rejoice that in all things you give me ground for courage.

viii. 1 I desire, brethren, to make known to you the manifestation of God's grace, which has been given
2 in [3] the churches of Macedonia. For in the heavy trial which has proved their stedfastness, the fulness of their joy has overflowed, out of the depth of their
3 poverty, in the richness of their liberality.[4] They have given (I bear them witness) not only according to their means, but beyond their means, and that of
4 their own free will; for they besought me with much entreaty that they might bear their part [5] in the grace
5 of ministering to the saints. And far beyond my hope, they gave their very selves to the Lord first, and
6 to me also by the will of God. So that I have desired Titus [to revisit you], that as he caused you to begin this work before, so he may lead you to finish it,
7 that this grace may not be wanting [6] in you; but that, as you abound in all gifts, in faith and utterance, and knowledge, and earnest zeal, and in the love which joins [7] your hearts with mine, so you may
8 abound in this grace also. I say not this by way of command; but by the zeal of others I would prove
9 the reality of your love. For you know the grace of our Lord Jesus Christ, how, though He was rich,

Explanations and directions concerning the collection for the poor Christians in Jerusalem.[2]

---

[1] For the meaning of this phrase, see 1 Cor. ii. 3.

[2] The great importance attached by St. Paul to this collection, as manifested in the present section of this Epistle, may be explained not merely by his desire to fulfil his share of the agreement mentioned, Gal. ii. 10, but also by his hope that such a practical proof of love would reconcile the Judaising Christians at Jerusalem to himself and his Gentile converts. See the conclusion of our preceding chapter.

[3] The original here cannot mean 'bestowed *on*' (A. V.).

[4] See note on 2 Cor. ix. 11.

[5] The omission here is required by the best MSS.

[6] Literally, *this grace as well as other graces.*

[7] If we follow the Received Text, this is literally, *the love which springs from you and dwells in me*; if with Lachmann's text we transpose the pronouns, it will be *the love which I have awakened in your hearts.* [Lachmann's second edition returns to the Received Text. II.]

yet for our sakes He became poor, that you, by His poverty might be made rich. And I give you my viii. advice in this matter; for it becomes you to do thus, inasmuch as you began not only the contribution, but the purpose of making it before others,[1] in the year which is passed. Now, therefore, fulfil your 11 purpose by your deeds, that as you then showed your readiness of will, so now you may finish the work, according to your means. For if there be a willing 12 mind, the [2] gift is acceptable when measured by the giver's power, and needs not to go beyond. Nor [is 13 this collection made] that others may be eased, and you distressed, but to make your burdens equal, that 14 as now your abundance supplies their need, your own need may [at another time] be relieved in equal measure by their abundance, as it is written,—'𝔥𝔢 15 𝔱𝔥𝔞𝔱 𝔤𝔞𝔱𝔥𝔢𝔯𝔢𝔡 𝔪𝔲𝔠𝔥 𝔥𝔞𝔡 𝔫𝔬𝔱𝔥𝔦𝔫𝔤 𝔬𝔳𝔢𝔯; 𝔞𝔫𝔡 𝔥𝔢 𝔱𝔥𝔞𝔱 𝔤𝔞𝔱𝔥𝔢𝔯𝔢𝔡 𝔩𝔦𝔱𝔱𝔩𝔢 𝔥𝔞𝔡 𝔫𝔬 𝔩𝔞𝔠𝔨.'[3]   But, thanks be to God, 16 by whose gift the heart of Titus has the same zeal as my own on your behalf; for he not only has con- 17 sented to my desire, but is himself very zealous in the matter, and departs [4] to you of his own accord. And 18 I have sent as his companion the brother who is with him, whose praise in publishing the Glad-tidings [5] is spread throughout all the churches; who has more- 19 over been chosen by the churches [of Macedonia] to accompany me in my journey (when I bear this gift, which I have undertaken to administer); that the Lord might be glorified, and that [6] I might undertake the task with more good will. For I guard myself 20 against all suspicion which might be cast upon me

---

[1] 'Began *before*; viz. before the Macedonian churches. The meaning is, that the Corinthians had been the first not only to make the collection, but to propose it.

[2] Literally, *it is acceptable according to that which it possesses, not that which it possesses not.*

[3] Exodus xvi. 18, quoted according to LXX. The subject is the gathering of the manna.

[4] The tense in the original is past, because the act is looked upon, according to the classical idiom, from the position of the reader.

[5] The word here cannot refer, as some have imagined, to a *written Gospel*; it is of constant occurrence in the New Testament (occurring sixty times in St. Paul's writings, and sixteen times in the other books), but never once in the supposed sense. Who the deputy here mentioned was, we have no means of ascertaining. Probably, however, he was either Luke (Acts xx. 6), or one of those, not Macedonians (ix. 4), mentioned Acts xx. 4; and possibly may have been Trophimus. See Acts xxi. 29. We may notice the coincidence between the phrase here and in Acts xix. 29.

[6] The reading of the best MSS. gives the sense as follows,—*to promote my willingness of mind,* i.e. *to render me more willing to undertake the administration of the alms,* which St. Paul would have been unwilling to do without coadjutors elected by the contributors, lest he should incur unworthy suspicions.

in my administration of this bounty with which I
viii. 21 am charged; being '𝔭𝔯𝔬𝔟𝔦𝔡𝔢𝔫𝔱 𝔬𝔣 𝔤𝔬𝔬𝔡 𝔯𝔢𝔭𝔬𝔯𝔱' not
only '𝔦𝔫 𝔱𝔥𝔢 𝔰𝔦𝔤𝔥𝔱 𝔬𝔣 𝔱𝔥𝔢 𝔏𝔬𝔯𝔡,' but also '𝔦𝔫 𝔱𝔥𝔢 𝔰𝔦𝔤𝔥𝔱
22 𝔬𝔣 𝔪𝔢𝔫.' [1] The brother [2] whom I have sent likewise
with them, is one whom I have put to the proof in
many trials, and found always zealous in the work,
but who is now yet more zealous from the full trust
23 which he has in you. Concerning Titus, then (on
the one hand), he is partner of my lot, and fellow-
labourer with me for your good; concerning our
brethren (on the other hand), they are ambassadors
of the churches—a manifestation of the glory of
24 Christ. Show them, therefore, the proof of your
love, and justify my boasting on your behalf, in the
ix. 1 sight of the churches.[3] For of your ministration to
the saints [at Jerusalem] it is needless that I should
2 write to you, since I know the forwardness of your
mind, and boast of it to the Macedonians on your
behalf, saying that Achaia has been ready ever since
last year, and the knowledge of your zeal has roused
3 the most of them. But I have sent the brethren,[4]
lest my report of you in this matter should be turned
into an empty boast; that you may be truly ready, as
4 I declared you to be. Lest perchance the Macedonians who may come with me to visit you, should
find you not yet ready, and so shame should fall upon
me (for I will not say upon you) in this ground of my
5 boasting.[5] Therefore, I thought it needful to desire
these brethren to visit you before my coming, and to
arrange beforehand the completion of this bounty
which you before promised to have in readiness; so
it be really given by your bounty, not wrung from
6 your covetousness. But remember, he [6] who sows
sparingly shall reap sparingly; and he who sows
7 bountifully, shall reap bountifully. Let each do ac-

---

[1] The quotation is from Prov. iii. 4
(LXX.), cited also Rom. xii. 17.

[2] There is even less to guide us in
our conjectures as to the person here
indicated, than in the case of the other
deputy mentioned above. Here, also,
the emissary was elected by some of the
Churches who had contributed to the
collection. He may have been either
Luke, Gaius, Tychicus, or Trophimus
(Acts xx. 4).

[3] 'To them' is contrasted with 'to
the saints' in the following verse; the
connection being *Show kindness to the
deputies; for as to the collection, I need
not ask you to show zeal for that,* &c.
The 'and' in the last clause is omitted
by all the best MSS.

[4] Viz. Titus and the other two.

[5] Literally, the word means, *the
groundwork on which some superstructure is founded.* His appeal to the
Macedonians was grounded on this
readiness of the Corinthians. If (with
the best MSS.) we omit 'of my boasting,' the meaning will be unaltered.
Compare xi. 17, and note on Heb. iii.
14.

[6] The same expression occurs Gal.
vi. 7.

cording to the free choice of his heart; not grudgingly, or of necessity; for '𝔊𝔬𝔡 𝔩𝔬𝔳𝔢𝔱𝔥 𝔞 𝔠𝔥𝔢𝔢𝔯𝔣𝔲𝔩 𝔤𝔦𝔳𝔢𝔯.' [1] And God is able to give you an overflowing **ix. 8** measure of all good gifts, that all your wants of every kind may be supplied at all times, and you may give of your abundance to every good work. As it is **9** written,—'𝔗𝔥𝔢 𝔤𝔬𝔬𝔡 𝔪𝔞𝔫 𝔥𝔞𝔱𝔥 𝔰𝔠𝔞𝔱𝔱𝔢𝔯𝔢𝔡 𝔞𝔟𝔯𝔬𝔞𝔡, 𝔥𝔢 𝔥𝔞𝔱𝔥 𝔤𝔦𝔳𝔢𝔫 𝔱𝔬 𝔱𝔥𝔢 𝔭𝔬𝔬𝔯 ; 𝔥𝔦𝔰 𝔯𝔦𝔤𝔥𝔱𝔢𝔬𝔲𝔰𝔫𝔢𝔰𝔰 𝔯𝔢𝔪𝔞𝔦𝔫𝔢𝔱𝔥 𝔣𝔬𝔯 𝔢𝔟𝔢𝔯.' [2] And He who furnisheth '𝔰𝔢𝔢𝔡 𝔱𝔬 𝔱𝔥𝔢 𝔰𝔬𝔴𝔢𝔯, **10** 𝔞𝔫𝔡 𝔟𝔯𝔢𝔞𝔡 𝔣𝔬𝔯 𝔱𝔥𝔢 𝔣𝔬𝔬𝔡 𝔬𝔣 𝔪𝔞𝔫,' [3] will furnish [4] you with plenteous store of seed, and bless your righteousness with fruits of increase ; being enriched with all **11** good things, that you may give ungrudgingly; [5] causing thanksgivings to God, from [6] those to whom I bear your gifts. For the ministration of this **12** service not only fills up the measure of the necessities of the saints, but also overflows beyond it, in many thanks to God ; while they [7] praise God for the **13** proof thus given of the obedience wherewith you have consented to the Glad-tidings of Christ, and for the single-mindedness of your liberality both to them, and to all. Moreover, in their prayers for you they **14** express the earnest longings of their love towards you, caused by the surpassing grace of God manifested in you. Thanks be to God for His unspeak- **15** able gift.

He contrasts his own character and services with those of the false teachers who depreciated him.

Now, I Paul, myself exhort you by the meekness **x. 1** and gentleness of Christ—(I, who am mean, forsooth, and lowly in outward presence,[8] while I am among you, yet treat you boldy when I am absent)—I **2** beseech you (I say), that you will not force me to

---

[1] Prov. xxii. 8 (according to LXX., with slight variation).

[2] Ps. cxii. 9 (LXX.). The subject of the verb 'scattered' in the psalm is 'the good man' (in the fifth verse), which St. Paul leaves to be supplied by the memory of his readers. To represent the quotation accurately to an English reader, it is necessary to insert this word, otherwise it would seem as if 'God' were the subject of the verb.

[3] These words are an exact quotation from Isaiah lv. 10 (LXX.). Ignorance of this fact has caused an inaccuracy in A. V. The literal translation of the remainder of the verse is,—' *Furnish and make plenteous your seed, and increase the fruits springing from your righteousness.*'

[4] In the best MSS. the verbs in this verse are future, not optative.

[5] The word here, probably denoting *singleness*, means, when applied to the mind, a disposition free from *arrières pensées*, either of duplicity, selfishness, or grudging; thus it might naturally acquire the meaning of *liberality*, which it has in the eighth and ninth chapters in this Epistle, and perhaps in Rom. xii. 9.

[6] Literally, *that you may give with liberality ; which works thanksgiving to God by my instrumentality.*

[7] Literally, *they, by the proof of this ministration, praising God,* i.e. *being caused to praise God for the obedience,* &c.

[8] The phraseology is similar here and in v. 12 and x. 7. Compare also x. 10.

show, when I am present, the bold confidence in my
power, wherewith I reckon to deal with some who
x. 3 reckon [1] me by the standard of the flesh. For, though
living in the flesh, my warfare is not waged accord-
4 ing to the flesh. For the weapons which I wield are
not of fleshly weakness, but mighty in the strength
of God to overthrow the strongholds of the adver-
5 saries. Thereby can I overthrow the reasonings of
the disputer, and pull down all lofty bulwarks that
raise themselves against the knowledge of God, and
bring every rebellious thought into captivity and
6 subjection to Christ. And when the obedience of
your [2] church shall be complete, I am ready to punish
all who may be disobedient.[3]

7   Do you look at matters of outward advantage?
If there be any among you who confidently assumes
that he belongs [above the rest] to Christ,[4] let him
reckon anew by his reason,[5] that if he belong to
8 Christ, so do I no less. For although I were to
boast somewhat highly concerning the authority
which the Lord has given me (not to cast you down,
but to build you up), my words would not be shamed
9 by the truth. I say this, lest you should imagine
10 that I am writing empty threats. 'For his letters,'
says one,[6] 'are weighty and powerful, but his bodily
11 presence is weak, and his speech contemptible.' Let
such a man assure himself that the words which I

[1] Literally, *who reckon me as walking according to the flesh.* The verses which follow explain the meaning of the expression.

[2] 'Your.' Compare ii. 5. He means that the disobedient minority would be chastised.

[3] [We should notice in verses 3–6 the completeness of the military allegory. The image is that of a campaign against rebels: rock-forts (such as those on St. Paul's own Cilician coast) must be cast down: and when the general obedience of the country is secured, those who are still rebellious must be summarily punished. We should observe, too, the new turn given to one phrase (not *casting down* but *building up*) in verse 8, and even in xiii. 10. See also xii. 19. H.]

[4] The party who said 'I of Christ.' (1 Cor. i. 12.) See Chap. XIII. As we have remarked above, p. 439, this party at Corinth seems to have been formed and led by an emissary from the Judaisers of Palestine, who is especially referred to in this chapter.

[5] In the former edition this phrase was translated *consider*; Dr. Alford has expressed an opinion that this translation is 'surely inadmissible,' and that it 'entirely omits *of himself.*' Yet it is in fact equivalent to his own translation, 'let him reckon out of his own mind,' for what is *considering* but *reckoning out of one's own mind*?). Nevertheless it must be admitted, that the former translation did not give sufficient *emphasis* to 'of himself.'

[6] Literally, '*says he*;' but it is occasionally used impersonally for 'they say:' yet as, in that sense, the plural would be more naturally used, the use of 'says he' and of 'such a man' in the next verse, seems to point to a single individual at the head of St. Paul's opponents. See last note, and p. 439, and compare the use of 'such a man' for the single incestuous person (2 Cor. ii. 7), and for St. Paul himself (2 Cor. xii. 2).

write while absent, I will bear out by my deeds when
present.[1] For I venture not to number or compare **x. 12**
myself with certain of the self-commenders; nay,
they, measuring themselves by themselves, and comparing themselves with themselves, are guilty of
folly.[2] But I, for my part, will not let my boasting **13**
carry me beyond measure, but will confine it within
that measure given me by God, who made my line
reach even to you. For I stretch not myself beyond **14**
due bounds (as though I reached you not); for I
have already come as far even as Corinth [3] to publish
the Glad-tidings of Christ. I am not boasting beyond **15**
measure, in the labours of others; [4] but, I hope that
as your faith goes on increasing, among [5] yourselves,
I shall be still further honoured within my appointed
limits, by bearing the Glad-tidings to the countries **16**
beyond you; not by boasting of work made ready to
my hand within another man's limit. Meantime, '𝕳𝖊 **17**
𝖙𝖍𝖆𝖙 𝖇𝖔𝖆𝖘𝖙𝖊𝖙𝖍, 𝖑𝖊𝖙 𝖍𝖎𝖒 𝖇𝖔𝖆𝖘𝖙 𝖎𝖓 𝖙𝖍𝖊 𝕷𝖔𝖗𝖉.' [6] For a man **18**
is proved worthy, not when he commends himself,
but when he is commended by the Lord.

Would that ye could bear with me a little in my **xi. 1**
folly! Yea, ye already bear with me. For I love **2**
you with a godly jealousy, because I betrothed you
to one only husband, even to Christ, that I might
present you unto Him in virgin purity; but I fear **3**
lest, as Eve was beguiled by the craftiness of the
serpent, so your imaginations should be corrupted,
and you should be seduced from your single-minded
faithfulness to Christ. For if he that comes among **4**
you is preaching another Jesus, whom I preached
not, or if you are receiving [from him] another Spirit,
which you received not before, or a new Glad-tidings,
which you accepted not before, you would do well to
bear with me; [7] for I reckon myself no whit behind **5**

---

[1] Literally, ' *Let such a man reckon,
that such as I am in word by letters while
absent, such will I be also in deed when
present.*'

[2] The Greek word here is an Hellenistic form of the 3rd pl. ind. present,
and occurs Mat. xiii. 13. Hence we
need not take it here for the dative
plural. If the latter view were correct,
the translation would be, ' but I measure myself by my own standard, and
compare myself with myself alone, unwise as I am.' But this translation
presents several difficulties, both in it-

self, and considered in reference to the
context. Lachmann's reading has apparently been caused by the difficulty
of the Hellenistic form.

[3] 'You.'

[4] This was the conduct of St. Paul's
Judaising antagonists.

[5] Instead of ' by you' we translate ' in
you,' and connect it with ' increased.'

[6] Quoted, according to the sense,
from Jer. ix. 24 (LXX.); 'in the
Lord' being substituted for a longer
phrase. Quoted also 1 Cor. i. 31.

[7] Lachmann (with the Vatican

xi. 6 your super-eminent Apostles.[1]   Yea, though I be
unskilled in the arts of speech, yet I am not wanting
in the gift of [2] knowledge ; but I have manifested [3] it
7 towards you in all things, and amongst all men.   Or
is it a sin [which must rob me of the name of
Apostle],[4] that I proclaimed to you, without fee or
reward, the Glad-tidings of God, and abased [5] myself
8 that you might be exalted ?   Other churches I spoiled,
9 and took their wages to do you service.   And when
I was with you, though I was in want, I pressed not
upon any of you ; for the brethren,[6] when they came
from Macedonia, supplied my needs ; and I kept, and
will keep myself altogether from casting a burden
10 upon you.   As the truth of Christ is in me, no deed
of mine shall rob me [7] of this boasting in the region
11 of Achaia.   And why ?   Because I love you not ?
12 God knows my love.   But what I do I will continue
to do, that I may cut off all ground from those who
wish to find some ground of slander ; and let them
show the same cause for their boasting as I for mine.[8]
13 For men like these are false Apostles, deceitful workmen, clothing themselves in the garb of Christ's
14 Apostles.   And no wonder ; for even Satan can trans-
15 form himself into an angel of light.   It is not strange,

Manuscript) has the verb in the present, which makes the coincidence
with ver. 1 more exact ; but if we keep
the aorist, it may bear the sense here
given it, on the same principle on which
erat is often used for *esset*, and *fuerat*
for *fuisset*.   We understand 'bear with
me' (not 'bear with *him*,' with most
commentators), because this agrees
better with the context (the preposition '*for*' following), and with the
first verse of the chapter.

[1] This phrase (which occurs only in
this Epistle) is ironical, as is evident
from the epithet '*the super-apostolic
Apostles.*'   He refers to the Judaising
emissaries from Palestine who had arrived at Corinth.

[2] The gift of 'Gnosis' was *a deep
insight into spiritual truth.*   See Chap.
XIII. p. 334, n. 1.

[3] This is according to the reading
supported by the preponderating weight
of MS. authority.

[4] See pp. 342, 343.

[5] i.e. by working with his hands for
his daily bread.   See p. 301.   In all
probability (judging from what we
know of other manufactories in those
times) his fellow-workmen in Aquila's
tent manufactory were slaves.   Compare Phil. iv. 12, 'I know how to be
abased.'

[6] Probably Timotheus and Silvanus,
who may have brought the contribution
sent by the Philippians.   The A. V.
'which came' is incorrect.

[7] According to the true reading here,
the literal English would be, *this boasting shall not be stopped for me.*

[8] The literal English of this difficult
passage is, '*that they, in the ground
of their boasting, may be found even as
I.*'   De Wette refers 'wherein they
glory' to *the Apostolic Office.*   We
take it more generally.   A more obvious way would be to take the phrase
(with Chrysostom and the older interpreters) to mean their *abstaining from
receiving maintenance* ; but we know
that the false teachers at Corinth did
not do this (compare ver. 20 below), but,
on the contrary, boasted of their privilege, and alleged that St. Paul, by not
claiming it, showed his consciousness
that he was not truly sent by Christ.
See 1 Cor. ix.

then, if his servants disguise themselves as servants of righteousness: but their end shall be according to their works.

I entreat you all once more [1] not to count me for a fool; or, if you think me such, yet bear with me in my folly, that I, too, may boast a little of myself. But, in so doing, I speak not in the spirit of the Lord, but, as it were, in folly, while we stand upon this ground [2] of boasting; for, since many are boasting in the spirit of the flesh, I will boast likewise. And I know that you bear kindly with fools as beseems the wise. [3] Nay, you bear with men, though they enslave you, though they devour you, though they entrap you, though they exalt themselves over you, though they smite you on the face, to degrade you. [4] I say that I was weak; [5] and yet, if any have ground of boldness, I too (I speak in folly) have ground to be as bold as they. Are they Hebrews? so am I. Are they sons of Israel? so am I. Are they the seed of Abraham? so am I. Are they servants of Christ? (I speak as though I were beside myself) such, far more am I. In labours more abundant, in stripes above measure, in prisons more frequent, in deaths oft. (Five times I received from Jews the forty stripes save one; thrice I was scourged with the Roman rods; once I was stoned; thrice I suffered shipwreck; [6] a night and a day have I spent in the open [7] sea.) In journeyings often; in perils of rivers, in perils of robbers; in perils from my countrymen, in perils from the heathen; in perils in the city, in perils in the wilderness, in perils in the sea; in perils among false brethren. In toil and weariness, often in sleepless watchings; in hunger

xi. ▶
17
18
19
20
21
22
23
24
25
26
27

---

[1] Literally, '*I say once more, let none count me,*' &c.

[2] See note on 2 Cor. ix. 4.

[3] This is ironical. So 'ye are wise,' in 1 Cor. iv. 10.

[4] Literally, *in the way of degradation.* The punctuation we adopt gives a simpler and more natural sense than that adopted in the first edition; and it also better suits the use of the pleonastic phrase here and in 2 Cor. v. 19 and 2 Thess. ii. 2.

[5] This refers to the acknowledgments he has previously made of weakness in outward advantages, e.g. at xi. 6 and x. i.

[6] The five Jewish scourgings, two of the three Roman beatings with rods (one being at Philippi), and the three shipwrecks, are all unrecorded in the Acts. The stoning was at Lystra. What a life of incessant adventure and peril is here disclosed to us! And when we remember that he who endured and dared all this was a man constantly suffering from infirm health (see 2 Cor. iv. 7–12, and 2 Cor. xii. 7–10, and Gal. iv. 13, 14), such heroic self-devotion seems almost superhuman.

[7] Probably in a small boat (or perhaps on a plank), escaping from one of the wrecks.

and thirst, often without bread to eat; in cold and
xi. 28 nakedness.   And besides all the rest,[1] there is the
crowd [2] which presses upon me daily, and the care of
29 all the churches.   Who is weak,[3] but I share his
weakness?   Who is caused to fall, but I burn with
30 indignation?   If I must needs boast, I will boast of
31 my weakness.   God, who is the Father of our Lord
Jesus Christ, He who is blessed for ever, knows that
I lie not.[4]

32   In Damascus, the governor under Aretas,[5] the
king, kept watch over the city with a garrison,
33 purposing to apprehend me; and I was let down
by the wall, through a window, in a basket, and
thus [not by my strength, but by my weakness]
xii. 1 I escaped his hands.   It is not for me, then, to
boast.[6]

But I will come also to visions and revelations
of the Lord.   I know [7] a man who was caught up
2 fourteen years ago (whether in the body or out of
the body, I cannot tell; God knoweth), caught up,
I say, in the power of Christ,[8] even to the third

---

[1] Not '*those things that are without*' as in A. V.

[2] For this meaning of the word compare Acts xxiv. 12. If we adopt another reading, which has the greater weight of existing MSS. in its favour, but patristic authority against it, the meaning will be nearly the same; see Canon Stanley's note.

[3] For the way in which St. Paul shared the weakness of the 'weaker brethren,' see p. 350, and the passages there referred to.

[4] This solemn oath, affirming his veracity, probably refers to the preceding statements of his labours and dangers. Compare Gal. i. 20. If, however, we should suppose that the next two verses were originally intended to be the beginning of a narrative of all his sufferings from the beginning, then we might refer the asseveration to such intended narrative.

[5] For the historical questions connected with this incident, see p. 83. [A note on the word Ethnarch will be found in p. 89. H.]

[6] We prefer the reading of the Textus Receptus (which is also adopted by Chrysostom and by Tischendorf) to that of the Vatican Manuscript, adopted by Lachmann. On the other hand, for what follows we take Lachmann's read-

ing, on the authority of the Codex Vaticanus, instead of the Textus Receptus. The whole passage is most perplexing, from the obscurity of its connection with what precedes and what follows. Why did St. Paul mention his escape from Damascus in so much detail? Was it merely as an event ignominious to himself? This seems the best view, but it is far from satisfactory. There is something most disappointing in his beginning thus to relate in detail the first in that series of wonderful escapes of which he had just before given a rapid sketch, and then suddenly and abruptly breaking off; leaving our curiosity roused and yet ungratified. We cannot agree with De Wette in considering the Damascene escape to be introduced as the climax of all the other perils mentioned, nor in referring to it the solemn attestation of ver. 31.

[7] The mistranslation of the verb in A. V. (*knew* for *know*) very seriously affects the sense: nor is there anything in the Greek corresponding to 'about.'

[8] We take 'in Christ' with 'caught up,' which would have come immediately after the date, had it not been intercepted by the parenthetic clause. To translate '*a Christian man*' (as some commentators have done) is

heaven,   And I know that such a man (whether
in the body or out of the body I cannot tell; God
knoweth) was caught up into Paradise,[1] and heard 4
unspeakable words, which it is not lawful for man to
utter.   Of such a man I will boast; but of myself I 5
will not boast, save in the tokens of my weakness.
If I should choose to boast, I should not be guilty of 6
empty vanity, for I should speak the truth; but I
forbear to speak, that I may not cause any man to
think of me more highly than when he sees my deeds
or hears my teaching.[2]   And lest, through the ex- 7
ceeding greatness of these revelations, I should be
lifted up with pride, there was given me a thorn in
the flesh,[3] a messenger of Satan, to buffet me, to keep
down my pride.   And thrice I besought the Lord [4] 8
concerning it, that it might depart from me.   But 9
He hath said to me, ' My grace is sufficient for thee;
for my strength is mighty [5] in weakness.'   Most
gladly, therefore, will I boast rather in my weakness
than in my strength, that the strength of Christ may
rest upon me and dwell in me.[6]   Therefore I rejoice 10
in signs of weakness, in outrage, in necessities, in
persecutions, in straitness of distress, endured for
Christ; for when I am weak, then am I strong.[7]

I have been guilty of folly, but you forced me to 11
it; for I ought myself to have been commended by
you: for I came no whit behind your super-eminent [8]
Apostles, though I be of no account.   The marks, at 12
least, of an Apostle were seen in the deeds which I
wrought among you, in signs, and wonders, and
miracles, with stedfast endurance of persecution.[9]
Wherein had you the disadvantage of other churches, 13

---

hardly justified by such analogies as
' they that are in Christ.'

[1] Compare Luke xxiii. 43, *To-day
shalt thou be with me in Paradise*, and
Rev. ii. 7.

[2] He alludes to the low opinion expressed by his adversaries at Corinth
of his personal qualifications and teaching; compare x. 10.

[3] The original is perhaps not adequately represented by the word *thorn*,
although the thorns of the East are far
more formidable than those of England.
Stake is probably a more accurate
translation. See Prof. Stanley's note
on the passage. *A painful bodily infirmity* is meant. See Gal. iv. 13, 14,
and p. 210.

[4] That is, the Lord Jesus, as appears
by ' Christ' in the next verse.

[5] *Has its full development.*

[6] The full meaning is, to *come to a
place for the purpose of fixing one's
tent there.* Compare (with the whole
verse) iv. 7.

[7] i.e. the more he was depressed by
suffering and persecution, the more was
he enabled to achieve by the aid of
Christ. See a very striking sermon of
A. Monod (in his *Discours sur St. Paul*)
on this text.

[8] See note on xi. 5.

[9] The word here (in St. Paul's language) means *stedfastness under persecution.* Some of the persecutions
referred to are recorded in Acts xviii.

unless, indeed, that I did not burden you with my
ii. 14 own maintenance ? forgive me this wrong.   Behold
I am now for the third time [1] preparing to visit you,
and I purpose to cast no burden upon you ; for I
seek not your substance, but yourselves.   Since
children should not lay up wealth for parents, but
parents for children.   Nay, rather, most gladly will
15 I spend, yea, and myself be spent, for your souls,
though the more abundantly I love you, the less I be
loved.

But though it be granted that I did not burden
16 you myself, yet perchance this was my cunning,
whereby I entrapped your simplicity.   Did I defraud
17 you of your wealth by some of the messengers whom
I sent to you ?   I desired Titus to visit you, and with
18 him I sent the brother, his fellow-traveller.   Did
Titus defraud you ?   Did we not act in the same
spirit ?   Did we not walk in the same steps ?

Do you again imagine that it is before you I de-
19 fend myself ?   Nay, before God I speak, in Christ ;
but all, beloved, for your sakes, that you may be
built up.   For I fear lest perchance when I come
20 I should find you not such as I could wish, and
that you also should fine me other than you desire.   I fear to find you full of strife, jealousies,
passions, intrigues,[2] slanderings, backbitings, vaunting, sedition.   I fear lest, when I come, my God
21 will again humble me [3] by your faults, and I shall
mourn over many among those who have sinned
before [4] and who have not repented of the uncleanness, and fornication, and wantonness which they
committed.

I now come to you for the third time.[5]   ' **Out**
iii. 1 **of the mouth of two or three witnesses shall every word
be confirmed.**' [6]   I have warned you formerly, and I
2 now forewarn you, as when [7] I was present the second

He warns the factious and immoral minority that he must be constrained to punish them if they persist in their disobedience.

---

[1] See note on xiii. 1.
[2] For the word here, see note on
Rom. ii. 8.
[3] Literally, *humble me in respect of
you.* See on this verse p. 375, note 1.
[4] Sinned 'before :' viz. before my
last visit.
[5] 'This third time I am coming to
you.' This could scarcely mean merely,
' I am for the third time *preparing* to
visit you,' although 2 Cor. xii. 14
might imply no more than that. See
p. 375, n. 1. Prof. Stanley, (who ignores

the intermediate visit,) can only get
over this argument by supposing that
St. Paul is here 'reckoning his Second
Epistle as virtually a second visit.
(Stanley's *Corinthians*, vol. ii. 265.)
[6] Deut. xix. 15 (from LXX. nearly
verbatim), meaning, ' I will judge not
without examination, nor will I abstain
from punishing upon due evidence.'
Or else (perhaps), ' I shall now assuredly fulfil my threats.'
[7] This passage, in which the word
for ' I write' is omitted by the best

time, so now, while I am absent, saying to those who had sinned before [my last visit], and to all the rest of the offenders,—'If I come again I will not spare.'[1] Thus you shall have the proof you seek of the power xii of Christ, who speaks in me; for He shows no weakness towards you, but works mightily among you. For although He died upon the cross through the 4 weakness of the flesh,[2] yet now He lives through the power of God. And so I, too, share the weakness of His body;[3] yet I shall share also the power of God, whereby He lives, when[4] I come to deal with you. Examine[5] [not me, but] yourselves, whether you 5 are truly in the faith; put yourselves to the proof [concerning Christ's presence with you which ye seek in me]. Know ye not of your own selves, that Jesus Christ is dwelling in you? unless, perchance, when thus proved, you fail to abide the proof.[6] But 6 I hope you will find that I, for my part, abide the proof.[7] Yet I pray to God that you may do no evil;[8] 7 desiring not that my own power may be clearly proved, but that you may do right, although I should seem unable to abide the proof: for I have no power 8 against the truth, but only for the truth's defence. I rejoice, I say, when I am powerless [against you], 9

MSS., seems conclusive for the intermediate journey. What would be the meaning of saying, 'I forewarn you as if I were present the second time, now also while I am absent?' which is the translation that we must adopt if we deny the intermediate visit. Also the 'they who had sinned before' contrasted with the 'all the rest' (ver. 2), seems inexplicable except on this hypothesis.

[1] The conjunction here (as frequently) is equivalent to a mark of quotation.

[2] The word here properly means *weakness of the body*.

[3] This is another reference to the disparaging reflections (see x. 10) cast upon him by his Corinthian opponents. He says virtually, 'You say that I am weak in bodily presence, and contemptible in personal accomplishments; so also Christ was weak in the flesh, and suffered a shameful death upon the cross; yet He triumphed over His adversaries, and now shows His victorious power; and so shall I do, in the same strength.' The sentiment is the same as in iv. 10.

[4] 'Towards you.' The literal English of the above passage is as follows: *For if He was crucified through weakness, yet He lives through the power of God; for I also am weak in Him, but I shall live with Him, through the power of God towards you.*

[5] 'Proof' and 'prove' would give the verbal connection between ver. 3 and ver. 5.

[6] The Greek means, *to fail when tested*; this was the orginal meaning of the English *to be reprobate* (A. V.). Observe here, again, the reference to the context (see preceding note). A paronomasia on the same words occurs Rom. i. 28.

[7] Viz. *the proof that Christ's power is with me.*

[8] This may be translated (as it is by Grotius and Billroth, and was in our former edition), '*that I may not harm you*;' for the verb used here sometimes takes a double accusative in N. T., e.g. Matt. xxvii. 22. Yet this construction so seldom occurs, that it seems better to adopt the more obvious meaning, although it does not so clearly suit the context.

and you are strong ; yea, the very end of my prayers
ii. 10 is your perfect reformation.   Therefore I write this
to you while absent, that, when present, I may not
deal harshly with you in the strength of that authority which the Lord has given me, not to cast down,[1]
but to build up.

11   Finally, brethren, farewell.   Reform what is amiss Conclusion.
in yourselves,[2] exhort one another, be of one mind,
live in peace ; so shall the God of love and peace be
12 with you.   Salute one another with the kiss of holi-
13 ness.[3]   All the saints here salute you.

14   The grace of the Lord Jesus Christ, and the love Autograph
of God, and the communion of the Holy Spirit, be benediction.
with you all.[4]

In this letter we find a considerable space devoted to subjects
connected with a collection now in progress for the poor Christians
in Judæa.[5]   It is not the first time that we have seen St. Paul
actively exerting himself in such a project.[6]   Nor is it the first
time that this particular contribution has been brought before our
notice.   At Ephesus, in the First Epistle to the Corinthians,
St. Paul gave special directions as to the method in which it
should be laid up in store (1 Cor. xvi. 1–4).   Even before this
period similar instructions had been given to the Churches of
Galatia (ib. 1).   And the whole project was in fact the fulfilment
of a promise made at a still earlier period, that in the course of
his preaching among the Gentiles, the poor in Judæa should be
remembered (Gal. ii. 10).

The collection was going on simultaneously in Macedonia and
Achaia ; and the same letter gives us information concerning the
manner in which it was conducted in both places.   The directions
given to the Corinthians were doubtless similar to those under
which the contribution was made at Thessalonica and Philippi.
Moreover, direct information is incidentally given of what was
actually done in Macedonia ; and thus we are furnished with
materials for depicting to ourselves a passage in the Apostle's life
which is not described by St. Luke.   There is much instruction to
be gathered from the method and principles according to which
these funds were collected by St. Paul and his associates, as well as
from the conduct of those who contributed for their distant and
suffering brethren.

Both from this passage of Scripture and from others we are fully

---

[1] Compare x. 8. [And see note on
x. 6.   This is the last echo of the military allegory; but with the threatening turned into encouragement. H.]
[2] The substantive corresponding to
this verb is found in verse 9 ; and see
1 Cor. i. 10.
[3] See note on 1 Thess. v. 25.

[4] The 'Amen' is not found in the
best MSS.
[5] The whole of the eighth and ninth
chapters.
[6] See the account of the mission of
Barnabas and Saul to Jerusalem in the
time of the famine, Chap. IV.

made aware of St. Paul's motives for urging this benevolent work. Besides his promise made long ago at Jerusalem, that in his preaching among the Gentiles the poor Jewish Christians should be remembered,[1] the poverty of the residents in Judæa would be a strong reason for his activity in collecting funds for their relief, among the wealthier communities who were now united with them in the same faith and hope.[2]   But there was a far higher motive, which lay at the root of the Apostle's anxious and energetic zeal in this cause.   It is that which is dwelt on in the closing verses of the ninth chapter of the Epistle which has just been read,[3] and is again alluded to in words less sanguine in the Epistle to the Romans.[4] A serious schism existed between the Gentile and Hebrew Christians,[5] which, though partially closed from time to time, seemed in danger of growing continually wider under the mischievous influence of the Judaisers.   The great labour of St. Paul's life at this time was directed to the healing of this division.   He·felt that if the Gentiles had been made partakers of the spiritual blessings of the Jews, their duty was to contribute to them in earthly blessings (Rom. xv. 27), and that nothing would be more likely to allay the prejudices of the Jewish party than charitable gifts freely contributed by the Heathen converts.[6]   According as cheerful or discouraging thoughts predominated in his mind,—and to such alternations of feeling even an Apostle was liable,—he hoped that ' the ministration of that service would not only fill up the measure of the necessities of Christ's people' in Judæa, but would ' overflow' in thanksgivings and prayers on their part for those whose hearts had been opened to bless them (2 Cor. ix. 12–15), or he feared that this charity might be rejected, and he entreated the prayers of others, ' that he might be delivered from the disobedient in Judæa, and that the service which he had undertaken for Jerusalem might be favourably received by Christ's people' (Rom. xv. 30, 31).

Influenced by these motives, he spared no pains in promoting the work ; but every step was conducted with the utmost prudence and delicacy of feeling.   He was well aware of the calumnies with which his enemies were ever ready to assail his character ; and, therefore, he took the most careful precautions against the possibility of being accused of mercenary motives.   At an early stage of the collection, we find him writing to the Corinthians, to suggest that ' whomsoever they should judge fitted for the trust, should be sent to carry their benevolence to Jerusalem' (1 Cor. xvi. 3) ; and again he alludes to the delegates commissioned with Titus, as ' guarding himself against all suspicion which might be cast on him in his administration of the bounty with which he was charged,' and as being ' careful to do all things in a seemly manner, not only in the sight of the Lord, but also in the sight of men' (2 Cor. viii. 20, 21).   This regard to what was seemly appears most strikingly

---

[1] Gal.ii. 10, above quoted. See p. 174.
[2] See the remarks on this subject, in reference to the early jealousy between the Christians of Aramaic and Hellenistic descent, p. 55.

[3] 2 Cor. ix. 12–15.
[4] Rom. xv. 30, 31.
[5] See the remarks on this subject in Chap. VII.
[6] See p. 107,

in his mode of bringing the subject before those to whom he wrote and spoke. He lays no constraint upon them. They are to give 'not grudgingly or of necessity,' but each 'according to the free choice of his heart ; for God loveth a cheerful giver' (2 Cor. ix. 7). 'If there is a willing mind, the gift is acceptable when measured by the giver's power, and needs not to go beyond' (2 Cor. viii. 12). He spoke rather as giving 'advice' (viii. 10), than a 'command ;'[1] and he sought to prove the reality of his converts' love, by reminding them of the zeal of others (viii. 8). In writing to the Corinthians, he delicately contrasts their wealth with the poverty of the Macedonians. In speaking to the Macedonians themselves, such a mode of appeal was less natural, for they were poorer and more generous. Yet them also he endeavoured to rouse to a generous rivalry, by telling them of the zeal of Achaia (viii. 24, ix. 2). To them also he would doubtless say that 'he who sows sparingly shall reap sparingly, and he who sows bountifully shall reap bountifully' (ix. 6), while he would gently remind them that God was ever able to give them an overflowing measure of all good gifts, supplying all their wants, and enabling them to be bountiful[2] to others (ib. 8). And that one overpowering argument could never be forgotten,—the example of Christ, and the debt of love we owe to Him,—'You know the grace of our Lord Jesus Christ, how, though He was rich, yet for our sakes He became poor, that you, by His poverty, might be made rich' (viii. 9). Nor ought we, when speaking of the instruction to be gathered from this charitable undertaking, to leave unnoticed the calmness and deliberation of the method which he recommends of laying aside, week by week,[3] what is devoted to God (1 Cor. xvi. 2),—a practice equally remote from the excitement of popular appeals, and the mere impulse of instinctive benevolence.

The Macedonian Christians responded nobly to the appeal which was made to them by St. Paul. The zeal of their brethren in Achaia 'roused the most of them to follow it' (2 Cor. ix. 2). God's grace was abundantly 'manifested in the Churches'[4] on the north of the Ægean (ib. viii. 1). Their conduct in this matter, as described to us by the Apostle's pen, rises to the point of the highest praise. It was a time, not of prosperity, but of great affliction, to the Macedonian Churches ; nor were they wealthy communities like the Church of Corinth ; yet, 'in their heavy trial, the fulness of their joy overflowed out of the depth of their poverty in the riches of their liberality' (ib. viii. 2). Their contribution was no niggardly gift, wrung from their covetousness (viii. 5); but they gave honestly 'according to their means' (ib. 3), and not only so, but even 'beyond their means' (ib.) ; nor did they give grudgingly, under the pressure of the Apostle's urgency, but 'of their own free will, beseeching him with much entreaty that they

---

[1] Compare his language to Philemon, whom he 'might have commanded,' but 'for love's sake he rather besought him,' ver. 9. See the Introduction.

[2] Compare what was said at Miletus, Acts xx. 35 ; also Eph. iv. 28.

[3] From 2 Cor. viii. 10, ix. 2, it would seem that the plan recommended in 1 Cor. xvi. 2, had been carried into effect. See Paley's remarks in the *Horæ Paulinæ* on 2 Cor. The same plan had been recommended in Galatia, and probably in Macedonia.

[4] See p. 453. n. 3.

might bear their part in the grace of ministering to Christ's people' (ib. 3, 4). And this liberality arose from that which is the basis of all true Christian charity. 'They gave themselves first to the Lord Jesus Christ, by the will of God' (ib. 5).

The Macedonian contribution, if not complete, was in a state of much forwardness,[1] when St. Paul wrote to Corinth. He speaks of liberal funds as being already pressed upon his acceptance (2 Cor. viii. 4), and the delegates who were to accompany him to Jerusalem had already been chosen (2 Cor. viii. 19, 23). We do not know how many of the Churches of Macedonia took part in this collection,[2] but we cannot doubt that that of Philippi held a conspicuous place in so benevolent a work. In the case of the Philippian Church, this bounty was only a continuation of the benevolence they had begun before, and an earnest of that which gladdened the Apostle's heart in his imprisonment at Rome. 'In the beginning of the Gospel' they and they only had sent once and again[3] to relieve his wants, both at Thessalonica and at Corinth (Phil. iv. 15, 16); and 'at the last' their care of their friend and teacher 'flourished again' (ib. 10), and they sent their gifts to him at Rome, as now they sent to their unknown brethren at Jerusalem. The Philippians are in the Epistles what that poor woman is in the Gospels, who placed two mites in the treasury. They gave much, because they gave of their poverty; and wherever the Gospel is preached throughout the whole world, there shall this liberality be told for a memorial of them.

If the principles enunciated by the Apostle in reference to the collection command our devout attention, and if the example of the Macedonian Christians is held out to the imitation of all future ages of the Church, the conduct of those who took an active part in the management of the business should not be unnoticed. Of two of these the names are unknown to us,[4] though their characters are described. One was a brother, 'whose praise in publishing the Gospel was spread throughout the Churches,' and who had been chosen by the Church of Macedonia to accompany St. Paul with the charitable fund to Jerusalem (2 Cor. viii. 18, 19). The other was one 'who had been put to the proof in many trials, and always found zealous in the work' (ib. 22). But concerning Titus, the third companion of these brethren, 'the partner of St. Paul's lot, and his fellow-labourer for the good of the Church,' we have fuller information; and this seems to be the right place to make a more particular allusion to him, for he was nearly concerned in all the steps of the collection now in progress.

---

[1] The aorist in 2 Cor. viii. 2 does not necessarily imply that the collection was closed; and the present in ix. 2 rather implies the contrary.

[2] In 2 Cor. xi. 9 we find Philippi used as equivalent to Macedonia (pp. 436, 437), and so it may be here. But it is not absolutely certain (ibid.) that the Second Epistle to the Corinthians was written at Philippi. The Churches in Macedonia were only few, and com-munication among them was easy along the Via Egnatia; as when the first contributions were sent from Philippi to St. Paul at Thessalonica. See pp. 253, 254.

[3] See above, p. 436. For the account of this relief being sent to St. Paul, see p. 254; and p. 301, n. 9, in reference to Phil. iv. 10, and 2 Cor. xi. 9.

[4] See the notes on 2 Cor. viii.

Titus does not, like Timothy, appear at intervals through all the passages of the Apostle's life. He is not mentioned in the Acts at all, and this is the only place where he comes conspicuously forward in the Epistles;[1] and all that is said of him is connected with the business of the collection.[2] Thus we have a detached portion of his biography, which is at once a thread that guides us through the main facts of the contribution for the Judæan Christians, and a source whence we can draw some knowledge of the character of that disciple, to whom St. Paul addressed one of his pastoral Epistles. At an early stage of the proceedings he seems to have been sent,—soon after the First Epistle was despatched from Ephesus to Corinth (or perhaps as its bearer)—not simply to enforce the Apostle's general injunctions, but[3] to labour also in forwarding the collection (2 Cor. xii. 18). Whilst he was at Corinth, we find that he took an active and zealous part at the outset of the good work (ib. viii. 6). And now that he had come to Macedonia, and brought the Apostle good news from Achaia, he was exhorted to return, that he might finish what was so well begun, taking with him (as we have seen) the Second Epistle to the Corinthians, and accompanied by the two deputies who have just been mentioned. It was a task which he was by no means unwilling to undertake. God 'put into his heart the same zeal' which Paul himself had ; he not only consented to the Apostle's desire, but was 'himself very zealous in the matter, and went of his own accord ' (2 Cor. viii. 16, 17). If we put together these notices, scanty as they are, of the conduct of Titus, they set before us a character which seems to claim our admiration for a remarkable union of enthusiasm, integrity, and discretion.

After the departure of Titus, St. Paul still continued to prosecute the labours of an evangelist in the regions to the north of Greece. He was unwilling as yet to visit the Corinthian Church, the disaffected members of which still caused him so much anxiety,—and he would doubtless gladly employ this period of delay to accomplish any plans he might have formed and left incomplete on his former visit to Macedonia. On that occasion he had been persecuted in Philippi,[4] and had been forced to make a precipitate retreat from Thessalonica ;[5] and from Berœa his course had been similarly urged to Athens and Corinth.[6] Now he was able to embrace a wider circumference in his Apostolic progress. Taking Jerusalem as his centre,[7] he had been perpetually enlarging the circle of his travels. In his first missionary journey he had preached in the southern

---

[1] See p. 167, n. 13. It is observed there that the only Epistles in which he is mentioned are Gal., 2 Cor., and 2 Tim. See also p. 418, note 6.

[2] The prominent appearance of Titus in this part of the history has been made an argument for placing the Epistle to Titus, as Wieseler and others have done, about this part of St. Paul's life. This question will be discussed afterwards.

[3] See above, p. 435. The fact that the mission of Titus had something to do with the collection, might be inferred from 2 Cor. xii. 18: 'Did Titus *defraud* you ? ' We do not know who the 'brother' was, that was sent with him on that occasion from Ephesus.

[4] p. 229.   [5] pp. 255, 256.
[6] pp. 262, 263.
[7] Notice the phrase, 'from Jerusalem, and *in a circle*,' &c. Rom. xv. 19; and see the *Horæ Paulinæ*.

parts of Asia Minor and the northern parts of Syria : in his second journey, he had visited the Macedonian towns which lay near the shores of the Ægean : and now on his third progress he would seem to have penetrated into the mountains of the interior, or even beyond them to the shores of the Adriatic, and 'fully preached the Gospel of Christ round about unto Illyricum' (Rom. xv. 19).

We here encounter a subject on which some difference of opinion must unavoidably exist. If we wish to lay down the exact route of the Apostle, we must first ascertain the meaning of the term 'Illyricum' as used by St. Paul in writing to the Romans : and if we find this impossible, we must be content to leave this part of the Apostle's travels in some degree of vagueness ; more especially as the preposition ('unto,' μέχρι) employed in the passage is evidently indeterminate.

The political import of the word 'Illyricum' will be seen by referring to what has been written on the province of Macedonia[1] in an earlier chapter. It has been there stated that the former province was contiguous to the north-western frontier of the latter. It must be observed, however, that a distinction was anciently drawn between *Greek Illyricum*, a district on the south, which was incorporated by the Romans with Macedonia, and formed the coast-line of that province where it touched the Adriatic,[2]—and *Barbarous*, or *Roman Illyricum*, which extended towards the head of that gulf, and was under the administration of a separate governor. This is ' one of those ill-fated portions of the earth which, though placed in immediate contact with civilisation, have remained perpetually barbarian.'[3] For a time it was in close connection, politically and afterwards ecclesiastically, with the capitals both of the Eastern and Western empires : but subsequently it relapsed almost into its former rude condition, and ' to this hour it is devoid of illustrious names and noble associations.'[4] Until the time of Augustus, the Romans were only in possession of a narrow portion along the coast, which had been torn during the wars of the Republic from the piratic inhabitants.[5] But under the first Emperor a large region, extending far inland towards the valleys of the Save and the Drave, was formed into a province, and contained some strong links of the chain of military posts, which was extended along the frontier of the Danube.[6] At first it was placed under the Senate : but it was soon found to require the presence of large masses of soldiers : the Emperor took it into his own hands, and inscriptions are still extant on which we can read the records of its occupation by the seventh and eleventh legions.[7] *Dalmatia*, which is also mentioned

---

[1] p. 243, &c. See our map of St. Paul's third missionary journey.

[2] For the seaboard of Macedonia on the Adriatic, see pp. 243, 244.

[3] Arnold's *Rome*, vol. i. p. 495.

[4] Ibid.

[5] It extended from the river Drilon to the Istrian peninsula.

[6] One of the most important of these military posts was Siscia, in the Pan-

nonian country, on the Save. The line was continued by Augustus through Mœsia, though the reduction of that region to a province was later. Six legions protected the frontier of the Danube.

[7] Josephus alludes to these legions, *War*, ii. 16. His language on geographical subjects is always important as an illustration of the Acts.

by St. Paul (2 Tim. iv. 10), was a district in the southern part of this province; and after the final reduction of the Dalmatian tribes, the province was more frequently called by this name than by that of Illyricum.[1] The limits of this political jurisdiction (to speak in general terms) may be said to have included Bosnia, and the modern[2] Dalmatia, with parts of Croatia and Albania.

But the term Illyricum was by no means always, or even generally, used in a strictly political sense. The extent of country included in the expression was various at various times. The Illyrians were loosely spoken of by the earlier Greek writers as the tribes which wandered on the eastern shore of the Adriatic. The Illyricum which engaged the arms of Rome under the Republic was only a narrow strip of that shore with the adjacent islands. But in the Imperial times it came to be used of a vast and vague extent of country lying to the south of the Danube, to the east of Italy, and to the west of Macedonia.[3] So it is used by Strabo in the reign of Augustus, and similarly by Tacitus in his account of the civil wars which preceded the fall of Jerusalem;[4] and the same phraseology continues to be applied to this region, till the third century of the Christian era. We need not enter into the geographical changes which depended on the new division of the empire under Constantine, or into the fresh significance which, in a later age, was given to the ancient names, when the rivalry of ecclesiastical jurisdictions led to the schism of Eastern and Western Christendom.[5] We have said enough to show that it is not possible to assume that the Illyricum of St. Paul was a definite district, ruled as a province by a governor from Rome.

It seems by far the most probable that the terms ' Illyricum ' and ' Dalmatia ' are both used by St. Paul in a vague and general sense: as we have before had occasion to remark in reference to Asia Minor, where many geographical expressions, such as ' Mysia,' ' Galatia,' and ' Phrygia,' were variously used, popularly and politically.[6] It is indeed quite possible that St. Paul, not deeming it right as yet to visit Corinth, may have pushed on by the Via Egnatia,[7] from Philippi and Thessalonica, across the central mountains which turn the streams eastward and westward, to Dyrrhachium, the landing-place of those who had come by the Appian Road from Rome to Brundusium.[8] Then, though still in the province of Macedonia, he would be in the district called Greek

---

[1] Dalmatia is a name unknown to the earlier Greek writers.

[2] The modern name of Illyria has again contracted to a district of no great extent in the northern part of the ancient province.

[3] See Gibbon's first chapter.

[4] Tac. *Hist.* i. 2, 76, &c., where under the term Illyricum are included Dalmatia, Pannonia, and Mœsia: and this, it must be remembered, is strictly cotemporaneous with the Apostle.

[5] A geographical account of Illyricum in its later ecclesiastical sense, and of the dioceses which were the subjects of the rival claims of Rome and Constantinople, will be found in Neale's *History of the Eastern Church*.

[6] See pp. 181, 182, 211.

[7] See the account of the Via Egnatia, p. 244.

[8] It has been said above (p. 292), that when St. Paul was on the Roman way at Philippi he was really on the road which led to Rome. The ordinary ferry was from Dyrrhachium to Brundusium.

Illyricum:[1] and he would be on a line of easy communication with Nicopolis[2] on the south, where, on a later occasion, he proposed to winter (Tit. iii. 12); and he could easily penetrate northwards into Roman or Barbarous Illyricum, where was that district of Dalmatia,[3] which was afterwards visited by his companion Titus, whom, in the present instance, he had despatched to Corinth. But we must admit that the expression in the Romans might have been legitimately[4] used, if he never passed beyond the limits of Macedonia, and even if his Apostolic labours were entirely to the eastward of the mountains, in the country watered by the Strymon and the Axius.[5]

Whether he travelled widely and rapidly in the regions to the north of Greece, or confined his exertions to the neighbourhood of those Churches which he had previously founded,—the time soon came when he determined to revisit that Church, which had caused him so much affliction not unmixed with joy. During the course of his stay at Ephesus, and in all parts of his subsequent journey in Troas and Macedonia, his heart had been continually at Corinth. He had been in frequent communication with his inconsistent and rebellious converts. Three letters[6] had been written to entreat or to threaten them. Besides his own personal visit[7] when the troubles were beginning, he had sent several messengers, who were authorised to speak in his name. Moreover, there was now a special subject in which his interest and affections were engaged, the contribution for the poor in Judæa, which he wished to ' seal ' to those for whom it was destined (Rom. xv. 28) before undertaking his journey to the West.[8]

Of the time and the route of this southward journey we can only say that the most probable calculation leads us to suppose that he was travelling with his companions towards Corinth at the approach of winter ; and this makes it likely that he went by land rather than by sea.[9] A good road to the south had long been formed from the neighbourhood of Berœa,[10] connecting the chief towns of Macedonia with those of Achaia. Opportunities would not be wanting for preaching the Gospel at every stage in his progress ; and perhaps we may infer from his own expression in writing to the Romans (xv. 23),—' I have no more place in those parts,'—either that Churches were formed in every chief city between Thessalonica and Corinth, or that the Glad-tidings had been unsuccessfully pro-

[1] See above, p. 470, comparing pp. 243, 244.

[2] Nicopolis was in Epirus, which, it will be remembered (see above under Macedonia), was in the *province of Achaia.*

[3] See above, p. 471. It is indeed possible that the word Dalmatia in this Epistle may be used for the *province* (of Illyricum or Dalmatia), and not a subordinate district of what was called Illyricum in the wider sense.

[4] The preposition need not denote anything more than that St. Paul came to the frontier.

[5] See what has been said of these rivers in Chap. IX.

[6] The question of the lost letter has been discussed above, Chap. XV. p. 377.

[7] See again, on this intermediate visit, the beginning of Chap. XV.

[8] For the project of this westward journey see the end of Chap. XV. above.

[9] See Acts xxvii. 9.

[10] The roads through Dium have been alluded to above, p. 264, and compare p. 261, n. 2.

claimed in Thessaly and Bœotia, as on the former journey they had found but little credence among the philosophers and triflers of Athens.[1]

[1] Athens is never mentioned again after Acts xviii. 1, 1 Thess. iii. 1. We do not know that it was ever revisited by the Apostle, and in the second century we find that Christianity was almost extinct there. See p. 295. At the same time nothing would be more easy than to visit Athens, with other 'Churches of Achaia,' during his residence at Corinth. See p. 302, note, and p. 439.

Coin of Macedonia.

CHAPTER XVIII.

St. Paul's Return to Corinth.—Contrast with his First Visit.—Bad News from
Galatia.—He writes *the Epistle to the Galatians.*

It was probably already winter, when St. Paul once more beheld
in the distance the lofty citadel of Corinth, towering above the
isthmus which it commands. The gloomy season must have harmonised with his feelings as he approached. The clouds which, at
the close of autumn, so often hang round the summit of the Acro-
Corinthus, and cast their shadow upon the city below, might have
seemed to typify the mists of vice and error which darkened the
minds even of its Christian citizens. Their father in the faith
knew that, for some of them at least, he had laboured in vain. He
was returning to converts who had cast off the morality of the
Gospel ; to friends who had forgotten his love ; to enemies who
disputed his divine commission. It is true, the majority of the
Corinthian Church had repented of their worst sins, and submitted
to his Apostolic commands. Yet what was forgiven could not
entirely be forgotten ; even towards the penitent he could not feel
all the confidence of earlier affection ; and there was still left an
obstinate minority, who would not give up their habits of impurity,
and who, when he spoke to them of righteousness and judgment to
come, replied either by openly defending their sins, or by denying
his authority and impugning his orthodoxy.

He now came prepared to put down this opposition by the most
decisive measures : resolved to cast out of the Church these antagonists of truth and goodness, by the plenitude of his Apostolic
power. Thus he warned them a few months before (as he had
threatened, when present on an earlier occasion), 'when I come
again, I will not spare' (2 Cor. xiii. 2). He declared his determi-
nation to punish the disobedient (2 Cor. x. 6). He 'boasted' of
the authority which Christ had given him (2 Cor. x. 8). He besought them not to compel him to use the weapons entrusted to him
(2 Cor. x. 2), weapons not of fleshly weakness, but endowed with
the might of God (2 Cor. x. 4). He pledged himself to execute by
his deeds when present, all he had threatened by his words when
absent (2 Cor. x. 11).

As we think of him, with these purposes of severity in his mind,
approaching the walls of Corinth, we are irresistibly reminded of
the eventful close of a former journey, when Saul, 'breathing out
threatenings and slaughter against the disciples of the Lord,' drew
nigh to Damascus. How strongly does this accidental resemblance
bring out the essential contrast between the weapons and the spirit

of Saul and Paul ! Then he wielded the sword of the secular power —he travelled as the proud representative of the Sanhedrin—the minister of human cruelty and injustice : he was the Jewish Inquisitor, the exterminator of heretics, seeking for victims to imprison or to stone. Now he is meek and lowly,[1] travelling in the humblest guise of poverty, with no outward marks of pre-eminence or power; he has no gaolers at his command to bind his captives, no executioners to carry out his sentence. All he can do is to exclude those who disobey him from a society of poor and ignorant outcasts, who are the objects of contempt to all the mighty, and wise, and noble, among their countrymen. His adversaries despise his apparent insignificance ; they know that he has no outward means of enforcing his will ; they see that his bodily presence is weak; they think his speech contemptible. Yet he is not so powerless as he seems. Though now he wields no carnal weapons, his arms are not weaker but stronger than they were of old. He cannot bind the bodies of men, but he can bind their souls. Truth and love are on his side; the Spirit of God bears witness with the spirits of men on his behalf. His weapons are 'mighty to overthrow the strongholds of the adversaries;' 'Thereby' he could 'overthrow the reasonings of the disputer, and pull down the lofty bulwarks which raise themselves against the knowledge of God, and bring every rebellious thought into captivity and subjection to Christ.'[2]

Nor is there less difference in the spirit of his warfare than in the character of his weapons. Then he 'breathed out threatenings and slaughter;' he 'made havoc of the Church;' he 'haled men and women into prison;' he 'compelled them to blaspheme.' When their sentence was doubtful, he gave his vote for their destruction;[3] he was 'exceedingly mad against them.' Then his heart was filled with pride and hate, uncharitableness and self-will. But now his proud and passionate nature is transformed by the Spirit of God ; he is crucified with Christ : the fervid impetuosity of his character is tempered by meekness and gentleness ; his very denunciations and threats of punishment are full of love ; he grieves over his contumacious opponents; the thought of their pain fills him with sadness. 'For if I cause you grief, who is there to cause me joy ?'[4] He implores them, even at the eleventh hour, to save him from the necessity of dealing harshly with them ; he had rather leave his authority doubtful, and still remain liable to the sneers of his adversaries, than establish it by their punishment (2 Cor. xiii. 7–9). He will condescend to the weakest prejudices, rather than cast a stumbling-block in a brother's path ; he is ready to become 'all things to all men,' that he may 'by all means save some.'

Yet all that was good and noble in the character of Saul remains in Paul, purified from its old alloy. The same zeal for God burns in his heart, though it is no longer misguided by ignorance or warped by party spirit. The same firm resolve is seen in carrying out his principles to their consequences, though he shows it not in persecuting but in suffering. The same restless energy, which carried him from Jerusalem to Damascus that he might extirpate

---

See 2 Cor. x. 1. 2 Cor. x. 4, 5. [3] Acts xxvi. 10.
[4] 2 Cor. ii. 2.

heresy, now urges him from one end of the world to the other,[1] that he may bear the tidings of salvation.

The painful anticipations which saddened his return to Corinth were not, however, altogether unrelieved by happier thoughts. As he approached the well-known gates, in the midst of that band of faithful friends who accompanied him from Macedonia, his memory could not but revert to the time when first he entered the same city, a friendless and lonely[2] stranger. He could not but recall the feelings of extreme depression with which he first began his missionary work at Corinth, after his unsuccessful visit to Athens. The very firmness and bold confidence which now animated him,— the assurance which he felt of victory over the opponents of truth, —must have reminded him by contrast of the anxiety and self-distrust[3] which weighed him down at his first intercourse with the Corinthians, and which needed a miraculous vision[4] for its removal. How could he allow discouragement to overcome his spirit, when he remembered the fruits borne by labours which had begun in so much sadness and timidity? It was surely something that hundreds of believers now called on the name of the Lord Jesus, who when he first came among them had worshipped nothing but the deification of their own lusts. Painful no doubt it was to find that their conversion had been so incomplete; that the pollutions of heathenism still defiled those who had once washed away the stains[5] of sin; yet the majority of the Church had repented of their offences; the number who obstinately persisted in sin was but small; and if many of the adult converts were so tied and bound by the chains of habit, that their complete deliverance could scarce be hoped for, yet at least their children might be brought up in the nurture and admonition of the Lord. Moreover, there were some, even in this erring Church, on whom St. Paul could think with unmingled satisfaction; some who walked in the Spirit, and did not fulfil the lust of the flesh : who were created anew in Christ Jesus; with whom old things had passed away, and all things had become new; who dwelt in Christ, and Christ in them. Such were Erastus the treasurer, and Stephanas, the first fruits of Achaia; such were Fortunatus and Achaicus, who had lately travelled to Ephesus on the errand of their brethren ; such was Gaius,[6] who was even now preparing to welcome beneath his hospitable roof the Apostle who had thrown open to himself the door of entrance into the Church of Christ. When St. Paul thought of 'them that were such,' and of the many others 'who worked with them and laboured,'[7] as he threaded the crowded streets on his way to the house of Gaius, doubtless he 'thanked God and took courage.'

[1] He was at this very time intending to go first to Jerusalem, thence to Rome, and thence to Spain ; that is, to travel from the Eastern to the Western extremities of the civilised world. See Rom. xv. 28. Compare the conclusion of Chap. XVII.

[2] He was left at Athens *alone* (1 Thess. iii. 1), and so remained till Timotheus and Silas rejoined him at Corinth. See p. 279.

[3] See 1 Cor. ii. 1-3.

[4] Acts xviii. 9.   [5] 1 Cor. vi. 11.

[6] It would be more correct to write this name Caius; but as the name under its Greek form of Gaius has become naturalised in the English language as a synonym of Christian hospitality, it seems undesirable to alter it.   [7] 1 Cor. xvi. 16.

But a painful surprise awaited him on his arrival. He found that intelligence had reached Corinth from Ephesus, by the direct route, of a more recent date than any which he had lately received; and the tidings brought by this channel concerning the state of the Galatian churches, excited both his astonishment and his indignation.[1] His converts there, whom he seems to have regarded with peculiar affection, and whose love and zeal for himself had formerly been so conspicuous, were rapidly forsaking his teaching, and falling an easy prey to the arts of Judaising missionaries from Palestine. We have seen the vigour and success with which the Judaising party at Jerusalem were at this period pursuing their new tactics, by carrying the war into the territory of their great opponent, and endeavouring to counterwork him in the very centre of his influence, in the bosom of those Gentile Churches which he had so lately founded. We know how great was the difficulty with which he had defeated (if, indeed, they were yet defeated) the agents of this restless party at Corinth; and now, on his reaching that city to crush the last remains of their opposition, he heard that they had been working the same mischief in Galatia, where he had least expected it. There, as in most of the early Christian communities, a portion of the Church had been Jews by birth; and this body would afford a natural fulcrum for the efforts of the Judaising teachers; yet we cannot suppose that the number of Jews resident in this inland district could have been very large.[2] And St. Paul in addressing the Galatians, although he assumes that there were some among them familiar with the Mosaic law, yet evidently implies that the majority were converts from heathenism.[3] It is remarkable, therefore, that the Judaising emissaries should so soon have gained so great a hold over a church consisting mainly of Gentile Christians; and the fact that they did so proves not only their indefatigable activity, but also their skill in the arts of conciliation and persuasion. It must be remembered, however, that they were by no means scrupulous as to the means which they employed to effect their objects. At any cost of falsehood and detraction, they resolved to loosen the hold of St. Paul upon the affection and respect of his converts. Thus to the Galatians they accused him of a want of uprightness, in observing the Law himself whilst among the Jews, yet persuading the Gentiles to renounce it;[4] they argued that his motive was to keep his converts in a subordinate state, excluded from the privileges of a full covenant with God, which was enjoyed by the circumcised alone;[5] they declared that he was an interested flatterer,[6] 'becoming all things to all men,' that he might make a party for himself; and above all, they insisted that he falsely represented himself as an apostle of Christ, for that he had not, like the Twelve, been a follower of

---

[1] This is on the assumption that the Epistle to the Galatians was written soon after St. Paul's arrival at Corinth on the present occasion. For the reasons in favour of this hypothesis, see the note upon the date of the Epistle below.

[2] On the probable character of the Jewish population of Galatia, see p. 189.

[3] See Gal. iv. 8.

[4] Gal. v. 11.

[5] Gal. iv. 16, compared with ii. 17.

[6] Ibid. i. 10.

Jesus when He was on earth, and had not received His commission; that, on the contrary, he was only a teacher sent out by the authority of the Twelve, whose teaching was only to be received so far as it agreed with theirs and was sanctioned by them; whereas his doctrine (they alleged) was now in opposition to that of Peter and James, and the other 'Pillars' of the Church.[1] By such representations they succeeded to a great extent in alienating the Galatian Christians from their father in the faith: already many of the recent converts submitted to circumcision,[2] and embraced the party of their new teachers with the same zeal which they had formerly shown for the Apostle of the Gentiles;[3] and the rest of the Church was thrown into a state of agitation and division.

On receiving the first intelligence of these occurrences, St. Paul hastened to check the evil before it should have become irremediable. He wrote to the Galatians an Epistle which begins with an abruptness and severity showing his sense of the urgency of the occasion, and the greatness of the danger. It is also frequently characterised by a tone of sadness, such as would naturally be felt by a man of such warm affections when he heard that those whom he loved were forsaking his cause and believing the calumnies of his enemies. In this letter his principal object is to show that the doctrine of the Judaisers did in fact destroy the very essence of Christianity, and reduced it from an inward and spiritual life to an outward and ceremonial system; but in order to remove the seeds of alienation and distrust which had been designedly planted in the minds of his converts, he begins by fully contradicting the falsehoods which had been propagated against himself by his opponents, and especially by vindicating his title to the Apostolic office as received directly from Christ, and exercised independently of the other Apostles. Such were the circumstances and such the objects which led him to write the following Epistle.

EPISTLE TO THE GALATIANS.[4]

Defence of his independent Apostolic au- PAUL,—an Apostle, sent not from men nor by man, i. 1 but by Jesus Christ, and God the Father, who

---

[1] See the whole of the first two chapters of the Epistle.

[2] Gal. vi. 13.

[3] Gal. iv. 14, 15.

[4] The date of this Epistle cannot be so clearly demonstrated as that of most of the others; but we conclude that it was written at the time assumed in the text on the following grounds:—

1st. It was not written till *after St. Paul's second visit to the Galatians.* This is proved (A) by his speaking of their conversion as having occurred at his *first* visit (iv. 13); implying that he had paid them a second visit. (B) (iv. 16): 'Am I now *become* your ene-

my by speaking truth among you?' implies that there had been a second visit, in which he had offended them, contrasted with the first when he was so welcome.

2ndly. It is maintained by many eminent authorities that it was written *soon* after his second visit. This St. Paul (they argue) expressly says; he marvels that the Galatians are *so soon* (i. 6) forsaking his teaching. The question is (according to these writers), within what interval of time would it have been possible for him to use this word '*soon?*' Now this depends on the length of their previous Christian

i.2   raised Him from the dead;—With all the brethren [1] thority against the Judaising in my company; To the Churches of Galatia.   teachers, and

life; for instance, had St. Paul known them as Christians for. twenty years, and then after an absence of four years heard of their perversion, he might have said their abandonment of the truth was marvellously *soon* after their possession of it; but if they had been only converted to Christianity for three years before his second visit (as was really the case), and he had heard of their perversion not till four years after his second visit, he could scarcely, in that case, speak of their perversion as having occurred *soon* after they had been in the right path, in reference to the whole time they had been Christians. He says virtually, 'You are wrong now, you were right a *short time ago.*' The natural impression conveyed by this language (considering that the time of their previous stedfastness in the true faith was only three years altogether) would certainly be, that St. Paul must have heard of their perversion within about a year from the time of his visit. At that time he was resident at Ephesus, where he would most naturally and easily receive tidings from Galatia. Hence they consider the Epistle to have been written at Ephesus during the first year of St. Paul's residence there. But in answer to these arguments it may be replied, that St. Paul does not say the Galatians were perverted *soon after his own last visit to them.* His words are. in fact, 'I wonder that you are so quickly shifting your ground.' The same word is used in 2 Thess. ii. 2, where he exhorts the Thessalonians 'not *rashly* to let themselves be shaken;' where the adverb refers not so much to the *time* as to the *manner* in which they were affected, like the English *hastily.* But even supposing it in Gal. i. 6, to refer simply to *time,* and to be translated *quickly* or *soon,* we still (if we would fix the date from it) must ask, 'quickly *after what event?*'—'soon *after what event?*' And it is more natural (especially as the verb is in the present tense) to understand 'soon *after the entrance of the Judaising teachers,*' than to understand 'soon *after my last visit.*'

Hence there seems nothing in this adverb to fix the date of the Epistle; nor is there any other *external* evidence of a decisive nature supplied by the Epistle. But

3rdly. The *internal* evidence that the Epistle was written nearly at the same time with that to the Romans is exceedingly strong. Examples of this are Rom. viii. 15 compared with Gal. iv. 6, Rom. vii. 14-25 compared with Gal. v. 17, Rom. i. 17 compared with Gal. iii. 11, and the argument about Abraham's faith in Rom. iv. compared with Gal. iii. But the comparison of single passages does not so forcibly impress on the mind the parallelism of the two Epistles, as the study of each Epistle as a whole. The more we examine them, the more we are struck by the resemblance; and it is exactly that resemblance which would exist between two Epistles written nearly at the same time, while the same line of argument was occupying the writer's mind, and the same phrases and illustrations were on his tongue. This resemblance, too, becomes more striking when we remember the very different circumstances which called forth the two Epistles; that to the Romans being a deliberate exposition of St. Paul's theology, addressed to a Church with which he was personally unacquainted; that to the Galatians being an indignant rebuke, written on the urgency of the occasion, to check the perversion of his children in the faith.

This internal evidence, therefore, leads us to suppose that the Epistle to the Galatians was written within a few months of that to the Romans; and most probably, therefore, from Corinth during the present visit (although there is nothing to show which of the two was written the first). The news of the arrival of the Judaisers in Galatia would reach St. Paul from Ephesus; and (considering the commercial relations between the two cities) there is no place where he would be so likely to hear tidings from Ephesus as at Corinth. And since, on his arrival at the latter city, he would probably find some intelligence from Ephesus waiting for him, we have supposed, in the text, that the tidings of the perversion of Galatia met him thus on his arrival at Corinth.

[1] Some of these 'brethren in St. Paul's company' are enumerated in Acts xx. 4: Sopater of Berœa; Aristarchus and Secundus of Thessalonica; Gaius of Derbe; Timotheus; and Ty-

historical
proofs that his
commission
was not de-
rived from the
other Apostles.
Grace be to you and peace from God our Father, i. 3
and our Lord Jesus Christ; who gave Himself for 4
our sins, that He might deliver us from this present
evil world, according to the will of our God and
Father; to whom be glory, even unto the ages of 5
ages. Amen.

I marvel that you are so soon shifting [1] your 6
ground, and forsaking Him [2] who called you [3] in the
grace of Christ, for a new Glad-tidings; which is 7
nothing else [4] but the device of certain men who are
troubling you, and who desire to pervert the Glad-
tidings of Christ. But even though I myself, or an 8
angel from heaven, should declare to you any other
Glad-tidings than that which I declared, let him be accursed. As I have said before, so now I say again, if 9
any man is come to you with a Glad-tidings different
from that which you received before, let him be accursed. Think ye that man's [5] assent, or God's, is 10
now my object? or is it that I seek favour with men?
Nay, if I still sought favour with men, I should not
be the bondsman of Christ.

For I certify you, brethren, that the Glad-tidings 11
which I brought you is not of man's devising. For 12
I myself received it not from man, nor was it taught
me by man's teaching; but by the revelation of Jesus
Christ. For you have heard of my former behaviour 13
in the days of my Judaism, how I persecuted beyond
measure the Church of God, and strove [6] to root it
out, and outran in Judaism many of my own age and 14

chicus and Trophimus from Proconsular
Asia. The junction of their names with
that of Paul in the salutation of this
Epistle, throws light on the junction of
the names of Timotheus, Sosthenes, Silvanus, &c. with Paul's in the salutation
at the head of some other Epistles;
showing us more clearly that these
names were not joined with that of St.
Paul as if they were *joint authors* of
the several Epistles referred to. This
clause also confirms the date we have
assigned to the Epistle, since it suits a
period when he had an unusual number
of travelling companions, in consequence of the collection which they and
he were jointly to bear to Jerusalem.
See the last chapter.

[1] For the translation of this, see the
note on the date of this Epistle, above.

[2] '*Him who called you.*' St. Paul probably means God. Compare Rom. ix. 24.

[3] 'In the grace of Christ.' The preposition here cannot mean *into*; Christians are called to salvation *in* the grace
of Christ.

[4] The Authorised Version, '*which is
not another*,' does not correctly represent the original; the word translated
'another' being not the same in the
two verses.

[5] This alludes to the accusations
brought against him. See above, pp.
477, 478; also 2 Cor. v. 11; and for
the words, compare Col. iii. 22. His
answer is, that had popularity and
power been his object, he would have
remained a member of the Sanhedrin.
The adverbs of time mark the reference
to this contrast between his position
before and since his conversion. Compare chap. v. 11.

[6] The verb is in the imperfect.

nation, being more exceedingly zealous[1] for the tra-
i. 15 ditions of my fathers.   But when it pleased Him, who
set me apart[2] from my mother's womb, and called
16 me by His grace, to reveal His Son in me, that I
might proclaim His Glad-tidings among the Gentiles,
17 I did not take counsel with flesh and blood, nor yet
did I go up to Jerusalem to those who were Apostles
before me, but I departed immediately into Arabia,[3]
18 and from thence returned to Damascus.   Afterwards,
when three years had passed, I went up to Jerusalem,
that I might know Cephas[4] and with him I remained
19 fifteen days;[5] but other of the Apostles saw I none,
20 save only James,[6] the brother of the Lord.   (Now in
this which I write to you, behold I testify before God
21 that I lie not.)   After this I came into the regions of
22 Syria and Cilicia;[7] but I was still unknown by face
23 to the Churches of Christ in Judæa: tidings only
were brought them from time to time,[8] saying, ' He
who was once our persecutor now bears the Glad-
tidings of that Faith, which formerly he laboured to
24 root out.'   And they glorified God in me.
ii. 1   Then fourteen[9] years after, I went up again to Je- The council of
rusalem with Barnabas, and took Titus with me also.   Jerusalem.
2 At that time I went up in obedience to a revelation,
and I communicated to the brethren in Jerusalem[10]
the Glad-tidings which I proclaimed among the Gentiles; but to the chief brethren I communicated it
privately,[11] lest perchance my labours, either past or
3 present, might be fruitless.[12] Yet not even Titus, my
own companion (being a Greek), was compelled to
4 be circumcised.   But this communication[13] [with the

---

[1] This term (' Zealot') was, perhaps, already adopted (as it was not long after, Joseph. *War*, iv. 6) by the Ultra-Pharisaical party.   Cf. Acts xxi. 20.

[2] Compare Rom. i. 1.

[3] The *immediately* belongs to *departed*, as if it were printed *immediately* (*I conferred not . . . . but*) *departed*.   On the events mentioned in this verse, see pp. 80, 81.

[4] *Cephas*, not *Peter*, is the reading of the best MSS. throughout this Epistle, as well as in the Epistles to Corinth; except in one passage, Gal. ii. 7, 8. St. Peter was ordinarily known up to this period by the Syro-Chaldaic form of his name (the name actually given by our Lord), and not by its Greek equivalent. It is remarkable that he himself, in his

Epistles, uses the Greek form, perhaps as a mark of his antagonism to the Judaisers, who naturally would cling to the Hebraic form.

[5] See pp. 84–86.

[6] See note on 1 Cor. ix. 5.

[7] See p. 87.

[8] Lit. ' They continued to hear.

[9] See the discussion of this passage, Appendix.

[10] ' To them.' Compare the preceding verse.

[11] On these private conferences preceding the public assembly of the Church, see p. 169.

[12] Literally, *lest perchance I should be running, or had run, in vain.*

[13] Something must be supplied here to complete the sense; we understand

Apostles in Judæa] I undertook on account of the
false brethren who gained entrance by fraud, for they
crept in among us to spy out our freedom[1] (which
we possess in Christ Jesus) that they might enslave
us under their own yoke.   To whom I yielded not ii. 5
the submission they demanded;[2] no, not for an
hour; that the truth of the Glad-tidings might stand
unaltered for your benefit.

But from those who were held in chief reputation— 6
it matters not to me of what account they were,—
God is no respecter of persons—those (I say) who
were the chief in reputation gave me no new instruction; but, on the contrary, when they saw that 7
I had[3] been charged to preach the Glad-tidings to
the uncircumcised, as Peter to the circumcised (for 8
He who wrought in Peter for the Apostleship of the
circumcision, wrought also in me for the Gentiles),
and when they had learned the grace which had been 9
given me,—James, Cephas, and John, who were accounted chief pillars, gave to me and Barnabas the
right hand of fellowship, purposing that we should
go to the Gentiles, and they to the Jews; provided 10
only, that we should remember the poor,[4] which I
have accordingly[5] endeavoured to do with diligence.

St. Peter at Antioch.

But when Cephas came to Antioch, I withstood 11
him to the face, because he had incurred[6] reproach;
for before the coming of certain [brethren] from 12
James, he was in the habit of eating with the Gentiles; but when they came, he began to draw back,
and to separate himself from the Gentiles, for fear of

'communicated' from ver. 2; others
supply 'was not circumcised,' 'but I
refused to circumcise him (which otherwise I would have done) on account of
the false brethren, that I might not
seem to yield to them.' Others again
supply 'was circumcised,' which gives
an opposite sense. The interpretation
here adopted agrees best with the narrative in Acts xv.

[1] Viz. from the ordinances of the
Mosaic law.

[2] The article implies this meaning.

[3] The perfect is used because the
charge still continued.

[4] Namely, *the poor Christians in
Judæa.* We have seen in the preceding chapters, how fully St. Paul had
carried out this part of his agreement.

[5] The A. V. here is probably incor-

rect. The aorist here seems to be used
for the perfect, as it often is in N. T.
[Mr. Ellicott, in his very valuable commentary on Galatians, disputes this, and
even calls the above assertion 'an oversight.' He expresses his opinion that
the aorist is never used for the perfect
in N. T. Yet Mr. Ellicott himself repeatedly translates the aorist as perfect,
for example in Gal. i. 13, iii. 3, iii. 27,
and many other passages. For the
proofs of this use of the aorist, see notes
on 2 Cor. vii. 2, and Rom. v. 5.] For
the phrase translated *accordingly* (to
which it is nearly equivalent), compare
2 Cor. ii. 3, and Phil. i. 6.

[6] The remarkable expression here is
not equivalent to the Authorised translation, ' *he was to be blamed.*' For the
history see Chap. VII.

ii. 13 the Jewish brethren. And he was joined in his dissimulation by the rest of the Jews [in the Church of Antioch], so that even Barnabas was drawn away 14 with them to dissemble in like manner. But when I saw that they were walking in a crooked path,[1] and forsaking the truth of the Glad-tidings, I said to Cephas before them all, 'if thou, being born a Jew, art wont to live according to the customs of the Gentiles, and not of the Jews, how is it that thou constrainest the Gentiles to keep the ordinances of the 15 Jews? We are Jews by birth, and not unhallowed 16 Gentiles; yet,[2] knowing that a man is not justified by the works of the Law, but by the faith of Jesus Christ, we ourselves also have put our faith in Christ Jesus, that we might be justified by the faith of Christ, and not by the works of the Law; for by the works of the Law "𝔰𝔥𝔞𝔩𝔩 𝔫𝔬 𝔣𝔩𝔢𝔰𝔥 𝔟𝔢 𝔧𝔲𝔰𝔱𝔦𝔣𝔦𝔢𝔡." [3]

The Jewish believers had renounced the righteousness of the law.

17 But what if,[4] while seeking to be justified in Christ, we have indeed reduced[5] ourselves also to the sinful state of unhallowed[6] Gentiles? Is Christ then a minister of sin? God forbid![7]

18 For if I again build up that [structure of the Law] which I have overthrown, then I represent myself as 19 a transgressor. Whereas[8] I, through the operation[9] of the Law, became dead to the Law, that I might 20 live to God. I am crucified with Christ; it is no more I that live, but Christ is living in me;[10] and my

---

[1] The Greek verb, found only here, means *to walk in a straight path.*

[2] We follow Tischendorf and the best MSS.

[3] Ps. cxliii. 2 (LXX.); quoted also more fully, Rom. iii. 20.

[4] The construction is like that in Rom. ix. 22.

[5] Literally, *been found sinners ourselves as well as other men.*

[6] 'Unhallowed.' Compare 'unhallowed Gentiles' above.

[7] Neander thinks that the 17th verse also ought to be included in the speech of St. Paul, and much might be said in favour of his view. Still, on the whole, we think the speech more naturally terminates with ver. 16. See p. 180, n. 1. The hypothesis in ver. 17 is that of the Judaisers, refuted (after St. Paul's manner) by an abrupt *reductio ad absurdum.* The Judaiser objects, ' *You say you seek righteousness in Christ, but in fact you reduce yourself to the state of*

a Gentile; you are farther from God, and therefore farther from righteousness, than you were before.' To which St. Paul only replies, ' *On your hypothesis then, we must conclude Christ to be the minister of sin! God forbid.'* This passage is illustrated by the similar mode in which he answers the objections of the same party, Rom. iii. 3–8. See note on the phrase rendered 'God forbid,' below, chap. iii. 21.

[8] In this '*for*' (A. V.) is virtually contained the suppressed clause '*but the abolition of the law does not make me a transgressor, for.*'

[9] This thought is fully expanded in the 7th of Romans.

[10] It is with great regret that we depart from the A. V. here, not only because of its extreme beauty, but because it must be so dear to the devotional feelings of all good men. Yet the words cannot be translated '*nevertheless I live, yet not I.*'

outward life which still remains, I live in the faith of the Son of God, who loved me and gave Himself for me. I frustrate not God's gift of grace [like those who seek righteousness in the Law]; for if the Law can make men righteous, then Christ died in vain. ii. 21

Appeal to the experience of the Galatians. O foolish Galatians, who has bewitched you ? [1]—iii. 1 You, before whose eyes was held up the picture [2] of Jesus Christ upon the cross. One question I would ask you. When you received the Spirit, was it from the works of the Law, or the preaching [3] of Faith ? 2 Are you so senseless ? Having begun in the Spirit, 3 would you now end in the Flesh ? Have you received 4 so many benefits [4] in vain—if indeed it has been in vain ? Whence, I say, are the gifts of Him who 5 furnishes you with the fulness of the Spirit, and works in you the power of miracles ? [5] From the deeds of the Law, or from the preaching of Faith ?

Faith, and not the Law, is the source of righteousness. So likewise ' 𝕬𝖇𝖗𝖆𝖍𝖆𝖒 𝖍𝖆𝖉 𝖋𝖆𝖎𝖙𝖍 𝖎𝖓 𝕲𝖔𝖉, 𝖆𝖓𝖉 𝖎𝖙 𝖜𝖆𝖘 6 𝖗𝖊𝖈𝖐𝖔𝖓𝖊𝖉 𝖚𝖓𝖙𝖔 𝖍𝖎𝖒 𝖋𝖔𝖗 𝖗𝖎𝖌𝖍𝖙𝖊𝖔𝖚𝖘𝖓𝖊𝖘𝖘.' [6] Know, there- 7 fore, that they only are the sons of Abraham who are children of Faith. And the Scripture, foreseeing 8 that God through Faith justifies [not the Jews only but] the Gentiles, declared beforehand to Abraham the Glad-tidings, saying, ' 𝕬𝖑𝖑 𝖙𝖍𝖊 𝖓𝖆𝖙𝖎𝖔𝖓𝖘 𝖔𝖋 𝖙𝖍𝖊 𝕲𝖊𝖓- 𝖙𝖎𝖑𝖊𝖘 𝖘𝖍𝖆𝖑𝖑 𝖇𝖊 𝖇𝖑𝖊𝖘𝖘𝖊𝖉 𝖎𝖓 𝖙𝖍𝖊𝖊.' [7] So then, they who are 9 children of Faith [whether they be Jews or Gentiles] are blessed with faithful Abraham.

For all they who rest upon [8] the works of the Law 10 are under a curse; for it is written, ' 𝕮𝖚𝖗𝖘𝖊𝖉 𝖎𝖘 𝖊𝖛𝖊𝖗𝖞 𝖔𝖓𝖊 𝖙𝖍𝖆𝖙 𝖈𝖔𝖓𝖙𝖎𝖓𝖚𝖊𝖙𝖍 𝖓𝖔𝖙 𝖎𝖓 𝖆𝖑𝖑 𝖙𝖍𝖎𝖓𝖌𝖘 𝖜𝖍𝖎𝖈𝖍 𝖆𝖗𝖊 𝖜𝖗𝖎𝖙𝖙𝖊𝖓 𝖎𝖓 𝖙𝖍𝖊 𝖇𝖔𝖔𝖐 𝖔𝖋 𝖙𝖍𝖊 𝕷𝖆𝖜 𝖙𝖔 𝖉𝖔 𝖙𝖍𝖊𝖒.' [9] And it is manifest 11 that no man is counted righteous in God's judgment under the conditions of the Law ; for it is written, ' 𝕭𝖞 𝖋𝖆𝖎𝖙𝖍 𝖘𝖍𝖆𝖑𝖑 𝖙𝖍𝖊 𝖗𝖎𝖌𝖍𝖙𝖊𝖔𝖚𝖘 𝖑𝖎𝖛𝖊.' [10] But the Law rests 12 not on Faith, but declares, ' 𝕿𝖍𝖊 𝖒𝖆𝖓 𝖙𝖍𝖆𝖙 𝖍𝖆𝖙𝖍 𝖉𝖔𝖓𝖊

[1] The words 'that ye should not obey the truth' are not found in the best MSS., and 'among you' is also omitted.

[2] This is the literal sense.

[3] Compare Rom. x. 17, and 1 Thess. ii. 13.

[4] Literally, *have you experienced so many things* [or, *such great things*]. The context is against the translation of the verb by *suffered*.

[5] The phrase is exactly similar in 1 Cor. xii. 10.

[6] Gen. xv. 6 (LXX.); quoted also Rom. iv. 3.

[7] Gen. xii. 3, from the LXX. but not verbatim. Compare the similar quotation, Rom. iv. 17.

[8] Literally, *who have their root in the works of the Law*, or, according to the Hebrew image, *the children of the works of the Law.*

[9] Deut. xxvii. 26. Nearly verbatim from LXX.

[10] Hab. ii. 4 (LXX.); quoted also Rom. i. 17, and Heb. x. 38.

iii. 13

14

15

16

7

18

19

20

𝖙𝖍𝖊𝖘𝖊 𝖙𝖍𝖎𝖓𝖌𝖘 𝖘𝖍𝖆𝖑𝖑 𝖑𝖎𝖛𝖊 𝖙𝖍𝖊𝖗𝖊𝖎𝖓.'[1]   Christ has redeemed us from the curse of the Law, having become accursed for our sakes[2] (for it is written, '𝕮𝖚𝖗𝖘𝖊𝖉 𝖎𝖘 𝖊𝖛𝖊𝖗𝖞 𝖔𝖓𝖊 𝖙𝖍𝖆𝖙 𝖍𝖆𝖓𝖌𝖊𝖙𝖍 𝖔𝖓 𝖆 𝖙𝖗𝖊𝖊'[3]), to the end that in Christ Jesus the blessing of Abraham might come unto the Gentiles; that through Faith we might receive the promise of the Spirit.

Brethren—I speak in man's language[4]—nevertheless,—a man's covenant, when ratified, cannot by its giver be annulled, or set aside by a later addition.

The Law could not abrogate the prior promise to Abraham.

Now God's promises were made to Abraham and to his seed; the scripture says not '𝖆𝖓𝖉 𝖙𝖔 𝖙𝖍𝖞 𝖘𝖊𝖊𝖉𝖘,' as if it spoke of many, but as of one, '𝖆𝖓𝖉 𝖙𝖔 𝖙𝖍𝖞 𝖘𝖊𝖊𝖉;'[5] and this seed is Christ. But this I say; a covenant which had been ratified before by God, to be fulfilled in Christ, the Law which was given four hundred and thirty[6] years afterwards, cannot make void, to the annulling of the promise. For if the inheritance comes from the Law, it comes no longer from promise; whereas God has given it to Abraham freely by promise.

To what end, then, was the Law? it was[7] added because of the transgressions[8] of men, till the Seed should come, to whom belongs the promise; and it was enacted by the ministration of angels[9] through the hands of [Moses,[10] who was] a mediator [between God and the people]. Now where[11] a mediator is,

---

[1] Levit. xviii. 5 (LXX.); quoted also Rom. x. 5.

[2] 'A curse for us.' The sentiment and expression strongly resembles 'sin for us,' 2 Cor. v. 21; which Epistle was very nearly cotemporaneous with this, if the date of the Galatians above adopted is correct.

[3] Deut. xxi. 23. Nearly verbatim from LXX.

[4] This parenthetical phrase here, in St. Paul's style, seems always to mean, *I use a comparison or illustration drawn from human affairs or human language.* Compare Rom. iii. 5, and 1 Cor. xv. 32.

[5] Gen. xiii. 15 (LXX.). The meaning of the argument is, that the recipients of God's promises are not to be looked on as an aggregate of different individuals, or of different races, but are all one body, whereof Christ is the head. Compare 'you are the seed,' ver. 29.

[6] With regard to the chronology, see p. 140, n. 2.

[7] This is according to the reading of the best MSS.

[8] Compare Rom. v. 20: 'The Law was added that sin might abound,' which must be taken with Rom. v. 13, and Rom. vii. 13.

[9] Compare Acts vii. 53.

[10] Moses is called 'the Mediator' by the Rabbinical writers. See several passages quoted by Schoettgen on this passage.

[11] St. Paul's argument here is left by him exceedingly elliptical, and therefore very obscure; as is evident from the fact that more than two hundred and fifty different explanations of the passage have been advocated by different commentators. The most natural meaning appears to be as follows: 'It is better to depend upon an unconditional promise of God, than upon a covenant made between God and man; for in the latter case the conditions of the covenant might be broken by man (as they had been), and so

there must be two parties. But God is one [and there is no second party to His promise].

Do I say then that the Law contradicts the pro- iii. 21 mises of God? that be far from me![1] For had a Law been given which could raise men from death to life, then would righteousness be truly from the Law. But[2] the Scripture (on the other hand) has 22 shut up the whole world together under sin, that from Faith in Jesus Christ the promise might be given to the faithful.

But before Faith came, we were shut up in prison, 23 in ward under the Law, in preparation for the Faith which should afterwards be revealed. Thus, even 24 as the slave[3] who leads a child to the house of the schoolmaster, so the Law has led us to [our teacher] Christ, that by Faith we might be justified : but 25 now that Faith is come, we are under the slave's care no longer. For you are all the sons of God, by 26 your faith in Christ Jesus : yea, whosoever among 27 you have been baptized unto Christ, have clothed yourselves with Christ.[4] In Him there is neither 28 Jew nor Gentile, neither slave nor freeman, neither male nor female ; for you all are one in Christ Jesus. And if you are Christ's, then you are Abraham's 29 seed, and heirs of the blessing by promise.

Now I say, that the heir, so long as he is a child, iv. 1 has no more freedom than a slave, though he is owner of the whole inheritance ; but he is under 2 overseers and stewards until the time appointed by his father. And so we also [who are Israelites] 3 when we were children, were in bondage, under our

the blessings forfeited ; whereas in the former case, God being immutable, the blessings derived from His promise remain stedfast for ever.' The passage is parallel with Rom. iv. 13–16.

[1] The expression occurs fourteen times in St. Paul ; viz. three times in Galatians, ten times in Romans (another example of the similarity between these Epistles), and once in 1 Corinthians. In one of these cases (Gal. vi. 14) it is not interjectional ; in another (1 Cor. vi. 15), it repels a direct hypothesis, ' *Shall I do* (*so and so*)*? God forbid.*' But in all the other instances it is interjectional, and rebuts *an inference deduced from St. Paul's doctrine by an opponent.* So that the question which precedes the phrase is equivalent to ' *Do I then infer that?* '

[2] The connection of the argument is, that if the Law could give men spiritual life, and so enable them to fulfil its precepts, it would give them righteousness ; but it does not pretend to do this ; on the contrary, it shows the impotence of their nature by the contrast of its requirements with their performance. This verse is parallel with Rom. xi. 32.

[3] The inadequate translation here in the Authorised Version has led to a misconception of the metaphor. See note on 1 Cor. iv. 15. Compare also Hor. *Sat.* i. 6 (81).

[4] The only other place where this expression occurs is Rom. xiii. 14 ; another instance of resemblance between the two Epistles.

iv. 4 childhood's lessons of outward ordinances.[1]   But
when the appointed time was fully come, God sent
forth His Son, who was born of a woman, and born
5 subject to the Law; that He might redeem from
their slavery the subjects of the Law, that we[2]
6 might be adopted as the sons of God.   And because
you are the sons of God, He has sent forth the Spirit
of His Son into your hearts, crying unto Him
7 ' 𝕱𝖆𝖙𝖍𝖊𝖗.' [3]   Wherefore thou [who canst so pray]
art no more a slave, but a son: and if a son, then
an heir of God through Christ.

8   But formerly, when you knew not God, you were
9 in bondage to gods that have no real being.[4]   Yet
now, when you have gained the knowledge of God,—
or rather, when God has acknowledged you,[5]—how
is it that you are turning backwards to those childish
lessons, weak and beggarly as they are ; [6] eager to
place yourselves once more in bondage under their
10 dominion ?   Are you observing days,[7] and months,[8]
11 and seasons,[9] and years.[10]   I am fearful for you, lest
12 I have spent my labour on you in vain.   I beseech
you, brethren, to become as I am, [and seek no more
a place among the circumcised;] for I too have become as you [11] are [and have cast away the pride of
my circumcision].   You have never wronged me: [12]
13 on the contrary, although it was sickness (as you

Appeal to the Heathen converts not to return to an outward and formal worship.

---

[1] The phrase literally means *the elementary lessons of outward things.* Compare Col. ii. 8 and 20.

[2] *We,* namely, *all Christians, whether Jews or Gentiles.* In other words, the Son of God, was *born of a woman,* that all the sons of women might by union with Him become the sons of God.

[3] ' Abba ' is the Syro-Chaldaic word for Father, and it is the actual word with which the Lord's prayer began, as it was uttered by our Lord Himself. The ' Father' which follows is only a translation of 'Abba,' inserted as translations of Aramaic words often are by the writers of the New Testament, but not used *along with* ' Abba.' This is rendered evident by Mark xiv. 36, when we remember that our Lord spoke in Syro-Chaldaic. Moreover, had it been used vocatively (as in A. V.) along with Abba, the Greek would have been different. Rom. viii. 15 is exactly parallel with the present passage.

[4] This is of course addressed to Heathen converts.

[5] Compare 1 Cor. viii. 3.

[6] Literally, *the weak and beggarly rudimentary lessons.*

[7] The Sabbath-days.   Compare Col. ii. 16.   [Also Rom. xiv. 6.   See notes on those passages.   H.]

[8] The seventh months.

[9] The seasons of the great Jewish feasts.

[10] The Sabbatical and Jubilee years. From this it has been supposed that this Epistle must have been written in a Sabbatical year.   But this does not necessarily follow, because the word may be merely inserted to complete the sentence ; and of course those who observed the Sabbaths, festivals, &c., would *intend* to observe also the Sabbatical years when they came.   The *plural* ' years ' favours this view.

[11] This is addressed (as above) to the Gentile converts.

[12] The aorist used as perf. (cf. notes on 2 Cor. vii. 2, and Rom. v. 5).   It might, however, perhaps be here rendered *ye did me no wrong* [*when I first came to you*].

know) which caused[1] me to preach the Glad-tidings
to you at my first visit, yet you neither scorned nor iv. 14
loathed the bodily infirmity which was my trial;[2]
but you welcomed me as an angel of God, yea, even
as Christ Jesus. Why, then, did you think your- 15
selves so happy? (for I bear you witness that, if it
had been possible, you would have torn out your
own eyes[3] and given them to me.) Am I then 16
become your enemy[4] because I tell you the truth?
They [who call me so] show zeal for you with no 17
good intent; they would shut you out from others
that your zeal may be for them alone. But it is 18
good to be zealous[5] in a good cause, and that at all
times, and not when zeal lasts only [like yours]
while I am present with you. My beloved children, 19
I am again bearing the pangs of travail for you, till
Christ be fully formed within you. I would that I 20
were present with you now, that I might change my
tone; for you fill me with perplexity.

The allegory of Hagar and Sarah teaches the same lesson to the Jew. , Tell me, ye that desire to be under the Law, will 21
you not hear the Law? For therein it is written 22
that Abraham had two sons;[6] one by the bond-

---

[1] i.e. by keeping him in their country against his previous intention. See p. 210. The literal English of this is, *You have injured me in nothing; but you know that because of bodily sickness I preached the Glad-tidings to you on the first occasion, and you neither,* &c. We are glad to find that Dean Ellicott, in his recent valuable and accurate commentary, expresses his opinion that, 'the only grammatically correct translation is *propter corporis infirmitatem.*' The contrary view of Professor Jowett, who translates, ' *amid* infirmity,' is defended only by a mistaken parallel from Phil. i. 15. See *Quarterly Review* for December 1855, p. 153, note 2.

[2] This was probably the same disease mentioned 2 Cor. xii. 7. It is very unfortunate that the word *temptation* has so changed its meaning in the last two hundred and fifty years, as to make the Authorised Version of this verse a great source of misapprehension to ignorant readers. Some have even been led to imagine that St. Paul spoke of a *sinful habit* in which he indulged, and to the dominion of which he was encouraged (2 Cor. xii. 9) contentedly to resign himself! We should add that if, with some of the best MSS., we read ' your,' it makes no very material difference in the sense; St. Paul's sickness would then be called *the trial of the Galatians.*

[3] This certainly seems to confirm the view of those who suppose St. Paul's malady to have been some disease in the eyes. The 'your' appears emphatic, as if he would say *you would have torn out your own eyes to supply the lack of mine.*

[4] The Judaisers accused St. Paul of desiring to keep the Gentile converts in an inferior position, excluded (by want of circumcision) from full covenant with God; and called him, therefore, their enemy.

[5] The expression would more naturally mean, ' to be the object of zeal,' as many interpreters take it; but, on the whole, the other interpretation (which is that of the older interpreters and of Olshausen) seems to suit the context better. Perhaps, also, there may be an allusion here to the peculiar use of the word ' Zealot.' Compare Gal. i. 14.

[6] With this passage compare Rom. ix. 7-9.

iv. 23 woman, the other by the free.   But the son of the
bond-woman was born to him after the flesh:
whereas the son of the free-woman was born by
24 virtue of the promise.   Now, all this is allegorical;
for these two women are the two covenants; the
first given from Mount Sinai, whose children are
25 born into bondage, which is Hagar (for the word
Hagar [1] in Arabia signifies Mount Sinai): and she
answers to the earthly Jerusalem, for [2] she is in
26 bondage with her children.   But [Sarah [3] is the
second covenant in Christ, and answers to the
heavenly Jerusalem; for] the heavenly Jerusalem is
free; which is the mother of us all.[4]   And so it is
27 written ' 𝕽𝖊𝖏𝖔𝖎𝖈𝖊, 𝖙𝖍𝖔𝖚 𝖇𝖆𝖗𝖗𝖊𝖓 𝖙𝖍𝖆𝖙 𝖇𝖊𝖆𝖗𝖊𝖘𝖙 𝖓𝖔𝖙; 𝖇𝖗𝖊𝖆𝖐
𝖋𝖔𝖗𝖙𝖍 𝖎𝖓𝖙𝖔 𝖘𝖍𝖔𝖚𝖙𝖎𝖓𝖌, 𝖙𝖍𝖔𝖚 𝖙𝖍𝖆𝖙 𝖙𝖗𝖆𝖛𝖆𝖎𝖑𝖊𝖘𝖙 𝖓𝖔𝖙; 𝖋𝖔𝖗 𝖙𝖍𝖊
𝖉𝖊𝖘𝖔𝖑𝖆𝖙𝖊 𝖍𝖆𝖙𝖍 𝖒𝖆𝖓𝖞 𝖒𝖔𝖗𝖊 𝖈𝖍𝖎𝖑𝖉𝖗𝖊𝖓 𝖙𝖍𝖆𝖓 𝖘𝖍𝖊 𝖜𝖍𝖎𝖈𝖍 𝖍𝖆𝖙𝖍
28 𝖙𝖍𝖊 𝖍𝖚𝖘𝖇𝖆𝖓𝖉.' [5]   Now, we, brethren, like Isaac, are
children [born not naturally, but] of God's promise.
29 Yet, as then the spiritual seed of Abraham was
persecuted by his natural seed, so it is also now.
30 Nevertheless, what says the Scripture?   ' 𝕮𝖆𝖘𝖙 𝖔𝖚𝖙
𝖙𝖍𝖊 𝖇𝖔𝖓𝖉-𝖜𝖔𝖒𝖆𝖓 𝖆𝖓𝖉 𝖍𝖊𝖗 𝖘𝖔𝖓; 𝖋𝖔𝖗 𝖙𝖍𝖊 𝖘𝖔𝖓 𝖔𝖋 𝖙𝖍𝖊 𝖇𝖔𝖓𝖉-
𝖜𝖔𝖒𝖆𝖓 𝖘𝖍𝖆𝖑𝖑 𝖓𝖔𝖙 𝖇𝖊 𝖍𝖊𝖎𝖗 𝖜𝖎𝖙𝖍 𝖙𝖍𝖊 𝖘𝖔𝖓 𝖔𝖋 𝖙𝖍𝖊 𝖋𝖗𝖊𝖊-
31 𝖜𝖔𝖒𝖆𝖓.'[6]   Wherefore, brethren, we are not children
v. 1 of the bond-woman, but of the free.   Stand fast,
then, in the freedom which Christ has given us, and
turn not back again, to entangle yourselves in the
yoke of bondage.
2   Lo, I Paul declare unto you, that if you cause
yourselves to be circumcised, Christ will profit you
3 nothing.   I testify again to every man who submits
to circumcision, that he thereby lays himself under

---

[1] The word Hagar in Arabic means
' a rock,' and some authorities tell us
that Mount Sinai is so called by the
Arabs. The lesson to be drawn from
this whole passage, as regards the
Christian use of the Old Testament, is
of an importance which can scarcely
be over-rated.

[2] All the best MSS. read ' for.' Hagar
being, both herself and her children, in
bondage, corresponds to *the earthly
Jerusalem*: by which latter expression
is denoted the whole system of the
Mosaic law, represented by its local
centre, the Holy City. To this latter
is opposed the 'city to come' (Heb.
xii. 22), where Christians have their
citizenship in heaven ' (Phil. iii 20).

[3] This clause in brackets is implied,
though not expressed, by St. Paul,
being necessary for the completion of
the parallel.

[4] The weight of MS. authority is
rather against the ' all ' of the received
text ; yet it bears an emphatic sense if
retained, viz. ' *us all, whether Jews or
Gentiles, who belong to the Israel of
God.*' Compare Gal. vi. 16.

[5] Isaiah liv. 1. (LXX.). Quoted as a
prophetic testimony to the fact that
the spiritual seed of Abraham should
be more numerous than his natural
seed.

[6] Gen. xxi. 10 from LXX., but not
quite verbatim.

obligation to fulfil the whole Law. If you rest your v. 4
righteousness on the Law, you are cut off from Christ,[1]
you are fallen from His gift of grace. For we, 5
through the Spirit [2] [not through the Flesh], from
Faith [not works], look eagerly for the hope [3] of
righteousness. For in Christ Jesus neither circum- 6
cision avails anything, nor uncircumcision; but
Faith, whose work is Love.

Warning against the Judaising teachers, and against party divisions.

You were running the race well: who has cast a 7
stumbling-block in your way? who has turned you
aside from your obedience to the truth? The counsel 8
which you have obeyed [4] came not from Him who
called [5] you. 'A little leaven leavens the whole 9
lump.' [6] As for me, I rely upon you, in the Lord, 10
that you will not be led astray; but he that is troubling you, whosoever he be, shall bear the blame.

But if I myself also [as they say] still preach cir- 11
cumcision,[7] why am I still persecuted? for if I preach
circumcision, then the cross, the stone at which they
stumble,[8] is done away.

I could wish that these agitators who disturb your 12
quiet, would execute upon themselves not only circumcision, but excision also.[9]

Exhortation to the more enlightened party not to

For you, brethren, have been called to freedom; [10] 13
only make not your freedom a vantage-ground for

---

[1] This phrase (meaning literally *to be cancelled from a thing*, i.e. *to have utterly lost all connection with it*) is only found in this passage and in Rom. vii. 2 and 6. Another instance of resemblance between the two Epistles.

[2] In the words 'spirit' and 'faith' a tacit reference is made to their antitheses (constantly present to St. Paul's mind) 'flesh' or 'letter,' and 'law' or 'works,' respectively.

[3] i.e. *the hope of eternal happiness promised to righteousness.* Compare Rom. viii. 24, 25, where the same verb is used.

[4] There is a paronomasia here, expressed by 'obedience' and 'obeyed.'

[5] The participle used substantively. Compare i. 6, and note.

[6] This proverb is quoted also 1 Cor. v. 6. Its application here may be 'Your seducers are few, but yet enough to corrupt you all;' or it may be 'Circumcision is a small part of the law, but yet its observance is sufficient to place you altogether under the legal yoke.'

[7] This accusation might naturally be made by St. Paul's opponents, on the ground of his circumcising Timothy, and himself still continuing several Jewish observances. See Acts xx. 6, and Acts xxi. 24. The first 'still' in this verse is omitted by some MSS. but retained by the best.

[8] Literally, *the stumbling-stone of the cross* ; i.e. *the cross which is their stumbling-stone.* Compare 1 Cor. i. 23. The doctrine of a crucified Messiah was a stumbling-block to the national pride of the Jews ; but if St. Paul would have consented to make Christianity a sect of Judaism (as he would by 'preaching circumcision'), their pride would have been satisfied. But then, if salvation were made to depend on outward ordinances, the death of Christ would be rendered unmeaning.

[9] Observe the force of the 'also' and of the middle voice here ; the A. V. is a mistranslation.

[10] Literally, *on terms of freedom.*

the Flesh, but rather enslave yourselves one to another abuse their
freedom. by the bondage of love. For all the Law is fulfilled in
14 by the bondage of love. For all the Law is fulfilled in
15 this one saying, '𝕿𝖍𝖔𝖚 𝖘𝖍𝖆𝖑𝖑 𝖑𝖔𝖛𝖊 𝖙𝖍𝖞 𝖓𝖊𝖎𝖌𝖍𝖇𝖔𝖚𝖗 𝖆𝖘 𝖙𝖍𝖞𝖘𝖊𝖑𝖋.'[1] But if you bite and devour one another, take heed lest you be utterly destroyed by one another's means.

16 But this I say, walk in the Spirit, and you shall Variance be-
tween the
17 not fulfil the desire of the Flesh; for the desire of the Spirit and the
Flesh. Flesh fights against the Spirit, and the desire of the Spirit fights against the Flesh; and this variance tends to hinder[2] you from doing what you wish to
18 do. But, if you be led by the Spirit, you are not
19 under the Law.[3] Now, the works of the Flesh are manifest, which are such as these; fornication, im-
20 purity, lasciviousness; idolatry, witchcraft;[4] enmities, strife, jealousy, passionate anger; intrigues,[5] divisions,
21 sectarian parties; envy, murder; drunkenness, revellings, and such like. Of which I forewarn you (as I told you also in times past), that they who do such things shall not inherit the kingdom of God.
22 But the fruit of the Spirit is love, joy, peace, long-
23 suffering, kindness, goodness, trustfulness,[6] gentleness, self-denial. Against such there is no Law.

24 But they who are Christ's have crucified[7] the Warning to
the more en-
25 Flesh, with its passions and its lusts. If we live by lightened
party against
26 the Spirit, let our steps be guided by the Spirit. Let spiritual
pride. us not become vainglorious, provoking one another

[1] Levit. xix. 18 (LXX).

[2] Not '*so that you cannot do*' (A. V.), but '*tending to prevent you from doing.*'

[3] 'To be 'under the yoke of the Law,' and ' under the yoke of the Flesh,' is in St. Paul's language the same; because, for those who are under the Spirit's guidance, the Law is dead (ver. 23); they do right, not from fear of the Law's penalties, but through the influence of the Spirit who dwells within them. This, at least, is the ideal state of Christians. Compare Rom. viii. 1–14. St. Paul here, and elsewhere in his Epistles, alludes thus briefly to important truths, because his readers were already familiar with them from his personal teaching. By the 'flesh' St. Paul denotes not merely the sensual tendency, but generally that which is earthly in man, as opposed to what is spiritual. It should be observed, that the 17th verse is a summary of the description of the struggle between flesh and spirit

in Rom. vii. 7–25; and verse 18th is a summary of the description of the Christian's deliverance from this struggle. Rom. viii. 1–14.

[4] The *profession of magical arts.* The history of the times in which St. Paul lived is full of the crimes committed by those who professed such arts. We have seen him brought into contact with such persons as Ephesus already. They dealt in poisons also, which accounts for the use of the term etymologically.

[5] For this word, compare Rom. ii. 8, and note. Also 2 Cor. xii. 20.

[6] The word seems to have this meaning here; for *faith* (in its larger sense) could not be classed as one among a number of the constituent parts of *love.* See 1 Cor. xiii.

[7] Some translate this aorist '*crucified the flesh* [at the time of their baptism or their conversion].' But it is more natural to take it as used for the perfect. See notes on 2 Cor. vii. 2, and Rom. v. 5.

to strife, regarding one another with envy. Brethren, vi.
—I speak to you who call yourselves the Spiritual,[1]
—even if any one be overtaken in a fault, do you
correct such a man in a spirit of meekness; and take
thou heed to thyself, lest thou also be tempted. Bear 2
ye one another's burdens, and so fulfil the law of
Christ. For, if any man exalts himself, thinking to 3
be something when he is nothing, he deceives himself
with vain imaginations. Rather let every man ex- 4
amine his own work, and then his boasting will concern himself alone and not his neighbour; for each 5
will bear the load [of sin] which is his own,[2] [instead
of magnifying the load which is his brother's].

Provision to be made for the mainte-nance of the presbyters (instructors). Moreover, let him who is receiving instruction in 6
the Word[3] give to his instructor a share in all the
good things which he possesses. Do not deceive 7
yourselves—God cannot be defrauded.[4] Every man
shall reap as he has sown. The man who now sows 8
for his own Flesh, shall reap therefrom a harvest
doomed[5] to perish; but he who sows for the Spirit,
shall from the Spirit reap the harvest of life eternal,
But let us continue in well-doing, and not be weary:[6] 9
for in due season we shall reap, if we faint not.
Therefore, as we have opportunity,[7] let us do good to 10
all men, but especially to our brethren in the household of Faith.

Autograph conclusion. Observe the size[8] of the characters in which I u
write[9] to you with my own hand.

[1] 'Ye that are spiritual.' See p. 351.

[2] The allusion here is apparently to Æsop's well-known fable. It is unfortunate that in the Authorised Version two words (ver. 2) are translated by the same term *burden*, which seems to make St. Paul contradict himself. His meaning is, that self-examination will prevent us from comparing ourselves boastfully with our neighbour; we shall have enough to do with our own sins, without scrutinising his.

[3] By *the Word* is meant *the doctrines of Christianity*.

[4] Literally, '*God is not mocked*, i.e. God is not really deceived by hypocrites, who think to reap where they have not sown.

[5] See Rom. viii. 21.

[6] Compare 2 Thess. iii. 13, where the expression is almost exactly the same.

[7] This *opportunity* (*time*) is suggested by the preceding *season* (*time*); but the verbal identity cannot with advantage be retained here in English.

[8] Thus we must understand the phrase, unless we suppose (with Tholuck) that 'how large' is used for 'what kind of,' as in the later Greek of the Byzantine writers. To take 'characters' as equivalent to 'letter' appears inadmissible. St. Paul does not here say that he wrote the whole Epistle with his own hand, but this is the beginning of his usual autograph postscript, and equivalent to the 'so I write' in 2 Thess. iii. 17. We may observe as a further confirmation of

[9] The past tense, used, according to the classical epistolatory style, from the position of the readers.

i. 12   I tell you that they who wish to have a good repute
in things pertaining to the Flesh, they, and they
alone [1] are forcing circumcision upon you; and that
only to save themselves from the persecution which [2]
13 Christ bore upon the cross. For even they who
circumcise themselves do not keep the Law; but they
wish to have you circumcised, that your obedience [3]
to the fleshly ordinance may give them a ground of
14 boasting. But as for me, far be it from me to boast,
save only in the cross [4] of our Lord Jesus Christ;
whereby the world is crucified unto me, and I unto
15 the world. For in Christ Jesus neither circumcision
is anything, nor uncircumcision; but a new creation. [5]
16 And whosoever shall walk by this rule, peace and
mercy be upon them, and upon all the Israel of God. [6]
17   Henceforth, let no man vex me; for I bear in my
body the scars [7] which mark my bondage to the Lord
Jesus.

18   Brethren, the grace of our Lord Jesus Christ be
with your spirit. Amen.

ΙΛΕΤΕ ΠΗΛΙΚΟΙΣ ΥΜΙΝ ΓΡΑΜΜΑΣΙΝ
ΕΓΡΑΨΑ ΤΗι ΕΜΗι ΧΕΙΡΙ. [8]

this view, that scarcely any Epistle bears more evident marks than this of having been written from dictation. The writer of this note received a letter from the venerable Neander a few months before his death, which illustrated this point in a manner the more interesting, because he (Neander) takes a different view of this passage. His letter is written in the fair and flowing hand of an amanuensis, but it ends with a few irregular lines in large and rugged characters, written by himself, and explaining the cause of his needing the services of an amanuensis, namely, the weakness of his eyes (probably the very malady of St. Paul). It was impossible to read this autograph without thinking of the present passage, and observing that he might have expressed himself in the very words of St. Paul: —'Behold! in what large characters I have written to thee with my own hand.' [The words are given in uncial characters above. H.]

[1] The 'they' is emphatic.

[2] Literally, *that they may not be persecuted with the cross of Christ.* Cf. 2 Cor. i. 5 (*the sufferings of Christ*).

[3] Literally, *that they may boast in your flesh.*

[4] To understand the full force of such expressions as ' to *boast* in the *cross*,' we must remember that the cross (the instrument of punishment of the vilest malefactors) was associated with all that was most odious, contemptible, and horrible, in the minds of that generation, just as the word *gibbet* would be now.

[5] Cf. 2 Cor. v. 17.

[6] Compare ch. iii. ver. 9.

[7] Literally, the scars of the wounds made upon the body of a slave by the branding-iron, by which he was marked as belonging to his master. Observe the emphatic 'I:' whatever others may do, I at least bear in my body the true marks which show that I belong to Christ; the scars, not of circumcision, but of wounds suffered for His sake. Therefore let no man vex me by denying that I am Christ's servant, and bear His commission. Cf. 2 Cor. xi. 23.

[8] [The words used by St. Paul (Gal. vi. 11), as they appear in the Uncial MSS. e.g. the Codex Ephræmi Rescriptus (C). H.]

CHAPTER XIX.

St. Paul at Corinth.—Punishment of contumacious Offenders.—Subsequent Character of the Corinthian Church.—Completion of the Collection.—Phœbe's Journey to Rome.—She bears *the Epistle to the Romans.*

IT was probably about the same time when St. Paul despatched to Ephesus the messengers who bore his energetic remonstrance to the Galatians, that he was called upon to inflict the punishment which he had threatened upon those obstinate offenders who still defied his censures at Corinth. We have already seen that these were divided into two classes : the larger consisted of those who justified their immoral practice by antinomian[1] doctrine, and, styling themselves 'the Spiritual,' considered the outward restrictions of morality as mere carnal ordinances, from which they were emancipated ; the other and smaller (but more obstinate and violent) class, who had been more recently formed into a party by emissaries from Palestine, were the extreme Judaisers,[2] who were taught to look on Paul as a heretic, and to deny his Apostleship. Although the principles of these two parties differed so widely, yet they both agreed in repudiating the authority of St. Paul ; and, apparently, the former party gladly availed themselves of the calumnies of the Judaising propagandists, and readily listened to their denial of Paul's divine commission ; while the Judaisers, on their part, would foster any opposition to the Apostle of the Gentiles, from whatever quarter it might arise.

But now the time was come when the peace and purity of the Corinthian Church was to be no longer destroyed (at least openly) by either of these parties. St. Paul's first duty was to silence and shame his leading opponents, by proving the reality of his Apostleship, which they denied. This he could only do by exhibiting 'the signs of an Apostle,' which consisted, as he himself informs us, mainly in the display of miraculous powers (2 Cor. xii. 12). The present was a crisis which required such an appeal to the direct judgment of God, who could alone decide between conflicting claimants to a Divine commission. It was a contest like that between Elijah and the prophets of Baal. St. Paul had already in his absence professed his readiness to stake the truth of his claims on this issue (2 Cor. x. 8, and xiii. 3-6) ; and we may be sure that

---

[1] In applying this term *Antinomian* to the 'all things lawful' party at Corinth, we do not of course mean that all their opinions were the same with those which have been held by modern (so-called) Antinomians. But their characteristic (which was a belief that the restraints of outward law were abolished for Christians) seems more accurately expressed by the term *Antinomian*, than by any other.

[2] See above, Chap. XVII.

now, when he was present, he did not shrink from the trial. And, doubtless, God, who had sent him forth, wrought such miracles by his agency as sufficed to convince or to silence the gainsayers. Perhaps the Judaising emissaries from Palestine had already left Corinth, after fulfilling their mission by founding an anti-Pauline party there. If they had remained, they must now have been driven to retreat in shame and confusion. All other opposition was quelled likewise, and the whole Church of Corinth were constrained to confess that God was on the side of Paul. Now, therefore, that 'their obedience was complete,' the painful task remained of 'punishing all the disobedient' (2 Cor. x. 6). It was not enough that those who had so often offended and so often been pardoned before, should now merely profess once more a repentance which was only the offspring of fear or of hypocrisy; unless they were willing to give proof of their sincerity by renouncing their guilty indulgences. They had long infected the Church by their immorality; they were not merely evil themselves, but they were doing harm to others, and causing the name of Christ to be blasphemed among the heathen. It was necessary that the salt which had lost its savour should be cast out, lest its putrescence should spread to that which still retained its purity (2 Cor. xii. 21). St. Paul no longer hesitated to stand between the living and the dead, that the plague might be stayed.[1] We know, from his own description (1 Cor. v. 3–5), the very form and manner of the punishment inflicted. A solemn assembly of the Church was convened; the presence and power of the Lord Jesus Christ was especially invoked; the cases of the worst offenders were separately considered, and those whose sins required so heavy a punishment were publicly cast out of the Church, and (in the awful phraseology of Scripture) delivered over to Satan. Yet we must not suppose that even in such extreme cases the object of the sentence was to consign the criminal to final reprobation. On the contrary, the purpose of this excommunication was so to work on the offender's mind as to bring him to sincere repentance, 'that his spirit might be saved in the day of the Lord Jesus.'[2] If it had this happy effect, and if he manifested true contrition, he was restored (as we have already seen in the case of the incestuous person[3]) to the love of the brethren and the communion of the Church.

We should naturally be glad to know whether the pacification and purification of the Corinthian Church thus effected was permanent; or whether the evils which were so deeply rooted, sprang up again after St. Paul's departure. On this point Scripture gives us no further information, nor can we find any mention of this Church (which has hitherto occupied so large a space in our narrative) after the date of the present chapter, either in the Acts or the Epistles. Such silence seems, so far as it goes, of favourable augury. And the subsequent testimony of Clement (the 'fellow-labourer' of Paul, mentioned Phil. iv. 3) confirms this interpretation of it. He speaks (evidently from his own personal experience) of the impression pro-

---

[1] We here assume that some of the Corinthian Church remained obstinate in their offences, as St. Paul expected that they would.
[2] 1 Cor. v. 5.
[3] 2 Cor. ii. 6–8.

duced upon every stranger who visited the Church of Corinth, by their exemplary conduct; and specifies particularly their possession of the virtues most opposite to their former faults. Thus, he says that they were distinguished for the *ripeness and soundness of their knowledge* in contrast to the unsound and false pretence of knowledge for which they were rebuked by St. Paul. Again, he praises the *pure and blameless lives of their women*; which must therefore have been greatly changed since the time when fornication, wantonness, and impurity (2 Cor. xii. 21) were the characteristics of their society. But especially he commends them for their entire freedom from *faction and party-spirit*, which had formerly been so conspicuous among their faults. Perhaps the picture which he draws of this golden age of Corinth may be too favourably coloured, as a contrast to the state of things which he deplored when he wrote. Yet we may believe it substantially true, and may therefore hope that some of the worst evils were permanently corrected; more particularly the impurity and licentiousness which had hitherto been the most flagrant of their vices. Their tendency to party-spirit, however (so characteristic of the Greek temper), was not cured; on the contrary, it blazed forth again with greater fury than ever, some years after the death of St. Paul. Their dissensions were the occasion of the letter of Clement already mentioned; he wrote in the hope of appeasing a violent and *long-continued schism* which had arisen (like their earlier divisions) from their being 'puffed up in the cause of one against another.'[1] He rebukes them for their *envy, strife, and party-spirit*; accuses them of being *devoted to the cause of their party-leaders rather than to the cause of God*; and declares that their divisions were *rending asunder the body of Christ*, and *casting a stumbling-block in the way of many*.[2] This is the last account which we have of the Corinthian Church in the Apostolic age; so that the curtain falls upon a scene of unchristian strife, too much like that upon which it rose. Yet, though this besetting sin was still unsubdued, the character of the Church, as a whole, was much improved since the days when some of them denied the resurrection, and others maintained their right to practise unchastity.

St. Paul continued three months[3] resident at Corinth; or, at least, he made that city his head-quarters during this period. Probably he made excursions thence to Athens and other neighbouring Churches, which (as we know[4]) he had established at his first visit throughout all the region of Achaia, and which, perhaps, needed his presence, his exhortations, and his correction, no less than the metropolitan Church. Meanwhile, he was employed in completing that great collection for the Christians of Palestine, upon which we have seen him so long engaged. The Christians of Achaia, from whose comparative wealth much seems to have been expected, had already prepared their contributions, by laying aside something for the fund on the first day of every week;[5] and, as this had been going on for more

[1] 1 Cor. iv. 6.

[2] The passages in italics are quotations from Clement's first epistle, ch. i., ii., iii., xiv., xlvi., liv.

[3] Acts xx. 3.

[4] See 2 Cor. i. 1, and 2 Cor. xi. 10 ('The regions of Achaia'). Compare, however, the remarks at the end of Chap. X. and Chap. XVII.

[5] 1 Cor. xvi. 2.

than a year,[1] the sum laid by must have been considerable. This was now collected from the individual contributors, and entrusted to certain treasurers elected by the whole Church,[2] who were to carry it to Jerusalem in company with St. Paul.

While the Apostle was preparing for this journey, destined to be so eventful, one of his converts was also departing from Corinth, in an opposite direction, charged with a commission which has immortalised her name. This was Phœbe, a Christian matron resident at Cenchreæ, the eastern port of Corinth. She was a widow[3] of consideration and wealth, who acted as one of the deaconesses[4] of the Church, and was now about to sail to Rome, upon some private business, apparently connected with a lawsuit in which she was engaged.[5] St. Paul availed himself of this opportunity to send a letter by her hands to the Roman Church. His reason for writing to them at this time was his intention of speedily visiting them, on his way from Jerusalem to Spain. He desired, before his personal intercourse with them should begin, to give them a proof of the affectionate interest which he felt for them, although they ' had not seen his face in the flesh.' We must not suppose, however, that they were hitherto altogether unknown to him; for we see, from the very numerous salutations at the close of the Epistle, that he was already well acquainted with many individual Christians at Rome. From the personal acquaintance he had thus formed, and the intelligence he had received, he had reason to entertain a very high opinion of the character of the Church;[6] and accordingly he tells them (Rom. xv. 14–16) that, in entering so fully in his letter upon the doctrines and rules of Christianity, he had done it not so much to teach as to remind them; and that he was justified in assuming the authority so to exhort them, by the special commission which Christ had given him to the Gentiles.

The latter expression shows us that a considerable proportion, if not the majority, of the Roman Christians were of Gentile origin,[7] which is also evident from several other passages in the Epistle. At the same time, we cannot doubt that the original nucleus of the Church there, as well as in all the other great cities of the Empire, was formed by converts (including more Gentile proselytes than Jews) who had separated themselves from the Jewish synagogue.[8] The name of the original founder of the Roman Church has not been preserved to us by history, nor even celebrated by tradition. This is a remarkable fact, when we consider how soon the Church of

---

[1] 2 Cor. viii. 10, and 2 Cor. ix. 2.

[2] 'Whomsoever ye shall approve.' 1 Cor. xvi. 3. (See the translation of the verse.)

[3] She could not (according to Greek manners) have been mentioned as acting in the independent manner described (Rom. xvi. 1, 2), either if her husband had been living or if she had been unmarried.

[4] On this appellation, however, see p. 341, n. 2; also p. 342, n. 1.

[5] See note on Rom. xvi. 1.

[6] Rom. i. 8: 'Your faith is spoken of throughout the whole world.'

[7] See also Rom. i. 13.

[8] This is evident from the familiarity with the Old Testament which St. Paul assumes in the readers of the Epistle to the Romans; also from the manifest reference to Jewish readers in the whole argument of chapters iii. and iv., and again of chapters ix., x., and xi. See moreover the note on Rom. iv. 18 below.

Rome attained great eminence in the Christian world, both from its numbers, and from the influence of its metropolitan rank. Had any of the Apostles laid its first foundation, the fact could scarcely fail to have been recorded. It is therefore probable that it was formed in the first instance, of private Christians converted in Palestine, who had come from the eastern[1] parts of the Empire to reside at Rome, or who had brought back Christianity with them, from some of their periodical visits to Jerusalem, as the ' Strangers of Rome,' from the great Pentecost. Indeed, among the immense multitudes whom political and commercial reasons constantly attracted to the metropolis of the world, there could not fail to be representatives of every religion which had established itself in any of the provinces.

On this hypothesis, the earliest of the Roman Christians were Jews by birth, who resided in Rome, from some of the causes above alluded to. By their efforts others of their friends and fellow-countrymen (who were very numerous at Rome[2]) would have been led to embrace the Gospel. But the Church so founded, though Jewish in its origin, was remarkably free from the predominance of Judaising tendencies. This is evident from the fact that so large a proportion of it at this early period were already of Gentile blood ; and it appears still more plainly from the tone assumed by St. Paul throughout the Epistle, so different from that in which he addresses the Galatians, although the subject-matter is often nearly identical. Yet, at the same time, the Judaising element, though not preponderating, was not entirely absent. We find that there were opponents of the Gospel at Rome, who argued against it on the ground of the immoral consequences which followed (as they thought) from the doctrine of Justification by Faith ; and even charged St. Paul himself with maintaining that the greater man's sin, the greater was God's glory. (See Rom. iii. 8.) Moreover, not all the Jewish members of the Church could bring themselves to acknowledge their uncircumcised Gentile brethren as their equals in the privileges of Christ's kingdom (Rom. iii. 9 and 29, xv. 7–11) ; and, on the other hand, the more enlightened Gentile converts were inclined to treat the lingering Jewish prejudices of weak consciences with scornful contempt (Rom. xiv. 3). It was the aim of St. Paul to win the former of these parties to Christian truth, and the latter to Christian love ; and to remove the stumbling-blocks out of the way of

---

[1] We cannot, perhaps, infer anything as to the composition of the Church at Rome, from the fact that St. Paul writes to them in Greek instead of Latin ; because Hellenistic Greek was (as we have seen, p. 32) his own native tongue, in which he seems always to have written ; and if any of the Roman Christians did not understand that language, interpreters were not wanting in their own body who could explain it to them. Unquestionably, however, he assumes that his readers are familiar with the Septuagint (Rom. iv. 18). It is rather remarkable

that Tertius, who acted as St. Paul's amanuensis, was apparently (to judge from his name) a Roman Christian of the Latin section of the Church. It cannot, of course, be supposed that *all* the Roman Christians were of Oriental origin and Grecian speech. Yet it is certain (as Dean Milman, in his ' *Latin Christianity*,' has lately observed) that Greek remained the prevailing language in the Church of Rome for several centuries.

[2] With regard to the Jews in Rome, see the beginning of Chap. XXIV.

both, by setting before them that grand summary of the doctrine and practice of Christianity which is contained in the following Epistle.

EPISTLE TO THE ROMANS.[1]

i. 1 PAUL, a bondsman of Jesus Christ, a called Apostle, Salutation.
set apart to publish the Glad-tidings of God————

2 which He promised of old by His Prophets in the
3 Holy Scriptures, concerning His Son (who was
   born of the seed of David according to the flesh,
4 but was marked out[2] as the Son of God with
   mighty power, according to the spirit of holiness,
   by resurrection from the dead),[3] even Jesus Christ,
5 our Lord and Master.[4] By whom I received grace
   and apostleship, that I might declare His name
   among all the Gentiles, and bring them to the
6 obedience of faith. Among whom ye also are
7 numbered, being called by Jesus Christ————TO
   ALL GOD'S BELOVED, CALLED TO BE SAINTS,[5] WHO
   DWELL IN ROME.[6]

Grace be to you, and peace from God our Father, and from our Lord Jesus Christ.

---

[1] The date of this Epistle is very precisely fixed by the following statements contained in it :—

(1.) St. Paul had never yet been to Rome (i. 11, 13, 15).

(2.) He was intending to go to Rome, after first visiting Jerusalem (xv. 23–28). This was exactly his purpose during his three months' residence at Corinth. See Acts xix. 21.

(3.) He was going to bear a collection of alms from Macedonia and Achaia to Jerusalem (xv. 26 and 31). This he did carry from Corinth to Jerusalem at the close of this three months' visit. See Acts xxiv. 17.

(4.) When he wrote the Epistle, Timotheus, Sosipater, Gaius, and Erastus were with him (xvi. 21, 23) ; of these, the first three are expressly mentioned in the Acts as having been with him at Corinth during the three months' visit (see Acts xx. 4) ; and the last, Erastus, was himself a Corinthian, and had been sent shortly before from Ephesus (Acts xix. 22) with Timotheus on the way to Corinth. Compare 1 Cor. xvi. 10, 11.

(5.) Phœbe, a deaconess of the Corinthian port of Cenchreæ, was the bearer of the Epistle (xvi. 1) to Rome.

[2] 'Defined,' here equivalent, as Chrysostom says, to 'marked out.' We may observe that the notes which marked Jesus as the Son of God, are here declared to be *power* and *holiness*. Neither would have been sufficient without the other.

[3] 'Resurrection of the dead' had already become a technical expression, used as we use 'Resurrection :' it cannot here mean the general resurrection of the dead (as Prof. Jowett supposes), because that event not having taken place could not 'define' our Lord to be the Son of God.

[4] 'Lord' seems to require this translation here, especially in connection with 'bondsman,' ver. 1.

[5] See note on 1 Cor. i. 2.

[6] If this introductory salutation appears involved and parenthetical, it the more forcibly recalls to our mind the manner in which it was written, namely, by dictation from the mouth of St. Paul. Of course an extemporary spoken composition will always be more full of parentheses, abrupt transitions, and broken sentences, than a treatise composed in writing by its author.

First I thank my God through Jesus Christ for i. 8
you all, because the tidings of your faith are told
throughout the whole world.   For God is my witness 9
(whom I serve with the worship [1] of my spirit, in
proclaiming the Glad-tidings of His Son), how unceasingly I make mention of you at all times in my
prayers, beseeching Him that, if it be possible, I 10
might now at length have a way open to me according
to the will of God, to come and visit you.   For I long 11
to see you, that I may impart to you some spiritual
gift, for the establishment of your stedfastness ; that 12
I may share with you (I would say) in mutual encouragement, through the faith both of you and me
together, one with another.   But I would not have 13
you ignorant, brethren, that I have often purposed
to come to you (though hitherto I have been hindered),
that I might have some fruit among you also, as I
have among the other Gentiles.   I am a debtor both 14
to Greeks and Barbarians, both to wise and foolish ;
therefore, as far as in me lies, I am ready to declare 15
the Glad-tidings to you that are in Rome, as well as
to others.   For [even in the chief city of the world] 16
I am not ashamed of the Glad-tidings of Christ,
seeing it is the mighty power whereby God brings
salvation to every man that has faith therein, to the

This Glad-
tidings con-
sists in the
revelation of
a new and
more perfect
moral state
(*God's righte-
ousness*), of
which faith is
the condition
and the reci-
pient.
For by God's
Jew first, and also to the Gentile. [2] For therein God's 17
righteousness [3] is revealed, a righteousness which
springs from Faith, and which Faith receives—as it
is written : '𝔅𝔶 𝔣𝔞𝔦𝔱𝔥 𝔰𝔥𝔞𝔩𝔩 𝔱𝔥𝔢 𝔯𝔦𝔤𝔥𝔱𝔢𝔬𝔲𝔰 𝔩𝔦𝔳𝔢.' [4]
For the wrath of God is revealed from heaven 18
against all ungodliness and unrighteousness of men,
who keep [5] down the truth [which they know] by the

---

[1] The addition of 'with my spirit'
qualifies the verb, which was generally
applied to acts of outward worship.
As much as to say, 'My worship of
God is not the outward service of the
temple, but the inward homage of the
spirit.' See the corresponding substantive similarly qualified, chap. xii. 1.

[2] St. Paul uses the word for 'Greek'
as the singular of the word for 'Gentiles,' because the singular of the latter
is not used in the sense of *a Gentile*.
Also the plural 'Greeks' is used when
individual Gentiles are meant ; 'Gentiles' when *Gentiles collectively* are
spoken of.

[3] *God's righteousness*. Not an attribute of God, but the righteousness

which God considers such ; and which
must, therefore, be the perfection of
man's moral nature. This righteousness may be looked on under two aspects : 1. *in itself*, as a moral condition
of man ; 2. *in its consequences*, as involving a freedom from guilt in the
sight of God. Under the first aspect
it is the possession of a certain disposition of mind called *faith*. Under
the second aspect it is regarded as
something reckoned by God to the
account of man—*an acquittal of past
offences*.

[4] Habakkuk ii. 4 (LXX.). Quoted
also Gal. iii. 11, and Heb. x. 38.

[5] For this meaning of the verb, compare 2 Thess. ii. 6.

i. 19 wickedness wherein they live.[1]   Because that which
can be known [2] of God is manifested in their hearts,
20 God Himself having shown it to them; for His eternal
power and Godhead, though they be invisible, yet
are seen ever since the world was made, being understood by His works, that they [who despised Him]
21 might have no excuse; because although they knew
God, they glorified Him not as God, nor gave Him
thanks, but in their reasonings they went astray
after vanity, and their senseless heart was darkened.
22 Calling themselves wise, they were turned into fools,
23 and forsook the glory [3] of the imperishable God for
idols graven in the likeness of perishable men, or of
24 birds and beasts, and creeping things.   Therefore
God also gave them up to work uncleanness according to their hearts' lust. to dishonour their bodies
25 one with another; seeing they had bartered the truth
of God for lies, and reverenced and worshipped the
things made instead of the Maker, who is blessed for
26 ever, Amen.   For this cause God gave them up to
shameful passions; for on the one hand their women
changed the natural use into that which is against
27 nature; and on the other hand their men, in like
manner, leaving the natural use of the woman, burned
in their lust one toward another, men with men
working abomination, and receiving in themselves
28 the due recompense of their transgression.   And as
they thought fit to cast out the acknowledgment of
God, God gave them over to an outcast [4] mind, to do
29 the things that are unseemly.   They are filled with
all unrighteousness, fornication, depravity, covetousness,[5] maliciousness.   They overflow with envy,
30 murder, strife, deceit, malignity.   They are whis-
perers, backbiters, God-haters;[6] outrageous, over-
weening, false boasters; inventors of wickedness;
31 undutiful to parents; bereft of wisdom; breakers of
covenanted faith; devoid of natural affection; ruthless,

previous re-
velations,
only His
prohibition of
sin had been
revealed.
Thus the law
of conscience
was God's re-
velation to the
Gentiles, and
had been
violated by
them, as was.
testified by the
utterly cor-
rupt state of
the heathen
world.

---

[1] *By living in wickedness.*

[2] That which can be known by men
as men; without special supernatural
communication.

[3] This is nearly a quotation from
Ps. cvi. 20 (LXX.)   The phrase used
there and here meaning *to forsake one
thing for another; to change one thing
against another.*

[4] There is a play upon the words
here (*cast out—outcast*).   A translation
should, if possible, retain such marked

characteristics of St. Paul's style.   **A**
paronomasia upon the same words is
found 2 Cor. xiii. 6, 7.

[5] Perhaps this may be here used for
lust, as it is at Eph. v. 3 and elsewhere;
see the notes there, and also see Hammond, and Jowett, *in loco.*

[6] We venture to consider this adjective active, against the opinion of
Winer, Meyer, and De Wette; relying
first, on the authority of Suidas, and
secondly, on the context.

merciless. Who knowing the decree of God,[1] whereby i. 32
all that do such things are worthy of death, not only
commit the sins, but delight in their fellowship with
the sinners.

Wherefore thou, O man, whosoever thou art that ii. 1
judgest others, art thyself without excuse;[2] for in
judging thy neighbour thou condemnest thyself,
since thy deeds are the same which in him thou dost
condemn. And we know that God judges them who 2
do such wickedness, not[3] by their words, but by
their deeds. But reckonest thou, O thou that con- 3
demnest such evil-doers, and doest the like thyself,
that thou shalt escape the judgment of God? or does 4
the rich abundance of His kindness and forbearance
and long-suffering cause thee to despise[4] Him? and
art thou ignorant that God, by His kindness [in
withholding punishment], strives to lead thee to repentance? But thou in the hardness and impenitence 5
of thy heart, art treasuring up against thyself a store
of wrath, which will be manifested in[5] the day of
wrath, even the day when God will reveal[6] to the
sight of men the righteousness of His judgment.
For He will pay to all their due, according to their 6
deeds; to those who with stedfast endurance in well 7
doing seek glory and honour[7] incorruptible, He will 8
give life eternal; but for men of guile,[8] who are
obedient to unrighteousness, and disobedient to the 9
truth, indignation and wrath, tribulation and anguish
shall[9] fall upon them; yea, upon every soul of man
that does the work of evil, upon the Jew first, and
also upon the Gentile. But glory and honour and 10

[1] How did they know this? By the
law of conscience (see ii. 14) confirmed
by the laws of nature (i. 20).

[2] Inexcusable *in doing evil* (not *in
judging*) is evidently meant, just as it
is before (i. 20) by the same word.
St. Paul does not here mean that 'cen-
soriousness is inexcusable;' but he
says 'thy power to judge the immoralities of others involves thy own guilt;
for thou also violatest the laws of thy
conscience.'

[3] This appears to be the meaning of
'according to truth.'

[4] Literally, '*is it the rich abundance
of His kindness, &c., which thou despisest?*'

[5] Not *against*, but *manifested in.*

[6] This means to *disclose to sight
what has been hidden*; the word *reveal*

does not by itself represent the full
force of the original term, although
etymologically it corresponds with it.

[7] 'Glory and honour and immortality,' an hendiadys for 'immortal
glory and honour.'

[8] This noun seems to mean *selfish
party intrigue, conducted in a mercenary spirit,* and more generally, *selfish
cunning;* being derived from a verb
denoting *to undertake a work for hire.*
It occurs also 2 Cor. xii. 20; Phil. i.
16, Phil. ii. 3; Gal. v. 20. The participle is used for *intriguing partisans*
by Aristotle (*Polit.* v. 3). The history
of this word seems to bear a strong
analogy to that of our term *job.*

[9] Observe the change of construction
here. The nouns in the latter clause
are in the nominative.

peace shall be given to every man who does the
work of good, to the Jew first, and also to the Gen-

11 tile; for there is no respect of persons with God.

12 For they who have sinned without [the knowledge
of] the Law, shall perish without [the punishment
of] the Law; and they who have sinned under the

13 Law, shall be judged by the Law.[1] For not the
hearers of the Law[2] are righteous in God's sight, but

14 the doers of the Law shall be counted righteous. For
when the Gentiles, having not the Law, do by nature
the works of the Law, they, though they have not

15 the Law, are a Law to themselves; since they manifest the work of the Law written in their hearts;
while their conscience also bears its witness, and
their inward thoughts answering one to the other,

16 accuse, or else defend them; [as will be seen][3] in
that day when God shall judge the secret counsels
of men by Jesus Christ, according to the Glad-tidings
which I preach.

17 Behold[4] thou callest thyself a Jew, and restest in

18 the Law, and boastest of God's favour, and knowest
the will of God, and givest[5] judgment upon good
or evil, being instructed by the teaching of the Law.

19 Thou deemest thyself a guide of the blind, a light to
those who are in darkness, an instructor of the simple,

20 a teacher of babes, possessing in the Law the perfect

21 pattern of knowledge and of truth. Thou therefore
that teachest thy neighbour, dost thou not teach
thyself? thou that preachest a man should not steal,

22 dost thou steal? thou that sayest a man should not
commit adultery, dost thou commit adultery? thou

Nor would the Jews be shielded by their boast in the Law, since they broke the Law; nor by their outward consecration to God, since true circumcision is that of the heart.

---

[1] We have remarked elsewhere (but
the remark may be here repeated with
advantage) that the attempts which
were formerly made to prove that νόμος,
when used with and without the article
by St. Paul, meant in the former case
a moral law in general, and in the latter
only *the Mosaic Law,* have now been
abandoned by the best interpreters.
See note on iii. 20.

[2] The Jews were 'hearers of the Law'
in their synagogues, every Sabbath.

[3] The clause in brackets (or some
equivalent) must be interpolated, to
render the connection clear to an English reader. The verbs are in the present, because the conscientious judgment described takes place in the present time; yet they are connected with

in the Day (as if they had been in the
future), because the manifestation and
confirmation of that judgment belongs
to 'the Day of the Lord.'

[4] If we follow some of the best
MSS., the translation must run thus:
'But what, if thou callest thyself,'
&c.; the apodosis beginning with verse
21.

[5] The verb means *to test (as a metal
by fire).* See 1 Peter i. 7. Hence *to
give judgment upon* (here). 'Things
that are excellent,' or rather 'things
that differ,' mean (as explained by
Theophylact), 'what we ought to do
and what we ought not to do.' The
same phrase occurs Phil. i. 10. See
also Rom. xii. 2.

that abhorrest idols, dost thou rob [1] temples? thou ii. 2
that makest thy boast in the Law, by breaking the
Law dost thou dishonour God? Yea, as it is written,
'𝕿𝖍𝖗𝖔𝖚𝖌𝖍 𝖞𝖔𝖚 𝖎𝖘 𝖙𝖍𝖊 𝖓𝖆𝖒𝖊 𝖔𝖋 𝕲𝖔𝖉 𝖇𝖑𝖆𝖘𝖕𝖍𝖊𝖒𝖊𝖉 𝖆𝖒𝖔𝖓𝖌 24
𝖙𝖍𝖊 𝕲𝖊𝖓𝖙𝖎𝖑𝖊𝖘.'[2]
For circumcision avails if thou keep the Law; but 25
if thou be a breaker of the Law, thy circumcision is
turned into uncircumcision. If then the uncircum- 26
cised Gentile keep the decrees of the Law, shall not
his uncircumcision be counted for circumcision?
And shall not he, though naturally uncircumcised, by 27
fulfilling the Law, condemn thee, who with Scripture
and circumcision dost break the Law? For he is not 28
a Jew, who is one outwardly; nor is that circumcision,
which is outward in the flesh; but he is a Jew who 29
is one inwardly, and circumcision is that of the heart,
in the spirit, not in the letter; whose praise comes
not from man[3] but from God.

'But if this be so, what advantage has the Jew, iii.
and what has been the profit of circumcision?' Much
every way. First, because to their keeping were en- 2
trusted the oracles of God. For what, though some 3
of them were faithless[4] to the trust? shall we say[5]
that their faithlessness destroys the faithfulness[6] of
God? That be far from us. Yea, be sure that God 4
is true, though all mankind be liars, as it is written:
'𝕿𝖍𝖆𝖙 𝖙𝖍𝖔𝖚 𝖒𝖎𝖌𝖍𝖙𝖊𝖘𝖙 𝖇𝖊 𝖏𝖚𝖘𝖙𝖎𝖋𝖎𝖊𝖉 𝖎𝖓 𝖙𝖍𝖞 𝖘𝖆𝖞𝖎𝖓𝖌𝖘, 𝖆𝖓𝖉
𝖒𝖎𝖌𝖍𝖙𝖊𝖘𝖙 𝖔𝖛𝖊𝖗𝖈𝖔𝖒𝖊 𝖜𝖍𝖊𝖓 𝖙𝖍𝖔𝖚 𝖆𝖗𝖙 𝖏𝖚𝖉𝖌𝖊𝖉.'[7] 'But if the 5
righteousness of God is established by our unrighteousness [His faithfulness being more clearly seen
by our faithlessness], must we not say that God is
unjust,' (I speak as men do),[8] 'in sending the punishment?' That be far from us; for [if this punishment 6

The advantage of the Jews consisted in their being entrusted with the outward revelation of God's will. Their faithlessness to this trust only established God's faithfulness, by furnishing the occasion for its display. Yet though this good resulted from their sin, its guilt is not thereby removed; since no consequences (however good) can make a wrong action right.

[1] Compare Acts xix. 37. [See above, p. 432. H.]
[2] Isaiah lii. 5 (LXX.).
[3] The Pharisees and Pharisaic Judaisers sought to gain the praise of men by their outward show of sanctity; which is here contrasted with the inward holiness which seeks no praise but that of God. The same contrast occurs in the Sermon on the Mount.
[4] 'Faithless to the trust' refers to the preceding 'entrusted.' For the meaning of the word, compare 2 Tim. ii. 13.
[5] See note on Gal. iii. 21.
[6] That is, shall we imagine that God

will break His covenant with the true Israel, because of the unfaithfulness of the false Israel? Compare Rom. xi. 1–5.
[7] Ps. li. 4 (LXX.). The whole context is as follows: '*I acknowledge my transgression, and my sin is ever before me; against Thee only have I sinned, and done this evil in Thy sight; that Thou mightest be justified in Thy sayings, and mightest overcome when Thou art judged.*'
[8] For this phrase see note on Gal. iii. 15. And compare also 1 Cor. xv. 32, and Rom. vi. 19,

i. 7 be unjust], how shall God judge the world? since [1]
[of that judgment also it might be said]: 'If God's
truth has by the occasion of my falsehood more fully
shown itself, to the greater manifestation of His glory,
8 why am I still condemned as a sinner? and why [2]
should we not say' (as I myself am slanderously
charged with saying) 'Let us do evil that good may
come?' Of such men [3] the doom is just.

9   What shall we say then? [having gifts above the *The privileges of the Jews*
Gentiles] have we the pre-eminence over them? No, *gave them no moral pre-*
in no wise; for we have already charged all, both *eminence over the hea-*
10 Jews and Gentiles, with the guilt of sin. And so it *then; their Law only*
11 is written, '𝕿𝖍𝖊𝖗𝖊 𝖎𝖘 𝖓𝖔𝖓𝖊 𝖗𝖎𝖌𝖍𝖙𝖊𝖔𝖚𝖘, 𝖓𝖔 𝖓𝖔𝖙 𝖔𝖓𝖊; 𝖙𝖍𝖊𝖗𝖊 *convicted them of sin.*
   𝖎𝖘 𝖓𝖔𝖓𝖊 𝖙𝖍𝖆𝖙 𝖚𝖓𝖉𝖊𝖗𝖘𝖙𝖆𝖓𝖉𝖊𝖙𝖍, 𝖙𝖍𝖊𝖗𝖊 𝖎𝖘 𝖓𝖔𝖓𝖊 𝖙𝖍𝖆𝖙 𝖘𝖊𝖊𝖐𝖊𝖙𝖍
12 𝖆𝖋𝖙𝖊𝖗 𝕲𝖔𝖉, 𝖙𝖍𝖊𝖞 𝖆𝖗𝖊 𝖆𝖑𝖑 𝖌𝖔𝖓𝖊 𝖔𝖚𝖙 𝖔𝖋 𝖙𝖍𝖊 𝖜𝖆𝖞, 𝖙𝖍𝖊𝖞 𝖆𝖗𝖊
   𝖆𝖑𝖙𝖔𝖌𝖊𝖙𝖍𝖊𝖗 𝖇𝖊𝖈𝖔𝖒𝖊 𝖚𝖓𝖕𝖗𝖔𝖋𝖎𝖙𝖆𝖇𝖑𝖊, 𝖙𝖍𝖊𝖗𝖊 𝖎𝖘 𝖓𝖔𝖓𝖊 𝖙𝖍𝖆𝖙
13 𝖉𝖔𝖊𝖙𝖍 𝖌𝖔𝖔𝖉, 𝖓𝖔 𝖓𝖔𝖙 𝖔𝖓𝖊. 𝕿𝖍𝖊𝖎𝖗 𝖙𝖍𝖗𝖔𝖆𝖙 𝖎𝖘 𝖆𝖓 𝖔𝖕𝖊𝖓 𝖘𝖊=
   𝖕𝖚𝖑𝖈𝖍𝖗𝖊, 𝖜𝖎𝖙𝖍 𝖙𝖍𝖊𝖎𝖗 𝖙𝖔𝖓𝖌𝖚𝖊 𝖙𝖍𝖊𝖞 𝖍𝖆𝖛𝖊 𝖚𝖘𝖊𝖉 𝖉𝖊𝖈𝖊𝖎𝖙, 𝖙𝖍𝖊
14 𝖕𝖔𝖎𝖘𝖔𝖓 𝖔𝖋 𝖆𝖘𝖕𝖘 𝖎𝖘 𝖚𝖓𝖉𝖊𝖗 𝖙𝖍𝖊𝖎𝖗 𝖑𝖎𝖕𝖘. 𝕿𝖍𝖊𝖎𝖗 𝖒𝖔𝖚𝖙𝖍 𝖎𝖘 𝖋𝖚𝖑𝖑
15 𝖔𝖋 𝖈𝖚𝖗𝖘𝖎𝖓𝖌 𝖆𝖓𝖉 𝖇𝖎𝖙𝖙𝖊𝖗𝖓𝖊𝖘𝖘. 𝕿𝖍𝖊𝖎𝖗 𝖋𝖊𝖊𝖙 𝖆𝖗𝖊 𝖘𝖜𝖎𝖋𝖙 𝖙𝖔 𝖘𝖍𝖊𝖉
,17 𝖇𝖑𝖔𝖔𝖉. 𝕯𝖊𝖘𝖙𝖗𝖚𝖈𝖙𝖎𝖔𝖓 𝖆𝖓𝖉 𝖒𝖎𝖘𝖊𝖗𝖞 𝖆𝖗𝖊 𝖎𝖓 𝖙𝖍𝖊𝖎𝖗 𝖕𝖆𝖙𝖍𝖘, 𝖆𝖓𝖉
18 𝖙𝖍𝖊 𝖜𝖆𝖞 𝖔𝖋 𝖕𝖊𝖆𝖈𝖊 𝖍𝖆𝖛𝖊 𝖙𝖍𝖊𝖞 𝖓𝖔𝖙 𝖐𝖓𝖔𝖜𝖓. 𝕿𝖍𝖊𝖗𝖊 𝖎𝖘 𝖓𝖔 𝖋𝖊𝖆𝖗
19 𝖔𝖋 𝕲𝖔𝖉 𝖇𝖊𝖋𝖔𝖗𝖊 𝖙𝖍𝖊𝖎𝖗 𝖊𝖞𝖊𝖘.' [4] Now we know that all the
sayings of the Law are spoken to those under the
Law; [these things therefore are spoken to the Jews]
that every mouth might be stopped, and the whole
world might be subjected to the judgment of God.
20 For [5] through the works of the Law, '𝖘𝖍𝖆𝖑𝖑 𝖓𝖔 𝖋𝖑𝖊𝖘𝖍
𝖇𝖊 𝖏𝖚𝖘𝖙𝖎𝖋𝖎𝖊𝖉 𝖎𝖓 𝕳𝖎𝖘 𝖘𝖎𝖌𝖍𝖙,' [6] because by the Law is
wrought [not the doing of righteousness, but] the
acknowledgment of sin.

21   But now, not by the Law, but by another way, [7] *Hence all men, being*

---

[1] In this most difficult passage we
must bear in mind that St. Paul is
constantly referring to the arguments
of his opponents, which were familiar
to his readers at Rome, but are not so
to ourselves. Hence the apparently
abrupt and elliptical character of the
argument, and the necessity of supplying something to make the connection
intelligible.

[2] The ellipsis is supplied by understanding 'why' from the preceding
clause, and 'say' from the following:
the complete expression would have
been, 'why should we not say?'

[3] Viz. men who deduce immoral consequences from sophistical arguments.

[4] This whole passage is quoted (and
all but verses 10 and 11 verbatim)
from Ps. xiv. 1, 2, 3. (LXX.) Portions of it also occur in Ps. liii. 3, Ps.
v. 9, Ps. cxl. 3, Ps. x. 7; Isaiah lix. 7;
Ps. xxxvi. 1.

[5] See note on ii. 12. That the absence of the article makes no difference
is shown by verses 28 and 29. At the
same time, it must be observed that
the Law is spoken of as a moral, not as
a ceremonial law.

[6] Ps. cxliii. 2, almost verbatim from
LXX. 'Enter not into judgment with
thy servant; for in thy sight shall no
man be justified.' No doubt the preceding words were in St. Paul's recollection, and are tacitly referred to,
being very suitable to his argument.

[7] *Not by the Law, but by something
else.* See iii. 28, and iv. 6.

condemned by the standard of moral law which they possessed, must be made righteous in God's sight in a way different from that of the Law; i.e. not by obeying precepts, and so escaping penalties, but by faith in Jesus Christ, and by receiving a gratuitous pardon for past offences. The sacrifice of Christ showed that this pardon proceeded not from God's indifference to sin.

God's righteousness is brought to light, whereto the Law.and the prophets bear witness; God's righteous- iii. ness (I say) which comes by faith in Jesus Christ, for all and upon all, who have faith;[1] for there is no difference [between Jew and Gentile], since all have 23 sinned, and none have attained the glorious likeness[2] of God. But they are justified freely by His grace 24 through the ransom which is paid in Christ Jesus. For Him hath God set forth, in His blood to be a 25 propitiatory sacrifice by means of Faith, thereby to manifest the righteousness of God; because in His forbearance God had passed over the former sins of men[3] in the times that are gone by. [Him (I say) 26 hath God set forth] in this present time to manifest His righteousness, that He might be just, and [yet] might justify[4] the children[5] of Faith. Where then is 27 the[6] boasting [of the Jew]? It has been[7] shut out. By what law? by the law of works? no, but by the law of Faith. For we reckon[8] that by Faith a man 28 is justified, and not by[9] the works of the Law; else

[1] In order to render more clear the connection between the words for 'faith' and 'believe,' it is desirable to translate the latter have faith (instead of believe) wherever it is possible.

[2] Literally, all fall short of the glory of God. We have 'God's glory' as analogous to 'Christ's glory' (2 Cor. viii. 23, or 2 Cor. iii. 18). It may also mean God's heavenly glory (Rom. v. 2, and 2 Thess. ii. 14). Meyer and others render it 'the praise which comes from God,' which is contrary to St. Paul's use of the phrase. Indeed St. John is the only writer in the New Testament who furnishes any analogy for this rendering (John xii. 43.)

[3] The A. V. here is a mistranslation. Cf. Acts xvii. 30, and the note on St. Paul's speech at Lystra, p. 154, n. 2.

[4] The first wish of a translator of St. Paul's Epistles would be to retain the same English root in all the words employed as translations of the various derivatives of δίκαιος, viz. δικαιοσύνη, δικαιοῦν, δικαίωμα, δικαίωσις, δικαίως, and δικαιοκρισία. But this is impossible, because no English root of the same meaning has these derivatives; for example, taking righteous to represent δίκαιος, we have righteousness for δικαιοσύνη, but no verb from the same root equivalent to δικαιοῦν. Again, taking just for δίκαιος, we have justify for δι-

καιοῦν, but no term for δικαιοσύνη, which is by no means equivalent to justice, nor even to justness, in many passages where it occurs. The only course which can be adopted, therefore, is to take that root in each case which seems best to suit the context, and bring out the connection of the argument.

[5] The original is not fully represented by the A. V. It means 'him whose essential characteristic is faith,' 'the child of faith.' Compare Gal. iii. 7, and Gal. iii. 9. The word 'Jesus' is omitted by some of the best MSS., and is introduced in others with variations, which look as if it had been originally an interpolation. It is omitted by Tischendorf.

[6] The Greek has the article before the word for 'boasting.'

[7] The aorist seems used here (as often) in a perfect tense. See note on 2 Cor. vii. 2, and on Rom. v. 5.

[8] We have adopted the reading 'for' instead of 'therefore,' because the authority of MSS. and Fathers is pretty equally divided between the two readings, and it suits the context better to make this clause a proposition supporting the preceding, and defended by the following, than to make it the conclusion from the preceding arguments.

[9] See note on verse 21.

iii.29 God must be the God of the Jews alone; but is He
   not likewise the God of the Gentiles? Yea, He is the
30 God of the Gentiles also. For God is one [for all
   men], and He will justify through Faith the circumcision of the Jews, and by their Faith will He justify
   also the uncircumcision of the Gentiles.

31 Do we then by Faith bring to nought the Law?
   That be far from us! Yea, we establish the Law.

iv. 1 What then[1] can we say that our father Abraham
 2 gained by[2] the fleshly ordinance? For, if Abraham
   was justified by works he has a ground of boasting.
 3 But he has no ground of boasting with God; for what
   says the Scripture : '𝔄𝔟𝔯𝔞𝔥𝔞𝔪 𝔥𝔞𝔡 𝔣𝔞𝔦𝔱𝔥 𝔦𝔫 𝔊𝔬𝔡, 𝔞𝔫𝔡 𝔦𝔱
 4 𝔴𝔞𝔰 𝔯𝔢𝔠𝔨𝔬𝔫𝔢𝔡 𝔲𝔫𝔱𝔬 𝔥𝔦𝔪 𝔣𝔬𝔯 𝔯𝔦𝔤𝔥𝔱𝔢𝔬𝔲𝔰𝔫𝔢𝔰𝔰.'[3] Now if a
   man earn his pay by his work, it is not 'reckoned to
 5 him' as a favour, but it is paid him as a debt; but if
   he earns nothing by his work, but puts faith in Him
   who justifies[4] the ungodly, then his faith is 'reckoned
 6 to him for righteousness.' In like manner David also
   tells the blessedness of the man, to whom God reckon-
   eth righteousness, not by works but by another way,[5]
 7 saying, '𝔅𝔩𝔢𝔰𝔰𝔢𝔡 𝔞𝔯𝔢 𝔱𝔥𝔢𝔶 𝔴𝔥𝔬𝔰𝔢 𝔦𝔫𝔦𝔮𝔲𝔦𝔱𝔦𝔢𝔰 𝔞𝔯𝔢 𝔣𝔬𝔯𝔤𝔦𝔳𝔢𝔫,
 8 𝔞𝔫𝔡 𝔴𝔥𝔬𝔰𝔢 𝔰𝔦𝔫𝔰 𝔞𝔯𝔢 𝔠𝔬𝔳𝔢𝔯𝔢𝔡. 𝔅𝔩𝔢𝔰𝔰𝔢𝔡 𝔦𝔰 𝔱𝔥𝔢 𝔪𝔞𝔫 𝔞𝔤𝔞𝔦𝔫𝔰𝔱
 9 𝔴𝔥𝔬𝔪 𝔱𝔥𝔢 𝔏𝔬𝔯𝔡 𝔰𝔥𝔞𝔩𝔩 𝔫𝔬𝔱 𝔯𝔢𝔠𝔨𝔬𝔫 𝔰𝔦𝔫.'[6] Is this blessing
   then for the circumcised alone? or does it not belong
   also to the uncircumcised? for we say, '𝔥𝔦𝔰 𝔣𝔞𝔦𝔱𝔥 𝔴𝔞𝔰
10 𝔯𝔢𝔠𝔨𝔬𝔫𝔢𝔡 𝔱𝔬 𝔄𝔟𝔯𝔞𝔥𝔞𝔪 𝔣𝔬𝔯 𝔯𝔦𝔤𝔥𝔱𝔢𝔬𝔲𝔰𝔫𝔢𝔰𝔰.'[7] How then
   was it reckoned to him? when he was circumcised,
   or uncircumcised? Not in circumcision but in un-
11 circumcision. And he received circumcision as an
   outward sign[8] of inward things, a seal to attest the
   righteousness which belonged to his Faith while he
   was yet uncircumcised. That so he might be father
   of all the faithful who are uncircumcised, that the
   righteousness [of Faith] might be reckoned to them
12 also ;—and father of circumcision to those[9] who are

Jewish objections met by appeal to the Old Testament and the example of Abraham, who was justified, not by circumcision, but before circumcision. Abraham's belief in God's promises foreshadows Christian faith, Christians being, by virtue of their faith, the spiritual children of Abraham and heirs of the promises.

---

[1] The 'therefore' here is very perplexing, as the argument seems to require 'for.' Nor is the difficulty removed by saying dogmatically that
this passage is 'not a proof but a consequence' of the preceding. For it is
unquestionably given by St. Paul as a
proof that the law is consistent with
his doctrine of faith. The 'therefore'
is probably repeated from the preceding
'therefore,' just as 'for' is repeated in
v. 7.

[2] Literally, *gained in the way of the
flesh.* The order of the Greek forbids
us to join 'after the flesh' with 'father,'
as in A. V.
[3] Gen. xv. 6 (LXX.).
[4] See note on iii. 26.
[5] See again note on iii. 21.
[6] Ps. xxxii. 1, 2 (LXX.).
[7] Gen. xv. 6 (LXX.) repeated.
[8] The full meaning of *sign* is *an outward sign of things unseen.*
[9] Viz., the faithful of Jewish birth.

not circumcised only in the flesh, but who also tread in the steps of that Faith which our father Abraham had while yet uncircumcised.

For the promise [1] to Abraham and his seed that he iv. 13 should inherit the world came not by the Law, but by the righteousness of Faith. For, if this inheritance 14 belong to the children of the Law, Faith is made of no account, and the promise is brought to nought; because the Law brings [not blessings but] punish- 15 ment,[2] (for where there is no law, there can be no law-breaking). Therefore the inheritance belongs to 16 Faith, that it might be a free gift; that so the promise [3] [not being capable of forfeiture] might stand firm to all the seed of Abraham, not to his children of the Law alone, but to the children of his Faith; for he is the Father of us all [both Jews and Gentiles], (as it is written, '𝔌 𝔥𝔞𝔳𝔢 𝔪𝔞𝔡𝔢 𝔱𝔥𝔢𝔢 𝔱𝔥𝔢 𝔣𝔞𝔱𝔥𝔢𝔯 𝔬𝔣 𝔪𝔞𝔫𝔶 𝔫𝔞= 17 𝔱𝔦𝔬𝔫𝔰,'[4]) in the sight of God, who saw his faith, even God who makes the dead to live, and calls the things that are not as though they were. For Abraham had 18 faith in hope beyond hope, that he might become 𝔱𝔥𝔢 𝔣𝔞𝔱𝔥𝔢𝔯 𝔬𝔣 𝔪𝔞𝔫𝔶 𝔫𝔞𝔱𝔦𝔬𝔫𝔰;[5] as it was said unto him, '𝔏𝔬𝔬𝔨 𝔱𝔬𝔴𝔞𝔯𝔡 𝔥𝔢𝔞𝔳𝔢𝔫 𝔞𝔫𝔡 𝔱𝔢𝔩𝔩 𝔱𝔥𝔢 𝔰𝔱𝔞𝔯𝔰 𝔦𝔣 𝔱𝔥𝔬𝔲 𝔟𝔢 𝔞𝔟𝔩𝔢 𝔱𝔬 𝔫𝔲𝔪𝔟𝔢𝔯 𝔱𝔥𝔢𝔪; 𝔢𝔳𝔢𝔫 𝔰𝔬 𝔰𝔥𝔞𝔩𝔩 𝔱𝔥𝔶 𝔰𝔢𝔢𝔡 𝔟𝔢.'[6] And 19 having no feebleness in his faith, he regarded not his own body which was already dead (being about a hundred years old), nor the deadness of Sarah's womb; at the promise of God (I say) he doubted not 20 faithlessly, but [7] was filled with the strength of Faith,

[1] ' *The land which thou seest, to thee will I give it, and to thy seed for ever,*' Gen. xiii. 15. St. Paul (according to his frequent practice in dealing with the Old Testament) allegorises this promise. So that, as Abraham is (allegorically viewed) the type of Christian faith, he is also the heir of the world, whereof the sovereignty belongs to his spiritual children, by virtue of their union with their Divine Head.

[2] Literally, *wrath*; i.e. the wrath of God punishing the transgressions of the Law.

[3] This passage throws light on Gal. iii. 18 and 20. It should be observed that St. Paul restricts ' *the seed of Abraham* ' to the *inheritors of his faith*; and *to all this seed* (he declares) *the promise must stand firm.*

[4] Gen. xvii. 5 (LXX.). It is impossible to represent in the English the

full force of the Greek, when the same word means *nations* and *Gentiles.*

[5] Gen. xvii. 5. See the previous note.

[6] Gen. xv. 5 (LXX.). In such quotations, a few words were sufficient to recall the whole passage to Jewish readers; therefore, to make them intelligible to modern readers, it is sometimes necessary to give the context. It should be observed that this quotation alone is sufficient to prove that the majority of those to whom St. Paul was writing were familiar with the Septuagint version; for to none others could such a curtailed citation be intelligible. The hypothesis that the Roman Christians had originally been Jewish proselytes, of Gentile birth, satisfies this condition. See the introductory remarks to this Epistle.

[7] Literally, *he was in-strengthened* (i.e. *strengthened inwardly*) *by faith,*

iv. 21 and gave glory to God; being fully persuaded that what
22 He has promised He is able also to perform. Therefore '𝔥𝔦𝔰 𝔣𝔞𝔦𝔱𝔥 𝔴𝔞𝔰 𝔯𝔢𝔠𝔨𝔬𝔫𝔢𝔡 𝔱𝔬 𝔥𝔦𝔪 𝔣𝔬𝔯 𝔯𝔦𝔤𝔥𝔱𝔢𝔬𝔲𝔰𝔫𝔢𝔰𝔰.'
23 But these words were not written for his sake only,
24 but for our sakes likewise; for it will be '𝔯𝔢𝔠𝔨𝔬𝔫𝔢𝔡
𝔣𝔬𝔯 𝔯𝔦𝔤𝔥𝔱𝔢𝔬𝔲𝔰𝔫𝔢𝔰𝔰,' to us also, who have faith in Him
25 that raised from the dead our Lord Jesus; who was
given up to death for our transgressions, and raised
again to life for our justification.[1]

v. 1   Therefore, being justified by Faith, we have peace
2 with God, through our Lord Jesus Christ, through
whom also we have received entrance into this grace [2]
wherein we stand; and we exult in hope of the glory
3 of God. And not only so, but we exult also in our
sufferings; for we know that by suffering is wrought
4 stedfastness, and stedfastness is the proof of sound-
5 ness, and proof gives rise to hope; and our hope
cannot shame us in the day of trial; because the love
of God is shed forth in our hearts by the Holy
6 Spirit, who has been [3] given unto us. For while we
were yet helpless [in our sins], Christ at the ap-
7 pointed time died for sinners. Now hardly for a
righteous man will any be found to die (although
some perchance would even endure death for the
8 good), but God gives proof of His own love to us,
because while we were yet sinners Christ died for us.
9 Much more, now that we have been justified in His
blood,[4] shall we be saved through Him from the
10 wrath[5] to come. For if, when we were His enemies,
we were reconciled to God by the death of His Son,
much more, being already reconciled, shall we be
11 saved, by sharing in[6] His life. Nor is this our hope

Through faith in Christ then Christians are justified; and they rejoice in the midst of their present sufferings, being filled with the consciousness of God's love in the sacrifice of Christ for them. For by partaking in the death of Christ, they are reconciled to God, and by partaking in the life of Christ they are saved.

---

[1] i.e. that we might have an ever-living Saviour as the object of our faith, and might through that faith be united with Him, and partake of His life, and thus be justified, or accounted righteous, and (for St. Paul does not, like later theologians, separate these ideas) have the seed of all true moral life implanted in us. Compare v. 10.

[2] 'By faith' is omitted in the best MSS.

[3] Olshausen translates 'was given unto us,' viz. on the day of Pentecost. But we have elsewhere shown the mistake of those who will never allow St. Paul to use the aorist in a perfect sense. See note on 2 Cor. vii. 2. Dr. Alford, who objects to translate one

aorist participle (in the 5th verse) '*having been given,*' is obliged himself inconsistently to translate another (in the 9th verse) '*having been justified,*' and an aorist verb (11th verse), '*we have received,*' and to consent to the junction of both these aorists with 'now,' a junction which is conclusive as to its perfect use.

[4] *Justified in His blood,* i.e. *by participation in His blood;* that is, *being made partakers of His death.* Compare Rom. vi. 3–8; also Gal. ii. 20.

[5] The original has the article before 'wrath.'

[6] This 'in' should be distinguished from the preceding 'by.'

only for the time to come; but also [in our present sufferings] we exult in God, through Jesus Christ our Lord, by whom we have now received reconciliation with God.

For Christ in His own person was the representative of all mankind for salvation, as Adam was for condemnation. The Mosaic Law was added to the law of conscience, in order that sin might be felt to be a transgression of acknowledged duty, and that thus the gift of spiritual life in Christ might be given to men prepared to feel their need of it, so that man's sin might be the occasion of God's mercy.

This, therefore, is like the case [1] when, through v. 12 one man [Adam], sin entered into the world, and by sin death; and so death spread to all mankind, because all committed sin. For before the Law was given 13 [by Moses] there was sin in the world; but sin is not reckoned against the sinner, when there is no law [forbidding it]; nevertheless death reigned from 14 Adam till Moses, even over those whose sin [not being the breach of law] did not resemble the sin of Adam. Now Adam is an image of Him that was to come. But far greater is the gift than was the 15 transgression; for if by the sin of the one man [Adam], death came upon the many,[2] much more in the grace of the one man Jesus Christ has the freeness of God's [3] bounty overflowed unto the many. Moreover the boon [of God] exceeds the fruit [4] of 16 Adam's sin; for the doom came, out of one offence, a sentence of condemnation; but the gift comes, out of many offences, a sentence of acquittal. For if the 17 reign of death was established by the one man [Adam], through the sin of him alone; far more shall the reign of life be established in those who receive the overflowing fulness of the free gift of righteousness, by the one man Jesus Christ. There- 18 fore, as the fruit of one offence reached to all men, and brought upon them condemnation [the source of death]; so likewise the fruit of one acquittal shall reach [5] to all, and shall bring justification, the source [6]

---

[1] Much difficulty has been caused to interpreters here by the '*as*' (which introduces the first member of the parallel) having no answering '*so*' (nor anything equivalent to it) to introduce the second. The best view of the passage is to consider '*as*' as used elliptically for [*the case is*] *as what follows*, in which sense it is used Matt. xxv. 14 : where it is similarly without any answering '*so*.' Another view is to suppose the regular construction lost sight of in the rapidity of dictation; the second member of the parallel being virtually supplied in verses 15 to 20.

[2] Not '*many*' (A. V.), but *the many*, nearly equivalent to *all*.

[3] We take *grace* and *gift* together. Compare the same expression below, in

verse 17; literally, *the free gift and the boon of God*, an hendiadys for *the freeness of God's bounty*.

[4] Literally, *the boon is not as* [*that which was*] *wrought by one man who sinned*.

[5] We take δικαίωμα here in the same sense as in verse 16, because, first, it is difficult to suppose the same word used in the very same passage in two such different meanings as *Recte factum*, and *Decretum absolutorium* (which Wahl and most of the commentators suppose it to be). And, secondly, because otherwise it is necessary to take '*one*' differently in two parallel phrases (masculine in the one, and neuter in the other), which is unnatural.

[6] Literally, *appertaining to life*.

v. 19 of life. For as, by the disobedience of the one, the
many were made sinners; so by the obedience of the
20 one, the many shall be made righteous. And the
Law was added, that sin might abound;[1] but where
sin abounded, the gift of grace has overflowed beyond
21 [the outbreak of sin]; that as sin has reigned in
death, so grace might reign through righteousness
unto life eternal, by the work of Jesus Christ our
Lord.

vi. 1   What shall we say then? shall we[2] persist in sin
2 that the gift of grace may be more abundant? God
forbid.   We who have died[3] to sin, how can we any
3 longer live in sin? or have you forgotten that all of
us, when we were baptized into fellowship with Christ
Jesus, were baptized into fellowship with His death?
4 With Him therefore we were buried by the baptism
wherein we shared His death [when we sank beneath
the waters];[4] that even as Christ was raised up from
the dead by the glory of the Father, so we likewise
5 might walk in newness of life.   For if we have been
grafted[5] into the likeness of His death, so shall we
6 also share His resurrection.   For we know that our
old man was crucified[6] with Christ, that the sinful
7 body [of the old man][7] might be destroyed, that we
might no longer be the slaves of sin; (for he that is
8 dead is justified[8] from sin).   Now if we have shared

It is a self-contradictory perversion of this truth to conclude from it that we should persist in sin in order to call forth a greater exhibition of God's grace; for spiritual life (which is the grace) cannot co-exist with spiritual death.

---

[1] A light is thrown on this very difficult expression by vii. 13; see note on that verse.

[2] This was probably an objection made by Judaising disputants (as it has been made by their successors in other ages of the Church) against St. Paul's doctrine. They argued that if (as he said) the sin of man called forth so glorious an exhibition of the pardoning grace of God, the necessary conclusion must be, that the more men sinned the more God was glorified. Compare iii. 7, 8, and verse 15 below. We know also, that this inference was actually deduced by the Antinomian party at Corinth (see p. 352), and therefore it was the more necessary for St. Paul to refute it.

[3] The A.V. '*are dead*' does not preserve the reference in the original to a past transaction. We might here keep the aorist to its classical use, by translating (as in our former edition) *who died to sin [when we became followers of Christ]*: but this render-

ing is less simple and natural than the other.

[4] This clause, which is here left elliptical, is fully expressed in Col. ii. 12. This passage cannot be understood unless it be borne in mind that the primitive baptism was by immersion. See p. 345.

[5] Literally, *have become partakers of a vital union* [as that of a graft with the tree into which it is grafted] *of the representation of his death* [in baptism]. The meaning appears to be, *if we have shared the reality of his death, whereof we have undergone the likeness.*

[6] Observe the mis-translation in the A. V. '*is crucified.*'

[7] With 'body of sin' compare 'body of flesh,' Col. ii. 11.

[8] *Is justified*, meaning that if a criminal charge is brought against a man who died before the perpetration of the crime, he must be acquitted, since he could not have committed the act charged against him.

the death of Christ, we believe that we shall also
share His life; knowing that Christ being raised vi. 9
from the dead, can die no more; death has no more
dominion over Him. For He died once, and once 10
only, unto sin; but He lives [for ever] unto God.
Likewise reckon ye also yourselves to be dead indeed 11
unto sin, but living unto God in Christ Jesus.[1] Let 12
not sin therefore reign in your dying body, causing
you to obey its lusts; nor give up your members
to sin, as instruments of unrighteousness; but give 13
yourselves to God, as being restored to life from the
dead, and your members to His service as instruments of righteousness; for sin shall not have the 14
mastery over you, since you are not under the Law,[2]
but under grace.

The Christian's freedom from the Law consists in living in the morality of the Law, not from fear of its penalties, but as necessary fruits of the spiritual life whereof Christians partake. Hence the slaves of sin can have no part in this freedom from the Law; since they are still subject to the penalties of the Law, which are the necessary results of sin.

What then? shall we sin[3] because we are not 15
under the Law, but under grace? God forbid. Know 16
ye not that He to whose service you give yourselves,
is your real master, whether sin, whose end is death,
or obedience, whose end is righteousness. But God 17
be thanked that you, who were once the slaves of
sin, obeyed from your hearts the teaching whereby
you were moulded anew;[4] and when you were freed 18
from the slavery of sin, you became the bondsmen of
righteousness. (I speak the language of common 19
life, to show the weakness of your fleshly nature[5]
[which must be in bondage either to the one, or to
the other].) For as once you gave up the members
of your body for slaves of uncleanness and licentiousness, to work the deeds of licence; so now must you
give them up for slaves of righteousness to work the
deeds of holiness. For when you were the slaves of 20
sin, you were free from the service of righteousness.
What fruit then had you[6] in those times, from the 21

---

[1] The best MSS. omit 'our Lord.'

[2] To be 'under the law,' in St. Paul's
language, means to avoid sin from fear
of penalties attached to sin by the law.
This principle of fear is not strong
enough to keep men in the path of duty.
Union with Christ can alone give man
the mastery over sin.

[3] See note on first verse of this chapter.

[4] Literally, *the mould of teaching
into which you were transmitted.* The
metaphor is from the casting of metals.

[5] There is a striking resemblance
between this passage and the words
of Socrates recorded by Xenophon,

Mem. I. 5. For the apologetic phrase
here compare Rom. iii. 5, and Gal. iii.
15.

[6] It has been alleged that 'fruit'
(in N. T.) always means '*actions;* the
fruit of a man considered as a tree;'
and that it never means 'the fruit of
his actions.' But in fact the metaphor
is used both ways : sometimes a man
is considered as *producing* fruit ; sometimes as *gathering* or *storing* fruit.
In the former case 'bear fruit,' in the
latter 'have fruit,' is appropriately
used. Compare Rom. i. 13, and also
Rom. xv. 28 ; Phil. i. 22 ; 2 Tim. ii. 6.

deeds whereof you are now ashamed? yea, the end of

vi. 22 them is death.   But now, being freed from the
bondage of sin, and enslaved to the service of God,
your fruit is growth in holiness,[1] and its end is life

23 eternal.   For the wage of sin is death; but the gift
of God is eternal life in Christ Jesus our Lord and
master.[2]

vii. 1 [I say that you are not under the Law]; or[3] are
you ignorant, brethren (for I speak to those who
know the Law), that the dominion of the Law over

2 men lasts only during their life? thus the married
woman is bound by the Law to her husband while
he lives, but if her husband be dead, the Law which

3 bound her to him has lost its hold upon her; so that
while her husband is living if she be joined to another
man, she will be counted an adulteress; but if her
husband be dead, she is free from the Law, so as to
be no adulteress although joined to another man.
Wherefore you also, my brethren, were made dead to
the Law, by [union with] the body of Christ; that
you might be married to another, even to Him who
was raised from the dead; that we might bring forth

5 fruit unto God.   For when we were in the flesh, the
sinful passions occasioned by the Law wrought in our
members, leading us to bring forth fruit unto death.

6 But now that we have died [with Christ][4] the Law
wherein we were formerly held fast, has lost its hold
upon us: so that we are no longer in the old bondage
of the letter, but in the new service of the spirit.

7   What shall we say then? that the Law is Sin? *The Law has*

As above said, Christians are not under the Law; for the Law belongs to that sinful earthly nature to which they have died by partaking in Christ's death, having been admitted to a better spiritual service by their union with Christ's life, so that the sins of which the Law was formerly the occasion over come them no more.

---

[1] Literally, *the fruit which you possess tends to produce holiness.* In other words, *the reward of serving God is growth in holiness.*

[2] We must give 'Lord' its full meaning here. Sin was our master (verses 16, 17), Christ is now our master.

[3] *Or are you ignorant?* the *or* (which is omitted in A. V.) referring to what has gone before, and implying, *if you deny what I have said, you must be ignorant of*, &c., or, in other words, *you must acknowledge what I say, or be ignorant of*, &c. The reference here is to the assertion in verses 14 and 15 of the preceding chapter, that Christians '*are not under the law.*' For the argument of the present passage, see the marginal summary. St. Paul's view of the Christian life throughout the sixth, seventh, and eighth chapters, is that it consists

of a death and a resurrection; the new-made Christian dies to sin, to the world, to the flesh, and to the Law; this death he undergoes at his first entrance into communion with Christ, and it is both typified and realised when he is buried beneath the baptismal waters. But no sooner is he thus dead with Christ, than he rises with Him; he is made partaker of Christ's resurrection; he is united to Christ's body; he lives in Christ, and to Christ; he is no longer 'in the flesh,' but 'in the spirit.'

[4] The best MSS. have the participle in the nom. plural. It is opposed to 'when we were in the flesh,' of the preceding verse. To make it clear, this verse should have a comma after the Greek participle. As to the sense in which Christians are '*dead*,' see the preceding note.

been above said to be the occasion of sin. For when its precepts awaken the conscience to a sense of duty, the sins which before were done in ignorance, are now done in spite of the resistance of conscience. For the carnal nature of the natural man fulfils the evil, which his spiritual nature condemns. Thus a struggle is produced, in which the worse part in man triumphs over the better, the law of his flesh over the law of his mind. And man in himself (*I myself*, ver. 25) without the help of Christ's Spirit, must continue the slave of his sinful earthly nature.

That be far from us! But then I should not have known what sin was, except through the Law; thus I should not have known the sin of coveting, unless the Law had said 𝕿𝖍𝖔𝖚 𝖘𝖍𝖆𝖑𝖙 𝖓𝖔𝖙 𝖈𝖔𝖛𝖊𝖙.[1] But when vii. 8 sin had gained by the commandment a vantage ground [against me], it wrought in me all manner of coveting; (for where there is no law, sin is dead). And 9 I felt [2] that I was alive before, when I knew no law; but when the commandment came, sin rose to life, and I died; and the very commandment whose end 10 is life, was found to me the cause of death; for sin, 11 when it had gained a vantage ground by the commandment, deceived me to my fall, and slew me by [3] the sentence of the Law.

Wherefore the Law indeed is holy, and its com- 12 mandments are holy, and just, and good. Do I say 13 then that Good became to me Death?[4] Far be that from me. But I say that sin wrought this; that so it might be made manifest as sin, in working Death to me through [the knowledge of] Good; that sin might become beyond measure [5] sinful, by the commandment.

For we know that the Law is spiritual;[6] but for 14 me, I am carnal,[7] a slave sold into the captivity of

---

[1] Exod. xx. 17 (LXX.). This illustration appears conclusive against the view of Erasmus and others who understood the following statement ('*without the Law, sin is dead*') to mean that the Law irritates and provokes sin into action, on the principle of 'nitimur in vetitum.' For the lust of concupiscence is quite as active in an ignorant Heathen as in an instructed Pharisee.

[2] For this meaning of 'live' see 1 Thess. iii. 8.

[3] Literally, *by the commandment*; which denounced death against its violators. See note on 1 Cor. xv. 56.

[4] Literally, *is it become*? equivalent to *do I say that it became*? If with several good MSS. we replace the perfect by the aorist, the difficulty is removed. We must supply ' become death' again after 'sin.'

[5] This explains Rom. v. 20. In both passages, St. Paul states the object of the law to be to lay down, as it were, a boundary line which should mark the limits of right and wrong; so that sin, by transgressing this line, might manifest its real nature, and be distinctly recognised for what it is. The Law was

not given to provoke man to sin (as some have understood, Rom. v. 20) but to stimulate the conscience into activity.

[6] It may be asked, how is this consistent with many passages where St. Paul speaks of the Law as a carnal ordinance, and opposes it as *letter* to *spirit*? The answer is, that here he speaks of the Law under its moral aspect, as is plain from the whole context.

[7] Scarcely anything in this Epistle has caused more controversy than the question whether St. Paul, in the following description of the struggle between the flesh and the spirit, wherein the flesh gains the victory, meant to describe his own actual state. The best answer to this question is a comparison between vi. 17 and 20 (where he tells the Roman Christians that they *are no longer the slaves of sin*), vii. 14 (where he says *I am* CARNAL, *a slave sold into the captivity of sin*), and viii. 4 (where he includes himself among those *who live not the life of the flesh, but the life of the spirit*, i.e. who are NOT CARNAL). It is surely clear that these descriptions

vii. 15 sin.   What I do, I acknowledge not; for I do not
16 what I would, but what I hate.   But if my will is
against my deeds, I thereby acknowledge the good-
17 ness of the Law.   And now it is no more I myself
who do the evil, but it is the sin which dwells in me.
18 For I know that in me, that is, in my flesh, good
abides not; for to will is present with me, but to do
19 the right is absent; the good that I would, I do not;
20 but the evil which I would not, that I do.   Now if
my own[1] will is against my deeds, it is no more I
myself who do them, but the sin which dwells in me.
21 I find then this law, that though my will is to do
22 good, yet evil is present with me; for I consent gladly
23 to the law of God in my inner man; but I behold
another law in my members, warring against the
law of my mind, and making me captive to the law
24 of sin which is in my members.   O wretched man
that I am! who shall deliver me from this body
of death?
25   I thank God [that He has now delivered me]
through Jesus Christ our Lord.

So then in myself,[2] though I am subject in my

---

cannot be meant to belong to the same person *at the same time.*   The best commentary on the whole passage (vii. 7 to viii. 13) is to be found in the condensed expression of the same truths contained in Gal. v. 16-18; *Walk in the spirit, and* YE SHALL NOT FULFIL THE DESIRE OF THE FLESH; *for the desire of the flesh fights against the spirit, and the desire of the spirit fights against the flesh; and this variance between the flesh and the spirit would hinder you from doing that which your will prefers; but if you be led by the spirit, you are not under the Law.*

[1] The 'I,' in I will is emphatic.

[2] Αὐτὸς ἐγώ, *I in myself,* i.e. without the help of God.   This expression is the key to the whole passage.   St. Paul, from verse 14 to verse 24, has been speaking of himself as he was *in himself,* i.e. in his natural state of helplessness, with a conscience enlightened, but a will enslaved; the better self struggling vainly against the worse.   Every man must continue in this state, unless he be redeemed from it by the Spirit of God.   Christians are (so far as God is concerned) redeemed already from this state; but *in themselves,* and so far as they live to themselves, they are still in

bondage.   The redemption which they (*potentially,* if not *actually*) possess, is the subject of the 8th chapter.   Leighton (though his view of the whole passage would not have entirely coincided with that given above) most beautifully expresses the contrast between these two states (of bondage and deliverance) in his sermon on Rom. viii. 35: 'Is this he that so lately cried out, *O wretched man that I am! who shall deliver me?* that now triumphs, O happy man! *who shall separate us from the love of Christ?* Yes, it is the same.   Pained then with the thoughts of that miserable conjunction with a body of death, and so crying out, who will deliver?   Now he hath found a deliverer to do that for him, to whom he is for ever united.   So vast a difference is there betwixt a Christian taken *in himself* and *in Christ.*'   Against the above view of verse 25, it may be said that the more natural and obvious meaning of αὐτὸς ἐγὼ is '*I Paul myself,*' '*I myself who write this;*' as has lately been urged with much force by Dean Alford.   He advocates the distinction between this verse and viii. 4, which is maintained by Olshausen and others, who think the spiritual man is described as 'serving the flesh

mind to the law of God, yet in my flesh I am subject
to the law of sin.

But with that
help this sin-
ful earthly
nature is van-
quished in the
Christian,
and he is en-
abled to live,
not according
to the *carnal*
part of his
nature, but
according to
the *spiritual*
part. God's
true children
are those only
who are thus
enabled, by
the *indwelling*
Spirit of
Christ, to
conquer their
earthly
nature.

Now, therefore, there is no condemnation to those viii. 1.
who are in Christ Jesus; [1] for the law of the Spirit of 2
life in Christ Jesus [2] has freed me from the law of
sin and death.   For God (which was impossible to 3
the Law, because by the flesh it had no power), by
sending His own Son in the likeness of sinful flesh,
and on behalf of sin, overcame [3] sin in the flesh; [4] to 4
the end, that the decrees of the Law might be fulfilled
in us, who walk not after the Flesh, but after the
Spirit.[5]   For they who live after the flesh, mind 5
fleshly things; but they who live after the Spirit
mind spiritual things, and [6] the fleshly mind is death; 6
but the spiritual mind is life and peace.   Because the 7
fleshly mind is enmity against God; for it is not subject to the law of God, nor can be; and they whose life 8
is in the Flesh cannot please God.   But your life is 9
not in the Flesh, but in the Spirit, if indeed the Spirit
of God be dwelling in you; and if any man has not
the Spirit of Christ, he is not Christ's.   But if Christ 10
be in you, though your body be dead, because of sin
[to which its nature tends], yet your spirit is life,[7]

by the law of sin,' but yet as 'not
walking after the flesh.'   According to
this interpretation, St. Paul here declares, that *he himself is in bondage to
the law of sin, in his flesh*; but means
only that 'the flesh is still, even in
the spiritual man, subject (*essentially*,
not practically) to the law of sin.' (Alford.) We would not venture dogmatically to pronounce this view untenable;
yet its advocates must acknowledge
that it is extremely difficult to reconcile it with the *slavery* of vi. 17–20.

[1] The clause which follows, from
'who walk' to 'Spirit,' is omitted in
the best MSS., having (it would seem)
been introduced by a clerical error
from verse 4.

[2] Winer wishes to join in 'Christ
Jesus' with the verb 'freed,' not
with the preceding words; but there
are so many examples of a similar construction in St. Paul's style, that we
think his reasons insufficient to justify
a departure from the more obvious
view.

[3] Literally, *condemned*, i.e. *put it to
rebuke, worsted it.*   Compare Heb. xi.
7.

[4] '*In the flesh*,' that is to say, *in the*

very seat of its power.

[5] The contrast between the victory
thus obtained by the spirit, with the
previous subjection of the soul to the
flesh, is thus beautifully described by
Tertullian:—'When the Soul is wedded
to the Spirit, the Flesh follows—like
the handmaid who follows her wedded
mistress to the husband's home—being
thenceforward no longer the servant of
the Soul, but of the Spirit.'   The whole
passage forms an excellent commentary
on this part of the Epistle.   See a
fuller extract in the larger editions.

[6] Winer sneers at Tholuck's remark
(which the latter has since modified),
that the conjunction (*for*, A. V.) is a
mere *transition particle* here; but yet
what else is it, when it does not introduce a reason for a preceding proposition?   In these cases of successive
clauses each connected thus with the
preceding, they all appear to refer back
to the first preceding clause, and therefore all but the first conjunction might
be represented by *and*.   Just in the same
way as *but* is used in English; as, for
example, 'But ye are washed, but ye
are sanctified.'

[7] The word here used is in St. Paul's

because of righteousness [which dwells within it];
viii. 11 yea, if the Spirit of Him who raised Jesus from the
dead be dwelling in you, He who raised Christ from
the dead shall endow with life also your dying bodies,
12 by His [1] Spirit which dwells within you. Therefore,
brethren, we are debtors bound not to the Flesh, that
13 we should live after the Flesh [but to the Spirit]; for
if you live after the Flesh, you are doomed to die;
but if by the Spirit you destroy the deeds of the body,
in their death[2] you will attain to life.

14 For all who are led by God's Spirit, and they alone,[3]
15 are the sons of God. For you have not received a
Spirit of bondage, that you should go back again to
the state of slavish fear,[4] but you have received a
Spirit of adoption wherein we cry [unto God] saying
16 '𝕱𝖆𝖙𝖍𝖊𝖗.'[5] The Spirit itself bears witness with our
17 own spirit, that we are the children of God. And if
children, then heirs: heirs of God, and joint heirs
with Christ; that if now we share His sufferings, we
18 should hereafter share His glory. For I reckon that
the sufferings of this present time are nothing worth,
when set against the glory which shall soon[6] be
19 revealed unto us. For the longing of the creation
looks eagerly for the time when [the glory of] the
20 sons of God shall be revealed. For the creation was
made subject to decay,[7] not by its own will, but
because of Him who subjected it thereto,[8] in hope:
21 for[9] the creation itself also shall be delivered from its

Such persons have an inward consciousness of child-like love to God (Abba), and they anticipate a future and more perfect state when this relation to God will have its full development (ἀπο-κάλυψις). And their longing for a future perfection is shared by all created beings upon earth, whose discontent at present imperfection points to another state freed from evil. And this feeling is (26, 27) implanted in

writings scarcely represented adequately by *life*; it generally means more than this, viz. *life triumphant over death.*

[1] The MSS. are divided here. One reading must be translated *because of* instead of *by*. This will make the clause exactly parallel with the end of verse 10. Tholuck gives an able summary of the arguments in favour of the accusative reading.

[2] This translation is necessary to represent the reference to *death* as expressed in the preceding verb (*mortify*, A. V.).

[3] *They and they alone, they and not the carnal seed of Abraham.*

[4] *Back again.* Compare Gal. iv. 9.

[5] See note on Gal. iv. 6.

[6] *Which is about to be revealed, which shall soon be revealed.*

[7] The word used here (*vanity*, A.V.) means *the transitory nature* which causes all the animated creation so

rapidly to pass away.

[8] God is probably meant by 'Him who subjected.' The difficulties which have been felt with regard to this expression are resolvable (like all the difficulties of Theism) into the permission of evil. This awful mystery St. Paul leaves unsolved; but he tells us to wait patiently for its solution, and encourages us to do so by his inspired declarations, in this and other places (as 1 Cor. xv. 25, &c.), that the reign of evil will not be eternal, but that good will ultimately and completely triumph. It should be observed that Evil is always represented in Scripture as in its nature opposed to God, not as included necessarily in His plan; even where God is represented as subjecting His creatures to its temporary dominion.

[9] We agree with Dean Alford that it is better here not to render, as some do, ' *in hope that*; ' for, were this

Christians by
the Spirit of
God, who sug-
gests their
prayers and
longings. slavery to death, and shall gain the freedom of the
sons of God when they are glorified.[1]　For we know viii. 2
that the whole creation is groaning together, and
suffering the pangs of labour, which[2] have not yet
brought forth the birth.　And not only they, but our- 23
selves also, who have received the Spirit for the first
fruits[3] [of our inheritance], even we ourselves are
groaning inwardly, longing for the adoption[4] which
shall ransom our body from its bondage.　For our 24
salvation[5] lies in hope; but hope possessed is not
hope, since a man cannot hope for what he sees in
his possession; but if we hope for things not seen, 25
we stedfastly[6] endure the present, and long earnestly
for the future.　And, even as[7] we long for our 26
redemption, so the Spirit gives help to our weakness;
for we know not what we should pray for as we
ought; but the Spirit itself makes intercession for
us, with groans [for deliverance] which words cannot
utter.　But He who searches our hearts knows 27
[though it be unspoken] what is the desire of the

---

correct, the words 'the creation itself' would not be so emphatically
repeated. See his commentary on the
passage.

[1] Literally, *the freedom which belongs
to the glorification of the sons of God.*

[2] Literally, *continuing to suffer the
pangs of labour even until now.* St. Paul
here suggests an argument as original
as it is profound. The very struggles
which all animated beings make against
pain and death, show (he says) that
pain and death are not a part of the
proper laws of their nature, but rather
a bondage imposed upon them from
without. Thus every groan and tear is
an unconscious prophecy of liberation
from the power of evil. St. Augustine
extends the same argument in the *Con-
fessions* (book XIII.) as follows:—'Even
in that miserable restlessness of the
spirits, who fell away and discovered
their own darkness when bared of the
clothing of Thy light, dost Thou sufficiently reveal how noble Thou madest
the reasonable creature; to which nothing will suffice to yield a happy rest,
less than Thee.' See also *De Civ.
Dei*, l. 22, c. 1:—'The nature which enjoyed God shows that it was formed
good, even by its very defect, in that
it is therefore miserable because it en-
joyeth not God.' (Oxford translation,
Library of Fathers.)

[3] See note on 1 Cor. i. 22.

[4] *Adoption to sonship*; by which a
slave was emancipated and made 'no
longer a slave but a son.' (Gal. iv. 7.)
In one sense St. Paul taught that Christians had already received this *adoption*
(compare Rom. viii. 15, Gal. iv. 5, Eph.
i. 5); they were already made the sons
of God in Christ. (Rom. viii. 16, Gal.
iii. 26.) So, in a yet lower sense, the
Jews under the old dispensation had
the *adoption to sonship*; see ix. 4.
But in this passage he teaches us that
this adoption is not perfect during the
present life; there is still a higher
sense, in which it is future, and the
object of earnest longing to those who
are already in the lower sense the sons
of God.

[5] Literally *we were saved*, i.e. at our
conversion; for the context does not
oblige us to take the aorist here as a
perfect. The exact translation would
be, ' *the salvation whereto we were called
lies in hope.*'

[6] The verb denotes, *we long earnestly
for the future*; the prepositional phrase
implies *with stedfast endurance of the
present.*

[7] After *in like manner*, we must
supply *as we long* from the preceding
clause; and the object of *long* is *our
redemption* (by verse 23).

Spirit,[1] because He intercedes for the saints according to the will of God.

iii. 28   Moreover, we know that all things[2] work together for good to those who love God, who have been called 29 according to His purpose.   For those whom He foreknew, He also predestined to be made like[3] to the pattern of His Son, that many brethren might be 30 joined to Him, the firstborn.   And those whom He predestined, them He also called; and whom He called, them He also justified; and whom he justified, them 31 He also glorified.   What shall we say then to these things?   If God be for us, who can be against us? 32 He that spared not His own Son, but gave Him up for us all, how shall He not with Him also freely give 33 us all things?   What accuser can harm God's chosen? 34 it is God who justifies them.[4]   What judge can doom us?   It is Christ who died, nay, rather, who is risen from the dead; yea, who is at the right hand of God, 35 who also makes intercession for us.   Who can separate us from the love of Christ?   Can suffering, or straitness of distress, or persecution, or famine, or nakedness, or the peril of our lives, or the swords of our enemies? [though we may say,] as it is written, 36 '𝕱𝖔𝖗 𝕿𝖍𝖞 𝖘𝖆𝖐𝖊 𝖜𝖊 𝖆𝖗𝖊 𝖐𝖎𝖑𝖑𝖊𝖉 𝖆𝖑𝖑 𝖙𝖍𝖊 𝖉𝖆𝖞 𝖑𝖔𝖓𝖌; 𝖜𝖊 𝖆𝖗𝖊 𝖆𝖈= 37 𝖈𝖔𝖚𝖓𝖙𝖊𝖉 𝖆𝖘 𝖘𝖍𝖊𝖊𝖕 𝖋𝖔𝖗 𝖙𝖍𝖊 𝖘𝖑𝖆𝖚𝖌𝖍𝖙𝖊𝖗.'[5]   Nay, in all these things we are more than conquerors through Him that 38 loved us.   For I am persuaded that neither death, nor life, nor all the[6] Principalities and Powers of Angels,

Hence in the midst of their persecutions Christians are more than conquerors; for they feel that all works together for their good. God has called them to share in His glory, and no human accusers or judges, no earthly sufferings, no power in the whole creation, can separate them from His love.

---

[1] This passage is well explained by Archbishop Leighton, in the following beautiful words: 'The work of the Spirit is in exciting the heart at times of prayer, to break forth in ardent desires to God, whatsoever the words be, whether new or old, yea possibly without words; and then most powerful when it *words it* least, but vents in sighs and groans that cannot be expressed. Our Lord understands the language of these perfectly, and likes it best; He knows and approves the meaning of His own Spirit; He looks not to the outward appearance, the shell of words, as men do.' Leighton's *Exposition of Lord's Prayer.*

[2] *All things*, viz. whether sad or joyful. We must remember that this was written in the midst of persecution, and in the expectation of bonds and imprisonment. See verses 17, 18, and 35, and Acts xx. 23.

[3] *Like in suffering* seems meant.

Compare Phil. iii. 10: 'The fellowship of His sufferings, being made conformable to His death.' [Does not this limit it too much? Compare 2 Cor. iii. 18: 'We are gradually transformed into the same likeness.' And see also 1 Cor. xv. 49. H.]

[4] St. Paul is here writing and thinking of his own case, and that of his brethren, liable daily to be dragged by their accusers before the tribunals. No accusers could harm them, because God acquitted them; no judicial condemnation could injure them, because Christ was the assessor of that tribunal before which they must be tried. The beauty and eloquence of the passage (as well as its personal reference to the circumstances of its writer and its readers) are much marred by placing marks of interrogation after *justifies* and *died.*

[5] Ps. xliv. 22 (LXX.).

[6] The expressions *principalities* and *powers* were terms applied in the

nor things present, nor things to come, nor things viii.39 above, nor things below, nor any power in the whole creation, shall be able to separate us from the love of God which is in Christ Jesus our Lord.

The fact that God has adopted Christians as His peculiar people, and rejected the Jews from their exclusive privileges, is in accordance with His former dealings. For not all the descendants of Abraham, but only a selected portion of them, were chosen by God.

I speak the truth in Christ—(and my conscience ix. 1 bears me witness, with the Holy Spirit's testimony, that I lie not)—I have great heaviness, and unceasing 2 sorrow in my heart; yea, I could wish that I myself 3 were cast out from Christ as an accursed thing, for the sake of my brethren, my kinsmen according to the flesh; who are the seed of Israel, whom God adopted 4 for His children, whose were the glory of the Shekinah, and the Covenants, and the Lawgiving, and the service of the temple, and the promises of blessing. Whose fathers were the Patriarchs, and of whom (as 5 to His flesh) was born the Christ who is over all, God blessed for ever.   Amen.

Yet I speak not as if the promise of God had fallen 6 to the ground; for not all are Israel who are of Israel, nor because all are the seed of Abraham, are they all 7 the children of Abraham; but '𝔍𝔫 𝔦𝔰𝔞𝔞𝔠 𝔰𝔥𝔞𝔩𝔩 𝔱𝔥𝔶 𝔰𝔢𝔢𝔡 𝔟𝔢 𝔠𝔞𝔩𝔩𝔢𝔡.'[1]   That is, not the children of the flesh of 8 Abraham are the sons of God, but his children of the promise are counted for his seed.   For thus spake the 9 word of promise, saying, '𝔄𝔱 𝔱𝔥𝔦𝔰 𝔱𝔦𝔪𝔢 𝔴𝔦𝔩𝔩 𝔍 𝔠𝔬𝔪𝔢, 𝔞𝔫𝔡 𝔖𝔞𝔯𝔞𝔥 𝔰𝔥𝔞𝔩𝔩 𝔥𝔞𝔳𝔢 𝔞 𝔰𝔬𝔫,'[2] [so that Ishmael, although the son of Abraham, had no part in the promise]. And not only so, but [Esau likewise was shut out; 10 for] when Rebekah had conceived two sons by the same husband, our forefather Isaac, yea, while they 11 were not yet born, and had done nothing either good or bad (that God's purpose according to election might abide, coming not from the works of the [3] called, but from the will of The Caller,) it was declared unto her '𝔗𝔥𝔢 𝔢𝔩𝔡𝔢𝔯 𝔰𝔥𝔞𝔩𝔩 𝔰𝔢𝔯𝔳𝔢 𝔱𝔥𝔢 𝔶𝔬𝔲𝔫𝔤𝔢𝔯;'[4] according to 12 that which is written, '𝔍𝔞𝔠𝔬𝔟 𝔍 𝔩𝔬𝔳𝔢𝔡, 𝔟𝔲𝔱 𝔈𝔰𝔞𝔲 𝔍 13 𝔥𝔞𝔱𝔢𝔡.'[5]

The Jews can-not deny

What shall we say, then?   Shall we call God unjust 14

Jewish theology to divisions of the hierarchy of angels, and, as such, were familiar to St. Paul's Jewish readers. Compare Eph. i. 21, and Col. i. 16.
[1] Gen. xxi. 12 (LXX.).   Compare Gal. iv. 22.   The context is, ' *Let it not be grievous in thy sight, because of the lad* [*Ishmael*] *and because of thy bondwoman* [*Hagar*], *for in Isaac shall thy*

seed be called.'
[2] Gen. xviii. 10, from LXX. not verbatim, but apparently from memory.
[3] Literally, *coming not from works, but from the Caller.*
[4] Gen. xxv. 23 (LXX.).   The context is, ' *Two nations are in thy womb, and the elder shall serve the younger.*'
[5] Mal. i. 2, 3 (LXX.).

[because He has cast off the seed of Abraham] ? That God's right to reject some
ix. 15 be far from us. For to Moses He saith, ' **I will have** and select others according to His will, since it is asserted in their own Scriptures in the case of Pharaoh. It may be objected that such a view represents God's will as the arbitrary cause of man's actions; the answer is, that the created being cannot investigate the causes which may have determined the will of his Creator.
mercy on whom I will have mercy, and I will have com-
16 **passion on whom I will have compassion.**' [1] So then,
the choice comes not from man's will, nor from man's
17 speed, but from God's mercy. And thus the Scripture
says to Pharaoh, ' **Even for this end did I raise thee up,**
that I might show my power in thee, and that my name
18 **might be declared throughout all the earth.**' [2] According to His will, therefore, He has mercy on one, and
19 hardens another. Thou wilt say to me, then, [3] 'Why
does God still blame us? for who can resist His will?'
20 Nay, rather, oh man, who art thou that disputest
against God ? ' **Shall the thing formed say to him that**
21 **formed it, Why hast thou made me thus?**' [4] '**Hath not**

[1] Exod. xxxiii. 19 (LXX.).

[2] Exod. ix. 16, according to LXX.,
with two slight changes.

[3] 'Thou wilt say' .... Here comes
the great question — no longer made
from the standing-point of the Jew, but
proceeding from the universal feeling of
justice. St. Paul answers the question
by treating the subject as one above the
comprehension of the human intellect,
when considered in itself objectively.
If it be once acknowledged that there
is any difference between the character
and ultimate fate of a good and a bad
man, the intellect is logically led, step
by step, to contemplate the will of the
Creator as the cause of this difference.
The question ' why hast thou made me
thus?' will equally occur and be
equally perplexing in any system of
religion, either natural or revealed. It
is, in fact, a difficulty springing at once
from the permitted existence of evil.
Scripture considers men under two
points of view ; first, as created by God,
and secondly, as free moral agents themselves. These two points of view are,
to the intellect of man, irreconcilable ;
yet both must be true, since the reason
convinces us of the one, and the conscience of the other. St. Paul here is
considering men under the first of these
aspects, as the creatures of God, entirely
dependent on God's will. It is to be
observed that he does not say that
God's will is arbitrary, but only that
men are entirely dependent on God's
will. The reasons by which God's will
itself is determined are left in the in-
scrutable mystery which conceals God's
nature from man.

The objection and the answer given

to it, partly here and partly chap. iii. 6,
may be stated as follows :—

Objector.—If men are so entirely dependent on God's will, how can He with
justice blame their actions ?

Answer.—By the very constitution
of thy nature thou art compelled to
acknowledge the blame-worthiness of
certain actions and the justice of their
punishment (iii. 6); therefore it is self-
contradictory to say that a certain intellectual view of man's dependence on
God would make these actions innocent ; thou art forced to feel them
guilty whether thou wilt or no, and
(ix. 20) it is vain to argue against
the constitution of thy nature, or its
Author.

The metaphysical questions relating
to this subject which have divided the
Christian world are left unsolved by
Scripture, which does not attempt to
reconcile the apparent inconsistency
between the objective and subjective
views of man and his actions. Hence
many have been led to neglect one side
of the truth for the sake of making a
consistent theory: thus the Pelagians
have denied the dependence of man's
will on God, and the Fatalists have
denied the freedom of man's moral
agency.

We may further observe that St.
Paul does not here explicitly refer to
eternal happiness or to its opposite.
His main subject is the national rejection of the Jews, and the above more
general topics are only incidentally
introduced.

[4] Isaiah xlv. 9. Not literally from
either LXX. or Hebrew: but apparently from memory out of LXX,

𝔱𝔥𝔢 𝔭𝔬𝔱𝔱𝔢𝔯 𝔭𝔬𝔴𝔢𝔯 𝔬𝔟𝔢𝔯 𝔱𝔥𝔢 𝔠𝔩𝔞𝔫,'[1] to make out of the same lump one vessel for honour and one for dishonour? But what if God (though willing to show forth His wrath, and to make known His power) endured with much long-suffering vessels of wrath, fitted for destruction, [and cast them not at once away]? And what if thus He purposed to make known the riches of His glory bestowed upon vessels of mercy, which He had before prepared for glory? And such are we, whom He has called not only from among the Jews, but from among the Gentiles, as He saith also in Hosea, ' 𝔍 𝔴𝔦𝔩𝔩 𝔠𝔞𝔩𝔩 𝔱𝔥𝔢𝔪 𝔪𝔶 𝔭𝔢𝔬𝔭𝔩𝔢 𝔴𝔥𝔦𝔠𝔥 𝔴𝔢𝔯𝔢 𝔫𝔬𝔱 𝔪𝔶 𝔭𝔢𝔬𝔭𝔩𝔢, 𝔞𝔫𝔡 𝔥𝔢𝔯 𝔟𝔢𝔩𝔬𝔳𝔢𝔡 𝔴𝔥𝔦𝔠𝔥 𝔴𝔞𝔰 𝔫𝔬𝔱 𝔟𝔢𝔩𝔬𝔳𝔢𝔡;[2] 𝔞𝔫𝔡 𝔦𝔱 𝔰𝔥𝔞𝔩𝔩 𝔠𝔬𝔪𝔢 𝔱𝔬 𝔭𝔞𝔰𝔰 𝔱𝔥𝔞𝔱 𝔦𝔫 𝔱𝔥𝔢 𝔭𝔩𝔞𝔠𝔢 𝔴𝔥𝔢𝔯𝔢 𝔦𝔱 𝔴𝔞𝔰 𝔰𝔞𝔦𝔡 𝔲𝔫𝔱𝔬 𝔱𝔥𝔢𝔪, 𝔜𝔢 𝔞𝔯𝔢 𝔫𝔬𝔱 𝔪𝔶 𝔭𝔢𝔬𝔭𝔩𝔢, 𝔱𝔥𝔢𝔯𝔢 𝔰𝔥𝔞𝔩𝔩 𝔱𝔥𝔢𝔶 𝔟𝔢 𝔠𝔞𝔩𝔩𝔢𝔡 𝔱𝔥𝔢 𝔰𝔬𝔫𝔰 𝔬𝔣 𝔱𝔥𝔢 𝔩𝔦𝔳𝔦𝔫𝔤 𝔊𝔬𝔡.'[3] But Esaias cries concerning Israel, saying, ' 𝔗𝔥𝔬𝔲𝔤𝔥 𝔱𝔥𝔢 𝔫𝔲𝔪𝔟𝔢𝔯 𝔬𝔣 𝔱𝔥𝔢 𝔰𝔬𝔫𝔰 𝔬𝔣 𝔍𝔰𝔯𝔞𝔢𝔩 𝔟𝔢 𝔞𝔰 𝔱𝔥𝔢 𝔰𝔞𝔫𝔡 𝔬𝔣 𝔱𝔥𝔢 𝔰𝔢𝔞, [𝔬𝔫𝔩𝔶] 𝔱𝔥𝔢 𝔯𝔢𝔪𝔫𝔞𝔫𝔱[4] 𝔰𝔥𝔞𝔩𝔩 𝔟𝔢 𝔰𝔞𝔳𝔢𝔡; 𝔣𝔬𝔯 𝔥𝔢 𝔡𝔬𝔱𝔥 𝔠𝔬𝔪𝔭𝔩𝔢𝔱𝔢 𝔥𝔦𝔰 𝔯𝔢𝔠𝔨𝔬𝔫𝔦𝔫𝔤, 𝔞𝔫𝔡 𝔠𝔲𝔱𝔱𝔢𝔱𝔥 𝔦𝔱 𝔰𝔥𝔬𝔯𝔱 𝔦𝔫 𝔯𝔦𝔤𝔥𝔱𝔢𝔬𝔲𝔰𝔫𝔢𝔰𝔰; 𝔶𝔢𝔞, 𝔞 𝔰𝔥𝔬𝔯𝔱 𝔯𝔢𝔠𝔨𝔬𝔫𝔦𝔫𝔤 𝔴𝔦𝔩𝔩 𝔱𝔥𝔢 𝔏𝔬𝔯𝔡 𝔪𝔞𝔨𝔢 𝔲𝔭𝔬𝔫 𝔱𝔥𝔢 𝔢𝔞𝔯𝔱𝔥.'[5] And as Esaias had said before, ' 𝔈𝔵𝔠𝔢𝔭𝔱 𝔱𝔥𝔢 𝔏𝔬𝔯𝔡 𝔬𝔣 𝔖𝔞𝔟𝔞𝔬𝔱𝔥 𝔥𝔞𝔡 𝔩𝔢𝔣𝔱 𝔲𝔰 𝔞 𝔰𝔢𝔢𝔡 𝔯𝔢𝔪𝔞𝔦𝔫𝔦𝔫𝔤, 𝔴𝔢 𝔥𝔞𝔡 𝔟𝔢𝔢𝔫 𝔞𝔰 𝔖𝔬𝔡𝔬𝔪, 𝔞𝔫𝔡 𝔥𝔞𝔡 𝔟𝔢𝔢𝔫 𝔪𝔞𝔡𝔢 𝔩𝔦𝔨𝔢 𝔲𝔫𝔱𝔬 𝔊𝔬𝔪𝔬𝔯𝔯𝔥𝔞.'[6] What shall we say, then? We say that the Gen-

Margin notes:
ix. 22

23

24

25

26

27

28

29

30

Also the Jewish Scriptures speak of the calling of the Gentiles and the rejection of the disobedient Jews.

The cause of this rejection

There is also a very similar passage in Isaiah xxix. 16, where, however, the context has less bearing on St. Paul's subject than in the place above cited.

[1] Jeremiah xviii. 6, not quoted literally, but according to the sense. In this and in other similar references to the Old Testament, a few words were sufficient to recall the whole passage to St. Paul's Jewish readers (compare Rom. iv. 18); therefore, to comprehend his argument, it is often necessary to refer to the context of the passage from which he quotes. The passage in Jeremiah referred to is as follows:—*Then I went down to the potter's house, and behold he wrought a work on the wheels. And the vessel that he made of clay was marred in the hands of the potter; so he made it again another vessel, as seemed good to the potter to make it. O house of Israel, cannot I do with you as this potter, saith the Lord. Behold, as the clay is in the potter's hand, so are ye in my hand, O house of Israel. At what instant I shall speak concerning a nation and concerning a kingdom, to pluck up and to pull down and to de-* stroy it; if that nation against whom I have pronounced turn from their evil, I will repent of the evil that I thought to do unto them. And at what instant I shall speak concerning a nation and concerning a kingdom, to build and to plant it; if it do evil in my sight, that it obey not my voice, then I will repent of the good wherewith I said I would benefit them. Similar passages might be quoted from the Apocryphal books; and it might be said that the above-cited passage of Isaiah was referred to here. Yet this from Jeremiah is so apposite to St. Paul's argument, that he probably refers especially to it.

[2] Hosea ii. 23 (LXX. almost verbatim).

[3] Hosea i. 10 (LXX.).

[4] Compare *remnant*, xi. 5, *left a remnant*, xi. 4, and *left a seed remaining*, ix. 29; all referring to the same subject, viz. the exclusion of the majority of the Israelites from God's favour.

[5] Isaiah x. 22, 23 (LXX. almost verbatim).

[6] Isaiah i. 9 (LXX.).

tiles, though they sought not after righteousness, have
attained to righteousness, even the righteousness of

x. 31 Faith; but that the house of Israel, though they sought
a law of righteousness, have not attained thereto.

32 And why? Because [1] they sought it not by Faith, but
33 thought to gain it by the works of the Law; for they
stumbled against the stone of stumbling, as it is written, '𝕭𝖊𝖍𝖔𝖑𝖉 𝕴 𝖑𝖆𝖞 𝖎𝖓 𝖅𝖎𝖔𝖓 𝖆 𝖘𝖙𝖔𝖓𝖊 𝖔𝖋 𝖘𝖙𝖚𝖒𝖇𝖑𝖎𝖓𝖌, 𝖆𝖓𝖉 𝖆
𝖗𝖔𝖈𝖐 𝖔𝖋 𝖔𝖋𝖋𝖊𝖓𝖈𝖊; 𝖆𝖓𝖉 𝖓𝖔 𝖒𝖆𝖓 𝖙𝖍𝖆𝖙 𝖍𝖆𝖙𝖍 𝖋𝖆𝖎𝖙𝖍 𝖎𝖓 𝕳𝖎𝖒 𝖘𝖍𝖆𝖑𝖑
𝖇𝖊 𝖈𝖔𝖓𝖋𝖔𝖚𝖓𝖉𝖊𝖉.' [2]

x. 1   Brethren, my heart's desire and my prayer to God
2 for Israel is, that they may be saved; for I bear them
witness that they have a zeal for God, yet not guided
3 by knowledge of God; [3] for because they knew not
the righteousness of God, and sought to establish their
own righteousness, therefore they submitted not to
4 the righteousness of God.   For the end of the Law is
Christ, that all may attain righteousness who have
5 faith in Him.   For Moses writes concerning the
righteousness of the Law, saying, '𝕿𝖍𝖊 𝖒𝖆𝖓 𝖙𝖍𝖆𝖙 𝖍𝖆𝖙𝖍
6 𝖉𝖔𝖓𝖊 𝖙𝖍𝖊𝖘𝖊 𝖙𝖍𝖎𝖓𝖌𝖘 𝖘𝖍𝖆𝖑𝖑 𝖑𝖎𝖛𝖊 𝖙𝖍𝖊𝖗𝖊𝖎𝖓;' [4] but the righteousness of Faith speaks in this wise.   Say not in thine
heart, '𝖂𝖍𝖔 𝖘𝖍𝖆𝖑𝖑 𝖆𝖘𝖈𝖊𝖓𝖉 𝖎𝖓𝖙𝖔 𝖍𝖊𝖆𝖛𝖊𝖓?' [5] that is, 'Who
7 can bring down Christ from heaven?' nor say, '𝖂𝖍𝖔
𝖘𝖍𝖆𝖑𝖑 𝖉𝖊𝖘𝖈𝖊𝖓𝖉 𝖎𝖓𝖙𝖔 𝖙𝖍𝖊 𝖆𝖇𝖞𝖘𝖘?' that is, 'Who can raise
8 up Christ from the dead?'   But how speaks it? '𝕿𝖍𝖊
𝖂𝖔𝖗𝖉 𝖎𝖘 𝖓𝖎𝖌𝖍 𝖙𝖍𝖊𝖊, 𝖊𝖛𝖊𝖓 𝖎𝖓 𝖙𝖍𝖞 𝖒𝖔𝖚𝖙𝖍 𝖆𝖓𝖉 𝖎𝖓 𝖙𝖍𝖞 𝖍𝖊𝖆𝖗𝖙;'

of the Jews was, that they persisted in a false idea of righteousness, as consisting in outward works and rites, and refused the true righteousness manifested to them in Christ, who was the end of the Law (x. 4). The Jew considers righteousness as the outward obedience to certain enactments (x. 5). The Christian considers righteousness as proceeding from the inward faith of the heart. Whoever has this faith, whether Jew or Gentile, shall be admitted into God's favour.

---

[1] Observe that in the preceding part of the chapter God is spoken of as rejecting the Jews according to His own will; whereas here a moral reason is given for their rejection. This illustrates what was said in a previous note of the difference between the objective and subjective points of view.

[2] Isaiah xxviii. 16, apparently from LXX., but not verbatim, 'stone of stumbling and rock of offence' being interpolated and not found exactly anywhere in Isaiah, though in viii. 14 there are words nearly similar.   Compare also Matt. xxi. 44.

[3] The word for *knowledge* here is very forcible; and is the same which is used in 1 Cor. xiii. 12, Rom. i. 28, and Col. i. 10.

[4] Levit. xviii. 5 (LXX.); quoted also Gal. iii. 12.

[5] Deut. xxx. 12.   St. Paul here, though he quotes from the LXX. (verse 8 is verbatim), yet slightly alters it, so as to adapt it better to illustrate his

meaning.   His main statement is, ' the Glad-tidings of salvation is offered, and needs only to be accepted;' to this he transfers the description which Moses has given of the Law, viz. 'the Word is nigh thee,' &c.; and the rest of the passage of Deuteronomy he applies in a higher sense than that in which Moses had written it (according to the true Christian mode of using the Old Testament), not to the Mosaic Law, but to the Gospel of Christ.   The passage in Deuteronomy is as follows:—
' *This commandment which I command thee this day is not hidden from thee, neither is it far off.   It is not in heaven that thou shouldst say, Who shall go up for us to heaven and bring it unto us, that we may hear it and do it?   Neither is it beyond the sea that thou shouldest say, who shall go over the sea for us and bring it unto us, that we may hear it and do it?   But the word is very nigh unto thee, in thy mouth and in thy heart, that thou mayest do it.*'

—that is, the Word Faith which we proclaim, saying, 'If with thy mouth thou shalt confess Jesus for thy x. 9 Lord, and shalt have faith in thy heart that God raised Him from the dead, thou shalt be saved.'   For faith 10 unto righteousness is in the heart, and confession unto salvation is from the mouth.   And so says the Scripture, 11 '𝕹𝕺 𝕸𝕬𝕹 that hath faith in 𝕳im shall be confounded;'[1] for there is no distinction between Jew and Gentile, 12 because the same [Jesus] is Lord over all, and He gives richly to all who call upon Him; for '𝕰𝖁𝕰𝕽𝖄 13 𝕸𝕬𝕹 who shall call upon the name of the Lord shall be saved.'[2]

In order, therefore, that all may be so admitted, the invitation to believe must be universally proclaimed; and it has already been enough so to deprive the Jews of the excuse of ignorance, especially as they had received warnings of rejection before in their own Scriptures.

How then shall they call on Him in whom they have 14 put no faith?   And how shall they put faith in Him whom they never heard?   And how shall they hear 15 of Him if no man bear the tidings?   And who shall bear the tidings if no messengers be sent forth?[3]   As it is written, '𝕳ow beautiful are the feet of them that bear 𝕲lad-tidings of peace, that bear 𝕲lad-tidings of good things.'[4]   Yet some have not hearkened to the Glad-16 tidings, as saith Esaias, '𝕷ord, who hath given faith to our teaching?'[5]   So, then, faith comes by teaching;[6] 17 and our teaching comes by the Word of God.   But 18 I say, have they not heard [the voice of the teachers]? Yea, '𝕿heir sound has gone forth into all the earth, and their words unto the ends of the world.'[7]   Again I say, 19 did not Israel know [the purpose of God]? yea, it is said first by Moses, '𝕴 will make you jealous against them which are no people, against a Gentile nation without understanding will 𝕴 make you wrath.'[8]   But Esaias 20 speaks boldly, saying, '𝕴 was found of them that sought me not; 𝕴 was made manifest unto them that asked not after me.'[9]   But unto Israel he says, '𝕬ll day long 21

---

[1] Isa. xxviii. 16 (LXX.).   See ix. 33.

[2] Joel ii. 32 (LXX.).

[3] This is a justification of the mission of the Apostles to *the Gentiles*, which was an offence to the Jews.   See Acts xxii. 22.

[4] Isaiah lii. 7, apparently from the Hebrew, and not LXX.

[5] Isaiah liii. 1 (LXX.).

[6] There is no English word which precisely represents ἀκοή in its subjective as well as objective meaning. See note on 1 Thess. ii. 13.

[7] Ps. xix. 4 (LXX.).   In the psalm this is said of 'the heavens,' which by their wonderful phenomena declare the glory of their Creator.   There

seems to be no *comparison* in the psalm (as some have thought) between *the heavens* and *the word of God*. St. Paul here quotes the Old Testament (as he so often does), not in its primary meaning, but applying it in a higher sense, or perhaps only as a poetical illustration.   As to the assertion of the universal preaching of the Gospel, Dean Alford well observes that it is not made in a *geographical* but in a *religious* sense.   The Gospel was now preached to all nations, and not to the Jews alone.

[8] Deut. xxxii. 21 (LXX.).

[9] Isa. lxv. 1 (LXX, with transposition).

𝔥𝔞𝔟𝔢 𝔛 𝔰𝔭𝔯𝔢𝔞𝔡 𝔣𝔬𝔯𝔱𝔥 𝔪𝔶 𝔞𝔯𝔪𝔰 [1] 𝔲𝔫𝔱𝔬 𝔞 𝔡𝔦𝔰𝔬𝔟𝔢𝔡𝔦𝔢𝔫𝔱 𝔞𝔫𝔡 𝔤𝔞𝔦𝔫𝔰𝔞𝔶𝔦𝔫𝔤 𝔭𝔢𝔬𝔭𝔩𝔢.' [2]

xi. 1 I say, then,—must we [3] think that God has cast off His people? [4] That be far from us; for I am myself also an Israelite, of the seed of Abraham, of the tribe 2 of Benjamin. God has not cast off His people whom He foreknew. Yea, know ye not what is said in the Scriptures of Elias, how he intercedes with God against 3 Israel, saying, '𝔏𝔬𝔯𝔡, 𝔱𝔥𝔢𝔶 𝔥𝔞𝔟𝔢 𝔨𝔦𝔩𝔩𝔢𝔡 𝔗𝔥𝔶 𝔭𝔯𝔬𝔭𝔥𝔢𝔱𝔰, 𝔞𝔫𝔡 𝔡𝔦𝔤𝔤𝔢𝔡 𝔡𝔬𝔴𝔫 𝔗𝔥𝔦𝔫𝔢 𝔞𝔩𝔱𝔞𝔯𝔰, 𝔞𝔫𝔡 𝔛 𝔬𝔫𝔩𝔶 𝔥𝔞𝔳𝔢 𝔟𝔢𝔢𝔫 𝔩𝔢𝔣𝔱, 4 𝔞𝔫𝔡 𝔱𝔥𝔢𝔶 𝔰𝔢𝔢𝔨 𝔪𝔶 𝔩𝔦𝔣𝔢 𝔞𝔩𝔰𝔬.' [5] But what says the answer of God to him? '𝔛 [6] 𝔥𝔞𝔳𝔢 𝔶𝔢𝔱 𝔩𝔢𝔣𝔱 𝔱𝔬 𝔪𝔶𝔰𝔢𝔩𝔣 𝔞 𝔯𝔢𝔪𝔫𝔞𝔫𝔱,' 𝔢𝔳𝔢𝔫 𝔰𝔢𝔳𝔢𝔫 𝔱𝔥𝔬𝔲𝔰𝔞𝔫𝔡 𝔪𝔢𝔫, 𝔴𝔥𝔬 𝔥𝔞𝔳𝔢 𝔫𝔬𝔱 𝔟𝔬𝔴𝔢𝔡 𝔱𝔥𝔢 𝔨𝔫𝔢𝔢 5 𝔱𝔬 𝔅𝔞𝔞𝔩.' So likewise at this present time there is a remnant [of the house of Israel] chosen by gift of 6 grace. But if their choice be the gift of grace, it can no more be deemed the wage of works; for the gift that is earned is no gift: or if it be gained by works, it is no longer the gift of grace; for work claims [8] 7 wages and not gifts. What follows then? That which Israel seeks, Israel has not won; but the chosen have won it, and the rest were blinded, as it is written, 8 '𝔊𝔬𝔡 𝔥𝔞𝔱𝔥 𝔤𝔦𝔳𝔢𝔫 𝔱𝔥𝔢𝔪 𝔞 𝔰𝔭𝔦𝔯𝔦𝔱 𝔬𝔣 𝔰𝔩𝔲𝔪𝔟𝔢𝔯, 𝔢𝔶𝔢𝔰 𝔱𝔥𝔞𝔱 𝔱𝔥𝔢𝔶 𝔰𝔥𝔬𝔲𝔩𝔡 𝔫𝔬𝔱 𝔰𝔢𝔢, 𝔞𝔫𝔡 𝔢𝔞𝔯𝔰 𝔱𝔥𝔞𝔱 𝔱𝔥𝔢𝔶 𝔰𝔥𝔬𝔲𝔩𝔡 𝔫𝔬𝔱 𝔥𝔢𝔞𝔯, 𝔲𝔫𝔱𝔬 9 𝔱𝔥𝔦𝔰 𝔡𝔞𝔶.' [9] And David says, '𝔏𝔢𝔱 𝔱𝔥𝔢𝔦𝔯 𝔱𝔞𝔟𝔩𝔢 𝔟𝔢 𝔪𝔞𝔡𝔢 𝔞 𝔰𝔫𝔞𝔯𝔢 𝔞𝔫𝔡 𝔞 𝔱𝔯𝔞𝔭, 𝔞𝔫𝔡 𝔞 𝔰𝔱𝔲𝔪𝔟𝔩𝔦𝔫𝔤-𝔟𝔩𝔬𝔠𝔨 𝔞𝔫𝔡 𝔞 𝔯𝔢𝔠𝔬𝔪- 10 𝔭𝔢𝔫𝔰𝔢 𝔲𝔫𝔱𝔬 𝔱𝔥𝔢𝔪. 𝔏𝔢𝔱 𝔱𝔥𝔢𝔦𝔯 𝔢𝔶𝔢𝔰 𝔟𝔢 𝔡𝔞𝔯𝔨𝔢𝔫𝔢𝔡 𝔱𝔥𝔞𝔱 𝔱𝔥𝔢𝔶 𝔪𝔞𝔶 𝔫𝔬𝔱 𝔰𝔢𝔢, 𝔞𝔫𝔡 𝔟𝔬𝔴 𝔡𝔬𝔴𝔫 𝔱𝔥𝔢𝔦𝔯 𝔟𝔞𝔠𝔨 𝔞𝔩𝔴𝔞𝔶.' [10] 11 Shall we say, [11] then, 'they have stumbled to the end that they might fall?' That be far from us; but rather their stumbling has brought salvation to the 12 Gentiles, '𝔱𝔬 [12] 𝔭𝔯𝔬𝔳𝔬𝔨𝔢 𝔛𝔰𝔯𝔞𝔢𝔩 𝔱𝔬 𝔧𝔢𝔞𝔩𝔬𝔲𝔰𝔶.' Now if

The Jews, however, are not all rejected; those who believe in Christ have been selected by God (ἐκλογή) as His people, and only the unbelieving portion rejected.

Nor is the rejection of the unbelieving Jews final, so as to exclude them and their

---

[1] The metaphor is of a mother opening her arms to call back her child to her embrace. In this attitude the hands are spread open, and hence the 'hands.'

[2] Isa. lxv. 2 (LXX.).

[3] The particle here asks a question expecting a negative answer = *is it true that? must we think that?* Also see note on Gal. iii. 21.

[4] Alluding to Psalm xciv. 14: '*Jehovah shall not utterly cast out his people.*' (LXX.) No doubt St. Paul's antagonists accused him of contradicting this prophecy.

[5] 1 Kings xix. 10 (LXX. but not verbatim).

[6] 1 Kings xix. 18, more nearly according to the Hebrew than LXX.

[7] The verb corresponds to the noun in the next verse and in ix. 27. See note there.

[8] By *work* is here meant *work which earns wages.* Compare iv. 4, 5. The latter clause of this verse, however, is omitted by the best MSS.

[9] This quotation seems to be compounded of Deut. xxix. 4, and Isaiah xxix. 10 (LXX.), though it does not correspond verbatim with either.

[10] Ps. lxix. 23, 24 (LXX. nearly verbatim).

[11] Literally, *I say then, shall we conclude that,* &c. See note on verse 1.

[12] Deut. xxxii. 21 (LXX.), quoted above, ch. x. 19.

descendants for ever from readmission into God's Church. As the Gentile unbelievers had on their belief been grafted into the Christian church which is the same original stock as the Jewish church, much more would Jewish unbelievers on their belief be grafted anew into that stock from which they had been broken off.

their stumbling enriches the world, and if the lessen-
ing of their gain gives wealth to the Gentiles, how
much more must their fulness do!

For to you who are Gentiles I say that, as Apostle xi. 13
of the Gentiles, I glorify my ministration for this end,
if perchance I might '**provoke to jealousy**' my kins- 14
men, and save some among them. For if the casting 15
of them out is the reconciliation of the world [to God],
what must the gathering of them in be, but life from
the dead?

Now, if the first of the dough be hallowed,[1] the 16
whole mass is thereby hallowed; and if the root be
hallowed, so are also the branches. But if some of 17
the branches were broken off, and thou being of the
wild olive stock wast grafted in amongst them, and
made to share the root and richness of the olive, yet 18
boast not over the branches: but—if thou art boastful
—thou bearest not the root, but the root thee. Thou 19
wilt say then, 'The branches were broken off that I
might be grafted in.' It is true,—for lack of faith 20
they were broken off, and by faith thou standest in
their place: be not high-minded, but fear; for if God 21
spared not the natural branches, take heed lest He
also spare not thee. Behold, therefore, the goodness 22
and the severity of God; towards them who fell, severity, but towards thee, goodness, if thou continue
stedfast to His goodness; for otherwise thou too shalt
be cut off. And they also, if they persist not in their 23
faithlessness, shall be grafted in: for God is able to
graft them in where they were before. For if thou 24
wast cut out from that which by nature was the wild
olive, and wast grafted against nature into the fruitful
olive, how much more shall these, the natural branches,
be grafted into the fruitful stock from whence they
sprang?

Thus God's object has been not to reject any, but to show mercy upon all mankind. His purpose has been to make use of the Jewish unbelief to call the Gentiles into His Church, and

For I would not have you ignorant, brethren, of 25
this mystery, lest you should be wise in your own
conceits; that blindness has fallen upon a part[2] of
Israel until the full body of the Gentiles shall have
come in. And so all Israel shall be saved, as it is 26
written, '**Out of Zion shall come the deliverer, and He** 27
shall turn away ungodliness from Jacob. And this is 28
my covenant with them,'[3] '**When I shall take away**

[1] St. Paul alludes to the *Heave-offering* prescribed Numbers xv. 20: '*Ye shall offer up a cake of the first of your dough for an heave-offering.*'

[2] For the phrase used here compare 2 Cor. i. 14, 2 Cor. ii. 5, Rom. xv. 15.

[3] Isaiah lix. 20 (LXX. almost verbatim).

their sins.'[1] In respect of the Glad-tidings, [that it might be borne to the Gentiles], they are God's enemies for your sakes; but in respect of God's choice,

i.29 they are His beloved for their fathers' sakes: for no
30 change of purpose can annul God's gifts and call. And as in times past you were yourselves [2] disobedient to God, but have now received mercy upon their disobe-
31 dience; so in this present time they have been disobedient, that upon your obtaining mercy they likewise
32 might obtain mercy. For God has shut up [3] all together under disobedience, that He might have mercy
33 upon all. O depth of the bounty, and the wisdom and the knowledge of God; how unfathomable are His
34 judgments, and how unsearchable His paths! Yea,
   '𝖂𝖍𝖔 𝖍𝖆𝖙𝖍 𝖐𝖓𝖔𝖜𝖓 𝖙𝖍𝖊 𝖒𝖎𝖓𝖉 𝖔𝖋 𝖙𝖍𝖊 𝕷𝖔𝖗𝖉, 𝖔𝖗 𝖜𝖍𝖔 𝖍𝖆𝖙𝖍
35 𝖇𝖊𝖊𝖓 𝕳𝖎𝖘 𝖈𝖔𝖚𝖓𝖘𝖊𝖑𝖑𝖔𝖗?'[4] Or '𝖂𝖍𝖔 𝖍𝖆𝖙𝖍 𝖋𝖎𝖗𝖘𝖙 𝖌𝖎𝖇𝖊𝖓 𝖚𝖓𝖙𝖔
36 𝕲𝖔𝖉, 𝖙𝖍𝖆𝖙 𝖍𝖊 𝖘𝖍𝖔𝖚𝖑𝖉 𝖉𝖊𝖘𝖊𝖗𝖇𝖊 𝖆 𝖗𝖊𝖈𝖔𝖒𝖕𝖊𝖓𝖘𝖊?'[5] For from Him is the beginning, and by Him the life, and in Him the end of all things.
   Unto Him be glory for ever. Amen.

ii.1 I EXHORT you, therefore, brethren, as you would acknowledge the mercies of God, to offer your bodies a living sacrifice, holy and well pleasing unto God, which
2 is your reasonable [6] worship. And be not conformed to the fashion of this [7] world, but be transformed by the renewing of your mind, that by an unerring test [8] you may discern the will of God, even that which is
3 good, and acceptable, and perfect. For through the grace bestowed upon me [as Christ's Apostle], I warn every man among you not to think of himself more highly than he ought to think, but to seek a sober mind, according to the measure of faith [9] which God

---

[1] Isaiah xxvii. 9 (LXX. nearly verbatim).

[2] Throughout this passage in the A. V., the word for *disobedience* is translated as if it were equivalent to *unbelief*, which it is not. Compare i. 30: '*disobedient to parents.*'

[3] 'Shut up.' Compare Gal. iii. 22.

[4] Isaiah xl. 13 (LXX. nearly verbatim). Quoted also (omitting the middle and adding the end of the verse) 1 Cor. ii. 16.

[5] Job xli. 11 (according to the sense of the Hebrew, but not LXX.).

[6] *Reasonable worship*, as contrasted with the unreasonable worship of those whose faith rested only on outward forms. See note on i. 9.

[7] See note on 1 Cor. i. 20.

[8] See note on ii. 18.

[9] 'Measure of faith' here seems (from the context of the following verses) equivalent to 'charism' as Chrysostom takes it. The particular talent given by God may be called a *measure of faith*, as being that by the use of which each man's faith will be tried. (Compare, as to the verbal expressions, 2 Cor. x. 13.) This explanation is, perhaps, not very satisfactory; but to understand measure as meaning *amount* is still less so, for a double *gift* of prophecy did not imply a double faith. The expression is so perplexing that

neighbour. All these duties should be performed (xiii. 11-14) as in the expectation of Christ's speedy coming.

has given him. For as we have many limbs, which xii. are all members of the same body, though they have not all the same office; so we ourselves are all [1] one 5 body in Christ, and fellow-members one of another; but we have gifts differing according to the grace 6 which God has given us.[2] He that has the gift of prophecy, let him exercise it [3] according to the proportion of his faith. He that has the gift of mini-7 stration, let him minister; let the teacher labour in teaching; the exhorter, in exhortation. He who gives, 8 let him give in singleness of mind. He who rules, let him rule diligently. He who shows pity, let him show it gladly. Let your love be without feigning. Abhor 9 that which is evil; cleave to that which is good. Be 10 kindly affectioned one to another in brotherly love; in honour let each set his neighbour above himself. Let your diligence be free from sloth, let your spirit 11 grow with zeal; be true bondsmen of your Lord. In 12 your hope be joyful; in your sufferings be stedfast; in your prayers be unwearied. Be liberal to the needs 13 of the saints. And show hospitality to the stranger. 14 Bless your persecutors; yea, bless, and curse not. 15 Rejoice with them that rejoice, and weep with them 16 that weep. Be of one mind amongst yourselves. Set not your heart on high things, but suffer yourselves to be borne along [4] with the lowly. Be not wise in your own conceits. Repay no man evil for evil. '𝔅𝔢 17 𝔭𝔯𝔬𝔟𝔦𝔡𝔢𝔫𝔱 𝔬𝔣 𝔤𝔬𝔬𝔡 𝔯𝔢𝔭𝔬𝔯𝔱 𝔦𝔫 𝔱𝔥𝔢 𝔰𝔦𝔤𝔥𝔱 𝔬𝔣 𝔞𝔩𝔩 𝔪𝔢𝔫.'[5] If it 18 be possible, as far as lies in yourselves, keep peace with all men. Revenge not yourselves, beloved, but 19 give place to the wrath [of God]; [6] for it is written, '𝔙𝔢𝔫𝔤𝔢𝔞𝔫𝔠𝔢 𝔦𝔰 𝔪𝔦𝔫𝔢; 𝔍 𝔴𝔦𝔩𝔩 𝔯𝔢𝔭𝔞𝔶, 𝔰𝔞𝔦𝔱𝔥 𝔱𝔥𝔢 𝔏𝔬𝔯𝔡.'[7] Therefore, '𝔍𝔣 𝔱𝔥𝔦𝔫𝔢 𝔢𝔫𝔢𝔪𝔶 𝔥𝔲𝔫𝔤𝔢𝔯, 𝔣𝔢𝔢𝔡 𝔥𝔦𝔪; 𝔦𝔣 𝔥𝔢 𝔱𝔥𝔦𝔯𝔰𝔱, 20 𝔤𝔦𝔳𝔢 𝔥𝔦𝔪 𝔡𝔯𝔦𝔫𝔨; 𝔣𝔬𝔯 𝔦𝔫 𝔰𝔬 𝔡𝔬𝔦𝔫𝔤, 𝔱𝔥𝔬𝔲 𝔰𝔥𝔞𝔩𝔱 𝔥𝔢𝔞𝔭 𝔠𝔬𝔞𝔩𝔰 𝔬𝔣

one is almost tempted to conjecture that the words crept into the text here by mistake, having been originally a marginal explanation of 'the proportion of faith' just below.

[1] Literally '*the* many.'

[2] The construction and the parallel both seem to require a comma at the end of verse 5, and a full stop in the middle of verse 6.

[3] We think it better to take these elliptical clauses as all imperative (with the A. V.) rather than to consider them (with De Wette and others) as 'descriptive of the sphere of the gift's operation'

up to a certain point, and then passing into the imperative. The participles in verses 9, 16, and 17 seem to refute De Wette's arguments.

[4] This is the literal translation.

[5] This is a quotation nearly verbatim from Prov. iii. 4 (LXX.). See note on 2 Cor. viii. 21.

[6] Such is the interpretation of Chrysostom, and is supported by the ablest modern interpreters. For 'wrath' in this sense, compare Rom. v. 9, 1 Thess. ii. 16.

[7] Deut. xxxii. 35 (LXX. but not verbatim); see note on Heb. x. 30.

i. 21 **fire upon his head.**' [1] Be not overcome by evil, but overcome evil with good.

ii. 1 Let every man submit himself to the authorities of government; for all authority comes from God, and the authorities which now are, have been set 2 in their place by God: therefore, he who sets himself against the authority, resists the ordinance of God; and they who resist will bring judgment upon 3 themselves. For the magistrate is not terrible to good works,[2] but to evil. Wilt thou be fearless of his authority? do what is good, and thou shalt have 4 its praise. For the magistrate is God's minister to thee for good. But if thou art an evil doer, be afraid; for not by chance does he bear the sword [of justice], being a minister of God, appointed to 5 do vengeance upon the guilty. Wherefore you must needs submit, not only for fear, but also for con- 6 science sake; for this also is the cause why you pay tribute, because the authorities of government are officers of God's will, and this is the very end of their 7 daily work. Pay, therefore, to all their dues; tribute to whom tribute is due; customs to whom customs; 8 fear to whom fear; honour to whom honour. Owe no debt to any man, save the debt of love alone; for 9 he who loves his neighbour has fulfilled the law. For the law which says, '**Thou shalt not commit adultery; Thou shalt do no murder; Thou shalt not steal; Thou shalt not bear false witness; Thou shalt not covet**'[3] (and whatsoever other commandment there be), is all contained in this one saying, '**Thou shalt love thy** 10 **neighbour as thyself.**'[4] Love works no ill to his neighbour; therefore Love is the fulfilment of the Law.

11 This do, knowing the season wherein we stand, and that for us it is high time to awake out of sleep, for our salvation is already nearer than when we first 12 believed. The night is far spent, the day is at hand; let us therefore cast off the works of darkness, and 13 let us put on the armour of light. Let us walk (as in the light of day) in seemly guise; not in rioting

[1] Prov. xxv. 21 (LXX.). There can be little doubt that the metaphor is taken from the melting of metals. It is obvious that 'thou shalt heap coals of fire on his head' could never have meant 'thou shalt destroy him;' because to feed an enemy could in no sense destroy him.

[2] We must remember that this was written before the Imperial government had begun to persecute Christianity. It is a testimony in favour of the general administration of the Roman criminal law.

[3] Exod. xx. 13–17 (LXX.).

[4] Levit. xix. 18 (LXX.).

and drunkenness, not in dalliance and wantonness, not in strife and envying. But clothe yourselves xiii. with the Lord Jesus Christ, and take no thought to please your fleshly lusts.

Him who is weak in his faith receive into your xiv. fellowship, -imposing no determinations of doubtful questions.[1] Some have faith that they may eat all 2 things : others, who are weak,[2] eat herbs alone. Let 3 not him who eats despise him who abstains, nor let him who abstains judge him who eats, for God has received him among[3] His people. Who art thou, that 4 judgest another's servant? To his own master he must stand or fall; but he shall be made to stand, for God is able to set him up. There are some who 5 esteem one day above another; and again there are some who esteem all days alike;[4] let each be fully persuaded in his own mind. He who regards the 6 day, regards it unto the Lord; and he who regards it not, disregards it unto the Lord.[5] He who eats, eats unto the Lord, for he gives God thanks ; and he who abstains, abstains unto the Lord, and gives thanks to God likewise. For not unto himself does any one of 7 us either live or die ; but whether we live, we live 8 unto the Lord, or whether we die, we die unto the Lord ; therefore, living or dying, we are the Lord's. For to this end Christ died, and [6] lived again, that He 9 might be Lord both of the dead and of the living. But thou, why judgest thou thy brother? Or thou, 10 why despisest thou thy brother? for we shall all stand 11 before the judgment-seat of Christ. And so it is written, '𝔄𝔰 𝔗 𝔩𝔦𝔟𝔢, 𝔰𝔞𝔦𝔱𝔥 𝔱𝔥𝔢 𝔏𝔬𝔯𝔡, 𝔢𝔟𝔢𝔯𝔶 𝔨𝔫𝔢𝔢 𝔰𝔥𝔞𝔩𝔩 𝔟𝔬𝔴 𝔱𝔬 𝔪𝔢, 𝔞𝔫𝔡 𝔢𝔟𝔢𝔯𝔶 𝔱𝔬𝔫𝔤𝔲𝔢 𝔰𝔥𝔞𝔩𝔩 𝔞𝔠𝔨𝔫𝔬𝔴𝔩𝔢𝔡𝔤𝔢 𝔊𝔬𝔡.'[7]

[1] Literally, *not acting so as to make distinctions* [or *determinations*] *which belong to disputatious reasonings*. The same word is used in Phil. ii. 14.

[2] These were probably Christians of Jewish birth, who so feared lest they should (without knowing it) eat meat which had been offered to idols or was otherwise ceremonially unclean (which might easily happen in such a place as Rome), that they abstained from meat altogether. Thus Josephus (*Life*, § 3, quoted by Tholuck) mentions some Jewish priests who, from such conscientious scruples, abstained while prisoners in Rome from all animal food. So Daniel and his fellow-captives in Babylon refused the king's meat and wine, and ate pulse alone, that they

might not defile themselves (Dan. i. 8–12). The tone and precepts of this 14th chapter of the Epistle correspond with 1 Cor. viii.

[3] Literally, *received him unto Himself*.

[4] Compare Col. ii. 16. Dean Alford has an excellent note on this verse. [Here, as at Gal. iv. 10, we may refer to the additional note on Col. ii. 16. H.]

[5] This negative clause is omitted by the majority of MSS., but is sanctioned by Chrysostom and other Fathers, and retained in the text by Tischendorf; Griesbach and Lachmann omit it.

[6] 'Rose again,' is omitted by the best MSS.

[7] Isaiah xlv. 23 (LXX. not accurately, but apparently from memory).

. 12 So, then, every one of us shall give account to God
13 [not of his brethren, but] of himself. Let us then
judge each other no more, but let this rather be your
judgment, to put no stumbling-block or cause of
14 falling in your brother's way. I know and am persuaded in the Lord Jesus, that nothing is in itself
unclean; but whatever a man thinks unclean, is
15 unclean to him. And if for meat thou grievest thy
brother, thou hast ceased to walk by the rule of
love. Destroy not him with thy meat for whom
Christ died.

16   I say then, let not your good be evil spoken of.[1]
17 For the kingdom of God is not meat and drink, but
righteousness, and peace, and joy in the Holy Spirit;
18 and he who lives in these things as Christ's bondsman is well-pleasing to God, and cannot be con-
19 demned[2] by men. Let us therefore follow the things
which make for peace, such as may build us up together into one. Destroy not thou the work of God
20 for a meal of meat. All things indeed [in them-
selves] are pure; but to him that eats with stum-
21 bling all is evil. It is good neither to eat flesh, nor to
drink[3] wine, nor to do any[4] other thing, whereby
22 thy brother is made to stumble.[5] Hast thou faith
[that nothing is unclean]? keep it for thine own
comfort before God. Happy is he who condemns
23 not himself by his own judgment.[6] But he who doubts,
is thereby condemned if he eats, because he has not
faith[7] that he may eat; and every faithless deed[8] is
v. 1 sin. And we, who are strong,[9] ought to bear the
infirmities of the weak, and not to please ourselves.
2 Let each of us please his neighbour for good ends,

---

[1] Compare 1 Cor. x. 29.

[2] Literally, *is capable of standing any test to which he may be put.*

[3] This does not necessarily imply that any of the weaker brethren actually did scruple to drink wine; it may be put only hypothetically. But it is possible that they may have feared to taste wine, part of which had been poured in libation to idols. Daniel (in the passage above referred to) refused wine.

[4] It is strange that no critic has hitherto proposed the simple emendation of reading ἓν instead of ἐν, which avoids the extreme awkwardness of the ellipsis necessitated by the Received Text. Compare John i. 3. The con-

struction of the last clause is similar to that in ix. 32.

[5] We adopt the reading sanctioned by Tischendorf, which omits one or two words.

[6] See note on ii. 18.

[7] Literally, *he eats not from faith.*

[8] Literally, *every deed which springs not from faith [that it is a right deed] is sin.*

[9] Literally, 'We the strong.' St. Paul here addresses the same party whom he so often exhorts to patience and forbearance; those who called themselves 'the spiritual' (Gal. vi. 1; 1 Cor. iii. 1), and boasted of their 'knowledge' (1 Cor. viii. 1). See p. 350.

to build him up.   For so [1] Christ pleased not Him- xv.
self, but in Him was fulfilled that which is written,
'𝕮𝖍𝖊 𝖗𝖊𝖕𝖗𝖔𝖆𝖈𝖍𝖊𝖘 𝖔𝖋 𝖙𝖍𝖊𝖒 𝖙𝖍𝖆𝖙 𝖗𝖊𝖕𝖗𝖔𝖆𝖈𝖍𝖊𝖉 𝖙𝖍𝖊𝖊 𝖋𝖊𝖑𝖑
𝖚𝖕𝖔𝖓 𝖒𝖊.' [2]   For our instruction is the end of all 4
which was written of old; that by stedfast endurance, and by the counsel of the Scriptures, we may
hold fast our hope.   Now may God, from whom both 5
counsel and endurance come, grant you to be of one
mind together, according to the will of Christ, that 6
you may all [both strong and weak], with one heart
and voice, glorify the God and Father of our Lord
Jesus Christ.   Wherefore, receive one another into 7
fellowship, to the glory of God, even as Christ also
received you.[3]

For [4] I say that Jesus Christ came to be a minister 8
of the circumcision, to maintain the truthfulness of
God, and confirm the promises made to our fathers;
and that the Gentiles should praise God for His 9
mercy, as it is written, '𝕱𝖔𝖗 𝖙𝖍𝖎𝖘 𝖈𝖆𝖚𝖘𝖊 𝕴 𝖜𝖎𝖑𝖑 𝖆𝖈𝖐𝖓𝖔𝖜-
𝖑𝖊𝖉𝖌𝖊 𝖙𝖍𝖊𝖊 𝖆𝖒𝖔𝖓𝖌 𝖙𝖍𝖊 𝕲𝖊𝖓𝖙𝖎𝖑𝖊𝖘, 𝖆𝖓𝖉 𝖜𝖎𝖑𝖑 𝖘𝖎𝖓𝖌 𝖚𝖓𝖙𝖔 𝖙𝖍𝖞
𝖓𝖆𝖒𝖊.' [5]   And again it is said, '𝕽𝖊𝖏𝖔𝖎𝖈𝖊, 𝖞𝖊 𝕲𝖊𝖓𝖙𝖎𝖑𝖊𝖘, 10
𝖜𝖎𝖙𝖍 𝕳𝖎𝖘 𝖕𝖊𝖔𝖕𝖑𝖊;' [6] and again, '𝕻𝖗𝖆𝖎𝖘𝖊 𝖙𝖍𝖊 𝕷𝖔𝖗𝖉, 𝖆𝖑𝖑 11
𝖞𝖊 𝕲𝖊𝖓𝖙𝖎𝖑𝖊𝖘, 𝖆𝖓𝖉 𝖑𝖆𝖚𝖉 𝕳𝖎𝖒, 𝖆𝖑𝖑 𝖞𝖊 𝖕𝖊𝖔𝖕𝖑𝖊𝖘;' [7] and
again Esaias saith, '𝕿𝖍𝖊𝖗𝖊 𝖘𝖍𝖆𝖑𝖑 𝖈𝖔𝖒𝖊 𝖙𝖍𝖊 𝖗𝖔𝖔𝖙 𝖔𝖋 12
𝕵𝖊𝖘𝖘𝖊, 𝖆𝖓𝖉 𝖍𝖊 𝖙𝖍𝖆𝖙 𝖘𝖍𝖆𝖑𝖑 𝖗𝖎𝖘𝖊 𝖙𝖔 𝖗𝖊𝖎𝖌𝖓 𝖔𝖛𝖊𝖗 𝖙𝖍𝖊 𝕲𝖊𝖓𝖙𝖎𝖑𝖊𝖘; 𝖎𝖓 𝖍𝖎𝖒 𝖘𝖍𝖆𝖑𝖑 𝖙𝖍𝖊 𝕲𝖊𝖓𝖙𝖎𝖑𝖊𝖘 𝖍𝖔𝖕𝖊.' [8]   Now may 13
the God of hope [9] fill you with all joy and peace in
believing, that you may abound in hope, through the
mighty working of the Holy Spirit.

St. Paul gives   But I am persuaded, my brethren, not only by the 14
these exhorta-
tions boldly to reports of others, [10] but by my own judgment, that
the Roman
Christians, as you are already full of goodness, filled with all know-
being the
Apostle of the ledge, and able, of yourselves, to admonish one an-
Gentiles. He
intends soon other.   Yet I have written to you somewhat boldly 15
to visit them
on his way to in parts [11] [of this letter], to remind you [rather than

---

[1] The '*even*' of A. V. is not in the
original.   '*For Christ also*' is the literal English.

[2] Ps. lxix. 9 (LXX.).

[3] 'You' (not 'us') is the reading of
the best MSS.

[4] The reading of the MSS. is 'for,'
not 'but.'

[5] Ps. xviii. 49 (LXX.).

[6] Deut. xxxii. 43 (LXX.).   See note
on ix. 25.

[7] Ps. cxvii. 1 (LXX.).

[8] Isaiah xi. 10 (LXX.).

[9] The reference of this to the pre-

ceding quotation is lost in A. V. through
the translation of the verb and noun for
'hope' by '*hope*' and '*trust*' respectively.

[10] Observe the force of the 'I myself
also.'

[11] For the meaning here, see 2 Cor. i.
14, 2 Cor. ii. 5.   It might here be translated *in some measure* (as Neander pro-
poses, compare ver. 24), but that
this is already expressed in 'somewhat
boldly.'   The word 'brethren,' is omitted in the best MSS.

to teach you], because of that gift of grace which

16 God bestowed upon me that I should be a minister of Jesus Christ to the Gentiles, serving in the Glad-tidings of God, that I might present the Gentiles to God, as a priest presents the offering,[1] a sacrifice well pleasing unto Him, hallowed by the working of the

17 Holy Spirit. I have therefore the power of boasting

18 in Christ Jesus, concerning the things of God ; for I will not dare [as some do] to glorify myself for the labours of others,[2] but I will speak only of the works which Christ has wrought by me, to bring the Gentiles to obedience, by word and deed, with the might

19 of signs and wonders, the might of the Spirit of God ; so that going forth from Jerusalem, and round about as far as[3] Illyricum, I have fulfilled my task in

20 bearing the Glad-tidings of Christ. And my ambition was to bear it according to this rule, [that I should go] not where the name of Christ was known (lest I should be building on another man's founda-

21 tion), but [where it was unheard] ; as it is written, ' 𝕿𝖔 𝖜𝖍𝖔𝖒 𝕳𝖊 𝖜𝖆𝖘 𝖓𝖔𝖙 𝖘𝖕𝖔𝖐𝖊𝖓 𝖔𝖋, 𝖙𝖍𝖊𝖞 𝖘𝖍𝖆𝖑𝖑 𝖘𝖊𝖊 ; 𝖆𝖓𝖉 𝖙𝖍𝖊 𝖕𝖊𝖔𝖕𝖑𝖊 𝖜𝖍𝖔 𝖍𝖆𝖛𝖊 𝖓𝖔𝖙 𝖍𝖊𝖆𝖗𝖉 𝖘𝖍𝖆𝖑𝖑 𝖚𝖓𝖉𝖊𝖗𝖘𝖙𝖆𝖓𝖉.'[4]

22 This is the cause why I have often been hindered

23 from coming to you. But now that I have no longer room enough [for my labours] in these regions, and have had a great desire to visit you these many years,

24 so soon as I take my journey into Spain, I will come to you ;[5] for I hope to see you on my way, and to be set forward on my journey thither by you, after I have in some measure satisfied my desire of your

25 company. But now I am going to Jerusalem, being

26 employed[6] in a ministration to the saints. For the provinces of Macedonia and Achaia have willingly undertaken to make a certain contribution for the

27 poor among the saints in Jerusalem. Willingly, I say, they have done this ; and indeed they are their debtors ; for since the Gentiles have shared in the spiritual goods of the brethren in Jerusalem, they

[Side note:] Spain ; for he had already executed his Apostolic commission in the eastern parts of the Empire, so far as the field was not occupied by other labourers. First, however, he must go to Jerusalem to convey the Greek contributions thither, in spite of the dangers which he expects to meet there.

---

[1] Literally, '*a minister of Jesus Christ unto the Gentiles, a priest presenting an offering in respect of the Glad-tidings of God, that the Gentiles might be offered up as an offering well-pleasing unto Him.*' The same thing is said under a somewhat different metaphor, 2 Cor. xi. 2.

[2] Compare 2 Cor. x. 15, the whole of which passage is parallel to this.

[3] See the remarks on this in the last chapter, p. 470.

[4] Isaiah lii. 15 (LXX.).

[5] This ' I will come to you,' is probably an interpolation, as it is omitted by the best MSS. ; but it makes no difference in the sense.

[6] The present participle, not (as in A. V.) the future.

owe it in return to minister to them in their earthly
goods. When, therefore, I have finished this task, xv.
and have given to them in safety the fruit of this
collection, I will come from thence, by you, into
Spain. And I am sure that when I come to you, 29
my coming will receive the fulness [1] of Christ's [2] blessing. But I beseech you, brethren, by our Lord Jesus 30
Christ, and by the love which the Spirit gives, to
help me in my conflict with your prayers to God on
my behalf, that I may be delivered from the disobe- 31
dient in Judæa, and that the service which I have
undertaken for Jerusalem may be favourably received
by the Saints; that so I may come to you in joy, by 32
God's will, and may be refreshed in your companionship. The God of peace be with you all. Amen. 33

Commenda-
tion of Phœbe,
and saluta-
tions to nume-
rous Roman
Christians. I commend to you Phœbe our sister, who is [3] a xvi
ministering servant of the Church at Cenchreæ; that 2
you may receive her in the Lord, as the saints should
receive one another, and aid her in any business [4]
wherein she needs your help; for she has herself
aided many, and me also among the rest.

Greet Priscilla and Aquila, [5] my fellow-labourers 3
in the work of Christ Jesus, who, to save my life, 4
laid down their own necks; who are thanked, not by
me alone, but by all the Churches of the Gentiles.
Greet likewise the Church which assembles at their
house.

Salute Epænetus my dearly-beloved, who is the 5
first fruits of Asia [6] unto Christ.

---

[1] Literally, *I shall come in the fulness,* &c.

[2] 'Gospel' is not in any of the best
MSS.

[3] Διάκονον (Deaconess). See p. 341,
n. 2; also p. 342, n. 1.

[4] From the use of legal terms here,
it would seem that the business on
which Phœbe was visiting Rome was
connected with some trial at law.

[5] The most ancient MSS. read *Prisca*
for *Priscilla* here; the names being the
same. Concerning these distinguished
Christians, see pp. 299, 300. When and
where they risked their lives for St.
Paul, we know not, but may conjecture
at Ephesus. We see here that they had
returned to Rome (whence they had
been driven by the edict of Claudius)
from Ephesus, where we left them last.
It is curious to observe the wife mentioned first, contrary to ancient usage.
Throughout this chapter we observe in-

stances of courtesy towards women sufficient to refute the calumnies of a recent
infidel writer, who accuses St. Paul of
speaking and feeling coarsely in reference to women; we cannot but add
our astonishment that the same writer
should complain that the standard of
St. Paul's ethics, in reference to the
sexual relations, is not sufficiently elevated, while at the same time he considers the instincts of the German race
to have first introduced into the world
the true morality of these relations.
One is inclined to ask whether the present facility of divorce in Germany is a
legitimate development of the Teutonic
instinct; and if so, whether the law of
Germany, or the law of our Saviour
(Mark x. 12) enforced by St. Paul (1
Cor. vii. 10), expresses the higher tone
of morality, and tends the more to ele
vate the female sex.

[6] *Asia,* not *Achaia,* is the reading of

vi. 6   Salute Mary, who laboured much for me.

7   Salute Andronicus and Junias, my kinsmen and fellow-prisoners,[1] who are well known among the Apostles, and who were also in Christ before me.

8   Salute Amplias, my dearly-beloved in the Lord.

9   Salute Urbanus, my fellow-workman in Christ's service, and Stachys my dearly-beloved.

10   Salute Apelles, who has been tried and found trustworthy in Christ's work.

Salute those who are of the household of Aristobulus.[2]

11   Salute Herodion, my kinsman.

Salute those of the household of Narcissus[3] who are in the Lord's fellowship.

12   Salute Tryphena and Tryphosa, the faithful labourers in the Lord's service.

Salute Persis the dearly-beloved, who has laboured much in the Lord.

13   Salute Rufus,[4] the chosen in the Lord and his mother, who is also mine.

14   Salute Asyncritus, Phlegon, Hermas, Patrobas, Hermes, and the brethren who are with them.

15   Salute Philologus, and Julia, Nereus and his sister, and Olympas, and all the saints who are with them.

the best MSS. Compare p. 374, note 1. The province of proconsular Asia is of course meant.

[1] When were they St. Paul's fellow-prisoners? Probably in some of those imprisonments not recorded in the Acts, to which he alludes 2 Cor. xi. 23. It is doubtful whether in calling them his 'kinsmen' St. Paul means that they were really related to him, or only that they were Jews. (Compare Rom. ix. 3.) The latter supposition seems improbable, because Aquila and Priscilla, and others in this chapter, mentioned without the epithet of kinsmen, were certainly Jews; yet, on the other hand, it seems unlikely that so many of St. Paul's relations as are here called 'kinsmen' (verses 7, 11, 21) should be mentioned in a single chapter. Perhaps we may take a middle course, and suppose the epithet to denote that the persons mentioned were of the tribe of Benjamin.

[2] This Aristobulus was probably the great-grandson of Herod the Great, mentioned by Josephus and Tacitus, to whom Nero in A.D. 55 gave the government of Lesser Armenia. He had very likely lived previously at Rome, and may still have kept up an establishment there, or perhaps had not yet gone to his government. See Tac. *Ann.* xiii. 7, and Joseph. *Ant.* xx. 5.

[3] There were two eminent persons of the name of Narcissus at Rome about this time; one the well-known favourite of Claudius (Suet. *Claud.* 28, Tac. *Ann.* xii. 57, 65, xiii. 1), who was put to death by Nero, A.D. 54, soon after the death of Claudius, and therefore before this Epistle was written: the other was a favourite of Nero's, and is probably the person here named. Some of his slaves or freedmen had become Christians. This Narcissus was put to death by Galba (Dio. lxiv. 3).

[4] St. Mark (xv. 21) mentions Simon of Cyrene as 'the father of Alexander and Rufus;' the latter therefore was a Christian well known to those for whom St. Mark wrote, and probably is the same here mentioned. It is gratifying to think that she whom St. Paul mentions here with such respectful affection, was the wife of that Simon who bore our Saviour's cross.

Salute one another with the kiss of holiness.[1]   xvi.
The Churches of Christ [in Achaia] salute you.

Warning against self-interested partizans.

I exhort you, brethren, to keep your eyes upon 17
those who cause divisions, and cast stumbling-blocks
in the way of others, contrary to the teaching which
you have learned.   Shun them that are such; for the 18
master whom they serve is not our Lord Jesus Christ,
but their own belly : and by their fair speaking and
flattery they deceive the hearts of the guileless.
I say this, because the tidings of your obedience have 19
been told throughout the world.   On your own behalf, therefore, I rejoice : but I wish you not only to
be simple in respect of evil, but to be wise for good.
And the God of peace shall bruise Satan under your 20
feet speedily.
The grace of our Lord Jesus Christ be with you.

Salutations from Christians at Corinth to those at Rome.

Timotheus, my fellow-labourer, and Lucius, and 21
Jason,[2] and Sosipater,[3] my kinsmen, salute you.
I, Tertius, who have written this letter, salute you 22
in the Lord.
Gaius,[4] who is the host, not of me alone, but also 23
of the whole Church, salutes you.
Erastus,[5] the treasurer of the city, and the brother
Quartus, salute you.

Autograph conclusion.

The grace of our Lord Jesus Christ be with you all. 24
Now I commend you [6] unto Him who is able to 25
keep you stedfast, according to my Glad-tidings, and
the preaching[7] of Jesus Christ————whereby is un-

---

[1] See note on 1 Thess. v. 26.

[2] Jason is mentioned as a Thessalonian, Acts xvii. 5; he had probably accompanied St. Paul from Thessalonica to Corinth.

[3] Sosipater is mentioned as leaving Corinth with St. Paul, soon after this Epistle was written (Acts xx. 4).

[4] This Gaius (or Caius) is no doubt the same mentioned (1 Cor. i. 14) as baptized at Corinth by St. Paul with his own hands.   In Acts xx. 4 we find 'Gaius of Derbe' leaving Corinth with St. Paul, soon after the writing of this Epistle, but this may perhaps have been a different person; although this is not certain, considering how the Jews migrated from one place to another, of which Aquila and Priscilla are an obvious example.

[5] Erastus is again mentioned (as stopping at Corinth) in 2 Tim. iv. 20. Probably the same Erastus who went with Timotheus from Ephesus to Macedonia, on the way towards Corinth (Acts xix. 22).

[6] If we retain the 'to whom' in verse 27 (with the great majority of MSS.) we must supply 'I commend' or something equivalent here, or else leave the whole passage anacoluthical.   Examples of a similar commendation to God at the conclusion of a letter or speech are frequent in St. Paul.   Compare 1 Thess. v. 23, 2 Thess. ii. 16, and especially the conclusion of the speech (so nearly cotemporaneous with this Epistle) at Miletus, Acts xx. 32.   The complicated and involved construction reminds us of the Salutation commencing this Epistle, and of Eph. i.

[7] Literally, *proclamation*.

veiled the mystery which was kept secret in eternal

i. 26 times [1] of old, but has now been brought to light, and made known to all the Gentiles by the Scriptures of the Prophets, by command of the eternal God : that the Gentiles might be led to the obedience of

27 faith————unto Him, the only wise God,[2] I commend you through Jesus Christ ; to whom be glory for ever. Amen.[3]

Corinthian Coin representing Cenchreæ.[4]

[1] Meaning probably, *the times of the Ancient Dispensation.* Compare the use of the same expression, Tit. i. 2. There is no inconsistency in saying that this mystery was 'kept secret' under the Old Dispensation, and yet confirmed by the Prophetical Scriptures ; for it was hidden *from the Gentiles* altogether, and the prophetical intimations of it were not understood by the Jews.

[2] If we were (on the authority of the Codex Vaticanus) to omit the 'to whom' in this passage, the last three verses would become a continuous doxology. The translators of the A. V. have tacitly omitted this 'to whom,' although professing to follow the Textus Receptus.

[3] Some MSS. insert the verses 25, 26, 27 after xiv. 23, instead of in this place ; but the greater weight of MS. authority is in favour of their present position. A good refutation of the objections which have been made against the authenticity of the last two chapters, is given by De Wette and Neander ; but, above all, by Paley's *Horæ Paulinæ,* inasmuch as these very chapters furnish four or five of the most striking undesigned coincidences there mentioned.

[4] Little has been said as yet concerning Cenchreæ, and some interest is given to the place both by the mention of its Church in the preceding Epistle (Rom. xvi. 1), and by the departure of St. Paul from that port at the close of his first visit to Achaia (Acts xviii. 18). We have seen (p. 324) that it was seventy stadia, or nearly nine miles distant from Corinth, and (p. 330) that its position is still pointed out by the modern *Kikries,* where some remains of the ancient town are visible. The road is described by Pausanias as leading from Corinth through an avenue of pine-trees, and past many tombs, among which, two of the most conspicuous were those of the cynic Diogenes and the profligate Thais. The coin here engraved is that to which allusion was made p. 330, n. 5. It is a colonial coin of Antoninus Pius, and represents the harbour of Cenchreæ exactly as it is described by Pausanias.

CHAPTER XX.

Isthmian Games.— Route through Macedonia.— Voyage from Philippi.—
Sunday at Troas.—Assos.—Voyage by Mitylene and Trogyllium to Miletus.
—*Speech to the Ephesian Presbyters.*—Voyage by Cos and Rhodes to Patara.
—Thence to Phœnicia.—Christians at Tyre.—Ptolemais.—Events at Cæsarea.
—Arrival at Jerusalem.

In the Epistles which have been already set before the reader in
the course of this biography, and again in some of those which are to
succeed, St. Paul makes frequent allusion to a topic which engrossed
the interest, and called forth the utmost energies, of the Greeks.
The periodical games were to them rather a passion than an amusement : and the Apostle often uses language drawn from these celebrations, when he wishes to enforce the zeal and the patience with
which a Christian ought to strain after his heavenly reward.   The
imagery he employs is sometimes varied.   In one instance, when he
describes the struggle of the spirit with the flesh, he seeks his illustration in the violent contest of the boxers (1 Cor. ix. 26).   In
another, when he would give a strong representation of the perils
he had encountered at Ephesus, he speaks as one who had contended
in that ferocious sport which the Romans had introduced among
the Greeks, the fighting of gladiators with wild beasts (ib. xv. 32).
But, usually, his reference is to the *foot-race* in the *stadium*, which,
as it was the most ancient, continued to be the most esteemed, among
the purely Greek athletic contests.[1]   If we compare the various
passages where this language is used, we find the whole scene in
the stadium brought vividly before us,—the *herald*[2] who summons
the contending runners,—the *course*, which rapidly diminishes in
front of them, as their footsteps advance to the goal,[3]—the *judge*[4]
who holds out the prize at the end of the course,—the *prize* itself,
a chaplet of fading leaves, which is compared with the strongest
emphasis of contrast to the unfading glory with which the faithful
Christian will be crowned,[5]— the *joy and exultation of the victor,*

[1] The victory in the stadium at
Olympia was used in the formula for
reckoning Olympiads. The stadium was
the Greek unit for the measurement of
distance.   With St. Paul's frequent reference to it in the Epistles, 1 Cor. ix.
24, Rom. ix. 16, Gal. ii. 2, v. 7, Phil.
ii. 16, 2 Tim. iv. 7, 8, should be compared two passages in the Acts, xx.
24 where he speaks of himself, and
xiii. 25 where he speaks of John the
Baptist.
[2] 'Having heralded.' 1 Cor. ix. 27.

Plato says that the herald summoned
the candidates for the foot-race first into
the stadium.
[3] 'Forgetting the things that are
behind and striving after the things
that are before.'   Phil. iii. 14.   For
the *Course*, see Phil. ii. 16 and 2 Tim.
iv. 7, besides Acts xx. 24, which is
particularly noticed below, p. 553, n. 14.
[4] 2 Tim. iv. 8.
[5] See 1 Cor. ix. 24, Phil. iii. 14.   It
was a chaplet of green leaves, ' a fading
crown.' 1 Cor. ix. 25. (Cf. 2 Tim. ii.

which the Apostle applies to his own case, when he speaks of his converts as his 'joy and crown,' the token of his victory and the subject of his boasting.[1] And under the same image he sets forth the heavenly prize, after which his converts themselves should struggle with strenuous and unswerving zeal,—with no hesitating step (1 Cor. ix. 26),—pressing forward and never looking back (Phil. iii. 13, 14),—even to the disregard of life itself (Acts xx. 24). And the metaphor extends itself beyond the mere struggle in the arena, to the preparations which were necessary to success,— to that severe and continued *training*,[2] which, being so great for so small a reward, was a fit image of that 'training unto godliness,' which has the promise not only of this life, but of that which is to come,—to the strict *regulations*[3] which presided over all the details, both of the contest and the preliminary discipline, and are used to warn the careless Christian of the peril of an undisciplined life,— to the careful *diet*,[4] which admonishes us that, if we would so run that we may obtain, we must be 'temperate in all things.'[5]

This imagery would be naturally and familiarly suggested to St. Paul by the scenes which he witnessed in every part of his travels. At his own native place on the banks of the Cydnus,[6] in every city throughout Asia Minor,[7] and more especially at Ephesus, the stadium, and the training for the stadium,[8] were among the chief subjects of interest to the whole population. Even in Palestine, and at Jerusalem itself, these busy amusements were well known.[9]

5, iv. 8 ; also 1 Pet. v. 4.) The leaves varied with the locality where the games were celebrated. At the Isthmus they were those of the indigenous pine. For a time parsley was substituted for them ; but in the Apostle's day the pine-leaves were used again.

[1] Phil. iv. 1. 1 Thess. ii. 19. This subject illustrates the frequent use of the word 'boast' by St. Paul.

[2] 1 Tim. iv. 7, 8. The *Gymnasium* or *training-ground* was an important feature of every Greek city. The word is not found in the New Testament, but we find it in 1 Macc. i. 14 and 2 Macc. iv. 9, where allusion is made to places of Greek amusement built at Jerusalem.

[3] 'Except a man strive lawfully.' 2 Tim. ii. 5. The following were among the regulations of the athletic contests. Every candidate was required to be of pure Hellenic descent. He was disqualified by certain moral and political offences. He was obliged to take an oath that he had been ten months in training, and that he would violate none of the regulations. Bribery was punished by a fine. The candidate was obliged to practise again in the gymnasium immediately before the games, under the direction of

judges or umpires, who were themselves required to be instructed for ten months in the details of the games.

[4] The physician Galen gives an account of this prescribed diet. See Hor. *A. P.* 414. Tertullian describes the self-restraint of the Athletes.

[5] In the larger editions is an energetic passage on this subject from St. Chrysostom, who was very familiar with all that related to public amusements both at Antioch and Constantinople.

[6] It is worth observing, that the only inscription from Tarsus published by Boeckh relates to the restoration of the stadium.

[7] Nothing is more remarkable than the number and magnitude of the theatres and stadia in the ruins of the great cities of Asia Minor. A vast number, too, of the inscriptions relate to the public amusements. It is evident, as a traveller remarks, that these amusements must have been one of the chief employments of the population.

[8] See above, n. 2.

[9] See the reference to Herod's theatre and amphitheatre, p. 2 Hence the significance of such a passage as Heb. xii. 1, 2, to the Hebrew Christians of Palestine.

But Greece was the very home from which these institutions drew their origin; and the Isthmus of Corinth was one of four sanctuaries, where the most celebrated games were periodically held. Now that we have reached the point where St. Paul is about to leave this city for the last time, we are naturally led to make this allusion : and an interesting question suggests itself here, viz., whether the Apostle was ever himself present during the Isthmian games. It might be argued *à priori* that this is highly probable ; for great numbers came at these seasons from all parts of the Mediterranean to witness or take part in the contests ; and the very fact that amusement and ambition brought some, makes it certain that gain attracted many others ; thus it is likely that the Apostle, just as he desired to be at Jerusalem during the Hebrew festivals, so would gladly preach the Gospel at a time when so vast a concourse met at the Isthmus,— whence, as from a centre, it might be carried to every shore with the dispersion of the strangers. But, further, it will be remembered, that on his first visit, St. Paul spent two years at Corinth ; and though there is some difficulty in determining the times at which the games were celebrated, yet it seems almost certain that they recurred every second year, at the end of spring, or the beginning of summer.[1] Thus it may be confidently concluded that he was there at one of the festivals. As regards the voyage undertaken from Ephesus (p. 375), the time devoted to it was short, yet that time may have coincided with the festive season ; and it is far from inconceivable that he may have sailed across the Ægean in the spring, with some company of Greeks who were proceeding to the Isthmian meeting. On the present occasion he spent only three of the winter months in Achaia, and it is hardly possible that he could have been present during the games. It is most likely that there were no crowds among the pine-trees[2] at the Isthmus, and that the stadium at the Sanctuary of Neptune was silent and unoccupied when St. Paul passed by it along the northern road, on his way to Macedonia.[3]

[1] Of the four great national festivals, the Olympian and Pythian games took place every fourth year, the Nemean and Isthmian every second ; the latter in the third and first year of each Olympiad. The festival was held in the year 53 A.D., which is the first of an Olympiad ; and (as we have seen), there is good reason for believing that the Apostle came to Corinth in the autumn of 52, and left it in the spring of 54.

[2] This pine (πευκή) still retains its ancient name. See Sibthorpe's *Flora Græca*, as referred to by Canon Stanley in his Introduction to 1 Cor.

[3] A full account, both of the description which Pausanias gives of the sanctuary and of present appearances, may be seen in Leake. In our account of Corinth (Chap. XI., XII.), we have entered into no inquiry concerning the topography of the scene of the Isthmian games. (See p. 325.) Since St. Paul (as we have seen) makes many allusions to the athletic contests of the Greeks, and since we are now come to the point in his life when he leaves Corinth for the last time, it seems right that we should state what is known on the subject.

No complete topographical delineation of the Isthmus exists. This district was omitted in the French *Expédition de la Morée*. We have given opposite the plan of the ground near the sanctuary from Col. Leake's third volume, which accurately represents the relative positions of the stadium, the theatre, and the temple. But we must add, that since our last edition was published, the ground has been more exactly examined by the Rev. W. G. Clark, and a careful plan given

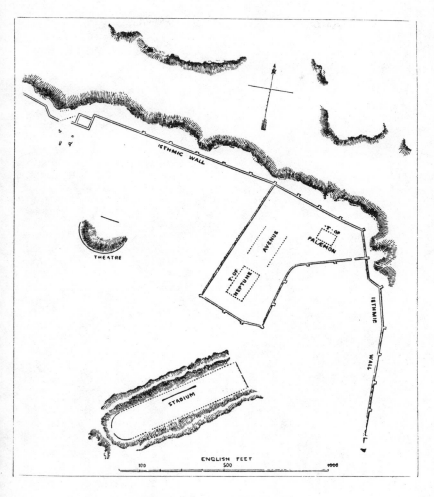

POSIDONIUM AT THE ISTHMUS.

(From Colonel Leake's *Morea.*)

His intention had been to go by sea to Syria,[1] as soon as the season of safe navigation should be come ; and in that case he would have embarked at Cenchreæ, whence he had sailed during his second missionary journey, and whence the Christian Phœbe had recently gone with the letter to the Romans.[2] He himself had prepared his mind for a journey to Rome ;[3] but first he was purposed to visit Jerusalem, that he might convey the alms which had been collected for the poorer brethren, in Macedonia and Achaia. He looked forward to this expedition with some misgiving; for he knew what danger was to be apprehended from his Jewish and Judaising enemies ; and even in his letter to the Roman Christians, he requested their prayers for his safety. And he had good reason to fear the Jews ; for ever since their discomfiture under Gallio they had been irritated by the progress of Christianity, and they organised a plot against the great preacher, when he was on the eve of departing for Syria. We are not informed of the exact nature of this plot ;[4] but it was probably a conspiracy against his life, like that which was formed at Damascus soon after his conversion (Acts ix. 23, 2 Cor. xi. 32), and at Jerusalem, both before and after the time of which we write (Acts ix. 29, xxiii. 12), and it necessitated a change of route, such as that which had once saved him on his departure from Berœa (Acts xvii. 14).

On that occasion his flight had been from Macedonia to Achaia ; now it was from Achaia to Macedonia. Nor would he regret the occasion which brought him once more among some of his dearest converts. Again he saw the Churches on the north of the Ægean, and again he went through the towns along the line of the Via Egnatia.[5] He reappeared in the scene of his persecution among the Jews of Thessalonica, and passed on by Apollonia and Amphipolis to the place where he had first landed on the European shore. The

---

in his *Peloponnesus* (1858).

The Posidonium, or Sanctuary of Neptune, is at the narrowest part of the Isthmus, close by Schœnus, the present Kalamaki (see p. 324, n. 3) ; and modern travellers may visit the ruins on their way between Kalamaki and Lutraki, from one steamboat to the other. St. Paul would also pass by this spot if he went by land from Athens (p. 319, n. 10). The distance from Corinth is about eight miles ; and at Hexamili, near Corinth, the road falls into that which lead to Cenchreæ. (See p. 537, and Leake, iii. 286.) The military wall, which crossed the Isthmus to Lechæum, abutted on the Sanctuary (p. 322, n. 1), and was for some space identical with the sacred enclosure. At no great distance are the traces of the canal which Nero left unfinished about the time of St. Paul's death (p. 324) ; and in many places along the shore, as any traveller may see on his way from Kalamaki to Lutraki, **are** those green pine-trees,

whose leaves wove the 'fading garlands' which the Apostle contrasts with the 'unfading crown,' the prize for which he fought.

[1] Acts xx. 3.

[2] For Cenchreæ, see the note at the end of the preceding chapter. Phœbe was a resident at Cenchreæ. When she went to Rome, she probably sailed from Lechæum.

[3] See the end of Chap. XV.

[4] 'The Jews generally settled in great numbers at seaports for the sake of commerce, and their occupation would give them peculiar influence over the captains and owners of merchant vessels, in which St. Paul must have sailed. They might, therefore, form the project of seizing him or murdering him at Cenchreæ with great probability of success.'—*Comm. on the Acts*, by Rev. F. C. Cook, 1850.

[5] For the Via Egnatia and the stages between Philippi and Berœa, see pp. 244, 245, 260, 261.

companions of his journey were Sopater the son of Pyrrhus,[1] a native of Berœa,—Aristarchus and Secundus, both of Thessalonica, —with Gaius of Derbe and Timotheus,—and two Christians from the province of Asia, Tychicus and Trophimus, whom we have mentioned before (p. 435), as his probable associates, when he last departed from Ephesus. From the order in which these disciples are mentioned, and the notice of the specific places to which they belonged, we should be inclined to conjecture that they had something to do with the collections which had been made at the various towns on the route. As St. Luke does not mention the collection,[2] we cannot expect to be able to ascertain all the facts. But since St. Paul left Corinth sooner than was intended, it seems likely that all the arrangements were not complete, and that Sopater was charged with the responsibility of gathering the funds from Berœa, while Aristarchus and Secundus took charge of those from Thessalonica. St. Luke himself was at Philippi : and the remaining four of the party were connected with the interior or the coast of Asia Minor.[3]

The whole of this company did not cross together from Europe to Asia ; but St. Paul and St. Luke lingered at Philippi, while the others preceded them to Troas.[4] The journey through Macedonia had been rapid, and the visits to the other Churches had been short. But the Church at Philippi had peculiar claims on St. Paul's attention : and the time of his arrival induced him to pause longer than in the earlier part of his journey. It was the time of the Jewish passover. And here our thoughts turn to the passover of the preceding year, when the Apostle was at Ephesus (p. 389). We remember the higher and Christian meaning which he gave to the Jewish festival. It was no longer an Israelitish ceremony, but it was the Easter of the New Dispensation. He was not now occupied with shadows ; for the substance was already in possession. Christ the Passover had been sacrificed, and the feast was to be kept with the unleavened bread of sincerity and truth. Such was the higher standing-point to which he sought to raise the Jews whom he met, in Asia or in Europe, at their annual celebrations.

Thus, while his other Christian companions had preceded him to Troas, he remained with Luke some time longer at Philippi, and did not leave Macedonia till the passover moon was waning. Notwith-

---

[1] Such seems to be the correct reading; and the addition may be made to distinguish him from Sosipater. (Rom. xvi. 21.)

[2] Except in one casual allusion at a later period. Acts xxiv. 17.

[3] Some would read 'and Timothy of Derbe,' in order to identify Gaius with the disciple of the same name who is mentioned before along with Aristarchus ('Gaius and Aristarchus, Macedonians,' xix. 29). But it is almost certain that Timotheus was a native of Lystra, and not Derbe (see p. 202, n. 5), and Gaius [or Caius, see above, p. 383] was so common a name, that this need cause us no difficulty.

[4] It is conceivable, but not at all probable, that these companions sailed direct from Corinth to Troas, while Paul went through Macedonia. Some would limit 'these' to Trophimus and Tychicus ; but this is quite unnatural. The expression 'as far as Asia' seems to imply that St. Paul's companions left him at Miletus, except St. Luke (who continues the narrative from this point in the first person) and Trophimus (who was with him at Jerusalem, xxi. 29), and whoever might be the other deputies who accompanied him with the alms. (2 Cor. viii. 19-21.)

standing this delay, they were anxious, if possible, to reach Jerusalem before Pentecost.[1] And we shall presently trace the successive days through which they were prosperously brought to the fulfilment of their wish.[2] Some doubt has been thrown on the possibility of this plan being accomplished in the interval; for they did not leave Philippi till the seventh day after the fourteenth of Nisan was past. It will be our business to show that the plan was perfectly practicable, and that it was actually accomplished, with some days to spare.

The voyage seemed to begin unfavourably. The space between Neapolis and Troas could easily be sailed over in two days with a fair wind : and this was the time occupied when the Apostle made the passage on his first coming to Europe.[3] On this occasion the same voyage occupied five days. We have no means of deciding

[1] Acts xx. 16.

[2] It may be well to point out here the general distribution of the time spent on the voyage. *Forty-nine* days intervened between Passover and Pentecost. The days of unleavened bread [Mark xiv. 12, Luke xxii. 7, Acts xii. 3, 1 Cor. v. 8] succeeded the Passover. Thus, St. Paul stayed at least *seven* days at Philippi after the Passover (ver. 6),—*five* days were spent on the passage to Troas (ib.),—*six* days (for so we may reckon them) were spent at Troas (ib.),—*four* were occupied on the voyage by Chios to Miletus (vv. 13 –15, see below),—*two* were spent at Miletus,—in *three* days St. Paul went by Cos and Rhode to Patara (xxi. 1, see below),—*two* days would suffice for the voyage to Tyre (vv. 2, 3),—*six* days were spent at Tyre (ver. 4), *two* were taken up in proceeding by Ptolemais to Cæsarea (vv. 7, 8). This calculation gives us *thirty-seven* days in all; thus leaving *thirteen* before the festival of Pentecost, after the arrival at Cæsarea, which is more than the conditions require. We may add, if necessary, two three or days more during the voyage in the cases where we have reckoned inclusively.

The mention of the *Sunday* spent at Troas fixes (though not quite absolutely) the day of the week on which the Apostle left Philippi. It was a Tuesday or a Wednesday. We might, with considerable probability, describe what was done *each day of the week* during the voyage; but we are not sure, in all cases, whether we are to reckon inclusively or exclusively, nor are we absolutely certain of the length of the stay at Miletus.

It will be observed, that all we have here said is independent of the parti-

cular year in which we suppose the voyage to have been made, and of the day of the week on which the 14th of Nisan occurred. Greswell and Wieseler have made the calculation for the years 56 and 58 respectively, and both have shown that the accomplishment of St. Paul's wish was practicable. Both too have allowed more time than needful for the voyage between Patara and Tyre.

We may observe here, that many commentators write on the nautical passages of the Acts as if the weather were always the same and the rate of sailing uniform, or as if the Apostle travelled in steam-boats. His motions were dependent on the wind. He might be detained in harbour by contrary weather. Nothing is more natural than that he should be five days on one occasion, and two on another, in passing between Philippi and Troas; just as Cicero was once fifteen, and once thirteen, in passing between Athens and Ephesus. So St. Paul might sail in two days from Patara to Tyre, though under less favourable circumstances, it might have required four or five, or even more. It is seldom that the same passage is twice made in exactly the same time by any vessel not a steamer.

Another remark may be added, that commentators often write as though St. Paul had chartered his own vessel, and had the full command of her movements. This would be highly unlikely for a person under the circumstances of St. Paul ; and we shall see that it was not the case in the present voyage, during which, as at other times, he availed himself of the opportunities offered by merchant vessels or coasters.

[3] Acts xvi. 11.

whether the ship's progress was retarded by calms, or by contrary winds.[1] Either of these causes of delay might equally be expected in the changeable weather of those seas. St. Luke seems to notice the time in both instances, in the manner of one who was familiar with the passages commonly made between Europe and Asia:[2] and something like an expression of disappointment is implied in the mention of the 'five days' which elapsed before the arrival at Troas.

The history of Alexandria Troas, first as a city of the Macedonian princes, and then as a favourite colony of the Romans,[3] has been given before; but little has been said as yet of its appearance. From the extent and magnitude of its present ruins (though for ages it has been a quarry both for Christian and Mahomedan edifices) we may infer what it was in its flourishing period. Among the oak-trees, which fill the vast enclosure of its walls, are fragments of colossal masonry. Huge columns of granite are seen lying in the harbour, and in the quarries on the neighbouring hills.[4] A theatre, commanding a view of Tenedos and the sea, shows where the Greeks once assembled in crowds to witness their favourite spectacles. Open arches of immense size, towering from the midst of other great masses of ruin, betray the hand of Roman builders. These last remains,—once doubtless belonging to a gymnasium or to baths, and in more ignorant ages, when the poetry of Homer was better remembered than the facts of history, popularly called 'The Palace of Priam,'[5]—are conspicuous from the sea. We cannot assert that these buildings existed in the day of St. Paul, but we may be certain that the city, both on the approach from the water, and to those who wandered through its streets, must have presented an appearance of grandeur and prosperity. Like Corinth, Ephesus, or Thessalonica, it was a place where the Apostle must have wished to

[1] The course is marked in our map with a zigzag line. If the wind was contrary, the vessel would have to beat. The delay might equally have been caused by calms.

[2] It has been remarked above (p. 241) that St. Luke's vocation as a physician may have caused him to reside at Philippi and Troas, and made him familiar with these coasts. The *autoptical* style (see p. 218, n. 4) is immediately resumed with the change of the pronoun.

[3] For the history of the foundation of the city under the successors of Alexander, and of the feelings of Romans towards it, see the concluding part of Chap. VIII.

[4] Alexandria Troas must have been, like Aberdeen, a city of granite. The hills which supplied this material were to the N.E. and S.E. Dr. Clarke (vol. ii. p. 149) mentions a stupendous column, which is concealed among some trees in the neighbourhood, and which he compares to the famous column of the Egyptian Alexandria. Fellows (p. 58) speaks of hundreds of columns, and says that many are bristling among the waves to a considerable distance out at sea. He saw seven columns lying with their chips in a quarry, which is connected by a paved road with the city. Thus granite seems to have been to Alexandria Troas what marble was to Athens. The granite columns of Troas have been used for making cannon-balls for the defence of the Dardanelles.

[5] Dr. Clarke regards these ruins as the remains of Alexandria Troas. He says that 'these three arches of the building make a conspicuous figure from a considerable distance at sea, like the front of a magnificent palace; and this circumstance, connected with the mistake so long prevalent concerning the city itself [viz. that it was the ancient Troy], gave rise to the appellation of "*The Palace of Priam,*" bestowed by mariners upon these ruins.' See p. 216, n. 3.

lay firmly and strongly the foundations of the Gospel. On his first visit, as we have seen (pp. 215–218), he was withheld by a supernatural revelation from remaining ; and on his second visit (pp. 434–436), though a door was opened to him, and he did gather together a community of Christian disciples, yet his impatience to see Titus compelled him to bid them a hasty farewell.[1] Now, therefore, he would be the more anxious to add new converts to the Church, and to impress deeply on those who were converted, the truths and the duties of Christianity : and he had valuable aid both in Luke, who accompanied him, and the other disciples who had preceded him.

The labours of the early days of the week that was spent at Troas are not related to us ; but concerning the last day we have a narrative which enters into details with all the minuteness of one of the Gospel histories. It was the evening which succeeded the Jewish Sabbath.[2] On the Sunday morning the vessel was about to sail.[3] The Christians of Troas were gathered together at this solemn time to celebrate that feast of love which the last commandment of Christ has enjoined on all His followers. The place was an upper room, with a recess or balcony[4] projecting over the street or the court. The night was dark : three weeks had not elapsed since the Passover,[5] and the moon only appeared as a faint crescent in the early part of the night. Many lamps were burning in the room where the congregation was assembled.[6] The place was hot and crowded. St. Paul, with the feeling strongly impressed on his mind that the next day was the day of his departure, and that souls might be lost by delay, was continuing in earnest discourse, and prolonging it even till midnight,[7] when an occurrence suddenly took place, which filled the assembly with alarm, though it was afterwards converted into an occasion of joy and thanksgiving. A young listener, whose name was Eutychus, was overcome by exhaustion, heat, and weariness, and sank into a deep slumber.[8] He was seated or leaning

---

[1] 2 Cor. ii. 13.

[2] 'The first day of the week,' ver. 7. This is a passage of the utmost importance, as showing that the observance of *Sunday* was customary. Cf. 1 Cor. xvi. 2. See p. 346.

[3] 'About to depart on the morrow,' ib. See ver. 13. By putting all these circumstances together, we can almost certainly infer the day of the week on which St. Paul left Troas. See above.

[4] The word used here denotes an aperture closed by a wooden door, doubtless open in this case because of the heat. See the note and the woodcut in the *Pictorial Bible*. These upper rooms of the ancients were usually connected with the street by outside stairs, such as those of which we see traces at Pompeii.

[5] See above, p. 543.

[6] Ver. 8. Various reasons have been suggested why this circumstance should

be mentioned. Meyer thinks it is given as the reason why the fate of the young man was perceived at once. But it has much more the appearance of having simply 'proceeded from an eye-witness, who mentions the incident, not for the purpose of obviating a difficulty which might occur to the reader, but because the entire scene to which he refers stood now with such minuteness and vividness before his mind.' Hackett *on the Acts*, Boston, U. S., 1852. [See a similar instance in the case of the mention of the proseucha at Philippi, Acts xvi. 13.]

[7] 'He continued his discourse till midnight,' ver. 7. 'While Paul was long discoursing,' ver. 9.

[8] The present participle in ver. 9 seems to denote the gradual sinking into sleep, as opposed to the sudden fall implied by the aorist participle in the next phrase.

in the balcony ; and, falling down in his sleep, was dashed upon the pavement below, and was taken up dead.[1] Confusion and terror followed, with loud lamentation.[2] But Paul was enabled to imitate the power of that Master whose doctrine he was proclaiming. As Jesus had once said[3] of the young maiden, who was taken by death from the society of her friends, 'She is not dead, but sleepeth,' so the Apostle of Jesus received power to restore the dead to life. He went down and fell upon the body, like Elisha of old,[4] and, embracing Eutychus, said to the bystanders, 'Do not lament ; for his life is in him.'

With minds solemnised and filled with thankfulness by this wonderful token of God's power and love, they celebrated the Eucharistic feast.[5] The act of Holy Communion was combined, as was usual in the Apostolic age, with a common meal :[6] and St. Paul now took some refreshment after the protracted labour of the evening,[7] and then continued his conversation till the dawning of the day.[8]

It was now time for the congregation to separate. The ship was about to sail, and the companions of Paul's journey took their departure to go on board.[9] It was arranged, however, that the Apostle himself should join the vessel at Assos, which was only about twenty miles[10] distant by the direct road, while the voyage round Cape Lectum was nearly twice as far. He thus secured a few more

[1] It is quite arbitrary to qualify the words by supposing that he was only apparently dead.

[2] This is implied in the 'Trouble not yourselves' below. The word denotes a loud and violent expression of grief, as in Matt. ix. 23, Mark v. 39.

[3] Matt. ix. 24 ; Mark v. 39.

[4] 2 Kings iv. 34. In each case, as Prof. Hackett remarks, the act appears to have been the sign of a miracle.

[5] Ver. 11, compared with ver. 7.

[6] See p. 345.

[7] *When he had eaten,* ver. 11. This is distinguished in the Greek from *the breaking bread.*

[8] *Having talked a long while.* This, again, is distinguished from the *preaching* mentioned above.

[9] We might illustrate what took place at this meeting by the sailing of the Bishop of Calcutta from Plymouth in 1829. 'He and his chaplain made impressive and profitable addresses to us, the first part of the meeting, as they had received orders to embark the same morning. I began then to speak, and in the middle of my speech the captain of the frigate sent for them, and they left the meeting.'—*Memoir of Rev. E. Bickersteth,* vol. i. p. 445.

[10] See p. 214. The impression derived from modern travellers through this neglected region is, that the distance between Assos and Troas is rather greater. Sir C. Fellows reckons it at 30 miles, and he was in the saddle from half-past eight to five. Dr. Hunt, in Walpole's *Memoirs,* was part of two days on the road, leaving Assos in the afternoon ; but he deviated to see the hot springs and salt works. Mr. Weston (MS. journal) left Assos at three in the afternoon, and reached Troas at ten the next morning ; but he adds, that it was almost impossible to find the road without a guide. In a paper on 'Recent Works on Asia Minor,' in the *Bibliotheca Sacra* for Oct. 1851, it is said that Assos is nine miles from Troas. This must be an oversight. It is, however, quite possible that Mitylene might have been reached, as we have assumed below, on the Sunday evening. If the vessel sailed from Troas at seven in the morning, she would easily be round Cape Lectum before noon. If St. Paul left Troas at ten, he might arrive at Assos at four in the afternoon ; and the vessel might be at anchor in the roads of Mitylene at seven. Greswell supposes that they sailed from Assos on the Monday. This would derange the days of the week as we have given them below, but would not affect the general conclusion.

precious hours with his converts at Troas ; and eagerly would they profit by his discourse, under the feeling that he was so soon to leave them : and we might suppose that the impression made under such circumstances, and with the recollection of what they had witnessed in the night, would never be effaced from the minds of any of them, did we not know, on the highest authority, that if men believe not the prophets of God, neither will they believe 'though one rose from the dead.'

But the time came when St. Paul too must depart. The vessel might arrive at Assos before him ; and, whatever influence he might have with the seamen, he could not count on any long delay. He hastened, therefore, through the southern gate, past the hot springs,[1] and through the oak woods,[2]—then in full foliage,[3]—which cover all that shore with greenness and shade, and across the wild water-courses on the western side of Ida.[4] Such is the scenery which now surrounds the traveller on his way from Troas to Assos. The great difference then was, that there was a good Roman road,[5] which made St. Paul's solitary journey both more safe and more rapid than it could have been now. We have seldom had occasion to think of the Apostle in the hours of his solitude. But such hours must have been sought and cherished by one whose whole strength was drawn from communion with God, and especially at a time when, as on this present journey, he was deeply conscious of his weakness, and filled with foreboding fears.[6] There may have been other reasons why he lingered at Troas after his companions : but the desire for solitude was (we may well believe) one reason among others. The discomfort of a crowded ship is unfavourable for devotion : and prayer and meditation are necessary for maintaining the religious life even of an Apostle. That Saviour to whose service he was devoted had often prayed in solitude on the mountain, and crossed the brook Kedron to kneel under the olives of Gethsemane. And strength and peace were surely sought and obtained by the Apostle from the Redeemer, as he pursued his lonely road that Sunday afternoon in spring, among the oak woods and the streams of Ida.

No delay seems to have occurred at Assos. He entered by the Sacred Way among the famous tombs,[7] and through the ancient

---

[1] Mentioned by Fellows and Hunt.

[2] All travellers make mention of the woods of Vallonea oaks in the neighbourhood of Troas. The acorns are used for dyeing, and form an important branch of trade. The collecting of the acorns, and shells, and gall-nuts, employs the people during a great part of the year. One traveller mentions an English vessel which he saw taking in a load of these acorns.

[3] The woods were in full foliage on the 18th of March. Hunt.

[4] For the streams of this mountain, see p. 214, n. 5.

[5] See note on the preceding page.

[6] Compare Rom. xv. 30, 31, Acts xx.

3. with Acts xx. 22–25, xxi. 4, 13.

This Street of Tombs (*Via Sacra*) is one of the most remarkable features of Assos. It is described by Fellows in his excellent account of Assos. The Street of Tombs extends to a great distance across the level ground to N.W. of the city. Some of the tombs are of vast dimensions, and formed each of one block of granite. These remains are the more worthy of notice because the word *sarcophagus* was first applied in Roman times to this stone of Assos (*lapis Assius*), from the peculiar power it was supposed to possess of aiding the natural decay of corpses.

gateway, and proceeded immediately to the shore. We may suppose
that the vessel was already hove to and waiting when he arrived ;
or that he saw her approaching from the west, through the channel
between Lesbos and the main.   He went on board without delay,
and the Greek sailors and the Apostolic missionaries continued their
voyage.   As to the city of Assos itself, we must conclude, if we
compare the description of the ancients with present appearances,
that its aspect as seen from the sea was sumptuous and grand.   A
terrace with a long portico was raised by a wall of rock above the
water-line.   Above this was a magnificent gate,[1] approached by a
flight of steps.   Higher still was the theatre, which commanded a
glorious view of Lesbos and the sea, and those various buildings
which are now a wilderness of broken columns, triglyphs, and
friezes.   The whole was crowned by a citadel of Greek masonry on
a cliff of granite.   Such was the view which gradually faded into
indistinctness as the vessel retired from the shore, and the summits
of Ida rose in the evening sky.[2]

The course of the voyagers was southwards, along the eastern
shore of Lesbos.   When Assos was lost, Mitylene, the chief city of
Lesbos, came gradually into view.   The beauty of the capital of
Sappho's island was celebrated by the architects, poets, and philosophers of Rome.   Like other Greek cities, which were ennobled
by old recollections, it was honoured by the Romans with the privilege of freedom.[3] Situated on the south-eastern coast of the island,
it would afford a good shelter from the north-westerly winds,
whether the vessel entered the harbour or lay at anchor in the
open roadstead.[4] It seems likely that the reason why they lay here

[1] The view opposite is from a drawing by the Rev. G. F. Weston, who
visited Assos in 1845. In his MS.
journal he speaks of it as follows:
'Proceeding 300 or 400 yards [from
the theatre] in a N.W. direction, you
come to the great gate of the city, a
very interesting specimen of Greek
architecture.   An arch is formed by
one stone overlapping that beneath it.
There are remains also of two flank-
ing towers with splayed loopholes, and
the wall running up to the precipices
of the Acropolis is almost perfect.
Higher up, towards the Acropolis, are
two more curious arches.   Running
N.W. from the great gate is the *Via
Sacra.*'   See the preceding note.

[2] The travellers above mentioned
speak in strong terms of the view from
the Acropolis towards Lesbos and the
sea.   Towards Ida and the land side
the eye ranges over the windings of a
river through a fruitful plain.

Fellows conceives that the remains
here mentioned have been preserved
from the depredations committed on
other towns near the coast, in consequence of the material being the 'same

grey stone as the neighbouring rock,
and not having intrinsic value as
marble.'   He observed 'no trace of
the Romans.'   Leake says that the
'hard granite of Mount Ida' has furnished the materials for many of the
buildings, and even the sculptures : and
he adds that 'the whole gives perhaps
the most perfect idea of a Greek city
that anywhere exists.'

[3] For a sketch of the history of
Mitylene, and for remarks on the or-
thography of the word, see Smith's
Dict. of Geography.   In our larger
editions is a view of the town with the
mountains behind.

[4] 'The chief town of Mitylene is on
the S.E. coast, and on a peninsula
(once an island) forming two small
harbours : of these the northern one is
sheltered by a pier to the north, and
admits small coasters. . . . . The
roadstead, which is about seven miles
N. from the S.E. end of the island,
is a good summer roadstead, but the
contrary in winter, being much exposed
to the S.E. and N.E. winds, which
blow with great violence.'—Purdy's
Sailing Directory, p. 154.   It should

GATEWAY OF ASSOS.

(See p. 548, n. 1.)

for the night was, because it was the time of dark moon,[1] and they would wish for daylight to accomplish safely the intricate navigation between the southern part of Lesbos and the mainland of Asia Minor.

In the course of Monday they were abreast of Chios (ver. 15). The weather in these seas is very variable : and, from the mode of expression employed by St. Luke, it is probable that they were becalmed. An English traveller under similar circumstances has described himself as 'engrossed from daylight till noon' by the beauty of the prospects with which he was surrounded, as his vessel floated idly on this channel between Scio and the continent.[2] On one side were the gigantic masses of the mainland : on the other were the richness and fertility of the island, with its gardens of oranges,[3] citrons, almonds, and pomegranates, and its white scattered houses overshadowed by evergreens. Until the time of its recent disasters, Scio was the paradise of the modern Greek : and a familiar proverb censured the levity of its inhabitants,[4] like that which in the Apostle's day described the coarser faults of the natives of Crete (Tit. i. 12).

The same English traveller passed the island of Samos after leaving that of Chios. So likewise did St. Paul (ver. 15). But the former sailed along the western side of Samos, and he describes how its towering cloud-capped heights are contrasted with the next low island to the west.[5] The Apostle's course lay along the eastern shore, where a much narrower 'marine pass' intervenes between it and a long mountainous ridge of the mainland, from which it appears to have been separated by some violent convulsion of nature.[6]

be particularly observed, that St. Paul's ship would be sheltered here from the N.W. We shall see, as we proceed, increasing reason for believing that the wind blew from this quarter.

[1] The moon would be about six days old (see above), and would set soon after midnight. We are indebted for this suggestion to Mr. Smith (author of the *Voyage and Shipwreck of St. Paul*), and we take this opportunity of acknowledging our obligations to his MS. notes, in various parts of this chapter.

[2] Dr. Clarke's *Travels*, vol. ii. p. 188. See the whole description. This applies to a period some years before the massacre of 1822. For notices of Scio, and a description of the scenery in its nautical aspect, see the *Sailing Directory*, pp. 124-128.

[3] It must be remembered that the vegetation, and with the vegetation the scenery, of the shores of the Mediterranean, have varied with the progress of civilisation. It seems that the Arabians introduced the orange in the early part of the middle ages. Other changes are subsequent to the

discovery of America. See p. 18, n. 1. The wines of Chios were always celebrated. Its coins display an amphora and a bunch of grapes.

[4] The proverb says that it is easier to find a green horse than a sober-minded Sciot.

[5] See the view which Dr. Clarke gives of this remarkable '*marine pass*,' vol. ii. p. 192. The summit of Samos was concealed by a thick covering of clouds, and he was told that its heights were rarely unveiled. See again vol. iii. pp. 364-367. Compare Norie's *Sailing Directory*, p. 150. 'Samos, being mountainous, becomes visible twenty leagues off; and the summit of Mount Kerki retains its snow throughout the year.' The strait through which Dr. Clarke sailed is called the *Great Boghaz*, and is ten miles broad. The island to the west is Icaria.

[6] This strait is the *Little Boghaz*, which is reckoned at about a mile in breadth both by Strabo and Chandler. We shall return presently to this ridge of Mycale in its relation to the interior, when we refer to the journey of the Ephesian elders to Miletus. It was

This high promontory is the ridge of Mycale, well known in the annals of Greek victory over the Persians. At its termination, not more than a mile from Samos, is the anchorage of Trogyllium. Here the night of Tuesday was spent; apparently for the same reason as that which caused the delay at Mitylene. The moon set early : and it was desirable to wait for the day before running into the harbour of Miletus.[1]

The short voyage from Chios to Trogyllium had carried St. Paul through familiar scenery. The bay across which the vessel had been passing was that into which the Cayster[2] flowed. The mountains on the mainland were the western branches of Messogis and Tmolus,[3] the ranges that enclose the primeval plain of ' Asia.' The city, towards which it is likely that some of the vessels in sight were directing their course, was Ephesus, where the Apostolic labours of three years had gathered a company of Christians in the midst of unbelievers. One whose solicitude was so great for his recent converts could not willingly pass by and leave them unvisited: and had he had the command of the movements of the vessel, we can hardly believe that he would have done so. He would surely have landed at Ephesus, rather than at Miletus. The same wind which carried him to the latter harbour, would have been equally advantageous for a quick passage to the former. And, even had the weather been unfavourable at the time for landing at Ephesus, he might easily have detained the vessel at Trogyllium; and a short journey by land northward would have taken him to the scene of his former labours.[4]

Yet every delay, whether voluntary or involuntary, might have been fatal to the plan he was desirous to accomplish. St. Luke informs us here (and the occurrence of the remark shows us how much regret was felt by the Apostle on passing by Ephesus) that his intention was, *if possible*, to be in Jerusalem at Pentecost (ver. 16). Even with a ship at his command, he could not calculate on favourable weather, if he lost his present opportunity : nor could he safely leave the ship which had conveyed him hitherto ;

evidently a place well known to sailors, from Strabo's reckoning the distance from hence to Sunium in Attica.

[1] We should observe here again that Trogyllium, though on the shore of the mainland, is protected by Samos from the north-westerly winds. With another wind it might have been better to have anchored in a port to the N.E. of Samos, now called Port Vathy, which is said, in the *Sailing Directory* (p. 119), to be ' protected from every wind but the N.W.' We may refer here to the clear description and map of Samos by Tournefort, *Voyage du Levant*, i. pp. 156, 157. But the Admiralty Charts (1530 and 1555) should be consulted for the soundings, &c. An anchorage will be seen just to the east of the extreme point of Trogyllium, bearing the name of '*St. Paul's Port.*'

[2] See what is said of the Cayster, pp. 368, 419, 420.

[3] See again, on these Ephesian mountains, pp. 419, 420.

[4] Trogyllium, as we have seen, is at the point where the coast projects and forms a narrow strait between Asia Minor and Samos. The coast recedes northwards towards Ephesus, and southwards towards Miletus, each of these places being about equidistant from Trogyllium. Up to this point from Chios St. Paul had been nearly following the line of the Ephesian merchant vessels up what is now called the gulf of Scala Nuova. By comparing the Admiralty Chart with Strabo and Chandler, a very good notion is obtained of the coast and country between Ephesus and Miletus.

for he was well aware that he could not be certain of meeting with another that would forward his progress. He determined, therefore, to proceed in the same vessel, on her southward course from Trogyllium to Miletus. Yet the same watchful zeal which had urged him to employ the last precious moments of the stay at Troas in his Master's cause, suggested to his prompt mind a method of re-impressing the lessons of eternal truth on the hearts of the Christians at Ephesus, though he was unable to revisit them in person. He found that the vessel would be detained at Miletus[1] a sufficient time to enable him to send for the presbyters of the Ephesian Church, with the hope of their meeting him there. The distance between the two cities was hardly thirty miles, and a good road connected them together.[2] Thus, though the stay at Miletus would be short, and it might be hazardous to attempt the journey himself, he could hope for one more interview,—if not with the whole Ephesian Church, at least with those members of it whose responsibility was the greatest.

The sail from Trogyllium, with a fair wind, would require but little time. If the vessel weighed anchor at daybreak on Wednesday, she would be in harbour long before noon.[3] The message was doubtless sent to Ephesus immediately on her arrival; and Paul remained at Miletus waiting for those whom the Holy Spirit, by his hands, had made 'overseers' over the flock of Christ (ver. 28). The city where we find the Christian Apostle now waiting, while those who had the care of the vessel were occupied with the business that detained them, has already been referred to as more ancient than Ephesus,[4] though in the age of St. Paul inferior to it in political and mercantile eminence. Even in Homer, the 'Carian Miletus' appears as a place of renown. Eighty colonies went forth from the banks of the Mæander, and some of them were spread even to the eastern shores of the Black Sea, and beyond the pillars of Hercules to the west. It received its first blow in the Persian war, when its inhabitants, like the Jews, had experience of a Babylonian captivity.[5] It suffered once more in Alexander's great campaign ;[6] and after his time it gradually began to sink towards its present condition of ruin and decay, from the influence, as it would seem, of

---

[1] It is surely quite a mistake to suppose, with some commentators, that St. Paul had the command of the movements of the vessel. His influence with the captain and the seamen might induce them to do all in their power to oblige him ; and perhaps we may trace some such feeling in the arrangements at Assos, just as afterwards at Sidon (Acts xxvii. 3), when on his voyage to Rome. But he must necessarily have been content to take advantage of such opportunities as were consistent with the business on which the vessel sailed. She evidently put in for business to Troas, Miletus, and Patara. At the other places she seems to have touched merely for convenience, in consequence of the state of the weather or the darkness.

[2] Pliny says that Magnesia is fifteen miles from Ephesus, and Magnesia was about equidistant from Ephesus, Tralles, and Miletus. For further notices of the roads we must refer to our larger editions.

[3] The distance is about seventeen nautical miles and a half. If the vessel sailed at six in the morning from Trogyllium, she would easily be in harbour at nine.

[4] See above, p. 368. Compare p. 420. Thus the imperial coins of Miletus are rare, and the autonomous coins begin very early.

[5] Herod. v. 30, vi. 18.

[6] Arrian, *Anab.* i. 19, 20.

mere natural causes,—the increase of alluvial soil in the delta having the effect of removing the city gradually further and further from the sea. Even in the Apostle's time, there was between the city and the shore a considerable space of level ground, through which the ancient river *meandered* in new windings, like the Forth at Stirling.[1] Few events connect the history of Miletus with the transactions of the Roman Empire. When St. Paul was there, it was simply one of the second-rate sea-ports on this populous coast, ranking, perhaps, with Adramyttium or Patara, but hardly with Ephesus or Smyrna.[2]

The excitement and joy must have been great among the Christians of Ephesus, when they heard that their honoured friend and teacher, to whom they had listened so often in the school of Tyrannus, was in the harbour[3] of Miletus, within the distance of a few miles. The presbyters must have gathered together in all haste to obey the summons, and gone with eager steps out of the southern gate, which leads to Miletus. By those who travel on such an errand, a journey of twenty or thirty miles is not regarded long and tedious, nor is much regard paid to the difference between day and night.[4] The presbyters of Ephesus might easily reach Miletus on the day after that on which the summons was received.[5] And though they might be weary when they arrived, their fatigue would soon be forgotten at the sight of their friend and instructor; and God also, 'who comforts them that are cast down' (2 Cor. vii. 6), comforted him by the sight of his disciples. They were gathered together—probably in some solitary spot upon the shore—to listen to his address. This little company formed a singular contrast with the crowds which used to assemble at the times of public amusement in the theatre of Miletus.[6] But that vast theatre is now

[1] This is the comparison of Sir C. Fellows. The Mæander was proverbial among the ancients, both for the sinuosities of its course, and the great quantity of alluvial soil brought down by the stream. Pliny tells us that islands near Miletus had been joined to the continent, and Strabo relates that Priene, once a sea-port, was in his time forty stadia from the sea. Fellows says that Miletus was once a headland in a bay, which is now a 'dead flat' ten miles in breadth. Chandler (p. 202), on looking down from Priene on the 'bare and marshy plain,' says, 'How different its aspect when the mountains were boundaries of a gulf, and Miletus, Myus, and Priene, maritime cities.'—And again (p. 207), he looks forward to the time when Samos and other islands will unite with the shore, and the present promontories will be seen inland. See Kiepert's *Hellas*, for a representation of the coast as it was in the early Greek times; and for a true delineation of its present state, see the Admiralty Chart,

No. 1555.
[2] For Smyrna, see again pp. 368, 420.
[3] Strabo says that Miletus had four harbours, one of which was for vessels of war. No trace of them is to be seen now.
[4] For a notion of the scenery of this journey of the presbyters over or round the ridge of Mycale, and by the windings of the Mæander, the reader may consult Chandler and Fellows. The latter describes the extensive view in each direction from the summit of the range. The former was travelling, like these presbyters, in April; and 'the weather was unsettled; the sky was blue and the sun shone, but a wet wintry north wind swept the clouds along the top of the range of Mycale.'
[5] We may remark here, in answer to those who think that the ἐπίσκοποι mentioned in this passage were the bishops of various places in the province of Asia, that there was evidently no time to summon them. On the convertibility of ἐπίσκοπος and πρεσβύτερος, see below.
[6] In our larger editions is a view of

a silent ruin,—while the words spoken by a careworn traveller to a few despised strangers are still living as they were that day, to teach lessons for all time, and to make known eternal truths to all who will hear them,—while they reveal to us, as though they were merely human words, all the tenderness and the affection of Paul, the individual speaker.

ACTS
XX.

18   Brethren,[1] ye know yourselves,[2] from the first day that I came into Asia, after what manner I have been
19 with you throughout all the time; serving the Lord Jesus[3] with all[4] lowliness of mind, and with many tears[5] and trials which befell me through the plotting[6]
20 of the Jews. And how I kept[7] back none of those things which are profitable for you, but declared them to you, and taught you both publicly and from house[8]
21 to house; testifying both to Jews and Gentiles their[9] need of repentance towards God, and faith in our
22 Lord Jesus Christ. And now as for me,[10] behold I go to Jerusalem[11] in spirit foredoomed to chains; yet I know not the things which shall befall me there,
23 save that in every city[12] the Holy Spirit gives the same testimony, that bonds and afflictions abide me.
24 But none of these things move me,[13] neither count I my life dear unto myself, so that I might finish my course with joy,[14] and the ministry which I received

He reminds them of his past labours among them.

Miletus from Laborde. The two conspicuous features are the great theatre and the windings of the Mæander towards the sea.

[1] 'Brethren' is found here in the Uncial Manuscript D (Codex Bezæ) and in some early versions; and we have adopted it, because it is nearly certain that St. Paul would not have begun his address abruptly without some such word. Compare all his other recorded speeches in the Acts.

[2] 'Ye yourselves,' emphatic.

[3] 'The Lord,' as Col. iii. 24. With this self-commendation Tholuck compares 1 Thess. ii. 10, and 2 Cor. vi. 3, 4. See note on verse 33 below. 'Felix,' says Bengel, 'qui sic exordiri potest conscientiam auditorum testando.'

[4] '*All*.' Tholuck remarks on the characteristic use of 'all' in St. Paul's Epistles.

[5] '*Tears*.' Compare 2 Cor. ii. 4, and Phil. iii. 18.

[6] '*Plotting of Jews*.' Compare 1 Cor. xv. 31.

[7] '*Kept back nothing*.' Compare 2 Cor. iv. 2, and 1 Thess. ii. 4.

[8] '*House to house*.' Compare 1 Thess. ii. 11.

[9] Observe that the definite article is used here. THE *repentance* (which they ought to have) *towards God*, &c.

[10] See next note.

[11] The order of the words, according to the true reading, gives this turn to the passage. St. Paul was '*bound*,' i.e. *a prisoner in chains*, but as yet only *in the spirit*, not in body. This is not the *Holy Spirit*, from which it is distinguished by the addition of 'Holy' in the verse below. This explanation of the passage (which agrees with that of Grotius and Chrysostom) seems the natural one, in spite of the objections of De Wette and others.

[12] We have two examples of this afterwards, namely, at Tyre (Acts xxi. 4) and at Cæsarea (Acts xxi. 10, 11). And from the present passage we learn that such warnings had been given in many places during this journey. St. Paul's own anticipations of danger appear Rom. xv. 31.

[13] The reading adopted by Tischendorf here, though shorter, is the same in sense.

[14] Compare 2 Tim. iv. 7 and Phil. ii. 16. See the remarks which have been

from the Lord Jesus to testify the Glad-tidings of the grace of God.

His farewell warning.

And now, behold I know that ye all,[1] among whom xx. 25 I have gone from city to city, proclaiming the kingdom of God, shall see my face no more. Wherefore 26 I take you to witness this day, that I am clear from the blood[2] of all. For I have not shunned to declare 27 unto you all the counsel of God. Take heed, therefore, 28 unto yourselves, and to all the flock in which the Holy Spirit has made you overseers,[3] to feed the Church of God,[4] which He purchased with His own blood. For this I know, that after my departure, 29 grievous wolves shall enter in among you, who will not spare the flock. And from your own selves will 30 men arise speaking perverted words, that they may draw away the disciples after themselves.[5] There- 31 fore, be watchful, and remember that for the space of three years [6] I ceased not to warn every one of you, night and day, with tears.[7]

Final commendation to God, and exhortation to disinterested exertion.

And [8] now, brethren, I commend you to God, and 32 to the word of His grace; even to Him who is able to build you up and to give you an inheritance among all them that are sanctified. When I was with you,[9] 33

made in the early part of this chapter on this favourite metaphor of St. Paul, especially p. 538, n. 1. [See also p. 140, n. 6. H.]

[1] This 'all' includes not only the Ephesian presbyters, but also the brethren from Macedonia. (See Acts xx. 4.) The 'gone' is, literally, 'gone *through*.' With regard to the expectation expressed by St. Paul, it must be regarded as a human inference from the danger which he knew to be before him. If (as we think) he was liberated after his first imprisonment at Rome, he did see some of his present audience again. Tholuck compares Phil. i. 20, 25, and ii. 24.

[2] See xviii. 6. 'Your blood be upon your own heads: I am clean.'

[3] Ἐπισκόπους. It is scarcely necessary to remark, that in the New Testament the words ἐπίσκοπος and πρεσβύτερος are convertible. Compare verse 17 and Tit. i. 5, 7, and see p. 340. Tholuck remarks that this reference to the Holy Spirit as the author of church government is in exact accordance with 1 Cor. xii. 8, 11, and 28.

[4] We have retained the T. R. here since the MSS. and Fathers are divided between the readings 'God' and 'Lord.'

At the same time we must acknowledge that the balance of authority is rather in favour of 'Lord.' A very candid and able outline of the evidence on each side of the question is given by Mr. Humphry. The sentiment exactly agrees with 1 Cor. vi. 20.

[5] We read 'themselves' with Lachmann on the authority of some of the best MSS.

[6] This *space of three years* may either be used (in the Jewish mode of reckoning) for the two years and upwards which St. Paul spent at Ephesus; or, if we suppose him to speak to the Macedonians and Corinthians also (who were present), it may refer to the whole time (about three years and a half), since he came to reside at Ephesus in the autumn of 54 A.D.

[7] See p. 553, n. 5. We have much satisfaction in referring here to the second of A. Monod's recently published sermons. (*Saint Paul, Cinq Discours.* Paris, 1851.)

[8] This conclusion reminds us of that of the letter to the Romans so recently written. Compare Rom. xvi. 25.

[9] This is the force of the aorist, unless we prefer to suppose it used (as often by St. Paul) for a perfect.

v. 34 I coveted no man's silver or gold, or raiment.   Yea,
ye know yourselves,[1] that these hands ministered to
my necessities, and to those who were with me.[2]

35 And all this I did for your example; to teach you
that so labouring ye ought to support the helpless,[3]
and to remember the words of the Lord Jesus, how
He said, 'IT IS MORE BLESSED TO GIVE THAN TO RE-
CEIVE.'

The close of this speech was followed by a solemn act of united
supplication (Acts xx. 36).   St. Paul knelt down on the shore with
all those who had listened to him, and offered up a prayer to that
God who was founding His Church in the midst of difficulties
apparently insuperable; and then followed an outbreak of natural
grief, which even Christian faith and resignation were not able to
restrain.   They fell on the Apostle's neck and clung to him, and
kissed him again and again,[4] sorrowing most because of his own
foreboding announcement, that they should never behold that countenance again, on which they had often gazed[5] with reverence and
love (ib. 37, 38).   But no long time could be devoted to the grief
of separation.   The wind was fair,[6] and the vessel must depart.
They accompanied the Apostle to the edge of the water (ib. 38).[7]
The Christian brethren were torn away from the embrace of their
friends;[8] and the ship sailed out into the open sea, while the presbyters prepared for their weary and melancholy return to Ephesus.

The narrative of the voyage is now resumed in detail.   It is quite
clear, from St. Luke's mode of expression, that the vessel sailed
from Miletus on the day of the interview.   With a fair wind she
would easily run down to Cos in the course of the same afternoon.
The distance is about forty nautical miles; the direction is due
south.   The phrase used implies a straight course and a fair wind,[9]
and we conclude, from the well-known phenomena of the Levant,
that the wind was north-westerly, which is the prevalent direction
in those seas.[10]   With this wind the vessel would make her passage

[1] This way of appealing to the recollection of his converts in proof of his
disinterestedness is highly characteristic of St. Paul.   Compare 1 Thess. ii.
5–11, 2 Thess. iii. 7–9, 1 Cor. ix.
4–15, 2 Cor. xii. 14, &c.

[2] This mention of his companions and
attendants is characteristic.   St. Paul
seems always to have been accompanied
by a band of disciples, who helped him
in the discharge of the many duties in
which he was involved by 'the care of
all the churches.'   Compare Gal. i. 2,
for the expression.

[3] 'The weak,' i.e. *the poor*.   This interpretation is defended by Chrysostom,
and confirmed by Aristophanes, quoted
by Wetstein.   The interpretation of
Calvin (who takes it as *the weak in
faith*), which is supported by Neander

and others, seems hardly consistent
with the context.

[4] The Greek verb (ver. 37) is in the
imperfect.

[5] '*Gaze on his face,*' ver. 38.   The
expression is stronger than that used
by St. Paul himself, ver. 25.

[6] See below.

[7] Prof. Hackett notices how the
phrase, *they accompanied him to the
ship,* suits the place, which had then a
long level between the town and the
anchorage.

[8] The English translation of xxi. 1,
' gotten from them ' is too weak.

[9] They *ran before the wind,* xxi. 1.
See what has been said before on this
nautical phrase, p. 219.

[10] For what relates to this prevalent
wind, see below.

from Miletus to Cos in six hours, passing the shores of Caria, with the high summits of Mount Latmus on the left, and with groups of small islands (among which Patmos (Rev. i. 9) would be seen at times[1]) studding the sea on the right. Cos is an island about twenty-three miles in length, extending from south-west to north-east, and separated by a narrow channel from the mainland.[2] But we should rather conceive the town to be referred to, which lay at the eastern extremity of the island. It is described by the ancients as a beautiful and well-built city: and it was surrounded with fortifications erected by Alcibiades towards the close of the Peloponnesian war. Its symmetry had been injured by an earthquake, and the restoration had not yet been effected; but the productiveness of the island to which it belonged, and its position in the Levant, made the city a place of no little consequence. The wine and the textile fabrics of Cos were well known among the imports of Italy. Even now no harbour is more frequented by the merchant vessels of the Levant.[3] The roadstead is sheltered by nature from all winds except the north-east, and the inner harbour was not then, as it is now, an unhealthy lagoon.[4] Moreover, Claudius had recently bestowed peculiar privileges on the city.[5] Another circumstance made it the resort of many strangers, and gave it additional renown. It was the seat of the medical school traditionally connected with Æsculapius; and the temple of the god of healing was crowded with votive models, so as to become in effect a museum of anatomy and pathology.[6] The Christian physician St. Luke, who knew these coasts so well, could hardly be ignorant of the scientific and religious celebrity of Cos. We can imagine the thankfulness with which he would reflect—as the vessel lay at anchor off the city of Hippocrates—that he had been emancipated from the bonds of superstition, without becoming a victim to that scepticism which often succeeds it, especially in minds familiar with the science of physical phenomena.[7]

On leaving the anchorage of Cos, the vessel would have to proceed through the channel which lies between the southern shore of the island and that tongue of the mainland which terminates in the

[1] Dr. Clarke describes a magnificent evening, with the sun setting behind Patmos, which he saw on the voyage from Samos to Cos.

[2] This is to be distinguished from the channel mentioned below, between the *southern* side of Cos and Cape Crio.

[3] 'No place in the Archipelago is more frequented by merchant vessels than this port.'—Purdy, p. 115.

[4] See the description of the town and anchorage in Purdy:—'The town is sheltered from westerly winds by very high mountains,' p. 114. 'The road is good in all winds except the E.N.E.,' p. 115. A view of the modern city of Cos from the anchorage, as well as the present soundings, and the traces of the ancient port, is given in the Admiralty Chart, No. 1550.

[5] Tac. *Ann.* xii. 61.

[6] See p. 241, n. 5. Perhaps the fullest account of Cos is that given by Dr. Clarke, vol. ii. pp. 196–213, and again after his return from Egypt, vol. iii. pp. 321–329. He describes the celebrated plane-tree, and from this island he brought the altar which is now in the Public Library at Cambridge. We may refer also to a paper on Cos by Col. Leake in the second vol. of the *Transactions of the Royal Society of Literature.* See Smith's *Dict. of Geog.*

[7] If we attached any importance to the tradition which represents St. Luke as a painter, we might add that Cos was the birthplace of Apelles as well as of Hippocrates.

Point of Cnidus. If the wind continued in the north-west, the vessel would be able to hold a straight course from Cos to Cape Crio (for such is the modern name of the promontory of Triopium, on which Cnidus was built), and after rounding the point she would run clear before the wind all the way to Rhodes.[1] Another of St. Paul's voyages will lead us to make mention of Cnidus.[2] We shall, therefore, only say, that the extremity of the promontory descends with a perpendicular precipice to the sea, and that this high rock is separated by a level space from the main, so that, at a distance, it appears like one of the numerous islands on the coast.[3] Its history, as well as its appearance, was well impressed on the mind of the Greek navigator of old; for it was the scene of Conon's victory: and the memory of their great admiral made the south-western corner of the Asiatic peninsula to the Athenians what the south-western corner of Spain is to us, through the memories of St. Vincent and Trafalgar.

We have supposed St. Paul's vessel to have rounded Cape Crio, to have left the western shore of Asia Minor, and to be proceeding along the southern shore. The current between Rhodes and the main runs strongly to the westward:[4] but the north-westerly wind[5] would soon carry the vessel through the space of fifty miles to the northern extremity of the island, where its famous and beautiful city was built.

Until the building of its metropolis, the name of this island was comparatively unknown. But from the time when the inhabitants

[1] We shall return again to the subject of the north-westerly winds which prevail during the fine season in the Archipelago, and especially in the neighbourhood of Rhodes. For the present the following authorities may suffice. Speaking of Rhodes, Dr. Clarke says (vol. ii. p. 223), 'The winds are liable to little variation; they are N. or N.W. during almost every month, but these winds blow with great violence:' and again, p. 230, 'A N. wind has prevailed from the time of our leaving the Dardanelles.' Again (vol. iii. p. 378), in the same seas he speaks of a gale from the N.W.:—'It is surprising for what a length of time, and how often, the N.W. rages in the Archipelago. It prevails almost unceasingly through the greater part of the year,' p. 380. And in a note he adds, 'Mr. Spencer Smith, brother of Sir Sidney Smith, informed the author that he was *an entire month employed in endeavouring to effect a passage from Rhodes to Stanchio [Cos]: the N.W. wind prevailed all the time with such force that the vessel in which he sailed could not double Cape Crio.*' We find the following in Norie's *Sailing Directory*, p. 127:—'The Etesian winds, which blow from the N.E. and N.W. quarters, are the monsoons of the Le-

vant, which blow constantly during the summer, and give to the climate of Greece so advantageous a temperature. At this season, the greatest part of the Mediterranean, but particularly the eastern half, including the Adriatic and Archipelago, are subject to N.W. winds. . . . When the sun, on advancing from the north, has begun to rarefy the atmosphere of southern Europe, the Etesians of spring commence in the Mediterranean Sea. These blow in Italy during March and April.' In Purdy's *Sailing Directory*, p. 122, it is said of the neighbourhood of Smyrna and Ephesus: 'The northerly winds hereabout continue all the summer, and sometimes blow with unremitting violence for several weeks.' See again what Admiral Beaufort says of the N.W. wind at *Patara*.

[2] See Acts xxvii. 7.

[3] In the Admiralty Chart of the gulf of Cos, &c. (No. 1604), a very good view of Cape Crio is given. We shall speak of Cnidus more fully hereafter. Meantime we may refer to a view in Laborde, which gives an admirable representation of the passage between Cos and Cape Crio.

[4] Purdy.

[5] See above.

of the earlier towns were brought to one centre,[1] and the new city, built by Hippodamus (the same architect who planned the streets of the Piræus), rose in the midst of its perfumed gardens and its amphitheatre of hills, with unity so symmetrical that it appeared like one house,[2]—Rhodes has held an illustrious place among the islands of the Mediterranean. From the very effect of its situation, lying as it did on the verge of two of the basins of that sea, it became the intermediate point of the eastern and western trade.[3] Even now it is the harbour at which most vessels touch on their progress to and from the Archipelago.[4] It was the point from which the Greek geographers reckoned their parallels of latitude and meridians of longitude. And we may assert that no place has been so long renowned for ship-building, if we may refer to the 'benches, and masts, and ship-boards' of 'Dodanim and Chittim' with the feeble constructions of the modern Turkish dockyard, as the earliest and latest efforts of that Rhodian skill, which was celebrated by Pliny in the time of St. Paul. To the copious supplies of ship-timber were added many other physical advantages. It was a proverb that the sun shone every day in Rhodes: and her inhabitants revelled in the luxuriance of the vegetation which surrounded them. We find this beauty and this brilliant atmosphere typified in her coins, on one side of which is the head of Apollo radiated like the sun, while the other exhibits the rose-flower, the conventional emblem which bore the name of the island.[5] But the interest of what is merely outward fades before the moral interest associated with its history. If we rapidly run over its annals, we find something in every period, with which elevated thoughts are connected. The Greek period is the first,—famous not merely for the great Temple of the Sun, and the Colossus, which, like the statue of Borromeo at Arona, seemed to stand over the city to protect it,[6]—but far more for the supremacy of the seas, which was

[1] Herodotus simply mentions Rhodes as forming part of the Dorian confederacy with Cos and Cnidus. It was about the time of the Peloponnesian war that the three earlier cities of Lindus, Ialysus, and Camirus were centralised in the new *city* of Rhodes. 'We find the Rhodian navy rising in strength and consequence towards the time of Demosthenes;' and, after this period, it 'makes nearly as great a figure in history as Venice does in the annals of Modern Europe.'

[2] This is the phrase of Diodorus Siculus.

[3] An interesting illustration of the trade of Rhodes will be found in vol. iii. of the *Trans. of the Royal Society of Literature,* in a paper on some inscribed handles of wine-vessels found at Alexandria. We shall refer to this paper again when we come to speak of Cnidus.

[4] 'Vessels bound to the ports of Karamania, as well as to those of Syria and Egypt, generally touch here for pilots or for intelligence.' Beaufort. 'The southern harbour is generally full of merchant-vessels.' Purdy, p. 232. 'The chief source of what little opulence it still enjoys is in the number of vessels which touch here on their passage from the Archipelago to the eastward.' Ib.

[5] One of these coins is given in the larger editions.

[6] The Colossus was in ruins, even in Strabo's time. It had been overthrown by an earthquake according to Polybius. It seems to be a popular mistake that this immense statue stood across the entrance of one of the harbours. The only parallel in modern times is the statue of San Carlo Borromeo, which has been alluded to before in reference to Athens, p. 291; and in height they were nearly identical, the latter being 106 feet, the former 105 (70 cubits). See the paper referred to, note 3, above.

employed to put down piracy, for the code of mercantile law, by which the commerce of later times was regulated, and for the legislative enactments, framed almost in the spirit of Christianity, for the protection of the poor. This is followed by the Roman period; when the faithful ally, which had aided by her naval power in subduing the East, was honoured by the Senate and the Emperors with the name and privileges of freedom ;[1] and this by the Byzantine, during which Christianity was established in the Levant, and the city of the Rhodians, as the metropolis of a province of islands, if no longer holding the empire of the Mediterranean, was at least recognised as the Queen of the Ægean.[2] During the earlier portion of the middle ages, while mosques were gradually taking the place of Byzantine churches, Rhodes was the last Christian city to make a stand against the advancing Saracens ; and again during their later portion, she reappears as a city ennobled by the deeds of Christian chivalry ; so that, ever since the successful siege of Solyman the Magnificent, her fortifications and her stately harbour, and the houses in her streets, continue to be the memorials of the Knights of St. John. Yet no point of Rhodian history ought to move our spirits with so much exultation as that day, when the vessel that conveyed St. Paul came round the low northern point[3] of the island to her moorings before the city. We do not know that he landed like other great conquerors who have visited Rhodes. It would not be necessary even to enter the harbour, for a safe anchorage would be found for the night in the open roadstead.[4] 'The kingdom of God cometh not with observation ;' and the vessel which was seen by the people of the city to weigh anchor in the morning, was probably undistinguished from the other coasting craft with which they were daily familiar.

No view in the Levant is more celebrated than that from Rhodes towards the opposite shore of Asia Minor. The last ranges of Mount Taurus[5] come down in magnificent forms to the sea ; and a long line of snowy summits is seen along the Lycian coast, while the sea between is often an unruffled expanse of water under a blue and brilliant sky. Across this expanse, and towards a harbour near the further edge of these Lycian mountains, the Apostle's course was now directed (Acts xxi. 1). To the eastward of Mount Cragus,—the steep sea-front of which is known to the pilots of the Levant by the name of the 'Seven Capes,'[6]—the river Xanthus

---

[1] After the defeat of Antiochus, Rhodes received from the Roman Senate some valuable possessions on the mainland, including part of Caria and the whole of Lycia. See what has been said on the province of Asia, p. 184, comparing p. 186. These continental possessions were afterwards withdrawn ; but the Rhodians were still regarded as among the allies of Rome. They rendered valuable aid in the war against Mithridates, and were not reduced to the form of a province till the reign of Vespasian.

[2] It was then the metropolis of the

'Province of the Islands.'

[3] Compare Purdy's *Sailing Directory* with the Admiralty Chart (No. 1639), attached to which is an excellent view of Rhodes.

[4] See Purdy, p. 231.

[5] Compare pp. 16, 17. For the appearance of this magnificent coast on a nearer approach, see Dr. Clarke. For a description of these south-western mountains of Asia Minor, the *Travels* of Spratt and Forbes may be consulted.

[6] 'These capes (called in Italian, the usual language of the pilots, *sette capi*) are the extremities of high and rugged

winds through a rich and magnificent valley, and past the ruins of an ancient city, the monuments of which, after a long concealment, have lately been made familiar to the British public.[1] The harbour of the city of Xanthus was situated a short distance from the left bank of the river. Patara was to Xanthus what the Piræus was to Athens;[2] and, though this comparison might seem to convey the idea of an importance which never belonged to the Lycian sea-port, yet ruins still remain to show that it was once a place of some magnitude and splendour. The bay, into which the river Xanthus flowed, is now a 'desert of moving sand,' which is blown by the westerly wind into ridges along the shore, and is gradually hiding the remains of the ancient city;[3] but a triple archway and a vast theatre have been described by travellers.[4] Some have even thought that they have discovered the seat of the oracle of Apollo, who was worshipped here, as his sister Diana was worshipped at Ephesus or Perga:[5] and the city-walls can be traced among the sand-hills with the castle[6] that commanded the harbour. In the war against Antiochus, this harbour was protected by a sudden storm from the Roman fleet, when Livius sailed from Rhodes.[7] Now we find the

mountains, occupying a space of ten miles.'—Purdy, p. 236.

[1] The allusion is of course to the Xanthian room in the British Museum.

[2] Thus Appian speaks of Patara as the port of Xanthus, *B. C.* iv. 81. In the following chapter he says that Andriace had the same relation to Myra (Acts xxvii. 5.)

[3] Admiral Beaufort was the first to describe Patara. *Karamania*, chap. i. It was also visited by the Dilettanti Society. It is described by Sir C. Fellows, both in his *Lycia* and his *Asia Minor*. In the *Travels* of Spratt and Forbes the destruction of the harbour and the great increase of sand are attributed to the rising of the coast. The following passage is transcribed at length from this work:—'A day was devoted to an excursion to Patara, which lies on the coast at some distance from the left bank of the river, about ten miles from Xanthus. We rode along the river-side to the sand-hills, passing large straw-thatched villages of gipsies on the way, and then crossed the sand-hills to the sea-side. . . . . At Patara is the triple arch which formed the gate of the city, the baths, and the theatre, admirably described long ago by Captain Beaufort. The latter is scooped out of the side of a hill, and is remarkable for the completeness of the proscenium and the steepness and narrowness of the marble seats. Above it is the singular pit excavated on the summit of the same hill, with its central square column, conjectured, with pro-

bability, by Admiral Beaufort, to have been the seat of the oracle of Apollo Patareus. The stones of which the column is built are displaced from each other in a singular manner, as if by the revolving motion of an earthquake. A fine group of palm trees rises among the ruins, and the aspect of the city when it was flourishing must have been very beautiful. Now its port is an inland marsh, generating poisonous malaria; and the mariner sailing along the coast would never guess that the sand-hills before him blocked up the harbour into which St. Paul sailed of old.'

[4] A drawing of the gateway is given by Beaufort, p. 1. Views of the theatre, &c. of Patara will be found in the first volume of the *Ionian Antiquities*, published by the Dilettanti Society.

[5] See pp. 127, 128, 422, &c. The coins of Patara show the ascendency of Apollo in the district. One is given in the larger editions.

[6] Beaufort, p. 3.

[7] The Roman fleet had followed nearly the same course as the Apostle from the neighbourhood of *Ephesus*, the following places being mentioned in order, *Miletus, Cnidus, Cos, Rhodes, Patara.* Liv. xxxvii. 16. We may add another illustration from Roman history, in Pompey's voyage, where the same places are mentioned in a similar order. After describing his departure from *Mitylene*, and his passing by *Asia* and *Chios*, Lucan proceeds to enumerate *Ephesus, Cos, Cnidus,* and *Rhodes. Phars.* viii.

Apostle Paul entering it with a fair wind, after a short sail from the same island.

It seems that the vessel in which St. Paul had been hitherto sailing either finished its voyage at Patara, or was proceeding further eastward along the southern coast of Asia Minor, and not to the ports of Phœnicia. St. Paul could not know in advance whether it would be 'possible' for him to arrive in Palestine in time for Pentecost (xx. 16); but an opportunity presented itself unexpectedly at Patara. Providential circumstances conspired with his own convictions to forward his journey, notwithstanding the discouragement which the fears of others had thrown across his path. In the harbour of Patara they found a vessel which was on the point of crossing the open sea to Phœnicia (xxi. 2). They went on board without a moment's delay; and it seems evident, from the mode of expression, that they sailed the very day of their arrival.[1] Since the voyage lay across the open sea,[2] with no shoals or rocks to be dreaded, and since the north-westerly winds often blow steadily for several days in the Levant during spring,[3] there could be no reason why the vessel should not weigh anchor in the evening, and sail through the night.[4]

We have now to think of St. Paul as no longer passing through narrow channels, or coasting along in the shadow of great mountains, but as sailing continuously through the midnight hours, with a prosperous breeze filling the canvas, and the waves curling and sounding round the bows of the vessel. There is a peculiar freshness and cheerfulness in the prosecution of a prosperous voyage with a fair wind by night. The sailors on the watch, and the passengers also, feel it, and the feeling is often expressed in songs or in long-continued conversation. Such cheerfulness might be felt by the Apostle and his companions, not without thankfulness to that God 'who giveth songs in the night' (Job xxxv. 10), and who hearkeneth to those who fear Him, and speak often to one another, and think upon His name (Mal. iii. 16). If we remember, too, that a month had now elapsed since the moon was shining on the snows of Hæmus,[5] and that the full moonlight would now be resting on the great sail[6] of the ship, we are not without an expressive imagery, which we may allowably throw round the Apostle's progress over the waters between Patara and Tyre.

The distance between these two points is three hundred and forty geographical miles; and if we bear in mind (what has been mentioned more than once) that the north-westerly winds in April often blow like monsoons in the Levant, and that the rig of ancient sailing vessels was peculiarly favourable to a quick run before the wind,[7] we come at once to the conclusion that the voyage might

---

[1] This is shown not only by the expression 'we went aboard,' but by the omission of any phrase for 'next day,' such as we find in xx. 15.

[2] It is said that the ship was on the point of sailing over or '*crossing*' to Phœnicia.

[3] See above, p. 557.

[4] For this and other points connected with the navigation of the ancients, we must refer to Chap. XXIII.

[5] See above, p. 542.

[6] See Smith's *Voyage and Shipwreck*, p. 151.

[7] Smith, p. 180.

easily be accomplished in forty-eight hours.[1] Everything in St.
Luke's account gives a strong impression that the weather was in
the highest degree favourable ; and there is one picturesque phrase
employed by the narrator, which sets vividly before us some of the
phenomena of a rapid voyage.[2] That which is said in the English
version concerning the 'discovering' of Cyprus, and 'leaving it
on the left hand,' is, in the original, a nautical expression, implying
that the land appeared to rise quickly,[3] as they sailed past it to the
southward.[4] It would be in the course of the second day (probably
in the evening) that 'the high blue eastern land appeared.' The
highest mountain of Cyprus is a rounded summit, and there would
be snow upon it at that season of the year.[5] After the second
night, the first land in sight would be the high range of Lebanon[6]
in Syria (xxi. 3), and they would easily arrive at Tyre before the
evening.

So much has been written concerning the past histoι and present
condition of Tyre, that these subjects are familiar to every reader,
and it is unnecessary to dwell upon them here.[7] When St. Paul
came to this city, it was neither in the glorious state described in
the prophecies of Ezekiel and Isaiah,[8] when 'its merchants were
princes, and its traffickers the honourable of the earth,' nor in the
abject desolation in which it now fulfils those prophecies, being
'a place to spread nets upon,' and showing only the traces of its
maritime supremacy in its ruined mole, and a port hardly deep
enough for boats.[9] It was in the condition in which it had been left
by the successors of Alexander,—the island, which once held the
city, being joined to the mainland by a causeway,—with a harbour
on the north, and another on the south.[10] In honour of its ancient

[1] i.e. the rate would be rather more
than seven knots an hour. The writer
once asked the captain of a vessel engaged in the Mediterranean trade, how
long it would take to sail with a fair
wind from the Seven Capes to Tyre ;
and the answer was, 'About thirty
hours, or perhaps it would be safer to
say forty-eight.' Now, vessels rigged
like those of the ancients, with one
large mainsail, would run *before the
wind* more quickly than our own merchantmen. Those who have sailed before the monsoons in the China seas
have seen junks (which are rigged in
this respect like Greek and Roman
merchantmen) behind them in the horizon in the morning, and before them
in the horizon in the evening.

[2] The word, in reference to sea-voyages, means ' to see land, to bring land
into view,' by a similar figure of speech
to that in which our sailors speak of
' *making* land.' So ' *aperire* ' is used
in Latin, and ' *open* ' by our own sailors.
The grammatical construction in the
Greek is peculiar ; but confusions of
grammar are common in the language

of sailors. Thus an English seaman
speaks of ' *rising* the land,' which is
exactly what is meant here.

[3] Mr. Smith says in a MS. note :
' The term indicates both the rapid approach to land, and that it was seen at
a distance by daylight.'

[4] We shall hereafter point out the
contrast between this voyage and that
which is mentioned afterwards in Acts
xxvii. 4.

[5] The island is traversed by two
chains running nearly east and west,
and they are covered with snow in winter. Norie, p. 144. The writer has
been informed by Captain Graves, R.N.,
that the highest part is of a rounded
form.

[6] Compare pp. 17, 44.

[7] One of the fullest accounts of Tyre
will be found in Dr. Robinson's third
volume.

[8] Ezek. xxvi. xxvii., Isa. xxiii.

[9] *Sailing Directory*, p. 259.

[10] *Old Tyre* was destroyed. *New
Tyre* was built on a small island, separated by a very narrow channel from
the mainland, with which it was united

greatness, the Romans gave it the name of a free city;[1] and it still commanded some commerce, for its manufactures of glass and purple were not yet decayed,[2] and the narrow belt of the Phœnician coast between the mountains and the sea required that the food for its population should be partly brought from without.[3] It is allowable to conjecture that the ship, which we have just seen crossing from Patara, may have brought grain from the Black Sea, or wine from the Archipelago,[4]—with the purpose of taking on from Tyre a cargo of Phœnician manufactures. We know that, whatever were the goods she brought, they were unladed at Tyre (ver. 3), and that the vessel was afterwards to proceed[5] to Ptolemais (ver. 7). For this task of unlading some days would be required. She would be taken into the inner dock;[6] and St. Paul had thus some time at his disposal, which he could spend in the active service of his Master. He and his companions lost no time in 'seeking out the disciples.' It is probable that the Christians at Tyre were not numerous;[7] but a Church had existed there ever since the dispersion consequent upon the death of Stephen (pp. 66, 97), and St. Paul had himself visited it, if not on his mission of charity from Antioch to Jerusalem (p. 105), yet doubtless on his way to the Council (p. 167). There were not only disciples at Tyre, but prophets. Some of those who had the prophetical power foresaw the danger which was hanging over St. Paul, and endeavoured to persuade him to desist from his purpose of going to Jerusalem. We see that different views of duty might be taken by those who had the same spiritual knowledge, though that knowledge were supernatural. St. Paul looked on the coming danger from a higher point. What to others was an overwhelming darkness, to him appeared only as a passing storm. And he resolved to face it, in the faith that He who had protected him hitherto, would still give him shelter and safety.

The time spent at Tyre in unlading the vessel, and probably taking in a new cargo, and possibly, also, waiting for a fair wind,[8]

by a dam in Alexander's siege; and thenceforward Tyre was on a *peninsula.*

[1] For the general notion of a free city (*libera civitas*) under the Empire, see p. 257. Tyre seems to have been honoured, like Athens, for the sake of the past.

[2] For the manufactures of Tyre at a much later period, see p. 168, n. 2.

[3] The dependence of Phœnicia on other countries for grain is alluded to in Acts xii. 20. (See p. 105, n. 11.)

[4] For the wine trade of the Archipelago, see what has been said in reference to Rhodes. We need not suppose that the vessel bound for Phœnicia sailed in the first instance from Patara. St. Paul afterwards found a westward-bound Alexandrian ship in one of the harbours of Lycia. Acts xxvii. 5, 6.

[5] We infer that St. Paul proceeded

in *the same vessel* to Ptolemais, partly because the phrase in ver. 6 means ''we went on board *the* ship,' and partly because it is not said that the vessel was *bound* for Tyre, but simply that she was to *unlade* there.

[6] Scylax mentions a harbour within the walls.

[7] 'Having sought out the disciples' is the literal translation. Some search was required before the Christians were found. Perhaps the first inquiries would be made at the synagogue. [See p. 302, note.] For a notice of the Jews at Tyre in later times, we may again refer to p. 168, n. 2.

[8] These suppositions, however, are not necessary; for the work of taking the cargo from the hold of a merchant-vessel might easily occupy six or seven days.

was 'seven days,' including a Sunday.[1] St. Paul 'broke bread' with the disciples, and discoursed as he had done at Troas (p. 214); and the week days, too, would afford many precious opportunities for confirming those who were already Christians, and for making the Gospel known to others, both Jews and Gentiles. When the time came for the ship to sail, a scene was witnessed on the Phœnician shore, like that which had made the Apostle's departure from Miletus so impressive and affecting.[2] There attended him through the city gate,[3] as he and his companions went out to join the vessel now ready to receive them, all the Christians of Tyre, and even their 'wives and children.' And there they knelt down and prayed together on the level shore.[4] We are not to imagine here any Jewish place of worship, like the *proseucha* at Philippi;[5] but simply that they were on their way to the ship. The last few moments were precious, and could not be so well employed as in praying to Him who alone can give true comfort and protection. The time spent in this prayer was soon passed. And then they tore themselves from each other's embrace; the strangers went on board,[6] and the Tyrian believers returned home sorrowful and anxious, while the ship sailed southwards on her way to Ptolemais.

There is a singular contrast in the history of those three cities on the Phœnician shore, which are mentioned in close succession in the concluding part of the narrative of this Apostolic journey. *Tyre*, the city from which St. Paul had just sailed, had been the sea-port whose destiny formed the burden of the sublimest prophecies in the last days of the Hebrew monarchy. *Cæsarea*, the city to which he was ultimately bound, was the work of the family of Herod, and rose with the rise of Christianity. Both are fallen now into utter decay. *Ptolemais*, which was the intermediate stage between them, is an older city than either, and has outlived them both. It has never been withdrawn from the field of history; and its interest has seemed to increase (at least in the eyes of Englishmen) with the progress of centuries. Under the ancient name of Acco it appears in the Book of Judges (i. 31) as one of the towns of the tribe of Assher. It was the pivot of the contests between Persia and Egypt. Not unknown in the Macedonian and Roman periods, it reappears with brilliant distinction in the middle ages, when the Crusaders called it St. Jean d'Acre. It is needless to allude to the events which have fixed on this sea-fortress, more than once, the attention of our own generation.[7] At the particular time when the Apostle Paul visited

[1] This, however, need not mean more than 'six days.' Some think that by 'accomplishing the days' is meant that they 'employed the time in making ready for the journey,' comparing 2 Tim. iii. 17. [See on ver. 15.]

[2] See above, p. 555.

[3] The Greek expresses this more fully and vividly than the English.

[4] The word here used is the same as in Acts xxvii. 39, 40, and denotes a sandy or pebbly beach, as opposed to a rocky shore.

[5] Hammond supposes that there was

a proseucha near the place of embarkation. But we need not suppose any reference to a Jewish place of worship either here or at Miletus, though it is interesting to bear in mind the *orationes littorales* of the Jews. See pp. 226–228.

[6] See above, p. 563.

[7] The events at the close of the last century, and others still more recent. It is surely well that we should be able to associate this place with the Apostle of the Gentiles as much as with Sir Sidney Smith and Sir Charles Napier.

this place, it bore the name of Ptolemais,[1]—most probably given to it by Ptolemy Lagi, who was long in possession of this part of Syria,[2]—and it had recently been made a Roman colony by the Emperor Claudius.[3] It shared with Tyre and Sidon,[4] Antioch and Cæsarea, the trade of the eastern coast of the Mediterranean Sea. With a fair wind, a short day's voyage separates it from Tyre. To speak in the language of our own sailors, there are thirteen miles from Tyre to Cape Blanco, and fifteen from thence to Cape Carmel ; and Acre—the ancient Ptolemais—is situated on the further extremity of that bay, which sweeps with a wide curvature of sand to the northwards, from the headland of Carmel.[5] It is evident that St. Paul's company sailed from Tyre to Ptolemais within the day.[6] At the latter city, as at the former, there were Christian disciples,[7] who had probably been converted at the same time and under the same circumstances as those of Tyre. Another opportunity was afforded for the salutations and encouragement of brotherly love ; but the missionary party stayed here only one day.[8] Though they had accomplished the voyage in abundant time to reach Jerusalem at Pentecost, they hastened onwards, that they might linger some days at Cæsarea.[9]

One day's travelling by land[10] was sufficient for this part of their journey. The distance is between thirty and forty miles.[11] At Cæsarea there was a Christian family, already known to us in the earlier passages of the Acts of the Apostles, with whom they were sure of receiving a welcome. The last time we made mention of Philip the Evangelist (p. 66), was when he was engaged in making the Gospel known on the road which leads southwards by Gaza towards Egypt, about the time when St. Paul himself was converted on the northern road, when travelling to Damascus. Now, after many years, the Apostle and the Evangelist are brought together under one roof. On the former occasion, we saw that Cæsarea was the place where the labours of Philip on that journey ended.[12] Thenceforward it became his residence if his life was stationary, or it was the centre from which he made other missionary circuits

---

[1] So it is called in 1 Macc. v. 15, x. 1, &c.
[2] See his life in Smith's *Dictionary of Biography.*
[3] Pliny, v. 19, 17.
[4] In the Acts of the Apostles, we find *Tyre* mentioned in connection with the voyages of merchantmen, xxi. 3, and *Sidon,* xxvii. 3.
[5] For a nautical delineation of this bay, with the anchorage, Kaifa, &c., see the Admiralty Chart. The travellers who have described the sweep of this bay from Carmel are so numerous, that they need not be specified.
[6] ver. 7. Instead of the words 'we that were of Paul's company,' the best MSS. have simply 'we,' which seems to have been altered into the longer phrase, as being the opening of a sepa-

rate section for reading in churches. The meaning of what begins the 7th verse seems to be 'thus accomplishing our voyage.' The rest of the journey was by land.
[7] Both here and in ver. 4 the Greek has the definite article.
[8] ver. 7.
[9] See below, ver. 10.
[10] 'The next day we departed,' ver. 8. We may observe, that the word used here is far more suitable to a departure by land than by sea.
[11] The Jerusalem Itinerary gives the distance as thirty-one miles, the stages being twelve, three, eight, and eight. The Antonine Itinerary makes the distance greater, viz. twenty-four and twenty.
[12] Acts viii. 40. See p. 66, n. 5,

through Judæa.[1] He is found, at least, residing in this city by the sea, when St. Paul arrives in the year 58 from Achaia and Macedonia. His family consisted of four daughters, who were an example of the fulfilment of that prediction of Joel, quoted by St. Peter, which said that at the opening of the new dispensation, God's Spirit should come on His 'handmaidens' as well as His bondsmen, and that the 'daughters,' as well as the sons, should prophesy.[2] The prophetic power was granted to these four women at Cæsarea, who seem to have been living that life of single devotedness[3] which is commended by St. Paul in his first letter to the Corinthians (1 Cor. vii.), and to have exercised their gift in concert for the benefit of the Church.

It is not improbable that these inspired women gave St. Paul some intimation of the sorrows which were hanging over him.[4] But soon a more explicit voice declared the very nature of the trial he was to expect. The stay of the Apostle at Cæsarea lasted some days (ver. 10). He had arrived in Judæa in good time before the festival, and haste was now unnecessary. Thus news reached Jerusalem of his arrival; and a prophet named Agabus—whom we have seen before (p. 104) coming from the same place on a similar errand—went down to Cæsarea, and communicated to St. Paul and the company of Christians by whom he was surrounded a clear knowledge of the impending danger. His revelation was made in that dramatic form which impresses the mind with a stronger sense of reality than mere words can do, and which was made familiar to the Jews of old by the practice of the Hebrew prophets. As Isaiah (ch. xx.) loosed the sackcloth from his loins, and put off his shoes from his feet, to declare how the Egyptian captives should be led away into Assyria naked and barefoot,—or as the girdle of Jeremiah (ch. xiii.), in its strength and its decay, was made a type of the people of Israel in their privilege and their fall,—Agabus, in like manner, using the imagery of action,[5] took the girdle of St. Paul, and fastened it round his own[6] hands and feet, and said, 'Thus saith the Holy Ghost: So shall the Jews at Jerusalem bind the man to whom this girdle belongs, and they shall deliver him into the hands of the Gentiles.'

The effect of this emphatic prophecy, both on Luke, Aristarchus, and Trophimus,[7] the companions of St. Paul's journey, and those

---

[1] The term 'Evangelist' seems to have been almost synonymous with our word 'Missionary.' It is applied to Philip and to Timothy. See p. 342; also p. 341, n. 3.

[2] Joel ii. 28, 29; Acts ii. 17, 18. Compare 1 Cor. xiv. 34; 1 Tim. ii. 12; and see p. 337.

[3] It is difficult not to see some emphasis in the word 'virgins.' See Matt. xix. 12.

[4] Perhaps the force of 'who did prophesy' (ver. 9) is to be found in the fact that they did foretell what was to come. The word, however, has not

necessarily any relation to the future. See p. 337.

[5] See another striking instance in Ezek. iv. Compare what has been said before in reference to the gestures of Paul and Barnabas when they departed from Antioch in Pisidia, p. 145.

[6] It would be a mistake to suppose that Agabus bound Paul's hands and feet. Besides, Agabus says, not 'the man whom I bind,' but 'the man whose girdle this is.'

[7] For the companions of St. Paul at this moment, see p. 542, and n. 4 on that page.

Christians of Cæsarea,[1] who, though they had not travelled with
him, had learnt to love him, was very great.   They wept,[2] and implored him not to go to Jerusalem.[3]   But the Apostle himself could
not so interpret the supernatural intimation.   He was placed in a
position of peculiar trial.   A voice of authentic prophecy had been
so uttered, that, had he been timid and wavering, it might easily
have been construed into a warning to deter him.   Nor was that
temptation unfelt which arises from the sympathetic grief of loving
friends.   His affectionate heart was almost broken[4] when he heard
their earnest supplications and saw the sorrow that was caused by
the prospect of his danger; but the mind of the Spirit had been so
revealed to him in his own inward convictions, that he could see
the Divine counsel through apparent hindrances.   His resolution
was 'no wavering between yea and nay, but was yea in Jesus
Christ.'[5]   His deliberate purpose did not falter for a moment.[6]   He
declared that he was 'ready not only to be bound, but to die at
Jerusalem for the name of the Lord Jesus.'   And then they desisted
from their entreaties.   Their respect for the Apostle made them
silent.   They recognised the will of God in the steady purpose of
His servant, and gave their acquiescence in those words in which
Christian resignation is best expressed: '*The will of the Lord be
done.*'

The time was now come for the completion of the journey.   The
festival was close at hand.   Having made the arrangements that
were necessary with regard to their luggage,[7]—and such notices in
Holy Scripture[8] should receive their due attention, for they help
to set before us all the reality of the Apostle's journeys,—he and
the companions who had attended him from Macedonia proceeded
to the Holy City.   Some of the Christians of Cæsarea went along
with them, not merely, as it would seem, to show their respect and
sympathy for the Apostolic company,[9] but to secure their comfort
on arriving, by taking him to the house of Mnason, a native of Cyprus, who had been long ago converted to Christianity,[10]—possibly
during the life of our Lord Himself,[11]—and who may have been one

---

[1] 'Both we and they of the place,'
ver. 12.

[2] 'What mean ye to weep,' &c. ver. 13.

[3] ver. 12.

[4] ver. 13.

[5] 2 Cor. i. See above, p. 442.

[6] This is implied in the present tense,
ver. 14.

[7] 'We weran made redi.' Wiclif.
'We made oure selfes redy.' Tyndale.
'Wee toke up oure burthens.' Cran-
mer. 'We trussed up our fardeles.'
Geneva. 'Being prepared.' Rheims.
The word 'carriage' in the Authorised
Version is used as in Judg. xviii. 21,
1 Sam. xvii. 22. Greswell sees, in the
allusion to the baggage, some indication
of haste; but the contrary seems rather
implied.

[8] See for instance 2 Tim. iv. 13.

[9] The frequent use of the word denoting 'to conduct' or 'to accompany,'
in the accounts of the movements of
the Apostles and their companions, is
worthy of observation. See Acts xv.
3, xx. 38; Rom. xv. 24, &c.

[10] 'An old disciple.'   The Greek adjective reminds us of Acts xi. 15.

[11] He can hardly have been converted
by St. Paul during his journey through
Cyprus, or St. Paul would have been
acquainted with him, which does not
appear to have been the case. He may
have been converted by Barnabas. (See
Acts xv. 39.) But he was most probably one of the earliest disciples of
Christ. As to the construction, see the
article on this name in the *Dict. of the
Bible.* [See p. 97, and Chap. V.]

of those Cyprian Jews who first made the Gospel known to the Greeks at Antioch.

Thus we have accompanied St. Paul on his last recorded journey to Jerusalem. It was a journey full of incident; and it is related more minutely than any other portion of his travels. We know all the places by which he passed, or at which he stayed; and we are able to connect them all with familiar recollections of history. We know, too, all the aspect of the scenery. He sailed along those coasts of Western Asia, and among those famous islands, the beauty of which is proverbial. The very time of the year is known to us. It was when the advancing season was clothing every low shore, and the edge of every broken cliff, with a beautiful and refreshing verdure; when the winter storms had ceased to be dangerous, and the small vessels could ply safely in shade and sunshine between neighbouring ports. Even the state of the weather and the direction of the wind are known. We can point to the places on the map where the vessel anchored for the night,[1] and trace across the chart the track that was followed, when the moon was full.[2] Yet more than this. We are made fully aware of the state of the Apostle's mind, and of the burdened feeling under which this journey was accomplished. The expression of this feeling strikes us the more from its contrast with all the outward circumstances of the voyage. He sailed in the finest season, by the brightest coasts, and in the fairest weather; and yet his mind was occupied with forebodings of evil from first to last;—so that a peculiar shade of sadness is thrown over the whole narration. If this be true, we should expect to find some indications of this pervading sadness in the letters written about this time; for we know how the deeper tones of feeling make themselves known in the correspondence of any man with his friends. Accordingly, we do find in *The Epistle written to the Romans* shortly before leaving Corinth, a remarkable indication of discouragement, and almost despondency, when he asked the Christians at Rome to pray that, on his arrival in Jerusalem, he might be delivered from the Jews who hated him, and be well received by those Christians who disregarded his authority.[3] The depressing anxiety with which he thus looked forward to the journey would not be diminished, when the very moment of his departure from *Corinth* was beset by a Jewish plot against his life.[4] And we find the cloud of gloom, which thus gathered at the first, increasing and becoming darker as we advance. At *Philippi* and at *Troas*, indeed, no direct intimation is given of coming calamities; but it is surely no fancy which sees a foreboding shadow thrown over that midnight meeting, where death so suddenly appeared among those that were assembled there with many lights in the upper chamber, while the Apostle seemed unable to intermit his discourse, as 'ready to depart on the morrow.'[5] For indeed at Miletus he said, that already '*in every city*'[5] the Spirit had ad-

---

[1] See pp. 549, 550.
[2] See p. 561.
[3] Rom. xv. 31. We should remember that he had two causes of apprehension, —one arising from the Jews, who persecuted him everywhere,—the other

from the Judaising Christians, who sought to depreciate his Apostolic authority.
[4] See p. 541.
[5] See p. 553.

monished him that bonds and imprisonment were before him. At *Miletus* it is clear that the heaviness of spirit, under which he started, had become a confirmed anticipation of evil. When he wrote to Rome, he hoped to be delivered from the danger he had too much reason to fear. Now his fear predominates over hope ;[1] and he looks forward, sadly but calmly, to some imprisonment not far distant. At *Tyre*, the first sounds that he hears on landing are the echo of his own thoughts. He is met by the same voice of warning, and the same bitter trial for himself and his friends. At *Cæsarea* his vague forebodings of captivity are finally made decisive and distinct, and he has a last struggle with the remonstrances of those whom he loved. Never had he gone to Jerusalem without a heart full of emotion,—neither in those early years, when he came an enthusiastic boy from Tarsus to the school of Gamaliel,—nor on his return from Damascus, after the greatest change that could have passed over an inquisitor's mind,—nor when he went with Barnabas from Antioch to the Council, which was to decide an anxious controversy. Now he had much new experience of the insidious progress of error, and of the sinfulness even of the converted. Yet his trust in God did not depend on the faithfulness of man ; and he went to Jerusalem calmly and resolutely, though doubtful of his reception among the Christian brethren, and not knowing what would happen on the morrow.

[1] Acts xx. 23 should be closely compared with Rom. xv. 30, 31. See also the note above (p. 553) on '*bound in spirit.*' St. Paul seems to have suffered extremely both from the anticipation and the experience of *imprisonment.*

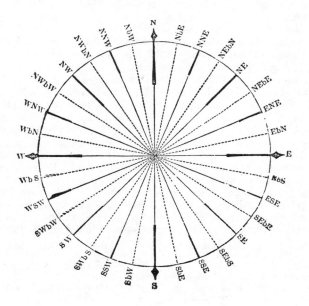

CHAPTER XXI.

Reception at Jerusalem.— Assembling of the Presbyters.—Advice given to
St. Paul.— The Four Nazarites. — St. Paul seized at the Festival.— The
Temple and the Garrison.—*Hebrew Speech on the Stairs.*— The Centurion
and the Chief Captain.—St. Paul before the Sanhedrin.—The Pharisees
and Sadducees.—Vision in the Castle.— Conspiracy.—St. Paul's Nephew.
— Letter of Claudias Lysias to Felix.— Night journey to Antipatris.—
Cæsarea.

' WHEN we were come to Jerusalem, the Brethren received us
gladly.' Such is St. Luke's description of the welcome which met
the Apostle of the Gentiles on his arrival in the metropolis of Judaism. So we shall find afterwards[1] ' the brethren ' hailing his
approach to Rome, and 'coming to meet him as far as Appii Forum.'
Thus, wherever he went, or whatever might be the strength of hostility and persecution which dogged his footsteps, he found some
Christian hearts who loved the Glad-tidings which he preached, and
loved himself as the messenger of the Grace of God.

The Apostle's spirit, which was much depressed, as we have seen,[2]
by anticipations of coldness and distrust on the part of the Church
at Jerusalem, must have been lightened by his kind reception. He
seems to have spent the evening of his arrival with these sympathising brethren ; but on the morrow, a more formidable ordeal
awaited him. He must encounter the assembled Presbyters of the
Church ; and he might well doubt whether even the substantial
proof of loving interest in their welfare, of which he was the bearer,
would overcome the antipathy with which (as he was fully aware)
too many of them regarded him. The experiment, however, must
be tried ; for this was the very end of his coming to Jerusalem at
all, at a time when his heart called him to Rome.[3] His purpose
was to endeavour to set himself right with the Church of Jerusalem,
to overcome the hostile prejudices which had already so much impeded his labours, and to endeavour, by the force of Christian love
and forbearance; to win the hearts of those whom he regarded, in
spite of all their weaknesses and errors, as brethren in Christ Jesus.
Accordingly, when the morning came,[4] the Presbyters or Elders of
the Church were called together by James,[5] (who as we have before
mentioned, presided over the Church of Jerusalem,) to receive Paul
and his fellow-travellers, the messengers of the Gentile Churches.

[1] Acts xxviii. 15. The same expression is used in both cases. This is
sufficient to refute the cavils which
have been made, as though this verse
(xxi. 17) implied unanimous cor-
diality on the part of the Church at
Jerusalem.

[2] See the preceding chapter, pp.
541, 553–555, 563, 566–569.
[3] See Acts xix. 21, Rom. i. 10–15,
xv. 22–29.
[4] 'The day following,' ver. 18.
[5] See pp. 169, 170.

We have already seen how carefully St. Paul had guarded himself from the possibility of suspicion in the administration of his trust, by causing deputies to be elected by the several churches whose alms he bore, as joint trustees with himself of the fund collected. These deputies now entered together with him [1] into the assembly of the Elders, and the offering was presented,—a proof of love from the Churches of the Gentiles to the mother Church, whence their spiritual blessings had been derived.

The travellers were received with that touching symbol of brotherhood, the kiss of peace,[2] which was exchanged between the Christians of those days on every occasion of public as well as private meeting. Then the main business of the assembly was commenced by an address from St. Paul. This was not the first occasion on which he had been called to take a similar part, in the same city, and before the same audience. Our thoughts are naturally carried back to the days of the Apostolic Council, when he first declared to the Church of Jerusalem the Gospel which he preached among the Gentiles, and the great things which God had wrought thereby.[3] The majority of the Church had then, under the influence of the Spirit of God, been brought over to his side, and had ratified his views by their decree. But the battle was not yet won; he had still to contend against the same foes with the same weapons.

We are told that he now gave a detailed account[4] of all that 'God had wrought among the Gentiles by his ministry' since he last parted from Jerusalem four years before.[5] The foundation of the great and flourishing Church of Ephesus doubtless furnished the main interest of his narrative; but he would also dwell on the progress of the several Churches in Phrygia, Galatia, and other parts of Asia Minor, and likewise those in Macedonia and Achaia, from whence he was just returned. In such a discourse, he could scarcely avoid touching on subjects which would excite painful feelings, and rouse bitter prejudice in many of his audience. He could hardly speak of Galatia without mentioning the attempted perversion of his converts there. He could not enter into the state of Corinth without alluding to the emissaries from Palestine, who had introduced confusion and strife among the Christians of that city. Yet we cannot doubt that St. Paul, with that graceful courtesy which distinguished both his writings and his speeches, softened all that was disagreeable, and avoided what was personally offensive to his audience, and dwelt, as far as he could, on topics in which all present would agree. Accordingly we find that the majority of the assembled Elders were favourably impressed by his address, and by the tidings which he brought of the progress of the Gospel. The first act of the assembly was to glorify God for the wonders He had wrought.[6] They joined in solemn thanksgiving with one accord; and the Amen (1 Cor. xiv. 16), which followed the utterance

---

[1] 'Paul with us,' pp. 169, 170.

[2] So we understand *when he had saluted them*, ver. 19. See 1 Thess. v. 26, and p. 311, n. 3.

[3] See pp. 170, 171.

[4] 'Particularly,' ver. 19.

[5] He had then endeavoured to reach Jerusalem by the feast of Pentecost (Acts xviii. 21, and see Wieseler), as on the present occasion.

[6] ver. 20.

of thanks and praise from Apostolic lips, was swelled by many voices.

Thus the hope expressed by St. Paul on a former occasion,[1] concerning the result of this visit to Jerusalem, was in a measure fulfilled. But beneath this superficial show of harmony there lurked elements of discord, which threatened to disturb it too soon. We have already had occasion to remark upon the peculiar composition of the Church at Jerusalem, and we have seen that a Pharisaic faction was sheltered in its bosom, which continually strove to turn Christianity into a sect of Judaism. We have seen that this faction had recently sent emissaries into the Gentile Churches, and had endeavoured to alienate the minds of St. Paul's converts from their converter. These men were restless agitators, animated by the bitterest sectarian spirit, and although they were numerically a small party, yet we know the power of a turbulent minority. But besides these Judaising zealots, there was a large proportion of the Christians at Jerusalem, whose Christianity, though more sincere than that of those just mentioned, was yet very weak and imperfect. The 'many thousands of Jews which believed' had by no means all attained to the fulness of Christian faith. Many of them still knew only a Christ after the flesh,—a Saviour of Israel,—a Jewish Messiah. Their minds were in a state of transition between the Law and the Gospel, and it was of great consequence not to shock their prejudices too rudely, lest they should be tempted to make shipwreck of their faith, and renounce their Christianity altogether. Their prejudices were most wisely consulted in things indifferent by St. James; who accommodated himself in all points to the strict requirements of the Law, and thus disarmed the hostility of the Judaising bigots. He was, indeed, divinely ordained to be the Apostle of this *transition-Church.* Had its councils been less wisely guided, had the Gospel of St. Paul been really repudiated by the Church of Jerusalem, it is difficult to estimate the evil which might have resulted. This class of Christians was naturally very much influenced by the declamation of the more violent partisans of Judaism. Their feelings would be easily excited by an appeal to their Jewish patriotism. They might without difficulty be roused to fury against one whom they were taught to regard as a despiser of the Law, and a reviler of the customs of their forefathers. Against St. Paul their dislike had been long and artfully fostered; and they would from the first have looked on him perhaps with some suspicion, as not being, like themselves, a Hebrew of the Holy City, but only a Hellenist of the Dispersion.

Such being the composition of the great body of the Church, we cannot doubt that the same elements were to be found amongst the Elders also. And this will explain the resolution to which the assembly came, at the close of their discussion on the matters brought before them. They began by calling St. Paul's attention to the strength of the Judaical party among the Christians of Jerusalem. They told him that the majority even of the Christian Church had been taught to hate his very name, and to believe that he went about the world 'teaching the Jews to forsake Moses, saying that

[1] 2 Cor. ix. 12.

they ought not to circumcise their children, neither to walk after the customs.' They further observed that it was impossible his arrival should remain unknown ; his renown was too great to allow him to be concealed : his public appearance in the streets of Jerusalem would attract a crowd[1] of curious spectators, most of whom would be violently hostile. It was therefore of importance that he should do something to disarm this hostility, and to refute the calumnies which had been circulated concerning him. The plan they recommended was, that he should take charge of four Jewish Christians,[2] who were under a Nazaritic vow, accompany them to the Temple, and pay for them the necessary expenses attending the termination of their vow. Agrippa I., not long before, had given the same public expression of his sympathy with the Jews, on his arrival from Rome to take possession of his throne.[3] And what the King had done for popularity, it was felt that the Apostle might do for the sake of truth and peace. His friends thought that he would thus, in the most public manner, exhibit himself as an observer of the Mosaic ceremonies, and refute the accusations of his enemies. They added that, by so doing, he would not countenance the errors of those who sought to impose the Law upon Gentile converts ; because it had been already decided by the Church of Jerusalem, that the ceremonial observances of the Law were not obligatory on the Gentiles.[4]

It is remarkable that this conclusion is attributed expressly, in the Scriptural narrative, not to James (who presided over the meeting), but to the assembly itself. The lurking shade of distrust implied in the terms of the admonition, was certainly not shared by that great Apostle, who had long ago given to St. Paul the right hand of fellowship. We have already seen indications that, however strict might be the Judaical observances of St. James, they did not satisfy the Judaising party at Jerusalem, who attempted, under the sanction of his name,[5] to teach doctrines and enforce practices of which he disapproved. The partisans of this faction, indeed, are called by St. Paul (while anticipating this very visit to Jerusalem), ' the *disobedient* party.'[6] It would seem that their influence was not unfelt in the discussion which terminated in the resolution recorded. And though St. James acquiesced (as did St. Paul) in the advice given, it appears not to have originated with himself.

The counsel, however, though it may have been suggested by suspicious prejudice, or even by designing enmity, was not in itself unwise. St. Paul's great object (as we have seen) in this visit to Jerusalem, was to conciliate the Church of Palestine. If he could win over that Church to the truth, or even could avert its open hostility to himself, he would be doing more for the diffusion of

---

[1] ' A multitude,' ver. 22. Not ' *the* multitude,' nor *the laity of the Church,* as some have imagined. Were such the meaning, the Greek would have had the definite article. There seems to be some doubt about the genuineness of the clause. See Tischendorf.

[2] That these Nazarites were Christians is evident from the words ' *We*

have.'

[3] ' On arriving at Jerusalem, he offered many sacrifices of thanksgiving : wherefore also he ordered that many of the Nazarites should have their heads shorn.' Joseph. *Ant.* xix. 6. 1.

[4] ver. 25, comparing xv. 28.

[5] Acts xv. See Gal. ii. 12.

[6] Rom. xv. 31.

Christianity than even by the conversion of Ephesus. Every lawful means for such an end he was ready gladly to adopt. His own principles, stated by himself in his Epistles, required this of him. He had recently declared that every compliance in ceremonial observances should be made, rather than cast a stumbling-block in a brother's way.[1] He had laid it down as his principle of action, to become a Jew to Jews, that he might gain the Jews ; as willingly as he became a Gentile to Gentiles, that he might gain the Gentiles.[2] He had given it as a rule, that no man should change his external observances because he became a Christian ; that the Jew should remain a Jew in things outward.[3] Nay more, he himself observed the Jewish festivals, had previously countenanced his friends in the practice of Nazaritic vows,[4] and had circumcised Timothy, the son of a Jewess. So false was the charge that he had forbidden the Jews to circumcise their children.[5] In fact, the great doctrine of St. Paul concerning the worthlessness of ceremonial observances, rendered him equally ready to practise as to forsake them. A mind so truly Catholic as his, was necessarily free from any repugnance to mere outward observances ; a repugnance equally superstitious with the formalism which clings to ritual. In his view, circumcision was nothing and uncircumcision was nothing ; but faith, which worketh by love. And this love rendered him willing to adopt the most burdensome ceremonies, if by so doing he could save a brother from stumbling. Hence he willingly complied with the advice of the assembly, and thereby, while he removed the prejudices of its more ingenuous members, doubtless exasperated the factious partisans who had hoped for his refusal.

Thus the meeting ended amicably, with no open manifestation of that hostile feeling towards St. Paul which lurked in the bosoms of some who were present. On the next day, which was the great feast of Pentecost,[6] St. Paul proceeded with the four Christian Nazarites to the Temple. It is necessary here to explain the nature of their vow, and of the office which he was to perform for them. It was

---

[1] Rom. xiv.

[2] See 1 Cor. ix. 20.

[3] 1 Cor. vii. 17–19. Such passages are the best refutation of those who endeavour to represent the conduct here assigned to St. Paul as inconsistent with his teaching. See the discussion pp. 204, 205.

[4] Acts xviii. 18, which we conceive to refer to Aquila. (See p. 394.) But many interpreters of the passage think that St. Paul himself made the vow. We cannot possibly assent to Mr. Lewin's view, that St. Paul was still, on his arrival at Jerusalem, under the obligation of a vow taken in consequence of his escape at Ephesus.

[5] It has been argued that this charge was true, because the logical inference from St. Paul's doctrines was the uselessness of circumcision. But it might as well be said that the logical inference from the decree of the Council of Jerusalem was the uselessness of circumcision. The continued observance of the Law was of course only transitional.

[6] This mode of settling the vexed question of the '*seven days*' entirely removes the difficulty arising out of the '*twelve days*,' of which St. Paul speaks (xxiv. 11) in his speech before Felix. Yet it cannot be denied that on reading consecutively the twenty-sixth and twenty-seventh verses of the twenty-first chapter, it is difficult (whether or not we identify 'the days of purification' with 'the seven days) to believe that the *same day* is referred to in each verse. And when we come to xxiv. 11, we shall see that other modes of reckoning the time are admissible.

customary among the Jews, for those who had received deliverance from any great peril, or who from other causes desired publicly to testify their dedication to God, to take upon themselves the vow of a Nazarite, the regulations of which are prescribed in the sixth chapter of the book of Numbers.[1] In that book no rule is laid down as to the time during which this life of ascetic rigour was to continue:[2] but we learn from the Talmud and Josephus,[3] that thirty days at least a customary period. During this time the Nazarite was bound to abstain from wine, and to suffer his hair to grow uncut. At the termination of the period, he was bound to present himself in the Temple, with certain offerings, and his hair was then cut off and burnt upon the altar. The offerings required[4] were beyond the means of the very poor, and consequently it was thought an act of piety for a rich man[5] to pay the necessary expenses, and thus enable his poorer countrymen to complete their vow. St. Paul was far from rich; he gained his daily bread by the work of his own hands; and we may therefore naturally ask how he was able to take upon himself the expenses of these four Nazarites. The answer probably is, that the assembled Elders had requested him to apply to this purpose a portion of the fund which he had placed at their disposal. However this may be, he now made himself responsible for these expenses, and accompanied the Nazarites to the Temple, after having first performed the necessary purifications together with them.[6] On entering the Temple he announced to the priests

[1] ' When either man or woman shall separate themselves to vow a vow of a Nazarite, to separate themselves unto the Lord ; he shall separate himself from wine and strong drink. . . . All the days of the vow of his separation there shall no razor come upon his head : until the days be fulfilled, in the which he separateth himself unto the Lord, he shall be holy, and shall let the locks of the hair of his head grow.'—*Numb.* vi. 2–5.

[2] Sometimes the obligation was for life, as in the cases of Samson, Samuel, and John the Baptist. That ' seven days' in the instance before us was the whole duration of the vow, seems impossible, for this simple reason, that so short a time could produce no perceptible effect on the hair. Hemsen makes a mistake here in referring to the ' seven days' in Numb. vi. 6, which contemplates only the exceptional case of defilement in the course of the vow.

[3] Josephus states this after mentioning Berenice's vow, *War*, ii. 15. 1.

[4] ' And this is the law of the Nazarite, when the days of his separation are fulfilled : he shall be brought unto the door of the tabernacle of the congregation ; and he shall offer his offering unto the Lord, one he lamb of the first year without blemish for a burnt offering, and one ewe lamb of the first year without blemish for a sin offering, and one ram without blemish for peace offerings, and a basket of unleavened bread, cakes of fine flour mingled with oil, and wafers of unleavened bread anointed with oil, and their meat offering, and their drink offerings. And the priest shall bring them before the Lord, and shall offer his sin offering and his burnt offering : and he shall offer the ram for a sacrifice of peace offerings unto the Lord, with the basket of unleavened bread : the priest shall offer also his meat offering, and his drink offering. And the Nazarite shall shave the head of his separation at the door of the tabernacle of the congregation, and shall take the hair of the head of his separation, and put it in the fire which is under the sacrifice of the peace offerings.'—*Numb.* vi. 13–18.

[5] Compare the case of Agrippa mentioned above.

[6] *Purify thyself with them* (xxi. 24). *when purified he went in* (26), *they found me purified* (xxiv. 18). We do not agree with those commentators who interpret the first expression to mean ' dedicate thyself as a Nazarite along with them.' We doubt whether it could bear this meaning. At all events, the other is by

that the period of the Nazaritic vow which his friends had taken was accomplished, and he waited [1] within the sacred enclosure till the necessary offerings were made for each of them, and their hair cut off and burnt in the sacred fire.

He might well have hoped, by thus complying with the legal ceremonial, to conciliate those, at least, who were only hostile to him because they believed him hostile to their national worship. And, so far as the great body of the Church at Jerusalem was concerned, he probably succeeded. But the celebration of the festival had attracted multitudes to the Holy City, and the Temple was thronged with worshippers from every land ; and amongst these were some of those Asiatic Jews who had been defeated by his arguments in the Synagogue of Ephesus, and irritated against him during the last few years daily more and more, by the continual growth of a Christian Church in that city, formed in great part of converts from among the Jewish Proselytes. These men, whom a zealous feeling of nationality had attracted from their distant home to the metropolis of their faith, now beheld, where they least expected to find him, the apostate Israelite, who had opposed their teaching and seduced their converts. An opportunity of revenge, which they could not have hoped for in the Gentile city where they dwelt, had suddenly presented itself. They sprang upon their enemy, and shouted while they held him fast, ' Men of Israel, help. This is the man that teacheth all men everywhere against the People and the Law, and this Place.' [2] Then as the crowd rushed tumultuously towards the spot, they excited them yet further by accusing Paul of introducing Greeks into the Holy Place, which was profaned by the presence of a Gentile. The vast multitude which was assembled on the spot, and in the immediate neighbourhood, was excited to madness by these tidings, which spread rapidly through the crowd. The pilgrims who flocked at such seasons to Jerusalem were of course the most zealous of their nation ; very Hebrews of the Hebrews. We may imagine the horror and indignation which would fill their minds when they heard that an apostate from the faith of Israel had been seized in the very act of profaning the Temple at this holy season. A furious multitude rushed upon the Apostle ; and it was

far the most natural and obvious, and it corresponds with the Septuagintal use of the same verb in Numbers xix. 12.

[1] The obvious translation of ver. 26 seems to be, ' He entered into the Temple, giving public notice that the days of purification were fulfilled [and staid there] till the offering for each one of the Nazarites was brought.' The emphatic force of *each one* should be noticed. Publicity is implied in the word for *giving notice*. The persons to whom notice was given were the priests.

This interpretation harmonises with Wieseler's view of the whole subject. If we believe that several days were yet to elapse before the expiration of the Na-

zaritic ceremonies, we must translate, with Mr. Humphry—' making it known that the days of separation which must be fulfilled before the offering should be made, were in the course of completion.'

[2] ' *This place*,' ver. 28, ' *this holy place*,'—ib. We should compare here the accusation against Stephen, vi. 13. ' He ceaseth not to speak blasphemous words *against this holy place.*' The two cases are in many respects parallel. We cannot but believe that Paul must have remembered Stephen, and felt as though this attack on himself were a retribution. See below on xxii. 20. Cf. p. 58.

only their reverence for the holy place which preserved him from being torn to pieces on the spot. They hurried him out of the sacred enclosure, and assailed him with violent blows.[1] Their next course might have been to stone him or to hurl him over the precipice into the valley below. They were already in the court of the Gentiles, and the heavy gates[2] which separated the inner from the outer enclosure were shut by the Levites,—when an unexpected interruption prevented the murderous purpose.

It becomes desirable here to give a more particular description than we have yet done of the Temple-area and the sanctuary which it enclosed. Some reference has been made to this subject in the account of St. Stephen's martyrdom (p. 58), especially to that 'Stone Chamber'—the Hall Gazith—where the Sanhedrin held their solemn conclave. Soon we shall see St. Paul himself summoned before this tribunal, and hear his voice in that hall where he had listened to the eloquence of the first martyr. But meantime other events came in rapid succession: for the better understanding of which it is well to form to ourselves a clear notion of the localities in which they occurred.

The position of the Temple on the eastern side of Jerusalem, the relation of Mount Moriah to the other eminences on which the city was built, the valley which separated it from the higher summit of Mount Zion, and the deeper ravine which formed a chasm between the whole city and the Mount of Olives,—these facts of general topography are too well known to require elucidation.[3] On the other hand, when we turn to the description of the Temple-area itself and that which it contained, we are met with considerable difficulties. It does not, however, belong to our present task to reconcile the statements in Josephus[4] and the Talmud[5] with each other and with present appearances.[6] Nor shall we attempt to trace the architectural changes by which the scene has been modified, in the long interval between the time when the Patriarch built the altar on Moriah for his mysterious sacrifice,[7] and our own day, when the same spot[8] is the 'wailing-place' of those who are his children after the flesh, but not yet the heirs of his faith. Keeping aloof from all difficult details, and withdrawing ourselves from the consideration of those events which have invested this hill with an interest unknown to any other spot on the earth, we confine our-

---

[1] See Acts xxi. 31, 32.

[2] For an account of these gates, see below.

[3] Among the materials used in our account of the Temple, we may particularly mention Dr. Robinson's *Researches*, the memoir on Jerusalem, with the plan of the Ordnance Survey, published separately by Mr. G. Williams, and Mr. Thrupp's *Ancient Jerusalem*.

[4] The two places in Josephus where Herod's Temple is described at length are *Ant.* xv. 11, and *War*, v. 5. See also *Ant.* xx. 9. 7.

[5] The tract *Middoth* (*Measures*) in the Mischna treats entirely of this sub-ject.

[6] Mr. Thrupp argues in favour of Josephus, because of his general accuracy, and against *Middoth*, because the Rabbis could write only from tradition.

[7] Gen. xxii.

[8] See Robinson, i. 350. 'It is the nearest point in which the Jews can venture to approach their ancient Temple; and, fortunately for them, it is sheltered from observation by the narrowness of the land and the dead walls around.' It seems that the custom is mentioned even by Benjamin of Tudela in the twelfth century.

selves to the simple task of depicting the Temple of Herod, as it was when St. Paul was arrested by the infuriated Jews.

That rocky summit, which was wide enough for the threshing-floor of Araunah,[1] was levelled after David's death, and enlarged by means of laborious substructions, till it presented the appearance of one broad uniform area.[2] On this level space the temples of Solomon and Zerubbabel were successively built : and in the time of the Apostles there were remains of the former work in the vast stones which formed the supporting wall on the side of the valley of Jehoshaphat,[3] and of the latter in the eastern gate, which in its name and its appearance continued to be a monument of the Persian power.[4] The architectural arrangements of Herod's Temple were, in their general form, similar to the two which had preceded it. When we think of the Jewish sanctuary, whether in its earlier or later periods, our impulse is to imagine to ourselves some building like a synagogue or a church : but the first effort of our imagination should be to realise the appearance of that wide open space, which is spoken of by the prophets as the ' Outer Court ' or the ' Court of the Lord's House ;'[5] and is named by Josephus the ' Outer Temple,' and both in the Apocrypha and the Talmud, the ' Mountain of the House.'[6] That which was the ' House ' itself, or the Temple, properly so called,[7] was erected on the highest of a series of successive terraces, which rose in an isolated mass from the centre of the Court, or rather nearer to its north-western corner.[8]

In form the Outer Court was a square ; a strong wall enclosed it ; the sides corresponded to the four quarters of the heavens, and each was a stadium or a furlong in length.[9] Its pavement of stone was of various colours:[10] and it was surrounded by a covered colonnade, the roof of which was of costly cedar, and was supported on lofty and massive columns of the Corinthian order, and of the whitest marble.[11] On three sides there were two rows of columns : but on

---

[1] 1 Chron. xxi. 18; 2 Chron. iii. 1.

[2] See the description of this work in Josephus, *War*, v. 5. 1. *Ant.* xv. 11. 3.

[3] The lower courses of these immense stones still remain, and are described by all travellers.

[4] The Shushan Gate, which had a sculptured representation of the city of Susa, and was preserved from the time of Zerubbabel. *Middoth*. That which is now called the *Golden Gate*, ' a highly ornamental double gateway of Roman construction,' is doubtless on the same spot.

[5] Ezek. xl. 17; Jer. xix. 14, xxvi. 2. In 2 Chron. iv. 9, it is called the Great Court.

[6] The term with which we are most familiar,—' The Court of the Gentiles,' —is never applied to this space by Jewish writers.

[7] In the LXX. we find οἶκος and ναὸς used for that which was properly the Temple. The expression τὸ ἱερόν,

in the N. T., is a general term, inclusive of the whole series of courts. So it is used by Josephus, who speaks of the Outer Court as *the first* ἱερόν, *the outer* ἱερόν, while he uses ναὸς for the Temple itself.

[8] In *Middoth* it is distinctly said that the space from the east and south is greater than that from the west and north.

[9] We do not venture to touch the difficulties connected with the dimension of the Temple. Josephus is inconsistent both with the Talmud and himself. In one of his estimates of the size of the whole area, the ground on which Antonia stood is included.

[10] *War*, v. 5. 2.

[11] *Ant.* xv. 11. 5. He adds that the height of the columns was 25 cubits (?), and their number 162, while each column was so wide that it required three men with outstretched arms to embrace it.

the southern side the cloister deepened into a fourfold colonnade, the innermost supports of the roof being pilasters in the enclosing wall. About the south-eastern angle, where the valley was most depressed below the plateau of the Temple, we are to look for that 'Porch of Solomon' (John x. 23, Acts iii. 11) which is familiar to us in the New Testament:[1] and under the colonnades, or on the open area in the midst, were the 'tables of the money-changers and the seats of them who sold doves,' which turned that which was intended for a house of prayer into a 'house of merchandise' (John ii. 16) and 'a den of thieves' (Matt. xxi. 13). Free access was afforded into this wide enclosure by gates[2] on each of the four sides, one of which on the east was called the Royal Gate, and was perhaps identical with the 'Beautiful Gate' of Sacred History,[3] while another on the west was connected with the crowded streets of Mount Zion by a bridge over the intervening valley.[4]

Nearer (as we have seen) to the north-western corner than the centre of the square, arose that series of enclosed terraces on the summit of which was the sanctuary. These more sacred limits were fenced off by a low balustrade of stone, with columns at intervals, on which inscriptions in Greek and Latin warned all Gentiles against advancing beyond them on pain of death.[5] It was within this boundary that St. Paul was accused of having brought his Heathen companions. Besides this balustrade, a separation was formed by a flight of fourteen steps leading up to the first platform,[6] which in its western portion was a narrow terrace of fifteen feet wide round the walls of the innermost sanctuary,—while the eastern portion expanded into a second court, called the *Court of the Women.*[7] By this term we are not to understand that it was exclusively devoted to that sex, but that no women were allowed to advance beyond it. This court seems to have contained the treasury[8] (Mark

---

[1] See Joseph. *Ant.* xx. 9. 7.

[2] The statements of Josephus and *Middoth* with regard to the gates into the Outer Court are absolutely irreconcilable.

[3] The Shushan Gate, mentioned above.

[4] The supposed remains of this bridge, with some of the different theories respecting them, have been alluded to before. See p. 22, and the engraving.

[5] Joseph. *War,* v. 5. 2. In the *Antiquities* (xv. 11. 7) he does not say that the inscription was in different languages, but he adds that it announced death as the penalty of transgression. A similar statement occurs in Philo. This fence is mentioned again by Josephus in a striking passage, where Titus says to the Jews, after a horrible scene of bloodshed within the sacred limits: 'Was it not yourselves, ye wretches, who raised this fence before your sanctuary? Was it not yourselves that set the pillars therein at in-

tervals, inscribed with Greek characters and *our* characters, and forbidding any one to pass the boundary? And was it not *we* that allowed you to kill any one so transgressing, though he were a Roman?' *War,* vi. 2. 4. From this it appears that the Jews had full permission from the Romans to kill even a Roman, if he went beyond the boundary. These inscriptions have been alluded to before in this work, p. 3.

[6] With this platform begins what is called 'the second ἱερὸν' by Josephus. For the fourteen steps see *War,* v. 5. 2. In *Middoth* the steps are twelve. Leaving aside the discordance as to numbers, we may remark that we are left in doubt as to whether the balustrade was above or below the steps. Mr. Thrupp places the steps within the barrier, p. 328.

[7] *War,* v. 5. 2. See *Ant.* xv. 11. 5.

[8] In Joseph. *War,* v. 5. 2, we find 'Treasuries' in the plural. Compare vi. 5. 2. L'Empereur, who edited the

xii. 41, Luke xxi. 1) and various chambers, of which that at the
south-eastern corner should be mentioned here, for there the Nazarites performed their vows;[1] and the whole court was surrounded
by a wall of its own, with gates on each side,—the easternmost of
which was of Corinthian brass, with folding-doors and strong bolts
and bars, requiring the force of twenty men to close them for the
night.[2] We conceive that it was the closing of these doors by the
Levites, which is so pointedly mentioned by St. Luke (Acts xxi.
30) ; and we must suppose that St. Paul had been first seized
within them, and was then dragged down the flight of steps into the
Outer Court.

The interest, then, of this particular moment is to be associated
with the eastern entrance of the Inner from the Outer Temple. But
to complete our description, we must now cross the Court of the
Women to its western gate. The Holy Place and the Holy of
Holies were still within and above the spaces we have mentioned.
Two courts yet intervened between the court last described and the
Holy House itself. The first was the *Court of Israel*, the ascent to
which was by a flight of fifteen semicircular steps ;[3] the second, the
Court of the Priests, separated from the former by a low balustrade.[4]
Where these spaces bordered on each other, to the south, was the
hall Gazith,[5] the meeting-place of the Sanhedrin, partly in one
court and partly in the other. A little further towards the north
were all those arrangements which we are hardly able to associate
with the thoughts of worship, but which daily reiterated in the sight
of the Israelites that awful truth that ' without shedding of blood
there is no remission,'—the rings at which the victims were slaugh-
tered,—the beams and hooks from which they were suspended when
dead,—and the marble tables at which the entrails were washed :[6]—
here, above all, was the *Altar*, the very place of which has been
plausibly identified by the bore in the sacred rock of the Moslems,
which appears to correspond exactly with the description given in
the Mischna of the drain and cesspool which communicated with
the sewer that ran off into the Kedron.[7]

tract *Middoth*, places the treasury, or
treasuries, in the wall of the Court of
the Women, but facing the Outer Court.

[1] *Middoth*.

[2] We can hardly doubt that this is
the gate mentioned by Josephus, *War*,
vi. 5. 3. ' The Eastern gate, made of
brass, and very strong, shut at night-
fall with difficulty by twenty men.'
And this, we think, must be identical
with that of *War*, v. 8. 3 : 'One gate
outside the Temple, made of Corinthian
brass.' This again is determined to be
the gate by which the Court of the
Women was *entered from the east*, by
Ant. xv. 11. Such is the position assigned to the gate of Corinthian brass
by L'Empereur and Winer. Others
(Lightfoot, De Wette, Williams) make
it the *western* gate of the Court of the
Women.

[3] *War*, v. 5. 3, also *Middoth*.

[4] The information which Josephus
gives concerning these two courts (or
rather two parts of one court) is scanty.
Under the Court of Israel were rooms
for the musical instruments of the
priests. *Middoth*.

[5] *Middoth*. Reference has been
made before to this hall, in the narrative of Stephen's trial. p. 58, n. 3.
See below, p. 590. Rabbinical authorities say that the boundary line of Judah
and Benjamin passed between Gazith
and the Holy Place.

[6] *Middoth*. The position of these
rings, &c., was on the north side of
the altar of burnt offering,—to which
the ascent was by a gradual slope on
the south side.

[7] This is the view of Prof. Willis.
See Williams' *Memoir*, p. 95. But it

The House itself remains to be described. It was divided into three parts, the Vestibule, the Holy Place, and the Holy of Holies. From the Altar and the Court of the Priests to the Vestibule was another flight of twelve steps, the last of the successive approaches by which the Temple was ascended from the east. The Vestibule was wider[1] than the rest of the House : its front was adorned with a golden vine of colossal proportions :[2] and it was separated by a richly-embroidered curtain or veil from the Holy Place, which contained the Table of Shew-bread, the Candlestick, and the Altar of Incense. After this was the 'second veil' (Heb. ix. 3), closing the access to the innermost shrine, which in the days of the Tabernacle had contained the golden censer and the ark of the covenant, but which in Herod's Temple was entirely empty, though still regarded as the 'Holiest of All.' (Ib.) The interior height of the Holy Place and the Holy of Holies was comparatively small : but above them and on each side were chambers so arranged that the general exterior effect was that of a clerestory[3] rising above aisles : and the whole was surmounted with gilded spikes,[4] to prevent the birds from settling on the sacred roof.

Such is a bare outline of the general plan of the Jewish Temple. Such was the arrangement of its parts, which could be traced as in a map, by those who looked down from the summit of the Mount of Olives, as the modern traveller looks now from the same place upon the mosque of Omar and its surrounding court. As seen from this eminence,—when the gilded front of the vestibule flashed back the rays of the sun, and all the courts glittered (to use the comparison of Josephus) with the whiteness of snow — while the column of smoke rose over all, as a perpetual token of acceptable sacrifice,— and worshippers were closely crowded on the eastern steps and terraces in front of the Holy House, and Pilgrims from all countries under heaven were moving through the Outer Court and flocking to the same point from all streets in the city,—the Temple at the time of a festival must have been a proud spectacle to the religious Jew. It must have been with sad and incredulous wonder that the four Disciples heard from Him who wept over Jerusalem, that all this magnificence was presently to pass away.[5] None but a Jew can understand the passionate enthusiasm inspired by the recollections and the glorious appearance of the national Sanctuary. And none

cannot be regarded as absolutely certain. Mr. Thrupp (p. 317) objects that it is difficult to understand how so elevated a rock can be identical with the threshing floor of Araunah, which must have been levelled. He thinks the perforation was the secret passage made by Herod from Antonia. Joseph. *Ant.* xv. 11. 7. The only authentic account of the 'Rock of the Sakrah' is that of Mr. Catherwood, given in Bartlett's *Walks about Jerusalem.* See Stanley's *Sinai and Palestine,* p. 177.

[1] Josephus says that there were shoulders on each side.

[2] *Ant.* xv. 11, 3. *War,* v. 5. 4. Compare *Middoth :* 'Vitis aurea expandebatur super portam templi ;' also Tacitus : 'Vitis aurea templo reperta.' *Hist.* v. 5.

[3] Williams, p. 97.

[4] *War,* v. 5. 6. Lightfoot (ch. xi.) thinks that the roof had pinnacles, 'as King's Colledge Chappelle in Cambridge is decked in like manner, to its great beauty :' and he adds that the roof was not flat, but rising in the middle, 'as King's Colledge Chapelle may be herein a parallel also.'

[5] Matt. xxiv. 2, 3 ; Mark xiii. 2, 3 ; Luke xxi. 6.

but a Jew can understand the bitter grief and deep hatred which grew out of the degradation in which his nation was sunk at that particular time. This ancient glory was now under the shadow of an alien power. The Sanctuary was all but trodden under foot by the Gentiles. The very worship was conducted under the surveillance of Roman soldiers. We cannot conclude this account of the Temple without describing the fortress which was contiguous, and almost a part of it.

If we were to remount to the earlier history of the Temple, we might perhaps identify the tower of Antonia with the 'palace' of which we read in the book of Nehemiah (ii. 8, vii. 2). It was certainly the building which the Asmonean princes erected for their own residence under the name of Baris.[1] Afterwards rebuilt with greater strength and splendour by the first Herod, it was named by him, after his Romanising fashion, in honour of Mark Antony.[2] Its situation is most distinctly marked out by Josephus, who tells us that it was at the north-western[3] corner of the Temple-area, with the cloisters of which it communicated by means of staircases (Acts xxi. 35, 40).[4] It is difficult, however, to define the exact extent of ground which it covered in its renewed form during the time of the Herods. There is good reason for believing that it extended along the whole northern side of the great Temple court, from the north-western corner where it abutted on the city, to the north-eastern where it was suddenly stopped by the precipice which fronted the valley : and that the tank, which is now popularly called the Pool of Bethesda, was part of the fosse which protected it on the north.[5] Though the ground on which the tower of Antonia stood was lower than that of the Temple itself, yet it was raised to such a height, that at least the south-eastern of its four turrets[6] commanded a view of all that went on within the Temple, and thus both in position and in elevation it was in ancient Jerusalem what the Turkish governor's house is now,—whence the best view is obtained over the enclosure of the mosque of Omar. But this is an inadequate comparison. If we wish to realise the influence of this fortress in reference to political and religious interests, we must turn rather to that which is the most humiliating spectacle in Christendom, the presence of the Turkish troops at the Church of the Holy Sepulchre, where they are stationed to control the fury of the Greeks and Latins at the most solemn festival of the Christian year. Such was the office of the Roman troops that were quartered at the Jewish festivals in the

[1] Joseph. *Ant.* xv. 11. 4.

[2] Josephus says of it:—'It was of old called *Baris*, but afterwards named Antonia during the time of Antony's ascendency, just as Sebaste and Agrippias gained their later names from Sebastus [Augustus] and Agrippa.' *War*, i. 5. 4. See pp. 22, 23.

[3] Compare *War*, v. 5. 8, with *Ant.* xv. 11. 4, and *War*, i. 5. 4; i. 21. 1; also v. 4. 2.

[4] See p. 583, n. 1, for the clear description which Josephus gives of this communication between the fortress and

the cloisters.

[5] This view is ably advocated by Dr. Robinson, in his account of Antonia (*Res.* i. pp. 431–436), and as Mr. Williams remarks (*Memoir*, p. 100), this reservoir (the Birket-Israel) may still be the Bethesda of the Gospel. See a confirmation of Dr. Robinson's hypothesis, from the observations of Mr. Walcott, *Bib. Sac.* i. p. 29.

[6] It had four smaller towers rising from its angles, like the Tower of London, save that that on the S.E. was higher than the others. *War*, v. 5. 8.

fortress of Antonia.[1] Within its walls there were barracks for at least a thousand soldiers.[2] Not that we are to suppose that all the garrison in Jerusalem was always posted there. It is probable that the usual quarters of the 'whole cohort' (Matt. xxvii. 27), or the greater part of it, were towards the western quarter of the city, in that 'prætorium' (John xviii. 28) or official residence[3] where JESUS was mocked by the soldiers, and on the tesselated pavement[4] in front of which Pilate sat, and condemned the Saviour of the world. But at the time of the greater festivals, when a vast concourse of people, full of religious fanaticism and embittered by hatred of their rulers, flocked into the Temple courts, it was found necessary to order a strong military force into Antonia, and to keep them under arms, so that they might act immediately and promptly in the case of any outbreak.

A striking illustration of the connection between the Fortress and the Temple is afforded by the history of the quarrels which arose in reference to the pontifical vestments. These robes were kept in Antonia during the time of Herod the Great. When he died, they came under the superintendence of the Roman Procurator. Agrippa I., during his short reign, exercised the right which had belonged to his grandfather. At his death the command that the Procurator Cuspius Fadus should take the vestments under his care raised a ferment among the whole Jewish people; and they were only kept from an outbreak by the presence of an overwhelming force under Longinus, the Governor of Syria. An embassy to Rome, with the aid of the younger Agrippa, who was then at the imperial court, obtained the desired relaxation: and the letter is still extant in which Claudius assigned to Herod, King of Chalcis, the privilege which had belonged to his brother.[5] But under the succeeding Procurators, the relation between the fortress Antonia and the religious ceremonies in the Temple became more significant and ominous. The hatred between the embittered Jews and those soldiers who were soon to take part in their destruction, grew deeper and more implacable. Under Ventidius Cumanus,[6] a frightful loss of life had taken place on one occasion at the pass-

[1] 'Where it joined the two colonnades of the Temple, it had passages leading down to them both, through which the guard (for a Roman legion was always quartered in the fort) went down, so as to take various positions along the colonnades, in arms, at festivals watching the people, lest any insurrectionary movement should arise.' *War.* v. 5. 8. [The word τάγμα seems to be loosely used in Josephus and elsewhere. See 1 Cor. xv. 23.]

[2] See below, p. 594, note on σπεῖρα.

[3] This Prætorium seems to have been the old palace of Herod, connected with the tower called Hippicus, which is identified by existing remains. It was on the western side of the city, and is one of our fixed points in tracing the course of the ancient walls.

[4] He took his seat on a tribunal at a place called 'the Pavement,' and in Hebrew, 'Gabbatha.' John xix. 13. Something has been said before (p. 328, n. 1) on the βῆμα or tribunal as the symbol of Roman power in the provinces.

[5] Joseph. *Ant.* xx. 1. 2. The letter is quoted in the fifteenth chapter of Mr. Lewin's work on the *Life and Epistles of St. Paul,* a chapter which contains much miscellaneous information concerning Jerusalem and the Jews at this time.

[6] Tiberius Alexander, a renegade Jew, intervened between Fadus and Cumanus. We shall recur to the series of Procurators in the beginning of the next chapter.

over, in consequence of an insult perpetrated by one of the military.[1] When Felix succeeded him, assassination became frequent in Jerusalem : the high priest Jonathan was murdered, like Becket, in the Temple itself, with the connivance of the Procurator :[2] and at the very moment of which we write, both the soldiers and the populace were in great excitement in consequence of the recent 'uproar' caused by an Egyptian impostor (Acts xxi. 38), who had led out a vast number of fanatic followers ' into the wilderness' to be slain or captured by the troops of Felix.[3]

This imperfect description of the Temple-area and of the relations subsisting between it and the contiguous fortress, is sufficient to set the scene before us, on which the events we are now to relate occurred in rapid succession. We left St. Paul at the moment when the Levites had closed the gates, lest the Holy Place should be polluted by murder,—and when the infuriated mob were violently beating the Apostle, with the full intention of putting him to death. The beginning and rapid progress of the commotion must have been seen by the sentries on the cloisters and the tower ; and news was sent up[4] immediately to Claudius Lysias, the commandant of the garrison, that ' all Jerusalem was in an uproar' (ver. 31). The spark had fallen on materials the most inflammable, and not a moment was to be lost, if a conflagration was to be averted. Lysias himself rushed down instantly, with some of his subordinate officers and a strong body of men,[5] into the Temple court. At the sight of the flashing arms and disciplined movements of the Imperial soldiers, the Jewish mob desisted from their murderous violence. ' They left off beating of Paul.' They had for a moment forgotten that the eyes of the sentries were upon them : but this sudden invasion by their hated and dreaded tyrants reminded them that they were ' in danger to be called in question for that day's uproar.' (Acts xix. 40.)

Claudius Lysias proceeded with the soldiers promptly and directly to St. Paul,[6] whom he perceived to be the central object of all the excitement in the Temple court : and in the first place he ordered him to be chained by each hand to a soldier :[7] for he suspected that he might be the Egyptian rebel,[8] who had himself baffled the pursuit of the Roman force, though his followers were dispersed. This being done, he proceeded to question the bystanders, who were watching this summary proceeding, half in disappointed rage at the loss of their victim, and half in satisfaction that they saw him at least in captivity. But ' when Lysias demanded who he was and what he had done, some cried one thing, and some another, among

---

[1] Joseph. *Ant.* xx. 5. 2. *War*, ii. 12. 1. In this narrative the tower of Antonia and its guards are particularly mentioned.

[2] *War*, ii. 13. 3.

[3] The passages in Josephus, which relate to this Egyptian, are *Ant.* xx. 8. 6. *War*, ii. 13. 5.

[4] Literally ' came *up*,' ver. 31. Compare this with ' ran *down*,' in the next verse, and the ' *stairs*,' mentioned

below.

[5] ver. 32. If the word (*chiliarch*) translated 'chief captain,' is to be understood literally of the commander of 1000 men, the full complement of *centurions* in the castle would be ten.

[6] ' Then the chief captain drew near.'

[7] ' Two chains.' So St. Peter was bound. Acts xii.

[8] This is evident from his question below, ver. 38,

the multitude' (vv. 33, 34); and when he found that he could obtain no certain information in consequence of the tumult, he gave orders that the prisoner should be conveyed into the barracks within the fortress.[1] The multitude pressed and crowded on the soldiers, as they proceeded to execute this order : so that the Apostle was actually 'carried up' the staircase, in consequence of the violent pressure from below.[2] And meanwhile deafening shouts arose from the stairs and from the court,—the same shouts which, nearly thirty years before, surrounded the prætorium of Pilate,[3]— 'Away with him, away with him.'

At this moment,[4] the Apostle, with the utmost presence of mind, turned to the commanding officer who was near him,—and, addressing him in Greek, said respectfully, 'May I speak with thee ?' Claudius Lysias was startled when he found himself addressed by his prisoner in Greek, and asked him whether he was then mistaken in supposing he was the Egyptian ringleader of the late rebellion. St. Paul replied calmly that he was no Egyptian, but a Jew ; and he readily explained his knowledge of Greek, and at the same time asserted his claim to respectful treatment,[5] by saying that he was a native of 'Tarsus in Cilicia, a citizen of no mean city :' and he proceeded to request that he might be allowed to address the people. The request was a bold one ; and we are almost surprised that Lysias should have granted it : but there seems to have been something in St. Paul's aspect and manner, which from the first gained an influence over the mind of the Roman officer : and his consent was not refused. And now the whole scene was changed in a moment. St. Paul stood upon the stairs and turned to the people, and made a motion with the hand,[6] as about to address them. And they too felt the influence of his presence. Tranquillity came on the sea of heads below : there was 'a great silence :' and he began, saying,

ACTS xxii. 1

Brethren and Fathers,[7] hear me, and let me now defend myself before you.

The language which he spoke was Hebrew.[8] Had he spoken in Greek, the majority of those who heard him would have understood his words : but the sound of the holy tongue in that holy place fell like a calm on the troubled waters. The silence became universal

---

[1] The word used here, ver. 34, and below, xxii. 24, xxiii. 16, denotes not 'the castle,' but soldiers' 'barracks' within it. It is the word used of the camp of the Israelites in the Wilderness. (LXX.)

[2] ver. 35.

[3] Compare Luke xxiii. 18, John xix. 15.

[4] 'When he was on the point of being led in.' ver. 37.

[5] We need not repeat all that has been said before concerning the importance of Tarsus. See pp. 18, 40–43, 87 88, 196, 197.

[6] ver. 40. Compare xiii. 16, xxvi. 1,

also xx. 34.

[7] To account for this peculiar mode of address, we must suppose that mixed with the crowd were men of venerable age and dignity, perhaps members of the Sanhedrin, ancient Scribes and Doctors of the Law, who were stirring up the people against the heretic. The phrase generally translated in A. V. '*Men and brethren*,' literally, '*Men who are my brethren*,' may be equally translated, '*Brethren*.'

[8] That is, it was the Hebraic dialect popularly spoken in Judæa, which we now call Syro-Chaldaic.

and breathless ; and the Apostle proceeded to address his countrymen as follows :—

education.

I am myself[1] an Israelite, born indeed at Tarsus, in xx
Cilicia, yet brought up in this city, and taught at the
feet of Gamaliel, in the strictest doctrine of the law

His persecution of the Christians.

of our fathers ; and was zealous[2] in the cause of
God, as ye all are this day. And I persecuted this sect 4
unto the death, binding with chains and casting into
prison both men and women. And of this the High 5
Priest is my witness, and all the[3] Sanhedrin ; from
whom, moreover, I received letters to the brethren,[4]
and went[5] to Damascus, to bring those also who
were there to Jerusalem, in chains, that they might
be punished.

His conversion.

But it came to pass that as I journeyed, when I 6
drew nigh to Damascus, about mid-day, suddenly
there shone from heaven a great light round about
me. And I fell to the ground, and heard a voice 7
saying unto me, *Saul, Saul, why persecutest thou me ?*
And I answered, *Who art thou, Lord ?* and He said 8
unto me, *I am Jesus of Nazareth,*[6] *whom thou persecutest.* And the men who were with me saw the light, 9
and were terrified ;[7] but they heard not the voice of
Him that spake unto me. And I said, *What shall I* 10
do, Lord ? And the Lord said unto me, *Arise and go
into Damascus, and there thou shalt be told of all
things which are appointed for thee to do.*

His blindness, cure, and baptism.

And when I could not see, from the brightness of 11
that light, my companions led me by the hand, and
so I entered into Damascus. And a certain Ananias, 12
a devout[8] man according to the law, well reported of
by all the Jews who dwelt there, came and stood beside me, and said to me, *Brother Saul, receive thy* 13
sight ; and in that instant I received my sight[9] and

---

[1] The pronoun is emphatic.

[2] See the note on Gal. i. 14.

[3] The Presbytery. Compare Luke
xxii. 66. The high priest here appealed
to was the person who held that office
at the time of St. Paul's conversion,
probably Theophilus, who was high
priest in 37 and 38 A.D.

[4] i.e. the Jews resident at Damascus.

[5] Literally, *I was on my road* (im-
perf.).

[6] Literally, *Jesus the Nazarene.* Saul
was going to cast the *Nazarenes* (so
the Christians were called, see Acts
xxiv. 5) into chains and dungeons
when he was stopped by the Lord, an-

nouncing Himself from heaven to be
Jesus the Nazarene.

[7] The clause 'and were terrified' is
omitted in some of the best MSS.

[8] The corresponding Greek word is
omitted in some of the best MSS. (and
altered in others), probably because
the copyists were perplexed at finding
it not here used in its usual technical
sense of a *Jewish Proselyte.*

[9] The verb here has the double
meaning of *to recover sight* and *to look
up*; in the former of which it is used
in the accounts of blind men healed in
the gospels. Here the A. V. translates
the same verb by two different words.

14 looked upon him. And he said, *The God of our Fathers hath ordained thee to know His will, and to behold the Just One, and to hear the voice of His mouth.*
15 *For thou shalt be His witness to all the world*[1] *of what*
16 *thou hast seen and heard. And now, why dost thou delay? Arise and be baptized*[2] *and wash away thy sins, calling on the name of Jesus.*[3]

17 And it came to pass, after I had returned to Jerusalem, and while I was praying in the Temple, that I was in a trance, and saw Him saying unto me, *His return to Jerusalem.*
18 *Make haste and go forth quickly from Jerusalem; for*
19 *they will not receive thy testimony concerning me.* And *He is commanded in a vision to go to the Gentiles.* I said,[4] *Lord, they themselves know that I continually*[5] *imprisoned and scourged in every synagogue the be-*
20 *lievers in Thee. And when the blood of thy martyr*[6] *Stephen was shed, I myself also was standing by and consenting gladly*[7] *to his death,*[8] *and keeping the raiment of them who slew him.* And He said unto
21 me, *Depart; for I will send thee far hence unto the Gentiles.*

At these words St. Paul's address to his countrymen was suddenly interrupted. Up to this point he had riveted their attention.[9] They listened, while he spoke to them of his early life, his persecution of the Church, his mission to Damascus. Many were present who could testify, on their own evidence, to the truth of what he said. Even when he told them of his miraculous conversion, his interview with Ananias, and his vision in the Temple, they listened still. With admirable judgment he deferred till the last all mention of the Gentiles.[10] He spoke of Ananias as a 'devout man according

[1] The meaning rather stronger than '*all men.*'

[2] Literally, *cause thyself to be baptized* (mid.). With the following compare 1 Cor. vi. 11.

[3] The best MSS. read 'His name,' and not 'the Lord's name.' The reference is to the confession of faith in Jesus, which preceded baptism.

[4] St. Paul expected at first that the Jews at Jerusalem (the members of his own party) would listen to him readily, because they could not be more violent against the Nazarenes than they knew him to have been: and he therefore thought that they must feel that nothing short of irresistible truth could have made him join the sect which he had hated.

[5] Literally, *I was imprisoning, I kept on imprisoning.*

[6] This word (literally *Witness*) had not yet acquired its technical sense, but here it may be translated *Martyr*, because the mode in which Stephen bore testimony was by his death.

[7] Compare Rom. i. 32.

[8] 'To his death,' though omitted in the best MSS., is implied in the sense.

[9] The verb for listening is in the imperfect, that for the outbreak is in the aorist. See the remarks on Stephen's speech, pp. 59, 60.

[10] As an illustration of St. Paul's wisdom, it is instructive to observe that in xxvi. 17 it is distinctly said that Jesus Himself announced from heaven Paul's mission to the Gentiles; and that in ix. 15 the same announcement is made to Ananias,—whereas in the address to the Jews this is kept out of view for the moment, and reserved till after the vision in the Temple is mentioned. And again we should observe that while in ix. 10, Ananias is spoken of as a *Christian* (see 13), here he is

to the law' (ver. 12), as one ' well reported of by all the Jews' (ib.), as one who addressed him in the name of ' the God of their Fathers' (ver. 14).   He showed how in his vision he had pleaded before that God the energy of his former persecution, as a proof that his countrymen must surely be convinced by his conversion : and when he alluded to the death of Stephen, and the part which he had taken himself in that cruel martyrdom (ver. 20), all the associations of the place where they stood [1] must (we should have thought) have brought the memory of that scene with pathetic force before their minds.   But when his *mission to the Gentiles* was announced,— though the words quoted were the words of Jehovah spoken in the Temple itself, even as the Lord had once spoken to Samuel,[2]—one outburst of frantic indignation rose from the Temple-area and silenced the speaker on the stairs.   Their national pride bore down every argument which could influence their reason or their reverence. They could not bear the thought of uncircumcised Heathens being made equal to the sons of Abraham.   They cried out that such a wretch ought not to pollute the earth with his presence—that it was a shame to have preserved his life :[3] and in their rage and impatience they tossed off their outer garments (as on that other occasion, when the garments were laid at the feet of Saul himself[4]), and threw up dust into the air with frantic violence.[5]   This commotion threw Lysias into new perplexity.   He had not been able to understand the Apostle's Hebrew speech : and, when he saw its results, he concluded that his prisoner must be guilty of some enormous crime.   He ordered him therefore to be taken immediately from the stairs into the barracks ;[6] and to be examined by torture,[7] in order to elicit a confession of his guilt.   Whatever instruments were necessary for this kind of scrutiny would be in readiness within a Roman fortress : and before long the body[8] of the Apostle was ' streched out,' like that of a common malefactor, ' to receive the lashes,' with the officer standing by,[9] to whom Lysias had entrusted the superintendence of this harsh examination.

described as *a strict and pious Jew.* He was, in fact, both the one and the other. But, for the purposes of persuasion, St. Paul lays stress here on the latter point.

[1] See above, p. 576, n. 2.

[2] 1 Sam. iii.

[3] The correct reading appears to put the verb in the past.   It will be remembered that they were on the point of killing St. Paul, when Claudius Lysias rescued him, xxi. 31.

[4] Compare xxii. 23, with vii. 58.   We need not, however, suppose that this tossing of the garments and throwing of dust was precisely symbolical of their desire to *stone* Paul.   It denoted simply impatience and disgust.

[5] ' Sir John Chardin, as quoted by Harmer (*Obs.* iv. 203), says that it is common for the peasants in Persia, when they have a complaint to lay before their governors, to repair to them by hundreds, or a thousand, at once.   They place themselves near the gate of the palace, where they suppose they are most likely to be seen and heard, and then set up a horrid outcry, rend their garments, and throw dust into the air, at the same time demanding justice.'—Hackett.

[6] See above, pp. 584, 585.

[7] ver. 24.

[8] We take the phrase to mean ' for the thongs,' i.e. the straps of which the scourges were made.   Others consider the words to denote the thongs or straps with which the offender was fastened to the post or pillar.   In either case, the use of the article is explained.

[9] We see this from ver. 25, ' he said to the centurion, who stood by.'   Claudius Lysias himself was not on the spot

Thus St. Paul was on the verge of adding another suffering and disgrace to that long catalogue of afflictions, which he had enumerated in the last letter he wrote to Corinth, before his recent visit to that city (2 Cor. xi. 23-25). Five times scourged by the Jews, once beaten with rods at Philippi, and twice on other unknown occasions, he had indeed been 'in stripes above measure.' And now he was in a Roman barrack, among rude soldiers, with a similar indignity[1] in prospect ; when he rescued himself, and at the same time gained a vantage-ground for the Gospel, by that appeal to his rights as a Roman citizen, under which he had before sheltered his sacred cause at Philippi.[2] He said these few words to the centurion who stood by. 'Is it lawful to torture one who is a Roman citizen and uncondemned ?' The magic of the Roman law produced its effect in a moment. The centurion immediately reported the words to his commanding-officer, and said significantly, 'Take heed what thou doest : for this man is a Roman citizen.' Lysias was both astonished and alarmed. He knew full well that no man would dare to assume the right of citizenship, if it did not really belong to him :[3] and he hastened in person to his prisoner. A hurried dialogue took place, from which it appeared, not only that St. Paul was indeed a Roman citizen, but that he held this privilege under circumstances far more honourable than his interrogator : for while Claudius Lysias had purchased[4] the right for 'a great sum,' Paul[5] 'was free-born.' Orders were instantly given[6] for the removal of the instruments of torture : and those who had been about to conduct the examination retired. Lysias was compelled to keep the Apostle still in custody ; for he was ignorant of the nature of his offence : and indeed this was evidently the only sure method of saving him from destruction by the Jews. But the Roman officer was full of alarm : for in his treatment of the prisoner[7] he had already been guilty of a flagrant violation of the law.

On the following day[8] the commandant of the garrison adopted a milder method of ascertaining the nature of his prisoner's offence.

(see ver. 26), but had handed over the Apostle to a centurion who 'stood by,' as in the case of a military flogging with us.

[1] We must distinguish between the *scourging* here (24, 25) and the *beating with rods* (Acts xvi. 22 ; 2 Cor. xi. 25). In the present instance the object was not punishment, but examination.

[2] See p. 239.

[3] Such pretensions were liable to capital punishment.

[4] We learn from Dio Cassius, that the *civitas* of Rome was, in the early part of the reign of Claudius, sold at a high rate and afterwards for a mere trifle.

[5] It is unnecessary to repeat here what has been said concerning the citizenship of Paul and his father. See

pp. 38, 39. For the laws relating to the privileges of citizens, see again p. 239.

[6] This is not expressed, but it is implied by what follows. 'Immediately they went away,' &c.

[7] Lysias was afraid, because he had so 'bound' the Apostle, as he could not have ventured to do, had he known he was a Roman citizen. It seems, that in any case it would have been illegal to have had immediate recourse to torture. Certainly it was contrary to the Roman law to put any Roman citizen to the torture, either by scourging or in any other way. Under the Imperial regime, however, so early as the time of Tiberius, this rule was violated ; and torture was applied to citizens of the highest rank, more and more freely.

[8] ver. 30.

He summoned a meeting of the Jewish Sanhedrin with the high priests, and brought St. Paul down from the fortress and set him before them,—doubtless taking due precautions to prevent the consequences which might result from a sudden attack upon his safety. Only a narrow space of the Great Temple Court intervened[1] between the steps which led down from the tower Antonia, and those which led up to the hall Gazith, the Sanhedrin's accustomed place of meeting. If that hall was used on this occasion, no Heathen soldiers would be allowed to enter it : for it was within the balustrade which separated the sanctuary from the Court. But the fear of pollution would keep the Apostle's life in safety within that enclosure. There is good reason for believing that the Sanhedrin met at that period in a place less sacred,[2] to which the soldiers would be admitted ; but this is a question into which we need not enter. Wherever the council sat, we are suddenly transferred from the interior of a Roman barrack to a scene entirely Jewish.

Paul was now in presence of that council, before which, when he was himself a member of it, Stephen had been judged. That moment could hardly be forgotten by him : but he looked steadily at his inquisitors,[3] among whom he would recognise many who had been his fellow-pupils in the school of Gamaliel, and his associates in the persecution of the Christians. That unflinching look of conscious integrity offended them,—and his confident words—'Brethren,[4] I have always lived a conscientious[5] life before God, up to this very day,'—so enraged the high priest, that he commanded those who stood near to strike him on the mouth. This brutal insult roused the Apostle's feelings, and he exclaimed, 'God shall smite thee, thou whited wall :[6] sittest thou to judge me according to the law, and then in defiance of the law dost thou command me to be struck?' If we consider these words as an outburst of natural indignation, we cannot severely blame them, when we remember St. Paul's temperament,[7] and how they were provoked. If we regard them as a prophetic denunciation, they were terribly fulfilled, when this hypocritical president of the Sanhedrin was murdered by the assassins in the Jewish war.[8] In whatever light we view them now, those who were present in the Sanhedrin treated them as profane and rebellious. 'Revilest thou God's high priest?' was the indignant exclamation of the bystanders. And then Paul recovered himself, and said, with Christian meekness and forbearance, that he did not consider[9] that Ananias was high priest; other-

---

[1] See above.

[2] See p. 58.

[3] Acts xxiii. 1. See p. 119, n. 6.

[4] It should be observed that, both here and below (vv. 5, 6) he addresses the Sanhedrin as equals,—'*Brethren*,' —whereas in xxii. 1 he says '*Brethren and Fathers.*'

[5] This assertion of habitual conscientiousness is peculiarly characteristic of St. Paul. See 2 Tim. i. 3, where there is also a reference to his forefathers, as in ver. 6 below. Compare ch. xxvi.

[6] With 'whited wall' compare our Saviour's comparison of hypocrites with 'whited sepulchres' (Matt. xxiii. 27). Lightfoot goes so far here, as to say that the words themselves mean that Ananias had the semblance of the high priest's office without the reality.

[7] See p. 41.

[8] He was killed by the Sicarii. Joseph. *War*, ii. 17. 9.

[9] The use of this English word retains something of the ambiguity of the original. It is difficult to decide positively on the meaning of the words.

wise he would not so have spoken, seeing that it is written in the Law,[1] '𝕿𝖍𝖔𝖚 𝖘𝖍𝖆𝖑𝖙 𝖓𝖔𝖙 𝖗𝖊𝖇𝖎𝖑𝖊 𝖙𝖍𝖊 𝖗𝖚𝖑𝖊𝖗 𝖔𝖋 𝖙𝖍𝖞 𝖕𝖊𝖔𝖕𝖑𝖊.' But the Apostle had seen enough to be convinced that there was no prospect before this tribunal of a fair inquiry and a just decision. He therefore adroitly adopted a prompt measure for enlisting the sympathies of those who agreed with him in one doctrine, which, though held to be an open question in Judaism, was an essential truth in Christianity.[2] He knew that both Pharisees and Sadducees were among his judges, and well aware that, however united they might be in the outward work of persecution, they were divided by an impassable line in the deeper matters of religious faith, he cried out, ' Brethren, I am a Pharisee, and all my forefathers were Pharisees :[3] it is for the hope of a resurrection from the dead that I am to be judged this day.' This exclamation produced an instantaneous effect on the assembly. It was the watchword which marshalled the opposing forces in antagonism to each other.[4] The Pharisees felt a momentary hope that they might use their ancient partisan as a new weapon against their rivals ; and their hatred against the Sadducees was even greater than their hatred of Christianity. They were vehement in their vociferations ;[5] and their language was that which Gamaliel had used more calmly many years before[6] (and possibly the aged Rabban may have been present himself in this very assembly) :[7] ' If this doctrine be of God, ye cannot destroy it : beware lest ye be found to be fighting against God.' ' We find no fault in this man : what, if (as he says[8]) an angel or a spirit have indeed spoken to him,——' The sentence was left incomplete or unheard

---

Some think that St. Paul meant to confess that he had been guilty of a want of due reflection,—others that he spoke ironically, as refusing to recognise a man like Ananias as high priest,—others have even thought that there was in the words an inspired reference to the abolition of the sacerdotal system of the Jews, and the sole priesthood of Christ. Another class of interpreters regard St. Paul as ignorant of the fact that Ananias was high priest, or argue that Ananias was not really installed in his office. And we know from Josephus, that there was the greatest irregularity in the appointments about this time. Lastly, it has been suggested p. 119, n. 6), that the imperfection of St. Paul's vision (supposed to be implied in xxiii. 1) was the cause of the mistake.

[1] Ex. xxii. 28.

[2] For these two sects, see the early part of Chap. II.

[3] 'Pharisees,' not 'Pharisee,' is the reading best supported by MSS., and the plural is far more forcible. See pp. 27, 28.

[4] 'There arose a *discussion*, . . . and the multitude was *divided*,' ver. 7. Compare 'they *strove*,' ver. 9.

[5] 'There arose a great cry,' ver. 9.

[6] Acts v. 39.

[7] It appears that he died about two years after this time. See p. 48. We may refer here to the observations of Mr. Birks in the *Horæ Apostolicæ* (No. xvi.) appended to his recent edition of the *Horæ Paulinæ*, where he applies the jealousy and mutual antipathy of the Sadducees and Pharisees, to explain the conduct of Gamaliel at the former trial, and thus traces 'an unobtrusive coincidence' between this passage and the narrative in Acts v. 'First, the leaders in the persecution were Sadducees (ver. 17). In the next place, it was a doctrinal offence which was charged upon them (ver. 28). Again, the answer of Peter, while an explicit testimony to the claims of Jesus, is an equally plain avowal of the doctrine of the resurrection (ver. 30). When Gamaliel interposes, it is noted that he was a Pharisee,' &c. (ver. 34).

[8] There is probably a tacit reference to what St. Paul had said, in his speech on the stairs, concerning his vision in the Temple.

in the uproar.[1] The judgment-hall became a scene of the most violent contention; and presently Claudius Lysias received information of what was taking place, and fearing lest the Roman citizen, whom he was bound to protect, should be torn in pieces between those who sought to protect him, and those who thirsted for his destruction, he ordered the troops to go down instantly, and bring him back into the soldiers' quarters within the fortress.[2]

So passed this morning of violent excitement. In the evening, when Paul was isolated both from Jewish enemies and Christian friends, and surrounded by the uncongenial sights and sounds of a soldiers' barrack,—when the agitation of his mind subsided, and he was no longer strung up by the presence of his persecutors, or supported by sympathising brethren,—can we wonder that his heart sank, and that he looked with dread on the vague future that was before him? Just then it was that he had one of those visions by night, which were sometimes vouchsafed to him, at critical seasons of his life, and in providential conformity with the circumstances in which he was placed. The last time when we were informed of such an event was when he was in the house of Aquila and Priscilla at Corinth, and when he was fortified against the intimidation of the Jews by the words, 'Fear not: for I am with thee.' (Acts xviii. 9, 10.) The next instance we shall have to relate is in the worst part of the storm at sea, between Fair Havens and Malta, when a similar assurance was given to him: 'Fear not: thou must stand before Cæsar.' (Ib. xxvii. 24.) On the present occasion events were not sufficiently matured for him to receive a prophetic intimation in this explicit form. He had, indeed, long looked forward to a visit to Rome: but the prospect now seemed further off than ever. And it was at this anxious time that he was miraculously comforted and strengthened by Him, who is 'the confidence of all the ends of the earth, and of them that are afar off upon the sea; who by His strength setteth fast the mountains; who stilleth the noise of the seas and the tumult of the people.' In the visions of the night, the Lord Himself stood by him and said: 'Be of good cheer, Paul; for as thou hast testified of me at Jerusalem, so must thou testify also at Rome.' (Ib. xxiii. 11.)

The contrast is great between the peaceful assurance thus secretly given to the faith of the Apostle in his place of imprisonment, and the active malignity of his enemies in the city. When it was day, more than forty of the Jews entered into a conspiracy to assassinate Paul:[3] and that they might fence round their crime with all the sanction of religion, they bound themselves by a curse, that they would eat and drink nothing till the deed was accomplished.[4] Thus

---

[1] There seems no doubt that the words 'let us not fight against God,' ought not to be in the text; and that there is an aposiopesis, either voluntary for the sake of emphasis, or compulsory because of the tumult. Perhaps the phrase 'fighters against God,' in Acts v. 39, may have led to the interpolation.

[2] Acts xxiii. 10.

[3] With the direct narrative, vv. 12 -15, we should compare closely the account given by St. Paul's nephew, vv. 20, 21.

[4] So we are told by Josephus that ten Jews bound themselves by a solemn oath, to assassinate Herod, and that before their execution they maintained 'that their oath had been well and piously taken.' *Ant.* xv. 8.3.4. Hackett

fortified by a dreadful oath, they came before the chief priests and members of the Sanhedrin,[1] and proposed the following plan, which seems to have been readily adopted. The Sanhedrists were to present themselves before Claudius Lysias, with the request that he would allow the prisoner to be brought once more before the Jewish Court, that they might enter into a further investigation:[2] and the assassins were to lie in wait, and murder the Apostle on his way down[3] from the fortress. The plea to be brought before Lysias was very plausible: and it is probable that, if he had received no further information, he would have acted on it: for he well knew that the proceedings of the Court had been suddenly interrupted the day before,[4] and he would be glad to have his perplexity removed by the results of a new inquiry.[5] The danger to which the Apostle was exposed was most imminent: and there has seldom been a more horrible example of crime masked under the show of religious zeal.

The plot was ready:[6] and the next day[7] it would have been carried into effect, when God was pleased to confound the schemes of the conspirators. The instrument of St. Paul's safety was one of his own relations,[8] the son of that sister whom we have before mentioned (p. 41) as the companion of his childhood at Tarsus. It is useless to attempt to draw that veil aside, which screens the history of this relationship from our view: though the narrative seems to give us hints of domestic intercourse at Jerusalem,[9] of which, if it were permitted to us, we would gladly know more. Enough is told to us to give a favourable impression, both of the affection and discretion of the Apostle's nephew: nor is he the only person, the traits of whose character are visible in the artless simplicity of the narrative. The young man came into the barracks,

quotes from Philo a formal justification of such assassinations of apostates. In illustration of the form of the oath, Lightfoot shows from the Talmud that those who were implicated in such an oath could obtain absolution.

[1] Most of the commentators are of opinion that only the Sadducean party is contemplated here, the Pharisees having espoused St. Paul's cause. But it is far more natural to suppose that their enthusiasm in his behalf had been only momentary, and that the temporary schism had been healed in the common wish to destroy him. The Pharisees really hated him the most. It would seem, moreover, from xxiv. 15, that Pharisees appeared as accusers before Felix.

[2] Or rather 'that *he* might enter,' &c. Such seems the true reading. See the next note but two.

[3] 'Bring *down*,' ver. 15 and ver. 20. So 'take *down*,' ver. 10, and 'bringing *down*,' xxii. 30. The accurate use of these words should be compared with what is said by Josephus and by St. Luke himself of the stairs between the Temple and the fortress. They present us with an undesigned consistency in a matter of topography; and they show that the writer was familiar with the place he is describing.

[4] See above.

[5] If the Sanhedrin were about to investigate (see ver. 15), it would be in order that Claudius Lysias might obtain more information: and it would be more natural for the young man to put the matter before him in this point of view.

[6] Observe the young man's words, ver. 21: 'and now are they ready, looking for a promise from thee.'

[7] 'To-morrow,' ver. 20. It is in the young man's statement that this precise reference to time occurs. In ver. 15 the word appears to be an interpolation.

[8] vv. 16–22.

[9] Two questions easily asked, but not easily answered, suggest themselves— whether St. Paul's sister and nephew resided at Jerusalem, and, if so, why he lodged not with them but with Mnason (above, p. 567).

and related what he knew of the conspiracy to his uncle; to whom he seems to have had perfect liberty of access.[1] Paul, with his usual promptitude and prudence, called one of the centurions to him, and requested him to take the youth[2] to the commandant, saying that he had a communication to make to him.[3] The officer complied at once, and took the young man with this message from 'the prisoner Paul,' to Claudius Lysias; who—partly from the interest he felt in the prisoner, and partly, we need not doubt, from the natural justice and benevolence of his disposition—received the stranger kindly, 'took him by the hand, and led him aside, and asked him in private' to tell him what he had to say. The young man related the story of the conspiracy in full detail, and with much feeling. Lysias listened to his statement and earnest entreaties;[4] then, with a soldier's promptitude, and yet with the caution of one who felt the difficulty of the situation, he decided at once on what he would do, but without communicating the plan to his informant. He simply dismissed him, with a significant admonition,—'Be careful that thou tell no man that thou hast laid this information before me.'

When the young man was gone, Claudius Lysias summoned one or two of his subordinate officers,[5] and ordered them to have in readiness two hundred of the legionary soldiers, with seventy of the cavalry, and two hundred spearmen;[6] so as to depart for Cæsarea at nine in the evening,[7] and take Paul in safety to Felix the governor. The journey was long, and it would be requisite to accomplish it as rapidly as possible. He therefore gave directions that more than one horse should be provided for the prisoner.[8] We may be surprised that so large a force was sent to secure the safety of one man; but we must remember that this man was a Roman citizen, while the garrison in Antonia, consisting of more than a thousand men,[9] could easily spare such a number for one day on such a service; and further, that assassinations, robberies, and rebellions were frequent occurrences at that time in Judæa,[10] and

[1] So afterwards at Cæsarea, xxiv. 23. 'Felix commanded to let him have liberty, and that he should forbid none of his acquaintance to minister or come to him.' See the next chapter for a description of the nature of the *Custodia*, in which St. Paul was kept, both at Jerusalem and Cæsarea.

[2] The word for 'young man' is indeterminate, but the whole narrative gives the impression that he was a very young man. See p. 88, n. 4.

[3] ver. 17, 18.

[4] 'But do not thou yield unto them,' ver. 21.

[5] The full complement of centurions would be ten. See below, p. 597, n. 9.

[6] The rendering in the Authorised Version is probably as near as any other to the true meaning. The singular word used here, distinguishes the soldiers in question from *legionary soldiers* and from *cavalry*, and therefore

doubtless means *light-armed troops.* Moreover the word seems to imply the use of some weapon simply carried in the right hand. As to the mixture of troops in the escort sent by Claudius Lysias, we may remark that he sent forces adapted to act on all kinds of ground, and from the imperfect nature of his information he could not be sure that an ambuscade might not be laid in the way; and at least banditti were to be feared. See p. 604.

[7] 'And at the third hour of the night,' ver. 23.

[8] ver. 24.

[9] The σπεῖρα was a cohort. There were ten cohorts in a legion; and each legion contained more than 6000 men, besides an equal number of auxiliaries and a squadron of horse: but see the next chapter, especially p. 604.

[10] See the next chapter.

that a conspiracy also wears a formidable aspect to those who are responsible for the public peace. The utmost secrecy, as well as promptitude, was evidently required ; and therefore an hour was chosen, when the earliest part of the night would be already past. At the time appointed, the troops, with St. Paul in the midst of them, marched out of the fortress, and at a rapid pace took the road to Cæsarea.

It is to the quick journey and energetic researches of an American traveller, that we owe the power of following the exact course of this night march from Jerusalem to Cæsarea.[1] In an earlier part of this work we have endeavoured to give an approximate representation of the Roman roads, as they existed in Palestine ;[2] and we have had occasion more than once to allude to the route which lay between the religious and political capitals of the country.[3] To the roads previously mentioned we must add another, which passes, not by Lydda[4] (or Diospolis), but more directly across the intermediate space from Gophna to Antipatris. We have thus the whole route to Cæsarea before us ; and we are enabled to picture to ourselves the entire progress of the little army which took St. Paul in safety from the conspiracies of the Jews, and placed him under the protection of Felix the governor.

The road lay, first, for about three hours, northwards,[5] along the high mountainous region which divides the valley of the Jordan from the great western plain of Judæa.[6] About midnight they would reach Gophna.[7] Here, after a short halt, they quitted the northern road which leads to Neapolis[8] and Damascus, once travelled by St. Paul under widely different circumstances,—and turned towards the coast on the left. Presently they began to descend among the western eminences and valleys of the mountain-country,[9] startling

---

[1] See 'A Visit to Antipatris,' by the Rev. Eli Smith, missionary in Palestine, in the *Bibliotheca Sacra*, vol. i. pp. 478 –496. The journey was expressly taken (on the way from Jerusalem to Joppa) for the purpose of ascertaining St. Paul's route to Antipatris ; and the whole of this circuitous route to Joppa was accomplished in two days. The article is followed by some valuable remarks by Dr. Robinson, who entirely agrees with Mr. E. Smith, though he had previously assumed (*Bibl. Res.* iii. 46, 60), that St. Paul's escort had gone by the pass of Bethoron, a route sometimes used, as by Cestius Gallus on his march from Cæsarea by Lydda to Jerusalem. Joseph. *War*, ii. 19. 1.

[2] Chap. III. In the larger editions these roads are shown in a map.

[3] pp. 44, 87, 332, 333, 567.

[4] See Acts ix. 32. For geographical illustration, we may refer to the movements of Peter in reference to Lydda, Joppa, Cæsarea, and Jerusalem (ix. 38, x. 23, 24, xi. 2), and also those of Philip in reference to Sebaste (?) in Samaria,

Azotus, Gaza, and Cæsarea (viii.).

[5] This part of the road has been mentioned before (p. 70) as one where Dr. Robinson followed the line of a Roman pavement. With the very full description in his third volume, pp. 75-80, the map in the first volume should be compared. Mr. E. Smith mentions this part of the route briefly, *B. S.* pp. 478, 479.

[6] p. 70.

[7] 'We rode hastily to Bireh. . . . reached Bireh in 2 h. 20 m. . . . 35 m. from Bireh, we came to ruins. Here we found we had mistaken our path. . . . 30 m. from hence we took the following bearings, &c. . . . . reached Jufna in 30 m.' *B. S.* 479. Compare the time in Dr. Robinson's account.

[8] pp. 69, 70.

[9] 'We started [from Jufna] by the *oldest* road to Kefr Saba. . . . In 20 m. reached Bir Zeit. In this distance, we found evident remains of the pavement of a Roman road, affording satisfactory proof that we had not mistaken our route.' *B. S.* 480. 'The whole of our way down the mountain was a very

the shepherd on the hills of Ephraim, and rousing the village peasant, who woke only to curse his oppressor, as he heard the hoofs of the horses on the pavement, and the well-known tramp of the Roman soldiers. A second resting-place might perhaps be found a Thamna,[1] a city mentioned by Josephus in the Jewish wars, and possibly the ' Timnath Heres,' where Joshua[2] was buried ' in mount Ephraim, in the border of his inheritance.' And then they proceeded, still descending over a rocky and thinly cultivated tract,[3] till about day-break they came to the ridge of the last hill,[4] and overlooked ' the great plain of Sharon coming quite up to its base on the west.' The road now turned northwards,[5] across the rich land of the plain of Sharon, through fields of wheat and barley,[6] just then almost ready for the harvest. ' On the east were

practicable, and, for the most part, a very easy descent. It seemed formed by nature for a road, and we had not descended far from the point where our observations were made, before we came again upon the Roman pavement. This we continued to find at intervals during the remainder of the day. In some places, for a considerable distance, it was nearly perfect; and then, again, it was entirely broken up, or a turn in our path made us lose sight of it. Yet we travelled hardly half an hour at any time without finding distinct traces of it. I do not remember observing anywhere before so extensive remains of a Roman road,' p. 482. 'A few minutes beyond the village [Um Sufah], a branch of the road led off to the right, where, according to our guides, it furnishes a more direct route to Kefr Saba. But just at this point the Roman road was fortunately seen following the path on the left; and thus informed us very distinctly that this was the direction for us to take,' p. 483.

[1] One of the collateral results of Mr. Eli Smith's journey is the identification of the site of this city—not the Timnath of Josh. xv. 10—but a place mentioned in the following passages of Josephus, *Ant.* xiv. 11. 2; *War,* iii. 3. 5, iv. 8. 1: also 1 Macc. ix. 50. The ruins are now called *Tibneh.*

[2] Josh. xix. 49, 50, xxiv. 30; Judg. ii. 8, 9. Mr. E. Smith observed some remarkable sepulchres at Tibneh.

[3] *B. S.* 486, 487. The traveller was still guided by the same indications of the ancient road. 'Hastening on [from Tibneh] and passing occasionally portions of the Roman road, we reached in 40 m. the large town of Abud. . . . To the left of our road we passed several sepulchral excavations, marking this as an ancient place. Our path led us for

a considerable distance down a gentle but very rocky descent, which was the beginning of a Wady. Through nearly the whole of it, we either rode upon or by the side of the Roman road. At length the Wady became broader, and with its declivities was chiefly occupied with fields of grain and other cultivation. . . . After clearing the cultivation in the neighbourhood we passed over a hilly tract, with little cultivation and thinly sprinkled with shrubbery. . . . In our descent, which was not great, we thought we could discern further traces of the Roman road. But it was nearly dark, and we may possibly have been mistaken.'

[4] At this point is the village of Mejdel Yaba in the province of Nablous. ' It stands on the top of a hill, with the valley of Belat on the south, a branch Wady running into it on the east, and the great plain of Sharon coming quite up to its base on the west,' p. 488. Mr. E. Smith arrived there at eight in the evening, having ridden about thirty miles since the morning. The next day he says : ' I was disappointed in not procuring so many bearings from Mejdel Yaba as I had hoped. The rising sun shooting his rays down the side of the mountain prevented our seeing much in that direction,' p. 490.

[5] From Mejdel Yaba Mr. E. Smith did not take the direct road to Kefr Saba, 'which would have led northward, probably in the direction of the Roman road,' but went more to the west, by Ras-el-Ain, and across the river Anjeh near its source, and then by Jiljulieh.

[6] ' Its soil is an inexhaustible black loam, and nearly the whole of it was now under cultivation, presenting a scene of fertility and rural beauty rarely equalled. Immense fields of wheat and

the mountains of Samaria, rising gradually above each other, and bounding the plain in that direction : on the left lay a line of low wooded hills, shutting it in from the sea.' Between this higher and lower range, but on the level ground, in a place well watered and richly wooded, was the town of Antipatris. Both its history and situation are described to us by Josephus. The ancient Caphar-Saba, from which one of the Asmonean princes had dug a trench and built a wall to Joppa, to protect the country from invasion,[1] was afterwards rebuilt by Herod, and named in honour of his father Antipater.[2] It is described in one passage as being near the mountains ;[3] and in another, as in the richest plain of his dominions, with abundance both of water and wood.[4] In the narrative of the Jewish war, Antipatris is mentioned as one of the scenes of Vespasian's first military proceedings.[5] It afterwards disappears from history :[6] but the ancient name is still familiarly used by the peasantry, and remains with the physical features of the neighbourhood to identify the site.[7]

The foot-soldiers proceeded no further than Antipatris, but returned from thence to Jerusalem (xxiii. 32). They were no longer necessary to secure St. Paul's safety ; for no plot by the way was now to be apprehended ; but they might very probably be required in the fortress of Antonia.[8] It would be in the course of the afternoon that the remaining soldiers with their weary horses entered the streets of Cæsarea. The centurion who remained in command of them[9] proceeded at once to the governor, and gave up his prisoner ; and at the same time presented the dispatch,[10] with which he was charged by the commandant of the garrison at Jerusalem.

We have no record of the personal appearance of Felix ; but if we may yield to the impression naturally left by what we know of his sensual and ferocious character,[11] we can imagine the countenance with which he read the following dispatch.[12] ' *Claudius Lysias sends greeting to the most Excellent* [13] *Felix the governor. This man was apprehended by the Jews, and on the point of being killed by*

barley waving in the breeze, were advancing rapidly to maturity,' p. 491. This was on the 27th of April, almost the exact time of St. Paul's journey.

[1] Joseph. *Ant.* xiii. 15. 1. *War*, i. 4. 7.

[2] *Ant.* xvi. 5. 2. *War*, i. 21. 9.

[3] *War*, i. 4. 7.

[4] *Ant.* xvi. 5. 2. *War*, i. 21. 9.

[5] Hearing of the revolt of Vindex from Nero, 'he moved his forces in spring from Cæsarea towards Antipatris.' *War*, iv. 8. 1.

[6] It is mentioned by Jerome as a 'small town half ruined.' It occurs in Jerusalem Itinerary between Cæsarea and Jerusalem ; and the distances are given.

[7] The existence of a place called Kafar Saba in this part of the plain was known to Prokesch, and its identity with Antipatris was suggested by Raumer, Rob. *Bib. Res.* iii. 45–47.

This identity may be considered now as proved beyond a doubt. For some remarks on minor difficulties, see our note here in the larger editions.

[8] It is explicitly stated that they came back to their quarters at Jerusalem.

[9] One centurion would remain, while the others returned. Possibly he is the same officer who is mentioned xxiv. 23.

[10] Acts xxiii. 33.

[11] See next chapter.

[12] Acts xxiii. 26.

[13] 'His Excellency the Governor.' This is apparently an official title. Tertullus uses the same style in addressing Felix, xxiv. 3, and Paul himself in addressing Festus, xxvi. 25. Hence we may suppose Theophilus (who is thus addressed, Luke i. 3) to have been a man holding official rank.

them, when I came and rescued him with my military guard:[1] *for I learnt that he was a Roman citizen.*[2]   *And wishing to ascertain the charge which they had to allege against him, I took him down*[3] *to their Sanhedrin: and there I found that the charge had reference to certain questions of their law, and that he was accused of no offence worthy of*

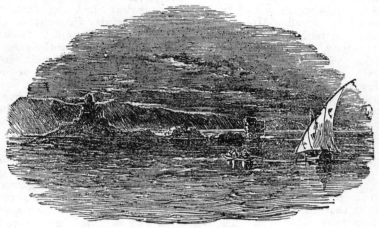

Cæsarea.

death or imprisonment.   And now having received information, that a plot is about to be formed against the man's life, I send[4] *him to thee forthwith, and I have told his accusers that they must bring their charge before thee.*[5]   *Farewell.'*[6]

Felix raised his eyes from the paper, and said, 'To what province does he belong?'   It was the first question which a Roman governor would naturally ask in such a case.   So Pilate had formerly paused, when he found he was likely to trespass on 'Herod's jurisdiction.' Besides the delicacy required by etiquette, the Roman law laid down strict rules for all inter-provincial communications.   In the present case there could be no great difficulty for the moment.   A Roman citizen with certain vague charges brought against him,

[1] In A. V. (through forgetfulness of the definite article) this is unfortunately translated 'with an army.'

[2] This statement was dexterously inserted by Claudius Lysias to save himself from disgrace.   But it was false: for it is impossible not to see 'I learnt' intends to convey the impression that Paul's Roman citizenship was the cause of the rescue, whereas this fact did not come to his knowledge till afterwards. Some of the commentators have justly observed that this dexterous falsehood is an incidental proof of the genuineness of the document.

[3] 'Took *down*.'   Here we may repeat what has been said above concerning

the topography of Antonia and the Temple.

[4] This is the natural English translation.   Our letters are expressed as from the writer's point of view, those of the ancients were adapted to the position of the reader.

[5] 'Before *thee*,' at the termination, emphatic.

[6] 'Farewell.'   The MSS. vary as to the genuineness of this word.   If the evidence is equally balanced, we should decide in its favour; for it is exactly the Latin 'Vale.'   Such despatches from a subordinate to a commanding officer would naturally be in Latin. See p. 2.

was placed under the protection of a provincial governor ; who was bound to keep him in safe custody till the cause should be heard. Having therefore ascertained that Paul was a native of the province of Cilicia,[1] Felix simply ordered him to be kept in 'Herod's prætorium,' and said to Paul himself, 'I will hear and decide thy cause,[2] when thy accusers are come.' Here then we leave the Apostle for a time. A relation of what befell him at Cæsarea will be given in another chapter, to which an account of the political state of Palestine, and a description of Herod's city, will form a suitable introduction.

[1] The word here is ἐπαρχία, ver. 34. It has already been observed (pp. 116, 117) that this is a general term for both the Emperor's and the Senate's provinces, just as ἡγεμών is a general term for the government of either. For the province of Cilicia, see p. 191.

[2] Such is the meaning of the phrase, ver. 35. So in xxiv. 22.

CHAPTER XXII.

History of Judæa resumed.—Roman Governors.—Felix.—Troops quartered in Palestine.—Description of Cæsarea.—St. Paul accused there.—*Speech before Felix.*—Continued Imprisonment.—Accession of Festus.—Appeal to the Emperor.—*Speech before Agrippa.*

WE have pursued a long and varied narrative, since we last took a general view of the political history of Judæa. The state of this part of the Empire in the year 44 was briefly summed up in a previous chapter (Chap. IV.). It was then remarked that this year and the year 60 were the two only points which we can regard as fixed in the annals of the earliest Church, and, therefore, the two best chronological pivots of the Apostolic history.[1] We have followed the life of the Apostle Paul through a space of fourteen years from the former of these dates: and now we are rapidly approaching the second. Then we recounted the miserable end of king Agrippa I. Now we are to speak of Agrippa II., who, like his father, had the title of King, though his kingdom was not identically the same.[2] The life of the second Agrippa ranges over the last period of national Jewish history, and the first age of the Christian Church: and both his life and that of his sisters Drusilla and Berenice are curiously connected, by manifold links, with the general history of the times. This Agrippa saw the destruction of Jerusalem, and lived till the first century was closed in the old age of St. John,—the last of a dynasty eminent for magnificence and intrigue. Berenice concluded a life of profligacy by a criminal connection with Titus, the conqueror of Jerusalem.[3] Drusilla became the wife of

---

[1] We assume that Festus succeeded Felix in the year 60. In support of this opinion we must refer to the note, (C) upon the Chronological Table in the Appendix.

[2] Agrippa II. was made king of Chalcis A.D. 48—he received a further accession of territory A.D. 53, and died, at the age of 70, A.D. 99. He was intimate with Josephus, and was the last prince of the Herodian house.

[3] Titus seems to have been only prevented from marrying this beautiful and profligate princess by the indignant feeling of the Romans. See Dio Cass. lxvi. 15. The name of Berenice is so mixed up with the history of the times, and she is so often mentioned, both by Josephus and by Roman writers, that it is desirable to put together here some of the principal notices of her life and

character. She was first married to her uncle, Herod, king of Chalcis; and after his death she lived with her brother, Agrippa, not without suspicion of the most criminal intimacy. (Joseph. *Ant.* xx. 7. 3.) Compare Juvenal, vi. 155.

It was during this period of her life that she made that marriage with Polemo, king of Cilicia, which has been alluded to in the earlier part of this work (p. 20). Soon she left Polemo and returned to her brother: and then it was that St. Paul was brought before them at Cæsarea. After this time, she became a partisan of Vespasian. Tac. *Hist.* ii. 81. Her connection with Vespasian's son is mentioned by Suetonius and by Tacitus, as well as by Dio Cassius. The one redeeming passage in her life is the patriotic feel-

Felix, and perished with the child of that union in the eruption of
Vesuvius.

We have said that the kingdom of this Agrippa was not coincident with that of his father. He was never, in fact, *King of Judæa.*
The three years, during which Agrippa I. reigned at Cæsarea, were
only an interpolation in the long series of Roman procurators, who
ruled Judæa in subordination to the governors of Syria, from the
death of Herod the Great to the final destruction of Jerusalem. In
the year 44, the second Agrippa was only sixteen years old, and he
was detained about the court of Claudius, while Cuspius Fadus
was sent out to direct the provincial affairs at Cæsarea.[1] It was
under the administration of Fadus that those religious movements
took place, which ended (as we have seen above, p. 583) in placing
under the care of the Jews the sacred vestments kept in the tower
of Antonia, and which gave to Herod king of Chalcis the management of the Temple and its treasury, and the appointment of the
high priests. And in other respects the Jews had reason to remember his administration with gratitude; for he put down the
banditti which had been the pest of the country under Agrippa;
and the slavish compliment of Tertullus to Felix (Acts xxiv. 2, 3)
might have been addressed to him with truth,—that 'by him the
Jews enjoyed great quietness, and that very worthy deeds had
been done to the nation by his providence.' He was succeeded by
Tiberius Alexander, a renegade Alexandrian Jew, and the nephew
of the celebrated Philo.[2] In relation to the life of this official in
Judæa, there are no incidents worth recording : at a later period
we see him at the siege of Jerusalem in command of Roman forces
under Titus :[3] and the consequent inscriptions in his honour at
Rome served to point the sarcasm of the Roman satirist.[4] Soon
after the arrival of Ventidius Cumanus to succeed him as governor[5]
in the year 48, Herod king of Chalcis died, and Agrippa II. was
placed on his throne, with the same privileges in reference to the
Temple and its worship, which had been possessed by his uncle.
' During the government of Cumanus, the low and sullen murmurs
which announced the approaching eruption of the dark volcano,
now gathering its strength in Palestine, became more distinct.
The people and the Roman soldiery began to display mutual animosity.'[6] One indication of this animosity has been alluded to
before,[7]—the dreadful loss of life in the Temple which resulted
from the wanton insolence of one of the soldiers in Antonia at the
time of a festival. Another was the excitement which ensued after
the burning of the Scriptures by the Roman troops at Beth-Horon,
on the road between Jerusalem and Cæsarea. An attack made by
the Samaritans on some Jews who were proceeding through their
country to a festival, led to wider results.[8] Appeal was made to
Quadratus, governor of Syria : and Cumanus was sent to Rome to

ing she displayed on the occasion alluded to, p. 575. (See Joseph. *War,*
ii. 15. 16.)

[1] Joseph. *Ant.* xix. 9, xx. 5. 1. *War,*
ii. 11. 6.

[2] Joseph. *Ant.* xx. 5. 2.

[3] *War,* v. 1. 6. Compare ii. 18. 7,

and iv. 10. 6.

[4] Juv. i. 129.

[5] *Ant.* xx. 5. 2. *War,* ii. 12. 1.

[6] Milman's *Hist. of the Jews,* ii. 203.

[7] See the preceding chapter, p. 583.
For Beth-Horon see p. 595, n. 1.

[8] *Ant.* xx. 6. *War,* ii. 12.

answer for his conduct to the Emperor. In the end he was deposed, and Felix, the brother of Pallas the freedman and favourite of Claudius, was (partly by the influence of Jonathan the high priest) appointed to succeed him.[1]

The mention of this governor, who was brought into such intimate relations with St. Paul, demands that we should enter now more closely into details. The origin of Felix and the mode of his elevation would prepare us to expect in him such a character as that which is condensed into a few words by Tacitus,[2]—that, 'in the practice of all kinds of lust and cruelty, he exercised the power of a king with the temper of a slave.' The Jews had, indeed, to thank him for some good services to their nation. He cleared various parts of the country from robbers ;[3] and he pursued and drove away that Egyptian fanatic,[4] with whom Claudius Lysias too hastily identified St. Paul.[5] But the same historian, from whom we derive this information, gives us a terrible illustration of his cruelty in the story of the murder of Jonathan, to whom Felix was partly indebted for his own elevation. The high priest had presumed to expostulate with the governor on some of his practices, and assassins were forthwith employed to murder him in the sanctuary of the Temple.[6] And as this crime illustrates one part of the sentence, in which Tacitus describes his character, so we may see the other parts of it justified and elucidated in the narrative of St. Luke :—that which speaks of him as a voluptuary, by his union with Drusilla, whom he had enticed from her husband by aid of a magician, who is not unreasonably identified by some with Simon Magus,[7]—and that which speaks of his servile meanness, by his trembling without repentance at the preaching of Paul, and by his detention of him in prison from the hope of a bribe. When he finally left the Apostle in bonds at Cæsarea, this also (as we shall see) was done from a mean desire to conciliate those who were about to accuse him at Rome of maladministration of the province. The final breach between him and the provincials seems to have arisen from a quarrel at Cæsarea, between the Jewish and Heathen population, which grew so serious, that the troops were called out into the streets, and both slaughter and plunder was the result.

The mention of this circumstance leads us to give some account of the troops quartered in Palestine and of the general distribution of the Roman army : without some notion of which no adequate idea can be obtained of the Empire and the Provinces. Moreover St. Paul is brought, about this part of his life, into such close relations with different parts of that military service, from which he draws some of his most forcible imagery,[8] that our narrative would be in-

---

[1] Josephus and Tacitus differ as to the circumstances of his first coming into the East. According to one account, he was joint-procurator for a time with Cumanus, the latter holding Galilee, the former Samaria. From the circumstance of his being called Antonius Felix, it has been supposed that he was manumitteb by Antonia, the mother of Claudius.

[2] *Hist.* v. 9. See *Ant.* xii. 54.
[3] *War*, ii. 13. 2.
[4] *Ant.* xx. 8. 6. *War*, ii. 13. 5.
[5] See the preceding chapter.
[6] *Ant.* xx. 8. 5. His treachery to Eleazar the arch-robber, mentioned by Josephus in the same section, should not be unnoticed.
[7] See p. 66, n. 1.
[8] See especially Eph. vi. 10–18; also

complete without some account both of the Prætorian guards and the legionary soldiers. The latter force may be fitly described in connection with Cæsarea, and we shall see that it is not out of place to allude here to the former also, though its natural association is with the city of Rome.

That division between the armed and unarmed provinces, to which attention has been called before (pp. 115–117),[1] will serve to direct us to the principle on which the Roman legions were distributed. They were chiefly posted in the outer provinces or along the frontier, the immediate neighbourhood of the Mediterranean being completely subdued under the sway of Rome. The military force required in Gaul and Spain was much smaller than it had been in the early days of Augustus. Even in Africa the frontier was easily maintained : for the Romans do not seem to have been engaged there in that interminable war with native tribes, which occupies the French in Algeria. The greatest accumulation of legions was on the northern and eastern boundaries of the Empire,—along the courses of the three frontier rivers, the Rhine, the Danube, and the Euphrates ;[2] and, finally, three legions were stationed in Britain and three in Judæa. We know the very names of these legions. Just as we find memorials of the second, the ninth, and the twentieth in connection with Chester[3] or York, so by the aid of historians or historic monuments we can trace the presence of the fifth, the tenth, and the fifteenth in Cæsarea, Ptolemais, or Jerusalem.[4] And here two principles must be borne in mind which regulated the stations of the legions. They did not move from province to province, as our troops are taken in succession from one colony to another ; but they remained on one station for a vast number of years. And they were recruited, for the most part, from the provinces where they were posted : for the time had long passed away when every legionary soldier was an Italian and a freeborn Roman citizen.[5] Thus Josephus tells us

---

1 Cor. xiv. 8 ; 1 Thess. v. 8 ; and 2 Tim. ii. 3, 4.

[1] We may add here, that the division of the provinces under the Emperors arose out of an earlier division under the Republic, when a Proconsul with a large military force was sent to some provinces, and a Proprætor with a smaller force to others.

[2] In the time of Augustus we find four legions in the neighbourhood of the Euphrates, eight on the Rhine-frontier, and six along the Danube (two in Mœsia, two in Panno nia, and two in Dalmatia). In that of Hadrian the force on each of these rivers was considerably greater.

[3] Antiquarians acquainted with the monuments of Chester are familiar with the letters LEG. XX. V. V. (Valens Victrix).

[4] In the *History* of Tacitus (v. 1) these three legions are expressly men-

tioned. Compare i. 10, ii. 4. The same legions are mentioned by Josephus. See, for instance, *War*, v. 1. 6, v. 2. 3. We have also notices of them on Syrian coins and inscriptions.

It should be noticed that the passages just adduced from Josephus and Tacitus refer to the time when the Jewish war was breaking out. Judæa may have been garrisoned, not by legions, but by detached cohorts, during the rule of Felix and Festus.

[5] At first under the Republic all Roman soldiers were Roman citizens. 'But in proportion as the public freedom was lost in extent of conquest, war was gradually improved into an art and degraded into a trade.' The change began with Marius. The *alauda* of Cæsar was formed of strangers : but these troops afterwards received the Roman citizenship. With the distinction between the Prætorian and legion-

repeatedly that the troops quartered in his native country were reinforced from thence ;[1] not indeed, from the Jews,—for they were exempt from the duty of serving,[2]—but from the Greek and Syrian population.

But what were these legions ? We must beware of comparing them too exactly with our own regiments of a few hundred men : for they ought rather to be called brigades, each consisting of more than 6000 infantry, with a regiment of cavalry attached. Here we see the explanation of one part of the force sent down by Claudius Lysias to Antipatris.[3] Within the fortress of Antonia were stables for the horses of the troopers, as well as quarters for a cohort of infantry. But, moreover, every legion had attached to it a body of auxiliaries levied in the province, of almost equal number : and here, perhaps, we find the true account of the 200 ‘ spearmen,’ who formed a part of St. Paul’s escort, with the 200 legionary soldiers. Thus we can form to ourselves some notion of those troops (amounting, perhaps, to 35,000 men), the presence of which was so familiar a thing in Judæa, that the mention of them appears in the most solemn passages of the Evangelic and Apostolic history,[4] while a Jewish historian gives us one of the best accounts of their discipline and exercises.[5]

But the legionary soldiers, with their cavalry and auxiliaries, were not the only military force in the Empire, and, as it seems, not the only one in Judæa itself. The great body of troops at Rome (as we shall see when we have followed St. Paul to the metropolis) were the Prætorian Guards, amounting at this period to 10,000 men.[6] These favoured forces were entirely recruited from Italy ; their pay was higher, and their time of service shorter ; and, for the most part, they were not called out on foreign service.[7] Yet there is much weight in the opinion which regards the *Augustan Cohort* of Acts xxvii. 1 as a part of this Imperial Guard.[8] Possibly it was

ary soldiers, all necessary connection between citizenship and military service ceased to exist. In strict conformity with this state of things we find that Claudius Lysias was a citizen by purchase, not because he was a military officer.

[1] *Ant.* xiv. 15. 10. *War,* i. 17. 1.

[2] Jos. *Ant.* xiv. 10. 11–19.

[3] What is written here and in the preceding chapter is based on the assumption that the cohort under the command of Claudius Lysias was a *legionary* cohort. But it is by no means certain that it was not an *independent* cohort, like those called ‘Augustan’ and ‘Italic.’ It appears that such cohorts really contained 1000 men each.

[4] It must be borne in mind that some of the soldiers mentioned in the Gospels belonged to Herod’s military force : but since his troops were disciplined on the Roman model, we need hardly make this distinction.

[5] *War,* iii. 5.

[6] Under Augustus there were nine cohorts. Under Tiberius they were raised to ten. The number was not increased again till after St. Paul’s time.

[7] Such a general rule would have exceptions,—as in the case of our own Guards at Waterloo and Sebastopol.

[8] This is a question of some difficulty. Two opinions held by various commentators may, we think, readily be dismissed. 1. This *cohors Augusta* was not a part of any *legio Augusta.* 2. It was not identical with the *Sebasteni* (so named from Sebaste in Samaria) mentioned by Josephus : for, in the first place, this was a troop of horse, and secondly, we should expect a different term to be used.

Wieseler thinks this cohort was a special corps enrolled by Nero under the name of *Augustani.* They were the *élite* of the Prætorians, and accompanied Nero to Greece. The date of their en-

identical[1] with the *Italic Cohort* of Acts x. 1. It might well be that
the same corps might be called 'Italic,' because its men were exclusively Italians; and 'Augustan,' because they were properly
part of the Emperor's guard, though some of them might occasionally be attached to the person of a provincial governor. And we
observe that, while Cornelius (x. 1) and Julius (xxvii. 1) are both
Roman names, it is at Cæsarea that each of these cohorts is said to
have been stationed. As regards the Augustan cohort, if the view
above given is correct, one result of it is singularly interesting: for
it seems that Julius the centurion, who conducted the Apostle Paul
to Rome, can be identified with a high degree of probability with
Julius Priscus, who was afterwards prefect of the Prætorian Guards
under the Emperor Vitellius.[2]

This brief notice may suffice, concerning the troops quartered
in Palestine, and especially at Cæsarea. The city itself remains to
be described. Little now survives on the spot to aid us in the
restoration of this handsome metropolis. On the wide area once
occupied by its busy population there is silence, interrupted only
by the monotonous washing of the sea; and no sign of human life,
save the occasional encampment of Bedouin Arabs, or the accident
of a small coasting vessel anchoring off the shore. The best of the
ruins are engulfed by the sand, or concealed by the encroaching
sea. The nearest road passes at some distance, so that comparatively few travellers have visited Cæsarea.[3] Its glory was short-
lived. Its decay has been complete, as its rise was arbitrary and
sudden. Strabo, in the reign of Augustus, describes at this part of
the inhospitable coast of Palestine nothing but a landing-place with
a castle called Strato's tower. Less than eighty years afterwards
we read in Tacitus and Pliny of a city here, which was in possession
of honourable privileges, which was the 'Head of Judæa,' as Antioch
was of Syria. Josephus explains to us the change which took place
in so short an interval, by describing the work which Herod the
Great began and completed in twelve years.[4] Before building Anti-

rolment constitutes a difficulty. But
might not the cohort in question be
some other detachment of the Prætorian
Guards?

It appears from Joseph. *War*, iii. 4.
2, that five cohorts (independently of
the legions) were regularly stationed
at Cæsarea, and the Augustan cohort
may very well have been one of them.
But we are not by any means limited
to those. Dean Alford remarks, very
justly, that we must not assume, as too
many commentators have done, that
this cohort was *resident* at Cæsarea.

[1] See p. 23, n. 5, also p. 96, n. 4, (in
the account of Cornelius,) where it is
shown that this corps cannot have been
a cohort of Nero's *Legio prima Italica*.
One objection to the view of Meyer,
who identifies the two, is that Judæa
was not under procurators at the time
of the conversion of Cornelius. But

there is great obscurity about the early
dates in the Acts. If the 'Augustan
cohort' is identical with the *Augustani*
of Nero, it is clear that the 'Italic cohort' is not the same.

[2] The argument is given in full by
Wieseler.

[3] Thus Dr. Robinson was prevented
from visiting or describing what remains. The fullest account is perhaps
that in Buckingham's *Travels* (i. 197–
215). See also Irby and Mangles, and
Lamartine. There is an excellent description of the place, with illustrations,
at the end of the first volume of Dr.
Traill's *Josephus*. Our illustration, at
the close of the preceding chapter, is
from Bartlett's *Footsteps of Our Lord
and His Apostles*. We may refer now
to the views in Van de Velde's *Pays
d'Israël*.

[4] *Antiq.* xv. 9. 6. *War*, i. 21. 5–8.

patris in honour of his father (see p. 597), he built on the shore between Dora and Joppa, where Strato's castle stood near the boundary of Galilee and Samaria, a city of sumptuous palaces in honour of Augustus Cæsar. The city was provided with everything that could contribute to magnificence,[1] amusement,[2] and health.[3] But its great boast was its harbour, which provided for the ships which visited that dangerous coast a safe basin, equal in extent to the Piræus.[4] Vast stones were sunk in the sea to the depth of twenty fathoms,[5] and thus a stupendous breakwater[6] was formed, curving round so as to afford complete protection from the south-westerly winds,[7] and open only on the north. Such is an imperfect description of that city, which in its rise and greatest eminence is exactly cotemporaneous with the events of which we read in the Gospels and the Acts of the Apostles. It has, indeed, some connection with later history. Vespasian was here declared Emperor, and he conferred on it the title of a colony, with the additional honour of being called by his own name. Here Eusebius[8] and Procopius were born, and thus it is linked with the recollections of Constantine and Justinian. After this time its annals are obscured, though the character of its remains—which have been aptly termed 'ruins of ruins,'—show that it must have long been a city of note under the successive occupants of Palestine.[9] Its chief association, however, must always be with the age of which we are writing. Its two great features were its close connection with Rome and the Emperors, and the large admixture of Heathen strangers in its population. Not only do we see here the residence of Roman procurators,[10] the quarters of imperial troops,[11] and the port by which Judæa was entered from

---

[1] The buildings were of white stone.

[2] It contained both a theatre and an amphitheatre. The former possesses great interest for us, as being the scene of the death of Agrippa (p. 106). Some traces of it are said to remain.

[3] The arrangement of the sewers is particularly mentioned by Josephus. The remains of the aqueducts are still visible.

[4] This is the comparison of Josephus, *Antiq.* In the '*War*' he says it was greater than the Piræus.

[5] Most of the stones were 50 feet long, 18 feet broad, and 9 feet deep. Josephus, however, is not quite consistent with himself in his statement of the dimensions.

[6] This breakwater has been compared to that of Plymouth: but it was more like that of Cherbourg, and the whole harbour may more fitly be compared to the harbours of refuge now (1852) in construction at Holyhead and Portland.

[7] Josephus particularly says that the places on this part of the coast were 'bad for anchorage on account of the swell towards (i.e. from) the S.W.'—a passage which deserves careful atten-

tion, as illustrating Acts xxvii. 12.

[8] He was the first biblical geographer (as Forbiger remarks in his account of Cæsarea), and to him we owe the *Onomasticon*, translated by Jerome. This place was also one of the scenes of Origen's theological labours.

[9] See the Appendix of Dr. Traill's *Josephus*, vol. i. xlix.–lvi., where a very copious account is given of the existing state of Cæsarea. Its ruins are described as 'remains from which obtrude the costly materials of a succession of structures, and which furnish a sort of condensed commentary upon that series of historical evidence which we derive from books.' Of late years they have been used as a quarry, furnishing shafts and ready-wrought blocks, &c., for public buildings at Acre and elsewhere.

[10] We are inclined to think that the 'prætorium' or 'palace' of Herod (Acts xxiii. 35) was a different building from the official residence of Felix and Festus. This seems to be implied in xxiv. 24 and xxv. 23. We shall have occasion again to refer to the word πραιτώριον, Chap. XXVI.

[11] See above on the Augustan cohort.

the west, but a Roman impress was ostentatiously given to everything that belonged to Cæsarea. The conspicuous object to those who approached from the sea was a temple dedicated to Cæsar and to Rome :[1] the harbour was called the 'Augustan harbour :'[2] the city itself was 'Augustan Cæsarea.'[3] And, finally, the foreign influence here was so great, that the Septuagint translation of the Scriptures was read in the synagogues.[4] There was a standing quarrel between the Greeks and the Jews, as to whether it was a Greek city or a Jewish city. The Jews appealed to the fact that it was built by a Jewish prince. The Greeks pointed to the temples and statues.[5] This quarrel was never appeased till the great war broke out, the first act of which was the slaughter of 20,000 Jews in the streets of Cæsarea.[6]

Such was the city in which St. Paul was kept in detention among the Roman soldiers, till the time should come for his trial before that unscrupulous governor, whose character has been above described. His accusers were not long in arriving. The law required that causes should be heard speedily ; and the Apostle's enemies at Jerusalem were not wanting in zeal. Thus, 'after five days,'[7] the high priest Ananias and certain members of the Sanhedrin[8] appeared, with one of those advocates who practised in the law courts of the provinces, where the forms of Roman law were imperfectly known, and the Latin language imperfectly understood.[9] The man, whose professional services were engaged on this occasion, was called Tertullus. The name is Roman, and there is little doubt that he was an Italian, and spoke on this occasion in Latin.[10] The criminal information was formally laid before the governor.[11] The prisoner was summoned,[12] and Tertullus brought forward the charges against him in a set speech, which we need not quote at length. He began by loading Felix with unmerited praises,[13] and then proceeded to allege

[1] This temple has been alluded to before, p. 96. Josephus says that in the temple were two statues, one of Rome and one of Cæsar. *Ant.* In *War*, he says that the statues were colossal, that of Cæsar equal in size to the Olympian Jupiter, and that of Rome to the Argive Juno.

[2] We find this term on coins of Agrippa I. One of them is given in our larger editions.

[3] So it is called by Josephus. *Ant.* xv. 1. 51.

[4] Lightfoot on Acts vi. 1. See p. 30, n. 4.

[5] *Ant.* xx. 8. 7. *War*, ii. 13. 7.

[6] *War*, ii. 18. i. See pp. 602, 603.

[7] It is most natural to reckon these five days from the time of St. Paul's departure from Jerusalem.

[8] 'With the Elders ;' by which we are to understand representatives or deputies from the Sanhedrin.

[9] The accuser and the accused could plead in person, as St. Paul did here : but *advocati* (ῥήτορες) were often employed. It was a common practice for young Roman lawyers to go with consuls and prætors to the provinces, and to 'qualify themselves by this provincial practice for the sharper struggles of the forum at home.' We have an instance in the case of Cælius, who spent his youth in this way in Africa. Cic. *pro Cæl.* 30. It must be remembered that *Latin* was the proper language of the law courts in every part of the Empire. See p. 2.

[10] See p. 3, for remarks on Tertullus and the peculiarly Latin character of the speech here given.

[11] 'They laid information before the governor against Paul,' xxiv. 1. See xxv. 2.

[12] 'When he was summoned,' ver. 2. The presence of the accused was required by the Roman law.

[13] See above. It is worth while to notice here one phrase which is exactly the Latin *tuâ providentiâ*. It may be illustrated by the inscription : PROVID. AUG. on the coin of Commodus in the title-page of this edition.

three distinct heads of accusation against St. Paul,—charging him, first, with causing factious disturbances among all the Jews throughout the Empire[1] (which was an offence against the Roman Government, and amounted to *Majestas* or treason against the Emperor),—secondly, with being a ringleader of ' the sect of the Nazarenes '[2] (which involved heresy against the Law of Moses),—and thirdly, with an attempt to profane the Temple at Jerusalem[3] (an offence not only against the Jewish, but also against the Roman Law, which protected the Jews in the exercise of their worship).   He concluded by asserting (with serious deviations from the truth) that Lysias, the commandant of the garrison, had forcibly taken the prisoner away, when the Jews were about to judge him by their own ecclesiastical law, and had thus improperly brought the matter before Felix.[4] The drift of this representation was evidently to persuade Felix to give up St. Paul to the Jewish courts, in which case his assassination would have been easily accomplished.[5] And the Jews who were present gave a vehement assent to the statements of Tertullus, making no secret of their animosity against St. Paul, and asserting that these things were indeed so.

The governor now made a gesture[6] to the prisoner to signify that he might make his defence.   The Jews were silent : and the Apostle, after briefly expressing his satisfaction that he had to plead his cause before one so well acquainted with Jewish customs, refuted Tertullus step by step.   He said that on his recent visit to Jerusalem at the festival (and he added that it was only ' twelve days ' since he had left Cæsarea for that purpose),[7] he had caused no disturbance in any part of Jerusalem,—that, as to heresy, he had never swerved from his belief in the Law and the Prophets, and that in conformity with that belief, he held the doctrine of a resurrection, and sought to live conscientiously before the God of his fathers,[8]—and, as to the Temple, so far from profaning it, he had been found in it delibe-

[1] *A mover of sedition among all the Jews throughout the world.*

[2] *A ringleader of the sect of the Nazarenes.* On the word for *sect* see below, note, on ver. 14. The Authorised Version unfortunately renders the same Greek word, in one case by 'sect,' in the other 'heresy,' and thus conceals the link of connection. As regards ' Nazarene,' this is the only place where it occurs in this sense. See pp. 116, 117. In the mouth of Tertullus it was a term of reproach, as ' Christian' below (xxvi. 28) in that of Agrippa.

[3] *Who hath also gone about to profane the Temple.*

[4] We have before observed that the Sanhedrin was still allowed to exercise criminal jurisdiction over ecclesiastical offenders.

[5] Compare the two attempts, xxiii. 15 and xxv. 3.

[6] Ver. 10. It is some help towards our realising the scene in our imagination, if we remember that Felix was seated

on the *tribunal* ($\beta\tilde{\eta}\mu\alpha$) like Gallio (xviii. 12) and Festus (xxv. 6).

[7] In reckoning these twelve days (ver. 11) it would be possible to begin with the arrival in Jerusalem instead of the departure for Cæsarea,—or we might exclude the days after the return to Cæsarea. Wieseler's arrangement of the time is as follows. 1st day: Departure from Cæsarea. 2nd: Arrival at Jerusalem. 3rd: Meeting of the Elders. 4th (*Pentecost*): Arrest in the Temple. 5th: Trial before the Sanhedrin. 6th. (at night): Departure to Cæsarea. 7th : Arrival. 12th (five days after): Ananias leaves Jerusalem. 13th : Ananias reaches Cæsarea. Trial before Felix.

[8] It has been well observed that the classical phrase ' our hereditary God ' (ver. 14) was judiciously employed before Felix. 'The Apostle asserts that, according to the Roman law which allowed all men to worship the gods of their own nation, he is not open to any charge of irreligion.' Humphry.

rately observing the very strictest ceremonies. The Jews of 'Asia,' he added, who had been his first accusers, ought to have been present as witnesses now. Those who were present knew full well that no other charge was brought home to him before the Sanhedrin, except what related to the belief that he held in common with the Pharisees. But, without further introduction, we quote St. Luke's summary of his own words.

ACTS
xxiv.

10 Knowing, as I do, that thou hast been judge over this nation for many years, I defend myself in the matters brought against me with greater confidence. He denies the charges against him.

11 For[1] it is in thy power to learn, that only twelve days have passed since I went up to Jerusalem to

12 worship. And neither in the Temple, nor in the synagogues, nor in the streets, did they find me disputing with any man, or causing any disorderly con-

13 course[2] of people; nor can they prove against me the things whereof they now accuse me.

14 But this I acknowledge to thee, that I follow the opinion,[3] which they call a sect,[4] and thus worship the God of my fathers. And I believe all things which are written in the Law and in the Prophets; His own statement of his case.

15 and I hold a hope towards God, which my accusers themselves[5] entertain, that there will be a resurrection of the dead, both of the just and of the unjust.

16 Wherefore[6] I myself also[7] strive earnestly to keep a conscience always void of offence[8] towards God and man.

17 Now after several[9] years I came[10] hither, to bring

---

[1] The connection of this with the preceding is that Felix, having so long governed the province, would know that Paul had not been resident there before, during several years; besides which he could easily ascertain the date of his recent arrival.

[2] This is a Pauline word found nowhere else in N. T. except 2 Cor. xi. 28. The literal translation would be *a mob.*

[3] *Way,* i.e. a *religious opinion* or *sect.* (See chap. xxii. 4.)

[4] Properly a *sect* or *religious party*; not used in a bad sense. See Acts v. 17 and xv. 5, and especially xxvi. 5, where the same word is used. St. Paul means to say (or rather did say in the argument of which St. Luke here gives the outlines): 'Our nation is divided into religious parties which are called *sects*; thus there is the sect of the Pharisees and the sect of the Sadducees,

and so now we are called the sect of the Nazarenes. I do not deny that I belong to the latter sect; but I claim for it the same toleration which is extended by the Roman law to the others. I claim the right which you allow to all the nations under your government, of worshipping their national gods.'

[5] This shows that the Pharisees were the principal accusers of St. Paul; and that the effect produced upon them by his speech before the Sanhedrin was only momentary.

[6] Compare 2 Cor. v. 9, where the same conclusion is derived from the same premises.

[7] The best MSS. have *also.*

[8] Literally, *containing no cause of stumbling.* This also is a Pauline word, occurring only 1 Cor. x. 32, and Phil. i. 10, in N. T.

[9] 'Several,' not so strong as 'many.'

[10] 'I came into this country.'

alms[1] to my nation, and offerings to the Temple.[2] And they found me so doing in the Temple, after I had undergone purification ; not gathering together a multitude, nor causing a tumult ; but certain Jews from Asia discovered me, who ought to have been here before thee to accuse me, if they had anything to object against me.

He appeals to his recent acquittal by the Sanhedrin.

Or let these my accusers themselves say whether they found me guilty of any offence, when I stood before the Sanhedrin ; except it be for these words only which I cried out as I stood in the midst of them : ' Concerning the resurrection of the dead, I am called in question before you this day.'

xxiv.

19

20

21

There was all the appearance of truthfulness in St. Paul's words ; and they harmonised entirely with the statement contained in the dispatch of Claudius Lysias. Moreover, Felix had resided so long in Cæsarea,[3] where the Christian religion had been known for many years,[4] and had penetrated even among the troops,[5] that ' he had a more accurate knowledge of their religion' (v. 22) than to be easily deceived by the misrepresentations of the Jews.[6] Thus a strong impression was made on the mind of this wicked man. But his was one of those characters, which are easily affected by feelings, but always drawn away from right action by the overpowering motive of self-interest. He could not make up his mind to acquit St. Paul. He deferred all inquiry into the case for the present. ' When Lysias comes down,' he said, ' I will decide finally[7] between you.' Meanwhile he placed the Apostle under the charge of the centurion who had brought him to Cæsarea,[8] with directions that he should be treated with kindness and consideration. Close confinement was indeed necessary, both to keep him in safety from the Jews, and because he was not yet acquitted : but orders were given that he should have every relaxation which could be permitted in such a

[1] This is the only mention of this collection in the Acts, and its occurrence here is a striking undesigned coincidence between the Acts and Epistles.

[2] *Offerings.* We need not infer that St. Paul brought offerings to the Temple with him from foreign parts ; this in itself would have been not unlikely, but it seems inconsistent with St. James's remarks (Acts xxi. 23, 24). The present is only a condensation for 'I came to Jerusalem to bring alms to my nation, and I entered the Temple to make offerings to the Temple.

[3] If these events took place in the year 58 A.D., he had been governor six years.

[4] See Acts viii. 40.

[5] Acts x. Besides other means of information, we must remember that

Drusilla, his present wife, was a Jewess.

[6] Such is the turn given to the words by some of the best commentators. Or they may be taken to denote that he was too well informed concerning the Christian religion to require any further information that might be elicited by the trial ; it was only needful to wait for the coming of Lysias.

[7] This is more correct than the A.V.

[8] Not ' *a* centurion,' as in A. V. A natural inference from the use of the article is, that it was the same centurion who had brought St. Paul from Antipatris (see above), and Mr. Birks traces here an undesigned coincidence. But no stress can be laid on this view. The officer might be simply the centurion who was present and on duty at the time.

case,[1] and that any of his friends should be allowed to visit him, and to minister to his comfort.[2]

We read nothing, however, of Lysias coming to Cæsarea, or of any further judicial proceedings. Some few days afterwards[3] Felix came into the audience-chamber[4] with his wife Drusilla, and the prisoner was summoned before them. Drusilla, 'being a Jewess' (v. 24), took a lively interest in what Felix told her of Paul, and was curious to hear something of this faith which had 'Christ' for its object.[5] Thus Paul had an opportunity in his bonds of preaching the Gospel, and such an opportunity as he could hardly otherwise have obtained. His audience consisted of a Roman libertine and a profligate Jewish princess : and he so preached, as a faithful Apostle must needs have preached to such hearers. In speaking of Christ, he spoke of 'righteousness and temperance and judgment to come,' and while he was so discoursing, 'Felix trembled.' Yet still we hear of no decisive result. 'Go thy way for this time : when I have a convenient season, I will send for thee,'—was the response of the conscience-stricken but impenitent sinner,—the response which the Divine Word has received ever since, when listened to in a like spirit.

We are explicitly informed why this governor shut his ears to conviction, and even neglected his official duty, and kept his prisoner in cruel suspense. 'He hoped that he might receive from Paul a bribe for his liberation.' He was not the only governor of Judæa, against whom a similar accusation is brought:[6] and Felix, well knowing how the Christians aided one another in distress, and possibly having some information of the funds with which St. Paul had recently been entrusted,[7] and ignorant of those principles which make it impossible for a true Christian to tamper by bribes with the course of law,—might naturally suppose that he had here a good prospect of enriching himself. 'Hence he frequently sent for Paul, and had many conversations[8] with him.' But his hopes were unfulfilled. Paul, who was ever ready to claim the protection of the law, would not seek to evade it by dishonourable means :[9] and the

---

[1] See below.

[2] v. 23.

[3] v. 24.

[4] We must understand that Felix and Drusilla *came* to some place convenient for an audience, probably the *hall* mentioned below (xxv. 23) where the Apostle spoke before Festus with Drusilla's brother and sister, Agrippa and Berenice.

[5] Observe the force of *being a Jewess*. We should also notice the phrase by which the Gospel is here described, *the faith in Christ* or *the Messiah*. The name 'Christian' was doubtless familiarly known at Cæsarea. And a Jewish princess must necessarily have been curious to hear some account of what professed to be the fulfilment of Jewish prophecy. Compare xxv. 22.

[6] Albinus, who succeeded Festus, is said to have released many prisoners, but those only from whom he received a bribe. Joseph. *Ant.* xx. 8. 5. *War*, ii. 14. 1.

[7] This suggestion is made by Mr. Birks. For the contributions which St. Paul had recently brought to Jerusalem, see above.

[8] We may contrast the verb here (v. 26) with that for continuous address (v. 25), as we have done before in the narrative of the night-service at Troas, xx. 9, 11.

[9] It is allowable here to refer to the words in which Socrates refused the aid of his friends, who urged him to escape from prison : while in comparing the two cases we cannot but contrast the vague though overpowering sense of

Christians, who knew how to pray for an Apostle in bonds (Acts xii.), would not forget the duty of ' rendering unto Cæsar the things that are Cæsar's.' Thus Paul remained in the Prætorium ; and the suspense continued ' two years.'

Such a pause in a career of such activity,—such an arrest of the Apostle's labours at so critical a time,—two years taken from the best part of a life of such importance to the world,—would seem to us a mysterious dispensation of Providence, if we did not know that God has an inner work to accomplish in those who are the chosen instruments for effecting His greatest purposes. As Paul might need the repose of preparation in Arabia, before he entered on his career,[1] so his prison at Cæsarea might be consecrated to the calm meditation, the less interrupted prayer,—which resulted in a deeper experience and knowledge of the power of the Gospel. Nor need we assume that his active exertions for others were entirely suspended. ' The care of all the churches ' might still be resting on him : many messages, and even letters,[2] of which we know nothing, may have been sent from Cæsarea to brethren at a distance. And a plausible conjecture fixes this period and place for the writing of St. Luke's Gospel under the superintendence of the Apostle of the Gentiles.

All positive information, however, is denied us concerning the employments of St. Paul while imprisoned at Cæsarea. We are the more disposed, therefore, to turn our thoughts to the consideration of the nature and outward circumstances of his confinement ; and this inquiry is indeed necessary for the due elucidation of the narrative.

When an accusation was brought against a Roman citizen, the magistrate, who had criminal jurisdiction in the case, appointed the time for hearing the cause, and detained the accused in custody during the interval. He was not bound to fix any definite time for the trial, but might defer it at his own arbitrary pleasure ; and he might also commit the prisoner at his discretion to any of the several kinds of custody recognised by the Roman law. These were as follows :—First, confinement in the public gaol (*custodia publica*), which was the most severe kind ; the common gaols throughout the Empire being dungeons of the worst description, where the prisoners were kept in chains, or even bound in positions of torture. Of this we have seen an example in the confinement of Paul and Silas at Philippi. Secondly, free custody (*custodia libera*), which was the mildest kind. Here the accused party was committed to the charge of a magistrate or senator, who became responsible for his appearance on the day of trial ; but this species of detention was only employed in the case of men of high rank. Thirdly, military custody (*custodia militaris*), which was introduced at the beginning of the Imperial regime. In this last species of custody the accused person was given in charge to a soldier, who was responsible with his own life for the safe keeping of his prisoner. This was further secured

---

moral duty in the Heathen philosopher, with the clear and lofty perception of eternal realities in the inspired Apostle.

[1] See pp. 79, 80.

[2] It is well known that some have thought that the Ephesians, Colossians, and Philemon were written here. This question will be considered hereafter

by chaining the prisoner's right hand to the soldier's left. The soldiers of course relieved one another in this duty. Their prisoner was usually kept in their barracks, but sometimes allowed to reside in a private house under their charge.

It was under this latter species of custody that St. Paul was now placed by Felix, who ' gave him in charge to the centurion, that he should be kept in custody' (Acts xxiv. 23); but (as we have seen) he added the direction, that he should be treated with such indulgence[1] as this kind of detention permitted. Josephus tells us that, when the severity of Agrippa's imprisonment at Rome was mitigated, his chain was relaxed at mealtimes.[2] This illustrates the nature of the alleviations which such confinement admitted ; and it is obvious that the centurion might render it more or less galling, according to his inclination, or the commands he had received. The most important alleviation of St. Paul's imprisonment consisted in the order, which Felix added, that his friends should be allowed free access to him.

Meantime, the political state of Judæa grew more embarrassing. The exasperation of the people under the mal-administration of Felix became increasingly implacable ; and the crisis was rapidly approaching. It was during the two years of St. Paul's imprisonment that the disturbances, to which allusion has been made before, took place in the streets of Cæsarea. The troops, who were chiefly recruited in the province, fraternised with the Heathen population, while the Jews trusted chiefly to the influence of their wealth. In the end Felix was summoned to Rome, and the Jews followed him with their accusations. Thus it was that he was anxious, even at his departure, ' to confer obligations upon them' (v. 27), and one effort to diminish his unpopularity was 'to leave Paul in bonds.' In so doing, he doubtless violated the law, and trifled with the rights of a Roman citizen ; but the favour of the provincial Jews was that which he needed ; and the Christians were weak in comparison with them ; nor were such delays in the administration of justice unprecedented, either at Rome or in the provinces. Thus it was, that, as another governor of Judæa[3] opened the prisons that

---

[1] Acts xxiv. 23. Meyer and De Wette have understood this as though St. Paul was committed to the *custodia libera*; but we have seen that this kind of detention was only employed in the case of men of rank ; and moreover, the mention of the centurion excludes it. But besides this, it is expressly stated (Acts xxiv. 27) that Felix left Paul *chained*. The same Greek word (meaning *relaxation*) is applied to the mitigation of Agrippa's imprisonment (Jos. *Ant.* xviii. 6. 10) on the accession of Caligula, although Agrippa was still left under *custodia militaris*, and still bound with a chain. We shall have occasion to refer again to this relaxation of Agrippa's imprisonment as illustrating that of St. Paul at Rome.

There, was, indeed, a lighter form of *custodia militaris* sometimes employed, under the name of *observatio*, when the soldier kept guard over his prisoner, and accompanied him wherever he went, but was not chained to him. To this we might have supposed St. Paul subjected, both at Cæsarea and at Rome, were not such an hypothesis excluded as to Cæsarea by Acts xxiv. 27, xxvi. 29, and as to Rome by Eph. vi. 20, Phil. i. 13. Compare Acts xxviii. 16, 31.

[2] Such seems the meaning of ' *relaxation as to eating* ' in the passage of Josephus, referred to in the preceding note.

[3] Albinus. See above, p. 611. Josephus says that, though he received bribes for opening the prisons, he wished

he might make himself popular, Felix, from the same motive, riveted the chains of an innocent man. The same enmity of the world against the Gospel which set Barabbas free, left Paul a prisoner.

No change seems to have taken place in the outward circumstances of the Apostle, when Festus came to take command of the province. He was still in confinement as before. But immediately on the accession of the new governor, the unsleeping hatred of the Jews made a fresh attempt upon his life ; and the course of their proceedings presently changed the whole aspect of his case, and led to unexpected results.

When a Roman governor came to his province—whether his character was coarse and cruel, like that of Felix, or reasonable and just, as that of Festus seems to have been,—his first step would be to make himself acquainted with the habits and prevalent feelings of the people he was come to rule, and to visit such places as might seem to be more peculiarly associated with national interests. The Jews were the most remarkable people in the whole extent of the Roman provinces : and no city was to any other people what Jerusalem was to the Jews. We are not surprised, therefore, to learn that ' three days' after his arrival at the political metropolis, Festus ' went up to Jerusalem.' Here he was immed tely met by an urgent request against St. Paul,[1] preferred by the chief priests and leading men among the Jews,[2] and seconded, as it seems, by a general concourse of the people, who came round him with no little vehemence and clamour.[3] They asked as a favour[4] (and they had good reason to hope that the new governor[5] on his accession would not refuse it), that he would allow St. Paul to be brought up to Jerusalem. The plea, doubtless, was, that he should be tried again before the Sanhedrin. But the real purpose was to assassinate him[6] on some part of the road, over which he had been safely brought by the escort two years before. So bitter and so enduring was their hatred against the apostate Pharisee. The answer of Festus was dignified and just, and worthy of his office. He said that Paul was in custody[7] at Cæsarea, and that he himself was shortly to return thither (v. 4), adding that it was not the custom of the Romans to give up an uncondemned person as a mere favour[8] (v. 16). The accused must have the accuser face to face,[9] and full opportunity must be given for a defence (ib.). Those, therefore,

by this act to make himself popular, when he found he was to be superseded by Gessius Florus.

[1] See v. 2 and v. 15. We should compare St. Luke's statement with the two accounts given by Festus himself to Agrippa, below.

[2] Again we should compare v. 2 and v. 15. Thus the accusers were again representatives of the Sanhedrin.

[3] See the second account given by Festus himself to Agrippa, below, v. 24. 'All the multitude of the Jews dealt with me, both at Jerusalem and also

here, crying that he ought not to live any longer.'

[4] v. 3. See v. 16.

[5] Compare the conduct of Albinus and Agrippa I., alluded to before.

[6] v. 3.

[7] The English version 'should be kept' is rather too peremptory. Festus doubtless expresses this decision, but in the most conciliating form.

[8] See above, v. 11. Compare the case of Pilate and Barabbas.

[9] v. 16. Compare the following passages : Acts xxiii. 30, xxiv. 19, xxv. 5.

who were competent to undertake the task of accusers,[1] should come down with him to Cæsarea, and there prefer the accusation (v. 5).

Festus remained 'eight or ten days' in Jerusalem, and then returned to Cæsarea ; and the accusers went down the same day.[2] No time was lost after their arrival. The very next day[3] Festus took his seat on the judicial tribunal,[4] with his Assessors near him (v. 12), and ordered Paul to be brought before him. 'The Jews who had come down from Jerusalem' stood round, bringing various heavy accusations against him (which, however, they could not establish),[5] and clamorously asserting that he was worthy of death.[6] We must not suppose that the charges now brought were different in substance from those urged by Tertullus. The Prosecutors were in fact the same now as then, namely, delegates from the Sanhedrin ; and the prisoner was still lying under the former accusation, which had never been withdrawn.[7] We see from what is said of Paul's defence, that the charges were still classed under the same three heads as before ; viz. Heresy, Sacrilege, and Treason.[8] But Festus saw very plainly that the offence was really connected with the religious opinions of the Jews, instead of relating, as he at first expected, to some political movement (ver. 18, 19) ; and he was soon convinced that Paul had done nothing worthy of death (v. 25). Being, therefore, in perplexity (v. 20), and at the same time desirous of ingratiating himself with the provincials (v. 9), he proposed to St. Paul that he should go up to Jerusalem, and be tried there in his presence, or at least under his protection.[9] But the Apostle knew full well the danger that lurked in this proposal, and, conscious of the rights which he possessed as a Roman citizen, he refused to accede to it, and said boldly to Festus :

ACTS
XXV.
10   I stand before Cæsar's tribunal, and there ought my trial to be. To the Jews I have done no wrong,
11 as thou knowest full well. If I am guilty, and have done anything worthy of death, I refuse not to die : but if the things whereof these men accuse me are nought, no man can give me up to them. I APPEAL UNTO CÆSAR

Festus was probably surprised by this termination of the proceedings ; but no choice was open to him. Paul had urged his prerogative as a Roman citizen, to be tried, not by the Jewish, but by the Roman law ;[10] a claim which, indeed, was already admitted

---

[1] v. 5.

[2] The course of the narrative shows that they went immediately. This is also asserted in the phrase 'go down with me,' which does not necessarily imply that they went down in the same company with Festus.

[3] 'The next day,' v. 6 ; 'without any delay on the morrow,' v. 17.

[4] See again ver. 6, 17.

[5] v. 7.

[6] See v. 24, where the demand for

his death is said to have taken place both at Jerusalem and Cæsarea.

[7] At this period, an accused person might be kept in prison indefinitely, by the delay of the accuser, or the procrastination of the magistrate. See our remarks on this subject, at the beginning of Chap. XXV.

[8] Acts xxv. 8, (1) 'the Law,' (2) 'the Temple,' (3) 'Cæsar.'

[9] v. 9. In v. 20 this is omitted.

[10] v. 10.

by the words of Festus, who only proposed to transfer him to the jurisdiction of the Sanhedrin with his own consent.[1] He ended by availing himself of one of the most important privileges of Roman citizenship, the right of appeal. By the mere pronunciation of these potent words, ' I appeal unto Cæsar,'[2] he instantly removed his cause from the jurisdiction of the magistrate before whom he stood, and transferred it to the supreme tribunal of the Emperor at Rome.

To explain the full effect of this proceeding, we must observe that in the provinces of Rome, the supreme criminal jurisdiction (both under the Republic and the Empire) was exercised by the Governors, whether they were Proconsuls, Proprætors, or (as in the case of Judæa) Procurators. To this jurisdiction the *provincials* were subject without appeal, and it is needless to say that it was often exercised in the most arbitrary manner. But the *Roman citizens* in the provinces, though also liable to be brought before the judgment-seat of the Governor, were protected from the abuse of his authority; for they had the right of stopping his proceedings against them by appealing to the Tribunes, whose intervention at once transferred the cognisance of the cause to the ordinary tribunals at Rome.[3] This power was only one branch of that prerogative of *intercession* (as it was called) by which the Tribunes could stop the execution of the sentences of all other magistrates. Under the Imperial regime, the Emperor stood in the place of the Tribunes ; Augustus and his successors being invested with the Tribunician power, as the most important of the many Republican offices which were concentrated in their persons. Hence the Emperors constitutionally exercised the right of *intercession*, by which they might stop the proceedings of inferior authorities. But they extended this prerogative much beyond the limits which had confined it during the Republican epoch. They not only arrested the execution of the sentences of other magistrates, but claimed and exercised the right of reversing or altering them, and of re-hearing[4] the causes themselves. In short, the Imperial tribunal was erected into a supreme court of appeal from all inferior courts, either in Rome or in the provinces.

Such was the state of things when St. Paul appealed from Festus

[1] ' Wilt thou,' &c.

[2] The expression here used (equivalent to the Latin *appellare*) was the regular technical phrase for lodging an appeal. The Roman law did not require any written appeal to be lodged in the hands of the Court ; pronunciation of the single word *Appello* was sufficient to suspend all further proceedings.

[3] We must not confound this right of *Appellatio* to the Tribunes with the right of appeal (*Provocatio*) to the Comitia, which belonged to every Roman citizen. This latter right was restricted, even in the Republican era, by the institution of the *Quæstiones Perpetuæ*; because, the judices appointed for those Quæstiones being regarded as representatives of the Comitia, there was no appeal from their decisions. In the time of the Emperors, the Comitia themselves being soon discontinued, this right of Provocatio could be no longer exercised.

[4] According to Dio, this was already the case as early as the time of Augustus. It may be doubted whether the Emperor at first claimed the right of reversing the sentences pronounced by the judices of the Quæstiones Perpetuæ, which were exempt from the Intercessio of the Tribune. But this question is of less importance, because the system of Quæstiones Perpetuæ was soon superseded under the Empire, as we shall afterwards have an opportunity of remarking.

to Cæsar. If the appeal was admissible, it at once suspended all further proceedings on the part of Festus. There were, however, a few cases in which the right of appeal was disallowed ; a bandit, or a pirate, for example, taken in the fact, might be condemned and executed by the Proconsul, notwithstanding his appeal to the Emperor. Accordingly, we read that Festus took counsel with his Assessors,[1] concerning the admissibility of Paul's appeal. But no doubt could be entertained on this head ; and he immediately pronounced the decision of the Court. 'Thou hast appealed[2] unto Cæsar : to Cæsar thou shalt be sent.'

Thus the hearing of the cause, as far as Festus was concerned, had terminated. There only remained for him the office of remitting to the supreme tribunal, before which it was to be carried, his official report[3] upon its previous progress. He was bound to forward to Rome all the acts and documents bearing upon the trial, the depositions of the witnesses on both sides, and the record of his own judgment on the case. And it was his further duty to keep the person of the accused in safe custody, and to send him to Rome for trial at the earliest opportunity.

Festus, however, was still in some perplexity. Though the appeal had been allowed, yet the information elicited on the trial was so vague, that he hardly knew what statement to insert in his dispatch to the Emperor : and it seemed ' a foolish thing to him to send a prisoner to Rome without at the same time specifying the charges against him' (v. 27). It happened about this time that Herod Agrippa II., King of Chalcis, with his sister Berenice, came on a complimentary visit to the new governor, and stayed ' some days' at Cæsarea.[4] This prince had been familiarly acquainted from his youth with all that related to the Jewish law, and moreover, was at this time (as we have seen)[5] superintendent of the Temple, with the power of appointing the high priest. Festus took advantage of this opportunity of consulting one better informed than himself on the points in question. He recounted to Agrippa what has been summarily related above :[6] confessing his ignorance of Jewish theology, and alluding especially to Paul's reiterated assertion[7] concerning ' one Jesus who had died and was alive again.' This cannot have been the first time that Agrippa had heard of the resurrection of Jesus, or of the Apostle Paul.[8] His curiosity was aroused, and he expressed a wish to see the prisoner. Festus readily acceded to the request, and fixed the next day for the interview.

At the time appointed Agrippa and Berenice came with great

---

[1] For a notice of such *consiliarii* in a province, see Sueton. *Tib.* 33. Their office was called *assessura*. Sueton. *Galb.* 14.

[2] The sentence is not interrogative, as in A.V., but the words express a solemn decision of the Procurator and his Assessors.

[3] This report was termed *Apostoli*, or *literæ dimissoriæ*.

[4] Some illustrations of peculiar interest from Josephus, as regards both the complimentary character of this visit and the position of Berenice in the matter, are pointed out by the lamented Prof. Blunt, in his *Scriptural Coincidences*, pp. 358–360.

[5] See above, p. 601.

[6] ver. 14–21.

[7] The form of the verb implies this reiteration.

[8] The tense (v. 22) might seem to imply that he had long wished to see St. Paul.

pomp and display and entered into the audience-chamber, with a suite of military officers and the chief men of Cæsarea :[1] and at the command of Festus, Paul was brought before them. The proceedings were opened by a ceremonious speech from Festus himself,[2] describing the circumstances under which the prisoner had been brought under his notice, and ending with a statement of his perplexity as to what he should write to 'his Lord'[3] the Emperor. This being concluded, Agrippa said condescendingly to St. Paul, that he was now permitted to speak for himself. And the Apostle, 'stretching out the hand' which was chained to the soldier who guarded him, spoke thus :—

ACTS xxvi.

Complimentary address to Agrippa.

I think myself happy, King Agrippa, that I shall 2 defend myself to-day, before thee, against all the charges of my Jewish accusers ; especially because 3 thou art expert in all Jewish customs and questions. Wherefore I pray thee to hear me patiently.

He defends himself against the charge of heresy.

My[4] life and conduct from my youth, as it was at 4 first among my own nation at Jerusalem, is known to all the Jews. They know me of old[5] (I say) from 5 the beginning, and can testify (if they would) that, following the strictest sect of our religion, I lived a Pharisee. And now I stand here to be judged, for 6 the hope of the promise[6] made by God unto our fathers. Which promise is the end whereto, in all 7 their zealous worship,[7] night and day, our twelve tribes hope to come. Yet this hope, O King Agrippa, is charged against me as a crime, and that by Jews.[8] What ![9] is it judged among you a thing incredible 8 that God should raise the dead ?[10]

---

[1] For the audience-hall see above. We may remark that the presence of several Chiliarchs implies that the military force at Cæsarea was considerable. The five resident cohorts mentioned by Josephus have been noticed above, p. 604, n. 8.

[2] ver. 24–27.

[3] The title *Lord* applied here to the Emperor should be noticed. Augustus and Tiberius declined a title which implied the relation of master and slave, but their successors sanctioned the use of it, and Julian tried in vain to break through the custom.

[4] The Greek particles here are rightly left untranslated in A. V. They form a conjunction, denoting that the speaker is beginning a new subject, used where no conjunction would be expressed in English.

[5] The tense is *present*.

[6] The promise meant is that of the

Messiah. Compare what St. Paul says in the speech at Antioch in Pisidia. Acts xiii. 32. Compare also Rom. xv. 8.

[7] This properly means to *perform the outward rites of worship* : see note on Rom. i. 19.

[8] Here again the best MSS. read *Jews* without *the*.

[9] The punctuation adopted is, a note of interrogation after *what*. Compare the use of the same word by St. Paul in Rom. iii. 3, iii. 9, vi. 15, Phil. i. 18.

[10] This is an *argumentum ad homines* to the Jews, whose own Scriptures furnished them with cases where the dead had been raised, as for example by Elisha. The Authorised Version is perfectly correct, notwithstanding the objections which have been made against it. The Greek idiom of '*if*' with an indicative cannot be better represented in English than by '*that*' with '*should.*'

vi. 9   Now I myself[1] determined, in my own mind, that I ought exceedingly to oppose the name of Jesus the

10 Nazarene.   And this I did in Jerusalem, and many of the saints[2] I myself shut up in prison, having received from the chief priests authority so to do;[3] and when they were condemned[4] to death, I gave

11 my vote against them.   And in every synagogue I continually punished them, and endeavoured[5] to compel them to blaspheme; and being exceedingly mad against them, I went even to foreign cities to persecute them.

12   With this purpose I was on my road to Damascus, bearing my authority and commission from the

13 chief[6] priests, when I saw in the way, O King, at midday[7] a light from heaven, above the brightness of the sun, shining round about me and those who

14 journeyed with me.   And when we all were fallen to the earth, I heard a voice speaking to me, and saying in the Hebrew tongue, *Saul, Saul, why persecutest*

15 *thou me? it is hard for thee to kick against the goad.* And I said, *Who art thou, Lord?*   And the Lord[8]

16 said, *I am Jesus whom thou persecutest.   But rise and stand upon thy feet; for to this end I have appeared unto thee, to ordain[9] thee a minister and a witness both of those things which thou hast seen, and of those things*

17 *wherein I shall appear unto thee.   And thee have I chosen[10] from the house of Israel,[11] and from among the Gentiles; unto whom now I send thee, to open their*

---

[1] The pronoun, from its position, must be emphatic.

[2] This speech should be carefully compared with that in chap. xxii., with the view of observing St. Paul's judicious adaptation of his statements to his audience.   Thus, here he calls the Christians '*Saints*,' which the Jews in the Temple would not have tolerated.   See some useful remarks on this subject by Mr. Birks.   *Hor. Ap.* vii. viii.

[3] '*The* authority,'—'*this* authority.'

[4] Literally, *when they were being destroyed*.   On the 'giving his vote see p. 64.

[5] Imperfect.

[6] By Chief Priests here and above, verse 10, is meant (as in Luke xxii. 52, Acts v. 24) the presidents of the 24 classes into which the priests were divided.   These were *ex officio* members of the Sanhedrin.   In the *speech*

on the stairs accordingly, St. Paul states that he had received his commission to Damascus from the high priest and Sanhedrin (Acts xxii. 5).

[7] The circumstance of the light overpowering even the blaze of the midday sun is mentioned before (Acts xxii. 6).

[8] All the best MSS. read '*the Lord* said.'   This also agrees better with what follows, where St. Paul relates all which the Lord had revealed to him, both at the moment of his conversion, and subsequently, by the voice of Ananias, and by the vision at Jerusalem.   See Acts xxii. 12–21.

[9] We have here the very words of Ananias (Acts xxii. 14, 15).   The same very unusual word for 'ordain' is used in both places.

[10] '*Choosing*,' not '*delivering*' (A.V.)

[11] '*The people*.'   See on the speech at Antioch, p. 141, note 3.

eyes, *that they may turn*[1] *from darkness to light, and* xx *from the power of Satan unto God; that they may receive forgiveness of sins, and an inheritance among the sanctified, by faith in me.*

His execution whereof had brought on him the hatred of the Jews.

Whereupon, O King Agrippa, I was not disobe- 19 dient to the heavenly vision.   But first[2] to those at 20 Damascus and Jerusalem, and throughout all the land of Judæa,[3] and also to the Gentiles, I proclaimed the tidings that they should repent and turn to God, and do works worthy of their repentance.

For these causes the Jews, when they caught me 21 in the Temple, endeavoured to kill me.

Yet his teaching accorded with the Jewish Scriptures.

Therefore,[4] through the succour which I have re- 22 ceived from God, I stand firm unto this day, and bear my testimony both to small and great; but I declare nothing else than what the Prophets and Moses foretold, That[5] the Messiah should suffer, and 23 that He should be the first[6] to rise from the dead, and should be the messenger[7] of light to the house of Israel, and also to the Gentiles.

Here Festus broke out into a loud exclamation,[8] expressive of ridicule and surprise.   To the cold man of the world, as to the inquisitive Athenians, the doctrine of the resurrection was foolishness: and he said, 'Paul, thou art mad: thy incessant study[9] is turning thee to madness.'   The Apostle had alluded in his speech to writings which had a mysterious sound, to the prophets and to Moses[10]

---

[1] Neuter, not active as in A. V. Compare, for the use of this word by St. Paul (to signify the conversion of the Gentiles), 1 Thess. i. 9, and Acts xiv. 15.   Also below, v. 20.

[2] This does not at all prove, as has sometimes been supposed, that Saul did not preach in Arabia when he went there soon after his conversion ; see p. 80.

[3] How are we to reconcile this with St. Paul's statement (Gal. i. 22) that he continued personally unknown to the Churches of Judæa for many years after his conversion ?   We must either suppose that, in the present passage, he means to speak not in the order of time, but of all which he had done up to the present date; or else we may perhaps suppose that St. Luke did not think it necessary to attend to a minute detail of this kind, relating to a period of St. Paul's life with which he was himself not personally acquainted, in giving the general outline of this speech.

[4] The conjunction here cannot mean '*however.*'

[5] The '*if*' in the original is equivalent to our '*that*' ('*if, as they assert*').   Compare note on Acts xxvi. 8 above.

[6] Compare Col. i. 18.   Also 1 Cor. xv. 20.

[7] 'Something more than merely 'show' (A. V.).

[8] Observe the mention of the 'loud voice' coupled with the fact that Paul 'was speaking for himself.'   Both expressions show that he was suddenly interrupted in the midst of his discourse.

[9] The original has the definite article here.

[10] See again v. 27, where St. Paul appeals again to the prophets, the *writings* to which he had alluded before.

(ver. 22, 23) : and it is reasonable to believe that in his imprisonment, such 'books and parchments,' as he afterwards wrote for in
his second letter to Timotheus,[1] were brought to him by his friends.
Thus Festus adopted the conclusion that he had before him a mad
enthusiast, whose head had been turned by poring over strange
learning.   The Apostle's reply was courteous and self-possessed,
but intensely earnest.

25   I am not mad, most noble Festus, but speak forth
26 the words of truth and soberness : For the king has·
knowledge of these matters ; and moreover I speak
to him with boldness ; because I am persuaded that
none of these things is unknown to him,—for this
has not been done in a corner.

Then turning to the Jewish voluptuary who sat beside the Governor, he made this solemn appeal to him :—

27   King Agrippa, believest thou the prophets ?   I
know that thou believest.

The King's reply was : 'Thou wilt soon[2] persuade me to be a
Christian.'   The words were doubtless spoken ironically and in
contempt : but Paul took them as though they had been spoken in
earnest, and made that noble answer, which expresses, as no other
words ever expressed them, that union of enthusiastic zeal with
genuine courtesy, which is the true characteristic of ' a Christian.'

29   I would to God, that whether soon or late, not
only thou, but also all who hear me to-day, were such
as I am ; excepting these chains.

This concluded the interview.   King Agrippa had no desire to
hear more ; and he rose from his seat,[3] with the Governor and
Berenice and those who sat with them.   As they retired, they discussed the case with one another,[4] and agreed that Paul was guilty
of nothing worthy of death or even imprisonment.   Agrippa said
positively to Festus, ' This man[5] might have been set at liberty,[6] if

---

[1] 2 Tim. iv. 13. These, we may well
believe, would especially be the Old
Testament Scriptures,—perhaps Jewish commentaries on them, and possibly
also the works of Heathen poets and
philosophers.

[2] The phrase here cannot mean
'almost,' as it is in the Authorised
Version.   It might mean either *'in
few words'* (Eph. iii. 3), or *'in a small
measure,'* or *'in a small time.'*   The
latter meaning agrees best with the
following, 'in little or in much.'   We
might render the passage thus : 'Thou

thinkest to make me a Christian with
little persuasion.'   We should observe
that the verb is in the present tense,
and that the title 'Christian' was one
of contempt.   See 1 Pet. iv. 16.

[3] v. 30.

[4] v. 31.

[5] Again the expression is contemptuous.   See the remarks on Acts xvi.
35 (p. 239).   Claudius Lysias uses a
similar expression in his letter to Felix,
xxiii. 27.

[6] Compare xxviii. 18.

he had not appealed to the Emperor.' But the appeal had been made. There was no retreat either for Festus or for Paul. On the new Governor's part there was no wish to continue the procrastination of Felix; and nothing now remained but to wait for a convenient opportunity of sending his prisoner to Rome.

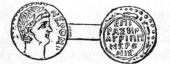

Coin of Nero and Herod Agrippa II.[1]

[1] From the British Museum. Mr. Akerman describes it thus: 'This prince, notwithstanding the troubles which now began to afflict his ill-fated country, spent large sums in improving and beautifying Jerusalem, Berytus, and Cæsarea Philippi. Of the latter there is a coin extant, bearing the head of Nero: *reverse* EΠI BAΣIΛE AΓPIΠΠA NEPΩNIE, within a laurel garland, confirming the account of Josephus (*Ant.* xx. 9. 8), who says Herod enlarged and called the city Neronias, in honour of the Emperor.' *Num. Ill.* p. 57.

CHAPTER XXIII.

Ships and Navigation of the Ancients.—Roman Commerce in the Mediterranean.—Corn Trade between Alexandria and Puteoli.—Travellers by Sea.—
St. Paul's Voyage from Cæsarea, by Sidon, to Myra.—From Myra, by Cnidus
and Cape Salmone, to Fair Havens.—Phœnix.—The Storm.—Seamanship
during the Gale.—St. Paul's Vision.—Anchoring in the Night.—Shipwreck.
—Proof that it took place in Malta.—Winter in the Island.—Objections considered.—Voyage, by Syracuse and Rhegium, to Puteoli.

BEFORE entering on the narrative of that voyage [1] which brought
the Apostle Paul, through manifold and imminent dangers, from
Cæsarea to Rome, it will be convenient to make a few introductory
remarks concerning the ships and navigation of the ancients. By
fixing clearly in the mind some of the principal facts relating to the
form and structure of Greek and Roman vessels, the manner in
which these vessels were worked, the prevalent lines of traffic in
the Mediterranean, and the opportunities afforded to travellers of
reaching their destination by sea,—we shall be better able to follow
this voyage without distractions or explanations, and with a clearer
perception of each event as it occurred.

With regard to the vessels and seamanship of the Greeks and
Romans, many popular mistakes have prevailed, to which it is
hardly necessary to allude, after the full illustration which the subject has now received. [2] We must not entertain the notion that all

[1] The nautical difficulties of this narrative have been successfully explained
by two independent inquirers ; and, so
far as we are aware, by no one else. A
practical knowledge of seamanship was
required for the elucidation of the whole
subject ; and none of the ordinary commentators seemed to have looked on it
with the eye of a sailor. The first who
examined St. Paul's voyage in a practical spirit was the late Admiral Sir
Charles Penrose, whose life has been
lately published (Murray, 1851). His
MSS. have been kindly placed in the
hands of the writer of this chapter, and
they are frequently referred to in the
notes. A similar investigation was
made subsequently, but independently,
and more minutely and elaborately, by
James Smith, Esq. of Jordanhill, whose
published work on the subject (Long-
mans, 1848) has already obtained an
European reputation. Besides other
valuable aid, Mr. Smith has examined

the sheets of this chapter, as they have
passed through the press. We have
also to express our acknowledgments
for much kind assistance received from
the late Admiral Moorsom and other
naval officers.

[2] The reference here is to the Dissertation on 'The Ships of the Ancients' in Mr. Smith's work on the
Voyage and Shipwreck of St. Paul, pp.
140–202. This treatise may be regarded as the standard work on the
subject, not only in England, but in
Europe. It has been translated into
German by H. Thiersch, and it is adduced in Hermann's well-known work
on Greek Antiquities, as the decisive
authority on the difficult points connected with the study of ancient ship-
building. It is hardly necessary to refer
to any of the older works on the subject. A full catalogue is given in Mr.
Smith's Appendix.

the commerce of the ancients was conducted merely by means or small craft, which proceeded timidly in the day time, and only in the summer season, along the coast from harbour to harbour,—and which were manned by mariners almost ignorant of the use of sails, and always trembling at the prospect of a storm. We cannot, indeed, assert that the arts either of ship-building or navigation were matured in the Mediterranean so early as the first century of the Christian era. The Greeks and Romans were ignorant of the use of the compass : [1] the instruments with which they took observations must have been rude compared with our modern quadrants and sextants : [2] and we have no reason to believe that their vessels were provided with nautical charts : [3] and thus, when ' neither sun nor stars appeared,' and the sky gave indications of danger, they hesitated to try the open sea. [4] But the ancient sailor was well skilled in the changeable weather of the Levant, and his very ignorance of the aids of modern science made him the more observant of external phenomena, and more familiar with his own coasts. [5] He was not less prompt and practical than a modern seaman in the handling of his ship, when overtaken by stormy weather on a dangerous coast.

The ship of the Greek and Roman mariner was comparatively rude, both in its build and its rig. The hull was not laid down with the fine lines, with which we are so familiar in the competing vessels of England and America, [6] and the arrangement of the sails exhibited little of that complicated distribution yet effective combination of mechanical forces, which we admire in the East-Indiaman or modern Frigate. With the war-ships [7] of the ancients we need not here occupy ourselves or the reader : but two peculiarities in the structure of Greek and Roman merchantmen must be carefully noticed ; for both of them are much concerned in the seamanship described in the narrative before us.

[1] See Humboldt's *Kosmos*, vol. ii., for the main facts relating to the history of the Compass.

[2] We have no information of any nautical instruments at the time when we read of Ptolemy's mural quadrant at Alexandria; nor is it likely that any more effectual means of taking exact observations at sea, than the simple quadrant held in the hand, were in use before the invention of the reflecting quadrants and sextants by Hooke and Hadley. The want of exact chronometers must also be borne in mind.

[3] The first nautical charts were perhaps those of Marinus of Tyre (A.D. 150), whom Forbiger regards as the founder of mathematical geography. See the life of Ptolemy in Dr. Smith's *Dictionary*.

[4] See Acts xxvii. 9–12, also xxviii. 11. ' We are apt to consider the ancients as timid and unskilful sailors, afraid to venture out of sight of land, or to make long voyages in the winter.

I can see no evidence that this was the case. The cause of their not making voyages after the end of summer arose, in a great measure, from the comparative obscurity of the sky during the winter, and not from the gales which prevail at that season. With no means of directing their course, except by observing the heavenly bodies, they were necessarily prevented from putting to sea when they could not depend on their being visible.'—Smith, p. 180.

[5] See again what is said below in reference to Acts xxvii. 12.

[6] ' As both ends were alike, if we suppose a full-built merchant-ship of the present day, cut in two, and the stern half replaced by one exactly the same as that of the bow, we shall have a pretty accurate notion of what these ships were.'—Smith, p. 141.

[7] For a full description and explanation of ancient triremes, &c., see Mr. Smith's Dissertation.

The ships of the Greeks and Romans, like those of the early Northmen,[1] were not steered by means of a single rudder, but by *two paddle-rudders*, one on each quarter. Hence 'rudders' are mentioned in the plural[2] by St. Luke (Acts xxvii. 40) as by Heathen writers : and the fact is made still more palpable by the representations of art, as in the coins of Imperial Rome or the tapestry of Bayeux : nor does the hinged-rudder appear on any of the remains of antiquity, till a late period in the Middle Ages.[3]

And as this mode of steering is common to the two sources, from which we must trace our present art of ship-building, so also is the same mode of rigging characteristic of the ships both of the North Sea and the Mediterranean.[4] We find in these ancient ships one large mast, with strong ropes rove through a block at the mast-head, and *one large sail*, fastened to an enormous yard.[5] We shall see the importance of attending to this arrangement, when we enter upon the incidents of St. Paul's voyage (xxvii. 17, 19). One consequence was, that instead of the strain being distributed over the hull, as in a modern ship, it was concentrated upon a smaller portion of it : and thus in ancient times there must have been a greater tendency to leakage than at present ;[6] and we have the testimony of ancient writers to the fact, that a vast proportion of the vessels lost were by foundering. Thus Virgil,[7] whose descriptions of everything which relates to the sea are peculiarly exact, speaks of the ships in the fleet of Æneas as lost in various ways, some on rocks and some on quicksands, but ' all with fastenings loosened :' and Josephus relates that the ship from which he so narrowly escaped, foundered[8] in 'Adria,' and that he and his companions saved themselves by swimming[9] through the night,—an escape which found its parallel in the experience of the Apostle, who in one of those shipwrecks, of

---

[1] See Vorsaee *on the Danes and Northmen in England.* He does not describe the structure of their ships; but this peculiarity is evident in the drawing given at p. 111, from the Bayeux tapestry.

[2] 'The fastenings of the rudders.' The fact of 'rudders' being in the plural is lost sight of in the English version ; and the impression is conveyed of a single rudder, worked by tiller-ropes, which, as we shall see, is quite erroneous. Compare the use of 'guberna' in Lucretius; and see Smith, p. 143, and Dr. Smith's *Dictionary of Antiquities*, under ' Gubernaculum.'

[3] Smith, p. 146. He traces the representation of ancient rudders from Trajan's column to the gold nobles of our king Edward III., and infers that 'the change in the mode of steering must have taken place about the end of the thirteenth, or early in the fourteenth century.'

[4] See Vorsaee, as above, and the representations of classical ships in Mr. Smith's work.

[5] By this it is not meant that topsails were not used, or that there were never more masts than one. Topsails (*suppara*) are frequently alluded to : and we shall have occasion hereafter to refer particularly to a second mast, besides the mainmast. See Mr. Smith's Dissertation, p. 151, and the engraving there given from M. Jal's *Archéologie Navale.*

[6] See Smith, p. 63.

[7]   ' Laxis laterum compagibus
            omnes
Accipiunt inimicum imbrem, rimisque
            fatiscunt.'

[8] *Life*, c. 3. Mr. Smith remarks here (p. 62) that, since Josephus and some of his companions saved themselves by swimming, ' the ship did not go down during the gale, but in consequence of the damage she received during its continuance.' For the meaning of the word ' Adria,' see below.

[9] Probably with the aid of floating spars, &c. See note on 2 Cor. xi. 25.

which no particular narration has been given to us, was 'a night and a day in the deep' (2 Cor. xi. 25). The same danger was apprehended in the ship of Jonah, from which 'they cast forth the wares that were in the ship into the sea to lighten it' (i. 5) ; as well as in the ship of St. Paul, from which, after having 'lightened' it the first day, they 'cast out the tackling' on the second day, and finally 'threw out the cargo of wheat into the sea' (xxvii. 18, 19, 38).

This leads us to notice what may be called a third peculiarity of the appointments of ancient ships, as compared with those of modern times. In consequence of the extreme danger to which they were exposed from leaking, it was customary to take to sea, as part of their ordinary gear, '*undergirders*' (ὑποζώματα), which were simply ropes for passing round the hull of the ship and thus preventing the planks from starting.[1] One of the most remarkable proofs of the truth of this statement is to be found in the inscribed marbles dug up within the last twenty years at the Piræus which give us an inventory of the Attic fleet in its flourishing period ;[2] as one of the most remarkable accounts of the application of these artificial 'helps' (xxvii. 17) in a storm, is to be found in the narrative before us.

If these differences between ancient ships and our own are borne in mind, the problems of early seamanship in the Mediterranean are nearly reduced to those with which the modern navigator has to deal in the same seas. The practical questions which remain to be asked are these : What were the dimensions of ancient ships ? How near the wind could they sail ? And, with a fair wind, at what rate ?

As regards the first of these questions, there seems no reason why we should suppose the old trading vessels of the Mediterranean to be much smaller than our own. We may rest this conclusion, both on the character of the cargoes with which they were freighted,[3] and on the number of persons we know them to have sometimes conveyed. Though the great ship of Ptolemy Philadelphus[4] may justly

[1] This is what is called '*frapping*' by seamen in the English navy, who are always taught how to frap a ship. The only difference is, that the practice is now resorted to much less frequently, and that modern ships are not supplied with 'undergirders' specially prepared. The operation and its use are thus described in Falconer's *Marine Dictionary* : ' To frap a ship is to pass four or five turns of a large cable-laid rope round the hull or frame of a ship, to support her in a great storm, or otherwise, when it is apprehended that she is not strong enough to resist the violent efforts of the sea.' In most of the European languages the nautical term is, like the Greek, expressive of the nature of the operation. Fr. *ceintrer*; Ital. *cingere* ; Germ. *umgürten* ; Dutch, *omgorden* ; Norw. *omgyrte* ; Portug. *cintrar*. In Spanish the word is *tortorar :* a circumstance which possesses some etymological interest, since the word used by Isidore of Seville for a rope used in this way is *tormentum*. See the next note.

[2] The excavations were made in the year 1834 ; and the inscriptions were published, in 1840, at Berlin, by A. Böckh. A complete account is given of everything with which the Athenian ships were supplied, with the name of each vessel, &c. ; and we find that they all carried 'undergirders,' which are classed among the *hanging gear*, as opposed to what was constructed of *timber*. In commenting on one passage having reference to the ships which were on service in the Adriatic, and which carried several 'undergirders,' Böckh shows that these were ropes passed round the body of the ship, but he strangely supposes that they were passed from stem to stern.

[3] See below on the traffic between the provinces and Rome.

[4] Described in Athenæus.

be regarded as built for ostentation rather than for use, the Alexandrian vessel, which forms the subject of one of Lucian's dialogues,[1] and is described as driven by stress of weather into the Piræus, furnishes us with satisfactory data for the calculation of the tonnage of ancient ships. Two hundred and seventy-six souls[2] were on board the ship in which St. Paul was wrecked (xxvii. 37), and the 'Castor and Pollux' conveyed them, in addition to her own crew, from Malta to Puteoli (xxviii. 11): while Josephus informs us[3] that there were six hundred on board the ship from which he, with about eighty others, escaped. Such considerations lead us to suppose that the burden of many ancient merchantmen may have been *from five hundred to a thousand tons.*

A second question of greater consequence in reference to the present subject, relates to the angle which the course of an ancient ship could be made to assume with the direction of the wind, or to use the language[4] of English sailors (who divide the compass into thirty-two points), *within how many points of the wind* she would sail? That ancient vessels could not work to windward, is one of the popular mistakes[5] which need not be refuted. They doubtless took advantage of the Etesian winds,[6] just as the traders in the Eastern Archipelago sail with the monsoons: but those who were accustomed to a seafaring life could not avoid discovering that a ship's course can be made to assume a less angle than a right angle with the direction of the wind, or, in other words, that she can be made to sail within less than eight points of the wind:[7] and Pliny distinctly says, that it is possible for a ship to sail on contrary tacks.[8] The limits of this possibility depend upon the character of the vessel and the violence of the gale. We shall find, below, that the vessel in which St. Paul was wrecked, 'could not *look at* the wind,'—for so the Greek word (xxvii. 15) may be literally translated in the language of English sailors,—though with a less violent gale, an English ship, well-managed, could easily have kept her course. A modern merchantman, in moderate weather, can sail within six points of the wind. In an ancient vessel the yard could not be braced so sharp, and the hull was more clumsy: and it

---

[1] From the length and breadth of this ship as given by Lucian, Mr. Smith infers that her burden was between 1000 and 1100 tons, pp. 147–150.

[2] 'The ship must have been of considerable burden, as we find there were no less than 276 persons embarked on board her. To afford fair accommodation for troops in a transport expressly fitted for the purpose, we should allow at the rate of a ton and a half to each man, and as the ship we are considering was not expressly fitted for passengers, we may conclude that her burden was fully, or at least nearly double, the number of tons, to the souls on board, or upwards of 500 tons.'—Penrose, MS.

[3] *Life*, c. 3.

[4] As it is essential, for the purpose of elucidating the narrative, that this

language should be clearly understod, a compass has been inserted at p. 569, and some words of explanation are given, both here and below. This will be readily excused by those who are familiar with nautical phraseology.

[5] Yet we sometimes find the mistake when we should hardly expect it. Thus, Hemsen says, in reference to Acts xxvii. 7, that it is 'doubtful whether the ancients were acquainted with the way of sailing against the wind.'

[6] The classical passages relating to these winds—the monsoons of the Levant—are collected in Forbiger's work on Ancient Geography.

[7] See Smith, p. 178.

[8] 'Iisdem ventis in contrarium navigatur prolatis pedibus.'—*H. N.* ii. 48.

would not be safe to say that she could sail nearer the wind than within *seven points*.[1]

To turn now to the third question, the *rate of sailing*,—the very nature of the rig, which was less adapted than our own for working to windward, was peculiarly favourable to a quick run before the wind. In the China seas, during the monsoons, junks have been seen from the deck of a British vessel behind in the horizon in the morning, and before in the horizon in the evening.[2] Thus we read of passages accomplished of old in the Mediterranean, which would do credit to a well-appointed modern ship. Pliny, who was himself a seaman, and in command of a fleet at the time of his death, might furnish us with several instances. We might quote the story of the fresh fig, which Cato produced in the senate at Rome, when he urged his countrymen to undertake the third Punic war, by impressing on them the imminent nearness of their enemy. ' This fruit,' he says, ' was gathered fresh at Carthage three days ago.'[3] Other voyages, which he adduces, are such as these,—seven days from Cadiz to Ostia,—seven days from the straits of Messina to Alexandria,—nine days from Puteoli to Alexandria. These instances are quite in harmony with what we read in other authors. Thus Rhodes and Cape Salmone, at the eastern extremity of Crete, are reckoned by Diodorus and Strabo as four days from Alexandria: Plutarch tells us of a voyage within the day from Brundusium to Corcyra: Procopius describes Belisarius as sailing on one day with his fleet from Malta, and landing on the next day some leagues to the south of Carthage.[4] A thousand stades (or between 100 and 150 miles), is reckoned by the geographers a common distance to accomplish in the twenty-four hours.[5] And the conclusion to which we are brought is, that with a fair wind an ancient merchantman would easily sail at the rate of *seven knots an hour*,—a conclusion in complete harmony both with what we have observed in a former voyage of St. Paul (Chap. XX.), and with what will demand our attention at the close of that voyage, which brought him at length from Malta by Rhegium to Puteoli (Acts xxviii. 13).

The remarks which have been made will convey to the reader a sufficient notion of the ships and navigation of the ancients. If to the above-mentioned peculiarities of build and rig we add the eye painted at the prow, the conventional ornaments at stem and stern, which are familiar to us in remaining works of art,[6] and the characteristic figures of Heathen divinities,[7] we shall gain a sufficient idea of an ancient merchantman. And a glance at the chart of the

---

[1] Smith, p. 178.

[2] See above, p. 562, n. 1.

[3] Plin. *H. N.* xv. 20. We may observe that the interval of time need not be regarded as so much as three entire days.

[4] This is one of the passages which will be referred to hereafter, in considering the boundaries of the sea called Adria (Acts xxvii. 27).

[5] Herodotus reckons a day and a night's sail in the summer time, and with a favourable wind, at 1300 stadia, or 162 Roman miles.

[6] For the χηνίσκος, a tall ornament at the stern or prow, in the form of the neck of a water-fowl, see Smith, p. 142, and the *Dictionary of Antiquities,* under 'Aplustre.'

[7] ' *Whose sign was Castor and Pollux,*' Acts xxviii. 11. This might be abundantly illustrated from classical authors.

Mediterranean will enable us to realise in our imagination the nature of the voyages that were most frequent in the ancient world. With the same view of elucidating the details of our subject beforehand, we may now devote a short space to the prevalent lines of traffic, and to the opportunities of travellers by sea, in the first century of the Christian era.

Though the Romans had no natural love for the sea, and though a commercial life was never regarded by them as an honourable occupation, and thus both experience of practical seamanship, and the business of the carrying trade remained in a great measure with the Greeks, yet a vast development had been given to commerce by the consolidation of the Roman Empire. Piracy had been effectually put down before the close of the Republic.[1] The annexation of Egypt drew towards Italy the rich trade of the Indian seas. After the effectual reduction of Gaul and Spain, Roman soldiers and Roman slave-dealers[2] invaded the shores of Britain. The trade of all the countries which surrounded the Mediterranean began to flow towards Rome. The great city herself was passive, for she had nothing to export. But the cravings of her luxury, and the necessities of her vast population, drew to one centre the converging lines of a busy traffic from a wide extent of provinces. To leave out of view what hardly concerns us here, the commerce by land from the North,[3] some of the principal directions of trade by sea may be briefly enumerated as follows. The harbours of Ostia and Puteoli were constantly full of ships from the West, which had brought wool and other articles from Cadiz :[4] a circumstance which possesses some interest for us here, as illustrating the mode in which St. Paul might hope to accomplish his voyage to Spain (Rom. xv. 24). On the South was Sicily, often called the Storehouse of Italy,—and Africa, which sent furniture-woods to Rome, and heavy cargoes of marble and granite. On the East, Asia Minor was the intermediate space through which the caravan-trade[5] passed, conveying silks and spices from beyond the Euphrates to the markets and wharves of Ephesus. We might extend this enumeration by alluding to the fisheries of the Black Sea, and the wine-trade of the Archipelago. But enough has been said to give some notion of the commercial activity of which Italy was the centre : and our particular attention here is required only to one branch of trade, one line of constant traffic across the waters of the Mediterranean to Rome.

Alexandria has been mentioned already as a city, which, next after Athens, exerted the strongest intellectual influence over the

---

[1] Compare pp. 17, 18.

[2] See the passage in Pitt's speeches, referred to in Milman's *Gibbon*, i. p. 70.

[3] For example, the amber trade of the Baltic, and the importing of provisions and rough cloths from Cisalpine Gaul.

[4] We may refer here, in illustration, to the coin representing Ostia below, p. 683. It was about this time that the new harbour of Portus (a city not unconnected with ecclesiastical history)

was completed by Nero on the north side of the mouth of the Tiber. See the article ' Ostia ' in Dr. Smith's *Dict. of Geography*.

[5] There seem to have been two great lines of inland trade through Asia Minor, one near the southern shore of the Black Sea, through the districts opened by the campaigns of Pompey, and the other through the centre of the country from Mazaca, on the Euphrates, to Ephesus.

age in which St. Paul's appointed work was done; and we have had occasion to notice some indirect connection between this city and the Apostle's own labours.[1] But it was eminent commercially not less than intellectually. The prophetic views of Alexander were at that time receiving an ampler fulfilment than at any former period. The trade with the Indian Seas, which had been encouraged under the Ptolemies, received a vast impulse in the reign of Augustus : and under the reigns of his successors, the valley of the Nile was the channel of an active transit trade in spices, dyes, jewels, and perfumes, which were brought by Arabian mariners from the far East, and poured into the markets of Italy.[2] But Egypt was not only the medium of transit trade. She had her own manufactures of linen, paper, and glass, which she exported in large quantities. And one natural product of her soil has been a staple commodity from the time of Pharaoh to our own. We have only to think of the fertilising inundations of the Nile, on the one hand, and, on the other, of the multitudes composing the free and slave population of Italy, in order to comprehend the activity and importance of the Alexandrian corn-trade. At a later period the Emperor Commodus established a company of merchants to convey the supplies from Egypt to Rome ; and the commendations which he gave himself for this forethought may still be read in the inscription round the ships represented on his coins.[3] The harbour, to which the Egyptian corn-vessels were usually bound, was Puteoli. At the close of this chapter we shall refer to some passages which give an animated picture of the arrival of these ships. Meanwhile, it is well to have called attention to this line of traffic between Alexandria and Puteoli ; for in so doing we have described the means which Divine Providence employed for bringing the Apostle to Rome.

The transition is easy from the commerce of the Mediterranean to the progress of travellers from point to point in that sea. If to this enumeration of the main lines of traffic by sea we add all the ramifications of the coasting-trade which depended on them, we have before us a full view of the opportunities which travellers possessed of accomplishing their voyages. Just in this way we have lately seen St. Paul completing the journey, on which his mind was set, from Philippi, by Miletus and Patara, to Cæsarea (Chap. XX.). We read of no periodical packets for the conveyance of passengers sailing between the great towns of the Mediterranean. Emperors themselves were usually compelled to take advantage of the same opportunities to which Jewish pilgrims and Christian Apostles were limited. When Vespasian went to Rome, leaving Titus to prosecute the siege of Jerusalem, 'he went on board a merchant-ship, and sailed from Alexandria to Rhodes,' and thence pursued his way through Greece to the Adriatic, and finally went to Rome through Italy by land.[4] And when the Jewish war was ended, and when, suspicions having arisen concerning the allegiance of Titus to Vespasian, the son was anxious 'to rejoin his father,' he also left

---

[1] See pp. 8, 9, 29, 365.

[2] See the history of this trade in Dean Vincent's *Commerce and Navigation of the Ancients.*

[3] One of them is given (from Mr. Smith's work) on the title-page.

[4] Joseph. *War,* vii. 2. 1.

Alexandria[1] in a 'merchant-ship,' and 'hastened to Italy,' touching at the very places at which St. Paul touched, first at Rhegium (xxviii. 13), and then at Puteoli (ib.).

If such was the mode in which even royal personages travelled from the provinces to the metropolis, we must of course conclude that those who travelled on the business of the state must often have been content to avail themselves of similar opportunities. The sending of state prisoners to Rome from various parts of the Empire was an event of frequent occurrence. Thus we are told by Josephus,[2] that Felix 'for some slight offence, bound and sent to Rome several priests of his acquaintance, honourable and good men, to answer for themselves to Cæsar.' Such groups must often have left Cæsarea and the other Eastern ports, in merchant-vessels bound for the West; and such was the departure of St. Paul, when the time at length came for that eventful journey, which had been so long and earnestly cherished in his own wishes;[3] so emphatically foretold by Divine revelation;[4] and which was destined to involve such great consequences to the whole future of Christianity.

The vessel in which he sailed, with certain other state prisoners, was 'a ship of Adramyttium' apparently engaged in the coasting trade,[5] and at that time (probably the end of summer or the beginning of autumn[6]) bound on her homeward voyage. Whatever might be the harbours at which she intended to touch, her course lay along the coast of the province of Asia.[7] Adramyttium was itself a seaport in Mysia, which (as we have seen) was a subdivision of that province : and we have already described it as situated in the deep gulf which recedes beyond the base of Mount Ida, over against the island of Lesbos, and as connected by good roads with Pergamus and Troas on the coast, and the various marts in the interior of the peninsula.[8] Since St. Paul never reached the place, no description

[1] Suet. *Tit.* c. 5.

[2] Joseph. *Life*, c. 3.

[3] Rom. xv. 23.

[4] Acts xix. 21; xxiii. 11. See xxvii. 24.

[5] The words 'meaning to sail by the coasts of Asia' (v. 2), should rather be applied to the ship ('about to sail,' &c.). They seem to imply that she was about to touch at several places on her way to Adramyttium. Probably she was a small coaster, similar to those of the modern Greeks in the same seas; and doubtless the Alexandrian corn-ship mentioned afterwards was much larger.

[6] This we infer, partly because it is reasonable to suppose that they expected to reach Italy before the winter, partly because of the delays which are expressly mentioned before the consultation at Fair Havens. See p. 639.

[7] For the meaning of the word 'Asia' in the New Testament, we need only refer again to p. 182, &c. It is of the utmost consequence to bear this in mind. If the *continent of Asia* were intended, the passage would be almost unmeaning. Yet Falconer says (*Diss. on St. Paul's Voyage, on the wind Euroclydon and the Apostle's shipwreck on the island Melita, by a Layman.* Oxf. 1817), 'They who conducted the ship, meant to sail on their return by the coasts of Asia; *accordingly*, the next day after they set sail, they touched at Sidon,' p. 4. Nor are we to suppose *Asia Minor* intended, which seems to be the supposition even of some of the most careful commentators.

[8] p. 214. See p. 548. We need hardly allude to the error of Grotius, who supposed Adrumetum, on the African coast, to be meant. Mr. Lewin assumes that the intention of Julius was to proceed (like those who afterwards took Ignatius to his martyrdom) by the Via Egnatia through Macedonia: but the narrative gives no indication of such a plan : and indeed the hypothesis is contradicted by the word in xxvii. 1.

of it is required.[1] It is only needful to observe that when the vessel reached the coast of ' Asia,' the travellers would be brought some considerable distance on their way to Rome; and there would be a good prospect of finding some other westward-bound vessel, in which they might complete their voyage,—more especially since the Alexandrian corn-ships (as we shall see) often touched at the harbours in that neighbourhood.

St. Paul's two companions—besides the soldiers, with Julius their commanding officer, the sailors, the other prisoners, and such occasional passengers as may have taken advantage of this opportunity of leaving Cæsarea,—were two Christians already familiar to us, Luke the Evangelist, whose name, like that of Timotheus, is almost inseparable from the Apostle, and whom we may conclude to have been with him since his arrival in Jerusalem,[2]—and ' Aristarchus the Macedonian, of Thessalonica,' whose native country and native city have been separately mentioned before (Acts xix. 29, xx. 4), and who seems, from the manner in which he is spoken of in the Epistles written from Rome (Philem. 24, Col. iv. 10), to have been, like St. Paul himself, a prisoner in the cause of the Gospel.

On the day after sailing from Cæarea the vessel put into Sidon (v. 3). This may be readily accounted for, by supposing that she touched there for the purposes of trade, or to land some passengers. Or another hypothesis is equally allowable. Westerly and north-westerly winds prevail in the Levant at the end of summer and the beginning of autumn ;[3] and we find that it did actually blow from these quarters soon afterwards, in the course of St. Paul's voyage. Such a wind would be sufficiently fair for a passage to Sidon : and the seamen might proceed to that port in the hope of the weather becoming more favourable, and be detained there by the wind continuing in the same quarter.[4] The passage from Cæsarea to Sidon is sixty-seven miles, a distance easily accomplished, under favour-

---

[1] A short notice of it is given by Sir C. Fellows (*A. M.* p. 39). Mr. Weston, in his MS. journal, describes it as a filthy town, of about 1500 houses, 150 of which are inhabited by Greeks, and he saw no remains of antiquity. It was a flourishing seaport in the time of the kings of Pergamus; and Pliny mentions it as the seat of a *conventus juridicus.* In Pococke's *Travels* (II. ii. 16), it is stated that there is much boat-building still at Adramyti.

[2] See above.

[3] See the quotation already given from Norie's *Sailing Directions*, p. 557, n. 1. A similar statement will be found in Purdy, p. 59. Mr. Smith (pp. 22, 23, 27, 41), gives very copious illustrat ons of this point, from the journal written by Lord de Saumarez, on his return from Aboukir, in the months of August and September 1798. He stood to the north towards Cyprus, and was compelled to run to the south of Crete. 'The wind

continues to the westward. I am sorry to find it almost as prevailing as the trade-winds (July 4) . . . We have just gained sight of Cyprus, nearly the track we followed six weeks ago ; so invariably do the westerly winds prevail at this season (Aug. 19). . . We are still off the island of Rhodes. Our present route is to the northward of Candia (Aug. 28). . . . After contending three days against the adverse winds which are almost invariably encountered here, and getting sufficiently to the northward to have weathered the small islands that lie more immediately between the Archipelago and Candia, the wind set in so strong from the westward, that I was compelled to desist from that passage, and to bear up between Scarpanto and Saxo.'

[4] 'They probably stopped at Sidon for the purposes of trade.'—Smith, p. 23. 'It may be concluded that they put in, because of contrary winds.'—Penrose, MS.

able circumstances, in less than twenty-four hours. In the course of the night they would pass by Ptolemais and Tyre, where St. Paul had visited the Christians two years before.[1] Sidon is the last city on the Phœnician shore in which the Apostle's presence can be traced. It is a city associated, from the earliest times, with patriarchal and Jewish History. The limit of 'the border of the Canaanites' in the description of the peopling of the earth after the Flood (Gen. x. 19),—'the haven of the sea, the haven of ships' in the dim vision of the dying Patriarch (ib. xlix. 13),—the 'great Sidon' of the wars of Joshua (Josh. xi. 8),—the city that never was conquered by the Israelites (Judg. i. 31),—the home of the merchants that 'passed over the sea' (Isa. xxiii.),—its history was linked with all the annals of the Hebrew race. Nor is it less familiarly known in the records of Heathen antiquity. Its name is celebrated both in the Iliad and the Odyssey, and Herodotus says that its sailors were the most expert of all the Phœnicians. Its strong and massive fortifications were pulled down when this coast fell under the sway of the Persians ; but its harbour remained uninjured till a far later period. The Prince of the Druses, with whose strange and brilliant career its more recent history is most closely connected, threw masses of stone and earth into the port, in order to protect himself from the Turks :[2]—and houses are now standing on the spot where the ships of King Louis anchored in the last Crusade,[3] and which was crowded with merchandise in that age, when the Geographer of the Roman Empire spoke of Sidon as the best harbour of Phœnicia.[4]

Nor is the history of Sidon without a close connection with those years in which Christianity was founded. Not only did its inhabitants, with those of Tyre, follow the footsteps of JESUS, to hear His words, and to be healed of their diseases (Luke vi. 17): but the Son of David Himself visited those coasts, and there rewarded the importunate faith of a Gentile suppliant (Matt. xv., Mark vii.) ; and soon the prophecy which lay, as it were, involved in this miracle, was fulfilled by the preaching of Evangelists and Apostles. Those who had been converted during the dispersion which followed the martyrdom of Stephen were presently visited by Barnabas and Saul (Acts xi.). Again, Paul with Barnabas passed through these cities on their return from the first victorious journey among the Gentiles (ib. xv. 3). Nor were these the only journeys which the Apostle had taken through Phœnicia ;[5] so that he well knew, on his arrival from Cæsarea, that Christian brethren were to be found in Sidon. He, doubtless, told Julius that he had 'friends' there, whom he wished to visit ; and, either from special commands which had been given by Festus in favour of St. Paul, or through an influence which the Apostle had already gained over the centurion's mind, the desired permission was granted. If we bear in our remembrance that St. Paul's health was naturally delicate, and that he must have

---

[1] See what has been said above on these two cities, Chap. XX. pp. 564, 565.

[2] A compendious account of Fakriddin will be found in the *Modern Traveller.*

[3] For the history of Sidon during the Middle Ages, see Dr. Robinson's third volume.

[4] Strabo, xvi.

[5] See pp. 332, 333.

suffered much during his long detention at Cæsarea, a new interest
is given to the touching incident, with which the narrative of this
voyage opens, that the Roman officer treated this one prisoner
'courteously, and gave him liberty to go unto his friends to refresh
himself.' We have already considered the military position of this
centurion, and seen that there are good grounds for identifying him
with an officer mentioned by a Heathen historian.[1] It gives an
additional pleasure to such investigations, when we can record our
grateful recollection of kindness shown by him to that Apostle, from
whom we have received our chief knowledge of the Gospel.

On going to sea from Sidon, the wind was unfavourable. Hence,
whatever the weather had been before, it certainly blew from the
westward now. The direct course from Sidon to the 'coasts of
Asia' would have been to the southward of Cyprus, across the sea
over which the Apostle had sailed so prosperously two years before.[2]
Thus when St. Luke says that 'they sailed *under the lee*[3] of Cyprus,
because the winds were contrary,' he means that they sailed to the
north-east and north of the island. If there were any doubt concerning his meaning, it would be made clear by what is said afterwards, that they '*sailed through*[4] the sea which is over against Cilicia
and Pamphylia.' The reasons why this course was taken will be
easily understood by those who have navigated those seas in modern
times. By standing to the north, the vessel would fall in with the
current which sets in a north-westerly direction past the eastern
extremity of Cyprus, and then westerly along the southern coast of
Asia Minor, till it is lost at the opening of the Archipelago.[5] And
besides this, as the land was neared, the wind would draw off the
shore, and the water would be smoother; and both these advantages
would aid the progress of the vessel.[6] Hence she would easily work

---

[1] See the preceding chapter.

[2] See Chap. XX.

[3] This is the strict meaning of the
term. So it is used below, v. 7, and the
sense is the same, v. 16. It is a confusion of geographical ideas to suppose
that a south shore is necessarily meant.
Falconer, who imagines the south coast
of Cyprus to be intended, was misled by
his view of the meaning of the word
'Asia.' They sailed, in fact, so that
the wind blew from the island towards
the ship. The idea of sailing *near* the
coast is no doubt included; but the two
things are distinct.

[4] *Through* or *across*. The meaning
is similar in v. 27. We should observe
the order in which the following words
occur. Cilicia is mentioned first.

[5] 'From Syria to the Archipelago
there is a constant current to the westward, slightly felt at sea, but very perceptible near the shore, along this part
of which [Lycia] it runs with considerable but irregular velocity: between Adratchan Cape and the small
adjacent island we found it one day
almost three miles an hour. . . .

The great body of water, as it moves
to the westward, is intercepted by the
western coast of the Gulf of Adalia;
thus pent up and accumulated, it rushes
with augmented violence towards Cape
Khelidonia, where, diffusing itself in the
open sea, it again becomes equalised.'
Beaufort's *Karamania*, p. 41. See pp.
113, 557. [Of two persons engaged in
the merchant-service, one says that he
has often 'tricked other fruit-vessels'
in sailing westward, by standing to the
north to get this current, while they
took the mid-channel course; the other,
that the current is sometimes so strong
between Cyprus and the main, that he
has known 'a steamer jammed' there,
in going to the East.]

[6] It is said in the *Sailing Directory*
(p. 243), that 'at night the great
northern valley conducts the land-wind
from the cold mountains of the interior
to the sea;' and again (p. 241), that
'Capt. Beaufort, on rounding Cape
Khelidonia, found the land-breezes,
which had generally been from the
west, or south-west, coming down the
Gulf of Adalia from the northward.'

to windward,[1] under the mountains of Cilicia, and through the bay of Pamphylia,—to Lycia, which was the first district in the province of Asia.[2] Thus we follow the Apostle once more across the sea over which he had first sailed with Barnabas from Antioch to Salamis,— and within sight of the summits of Taurus, which rise above his native city,—and close by Perga and Attaleia,—till he came to a Lycian harbour not far from Patara, the last point at which he had touched on his return from the third Missionary journey.

The Lycian harbour, in which the Adramyttian ship came to anchor on this occasion, after her voyage from Sidon, was Myra, a city which has been fully illustrated by some of those travellers whose researches have, within these few years, for the first time provided materials for a detailed geographical Commentary on the Acts of the Apostles.[3] Its situation was at the opening of a long and wonderful gorge, which conducts the traveller from the interior of the mountain-region of Lycia to the sea.[4] A wide space of plain intervened between the city and the port. Strabo says that the distance was twenty stadia, or more than two miles.[5] If we draw a natural inference from the magnitude of the theatre,[6] which remains at the base of the cliffs, and the traces of ruins to some distance across the plain, we should conclude that Myra once held a considerable population : while the Lycian tombs, still conspicuous in the rocks, seem to connect it with a remote period of Asiatic history.[7] We trace it, on the other hand, in a later though hardly less obscure period of history : for in the Middle Ages it was called the port of the Adriatic, and was visited by Anglo-Saxon travellers.[8] This was the period when St. Nicholas, the saint of the modern Greek sailors,—born at Patara, and buried at Myra,—had usurped the honour which those two cities might more naturally have given to the Apostle who anchored in their harbours.[9] In the seclusion of the deep gorge of Dembra is a magnificent Byzantine church,[10]—

---

[1] The vessel would [probably] have to beat up to Myra. This is indicated in the map. The wind is assumed to be N.W.; and the alternate courses marked are about N.N.E. on the larboard tack, and W.S.W. on the starboard tack.

[2] Lycia was once virtually a part of the province of Asia (p. 184); but shortly before the time of St. Paul's voyage to Rome it seems to have been united under one jurisdiction with Pamphylia (p. 186). The period when it was a separate province, with Myra for its metropolis, was much later.

[3] The two best accounts of Myra will be found in Fellows's *Asia Minor*, pp. 194, &c., and Spratt and Forbes's *Lycia*, vol. i. ch. iii.

[4] This gorge is described in striking language, both by Sir C. Fellows and by Spratt and Forbes.

[5] See note 8.

[6] Mr. Cockerell remarks that we may infer something in reference to the population of an ancient city from the size of its theatre. A plan of this theatre is given in Leake's *Asia Minor*, and also in Texier's *Asie Mineure*.

[7] It is well known that there is much difference of opinion concerning the history of Lycian civilisation, and the date of the existing remains.

[8] *Early Travels in Palestine*, quoted by Mr. Lewin, vol. ii. p. 716. It is erroneously said there that Myra was *at that time* the metropolis of Lycia, on the authority of the *Synecdemus*, which belongs to a period much later. The river Andriaki is also incorrectly identified with the Limyrus.

[9] The relics of St. Nicholas were taken to St. Petersburg by a Russian frigate during the Greek revolution, and a gaudy picture sent instead. Sp. & F. Compare Fellows.

[10] See the description of this grand and solitary building, and the vignette,

probably the cathedral of the diocese, when Myra was the ecclesiastical and political metropolis of Lycia.[1] Another building, hardly less conspicuous, is a granary erected by Trajan near the mouth of the little river Andraki.[2] This is the ancient Andriace, which Pliny mentions as the port of Myra, and which is described to us by Appian, in his narrative of the Civil Wars of Rome, as closed and protected by a chain.[3]

Andriace, the port of Myra, was one of the many excellent harbours which abound in the south-western part of Asia Minor. From this circumstance, and from the fact that the coast is high and visible to a great distance,—in addition to the local advantages which we have mentioned above, the westerly current, and the off-shore wind,—it was common for ships bound from Egypt to the westward to be found in this neighbourhood when the winds were contrary.[4] It was therefore a natural occurrence, and one which could have caused no surprise, when the centurion met in the harbour at Myra with an Alexandrian corn-ship on her voyage to Italy (v. 6). Even if business had not brought ther to this coast, she was not really out of her track in a harbour in the same meridian as that of her own port.[5] It is probable that the same westerly winds which had hindered St. Paul's progress from Cæsarea to Myra, had caused the Alexandrian ship to stand to the north.

Thus the expectation was fulfilled, which had induced the centurion to place his prisoners on board the vessel of Adramyttium.[6] That vessel proceeded on her homeward route up the coast of the Ægean, if the weather permitted : and we now follow the Apostle through a more eventful part of his voyage, in a ship which was probably much larger than those that were simply engaged in the coasting trade. From the total number of souls on board (v. 37), and the known fact that the Egyptian merchantmen were among the largest in the Mediterranean,[7] we conclude that she was a vessel of considerable size. Everything that relates to her construction is interesting to us, through the minute account which is given of her misfortunes, from the moment of her leaving Myra. The weather was unfavourable from the first. They were '*many days*' before reaching Cnidus (v. 7) : and since the distance from Myra to this

in Spratt and Forbes. They remark, that ' as Myra was the capital of the bishopric of Lycia for many centuries afterwards, and as there are no remains at Myra itself indicating the existence of a cathedral, we probably behold in this ruin the head-church of the diocese, planted here from motives of seclusion and security.' — vol. i. p. 107.

[1] Hierocl. *Synecd.* See Wesseling's note, p. 684.

[2] The inscription on the granary is given by Beaufort.

[3] See above p. 560, n. 2.

[4] See the references to Socrates, Sozomen, and Philo, in Wetstein. It is possible, as Kuinoel suggests, that the ship might have brought goods from Alexandria to Lycia, and then taken in a fresh cargo for Italy : but not very probable, since she was full of wheat when the gale caught her. [A captain in the merchant-service told the writer, that in coming *from Alexandria in August* he has stood to the north towards Asia Minor, for the sake of the current, and that this is a very common course.]

[5] Mr. Lewin supposes that the plan of Julius was changed, in consequence of this ship being found in harbour here. ' At Myra the centurion most unluckily changed his plan,' &c., vol. ii. p. 716.

[6] See above, p. 631.

[7] A quotation to this effect is given by Wetstein.

place is only a hundred and thirty miles, it is certain that they must have sailed '*slowly*' (ib.). The delay was of course occasioned by one of two causes, by calms or by contrary winds. There can be no doubt that the latter was the real cause, not only because the sacred narrative states that they reached Cnidus[1] '*with difficulty,*' but because we are informed that, when Cnidus was reached, they could not make good their course[2] any further, '*the wind not suffering them*' (ib.). At this point they lost the advantages of a favouring current, a weather shore and smooth water, and were met by all the force of the sea from the westward; and it was judged the most prudent course, instead of contending with a head sea and contrary winds, to run down to the southward, and, after rounding Cape Salmone, the easternmost point of Crete, to pursue the voyage under the lee of that island.[3]

Knowing, as we do, the consequences which followed this step, we are inclined to blame it as imprudent, unless, indeed, it was absolutely necessary. For while the south coast of Crete was deficient in good harbours, that of Cnidus was excellent,—well sheltered from the north-westerly winds, fully supplied with all kinds of stores, and in every way commodious, if needful, for wintering.[4]

And here, according to our custom, we pause again in the narrative, that we may devote a few lines to the history and description of the place. In early times it was the metropolis of the Asiatic Dorians, who worshipped Apollo, their national Deity, on the rugged headland called the Triopian[5] promontory (the modern Cape Crio), which juts out beyond the city to the West. From these heights the people of Cnidus saw that engagement between the fleets of Pisander and Conon, which resulted in the maritime supremacy of

---

[1] The Greek word here is only imperfectly rendered by 'scarce' in the English version. It is the same word which is translated 'hardly' in v. 8, and it occurs again in v. 16.

[2] Their direct course was about W. by S.: and, when they opened the point, they were under very unfavourable circumstances even for beating. The words 'the wind not suffering us,' Mr. Smith understands to mean that the wind would not allow the vessel to hold on her course towards Italy, after Cnidus was passed. So Sir C. Penrose, in whose MS. we find the following: 'The course from Myra towards Italy was to pass close to the Island of Cythera (Cerigo), or the south point of the Morea; the island of Rhodes lying in the direct track. It appears that the ship passed to the northward of that island, having sailed slowly many days from the light and baffling winds, usual in those seas and at that season. Having at last got over against Cnidus (C. Crio), *the wind not suffering them to get on in the direct course*, it having become steady from the west or north-

west, they sailed southwards, till, coming near to the east end of Crete, they passed,' &c.

The words at first sight seem to mean that the wind would not allow them *to put into the harbour of Cnidus*: and so they are understood by Meyer, De Wette, Humphry, and Hackett. But in a case of this kind nautical considerations must be taken into account. A friend remarks in a letter that 'a ship on a weather shore could come to and warp it.' If, however, it were true that they could not get into Cnidus, it would equally follow that the wind was blowing hard from the N.W.

[3] See above.

[4] If the words 'the wind not suffering us' really mean that the wind would not allow them to enter the harbour of Cnidus, these remarks become unnecessary.

[5] For a view of this remarkable promontory, which is the more worthy of notice, since St. Paul passed it twice (Acts xxi. 1, xxvii. 7), see the engraving in the Admiralty Chart, No. 1604.

Athens.[1] To the north-west is seen the island of Cos (pp. 555, 556);
to the south-east, across a wider reach of sea, is the larger island of
Rhodes (p. 557), with which, in their weaker and more voluptuous
days,[2] Cnidus was united in alliance with Rome, at the beginning
of the struggle between Italy and the East.[3] The position of the
city of Cnidus is to the east of the Triopian headland, where a
narrow isthmus unites the promontory with the continent, and
separates the two harbours which Strabo has described.[4] 'Few
places bear more incontestable proofs of former magnificence ; and
fewer still of the ruffian industry of their destroyers. The whole
area of the city is one promiscuous mass of ruins ; among which
may be traced streets and gateways, porticoes and theatres.'[5] But
the remains which are the most worthy to arrest our attention are
those of the harbours : not only because Cnidus was a city peculiarly
associated with maritime enterprise,[6] but because these remains
have been less obliterated by violence or decay. 'The smallest
harbour has a narrow entrance between high piers, and was evidently
the closed basin for triremes, which Strabo mentions.' But it was
the southern and larger port which lay in St. Paul's course from
Myra, and in which the Alexandrian ship must necessarily have
come to anchor, if she had touched at Cnidus. 'This port is formed
by two transverse moles ; these noble works were carried into the
sea to a depth of nearly a hundred feet ; one of them is almost
perfect: the other, which is more exposed to the south-west swell,
can only be seen under water.'[7] And we may conclude our description by quoting from another traveller, who speaks of 'the remains
of an ancient quay on the S.W., supported by Cyclopian walls, and
in some places cut out of the steep limestone rocks, which rise
abruptly from the water's edge.'[8]

This excellent harbour then, from choice or from necessity, was
left behind by the seamen of the Alexandrian vessel. Instead of
putting back there for shelter, they yielded to the expectation of
being able to pursue their voyage under the lee of Crete, and ran
down to Cape Salmone : after rounding which, the same 'difficulty'
would indeed recur (v. 8), but still with the advantage of a weather

---

[1] See above, p. 556.

[2] We can hardly avoid making some
allusion here to the celebrated Venus of
Praxiteles. This object of universal
admiration was at Cnidus when St. Paul
passed by.

[3] It was afterwards made 'a free
city.'

[4] The ruins are chiefly on the east
side of the Isthmus (see Hamilton, as
referred to below). Pausanias says
that the city was divided into two parts
by an *Euripus*, over which a bridge
was thrown; one half being towards
the Triopian promontory, the other towards the east.

[5] Beaufort's *Karamania*, p. 81. The
fullest account of the ruins will be
found in the third volume of the *Transactions of the Dilettanti Society*, and in

Hamilton's *Asia Minor*, vol. i. pp. 39–
45.

[6] It was Sostratus of Cnidus who
built the Pharos of Alexandria. The
same place gave birth to Ctesias and
Agatharchides, and others who have
contributed much to geographical
knowledge.

[7] Here and above we quote from
Beaufort. See his Sketch of the Harbour. The same may be seen in the
Admiralty Chart, No. 1533. Another
chart gives a larger plan of the ruins,
&c. Other references might easily be
given. Perhaps there is no city in Asia
Minor which has been more clearly
displayed, both by description and engravings.

[8] Hamilton, p. 39.

shore. The statements at this particular point of St. Luke's narrative enable us to ascertain, with singular minuteness, the direction of the wind : and it is deeply interesting to observe how this direction, once ascertained, harmonises all the inferences which we should naturally draw from other parts of the context. But the argument has been so well stated by the first writer who has called attention to this question, that we will present it in his words rather than our own.[1] 'The course of a ship on her voyage from Myra to Italy, after she has reached Cnidus, is by the north side of Crete, through the Archipelago, W. by S. Hence a ship which can make good a course of less than seven points from the wind, would not have been prevented from proceeding on her course, unless the wind had been to the west of N.N.W. But we are told that she "ran under Crete, over against Salmone," which implies that she was able to fetch that cape, which bears about S.W. by S. from Cnidus ; but, unless the wind had been to the north of W.N.W., she could not have done so. The middle point between N.N.W. and W.N.W. is north-west, which cannot be more than two points, and is probably not more than one, from the true direction. The wind, therefore, would in common language have been termed north-west.'[2] And then the author proceeds to quote, what we have quoted elsewhere (p. 557, n. 1), a statement from the English Sailing Directions regarding the prevalence of north-westerly winds in these seas during the summer months : and to point out that the statement is in complete harmony with what Pliny says of the Etesian monsoons.

Under these circumstances of weather, a consideration of what has been said above, with the chart of Crete before us, will show that the voyage could have been continued some distance from Cape Salmone under the lee of the island, as it had been from Myra to Cnidus,[3]—but that at a certain point (now called Cape Matala), where the coast trends suddenly to the north, and where the full force of the wind and sea from the westward must have been met, this possibility would have ceased once more, as it had ceased at the south-western corner of the Peninsula. At a short distance to the east of Cape Matala is a roadstead,[4] which was then called 'Fair Havens,' and still retains the same name,[5] and which the voyagers successfully reached and came to anchor. There seems to have been no town at Fair Havens ; but there was a town near it called

[1] For what may be necessary to explain the nautical terms, see the compass on p. 569.

[2] Smith, p. 35.

[3] See above. It is of importance to observe here that the pronoun '*it*' in v. 8 refers not to Salmone, but to *Crete*. With the wind from the N.W. they would easily round the point : but after this they would '*beat up with difficulty along the coast*' to the neighbourhood of Cape Matala.

[4] In our larger editions, a view is given from Schranz's drawing, in Mr. Smith's work.

[5] It is no doubt the same place which

is mentioned by Pococke (ii. 250) under the name of Λιμέονες Κάλους, and also the *Calismene* spoken of in the voyage of Rauwolf (in Ray's Collection), and the *Calis Miniones* of Fynes Morison. In ancient sailing directions, Dutch and French, it is described as 'een schoone baய,—une belle baie.' See all these references in Smith, pp. 30, 38, 44. The place was visited by Mr. Pashley, but is not described by him. Meyer considers the name euphemistic. As regards wintering, the place was certainly 'not commodious,' but as regards shelter from some winds (including N.W.), it was a good anchorage.

Lasæa,[1] a circumstance which St. Luke mentions (if we may presume to say so), not with any view of fixing the locality of the roadstead, but simply because the fact was impressed on his memory.[2] If the vessel was detained long at this anchorage, the sailors must have had frequent intercourse with Lasæa, and the soldiers too might obtain leave to visit it ; and possibly also the prisoners, each with a soldier chained to his arm. We are not informed of the length of the delay at Fair Havens : but before they left the place, a 'considerable time' had elapsed since they had sailed from Cæsarea[3] (v. 9); and they had arrived at that season of the year when it was considered imprudent to try the open sea. This is expressed by St. Luke by saying that 'the fast was already past ;' a proverbial phrase among the Jews, employed as we should employ the phrase ' about Michaelmas,' and indicating precisely that period of the year.[4] The fast of expiation was on the tenth of Tisri, and corresponded to the close of September or the beginning of October ;[5] and is exactly the time when seafaring is pronounced to be dangerous by Greek and Roman writers.[6] It became then a very serious matter of consultation whether they should remain at Fair Havens for the winter, or seek some better harbour. St. Paul's advice was very strongly given that they should remain where they were. He warned them that if they ventured to pursue their voyage they would meet with violent weather,[7] with great injury to the cargo and the ship, and much risk to the lives of those on board. It is sufficient if we trace in this warning rather the natural prudence and judgment of St. Paul than the result of any supernatural revelation : though it is possible that a prophetic power was acting[8] in combination with the insight derived from long experience of ' perils in the sea' (2 Cor.

---

[1] Mr. Smith says that Lasæa is not mentioned by any ancient writer. It is however, probably the Lasia of the Peutingerian Tables, stated there to be sixteen miles to the east of Gortyna.

[We are now able with great satisfaction to state that the city of Lasæa has been discovered. The Rev. G. Brown, with some companions, has recently visited this coast in the yacht St. Ursula ; and a letter written by him from Fair Havens on January 18th, 1856, supplies the following facts. When the party landed at Fair Havens the question was asked, ' Where is Lasæa ? ' to which it was answered at once, that it was now a deserted place about two hours to the eastward, close to Cape Leonda. On receiving this information they ran along the coast before a S.W. wind: and, just after passing the Cape, the eye of one of the party was caught by ' two white pillars standing on a brae-side near the shore.' On approaching and landing, the beach was found to be lined with masses of masonry, and various remains of a considerable town were discovered. The peasants, who came down from the hills, said that the name of the place was Lasea. Cape Leonda lies five miles east of Fair Havens. Mr. Brown's letter has been placed at our disposal by Mr. Smith, who will give fuller details in the second edition of his work on St. Paul's Shipwreck. (This edition is now published. 1861.)]

[2] The allusion is, in truth, an instance of the autoptic style of St. Luke, on which we have remarked in the narrative of what took place at Philippi.

[3] When they left Cæsarea they had every reasonable prospect of reaching Italy before the stormy season : but since then ' much time had been spent.'

[4] Just so Theophrastus reckons from a Heathen festival, when he says 'that the sea is navigable *after the Dionysia.*'

[5] Levit. xvi. 29, xxiii. 27.

[6] Authorities are given in the larger editions.

[7] See v. 10, and v. 21.

[8] Observe the vagueness of the words ' a certain island.'

xi. 26).   He addressed such arguments to his fellow-voyagers as would be likely to influence all : the master[1] would naturally avoid what might endanger the ship : the owner[2] (who was also on board) would be anxious for the cargo : to the centurion and to all, the risk of perilling their lives was a prospect that could not lightly be regarded.   That St. Paul was allowed to give advice at all, implies that he was already held in a consideration very unusual for a prisoner in the custody of soldiers ; and the time came when his words held a commanding sway over the whole crew: yet we cannot be surprised that on this occasion the centurion was more influenced[3] by the words of the owner and the master than those of the Apostle. There could be no doubt that their present anchorage was ' incommodious to winter in' (v. 12), and the decision of ' the majority' was to leave it so soon as the weather should permit.

On the south coast of the island, somewhat farther to the west, was a harbour called Phœnix,[4] with which it seems that some of the sailors were familiar.[5]   They spoke of it in their conversation during

---

[1] The same word is translated ' shipmaster,' in Rev. xviii. 17.

[2] He might be the skipper, or little more than supercargo.

[3] The imperfect tense is used here. [It appears from Mr. Brown's letter that St. Paul's counsel was not unwise, even in the nautical sense. For further details we must again refer to Mr. Smith's second edition. We may just add that Mr. Brown was told at Lutro, that the 'Holy Apostle Paul' had visited *Calolimounias* and baptized many people there ; and that near the latter place he saw the ruins of a monastery bearing the Apostle's name.]

[4] So the name is written by St. Luke and by Strabo.   See below.   The name was probably derived from the palmtrees, which are said by Theophrastus and Pliny to be indigenous in Crete.

[5] At the time when Mr. Smith's work was published, our information regarding the coast of Crete was very imperfect ; and he found it to be the general impression of several officers acquainted with the navigation of those seas [and the writer of this note may add that he has received the same impression from persons engaged in the merchant-service, and familiar with that part of the Levant], that there are no ship-harbours on the south side of the island. Mr. Smith's conviction, however, was that at Lutro there was a harbour satisfying all the conditions, and the writer of this note was enabled, in April 1852, to confirm this conviction in a very satisfactory manner.   The Admiralty drawings of the south coast of Crete had just then arrived, and the soundings of Lutro were decisive.   These were exhibited in our earlier editions from a tracing made at the Admiralty. The position of the harbour is shown by the anchor in the chart opposite p. 642.

Previously, however, Mr. Smith had received a letter from Mr. Urquhart, M.P., alluding to what occurred to him, when on board a Greek ship of war and chasing a pirate.   ' Lutro is an admirable harbour.   You open it like a box; unexpectedly, the rocks stand apart, and the town appears within . . . . We thought we had cut him off, and that we were driving him right upon the rocks.   Suddenly he disappeared ;— and, rounding in after him, like a change of scenery, the little basin, its shipping and the town presented themselves. . . . Excepting Lutro, all the roadsteads looking to the southward are perfectly exposed to the south or east.' For a view of Lutro, see Pashley's *Travels in Crete.*

[The earlier part of this note remains as it was in the first edition.   It is confirmed in every particular by Mr. Brown's letter.   In the first place, when they were in search of Lutro, *they ran past it,* partly because of an error in the chart, and partly because ' *the port in question makes no appearance from the sea.*'   Next, on reaching the place and inquiring from an old Greek what was its ancient name, ' he replied, without hesitation, *Phœniki,* but that the old city exists no longer.'   A Latin inscription relating to the Emperor Nerva (who was of Cretan extraction), is mentioned as being found on the

the delay at Fair Havens, and they described it as ' looking[1] toward the south-west wind and the north-west wind.' If they meant to recommend a harbour, into which these winds blew dead on shore, it would appear to have been unsailorlike advice : and we are tempted to examine more closely whether the expression really means what at first sight it appears to mean, and then to inquire further whether we can identify this description with any existing harbour. This might indeed be considered a question of mere curiosity,—since the vessel never reached Phœnix,—and since the description of the place is evidently not that of St. Luke, but of the sailors, whose conversation he heard.[2] But everything has a deep interest for us which tends to elucidate this voyage. And, first, we think there cannot be a doubt, both from the notices in ancient writers and the continuance of ancient names upon the spot, that Phœnix is to be identified with the modern Lutro.[3] This is a harbour which is *sheltered* from the winds above-mentioned : and without entering fully into the discussions which have arisen upon this subject, we give it as our opinion that the difficulty is to be explained, simply by remembering that sailors speak of everything from their own point of view, and that such a harbour does ' look '

point which defends the harbour on the south. The harbour itself is described thus : ' We found the shores steep and perfectly clean. There are fifteen fathoms in the middle of the harbour, diminishing gradually to two close to the village. As the beach is extremely narrow, and the hills immediately behind steep and rocky, the harbour cannot have altered its form materially since the days of the Apostle.' The health-officer said, that ' though the harbour is open to the East, yet the easterly gales never blow home, being *lifted* by the high land behind ; and that even in storms the sea rolls in gently (*piano, piano*) . . . . *it is the only secure harbour, in all winds, on the south coast of Crete* ; and, during the wars between the Venetians and the Turks, as many as twenty and twenty-five war galleys have found shelter in its waters.'

Further interest is given to this narrative by the circumstance that this yachting party was caught by the Euroclydon (see below, p. 644), so that some of them who landed were unable to rejoin the vessel, and detained a night on shore. The sailors said that it was ' no wonder that St. Paul was blown off the coast in such weather' (see p. 644), and they added that ' no boat could have boarded them in such a sea ' (see p. 645).

It is a curious fact that this same party, on returning from Alexandria, were again caught in a gale on this coast, on February 19th, 1856, and obliged to run with three-reefed mainsail and fore-staysail into the harbour of Lutro, where, the writer says, ' we spent as quiet a night as if we were in a mill-pond. It is a small place,' he continues, ' and it was queer, in looking up the after companion, to see olive-trees and high rocks overhanging the taffrail.']

[1] This is the literal meaning of the original, which is inadequately translated in the English version.

[2] Observe the parenthetic way in which the description of Phœnix is introduced, v. 12.

[3] The details are given in the larger editions. Moreover Strabo says that Phœnix is in the narrowest part of Crete, which is precisely true of Lutro; and the longitudes of Ptolemy harmonise with the same result. See Smith, p. 51.

The chart on the opposite page is taken from Mr. Smith's work, with some modifications. The part near Lutro is corrected from the tracing mentioned above. The spot marked ' Spring and Church of St. Paul' is from the English Admiralty survey. The cape marked ' C. St. Paul' is so named on the authority of Lapie's map and last French government chart of the eastern part of the Mediterranean. The physical features are after Lapie and Pashley. For a notice of St. Paul's fountain, see Pashley, ii. 259.

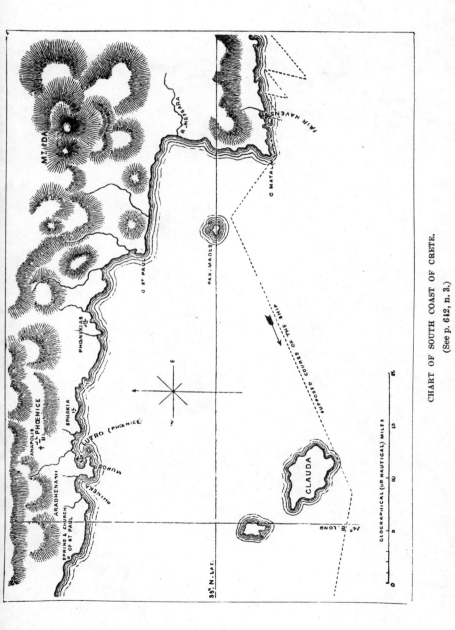

CHART OF SOUTH COAST OF CRETE.

(See p. 612, n. 3.)

—from the water towards the land which incloses it—in the direction
of ' south-west and north-west.'[1]

With a sudden change of weather, the north-westerly wind
ceasing, and a light air springing up from the south, the sanguine
sailors ' thought that their purpose was already accomplished'
(v. 13). They weighed anchor : and the vessel bore round Cape
Matala. The distance to this point from Fair Havens is four or five
miles : the bearing is W. by S. With a gentle southerly wind she
would be able to weather the cape : and then the wind was fair to
Phœnix, which was thirty-five miles distant from the cape, and bore
from thence about W.N.W. The sailors already saw the high land
above Lutro, and were proceeding in high spirits,—perhaps with
fair-weather sails set,[2]—certainly with the boat towing astern,[3]—
forgetful of past difficulties, and blind to impending dangers.

The change in the fortunes of these mariners came without a
moment's warning.[4] Soon after weathering Cape Matala, and, while
they were pursuing their course in full confidence, close by the coast
of Crete[5] (v. 13), a violent wind came down[6] from the mountains,
and struck the ship (seizing her, according to the Greek expression,
and whirling her round), so that it was impossible for the helmsman
to make her keep her course.[7] The character of the wind is described in terms expressive of the utmost violence. It came with all
the appearance of a hurricane :[8] and the name ' Euroclydon,' which

---

[1] It seems strange that this view
should not have occurred to the commentators. For discussion regarding
the Greek preposition used here, we
must refer to the larger editions.

Such a harbour would have been very
' commodious to winter in ; ' and it
agrees perfectly with Lutro, as de-
lineated in the recent survey. To have
recommended a harbour *because* the
south-west and north-west winds blew
into it would have been folly. But
whether the commentators felt this or
not, they have generally assumed that
the harbour was open to these winds.

[2] See what is said below in reference
to *lowering the gear*, v. 17.

[3] This is certain, from v. 16.

[4] Their experience, however, might
have taught them that there was some
cause for fear. Capt. J. Stewart, R.N.
(as quoted by Mr. Smith, p. 60) observes, in his remarks on the Archipelago : ' It is always safe to anchor
under the lee of an island with a
northerly wind, as it dies away gradually ; but it would be extremely dangerous *with southerly winds, as they
almost invariably shift to a violent
northerly wind.*' [During the revision
of these pages for the press (March 4,
1856), the following communication
from Capt. Spratt was received in a
letter from Mr. Smith : ' We left Fair

Havens with a light southerly wind
and clear sky—everything indicative
of a fine day, until we rounded the
cape to haul up for the head of the bay.
Then we saw Mount Ida covered with
a dense cloud, and met a strong northerly breeze (one of the summer gales,
in fact, so frequent in the Levant, but
which in general are accompanied by
terrific gusts and squalls from those
high mountains), the wind blowing
direct from Mount Ida.']

[5] The verb is in the imperfect.

[6] The Greek here denotes that the
wind came ' *down from it,*' i.e. *Crete,*
not ' *against it,*' i.e. the ship. [Sir
C. Penrose, without reference to the
Greek, speaks of the wind as ' *descending from the lofty hills* in heavy squalls
and eddies, and driving the now almost
helpless ship far from the shore, with
which her pilots vainly attempted to
close.']

[7] Literally ' to look at the wind.'
See above, p. 627. We see the additional emphasis in the expression, if
we remember that an eye was painted
on each side of the bow, as we have
mentioned above. Even now the '*eyes*'
of a ship is a phrase used by English
sailors for the bow.

[8] ' A *typhonic* wind.' [See above,
n. 4.]

was given to it by the sailors, indicates the commotion in the sea which presently resulted.[1] The consequence was, that, in the first instance, they were compelled to scud before the gale.[2]

If we wish to understand the events which followed, it is of the utmost consequence that we should ascertain, in the first place, the direction of this gale. Though there is a great weight of opinion in favour of the reading *Euroaquilo*, in place of *Euroclydon*,[3]—a view which would determine, on critical grounds, that the wind was E.N.E.,—we need not consider ourselves compelled to yield absolutely to this authority : and the mere context of the narrative enables us to determine the question with great exactitude. The wind came *down from the island* and drove the vessel *off the island* : whence it is evident that it could not have been southerly.[4] If we consider further that the wind struck the vessel when she was *not far*[5] from Cape Matala (v. 14),—that it drove her *towards Clauda*[6] (v. 16), which is an island about twenty miles to the S.W. of that point,—and that the sailors 'feared' lest it should drive them *into the Syrtis*[7] on the African coast (v. 17),—all which facts are mentioned in rapid succession,—an inspection of the chart will suffice to show us that the point from which the storm came must have been N.E., or rather to the East of N.E.,—and thus we may safely speak of it as coming from the E.N.E.[8]

---

[1] Whatever we may determine as to the etymology of the word *Euroclydon*, it seems clear that the term implies a violent agitation of the water.

[2] 'We let her drive.'

[3] Mr. Smith argues in favour of another reading which denotes a N.E. wind. But we have a strong impression that *Euroclydon* is the correct reading. The addition of the words 'which was called' seems to us to show that it was a name popularly given by the sailors to the wind; and nothing is more natural than that St. Luke should use the word which he heard the seamen employ on the occasion. Besides it is the more difficult reading.

[4] Falconer supposes that the wind came from the southward, and clumsily attempts to explain why (on this supposition) the vessel was not driven on the Cretan coast.

[5] The use of the imperfect shows that they were sailing near the shore when the gale seized the vessel. Thus we do not agree with Mr. Smith in referring 'not long after' to the time when they were passing round Cape Matala, but to the time of leaving Fair Havens. The general result, however, is the same. [It appears from Capt. Spratt's information, that a ship can stand quite close to Cape Matala.]

[6] There is no difficulty in identifying Clauda. It is the Claudos of Ptolemy and the *Synecdemus*, and the Gaudus of Pomponius Mela. Hence the modern Greek *Gaudonesi*, and the Italian corruption into *Gozo*.

[7] We may observe here, once for all, that the Authorised Version, 'the quicksands,' does not convey the accurate meaning. The word denotes the notoriously dangerous bay between Tunis and the eastern part of Tripoli.

[8] These arguments are exhibited with the utmost clearness by Mr. Smith. Adopting the reading Εὐρακύλων, he has three independent arguments in proof that the wind was E.N.E.¼N. ; (1) the etymological meaning of the word; (2) the fact that the vessel was driven to Clauda, from a point a little west of C. Matala ; (3) the fear of the sailors lest they might be driven into the Syrtis.

The view of Admiral Penrose is slightly different. He supposes that the wind began from some of the northern points, and drew gradually to the eastward, as the ship gained an offing ; and continued nearly at East, varying occasionally a point or two to the North or South. He adds that a Levanter, when it blows with peculiar violence some points to the North of East, is called a Gregalia [compare '*which is called* Euroclydon '], and that he had seen many such.

We proceed now to inquire what was done with the vessel under these perilous circumstances. She was compelled at first (as we have seen) to scud before the gale. But three things are mentioned in close connection with her coming near to Clauda, and *running under the lee of it.*[1] Here they would have the advantage of a temporary lull and of comparatively smooth water for a few miles :[2] and the most urgent necessity was attended to first. *The boat was hoisted on board* : but after towing so long, it must have been nearly filled with water : and under any circumstances the hoisting of a boat on board in a gale of wind is a work accomplished ' *with difficulty.*' So it was in this instance, as St. Luke informs us. To effect it at all, it would be necessary for the vessel to be rounded-to, with her head brought towards the wind ;[3] a circumstance which, for other reasons (as we shall see presently), it is important to bear in mind. The next precaution that was adopted betrays an apprehension less the vessel should spring a leak, and so be in danger of foundering at sea.[4]

---

[1] See ver. 16, 17.

[2] ' The ship, still with her boat towing at her stern, was however enabled to run under the lee of Clauda, a small island about twenty miles from the south coast of Crete, and with some rocks adjacent, affording the advantage of smooth water for about twelve or fifteen miles, while the ship continued under their lee. Advantage was taken of this comparative smooth water, with some difficulty to hoist the boat into the ship, and also to take the further precaution of undergirding her by passing cables or other large ropes under the keel and over the gunwales, and then drawing them tight by means of pullies and levers.'—Penrose, MS. It is interesting to observe the coincidence of this passage with what is said by Mr. Smith.

Sir C. Penrose proceeds to mention another reason for the vessel being undergirded. ' This wise precaution was taken, not only because the ship, less strongly built than those in modern days, might strain her planks and timbers and become leaky, but from the fears, that if the gale continued from the North-East, as it probably began, they might be driven into the deep bight on the coast of Africa, where were situated the greater and lesser Syrtis, so much dreaded by the ancients, and by these means of security be enabled to keep together longer, should they be involved in the quicksands.'

[3] Smith, p. 64.

[4] Frapping would be of little use in stopping a leak. It was rather a precaution to prevent the working of the planks and timbers : and thus, since the extensive application of iron in modern ship-building, this contrivance has rarely been resorted to. Besides the modern instances adduced by Mr. Smith, the writer has heard of the following : (1) A Canadian timber vessel in the year 1846 came frapped to Aberdeen. (2) In 1809 or 1810, a frigate (the ' Venus ? ') came home from India with hawsers round her. (3) The same happened to a merchant vessel which came from India, apparently in the same convoy. (4) Lord Exmouth (then Captain Pellew) brought home the 'Arethusa' in this state from Newfoundland. (5) At the battle of Navarin, the ' Albion ' man-of-war received so much damage during the action, that it became necessary to have recourse to frapping, and the vessel had chain cables passed round her under the keel, which were tightened by others passed horizontally along the sides interlacing them; and she was brought home in this state to Portsmouth. See the next note.

[Since the publication of the first edition, two other instances have come to the writer's knowledge. One is that of the barque 'Highbury,' which is stated in the *Royal Cornwall Gazette* of May 26, 1854, to have just arrived in this state, i.e. ' with a chain cable round the ship's bottom,' off the Lizard Point, after a voyage of five months, from Port Adelaide, with a cargo of copper ore, wool, and gold. The other case is described by the captain of the ship, as follows : ' I sailed from St. Stephen, New Brunswick, on the 12th Dec. 1837, in the schooner "St. Croix,' 53 tons, bound for Kingston, Jamaica with cargo of boards in the hold and shingles on deck, with a few spars. On

They used the tackling, which we have described above, and which provided 'helps' in such an emergency. They '*undergirded*' the ship with ropes passed round her frame and tightly secured on deck.[1] And after this, or rather simultaneously (for, as there were many hands on board, these operations might all be proceeding together), they '*lowered the gear.*' This is the most literal translation of the Greek expression.[2] In itself it is indeterminate : but it doubtless implies careful preparation for weathering out the storm. What precise change was made we are not able to determine, in our ignorance of the exact state of the ship's gear at the moment. It might mean that the mainsail was reefed and set ;[3] or that the great yard[4] was lowered upon deck and a small storm sail hoisted. It is certain that what English seamen call the top-hamper[5] would be sent down on deck. As to those fair-weather sails themselves, which may have been too hastily used on leaving Fair Havens, if not taken in at the beginning of the gale they must have been already blown to pieces.

the 20th of same month encountered a severe gale from S.W., and *lay to for seven days* [see below, p. 647]. On the 26th shipped a heavy sea, which took away about one third of deck load; found the balance shifting from side to side, top of vessel spreading, that the seams in water-ways were open from one and a half to two inches, much water running down the seams. Found it necessary, for the preservation of crew and vessel, and balance of deck load, to secure top of ship; took a coil of four-inch Manilla rope, commenced forward, passing it round and round the vessel, after which cut up some spars, made heavers, and hove the warp as tight as possible. Fearing the warp would chafe off and part, took one of the chains, passed it round and before with tackles and heavers, and secured the top of the vessel, so that the leak in the water-ways was partially stopped. In this state I reached Port Royal, when I took off the warp and chain, and arrived at Kingston on the 12th Jan. 1838. Had I not taken the means I did, I am of opinion the vessel could not have been got into port.']

[1] Among classical instances we may select Thucyd. i. 29, where Dr. Arnold says, in his note, that 'the Russian ships taken in the Tagus in 1808 were kept together in this manner, in consequence of their age and unsound condition.'

[2] The same verb is used below (v. 30) in reference to lowering the boat into the water.

[3] This suggestion is partly due to a criticism in the *English Review* (June 1850, Notice of Mr. Smith's work),

based on Isaiah xxxiii. 23 (LXX.). In reference to which passage, we may remark that the verb is equally applicable to the spreading of a sail which is lowered from a yard, and to the lowering of a yard with whatever belongs to it. The reviewer lays stress on the circumstance that St. Paul's ship had probably no sail set when she reached Clauda ; and, as he justly remarks, the Alexandrian origin o í the Septuagint version should be recollected.

[4] Such is Mr. Smith's view.

[5] i.e. the gear connected with the fair-weather sails. See Smith, p. 69. We are here allowed to quote from a letter addressed to Mr. Smith by Capt. Spratt, R.N. After saying that the translation of the word into 'gear' is borne out by its application among the modern Greek sailors to the ropes, &c., he proceeds: 'Ships so rigged as those of the ancients, with only one large square sail, would require very heavy mast-head gear ; i.e. very large ropes rove there, to support the yard and sail ; so that, even when the latter was lowered, considerable top-weight would remain, to produce much uneasiness of motion as well as resistance to the wind. Two such combined evils would not be overlooked by sailors, who had a thought about drifting on a lee shore. Presuming the main-sail and yard to be down, and the vessel snug under a storm-sail, the heavy σκευή, or ropes, being no longer of use aloft, would naturally be unrove or lowered, to prevent drift, as a final resource, when the sailors saw that the gale was likely to be strong and lasting.'

But the mention of one particular apprehension, as the motive of this last precaution, informs us of something further. It was because they *feared lest they ' should be driven into the Syrtis,'* that they ' lowered the gear.' Now to avoid this danger, the head of the vessel must necessarily have been turned away from the African coast, in the direction (more or less) from which the wind came. To have scudded before the gale under bare poles, or under storm-sails, would infallibly have stranded them in the Syrtis,—not to mention the danger of pooping, or being swamped by the sea break-ing over her stern. To have anchored was evidently impossible. Only one course remained : and this was what is technically called by sailors *lying-to.* To effect this arrangement, the head of the vessel is brought as near to the wind as possible : a small amount of canvas is set, and so adjusted, as to prevent the vessel from falling off into the trough of the sea.[1] This plan (as is well known to all who have made long voyages) is constantly resorted to when the object is not so much to make progress, as to weather out a gale.

We are here brought to the critical point of the whole nautical difficulty in the narrative of St. Paul's voyage and shipwreck, and it is desirable to notice very carefully both the ship's position in re-ference to the wind and its consequent motion through the water. Assuming that the vessel was *laid-to,* the questions to be answered in reference to its position are these : How near the wind did she lie ? and which side did she present to the wind? The first question is answered in some degree by a reference to what was said in the early part of this chapter.[2] If an ancient merchantman could go ahead in moderate weather, when within seven points of the wind, we may assume that she would make about the same angle with it when lying-to in a gale.[3] The second question would be practically determined by the circumstances of the case and the judgment of the sailors. It will be seen very clearly by what follows, that if the ship had been laid-to with her left or port side to the wind, she must have drifted far out of her course, and also in the direction of another part of the African coast. In order to make sure of sea-room, and at the same time to drift to the westward, she must have been laid-to with her right side to the wind, or *on the starboard tack,*—the position which she was probably made to assume at the moment of taking the boat on board.[4]

[1] i.e. the hull of the vessel is in a direction oblique to the length of the wave. The following extract from Falconer's *Marine Dictionary,* under the article *Trying* (an equivalent term), may be useful to those who are not familiar with sea-phrases:—'The in-tent of spreading a sail at this time is to keep the ship more steady ; and, by pressing her side down in the water, to prevent her from rolling violently ; and also to turn her bow towards the direc-tion of the wind, so that the shock of the waves may fall more obliquely on her flank than when she lies along the trough of the sea. . . . . In this position she advances very little ac-cording to the line of her length, but is driven considerably to the leeward.'

[2] See p. 627.

[3] It is not to be understood, how-ever, that the same absolute position in reference to the wind is continually maintained. When a ship is laid-to in a gale, a kind of vibration takes place. To use the technical expression, *she comes up and falls off*—oscillating per-haps between five points and nine points.

[4] See Smith, pp. 64, 68, and compare

We have hitherto considered only the ship's position in reference to the wind. We must now consider its motion. When a vessel is laid-to, she does not remain stationary, but *drifts*: and our inquiries of course have reference to the rate and direction of the drift. The *rate* of drift may vary, within certain limits, according to the build of the vessel and the intensity of the gale : but all seamen would agree, that, under the circumstances before us, a mile and a half in the hour, or thirty-six miles in twenty-four hours, may be taken as a fair average. [1] The *direction* in which she drifts is not that in which she appears to sail, or towards which her bows are turned : but she falls off to leeward : and to the angle formed by the line of the ship's keel and the line in which the wind blows we must add another, to include what the sailors call *lee-way* : [2] and this may be estimated on an average at six points (67°). Thus we come to the conclusion that the direction of drift would make an angle of thirteen points (147°) with the direction of the wind. If the wind was E. N. E., the course of the vessel would be W. by N. [3]

We have been minute in describing the circumstances of the ship at this moment ; for it is the point upon which all our subsequent conclusions must turn. [4] Assuming now that the vessel was, as we

the following: ' I ought to assign the reason why I consider the ship to have drifted with her starboard side toward the wind, or on the starboard tack, as a sailor expresses it. When the South wind blew softly, the ship was slowly sailing along the coast of Crete, with her starboard side towards the land, or to the North. . . . . The storm came on her starboard side, and in this manner, with her head to the West-ward, she drifted, first to the South-West under Clauda, and as the wind drew more to the Eastward her head pointed more towards the North, the proper tack to keep farther from the quicksands, whether adopted from ne-cessity or from choice.'—Penrose, MS.

[1] See the two naval authorities quo-ted by Mr. Smith, p. 84. The same estimate is given in the MS. of Admiral Penrose. 'Allowing the degree of strength of the gale to vary a little occasionally, I consider that a ship would drift at the rate of about a mile and a half per hour.'

[2] A reference to the compass on p. 569, with the following extracts from Falconer's *Marine Dictionary*, will make the meaning clear. ' LEE-WAY is the lateral movement of a ship to lee-ward of her course, or the angle which the line of her way makes with the keel when she is closehauled. This movement is produced by the mutual effort of the wind and sea upon her side, forcing her to leeward of the line on which she appears to sail.' ' CLOSE-

HAULED (*au plus près*, Fr.). The gene-ral arrangement of a ship's sails, when she endeavours to make a progress in the nearest direction possible towards that point of the compass from which the wind bloweth. . . . . In this manner of sailing the keel commonly makes an angle of six points with the line of the wind. The angle of leeway, however, enlarges in proportion to the increase of the wind and sea.'

[3] Again, our two authorities are in substantial agreement. ' Supposing the Levanter (as is most probable, it being most usual) after the heavy Gregalia, which first drove the ship off the coast of Crete, and under the lee of Clauda, took upon the average the direction of East,—the mean direction of the drift of such a ship, lying-to, as before de-scribed, would be between W.N.W. and W. by N.; and such is nearly the bearing of the North coast of Malta from the South side of Clauda.'—Pen-rose, MS. Compare Smith.

[4] It is at this point especially that we feel the importance of having St. Paul's voyage examined in the light of practical seamanship. The two inves-tigators, who have so examined it, have now enabled us to understand it clearly, though all previous commentators were at fault, and while the ordinary charts are still full of error and confusion. The sinuosities in this part of the voy-age, as exhibited in the common maps of St. Paul's travels, are only an indi-cation of the perplexity of the com-

have said, laid-to on the larboard tack, with the boat on board and
the hull undergirded, drifting from Clauda in a direction W. by N.
at the rate of thirty-six miles in twenty-four hours, we pursue the
narrative of the voyage, without anticipating the results to which we
shall be brought.   The more marked incidents of the second and
third days of the gale are related to us (ver. 18, 19).   The violence
of the storm continued without any intermission.[1]   On 'the day
after' they left Clauda, 'they proceeded to lighten[2] the ship' by
throwing overboard whatever could be most easily spared.   From
this we should infer that the precaution of undergirding had been
only partially successful, and that the vessel had already sprung a
leak.   This is made still more probable by what occurred on the
'third day.'   Both sailors and passengers united[3] in throwing out
all the 'spare gear' into the sea.[4]   Then followed 'several days'
of continued hardship and anxiety.[5]   No one who has never been in
a leaking ship in a continued gale[6] can know what is suffered under
such circumstances.   The strain both of mind and body—the incessant demand for the labour of all the crew—the terror of the
passengers—the hopeless working at the pumps—the labouring of
the ship's frame and cordage—the driving of the storm—the be-
numbing effect of the cold and wet,—make up a scene of no ordinary confusion, anxiety, and fatigue.   But in the present case these
evils were much aggravated by the continued overclouding of the sky
(a circumstance not unusual during a Levanter), which prevented the

pilers.   The course from Clauda to
Malta did not deviate far from a
straight line.

[1] 'We being exceedingly tossed with
the tempest.'

[2] We should observe that the tense
is imperfect here, as contrasted with
the aorist in the next verse.   It denotes
'they began to lighten,' or perhaps,
'they kept lightening.'

[3] 'We cast out with our own hands.'
Observe the change from the third
person to the first.   St. Luke's hands,
and probably St. Paul's, aided in this
work.

[4] We cannot determine precisely
what is meant here by the 'tackle' or
'gear' of the ship.   Mr. Smith thinks
the mainyard is meant, 'an immense
spar, probably as long as the ship, and
which would require the united efforts
of passengers and crew to launch overboard,'—adding that 'the relief which
a ship would experience by this would
be of the same kind as in a modern
ship when the guns are thrown overboard.'   But would sailors in danger
of foundering willingly lose sight of
such a spar as this, which would be
capable of supporting thirty or forty
men in the water ?

[5] The narrative of the loss of the
'Ramillies' supplies a very good illus-

tration of the state of things on board
St. Paul's vessel during these two days.
'At this time she had six feet of water
in the hold, and the pumps would not
free her, the water having worked out
all the oakum.   The admiral therefore
gave orders for all the buckets to be
remanned, and *every officer to help* towards freeing the ship: this enabled
her to sail on. . . . . . *In the
evening* it was found necessary to dis-
pose of the forecastle and aftermost
quarter-deck guns, together with some
of the shot and other articles of very
great weight ; and *the frame of the
ship having opened during the night,*
the admiral was next morning prevailed
upon, by the renewed and pressing remonstrances of his officers, to allow *ten
guns more* to be thrown overboard.   The
ship still continuing to open very much,
the admiral ordered tarred canvas and
hides to be nailed fore and aft, from
under the cills of the ports on the main
deck and on the lower deck.   *Her increasing damage requiring still more to
be done,* the admiral directed all the
guns on the upper deck, the shot, both
on that and the lower deck, *with various heavy stores,* to be thrown overboard.'

[6] 'No small tempest lay on us.'

navigators from taking the necessary observations of the heavenly bodies. In a modern ship, however dark the weather might be, there would always be a light in the binnacle, and the ship's course would always be known : but in an ancient vessel, 'when neither sun nor stars were seen for many days,' the case would be far more hopeless. It was impossible to know how near they might be to the most dangerous coast. And yet the worst danger was that which arose from the leaky state of the vessel. This was so bad, that at length they gave up all hope of being saved, thinking that nothing could prevent her foundering.[1] To this despair was added a further suffering from want of food,[2] in consequence of the injury done to the provisions, and the impossibility of preparing any regular meal. Hence we see the force of the phrase[3] which alludes to what a casual reader might suppose an unimportant part of the suffering, the fact that there was 'much abstinence.' It was in this time of utter weariness and despair that to the Apostle there rose up 'light in the darkness :' and that light was made the means of encouraging and saving the rest. While the Heathen sailors were vainly struggling to subdue the leak, Paul was praying ; and God granted to him the lives of all who sailed with him. A vision was vouchsafed to him in the night, as formerly, when he was on the eve of conveying the

---

[1] 'All hope that we should be saved was then taken away.'

[2] Mr. Smith illustrates this by several examples. We may quote an instance from a very ordinary modern voyage between Alexandria and Malta, which presents some points of close resemblance in a very mitigated form :—

'The commander came down, saying the night was pitch dark and rainy, with symptoms of a regular gale of wind. This prediction was very speedily verified. A violent shower of hail was the precursor, followed by loud peals of thunder, with vivid flashes of forked lightning, which played up and down the iron rigging with fearful rapidity. . . . . She presently was struck by a sea which came over the paddle-boxes, soon followed by another, which, coming over the forecastle, effected an entrance through the sky-lights, and left four feet of water in the officers' cabin. *The vessel seemed disabled by this stunning blow* ; the bowsprit and fore part of the ship were for some moments under water, and the officer stationed at that part of the ship described her as appearing during that time to be evidently sinking, and declared that for many seconds he saw only sea. The natural buoyancy of the ship at last allowed her to right herself, and *during the short lull* (of three minutes) *her head was turned, to avoid the danger of running too near*

the coast of Lybia, *which to the more experienced was the principal cause of alarm* ; for had the wheels given way, which was not improbable from the strain they had undergone, nothing could have saved us, though we had been spared all other causes for apprehension. . . . . With daylight the fearful part of the hurricane gave way, and we were now in the direction of Candia, no longer indeed contending against the wind, but the sea still surging and impetuous, and no lull taking place during twelve hours, to afford the opportunity of regaining our tack, from which we had deviated about 150 miles. *The sea had so completely deluged the lower part of the ship, that it was with difficulty that sufficient fire could be made to afford us even coffee for breakfast. Dinner was not to be thought of.*' —Mrs. Damer's *Diary in the Holy Land*, vol. ii.

[3] 'After long abstinence.' See below, the narrative of the meal at daybreak, ver. 33, 34. The commentators have done little to elucidate this, which is in fact no difficulty to those who are acquainted with sea-voyages. The strangest comment is in a book, which devotionally is very useful,—*Lectures on St. Paul*, by the late Rev. H. Blunt, of Chelsea,—who supposes that a *religious fast* was observed by the crew during the storm.

Gospel from Asia to Europe, and more recently in the midst of those harassing events, which resulted in his voyage from Jerusalem to Rome. When the cheerless day came, he gathered the sailors round him[1] on the deck of the labouring vessel, and, raising his voice above the storm, said :—

Acts xxvii.

21 Sirs, ye should have hearkened to my counsel, and not have set sail from Crete : thus would you have been spared[2] this harm[3] and loss.

22 And now I exhort you to be of good cheer : for there shall be no loss of any man's life among you, 23 but only of the ship. For there stood by me this night an angel of God, whose I am, and whom I 24 serve,[4] saying, '*Fear not, Paul ; thou must stand before Cæsar : and, lo ! God hath given thee all who sail* 25 *with thee.*' Wherefore, Sirs, be of good cheer : for I believe God, that what hath been declared unto me 26 shall come to pass. Nevertheless, we must be cast upon a certain island.

We are not told how this address was received. But sailors, however reckless they may be in the absence of danger, are peculiarly open to religious impressions : and we cannot doubt that they gathered anxiously round the Apostle, and heard his words as an admonition and encouragement from the other world ; that they were nerved for the toil and difficulty which was immediately before them, and prepared thenceforward to listen to the Jewish prisoner as to a teacher sent with a divine commission.

The gale still continued without abatement. Day and night succeeded, and the danger seemed only to increase : till fourteen days had elapsed, during which they had been ' drifting through the sea of Adria'[5] (v. 27). A gale of such duration, though not very frequent, is by no means unprecedented in that part of the Mediterranean, especially towards winter.[6] At the close of the

---

[1] 'Paul stood forth in the midst of them.'

[2] The verb means '*to be spared,*' not '*to gain.*' (A. V.) We should observe that St. Paul's object in alluding to the correctness of his former advice, is not to taunt those who had rejected it, but to induce them to give credit to his present assertions.

[3] The *harm* was to their persons, the *loss* to their property.

[4] Compare Rom. i. 9, and note.

[5] By this is meant, as we shall see presently, that division of the Mediterranean which lies between Sicily and Malta on the west, and Greece with Crete on the east. See above, p. 625, n. 8, and p. 628, n. 4.

[6] The writer has heard of easterly and north-easterly gales lasting for a

still longer period, both in the neighbourhood of Gibraltar and to the eastward of Malta. A captain in the merchant service mentions a fruit vessel near Smyrna hindered for a fortnight from loading by a gale from the N.E. She was two days in beating up a little bay a mile deep. He adds, that such gales are prevalent there winter. Another case is that of a vessel bound for Odessa, which was kept three weeks at Milo with an easterly gale. This, also, was late in the year (October). A naval officer writes thus : —'About the same time of the year, in 1839, I left Malta for the Levant in the "Hydra," a powerful steam frigate, and encountered *Euroclydon* (or, as we call it, a Levanter) in full force. I think we were four days without

fourteenth day, about the middle of the night the sailors suspected that they were nearing land.[1] There is little doubt as to
what were the indications of land. The roar of breakers is a
peculiar sound, which can be detected by a practised ear,[2] though
not distinguishable from the other sounds of a storm by those who
have not 'their senses exercised' by experience of the sea. When
it was reported that this sound was heard by some of the crew,
orders were immediately given to heave the lead, and they found
that the depth of the water was 'twenty fathoms.' After a short
interval, they sounded again, and found ' fifteen fathoms.' Though
the vicinity of land could not but inspire some hope, as holding out
the prospect of running the ship ashore[3] and so being saved, yet the
alarm of the sailors was great when they perceived how rapidly they
were shoaling the water. It seems also that they now heard breakers
ahead.[4] However this might be, there was the utmost danger lest
the vessel should strike and go to pieces. No time was to be lost.
Orders were immediately given to clear the anchors. But, if they
had anchored by the bow, there was good ground for apprehending
that the vessel would have swung round and gone upon the rocks.
They therefore let go ' four anchors *by the stern.*' For a time, the
vessel's way was arrested: but there was too much reason to fear
that she might part from her anchors and go ashore, if indeed
she did not founder in the night : and ' they waited anxiously for
the day.'

The reasons are obvious why she anchored by the stern, rather
than in the usual mode. Besides what has been said above, her

being able to sit down at table to a
meal; during which time we saw
"neither sun nor stars." Happily she
was a powerful vessel, and we forced
her through it, being charged with despatches, though with much injury to
the vessel. Had we been a mere log
on the water, like St. Paul's ship, we
should have drifted many days.'

[We extract the following from the
Christian Observer for May 1853, pp.
324, 325 : 'Late in the autumn of 1848
we were returning from Alexandria to
Malta, and met the wild Euroclydon.
The sea was crested with foam over all
the wide waste of waters, and a dull
impervious canopy of misty cloud was
drawn over the sky. A vessel which
preceded us had been *fifty-six days
from Alexandria to Malta*; and just in
the same way St. Paul's vessel was reduced to lie-to in the gale and drifted
for fourteen days across the sea which
separates Crete from Malta. . . . .
Under the modern name of a Levanter,
the same Euroclydon which dashed
down from the gullies of the Cretan Ida
in the autumn of 60 A.D., swept the sea
in the autumn of 1848, ...
just in the same way veering round

from North to Easterly. . . . . .
Just in the same way, likewise, did our
Euroclydon exhaust itself in a violent
fall of rain.']

[1] This might be translated literally :
' The sailors thought they were about
to *fetch* some land.' Mr. Smith (p. 78)
truly remarks, that this is an instance
of ' the graphic language of seamen,
to whom the ship is the principal object.'

[2] It is hardly likely that they *saw*
the breakers. To suppose that they became aware of the land by the smell of
fragrant gardens (an error found in a
recent work) is absurd; for the wind
blew from the ship towards the land.

[3] ' They can now adopt the last resource for a sinking ship and run her
ashore : but to do so before it was day
would have been to have rushed on certain destruction : they must bring the
ship, if it be possible, to anchor, and
hold on till daybreak,' &c.—Smith,
p. 88.

[4] Mr. Smith (p. 91) seems to infer
this from the words ' fearing lest we
should have fallen upon rocks.' But
the words would rather imply that the
fear was a general one.

way would be more easily arrested, and she would be in a better position for being run ashore[1] next day. But since this mode of anchoring has raised some questions, it may be desirable, in passing, to make a remark on the subject. That a vessel *can* anchor by the stern is sufficiently proved (if proof were needed) by the history of some of our own naval engagements. So it was at the battle of the Nile. And when ships are about to attack batteries, it is customary for them to go into action prepared to anchor in this way. This was the case at Algiers. There is still greater interest in quoting the instance of Copenhagen, not only from the accounts we have of the precision with which each ship let go her anchors astern as she arrived nearly opposite her appointed station,[2] but because it is said that Nelson stated after the battle, that he had that morning been reading the twenty-seventh chapter of the Acts of the Apostles.[3] But, though it will be granted that this manœuvre is possible with due preparation, it may be doubted whether it could be accomplished in a gale of wind on a lee shore, without any previous notice. The question in fact is, whether ancient ships in the Mediterranean were always *prepared* to anchor in this way. Some answer to this doubt is supplied by the present practice of the Levantine caiques, which preserve in great measure the traditionary build and rig of ancient merchantmen. These modern Greek vessels may still be seen anchoring by the stern in the Golden Horn at Constantinople, or on the coast of Patmos.[4] But the best illustration is afforded by one of the paintings of Herculaneum, which represents 'a ship so strictly cotemporaneous with that of St. Paul, that there is nothing impossible in the supposition, that the artist had taken his subject from that very ship, on loosing from the pier at Puteoli.'[5] There is this additional advantage to be obtained from an inspection of this rude drawing, that we see very clearly how the rudders would be in danger of interfering with this mode of anchoring,—a subject to which our attention will presently be required.[6] Our supposed objector, if he had a keen sense of practical difficulties, might still insist that to have anchored in this way (or indeed in the ordinary way) would have been of little avail in St. Paul's ship: since it could not be supposed that the anchors would have held in such a gale of wind. To this we can only reply, that this course was adopted to meet a dangerous emergency. The sailors could not have been certain of the result.

[1] We must carefully observe that, in anchoring,—besides the proximate cause, viz. the fear of falling on rocks to leeward,—'they had also an ulterior object in view, which was to run the ship ashore as soon as daylight enabled them to select a spot where it could be done with a prospect of safety : for this purpose the very best position in which the ship could be was to be anchored by the stern.'—Smith, p. 92.

[2] See Southey's *Life of Nelson* : ' All the line-of-battle ships were to anchor by the stern, abreast of the different vessels composing the enemy's line·

and for this purpose they had already prepared themselves with cables out of their stern ports.'

[3] This anecdote is from a private source, and does not appear in any of the printed narratives of the battle.

[4] The first of these instances is supplied by a naval officer ; the second by a captain who has spent a long life in the merchant-service.

[5] A drawing of this is given by Mr. Smith (p. 94), and from him in our larger editions.

[6] See v. 40.

They might indeed have had confidence in their cables : but they could not be sure of their holding ground.

This is one of the circumstances which must be taken into account, when we sum up the evidence in proof that the place of shipwreck was Malta. At present we make no such assumption. We will not anticipate the conclusion, till we have proceeded somewhat further with the narrative. We may, however, ask the reader to pause for a moment, and reconsider what was said of the circumstances of the vessel, when we described what was done under the lee of Clauda. We then saw that the direction in which she was drifting was W. by N. Now an inspection of the chart will show us that this is exactly the bearing of the northern part of Malta from the south of Clauda. We saw, moreover, that she was drifting at the rate of about a mile and a half in every hour, or thirty-six miles in the twenty-four hours. Since that time thirteen days had elapsed : for the first of the 'fourteen days' would be taken up on the way from Fair Havens to Clauda.[1] The ship therefore had passed over a distance of about 468 miles. The distance between Clauda and Malta is rather less than 480 miles. The coincidence[2] is so remarkable, that it seems hardly possible to believe that the land, to which the sailors on the fourteenth night 'deemed that they drew nigh,'—the 'certain island' on which it was prophesied that they should be cast,—could be any other place than Malta. The probability is overwhelming. But we must not yet assume the fact as certain : for we shall find, as we proceed, that the conditions are very numerous, which the true place of shipwreck will be required to satisfy.

We return then to the ship, which we left labouring at her four anchors. The coast was invisible, but the breakers were heard in every pause of the storm. The rain was falling in torrents ;[3] and all hands were weakened by want of food. But the greatest danger was lest the vessel should founder before daybreak. The leak was rapidly gaining, and it was expected that each moment might be the last. Under these circumstances we find the sailors making a selfish attempt to save themselves, and leave the ship and the passengers to their fate. Under the pretence of carrying out some anchors

---

[1] All that happened after leaving Fair Havens before the ship was undergirded and laid-to, must evidently have occupied a great part of the day.

[2] In the general calculation Mr. Smith and Sir C. Penrose agree with one another ; and the argument derives great force from the slight difference between them. Mr. Smith (pp. 83–89) makes the distance 476·6 miles, and the time occupied thirteen days one hour and twenty-one minutes. With this compare the following : 'Now, with respect to the distance, allowing the degree of strength of the gale to vary a little occasionally, I consider that a ship would drift at the rate of about one mile and a half per hour, which, at the

end of fourteen complete days, would amount to 504 miles ; but it does not appear that the calculation is to be made for fourteen entire days ; it was on the fourteenth night the anchors were cast off the shores of Melita. The distance from the S. of Clauda to the N. of Malta, measured on the best chart I have, is about 490 miles ; and is it possible for coincident calculations, of such a nature, to be more exact ? In fact, on one chart, after I had calculated the supposed drift, as a seaman, to be 504 miles, I measured the distance to be 503.'

[3] See xxviii. 2, 'because of the present rain.'

from the bow, they lowered the boat over the ship's side (v. 30). The excuse was very plausible, for there is no doubt that the vessel would have been more steady if this had been done ; and, in order to effect it, it would be necessary to take out anchors in the boat. But their real intention was to save their own lives and leave the passengers.[1] St. Paul penetrated their design, and either from some divine intimation of the instruments which were to be providentially employed for the safety of all on board,—or from an intuitive judgment, which showed him that those who would be thus left behind, the passengers and soldiers, would not be able to work the ship in any emergency that might arise,—he saw that, if the sailors accomplished their purpose, all hope of being saved would be gone.[2] With his usual tact, he addressed not a word to the sailors, but spoke to the soldiers and his friend the centurion ;[3] and they, with military promptitude, held no discussion on the subject, but decided the question by immediate action. With that short sword, with which the Roman legions cleft their way through every obstacle to universal victory, they 'cut the ropes ;' and the boat fell off,[4] and, if not instantly swamped, drifted off to leeward into the darkness, and was dashed to pieces on the rocks.

Thus the prudent counsel of the Apostle, seconded by the prompt action of the soldiers, had been the means of saving all on board. Each successive incident tended to raise him, more and more, into a position of overpowering influence.[5] Not the captain or the ship's crew, but the passenger and the prisoner, is looked to now as the source of wisdom and safety. We find him using this influence for the renewal of their bodily strength, while at the same time he turned their thoughts to the providential care of God. By this time the dawn of day was approaching.[6] A faint light showed more of the terrors of the storm, and the objects on board the ship began to be more distinctly visible. Still, towards the land, all was darkness, and their eyes followed the spray in vain as it drifted off to leeward. A slight effort of imagination suffices to bring before us an impressive spectacle, as we think of the dim light just showing the haggard faces of the 276 persons,[7] clustered on the deck, and holding on by the bulwarks of the sinking vessel. In this hour of

---

[1] 'About to (seeking to) flee out of the ship.'

[2] 'Unless these remain in the ship, ye cannot be saved.' We observe that in the '*ye*' the soldiers are judiciously appealed to on the source of their own safety. Much has been very unnecessarily written on the mode in which this verse is to be harmonised with the unconditional assurance of safety in ver. 22–24. The same difficulty is connected with every action of our lives. The only difference is, that, in the narrative before us, the Divine purpose is more clearly indicated, whereas we usually see only the instrumentality employed.

[3] 'To the centurion and to the soldiers.'

[4] 'Let her fall off.' In the words above ('when they had lowered the boat into the sea') it is clear that the boat, which was hoisted on deck at the beginning of the gale, had been half-lowered from the davits.

[5] The commanding attitude of St. Paul in this and other scenes of the narrative is forcibly pointed out by the Reviewer of Mr. Smith's work in the *North British Review* for May 1849.

[6] 'While the day was coming on,' v. 39.

[7] It is at this point of the narrative that the total number of souls on board is mentioned.

anxiety the Apostle stands forward to give them courage. He reminds them that they had 'eaten nothing' for fourteen days ; and exhorts them now to partake of a hearty meal, pointing out to them that this was indeed essential to their safety,[1] and encouraging them by the assurance that 'not a hair[2] of their head' should perish. So speaking, he set the example of the cheerful use of God's gifts and grateful acknowledgment of the Giver, by taking bread, 'giving thanks to God before all,' and beginning to eat. Thus encouraged by his calm and religious example, they felt their spirits revive,[3] and 'they also partook of food,' and made themselves ready for the labour which awaited them.[4]

Instead of abandoning themselves to despair, they proceeded actively to adopt the last means for relieving the still sinking vessel. The cargo of wheat was now of no use. It was probably spoilt by the salt water. And however this might be, it was not worth a thought ; since it was well known that the vessel would be lost. Their hope now was to run her on shore and so escape to land. Besides this, it is probable that, the ship having been so long in one position, the wheat had shifted over to the port side, and prevented the vessel from keeping that upright position, which would be most advantageous when they came to steer her towards the shore.[5] The hatchways were therefore opened, and they proceeded to throw the grain into the sea. This work would occupy some time ; and when it was accomplished, the day had dawned, and the land was visible.[6]

The sailors looked hard at the shore, but they could not recognise it.[7] Though ignorant, however, of the name of the coast, off which they were anchored, they saw one feature in it which gave them a hope that they might accomplish their purpose of running the ship

---

[1] 'This is for your safety.'

[2] Our Lord uses the same proverbial expression, Luke xxi. 18.

[3] 'Then were they all of good cheer.'

[4] 'All hands now, crew and passengers, bond or free, are assembled on the deck, anxiously wishing for day, when Paul, taking advantage of a smaller degree of motion [would this necessarily be the case ?] in the ship than when drifting with her side to the waves, recommends to them to make use of this time, before the dawn would require fresh exertions, in making a regular and comfortable meal, in order to refresh them after having so long taken their precarious repasts, probably without fire or any kind of cooking. He begins by example, but first, by giving God thanks for their preservation hitherto, and hopes of speedy relief. Having thus refreshed themselves, they cast out as much of the remaining part of the cargo (wheat) as they could, to enable them by a lighter draft of water either to run into any small harbour, or at least closer in with dry land, should they be obliged to run the ship on the rocks or beach.'—Penrose, MS.

[5] The following extract from Sir C. Penrose's papers supplies an addition to Mr. Smith's remarks: 'With respect to throwing the wheat into the sea after anchoring, it may be remarked, that it was not likely that, while drifting, the hatchways could have been opened for that purpose ; and, when anchored by the stern, I doubt not that it was found, that, from the ship having been so long pressed down on one side, the cargo had shifted, i.e. the wheat had pressed over towards the larboard side, so that the ship, instead of being upright, heeled to the larboard, and made it useful to throw out as much of the wheat as time allowed, not only to make her specifically lighter, but to bring her upright, and enable her to be more accurately steered and navigated towards the land at daybreak.'

[6] 'When it was day.'

[7] The tense is imperfect (v. 39). 'They tried to recognise it, but could not.' The aorist is used below in xxviii. 1, from which it appears that the island was recognised immediately on landing.

aground. They perceived a small bay or indentation, with a sandy or pebbly beach :[1] and their object was, 'if possible,' so to steer the vessel that she might take the ground at that point. To effect this, every necessary step was carefully taken. While cutting the anchors adrift, they unloosed the lashings with which the rudders had been secured,[2] and hoisted the foresail.[3] These three things would be done simultaneously,[4] as indeed is implied by St. Luke ; and there were a sufficient number of hands on board for the purpose. The free use of the rudders would be absolutely necessary : nor would this be sufficient without the employment of some sail.[5] It does not appear quite certain whether they exactly hit the point at which they aimed.[6] We are told that they fell into 'a place between two seas' (a feature of the coast, which will require our consideration presently), and there stranded the ship. The bow stuck fast in the shore and remained unmoved ; but the stern began immediately to go to pieces[7] under the action of the sea.

And now another characteristic incident is related. The soldiers, who were answerable with their lives for the detention of their prisoners, were afraid lest some of them should swim out and escape ; and therefore, in the spirit of true Roman cruelty, they proposed to kill them at once. Now again the influence of St. Paul over the centurion's mind[8] was made the means of saving both his own life and that of his fellow-prisoners. For the rest he might care but little ; but he was determined to secure Paul's safety.[9] He therefore prevented the soldiers from accomplishing their heartless intention, and directed[10] those who could swim to 'cast themselves into the sea' first, while the rest made use of spars and broken pieces of the wreck. Thus it came to pass that all escaped safely[11] through the breakers to the shore.

When the land was safely reached, it was ascertained that the

---

[1] It is important to observe that the word for '*shore*' here has this meaning, as opposed to a rocky coast. We may refer in illustration to Matt. xiii. 2 ; Acts xxi. 5.

[2] When they anchored, no doubt the paddle rudders had been hoisted up and lashed, lest they should foul the anchors.

[3] For the proof that ἀρτέμων is the foresail, we must refer to the able and thorough investigation in Mr. Smith's Dissertation on Ancient Ships, pp. 153–162. The word does not occur in any other Greek writer, but it is found in the old nautical phraseology of the Venetians and Genoese, and it is used by Dante and Ariosto. The French still employ the word, but with them it has become the mizensail, while the mizen has become the foresail. [See the woodcut on the title-page.]

[4] The word, which implies this in the original, is omitted in A.V.

[5] 'The mainsail [foresail] being hoisted showed good judgment, though

the distance was so small, as it would not only enable them to steer more correctly than without it, but would press the ship further on upon the land, and thus enable them the more easily to get to the shore.'—Penrose, MS. [See the following passage in a naval officer's letter, dated 'H.M.S. ——, off the Katcha, Nov. 15,' in the *Times* of Dec. 5, 1855. 'The *Lord Raglan* (merchant-ship) is on shore, but taken there in a most sailor-like manner. Directly her captain found he could not save her, he cut away his mainmast and mizen, and, *setting a topsail on her foremast, ran her ashore stem on.*']

[6] See below.

[7] Imperfect.

[8] See v. 43.

[9] 'To save Paul to the end,' literally.

[10] The military officer gives the order. The ship's company are not mentioned. Are we to infer that they fell into the back-ground, in consequence of their cowardly attempt to save themselves ?

[11] The same strong verb is used in xxvii. 44, xxviii. 1, 4, as in xxvii. 43.

island on which they were wrecked was Melita. The mere word does not absolutely establish the identity of the place: for two islands were anciently called alike by this name. This, therefore, is the proper place for summing up the evidence which has been gradually accumulating in proof that it was the modern Malta. We have already seen (p. 654) the almost irresistible inference which follows from the consideration of the direction and rate of drift since the vessel was laid-to under the lee of Clauda. But we shall find that every succeeding indication not only tends to bring us to the shore of this island, but to the very bay (the Cala di San Paolo) which has always been the traditionary scene of the wreck.

In the first place we are told that they became aware of land *by the presence of breakers, and yet without striking.* Now, an inspection of the chart will show us that a ship drifting W. by N. might approach Koura point, the eastern boundary of St. Paul's Bay, without having fallen in previously with any other part of the coast: for, towards the neighbourhood of Valetta, the shore trends rapidly to the southward.[1] Again, the character of this point, as described in the Sailing Directions, is such that there must infallibly have been violent breakers upon it that night.[2] Yet a vessel drifting W. by N. might pass it, within a quarter of a mile, without striking on the rocks. But what are the soundings at this point? They are now *twenty fathoms.* If we proceed a little further we find *fifteen fathoms.* It may be said that this, in itself, is nothing remarkable. But if we add, that the fifteen fathom depth is *in the direction of the vessel's drift* (W. by N.) from the twenty fathom depth, the coincidence is startling.[3] But at this point we observe, on looking at the chart, that now there would be *breakers ahead,*—and yet at such a distance ahead, that there would be *time for the vessel to anchor,* before actually striking on the rocks.[4] All these conditions must necessarily be fulfilled ; and we see that they are fulfilled without any attempt at ingenious explanation. But we may proceed further. The character of the coast on the farther side of the bay is such, that though the greater part of it is fronted with mural precipices, there are one or two indentations,[5] which exhibit the appearance of ' *a creek with a [sandy or pebbly] shore.'* And again we observe that the island of Salmonetta is so placed, that the sailors, looking from the deck when the vessel was at anchor, could not possibly be aware that it was not a continuous part of the mainland'; whereas, while they were running her aground, they could not help observing the opening of the channel, which would thus appear (like the Bosphorus[6]) ' *a place between two seas,'* and would be more likely to

---

[1] See the chart opposite.

[2] Smith, pp. 79, 89. ' With north-easterly gales, the sea breaks upon this point with such violence, that Capt. Smyth, in his view of the headland, has made the breakers its distinctive character.'

[3] Smith, p. 91.

[4] Ibid.

[5] One place, at the opening of the Mestara Valley (see chart) has still this character. At another place there

has been a beach, though it is now obliterated. See the remarks of Mr. Smith, who has carefully examined the bay, and whose authority in any question relating to the geology of coasts is of great weight.

[6] This illustration is from Strabo, who uses the very word of the Bosphorus. It would, of course, be equally applicable to a neck of land between two seas, like the Isthmus of Corinth.

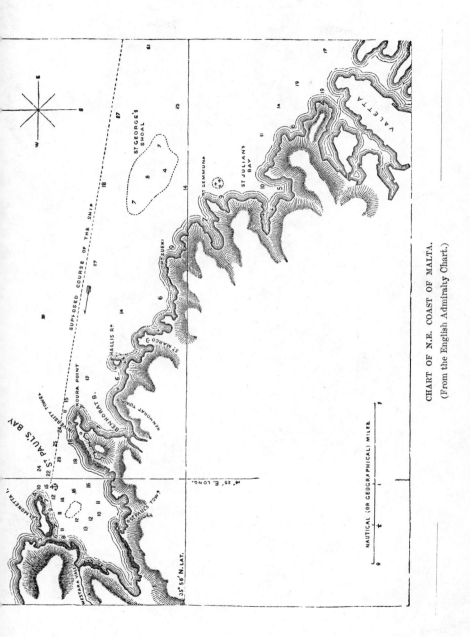

CHART OF N.E. COAST OF MALTA.

(From the English Admiralty Chart.)

attract their attention if some current resulting from this juxta-position of the island and the coast interfered with the accuracy of their steering.[1]   And finally, to revert to the fact of the anchors holding through the night (a result which could not confidently be predicted), we find it stated, in our English Sailing Directions,[2] that the ground in St. Paul's Bay is so good, that, '*while the cables hold, there is no danger, as the anchors will never start.*'

Malta was not then the densely crowded island which it has become during the last half-century.[3]   Though it was well known to the Romans as a dependency of the province of Sicily,[4] and though the harbour now called Valetta must have been familiar to the Greek mariners who traded between the East and the West,[5]— much of the island was doubtless uncultivated and overrun with wood.   Its population was of Phœnician origin,—speaking a language which, as regards social intercourse, had the same relation to Latin and Greek, which modern Maltese has to English and Italian.[6]   The inhabitants, however, though in this sense[7] 'barbarians,' were favourably contrasted with many Christian wreckers in their reception of those who had been cast on their coast.   They showed them no 'ordinary kindness;' for they lighted a fire and welcomed them all to the warmth, drenched and shivering as they were in the rain and the cold.   The whole scene is brought very vividly before us in the sacred narrative.   One incident has become a picture in St. Paul's life, with which every Christian child is familiar.   The Apostle had gathered with his own hand a heap of sticks and placed them on the fire, when a viper came 'out of the heat' and fastened on his hand.   The poor superstitious people, when they saw this, said to one another, 'This man must be a murderer : he has escaped from the sea : but still vengeance suffers him not to live.'   But Paul threw off the animal into the fire and suffered no harm.   Then they watched him, expecting that his body would become swollen, or

[1] Though we are not to suppose that by 'two seas' two moving bodies of water, or two opposite currents, are meant, yet it is very possible that there might be a current between Salmonetta and the coast, and that this affected the steering of the vessel.

[2] Purdy, p. 180.   In reference to what happened to the ship when she came aground (v. 4), Mr. Smith lays stress upon the character of the deposits on the Maltese coast.   The ship 'would strike a bottom of mud, graduating into tenacious clay, into which the fore-part would fix itself, and be held fast, whilst the stern was exposed to the force of the waves.'—p. 104.

[3] The density of the Maltese popula-tion, at the present day, is extraordi-nary ; but this state of things is quite recent.   In Boisgelin (*Ancient and Modern Malta*, 1805) we find it stated that in 1530 the island did not contain quite 15,000 inhabitants, and that they were reduced to 10,000 at the raising

of the siege in the grand-mastership of La Valetta.   Notwithstanding the subsequent wars, and the plagues of 1592 and 1676, the numbers in 1798 were 90,000. (vol. i. pp. 107, 108.) Simi-lar statements are in Miège, *Histoire de Malte.*

[4] The mention of it in Cicero's *Ver-rine Orations* is well known.

[5] Diodorus Siculus speaks of the manufactures of Malta, of the wealth of its inhabitants, and of its handsome buildings, such as those which are now characteristic of the place.   We might also refer to Ovid and Cicero.

[6] See the Essay on Mr. Smith's work in the *North British Review* (p. 208) for some remarks on the Maltese lan-guage, especially on the Arabic name of what is still called the Apostle's foun-tain (*Ayn-tal-Ruzzul*).

[7] It is sufficient to refer to Rom. i. 14 ; 1 Cor. xiv. 11 ; Col. iii. 11 ; for the meaning of the word in the N. T

that he would suddenly fall down dead. At length, after they had watched for a long time in vain, and saw nothing happen to him, their feelings changed as violently as those of the Lystrians had done in an opposite direction ;[1] and they said that he was a god. We are not told of the results to which this occurrence led, but we cannot doubt that while Paul repudiated, as formerly at Lystra, [2] all the homage which idolatry would pay to him, he would make use of the influence acquired by this miracle, for making the Saviour known to his uncivilised benefactors.

St. Paul was enabled to work many miracles during his stay in Malta. The first which is recorded is the healing of the father of Publius, the governor of the island,[3] who had some possessions[4] near the place where the vessel was lost, and who had given a hospitable reception to the shipwrecked strangers, and supplied their wants for three days. The disease under which the father of Publius was suffering was dysentery in an aggravated form.[5] St. Paul went in to him and prayed, and laid his hands on him : and he recovered. This being noised through the island, other sufferers came to the Apostle and were healed. Thus he was empowered to repay the kindness of these islanders by temporal services intended to lead their minds to blessings of a still higher kind. And they were not wanting in gratitude to those, whose unexpected visit had brought so much good among them. They loaded them with every honour in their power, and, when they put to sea again, supplied them with everything that was needful for their wants (v. 10).

Before we pursue the concluding part of the voyage, which was so prosperous that hardly any incident in the course of it is recorded, it may be useful to complete the argument by which Malta is proved to be the scene of St. Paul's shipwreck, by briefly noticing some objections which have been brought against this view. It is true that the positive evidence already adduced is the strongest refutation of mere objections ; but it is desirable not to leave unnoticed any of the arguments which appear to have weight on the other side. Some of them have been carelessly brought together by a great writer, to whom, on many subjects, we might be glad to yield our assent.[6] Thus it is argued, that, because the

---

[1] See p. 155.　　[2] p. 153.

[3] We observe that the name is Roman. In the phrase used here there is every appearance of an official title, more especially as the father of the person called ' first of the island ' was alive. And inscriptions containing this exact title are said to have been found in the island.

[4] Acts xxviii. 7. These possessions must therefore have been very near the present country residence of the English Governor, near Citta Vecchia.

[5] xxviii. 8.

[6] 'The belief that Malta is the island on which St. Paul was wrecked is so rooted in the common Maltese, and is

cherished with such a superstitious nationality, that the government would run the chance of exciting a tumult, if it, or its representatives, unwarily ridiculed it. The supposition itself is quite absurd. Not to argue the matter at length, consider these few conclusive facts :—The narrative speaks of the " barbarous people," and " barbarians," of the island. Now, our Malta was at that time fully peopled and highly civilised, as we may surely infer from Cicero and other writers. A viper comes out from the sticks upon the fire being lighted : the men are not surprised at the appearance of the snake, but imagine first a murderer, and then a

ST. PAUL'S BAY, MALTA.

(From a Drawing by J. Smith, Esq., of Jordan Hill.)

vessel is said to have been drifting in the Adriatic, the place of shipwreck must have been, not Malta to the south of Sicily, but Meleda in the Gulf of Venice. It is no wonder that the Benedictine of Ragusa[1] should have been jealous of the honour of his order, which had a convent on that small island. But it is more surprising that the view should have been maintained by other writers since.[2] For not only do the classical poets[3] use the name 'Adria' for all that natural division of the Mediterranean which lies between Sicily and Greece, but the same phraseology is found in historians and geographers. Thus Ptolemy distinguishes clearly between the Adriatic Sea and the Adriatic Gulf. Pausanias says that the Straits of Messina unite the Tyrrhene Sea with the Adriatic Sea; and Procopius[4] considers Malta as lying on the boundary of the latter. Nor are the other objections more successful. It is argued that Alexandrian sailors could not possibly have been ignorant of an island so well known as Malta was then. But surely they might have been very familiar with the harbour of Valetta, without being able to recognise that part of the coast on which they came during the storm. A modern sailor who had made many passages between New York and Liverpool might yet be perplexed if he found himself in hazy weather on some part of the coast of Wales.[5] Besides, we are told that the seamen did recognise the island as soon as they were ashore.[6] It is contended also that the people of Malta would not have been called barbarians. But, if the sailors were Greeks (as they probably were), they would have employed this term, as a matter of course, of those who spoke a different language from their own.[7] Again it is argued that there are no vipers—that there is hardly any wood—in Malta. But who does not recognise here the natural changes which result from the increase of inhabitants[8] and cultivation? Within a very few years there was wood

god, from the harmless attack. Now, in our Malta, there are, I may say, no snakes at all; which, to be sure, the Maltese attribute to St. Paul's having cursed them away. Melita in the Adriatic was a perfectly barbarous island as to its native population, and was, and is now, infested with serpents. Besides, the context shows that the scene is in the Adriatic.'—Coleridge's *Table Talk*, p. 185.

[1] Padre Georgi, however, was not the first who suggested that the Apostle was wrecked on Melida in the Adriatic. We find this mistaken theory in a Byzantine writer of the tenth century. [Very recently the same view has been advocated, but quite inconclusively, in Mr. Neale's *Ecclesiological Notes on Dalmatia*, 1861.]

[2] Mr. Smith has effectually disposed of all Bryant's arguments, if such they can be called. See especially his Dissertation on the island Melita. Among those who have adopted Bryant's view,

we have referred by name only to Falconer.

[3] Ovid, for instance, and Horace.

[4] Thucydides speaks of the Adriatic Sea in the same way. We should also bear in mind the shipwreck of Josephus, which took place in 'Adria.' Some (e.g. Mr. Sharpe, the author of the *History of Egypt*) have identified the two shipwrecks: but it is difficult to harmonise the narratives.

[5] Even with charts he might have a difficulty in recognising a part of the coast, which he had never seen before. And we must recollect that the ancient mariner had no charts.

[6] xxviii. 1.

[7] See above, p. 659, n. 7.

[8] See above, note on the population of Malta. Sir C. Penrose adds a circumstance, which it is important to take into account in considering this question, viz. that, in the time of the Knights, the bulk of the population was at the east end of the island, and that the neighbourhood of St. Paul's

close to St. Paul's Bay;[1] and it is well known how the Fauna of any country varies with the vegetation.[2] An argument has even been built on the supposed fact, that the disease of Publius is unknown in the island. To this it is sufficient to reply by a simple denial.[3] Nor can we close this rapid survey of objections without noticing the insuperable difficulties which lie against the hypothesis of the Venetian Meleda, from the impossibility of reaching it, except by a miracle, under the above-related circumstances of weather,[4]—from the disagreement of its soundings with what is required by the narrative of the shipwreck,[5]—and from the inconsistency of its position with what is related of the subsequent voyage.[6]

To this part of the voyage we must now proceed. After three months they sailed again for Italy in a ship called the 'Castor and Pollux.'[7] Syracuse was in their track, and the ship put into that famous harbour, and stayed there three days. Thus St. Paul was in a great historic city of the West, after spending much time in those of greatest note in the East. We are able to associate the Apostle of the Gentiles and the thoughts of Christianity with the scenes of that disastrous expedition which closed the progress of the Athenians towards our part of Europe,—and with those Punic Wars, which

---

Bay was separated off by a line of fortification, built for fear of descents from Barbary cruisers.

[1] This statement rests on the authority of an English resident on the island.

[2] Some instances are given by Mr. Smith.

[3] It happens that the writer once spent an anxious night in Malta with a fellow-traveller, who was suffering precisely in the same way.

[4] 'If Euroclydon blew in such a direction as to make the pilots afraid of being driven on the quicksands (and there were no such dangers but to the south-west of them), how could it be supposed that they could be driven north towards the Adriatic? In truth, it is very difficult for a well-appointed ship of modern days to get from Crete into and up the Adriatic at the season named in the narrative, the north winds being then prevalent, and strong. We find the ship certainly driven from the south coast of Crete, from the Fair Havens towards Clauda (now Gozzi), on the south-west, and during the fourteen days' continuance of the gale, we are never told that Euroclydon ceased to blow; and with either a Gregalia or Levanter blowing hard, St. Paul's ship could not possibly have proceeded up the Adriatic.'—Penrose, MS. He says again: 'How is it possible that a ship at that time, and so circumstanced,

could have got up the difficult navigation of the Adriatic? To have *drifted* up the Adriatic to the island of Melita or Melida, in the requisite curve, and to have passed so many islands and other dangers in the route, would, humanly speaking, have been impossible. The distance from Clauda to this Melita is not less than 780 geographical miles, and the wind must have long been from the south to make this voyage in fourteen days. Now, from Clauda to Malta, there is not any one danger in a direct line, and we see that the distance and direction of drift will both agree.'

[5] This is clearly shown on the Austrian chart of that part of the Adriatic.

[6] From the Adriatic Melida it would have been more natural to have gone to Brundusium or Ancona, and thence by land to Rome; and, even in going by sea, Syracuse would have been out of the course, whereas it is in the direct track from Malta.

[7] It is natural to assume that such was its name, if such was its 'sign,' i.e. the sculptured or painted figures at the prow. It was natural to dedicate ships to the Dioscuri, who were the hero-patrons of sailors. They were supposed to appear in those lights which are called by modern sailors the fires of St. Elmo; and in art they are represented as stars. See below on the coins of Rhegium.

ended in bringing Africa under the yoke of Rome. We are not told whether St. Paul was permitted to go on shore at Syracuse; but from the courtesy shown him by Julius, it is probable that this permission was not refused. If he landed, he would doubtless find Jews and Jewish proselytes in abundance, in so great a mercantile emporium ; and would announce to them the Glad-tidings which he was commissioned to proclaim 'to the Jew first and also to the Gentile.' Hence we may without difficulty give credit to the local tradition, which regards St. Paul as the first founder of the Sicilian church.

Sailing out of that beautiful land-locked basin, and past Ortygia, once an island,[1] but then united in one continuous town with the buildings under the ridge of Epipolæ,—the ship which carried St. Paul to Rome shaped her course northwards towards the straits of Messina. The weather was not favourable at first : they were compelled to take an indirect course,[2] and they put into Rhegium, a city whose patron divinities were, by a curious coincidence, the same hero-protectors of seafaring men, 'the Great Twin Brethren,' to whom the ship itself was dedicated.[3]

Here they remained one day (v. 13), evidently waiting for a fair wind to take them through the Faro ; for the springing up of a wind from the south is expressly mentioned in the following words. This wind would be favourable, not only for carrying the ship through the straits, but for all the remainder of the voyage. If the vessel was single-masted,[4] with one large square sail, this wind was the best that could blow: for to such a vessel the most advantageous point of sailing is to run right before the wind ;[5] and Puteoli lies nearly due north from Rhegium. The distance is about 182 miles. If then we assume, in accordance with what has been stated above (p. 628), that she sailed at the rate of seven knots an hour,[6] the passage would be accomplished in about twenty-six hours, which agrees perfectly with the account of St. Luke, who says that, after leaving Rhegium, they came, ' *the next day*,' to Puteoli.

Before the close of the first day they would see on the left the volcanic cone and smoke of Stromboli, the nearest of the Liparian islands. In the course of the night they would have neared that projecting part of the mainland which forms the southern limit of

---

[1] The city has now shrunk to its old limit.

[2] Mr. Smith's view that the word here (rendered in A. V. 'fetching a compass,' i.e. 'going round ') means simply 'beating,' is more likely to be correct than that of Mr. Lewin, who supposes that 'as the wind was westerly, and they were under shelter of the high mountainous range of Etna on their left, they were obliged to stand out to sea in order to fill their sails, and so come to Rhegium by a circuitous sweep.' He adds in a note, that he 'was informed by a friend that when he made the voyage from Syracuse to Rhegium, the vessel in which he sailed took a similar circuit for a similar reason.'

[3] Macaulay's *Lays of Rome* (Battle of Lake Regillus). One of these coins, exhibiting the heads of the twin-divinities with the stars, is given at the end of the chapter.

[4] We cannot assume this to have been the case, but it is highly probable. See above. We may refer here to the representation of the harbour of Ostia on the coin of Nero, given below, p. 683. It will be observed that all the ships in the harbour are single-masted.

[5] Smith, p. 180.

[6] We cannot agree with the N. Brit. Reviewer in doubting the correctness of Mr. Smith's conclusion on this point.

the bay of Salerno.[1] Sailing across the wide opening of this gulf, they would, in a few hours, enter that other bay, the bay of Naples, in the northern part of which Puteoli was situated. No long description need be given of that bay, which has been made familiar, by every kind of illustration, even to those who have never seen it. Its south-eastern limit is the promontory of Minerva, with the island of Capreæ opposite, which is so associated with the memory of Tiberius, that its cliffs still seem to rise from the blue waters as a monument of hideous vice in the midst of the fairest scenes of nature. The opposite boundary was the promontory of Misenum, where one of the imperial fleets[2] lay at anchor under the shelter of the islands of Ischia and Procida. In the intermediate space the Campanian coast curves round in the loveliest forms, with Vesuvius as the prominent feature of the view. But here one difference must be marked between St. Paul's day and our own. The angry neighbour of Naples was not then an unsleeping volcano, but a green and sunny background to the bay, with its westward slope covered with vines.[3] No one could have suspected that the time was so near, when the admiral of the fleet at Misenum would be lost in its fiery eruption;[4] and little did the Apostle dream, when he looked from the vessel's deck across the bay to the right, that a ruin, like that of Sodom and Gomorrah, hung over the fair cities at the base of the mountain, and that the Jewish princess, who had so lately conversed with him in his prison at Cæsarea, would find her tomb in that ruin, with the child she had borne to Felix.[5]

By this time the vessel was well within the island of Capreæ and the promontory of Minerva, and the idlers of Puteoli were already crowding to the pier to watch the arrival of the Alexandrian corn-ship. So we may safely infer from a vivid and descriptive letter preserved among the correspondence of the philosopher Seneca. He says that all ships, on rounding into the bay within the above-mentioned island and promontory, were obliged to strike their topsails, with the exception of the Alexandrian corn-vessels, which were thus easily recognised, as soon as they hove in sight: and then he proceeds to moralise on the gathering and crowding of the people of Puteoli, to watch these vessels coming in. Thus we are furnished with new circumstances to aid our efforts to realise the arrival of the 'Castor and Pollux,' on the coast of Italy, with St. Paul on board. And if we wish still further to associate this event with the history and the feeling of the times, we may turn to an anecdote of the Emperor Augustus, which is preserved to us by Suetonius. The Emperor had been seized with a feverish attack—it was the beginning of his last illness—and was cruising about the bay for the benefit of his health, when an Alexandrian corn-ship was coming to her moorings, and passed close by. The sailors recognised the old man, whom the

---

[1] See the *Sailing Directions*, 129–133, with the Admiralty Charts, for the appearance of the coast between Cape Spartivento (Pr. Palinurum) and Cape Campanella (Pr. Minervæ).

[2] The fleet of the 'Upper Sea' was stationed at Ravenna, of the 'Lower' at Misenum.

[3] So it is described by Martial and others. Strabo describes the mountain as very fertile at its base, though its summit was barren, and full of apertures, which showed the traces of earlier volcanic action.

[4] See the younger Pliny's description of his uncle's death, *Ep.* vi. 16.

[5] Josephus. See above, pp. 600, 601.

civilised world obeyed as master and was learning to worship as
God : and they brought out garlands and incense, that they might
pay him divine honours, saying that it was by his providence that
their voyages were made safe and that their trade was prosperous.
Augustus was so gratified by this worship, that he immediately
distributed an immense sum of gold among his suite, exacting from
them the promise that they would expend it all in the purchase of
Alexandrian goods. Such was the interest connected in the first
century with the trade between Alexandria and Puteoli. Such was
the idolatrous homage paid to the Roman Emperor. The only difference, when the Apostle of Christ came, was that the vice and
corruption of the Empire had increased with the growth of its trade,
and that the Emperor now was not Augustus but Nero.

In this wide and sunny expanse of blue waters, no part was calmer
or more beautiful than the recess in the northern part of the bay,
between Baiæ and Puteoli. It was naturally sheltered by the surrounding coasts, and seemed of itself to invite both the gratification
of luxurious ease, and the formation of a mercantile harbour. Baiæ
was devoted to the former purpose ; it was to the invalids and
fashionable idlers of Rome like a combination of Brighton and
Cheltenham. Puteoli, on the opposite side of this inner bay, was
the Liverpool of Italy. Between them was that inclosed reach of
water, called the Lucrine Lake, which contained the oyster-beds for
the luxurious tables of Rome, and on the surface of which the small
yachts of fashionable visitors displayed their coloured sails. Still
further inland was that other calm basin, the Lacus Avernus, which
an artificial passage connected with the former, and thus converted
into a harbour. Not far beyond was Cumæ, once a flourishing
Greek city, but when the Apostle visited this coast, a decayed country
town, famous only for the recollections of the Sibyl.[1]

We must return to Puteoli. We have seen above (p. 629) how
it divided with Ostia the chief commerce by sea between Rome and
the provinces. Its early name, when the Campanian shore was
Greek rather than Italian, was Dicæarchia. Under its new appellation (which seems to have had reference to the mineral springs of
the neighbourhood[2]) it first began to have an important connection
with Rome in the second Punic war. It was the place of embarkation for armies proceeding to Spain, and the landing-place of ambassadors from Carthage. Ever afterwards it was an Italian town
of the first rank. In the time of Vespasian it became the Flavian
Colony, like the city in Palestine from which St. Paul had sailed ;[3]
but even from an earlier period it had colonial privileges, and these
had just been renewed under Nero. It was intimately associated
both with this Emperor and with two others who preceded him in
power and in crime. Close by Baiæ, across the bay, was Bauli,
where the plot was laid for the murder of Agrippina.[4] Across these
waters Caligula built his fantastic bridge ; and the remains of it were
probably visible when St. Paul landed.[5] Tiberius had a more

---

[1] See Juv. *Sat.* iii. 1.

[2] It was named either from the
springs (*a puteis*), or from their stench
(*a putendo*).

[3] See above on Cæsarea, pp. 605, 606.

[4] Nero had murdered his mother

about two years before St. Paul's coming.

[5] Some travellers have mistaken the
remains of the mole for those of Caligula's bridge. But that was only a
wooden structure.

honourable monument in a statue (of which a fragment is still seen by English travellers at Pozzuoli), erected during St. Paul's life to commemorate the restitution of the Asiatic cities overthrown by an earthquake.[1] But the ruins which are the most interesting to us are the seventeen piers of the ancient mole, on which the lighthouse stood, and within which the merchant-men were moored. Such is the proverbial tenacity of the concrete which was used in this structure,[2] that it is the most perfect ruin existing of any ancient Roman harbour. In the early part of this chapter, we spoke of the close mercantile relationship which subsisted between Egypt and this city. And this remains on our minds as the prominent and significant fact of its history,—whether we look upon the ruins of the mole and think of such voyages as those of Titus and Vespasian,[3] or wander among the broken columns of the Temple of Serapis,[4] or read the account which Philo gives of the singular interview of the Emperor Caligula with the Jewish ambassadors from Alexandria.[5]

Puteoli, from its trade with Alexandria and the East, must necessarily have contained a colony of Jews, and they must have had a close connection with the Jews of Rome. What was true of the Jews would probably find its parallel in the Christians. St. Paul met with disciples here;[6] and, as soon as he was among them, they were in prompt communication on the subject with their brethren in Rome.[7] The Italian Christians had long been looking for a visit from the famous Apostle, though they had not expected to see him arrive thus, a prisoner in chains, hardly saved from shipwreck. But these sufferings would only draw their hearts more closely towards him. They earnestly besought him to stay some days with them, and Julius was able to allow this request to be complied with.[8] Even when the voyage began, we saw that he was courteous and kind towards his prisoner; and, after all the varied and impressive incidents which have been recounted in this chapter, we should indeed be surprised if we found him unwilling to contribute to the comfort of one by whom his own life had been preserved.

Coin of Rhegium.[9]

---

[1] The pedestal of this statue, with the allegorical representations of the towns, is still extant.

[2] The well-known *Pozzolana*, which is mentioned by Pliny.

[3] See p. 630.

[4] This is one of the most remarkable ruins at Pozzuoli. It is described in the guide-books.

[5] Philo *Leg. ad Caium.*

[6] Acts xxviii. 14.

[7] See v. 15.

[8] It is not clearly stated who urged this stay. Possibly it was Julius himself. It is at all events evident from v. 15 that they did stay; otherwise there would not have been time for the intelligence of St. Paul's landing to reach Rome so long before his own arrival there.

[9] From the British Museum. The heads and stars are those of Castor and Pollux. See pp. 662, n. 7. and 663, n. 3.

CHAPTER XXIV.

The Appian Way.—Appii Forum and the Three Taverns.—Entrance into Rome.—The Prætorian Prefect.—Description of the City.—Its Population. —The Jews in Rome.—The Roman Church.—St. Paul's Interview with the Jews.—His Residence in Rome.

THE last chapter began with a description of the facilities possessed by the ancients for travelling by sea : this must begin with a reference to their best opportunities of travelling by land. We have before spoken of some of the most important roads through the provinces of the Empire: now we are about to trace the Apostle's footsteps along that road, which was at once the oldest and most frequented in Italy,[1] and which was called, in comparison with all others, the ' Queen of Roads.'   We are no longer following the narrow line of compact pavement across Macedonian plains and mountains,[2] or through the varied scenery in the interior of Asia Minor:[3] but we are on the most crowded approach to the metropolis of the world, in the midst of prætors and proconsuls, embassies, legions, and turms of horse, ' to their provinces hasting or on return,' which Milton,[4]—in his description of the City enriched with the spoils of nations,—has called us to behold ' in various habits on the Appian road.'

Leaving then all consideration of Puteoli, as it was related to the sea and to the various places on the coast, we proceed to consider its communications by land with the towns of Campania and Latium. The great line of communication between Rome and the southern part of the peninsula was the Way constructed by Appius Claudius, which passed through Capua,[5] and thence to Brundusium on the shore of the Adriatic.[6]   Puteoli and its neighbourhood lay some

---

[1] '*Appia* longarum teritur *Regina viarum.*'—Stat. *Silv.* ii. 2. See below.

[2] For the Via Egnatia, see pp. 244, 245.

[3] In making our last allusion to Asia Minor, we may refer to the description which Basil gives of the scenery round his residence, a little to the east of the inland region thrice traversed by St. Paul. See Humboldt's *Kosmos*, vol. ii. p. 26. (Sabine's Eng. Trans.)

[4] *Paradise Regained*, book iv.

[5] The Via Appia, the oldest and most celebrated of Roman roads, was constructed as far as Capua, A. U. C. 442, by the censor Appius Claudius. Eight hundred years afterwards, Procopius was astonished at its appearance. He describes it as broad enough for two carriages to pass each other, and as made of stones brought from some distant quarry, and so fitted to each other, that they seemed to be thus formed by nature, rather than cemented by art. He adds that, notwithstanding the traffic of so many ages, the stones were not displaced, nor had they lost their original smoothness.   There is great doubt as to the date of the continuation by Beneventum to Brundusium, nor is the course of it absolutely ascertained.

[6] Here it came to the customary ferry between the Greek and Italian peninsulas, and was succeeded on the other side by the Via Egnatia. Strabo, v. 3 ; vi. 3.   Compare pp. 244, 245.

miles to the westward of this main road: but communicated with it easily by well-travelled cross-roads. One of them followed the coast from Puteoli northwards, till it joined the Appian Way at Sinuessa, on the borders of Latium and Campania.[1] It appears, however, that this road was not constructed till the reign of Domitian.[2] Our attention, therefore, is called to the other cross-road which led directly to Capua. One branch of it left the coast at Cumæ, another at Puteoli. It was called the ' Campanian Way,' and also the ' Consular Way.' It seems to have been constructed during the Republic, and was doubtless the road which is mentioned, in an animated passage of Horace's Epistles, as communicating with the baths and villas of Baiæ.[3]

The first part then of the route which Julius took with his prisoners was probably from Puteoli to Capua. All the region near the coast, however transformed in the course of ages by the volcanic forces which are still at work, is recognised as the scene of the earliest Italian mythology, and must ever be impressive from the poetic images, partly of this world and partly of the next, with which Virgil has filled it. From Cumæ to Capua, the road traverses a more prosaic district:[4] the ' Phlegræan fields ' are left behind, and we pass from the scene of Italy's dim mythology to the theatre of the most exciting passages of her history. The whole line of the road can be traced at intervals, not only in the close neighbourhood of Puteoli and Capua, but through the intermediate villages, by fragments of pavement, tombs, and ancient milestones.[5]

Capua, after a time of disgrace had expiated its friendship with Hannibal, was raised by Julius Cæsar to the rank of a colony: in the reign of Augustus it had resumed all its former splendour: and about the very time of which we are writing, it received accessions of dignity from the Emperor Nero. It was the most important city on the whole line of the Appian Way, between Rome and Brundusium. That part of the line with which we are concerned, is the northerly and most ancient portion. The distance is about 125 miles: and it may be naturally divided into two equal parts. The division is appropriate, whether in regard to the physical configuration of the country, or the modern political boundaries. The point of division is where Terracina is built at the base of those cliffs,[6] on which the city of Anxur was of old proudly situ-

[1] The stages of this road from Sinuessa appear as follows in the Peutingerian Table:—Savonem Fl. III.; Vulturnum, VII.; Liternum, VII.; Cumas, VI.; Lacum Avernum, II.; Puteolos, III. Thence it proceeds by Naples to Herculaneum, Pompeii, Stabiæ, and Surrentum. In the *Antonine Itinerary* it is entitled, ' Iter a Terracinâ Neapolim,' and the distances are slightly different. A direct road from Capua to Neapolis, by Atella, is mentioned in the *Tab. Peut.*

[2] This is the road which is the subject of the pompous yet very interesting poem of Statius, *Silv.* iv.

[3] See the vivid passage in the be-

ginning of *Ep.* i. xv., where we see that the road was well travelled at that period, and where its turning out of the Via Appia is clearly indicated.

[4] On the left was a district of pine woods, notorious for banditti (*Gallinaria pinus*), Juv. iii. 305 : now Pineta di Castel Volturno.

[5] The road seems to have left Puteoli by the Solfatara, where Romanelli says that the old pavement is visible.

[6] The modern Terracina is by the sea at the base of the cliffs, and the present road passes that way. The ancient road ascended to Anxur, which was on the summit.

ated, and where a narrow pass between the mountain and the sea, unites (or united recently) the Papal States to the kingdom of Naples.

The distance from Capua to Terracina [1] is about seventy Roman miles. At the third mile the road crossed the river Vulturnus at Casilinum, a town then falling into decay.[2] Fifteen miles further it crossed the river Savo, by what was then called the Campanian Bridge.[3] Thence, after three miles, it came to Sinuessa on the sea,[4] which in St. Paul's day was reckoned the first town in Latium. But the old rich Campania extended farther to the northward, including the vine-clad hills of the famous Falernian district through which we pass, after crossing the Savo.[5] The last of these hills (where the vines may be seen trained on elms, as of old) is the range of Massicus, which stretches from the coast towards the Apennines, and finally shuts out from the traveller, as he descends on the farther side, all the prospect of Vesuvius and the coast near Puteoli.[6] At that season, both vines and elms would have a winterly appearance. But the traces of spring would be visible in the willows;[7] among which the Liris flows in many silent windings—from the birthplace of Marius in the mountains [8]—to the city and the swamps by the sea, which the ferocity of his mature life has rendered illustrious. After leaving Minturnæ, the Appian Way passes on to another place, which has different associations with the later years of the Republic. We speak of Formiæ,[9] with its long street by the shore of its beautiful bay, and with its villas on the sea-side, and above it ; among which was one of Cicero's favourite retreats from the turmoil of the political world, and where at last he fell by the hand of assassins.[10] Many a *lectica*,[11] or palanquin, such as that in which he was reclining when overtaken by his murderers, may have been met by St. Paul in his progress,—with other carriages, with which the road would become more and more crowded,—the

[1] The stages are as follows (reckoning from Terracina) in the *Antonine Itinerary*: FUNDIS. XVI. FORMIS. XIII. MINTURNIS. IX. SINUESSA. IX. CAPUA. XXVI. The distances are rather smaller in the Jerusalem Itinerary, where a *mutatio Ponte Campano* and a *mutatio ad octavum* are inserted between Sinuessa and Capua. *Casilinum* is mentioned only in the Peutingerian Table.

[2] The operations on the *Volturno* in Garibaldi's recent campaign are very fresh in our recollection.

[3] Campano Ponti. Hor. *Sat.* i. v. 45.

[4] 'Plotius et Varius Sinuessæ, Virgiliusque
Occurrunt.' Ib. 40.

[5] Pliny extends Campania to the Liris or *Garigliano*. It is difficult to fix the limits of the *Falernus ager*, which extended from the Massic Hills towards the Volturnus.

[6] The ancient road, however, seems

to have followed the coast.

[7] 'March 22. We cross the *Liris* by a suspension bridge. It is a large stream—truly a *taciturnus amnis*—winding like the Trent among willow-trees, which showed nearly the first symptoms of spring we had seen.' (Extract from a private journal.) We have already seen that St. Paul's journey through Campania and Latium was very early in the spring.

[8] The Garigliano rises near Arpinum, which was also the birth-place of Cicero.

[9] This is *Mola di Gaeta*, just opposite the fortress which has been so notorious in recent passages of Italian history.

[10] See Plutarch's description of his death.

[11] The *lecticæ*, or couches carried by bearers were in constant use both for men and women ; and a traveller could hardly go from Puteoli to Rome without seeing many of them.

cisium,[1] or light cabriolet, of some gay reveller, on his way to Baiæ,
—or the four-wheeled *rheda*,[2] full of the family of some wealthy
senator quitting the town for the country.   At no great distance
from Formiæ the road left the sea again, and passed, where the
substructions of it still remain, through the defiles [3] of the Cæcuban
hills, with their stony but productive vineyards.   Thence the
traveller looked down upon the plain of Fundi, which retreats like
a bay into the mountains, with the low lake of Amyclæ between the
town and the sea.   Through the capricious care, with which time
has preserved in one place what is lost in another, the pavement of
the ancient way is still the street of this, the most northerly town
of the Neapolitan kingdom in this direction.   We have now in front
of us the mountain line, which is both the frontier of the Papal
States,[4] and the natural division of the Apostle's journey from
Capua to Rome.   Where it reaches the coast, in bold limestone
precipices, there Anxur was situated, with its houses and temples
high above the sea.[5]

After leaving Anxur,[6] the traveller observes the high land retreating again from the coast, and presently finds himself in a wide
and remarkable plain, enclosed towards the interior by the sweep of
the blue Volscian mountains, and separated by a belt of forest from
the sea.   Here are the Pomptine marshes,—' the only marshes ever
dignified by classic celebrity.'   The descriptive lines of the Roman
satirist have wonderfully concurred with the continued unhealthi-
ness of the half-drained morass, in preserving a living commentary
on that fifteenth verse in the last chapter of the Acts, which exhibits to us one of the most touching passages in the Apostle's life.
A few miles beyond Terracina, where a fountain, grateful to travellers, welled up near the sanctuary of Feronia,[7] was the termination
of a canal, which was formed by Augustus for the purpose of drain-
ing the marshes, and which continued for twenty miles by the side
of the road.[8]   Over this distance, travellers had their choice, whether
to proceed by barges dragged by mules, or on the pavement of the
way itself.[9]   It is impossible to know which plan was adopted by
Julius and his prisoners.   If we suppose the former to have been
chosen, we have the aid of Horace's Satire to enable us to imagine

---

[1] Seneca says you could write in the
cisium, whence we must infer that such
carriages [if they had springs] were
often as comfortable as those of modern
times.

[2] 'Tota domus *rheda* componitur una.'
(Juv. iii. 10.)   The remark just made
on the cisium is equally applicable to
the larger carriage.   Cicero says in
one of his Cilician letters that he dictated it while seated in his rheda.

[3] Itri is in one of these defiles.   The
substructions of the ancient way show
that it nearly followed the line of the
modern road between Rome and Naples.

[4] Or of what were till lately the
Papal States.

[5] See Hor. *Sat.* I. v. 25, 26, and many
other passages in Roman poets.   There
are here still the substructions of large
temples, one of them probably that of
Jupiter, to whom the town was dedicated.

[6] The stages during the latter half
of the journey, reckoning from Rome,
appear thus in the *Antonine Itinerary*:
ARICIAM. XVI.   TRES TABERNAS. XVII.
APPI FORO. X.   TARRACINA. XVIII.   The
other Itineraries give some intermediate
details.

[7] Hor. *Sat.* I. 24.

[8] 'Qua Pomptinas via dividit uda
paludes.' (Lucan, iii. 85.)   The length
of the canal was nineteen miles.

[9] With Horace's account of his night-
journey on the canal we may compare
Strabo.

the incidents and the company, in the midst of which the Apostle came, unknown and unfriended, to the corrupt metropolis of the world. And yet he was not so unfriended as he may possibly have thought himself that day, in his progress from Anxur across the watery, unhealthy plain. On the arrival of the party at Appii Forum, which was a town where the mules were unfastened, at the other end of the canal, and is described by the satirist as full of low tavern-keepers and bargemen,[1]—at that meeting-place where travellers from all parts of the Empire had often crossed one another's path,—on that day, in the motley and vulgar crowd, some of the few Christians who were then in the world suddenly recognised one another, and emotions of holy joy and thanksgiving, sanctified the place of coarse vice and vulgar traffic. The disciples at Rome had heard of the Apostle's arrival at Puteoli, and hastened to meet him on the way; and the prisoner was startled to recognise some of those among whom he had laboured, and whom he had loved, in the distant cities of the East. Whether Aquila and Priscilla were there it is needless to speculate. Whoever might be the persons, they were brethren in Christ, and their presence would be an instantaneous source of comfort and strength. We have already seen on other occasions of his life,[2] how the Apostle's heart was lightened by the presence of his friends.

About ten miles farther he received a second welcome from a similar group of Christian brethren. Two independent companies had gone to meet him; or the zeal and strength of one party had outstripped the other. At a place called the Three Taverns,[3] where a cross road from the coast at Antium came in from the left, this second party of Christians was waiting to welcome and to honour 'the ambassador in bonds.' With a lighter heart and a more cheerful countenance, he travelled the remaining seventeen miles, which brought him along the base of the Alban Hills, in the midst of places well known and famous in early Roman legends, to the town of Aricia. The Great Apostle had the sympathies of human nature; he was dejected and encouraged by the same causes which act on our spirits; he too saw all outward objects in 'hues borrowed from the heart.' The diminution of fatigue—the more hopeful prospect of the future—the renewed elasticity of religious trust—the sense of a brighter light on all the scenery round him—on the foliage which overshadowed the road—on the wide expanse of the plain to the left—on the high summit of the Alban Mount,—all this, and more than this, is involved in St. Luke's sentence,—'*When Paul saw the brethren, he thanked God, and took courage.*'

The mention of the Alban Mount reminds us that we are approaching the end of our journey. The isolated group of hills, which is called by this collective name, stands between the plain which has just been traversed and that other plain which is the Campagna of Rome. All the bases of the mountain were then (as

---

[1] This place is also mentioned by Cicero. *Att.* ii. 10. Its situation was near the present *Treponti*.

[2] See especially p 279.

[3] This place is mentioned by Cicero when on a journey from Antium to Rome. *Att.* ii. 12. From the distances in the Itineraries it seems to have been not very far from the modern Cisterna.

indeed they are partially now) clustered round with the villas and gardens of wealthy citizens. The Appian Way climbs and then descends along its southern slope. After passing Lanuvium [1] it crossed a crater-like valley on immense substructions, which still remain.[2] Here is Aricia, an easy stage from Rome.[3] The town was above the road; and on the hill-side swarms of beggars beset travellers as they passed.[4] On the summit of the next rise, Paul of Tarsus would obtain his first view of Rome. There is no doubt that the prospect was, in many respects, very different from the view which is now obtained from the same spot. It is true that the natural features of the scene are unaltered. The long wall of blue Sabine mountains, with Soracte in the distance, closed in the Campagna, which stretched far across to the sea and round the base of the Alban hills. But ancient Rome was not, like modern Rome, impressive from its solitude, standing alone, with its one conspicuous cupola, in the midst of a desolate though beautiful waste. St. Paul would see a vast city, covering the Campagna, and almost continuously connected by its suburbs with the villas on the hill where he stood, and with the bright towns which clustered on the sides of the mountains opposite. Over all the intermediate space were the houses and gardens, through which aqueducts and roads might be traced in converging lines towards the confused mass of edifices which formed the city of Rome. Here no conspicuous building, elevated above the rest, attracted the eye or the imagination. Ancient Rome had neither cupola[5] nor campanile. Still less had it any of those spires, which give life to all the landscapes of Northern Christendom. It was a wide-spread aggregate of buildings, which, though separated by narrow streets and open squares, appeared, when seen from near Aricia, blended into one indiscriminate mass: for distance concealed the contrasts[6] which divided the crowded habitations of the poor, and the dark haunts of filth and misery,—from the theatres and colonnades, the baths, the temples and palaces with gilded roofs, flashing back the sun.

The road descended into the plain at Bovillæ, six miles from Aricia,[7] and thence it proceeded in a straight line,[8] with the se-

[1] Sub Lanuvio is one of the stations in the *Tab. Peut.* (See above.) The ancient Lanuvium was on a hill on the left, near where the Via Appia (which can be traced here, by means of the tombs, as it descends from the plain) strikes the modern road by Velletri.

[2] The present road is carried through the modern town of Laricia, which occupies the site of the citadel of ancient Aricia. The Appian Way went across the valley below. See Sir W. Gell's *Campagna*, under Aricia and Laricia: see also an article, entitled 'Excursions from Rome in 1843,' in the first volume of the *Classical Museum*, p. 322. The magnificent causeway or viaduct, mentioned in the text, is 700 feet long, and in some places 70 feet high. It is built of enormous

squared blocks of peperino, with arches for the water of the torrents to pass through.

[3] It was Horace's first halting-place. The distance from Rome was sixteen miles.

[4] The *clivus Aricinus* is repeatedly mentioned by the Roman satirists as swarming with beggars.

[5] The Pantheon was indeed built; but the world had not seen any instance of an elevated dome, like that of St. Sophia, St. Peter's, or St. Paul's.

[6] See below, p. 675, and the reference to 1 Cor.

[7] Bovillæ (not far from *Fratocchie*) is memorable as the place where Clodius was killed.

[8] The modern road deviates slightly from the Via Appia; but by aid of the

pulchres of illustrious families on either hand.[1] One of these was the burial-place of the Julian gens,[2] with which the centurion who had charge of the prisoners was in some way connected.[3] As they proceeded over the old pavement, among gardens and modern houses,[4] and approached nearer the busy metropolis—the 'conflux issuing forth or entering in'[5] on various errands and in various costumes, —vehicles, horsemen, and foot-passengers, soldiers and labourers, Romans and foreigners,—became more crowded and confusing. The houses grew closer. They were already in Rome. It was impossible to define the commencement of the city. Its populous portions extended far beyond the limits marked out by Servius. The ancient wall, with its once sacred pomœrium, was rather an object for antiquarian interest, like the walls of York or Chester, than any protection against the enemies, who were kept far aloof by the legions on the frontier.

Yet the Porta Capena is a spot which we can hardly leave without lingering for a moment. Under this arch—which was perpetually dripping[6] with the water of the aqueduct that went over it[7]—had passed all those who, since a remote period of the Republic, had travelled by the Appian Way,—victorious generals with their legions, returning from foreign service,—emperors and courtiers, vagrant representatives of every form of Heathenism, Greeks and Asiatics, Jews and Christians.[8] From this point entering within the city, Julius and his prisoners moved on, with the Aventine on their left close round the base of the Cœlian, and through the hollow ground which lay between this hill and the Palatine : thence over the low ridge called Velia,[9] where afterwards was built the

tombs the eye can easily trace the course of the ancient way. Recent excavations have brought the whole line of the Via Appia more clearly into view than formerly.

[1] There is a well-known sentence in Cicero having reference to these sepulchres. That of Cecilia Metella is familiar to all travellers. Pompey's tomb was also on the Appian Way, but nearer to Aricia.

[2] Sir W. Gell, on what appears to be a memorial of the burying-place of the Gens Julia, near Bovillæ. See Tac. *Ann.* ii. 41, xv. 33.

[3] He might be a free-born Italian (like Cornelius, see p. 96), or he might be a freedman, or the descendant of a freedman, manumitted by some members of the Julian house.

[4] Much building must have been continually going on. Juvenal mentions the carrying of building materials as one of the annoyances of Rome.

[5] *Paradise Regained*, iv. 62.

[6] Mart. iii. 47. Hence called the moist gate by Juvenal, iii. 10. Compare Mart. iv. 18. It was doubtless called Capena, as being the gate of Capua. Its position is fully ascertained to have

been at the point of union of the valleys dividing the Aventine, Cœlian, and Palatine. Both the Via Latina and Via Appia issued from this gate. The first milestone on the latter was found in the first vineyard beyond the Porta S. Sebastiano (see map).

[7] This was a branch of the Marcian aqueduct.

[8] We must not forget that close by this gate was the old sanctuary of Egeria, which in Juvenal's time was occupied by Jewish beggars. See *Sat.* iii. 13, vi. 542, already referred to in p. 118.

[9] 'The ridge, on which the arch of Titus stands, was much more considerable than the modern traveller would suppose : the pavement, which has been excavated at this point, is fifty-three feet above the level of the pavement in the Forum. This ridge ran from the Palatine to the Esquiline, dividing the basin in which the Colosseum stands, from that which contained the Forum : it was called Velia. Publicola excited popular suspicion and alarm by building his house on the elevated part of this ridge.'—Companion-Volume to Mr. Cookesley's *Map of Rome*, p. 30.

arch of Titus to commemorate the destruction of Jerusalem ; and then descending,[1] by the *Sacra Via*, into that space which was the centre of imperial power and imperial magnificence, and associated also with the most glorious recollections of the Republic. The Forum was to Rome what the Acropolis[2] was to Athens, the heart of all the characteristic interest of the place. Here was the *Milliarium Aureum*, to which the roads of all the provinces converged. All around were the stately buildings, which were raised in the closing years of the Republic, and by the earlier Emperors. In front was the Capitoline Hill, illustrious long before the invasion of the Gauls. Close on the left, covering that hill, whose name is associated in every modern European language with the notion of imperial splendour, were the vast ranges of the *palace*—the ' house of Cæsar' (Phil. iv. 22). Here were the household troops quartered in a *prætorium*[3] attached to the palace. And here (unless, indeed, it was in the great *Prætorian camp*[4] outside the city wall) Julius gave up his prisoner to Burrus, the *Prætorian Præfect*,[5] whose official duty it was to keep in custody all accused persons who were to be tried before the Emperor.[6]

This doubt, which of two places, somewhat distant from each other, was the scene of St. Paul's meeting with the commander-in-chief of the Prætorian guards, gives us the occasion for entering on a general description of the different parts of the city of Rome. It would be nugatory to lay much stress, as is too often done, on its ' seven hills :' for a great city at length obliterates the original features of the ground, especially where those features were naturally not very strongly marked. The description, which is easy in reference to Athens or Edinburgh, is hard in the instance of modern London or ancient Rome. Nor is it easy, in the case of one of the larger cities of the world, to draw any marked lines of distinction among the different classes of buildings. It is true the contrasts are really great ; but details are lost in a distant view of so vast an aggregate. The two scourges to which ancient Rome was most exposed, revealed very palpably the contrast, both of the natural ground and the human structures, which by the general observer might be unnoticed or forgotten. When the Tiber was flooded, and the muddy waters converted all the streets and open places of the lower part of the city into lakes and canals,[7] it would be seen very clearly how much

---

[1] This slope, from the Arch of Titus down to the Forum, was called the Sacer Clivus.

[2] See p. 275.

[3] We think that Wieseler has proved that the πραιτώριον in Phil. i. 13, denotes the quarters of the household troops attached to the Emperor's residence on the Palatine. See the beginning of Chap. XXVI.

[4] The establishment of this camp was the work of Tiberius. Its place is still clearly visible in the great rectangular projection in the walls, on the north of the city. In St. Paul's time it was strictly outside the city. The inner wall was pulled down by Constantine.

[5] This is the accurate translation of Acts xxviii. 16. The *Præfectus Prætorio* was already the most important subject of the Emperor, though he had not yet acquired all that extensive jurisdiction which was subsequently conferred upon him. At this time (A.D. 61) Burrus, one of the best of Nero's advisers, was Prætorian Præfect.

[6] Trajan says (Plin. *Ep.* x. 65) of such a prisoner, 'vinctus mitti ad Præfectos Prætorii mei debet.' Compare also Joseph. *Ant.* xviii. 6, quoted by Wieseler, p. 393.

[7] The writer has known visits paid

lower were the Forum and the Campus Martius than those three detached hills (the Capitoline, the Palatine, and the Aventine) which rose near the river; and those four ridges (the Cœlian, the Esquiline, the Viminal, and the Quirinal) which ascended and united together in the higher ground on which the Prætorian camp was situated. And when fires swept rapidly from roof to roof,[1] and vast ranges of buildings were buried in the ruins of one night, that contrast between the dwellings of the poor and the palaces of the rich, which has supplied the Apostle with one of his most forcible images, would be clearly revealed,—the difference between structures of 'sumptuous marbles, with silver and gold,' which abide after the fire, and the hovels of 'wood, hay, stubble,' which are burnt (1 Cor. iii. 10–15).

If we look at a map of modern Rome, with a desire of realising to ourselves the appearance of the city of Augustus and Nero, we must in the first place obliterate from our view that circuit of walls, which is due in various proportions, to Aurelian, Belisarius, and Pope Leo IV.[2] The wall through which the Porta Capena gave admission, was the old Servian enclosure, which embraced a much smaller area : though we must bear in mind, as we have remarked above, that the city had extended itself beyond this limit, and spread through various suburbs, far into the country. In the next place we must observe that the hilly part of Rome, which is now half occupied by gardens, was then the most populous, while the Campus Martius, now covered with crowded streets, was comparatively open. It was only about the close of the Republic that many buildings were raised on the Campus Martius, and these were chiefly of a public or decorative character. One of these, the Pantheon, still remains, as a monument of the reign of Augustus. This, indeed, is the period from which we must trace the beginning of all the grandeur of Roman buildings. Till the civil war between Pompey and Cæsar, the private houses of the citizens had been mean, and the only public structures of note were the cloacæ and the aqueducts. But in proportion as the ancient fabric of the constitution broke down, and while successful generals brought home wealth from provinces conquered and plundered on every shore of the Mediterranean, the City began to assume the appearance of a new and imperial magnificence. To leave out of view the luxurious and splendid residences which wealthy citizens raised for their own uses,[3] Pompey erected the first theatre of stone,[4] and Julius Cæsar surrounded the great Circus with a portico. From

in the Ripetta (in the Campus Martius) by means of boats brought to the windows of the first story. Dio Cassius makes three distinct references to a similar state of things.

[1] Suetonius mentions floods and fires together, *Aug.* 29, 30. The *fire-police* of Augustus seems to have been organised with great care. The care of the river, as we learn from inscriptions, was committed to a *Curator alvei Tiberis.*

[2] The wall of Leo IV. is that which encloses the Borgo (said to be so called

from the word *burgh*, used by Anglo-Saxon pilgrims) where St. Peter's and the Vatican are situated.

[3] Till the reign of Augustus, the houses of private citizens had been for the most part of sun-dried bricks, on a basement of stone. The houses of Crassus and Lepidus were among the earlier exceptions.

[4] This theatre was one of the principal ornaments of the Campus Martius. Some parts of it still remain.

this time the change went on rapidly and incessantly. The increase of public business led to the erection of enormous Basilicas.[1] The Forum was embellished on all sides.[2] The Temple of Apollo on the Palatine, and those other temples the remains of which are still conspicuous at the base of the Capitoline,[3] were only a small part of similar buildings raised by Augustus. The triumphal arch erected by Tiberius, near the same place[4] was only one of many structures, which rose in rapid succession to decorate that busy neighbourhood. And if we wish to take a wider view, we have only to think of the aqueducts, which were built, one by one, between the private enterprises of Agrippa in the reign of Augustus, and the recent structures of the Emperor Claudius, just before the arrival of the Apostle Paul. We may not go farther in the order of chronology. We must remember that the Colosseum, the Basilica of Constantine, and the baths of other emperors, and many other buildings which are now regarded as the conspicuous features of ancient Rome, did not then exist. We are describing a period which is anterior to the time of Nero's fire. Even after the opportunity which that calamity afforded for reconstructing the city, Juvenal complains of the narrowness of the streets. Were we to attempt to extend our description to any of these streets—whether the old Vicus Tuscus, with its cheating shopkeepers, which led round the base of the Palatine, from the Forum to the Circus,—or the aristocratic Carinæ along the slope of the Esquiline,—or the noisy Suburra, in the hollow between the Viminal and Quirinal, which had sunk into disrepute, though once the residence of Julius Cæsar,—we should only wander into endless perplexity. And we should be equally lost, if we were to attempt to discriminate the mixed multitude, which were crowded on the various landings of those *insulæ*,[5] or piles of lodging-houses, which are perhaps best described by comparing them to the houses in the old town of Edinburgh. If it is difficult to describe the outward appearance of the city, it is still more difficult to trace the distinctive features of all the parts of that colossal population which filled it. Within a circuit of little more than twelve miles[6] more than two millions[7] of inhabitants were crowded. It is evident that this fact is only explicable by the

---

[1] The Roman Basilica is peculiarly interesting to us, since it contains the germ of the Christian cathedral. Originally these Basilicas were rather open colonnades than enclosed halls ; but, before the reign of Nero, they had assumed their ultimate form of a nave with aisles. We shall refer again to them in our account of St. Paul's last trial. See p. 769.

[2] Three well-known Corinthian columns, of the best period of art under the Emperors, remain near the base of the Palatine. They are popularly called the remains of the Temple of Jupiter Stator : perhaps they are part of the Temple of Castor and Pollux.

[3] The larger ruin, on the lower side of the Clivus Capitolinus, is believed to be the Temple of Vespasian, and was not built till after St. Paul's death. The Temples of Concord and of Saturn were of earlier date.

[4] It was built in commemoration of the recovery of the standards of Varus.

[5] A decree was issued by Augustus, defining the height to which these *insulæ* might be raised.

[6] This is of course a much wider circuit than that of the Servian wall. The present wall, as we have said above, did not then exist.

[7] See Milman's note on Gibbon's thirty-first chapter. The estimate of 2,000,000 agrees with that of the writer of the article 'Rome' in Smith's *Dict*.

narrowness of the streets, with that peculiarity of the houses which has been alluded to above.   In this prodigious collection of human beings, there were of course all the contrasts which are seen in a modern city,—all the painful lines of separation between luxury and squalor, wealth and want.   But in Rome all these differences were on an exaggerated scale, and the institution of slavery modified further all social relations.   The free citizens were more than a million : of these, the senators were so few in number, as to be hardly appreciable : [1] the knights, who filled a great proportion of the public offices, were not more than 10,000 : the troops quartered in the city may be reckoned at 15,000: the rest were the *Plebs urbana.*   That a vast number of these would be poor, is an obvious result of the most ordinary causes.   But, in ancient Rome, the luxury of the wealthier classes did not produce a general diffusion of trade, as it does in a modern city.   The handicraft employments, and many of what we should call professions,[2] were in the hands of slaves ; and the consequence was, that a vast proportion of the Plebs urbana lived on public or private charity.   Yet were these pauper citizens proud of their citizenship, though many of them had no better sleeping-place for the night than the public porticoes or the vestibules of temples.   They cared for nothing beyond bread for the day, the games of the Circus,[3] and the savage delight of gladiatorial shows.   Manufactures and trade they regarded as the business of the slave and the foreigner.   The number of the slaves was perhaps about a million.   The number of the strangers or *peregrini* was much smaller ; but it is impossible to describe their varieties.   Every kind of nationality and religion found its representative in Rome.   But it is needless to pursue these details.   The most obvious comparison is better than an elaborate description. Rome was like London with all its miseries, vices, and follies exaggerated, and without Christianity.

One part of Rome still remains to be described, the ' Trastevere ' or district beyond the river.[4]   This portion of the city has been known in modern times for the energetic and intractable character of its population.   In earlier times it was equally notorious, though not quite for the same reason. It was the residence of a low rabble, and the place of the meanest merchandise.[5]   There is, however, one reason why our attention is particularly called to it.   It was the ordinary residence of the Jews, the ' Ghetto' of ancient Rome : [6] and great part of it was doubtless squalid and miserable, like the Ghetto of modern Rome,[7] though the Jews were often less oppressed

of Geog. vol. ii. p. 748.   Mr. Merivale thinks it far too high.   *Hist. of Rom. under Emp.* vol. iv. pp. 515-528.

[1] Before Augustus there were 1000 senators ; he reduced them to about 700.

[2] Some were physicians, others were engaged in education, &c.

[3] ' Panem et Circenses ;' such is the satirist's account of the only two things for which the Roman populace was really anxious.

[4] Whether the wall of Servius in-

cluded any portion of the opposite side of the river or not (a question which is disputed among the topographers of the Italian and German schools), a suburb existed there under the imperial régime.

[5] Juv. xiv. 202 ; Mart. i. 42, 109 ; vi. 93.

[6] We learn this from Philo.

[7] The modern Ghetto is in the filthy quarter between the Capitoline Hill and the old Fabrician Bridge, which

under the Cæsars than under the Popes. Here then, on the level ground, between the windings of the muddy river, and the base of that hill [1] from the brow of which Porsena looked down on early Rome, and where the French within these few years have planted their cannon,—we must place the home of those Israelitish families among whom the Gospel bore its first-fruits in the metropolis of the world : and it was on these bridges,[2]—which formed an immediate communication from the district beyond the Tiber to the Emperor's household and the guards on the Palatine,—that those despised Jewish beggars took their stand, to whom in the place of their exile had come the hopes of a better citizenship than that which they had lost.

The Jewish community thus established in Rome, had its first beginnings in the captives brought by Pompey after his eastern campaign.[3] Many of them were manumitted; and thus a great proportion of the Jews in Rome were freedmen.[4] Frequent accessions to their numbers were made as years went on,—chiefly from the mercantile relations which subsisted between Rome and the East. Many of them were wealthy, and large sums were sent annually for religious purposes from Italy to the mother country.[5] Even the proselytes contributed to these sacred funds.[6] It is difficult to estimate the amount of the religious influence exerted by the Roman Jews upon the various Heathens around them : but all our sources of information lead us to conclude that it was very considerable.[7] So long as this influence was purely religious, we have no reason to suppose that any persecution from the civil power resulted. It was when commotions took place in consequence of expectations of a temporal Messiah, or when vague suspicions of this mysterious people were more than usually excited, that the Jews of Rome were cruelly treated, or peremptorily banished. Yet from all these cruelties they recovered with elastic force, and from all these exiles they returned; and in the early years of Nero, which were distinguished for a mild and lenient government of the Empire,[8] the Jews in Rome seem to have enjoyed complete tolera-

leads to the island, and thence to the Trastevere. It is surrounded by walls, and the gates are closed every night by the police. The number of Jews is about 8000, in a total population of 150,000.

[1] The Janiculum.

[2] Mart. x. 5. See Juv. iv. 116 ; v. 8 ; xiv. 134.

[3] See p. 15. The first introduction of the Jews to Rome was probably the embassy of the Maccabees.

[4] This we have on the authority of Philo.

[5] Here again Cicero confirms what we learn from Philo.

[6] Tac. *Hist.* v. 6.

[7] The very passages (and they are numerous) which express hatred of the Jews imply a sense of their influence.

Again, many Jews were Roman citizens, like Josephus and St. Paul : and there were numerous proselytes at Rome, especially among the women (see for instance Joseph. *Ant.* xviii. 3. 5). As in the case of Greece, the conquest of Judæa brought Rome under the influence of her captive. Hence Seneca's remark, in reference to the Jews : 'The conquered gave laws to their conquerors.'

[8] The good period of Nero's reign— the first *quinquennium*—had not yet expired. The full toleration of the Jews in Rome is implied in the narration of St. Paul's meeting with the elders, as well as in a passage which might be quoted from the satirist Persius.

tion, and to have been a numerous, wealthy, and influential community.

The Christians doubtless shared the protection which was extended to the Jews. They were hardly yet sufficiently distinguished as a self-existent community, to provoke any independent hostility. It is even possible that the Christians, so far as they were known as separate, were more tolerated than the Jews ; for, not having the same expectation of an earthly hero to deliver them, they had no political ends in view, and would not be in the same danger of exciting the suspicion of the government. Yet we should fall into a serious error, if we were to suppose that all the Christians in Rome, or the majority of them, had formerly been Jews or Proselytes; though this was doubtless true of its earliest members, who may have been of the number that were dispersed after the first Pentecost, or, possibly, disciples of our Lord Himself. It is impossible to arrive at any certain conclusion concerning the first origin and early growth of the Church in Rome ;[1] though, from the manifold links between the city and the provinces, it is easy to account for the formation of a large and flourishing community. Its history before the year 61 might be divided into three periods, separated from each other by the banishment of the Jews from Rome in the reign of Claudius,[2] and the writing of St. Paul's letter from Corinth.[3] Even in the first of these periods there might be points of connection between the Roman Church and St. Paul ; for some of those whom he salutes (Rom. xvi. 7, 11) as ' kinsmen,' are also said to have been ' Christians before him.' In the second period it cannot well be doubted that a very close connection began between St. Paul and some of the conspicuous members and principal teachers of the Roman Church. The expulsion of the Jews in consequence of the edict of Claudius, brought them in large numbers to the chief towns of the Levant; and there St. Paul met them in the synagogues. We have seen what results followed from his meeting with Aquila and Priscilla at Corinth. They returned to Rome with all the stores of spiritual instruction which he had given them ; and in the Epistle to the Romans we find him, as is natural, saluting them thus :—' Greet Priscilla and Aquila, my helpers in Christ Jesus : who have for my sake laid down their own necks : unto whom not only I give thanks, but also all the Churches of the Gentiles. Likewise greet the Church that is in their house.' All this reveals to us a great amount of devoted exertion on behalf of one large congregation in Rome ; and all of it distinctly connected with St. Paul. And this is perhaps only a specimen of other cases of the like kind Thus he sends a greeting to Epænetus, whom he names ' the firstfruits of Asia'[4] (v. 5), and who may have had the same close relation to him during his long ministration at Ephesus (Acts xix.), which Aquila and Priscilla had at Corinth. Nor must we forget those women, whom he singles out for special mention,—' Mary, who bestowed much labour on him' (v. 6); 'the beloved Persis, who laboured much in the Lord ' (v. 12); with Tryphæna and

---

[1] See pp. 497, 498.
[2] p. 299.
[3] p. 497.

[4] For the reading here, see p. 534 n. 6.

Tryphosa, and the unknown mother of Rufus (v. 13). We cannot doubt, that, though the Church of Rome may have received its growth and instruction through various channels, many of them were connected, directly or indirectly, with St. Paul; and accordingly he writes, in the whole of the letter, as one already in intimate relation with a Church which he has never seen. And whatever bonds subsisted between this Apostle and the Roman Christians must have been drawn still closer when the letter had been received ; for from that time they were looking forward to a personal visit from him, in his projected journey to the West. Thenceforward they must have taken the deepest interest in all his movements, and received with eager anxiety the news of his imprisonment at Cæsarea, and waited (as we have already seen) for his arrival in Italy. It is indeed but too true that there were parties among the Christians in Rome, and that some had a hostile feeling against St. Paul himself;[1] yet it is probable that the animosity of the Judaisers was less developed than it was in those regions which he had personally visited, and to which they had actually followed him. As to the unconverted Jews, the name of St. Paul was doubtless known to them; yet were they comparatively little interested in his movements. Their proud contempt of the Christian heresy would make them indifferent. The leaven of the Gospel was working around them to an extent of which they were hardly aware. The very magnitude of the population of Rome had a tendency to neutralise the currents of party feeling. For these reasons the hostility of the Jews was probably less violent than in any other part of the Empire.

Yet St. Paul could not possibly be aware of the exact extent of their enmity against himself. Independently, therefore, of his general principle of preaching, first to the Jew and then to the Gentile, he had an additional reason for losing no time in addressing himself to his countrymen. Thus, after the mention of St. Paul's being delivered up to Burrus, and allowed by him to be separate from the other prisoners,[2] the next scene to which the sacred historian introduces us is among the Jews. After three days[3] he sent for the principal men among them to his lodging,[4] and endeavoured to conciliate their feelings towards himself and the Gospel.

It is highly probable that the prejudices of these Roman Jews were already roused against the Apostle of the Gentiles; or if they

---

[1] See Phil. i. 15.

[2] 'By himself,' v. 16 ; an indulgence probably due to the influence of Julius.

[3] v. 17. This need not mean three complete days.

[4] 'Paul called the chief of the Jews together,' v. 17. With regard to the 'lodging,' v. 23, we are convinced, with Wieseler, that it is to be distinguished from ' his own hired house,' v. 30, mentioned below. The latter was a *hired lodging*, which he took for his permanent residence ; and the mention of the money he received from the Philippians (Phil. iv.) serves to show that he would not need the means of hiring a lodging. The former phrase implies the temporary residence of a guest with friends, as in Philemon 22. Nothing is more likely than that Aquila and Priscilla were his hosts at Rome, as formerly at Corinth.

had not yet conceived an unfavourable opinion of him, there was a danger that they would now look upon him as a traitor to his country, from the mere fact that he had appealed to the Roman power. He might even have been represented to them in the odious light of one who had come to Rome as an accuser of the Sanhedrin before the Emperor. St. Paul, therefore, addressed his auditors on this point at once, and showed that his enemies were guilty of this very appeal to the foreign power, of which he had himself been suspected. He had committed no offence against the holy nation, or the customs of their fathers; yet his enemies at Jerusalem had delivered him,—one of their brethren—of the seed of Abraham—of the tribe of Benjamin—a Hebrew of the Hebrews,—into the hands of the Romans. So unfounded was the accusation, that even the Roman governor had been ready to liberate the prisoner; but his Jewish enemies opposed his liberation. They strove to keep a child of Israel in Roman chains. So that he was compelled, as his only hope of safety, to appeal unto Cæsar. He brought no accusation against his countrymen before the tribunal of the stranger: that was the deed of his antagonists. In fact, his only crime had been his firm faith in God's deliverance of his people through the Messiah promised by the Prophets. '*For the hope of Israel,*' he concluded, '*I am bound with this chain.*' [1]

Their answer to this address was reassuring. They said that they had received no written communication from Judæa concerning St. Paul, and that none of 'the brethren' who had arrived from the East had spoken any evil of him. They further expressed a wish to hear from himself a statement of his religious sentiments, adding that the Christian sect was everywhere spoken against.[2] There was perhaps something hardly honest in this answer; for it seems to imply a greater ignorance with regard to Christianity than we can suppose to have prevailed among the Roman Jews. But with regard to Paul himself, it might well be true that they had little information concerning him. Though he had been imprisoned long at Cæsarea, his appeal had been made only a short time before winter. After that time (to use the popular expression), the sea was shut; and the winter had been a stormy one; so that it was natural enough that his case should be first made known to the Jews by himself. All these circumstances gave a favourable opening for the preaching of the Gospel, and Paul hastened to take advantage of it. A day was fixed for a meeting at his own private lodging.[3]

They came in great numbers[4] at the appointed time. Then followed an impressive scene, like that at Troas (Acts xxi.)—the Apostle pleading long and earnestly,—bearing testimony concerning the kingdom of God,—and endeavouring to persuade them by arguments drawn from their own Scriptures,—'from morning till evening.'[5] The result was a division among the auditors[6]—'not

---

[1] ver. 17–20.   [2] ver. 21, 22.

[3] 'When they had appointed him a day.'

[4] 'Then came many.'

[5] v. 23.

[6] 'Some believed the things which

peace but a sword,'—the division which has resulted ever since, when the Truth of God has encountered, side by side, earnest conviction with worldly indifference, honest investigation with bigoted prejudice, trustful faith with the pride of scepticism. After a long and stormy discussion, the unbelieving portion departed; but not until St. Paul had warned them, in one last address, that they were bringing upon themselves that awful doom of judicial blindness, which was denounced in their own Scriptures against obstinate unbelievers; that the salvation which they rejected would be withdrawn from them, and the inheritance they renounced would be given to the Gentiles.[1] The sentence with which he gave emphasis to this warning was that passage in Isaiah, which is more often quoted in the New Testament than any other words from the Old,[2]—which recurring thus with solemn force at the very close of the Apostolic history, seems to bring very strikingly together the Old Dispensation and the New, and to connect the ministry of Our Lord with that of His Apostles :—' 𝔊𝔬 𝔲𝔫𝔱𝔬 𝔱𝔥𝔦𝔰 𝔭𝔢𝔬𝔭𝔩𝔢 𝔞𝔫𝔡 𝔰𝔞𝔶: 𝔥𝔢𝔞𝔯𝔦𝔫𝔤 𝔶𝔢 𝔰𝔥𝔞𝔩𝔩 𝔥𝔢𝔞𝔯 𝔞𝔫𝔡 𝔰𝔥𝔞𝔩𝔩 𝔫𝔬𝔱 𝔲𝔫𝔡𝔢𝔯𝔰𝔱𝔞𝔫𝔡, 𝔞𝔫𝔡 𝔰𝔢𝔢𝔦𝔫𝔤 𝔶𝔢 𝔰𝔥𝔞𝔩𝔩 𝔰𝔢𝔢 𝔞𝔫𝔡 𝔰𝔥𝔞𝔩𝔩 𝔫𝔬𝔱 𝔭𝔢𝔯𝔠𝔢𝔦𝔳𝔢: 𝔣𝔬𝔯 𝔱𝔥𝔢 𝔥𝔢𝔞𝔯𝔱 𝔬𝔣 𝔱𝔥𝔦𝔰 𝔭𝔢𝔬𝔭𝔩𝔢 𝔦𝔰 𝔴𝔞𝔵𝔢𝔡 𝔤𝔯𝔬𝔰𝔰, 𝔞𝔫𝔡 𝔱𝔥𝔢𝔦𝔯 𝔢𝔞𝔯𝔰 𝔞𝔯𝔢 𝔡𝔲𝔩𝔩 𝔬𝔣 𝔥𝔢𝔞𝔯𝔦𝔫𝔤, 𝔞𝔫𝔡 𝔱𝔥𝔢𝔦𝔯 𝔢𝔶𝔢𝔰 𝔥𝔞𝔳𝔢 𝔱𝔥𝔢𝔶 𝔠𝔩𝔬𝔰𝔢𝔡; 𝔩𝔢𝔰𝔱 𝔱𝔥𝔢𝔶 𝔰𝔥𝔬𝔲𝔩𝔡 𝔰𝔢𝔢 𝔴𝔦𝔱𝔥 𝔱𝔥𝔢𝔦𝔯 𝔢𝔶𝔢𝔰, 𝔞𝔫𝔡 𝔥𝔢𝔞𝔯 𝔴𝔦𝔱𝔥 𝔱𝔥𝔢𝔦𝔯 𝔢𝔞𝔯𝔰, 𝔞𝔫𝔡 𝔲𝔫𝔡𝔢𝔯𝔰𝔱𝔞𝔫𝔡 𝔴𝔦𝔱𝔥 𝔱𝔥𝔢𝔦𝔯 𝔥𝔢𝔞𝔯𝔱, 𝔞𝔫𝔡 𝔰𝔥𝔬𝔲𝔩𝔡 𝔟𝔢 𝔠𝔬𝔫𝔳𝔢𝔯𝔱𝔢𝔡, 𝔞𝔫𝔡 𝔍 𝔰𝔥𝔬𝔲𝔩𝔡 𝔥𝔢𝔞𝔩 𝔱𝔥𝔢𝔪.'[3]

A formal separation was now made between the Apostle of the Gentiles and the Jews of Rome. They withdrew to dispute concerning the 'sect' which was making such inroads on their prejudices (v. 29). He remained in his own hired house[4]—where the indulgence of Burrus permitted him to reside, instead of confining him within the walls of the Prætorian barrack. We must not forget, however, that he was still a prisoner under military custody, —chained by the arm,[5] both day and night, to one of the imperial body-guard,—and thus subjected to the rudeness and caprice of an insolent soldiery. This severity, however, was indispensable according to the Roman law; and he received every indulgence which it was in the power of the Præfect to grant. He was allowed to receive all who came to him (v. 30), and was permitted,. without hindrance, to preach boldly the kingdom of God, and teach the things of the LORD JESUS CHRIST (v. 31).

Thus was fulfilled his long cherished desire 'to proclaim the Gospel to them that were in Rome also' (Rom. i. 15). Thus ends the Apostolic History, so far as it has been directly revealed. Here the thread of sacred narrative, which we have followed so long, is

---

were spoken, and some believed not. And when they agreed not among themselves,' &c.

[1] v. 28.

[2] ver. 24–28.

[3] Isa. vi. 9, 10 (LXX.). Quoted also by our Lord (Matt. xiii. 15), and referred to by St. John (John xii. 40).

[4] See above.

[5] 'With *the* soldier that kept him,' Acts xxviii. 16. See above, pp. 612, 613, and compare Eph. vi. 20 ('an ambassador in bonds'), Col. iv. 18, Phil. i. 13. Possibly two soldiers guarded him by night, according to the sentence of the Roman law—'nox custodiam geminat,'—quoted by Wieseler.

suddenly broken. Our knowledge of the incidents of his residence in Rome, and of his subsequent history, must be gathered almost exclusively from the letters of the Apostle himself.

Coin of Nero (with the Harbour of Ostia).[1]

·[1] From the British Museum. This is one of the large brass coins of Nero's reign, which exhibit admirable portraits of the Emperor. We notice here that peculiar rig of ancient ships which was mentioned above, pp. 626 and 663.

CHAPTER XXV.

Delay of St. Paul's Trial.—His Occupations and Companions during his Imprisonment.—He writes *The Epistle to Philemon, The Epistle to the Colossians,*
and *The Epistle to the Ephesians (so called).*

WE have seen that St. Paul's accusers had not yet arrived from
Palestine, and that their coming was not even expected by the
Roman Jews. This proves that they had not left Syria before the
preceding winter, and consequently that they could not have set
out on their journey till the following spring, when the navigation
of the Mediterranean was again open. Thus, they would not reach
Rome till the summer or autumn of the year 61 A.D.[1] Meanwhile,
the progress of the trial was necessarily suspended, for the Roman
courts required[2] the personal presence of the prosecutor. It would
seem that, at this time,[3] an accused person might be thus kept in
prison for an indefinite period, merely by the delay of the prosecutor to proceed with his accusation; nor need this surprise us, if
we consider how harshly the law has dealt with supposed offenders,
and with what indifference it has treated the rights of the accused,
even in periods whose civilisation was not only more advanced than
that of the Roman Empire, but also imbued with the merciful
spirit of Christianity. And even when the prosecutors were present,
and no ground alleged for the delay of the trial, a corrupt judge
might postpone it, as Felix did, for months and years, to gratify
the enemies of the prisoner. And if a provincial Governor, though
responsible for such abuse of power to his master, might venture
to act in this arbitrary manner, much more might the Emperor
himself, who was responsible to no man. Thus, we find that Tibe-

[1] About this period (as we learn
from Josephus) there were two embassies sent from Jerusalem to Rome ;
viz., that which was charged to conduct
the impeachment of Felix, and that
which was sent to intercede with Nero
on the subject of Agrippa's palace,
which overlooked the Temple. The
former seems to have arrived in Rome
in A.D. 60, the latter in A.D. 61. (See
note on the Chronological Table in Appendix.) It is not impossible that the
latter embassy, in which was included
Ishmael the high priest, may have been
entrusted with the prosecution of St.
Paul, in addition to their other business.

[2] It should be observed that the
prosecutor on a criminal charge, under

the Roman law, was not the State (as
with us the Crown), but any private
individual who chose to bring an accusation.

[3] At a later period the suspension
on the part of the prosecutor of the
proceedings during a year, was made
equivalent to an abandonment of it,
and amounted to an *abolitio* of the
process. In the time of Nero the prosecutors on a public charge were liable
to punishment if they abandoned it
from corrupt motives, by the Senatus
Consultum Turpilianum. See Tacitus,
Ann. xiv. 41. This law was passed
A.D. 61, and was afterwards interpreted
by the juriconsults as forbidding an
accuser to withdraw his accusation.

rius was in the habit of delaying the hearing of causes, and retaining the accused in prison unheard, merely out of procrastination.[1] So that, even after St. Paul's prosecutors had arrived, and though we were to suppose them anxious for the progress of the trial, it might still have been long delayed by the Emperor's caprice. But there is no reason to think that, when they came, they would have wished to press on the cause. From what had already occurred they had every reason to expect the failure of the prosecution. In fact it had already broken down at its first stage, and Festus had strongly pronounced his opinion of the innocence[2] of the accused. Their hope of success at Rome must have been grounded either on influencing the Emperor's judgment by private intrigue, or on producing further evidence in support of their accusation. For both these objects delay would be necessary. Moreover, it was quite in accordance with the regular course of Roman jurisprudence, that the Court should grant a long suspension of the cause, on the petition of the prosecutor, that he might be allowed time to procure the attendance of witnesses[3] from a distance. The length of time thus granted would depend upon the remoteness of the place where the alleged crimes had been committed. We read of an interval of twelve months permitted during Nero's reign, in the case of an accusation against Suilius,[4] for misdemeanours committed during his government of Proconsular Asia. The accusers of St. Paul might fairly demand a longer suspension; for they accused him of offences committed not only in Palestine (which was far more remote than Proconsular Asia from Rome), but also over the whole[5] Empire. Their witnesses must be summoned from Judæa, from Syria, from Cilicia, from Pisidia, from Macedonia. In all cities, from Damascus to Corinth, in all countries, 'from Jerusalem round about unto Illyricum,' must testimony be sought to prove the seditious turbulence of the ringleader of the Nazarenes. The interval granted them for such a purpose could not be less than a year, and might well be more.[6] Supposing it to be the shortest possible, and assuming that the prosecutors reached Rome in August A.D. 61, the first stage of the trial would be appointed to commence not before August A.D. 62. And when this period arrived, the prosecutors and the accused, with their witnesses, must have been heard on each of the charges separately (according to Nero's regulations,)[7] and sentence pronounced on the first charge before

[1] Joseph. *Ant.* xviii. 6. 5.

[2] Acts xxv. 25, and xxvi. 32.

[3] A good instance is given in Tacitus, *Ann.* xiii. 52. This was in a case where the accused had been proconsul in Africa. We may observe that the attendance of the witnesses for the prosecution could be legally enforced.

[4] Tac. *Ann.* xiii. 43.

[5] 'A mover of sedition among the Jews throughout the world,' Acts xxiv. 5.

[6] Another cause of delay, even if the prosecutors did not make the demand for suspension, would have been the loss of the official notice of the case forwarded by Festus. No appeal (as we have before observed) could be tried without a rescript (called *Apostoli* or *literæ dimissoriæ*) from the inferior to the superior judge, stating full particulars of the case. Such documents might well have been lost in the wreck at Malta.

[7] It was Nero's practice, as Suetonius tells us (*Nero*, 15), 'to take the heads of accusation singly.'

the second was entered into.   Now, the charges against St. Paul were divided (as we have seen) into three[1] separate heads of accusation.   Consequently, the proceedings, which would of course be adjourned from time to time to suit the Emperor's convenience, may well have lasted till the beginning of 63, at which time St. Luke's narrative would lead us to fix their termination.[2]

During the long delay of his trial, St. Paul was not reduced, as he had been at Cæsarea, to a forced inactivity.   On the contrary he was permitted the freest intercourse with his friends, and was allowed to reside in a house of a sufficient size to accommodate the congregation which flocked together to listen to his teaching.   The freest scope was given to his labours, consistent with the military custody under which he was placed.   We are told, in language peculiarly emphatic, that this preaching was subjected to no restraint whatever.[3]   And that which seemed at first to impede, must really have deepened the impression of his eloquence; for who could see without emotion that venerable form subjected by iron links to the coarse control of the soldier who stood beside him? how often must the tears of the assembly have been called forth by the upraising of that fettered hand, and the clanking of the chain which checked its energetic action!

We shall see hereafter that these labours of the imprisoned Confessor were not fruitless; in his own words, he begot many children in his chains.[4]   Meanwhile, he had a wider sphere of action than even the metropolis of the world.   Not only 'the crowd which pressed upon him daily,'[5] but also 'the care of all the Churches,' demanded his constant vigilance and exertion.   Though himself tied down to a single spot, he kept up a constant intercourse, by his delegates, with his converts throughout the Empire; and not only with his own converts, but with the other Gentile Churches, who, as yet, had not seen his face in the flesh.   To enable him to maintain this superintendence, he manifestly needed many faithful messengers; men who (as he says of one of them) rendered him profitable service;[6] and by some of whom he seems to have been constantly accompanied, wheresoever he went.[7]   Accordingly, we find him, during this Roman imprisonment, surrounded by many of his oldest and most valued attendants.   Luke,[8] his fellow-traveller, remained with him during his bondage; Timotheus,[9] his beloved son in the faith, ministered to him at Rome, as he had done in Asia, in Macedonia, and in Achaia.   Tychicus,[10] who had formerly borne him company from Corinth to Ephesus, is now at hand to

---

[1] See above, p. 608.

[2] We need not notice the hypothesis of Böttger, that St. Paul's imprisonment at Rome only lasted five days. It has already been refuted by Neander and Wieseler.

[3] Acts xxviii. 31: 'teaching . . . . with all confidence, no man forbidding him.'   [4] Philem. 10.

[5] 2 Cor. xi. 28.   [6] 2 Tim. iv. 11.

[7] Comp. Acts xix. 22: 'two of them that ministered to him.'

[8] Col. iv. 14; Philem. 24. Luke seems, however, to have been absent from Rome when the Epistle to the Philippians was written.

[9] Philem. 1; Col. i. 1; Phil. i. 1.

[10] Col. iv. 7; Eph. vi. 21; cf. Acts xx. 4; and Tit. iii. 12.   [St. Paul himself was not actually at Ephesus. It is very possible that Tychicus went thither from Miletus. See Acts xx. 16, 38.   H.]

carry his letters to the shores which they had visited together. But there are two names amongst his Roman companions which excite a peculiar interest, though from opposite reasons,—the names of Demas and of Mark. The latter, when last we heard of him, was the unhappy cause of the separation of Barnabas and Paul. He was rejected by Paul, as unworthy to attend him, because he had previously abandoned the work of the Gospel out of timidity or indolence.[1] It is delightful to find him now ministering obediently to the very Apostle who had then repudiated his services; still more, to know that he persevered in this fidelity even to the end,[2] and was sent for by St. Paul to cheer his dying hours. Demas, on the other hand, is now a faithful ' fellow-labourer '[3] of the Apostle; but in a few years we shall find that he had ' forsaken ' him, ' having loved this present world.' Perhaps we may be allowed to hope, that, as the fault of Demas was the same with that of Mark, so the repentance of Mark may have been paralleled by that of Demas.

Amongst the rest of St. Paul's companions at this time, there were two whom he distinguishes by the honourable title of his 'fellow-prisoners.' One of these is Aristarchus,[4] the other Epaphras.[5] With regard to the former, we know that he was a Macedonian of Thessalonica, one of 'Paul's companions in travel,' whose life was endangered by the mob at Ephesus, and who embarked with St. Paul at Cæsarea when he set sail for Rome. The other, Epaphras, was a Colossian, who must not be identified with the Philippian Epaphroditus, another of St. Paul's fellow-labourers during this time. It is not easy to say what was the exact sense in which these two disciples were peculiarly *fellow-prisoners*[6] of St. Paul. Perhaps it only implies that they dwelt in his house, which was also his prison.

But of all the disciples now ministering to St. Paul at Rome, none has for us a greater interest than the fugitive Asiatic slave Onesimus. He belonged to a Christian named Philemon, a member of the Colossian[7] Church. But he had robbed[8] his master, and fled from Colossæ, and at last found his way to Rome. It is difficult to imagine any portion of mankind more utterly depraved than the associates among whom a runaway pagan slave must have found himself in the capital. Profligate and unprincipled as we know even the highest and most educated society to have then been, what must have been its dregs and offal? Yet from this lowest depth Onesimus was dragged forth by the hand of Christian love. Perhaps some Asiatic Christian, who had seen him formerly at his master's house, recognised him in the streets of Rome destitute and starving, and had compassion on him; and thus he might have been brought to hear the preaching of the illustrious prisoner. Or

---

[1] pp. 128, 129, 192, 193.

[2] 2 Tim. iv. 11 : ' Take Mark, and bring him with thee; for his services are profitable to me.'

[3] Philem. 24; cf. Col. iv. 14.

[4] Col. iv. 10; cf. Acts xix. 29, and Acts xxvii. 2, and Philem. 24.

[5] Col. i. 7; Philem. 23.

[6] The same expression is used of Andronicus and Junias (Rom. xvi. 7), but of no others except these four.

[7] For the proof of this see Paley's *Horæ Paulinæ* on Philemon (10–12).

[8] Philem. 18.

it is not impossible that he may have already known St. Paul at Ephesus, where his master Philemon had formerly been himself converted [1] by the Apostle. However this may be, it is certain that Onesimus was led by the providence of God to listen to that preaching now which he had formerly despised. He was converted to the faith of Christ, and therefore to the morality of Christ. He confessed to St. Paul his sins against his master. The Apostle seems to have been peculiarly attracted by the character of Onesimus; and he perceived in him the indications of gifts which fitted him for a more important post than any which he could hold as the slave of Philemon. He wished [2] to keep him at Rome, and employ him in the service of the Gospel. Yet he would not transgress the law, nor violate the rights of Philemon, by acting in this matter without his consent. He therefore decided that Onesimus must immediately return to his master ; and, to make this duty less painful, he undertook himself to discharge the sum of which Philemon had been defrauded. An opportunity now offered itself for Onesimus to return in good company; for St. Paul was sending Tychicus to Asia Minor, charged, amongst other commissions, with an epistle to Colossæ, the home of Philemon. Under his care, therefore, he placed the penitent slave, who was now willing to surrender himself to his offended master. Nevertheless, he did not give up the hope of placing his new convert in a position wherein he might minister no longer to a private individual, but to the Church at large. He intimated his wishes on the subject to Philemon himself, with characteristic delicacy, in a letter which he charged Onesimus to deliver on his arrival at Colossæ. This letter is not only a beautiful illustration of the character of St. Paul, but also a practical commentary upon the precepts concerning the mutual relations of slaves [3] and masters given in his cotemporary Epistles. We see here one of the earliest examples of the mode in which Christianity operated upon these relations ; not by any violent disruption of the organisation of society, such as could only have produced another Servile War, but by gradually leavening and interpenetrating society with the spirit of a religion which recognised the equality of all men in the sight of God. The letter was as follows :—

[1] Philem. 10 appears to state this. (See p. 371.)

[2] Philem. 13.

[3] See Col. iii. 22 and Eph. vi. 5. St. Paul's attention seems to have been especially drawn to this subject at the present time ; and he might well feel the need there was for a fundamental change in this part of the social system of antiquity, such as the spirit of Christ alone could give. In the very year of his arrival at Rome, a most frightful example was given of the atrocity of the laws which regulated the relations of slave to master. The prefect of the city (Pedanius Secundus) was killed by one of his slaves ; and in accordance with the ancient law, the whole body of slaves belonging to Pedanius at Rome, amounting to a vast multitude, and including many women and children, were executed together, although confessedly innocent of all participation in the crime. Tac. *Ann.* xiv. 42–45.

THE EPISTLE TO PHILEMON.[1]

Salutation.

1 PAUL, a prisoner of Christ Jesus, and Timotheus the
   brother, To PHILEMON OUR BELOVED FRIEND AND
2 FELLOW LABOURER ; AND TO APPIA[2] OUR BELOVED
   SISTER,[3] AND TO ARCHIPPUS[4] OUR FELLOW SOLDIER,
   AND TO THE CHURCH AT THY HOUSE.
3 Grace be to you and peace, from God our Father and
   our Lord Jesus Christ.

Thanksgivings and prayers for Philemon.

4 I thank my God, making mention of thee always
5 in my prayers, because I hear of thy love and faith
   towards the Lord Jesus, and towards all the saints ;
6 praying[5] that thy faith may communicate itself to
   others, and may become workful, in causing true
   knowledge of all the good which is in us, for Christ's
7 service.   For I have great joy and consolation in thy
   love, because the hearts of the saints have been comforted by thee, brother.

Request for the favourable reception of Onesimus.

8 Wherefore, although in the authority of Christ I
9 might boldly enjoin upon thee that which is befit-
   ting, yet for love's sake I rather beseech thee as Paul
10 the aged, and now also prisoner of Jesus Christ.   I
   beseech thee for my son, whom I have begotten in
11 my chains, Onesimus; who formerly was to thee unprofitable,[6] but now is profitable both to thee and
12 me.   Whom I have sent back to thee ;[7] but do thou

---

[1] With respect to the date of this Epistle, the fact that it was conveyed by Onesimus (compare Col. iv. 9), and the persons mentioned as with St. Paul at the time (Philem. 23, 24, compared with Col. iv. 12-14), prove that it was sent to Asia Minor, together with the Epistle to the Colossians, the date of which is discussed in a note on the begining of that Epistle.

[2] We are told by Chrysostom that she was the wife of Philemon, which seems probable from the juxtaposition of their names.

[3] 'Sister' is added in many of the best MSS.

[4] Archippus was apparently a presbyter of the church at Colossæ, or perhaps an *evangelist* resident there on a special mission (compare Col. iv. 17) : from the present passage he seems to have lived in the house of Philemon.

[5] 'That' is to be joined with verse 4, as stating the object of the prayer there mentioned, while verse 5 gives the subject of the thanksgiving.   This is Chrysostom's view, against which Meyer's objections appear inconclusive. The literal English of verse 6 is as follows : *that the communication of thy faith may become workful, in true knowledge of all good which is in us, for Christ.*   The latter words are very obscure, but the rendering adopted in the text appears to make the best sense.   The best MSS. are divided between Christ and Christ Jesus ; but agree in reading ' in *us*,' not ' in *you*.'

[6] Most modern commentators suppose a play on the name *Onesimus*, which means *useful* ; but there seems scarcely sufficient ground for this, and it was never remarked by the ancient Greek commentators, whose judgment on such a point would be entitled to most deference.

[7] Many of the best MSS. add ' to thee.' The omission of the imperative makes no difference in the sense ; but it is characteristic of St. Paul's abrupt

receive him as my own[1] flesh and blood. For I 13
would gladly[2] retain him with myself, that he might
render service to me in thy stead, while I am a prisoner for declaring the Glad-tidings ; but I am un- 14
willing to do anything without thy decision, that thy
kindness may not be constrained, but voluntary.
For perhaps to this very end he was parted from 15
thee for a time, that thou mightest possess him for
ever ; no longer as a bondsman, but above a bonds- 16
man, a brother beloved ; very dear to me, but how
much more to thee, being thine both in the flesh and
in the Lord. If, then, thou count me in fellowship 17
with thee, receive him as myself. But whatsoever 18
he has wronged thee of, or owes thee, reckon it to 19
my account (I, Paul, write[3] this with my own hand);
I will repay it ; for I would not say to thee that thou 20
owest me even thine own self besides. Yea, brother,
let me have joy of thee in the Lord ; comfort my
heart in Christ.[4]

Announcement of a visit from Paul to Asia Minor on his acquittal.

I write to thee with full confidence in thy obedi- 21
ence, knowing that thou wilt do even more than I
say. But, moreover, prepare to receive me as thy 22
guest ; for I trust that through your[5] prayers I shall
be given to you.

Salutations from Rome.

There salute thee Epaphras my fellow-prisoner[6] 23
in Christ Jesus, Marcus, Aristarchus, Demas, and 24
Luke, my fellow-labourers.

Concluding benediction.

The Grace of our Lord Jesus Christ be with your 25
spirits.[7]

While Onesimus, on the arrival of the two companions at Colossæ,[8] hurried to the house of his master with the letter which we

and rapid dictation. [If, with the best MSS., we omit the imperative, we find it in v. 17 : and the intermediate matter is practically parenthetic. H.]

[1] Children were called the σπλάγχνα of their parents.

[2] The imperfect here, and aorist in the preceding and following verse, are used, according to classical idiom, from the position of the *reader* of the letter.

[3] See the preceeding note.

[4] 'Christ' is the reading of the best MSS.

[5] Observe the change from singular to plural here, and in verse 25.

[6] 'Fellow-soldier,' as we have be-

fore remarked, perhaps means only that Epaphras had voluntarily shared Paul's imprisonment at Rome by taking up his residence with him, in the lodging where he was guarded by the 'soldier that kept him.'

[7] The *Amen* as usual is interpolated.

[8] Though we have come to the conclusion that St. Paul had not himself (at this time) visited Colossæ, yet it is hardly possible to read these Epistles without feeling an interest in the scenery and topography of its vicinity. The upper part of the valley of the Mæander, where this city, with its neighbour-cities Hierapolis and Laodicea (Col. ii. 1, iv. 13 ; Rev. iii. 14), was situated, has been described by

have just read, Tychicus proceeded to discharge his commission likewise, by delivering to the Presbyters the Epistle with which he was charged, that it might be read to the whole Colossian Church at their next meeting. The letter to the Colossians itself gives us distinct information as to the cause which induced St. Paul to write it. Epaphras, the probable founder of that Church (Col. i. 7), was now at Rome, and he had communicated to the Apostle the unwelcome tidings, that the faith of the Colossians was in danger of being perverted by false teaching. It has been questioned whether several different systems of error had been introduced among them, or whether the several errors combated in the Epistle were parts of one system, and taught by the same teachers. On the one side we find that in the Epistle, St. Paul warns the Colossians *separately* against the following different errors :—First, A combination of angel-worship and asceticism; Secondly, A self-styled *philosophy* or *gnosis* which depreciated Christ; Thirdly, A rigid observance of Jewish festivals and Sabbaths. On the other side, First, the Epistle seems distinctly (though with an indirectness caused by obvious motives) to point to a single source, and even a single individual, as the origin of the errors introduced ; and, Secondly, we know that at any rate the two first of these errors, and apparently the third also, were combined by some of the early Gnostics. The most probable view, therefore, seems to be, that some Alexandrian Jew had appeared at Colossæ, professing a belief in Christianity, and imbued with the Greek 'philosophy' of the school of Philo, but combining with it the Rabbinical theosophy and angelology, which afterwards was embodied in the Cabbala, and an extravagant asceticism, which also afterwards distinguished several sects of the Gnostics.[1] In short, one of the first heresiarchs of the incipient Gnosticism had begun to pervert the Colossians from the simplicity of their faith. We have seen in a former chapter[2] how great was the danger to be apprehended from this source, at the stage which the Church had now reached ; especially in a church which consisted, as that at Colossæ did, principally of Gentiles (Col. i. 25–27, Col. ii. 11) ; and that, too, in Phrygia,[3] where the national character was so prone to a mystic fanaticism. We need not wonder, therefore, that St. Paul, acting under the inspiration of the Holy Spirit, should have thought it needful to use every effort to counteract the growing evil. This he does, both by

many travellers ; and the illustrated works on Asia Minor contain several views, especially of the vast and singular petrifactions of Hierapolis (Pambouk-Kalessi). Colossæ was older than either Laodicea or Hierapolis, and it fell into comparative insignificance as they rose into importance. In the Middle Ages it became a place of some consequence, and was the birthplace of the Byzantine writer Nicetas Choniates, who tells us that Chonæ and Colossæ were the same place. A village called *Chonas* still remains, the proximity of which to the ancient Colossæ is proved

by the correspondence of the observed phenomena with what Herodotus says of the river Lycus. The neighbourhood was explored by Mr. Arundel (*Seven Churches*, p. 158. *Asia Minor*, II. 160), but Mr. Hamilton was the first to determine the actual site of the ancient city. (*Researches*, I. 508.)

[1] See pp. 30 and 355, 356.

[2] Chap. XIII.

[3] See pp. 181–184 ; and also the account of the early Phrygian Gnostics in the lately discovered '*Refutation of Heresies*,' book v.

contradicting the doctrinal errors of the new system, and by inculcating, as essential to Christianity, that pure morality which these early heretics despised. Such appears to have been the main purpose of the following Epistle.

THE EPISTLE TO THE COLOSSIANS.[1]

Salutation. PAUL, an apostle of Jesus Christ, by the will of God, i. 1 and Timotheus the brother, TO THE HOLY AND 2 FAITHFUL BRETHREN IN CHRIST WHO ARE AT CO-LOSSÆ,[2]

Grace be to you, and peace from God our Father.[3]

Thanksgiving for their conversion. I[4] give continual thanks to God[5] the Father of 3 our Lord Jesus Christ, in my prayers for you (since 4 I heard of your faith in Christ Jesus, and your love to all the saints), because[6] of the hope laid up for 5 you in the heavens, whereof you heard the promise[7] in the truthful Word of the Glad-tidings; which is 6 come to you, as it is through all the world; and everywhere it bears fruit and[8] grows, as it does also among you, since the day when first you heard it, and learned to know truly the grace of God. And 7 thus you were taught by Epaphras my beloved fellow-bondsman,[9] who is a faithful servant of Christ on your behalf. And it is he who has declared to me 8 your love for me[10] in the Spirit.

---

[1] The following are the grounds for the date assigned to this Epistle.

(1.) It was written in prison at the same time as that to Philemon, and sent by the same messenger (iv. 7–9).

(2.) It was not written in Cæsarea—
(A) Because while writing St. Paul was labouring for the Gospel (iv. 3, 4), which he did not at Cæsarea (Acts xxviii. 31).
(B) Because he could not have expected at Cæsarea to be soon coming to Phrygia (Acts xxiii. 11, xix. 21; Rom. i. 13; Acts xx. 25), whereas while writing this he expected soon to visit Phrygia (Philem. 22).

(3.) The indications above mentioned all correspond with Rome. Moreover Timotheus was with him, as we know he was at Rome, from Phil. i. 1.

[2] Many of the best MSS. have Colassæ; and this form is found in some of the later Greek writers.

[3] The words 'And our Lord Jesus Christ,' with which St. Paul in all other cases concludes this formula of benediction, are omitted here in the best MSS. Chrysostom remarks on the omission.

[4] See note on 1 Thess. i. 2.

[5] 'And' is omitted by the best MSS.

[6] It seems more natural to take the preposition thus, as in v. 9, than to connect it with the preceding verse.

[7] '*Before.*' The information regarding the hope had been received by them *before its fulfilment.* Olshausen.

[8] The MSS. add this to the T. R.

[9] *Epaphras* is the same name with *Epaphroditus*; but this can scarcely be the same person with that Epaphroditus who brought the contribution from Philippi to Rome about this time. This was a native of Colossæ (see iv. 12), the other was settled at Philippi, and held office in the Philippian Church.

[10] This interpretation (which is Chrysostom's) seems the most natural. Their love for St. Paul was *in the Spirit* because they had never seen him *in the flesh.*

i. 9   Wherefore I also, since the day when first I heard it, cease not to pray for you, and to ask of God that

10 you may fully attain to the knowledge of His will; that[1] in all wisdom and spiritual understanding you may walk worthy of the Lord, to please Him in all things; that you may bear fruit in all good works

11 and grow continually in the knowledge of God; that you may be strengthened to the uttermost in the strength of His glorious power, to bear all sufferings

12 with stedfastness and with joy, giving thanks[2] to the Father who has fitted us to share the portion of the saints in the light.

13   For He has delivered us from the dominion of darkness, and transplanted us into the kingdom of

14 His beloved Son, in whom we have our redemption,[3]

15 the forgiveness of our sins. Who is a visible[4] image

16 of the invisible God, the firstborn of all creation; for in[5] Him were all things created, both in the heavens and on the earth, both visible and invisible, whether they be Thrones, or Dominations, or Principalities, or Powers;[6] by him and for Him[7] were all created.

17 And He is before all things, and in Him all things

18 subsist.[8] And He is the head of the body, the Church; whereof He is the beginning, as firstborn

---

[1] The punctuation here adopted connects 'in all wisdom,' &c. with the following verb.

[2] The 'giving thanks' here seems parallel to the preceding participles, and consequently the '*us*' is used, not with reference to the writer, but generally, as including both writer and readers; and the particular case of the readers (as formerly Heathens) referred to in v. 21 ('and *you*').

[3] 'Through His blood' has been introduced here by mistake from Eph. i. 7, and is not found in the best MSS.

[4] It is important to observe here, that St. Paul says not merely that our Lord *was*, when on earth, the visible image of God, but that He *is* so still. In Him only God manifests Himself to man, and He is still visible to the eye of faith.

[5] 'In' here must not be confounded with 'through' or 'by.' The existence of Christ, the λόγος, is the condition of all Creation; in Him the Godhead is manifested.

[6] St. Paul here appears to allude to the doctrines of the Colossian heretics, who taught a system of angel-worship,

based upon a systematic classification of the angelic hierarchy (probably similar to that found in the Cabbala), and who seem to have represented our Lord as only one (and perhaps not the highest) of this hierarchy. Other allusions to a hierarchy of angels (which was taught in the Rabbinical theology) may be found Rom. viii. 38; Eph. i. 21, iii. 10; 1 Pet. iii. 22, joined with the assertion of their subjection to Christ.

[7] Compare Rom. xi. 36, where exactly the same thing is said concerning *God*; from which the inference is plain. It appears evident that St. Paul insists here thus strongly on the creation by Jesus Christ, in opposition to some erroneous system which ascribed the creation to some other source; and this was the case with the early Gnosticism, which ascribed the creation of the world to a Demiurge, who was distinct from the man Jesus.

[8] i.e. the life of the universe is conditioned by His existence. See the last note but two.

from the dead ; that in all things His place might be the first.

For He willed[1] that in Himself all the Fulness of the universe[2] should dwell; and by Himself he willed i. 19 to reconcile all things to Himself, having made peace 20 by the blood of His cross ; by Himself (I say) to reconcile all things, whether on the earth, or in the heavens.[3]

The Colossians had been called from Heathenism and reconciled to God by Christ.

And you, likewise, who once were estranged from 21 Him, and with your mind at war with Him, when you lived in wickedness, yet now He has reconciled 22 in the body of his flesh[4] through death, that He might bring you to His presence in holiness, without blemish and without reproach ; if, indeed, you be 23 stedfast in your faith, with your foundation firmly grounded and immovably fixed, and not suffering yourselves to be shifted away from the hope of the Glad-tidings which you heard, which has been published throughout all the earth,[5] whereof I, Paul, was made a ministering servant.

St. Paul's commission to reveal the Christian mystery of

And even now I rejoice in the afflictions which I 24 bear for your[6] sake, and I fill up what yet is lacking of the sufferings[7] of Christ in my flesh, on behalf of

---

[1] ' He willed.' Most commentators suppose an ellipsis of ' God,' but the instances adduced by De Wette and others to justify this seem insufficient ; and there seems no reason to seek a new subject for the verb, when there is one already expressed in the preceding verse.

[2] The word *Pleroma* is here used by St. Paul in a technical sense, with a manifest allusion to the errors against which he is writing. The early Gnostics used the same word to represent the assemblage of emanations (conceived as angelic powers) proceeding from the Deity. St. Paul therefore appears to say, that the true *Fulness of the universe* (or, as he calls it, chap. ii. 9, *Fulness of the Godhead*), is to be found, not in any angelic hierarchy (see the remarks introductory to this Epistle, page 691), but in Christ alone.

[3] This statement of the infinite extent of the results of Christ's redemption (which may well fill us with reverential awe), has been a sore stumbling-block to many commentators, who have devised various (and some very ingenious) modes of explaining it away.

Into these this is not the place to enter. It is sufficient to observe that St. Paul is still led to set forth the true greatness of Christ in opposition to the angelolatry of the Colossian heretics ; intimating that, far from Christ being one only of the angelic hierarchy, the heavenly hosts themselves stood in need of His atonement. Compare Heb. ix. 23.

[4] Here again is perhaps a reference to the Gnostic element in the Colossian theosophy. It was Christ Himself who suffered death, in the body of His flesh ; He was perfect man ; and not (as the Docetæ taught) an angelic emanation, who withdrew from the man Jesus before He suffered.

[5] Literally *throughout all the creation under the sky*, which is exactly equivalent to *throughout all the earth.* St. Paul of course speaks here hyperbolically, meaning, *the teaching which you heard from Epaphras is the same which has been published universally by the Apostles.*

[6] St. Paul's sufferings were caused by his zeal on behalf of the *Gentile* converts.

[7] Compare 2 Cor. i. 5. 'The suf-

i. 25 His body, which is the Church ; whereof I was made
a servant, to minister in the stewardship which God
26 gave me for you [Gentiles], that I might fulfil it by
declaring the Word of God, the mystery which has
been hid for ages and generations,[1] but has now been
27 shown openly to His saints ; to whom God willed to
mánifest how rich, among the Gentiles, is the glory
of this mystery, which[2] is CHRIST IN YOU THE HOPE OF
GLORY.

28   Him, therefore, I proclaim, warning every man,
and teaching every man, in all wisdom ; that I may
bring every man into His presence full grown in
29 Christ.[3] And to this end I labour in earnest conflict, according to His working which works in me
with mighty power.

ii. 1   For I would have you know how great[4] a conflict
I sustain for you, and for those at Laodicea, and for
2 all[5] who have not seen my face in the flesh ; that
their hearts may be comforted, and that they may be
knit together in love, and may gain in all its richness
3 the full assurance of understanding ;[6] truly to know
the mystery of God,[7] wherein are all the treasures of
wisdom and of knowledge[8] hidden.

4   I say this, lest any man should mislead you with
5 enticing words. For though I am absent from you
in the flesh, yet I am present with you in the spirit,

He prays that they may grow in true wisdom;

and warns them against those who would mislead them

---

ferings *of Christ* have come upon me
above measure ; ' and also Acts ix. 4,
' Why persecutest thou *me.*' St. Paul
doubtless recollected those words when
he called his sufferings ' the sufferings
of Christ in his flesh.'

[1] Literally, *from* (i.e. *since*) *the ages
and the generations,* meaning *from the
remotest times,* with special reference
to the times of the Mosaic Dispensation. Compare Rom. xvi. 25 ; and
Titus i. 2.

[2] The best MSS are here divided,
so as to leave it doubtful whether the
relative belongs to *mystery* or *riches* ;
in either case the sense is the same,
the *riches* are the rich abundance contained in the *mystery.*

[3] *Jesus* is omitted here in the best
MSS. *Perfect* denotes *grown to the
ripeness of maturity.*

[4] Alluding to what has just preceded.

[5] Viz. all *Christians.* By the plain
natural sense of this passage, the
Colossians are classed among those

personally unknown to St. Paul. For
the 'they' of verse 2 comprehends
and binds together the Colossians, and
the Laodiceans, with the ' all who,' &c.
This view is confirmed by i. 4 (where
Paul had *heard of,* not witnessed, their
faith) ; by i. 7 (where *Epaphras* is described as their founder) ; and by i. 8
(where their love for Paul has been
declared to him by Epaphras, not personally known by himself.

[6] Compare 'spiritual understanding'
(i. 9).

[7] The reading of the MSS. here is
very doubtful. The reading we have
adopted is that of Tischendorf's 2nd
edition.

[8] St. Paul here alludes, as we see
from the next verse, to those who (like
the Colossian false teachers) professed
to be in possession of a higher *Gnosis.*
In opposition to them he asserts that
the depths of *Gnosis* are to be found
only in the 'Mystery of God,' viz. the
Gospel, or (as he defines it above)
' Christ in you.'

rejoicing when I behold your good order, and the
firmness of your faith in Christ. As, therefore, you ii. 6
first received Christ Jesus the Lord, so walk in
Him ; having in Him your root, and in Him the 7
foundation whereon you are continually[1] built up ;
persevering stedfastly in your faith, as you were
taught ; and abounding[2] in thanksgiving.

by a system
of misnamed
philosophy,
which de-
preciates
Christ,
Beware[3] lest there be any man who leads you 8
captive[4] by his philosophy, which is a vain deceit,
following the tradition of men,[5] the outward lessons[6]
of childhood, not the teaching of Christ. For in 9
Him dwells all the Fulness[7] of the Godhead in
bodily form, and in Him[8] you have your fulness ; 10
for He is the head of all the Principalities and 11
Powers. In Him, also, you were circumcised with a
circumcision not made by hands, even the offcasting
of the[9] whole body of the flesh, the circumcision
of Christ ; for with Him you were buried in your 12
baptism, wherein also you were made partakers of
His resurrection, through the faith wrought in you

---

[1] Observe the present tense, and compare 1 Cor. iii. 10.

[2] 'Therein' is omitted here, as in
Tischendorf's text.

[3] The following paraphrase of this
part of the Epistle is given by Neander:—' How can you still fear evil
spirits, when the Father Himself has
delivered you from the kingdom of
darkness, and transplanted you into
the kingdom of His dear Son, who has
victoriously ascended to heaven to
share the divine might of His Father,
with whom He now works in man ;
when, moreover, He by His sufferings
has united you with the Father, and
freed you from the dominion of all the
powers of darkness, whom He exhibits
(as it were) as captives in His triumphal pomp, and shows their impotence
to harm His kingdom established among
men ? How can you still let the doubts
and fears of your conscience bring you
into slavery to superstition, when Christ
has nailed to His cross, and blotted out
the record of guilt which testified against
you in your conscience, and has assured
to you the forgiveness of all your sins ?
Again, how can you fear to be polluted
by outward things, how can you suffer
yourselves to be in captivity to outward ordinances, when you have died
with Christ to all earthly things, and
are risen with Christ, and live (ac-

cording to your true, inward life) with
Christ in heaven ? Your faith must
be fixed on things above, where Christ
is, at the right hand of God. Your
life is hid with Christ in God, and belongs no more to earth.'

[4] Literally, *who drags you away as
his spoil.* The peculiar form of expression employed (similar to ' there
are some that trouble you,' Gal. i. 7)
shows that St. Paul alludes to some
particular individual at Colossæ, who
professed to teach a ' Philosophy.'

[5] ' The tradition of men' is applied
to the Rabbinical theology (Mark vii.
8).

[6] ' Elements of the world' (cf. Gal.
iv. 3), referring to the Jewish ordinances, as ' a shadow of things to come'
(v. 17).

[7] See note on i. 19.

[8] i. e. by union with Him alone, you
can partake of the Pleroma of the Godhead, and not (as the Gnostics taught)
by initiation into an esoteric system of
theosophy, whereby men might attain
to closer connection with some of the
' Principalities and Powers' of the angelic hierarchy.

[9] The casting off, not (as in outward
circumcision) of a part, but of the
whole body of the flesh, the whole
carnal nature. *Of the sins* in the T. R.
is an interpolation.

by God, who raised Him from the dead; and you
ii. 13 also, when you were dead in the transgressions and
uncircumcision of your flesh, God raised to share His
14 life.   For He forgave us[1] all our transgressions, and
blotted out the Writing against us which opposed us
with its decrees,[2] having taken it out of our way,
15 and nailed it to the cross.   And He disarmed the
Principalities and the Powers[3] [which fought against
Him], and put them to open shame, leading them
captive in the triumph of Christ.[4]

16   Therefore, suffer not any man to condemn you for ‹and unites
what you eat or drink,[5] nor in respect of feast-days, ‹Jewish ob-
17 or new moons,[6] or sabbaths; for these are a shadow ‹with angel-
18 of things to come, but the body is Christ's.   Let no ‹worship and
man succeed in his wish[7] to defraud you of your ‹asceticism.
prize, persuading you to self humiliation,[8] and worship of the angels,[9] intruding[10] rashly into things
which he has not seen, puffed up by his fleshly mind,
19 and not holding fast the Head, from whom[11] the
whole body, by the joints which bind it, draws full
supplies[12] for all its needs, and is knit together, and
increases in godly growth.

[1] 'Us' is the reading of the best
MSS.
[2] The parallel passage (Eph. ii. 15)
is more explicit, 'the law of enacted
ordinances.'
[3] Cf. Eph. vi. 12; and see Neander's
paraphrase quoted above.
[4] 'In Him,' i.e. 'Christ,' the subject
being 'God.' For the metaphor, compare 2 Cor. ii. 14.
[5] Compare Rom. xiv. 1-17.
[6] The same three Mosaic observances
are joined together, 1 Chron. xxiii. 31.
Compare also Gal. iv. 10.
[7] *Let no man, though he wishes it*;
this seems the most natural explanation of this difficult expression; it is
that adopted by Theodoret and Theophylact. We observe again the reference to some individual false teacher.
[8] From the combination of this with
'chastening of the body,' in v. 23, it
seems to mean an exaggerated self-
humiliation, like that which has often
been joined with ascetic practices, and
has shown itself by the devotee wearing rags, exposing himself to insult,
living by beggary, &c.
[9] Mr. Hartley mentions a fact in
the later *Christian* history of Colossæ
which is at least curious when consi-

dered in connection with St. Paul's
warning concerning angels, and the
statement of Herodotus regarding the
river Lycus. The modern Greeks have
a legend to this effect:—'An overwhelming inundation threatened to
destroy the Christian population of
that city. They were fleeing before it
in the utmost consternation, and imploring superior succour for their deliverance. At this critical moment,
the Archangel Michael descended from
heaven, *opened the chasm in the earth to
which they still point,* and at this opening the waters of the inundation were
swallowed up and the multitude was
saved.' (*Res. in Greece,* p. 52.) A
church in honour of the archangel was
built at the entrance of the chasm. A
council held at the neighbouring town
of Laodicea, in the 4th century, condemned this Angel worship; and
Theodoret speaks of it as existing in
the same region.
[10] We join *vainly (rashly)* with what
precedes.
[11] *From whom,* not *from which,* as in
A. V.
[12] Literally, *furnished with all things
necessary to its support.*

If, then,[1] when you died with Christ, you put away ii. 20
the childish lessons of outward things, why, as
though you still lived in outward things, do you
submit yourselves to decrees ('hold[2] not, taste not, 21
touch not'—forbidding the use of things which
are all made to be consumed in the using[3]) founded 22
on the precepts and doctrines of men? For these 23
precepts, though they have a show of wisdom, in a
self-chosen worship, and in humiliation, and chastening of the body, are of no value to check[4] the
indulgence of fleshly passions.

Exhortation to heaven-ward affec-tions. If, then,[5] you were made partakers of Christ's iii. 1
resurrection, seek those things which are above,
where Christ abides,[6] seated on the right hand of
God. Set your heart on things above, not on things 2
earthly; for ye are dead,[7] and your life is hid with 3
Christ in God. When Christ, who is our life, shall 4
be made manifest, then shall ye also be made manifest[8] with Him in glory.

Against Heathen im-purity and other vices. Give, therefore, unto death your earthly members; 5
fornication, uncleanness,[9] shameful appetites, un-
natural desires, and the lust of concupiscence,[10]

---

[1] The reference is to verse 12. The literal translation is, *if you died with Christ, putting away*, &c.

[2] *Hold* is distinguished from *touch*, the former conveying (according to its original sense) the notion of *close contact and retention*, the latter of only *momentary contact*: compare 1 Cor. vii. 1, and also John xx. 17, where the words should probably be translated 'hold me not,' or 'cling not to me.'

[3] This appears to be the best view of this very difficult passage, on a comparison with 1 Cor. vi. 13, and with St. Paul's general use of this verb.

[4] Literally this is, *in reference to the indulgence of the flesh.* The difficulty of this verse is well known. The interpretation which leaves the verse a mere statement of the favourable side of this Colossian asceticism, unbalanced by any contrary conclusion, and with nothing to answer to 'having a show,' &c. appears very untenable. We consider 'in no honour' here to be used as 'of no value.' See Acts xx. 24, Rev. xvii. 4. Since the first edition of this work was published, we have ascertained that the view above taken of this verse was proposed by Archbishop Sumner (*Practical Expos. in loco*), who interprets it: 'These

things are of little honour or value *against the fulness of the flesh,* the motions of sin in the members;' and quotes the LXX. in illustration.

[5] The reference is to ii. 12.

[6] Stronger than 'is seated.'

[7] Literally, *you have died*; for the aorist must here be used for a perfect, since it is coupled with a perfect following.

[8] So also in Rom. viii. 19 the coming of Christ in glory is identified with the *manifestation of the sons of God.* St. Paul declares, that the real nature and glory of Christ's people (which is now hidden) will be manifested to all mankind when Christ shall come again, and force the world to recognise Him, by an open display of His majesty. The Authorised Version (though so beautiful in this passage that it is impossible to deviate from it without regret), yet does not adequately represent the original.

[9] Viz. of word as well as deed.

[10] *Lust of concupiscence,* whence the beforenamed special sins spring, as branches from the root. For the meaning of the original word see note on 1 Cor. v. 11. Lust is called idolatry, either because impurity was so closely connected with the Heathen

iii. 6 which is idolatry. For these things bring the wrath
7 of God upon the children of disobedience ; among
whom you also walked in former times, when you
lived therein ; but now, with us,[1] you likewise must
8 renounce them all. Anger, passion and malice must _{Exhortation to put on the}
be cast away, evil-speaking and reviling put out of _{Christian character in}
9 your mouth. Lie not one to another, but[2] put off _{all its various perfections.}
the old man with his deeds, and put on the new[3]
10 man, who grows continually to a more perfect know-
11 ledge and likeness of his Creator.[4]   Wherein there is
not 'Greek and Jew,' ' circumcision and uncircumcision,' 'barbarian,' 'Scythian,' ' bondsman,' 'freeman ;'
12 but Christ is all, and in all. Therefore, as God's chosen
people, holy and beloved, put on tenderness of heart,
kindness, self-humiliation,[5] gentleness, long-suffering,
13 forbearing one another, and forgiving one another,
if any thinks himself aggrieved by his neighbour ;
14 even as Christ forgave you, so also do ye. And over
all the rest put on the robe[6] of love, which binds
15 together and completes the whole.[7]   Let the peace of
Christ[8] rule in your hearts, to which also you were
called in one body ; and be thankful one[9] to another.
16 Let the Word of Christ dwell in you richly. Teach
and admonish one another in all wisdom.[10]

Let your singing be of psalms, and hymns, and _{Festive meetings, how to}
spiritual songs,[11] sung in thanksgiving, with your _{be celebrated.}

---

idol-worship, or because it alienates
the heart from God.

[1] *You also,—you as well as other
Christians.* There should be a comma
after v. 7, and a full stop in the middle
of v. 8. Then the exhortation beginning *anger*, &c., follows abruptly, a
repetition of *renounce* being understood
from the sense.

[2] '*Put off.*' The participle is equivalent to the imperative. Compare
'put *on*,' v. 12.

[3] For this use of *new* compare Heb.
xii. 24.

[4] Literally, *who is continually renewed* [present participle] *to the attainment of a true knowledge according to
the likeness of his Creator.*

[5] It is remarkable that the very
same quality which is condemned in
the false teachers, is here enjoined ;
showing that it was not their self-
humiliation which was condemned,
but their exaggerated way of showing
it, and the false system on which it
was engrafted.

[6] *Above all* in the sense of *over all.*
See Eph. vi. 16.

[7] Literally, *which is the bond of completeness.*

[8] The great majority of MSS. read
Christ.

[9] This is most naturally understood
of gratitude towards one another, especially as the context treats of their
love towards their brethren ; for ingra-
titude destroys mutual love.

[10] The punctuation here adopted
connects ' in all wisdom ' with what
follows. The participles are used imperatively, as in Rom. xii. 9–16.

[11] The reading adopted is Tischendorf's, a stop being put after the preceding. St. Paul appears to intend (as
in Eph. v. 18, 19, which throws light
on the present passage) to contrast the
songs which the Christians were to
employ at their meetings, with those
impure or bacchanalian strains which
they formerly sang at their heathen
revels. It should be remembered that
singing always formed a part of the

heart, unto[1] God. And whatsover you do, in word iii. 17 or deed, do all in the name of the Lord Jesus, giving thanks to God our Father through Him.

Wives, submit yourselves to your husbands, as 18 it is fit in the Lord.

Husbands, love your wives, and deal not harshly 19 with them.

Children, obey your parents in all things; for 20 this is acceptable in the Lord.[2]

Fathers, vex not your children, lest their spirit 21 should be broken.

Bondsmen, obey in all things your earthly mas- 22 ter; not in eye-service, as men pleasers, but in singleness of heart, fearing the Lord.[3] And what- 23 soever you do, do it heartily, as for the Lord, and not for men; knowing that from the Lord you will 24 receive the reward of the inheritance; for you are the bondsmen of Christ, our Lord and Master.[4] But 25 he who wrongs another will be requited for the wrong which he has done, and [in that judgment] there is no respect of persons.[5]

Masters, deal rightly and justly with your iv. 1 bondsmen, knowing that you also have a Master in heaven.

Persevere in prayer, and join thanksgiving with 2 your watchfulness therein; and pray for me like- 3 wise, that God would open to me a door of entrance[6] for His Word, that I may declare the mystery of Christ,[7] which is the very cause of my imprisonment: pray for me that I may declare it openly, as I 4 ought to speak.

Conduct yourselves with wisdom towards those 5 without the Church,[8] and forestal opportunity.[9] Let 6 your speech be always gracious, with a seasoning

---

entertainment at the banquets of the Greeks. Compare also James v. 13, 'Is any man merry? Let him sing psalms.' For the '*Thanksgiving*' see 1 Cor. x. 30, where the same word is used.

[1] *God* is the reading of the best MSS.

[2] 'Acceptable *in* the Lord' is the reading of the MSS.

[3] 'The Lord' is the reading of the MSS.

[4] The correlative meanings of *Lord* (*Master*) and *Servant* (*Slave*) give a

force to this in Greek, which cannot be fully expressed in English.

[5] i.e. slaves and masters are equal at Christ's judgment seat.

[6] Compare 2 Cor. ii. 12.

[7] See above, i. 27.

[8] Compare 1 Thess. iv. 12 and 1 Cor. v. 12.

[9] This is the literal translation. Like the English *forestal*, the verb means *to buy up an article out of the market*, in order to make the largest possible profit from it.

of salt,[1] understanding how to give to every man a fitting answer.

iv. 7   All that concerns me will be made known to you by Tychicus, my beloved brother and faithful servant 8 and fellow-bondsman in the Lord, whom I have sent to you for this very end, that he might learn your 9 state, and comfort your hearts; with Onesimus, the faithful and beloved brother, your fellow-country-man; they will tell you all which has happened here. *Mission of Tychicus and Onesimus.*

10   Aristarchus, my fellow-prisoner, salutes you, and Marcus, the cousin[2] of Barnabas, concerning whom 11 you received instructions (if he come to you, receive him), and Jesus surnamed Justus. Of the circumcision[3] these only are my fellow-labourers for the kingdom of God, who have been a comfort to me. *Greetings from Christians in Rome.*

12   Epaphras your fellow-countryman salutes you; a bondsman of Christ, who is ever contending on your behalf in his prayers, that in ripeness of understanding and full assurance of belief,[4] you may abide 13 stedfast in all the will of God; for I bear him witness that he is filled with zeal[5] for you, and for those in Laodicea and Hierapolis.

14   Luke, the beloved physician, and Demas, salute you.

15   Salute the brethren in Laodicea, and Nymphas, 16 with the Church at his house. And when this letter has been read among you, provide that it be read also in the Church of the Laodiceans, and that you 17 also read the letter from Laodicea. And say to Archippus, ' Take heed to the ministration which thou hast received in the Lord's service, that thou fulfil it.' *Messages to Colossian and Laodicean Christians.*

18   The salutation of me, Paul, with my own hand. Remember my chains.[6]   Grace be with you.[7] *Autograph salutation and benediction.*

---

[1] i.e. *free from insipidity.* It would be well if religious speakers and writers had always kept this precept in mind.

[2] The original word has the meaning of *cousin* (not *nephew*) both in classical and Hellenistic Greek.

[3] We adopt the punctuation of Lachmann and Meyer. Literally, *these, who are of the circumcision, are alone fellow-workers*; i.e. alone among those of the circumcision; for other fellow-workers are mentioned below.

[4] We adopt Lachmann and Tischendorf's reading. For the meaning of the word, see Rom. iv. 21.

[5] If, with some MSS., we read *toil* here, it will not materially alter the sense.

[6] We have before remarked that the right hand, with which he wrote these words, was fastened by a chain to the left hand of the soldier who was on guard over him.

[7] The *Amen* (as usual) was added by the copyists, and is absent from the best MSS.

We have seen that the above Epistle to the Colossians, and that to Philemon, were conveyed by Tychicus and Onesimus, who travelled together from Rome to Asia Minor. But these two were not the only letters with which Tychicus was charged. We know that he carried a third letter also; but it is not equally certain to whom it was addressed. This third letter was that which is now entitled the Epistle to the Ephesians; [1] concerning the destination of which (disputed as it is) perhaps the least disputable fact is, that it was not addressed to the Church of Ephesus. [2]

This point is established by strong evidence, both internal and external. To begin with the former, we remark, First, that it would be inexplicable that St. Paul, when he wrote to the Ephesians, amongst whom he had spent so long a time, and to whom he was bound by ties of such close affection (Acts xx. 17, &c.), should not have a single message of personal greeting to send. Yet none such are found in this Epistle. Secondly, He could not have described the Ephesians as a Church whose conversion he knew only by report (i. 15). Thirdly, He could not speak to them, as only knowing himself (the founder of their Church) to be an Apostle *by hearsay* (iii. 2), so as to need *credentials* to accredit him with them (iii. 4). Fourthly, He could not describe the Ephesians as so exclusively Gentiles (ii. 11, iv. 17), and so recently converted (v. 8, i. 13, ii. 13).

This internal evidence is confirmed by the following external evidence also.

(1.) St. Basil distinctly asserts, that the early writers whom he had consulted declared that the manuscripts of this Epistle in their time did not contain the name of Ephesus, but left out altogether the name of the Church to which the Epistle was addressed. He adds, that the most ancient manuscripts which he had himself seen gave the same testimony. This assertion of Basil's is confirmed by Jerome, Epiphanius, and Tertullian. [3]

(2.) The most ancient manuscript now known to exist, namely, that of the Vatican Library, fully bears out Basil's words; for in its text it does not contain the words 'in Ephesus' at all; and they are only added in its margin by a much later hand. [4]

(3.) We know, from the testimony of Marcion, that this Epistle was entitled in his collection 'the Epistle to the Laodiceans.' And his authority on this point is entitled to greater weight from the fact, that he was himself a native of the district where we should expect the earlier copies of the Epistle to exist. [5]

---

[1] See Eph. vi. 21, 22.

[2] [This statement has been blamed, as extreme; and perhaps it is too strong; but the omission of the words 'in Ephesus' from the recently discovered Sinaitic MS. is a strong confirmation of the view here expressed. H.]

[3] Tertullian accuses Marcion of *adding* the title 'to the Laodiceans,' but not of altering the salutation; whence it is clear that the MSS. used by Tertullian did not contain the words 'in

Ephesus.' It is scarcely necessary here to notice the apocryphal *Epistola ad Laodicenses*, which only exists in Latin MSS. It is a mere cento compiled from the Epistles to the Galatians and Philippians; and was evidently a forgery of a very late date, originating from the wish to represent the Epistle mentioned Col. iv. 16, as not lost.

[4] [See remark above, n. 2, on the Sinaitic MS. H.]

[5] Many critics object to receive Marcion's evidence, on the ground

The above arguments have convinced the ablest modern critics that this Epistle was not addressed to the Ephesians. But there has not been by any means the same approach to unanimity on the question, who were its intended readers. In the most ancient manuscripts of it (as we have said) no Church is mentioned by name, except in those consulted by Marcion, according to which it was addressed to the Laodiceans. Now the internal evidence above mentioned proves that the Epistle was addressed to some particular church or churches, who were to receive intelligence of St. Paul through Tychicus, and that it was not a *treatise* addressed to the whole Christian world ; and the form of the salutation shows that the name of *some* place[1] must originally have been inserted in it. Again : the very passages in the Epistle which have been above referred to, as proving that it could not have been directed to the Ephesians, agree perfectly with the hypothesis that it was addressed to the Laodiceans. Lastly, we know from the Epistle to the Colossians, that St. Paul did write a letter to Laodicea (Col. iv. 16) about the same time with that to Colossæ.[2]   On these grounds, then, it appears the safest course to assume (with Paley, in the *Horæ Paulinæ*) that the testimony of Marcion (uncontradicted by any other positive evidence) is correct, and that Laodicea was one at least of the Churches to which this Epistle was addressed. And, consequently, as we know not the name of any other Church to which it was written, that of Laodicea should be inserted in the place which the most ancient manuscripts leave vacant.

Still, it must be obvious, that this does not remove all the difficulties of the question. For, first it will be asked, how came the name of Laodicea (if originally inserted) to have slipped out of

that he often made arbitrary alterations in the text of the New Testament. But this he did on doctrinal grounds, which could not induce him to alter the *title* of an Epistle.

[1] Compare the salutations at Rom. i. 7; 2 Cor. i. 1; Phil. i. 1; the analogy of which renders it impossible to suppose 'those who are' used emphatically ('those who are *really Saints*'), as some commentators mentioned by Jerome took it. It is true that this (the oldest known form of the text) might be translated 'to God's people who are also faithful in Christ Jesus;' but this would make the Epistle addressed (like the 2nd of Peter) to the whole Christian world; which is inconsistent with its contents, as above remarked.

[2] De Wette argues that the letter to Laodicea, mentioned Col. iv. 16, must have been written some time *before* that to Colossæ, and not sent by the same messenger, because St. Paul in the Colossian Epistle sends greetings to Laodicea (Col. iv. 15), which he would

have sent directly if he had written to Laodicea at the same time. But there is not much weight in this objection, for it was agreeable to St. Paul's manner to charge one part of the church to salute the other; see Rom. xvi. 3, where he says 'salute ye,' not 'I salute.' Moreover it seems most probable that Col. iv. 16–18 was a postscript, added to the Epistle after the Epistle to Laodicea was written. It is difficult to imagine that the 'letter from Laodicea' (Col. iv. 16) could have been received much before that to the Colossians, from the manner in which it is mentioned, and the frequent intercourse which must have occurred between such neighbouring churches. The hypothesis of Wieseler, that the Laodicean Epistle was that to Philemon, is quite arbitrary, and appears irreconcilable with the fact that Onesimus is expressly called a Colossian; and was sent to Colossæ on this very occasion. See also *Horæ Paulinæ (in loco).*

these ancient manuscripts? and again, how came it that the majority of more recent manuscripts inserted the name of Ephesus? These perplexing questions are in some measure answered by the hypothesis originated by Archbishop Ussher, that this Epistle was a circular letter, addressed not to one only, but to several Churches, in the same way as the Epistle to the Galatians was addressed to all the Churches in Galatia, and those to Corinth were addressed to the Christians 'in the whole province of Achaia.'[1] On this view, Tychicus would have carried several copies of it, differently superscribed, one for Laodicea, another, perhaps, for Hierapolis, another for Philadelphia, and so on. Hence the early copyists, perplexed by this diversity in their copies, might many of them be led to omit the words in which the variation consisted: and thus the state of the earliest known text[2] of the Epistle would be explained. Afterwards, however, as copies of the Epistle became spread over the world, all imported from Ephesus (the commercial capital of the district where the Epistle was originally circulated), it would be called (in default of any other name) the *Epistle from Ephesus*; and the manuscripts of it would be so entitled; and thence the next step, of inserting the name of Ephesus into the text, in a place where some local designation was plainly wanted, would be a very easy one. And this designation of the Epistle would the more readily prevail, from the natural feeling that St. Paul must have written[3] *some* Epistle to so great a Church of his own founding as Ephesus.

Thus the most plausible account of the origin of this Epistle seems to be as follows. Tychicus was about to take his departure from Rome for Asia Minor. St. Paul had already written[4] his Epistle to the Colossians at the request of Epaphras, who had informed him of their danger. But Tychicus was about to visit other places, which, though not requiring the same warning with Colossæ, yet abounded in Christian converts. Most of these had been Heathens, and their hearts might be cheered and strengthened by words addressed directly to themselves from the great Apostle of the Gentiles, whose face they had never seen, but whose name they had learned to reverence, and whose sufferings had endeared

---

[1] See 2 Cor. i. 1, and p. 440, above.

[2] That of the Codex Vaticanus, above described as agreeing with the most ancient MSS. seen by Basil.

[3] We cannot doubt that St. Paul did write many Epistles which are now lost. He himself mentions one such to the Corinthians (see pp. 377, 378); and it is a mysterious dispensation of Providence that his Epistles to the two great metropolitan churches of Antioch and Ephesus, with which he was himself so peculiarly connected, should not have been preserved to us.

[4] It is here assumed that the Epistle to the Colossians was written before that (so called) to the Ephesians. This appears probable from a close examina-

tion of the parallel passages in the two Epistles; the passages in Ephesians bear marks of being expanded from those in Colossians; and the passages in Colossians could not be so well explained on the converse hypothesis, that they were a condensation of those in Ephesians. We have remarked, however, in a previous note, that we must assume the reference in Colossians to the other Epistle (Col. iv. 16), to have been added as a postscript; unless we suppose that St. Paul there refers to 'the letter from Laodicea' before it was actually written (as intending to write it, and send it by the same messenger), which he might very well have done.

him to their love. The scattered Churches (one of which was Laodicea)[1] had very much in common, and would all be benefited by the same instruction and exhortation. Since it was not necessary to meet the individual case of any one of them, as distinct from the rest, St. Paul wrote the same letter to them all, but sent to each a separate copy authenticated by the precious stamp of his own autograph benediction. And the contents of this circular epistle naturally bore a strong resemblance to those of the letter which he had just concluded to the Colossians, because the thoughts which filled his heart at the time would necessarily find utterance in similar language, and because the circumstances of these Churches were in themselves very similar to those of the Colossian Church, except that they were not infected with the peculiar errors which had crept in at Colossæ.[2] The Epistle which he thus wrote consists of two parts : first, a doctrinal, and, secondly, a hortatory portion. The first part contains a summary, very indirectly conveyed (chiefly in the form of thanksgiving), of the Christian doctrines taught by St. Paul, and is especially remarkable for the great prominence given to the abolition of the Mosaic Law. The hortatory part, which has been so dear to Christians of every age and country, enjoins unity (especially between Jewish and Gentile Christians), the renunciation of Heathen vices, and the practice of Christian purity. It lays down rules (the same as those in the Epistle to Colossæ, only in an expanded form) for the performance of the duties of domestic life, and urges these new converts, in the midst of the perils which surrounded them, to continue stedfast in watchfulness and prayer. Such is the substance, and such was most probably the history, of the following Epistle.

THE EPISTLE TO THE EPHESIANS
(SO CALLED).[3]

1. 1 PAUL, an Apostle of Jesus Christ, by the will of God, Salutation.

[1] It has been objected to the circular hypothesis, that the Epistle, if meant as a circular, would have been addressed 'to those who are in *Asia.*' But to this it may be replied that on our hypothesis the Epistle was *not* addressed to *all* the churches in Proconsular Asia, and that it *was* addressed to some churches *not* in that province.

[2] On this part of the subject see the Appendix.

[3] In the above introductory remarks it is assumed that this Epistle was cotemporary with that to the Colossians, which is stated in the Epistle itself (vi. 21. Compare Col. iv. 7). Its date, therefore, is fixed by the arguments in p. 692. We may here shortly notice the arguments which have been advanced by some German critics, for rejecting the Epistle altogether as a forgery. Their objections against its authenticity are principally the following. First, The difficulties respecting its destination, which have been already noticed. Secondly, The want of originality in its matter, the substance of its contents being found also in the Colossians, or others of St. Paul's Epistles. This phenomenon has been accounted for above (p. 705), and is well explained by Paley (*Horæ Paulinæ*). Thirdly, certain portions of the doctrinal contents are thought to indicate a later origin, e.g., the Demonology (ii. 2, and vi. 12). Fourthly, Some portions of the style are considered un-Pauline. Fifthly, Several words are used in a sense different from that

TO THE SAINTS[1] WHO ARE [IN LAODICEA[2]], AND WHO
HAVE FAITH IN CHRIST JESUS.

Grace be to you and peace, from God our Father, i. 2
and from our Lord Jesus Christ.

Blessed be God, the Father of our Lord Jesus 3
Christ, who has given us[3] in Christ all spiritual
blessings in the heavens.[4]   Even as He chose us in 4
Him, before the foundation of the world, that we
should be holy and spotless in His sight.   For in 5
His love[5] He predestined us to be adopted among
His children through Jesus Christ, according to the
good pleasure of His will, that we might praise and 6
glorify His grace, wherewith He favoured[6] us in His
beloved.   For in Him we have our redemption 7
through His blood, even the forgiveness of our sins,
in the richness of His grace,[7] which he bestowed upon us above measure ;   and he made known[8] to us, in 8
the fulness of wisdom and understanding, the mys- 9
tery of His will, according to His good pleasure,
which He had purposed in Himself to fulfil, that it
should be dispensed[9] in the fulness of time ;[10] to make 10

which they bear in St. Paul's other
writings. These three last classes of
difficulties we cannot pretend fully to
explain, nor is this the place for their
discussion ; but as a general answer to
them we may remark : First, That if we
had a fuller knowledge of the persons to
whom, and especially of the amanuensis
by whom, the letter was written, they
would probably vanish. Secondly, That
no objector has yet suggested a satisfactory explanation of the origin of the
Epistle, if it were a forgery ; no motive
for forgery can be detected in it ; it contains no attack on post-apostolic forms
of heresy, no indication of a later development of church government. The
very want of originality alleged against
it would not leave any motive for its
forgery. Thirdly, It was unanimously
received as St. Paul's Epistle by the
early Church, and is quoted by Polycarp
and Irenæus ; and, as appears by the
lately discovered work of Hippolytus
against heresies (which has appeared
since this was first published), it is
also quoted most distinctly by Valentinus (about 120 A.D.), who cites Eph.
iii. 14, 16, 17, and 18, verbatim.

[1] For the translation here see note
on 1 Cor. i. 2.

[2] See the preceding remarks, p. 703.

[3] ' Us ' (here) includes both *the
writer and (apparently) the other Apostles*; while ' you likewise ' (v. 13) addresses *the readers as distinguished from
the writer.*

[4] Literally, *in the heavenly places.*
This expression is peculiar to the present Epistle, in which it occurs five
times.

[5] We join ' in love ' with v. 5.

[6] The verbal connection would be
more literally given thus: *His favour
wherewith he favoured us.*

[7] Comma at the end of verse 7, colon
in the middle of v. 8, and no stop at
the end of v. 8, taking the verb transitively.

[8] This is referred to in iii. 3. Compare ' made known to us the mystery,
&c.,' with ' made known to me the
mystery,' which proves ' us ' here to
correspond with ' me ' there.

[9] *Dispensation.* According to most
interpreters this expression is used in
this Epistle in the sense of adjustment,
or *preparation* ; but as the meaning it

[10] Literally, *for a dispensation* [*of it*], *which belongs to the fulness of time.*

all things one[1] in Christ as head, yea, both things in
i. 11 heaven and things on earth in Him; in whom we
also receive the portion of our lot,[2] having been predestined thereto according to His purpose, whose
working makes all fulfil the counsel of His own will;
12 that unto His praise and glory[3] we might live, who
have hoped in Christ before[4] you.

13   And you, likewise, have hoped in Him, since you
heard the message of the truth, the Glad-tidings of
your salvation; and you believed in Him, and received
14 His seal, the holy Spirit of promise; who is an[5]
earnest of our inheritance, given to[6] redeem that
which He hath purchased,[7] to the praise of His
glory.

15   Wherefore I, also, since I heard of your faith in
16 our Lord Jesus, and your love to all the saints, give
thanks for you without ceasing, and make mention
17 of you in my prayers, beseeching the God of our
Lord Jesus Christ, the Father of Glory, to give you
a spirit of wisdom and of insight, in the knowledge
18 of Himself; the eyes of your understanding[8] being
filled with light, that you may know what is the hope
of His calling, and how rich is the glory of His in-
19 heritance among the saints, and how surpassing is
the power which He has shown toward us who believe; [for He has dealt with us] in the strength of
20 that might wherewith He wrought in Christ, when
He raised Him from the dead; and set Him on His
own right hand in the heavens, far above every[9]
21 Principality and Power, and Might, and Domination,
and every name which is named, not only in this

Thanks for their conversion, and prayer for their enlightenment.

Office and dignity of Christ.

---

bears elsewhere in St. Paul's writings
(viz. *the office of a steward in dispensing
his master's goods*; see 1 Cor. ix. 17, and
cf. Col. i. 25) gives a very intelligible
sense to the passages in this Epistle, it
seems needless to depart from it.   The
meaning of the present passage is best
illustrated by iii. 2, 3.

[1] Literally, *to unite all things under
one head, in union with Christ*: so
Chrysostum explains it.   For the doctrine compare 1 Cor. xv. 24.

[2] Literally, *were portioned with our
lot.*

[3] The original may be considered as
a Hebraism; literally, *that we should
be for the glory-praise of Him*; compare
v. 6.

[4] This might mean, as some take it,
to look forward with hope: but the

other meaning appears most obvious,
and best suits the context   Compare
'went before to ship,' Acts xx. 13.

[5] Compare Rom. viii. 2 ; and note
on 1 Cor. i. 22.

[6] Not *until* (A. V.).

[7] Used in the same sense here as
'the church which He purchased'
(Acts xx. 28).   The metaphor is, that
the gift of the Holy Spirit was an
earnest (that is, *a part payment in
advance*) of the price required for the
full deliverance of those who had been
slaves of sin, but now were purchased
for the service of God.

[8] The majority of MSS. read 'heart,'
which would give the less usual sense,
the eyes of your heart.

[9] See Col. i. 16, and note.

world, but also in that which is to come. And '𝕳𝕖 i. 22 put all things under 𝕳is feet,'[1] and gave Him to be sovereign head of the Church, which is His body; the[2] Fulness of Him who fills all things everywhere 23 with Himself. And you, likewise, He raised from ii. 1 death[3] to life, when you were dead in transgressions and sins; wherein once you walked according to the 2 course of this[4] world, and obeyed the Ruler of the Powers of the Air,[5] even the Spirit who is now working in the children of disobedience; amongst whom 3 we also, in times past, lived, all of us, in fleshy lusts, fulfilling the desires of our flesh and of our imagination, and were by nature children of wrath, no less than others.[6] But God, who is rich in mercy, be-4 cause of the great love wherewith He loved us, even 5 when we were dead in sin, called us to share the life of Christ—(by grace you are saved),—and in[7] Christ Jesus, He raised us up with Him from the dead, and 6 seated us with Him in the heavens; that, in the ages 7 which are coming,[8] He might manifest the surpassing riches of His grace, showing kindness toward us in Christ Jesus. For by grace you are saved, through 8 faith; and that not of yourselves, it is the gift of God; not won by works, lest any man should boast. 9 For we are His workmanship, created in Christ 10 Jesus to do good works, which God has prepared[9] that we should walk therein.

Wherefore remember that you, who once were 11 reckoned among carnal Gentiles, who are called the Uncircumcision by that which calls itself the Cir-

They had been awakened from Heathenism by God's grace,

and incorporated into God's Israel.

---

[1] Ps. viii. 6 (LXX.), quoted in the same Messianic sense, 1 Cor. xv. 27, and Heb. ii. 8. Compare also Ps. cx. 1.

[2] We see here again the same allusion to the technical use of the word *Pleroma* by false teachers, as in Col. ii. 9, 10. St. Paul there asserts that, not the angelic hierarchy, but Christ Himself is the true *fulness of the Godhead*; and here that the Church is the *fulness of Christ*, that is, the full manifestation of His being, because penetrated by His life, and living only in Him. It should be observed that the Church is here spoken of so far forth as it corresponds to its ideal.

[3] The sentence (in the original) is left unfinished in the rapidity of dictation; but the verb is easily supplied from the context.

[4] Compare 2 Cor. iv. 4, 1 Cor. i. 20, &c.

[5] In the Rabbinical theology evil spirits were designated as the 'Powers of the Air.' St. Paul is here again probably alluding to the language of those teachers against whom he wrote to the Colossians.

[6] Literally, *the rest of mankind*, i.e. *unbelievers*. Compare 1 Thess. iv. 13.

[7] The meaning is, that Christians share in their Lord's glorification, and dwell with Him in heaven, in so far as they are united with Him.

[8] Viz. the time of Christ's perfect triumph over evil, always contemplated in the New Testament as near at hand.

[9] i.e. God, by the laws of His Providence, has prepared opportunities of doing good for every Christian.

cumcision (a circumcision of the flesh,[1] made by the
i. 12 hands of man)—that in those times you were shut
out from Christ, aliens from the commonwealth of
Israel, and strangers from the covenants[2] of the promise, having no hope, and without God in the world.
13 But now, in Christ Jesus, ye, who were once far off,
have been brought near through the blood of Christ.
14 For He is our peace, who has made both one,[3] and
has broken down the[4] wall which parted us; for, in
15 His[5] flesh, He destroyed the ground of our enmity,
16 the law of enacted ordinances; that so, making peace
between us, out of both He might create[6] in Himself
17 one new man; and that, by His cross, He might reconcile both, in one body, unto God, having slain
their enmity thereby. And when He came, He published the Glad-tidings of peace to you that were far
18 off, and to them that were near. For through Him
we both have power to approach the Father in the
19 fellowship[7] of one Spirit. Now, therefore, you are
no more strangers and sojourners, but fellow-citizens
20 of the saints, and members of God's household. You
are built upon the foundation of the Apostles and
Prophets, Jesus Christ Himself being the chief
21 corner-stone; in whom all the building, fitly framed
together, grows into a temple hallowed by the[8] in-
22 dwelling of the Lord. And in Him, not others only,[9]
but you also, are built up together, to make a house
wherein God may dwell by the[10] presence of His
Spirit.

i. 1   Wherefore I, Paul, who, for maintaining the cause
2 of you Gentiles, am the prisoner of Jesus Christ[11]—
for[12] I suppose that you have heard of the steward-

The Law which divided Jews from Gentiles abolished.

They are built into the Temple of God.

The mystery of universal salvation proclaimed by Paul, a prisoner for it.

---

[1] Meaning *a circumcision of the flesh, not of the spirit,—made by man's hands, not by God's.*

[2] *Covenants of the promise.* Compare Gal. iii. 16, and Rom. ix. 4,

[3] *Both*, viz. Jews and Gentiles.

[4] The allusion is evidently to that 'balustrade of stone' described by Josephus, which separated the Court of the Gentiles from the holier portion of the Temple, and which it was death for a Gentile to pass. See Chap. XXI. p. 579.

[5] i.e. by His death, as explained by the parallel passage, Col. i. 22.

[6] Christians are *created in Christ* (see above, v. 10), i.e. their union with Christ is the essential condition of

their Christian existence.

[7] '*In* one spirit.' It is sometimes impossible to translate such expressions accurately, except by a periphrasis.

[8] 'Holy *in* the Lord.' See the preceding note.

[9] *You as well as others.*

[10] Compare 1 Cor. iii. 16; and see note 1. 'In the spirit,' might, however, be taken (with Olshausen and others) merely as an antithesis to 'in the flesh.'

[11] The sentence is abruptly broken off here, but carried on again at v. 13. The whole passage bears evident marks of the rapidity of dictation.

[12] Literally, *if, as I suppose, you have heard of the office of dispensing*

ship of God's grace, which was given me for you; iii. and how, by revelation, was [1] made known to me the mystery (as I have already shortly [2] written 4 to you; so that, when you read, you may perceive my understanding in the mystery of Christ), which, 5 in the generations of old, was not made known to the sons of men, as it has now been revealed by the indwelling [3] of the Spirit, to His holy Apostles and Prophets; to wit, that the Gentiles are heirs of the 6 same inheritance, and members of the same body, and partakers of the [4] same promise in Christ, by means of the Glad-tidings.

And of this Glad-tidings I was made a ministering 7 servant, according to the gift of the grace of God, which was given me in the full measure of His mighty working; to me, I say, who am less than the 8 least of all the saints, this grace was given, to bear among the Gentiles the Glad-tidings of the unsearchable riches of Christ, and to bring light to all, that 9 they might behold what is the stewardship [5] of the mystery which, from the ages of old, has been hid in 10 God, the maker of all things; [6] that now, by the Church, [7] the manifold wisdom of God might be made 11 known to the Principalities and Powers in the heavens, according to His eternal purpose, which He 12 wrought in Jesus Christ our Lord; in whom we can approach without fear to God, in trustful confidence, through faith in Him.

He prays for himself and them, that they may be strengthened

Wherefore I pray that I may not faint under my 13 sufferings for you, which are your glory. For this 14 cause I bend my knees before the Father, [8] whose 15 children [9] all are called in heaven and in earth, be- 16

(see note on 1. 10) *the grace of God which was given me for you.*

[1] In the MSS. the verb is passive.

[2] The reference is to chap. i. 9, 10.

[3] See notes on ch. ii. ver. 18 and 21 above.

[4] 'His' is omitted by the best MSS.

[5] The best MSS. have *stewardship*, not *fellowship.* See note on i. 10. St. Paul displayed the nature of his 'stewardship' by the manner in which he discharged its duties. Compare 1 Cor. ix. 17, and 2 Cor. iv. and v.

[6] 'By Jesus Christ' is not in the best MSS

[7] i.e. by the union of all mankind in the Church. That which calls forth the expressions of rapturous admiration here, and in the similar passage in

Romans (xi. 33), is the divine plan of including all mankind in a universal redemption.

[8] The words 'of our Lord Jesus Christ' are not in the best MSS.

[9] The sense depends on a paronomasia, the word for 'family' (A. V.) meaning *a race descended from a common ancestor.* Compare Luke ii. 4. If *fatherhood* had this meaning in English (as it might have had, according to the analogy of '*a brotherhood*'), the verse might be literally rendered *from whom every fatherhood in heaven and earth is named*; i.e. the very name of *fatherhood* refers us back to God as the *father of all.* The A. V. is incorrect, and would require the definite article.

seeching Him, that, in the richness of His glory, He
would grant you strength by the entrance of His

i. 17 Spirit into your inner man, that Christ may dwell in *and enlight-*
your hearts by faith; that having your root and your *ened.*

18 foundation in love, you may be enabled, with all the
saints, to comprehend the breadth and length, and

19 depth and height thereof; and to know the love of
Christ which passeth knowledge,[1] that you may be
filled therewith, even to the measure of[2] the Fulness

20 of God.   Now unto Him who is able to do exceeding *Doxology.*

21 abundantly, above all that we ask or think, in the
power of His might which works within us,—unto
Him, in Christ Jesus, be glory in the Church, even
to all the generations of the age of ages.   Amen.

v. 1   I, therefore, the Lord's prisoner, exhort you to *Exhortation*
walk worthy of the calling wherewith you were *to unity.*
Different gifts

2 called; with all lowliness,[3] and gentleness, and long- *and offices*
must combine
suffering, forbearing one another in love, striving to *to build up*
the Church.

3 maintain the unity of the Spirit, bound together with

4 the bond of peace.   You are one body and one spirit,
even as you were called to share one common hope;

5 you have one Lord, you have one faith, you have one

6 baptism; you have one God and Father of all, who is

7 over all, and works through all, and dwells in all.[4]
But each one of us received the gift of grace which
he possesses according to the measure[5] wherein it
it was given by Christ.   Wherefore it is[6] written:

8 '𝔚𝔥𝔢𝔫 𝔥𝔢 𝔴𝔢𝔫𝔱 𝔲𝔭 𝔬𝔫 𝔥𝔦𝔤𝔥, 𝔥𝔢 𝔩𝔢𝔡 𝔠𝔞𝔭𝔱𝔦𝔟𝔦𝔱𝔶 𝔠𝔞𝔭𝔱𝔦𝔟𝔢,

9 𝔞𝔫𝔡 𝔤𝔞𝔟𝔢 𝔤𝔦𝔣𝔱𝔰 𝔲𝔫𝔱𝔬 𝔪𝔢𝔫.'   Now that word '𝔥𝔢 𝔴𝔢𝔫𝔱
𝔲𝔭,' what saith it, but that He first came down to

10 the earth below?   Yea, He who came down is the
same who is gone up, far above all the heavens, that

11 He might fill all things.[7]   And He gave some to be
apostles,[8] and some prophets, and some evangelists,

12 and some pastors and teachers; for the perfecting of

---

[1] Again we observe an apparent
allusion to the technical employment
of the words *Gnosis* and *Pleroma.*

[2] *Unto,* not *with* (A. V.).

[3] See note on Col. iii. 12.

[4] *You* omitted in best MSS.

[5] This verse is parallel to Rom. xii.
6, 'having gifts differing according
to the grace which God has given us.'
The whole context of the two passages
also throws light on both.

[6] Literally, *it says,* i.e. *the Scripture
says.*   The quotation is from Ps. lxviii.

18, but slightly altered, so as to correspond neither with the Hebrew nor
with the Septuagint.   Our two authorised versions of the Psalms have here
departed from the original, in order to
follow the present passage; probably
on the supposition that St. Paul quoted
from some older reading.

[7] Again we remark an allusion to
the doctrine of the *Pleroma.*   Compare
i. 23.

[8] On this classification of church offices, see p. 342.

the saints, to labour[1] in their appointed service, to iv. build up the body of Christ; till we all attain the same[2] faith and knowledge of the Son of God, and reach the stature of manhood,[3] and be of ripe age to receive the Fulness of Christ;[4] that we should no 14 longer be children, tossed to and fro, and blown round by every shifting current of teaching, tricked by the sleight of men, and led astray into the snares[5] of the cunning; but that we should live in truth and 15 love, and should grow up in every part[6] to the measure of His[7] growth, who is our head, even Christ. From whom[8] the whole body (being knit together, 16 and compacted by all its joints) derives its continued growth in the working of His bounty, which supplies its needs, according to the measure of each several part, that it may build itself up in love.

Exhortation to the rejection of Heathen vice and to moral renewal.

This I say, therefore, and adjure you in the Lord, 17 to live no longer like other Gentiles, whose minds are filled with folly, whose understanding is dark- 18 ened, who are estranged from the life of God because of the ignorance which is in them, through the blindness of their hearts; who, being past feeling, 19 have given themselves over to lasciviousness, to work all uncleanness in lust.[9]   But you have not 20 so learned Christ; if, indeed, you have heard His voice, and been taught in Him, as the truth is in 21 Jesus; to forsake your former life, and put off the 22 old man, whose way is[10] destruction, following the desires which deceive; and to be renewed in the 23 spirit of your mind, and to put on the new man, created after God's likeness, in the righteousness and 24

Against several specified vices.

holiness of the Truth.   Wherefore, putting away 25 lying, speak every man truth with his neighbour; for we are members one of another.   ' 𝕭𝖊 𝖞𝖊 𝖆𝖓𝖌𝖗𝖞, 26

---

[1] The word does not mean *the ministry*' (A. V.).

[2] Literally, *the oneness of the faith and of the knowledge.*

[3] Literally, *a man of mature age.*

[4] See again note on iii. 19.

[5] Literally, *cunningly toward the snares of misleading error.*

[6] 'In every part.' See following verse.

[7] *To grow into Him,* is *to grow to the standard of His growth.*

[8] Literally rendered, this is *from whom all the body (being knit together and compacted by every joint)* accord-

ing to the working of his bounteous providing in the measure of each several part, continues the growth of the body. Compare the parallel passage, Col. ii. 19, *from whom the whole body, by the joints which bind it, draws full supplies for its needs, and is knit together and increases in godly growth.* A child derives its life *from* its father, and grows *up to* the standard of its father's growth.

[9] For this see note on 1 Cor. v. 11; and compare chap. v. 3.

[10] Not ' *corrupt*' (A.V.), but *going on in the way of ruin.*

7. 27 𝖆𝖓𝖉 𝖘𝖎𝖓 𝖓𝖔𝖙.'[1]   Let not the sun go down upon your
28 wrath, nor give away to the Devil.   Let the robber[2] rob no more, but rather let him labour, working to good purpose with his hands, that he may have
29 somewhat to share with the needy.   From your mouth let no filthy words come forth, but such as may build up[3] the Church according to its need, and
30 give a blessing to the hearers.   And grieve not the Holy Spirit of God, who was given to seal you[4] for
31 the day of redemption.   Let all bitterness, and passion, and anger, and clamour, and evil speaking be put away from you, with all malice; and be[5]
32 kind one to another, tender-hearted, forgiving one another, even as God in Christ has forgiven you.

Exhortation to Christ-like forgiveness and love.

7. 1 Therefore be followers of God's example, as the
2 children of His love. And walk in love, as Christ also loved us, and gave Himself for us, an offering and a sacrifice unto God, for ' 𝖆𝖓 𝖔𝖉𝖔𝖚𝖗 𝖔𝖋 𝖘𝖜𝖊𝖊𝖙𝖓𝖊𝖘𝖘.'[6]

3   But, as befits the saints, let not fornication or any kind of uncleanness or lust[7] be so much as
4 named among you; nor filthiness, nor buffoonery, nor ribald jesting, for such speech beseems you not, but rather thanksgiving. Yea, this you know; for
5 you have learned that no fornicator, or impure or lustful man, who is nothing better than an[8] idolater, has any inheritance in the kingdom of Christ and

Against impurity and other sins of Heathen darkness;

---

[1] Ps. iv. 4 (LXX.).

[2] Him that steals (present). The A. V. would require the aorist. It should be remembered that the *stealers* (*klephts*) of the N. T. were not what we should now call *thieves* (as the word is generally rendered in A. V.), but *bandits*; and there is nothing strange in finding such persons numerous in the provincial towns among the mountains of Asia Minor. See p. 129.

[3] Literally, *such as is good for needful building up* ('building' always implies 'the Church' or something equivalent), *that it may give a blessing to the hearers.*

[4] The tense is mistranslated in A.V. Literally, *in whom you were sealed.* The meaning is rendered evident by i. 13, 14. It is the constant doctrine of St. Paul, that the gift of the Holy Spirit is a seal or mark of Christ's redeemed, which was given them at their conversion and reception into the Church, as a foretaste of their full redemption. Compare Rom. viii. 23.

[5] Literally, 'become ye.' This word is sometimes used as simply equivalent to 'be ye.' Compare v. 17.

[6] Gen. viii. 21 (LXX.); see Phil. iv. 18, where it is also quoted.

[7] It has been before remarked that this passage is conclusive as to the use of this particular Greek word by St. Paul; for what intelligible sense is there in saying that ' *covetousness* ' must not be so much as *named* ? See note on 1 Cor. v. 11. It was there remarked that the use of *concupiscence* in English is an analogous case; it might be added that the word *lust* itself is likewise used in both senses; e.g. ' the lust of gold.'

[Since our first edition, we are glad to see that this old view of the Pauline usage of the word has been adopted by Prof. Jowett and Prof. Stanley, in their notes on Rom. i. 29, and 1 Cor. v. 11, respectively, and by Dean Trench in his *Synonyms.*]

[8] See note on Col. iii. 5.

God. Let no man mislead you by empty[1] words; v. for these are the deeds[2] which bring the wrath of God upon the children of disobedience. Be not ye, 7 therefore, partakers with them; for you once were 8 darkness, but now are light in the Lord. Walk 9 as children of light; for the fruits of light[3] are in all goodness, and righteousness, and truth. Ex- 10 amine well what is acceptable to the Lord, and have 11 no fellowship with the unfruitful works of darkness, yea, rather expose their foulness.[4] For, concerning 12 the secret deeds of the Heathen,[5] it is shameful even to speak; yet all these things, when exposed, are 13 made manifest by the shining of the light; for whatsoever is made manifest becomes light.[6] Where- 14 fore it is written,[7] '𝔄𝔴𝔞𝔨𝔢, 𝔱𝔥𝔬𝔲 𝔱𝔥𝔞𝔱 𝔰𝔩𝔢𝔢𝔭𝔢𝔰𝔱, 𝔞𝔫𝔡 𝔞𝔯𝔦𝔰𝔢 𝔣𝔯𝔬𝔪 𝔱𝔥𝔢 𝔡𝔢𝔞𝔡, 𝔞𝔫𝔡 𝔠𝔥𝔯𝔦𝔰𝔱 𝔰𝔥𝔞𝔩𝔩 𝔰𝔥𝔦𝔫𝔢 𝔲𝔭𝔬𝔫 𝔱𝔥𝔢𝔢.'[8]

See, then, that you walk[9] without stumbling, not 15 in folly but in wisdom, forestalling[10] opportunity, be- 16 cause the times are evil. Therefore, be not without 17 understanding, but learn to know what the will of the Lord is.

Be not drunk with wine, like those[11] who live 18 riotously; but be filled with the indwelling of the Spirit, when you speak one to another.[12] Let your 19 singing be of psalms and hymns and spiritual songs, and make melody with the music of your hearts, to the Lord.[13] And at all times, for all things which 20

[marginal notes]
which must be rebuked by the example and watchfulness of Christians.

Festive meetings, how to be celebrated.

---

[1] Namely, reasonings to prove the sins of impurity innocent. See 1 Cor. vi. 12–20, and the note.

[2] Viz., the sins of impurity. Compare Rom. i. 24–27.

[3] *Light*, not *Spirit*, is the reading of the best MSS.

[4] The verb means *to lay bare the real character of a thing by exposing it to open scrutiny.*

[5] 'What is done by *them*,' i.e. *the Heathen.*

[6] Such appears to be the meaning of this difficult verse, viz., that when the light falls on any object, the object itself reflects the rays; implying that moral evil will be recognised as evil by the conscience, if it is shown in its true colours by being brought into contrast with the laws of pure morality. The preceding 'is made manifest' does not allow us to translate the same form immediately following as active (as A. V.).

[7] See note on iv. 8.

[8] There is no verse exactly corresponding with this in the O. T. But Isaiah lx. 1 is perhaps referred to. We must remember, however, that there is no proof that St. Paul intends (either here, or 1 Cor. ii. 9) to quote the Old Testament. Some have supposed that he is quoting a Christian hymn; others, a saying of our Lord (as at Acts xx. 35).

[9] Dean Ellicott's translation, 'See then how ye walk with exactness,' literally accurate, though scarcely intelligible to an English reader.

[10] See Col. iv. 5, and note.

[11] Literally, *in doing which is riotous living.*

[12] We put a full stop after *to one another* (here), as Col. iii. 16.

[13] Throughout the whole passage there is a contrast implied between the Heathen and the Christian practice, q. d. *When you meet, let your enjoyment consist not in fulness of wine, but fulness of the Spirit; let your songs be,*

befal you, give thanks to our God and Father, in the name of our Lord Jesus Christ.

21 Submit yourselves one to another in the fear of **Duties of**
22 Christ.[1] Wives, submit yourselves to your hus-**wives and husbands.**
23 bands, as unto the Lord; for the husband is head of the wife, even as Christ is head of the Church,[2]
24 His body, which He saves.[3] But,[4] as the Church submits itself to Christ, so let the wives submit themselves to their husbands in all things.

25 Husbands, love your wives, as Christ also loved
26 the Church, and gave Himself for it, that having purified it by the water wherein it is washed,[5] He might hallow it by the indwelling of the word of
27 God; that He might Himself[6] present unto Himself[7] the Church in stainless glory, not having spot or wrinkle, or any such thing; but that it should
28 be holy and unblemished. In like manner, husbands ought to love their wives as they love their own bodies; for he that loves his wife does but love
29 himself: and a man never hated his own flesh, but
30 nourishes and cherishes it, as Christ[8] also the
31 Church; for we are members of His body.[9] '**For this cause shall a man leave his father and his mother, and shall cleave unto his wife, and they two shall be one**

---

not the drinking-songs of heathen feasts, but psalms and hymns; and their accompaniment, not the music of the lyre, but the melody of the heart; while you sing them to the praise, not of Bacchus or Venus, but of the Lord Jesus Christ. For the construction and punctua on see Col. iii. 16.

[1] *Christ* is the reading of the best MSS. That this comprehends all the special relations of subjection which follow (and should be joined with what follows) is shown by the omission of *submit yourselves* (in the next verse) by the best MSS.; an omission to which Jerome testifies. The transition of participial into imperative clauses is according to the analogy of the similar hortatory passage, Rom. xii. 8. to 19.

[2] This statement occurs 1 Cor. ii. 3, almost verbatim.

[3] The literal English is, *he is the de liverer of his body*; and an analogy is implied to the conjugal relation, in which the husband maintains and cherishes the wife.

[4] The conjunction cannot be translated '*therefore*' (A. V.).

[5] '*The* water' (not simply 'water'); literally, *by the laver of the water*, equi-

valent to *laver of regeneration* (Titus iii. 5). The following *in the word* is exceedingly difficult. Chrysostom and the patristic commentators generally explain it of the formula of baptism; De Wette takes the same view. But see St. Paul's use of the same expression elsewhere, Rom. x. 8, x. 17, also Eph. vi. 17; and moreover, as Winer and Meyer have remarked, the junction of 'in the word' with the verb better suits the Greek. On this view, the meaning is that the Church, having been purified by the waters of baptism, is hallowed by the revelation of the mind of God imparted to it, whether mediately or immediately. Compare Heb. iv. 12, 13.

[6] The best MSS. read thus.

[7] The Church is compared to a bride, as 2 Cor. xi. 2.

[8] The best MSS. read *Christ*.

[9] The words 'of his flesh and of his bones' are not found in the MSS. of highest authority (A and B.). They may have easily been introduced from the Septuagint, where they occur immediately before the following quotation, viz. at Gen. ii. 23.

flesh.'[1] This mystery is great, but I[2] speak of Christ v. 3
and of the Church. Nevertheless, let every one of 33
you individually[3] so love his wife even as himself,
and let the wife see that she reverence her husband.

Duties of children and parents.

Children, obey your parents in the Lord; for this vi. 1
is right. 'Honour thy father and thy mother,'[4] which 2
is the first commandment with[5] promise: 'That it 3
may be well with thee, and thou shalt live long upon
the earth.'[6]

And ye, fathers, vex not your children; but bring 4
them up in such training and correction as befits the
servants of the Lord.[7]

Duties of slaves and masters.

Bondsmen, obey your earthly masters with 5
anxiety and self-distrust,[8] in singleness of heart, as
unto Christ; not with eye-service, as men-pleasers, 6
but as bondsmen of Christ, doing the will of God
from the soul. With good will fulfilling your ser- 7
vice, as to the Lord our Master[9] and not to men.
For you know that whatever good any man does, the 8
same shall he receive from the Lord, whether he
be bond or free.

And ye, masters, do in like manner by them, and 9
abstain from threats; knowing that your own [10]
Master is in heaven, and that with Him is no respect of persons.

Exhortation to fight in the Christian armour.

Finally, my brethren, let your hearts be strength- 10
ened in the Lord[11] and in the conquering power of
His might. Put on the whole armour of God, that 11
you may be able to stand firm against the wiles
of the Devil. For the adversaries with whom we 12
wrestle are not flesh and blood, but they are[12] the
Principalities, the Powers, and the Sovereigns of
this[13] present darkness, the spirits of evil in the
heavens. Wherefore, take up with you to the 13
battle[14] the whole armour of God, that you may be

---

[1] Gen. ii. 24 (LXX.).

[2] The pronoun is emphatic: *but I, while I quote these words out of the Scriptures, use them in an higher sense.*

[3] *In your individual capacity*, contrasted with the previous *collective* view of the members of the Church as the bride of Christ.

[4] Exodus xx. 12, and Deut. v. 16 (LXX.).

[5] Literally, *in a promise*. The command being (as it were) set in a promise.

[6] Exodus xx. 12, and Deut. v. 16 (LXX. not exactly verbatim).

[7] The word *lord* implies the idea of *servants*.

[8] 'With fear and trembling' has this meaning in St. Paul's language. Compare 1 Cor. ii. 3.

[9] See note on Col. iii. 25.

[10] Some of the best MSS. read 'both their and your,' which brings out still more forcibly the equality of slaves and masters in the sight of Christ.

[11] This is the literal meaning.

[12] Compare Col. ii. 15, and the note; also John xii. 31.

[13] '*This world*' is omitted in the best MSS.

[14] 'Take up,' literally.

able to withstand them in the evil day, and having[1]
i. 14 overthrown them all, to stand unshaken. Stand,
therefore, girt with the belt of truth, and wearing
15 the breastplate of righteousness, and shod as ready
16 messengers of the Glad-tidings of peace : and take
up to cover you[2] the shield of faith, wherewith you
shall be able to quench all the fiery darts of the
17 Evil One. Take, likewise, the helmet of salvation,[3]
and the sword of the Spirit, which is the word of God.[4]

18 Continue to pray at every season with all earnestness of supplication in the Spirit; and to this end
be watchful with all perseverance in prayer for
19 all the saints ; and for me, that utterance may be
20 given me, to open my mouth and make known
with boldness the mystery of the Glad-tidings, for
which I am an ambassador in fetters.[5] Pray that I
may declare it boldly, as I ought to speak.

To pray for others and for Paul.

21 But that you, as well as[6] others, may be informed
of my concerns, and how I fare, Tychicus, my[7]
beloved brother, and faithful servant in the Lord,
22 will make all known to you. And I have sent him
to you for this very end, that you may learn what
concerns me, and that he may comfort your hearts.

Tychicus the messenger.

23 Peace be to the brethren, and love with faith, from
God our Father, and our Lord Jesus Christ.

Concluding benediction.

24 Grace be with all who love our Lord Jesus Christ
in[8] sincerity.[9]

---

[1] Not ‘*done*’ (A. V.), but ‘*overthrown*.’

[2] *To cover all*. If it meant *in addition to all* (Ellicott), it would surely have come last in the list.

[3] The head of the Christian is defended against hostile weapons by his knowledge of the salvation won for him by Christ.

[4] For the meaning of ‘word of God,’ see note on chap. v. 26. It is here represented as the only *offensive* weapon of Christian warfare. The Roman pilum (Joh. xix. 34) is not mentioned. For a commentary on this military imagery, and the circumstances which naturally suggested it, see the begin-

ning of the next chapter.

[5] See Paley’s observations (*Horæ Paulinæ*, in loco), and our preceding remarks on *Custodia Militaris*.

[6] ‘You *also*.’

[7] See the parallel passage, Col. iv. 7.

[8] The difficulty of the concluding words is well known : the phrase might also be translated *in immortality*, with the meaning *whose love endures immortally*. Olshausen supposes the expression elliptical, for ‘ that they may have life in immortality ; ’ but this can scarcely be justified.

[9] ‘Amen,’ as usual, is omitted in the best MSS.

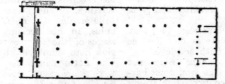

Ground plan of the Basilica of Pompeii. (From Gell's Pompeii.)

CHAPTER XXVI.

The Prætorium and the Palatine.—Arrival of Epaphroditus,—Political Events at Rome.—Octavia and Poppæa.—St. Paul writes *the Epistle to the Philippians.*—He makes Converts in the Imperial Household.

THE close of the Epistle to which our attention has just been turned contains a remarkable example of the forcible imagery of St. Paul.[1] Considered simply in itself, this description of the Christian's armour is one of the most striking passages in the Sacred Volume. But if we view it in connection with the circumstances with which the Apostle was surrounded, we find a new and living emphasis in his enumeration of all the parts of the heavenly panoply,[2]—the belt of sincerity and truth, with which the loins[3] are girded for the spiritual war,—the breastplate of that righteousness,[4] the inseparable links whereof are faith and love,[5]—the strong sandals,[6] with which the feet of Christ's soldiers are made ready,[7] not for such errands of death and despair as those on which the Prætorian soldiers were daily sent, but for the universal message of the Gospel of peace,—the large shield[8] of confident trust,[9] wherewith the whole man is protected,[10] and whereon the fiery arrows[11] of the Wicked One fall harmless and dead,—the

---

[1] Eph. vi. 14–17.

[2] 'The whole armour of God.' For authentic information regarding the actual Roman armour of the time, we may refer to Piranesi's fine illustrations of the columns of Trajan and Marcus Aurelius. There are also many useful engravings in Dr. Smith's *Dictionary of Antiquities*.

[3] 'Your loins girt about with truth.' The belt or *zona* passed round the lower part of the body, below the 'breastplate,' and is to be distinguished from the *balteus,* which went over the shoulder.

[4] 'Wearing the breastplate of righteousness.' The 'breastplate' was a cuirass or corslet, reaching nearly to the loins.

[5] In the parallel passage (1 Thess. v. 8), the breastplate is described as 'the breastplate of faith and love.'

[6] The Roman *caligæ* were not greaves, which in fact would not harmonise with the context, but strong

and heavy sandals. See the anecdote of the death of the centurion Julian in the Temple at Jerusalem. Joseph. *War,* vi. 1. 8.

[7] 'Shod as ready messengers,' &c.

[8] The 'shield' here is the large oblong or oval Roman shield—the *scutum* not the *clipeus,*—specimens of which may be seen in Piranesi. See especially the pedestal of Trajan's column.

[9] 'The shield of faith.'

[10] Observe 'over all,' which is not clearly translated in the Authorised Version.

[11] Part of the artillery in an ancient siege consisted of darts and heavier missiles, in the heads of which were inflammable materials. Diodorus Siculus, in his account of one of the sieges of Rhodes, uses the very expression here employed by the Apostle. The Latin names for these missiles were *fularicæ* and *malleoli.* Liv. xxi. 8 ; Cic. *Cat.* i. 13.

close-fitting, helmet,[1] with which the hope of salvation[2] invests the head of the believer,—and finally the sword of the Spirit, the Word of God,[3] which, when wielded by the Great Captain of our Salvation, turned the tempter in the wilderness to flight, while in the hands of His chosen Apostle (with whose memory the sword seems inseparably associated)[4] it became the means of establishing Christianity on the earth.

All this imagery becomes doubly forcible, if we remember that when St. Paul wrote the words he was chained to a soldier, and in the close neighbourhood of military sights and sounds. The appearance of the Prætorian guards was daily familiar to him;—as his ‘chains’ on the other hand (so he tells us in the succeeding Epistle) became ‘well known throughout the whole *Prætorium.*’ (Phil. i. 13.)   A difference of opinion has existed as to the precise meaning of the word in this passage.   Some have identified it, as in the Authorised Version, with the ‘house of Cæsar’ on the Palatine :[5] more commonly it has been supposed to mean that permanent camp of the Prætorian guards, which Tiberius established on the north of the city, outside the walls.[6]   As regards the former opinion, it is true that the word came to be used, almost as we use the word ‘palace,’ for royal residences generally, or for any residences of a princely splendour,[7] and that thus we read, in other parts of the New Testament, of the Prætorium of Pilate at Jerusalem[8] and the Prætorium of Herod at Cæsarea.[9]   Yet we never find the word employed for the Imperial house at Rome : and we believe the truer view to be that which has been recently advocated,[10] namely, that it denotes here, not the palace itself, but the quarters of that part of the Imperial guards which was in immediate attendance upon the Emperor.   Such a military establishment is mentioned in the fullest account which we possess of the first residence of Augustus on the Palatine :[11] and it is in harmony with the general ideas on which the monarchy was founded.   The Emperor was *prætor*[12] or commander-in-chief of the troops, and it was natural

[1] One of these compact Roman helmets, preserved in England, at Goodrich Court, is engraved in Dr. Smith's *Dictionary.* (See under *Galea.*)

[2] With ‘helmet of salvation’ (Eph. vi. 17) we should compare ‘as a helmet the hope of salvation’ (1 Thess. v. 8).

[3] See note on the passage.

[4] It is the emblem of his martyrdom : and we can hardly help associating it also with this passage. The small short sword of the Romans was worn like a dagger on the right side. Specimens may be seen in Piranesi. Those readers who have been in Rome will remember that Pope Sixtus V. dedicated the column of Aurelius (ab omni impietate purgatam) to St. Paul, and that statue of the Apostle, bearing the sword, is on the summit.

[5] With Phil. i. 13 we should compare iv. 22 in the Authorised Version.

[6] See above, in the description of Rome, and compare the map.

[7] We find the word used in Suetonius for the Imperial castles out of Rome. Elsewhere it is applied to the palaces of foreign princes and even private persons.

[8] See above, p. 583.

[9] See above, p. 606, n. 10.

[10] In Wieseler's note, p. 403.

[11] ‘The Imperial residence is called *Palatium* . . . . because the Emperor dwelt on Mount Palatine, and there he had his military force (*Prætorium*). . . hence it comes that wherever the Emperor is living it is called *Palatium.*’ Dio Cass. liii. 16.

[12] See what has been said (pp. 115, 116), in reference to the term *proprætor* in the provinces.

that his immediate guard should be in a *prætorium* near him. It might, indeed, be argued that this military establishment on the Palatine would cease to be necessary, when the Prætorian camp was established : but the purpose of that establishment was to concentrate near the city those cohorts, which had previously been dispersed in other parts of Italy : a local body-guard near the palace would not cease to be necessary : and Josephus, in his account of the imprisonment of Agrippa,[1] speaks of a ' camp' in connection with the ' royal house.' Such we conceive to have been the barrack immediately alluded to by St. Paul : though the connection of these smaller quarters with the general camp was such, that he would naturally become known to ' *all the rest* '[2] of the guards, as well as those who might for the time be connected with the Imperial household.

What has just been said of the word ' prætorium,' applied still more extensively to the word '*palatium.*' Originally denoting the hill on which the twin-brothers were left by the retreating river, it grew to be, and it still remains, the symbol of Imperial power. Augustus was born on the Palatine ;[3] and he fixed his official residence there when the Civil Wars were terminated. Thus, it may be truly said that ' after the Capital and the Forum, no locality in the ancient city claims so much of our interest as the Palatine hill—at once the birth-place of the infant city, and the abode of her rulers during the days of her greatest splendour,—where the red-thatched cottage of Romulus was still preserved in the midst of the gorgeous structures of Caligula and Nero.'[4] About the close of the Republic, this hill was the residence of many distinguished citizens, such as Crassus, Cicero, Catiline, Clodius, and Antony. Augustus himself simply bought the house of Hortensius, and lived there in modest state.[5] But the new era was begun for the Palatine, when the first Emperor, soon after the battle of Actium, raised the temple of Apollo, with its celebrated Greek and Latin libraries,[6] on the side near the Forum. Tiberius erected a new palace, or an addition to the old one, on the opposite side of the hill, immediately above the Circus Maximus.[7] It remained for subsequent Emperors to cover the whole area of the hill with structures connected with the palace. Caligula extended the Imperial buildings by a bridge (as fantastic as that at Baiæ),[8] which joined the Palatine with the Capitol. Nero made a similar extension in the direction of the Esquiline; and this is the point at which we must arrest our series of historical notices ; for the burning of Rome and the erection of the Golden

---

[1] Joseph. *Ant.* xviii. 6. He uses στρατόπεδον for the *prætorium*, and βασίλειον for the *palatium*. Compare what is said of Drusus, Suet. *Tib.* 54.

[2] Ibid.

[3] Suet. *Aug.* 5.

[4] Bunbury in the *Classical Museum*, vol. v. p. 229. We learn from Plutarch and Dionysius, that this 'wooden hut thatched with reeds, which was preserved as a memorial of the simple habitation of the Shepherd-king,' was on the side of the hill towards the Circus, p. 232.

[5] Suet. *Aug.* 72.

[6] Hor. *Ep.* I. iii. 17. Suet. *Aug.* 29.

[7] The position of the ' Domus Tiberiana' is determined by the notices of it in the account of the murder of Galba.

[8] See above, p. 665.

House intervened between the first and second imprisonments of the Apostle Paul. The fire, moreover, which is so closely associated with the first sufferings of the Church, has made it impossible to identify any of the existing ruins on the Palatine with buildings that were standing when the Apostle was among the Prætorian guards. Nor indeed it is possible to assign the ruins to their proper epochs. All is now confusion on the hill of Romulus and Augustus. Palace after palace succeeded, till the Empire was lost in the mist of the Middle Ages. As we explore the subterraneous chambers, where classical paintings are still visible on the plaster, or look out through broken arches over the Campagna and its aqueducts, the mind is filled with blending recollections, not merely of a long line of Roman Cæsars, but of Ravenna and Constantinople, Charlemagne and Rienzi. This royal part of the Western Babylon has almost shared the fate of the city of the Euphrates. The Palatine contains gardens and vineyards,[1] and half cultivated spaces of ground, where the acanthus-weed grows in wild luxuriance: but its population has shrunk to one small convent;[2] and the unhealthy air seems to brood like a curse over the scene of Nero's tyranny and crime.

St. Paul was at Rome precisely at that time when the Palatine was the most conspicuous spot on the earth, not merely for crime, but for splendour and power. This was the centre of all the movements of the Empire.[3] Here were heard the causes of all Roman citizens who had appealed to Cæsar.[4] Hence were issued the orders to the governors of provinces, and to the legions on the frontier. From the 'Golden Mile-stone' (Milliarium Aureum)[5] below the palace, the roads radiated in all directions to the remotest verge of civilisation. The official messages of the Emperor were communicated along them by means of posts established by the government:[6] but these roads afforded also the means of transmitting the letters of private citizens, whether sent by means of *tabellarii*,[7] or by the voluntary aid of accidental travellers. To such communications between the metropolis and the provinces others were now added of a kind hitherto unknown in the world,—not different indeed in outward appearance[8] from common letters,—but contain-

---

[1] The Farnese gardens and the Villa Mills (formerly Villa Spada) are well known to travellers. Some of the finest arches are in the Vigna del Collegio Inglese.

[2] The Franciscan convent of St. Bonaventura, facing the Forum.

[3] Tac. *Hist.* iii. 70.

[4] See the account of St. Paul's trial in the next chapter.

[5] The *Milliarium Aureum* (afterwards called the *Umbilicus Romæ*) is believed to have been discovered at the base of the Capitol, near the Temples of Saturn and Concord.

[6] So far as related to government despatches, Augustus established posts similar to those of King Ahasuerus. Compare Suet. *Aug.* 49 with Esther

viii. 13, 14.

[7] See Becker's *Gallus*, p. 250 (Eng. Trans.)

[8] In p. 321, a general reference was made to the interest connected even with the writing materials employed by St. Paul. There is little doubt that these were reed-pens, Egyptian paper, and black ink. All these are mentioned by St. John (*paper and ink*, 2 John 12 ; *ink and pen*, 3 John 13); and St. Paul himself, in a passage where there is a blended allusion to inscriptions on stone and to letter-writing (2 Cor. iii. 3), speaks of *ink*. Representations of ancient inkstands found at Pompeii, with reed-pens, may be seen in Dr. Smith's *Dictionary*, under *Atramentum*. Allusion

ing commands more powerful in their effects than the despatches of Nero,—touching more closely the private relations of life than all the correspondence of Seneca [1] or Pliny,—and proclaiming, in the very form of their salutations, the perpetual union of the Jew, the Greek, and the Roman. [2]

It seems probable that the three letters which we have last read were despatched from Rome when St. Paul had been resident there about a year, [3] that is, in the spring of the year 62 A.D. After the departure of Tychicus and Onesimus, the Apostle's prison was cheered by the arrival of Epaphroditus, who bore a contribution from the Christians of Philippi. We have before seen instances [4] of the noble liberality of that Church, and now once more we find them ministering to the necessities of their beloved teacher. Epaphroditus, apparently a leading presbyter among the Philippians, had brought on himself, by the fatigues or perils of his journey, a dangerous illness. St. Paul speaks of him with touching affection. He calls him his 'brother, and companion in labour, and fellow soldier' (ii. 25); declares that 'his labour in the cause of Christ had brought him near to death' (ii. 30), and that he had 'hazarded his life' in order to supply the means of communication between the Philippians and himself. And when speaking of his recovery, he says, 'God had compassion on him, and not on him only, but on me also, that I might not have sorrow upon sorrow' (ii. 27). We must suppose, from these expressions, that Epaphroditus had exposed himself to some unusual risk in his journey. Perhaps his health was already feeble when he set out, so that he showed self-devotion in encountering fatigues which were certain to injure him.

Meanwhile St. Paul continued to preach, and his converts to multiply. We shall find that when he wrote to the Philippians, either towards the close of this year, or at the beginning of the next, great effects had already been produced; and that the Church of Rome was not only enlarged, but encouraged to act with greater boldness upon the surrounding masses of Heathenism, [5] by the successful energy of the apostolic prisoner. Yet the political occurrences of the year might well have alarmed him for his safety,

---

has been made before (p. 630) to the paper trade of Egypt. *Parchment* (2 Tim. iv. 13) was of course used for the secondary MSS. in which the Epistles were preserved. Letters were written in the large or uncial character, though of course the handwriting of different persons would vary. See Gal. vi. 11.

[1] We must not pass by the name of Seneca without some allusion to the so-called correspondence between him and St. Paul; but a mere allusion is enough for so vapid and meaningless a forgery. These Epistles (with that which is called the Ep. to the Laodiceans, described p. 702, n. 3) will be found in Jones *on the Canon* (vol. ii.).

[2] We allude to the combination of the Oriental '*peace*' with the Greek '*grace*' or '*joy*' in the opening saluta-

tions of all St. Paul's Epistles. We may compare Horace's 'Celso *gaudere*,' &c., *Ep.* I. viii., with the opening of the letter of Lysias to Felix, Acts xxiii. 26.

[3] The state of things described in the 4th chapter of Colossians, the conversion of Onesimus and his usefulness to St. Paul (Philem. 11-13), imply the continuance of St. Paul's ministry at Rome during a period which can hardly have been less than a year. Nor would St. Paul, at the beginning of his imprisonment, have written as he does (Philem. 22) of his captivity as verging towards its termination.

[4] See the account of the Macedonian collection, pp. 436, 437.

[5] Phil. i. 12-14.

and counselled a more timid course. We have seen that prisoners in St. Paul's position were under the charge of the Prætorian Præfect; and in this year occurred the death of the virtuous Burrus,[1] under whose authority his imprisonment had been so unusually mild. Upon this event the præfecture was put into commission, and bestowed on Fenius Rufus and Sofonius Tigellinus. The former was respectable,[2] but wanting in force of character, and quite unable to cope with his colleague, who was already notorious for that energetic wickedness which has since made his name proverbial. St. Paul's Christian friends in Rome must have trembled to think of him as subject to the caprice of this most detestable of Nero's satellites. It does not seem, however, that his situation was altered for the worse; possibly he was never brought under the special notice of Tigellinus, who was too intent on court intrigues, at this period, to attend to so trifling a matter as the concerns of a Jewish prisoner.

Another circumstance occurred about the same time, which seemed to threaten still graver mischief to the cause of Paul. This was the marriage of Nero to his adulterous mistress Poppæa, who had become a proselyte to Judaism. This infamous woman, not content with inducing her paramour to divorce his young wife Octavia, had demanded and obtained the death of her rival; and had gloated over the head of the murdered victim,[3] which was forwarded from Pandataria to Rome for her inspection. Her power seemed now to have reached its zenith, but rose still higher at the beginning of the following year, upon the birth of a daughter, when temples were erected to her and her infant,[4] and divine honours paid them. We know from Josephus[5] that she exerted her influence over Nero in favour of the Jews, and that she patronised their emissaries at Rome; and assuredly no scruples of humanity would prevent her from seconding their demand for the punishment of their most detested antagonist.

These changed circumstances fully account for the anticipations of an unfavourable issue to his trial, which we shall find St. Paul now expressing;[6] and which contrast remarkably with the confident expectation of release entertained by him when he wrote the letter[7] to Philemon. When we come to discuss the trial of St. Paul, we shall see reason to believe that the providence of God did in fact avert this danger; but at present all things seemed to wear a

---

[1] Tac. *Ann.* xiv. 51. The death of Burrus was an important epoch in Nero's reign. Tacitus tells us in the following chapter, that it broke the power of Seneca and established the influence of Tigellinus; and from this period Nero's public administration became gradually worse and worse, till at length his infamy rivalled that of his private life.

[2] Fenius Rufus was afterwards executed for his share in Piso's conspiracy (Tac. *Ann.* xv. 66, 68), in which he showed lamentable imbecility.

[3] Tac. *Ann.* xiv. 64.

[4] Tac. *Ann.* xv. 23. The temples to Poppæa are mentioned in a fragment of Dio.

[5] Josephus, *Antiq.* xx. 8. 11, speaks of Nero as 'granting favours to the Jews to please Poppæa, who was a religious woman.' This was on the occasion of the wall which the Jews built to intercept Agrippa's view of the Temple. They sent ambassadors to Rome, who succeeded by Poppæa's intercession in carrying their point.

[6] Phil. ii. 17, and iii. 11.

[7] Philem. 22, 23.

most threatening aspect. Perhaps the death of Pallas [1] (which also happened this year) may be considered, on the other hand, as removing an unfavourable influence; for, as the brother of Felix, he would have been willing to soften the Jewish accusers of that profligate governor, by co-operating with their designs against St. Paul. But his power had ceased to be formidable, either for good or evil, some time before his death.

Meanwhile Epaphroditus was fully recovered from his sickness, and able once more to travel; and he willingly prepared to comply with St. Paul's request that he would return to Philippi. We are told that he was 'filled with longing' to see his friends again, and the more so when he heard that great anxiety had been caused among them by the news of his sickness.[2] Probably he occupied an influential post in the Philippian Church, and St. Paul was unwilling to detain him any longer from his duties there. He took the occasion of his return, to send a letter of grateful acknowledgment to his Philippian converts.

It has been often remarked, that this Epistle contains less of censure and more of praise than any other of St. Paul's extant letters. It gives us a very high idea of the Christian state of the Philippians, as shown by the firmness of their faith under persecution,[3] their constant obedience and attachment to St. Paul,[4] and the liberality which distinguished them above all other Churches.[5] They were also free from doctrinal errors, and no schism had as yet been created among them by the Judaising party. They are warned, however, against these active propagandists, who were probably busy in their neighbourhood, or (at least) might at any time appear among them. The only blemish recorded as existing in the Church of Philippi is, that certain of its members were deficient in lowliness of mind, and were thus led into disputes and altercations with their brethren. Two women of consideration amongst the converts, Euodia and Syntyche by name, had been especially guilty of this fault; and their variance was the more to be regretted, because they had both laboured earnestly for the propagation of the faith. St. Paul exhorts the Church, with great solemnity and earnestness,[6] to let these disgraceful bickerings cease, and to be all 'of one soul and one mind.' He also gives them very full particulars about his own condition, and the spread of the Gospel at Rome. He writes in a tone of most affectionate remembrance, and, while anticipating the speedily approaching crisis of his fate, he expresses his faith, hope, and joy with peculiar fervency.

---

[1] Pallas was put to death by poison soon after the marriage of Poppæa, and in the same year. Tac. *Ann.* xiv. 65.

[2] Phil. ii. 26.

[3] Phil. i. 28, 29.

[4] Phil. ii. 12.

[5] Phil. iv. 15.

[6] Phil. ii. 1, 2, and iv. 2.

THE EPISTLE TO THE PHILIPPIANS.[1]

i. 1 PAUL and Timotheus, bondsmen of Jesus Christ Salutation. TO ALL THE SAINTS[2] IN CHRIST JESUS WHO ARE AT PHILIPPI, WITH THE BISHOPS[3] AND DEACONS.[4]

2 Grace be to you and Peace, from God our Father, and from our Lord Jesus Christ.

3 I[5] thank my God upon every remembrance of you Thanksgiv- 4 (continually in all my prayers making my supplication ings and prayers for 5 for you all[6] with joy), for your fellowship in for- them. warding[7] the Glad-tidings, from the first day until 6 now. And I am confident accordingly,[8] that He who has begun a good work in you will perfect it, 7 even until the day of Jesus Christ. And it is just that I should be thus mindful[9] of you all, because you have me in your hearts, and both in my im- prisonment and in my defence and confirmation[10] of the Glad-tidings, you all share in the grace[11]

---

[1] The following are the grounds of the date assigned to this Epistle :—

(1.) It was written during an im- prisonment at Rome, because (A) the *Prætorium* (i. 13) was at Rome; (B) So was the Emperor's household (iv. 22); (C) He expects the immediate decision of his cause (i. 19, ii. 24), which could only have been given at Rome.

(2.) It was written during the *first* imprisonment at Rome, because (A) the mention of the Prætorium agrees with the fact that, during his first imprisonment, he was in the custody of the Prætorian Præfect; (B) His situation described (i. 12–14) agrees with his situation in the first two years of his imprisonment (Acts xxviii. 30, 31).

(3.) It was written *towards the con- clusion* of this first imprisonment, because (A) he expects the immediate decision of his cause; (B) Enough time had elapsed for the Philippians to hear of his imprisonment, send Epaphroditus to him, hear of Epa- phroditus's arrival and sickness, and send back word to Rome of their distress (ii. 26).

(4.) It was written *after* Colossians and Philemon ; both for the preceding reason, and because Luke was no longer at Rome, as he was when those were written ; otherwise he would

have *saluted* a Church in which he had laboured, and would have 'cared in earnest for their concerns' (see ii. 20).

[2] For *Saints*, see note on 1 Cor. i. 2.

[3] *Bishops.* This term was at this early period applied to all the presby- ters : see p. 340.

[4] *Deacons:* see p. 341. It is sin- gular that the presbyters and deacons should be mentioned separately in the address of this Epistle only. It has been suggested that they had col- lected and forwarded the contribution sent by Epaphroditus.

[5] Observe 'Paul and Timotheus' followed immediately by 'I,' in con- firmation of the remarks in the note on 1 Thess. i. 2.

[6] The constant repetition of 'all' in connection with 'you' in this Epistle is remarkable. It seems as if St. Paul implied that he (at least) would not recognise any divisions among them. See above.

[7] Not '*in* the Gospel' (A. V.)

[8] *Accordingly*: compare 2 Cor. ii. 3, and Gal. ii. 10.

[9] *Mindful*, &c. This refers to the preceding mention of his prayers for them.

[10] St. Paul *defended* his doctrine by his words, and *confirmed* it by his life.

[11] The *grace* or *gift* bestowed on St. Paul, and also on the Philippians, was

bestowed upon me. God is my witness how I i. 8
long after you all, in the tender affection of Christ
Jesus.

And this I pray, that your love may abound yet 9
more and more, in true knowledge, and in all understanding, teaching you to distinguish good[1] from
evil ; that you may be pure, and may walk without[2] 10
stumbling until the day of Christ; being filled with 11
the fruits of righteousness which are by Jesus
Christ, unto the glory and praise of God.

Intelligence of his condition at Rome.   I would have you know, brethren, that the things 12
which have befallen me have tended rather to the
furtherance than hindrance of the Glad-tidings. So 13
that my chains have become well known in the name
of Christ, throughout the whole Prætorium,[3] and
to all the rest.[4]   And thus most[5] of the brethren in 14
the Lord, rendered confident by my chains, are very
much emboldened to speak the Word fearlessly.
Some, indeed, proclaim Christ[6] even out of envy 15
and contention;[7] but some, also, out[8] of good-will.
These do it from love,[9] knowing that I am appointed 16
to defend the Glad-tidings ; but those announce 17
Christ from a spirit of intrigue,[10] not sincerely,
thinking to stir[11] up persecution against me in my
imprisonment. What then ? nevertheless, every 18
way, whether in pretence or in truth, Christ is
announced ; and herein I rejoice now, yea, and I

---

the power of confirming the Gospel by
their sufferings ; the corresponding verb
is used in v. 29.

[1] Compare Rom. ii. 18.

[2] ' Without offence ' seems used here
intransitively ; at 1 Cor. x. 32, the
same word is active.

[3] *Prætorium.* For the explanation
of this, see above, p. 719. We have
seen that St. Paul was committed to the
custody of the *Præfectus Prætorio,*
and guarded by different Prætorian
soldiers, who relieved one another.
Hence his condition would be soon
known throughout the Prætorian
quarters.

[4] This expression is very obscure ;
it may mean either *to the Prætorian
soldiers who guard me, and to all the
rest of those who visit me* ; or *to all the
rest of the Prætorian Guards.* The
latter view gives the best sense.

[5] '*Most,*' not ' *many* ' (A.V.).

[6] ' Christ ' has the article, which

perhaps may indicate that they were
Jews, who proclaimed Jesus as the
Messiah. The verb in v. 15 denotes
to proclaim (as a herald) ; that in v.
17, *to declare tidings of (as a messenger).*

[7] These were probably Judaisers.

[8] We can by no means assent to
Professor Jowett's proposal to translate the preposition here ' amid.' See
his note on Gal. iv. 13.

[9] The order of ver. 16 and 17 (as
given in the best MSS.) is transposed
in the Received Text.

[10] See note on Rom. ii. 8.

[11] Such is the reading of the best
MSS. The Judaisers probably, by professing to teach the true version of
Christianity, and accusing Paul of
teaching a false and anti-national
doctrine, excited odium against him
among the Christians of Jewish birth
at Rome.

i. 19 shall rejoice hereafter. For I know that '𝖙𝖍𝖊𝖘𝖊 𝖙𝖍𝖎𝖓𝖌𝖘 [1]
𝖘𝖍𝖆𝖑𝖑 𝖋𝖆𝖑𝖑 𝖔𝖚𝖙 𝖙𝖔 𝖒𝖞 𝖘𝖆𝖑𝖛𝖆𝖙𝖎𝖔𝖓,' [2] through your prayers,
and through the supply of all my needs [3] by the
20 Spirit of Jesus Christ; according to my earnest
expectation and hope, that I shall in no wise be
put to shame, [4] but that with all boldness, as at
all other times, so now also, Christ will be magnified
in my body, whether by my life or by my death.
21,22 For to me life is Christ, and death is gain. But
whether this life [5] in the flesh shall be the fruit of
my labour, and what I should choose, I know not.
23 But [6] between the two I am in perplexity; having
the desire to depart and be with Christ, which is far
24 better; yet to remain in the flesh is more needful,
25 for your sake. And in this confidence, I know that
I shall remain, [7] and shall continue with you all, to
26 your furtherance and joy in faith; that you may
have more abundant cause for your boasting [8] in
Christ Jesus on my account, by my presence again
among you.

27   Only live [9] worthy of the Glad-tidings of Christ, *Exhortations*
that whether I come and see you, or be absent, I *to stedfast endurance,*
28 may hear concerning you, that you stand firmly in *concord, and lowliness.*
one spirit, contending together with one mind for
the faith of the Glad-tidings, and nowise terrified
by its enemies; [10] for their enmity is to them an
evidence of perdition, but to you of salvation, and
29 that from God. For to you it has been given, on

---

[1] *These things,* viz. the sufferings resulting from the conduct of these Judaisers.

[2] The words are quoted verbatim from Job xiii. 16 (LXX.). Yet perhaps St. Paul did not so much deliberately quote them, as use an expression which floated in his memory.

[3] The words literally applied would mean *the supplying of all needs [of the chorus] by the Choregus.* So the words here mean *the supplying of all needs [of the Christian] by the Spirit.* Compare Eph. iv. 16, and Col. ii. 19.

[4] St. Paul was confident that his faith and hope would not fail him in the day of trial. Compare Rom. v. 5 'our hope cannot shame us.' He was looking forward to his final hearing, as we have already seen, p. 723.

[5] We punctuate this very difficult verse so that the meaning is literally, *but whether this life in the flesh* (com-

pare *this mortal,* 1 Cor. xv. 54, and *my present life in the flesh,* Gal. ii. 20) *be my labour's fruit, and what I shall choose, I know not.* The A. V. assumes an ellipsis, and gives no intelligible meaning to *fruit of my labour.* On the other hand, De Wette's translation, *if life in the flesh,—if this be my labour's fruit, what I shall choose I know not,* causes a redundancy, and is otherwise objectionable. Beza's translation, 'an vero vivere in carne mihi operæ pretium sit, et quid eligam ignoro,' comes nearest to that which we adopt.

[6] The MSS. read 'but' and not 'for' here.

[7] *Shall remain,* i.e. alive.

[8] 'Whose boasting is in Christ.' Compare iii. 3.

[9] See note on iii. 20.

[10] Compare 'many adversaries,' 1 Cor. xvi. 9.

behalf of Christ, not only to believe on Him, but also to suffer for His sake; having the same conflict which once you saw [1] in me, and which now you hear that I endure.

If, then, you can be entreated [2] in Christ, if you ii. 1 can be persuaded by love, if you have any fellowship in the Spirit, if you have any tenderness or compassion, I pray you make my joy full, [3] be of one 2 accord, filled with the same love, of one soul, of one mind. Do nothing in a spirit of intrigue [4] or vanity, 3 but in lowliness of mind let each account others above himself. Seek not your private ends alone, 4 but let every man seek likewise his neighbour's good.

Let this mind be in you, which was also in Christ 5 Jesus; who, being in the form of God, thought it 6 not robbery [5] to be equal with God, but stripped [6] Himself [of His glory] and took upon Him the form 7 of a slave, [7] being changed [8] into the likeness of man. And having appeared in the guise of men, He abased 8 Himself and shewed obedience, [9] even unto death, yea, death upon the cross. Wherefore God also 9 exalted Him above measure, and gave Him the [10] name which is above every name; that in the name 10 of Jesus '𝔢𝔳𝔢𝔯𝔶 𝔨𝔫𝔢𝔢 𝔰𝔥𝔬𝔲𝔩𝔡 𝔟𝔬𝔴,' [11] of all who dwell in

---

[1] They had seen him sent to prison, Acts xvi. 23.

[2] The first word means *to entreat*, see Matt. xviii. 32; the second *to urge by persuasion or entreaty*, see 1 Thess. ii. 11.

[3] The extreme earnestness of this exhortation to unity shows that the Philippians were guilty of dissension; perhaps Euodia and Syntyche, whose opposition to each other is mentioned iv. 2, had partisans who shared their quarrel.

[4] See above, i. 17.

[5] This very difficult expression admits of the translation adopted in the Authorised Version, from which therefore we have not thought it right to deviate. The majority of modern interpreters, however, take it as meaning *to reckon a thing as a booty, to look on a thing as a robber would look on spoil*. It is a considerable (though not a fatal) objection to this view, that it makes a word denoting *the act of seizing* identical with one denoting *the thing seized*. The Authorised Version is free from this objection, but it is liable to the charge of rendering the connection with the following verse less natural than the other interpretation. If the latter be correct, the translation would be, *He thought not equality with God a thing to be seized upon*, i.e. *though, essentially, even while on earth, He was in the form of God, yet He did not think fit to claim equality with God until He had accomplished His mission*.

[6] Literally, *emptied Himself*.

[7] The *likeness of man* was the *form of a slave* to Him, contrasted with the *form of God* which essentially belonged to Him.

[8] Literally, *having become in the likeness*, which in English is expressed by *being changed into the likeness*.

[9] He 'showed obedience' to the laws of human society, to His parents, and to the civil magistrate; and carried that self-humiliating obedience even to the point of submitting to death, when He might have summoned 'twelve legions of angels' to His rescue.

[10] The best MSS. have '*the* name.'

[11] Isaiah xlv. 23 (LXX.), quoted Rom. xiv. 11. It is strange that this

ii. 11 heaven, in earth, or under the earth, and every
tongue should confess that Jesus Christ is Lord, to
the glory of God the Father.

12   Wherefore, my beloved, as you have always obeyed
me, not as in my presence only, but now much more
in my absence, work out your own salvation with
13 fear and trembling;[1] for it is God who works in you
14 both will and deed.   Do all things for the sake of
15 goodwill,[2] without murmurings and disputings, that
you may be blameless and guileless, the sons of God
without rebuke, in the midst of ' 𝔞 𝔠𝔯𝔬𝔬𝔨𝔢𝔡 𝔞𝔫𝔡 𝔭𝔢𝔯-
𝔟𝔢𝔯𝔰𝔢 𝔤𝔢𝔫𝔢𝔯𝔞𝔱𝔦𝔬𝔫,'[3] among whom ye shine like stars[4]
16 in the world; holding fast the Word of Life; that
you may give me ground of boasting, even to the
day of Christ, that I have not run in vain, nor
laboured in vain.

17   But[5] though my blood[6] be poured forth upon the St. Paul's ex-
ministration of the sacrifice of your faith, I rejoice pectations and
intentions.
18 for myself, and rejoice with you all; and do ye like-
19 wise rejoice, both for yourselves and with me.   But
I hope in the Lord Jesus to send Timotheus to you[7]
shortly, that I also may be cheered, by learning your
20 state; for I have no other like-minded with me, who
21 would care in earnest for your concerns; for all seek

verse should often have been quoted as
commanding the practice of *bowing the
head* at the name of Jesus; a practice
most proper in itself, but not here referred to: what it really prescribes is,
kneeling in adoration of Him.

[1] We have already remarked, that
with anxiety and self-distrust is a
nearer representation of this Pauline
phrase than the literal English, as
appears by the use of the same phrase
1 Cor. ii. 3; 2 Cor. vii. 15; Eph. vi. 5.
The 'fear' is *a fear of failure*, the
'trembling' *an eager anxiety.*

[2] This phrase has perplexed the
interpreters, because they have all
joined it with the preceding words.
We put a stop after the preceding
verb, and take the noun in the same
sense as at i. 15 above, and Luke ii.
14. It is strange that so clear and
simple a construction, involving no
alteration in the text, should not have
been before suggested.

Since the above was first published,
it has been objected that the position
of the Greek article negatives the
above rendering; because the insertion
of the article (where it is generally
omitted) between a preposition and an

abstract noun, gives to the latter a
reflective sense; so that the phrase
would mean '*your* goodwill,' not goodwill in the abstract. This grammatical
statement is not universally true; but
even if the objection were valid, it would
not negative the construction proposed,
nor materially alter the meaning. The
translation would then stand :—' *Do all
things for the sake of maintaining your
mutual goodwill.*'
[It seems very doubtful whether this
view is tenable: and the ordinary rendering gives a very forcible sense. H.]

[3] Deut. xxxii. 5 (LXX.). The preceding 'without rebuke' calls up a corresponding word in the Greek context
of the LXX.

[4] Compare Gen. i. 14 (LXX.).

[5] This *but* seems to connect what
follows with i. 25, 26.

[6] Literally, *I be poured forth.* The
metaphor is probably from the Jewish
drink-offerings (Numb. xxviii. 7), rather than from the Heathen libations.
The Heathen converts are spoken of as
a sacrifice offered up by St. Paul as the
ministering priest, in Rom. xv. 16.

[7] The Greek construction is the same
as in 1 Cor. iv. 17.

their own, not the things of Jesus Christ. But you ii. 22 know[1] the trials which have proved his worth, and that, as a son with a father, he has shared my servitude, to proclaim the Glad-tidings. Him, then, I 23 hope to send without delay, as soon as I see how it will go with me; but I trust in the Lord that I also 24 myself shall come shortly.

Return of Epaphroditus. Epaphroditus, who is my brother and companion 25 in labour and fellow-soldier, and your messenger to minister[2] to my wants, I have thought it needful to send to you. For he was filled with longing for you 26 all, and with sadness, because you had heard that he was sick. And, indeed, he had a sickness which 27 brought him almost to death, but God had compassion on him; and not on him only but on me, that I might not have sorrow upon sorrow. Therefore I 28 have been[3] the more anxious to send him, that you may have the joy of seeing him again, and that I may have one sorrow the less. Receive him, there- 29 fore, in the Lord, with all gladness, and hold such men in honour; because his labour in the cause of 30 Christ brought him near to death; for he hazarded[4] his life that he might supply all which you could not do,[5] in ministering to me.

Finally, my brethren, rejoice in the Lord. iii. 1

Warning against Judaisers and exhortation to perseverance in the Christian race. To repeat the same[6] warnings is not wearisome to me, and it is safe for you. Beware of the Dogs,[7] 2 beware of the Evil Workmen, beware of the Concision. For we are the Circumcision, who worship 3 God[8] with the spirit, whose boasting[9] is in Christ

[1] Timotheus had laboured among them at the first. See Acts xvi.

[2] *Minister.* We have the corresponding abstract noun in v. 30.

[3] The aorist used from the position of the reader, according to classical usage.

[4] This is the meaning of the reading of the best MSS.

[5] The same expression is used of the messengers of the Corinthian Church. 1 Cor. xvi. 17. The English reader must not understand the A. V. '*lack of service*' to convey a reproach. From this verse we learn that the illness of Epaphroditus was caused by some casualty of his journey, or perhaps by over-fatigue.

[6] Literally, *to write the same things to you.* St. Paul must here refer either to some previous Epistle to the Philippians (now lost), or to his former conversations with them.

[7] The Judaisers are here described

by three epithets: 'the dogs' because of their uncleanness (of which that animal was the type: compare 2 Pet. ii. 22); 'the evil workmen' (not equivalent to '*evil workers*'), for the same reason that they are called 'deceitful workmen' in 2 Cor. xi. 13; and 'the concision,' to distinguish them from the true circumcision, the spiritual Israel.

[8] We retain 'God' here, with the Textus Receptus, and a minority of MSS., because of the analogy of Rom. i. 9 (see note there). The true Christians are here described by contrast with the Judaisers, whose *worship* was the carnal worship of the Temple, whose *boasting* was in the Law, and whose *confidence* was in the circumcision of their flesh.

[9] Apparently alluding to Jer. ix. 24, '*He that boasteth let him boast in the Lord,*' which is quoted 1 Cor. i. 31 and 2 Cor. x. 7.

Jesus, and whose confidence is not in the flesh.
iii. 4 Although I might have confidence in the flesh also.
If any other man thinks that he has ground of confi-
5 dence in the flesh, I have more. Circumcised the
eighth day, of the stock of Israel, of the tribe of
6 Benjamin, a Hebrew of the Hebrews; as to the
Law, a Pharisee; as to zeal a persecutor of the
Church; as to the righteousness of the Law, un-
7 blameable. But what once was gain to me, that I
8 have counted loss for Christ. Yea, doubtless, and I
count all things but loss, because all are nothing-
worth in comparison[1] with the knowledge of Christ
Jesus my Lord; for whom I have suffered the loss of
all things, and count them but as dung that I may
9 gain Christ, and be found in Him; not having my
own righteousness of the Law, but the righteousness
of faith in Christ, the righteousness which God be-
10 stows on Faith;[2] that I may know Him, and the
power of His resurrection, and the fellowship of His
11 sufferings, sharing the likeness of His death; if by
any means I might attain to the resurrection from
the dead.

12 Not that I have already won,[3] or am already perfect; but I press onward, if indeed, I might lay hold
on that, for which Christ also laid hold on me.[4]

13 Brethren, I count not myself to have laid hold
thereon; but this one thing I do—forgetting that
which is behind, and reaching[5] forth to that which
14 is before, I press onward towards the mark, for the
prize of God's heavenly calling in Christ Jesus.

15 Let us all, then, who are ripe[6] in understanding,
be thus minded; and if in anything you are otherwise minded, that also shall be revealed to you by
16 God [in due time]. Nevertheless, let us walk according to that which we have attained.[7]

[1] Literally, *because of the supereminence of the knowledge of Christ,* i.e. *because the knowledge of Christ surpasses all things else.*

[2] *Of God* (i.e. which He bestows) *on condition of faith.* Compare Acts iii. 16.

[3] 'Won,' i.e. 'the prize' (v. 14). Compare 1 Cor. ix. 24, 'So run that ye may win.' It is unfortunate that in A. V. this is translated by the same verb *attain,* which is used for another verb in the preceding verse, so as to make it seem to refer to that.

[4] Our Lord had 'laid hold on' Paul, in order to bring him to the attainment of 'the prize of God's heavenly calling.' 'Jesus' is omitted by the best MSS.

[5] The image is that of the runner in a foot race, whose body is bent forwards in the direction towards which he runs. See beginning of Chap. XX.

[6] The translation in A. V. (here and in v. 12) by the same word, makes St. Paul seem to contradict himself. 'Perfect' is the antithesis of 'babe.' Compare 1 Cor. xiv. 20.

[7] The precept is the same given Rom. xiv. 5. The words 'think the same thing' are omitted in the best MSS.

Brethren, be imitators of me with one consent, iii. 17
and mark those who walk according to my example.
For many walk, of whom I told you often in times[1] 18
past, and now tell you even weeping, that they are
the enemies[2] of the cross of Christ; whose end is 19
destruction, whose God is their belly,[3] and whose
glory is in their shame; whose mind is set on earthly
things. For my[4] life[5] abides in heaven; from whence 20
also I look for a Saviour, the Lord Jesus Christ; 21
who shall change my vile[6] body into the likeness of 22
His glorious body; according to the working whereby
He is able even to subdue all things unto Himself.
Therefore, my brethren, dearly beloved and longed iv. 1
for, my joy and crown, so stand fast in the Lord, my
dearly beloved.

Euodia and Syntyche must be reconciled.

I exhort Euodia, and I exhort Syntyche,[7] to be of 2
one mind in the Lord. Yea, and I beseech thee also, 3
my true yoke-fellow,[8] to help them [to be reconciled];
for they strove earnestly in the work of the Glad-
tidings with me, together with Clemens[9] and my

---

[1] Literally, *I used to tell you.*

[2] For the construction, compare 1 John ii. 25. The persons meant were men who led licentious lives (like the Corinthian freethinkers), and they are called 'enemies of the *cross*' because the cross was the symbol of mortification.

[3] Cf. Rom. xvi. 18.

[4] On St. Paul's use of 'we' see note on 1 Thess. i. 3. An objection has been made to translating it in the singular in this passage, on the ground that this seems to limit St. Paul's expression of Christian hope and faith to himself; but a very little consideration will suffice to show the futility of such an objection. Where St. Paul speaks of his hopes and faith *as a Christian*, his words are necessarily applicable to other Christians as well as to himself. And, in fact, some of the passages to which Christians in general have ever turned with the most fervent sympathy, and which they have most undoubtingly appropriated, are those very passages where St. Paul uses the 'singular:' as, for example, 'for *me*,' Gal. ii. 20.

[5] This noun must not be translated *citizenship* (as has been proposed), which would be a different word (cf. Acts xxii. 28). The corresponding verb means *to perform the functions of civil life*, and is used simply for *to live*; see Acts xxiii. 1, and Phil. i. 27. Hence the noun means *the tenor of life.* It should

be also observed, that the verb here means more than simply '*is*,' though it is difficult here to express the shade of difference in English.

[6] Literally, *the body of my humiliation.*

[7] These were two women (the pronoun is feminine in v. 3, which is mistranslated in A. V.) who were at variance.

[8] We have no means of knowing who was the person thus addressed. Apparently some eminent Christian at Philippi, to whom the Epistle was to be presented in the first instance. The old hypothesis (mentioned by Chrysostom) that the word is a proper name, is not without plausibility; 'who art *Syzygus* in name and in fact,' as a commentator says.

[9] We learn from Origen (*Comm.* on John i. 29) that this Clemens (commonly called Clement) was the same who was afterwards Bishop of Rome, and who wrote the Epistles to the Corinthians which we have before referred to (pp. 495, 496). Eusebius quotes the following statement concerning him from Irenæus: 'In the third place after the Apostles the episcopal office was held by Clemens, who also saw the blessed Apostles, and lived with them.' *Hist. Eccl.* v. 6. It appears from the present passage that he had formerly laboured successfully at Philippi.

other fellow-labourers, whose names are in the Book[1]
of Life.

iv. 4   Rejoice in the Lord at all times.   Again will[2] I
5 say, rejoice.   Let your forbearance be known to all
6 men.   The[3] Lord is at hand.   Let no care trouble
you, but in all things, by prayer and supplication
with thanksgiving, let your requests be made known
7 to God.   And the peace of God, which passeth all
understanding, shall keep[4] your hearts and minds in
8 Christ Jesus.   Finally, brethren, whatsoever is true,
whatsoever is venerable, whatsoever is just, whatsoever is pure, whatsoever is endearing, whatsoever
is of good report,—if there be any virtue, and if there
9 be any praise—be such your treasures.[5]   That which
you were taught and learned, and which you heard
and saw in me,—be that your practice.   So shall the
God of peace be with you.

10   I rejoiced in the Lord greatly when I found that
now, after so long a time, your care for me had borne
fruit again;[6] though your care indeed never failed,
11 but you lacked opportunity.   Not that I speak as if I
were in want; for I[7] have learnt, in whatsoever state
12 I am, to be content.   I can bear either abasement or
abundance.   In all things, and amongst all men, I
have been taught the secret,[8] to be full or to be
hungry, to want or to abound.   I can do all things
13 in Him[9] who strengthens me.   Nevertheless, you
have done well, in contributing to the help of my
14 affliction.   And you know yourselves, Philippians,
15 that, in the beginning of the Glad-tidings, after I had
left Macedonia,[10] no Church communicated with me
on account of giving and receiving, but you alone.
16 For even while I was [still] in Thessalonica,[11] you
17 sent once and again to relieve my need.   Not that I
seek your gifts, but I seek the fruit which accrues
18 therefrom, to your account.   But I have all which I
require, and more than I require.   I am fully supplied, having received from Epaphroditus your gifts,

Marginal notes:

Exhortation to rejoice in tribulation, and to love and follow goodness.

Liberality of the Philippian Church.

[1] Compare 'Book of the living,' Ps. lxix. 28 (LXX.), and also Luke x. 20, and Heb. xii. 23.

[2] The verb is future.   He refers to iii. 1.

[3] They are exhorted to be joyful under persecution, and show gentleness to their persecutors, because the Lord's coming would soon deliver them from all their afflictions.   Compare note on 1 Cor. xvi. 22.

[4] Literally, *garrison.*

[5] Literally, *reckon these things in account.*   Compare 1 Cor. xiii. 5.

[6] The literal meaning is *to put forth fresh shoots.*

[7] This 'I' is emphatic.

[8] Literally, 'I have been initiated.'

[9] 'Christ' is omitted in the best MSS.   For 'strengthen,' cf. Rom. iv. 20.

[10] Compare 2 Cor. xi. 9, and p. 301.

[11] See pp. 253, 254.

' **An odour of sweetness**,'[1] an acceptable sacrifice well pleasing to God. And your own needs[2] shall be all iv. 19 supplied by my God, in the fulness of His glorious riches in Christ Jesus. Now to our God and Father 20 be glory unto the ages of ages. Amen.

Salutations.   Salute every saint in Christ Jesus. The brethren 21 who are with me[3] salute you.

All the saints here salute you, especially those who 22 belong to the house of Cæsar.[4]

Autograph   The Grace of our Lord Jesus Christ be with your 23
benediction.   spirits.[5]

The above Epistle gives us an unusual amount of information concerning the personal situation of its writer, which we have already endeavoured to incorporate into our narrative. But nothing in it is more suggestive than St. Paul's allusion to the Prætorian guards, and to the converts he had gained in the household of Nero. He tells us (as we have just read) that throughout the Prætorian quarters he was well known as a prisoner for the cause of Christ,[6] and he sends special salutations to the Philippian Church from the Christians in the Imperial household.[7] These notices bring before us very vividly the moral contrast by which the Apostle was surrounded. The soldier to whom he was chained to-day might have been in Nero's body-guard yesterday ; his comrade who next relieved guard upon the prisoner, might have been one of the executioners of Octavia, and might have carried her head to Poppæa a few weeks before. Such were the ordinary employments of the fierce and blood-stained veterans who were daily present, like wolves in the midst of sheep, at the meetings of the Christian brotherhood. If there were any of these soldiers not utterly hardened by a life of cruelty, their hearts must surely have been touched by the character of their prisoner, brought as they were into so close a contact with him. They must have been at least astonished to see a man, under such circumstances, so utterly careless of selfish interests, and devoting himself with an energy so unaccountable to the teaching of others. Strange indeed to their ears, fresh from the brutality of a Roman barrack, must have been the sound of Christian exhortation, of prayers, and of hymns ; stranger still, perhaps, the tender love which bound the converts

[1] Gen. viii. 21 (LXX.). Compare also Levit. i. 9, and Eph. v. 2.

[2] The *your* is emphatic.

[3] This *brethren with me*, distinguished from *all the saints* in the next verse, seems to denote St. Paul's special attendants, such as Aristarchus, Epaphras, Demas, Timotheus, &c. Cf. Gal. i. 2.

[4] These members of the Imperial household were probably slaves ; so the same expression is used by Josephus

(*Ant.* xviii. 5. 8). If St. Paul was at this time confined in the neighbourhood of the Prætorian quarters attached to the palace, we can more readily account for the conversion of some of those who lived in the buildings immediately contiguous.

[5] The majority of uncial MSS. read 'spirit,' and omit the 'amen.'

[6] Phil. i. 1.

[7] Phil. iv. 22.

to their teacher and to one another, and showed itself in every look and tone.

But if the agent's of Nero's tyranny seem out of place in such a scene, still more repugnant to the assembled worshippers must have been the instruments of his pleasures, the ministers of his lust. Yet some even among these, the depraved servants of the palace, were redeemed from their degradation by the Spirit of Christ, which spoke to them in the words of Paul. How deep their degradation was, we know from authentic records. We are not left to conjecture the services required from the attendants of Nero. The ancient historians have polluted their pages[1] with details of infamy which no writer in the languages of Christendom may dare to repeat. Thus, the very immensity of moral amelioration wrought, operates to disguise its own extent ; and hides from inexperienced eyes the gulf which separates Heathenism from Christianity. Suffice it to say, that the courtiers of Nero were the spectators, and the members of his household the instruments, of vices so monstrous and so unnatural, that they shocked even the men of that generation, steeped as it was in every species of obscenity. But we must remember that many of those who took part in such abominations were involuntary agents, forced by the compulsion of slavery to do their master's bidding. And the very depth of vileness in which they were plunged, must have excited in some of them an indignant disgust and revulsion against vice. Under such feelings, if curiosity led them to visit the Apostle's prison, they were well qualified to appreciate the purity of its moral atmosphere. And there it was that some of these unhappy bondsmen first tasted of spiritual freedom ; and were prepared to brave with patient heroism the tortures under which they soon[2] were destined to expire in the gardens of the Vatican.

History has few stranger contrasts than when it shows us Paul preaching Christ under the walls of Nero's palace. Thenceforward, there were but two religions in the Roman world : the worship of the Emperor, and the worship of the Saviour. The old superstitions had been long worn out ; they had lost all hold on educated minds. There remained to civilised Heathens no other worship possible but the worship of power; and the incarnation of power which they chose was, very naturally, the sovereign of the world. This, then, was the ultimate result of the noble intuitions of Plato, the methodical reasonings of Aristotle, the pure morality of Socrates. All had failed, for want of external sanction and authority. The residuum they left was the philosophy of Epicurus, and the religion of Nerolatry. But a new doctrine was already taught in the Forum, and believed even on the Palatine. Over against the altars of Nero and Poppæa, the voice of a prisoner was daily heard, and daily woke in grovelling souls the consciousness of their divine destiny. Men listened, and knew that self-sacrifice was better than ease, humiliation more exalted than pride, to suffer nobler than to reign.

---

[1] See Tac. *Ann.* xv. 37, Dio. lxiii. 13, and especially Suetonius, *Nero*, 28, 29.

[2] The Neronian persecution, in which such vast multitudes of Christians perished, occurred in the summer of 64 A.D., that is, within less than two years of the time when the Epistle to Philippi was written. See the next chapter.

They felt that the only religion which satisfied the needs of man was the religion of sorrow, the religion of self-devotion, the religion of the cross.

There are some amongst us now who think that the doctrine which Paul preached was a retrograde movement in the course of humanity ; there are others who, with greater plausibility, acknowledge that it was useful in its season, but tell us that it is now worn out and obsolete. The former are far more consistent than the latter ; for both schools of infidelity agree in virtually advising us to return to that effete philosophy which had been already tried and found wanting, when Christianity was winning the first triumphs of its immortal youth. This might well surprise us, did we not know that the progress of human reason in the paths of ethical discovery is merely the progress of man in a treadmill, doomed for ever to retrace his own steps. Had it been otherwise, we might have hoped that mankind could not again be duped by an old and useless remedy, which was compounded and recompounded in every possible shape and combination, two thousand years ago, and at last utterly rejected by a nauseated world. Yet for this antiquated anodyne, disguised under a new label, many are once more bartering the only true medicine that can head the diseases of the soul.

For such mistakes there is, indeed, no real cure, except prayer to Him who giveth sight to the blind ; but a partial antidote may be supplied by the history of the Imperial Commonwealth. The true wants of the Apostolic age can best be learned from the *Annals* of Tacitus. There men may still see the picture of that Rome to which Paul preached ; and thence they may comprehend the results of civilisation without Christianity, and the impotence of a moral philosophy destitute of supernatural attestation.[1]

Coin of Philippi.[2]

---

[1] Had Arnold lived to complete his task, how nobly would his history of the Empire have worked out this great argument! His indignant abhorrence of wickedness, and his enthusiastic love of moral beauty, made him worthy of such a theme.

[2] From the British Museum.

CHAPTER XXVII.

Authorities for St. Paul's subsequent History. — His Appeal is heard. — His Acquittal. — He goes from Rome to Asia Minor. — Thence to Spain, where he resides two years. — He returns to Asia Minor and Macedonia. — Writes *The First Epistle to Timotheus.* — Visits Crete. — Writes *The Epistle to Titus.* — He winters at Nicopolis. — He is again imprisoned at Rome. — Progress of his Trial. — He writes *The Second Epistle to Timotheus.* — His Condemnation and Death.

WE have already remarked that the light concentrated upon that portion of St. Paul's life which is related in the latter chapters of the Acts, makes darker by contrasts the obscurity which rests upon the remainder of his course. The progress of the historian who attempts to trace the footsteps of the Apostles beyond the limits of the Scriptural narrative must, at best, be hesitating and uncertain. It has been compared[1] to the descent of one who passes from the clear sunshine which rests upon a mountain's top into the mist which wraps its side. But this is an inadequate comparison ; for such a wayfarer loses the daylight gradually, and experiences no abrupt transition, from the bright prospect and the distinctness of the onward path, into darkness and bewilderment. Our case should rather be compared with that of the traveller on the Chinese frontier, who has just reached a turn in the valley along which his course has led him, and has come to a point whence he expected to enjoy the view of a new and brilliant landscape ; when he suddenly finds all farther prospect cut off by an enormous wall, filling up all the space between precipices on either hand, and opposing a blank and insuperable barrier to his onward progress. And if a chink here and there should allow some glimpses of the rich territory beyond, they are only enough to tantalise, without gratifying his curiosity.

Doubtless, however, it was a Providential design which has thus limited our knowledge. The wall of separation, which for ever cuts off the Apostolic age from that which followed it, was built by the hand of God. That age of miracles was not to be revealed to us as passing by any gradual transition into the common life of the Church ; it was intentionally isolated from all succeeding time, that we might learn to appreciate more fully its extraordinary character, and see, by the sharpness of the abruptest contrast the difference between the human and the divine.

A few faint rays of light, however, have been permitted to penetrate beyond the dividing barrier, and of these we must make the best use we can : for it is now our task to trace the history of St. Paul beyond the period where the narrative of his fellow-traveller

---

[1] The comparison occurs somewhere in Arnold's works.

so suddenly terminates.[1]   The only cotemporary materials for this
purpose are his own letters to Titus and Timotheus, and a single
sentence of his disciple, Clement of Rome ; and during the three
centuries which followed we can gather but a few scattered and unsatisfactory notices from the writers who have handed down to us
the traditions of the Church.

The great question which we have to answer concerns the termination of that long imprisonment whose history has occupied the
preceding chapters.   St. Luke tells us that Paul remained under
military custody in Rome for 'two whole years' (Acts xxviii. 16
and 30) ; but he does not say what followed, at the close of that
period.   Was it ended, we are left to ask, by the Apostle's condemnation and death, or by his acquittal and liberation ?   Although
the answer to this question has been a subject of dispute in modern
times, no doubt was entertained about it by the ancient Church.[2]
It was universally believed that St. Paul's appeal to Cæsar terminated successfully ; that he was acquitted of the charges laid against
him ; and that he spent some years in freedom before he was again
imprisoned and condemned.   The evidence on this subject, though
(as we have said) not copious, is yet conclusive so far as it goes, and
it is all one way.[3]

The most important portion of it is supplied by Clement, the
disciple of St. Paul, mentioned Phil. iv. 3,[4] who was afterwards
Bishop of Rome.   This author, writing *from Rome* to Corinth, expressly asserts that Paul had preached the Gospel 'IN THE EAST
AND IN THE WEST ;' that 'he had instructed *the whole world* [i.e.
the *Roman Empire*, which was commonly so called] in righteousness ;' and that he 'had gone to THE EXTREMITY OF THE WEST'
before his martyrdom.[5]

[1] Numerous explanations have been
attempted of the sudden and abrupt
termination of the Acts, which breaks
off the narrative of St. Paul's appeal to
Cæsar (up to that point so minutely
detailed) just as we are expecting its
conclusion.   The most plausible explanations are — (1) That Theophilus
already knew of the conclusion of the
Roman imprisonment ; whether it was
ended by St. Paul's death or by his
liberation.   (2) That St. Luke wrote
before the conclusion of the imprisonment, and carried his narrative up to
the point at which he wrote.   But
neither of these theories is fully satisfactory.   We may take this opportunity to remark that the 'dwelt' and
'received' (Acts xxviii. 30) by no
means imply (as Wieseler asserts) that
a *changed state* of things had succeeded to that there described.   In writing historically, the historical tenses
would be used by an ancient writer,
even though (when he wrote) the
events described by him were still
going on.

[2] If the Epistle to the Hebrews was

written by St. Paul, it proves conclusively that he was liberated from his
Roman imprisonment ; for its writer is
in Italy and *at liberty.*   (Heb. xiii. 23,
24.)   But we are precluded from using
this as an argument, in consequence of
the doubts concerning the authorship
of that Epistle.   See the next chapter.

[3] Since the above was published, the
same opinion has been expressed yet
more strongly by Chevalier Bunsen,
whose judgment on such a point is entitled to the greatest weight.   He says,
' Some German critics have a peculiar
idiosyncracy which leads them to dis-
believe the second captivity of Paul.
Yet it appears to me very arbitrary to
deny a fact for which we have the explicit evidence of Paul's disciple and
companion Clemens.'   (Bunsen's *Hippolytus,* second ed. vol. i. p. 27.)

[4] For the identity of St. Paul's disciple Clemens with Clemens Romanus,
see the note on Phil. iv. 3.   We may
add, that even those who doubt this
identity acknowledge that Clemens Romanus wrote in the first century.

[5] Clem. Rom. i. chap. v.   We need

Now, in a Roman author, *the extremity of the West* could mean nothing short of Spain, and the expression is often used by Roman writers to denote Spain.   Here, then, we have the express testimony of St. Paul's own disciple that he fulfilled his original intention (mentioned Rom. xv. 24–28) of visiting the Spanish peninsula ; and consequently that he was liberated from his first imprisonment at Rome.

The next piece of evidence which we possess on the subject is contained in the canon of the New Testament, compiled by an unknown Christian about the year A.D. 170, which is commonly called 'Muratori's Canon.'   In this document it is said, in the account of the *Acts of the Apostles*, that '*Luke relates to Theophilus events of which he was an eye-witness, as also, in a separate place* (semote) [viz. Luke xxii. 31–33], *he evidently declares the martyrdom of Peter, but* [*omits*] THE JOURNEY OF PAUL FROM ROME TO SPAIN.'[1]

In the next place, Eusebius tells us, '*after defending himself successfully, it is currently reported that the Apostle again went forth to proclaim the Gospel, and afterwards came to Rome a second time, and was martyred under Nero.*'[2]

Next we have the statement of Chrysostom, who mentions it as an undoubted historical fact, that '*St. Paul after his residence in Rome departed to Spain.*'[3]

About the same time St. Jerome bears the same testimony, saying that '*Paul was dismissed by Nero, that he might preach Christ's Gospel in the West.*'[4]

Against this unanimous testimony of the primitive Church there is no external evidence[5] whatever to oppose.   Those who doubt the liberation of St. Paul from his imprisonment are obliged to resort

scarcely remark upon Wieseler's proposal to translate the words for *the extremity of the West* (το τέρμα τῆς δύσεως), *the Sovereign of Rome*!   That ingenious writer has been here evidently misled by his desire to wrest the passage (quocunque modo) into conformity with his theory.   Schrader translates one phrase 'having been martyred *there*,' and then argues that the *extremity of the West* cannot mean Spain, because St. Paul was not martyred in Spain ; but his 'there' is a mere interpolation of his own.

[1] For an account of this fragment, see Routh's *Reliquiæ Sacræ*, vol. iv. p. 1–12.

[2] *Hist. Eccl.* ii. 22.

[3] He adds, 'whether he went to the Eastern part of the Empire, we know not.'   This does not imply a doubt of his return to Rome.

[4] Hieron. *Catal. Script.*

[5] It has indeed been urged that Origen knew nothing of the journey to Spain, because Eusebius tells us that he speaks of Paul 'preaching from Jerusalem to Illyricum,'—a manifest allusion to Rom. xv. 19.   It is strange that those who use this argument should not have perceived that they might, with equal justice, infer that Origen was ignorant of St. Paul's preaching at Malta.   Sill more extraordinary is it to find Wieseler relying on the testimony of Pope Innocent I., who asserts (in the true spirit of the Papacy) that 'all the churches in Italy, Gaul, Spain, Africa, Sicily, and the interjacent islands, were founded by emissaries of St. Peter or his successors:' an assertion manifestly contradicting the Acts of the Apostles, and the known history of the Gallican Church, and made by a writer of the fifth century !   It has been also argued by Wieseler that Eusebius and Chrysostom were led to the hypothesis of a second imprisonment by their mistaken view of 2 Tim. iv. 20.   But it is equally probable that they were led to that view of the passage by their previous belief in the tradition of the second imprisonment.   Nor is their view of that passage untenable, though we think it mistaken.

to a gratuitous hypothesis, or to inconclusive arguments from probability. Thus they try to account for the tradition of the Spanish journey, by the arbitrary supposition that it arose from a wish to represent St. Paul as having fulfilled his expressed intentions (Rom. xv. 19) of visiting Spain. Or they say that it is *improbable* Nero would have liberated St. Paul after he had fallen under the influence of Poppæa, the Jewish proselyte. Or, lastly, they urge that, if St. Paul had really been liberated, we must have had some account of his subsequent labours. The first argument needs no answer, being a mere hypothesis. The second, as to the probability of the matter, may be met by the remark that we know far too little of the circumstances, and of the motives which weighed with Nero, to judge how he would have been likely to act in the case. To the third argument we may oppose the fact, that we have no account whatever of St. Paul's labours, toils, and sufferings, during several of the most active years of his life, and only learn their existence by a casual allusion in a letter to the Corinthians (2 Cor. xi. 24, 25). Moreover, if this argument be worth anything, it would prove that none of the Apostles except St. Paul took any part whatever in the propagation of the Gospel after the first few years ; since we have no testimony to their subsequent labours at all more definite than that which we have above quoted concerning the work of St. Paul after his liberation.

But further, unless we are prepared to dispute the genuineness of the Pastoral Epistles,[1] we must admit not only that St. Paul was liberated from his Roman imprisonment, but also that he continued his Apostolic labours for at least some years afterwards. For it is now admitted, by nearly all those who are competent to decide on such a question,[2] first, that the historical facts mentioned in the Epistles to Timotheus and Titus cannot be placed in any portion of St. Paul's life before or during his first imprisonment in Rome ; and, secondly, that the style in which those Epistles are written, and the condition of the Church described in them, forbid the supposition of such a date. Consequently we must acknowledge (unless we deny the authenticity of the Pastoral Epistles) that after St. Paul's Roman imprisonment he was travelling at liberty in Ephesus,[3] Crete,[4] Macedonia,[5] Miletus,[6] and Nicopolis,[7] and that he was afterwards a second time in prison in Rome.[8]

But when we have said this, we have told nearly all that we know of the Apostle's personal history, from his liberation to his

---

[1] On the question of the date of the Pastoral Epistles, see Appendix II.

[2] Dr. Davidson is an exception, and has summed up all that can be said on the opposite side of the question with his usual ability and fairness. With regard to Wieseler, see the note in the Appendix, above referred to. [In an able and candid review of this work, which appeared in Kitto's *Journal of Sacred Literature*, the reviewer has misunderstood our assertion in the text, on which this is a note. He states that

we have there asserted that competent judges are nearly unanimous in agreeing with our view of the second imprisonment. But any one who reads carefully what we have written above, will perceive that this is not what we have said. We have only asserted that most competent judges are agreed in thinking *that the Pastoral Epistles cannot be placed before the first captivity.*]

[3] 1 Tim. i. 3.   [4] Titus i. 5.
[5] 1 Tim. i. 3.   [6] 2 Tim. iv. 20.
[7] Titus iii. 12.   [8] 2 Tim. i. 16, 17.

death.   We cannot fix with certainty the length of the time which
intervened, nor the order in which he visited the different places
where he is recorded to have laboured.   The following data, however, we have.   In the first place, his martyrdom is universally said
to have occurred[1] in the reign of Nero.   Secondly, Timotheus was
still *a young man* (i.e. young for the charge committed to him)[2] at
the time of Paul's second imprisonment at Rome.   Thirdly, the
three Pastoral Epistles were written within a few months of one
another.[3]   Fourthly, their style differs so much from the style of the
earlier Epistles, that we must suppose as long an interval between
their date and that of the Epistle to Philippi as is consistent with
the preceding conditions.

These reasons concur in leading us to fix *the last year of Nero* as
that of St. Paul's martyrdom.   And this is the very year assigned
to it by Jerome, and the next to that assigned by Eusebius; the
two earliest writers who mention the date of St. Paul's death at all.
We have already seen that St. Paul first arrived in Rome in the
spring of A.D. 61: we therefore have, on our hypothesis, an interval
of five years between the period with which St. Luke concludes
(A.D. 63), and the Apostle's martyrdom.[4]   And the grounds above
mentioned lead us to the conclusion that this interval was occupied
in the following manner.

In the first place, after the long delay which we have before endeavoured to explain, St. Paul's appeal came on for hearing before
the Emperor.   The appeals from the provinces in civil causes were
heard, not by the Emperor himself, but by his delegates, who were
persons of consular rank: Augustus had appointed one such dele-
gate to hear appeals from each province respectively.[5]   But criminal
appeals appear generally to have been heard by the Emperor in
person,[6] assisted by his council of Assessors.   Tiberius and Claudius
had usually sat for this purpose in the Forum;[7] but Nero, after the
example of Augustus, heard these causes in the Imperial Palace,[8]
whose ruins still crown the Palatine.   Here, at one end of a splendid
hall,[9] lined with the precious marbles[10] of Egypt and of Lybia, we
must imagine the Cæsar seated, in the midst of his Assessors.
These councillors, twenty in number, were men of the highest rank

---

[1] See the references to Tertullian,
Eusebius, Jerome, &c. given below, p.
782, n. 2.

[2] 1 Tim. iii. 2, 2 Tim. ii. 22.

[3] See remarks on the date of the
Pastoral Epistles, in the Appendix.

[4] The above data show us the necessity of supposing as long an interval
as possible between St. Paul's liberation
and his second imprisonment.   Therefore we must assume that his appeal
was finally decided at the end of the
'two years' mentioned in Acts xxviii.
30,—that is, in the spring of A.D. 63.

[5] Sueton. *Oct.* 33; but Geib thinks
this arrangement was not of long duration.

[6] 'Other matters he himself examined
and decided with his Assessors, sitting

on the tribunal in the Palatium.' (Dio,
lv. 27.)   This is said of Augustus.

[7] As to Tiberius, see Dio, lvii. 7; and
as to Claudius, Dio, lx. 4.

[8] Tiberius built a tribunal on the
Palatine (Dio, lvii. 7).

[9] Dio mentions that the ceilings of
the Halls of Justice in the Palatine
were painted by Severus to represent
the starry sky.   The old Roman practice was for the magistrate to sit under
the open sky, which probably suggested
this kind of ceiling.   Even the Basilicas were not roofed over (as to their
central nave) till a late period.

[10] Those who are acquainted with
Rome will remember how the interior
of many of the ruined buildings is lined
with a coating of these precious marbles.

and greatest influence. Among them were the two consuls,[1] and selected representatives of each of the other great magistracies of Rome.[2] The remainder consisted of Senators chosen by lot. Over this distinguished bench of judges presided the representative of the most powerful monarchy which has ever existed,—the absolute ruler of the whole civilised world. But the reverential awe which his position naturally suggested, was changed into contempt and loathing by the character of the Sovereign who now presided over that supreme tribunal. For Nero was a man whom even the awful attribute of 'power equal to the gods,'[3] could not render august, except in title. The fear and horror excited by his omnipotence and his cruelty, were blended with contempt for his ignoble lust of praise, and his shameless licentiousness. He had not as yet plunged into that extravagance of tyranny which, at a later period, exhausted the patience of his subjects, and brought him to destruction. Hitherto his public measures had been guided by sage advisers, and his cruelty had injured his own family rather than the State. But already, at the age of twenty-five, he had murdered his innocent wife and his adopted brother, and had dyed his hands in the blood of his mother. Yet even these enormities seem to have disgusted the Romans less than his prostitution of the Imperial purple, by publicly performing as a musician on the stage and a charioteer in the circus. His degrading want of dignity and insatiable appetite for vulgar applause, drew tears from the councillors and servants of his house, who could see him slaughter his nearest relatives without remonstrance.

Before the tribunal of this blood-stained adulterer, Paul the Apostle was now brought in fetters, under the custody of his military guard. We may be sure that he, who had so often stood undaunted before the delegates of the Imperial throne did not quail when he was at last confronted with their master. His life was not in the hands of Nero; he knew that while his Lord had work for him on earth, HE would shield him from the tyrant's sword; and if his work was over, how gladly would he 'depart and be with Christ, which was far better.'[4] To him all the majesty of Roman despotism was nothing more than an empty pageant; the Imperial demigod himself was but one of 'the princes of this world, that come to nought.'[5] Thus he stood, calm and collected, ready to answer the charges of his accusers, and knowing that in the hour of his need it should be given him what to speak.

The prosecutors and their witnesses were now called forward, to support their accusation:[6] for although the subject-matter for de-

[1] Memmius Regulus and Virginius Rufus were the consuls of the year A.D. 63 (A.U.C. 816). Under some of the Emperors, the consuls were often changed several times during the year; but Nero allowed them to hold office for six months. So that these consuls would still be in office till July.

[2] Such, at least, was the constitution of the council of Assessors, according to the ordinance of Augustus, which ap-

pears to have remained unaltered. See Dio, liii. 21. Also see Sueton. *Tiber.* 55, and the passages of Dio referred to in the notes above.

[3] 'Diis æqua potestas' was the attribute of the Emperors. (Juv. iv.)

[4] See his anticipations of his trial. Phil. i. 20–25, and Phil. ii. 17.

[5] 1 Cor. ii. 6.

[6] The order of the proceedings was, (1) Speech of the prosecutor; (2) Ex

cision was contained in the written depositions forwarded from
Judæa by Festus, yet the Roman law required the personal presence
of the accusers and the witnesses, whenever it could be obtained.[1]
We already know the charges [2] brought against the Apostle. He
was accused of disturbing the Jews in the exercise of their worship,
which was secured to them by law ; of desecrating their Temple ;
and, above all, of violating the public peace of the Empire by perpetual agitation, as the ringleader of a new and factious sect. This
charge [3] was the most serious in the view of a Roman statesman ;
for the crime alleged amounted to *majestas*, or treason against the
Commonwealth, and was punishable with death.

These accusations were supported by the emissaries of the Sanhedrin, and probably by the testimony of witnesses from Judæa,
Ephesus, Corinth, and the other scenes of Paul's activity. The
foreign accusers, however, did not rely on the support of their own
unaided eloquence. They doubtless hired the rhetoric of some
accomplished Roman pleader (as they had done even before the
provincial tribunal of Felix) to set off their cause to the best advantage, and paint the dangerous character of their antagonist in
the darkest colours. Nor would it have been difficult to represent
the missionary labours of Paul as dangerous to the security of the
Roman state, when we remember how ill-informed the Roman
magistrates, who listened, must have been concerning the questions
really at issue between Paul and his opponents ; and when we consider how easily the Jews were excited against the government by
any fanatical leader who appealed to their nationality, and how
readily the kingdom of the Messiah, which Paul proclaimed, might
be misrepresented as a temporal monarchy, set up in opposition to
the foreign domination of Rome.

We cannot suppose that St. Paul had secured the services of any
professional advocate to repel such false accusations,[4] and put the
truth clearly before his Roman judges. We know that he resorted
to no such method on former occasions of a similar kind. And
it seems more consistent with his character, and his unwavering

---

amination and cross-examination of
witnesses for the prosecution ; (3)
Speech of the prisoner ; (4) Examination
and cross-examination of the witnesses
for the defence. The introduction of
cross-examination was an innovation
upon the old Republican procedure.

[1] As to the accusers, see above, p.
614, n. 9. Written depositions were
received at this period by the Roman
Courts, but not where the personal
presence of the witnesses could be obtained. See also Acts xxiv. 19, ' who
ought to have been here present before
thee.'

[2] See Acts xxiv. 5, 6, and xxv. 7, 8,
and pp. 607, 608, and 615.

[3] It must be remembered that the
old Republican system of criminal procedure had undergone a great change
before the time of Nero. Under the

old law (the system of *Quæstiones Perpetuæ*) different *charges* were tried in
distinct *courts*, and by different magistrates. In modern language a criminal
indictment could then only contain one
count. But this was altered under the
Emperors ; ' ut si quis sacrilegii simul
et homicidii accusetur ; quod nunc in
publicis judiciis [i.e. those of the *Quæstiones Perpetuæ*, which were still not
entirely obsolete] non accidit, quoniam
Prætor certâ lege sortitur ; Principum
autem et Senatûs cognitionibus fre-
quens est.' (Quintil. *Inst. Orat.* iii.
10.)

[4] It was most usual, at this period,
that both parties should be represented
by advocates ; but the parties were allowed to conduct their cause themselves,
if they preferred doing so.

reliance on his Master's promised aid, to suppose that he answered [1] the elaborate harangue of the hostile pleader by a plain and simple statement of facts, like that which he addressed to Felix, Festus, and Agrippa. He could easily prove the falsehood of the charge of sacrilege, by the testimony of those who were present in the Temple ; and perhaps the refutation of this more definite accusation might incline his judges more readily to attribute the vaguer charges to the malice of his opponents. He would then proceed to show that, far from disturbing the exercise of the *religio licita* of Judaism, he himself adhered to that religion, rightly understood. He would show that, far from being a seditious agitator against the state, he taught his converts everywhere to honour the Imperial Government, and submit to the ordinances [2] of the magistrate for conscience' sake. And, though he would admit the charge of belonging to the sect of the Nazarenes, yet he would remind his opponents that they themselves acknowledged the division of their nation into various sects, which were equally entitled to the protection of the law ; and that the sect of the Nazarenes had a right to the same toleration which was extended to those of the Pharisees and the Sadducees.

We know not whether he entered on this occasion into the peculiar doctrines of that 'sect' to which he belonged ; basing them, as he ever did, on the resurrection of the dead ; [3] and reasoning of righteousness, temperance, and judgment to come. If so, he had one auditor at least who had more need to tremble than even Felix. But doubtless a seared conscience, and a universal frivolity of character, rendered Nero proof against emotions which for a moment shook the nerves of a less audacious criminal.

When the parties on both sides had been heard, [4] and the witnesses all examined and cross-examined (a process which perhaps occupied several days [5]), the judgment of the court was taken. Each of the Assessors gave his opinion in writing to the Emperor, who never discussed the judgment with his Assessors, as had been the practice of better emperors, but after reading their opinions gave sentence according to his own pleasure, [6] without reference to the judgment of the majority. On this occasion it might have

---

[1] Probably all St. Paul's judges, on this occasion, were familiar with Greek, and therefore he might address them in his own native tongue, without the need of an interpreter.

[2] Compare Rom. xiii. 1–7.

[3] Compare the prominence given to the Resurrection in the statement before the Sanhedrin (Acts xxiii. 6), before Felix (Acts xxiv. 15), before Festus (Acts xxv. 19), and before Agrippa (Acts xxvi. 8).

[4] We are told by Suetonius, as we have mentioned before, that Nero heard both parties on each of the counts of the indictment separately; and gave his decision on one count before he proceeded to the next. (Sueton. *Nero*, 15.) The proceedings, therefore, which we

have described in the text, must have been repeated as many times as there were separate charges against St. Paul.

[5] Plin. *Epist.* ii. 11. 'The giving of the proofs continued till the third day ; ' and again, *Ep.* iv. 9, 'On the following day Titius, Homullus, and Fronto pleaded admirably for Bassus : the proofs occupied four days.'

[6] Suet. *Nero*. 15. This judgment was not pronounced by Nero till the next day. The sentence of a magistrate was always given in writing at this period and generally delivered by the magistrate himself. But in the case of the Emperor, he did not read his own sentence, but caused it to be read in his presence by his Quæstor.

been expected that he would have pronounced the condemnation of the accused; for the influence of Poppæa had now[1] reached its culminating point, and she was, as we have said, a Jewish proselyte. We can scarcely doubt that the emissaries from Palestine would have sought access to so powerful a protectress, and demanded her aid[2] for the destruction of a traitor to the Jewish faith; nor would any scruples have prevented her from listening to their request, backed as it probably was, according to the Roman usage, by a bribe. If such influence was exerted upon Nero, it might have been expected easily to prevail. But we know not all the complicated intrigues of the Imperial Court. Perhaps some Christian freedman of Narcissus[3] may have counteracted, through the interest of that powerful favourite, the devices of St. Paul's antagonists; or possibly Nero may have been capriciously inclined to act upon his own independent view of the law and justice of the case, or to show his contempt for what he regarded as the petty squabbles of a superstitious people, by 'driving the accusers from his judgment seat' with the same feelings which Gallio had shown on a similar occasion.

However this may be, the trial resulted in the acquittal of St. Paul. He was pronounced guiltless of the charges brought against him, his fetters were struck off, and he was liberated from his lengthened captivity. And now at last he was free to realise his long-cherished purpose of evangelising the West. But the immediate execution of this design was for the present postponed, in order that he might first revisit some of his earlier converts, who again needed his presence.

Immediately on his liberation it may reasonably be supposed that he fulfilled the intention which he had lately expressed (Philem. 22, and Phil. ii. 24), of travelling eastward through Macedonia, and seeking the churches of Asia Minor, some of which, as yet, had not seen his face in the flesh. We have already learnt, from the Epistle to the Colossians, how much his influence and authority were required among those Asiatic Churches. We must suppose him, therefore, to have gone from Rome by the usual route, crossing the Adriatic from Brundusium to Apollonia, or Dyrrhachium, and proceeding by the great Egnatian road through Macedonia; and we can imagine the joy wherewith he was welcomed by his beloved children at Philippi, when he thus gratified the expectation which he had encouraged them to form. There is no reason to suppose, however, that he lingered in Macedonia. It is more likely that he hastened on to Ephesus, and made that city once more his centre of operations. If he effected his purpose,[4] he now for the first time visited Colossæ, Laodicea, and other churches in that region.

Having accomplished the objects of his visit to Asia Minor, he was at length enabled (perhaps in the year following that of his

---

[1] Poppæa's influence was at its height from the birth to the death of her daughter Claudia, who was born at the beginning of A.D. 63, and lived four months.

[2] See last chapter, p. 723, n. 5.

[3] This Narcissus must not be confounded with the more celebrated favourite of Claudius. See Dio, lxiv. 3. The Narcissus here mentioned had Christian converts in his establishment; see Rom. xvi. 11 and note.

[4] See Philem. 22.

liberation) to undertake his long-meditated journey to Spain. By what route he went, we know not; he may either have travelled by way of Rome, which had been his original intention, or more probably, avoiding the dangers which at this period (in the height of the Neronian persecution) would have beset him there, he may have gone by sea. There was constant commercial intercourse between the East and Massilia (the modern Marseilles); and Massilia was in daily communication with the Peninsula. We may suppose him to have reached Spain in the year 64, and to have remained there about two years; which would allow him time to establish the germs of Christian Churches among the Jewish proselytes who were to be found in all the great cities, from Tarraco to Gades, along the Spanish coast.[1]

From Spain St. Paul seems to have returned, in A.D. 66,[2] to Ephesus; and here he found that the predictions which he had long ago uttered to the Ephesian presbyters were already receiving their fulfilment. Heretical teachers had arisen in the very bosom of the Church, and were leading away the believers after themselves. Hymenæus and Philetus were sowing, in a congenial soil, the seed which was destined in another century to bear so ripe a crop of error. The East and West were infusing their several elements of poison into the pure cup of Gospel truth. In Asia Minor, as at Alexandria, Hellenic philosophism did not refuse to blend with Oriental theosophy; the Jewish superstitions of the Cabbala, and the wild speculations of the Persian magi, were combined with the Greek craving for an enlightened and esoteric religion. The outward forms of superstition were ready for the vulgar multitude; the interpretation was confined to the aristocracy of knowledge, the self-styled Gnostics (1 Tim. vi. 20); and we see the tendencies at work among the latter, when we learn that, like their prototypes at Corinth, they denied the future resurrection of the dead, and taught that the only true resurrection was that which took place when the soul awoke from the death of ignorance to the life of knowledge.[3] We recognise already the germ of those heresies which convulsed the Church in the succeeding century; and we may imagine the grief and indignation aroused in the breast of St. Paul, when he found the extent of the evil, and the number of Christian converts already infected by the spreading plague.

Nevertheless, it is evident from the Epistles to Timotheus and Titus, written about this time, that he was prevented by other duties from staying in this oriental region so long as his presence was required. He left his disciples to do that which, had circumstances permitted, he would have done himself. He was plainly hurried from one point to another. Perhaps also he had lost some of his former energy. This might well be the case, if we consider all he had endured during thirty years of labour. The physical hardships which he had undergone were of themselves sufficient to wear out the most robust constitution; and we know that his health

---

[1] See p. 15.

[2] This hypothesis best explains the subsequent transactions recorded in the Pastoral Epistles. See remarks in Appendix II. on their date, and the Chronological Table given in Appendix III.

[3] See pp. 353, 354.

was already broken many years before.[1] But in addition to these bodily trials, the moral conflicts which he continually encountered could not fail to tire down the elasticity of his spirit. The hatred manifested by so large and powerful a section even of the Christian Church; the destruction of so many early friendships; the faithless desertion of followers; the crowd of anxieties which pressed upon him daily, and 'the care of all the Churches;' must needs have preyed upon the mental energy of any man, but especially of one whose temperament was so ardent and impetuous. When approaching the age of seventy,[2] he might well be worn out both in body and mind. And this will account for the comparative want of vigour and energy which has been attributed to the Pastoral Epistles, if there be any such deficiency; and may perhaps also be in part the cause of his opposing those errors by deputy, which we might rather have expected him to uproot by his own personal exertions.

However this may be, he seems not to have remained for any long time together at Ephesus, but to have been called away from thence, first to Macedonia,[3] and afterwards to Crete;[4] and immediately on his return from thence, he appears finally to have left Ephesus for Rome, by way of Corinth.[5] But here we are anticipating our narrative: we must return to the first of these hurried journeys, when he departed from Ephesus to Macedonia, leaving the care of the Ephesian Church to Timotheus, and charging him especially with the duty of counteracting the efforts of those heretical teachers whose dangerous character we have described.

When he arrived in Macedonia, he found that his absence might possibly be prolonged beyond what he had expected; and he probably felt that Timotheus might need some more explicit credential from himself than a mere verbal commission, to enable him for a longer period to exercise that Apostolic authority over the Ephesian Church, wherewith he had invested him. It would also be desirable that Timotheus should be able, in his struggle with the heretical teachers, to exhibit documentary proof of St. Paul's agreement with himself, and condemnation of the opposing doctrines. Such seem to have been the principal motives which led St. Paul to despatch from Macedonia that which is known as 'the First Epistle to Timothy;' in which are contained various rules for the government of the Ephesian Church, such as would be received with submission when thus seen to proceed directly from its Apostolic founder, while they would perhaps have been less readily obeyed, if seeming to be the spontaneous injunctions of the youthful Timotheus. In the same manner it abounds with impressive denunciations against the false teachers at Ephesus, which might command the assent of some who turned a deaf ear to the remonstrances of the Apostolic deputy. There are also exhortations to Timotheus himself, some of which perhaps were rather meant to bear an indirect application to others, at the time, as they have ever since furnished a treasury of practical precepts for the Christian Church.

---

[1] See Gal. iv. 13, 14, and 2 Cor. xii. 7-9.
[2] See p. 53, and compare Philem. 9 and the Chronological Table in the Appendix.
[3] 1 Tim. i. 3.
[4] Titus i. 5.
[5] 2 Tim. iv. 20.

THE FIRST EPISTLE TO TIMOTHEUS.[1]

Salutation.

PAUL, an Apostle of Jesus Christ, by command of i. 1 God our Saviour and Christ Jesus[2] our hope, TO 2 TIMOTHEUS MY TRUE SON IN[3] FAITH.

Grace, Mercy, and Peace, from God our Father, and Christ Jesus our Lord.

Timotheus is reminded of the commission given him to oppose the false teachers.

As I desired thee to remain in Ephesus,[4] when I 3 was setting out for Macedonia, that thou mightest command certain persons not to teach[5] falsely, nor to regard fables and endless[6] genealogies, which fur- 4 nish ground for disputation, rather than for the exercising of the stewardship[7] of God in faith.

Now the end of the commandment is love, pro- 5 ceeding from a pure heart, and good conscience, and undissembled faith. Which some have missed, and 6 have turned aside to vain babbling, desiring to be teachers of the Law,[8] understanding neither what 7 they say nor whereof they affirm. But we know that 8 the Law is good, if a man use it lawfully; knowing 9 this, that the[9] Law is not made for a[10] righteous man, but for the lawless and disobedient, for the impious and sinful, for the unholy and profane, for parricides[11] and murderers, for fornicators, sodomites, slavedealers,[12] liars, perjurers, and whatsoever else is con- 10 trary to sound doctrine. Such is the glorious Glad- 11

---

[1] For the date of this Epistle see the Appendix.

[2] ' Lord ' is omitted in the best MSS.

[3] Not '*the* faith' (A. V.), which would require the definite article.

[4] This sentence is left incomplete. Probably St. Paul meant to complete it by ' so I still desire thee,' or something to that effect; but forgot to express this, as he continued to dictate the subject of his charge to Timotheus.

[5] This Greek word occurs nowhere but in this Epistle.

[6] See pp. 355, 356, and Titus iii. 9.

[7] 'Stewardship' (not ' edifying') is the reading of the MSS. Compare 1 Cor. ix. 17. It would seem from this expression, that the false teachers in Ephesus were among the number of the presbyters, which would agree with the anticipation expressed in Acts xx. 30.

[8] We must observe that this expression may be taken in two ways; either

to denote Judaisers, who insisted on the permanent obligation of the Mosaic Law (which seems to suit the context best), or to denote Platonising expounders of the Law, like Philo, who professed to teach the true and deep view of the Law. To suppose (with Baur) that a Gnostic like Marcion, who rejected the Law altogether, could be called ' a teacher of the Law ' is (to say the least of it) a very unnatural hypothesis.

[9] The noun in the original is without the article here, as often when thus used. Compare Rom. ii. 12, iii. 31, iv. 13, &c.

[10] Compare Gal. v. 18, ' If ye are led by the Spirit, ye are not under the Law,' and the note on that passage.

[11] This word in English includes *parricides* and *matricides*, both of which are expressed in the original.

[12] This is the literal translation.

tidings of the blessed God, which was committed to my trust.

i. 12 And I thank Him who has given me strength, Christ Jesus our Lord, that He accounted me faith-

13 ful, and appointed me to minister unto His service, who was before a blasphemer and persecutor, and doer of outrage; but I received mercy, because I

14 acted ignorantly, in unbelief. And the grace of our Lord abounded beyond[1] measure, with faith and love

15 which is in Christ Jesus. Faithful is the saying,[2] and worthy of all acceptation, ' *Christ Jesus came into the world to save sinners*;' of whom I am first.

16 But for this cause I received mercy, that in me first Jesus Christ might shew forth all His long suffering, for a pattern of those who should hereafter believe

17 on Him unto life everlasting. Now to the king eternal,[3] immortal, invisible, the only[4] God, be honour and glory unto the ages of ages. Amen.

18 This charge I commit unto thee, son Timotheus, according to the former prophecies[5] concerning thee;

19 that in the strength thereof thou mayest fight the good fight, holding faith and a good conscience, which some have cast away, and made shipwreck

20 concerning the faith. Among whom are Hymenæus[6] and Alexander, whom I delivered over unto Satan[7] that they might be taught by[8] punishment not to blaspheme.

ii. 1 I exhort therefore, that first of all,[9] supplications,

The commission and calling of Paul.

Timotheus is enjoined to fulfil his commission.

Directions for

---

[1] Compare Rom. v. 20, 'the gift of grace overflowed beyond.'

[2] See note on iii. 16.

[3] This seems the best interpretation of 'king of the ages;' compare Apoc. xi. 15.

[4] 'Wise' is omitted in the best MSS.

[5] These prophecies were probably made at the time when Timotheus was first called to the service of Christ. Compare Acts xiii. 1, 2, when the will of God for the mission of Paul and Barnabas was indicated by the Prophets of the Church of Antioch.

[6] These are probably the same mentioned in the second Epistle (2 Tim. ii. 17, and iv. 14). Baur and De Wette argue that this passage is inconsistent with the hypothesis that 2 Tim. was written after 1 Tim.; because Hymenæus (who in this place is described as excommunicated and cut off from the Church) appears in 2 Tim. as a false teacher still active in the Church. But

there is nothing at all inconsistent in this; for example, the incestuous man at Corinth, who had the very same sentence passed on him (1 Cor. v. 5), was restored to the Church in a few months, on his repentance. De Wette also says that in 2 Tim. ii. 17, Hymenæus appears to be mentioned to Timotheus *for the first time*; but this (we think) will not be the opinion of any one who takes an unprejudiced view of that passage.

[7] On this expression, see the note on 1 Cor. v. 5.

[8] The Greek verb has this meaning. Cf. Luke xxiii. 16, and 2 Cor. vi. 9.

[9] 'First of all,' namely, before the other prayers. This explanation, which is Chrysostom's, seems preferable to that adopted by De Wette, Huther, and others, who take it to mean 'above all things.' It is clear from what follows (v. 8) that St. Paul is speaking of public prayer, which he here directs

public worship
and the beha-
viour of men
and women.
thereat. prayers, intercessions, and thanksgivings be made
for all men ; for kings [1] and all that are in authority, ii. 2
that we may lead a quiet and peaceable life in all
godliness [2] and gravity. For this is good and accept- 3
able in the sight of God our Saviour, who wills that 4
all men should be saved, and should come to the
knowledge [3] of the truth. For [over all] there is but [4] 5
one God, and one mediator between God and men,
the man [5] Christ Jesus, who gave Himself a ransom 6
for all men, to be testified in due time. And of this 7
testimony I was appointed herald and apostle (I
speak the truth in Christ, I lie not), a teacher of the
Gentiles, in faith and truth. I desire, then, that in 8
every place [6] the men [7] should offer up prayers, lifting
up their hands [8] in holiness, putting away anger and
disputation. Likewise, also, that the women should 9
come [9] in seemly apparel, and adorn themselves with
modesty and self-restraint ; [10] not in braided hair, or
gold, or pearls, or costly garments, but (as befits 10
women professing godliness) with the ornament of
good works. Let women learn in silence, with entire 11
submission. But I permit not a woman to teach, nor 12
to claim authority over the man, but to keep silence.
(For Adam was first formed, then Eve. And Adam 13
was not deceived ; but the woman was deceived, and 14
became a transgressor.) But women will be saved [11] 15

to be commenced by intercessory
prayer.

[1] Here we see a precept directed
against the seditious temper which prevailed (as we have already seen, p. 358)
among some of the early heretics
Compare Jude 8, and 2 Pet. ii. 9, and
Rom. xiii. 1.

[2] This term for *Christian piety* is not
used by St. Paul except in the Pastoral
Epistles. We must refer here to the
Appendix in the larger editions. See
note on Tit. i. 9. It is used by St.
Peter (2 Pet. i. 6) and by Clemens Romanus in the same sense.

[3] For the meaning of this, compare
2 Tim. iii. 7, and Rom. x. 2, and 1 Cor.
xiii. 12.

[4] This is the same sentiment as Rom.
iii. 29, 30.

[5] The *manhood* of our Lord is here
insisted on, because thereon rests His
mediation. Compare Heb. ii. 14, and
iv. 15.

[6] Chrysostom thinks that there is
a contrast between Christian worship,

which could be offered in *every place*
and the *Jewish* sacrifices, which could
only be offered in the Temple.

[7] The *men*, not the *women*, were to
officiate.

[8] This was the Jewish attitude in
prayer. Cf. Ps. lxiii. 4.

[9] After *women* we must supply *pray*
(as Chrysostom does), or something
equivalent (*to take part in the worship,*
&c.) from the preceding context.

[10] It is a peculiarity of the Pastoral
Epistles to dwell very frequently on this
virtue of *self-restraint.* A list of such
peculiarities is given in the Appendix
in the larger editions.

[11] The Greek here cannot mean ' *in
child-bearing.*' (A. V.) The Apostle's
meaning is, that women are to be kept
in the path of safety, not by taking
upon themselves the office of the man
(by taking a public part in the assemblies of the Church, &c.), but by
the performance of the peculiar functions which God has assigned to their
sex.

by the bearing of children; if they continue in faith
and love and holiness, with self-restraint.

iii. 1 Faithful is the saying, '*if a man seeks the office of* Directions for the appoint-
2 *a Bishop*[1] *he desires a good work.*' A Bishop,[2] then, ment of Presbyters.
must be free from reproach, the husband[3] of one
wife, sober, self-restrained, orderly, hospitable,[4]
3 skilled in teaching; not given to wine or brawls,[5]
4 but gentle, peaceable, and liberal; ruling his own
household well, keeping his children in subjection
5 with all gravity—(but if a man knows not how to
rule his own household, how can he take charge of the
6 Church of God?)—not a novice, lest he be blinded
with pride and fall into the condemnation of the
7 Devil. Moreover, he ought to have a good reputation among those who are without the Church; lest
he fall into reproach, and into a snare of the Devil.[6]

8 Likewise, the Deacons must be men of gravity, Directions for the appoint-
not double-tongued, not given to much wine, not ment of Deacons.
greedy of gain, holding the mystery of the faith in a
9 pure conscience. And let these also be first tried,
10 and after trial be made Deacons, if they are found
11 irreproachable. Their wives,[7] likewise, must be

[1] It should not be forgotten that the word ἐπίσκοπος is used in the Pastoral Epistles as synonymous with πρεσβύτερος. See p. 340 and Tit. i. 5, compared with i. 7.

[2] Rightly translated in A. V. '*a* bishop,' not '*the* bishop,' in spite of the article. See note on Tit. i. 7.

[3] 'Husband of one wife.' Compare iii. 12, v. 9, and Tit. i. 6. Many different interpretations have been given to this precept. It has been supposed (1) to prescribe marriage, (2) to forbid polygamy, (3) to forbid second marriages. The true interpretation seems to be as follows:—In the corrupt facility of divorce allowed both by the Greek and Roman law, it was very common for man and wife to separate, and marry other parties, during the life of one another. Thus a man might have three or four living wives; or, rather, women who had all successively been his wives. An example of the operation of a similar code is unhappily to be found in our own colony of Mauritius: there the French Revolutionary law of divorce has been suffered by the English government to remain unrepealed; and it is not uncommon to meet in society three or four women who have all been the wives of the same man, and three or

four men who have all been the husbands of the same woman. We believe it is this kind of *successive* polygamy, rather than *simultaneous* polygamy, which is here spoken of as disqualifying for the Presbyterate. So Beza.

[4] 'Hospitable.' Compare Heb. xiii. 2, and v. 10.

[5] The allusion to 'filthy lucre' is omitted in the best MSS.

[6] See note on 2 Tim. ii. 26.

[7] We agree with Huther in thinking the Authorised Version correct here, notwithstanding the great authority of Chrysostom in ancient, and De Wette and others in modern times, who interpret '*women*' here to mean '*deaconesses*.' On that view, the verse is most unnaturally interpolated in the midst of the discussion concerning the Deacons. [This is hardly so, if we view the Primitive Diaconate as consisting of two co-ordinate branches, a diaconate of men and a diaconate of women. We observe too, that nothing is said above of the duties of the wives of the Bishops. Our three chief modern commentators in England, Alford, Ellicott, and Wordsworth, interpret the verse before us as it was interpreted by Chrysostom and Jerome. H.]

women of gravity, not slanderers, sober and faithful,
in all things.   Let the Deacons be husbands of one iii.
wife, fitly ruling their children and their own households. For those who have well performed the office 13
of a Deacon, gain for themselves a good position,[1]
and great boldness in the faith of Christ Jesus.

Reason for
writing these
directions to
Timotheus. These things I write to thee, although I hope to 14
come to thee shortly; but in order that (if I should 15
be delayed) thou mayst know how to conduct thyself
in the house of God (for such is the Church of the
living God)[2] as a pillar and main-stay of the truth.
And, without contradiction, great is the mystery of 16
godliness—'*God*[3] *was manifested in the flesh, justified*[4]
*in the Spirit; beheld by angels, preached among the
Gentiles; believed on in the world, received up in
Glory.*'[5]

False teachers
to be expelled;
their charac-
teristics and
the mode of
resisting
them. Now the Spirit declares expressly, that in after iv.
times some will depart from the faith, giving heed to
seducing spirits, and teachings of dæmons, speaking[5]
lies in hypocrisy, having their conscience seared; 2
hindering marriage,[7] enjoining abstinence from meats, 3

---

[1] This verse is introduced by 'for' as giving a reason for the previous directions, viz. the great importance of having *good* deacons; such men, by the fit performance of the office, gained a high position in the community, and acquired (by constant intercourse with different classes of men) a boldness in maintaining their principles, which was of great advantage to them afterwards, and to the Church of which they were subsequently to become Presbyters.

[2] In this much disputed passage, we adopt the interpretation given by Gregory of Nyssa. So the passage was understood (as Canon Stanley observes) by the Church of Lyons (A.D. 177), for in their Epistle the same expression is applied to Attalus the Martyr. So, also, St. Paul speaks of the chief Apostles at Jerusalem as 'pillars' (Gal. ii. 9); and so, in Apoc. iii. 12, we find the Christian who is undaunted by persecution described as 'a pillar in the temple of God.' The grammatical objection to Gregory's view is untenable; and a Greek writer of the 4th century may be at least as good a judge on this point as his modern opponents.

[3] We retain the Received Text here, considering, that when the testimony of the MSS. is so divided, we are justified in retaining the text most familiar

to English readers.

[4] i.e. justified against gainsayers, as being what He claimed to be.

[5] There can be little doubt that this is a quotation from some Christian hymn or creed. Such quotations in the Pastoral Epistles (of which there are five introduced by the same expression, 'faithful is the saying') correspond with the hypothesis that these Epistles were among the last written by St. Paul.

[6] 'Speaking lies' is most naturally taken with 'dæmons;' but St. Paul, while grammatically speaking of the dæmons, is really speaking of the false teachers who acted under their impulse.

[7] With regard to the nature of the heresies here spoken of, see pp. 353–356. We observe a strong admixture of the Jewish element (exactly like that which prevailed, as we have seen, in the Colossian heresies) in the prohibition of *particular kinds of food*; compare v. 4, and Col. ii. 16 and Col. ii. 21, 22. This shows the very early date of this Epistle, and contradicts the hypothesis of Baur as to its origin. At the same time there is also an Anti-Judaical element, as we have remarked above, p. 356, n. 7,

which God created to be received with thanksgiving by those who believe and have [1] knowledge of the iv. 4 truth. For all things created by God are good, and nothing is to be rejected, if it be received with 5 thanksgiving. For it is sanctified by the Word of God [2] and prayer.

6 In thus instructing the brethren, thou wilt be a good servant of Jesus Christ, nourishing thyself with the words of the faith and good doctrine which thou 7 hast followed. Reject the fables of profane and doting teachers, but train thyself [3] for the contests of 8 godliness. For the training of the body is profitable for a little ; but godliness is profitable for all things, having promise of the present life, and of the life to 9 come. Faithful is the saying, and worthy of all ac-10 ceptation,—‘ *For to this end we endure labour and reproach, because we have set our hope on the living God, who is the saviour of all* [4] *mankind, specially of the faithful.*’

11 These things enjoin and teach ; let no man despise 12 thy youth, [5] but make thyself a pattern of the faith-13 ful, in word, in life, in love, [6] in faith, in purity. Until I come, apply thyself to public [7] reading, exhortation, 14 and teaching. Neglect not the gift that is in thee, which was given thee by prophecy [8] with the laying 15 on of the hands of the Presbytery. Let these things be thy care ; give thyself wholly to them ; that thy 16 improvement may be manifest to all men. Give heed

Duties of Timotheus.

[1] See note on 1 Tim. ii. 4.

[2] We have a specimen of what is meant by this verse, in the following beautiful ‘ Grace before Meat,’ which was used in the primitive Church : ‘Blessed art Thou, O Lord, who feedest me from my youth, who givest food unto all flesh. Fill our hearts with joy and gladness, that always having all sufficiency we may abound unto every good work, in Christ Jesus our Lord, through whom be glory, honour, and might unto Thee for ever. Amen.’ (*Apostolical Constitutions*, vii. 49.) The expression ‘ Word of God ’ probably implies that the thanksgiving was commonly made in some Scriptural words, taken, for example, out of the Psalms, as are several expressions in the above *Grace.*

[3] It seems, from a comparison of this with the following verse, that the false teachers laid great stress on a training of the body by ascetic prac-

tices. For the metaphorical language, borrowed from the contests of the Palæstra, compare 1 Cor. ix. 27, and pp. 538, 539.

[4] The prominence given to this truth of the universality of salvation in this Epistle (compare ii. 4) seems to imply that it was denied by the Ephesian false teachers. So the Gnostics considered salvation as belonging only to the enlightened few, who, in their system, constituted a kind of spiritual aristocracy. See p. 354.

[5] Compare 2 Tim. ii. 22 and the remarks in Appendix II.

[6] The words ‘ in spirit’ are omitted in the best MSS.

[7] This does not mean reading in the sense of *study*, but *reading aloud to others* ; the books so read were (at this period) probably those of the Old Testament, and perhaps the earlier gospels.

[8] Compare with this passage 1 Tim. i. 18 and the note.

to thyself and to thy teaching; continue stedfast therein.[1] For in so doing, thou shalt save both thyself and thy hearers.

Rebuke not an aged[2] man, but exhort him as thou wouldest a father; treat young men as brothers; the aged women as mothers; the young as sisters, in all purity.   v. 1   2

Widows are to be supported. Pay due regard[3] to the widows who are friendless in their widowhood. But if any widow has children or grandchildren, let them learn to shew their godliness first[4] towards their own household, and to requite their parents: for this is acceptable[5] in the sight of God. The widow who is friendless and desolate in her widowhood, sets her hope on God, and continues in supplications and prayers night and day; but she who lives in wantonness is dead while she lives: and hereof do thou admonish them, that they may be irreproachable. But if any man provide not for his own,[6] and especially for his kindred, he has denied the faith, and is worse than an unbeliever.   3   4   5   6   7   8

Qualifications of widows on the list. A widow, to be placed upon the[7] list, must be not less than sixty years of age, having been the wife of one husband;[8] she must be well reported of for good deeds, as one who has brought up children, received   9   10

[1] This *in them* is very perplexing; but it may most naturally be referred to the preceding *these things*.

[2] Chrysostom has remarked that we must not take 'elder' here in its official sense; compare the following 'elder women.'

[3] The *widows* were from the first supported out of the funds of the Church. See Acts vi. 1.

[4] *First*: i.e. before they pretend to make professions of godliness in other matters, let them show its fruits towards their own kindred.

[5] The best MSS. omit 'good and.'

[6] *His own* would include his slaves and dependants. So Cyprian requires the Christian masters to tend their sick slaves in a pestilence.

[7] It is a disputed point *what list* is referred to in this word; whether (1) it means the *list of widows to be supported out of the charitable fund*, or (2) the *list of deaconesses* (for which office the age of sixty seems too old), or (3) the *body of church-widows* mentioned by Tertullian and by other writers, as a kind of female Presbyters, having a distinct ecclesiastical position and duties The point is discussed by De Wette, Huther, and Wiesinger. We are disposed to take a middle course between the first and third hypotheses; by supposing, viz., that the *list* here mentioned was that of all the widows who were *officially recognised* as supported by the Church; but was not confined to such persons, but included also richer widows, who were willing to devote themselves to the offices assigned to the pauper widows. It has been argued that we cannot suppose that needy widows who did not satisfy the conditions of verse 9 would be *excluded* from the benefit of the fund; nor need we suppose this; but since *all* could scarcely be supported, certain conditions were prescribed, which must be satisfied before any one could be considered as officially *entitled* to a place on the list. From the class of widows thus formed, the subsequent 'body of widows' would naturally result. There is not the slightest ground for supposing that *widows* here means *virgins*, as Baur has imagined. His opinion is well refuted by Wiesinger and De Wette.

[8] For the meaning of this, see note on iii. 2.

strangers with hospitality, washed the feet of the saints, relieved the distressed, and diligently followed

v. 11 every good work. But younger widows reject; for when they have become wanton against Christ, they

12 desire to marry; and thereby incur condemnation, because they have broken their former[1] promise.

13 Moreover, they learn[2] to be idle, wandering about from house to house ; and not only idle, but tattlers also and busy-bodies, speaking things which ought not

14 to be spoken. I wish therefore that younger widows should marry, bear children, rule their households, and give no occasion to the adversary for reproach.

15 For already some of them have gone astray after Satan.

16 If there are widows dependent on any believer (whether man or woman), let those on whom they depend relieve them, and let not the Church be burdened with them; that it may relieve the widows who are destitute.

17 Let the Presbyters who perform their office well be counted worthy of a twofold honour,[3] especially

18 those[4] who labour in speaking and teaching. For the Scripture saith, ' 𝕿𝖍𝖔𝖚 𝖘𝖍𝖆𝖑𝖙 𝖓𝖔𝖙 𝖒𝖚𝖟𝖟𝖑𝖊 𝖙𝖍𝖊 𝖔𝖗 𝖙𝖍𝖆𝖙 𝖙𝖗𝖊𝖆𝖉𝖊𝖙𝖍 𝖔𝖚𝖙 𝖙𝖍𝖊 𝖈𝖔𝖗𝖓; '[5] and ' *the labourer is worthy of his hire.*'[6]

Government of the Presbyters.

19 Against a Presbyter receive no accusation except

20 on the testimony[7] of two or three witnesses. Rebuke

---

[1] The phrase means *to break a promise,* and is so explained by Chrysostom, and by Augustine. Hence we see that, when a widow was received into the number of *church-widows,* a promise was required from her (or virtually understood) that she would devote herself for life to the employments which these widows undertook ; viz. the education of orphans, and superintendence of the younger women. There is no trace here of the subsequent ascetic *disapprobation* of second marriages, as is evident from verse 14, where the younger widows are expressly desired to marry again. This also confirms our view of the ' wife of one husband.' See note on iii. 2.

[2] The construction is peculiar, but not unexampled in classical Greek.

[3] *Honour* here seems (from the next verse) to imply the notion of *reward.* Compare the verb *honour* in verse 3 above. Upon a misinterpretation of this verse was founded the disgusting practice, which prevailed in the third century, of setting a double portion of meat before the Presbyters, in the feasts of love.

[4] In pp. 340, 341, we observe that the offices of *presbyter* and *teacher* were united, at the date of the Pastoral Epistles, in the same persons ; which is shown by *apt to teach* being a qualification required in a Presbyter, 1 Tim. iii. 2. But though this union must in all cases have been desirable, we find, from this passage, that there were still some *presbyters* who were not *teachers,* i.e. who did not perform the office of public instruction in the congregation. This is another strong proof of the early date of the Epistle.

[5] This quotation (Deut. xxv. 4) is applied to the same purpose, 1 Cor. ix. 9 (where the words are quoted in a reverse order). The LXX. agrees with 1 Cor. ix. 9.

[6] Luke x. 7.

[7] This rule is founded on the Mosaic jurisprudence, Deut. xix. 5, and appealed to by St. Paul, 2 Cor. xiii. 1.

the offenders in the presence of all, that others also may fear. I adjure thee, before God and[1] Christ v. 21 Jesus and the chosen[2] angels, that thou observe these things without prejudice against any man, and do nothing out of partiality.

Ordination.

Lay hands hastily on no man, nor make thyself[3] a 22 partaker in the sins committed by another. Keep thyself pure.

Particular and general cautions.

Drink no longer water only, but use a little wine 23 for the sake of thy stomach, and thy frequent maladies.

[In thy decisions remember that] the sins of some 24 men are manifest beforehand, and lead the way to their condemnation; but the sins of others are not seen till afterwards. Likewise, also the good deeds 25 of some men are conspicuous; and those which they conceal cannot be kept hidden.

Duties of slaves.

Let those who are under the yoke as bondsmen vi. 1 esteem their masters worthy of all honour, lest reproach be brought upon the name of God and His doctrine. And let those whose masters are believers 2 not despise them because they are brethren, but serve them with the more subjection, because they who claim[4] the benefit are believing and beloved. Thus teach thou, and exhort.

False teachers rebuked; their covetousness.

If any man teach falsely,[5] and consent not to the 3 sound words of our Lord Jesus Christ, and to the godly doctrine, he is blinded with pride, and under- 4 stands nothing, but is filled with a sickly[6] appetite

---

[1] *Lord* is omitted by the best MSS.

[2] By the *chosen* angels are probably meant those especially selected by God as His messengers to the human race, such as Gabriel.

[3] The meaning of the latter part of this verse is, that Timotheus, if he ordained unfit persons (e.g. friends or relations) out of partiality, would thereby make himself a participator in their sins.

[4] The A. V. is inconsistent with the presence of the Greek definite article. The verb here used has the sense of *claim* in classical Greek, though not elsewhere in the N. T.

[5] The section from ver. 3 to 10 is a general warning against the false teachers, as is evident from the whole context. It is a mistake to refer the 'false teaching' to some (imaginary) teachers who are supposed by some to

have preached the abolition of slavery. There is no evidence or probability whatever that such teachers existed; although it was natural that some of the Christian slaves themselves should have been tempted to 'despise' their believing masters, with whom they were now united by so holy a bond of brotherhood; a bond which contained in itself the seeds of liberty for the slave, destined to ripen in due time. It would scarcely have been necessary to say this, but that a teacher of Divinity has lately published a statement that 'St. Paul's epistles condemn attempts to abolish slavery, as the work of men *"proud, knowing nothing"* (1 Tim. vi. 2–4).' See *Rational Godliness*: by R. Williams, D.D., p. 303.

[6] *Sickly* is the antithesis to *sound* above. Similar phraseology is found in Plato.

for disputations and contentions about words, whence
vi. 5 arise envy, strife, reproaches, evil suspicions, violent
collisions[1] of men whose mind is corrupted, and who
are destitute of the truth ; who think that godliness[2]
6 is a gainful trade.[3]   But godliness with contentment
7 is truly gainful ; for we brought nothing into the
world, and it is certain we can carry nothing out ;
8 but having food and shelter, let us be therewith con-
9 tent.   They who seek for riches fall into temptations
and snares and many foolish and hurtful desires,
10 which drown men in ruin and destruction.   For the
love of money is the root of all evils ; and some
coveting it, have been led astray from the faith, and
pierced themselves through with many sorrows.

11   But thou, O man of God, flee these things ; and   Exhortations
12 follow after righteousness, godliness, faith, love, sted-   to Timotheus.
fastness,[4] meekness.   Fight the good fight[5] of faith,
lay hold on eternal life, to which thou[6] wast called,
and didst confess the good[7] confession before many
13 witnesses.   I charge thee in the presence of God who
gives life to all things, and Christ Jesus who bore
testimony under Pontius Pilate[8] to the good confes-
14 sion, that thou keep that which thou art commanded,
spotlessly and irreproachably, until the appearing of
15 our Lord Jesus Christ ; which shall in due time be
made manifest by the blessed and only[9] potentate,
16 the King of kings, and Lord of lords ; who only hath
immortality, dwelling in light unapproachable ; whom
no man hath seen, nor can see ; to whom be honour
and power everlasting.   Amen.

17   Charge those who are rich in this present world,   Duties of the
not to be high-minded, nor to trust in uncertain   rich.
riches, but in[10] God, who provides all things richly

---

[1] The original meaning of the un-compounded word (taking the reading of the best MSS.) is *friction*.

[2] The A. V. here reverses the true order, and violates the law of the article.

[3] The words 'From such withdraw thyself' are not found here in the best MSS.

[4] The meaning is, *stedfast endurance under persecution.*

[5] Here we have another of those metaphors from the Greek games, so frequent with St. Paul. See 2 Tim. iv. 7.

[6] 'Also' is omitted by the best MSS.

[7] '*The* (not *a*) good confession' means the confession of faith in Jesus

as the Christ.   (Compare Rom. x. 10.) Timotheus had probably been a confessor of Christ in persecutions, either at Rome or elsewhere ; or it is possible that the allusion here may be to his baptism.

[8] For this use of 'witness' or 'testify' with the accusative, compare John iii. 32, 'What he hath seen, that he testifieth.'   Our Lord testified before Pontius Pilate that He was the Messiah.

[9] *Only.* This seems to allude to the same polytheistic notions of incipient Gnosticism which are opposed in Col. i. 16.

[10] 'Living' is omitted by the best MSS.

for our use. Charge them to practise benevolence, vi.18
to be rich in good works, to be bountiful and generous, storing up for themselves a good foundation for 19
the time to come, that they may lay hold on eternal [1]
life.

Timotheus again reminded of his commission. O Timotheus, guard [2] the treasure which is com- 20
mitted to thy trust, and avoid the profane babblings
and antitheses [3] of the falsely-named ' Knowledge ; [4]
which some professing, have erred concerning the 21
faith.

Concluding benediction. Grace be with thee. [5]

The expectations which St. Paul expressed in the above letter of
a more prolonged absence from Ephesus, could scarcely have been
fulfilled ; for soon after [6] we find that he had been in Crete (which
seems to imply that, on his way thither, he had passed through
Ephesus), and was now again on his way westwards. We must
suppose, then, that he returned shortly from Macedonia to Ephesus,
as he hoped, though doubtfully, to be able to do when he wrote to
Timotheus. From Ephesus, as we have just said, he soon afterwards made an expedition to Crete. It can scarcely be supposed
that the Christian Churches of Crete were first founded during this
visit of St. Paul ; on the contrary, many indications in the Epistle
to Titus show that they had already lasted for a considerable time.
But they were troubled by false teachers, and probably had never
yet been properly organised, having originated, perhaps, in the
private efforts of individual Christians, who would have been supplied with a centre of operations and nucleus of Churches by the
numerous colonies of Jews established in the island. [7] St. Paul now

[1] The majority of MSS. read *the true life*, which is equivalent to the Received Text.

[2] The *treasure* here mentioned is probably the pastoral office of superin-
tending the Church of Ephesus, which was committed by St. Paul to Timotheus. Cf. 2 Tim. i. 14.

[3] 'Antitheses.' There is not the slightest ground (as even De Wette allows) for supposing, with Baur, that this expression is to be understood of the *contrariæ oppositiones* (or contrasts between Law and Gospel) of Marcion. If there be an allusion to any Gnostic *doctrines* at all, it is more probable that it is to the *dualistic* opposition between the principles of good and evil in the world, which was an Oriental element in the philosophy of some of the early Gnostics. But the most natural interpretation (considering the junc-
tion with ' babblings ' and the ' conten-
tions about words ' ascribed to the heretics above, vi. 4) is to suppose that

St. Paul here speaks, not of the *doctrines*, but of the dialectical and rhetorical arts of the false teachers.

[4] From this passage we see that the heretics here opposed by St. Paul laid claim to a peculiar philosophy, or ' Gnosis.' Thus they were *Gnostics*, at all events *in name*; how far their *doctrines* agreed with those of later Gnostics is a further question. We have before seen that there were those at Corinth (1 Cor. viii. 1, 10, 11) who were blamed by St. Paul for claiming a high degree of ' gnosis ;' and we have seen him condemn the ' philosophy ' of the heretics at Colossæ (Col. ii. 8), who appear to bear the closest resemblance to those condemned in the Pastoral Epistles. See pp. 353–360.

[5] 'Amen ' is not found in the best MSS.

[6] See remarks on the date of the Pastoral Epistles in the Appendix.

[7] Philo mentions Crete as one of the seats of the Jewish dispersion ; see

visited them in company with Titus,[1] whom he left in Crete as his representative on his departure.   He himself was unable to remain long enough to do what was needful, either in silencing error, or in selecting fit persons as presbyters of the numerous scattered Churches, which would manifestly be a work of time.   Probably he confined his efforts to a few of the principal places, and empowered Titus to do the rest.   Thus, Titus was left at Crete in the same position which Timotheus had occupied at Ephesus during St. Paul's recent absence; and there would, consequently, be the same advantage in his receiving written directions from St. Paul concerning the government and organisation of the Church, which we have before mentioned in the case of Timotheus.   Accordingly, shortly after leaving Crete, St. Paul sent a letter to Titus, the outline of which would equally serve for that of the preceding Epistle.   But St. Paul's letter to Titus seems to have been still further called for, to meet some strong opposition which that disciple had encountered while attempting to carry out his master's directions.   This may be inferred from the very severe remarks against the Cretans which occur in the Epistle, and from the statement, at its commencement, that the very object which its writer had in view, in leaving Titus in Crete, was that he might appoint Presbyters in the Cretan Churches; an indication that his claim to exercise this authority had been disputed.   This Epistle seems to have been despatched from Ephesus at the moment when St. Paul was on the eve of departure on a westward journey, which was to take him as far as Nicopolis[2] (in Epirus) before the winter.   The following is a translation of this Epistle.

THE EPISTLE TO TITUS.[3]

i. 1 PAUL, a bondsman of God, and an apostle of Jesus Salutation. Christ—sent forth [4] to bring God's chosen to faith,

p. 15. [For the introduction of Christianity into the island in connection with St. Paul, see the art. 'Crete' in the *Dict. of the Bible.* H.]

[1] For the earlier mention of Titus, see above, pp. 468, 469. There is some interest in mentioning the traditionary recollections of him, which remain in the island of Crete. One Greek legend says that he was the nephew of a proconsul of Crete, another that he was descended from Minos. The cathedral of Megalo-Castron on the north of the island was dedicated to him. His name was the watchword of the Cretans, when they fought against the Venetians, who came under the standard of St. Mark. The Venetians themselves, when here, 'seem to have transferred to him part of that respect, which, elsewhere, would probably have been manifested for Mark alone. During the

celebration of several great festivals of the Church, the response of the Latin clergy of Crete, after the prayer for the Doge of Venice, was *Sancte Marce, tu nos adjuva* ; but, after that for the Duke of Candia, *Sancte Tite, tu nos adjuva.*' Pashley's *Travels in Crete*, vol. i. pp. 6 and 165.

[2] See below, p. 763, n. 10.

[3] For the date of this Epistle, see the Appendix.

[4] The original here is perplexing, but seems to admit of no other sense than this, *an apostle sent forth on an errand of faith.* Compare 2 Tim. i. 1, 'an apostle sent forth to proclaim the promise of life.' The involved and parenthetical style of this salutation reminds us of that to the Romans, and is a strong evidence of the genuineness of this Epistle.

and to the [1] knowledge of the truth which is accord- i. 2
ing to godliness,[2] with hope of eternal life, which
God, who cannot lie, promised before eternal times;[3] 3
(but He made known His word in due season, in
the message[4] committed to my trust by the command of God our Saviour),—TO TITUS, MY TRUE SON 4
IN OUR COMMON FAITH.

Grace and Peace[5] from God our Father, and the
Lord Jesus Christ our Saviour.

Commission of Titus to regulate the Cretan Churches.

This was the [very] cause[6] why I left thee in Crete, 5
that thou mightest farther[7] correct what is deficient,
and appoint Presbyters in every city, as I gave thee

Qualifications of Presbyters.

commission. No man must be appointed a Presbyter, 6
but he who is without reproach, the husband of one
wife,[8] having believing children who are not accused
of riotous living, nor disobedient; for a[9] Bishop must 7
be free from reproach, as being a steward of God;
not self-willed, not easily provoked, not a lover of wine,
not given to brawls, not greedy of gain; but hospi- 8
table to[10] strangers, a lover of good men, self-
restrained,[11] just, holy, continent; holding fast the 9
words which are faithful to our teaching, that he may
be able both to exhort others in the sound[11] doctrine,
and to rebuke the gainsayers.

Titus must oppose the false teachers.

For there are many disobedient babblers and de- 10
ceivers, specially they of the Circumcision, whose
mouths need[12] bit and bridle; for they subvert whole 11
houses, by teaching evil, for the love of shameful gain.

---

[1] See note on 1 Tim. ii. 4.

[2] *Godliness.* See note on 1 Tim. ii. 2.

[3] *Before eternal times*: meaning probably, *in the old dispensation*; cf. Rom. xvi. 25, and note on 2 Tim. i. 9.

[4] Literally, *proclamation.*

[5] The best MSS. omit *mercy* here.

[6] This commencement seems to indicate (as we have above remarked) that, in exercising the commission given to him by St. Paul for reforming the Cretan Church, Titus had been resisted.

[7] Not simply 'set in order' (as in A. V.), but 'set in order *farther.*'

[8] This part of the Presbyter's qualifications has been very variously interpreted. See note on 1 Tim. iii. 2.

[9] Rightly translated in A. V. '*a*' (not *the*) 'bishop,' because the article is only used generically. So, in English, 'the reformer must be patient:' equivalent to '*a* reformer,' &c. We see here a proof of the early date of this Epistle,

in the synonymous use of ἐπίσκοπος and πρεσβύτερος ; the latter word designating the *rank*, the former the *duties*, of the Presbyter. The best translation here would be the term *overseer*, which is employed in the A. V. as a translation of ἐπίσκοπος, Acts xx. 28; but, unfortunately, the term has associations in modern English which do not permit of its being thus used here. Compare with this passage 1 Tim. iii. 2.

[10] Cf. 3 John, 5, 6. In the early Church, Christians travelling from one place to another were received and forwarded on their journey by their brethren; this is the 'hospitality' so often commended in the N. T.

[11] The Appendix in the larger editions contains a list of words peculiarly used in the Pastoral Epistles. Among them are these words.

[12] The word literally denotes *to put a bit and bridle upon* a horse.

i. 12 It was said by one of themselves, a prophet [1] of their own,—

'Always liars and beasts are the Cretans, and inwardly sluggish.'

13 This testimony is true. Wherefore rebuke [2] them 14 sharply, that they may be sound in faith, and may no more give heed to Jewish fables,[3] and precepts [4] of men who turn away from the truth. To the pure all 15 things are pure; [5] but to the polluted and unbelieving nothing is pure, but both their understanding and 16 their conscience is polluted. They profess to know God, but by their works they deny Him, being abominable and disobedient, and worthless [6] for any good work.

ii. 1 But do thou speak conformably to the sound doc- 2 trine. Exhort the aged men to be sober, grave, self-restrained, sound in faith, in love, in stedfastness. 3 Exhort the aged women likewise, to let their deportment testify of holiness, not to be slanderers, not to be enslaved by drunkenness, but to give good instruc- 4 tion; that they may teach discretion to the younger women, leading them to be loving wives and loving 5 mothers, self-restrained, chaste, keepers at home, amiable and obedient to their husbands, lest reproach 6 be brought upon the Word of God. In like manner, 7 do thou exhort the young men to self-restraint. And show thyself in all things a pattern of good works; manifesting in thy teaching uncorruptness, gravity,[7] 8 soundness of doctrine not to be condemned, that our adversaries may be shamed, having no evil to say

Directions to Titus how he is to instruct those of different ages and sexes.

His own conduct.

[1] Epimenides of Crete, a poet who lived in the 6th century B.C., is the author quoted. His verses were reckoned oracular, whence the title ' prophet.' So by Plato he is called ' a divinely-inspired man,' and by Plutarch, ' a man dear to the gods.'

[2] *Rebuke*: this seems to refer to the same word in v. 9.

[3] *Fables.* See note on 1 Tim. iv. 7.

[4] These *precepts* were probably those mentioned 1 Tim. iv. 3, and Col. ii. 16–22. The ' Jewish' element appears distinctly in the Colossian heretics ('Sabbaths,' Col. ii. 16), although it is not seen in the Epistles to Timothy. Comp. iii. 9, and see pp. 356, 357.

[5] It would seem from this that the heretics attacked taught their followers to abstain from certain acts, or certain kinds of food, as being *impure*. We must not, however, conclude from this that they were *Ascetics*. Superstitious abstinence from certain material acts is quite compatible with gross impurity of teaching and of practice, as we see in the case of Hindoo devotees, and in those impure votaries of Cybele and of Isis, mentioned so often in Juvenal and other writers of the same date. The early Gnostics, here attacked, belonged apparently to that class who borrowed their theosophy from Jewish sources, and the *precepts of abstinence* which they imposed may probably have been derived from the Mosaic law. Their immorality is plainly indicated by the following words.

[6] Literally, *unable to stand the test*: i.e. when tested by the call of duty, they fail.

[7] The best MSS. omit the word translated 'sincerity' in A. V.

Duties of slaves. against us.[1]   Exhort bondsmen to obey their masters, ii. 9 and to strive to please them in all things, without gainsaying; not purloining, but showing all good fide- 10 lity, that they may adorn the doctrine of God our General motives of Christianity. Saviour in all things.   For the grace of God has been 11 made manifest, bringing salvation to all [2] mankind; teaching us to deny ungodliness and earthly lusts, 12 and to live temperately, justly, and godly in this present world ; looking for that blessed hope,[3] the appear- 13 ing of the glory of the great God, and our [4] Saviour Jesus Christ ; who gave Himself for us, that He might 14 redeem us from all iniquity, and purify us unto Himself, as a ‘ 𝖕𝖊𝖈𝖚𝖑𝖎𝖆𝖗 𝖕𝖊𝖔𝖕𝖑𝖊,’ [5] zealous of good works. These things speak, and exhort and rebuke with all 15 authority.   Let no man despise thee.

Duty towards Government and towards unbelievers generally. Remind [6] them to render submission to magistrates iii. 1 and authorities, to obey the Government, to be ready for every good work, to speak evil of no man, to avoid 2 strife, to act with forbearance, and to show all meekness to all men.   For we ourselves also were formerly 3 without understanding, disobedient and led astray, enslaved to all kinds of lusts and pleasures, living in malice and in envy, hateful and hating one another. But when God our Saviour made manifest His kind- 4 ness and love of men, He saved us, not through the 5 works of righteousness which we have done, but according to His own mercy, by the laver [7] of regeneration, and the renewing of the Holy Spirit, which He 6 richly poured forth upon us, by Jesus Christ our Saviour ; that, being justified by His grace, we might 7 Titus must enforce good works and re- become heirs, through [8] hope, of life eternal.   Faith- 8 ful is the saying,[9] and these things I desire thee to

---

[1] *Us* (not *you*) is the reading of the best MSS.

[2] This statement seems intended to contradict the Gnostic notion that salvation was given to the enlightened alone.   It should be observed that the definite article of T. R. is omitted by some of the best MSS.

[3] Compare the same expectation expressed Rom. viii. 18–25.

[4] The A. V. here is probably correct, notwithstanding the omission of the article before ‘ Saviour.’   We must not be guided entirely by the rules of classical Greek, in this matter.   Comp. 2 Thess. i. 12.

[5] This expression is borrowed from the Old Testament, Deut. vii. 6, Deut.

xiv. 2, and other places (LXX.).

[6] St. Paul himself had no doubt insisted on the duty of obedience to the civil magistrate, when he was in Crete. The Jews throughout the Empire were much disposed to insubordination at this period.

[7] The word does not mean *‘ washing’* (A. V.), but *laver* ; i.e. *a vessel in which washing takes place.*

[8] *Through hope* is explained by Rom. viii. 24, 25.

[9] The ‘ saying’ referred to is supposed by some interpreters to be the statement which precedes (from 3 to 7). These writers maintain that it is ungrammatical to refer ‘ *Faithful is the saying’* to the following, as is done in

affirm, *' let them that have believed in God be careful* sist the false teachers.
iii. 9 *to practise good works.''* These things are good and
profitable to men: but avoid foolish disputations,[1]
and genealogies,[2] and strifes and contentions concern-
10, 11 ing the [3] Law, for they are profitless and vain. A
sectarian,[4] after two admonitions, reject, knowing that
such a man is perverted, and by his sins is self-condemned.

12　When I send Artemas or Tychicus [5] to thee, endea- Special direc-
vour to come to me to Nicopolis; [6] for there I have tions for Ti-
tus's journey
13 determined to winter. Forward Zenas the lawyer to Nicopolis.
and Apollos on their journey zealously, that they may
14 want for nothing. And let our people also [7] learn to
practise good works, ministering to the necessities of
others, that they may not be unfruitful.

15　All that are with me salute thee. Salute those who Salutations.
love us in faith.

Grace be with you all.[8] Concluding
benediction.

We see from the above letter that Titus was desired to join St.
Paul at Nicopolis, where the Apostle designed to winter. We learn
from an incidental notice elsewhere,[9] that the route he pursued was
from Ephesus to Miletus, where his old companion Trophimus remained behind from sickness, and thence to Corinth, where he left
Erastus, the former Treasurer of that city, whom, perhaps, he had
expected, or wished, to accompany him in his farther progress. The
position of Nicopolis[10] would render it a good centre for operating
upon the surrounding province; and thence St. Paul might make excursions to those Churches of Illyricum which he perhaps[11] founded

A. V. But this objection is avoided
by taking *'that'* as a part of the quotation. The usuage is similar in Eph.
v. 33.

[1] *Disputations*: see 1 Tim. vi. 4, and
2 Tim. ii. 23.

[2] See 1 Tim. i. 4.

[3] Compare *precepts* (i. 14), and
teachers of the Law. 1 Tim. i. 7.

[4] *Sectarian.* We have seen that the
word from which our term 'heresy'
comes is used by St. Paul, in his
earlier writings, simply for *a religious
sect*, sometimes (as Acts xxvi. 5) without disapprobation, sometimes (as 1
Cor. xi. 19) in a bad sense; here we
find its derivative (which occurs here
and nowhere else in the N. T.) already
assuming a bad sense, akin to that
which it afterwards bore. It should be
also observed that these early heretics

united *moral depravity* with erroneous
teaching; their works bore witness
against their doctrine; and this explains the subsequent 'by his sins he
is self-condemned.' See pp. 356–358.

[5] Cf. Col. iv. 7.

[6] See n. 10 below.

[7] i.e. the Cretan Christians were to
aid in furnishing Zenas and Apollos
with all that they needed.

[8] The 'Amen' is omitted in the best
MSS.

[9] 2 Tim. iv. 20.

[10] It is here assumed that the Nicopolis spoken of Titus iii. 12, was the
city of that name in Epirus. There
were other places of the same name,
but they were comparatively insignificant.

[11] See above, pp. 471 and 533.

himself at an earlier period. The city which was thus chosen as the
last scene of the Apostle's labours, before his final imprisonment, is
more celebrated for its origin than for its subsequent history.   It
was founded by Augustus, as a permanent memorial of the victory
of Actium, and stood upon the site of the camp occupied by his land
forces before that battle.   We learn, from the accounts of modern
travellers, that the remains upon the spot still attest the extent and
importance of the ' City of Victory.' ' A long lofty wall spans a desolate plain; to the north of it rises, on a distant hill, the shattered
scena of a theatre; and, to the west, the extended though broken
line of an aqueduct connects the distant mountains, from which it
tends, with the main subject of the picture, the city itself.' [1]   To
people this city, Augustus uprooted the neighbouring mountaineers
from their native homes, dragging them by his arbitrary compulsion
' from their healthy hills to this low and swampy plain.'   It is satisfactory to think (with the accomplished traveller from whom the
above description is borrowed) that, ' in lieu of the blessings of which
they were deprived, the Greek colonists of Nicopolis were consoled
with one greater than all, when they saw, heard, and talked with
the Apostle who was debtor to the Greeks.'

It seems most probable, however, that St. Paul was not permitted
to spend the whole of this winter in security at Nicopolis.   The
Christians were now far more obnoxious to the Roman authorities
than formerly.   They were already distinguished from the Jews, and
could no longer shelter themselves under the toleration extended
to the Mosaic religion.   So eminent a leader of the proscribed sect
was sure to find enemies everywhere, especially among his fellow-
countrymen; and there is nothing improbable in supposing that,
upon the testimony of some informer, he was arrested [2] by the magistrates of Nicopolis, and forwarded to Rome [3] for trial.   The indications which we gather from the Second Epistle to Timotheus
render it probable that this arrest took place not later than [4] mid-
winter, and the authorities may have thought to gratify the Emperor
by forwarding so important a criminal immediately to Rome.   It is
true that the navigation of the Mediterranean was in those times
suspended during the winter; but this rule would apply only to

[1] See Wordsworth's *Greece*, pp. 229–
232, where a map of Nicopolis will be
found, and an interesting description
of the ruins.   See also Leake's *Northern Greece*, vol. i. p. 178, and vol. iii.
p. 491; and Merivale's *Rome*, vol. iii.
pp. 327, 328.   In Bowen's *Mount Athos
and Epirus* (p. 211) there is also a
notice of its present desolate aspect.

[2] It may be asked, why was he
not arrested sooner, in Spain or Asia
Minor?   The explanation probably is,
that he had not before ventured so
near Italy as Nicopolis.

[3] The law required that a prisoner
should be tried by the magistrates
within whose jurisdiction the offence
was alleged to have been committed;

therefore, a prisoner accused of conspiring to set fire to Rome must be
tried at Rome.   There can be no doubt
that this charge must have formed one
part of any accusation brought against
St. Paul, after 64 A.D.   Another part
(as we have suggested below) may
have been the charge of introducing a
religio nova et illicita.

[4] The reason for supposing this is,
that it leaves more time for the events
which intervened between St. Paul's
arrest and his death, which took place
(if in Nero's reign) not later than June.
If he had not been arrested till the
spring, we must crowd the occurrences
mentioned in the Second Epistle to
Timothy into a very short space.

longer voyages, and not to the short passage[1] from Apollonia to Brundusium. Hence, it is not unlikely that St. Paul may have arrived at Rome some time before spring.

In this melancholy journey he had but few friends to cheer him. Titus had reached Nicopolis, in obedience to his summons; and there were others, also, it would seem, in attendance on him; but they were scattered by the terror of his arrest. Demas forsook him, 'for love of this present world,'[2] and departed to Thessalonica; Crescens[3] went to Galatia on the same occasion. We are unwilling to suppose that Titus could have yielded to such unworthy fears, and may be allowed to hope that his journey to the neighbouring Dalmatia[4] was undertaken by the desire of St. Paul. Luke,[5] at any rate, remained faithful, accompanied his master once more over the wintry sea, and shared the dangers of his imprisonment at Rome.

This imprisonment was evidently more severe than it had been five years before. Then, though necessarily fettered to his military guard, he had been allowed to live in his own lodgings, and had been suffered to preach the Gospel to a numerous company who came to hear him. Now, he is not only chained, but treated 'as a malefactor.'[6] His friends, indeed, are still suffered to visit him in his confinement, but we hear nothing of his preaching. It is dangerous and difficult[7] to seek his prison; so perilous to show any public sympathy with him, that no Christian ventures to stand by him in the court of justice.[8] And as the final stage of his trial approaches, he looks forward to death as his certain sentence.[9]

This alteration in the treatment of St. Paul exactly corresponds with that which the history of the times would have led us to expect. We have concluded that his liberation took place early in A.D. 63: he was therefore far distant from Rome when the first imperial persecution of Christianity broke out, in consequence of the great fire in the summer of the following year. Then first, as it appears, Christians were recognised as a distinct body, separate both from Jews and heathens; and their number must have been already very great at Rome, to account for the public notice attracted towards a sect whose members were, most of them, individually so obscure in social position.[10] When the alarm and indignation of the people was excited by the tremendous ruin of a conflagration, which burnt down almost half the city, it answered

[1] Even an army was transported across the Hadriatic by Cæsar, during the season of the 'Mare Clausum,' before the battle of Philippi. See also p 245.
[2] 2 Tim. iv. 10.
[3] Ibid.
[4] Ibid. See above, p. 470.
[5] 2 Tim. iv. 11.
[6] 2 Tim. ii. 9. According to the legends of the Mediæval Church, St. Paul was imprisoned in the Mamertine prison, together with St. Peter; see the Martyrology of Baronius, under March 14. But there is no early authority for this story, which seems

irreconcilable with the fact that Onesiphorus, Claudia, Linus, Pudens, &c., had free access to St. Paul during his imprisonment. It seems more likely [see 2 Tim. i. 16] that he was again under military custody, though of a severer nature than that of his former imprisonment. We have given a view of the Tullianum, or dungeon of the Mamertine prison, p. 265. Very full details will be found in Sir W. Gell's work on Rome and its neighbourhood.
[7] 2 Tim. i. 16.
[8] 2 Tim. iv. 16.
[9] 2 Tim. iv. 6–8.
[10] 1 Cor. i. 26.

the purpose of Nero (who was accused of causing the fire) to avert the rage of the populace from himself to the already hated votaries of a new religion. Tacitus[1] describes the success of this expedient, and relates the sufferings of the Christian martyrs, who were put to death with circumstances of the most aggravated cruelty. Some were crucified; some disguised in the skins of beasts, and hunted to death with dogs; some were wrapped in robes impregnated with inflammable materials, and set on fire at night, that they might serve to illuminate the circus of the Vatican and the gardens of Nero, where this diabolical monster exhibited the agonies of his victims to the public, and gloated over them himself, mixing among the spectators in the costume of a charioteer. Brutalised as the Romans were, by the perpetual spectacle of human combats in the amphitheatre, and hardened by popular prejudice against the 'atheistical' sect, yet the tortures of the victims excited even their compassion. 'A very great multitude,' as Tacitus informs us, perished in this manner; and it appears from his statement that the mere fact of professing Christianity was accounted sufficient[2] to jus-

---

[1] Tac. *Ann.* xv. 44. We give the well-known passage from a popular translation:—' But neither these religious ceremonies, nor the liberal donations of the prince, could efface from the minds of men the prevailing opinion, that Rome was set on fire by his own orders. The infamy of that horrible transaction still adhered to him. In order, if possible, to remove the imputation, he determined to transfer the guilt to others. For this purpose he punished, with exquisite torture, a race of men detested for their evil practices, by vulgar appellation commonly called Christians. The name was derived from Christ, who, in the reign of Tiberius, suffered under Pontius Pilate, the procurator of Judæa. By that event the sect, of which he was the founder, received a blow which, for a time, checked the growth of a dangerous superstition; but it revived soon after, and spread with recruited vigour, not only in Judæa, the soil that gave it birth, but even in the city of Rome, the common sink into which everything infamous and abominable flows like a torrent from all quarters of the world. Nero proceeded with his usual artifice. He found a set of profligate and abandoned wretches, who were induced to confess themselves guilty, and, on the evidence of such men, a number of Christians were convicted, not, indeed, upon clear evidence of their having set the city on fire, but rather on account of their sullen hatred of the whole Roman race. They were put to death with exquisite cruelty,

and to their sufferings Nero added mockery and derision. Some were covered with the skins of wild beasts, and left to be devoured by dogs; others were nailed to the cross; numbers were burnt alive; and many, covered over with inflammable matter, were lighted up, when the day declined, to serve as torches during the night. For the convenience of seeing this tragic spectacle, the Emperor lent his own gardens. He added the sports of the circus, and assisted in person, sometimes driving a curricle, and occasionally mixing with the rabble in his coachman's dress. At length the cruelty of these proceedings filled every breast with compassion. Humanity relented in favour of the Christians. The manners of that people were, no doubt, of a pernicious tendency, and their crimes called for the hand of justice; but it was evident that they fell a sacrifice, not for the public good, but to glut the rage and cruelty of one man only.'

[2] It was criminal, according to the Roman law, to introduce into Rome any *religio nova et illicita.* Yet, practically, this law was seldom enforced, as we see by the multitude of foreign superstitions continually introduced into Rome, and the occasional and feeble efforts of the Senate or the Emperor to enforce the law. Moreover, the punishment of those who offended against it seems only to have been expulsion from the city, unless their offence had been accompanied by aggravating circumstances. It was not, therefore, under this law that the

tify their execution; the whole body of Christians being considered as involved in the crime of firing the city. This, however, was in the first excitement which followed the fire, and even then, probably but few among those who perished were Roman citizens.[1] Since that time some years had passed, and now a decent respect would be paid to the forms of law, in dealing with one who, like St. Paul, possessed the privilege of citizenship. Yet we can quite understand that a leader of so abhorred a sect would be subjected to a severe imprisonment.

We have no means of knowing the precise charge now made against the Apostle. He might certainly be regarded as an offender against the law which prohibited the propagation of a new and illicit religion (*religio nova et illicita*) among the citizens of Rome. But, at this period, one article of accusation against him must have been the more serious charge, of having instigated the Roman Christians to their supposed act of incendiarism, before his last departure from the capital. It appears that 'Alexander the brass-founder' (2 Tim. iv. 14) was either one of his accusers, or, at least, a witness against him. If this was the same with the Jewish[2] Alexander of Ephesus (Acts xix. 33), it would be probable that his testimony related to the former charge. But there is no proof that these two Alexanders were identical. We may add, that the employment of Informer (*delator*) was now become quite a profession at Rome, and that there would be no lack of accusations against an unpopular prisoner as soon as his arrest became known.

Probably no long time elapsed, after St. Paul's arrival, before his cause came on for hearing. The accusers, with their witnesses, would be already on the spot; and on this occasion he was not to be tried by the Emperor in person,[3] so that another cause of delay,[4] which was often interposed by the carelessness or indolence of the Emperor, would be removed. The charge now alleged against him, probably fell under the cognisance of the City Præfect (Præfectus Urbi), whose jurisdiction daily encroached, at this period, on that of the ancient magistracies.[5] For we must remember that, since the

Christians were executed; and, when Suetonius tells us that they were punished as professors of a *superstitio nova et malefica*, we must interpret his asssertion in accordance with the more detailed and accurate statement of Tacitus, who expressly says that the victims of the Neronian persecution were condemned on the charge of *arson*. Hence the extreme cruelty of their punishment, and especially the setting them on fire.

[1] No doubt most of the victims who perished in the Neronian persecution were foreigners, slaves, or freedmen; we have already seen how large a portion of the Roman Church was of Jewish extraction (see p. 497, n. 8). It was illegal to subject a Roman citizen to the ignominious punishments mentioned by Tacitus; but probably Nero would not have regarded this privilege in the case of freedmen, although by their emancipation they had become Roman citizens. And we know that the Jewish population of Rome had, for the most part, a Servile origin; see pp. 299 and 679.

[2] An Alexander is also mentioned, 1 Tim. i. 20, as a heretic, who had been excommunicated by St. Paul. This is, probably, the same person with the Alexander of 2 Tim. iv. 14; and if so, motives of personal malice would account for his conduct.

[3] Clemens Romanus says that Paul, on this occasion, was tried 'before the presiding magistrates.' Had the Emperor presided, he would probably have said 'before Cæsar.'

[4] See above, pp. 684-686.

[5] The authority for this, and for all

time of Augustus, a great though silent change had taken place in the Roman system of criminal procedure. The ancient method, though still the regular and legal system, was rapidly becoming obsolete in practice. Under the Republic, a Roman citizen could theoretically be tried on a criminal charge only by the Sovereign People; but the judicial power of the people was delegated, by special laws, to certain bodies of Judges, superintended by the several Prætors. Thus one Prætor presided at trials for homicide, another at trials for treason, and so on.[1] But the presiding Magistrate did not give the sentence; his function was merely to secure the legal formality of the proceedings. The judgment was pronounced by the Judices, a large body of judges (or rather jurors), chosen (generally by lot) from amongst the senators or knights, who gave their vote, by ballot, for acquittal or condemnation. But under the Empire this ancient system, though not formally abolished, was gradually superseded. The Emperors from the first claimed supreme[2] judicial authority, both civil and criminal. And this jurisdiction was exercised not only by themselves, but by the delegates whom they appointed. It was at first delegated chiefly to the Præfect of the city; and though causes might, up to the beginning of the second century, be tried by the Prætors in the old way, yet this became more and more unusual. In the reign of Nero it was even dangerous for an accuser to prosecute an offender in the Prætor's instead of the Præfect's court.[3] Thus the trial of criminal charges was transferred from a jury of independent Judices to a single magistrate appointed by a despot, and controlled only by a Council of Assessors, to whom he was not bound to attend.

Such was the court before which St. Paul was now cited. We have an account of the first hearing of the cause from his own pen. He writes thus to Timotheus immediately after :—'When I was first heard in my defence, no man stood by me, but all forsook me,—I pray that it be not laid to their charge.—Nevertheless the Lord Jesus stood by me, and strengthened my heart; that by me the proclamation of the Glad-tidings might be accomplished in full measure, and that all the Gentiles might hear; and I was delivered out of the lion's mouth.' We see from this statement, that it was dangerous even to appear in public as the friend or adviser of the Apostle. No advocate would venture to plead his cause, no *pro-*

the points of Roman Law referred to in this chapter, is given in our larger editions.

[1] This was the system of *Quæstiones Perpetuæ*.

[2] The origin of this jurisdiction is not so clear as that of their *appellate* jurisdiction, which we have explained above. Some writers hold that the Emperor assumed the supreme judicial power as an incident of his quasi-dictatorial authority. Others think that it was theoretically based upon a revival of that summary jurisdiction which was formerly (in the earliest ages of the Commonwealth) exercised by the great

magistrates whose functions were now concentrated in the Emperor. Others again refer it to the Tribunitian power conferred upon the Emperor, which was extended (as we have seen) so as to give him a supreme appellate jurisdiction; and by virtue of which he might perhaps bring before his tribunal any cause in the first instance, which would ultimately come under his judgement by appeal.

[3] Tacitus relates that Valerius Ponticus was banished under Nero, because he had brought some accused persons before the Prætor instead of the Præfect. *Ann.* xiv. 41.

curator[1] to aid him in arranging the evidence, no *patronus* (such as he might have found, perhaps, in the powerful Æmilian[2] house) to appear as his supporter, and to deprecate,[3] according to ancient usage, the severity of the sentence. But he had a more powerful intercessor, and a wiser advocate, who could never leave him nor forsake him. The Lord Jesus was always near him, but now was felt almost visibly present in the hour of his need.

From the above description we can realise in some measure the external features of his last trial. He evidently intimates that he spoke before a crowded audience, so that ' all the Gentiles might hear;' and this corresponds with the supposition, which historically we should be led to make, that he was tried in one of those great basilicas which stood in the Forum. Two of the most celebrated of these edifices were called the Pauline Basilicas, from the well-known Lucius Æmilius Paulus, who had built one of them and restored the other. It is not improbable that the greatest man who ever bore the Pauline name was tried in one of these. From specimens which still exist, as well as from the descriptions of Vitruvius, we have an accurate knowledge of the character of these halls of justice. They were rectangular buildings, consisting of a central nave and two aisles, separated from the nave by rows of columns. At one end of the nave was the tribune,[4] in the centre of which was placed the magistrate's curule chair of ivory, elevated on a platform called the tribunal. Here also sat the Council of Assessors, who advised the Præfect upon the law, though they had no voice in the judgment. On the sides of the tribune were seats for distinguished persons, as well as for parties engaged in the proceedings. Fronting the presiding magistrate stood the prisoner, with his accusers and his advocates. The public was admitted into the remainder of the nave and aisles (which was railed off from the portion devoted to the judicial proceedings); and there were also galleries along the whole length of the aisles, one for men, the other for women.[5] The aisles were roofed over; as was the tribune. The nave was originally left open to the sky. The basilicas were buildings of great size, so that a vast multitude of spectators was always present at any trial which excited public interest.

Before such an audience it was, that Paul was now called to speak in his defence. His earthly friends had deserted him, but his Heavenly Friend stood by him. He was strengthened by the

[1] The procurator performed the functions of our attorney.

[2] We have already (p. 123) suggested the possibility of a connection of clientship between Paul's family and this noble Roman house.

[3] It was the custom, both in the Greek and Roman courts of justice, to allow the friends of the accused to intercede for him, and to endeavour by their prayers and tears to move the feelings of his judges. This practice was gradually limited under the Imperial régime.

[4] The features of the basilica will be best understood by the ground-plan of that of Pompeii, which is given at the end of Chap. XXV. Here the tribune is rectangular; in others it was semicircular.

[5] Pliny gives a lively description of the scene presented by a basilica at an interesting trial: 'A dense ring, many circles deep, surrounded the scene of trial. They crowded close to the judgment-seat itself, and even in the upper part of the basilica both men and women pressed close in the eager desire to see (which was easy) and to hear (which was difficult).' Plin. *Ep.* vi. 33.

power of Christ's Spirit, and pleaded the cause not of himself only, but of the Gospel. He spoke of Jesus, of His death and His resurrection, so that all the Heathen multitude might hear. At the same time, he successfully defended himself from the first[1] of the charges brought against him, which perhaps accused him of conspiring with the incendiaries of Rome. He was delivered from the immediate peril, and saved from the ignominious and painful death[2] which might have been his doom had he been convicted on such a charge.

He was now remanded to prison to wait for the second stage of his trial. It seems that he himself expected this not to come on so soon as it really did; or, at any rate, he did not think the final decision would be given till the following[3] winter, whereas it actually took place about midsummer. Perhaps he judged from the long delay of his former trial; or he may have expected (from the issue of his first hearing) to be again acquitted on a second charge, and to be convicted on a third. He certainly did not expect a final acquittal, but felt no doubt that the cause would ultimately result in his condemnation. We are not left to conjecture the feelings with which he awaited this consummation; for he has himself expressed them in that sublime strain of triumphant hope which is familiar to the memory of every Christian, and which has nerved the hearts of a thousand martyrs. 'I am now ready to be offered, and the time of my departure is at hand. I have fought the good fight, I have finished my course, I have kept the faith. Henceforth is laid up for me the crown of righteousness, which the Lord, the righteous judge, shall give me in that day.' He saw before him, at a little distance, the doom of an unrighteous magistrate, and the sword of a bloodstained executioner; but he appealed to the sentence of a juster Judge, who would soon change the fetters of the criminal into the wreath of the conqueror; he looked beyond the transitory present; the tribunal of Nero faded from his sight; and the vista was closed by the judgment-seat of Christ.

Sustained by such a blessed and glorious hope—knowing, as he did, that nothing in heaven or in earth could separate him from the love of Christ—it mattered to him but little, if he was destitute of earthly sympathy. Yet still, even in these last hours, he clung to the friendships of early years; still the faithful companionship of

[1] The hypothesis of an aquittal on the first charge agrees best with the being *delivered from the mouth of the lion* (2 Tim. iv. 17). We have seen that it was Nero's practice (and therefore, we may suppose, the practice of the Præfects under Nero) to hear and decide each branch of the accusation separately (Suet. *Ner.* 15, before cited). Had the trial taken place under the ancient system, we might have supposed an *Ampliatio,* which took place when the judices held the evidence insufficient, and gave the verdict *Non liquet,* in which case the trial was commenced *de novo;* but Geib has shown that under the imperial system the practice of *Ampliatio* was discontinued. So also was the *Comperendinatio* abolished, by which certain trials were formerly divided into a *prima actio* and *secunda actio.* We cannot therefore agree with Wieseler in supposing this 'first defence' to indicate an *Ampliatio* or *Comperendinatio.*

[2] See the account given by Tacitus (above quoted) of the punishment of the supposed incendaries. In the case of such a crime, probably, even a Roman citizen would not have been exempted from such punishments.

[3] 2 Tim. iv. 21.

Luke consoled him, in the weary hours of constrained inactivity, which, to a temper like his, must have made the most painful part of imprisonment.　Luke was the only one[1] of his habitual attendants who now remained to minister to him: his other companions had left him, probably before his arrival at Rome.　But one friend from Asia, Onesiphorus[2] had diligently sought him out, and visited him in his prison, undeterred by the fear of danger or of shame. And there were others, some of them high in station, who came to receive from the chained malefactor blessings infinitely greater than all the favours of the Emperor of the world.　Among these were Linus, afterwards a bishop of the Roman Church; Pudens, the son of a senator; and Claudia, his bride, perhaps the daughter of a British king.[3]　But however he may have valued these more recent friends, their society could not console him for the absence of one far dearer to him: he longed with a paternal longing to see once more the face of Timotheus, his beloved son.　The disciple who had so long ministered to him with filial affection might still (he hoped) arrive in time to receive his parting words, and be with him in his dying hour.　But Timotheus was far distant, in Asia Minor, exercising apparently the same function with which he had before been temporarily invested.　Thither then he wrote to him, desiring him to come with all speed to Rome, yet feeling how uncertain it was whether he might not arrive too late.　He was haunted also by another fear, far more distressing.　Either from his experience of the desertion of other friends, or from some signs of timidity which Timotheus[4] himself had shown, he doubted whether he might not shrink from the perils which would surround

---

[1] 2 Tim. iv. 11.　If we suppose Tychicus the bearer of the Second Epistle to Timothy (2 Tim. iv. 12), he also would have been with St. Paul at Rome, till he was despatched to Ephesus.

[2] 2 Tim. i. 16.

[3] For the evidence of these assertions, see note on 2 Tim. iv. 21.　We may take this opportunity of saying that the tradition of St. Paul's visit to Britain rests on no sufficient authority.　Probably all that can be said in its favour will be found in the Tracts of the late Bishop Burgess on the origin of the ancient British Church.　See especially pp. 21–54, 77–83, and 108–120.

[4] We cannot say with certainty where Timotheus was at this time ; as there is no direct mention of his locality in the Second Epistle.　It would seem, at first sight, probable that he was still at Ephesus, from the salutation to Priscilla and Aquila, who appear to have principally resided there.　Still this is not decisive, since we know that they were occasional residents both at Rome and Corinth, and Aquila was himself a native of Pontus, where he

and Timotheus may perhaps have been. Again, it is difficult, on the hypothesis of Timotheus being at Ephesus, to account for 2 Tim. iv. 12, 'Tychicus I sent to Ephesus,' which Timotheus need not have been told if himself at Ephesus.　Also, it appears strange that St Paul should have told Timotheus that he had left Trophimus sick at Miletus, if Timotheus was himself at Ephesus, within thirty miles of Miletus. Yet both these objections may be explained away, as we have shown in the notes on 2 Tim. iv. 12, and 2 Tim. iv. 20.　The message about bringing the articles from Troas shows only that Timotheus was in a place whence the road to Rome lay through Troas ; and this would agree either with Ephesus, or Pontus, or any other place in the north or north-west of Asia Minor.　It is most probable that Timotheus was not fixed to any one spot, but employed in the general superintendence of the Pauline Churches throughout Asia Minor.　This hypothesis agrees best with his designation as an *Evangelist* (2 Tim. iv. 5), a term equivalent to *itinerant missionary.*

him in the city of Nero. He therefore urges on him very emphatically the duty of boldness in Christ's cause, of stedfastness under persecution, and of taking his share in the sufferings of the Saints. And, lest he should be prevented from giving him his last instructions face to face, he impresses on him, with the earnestness of a dying man, the various duties of his Ecclesiastical office, and especially that of opposing the heresies which now threatened to destroy the very essence of Christianity. But no summary of its contents can give any notion of the pathetic tenderness and deep solemnity of this Epistle.

THE SECOND EPISTLE TO TIMOTHEUS.[1]

Salutation. PAUL, an Apostle of Jesus Christ by the will of God i. 1 —sent forth [2] to proclaim the promise of the life which is in Christ Jesus—TO TIMOTHEUS MY BELOVED SON. 2 Grace, Mercy, and Peace from God our Father. and Christ Jesus our Lord.

Timotheus is reminded of his past history, and exhorted to perseverance and courage by the hope of immortality. I thank God (whom I worship, as [3] did my fore- 3 fathers, with a pure conscience) whenever [4] I make mention of thee, as I do continually, in my prayers night and day. And I long to see thee, remembering 4 thy [parting] tears, that I may be filled with joy. For I have been [5] reminded of thy undissembled faith, 5 which dwelt first in thy grandmother Lois, and thy mother Eunice, and (I am persuaded) dwells in thee also. Wherefore I call thee to remembrance, that 6 thou mayest stir up the gift of God, which is in thee by the laying on of my [6] hands. For God gave us not 7

[1] For the date of this Epistle, see the Appendix.

[2] 'An Apostle according to the promise of life.' See note on Tit. i. 1.

[3] Some interpreters have found a difficulty here, as though it were inconsistent with St. Paul's bitter repentance for the sins he had committed in the time of his Judaism. (Cf. 1 Tim. i. 13.) But there is no inconsistency. All that is said here is, that the *worship* of God was handed down to St. Paul from his forefathers, or, in other words, that his religion was hereditary. This is exactly the view taken of the religion of *all* converted Jews in Rom. xi. 23, 24, 28. Compare also 'the God of my fathers' (Acts xxiv. 14), and 'I have always lived a conscientious life' (Acts xxiii. 1). These latter passages remind us that the topic was one on which St. Paul had probably insisted, in his recent defence; and this ac-

counts for its parenthetical introduction here.

[4] Literally, *as the mention which I make of thee in my prayers is continual.*

[5] '*Have been* reminded.' Such is the reading of the best MSS. Perhaps a message or other incident had reminded St. Paul of some proof which Timotheus had given of the sincerity of his faith (as Bengel thinks); or, still more probably, he was reminded of the faith of Timotheus by its contrast with the cowardice of Demas and others. He mentions it here obviously as a motive to encourage him to persevere in courageous stedfastness.

[6] The grace of God required for any particular office in the early Church, was conferred after prayer and the laying on of hands. This imposition of hands was repeated whenever any one was appointed to a new office or commission. The reference here may,

a spirit of cowardice, but a spirit of power and love
i. 8 and self-restraint.[1] Be not therefore ashamed of the
testimony of our Lord, nor of me His prisoner; but
share the affliction [2] of them who publish the Glad-
9 tidings, according to the power of God. For He saved
us, and called us with a holy calling, not dealing
with us according to our own works, but according
to His own purpose and grace, which was bestowed
10 upon us in Christ Jesus before eternal times,[3] but
is now made manifest by the appearing of our Saviour
Jesus Christ, who has put an end to death, and
brought life and immortality from darkness into
11 light; by the Glad-tidings, whereunto I was appointed
herald and apostle, and teacher of the Gentiles.
12 Which also is the cause of these sufferings that I now
endure; nevertheless I am not ashamed; for I know
in whom I have trusted, and I am persuaded that He
is able to guard the treasure [4] which I have committed
to Him, even unto that day.

13   Hold fast the pattern of sound [5] words which thou
hast heard from me, in the faith and love which is in
14 Christ Jesus.   That goodly treasure which is committed to thy charge, guard by the Holy Spirit who
dwelleth in us.

Exhortation to fulfil his commission faithfully.

15   Thou already knowest that I was abandoned [6] by
all the Asiatics, among whom are Phygellus and
16 Hermogenes.   The Lord give mercy to the house of

Conduct of certain Asiatic Christians at Rome.

therefore, be to the original 'ordination'
of Timotheus, or to his appointment to
the superintendence of the Ephesian
Church.   See p. 343, and compare Acts
viii. 18, and 1 Tim. iv. 14; also p. 207,
n. 1.
    [1] *Self-restraint* would control the
passion of *fear*.
    [2] Literally, *share affliction for the
Glad-tidings*.   The dative used as in
Phil. i. 27.
    [3] ' Before eternal times ' (which
phrase also occurs in Titus i. 2) appears to mean the period of the Jewish
(including the Patriarchal) dispensation.   The grace of Christ was *virtually* bestowed on mankind in the
Patriarchal covenant, though only
made manifest in the Gospel.
    [4] 'That which I have committed
unto Him.'   It is strange that so acute
an interpreter as De Wette should
maintain that this expression must
necessarily mean the same thing as
' that which is committed unto thee '

in verse 14.   Supposing St. Paul to
have said ' God will keep the trust
committed to Him; do thou keep the
trust committed to thee,' it would not
follow that the *same* trust was meant
in each case.   Paul had committed
himself, his soul and body, his true
life, to God's keeping; this was the
treasure which he trusted to God's care.
On the other hand, the treasure committed to the charge of Timotheus was
the ecclesiastical office entrusted to
him.   (Compare 1 Tim. vi. 20.)
    [5] *Sound words.* The want of the
article shows that this expression had
become almost a technical expression
at the date of the Pastoral Epistles.
    [6] This appears to refer to the con-
duct of certain Christians belonging to
the province of Asia, who deserted St.
Paul at Rome when he needed their
assistance.   ' They in Asia ' is used instead of ' they of Asia,' because these
persons had probably now returned
home,

Onesiphorus; [1] for he often refreshed me, and was not ashamed of my chain; [2] but when he was in Rome, i. 17 sought me out very diligently and found me. The 18 Lord grant unto him that he may find mercy from the Lord in that day. And all his services [3] at Ephesus, thou knowest better [4] than I.

Duty of Timotheus in Church government. Thou, therefore, my son, strengthen thy heart [5] ii. 1 with the grace that is in Christ Jesus. And those 2 things which thou hast heard from me attested [6] by many witnesses, deliver into the keeping of faithful men, who shall be able to teach others in their turn. [7]

He is exhorted not to shrink from suffering. Take thy [8] share in suffering, as a good soldier of 3 Jesus Christ. The soldier when [9] on service abstains 4 from entangling himself in the business of life, that he may please his commander. And again, the 5 wrestler does not win the crown, unless he wrestles lawfully. [10] The husbandman who toils must share the 6 fruits of the ground before [11] the idler. Consider what 7 I say; for the Lord will [12] give thee understanding in all things. Remember that Jesus Christ, of the seed [13] 8

[1] An undesigned coincidence should be observed here, which is not noticed by Paley. Blessings are invoked on the *house* of Onesiphorus, *not on himself*; and in verse 18 a hope is expressed that he may find mercy *at the last day*. This seems to show that Onesiphorus was dead; and so, in iv. 19, greetings are addressed *not to himself, but to his house.*

[2] 'My chain.' Hence we see that St. Paul was, in this second imprisonment, as in the first, under Custodia Militaris, and therefore bound to the soldier who guarded him by a chain. See above, pp. 612, 613.

[3] 'Unto me' is omitted by the best MSS.

[4] *Better,* because Timotheus had been more constantly resident at Ephesus than St. Paul.

[5] Compare Rom. iv. 20, and Eph. vi. 10.

[6] We agree with De Wette, Huther, and Wiesinger as to the construction here, but cannot agree with them in referring this passage to Timothy's ordination or baptism. The literal English must be, *those things which thou hast heard from me by the intervention of many witnesses,* which is surely equivalent to ' *by the attestation* of many witnesses.' In a similar way St. Paul appeals to the attestation of other witnesses in 1 Cor. xv. 3–7.

[7] The 'also' seems to have this meaning here.

[8] 'Take thy share in suffering.' This is according to the reading of the best MSS.

[9] This is the force of the present participle. Cf. Luke iii. 14.

[10] 'Lawfully.' See pp. 538, 539. The verb here used is not confined to *wrestling,* but includes the other exercises of the athletic contests also; but there is no English verb co-extensive with it. With this passage (ver. 3–6) compare 1 Cor. ix. 7.

[11] This is the sense of 'first.' The Authorised Version, and not its margin, is here correct.

[12] The future, not the optative, is the reading of the best MSS. De Wette and others object to this verse, that it is impossible to suppose that St. Paul would imagine Timotheus so dull of apprehension as not to comprehend such obvious metaphors. But they have missed the sense of the verse, which is not meant to enlighten the understanding of Timotheus as to the *meaning* of the metaphors, but as to the *personal application* of them.

[13] i.e. though a man in flesh and blood; therefore His resurrection is an encouragement to His followers to be fearless.

of David, is[1] raised from the dead, according to the
ii. 9 Glad-tidings which I proclaim.   Wherein I suffer
even unto chains, as a malefactor; nevertheless the
10 Word of God is bound by no chains.   Wherefore I
endure all for the sake of the chosen, that they also
may obtain the salvation which is in Christ Jesus,
11 with glory everlasting.   Faithful is the saying, '*For*[2]
if we have died with Him,[3] *we shall also live with Him;*
12 *if we suffer, we shall also reign with Him; if we deny*
Him, He also will deny us; if we be faithless, yet He
13 *abideth faithful; He cannot deny Himself.*'

14   Call men to remembrance of these things, and
adjure them before the Lord not to contend[4] about
words, with no profitable end, but for the subversion
15 of their hearers.   Be diligent to present thyself unto
God as one proved trustworthy[5] by trial, a workman
not to be ashamed, declaring the word of truth with-
16 out distortion.[6]   But avoid the discussions of pro-
17 fane babblers; for they will go farther and farther in
ungodliness, and their word will eat like a cancer.
18 Among whom are Hymenæus and Philetus; who concerning the truth have erred, for they say that the
resurrection is past[7] already, and overthrow the faith
of some.

19   Nevertheless the firm[8] foundation of God stands
unshaken, having this seal, ' 𝕮𝖍𝖊 𝕷𝖔𝖗𝖉 𝖐𝖓𝖊𝖜 𝖙𝖍𝖊𝖒 𝖙𝖍𝖆𝖙
𝖜𝖊𝖗𝖊 𝕳𝖎𝖘,'[9] and '*Let every one that nameth the name*

*He must op-
pose the false
teachers and
their immo-
ralities, and
carefully pre-
serve his own
purity.*

[1] Perfect, not aorist.

[2] This is another of those quotations so characteristic of the Pastoral
Epistles.   It appears to be taken from
a Christian hymn.   The Greek may be
easily sung to the music of one of the
ancient ecclesiastical chants.

[3] Rom. vi. 8, 'If we died with
Christ, we believe that we shall also
live with Him.'

[4] Compare 1 Tim. vi. 4.

[5] The meaning is, *tested and proved
worthy by trial.*   Cf. 2 Cor. xiii. 7.

[6] The verb used here (not found elsewhere in New Testament) means *to cut
straight.*   So in the LXX. 'righteousness cuts straight paths' (Prov. xi. 5).
The metaphor here, being connected
with the previous 'workman,' appears
to be taken from the work of a car-
penter.

[7] See p. 355.   In the larger editions
a passage is there quoted from Tertullian, which shows that the Gnostics
taught that the *Resurrection* was to be

understood of the rising of the soul from
the death of ignorance to the light of
knowledge.   There is nothing here to
render doubtful the date of this Epistle,
for we have already seen that even so
early as the First Epistle to Corinth,
there were heretics who denied the
resurrection of the dead.   Baur's view
— that the Pastoral Epistles were
written against Marcion — is inconsistent with the present passage; for
Marcion did *not* deny the resurrection
of the *dead,* but only the resurrection
of the *flesh.*   (See Tertull. *adv. Marcion.* v. 10.)

[8] The Authorised Version here violates the law of the article.

[9] Numbers xvi. 5 (LXX. with *Lord*
for *God*).   We must not translate the
verb '*knoweth,*' as in A. V.   The context of the passage, according to LXX.
(which differs from the present Hebrew text), is, '*Moses spake unto Core,
saying . . . The Lord knew them that
were His, and that were holy, and*

of the Lord depart from iniquity.' [1] But in a great ii. 20
house there are not [2] only vessels of gold and silver,
but also of wood and clay; and some for honour, 21
others for dishonour. If a man therefore purify himself from these, he shall be a vessel for honour, sanctified, and fitted for the master's use, being prepared
for every good work.

Flee the lusts of youth; [3] and follow righteousness, 22
faith, love, and peace with those who call on the Lord
out of a pure heart; but shun the disputations of the 23
foolish and ignorant, knowing that they breed strife;
and the bondsman of the Lord [4] ought not to strive, 24
but to be gentle towards all, skilful in teaching, patient
of wrong, instructing opponents with meekness; if 25
God perchance may give them repentance, that they
may attain the knowledge of the truth, and may escape,
restored, [5] to soberness, out of the snare of the Devil, [6] 26
by whom [7] they have been taken captive to do his
will.

Dangerous errors of the 'last days.' Know this, that in the last [8] days evil times shall iii. 1
come. For men shall be selfish, covetous, false boast- 2
ers, [9] haughty, blasphemous, disobedient to parents,
ungrateful, unholy, without natural affection, ruthless, 3
calumnious, incontinent, merciless, haters of the good,

brought them near unto Himself; and whom He chose unto Himself, He brought near unto Himself.'

[1] This quotation is not from the Old Testament; Isaiah lii. 11 is near it in sentiment, but can scarcely be referred to, because it is quoted exactly at 2 Cor. vi. 17. The MSS. read *Lord* instead of the *Christ* of T. R.

[2] The thought here is the same as that expressed in the parable of the fishes and of the tares,—viz. that the visible church will never be perfect. We are reminded of Rom. ix. 21, by the ' vessels for dishonour.'

[3] Compare 1 Tim. iii. 2, and the remarks upon the age of Timotheus in the Essay in the Appendix on the date of these Epistles.

[4] *Lord,* viz. the Lord Jesus. Compare 'bondsman of Christ,' 1 Cor. vii. 22.

[5] ' *Restored* to soberness.' See 1 Cor. xv. 34.

[6] This expression appears to be used here, and in Eph. iv. 27, and Eph. vi. 11, for *the Devil,* who is elsewhere called 'Satan' by St. Paul. In the Gospels and Acts the two expressions are used with nearly equal frequency.

[7] The interpretation of this last clause is disputable. The construction is awkward, and there is a difficulty in referring the two pronouns to the same subject; but De Wette shows that this is admissible by a citation from Plato.

[8] This phrase (used without the article, as having become a familiar expression) generally denotes the termination of the Mosaic dispensation: see Acts ii. 17; 1 Pet. i. 5, 20; Heb. i. 2. Thus the expression generally denotes (in the Apostolic age) the 'time present; but here it points to a future immediately at hand, which is however, blended with the present (see ver. 6, 8), and was, in fact, the end of the Apostolic age. Compare 1 John ii. 18. ' it is the last hour.' The *long duration* of this last period of the world's development was not revealed to the Apostles; they expected that their Lord's return would end it, in their own generation; and thus His words were fulfilled, that none should foresee the time of His coming. (Matt. xxiv. 36.)

[9] Several of the classes of sinners here mentioned occur also Rom. i, 30,

ii. 4 treacherous, headlong with passion, blinded with
pride, lovers of pleasure rather than lovers of God;
5 having an outward form of godliness, but renouncing
6 its power. From such turn away. Of these are they
who creep into houses, and lead captive silly women,
7 laden with sins, led away by lusts of all kinds, perpetually learning, yet never able to attain the know-
8 ledge [1] of the truth. And as Iannes and Iambres,[2]
resisted Moses, so do these men resist the truth, being
corrupt in mind, and worthless [3] in all that concerns
9 the faith. But they [4] shall not advance farther, for
their folly shall be made openly manifest to all, as
was that of Iannes and Iambres.

10   But thou hast been the follower [5] of my teaching
and behaviour,[6] my resolution,[7] faith, patience, love,
11 and stedfastness; my persecutions and sufferings,
such as befel me at Antioch, Iconium, and Lystra.[8]
12 [Thou hast seen] what persecutions I endured; and
out of them all the Lord delivered me. Yea, and all
who determine to live a godly life in Christ Jesus,
13 will suffer persecution. But wicked men and impostors will advance from bad to worse, deceiving and
14 being deceived. But do thou continue in that which
was taught thee, and whereof thou wast persuaded;
knowing who were [9] thy teachers, and remembering
that from a child thou hast known the Holy Scrip-
15 tures, which are able to make thee wise unto salva-
16 tion, by the faith which is in Christ Jesus. All
Scripture is inspired by God, and may profitably be
used for teaching,[10] for confutation,[11] for correction,[12]

Exhortation to be stedfast in Paul's doctrine.

---

[1] For the meaning of this word (cf. above, ii. 25), see Rom. x. 2, and 1 Cor. xiii. 12.

[2] These, as we find in the Targum of Jonathan, were the traditional names of the Egyptian sorcerers who opposed Moses.

[3] *Worthless*; see Tit. i. 16, and note.

[4] It has been thought that this 'they shall not advance farther' contradicts the assertion in ii. 16, 'they will go farther and farther in ungodliness;' but there is no contradiction, for the present passage speaks of *outward success*, the former of *inward deterioration*. Impostors will usually go on *from bad to worse* (as it is said just below, v. 13), and yet their success in deceiving others is generally soon ended by detection.

[5] This verb cannot be accurately translated '*hast fully known*' (Author-ised Version), but its meaning is not very different. Chrysostom explains it, ' of these things thou art the wit-ness.'

[6] In this meaning the word is found in LXX.

[7] Compare Acts xi. 23.

[8] It has been before remarked how appropriate this reference is. See p. 156.

[9] This is plural in the best MSS.

[10] St. Paul frequently uses the Old Testament for *teaching*, i.e. to enforce or illustrate his doctrine; e.g. Rom. i. 17.

[11] The numerous quotations from the Old Testament, in the Romans and Ga-latians, are mostly examples of its use for *confutation*.

[12] The word means *the setting right of that which is wrong*. The Old Testa-

and for righteous discipline;[1] that the man of God iii.1 may be fully prepared, and thoroughly furnished for every good work.

I[2] adjure thee before God and Jesus Christ, who is iv. about to judge the living and the dead—I adjure thee by His appearing and His kingdom—proclaim the 2 tidings, be urgent in season and out of season, convince, rebuke, exhort, with all forbearance and perseverance in teaching. For a time will come when they 3 will not endure the sound doctrine, but according to their own inclinations they will heap up for themselves teachers upon teachers, to please their itching ears. And they will turn away their ears from the 4 truth, and turn aside to fables.

But thou in all things be sober,[3] endure affliction, 5 do the work of an evangelist,[4] accomplish thy ministration in full measure. For I am now ready[5] to be 6 offered, and the time of my departure is at hand. I 7 have fought[6] the good fight, I have finished my[7] course, I have kept the faith. Henceforth is laid up 8 for me the crown of righteousness, which the Lord, the righteous[8] judge, shall give me in that day; and not to me only, but to all who love His appearing.

Do thy utmost to come to me speedily; for Demas 9 has forsaken me, for love of this present world, and has departed to Thessalonica;[9] Crescens is gone to 10 Galatia, Titus to Dalmatia; Luke alone is with me. 11

ment is applied to this purpose by St. Paul in 1 Cor. xiv. 21, 1 Cor. x. 1–10, and, generally, wherever he applies it to enforce precepts of morality.

[1] 'Chastisement that is in righteousness.' The word used here has the meaning of *chastisement* or *discipline*; compare Heb. xii. 7. Thus the Old Testament is applied in 1 Cor. v. 13.

[2] The best MSS. omit *therefore* and *Lord*, and read *'and'* instead of *'at'* in this verse.

[3] Not *'watch,'* as in A. V.

[4] Compare Eph. iv. 11. And see p. 342.

[5] Literally, *I am already in the very act of being poured out as a sacrificial offering.* Compare Phil. ii. 17.

[6] It is impossible to translate this fully in English. It is not strictly correct to render it 'I have fought the *fight,'* and seems to introduce a new metaphor. The noun means *a contest for a prize,* and the metaphor is taken from the Greek foot-races. *I*

have *run the good race* would be perhaps more exact. The literal English is, *I have completed the glorious contest.* See pp. 538–540 above, and 1 Tim. vi. 12.

[7] Strictly, *the course marked out for the race.* This expression occurs only in two other places in the New Testament, both being in speeches of St. Paul.

[8] 'The *righteous* Judge' contrasted with the *unrighteous* judge, by whose sentence he was soon to be condemned.

[9] Demas is mentioned as a 'fellow-labourer,' at Rome with St.Paul,Philem. 24, and joined with Luke, Col. iv. 14. Nothing further is known of him. Crescens is not mentioned elsewhere. In saying here that he was deserted by all but Luke, St. Paul speaks of his own companions and attendants; he had still friends among the Roman Christians who visited him (iv. 21), though they were afraid to stand by him at his trial.

v. 12 Take Mark [1] and bring him with thee, for his services [2] are profitable to me; but Tychicus [3] I have sent to Ephesus.

13   When thou comest, bring with thee the case [4] which I left at Troas with Carpus, and the books, but especially the parchments.

14   Alexander, the brass-founder [5] charged [6] me with much evil in his declaration; the Lord shall [7] reward

Intelligence of the progress of Paul's trial.

15 him according to his works. Be thou also on thy guard against him, for he has been a great opponent

16 of my arguments.[8] When I was first heard in my defence [9] no man stood by me, but all forsook me;

17 (I pray that it be not laid to their charge). Nevertheless the Lord Jesus [10] stood by me, and strengthened my heart,[11] that by me the proclamation of the [12] Gladtidings might be accomplished in full measure, and that all the Gentiles might hear; and I was delivered

18 out of the lion's mouth.[13]   And the Lord shall deliver

---

[1] Mark was in Rome during a part of the former imprisonment, Col. iv. 10 ; Philem. 24.

[2] Not (as in A. V.) '*the* ministry.'

[3] If we suppose (see above, p. 771, note 4) that Timotheus was at Ephesus, we must conclude that Tychicus was the bearer of this Epistle, and the aorist, '*I send herewith,*' used according to the idiom of classical letter-writers.

[4] This word means either a travelling-case (for carrying clothes, books, &c.), or a travelling-cloak. The former seems the more probable meaning here, from the mention of *the books.*

[5] *Brass-founder.* Whether this Alexander is the same mentioned as put forward by the Jews at Ephesus in the theatre (Acts xix. 33), and as excommunicated by St. Paul (1 Tim. i. 20), we do not know. If these names all belong to the same person, he was probably of the Judaising faction. See above, p. 431.

[6] '*Charged me with,*' not '*did*' (A.V.). This verb, though of frequent occurrence in the New Testament (in the sense of *exhibit, display, manifest*), does not elsewhere occur in the same construction as here, with an accusative of the thing, and a dative of the person. The active form of the verb in classical Greek has a forensic sense,—viz. to *make a declaration against* ; and as the verb is here used in an active sense (the active *form* of it not occurring in the New Testament), we may not unnaturally suppose that it is so used here. At any rate, the literal English is, '*Alexander manifested many evil things against me.*'

[7] The MSS. are divided here between the optative and the future ; the latter is adopted by Lachmann, and has rather the greatest weight of MS. authority in its favour. We have, therefore, adopted it in the translation in the present edition. Yet it must be acknowledged that there are obvious reasons why the optative (if it was the original reading) should have been altered into the future.

[8] The 'arguments' here mentioned are probably those used by St. Paul in his defence.

[9] On this *first defence,* see above, pp. 769, 770. The ancient interpreters, Eusebius, Jerome, and others, understood St. Paul here to refer to his acquittal at the end of his *first imprisonment* at Rome, and his subsequent preaching in Spain ; but while we must acknowledge that the strength of the expressions *accomplished in full measure* and *all the Gentiles* are in favour of this view, we think that on the whole the context renders it unnatural.

[10] *The Lord,* viz. *Jesus.*

[11] Cf. Rom. iv. 20 ; Eph. vi. 10.

[12] *The proclamation,* i.e. *of the Gladtidings.*

[13] By *the lion's mouth* may be only meant *the imminence of the immediate*

me from every evil, and shall preserve me unto His heavenly kingdom. To Him be glory unto the ages of ages. Amen.

Salutations and personal intelligence.

Salute Prisca and Aquila, and the household of iv. 1 Onesiphorus.

Erastus[1] remained at Corinth; but Trophimus I 20 left sick at Miletus.

Do thy utmost to come before winter.   21

There salute thee, Eubulus, and Pudens, and Linus,[2] and Claudia,[3] and all the brethren.

Concluding benedictions.

The Lord Jesus Christ be with thy spirit. Grace 22 be with you[4] all.

peril; but it *may* mean that St. Paul, at his first hearing, established his right, as a Roman citizen, to be exempted from the punishment of exposure to wild beasts, which was inflicted during the Neronian persecution on so many Christians. On the historical inferences drawn from this verse, see the preceding remarks.

[1] This verse is an insuperable difficulty to those who suppose this Epistle written in the first imprisonment at Rome; since it implies a recent journey, in which St. Paul had passed through Miletus and Corinth. It has been also thought inexplicable that Paul should mention to Timotheus (who was at Ephesus, so near Miletus) the fact that Trophimus was left there. But many suppositions might be made to account for this. For instance, Trophimus may have only stayed a short time at Miletus, and come on by the first ship after his recovery. This was probably the first communication from St. Paul to Timotheus since they parted; and there would be nothing unnatural even if it mentioned a circumstance which Timotheus knew already. For example, *A.* at Calcutta writes to *B.* in London, ' *I left C. dangerously ill at Southampton,*' although he may be sure that *B.* has heard of *C*'s illness long before he can receive the letter.

[2] Linus is probably the same person who was afterwards bishop of Rome, and is mentioned by Irenæus and Eusebius.

[3] *Pudens and Claudia.* The following facts relating to these names are taken from an ingenious essay on the subject, entitled ' *Claudia and Pudens*, by J. Williams, M.A. (London, 1848).'

There are two epigrams of Martial,

the former of which describes the marriage of a distinguished Roman named *Pudens* to a foreign lady named *Claudia*, and the latter of which tells us that this *Claudia* was a *Briton*, and gives her the cognomen of *Rufina*. When the latter epigram was written, she had grown-up sons and daughters, but herself still retained the charms of youth. Both these epigrams were written during Martial's residence at Rome; and, therefore, their date must be between A.D. 66 and A.D. 100. The former of the two epigrams was not *published* till the reign of Domitian, but it may very probably have been *written* many years earlier. Thus the Claudia and Pudens of Martial *may* be the same with the Claudia and Pudens who are here seen as friends of St. Paul, in A.D. 68.

But, further, Tacitus mentions (*Agric.* 14) that certain territories in the south-east of Britain were given to a British king *Cogidunus* as a reward for his fidelity to Rome : this occurred about A.D. 52, while *Tiberius Claudius Nero*, commonly called *Claudius*, was emperor.

Again, in 1723, a marble was dug up at Chichester, with an inscription making mention of a British king bearing the title of *Tiberius Claudius Cogidubnus*. His daughter would, according to Roman usage, have been called *Claudia*. And in the same inscription we find the name *Pudens*. Other details are given in our larger editions. See the *Quarterly Review* for July 1858.

[4] *You* (not *thee*) is the reading of the best MSS., which also omit ' amen.' In English we are compelled to insert *all* here, in order to shew that *you* is plural,

We know not whether Timotheus was able to fulfil these last requests of the dying Apostle ; it is doubtful whether he reached Rome in time to receive his parting commands, and cheer his latest earthly sufferings. The only intimation which seems to throw any light on the question, is the statement in the Epistle to the Hebrews, that Timotheus had been liberated from imprisonment in Italy. If, as appears not improbable,[1] that Epistle was written shortly after St. Paul's death, it would be proved not only that the disciple fearlessly obeyed his master's summons, but that he actually shared his chains, though he escaped his fate. This, also, would lead us to think that he must have arrived before the execution of St. Paul, for otherwise there would be no reason to account for his being himself arrested in Rome ; since, had he come too late, he would naturally have returned to Asia at once, without attracting the notice of the authorities.

We may, therefore, hope that Paul's last earthly wish was fulfilled. Yet if Timotheus did indeed arrive before the closing scene, there could have been but a very brief interval between his coming and his master's death. For the letter which summoned him[2] could not have been despatched from Rome till the end of winter, and St. Paul's martyrdom took place in the middle of summer.[3] We have seen that this was sooner than he had expected ; but we have no record of the final stage of his trial, and cannot tell the cause of its speedy conclusion. We only know that it resulted in a sentence of capital punishment.

The privileges of Roman citizenship exempted St. Paul from the ignominious death of lingering torture, which had been lately inflicted on so many of his brethren. He was to die by decapitation ;[4] and he was led out to execution beyond the city walls, upon the road to Ostia, the port of Rome. As he issued forth from the gate, his eyes must have rested for a moment on that sepulchral pyramid which stood beside the road, and still stands unshattered, amid the wreck of so many centuries, upon the same spot. That spot was

---

[1] See the next chapter. If our Chronology be right, Timothy's escape would be accounted for by the death of Nero, which immediately followed that of St. Paul.

[2] Supposing the letter to have been despatched to Timotheus on the 1st of March, he could scarcely have arrived at Rome from Asia Minor before the end of May.

[3] Nero's death occurred in June, A.D. 68. Accepting therefore, as we do, the universal tradition that St. Paul was executed in the reign of Nero, his execution must have taken place not later than the beginning of June. We have endeavoured to show (in the article on the Pastoral Epistles in the Appendix) that this date satisfies all the necessary conditions.

[4] Such is the universal tradition ; see note 2 in page 782. The consti-

tutional mode of inflicting capital punishment on a Roman citizen was by the lictor's axe. The criminal was tied to a stake ; cruelly scourged with the rods, and then beheaded. See Livy, ii. 6. ' *Missi lictores ad sumendum supplicium, nudatos virgis cædunt, securique feriunt.*' Compare Juv. 8, '*legum prima securis.*' But the military mode of execution—decapitation by the sword—was more usual under Nero. Many examples may be found in Tacitus ; for instance, the execution of Subrius Flavius (Tac. *Ann.* xv. 67). The executioner was generally one of the *speculatores*, or imperial body-guards, under the command of a centurion, who was responsible for the execution of the sentence. See the interesting story in Seneca *de Irâ*, lib. i. cap. 16

then only. the burial-place of a single Roman; it is now the burial place of many Britons. The mausoleum of Caius Cestius[1] rises conspicuously amongst humbler graves, and marks the site where Papal Rome suffers her Protestant sojourners to bury their dead. In England and in Germany, in Scandinavia and in America, there are hearts which turn to that lofty cenotaph as the Sacred Point of their whole horizon; even as the English villager turns to the grey church tower, which overlooks the grave-stones of his kindred. Among the works of man, that pyramid is the only surviving witness of the martyrdom of St. Paul; and we may thus regard it with yet deeper interest, as a monument unconsciously erected by a pagan to the memory of a martyr. Nor let us think that they who lie beneath its shadow are indeed resting (as degenerate Italians fancy) in unconsecrated ground. Rather let us say, that a spot where the disciples of Paul's faith now sleep in Christ, so near the soil once watered by his blood, is doubly hallowed; and that their resting-place is most fitly identified with the last earthly journey and the dying glance of their own Patron Saint, the Apostle of the Gentiles.

As the martyr and his executioners passed on, their way was crowded with a motley multitude of goers and comers between the metropolis and its harbour—merchants hastening to superintend the unloading of their cargoes—sailors eager to squander the profits of their last voyage in the dissipations of the capital—officials of the government, charged with the administration of the Provinces, or the command of the legions on the Euphrates or the Rhine—Chaldean astrologers — Phrygian eunuchs — dancing-girls from Syria with their painted turbans—mendicant priests from Egypt howling for Osiris—Greek adventurers, eager to coin their national cunning into Roman gold—representatives of the avarice and ambition, the fraud and lust, the superstition and intelligence, of the Imperial world. Through the dust and tumult of that busy throng, the small troop of soldiers threaded their way silently, under the bright sky of an Italian midsummer. They were marching, though they knew it not, in a procession more truly triumphal than any they had ever followed, in the train of General or Emperor, along the Sacred Way. Their prisoner, now at last and for ever delivered from his captivity, rejoiced to follow his Lord 'without the gate.'[2] The place of execution was not far distant; and there the sword of the headsman[3] ended his long course of sufferings, and released

[1] The pyramid of Caius Cestius, which now marks the site of the Protestant burying-ground, was erected in, or just before, the reign of Augustus. It was outside the walls in the time of Nero, though within the present Aurelianic walls.

[2] Heb. xiii. 12, 'He suffered without the gate.'

[3] The death of St. Paul is recorded by his cotemporary Clement, in a passage already quoted; also by the Roman presbyter Caius (about 200 A.D.) (who alludes to the Ostian road as the site of St. Paul's martyrdom), by Tertullian, Eusebius (in the passage above cited), Jerome, and many subsequent writers. The statement of Caius is quoted by Eusebius. That of Jerome is the most explicit.

The statement that Paul was beheaded on the Ostian road agrees with the usage of the period, and with the tradition that his decapitation was by the sword not the axe. We have this tradition in Orosius and Lactantius. It was not uncommon to send prisoners whose death might attract too much notice in Rome, to some distance from the city, under a military escort, for

that heroic soul from that feeble body. Weeping friends took up his corpse, and carried it for burial to those subterranean labyrinths,[1] where, through many ages of oppression, the persecuted Church found refuge for the living, and sepulchres for the dead.

Thus died the Apostle, the Prophet, and the Martyr; bequeathing to the Church, in her government and her discipline, the legacy of his Apostolic labours; leaving his Prophetic words to be her living oracles; pouring forth his blood to be the seed of a thousand Martyrdoms. Thenceforth, among the glorious company of the Apostles, among the goodly fellowship of the Prophets, among the noble army of Martyrs, his name has stood pre-eminent. And wheresoever the Holy Church throughout all the world doth acknowledge God, there Paul of Tarsus is revered, as the great teacher of a universal redemption and a catholic religion—the herald of Glad-tidings to all mankind.

execution. Wieseler compares the execution of Calpurnius Galerianus, as recorded by Tacitus, ' who was sent under a military escort some distance along the Appian road.' (Tac. *Hist.* iv. 11.) This happened A.D. 70.

The great Basilica of St. Paul now stands outside the walls of Rome, on the road to Ostia, in commemoration of his martyrdom, and the Porta Ostiensis (in the present Aurelianic wall) is called the gate of St. Paul. The traditional spot of the martyrdom is the *Tre Fontane* not far from the basilica. The basilica itself (S. Paolo-fuori-le-mura) was first built by Constantine. Till the Reformation it was under the protection of the Kings of England, and the emblem of the Order of the Garter is still to be seen among its decorations.

[1] Eusebius (ii. 25) says that the original burial-places of Peter and Paul, in the Catacombs, were still shown in his time. This shows the tradition on the subject. Jerome, however, in the passage above cited, seems to make the place of burial and execution the same.

Coin of Antioch in Pisidia.

CHAPTER XXVIII.

The Epistle to the Hebrews.—Its Inspiration not affected by the Doubts concerning its Authorship.—Its original Readers.—Conflicting Testimony of the Primitive Church concerning its Author.—His Object in writing it.—Translation of the Epistle.

THE origin and history of the Epistle to the Hebrews was a subject of controversy even in the second century. There is no portion of the New Testament whose authorship is so disputed; nor any of which the inspiration is more indisputable. The early Church could not determine whether it was written by Barnabas, by Luke, by Clement, or by Paul. Since the Reformation still greater diversity of opinion has prevailed. Luther assigned it to Apollos, Calvin to a disciple of the Apostles. The church of Rome now maintains by its infallibility the Pauline authorship of the Epistle, which in the second, third, and fourth centuries, the same Church, with the same infallibility, denied. But notwithstanding these doubts concerning the origin of this canonical book, its inspired authority is beyond all doubt. It is certain, from internal evidence, that it was written by a cotemporary of the Apostles, and before the destruction of Jerusalem;[1] that its writer was the friend of Timotheus;[2] and that he was the teacher[3] of one of the Apostolic Churches. Moreover the Epistle was received by the Oriental Church as canonical from the first.[4] Every sound reasoner must agree with St. Jerome, that it matters nothing whether it were written by Luke, by Barnabas, or by Paul, since it is allowed to be the production of the Apostolic age, and has been read in the public service of the Church from the earliest times. Those, therefore, who conclude with Calvin, that it was not written by St. Paul, must also join with him in thinking the question of its authorship a question of little moment, and in 'embracing it without controversy as one of the Apostolical Epistles.'

But when we call it an *Epistle*, we must observe that it is distinguished, by one remarkable peculiarity, from other compositions which bear that name. In ancient no less than in modern times, it was an essential feature of an epistle, that it should be distinctly addressed, by the writer, to some definite individual, or body of individuals; and a composition which bore on its surface neither the name of its writer, nor an address to any particular readers, would

---

[1] See Heb. vii. 25, xiii. 11–13, and other passages which speak of the Temple services as going on.

[2] See xiii. 23.

[3] See xiii. 19. *Restored to you.*

[4] For this we can refer to Clemens Alexandrinus and Origen, also to passages of Jerome. Our larger editions give at length in the notes the passages from the Fathers referred to in the introductory part of this chapter.

then, as now, have been called rather a treatise than a letter. It was this peculiarity[1] in the portion of Scripture now before us, which led to some of the doubts and perplexities concerning it which existed in the earliest times. Yet, on the other hand, we cannot consider it merely as a treatise or discourse ; because we find certain indications of an epistolary nature, which show that it was originally addressed not to the world in general, nor to all Christians, nor even to all Jewish Christians, but to certain individual readers closely and personally connected with the writer.

Let us first examine these indications, and consider how far they tend to ascertain the *readers* for whom this Epistle was originally designed.

In the first place, it may be held as certain that the Epistle was addressed to *Hebrew* Christians. Throughout its pages there is not a single reference to any other class of converts. Its readers are assumed to be familiar with the Levitical worship, the Temple services, and all the institutions of the Mosaic ritual. They are in danger of apostasy to Judaism, yet are not warned (like the Galatians and others) against circumcision ; plainly because they were already circumcised. They are called to view in Christianity the completion and perfect consummation of Judaism. They are called to behold in Christ the fulfilment of the Law, in His person the antitype of the priesthood, in his offices the eternal realisation of the sacrificial and mediatorial functions of the Jewish hierarchy.

Yet, as we have said above, this work is not a treatise addressed to all Jewish Christians throughout the world, but to one particular Church, concerning which we learn the following facts :—First, its members had stedfastly endured persecution and the loss of property ; secondly, they had shown sympathy to their imprisoned brethren and to Christians generally (x. 32–34, and vi. 10); thirdly, they were now in danger of apostasy, and had not yet resisted unto blood (xii. 3, 4 ; see also v. 11, &c., vi. 9, &c.) ; fourthly, their Church had existed for a considerable length of time (v. 12), and some of its chief pastors were dead (xiii. 7) ; fifthly, their prayers are demanded for the *restoration to them* of the writer of the Epistle, who was therefore personally connected with them (xiii. 19); sixthly, they were acquainted with Timotheus, who was about to visit them (xiii. 23) ; seventhly, the arguments addressed to them presuppose a power on their part of appreciating that spiritualising and allegorical interpretation of the Old Testament which distinguished the Alexandrian[2] School of Jewish Theology ; eighthly, they must have been familiar with the Scriptures in the Septuagint version, because every one of the numerous quotations is taken from that version, even where it differs materially from the

---

[1] We need scarcely remark that the inscription which the Epistle at present bears was not a part of the original document. It is well known that the titles of all the Epistles were of later origin; and the title by which this was first known was merely 'to the Hebrews,' and not 'of Paul to the Hebrews.'

[2] The resemblance between the Epistle to the Hebrews and the writings of Philo is most striking. It extends not only to the general points mentioned in the text, but to particular doctrines and expressions : the parallel passages are enumerated by Bleek.

Hebrew; ninthly, the language in which they are addressed is Hellenistic Greek, and not Aramaic.[1]

It has been concluded by the majority, both of ancient and modern critics, that the church addressed was that of Jerusalem, or at least was situate in Palestine. In favour of this view it is urged, *first*, that no church out of Palestine could have consisted so exclusively of Jewish converts. To this it may be replied that the Epistle, though *addressed* only to Jewish converts, and contemplating their position and their dangers exclusively, might still have been sent to a church which contained Gentile converts also. In fact, even in the church of Jerusalem itself there must have been some converts from among the Gentile sojourners who lived in that city; so that the argument proves too much. Moreover, it is not necessary that every discourse addressed to a mixed congregation should discuss the position of every individual member. If an overwhelming majority belong to a particular class, the minority is often passed over in addresses directed to the whole body. Again, the Epistle may have been intended for the Hebrew members only of some particular church, which contained also Gentile members; and this would perhaps explain the absence of the usual address and salutation at the commencement. *Secondly*, it is urged that none but Palestinian Jews would have felt the attachment to the Levitical ritual implied in the readers of this Epistle. But we do not see why the same attachment may not have been felt in every great community of Hebrews; nay, we know historically, that no Jews were more devotedly attached to the Temple worship than those of the dispersion, who were only able to visit the Temple itself at distant intervals, but who still looked to it as the central point of their religious unity and of their national existence.[2] *Thirdly*, it is alleged that many passages seem to imply readers who had the Temple services going on continually under their eyes. The whole of the ninth and tenth chapters speak of the Levitical ritual in a manner which naturally suggests this idea. On the other hand it may be argued, that such passages imply no more than that amount of familiarity which might be presupposed, in those who were often in the habit of going up to the great feasts at Jerusalem.[3]

[1] It may be considered as an established point, that the Greek Epistle which we now have is the original. Some of the early Fathers thought that the original had been written in Aramaic; but the origin of this tradition seems to have been, 1st, the belief that the Epistle was written by St. Paul, combined with the perception of its dissimilarity in style to his writings; and 2ndly, the belief that it was addressed to the Palestinian Church. That the present Epistle is *not* a translation from an Aramaic original is proved, 1st, by the quotation of the Septuagint *argumentatively*, where it differs from the Hebrew; for instance, Heb. x. 38: 2ndly, by the *paronomasias* upon Greek words, which could not be translated into Aramaic, e.g. that on διαθήκη (ix. 16); 3rdly, by the free use of Greek compounds, &c., which could only be expressed in Aramaic by awkward periphrases; 4th, by the fact that even the earliest Christian writers had never seen a copy of the supposed Aramaic original. Its existence was only hypothetical from the first.

[2] They showed this by the large contributions which they sent to the Temple from all countries where they were dispersed; see above, p. 678.

[3] We cannot agree with Ebrard, that the Epistle contains indications that the Christians addressed had been excluded from the Temple.

Thus, then, we cannot see that the Epistle must necessarily have been addressed to Jews of *Palestine,* because addressed to *Hebrews.*[1] And, moreover, if we examine the preceding nine conditions which must be satisfied by its readers, we shall find some of them which could scarcely apply to the church of Jerusalem, or any other church in Palestine. Thus the Palestinian Church was remarkable for its poverty, and was the recipient of the bounty of other churches ; whereas those addressed here are themselves the liberal benefactors of others. Again, those here addressed have not yet *resisted unto blood* ; whereas the Palestinian Church had produced many martyrs, in several persecutions. Moreover, the Palestinian[2] Jews would hardly be addressed in a style of reasoning adapted to minds imbued with Alexandrian culture. Finally, a letter to the church of Palestine would surely have been written in the language of Palestine ; or, at least, when the Scriptures of Hebraism were appealed to, they would not have been quoted from the Septuagint version, *where it differs from the Hebrew.*

These considerations (above all, the last) seem to negative the hypothesis that this Epistle was addressed to a church situate in the Holy Land ; and the latter portion of them point to another church, for which we may more plausibly conceive it to have been intended, namely, that of Alexandria.[3] Such a supposition would at once account for the Alexandrian tone of thought and reasoning, and for the quotations from the Septuagint ;[4] while the wealth of the Alexandrian Jews would explain the liberality here commended ; and the immense Hebrew population of Alexandria would render it natural that the Epistle should contemplate the Hebrew Christians alone in that church, wherein there may perhaps at first have been as few Gentile converts as in Jerusalem itself. It must be remembered, however, that this is only an hypothesis,[5] offered as being embarrassed with fewer difficulties than any other which has been proposed.

[1] Bleek and De Wette have urged the title 'to the Hebrews,' to prove the same point. But Wieseler has conclusively shown that '*Hebrew*' was applied as properly to Jews of the dispersion, as to Jews of Palestine.

[2] Cultivated individuals at Jerusalem (as, for instance, the pupils of Gamaliel) would have fully entered into such reasoning ; but it would scarcely have been addressed to the mass of Jewish believers. Bleek (as we have before observed) has shown many instances of parallelism between the Epistle to the Hebrews and the writings of Philo, the representative of Alexandrian Judaism.

[3] The canon of Muratori mentions an epistle *ad Alexandrinos* (which it rejects), and takes no notice of any epistle *ad Hebræos.* We cannot prove, however, that this epistle *ad Alexandrinos* was the same with our Epistle to the Hebrews.

[4] Bleek has endeavoured to prove (and we think successfully) that these are not only from the LXX., but from the Alexandrian MSS. of the LXX. But we do not insist on this argument, as it is liable to some doubt.

[5] Since the above remarks were published, this hypothesis has been advocated by Bunsen in his '*Hippo-lytus.*' It is to be regretted that Wieseler should have encumbered his able arguments in defence of this hypothesis (originally suggested by Schmidt) by maintaining that the constant allusions to the Temple and hierarchy in this Epistle refer to the Egyptian temple built by Onias at Leontopolis. This notion is sufficiently refuted by Wieseler's own admission, that even Philo the Alexandrian, when speaking of *the Temple,* knows but one, viz. the Temple on Mount Zion.

Such then being the utmost which we can ascertain concerning the readers of the Epistle, what can we learn of its writer? Let us first examine the testimony of the Primitive Church on this question. It is well summed up by St. Jerome in the following passage :[1]—'That which is called the Epistle *to the Hebrews* is thought not to be Paul's, because of the difference of style and language, but is ascribed either to Barnabas (according to Tertullian) ; or to Luke the Evangelist (according to some authorities); or to Clement (afterwards Bishop of Rome), who is said to have arranged and adorned Paul's sentiments in his own language ; or at least it is thought that Paul abstained from the inscription of his name at its commencement because it was addressed to the Hebrews, among whom he was unpopular.' Here then we find that the Epistle was ascribed to four different writers—St. Barnabas, St. Luke, St. Clement, or St. Paul. With regard to the first, Tertullian expressly says that copies of the Epistle in his day bore the inscription, 'the Epistle of Barnabas to the Hebrews.' The same tradition is mentioned by Philastrius. The opinion that either Luke or Clement was the writer is mentioned by Clement of Alexandria, Origen,[2] and others ; but they seem not to have considered Luke or Clement as the independent authors of the Epistle, but only as editors of the sentiments of Paul. Some held that Luke had only translated the Pauline original; others that he or Clement had systematised the teaching of their master with a commentary[3] of their own. Fourthly, St. Paul was held to be, in some sense, the *author* of the Epistle, by the Greek ecclesiastical writers generally ; though no one, so far as we know, maintained that he had *written* it in its present form. On the other hand, the Latin Church, till the fourth century, refused to acknowledge the Epistle[4] as Paul's in any sense.

Thus there were, in fact, only two persons whose claim to the *independent authorship* of the Epistle was maintained in the Primitive Church, viz. St. Barnabas and St. Paul. Those who contend that Barnabas was the author, confirm the testimony of Tertullian by the following arguments from internal evidence. First, Barnabas was a Levite, and therefore would naturally dwell on the Levitical worship which forms so prominent a topic of this Epistle. Secondly, Barnabas was a native of Cyprus, and Cyprus was peculiarly connected with Alexandria ; so that a Cyprian Levite would most probably receive his theological education at Alexandria. This would agree with the Alexandrian character of the argumentation of this Epistle. Thirdly, this is further confirmed by the ancient tradition which connects Barnabas and his kinsman Mark with the church of Alexandria.[5] Fourthly, the writer of the Epistle was a

---

[1] See p. 784, n. 4.

[2] After stating that the style is admitted not to be that of St. Paul, Origen adds his own opinion that the Epistle was written by some disciple of St. Paul, who recorded the *sentiments* of the Apostle, and commented *like a scholiast* upon the teaching of his master. Then follows the passage which is quoted below; after which

he mentions the tradition about Clement and Luke.—Origen in Euseb. *Hist. Ecc.* vi. 25.

[3] See the preceding note.

[4] Even Cyprian rejected it, and Hilary is the first writer of the Western Church who received it as St. Paul's.

[5] Bunsen acknowledges the force of the arguments in favour of Barnabas,

friend of Timotheus (see above, pp. 781, 785); so was Barnabas (cf. Acts xiii. and xiv. with 2 Tim. iii. 11). Fifthly, the Hebraic appellation which Barnabas received from the Apostles—'*Son of Exhortation*'[1]—shows that he possessed the gift necessary for writing a composition distinguished for the power of its hortatory admonitions.

The advocates of the Pauline authorship urge, in addition to the external testimony which we have before mentioned, the following arguments from internal evidence. First, that the general plan of the Epistle is similar to that of Paul's other writings; secondly, that its doctrinal statements are identical with Paul's; thirdly, that there are many points of similarity between its phraseology and diction and those of Paul.[2] On the other hand, the opponents of the Pauline origin argue, first, that the rhetorical character of the composition is altogether unlike Paul's other writings; secondly, that there are many points of difference in the phraseology and diction; thirdly, that the quotations of the Old Testatment are not made in the same form as Paul's;[3] fourthly, that the writer includes himself among those *who had received the Gospel from the original disciples of the Lord Jesus* (ii. 3),[4] whereas St. Paul declares that the Gospel *was not taught him by man, but by the revelation of Jesus Christ* (Gal. i. 11, 12); fifthly, that St. Paul's Epistles always begin with his name, and always specify in the salutation the persons to whom they are addressed.[5]

Several very able modern critics have agreed with Luther in assigning the authorship of this Epistle to Apollos, chiefly because we know him to have been a learned Alexandrian Jew,[6] and

but thinks that if he had been the author 'his authorship could not easily have been forgotten,' and also that 'we should not expect in Barnabas so Pauline a turn of mind.' On these grounds he assigns the Epistle to Apollos.

[1] So the word is translated by some of the best authorities. See p. 98, n. 1.

[2] The ablest English champion of the Pauline authorship is Dr. Davidson, who has stated the arguments on both sides with that perfect candour which so peculiarly distinguishes him among theological writers. See Davidson's *Introduction*, vol. iii. pp. 163–259. Ebrard, in his recent work on the Epistle, argues plausibly in favour of the hypothesis mentioned above, that it was written by St. Luke, under the direction of St. Paul. He modifies this hypothesis by supposing Luke to receive Paul's instructions at Rome, and then to write the Epistle in some other part of Italy. We think, however, that the argument on which he mainly relies (viz. that the writer of xiii. 19 could not have been the writer of xiii. 23), is untenable.

[3] It should be observed, that the three preceding arguments do not contradict the primitive opinion that the Epistle contained the embodiment of St. Paul's sentiments by the pen of Luke or Clement.

[4] Some have argued that this could not have been said by Barnabas, because they receive the tradition mentioned by Clement of Alexandria, that Barnabas was one of the seventy disciples of Christ. But this tradition seems to have arisen from a confusion between Barnabas and Barsabas (Acts i. 23). Tertullian speaks of Barnabas as a disciple of the Apostles, 'qui ab Apostolis didicit.'—*De Pudic.* c. 20.

[5] We have not mentioned here the mistakes which some suppose the writer to have made concerning the internal arrangements of the Temple and the official duties of the High Priest. These difficulties will be discussed in the notes upon the passages where they occur. They are not of a kind which tend to fix the authorship of the Epistle upon one more than upon another of those to whom it has been assigned.

[6] Acts xviii. 24.

because he fulfils the other conditions mentioned above, as required by the internal evidence. But we need not dwell on this opinion, since it is not based on external testimony, and since Barnabas fulfils the requisite conditions almost equally well.

Finally, we may observe that, notwithstanding the doubts which we have recorded, we need not scruple to speak of this portion of Scripture by its canonical designation, as 'the Epistle of Paul the Apostle to the Hebrews.' We have seen that Jerome expresses the greatest doubts concerning its authorship: Origen also says, 'the writer is known to God alone:' the same doubts are expressed by Eusebius and by Augustine: yet all these great writers refer to the words of the Epistle as *the words of Paul.* In fact, whether written by Barnabas, by Luke, by Clement, or by Apollos, it represented the views, and was impregnated by the influence, of the great Apostle, whose disciples even the chief of these Apostolic men might well be called. By their writings, no less than by his own, he being dead yet spake.

We have seen that the Epistle to the Hebrews was addressed to Jewish converts, who were tempted to apostatise from Christianity, and return to Judaism. Its primary object was to check this apostasy, by showing them the true end and meaning of the Mosaic system, and its symbolical and transitory character. They are taught to look through the shadow to the substance, through the type to the antitype. But the treatise, though first called forth to meet the needs of Hebrew converts, was not designed for their instruction only. The Spirit of God has chosen this occasion to enlighten the Universal Church concerning the design of the ancient covenant, and the interpretation of the Jewish Scriptures. Nor could the memory of St. Paul be enshrined in a nobler monument, nor his. mission on earth be more fitly closed, than by this inspired record of the true subordination of Judaism to Christianity.

THE EPISTLE TO THE HEBREWS.[1]

God has revealed Himself finally to man, in the   GOD,[2] who at sundry times and in divers manners i. 1 spake of old to our fathers by the prophets, hath[3] in

[1] We have the following circumstances to fix the date of this Epistle:—

(1) The Temple of Jerusalem was standing, and the services going on undisturbed (vii. 23, xiii. 11–13). Hence it was written before the destruction of the Temple in A.D. 70.

(2) Its author was at liberty in Italy; and Timotheus was just liberated from imprisonment (xiii. 23, 24). If St. Paul wrote it, this would fix the date at 63; but as we do not hear that Timotheus was then imprisoned in Italy (either in Acts, or in the Epistles to Timothy, where allusions might be expected to the fact), it would seem more probable that his imprisonment here mentioned took place about the time of St. Paul's death; and that he

was liberated after the death of Nero. This would place the date of the Epistle in A.D. 68 or 69, if our chronology be correct: see Chronol. Table in Appendix.

(3) This date agrees with ii. 3, which places the readers of the Epistle among those who had not seen our Lord in the flesh; for the 'we' there plainly includes the readers as well as the writer.

[2] In order to mark the difference of style and character between this and the preceding Epistles, the translator has in this Epistle adhered as closely as possible to the language of the Authorised Version.

[3] The Hellenistic peculiarity of using the aorist for the perfect (which is not

these last days[1] spoken unto us by[2] His Son, whom person of His Son,
He appointed heir of all things, by whom also He
i. 3 made the universe;[3] who being an emanation[4] of
His glory, and an express[5] image of his substance,[6]
and upholding all things by the word of His
power, when He had by Himself made purification[7] for our sins, sat down on the right hand of the
4 Majesty on high; being made so much greater than
the Angels, as He hath by inheritance obtained a
more excellent name than they.

5   For to which of the Angels[8] said He at any time, who is higher than the Angels.
'𝕿𝖍𝖔𝖚 𝖆𝖗𝖙 𝖒𝖞 𝖘𝖔𝖓, 𝖙𝖍𝖎𝖘 𝖉𝖆𝖞 𝖍𝖆𝖛𝖊 𝕴 𝖇𝖊𝖌𝖔𝖙𝖙𝖊𝖓 𝖙𝖍𝖊𝖊;'[9]
and again, '𝕴 𝖜𝖎𝖑𝖑 𝖇𝖊 𝖙𝖔 𝖍𝖎𝖒 𝖆 𝖋𝖆𝖙𝖍𝖊𝖗, 𝖆𝖓𝖉 𝖍𝖊 𝖘𝖍𝖆𝖑𝖑 𝖇𝖊 𝖙𝖔
6 𝖒𝖊 𝖆 𝖘𝖔𝖓?'[10] But when he bringeth back[11] the First-
begotten into the world, He saith, '𝕬𝖓𝖉 𝖑𝖊𝖙 𝖆𝖑𝖑 𝖙𝖍𝖊
7 𝕬𝖓𝖌𝖊𝖑𝖘 𝖔𝖋 𝕲𝖔𝖉 𝖜𝖔𝖗𝖘𝖍𝖎𝖕 𝖍𝖎𝖒.'[12] And of the angels He
saith, '𝖂𝖍𝖔 𝖒𝖆𝖐𝖊𝖙𝖍 𝖍𝖎𝖘 𝖆𝖓𝖌𝖊𝖑𝖘 𝖘𝖕𝖎𝖗𝖎𝖙𝖘, 𝖆𝖓𝖉 𝖍𝖎𝖘 𝖒𝖎𝖓𝖎𝖘-
𝖙𝖊𝖗𝖘 𝖋𝖑𝖆𝖒𝖊𝖘 𝖔𝖋 𝖋𝖎𝖗𝖊.'[13]   But unto the Son He saith,
8 '𝕿𝖍𝖞 𝖙𝖍𝖗𝖔𝖓𝖊, 𝕺 𝕲𝖔𝖉, 𝖎𝖘 𝖋𝖔𝖗 𝖊𝖛𝖊𝖗 𝖆𝖓𝖉 𝖊𝖛𝖊𝖗; 𝖆 𝖘𝖈𝖊𝖕𝖙𝖗𝖊 𝖔𝖋
𝖗𝖎𝖌𝖍𝖙𝖊𝖔𝖚𝖘𝖓𝖊𝖘𝖘 𝖎𝖘 𝖙𝖍𝖊 𝖘𝖈𝖊𝖕𝖙𝖗𝖊 𝖔𝖋 𝖙𝖍𝖞 𝖐𝖎𝖓𝖌𝖉𝖔𝖒. 𝕿𝖍𝖔𝖚 𝖍𝖆𝖘𝖙
9 𝖑𝖔𝖛𝖊𝖉 𝖗𝖎𝖌𝖍𝖙𝖊𝖔𝖚𝖘𝖓𝖊𝖘𝖘 𝖆𝖓𝖉 𝖍𝖆𝖙𝖊𝖉 𝖎𝖓𝖎𝖖𝖚𝖎𝖙𝖞. 𝕿𝖍𝖊𝖗𝖊𝖋𝖔𝖗𝖊 𝕲𝖔𝖉,

uncommon in St. Paul's writings, see
Rom. xi. 30, and Phil. iii. 12) is very
frequent in this Epistle.

[1] The best MSS. have the singular.
It should perhaps rather be translated
'*in the end of these days,*' *these days*
being contrasted with the future period,
the world to come.

[2] The preposition means more than
'*by*' (so in preceding verse); *in the
person of His Son* would be more
accurate.

[3] 'The worlds:' so xi. 3.

[4] Not '*brightness*' (A. V.), but *emanation,* as of light from the sun. The
word and idea occur in Philo.

[5] Literally, *impression,* as of a seal
on wax. The same expression is used
by Philo concerning 'the Eternal
Word.'

[6] Not '*person*' (A. V.), but *substance.* Cf. xi. 1; and see note on
iii. 14.

[7] The 'by Himself' and 'our' of
T. R. are not found in some of the best
MSS.

[8] The Law (according to a Jewish
tradition frequently confirmed in the
New Testament) was delivered by
angels (Acts vii. 53; Gal. iii. 19; Heb.
ii. 3). Hence the emphasis here laid
upon the inferiority of the angels to
the Messiah, whence follows the inferiority of the Law to the Gospel.
This inference is expressed ii. 3.

[9] Ps. ii. 7 (LXX.).

[10] 2 Sam. vii. 14 (LXX.) (originally
spoken of Solomon, in whom we see a
type of Christ. Cf. Ps. lxxii.).

[11] This is, literally translated, *when
He shall have brought back,* not *again,
when He has brought back.* The *ascension* of Christ having been mentioned,
His *return* to judge the world follows.

[12] This quotation forms an exception
to Bleek's assertion that the quotations
in this Epistle are always from the
Alexandrian text of the LXX. It is
from Deut. xxxii. 43, verbatim according to the MSS. followed by the T. R.;
but not according to the Codex Alex.,
which reads 'sons,' instead of 'angels.'
The LXX. here differs from the Hebrew, which entirely omits the words
here quoted. The passage where the
quotation occurs is at the conclusion of the final song of Moses, where
he is describing God's vengeance upon
His enemies. It seems here to be applied in a higher sense to the last
judgment.

[13] Ps. civ. 4. Quoted according to
LXX. The Hebrew is, 'Who maketh
the winds His messengers, and the
flames His ministers.' But the
thought expressed here is, that God
employs His angels in the physical
operations of the universe. 'Spirits'
is equivalent to 'winds,' as at John iii.
8, and Gen. viii. 1 (LXX.).

even thy God, hath anointed thee with the oil of gladness above thy fellows.'[1] And 'Thou, Lord, in the begin- i. 10 ning didst lay the foundation of the earth, and the heavens are the works of thine hands. They shall perish, 11 but thou remainest ; and they all shall wax old, as doth a 12 garment, and as a vesture shalt thou fold them up and they shall be changed; but thou art the same, and thy years shall not fail.'[2]

But to which of the angels hath He said at any 13 time, ' Sit thou on my right hand, until I make thine enemies thy footstool?'[3] Are they not all ministering 14 spirits, sent forth to execute [His] service, for[4] the sake of those who shall inherit salvation ?

Therefore, we ought to give the more earnest heed ii. 1 to the things which we have heard, lest at any time we should let them slip.[5] For if the word declared 2 by angels[6] was stedfast, and every transgression and disobedience received a due requital; how shall we 3 escape, if we neglect so great salvation ? which was declared at first by the Lord, and was established[7] unto us[8] on firm foundations by those who heard Him, God also bearing them witness both with signs and 4 wonders and divers miracles, and with gifts of the Holy Spirit, which He distributed[9] according to His own will.

For not unto angels hath He subjected the world[10] 5 to come, whereof we speak. But one in a certain 6 place testified, saying, ' What is man that thou art mindful of him, or the son of man that thou regardest him? For a little while[11] thou hast made him lower than 7 the angels; thou hast crowned him with glory and honour,[12] thou hast put all things in subjection under 8

---

[1] Ps. xlv. 6, 7 (LXX.).

[2] Ps. cii. 26–28 (LXX.). It is most important to observe that this description, applied in the original to God, is here without hesitation applied to Christ.

[3] Ps. cx. 1 (LXX.). Applied to the Messiah by our Lord Himself, by St. Peter (Acts ii. 35), and by St. Paul (1 Cor. xv. 25).

[4] The A. V. '*to minister for them*,' is incorrect.

[5] The active signification here given in A. V. is defended by Buttmann and Wahl.

[6] Viz. the Mosaic Law. See the note on i. 5.

[7] The verb means, *was established on firm ground.*

[8] On the inferences from this verse, see above, p. 789.

[9] 'Distributed.' Compare 1 Cor. xii. 11.

[10] The *world to come* here corresponds with the *city to come* of xiii. 14. The subjection of this to the Messiah (though not yet accomplished, see v. 9) was another proof of His superiority to the angels.

[11] The phrase may mean *in a small degree*, or *for a short time* ; the former is the meaning of the Hebrew original, but the latter meaning is taken here, as we see from v. 9.

[12] The T. R. inserts here what we find in A. V., *and hast set him over the works of thy hands*, but this is not found in the best MSS.

𝔥𝔦𝔰 𝔣𝔢𝔢𝔱.' [1] For in that He '𝔭𝔲𝔱 𝔞𝔩𝔩 𝔱𝔥𝔦𝔫𝔤𝔰 𝔦𝔫 𝔰𝔲𝔟𝔧𝔢𝔠𝔱𝔦𝔬𝔫' under Him, He left nothing that should not be put under Him.

But now we see not yet all things in subjection
ii. 9 under Him. But we behold Jesus, who was '𝔣𝔬𝔯 𝔞 𝔩𝔦𝔱𝔱𝔩𝔢 𝔴𝔥𝔦𝔩𝔢 𝔪𝔞𝔡𝔢 𝔩𝔬𝔴𝔢𝔯 𝔱𝔥𝔞𝔫 𝔱𝔥𝔢 𝔞𝔫𝔤𝔢𝔩𝔰,' crowned through [2] the suffering of death with glory and honour; that by the free gift of God He might taste
10 death for all men. For it became Him, through [3] whom are all things, and by whom are all things, in bringing [4] many sons unto glory, to consecrate [5] by sufferings the captain [6] of their salvation.
11 For both He that sanctifieth, and they that are [7] sanctified, have all one Father; wherefore, He is not
12 ashamed to call them brethren, saying, '𝔍 𝔴𝔦𝔩𝔩 𝔡𝔢𝔠𝔩𝔞𝔯𝔢 𝔱𝔥𝔶 𝔫𝔞𝔪𝔢 𝔱𝔬 𝔪𝔶 𝔟𝔯𝔢𝔱𝔥𝔯𝔢𝔫, 𝔦𝔫 𝔱𝔥𝔢 𝔪𝔦𝔡𝔰𝔱 𝔬𝔣 𝔱𝔥𝔢 𝔠𝔬𝔫𝔤𝔯𝔢𝔤𝔞-
13 𝔱𝔦𝔬𝔫 𝔴𝔦𝔩𝔩 𝔍 𝔰𝔦𝔫𝔤 𝔭𝔯𝔞𝔦𝔰𝔢𝔰 𝔲𝔫𝔱𝔬 𝔱𝔥𝔢𝔢.' [8] And again, '𝔍 𝔴𝔦𝔩𝔩 𝔭𝔲𝔱 𝔪𝔶 𝔱𝔯𝔲𝔰𝔱 𝔦𝔫 𝔥𝔦𝔪; 𝔩𝔬, 𝔍 𝔞𝔫𝔡 𝔱𝔥𝔢 𝔠𝔥𝔦𝔩𝔡𝔯𝔢𝔫 𝔴𝔥𝔦𝔠𝔥 𝔊𝔬𝔡
14 𝔥𝔞𝔱𝔥 𝔤𝔦𝔳𝔢𝔫 𝔪𝔢.' [9] Forasmuch then as '𝔱𝔥𝔢 𝔠𝔥𝔦𝔩𝔡𝔯𝔢𝔫' are partakers of flesh and blood, He also Himself likewise took part of the same, that by death He might destroy the lord of death, that is, the Devil;
15 and might deliver them who through fear of death
16 were all their lifetime subject to bondage. For truly, He giveth His aid, [10] not unto angels, but unto the
17 seed of Abraham. Wherefore, it behoved Him in all things to be made like unto His brethren, that He

[1] Ps. viii. 5-7 (LXX). Quoted also (with a slight variation) as referring to our Lord, 1 Cor. xv. 27, and Eph. i. 22. The Hebrew Psalmist speaks of mankind, the New Testament teaches us to apply his words in a higher sense to Christ, the representative of glorified humanity.

[2] Compare Phil. ii. 8, 9.

[3] Compare Rom. xi. 36, and 1 Cor. viii. 6. God is here described as the First Cause ('by whom'), and the Sustainer ('through whom') of the Universe.

[4] For the grammar here we may refer to Acts xi. 12.

[5] Literally, *to bring to the appointed accomplishment, to develop the full idea of the character, to consummate.* The latter word would be the best translation, if it were not so unusual as applied to persons; but the word *consecrate* is often used in the same sense, and is employed in the A. V. as a translation of this verb, vii. 28.

[6] *Captain.* Those who are being saved are here represented as an army, with Jesus leading them on. Compare xii. 2.

[7] Literally, *who are in the process of sanctification.*

[8] Ps. xxii. 23 (LXX. with a slight change in the verb for 'declare'). Here again the Messianic application of this Psalm (which is not apparent in the original) is very instructive.

[9] This quotation from Isa. viii. 17, 18 (LXX.) appears in English to be broken into two (which destroys the sense), if the intermediate words 'and again' (which are not in the LXX.) be inserted. Indeed, it may well be suspected that they have here been introduced into the MSS., by an error of transcription, from the line above.

[10] The verb means *to assist* here. So it is used in Sirach iv. 12. The A. V. mistranslates the *present* tense as *past.*

might become a merciful[1] and faithful High Priest in the things of God, to make expiation for the sins of the people. For whereas He hath Himself been tried[2] ii. 18 by suffering, He is able to succour them that are in trial.

Christ is higher than Moses. Wherefore, holy brethren, partakers of a heavenly iii. 1 calling, consider the apostle[3] and High Priest of our Confession,[4] Christ[5] Jesus; who was faithful to Him 2 that appointed Him, as Moses also was '𝔣𝔞𝔦𝔱𝔥𝔣𝔲𝔩 𝔦𝔫 𝔞𝔩𝔩 𝔱𝔥𝔢 𝔥𝔬𝔲𝔰𝔢𝔥𝔬𝔩𝔡 𝔬𝔣 𝔊𝔬𝔡.'[6] For greater glory is due to 3 Him than unto Moses, inasmuch as the founder of the household is honoured above the household. For 4 every household hath some founder; but He that hath founded all things is God. And Moses indeed was 5 '𝔣𝔞𝔦𝔱𝔥𝔣𝔲𝔩 𝔦𝔫 𝔞𝔩𝔩 𝔱𝔥𝔢 𝔥𝔬𝔲𝔰𝔢𝔥𝔬𝔩𝔡 𝔬𝔣 𝔊𝔬𝔡' as '𝔞 𝔖𝔢𝔯𝔳𝔞𝔫𝔱'[7] appointed to testify the words that should be spoken [unto him]: but Christ as '𝔞 𝔖𝔬𝔫'[8] over His own 6 household.

Warning against apostasy, And His household are we, if we hold fast our confidence, and the rejoicing of our hope, firmly unto the end. Wherefore, as the Holy Spirit saith, '𝔗𝔬-𝔡𝔞𝔶 𝔦𝔣 𝔶𝔢 𝔥𝔢𝔞𝔯 𝔥𝔦𝔰 𝔳𝔬𝔦𝔠𝔢, 𝔥𝔞𝔯𝔡𝔢𝔫 𝔫𝔬𝔱 𝔶𝔬𝔲𝔯 𝔥𝔢𝔞𝔯𝔱𝔰 𝔞𝔰 7 𝔦𝔫 𝔱𝔥𝔢 𝔭𝔯𝔬𝔳𝔬𝔠𝔞𝔱𝔦𝔬𝔫, 𝔦𝔫 𝔱𝔥𝔢 𝔡𝔞𝔶 𝔬𝔣 𝔱𝔢𝔪𝔭𝔱𝔞𝔱𝔦𝔬𝔫 𝔦𝔫 𝔱𝔥𝔢 𝔴𝔦𝔩= 8 𝔡𝔢𝔯𝔫𝔢𝔰𝔰; 𝔴𝔥𝔢𝔫 𝔶𝔬𝔲𝔯 𝔣𝔞𝔱𝔥𝔢𝔯𝔰 𝔱𝔢𝔪𝔭𝔱𝔢𝔡 𝔪𝔢, 𝔭𝔯𝔬𝔳𝔢𝔡 𝔪𝔢, 𝔞𝔫𝔡 9 𝔰𝔞𝔴 𝔪𝔶 𝔴𝔬𝔯𝔨𝔰 𝔣𝔬𝔯𝔱𝔶 𝔶𝔢𝔞𝔯𝔰. 𝔚𝔥𝔢𝔯𝔢𝔣𝔬𝔯𝔢 𝔍 𝔴𝔞𝔰 𝔤𝔯𝔦𝔢𝔳𝔢𝔡 10 𝔴𝔦𝔱𝔥 𝔱𝔥𝔞𝔱 𝔤𝔢𝔫𝔢𝔯𝔞𝔱𝔦𝔬𝔫, 𝔞𝔫𝔡 𝔰𝔞𝔦𝔡, 𝔗𝔥𝔢𝔶 𝔡𝔬 𝔞𝔩𝔴𝔞𝔶 𝔢𝔯𝔯 𝔦𝔫 𝔱𝔥𝔢𝔦𝔯 𝔥𝔢𝔞𝔯𝔱𝔰, 𝔞𝔫𝔡 𝔱𝔥𝔢𝔶[9] 𝔥𝔞𝔳𝔢 𝔫𝔬𝔱 𝔨𝔫𝔬𝔴𝔫 𝔪𝔶 𝔴𝔞𝔶𝔰. 𝔖𝔬 𝔍 11 𝔰𝔴𝔞𝔯𝔢 𝔦𝔫 𝔪𝔶 𝔴𝔯𝔞𝔱𝔥, 𝔗𝔥𝔢𝔶 𝔰𝔥𝔞𝔩𝔩 𝔫𝔬𝔱 𝔢𝔫𝔱𝔢𝔯 𝔦𝔫𝔱𝔬 𝔪𝔶 𝔯𝔢𝔰𝔱.'[10] Take heed, brethren, lest there be in any of you an 12 evil heart of unbelief, in departing from the living

---

[1] Perhaps it would be more correct to translate *that he might become merciful, and a faithful*, &c.

[2] Literally, *hath suffered when in trial* This verb does not mean usually *to be tempted to sin*, but *to be tried by affliction*. Cf. 1 Cor. x. 13, and James i. 2. Hence it is better not to translate it by *temptation*, which, in modern English, conveys only the former idea. A perplexity may perhaps be removed from some English readers by the information that St. James's direction to 'count it all joy when we fall into divers *temptations*,' is, in reality, an admonition to rejoice in suffering for Christ's sake.

[3] *Apostle* is here used in its etymological sense for *one sent forth*.

[4] For 'confession' compare iv. 14 and x. 23.

[5] We have not departed here from the T. R.; but the best MSS. omit 'Christ.'

[6] Numbers xii. 7 (LXX). 'My servant Moses is faithful in all my household.' The metaphor is of a *faithful steward* presiding over his master's household.

[7] 'Servant,' quoted from the same verse, Numbers xii. 7 (LXX.). (See above.)

[8] See the quotations in i. 5.

[9] *They* is emphatic.

[10] The above quotation is from Ps. xcv. 7–11, mainly according to the Codex Alexandrinus of the LXX., but not entirely so, the *forty years* interpolated in v. 9th being the principal, though not the only variation. The peculiar use of 'if' here (and iv. 3) is a Hebraism.

iii. 13 God.   But exhort one another daily while it is called
To-day, lest any of you be hardened through the
14 deceitfulness of sin.   For we are made partakers[1] of
Christ, if we hold our first foundation[2] firmly unto
the end.

15   When it is said, '𝕿𝖔=𝖉𝖆𝖞, 𝖎𝖋 𝖞𝖊 𝖍𝖊𝖆𝖗 𝖍𝖎𝖘 𝖛𝖔𝖎𝖈𝖊, 𝖍𝖆𝖗𝖉𝖊𝖓
16 𝖓𝖔𝖙 𝖞𝖔𝖚𝖗 𝖍𝖊𝖆𝖗𝖙𝖘 𝖆𝖘 𝖎𝖓 𝖙𝖍𝖊 𝖕𝖗𝖔𝖛𝖔𝖈𝖆𝖙𝖎𝖔𝖓,'—who[3] were they
that, though they had heard, did provoke?   Were
they not all[4] whom Moses brought forth out of
17 Egypt? And with whom was He grieved forty years?
Was it not with them that had sinned, whose car-
18 cases[5] fell in the wilderness?   And to whom sware
He that they should not enter into His rest, but to
19 them that were disobedient?[6]   And[7] we see that
they could not enter, because of unbelief.[8]

iv. 1   Therefore let us fear, since a promise still[9] remaineth of entering into His rest, lest any of you
2 should be found[10] to come short of it.   For we have
received glad tidings as well as they; but the report
which they heard did not profit them, because it[11]
3 met no belief in the hearers.   For we, THAT HAVE
BELIEVED, are entering into the [promised] rest.   And
thus He hath said, '𝕾𝖔 𝕴 𝖘𝖜𝖆𝖗𝖊 𝖎𝖓 𝖒𝖞 𝖜𝖗𝖆𝖙𝖍, 𝕿𝖍𝖊𝖞
𝖘𝖍𝖆𝖑𝖑 𝕹𝕺𝕿 𝖊𝖓𝖙𝖊𝖗 𝖎𝖓𝖙𝖔 𝖒𝖞 𝖗𝖊𝖘𝖙.'[12]   Although His works
were finished, ever since the foundation of the world;
4 for He hath spoken in a certain place of the seventh

[1] 'Partakers.'   Compare iii. 1 and vi. 4 ('partakers of the Holy Spirit').

[2] Literally, *the beginning of our foundation.*   The original meaning of the latter word is *that whereon anything else stands, or is supported*; hence it acquired the meaning of *substantia,* or *substance* (in the metaphysical sense of the term).   Cf. Heb. i. 3, and xi. 1; hence, again that of *ground,* nearly in the sense of *subject-matter* (2 Cor. ix. 4; 2 Cor. xi. 17).   There is no passage of the New Testament where it need necessarily be translated ' *confidence*;' although it seems to have the latter meaning in some passages of the LXX. cited by Bleek; and it is also so used by Diodorus Siculus, and by Polybius.

[3] We follow the accentuation adopted by Chrysostom, Griesbach, &c.

[4] The inference is that Christians, though delivered by Christ from bondage, would nevertheless perish if they did not persevere (see ver. 6 and 14).   The interrogation is not observed in A. V

[5] Literally, *limbs;* but the word is used by the LXX. for *carcases.*   Numbers xiv. 32.

[6] Not ' *that believed not*' (A. V.).   See note on Rom. xi. 30.

[7] ' *And,*' not ' *So*' (A. V.).

[8] The allusion is to the refusal of the Israelites to believe in the good report of the land of Canaan brought by the spies.   (Numbers xiii. and xiv.)

[9] 'Still remaineth.'   Compare 'remaineth,' ver. 6 and 9.   The reasoning is explained by what follows, especially ver. 6–8.

[10] *Should be seen.*

[11] Literally, *it was not mixed with belief.*   The other reading would mean, 'they were not united by belief to its hearers,' where *its hearers* must mean the spies, who reported *what they had heard* of the richness of the land. Tischendorf, in his second edition, retains the T. R.

[12] The A. V. here strangely departs from the correct translation which it adopts above (iii. 11).

day in this wise, '𝕬𝖓𝖉 𝕲𝖔𝖉 𝖉𝖎𝖉 𝕽𝕰𝕾𝕿 𝖔𝖓 𝖙𝖍𝖊 𝖘𝖊𝖛𝖊𝖓𝖙𝖍 iv. 5 𝖉𝖆𝖞 𝖋𝖗𝖔𝖒 𝖆𝖑𝖑 𝖍𝖎𝖘 𝖜𝖔𝖗𝖐𝖘;'[1] and in this place again '𝖙𝖍𝖊𝖞 𝖘𝖍𝖆𝖑𝖑 𝕹𝕺𝕿 𝖊𝖓𝖙𝖊𝖗 𝖎𝖓𝖙𝖔 𝖒𝖞 𝖗𝖊𝖘𝖙.'[2]   Since there- 6 fore it still remaineth that some must enter therein, and they who first received the glad tidings thereof entered not, because of disobedience,[3] He AGAIN fixeth 7 a certain day,—'𝕿𝕺-𝕯𝕬𝖄'—declaring in David, after so long a time (as hath been said), '𝕿𝖔-𝖉𝖆𝖞, 𝖎𝖋 𝖞𝖊 𝖍𝖊𝖆𝖗 𝖍𝖎𝖘 𝖛𝖔𝖎𝖈𝖊, 𝖍𝖆𝖗𝖉𝖊𝖓 𝖓𝖔𝖙 𝖞𝖔𝖚𝖗 𝖍𝖊𝖆𝖗𝖙𝖘.' For if Joshua had 8 given them rest, God would not speak afterwards of ANOTHER day.   Therefore there still remaineth a Sab- 9 bath-rest[4] for the people of God.   For he that is 10 entered into God's rest, must[5] himself also rest from his labours, as God did from His.   Let us therefore 11 strive to enter into that rest, lest any man fall after the same example of disobedience.[6]

forGod'sjudg-
ment cannot
be evaded.   For the word of God[7] liveth and worketh, and is 12 sharper than any two-edged sword, piercing even to the dividing asunder of soul and spirit, yea, to the[8] inmost parts thereof, and judging the thoughts and imaginations of the heart.   Neither is there any crea- 13 ture that is not manifest in His sight.   But all things are naked and opened unto the eyes of Him with whom we have to do.

Christ is a
High Priest
who can be
touched with
a feeling of
our infirmities   Seeing, then, that we have a great High Priest, 14 who hath passed[9] through the heavens, Jesus the Son of God, let us hold fast our confession.   For 15 we have not an High Priest that cannot be touched

[1] Gen. ii. 2 (LXX. slightly altered).

[2] The meaning of this is,—God's rest was a perfect rest,—He declared His intention that His people should enjoy His rest,—that intention has not yet been fulfilled,—its fulfilment therefore is still to come.

[3] Here it is said they entered not *because of disobedience*; in iii. 19, *because of unbelief*; but this does not justify us in translating these different Greek expressions (as in A. V.) by the same English word. The rejection of the Israelites was caused both by *unbelief* and by *disobedience*; the former being the source of the latter.

[4] Strictly, *a keeping of Sabbatical rest*.

[5] Literally, *hath rested*, the aorist used for perfect. To complete the argument of this verse, we must supply the minor premiss, *but God's people have never yet enjoyed this perfect rest*; whence the conclusion follows, *there-*

fore its enjoyment is still future, as before.

[6] The reasoning of the above passage rests upon the truth that the unbelief of the Israelites, and the repose of Canaan, were typical of higher realities ; and that this fact had been divinely intimated in the words of the Psalmist.

[7] The *word of God* is *the revelation of the mind of God, imparted to man*. See note on Eph. v. 26. Here it denotes *the revelation of God's judgment to the conscience*.

[8] The expression is literally, *of soul and spirit, both joint and marrow*; the latter being a proverbial expression for *utterly, even to the inmost parts*.

[9] ' *Through*,' not ' *into*' (A. V.). The allusion is to the high priest passing through the courts of the Temple to the Holy of Holies. Compare ix. 11 and 24.

with a feeling of our infirmities, but who bore in
all things the likeness of our trials,[1] yet without sin.
iv. 16 Let us therefore come boldly to the throne of grace,
that we may obtain mercy, and find grace to help
v. 1 in time of need.   For every High Priest taken from
among men, is ordained to act on behalf of men in
the things of God, that he may offer gifts and sacri-
2 fices for sins; and is able to bear with the ignorant [2]
and erring, being himself also encompassed with in-
3 firmity.   And by reason thereof, he is bound, as for
the people,[3] so also for himself, to make offering for
4 sins.   And no man taketh this honour on himself,
5 but he that is[4] called by God, as was Aaron.   So also
Christ glorified not Himself, to be made an High
6 Priest; but He that said unto Him, ' 𝕮𝖍𝖔𝖚 𝖆𝖗𝖙 𝖒𝖞 𝖘𝖔𝖓,
𝖙𝖔-𝖉𝖆𝖞 𝖍𝖆𝖇𝖊 𝕴 𝖇𝖊𝖌𝖔𝖙𝖙𝖊𝖓 𝖙𝖍𝖊𝖊.' [5]   As He saith also in
another place, ' 𝕮𝖍𝖔𝖚 𝖆𝖗𝖙 𝖆 𝖕𝖗𝖎𝖊𝖘𝖙 𝖋𝖔𝖗 𝖊𝖇𝖊𝖗 𝖆𝖋𝖙𝖊𝖗 𝖙𝖍𝖊 𝖔𝖗𝖉𝖊𝖗
7 𝖔𝖋 𝕸𝖊𝖑𝖈𝖍𝖎𝖘𝖊𝖉𝖊𝖈.' [6]   Who in the days of His flesh offered
up prayers and supplications with strong crying and
tears, unto Him that could save Him from death,
8 and was heard because He feared God,[7] and though
He was a Son, yet learned He obedience [8] by suf-
9 fering.   And when His consecration [9] was accomplished, He became the author of eternal salvation
0 to all them that obey Him; having been named by
God an High Priest ' 𝖆𝖋𝖙𝖊𝖗 𝖙𝖍𝖊 𝖔𝖗𝖉𝖊𝖗 𝖔𝖋 𝕸𝖊𝖑𝖈𝖍𝖎𝖘𝖊𝖉𝖊𝖈.'
11   Of whom I have many things to say, and hard of   *The readers*
interpretation, since ye have grown [10] dull in under-   *are reproached for their de-*
12 standing.[11]   For when ye ought, after so long a time,[12]   *cline in spiri-*
to be teachers, ye need again to be taught yourselves,   *tual under-standing,*
what[13] are the first principles of the oracles of God;
and ye have come to need milk, instead of meat.[14]
13 For every one that feeds on milk is ignorant of the

[1] See note on ii. 18.
[2] The sin-offerings were mostly for
sins of ignorance. See Leviticus, chap. v.
[3] See Levit. chap. iv. and chap. ix.
[4] If (with the best MSS.) we omit
the article, the translation will be ' *but
when called by God,*' which does not
alter the sense.
[5] Ps. ii. 7 (LXX.).
[6] Ps. cx. 4 (LXX.).
[7] ' Fear ' here means *the fear of God.*
Compare ' God-fearing men,' Acts ii. 5.
The sentiment corresponds remarkably
with that of chap. xii. 5–11.
[8] There is a junction here of words
of similar sound and parallel meaning,
with which the readers of Æschylus

and Herodotus are familiar. See Æsch.
Agam. and Herod. i. 207.
[9] Compare ii. 10, and the note there.
[10] ' Have grown,' implying that they
had declined from a more advanced
state of Christian attainment.
[11] Literally, ' in their hearing.' Compare Acts xvii. 20, and Matt. xiii. 15.
[12] Literally, *because of the time,* viz.,
the length of time elapsed since your
conversion.   See the preceding introductory remarks, p. 785.
[13] We accentuate with Griesbach,
Tischendorf, &c.
[14] The adjective does not mean '*strong*'
(A. V.), but *solid,* opposed to *liquid.*
We use *meat* for *solid food* in general.

doctrine of righteousness, for he is a babe ; but meat v. 14
is for men full grown, who, through habit, have their
senses exercised to know good from evil.   Therefore vi. 1
let me leave[1] the rudiments of the doctrine of Christ,
and go on to its maturity ; not laying again the foundation,—of Repentance from dead works,[2] and Faith
towards God ;—Baptism,[3] Instruction,[4] and Laying 2
on of hands ;[5]—and Resurrection of the dead, and
Judgment everlasting.

warned of the
danger of
apostasy,   And this I will do[6] if God permit.   For it is im- 3, 4
possible[7] again to renew unto repentance those who
have been once enlightened, and have tasted of the
heavenly gift, and been made partakers of the Holy
Spirit, and have tasted the goodness of the word of 5
God,[8] and the powers of the world to come,[9] and
afterwards have fallen away ; seeing they[10] crucify to 6
themselves the Son of God afresh, and put Him to an
open shame.   For the earth, when it hath drunk in 7
the rain that falleth oft upon it, if it bear herbs profitable to those for whom it is tilled, partaketh of
God's blessing; but if it bear thorns and thistles, it 8
is counted worthless and is nigh unto cursing, and its
and reminded
of their mo-
tives to perse-
verance. end is to be burned.   But, beloved, I am persuaded 9
better things of you, and things that accompany sal-

[1] The 1st person plural here, as at
v. 11, vi. 3, vi. 9, vi. 11, is used by the
writer ; it is translated by the 1st person singular in English according to
the principle laid down, p. 304, n. 5.

[2] *Dead works* here may mean either
sinful works (cf. Eph. ii. 1, 'dead in
sins'), or *legal* works ; but the former
meaning seems to correspond better
with the 'repentance' here, and with
ix. 14.

[3] We take the punctuation sanctioned
by Chrysostom.

[4] This was the *Catechetical Instruction* which, in the Apostolic age, *.fol-
lowed* baptism, as we have already
mentioned, p. 344.

[5] This is mentioned as following
baptism, Acts viii. 17–19, xix. 6, and
other places.

[6] Or, *let me do,* if we read with the
best MSS.

[7] A reason is here given by the
writer, why he will not attempt to
teach his readers the rudiments of
Christianity over again ; namely, that
it is useless to attempt, by the repetition of such instruction to recall those
who have renounced Christianity to

repentance.   The *impossibility* which
he speaks of, has reference (it should
be observed) only to *human agents*; it
is only said that *all human means of
acting on the heart* have been exhausted
in such a case.   Of course no limit is
placed on the Divine power.   Even in
the passage, x. 26–31 (which is much
stronger than the present passage) it
is not said that such apostates are
never brought to repentance ; but only
that it cannot be *expected* they ever
should be.   Both passages were much
appealed to by the Novatians, and some
have thought that this was the cause
which so long prevented the Latin
Church from receiving this Epistle into
the Canon.

[8] i.e. have experienced the fulfilment
of God's promises.

[9] *The powers of the world to come*
appear to denote the miraculous operations of the spiritual gifts.   They
properly belonged to the 'world to
come.'

[10] These apostates to Judaism *crucified Christ afresh,* inasmuch as they
virtually gave their approbation to His
crucifixion, by joining His crucifiers.

vi. 10 vation, though I thus speak. For God is not unrighteous to forget your labour, and the love[1] which
ye have shown to His name, in the services ye have
11 rendered and still render[2] to the saints. But I desire
earnestly that every cne of you might show the same
zeal, to secure the full possession[3] of your hope unto
12 the end ; that ye be not slothful, but follow the example of them who through faith and stedfastness
13 inherit the promises. For God when He made promise
to Abraham, because He could swear by no greater,
14 sware by Himself, saying, ' 𝕺𝖊𝖗𝖎𝖑𝖞, 𝖇𝖑𝖊𝖘𝖘𝖎𝖓𝖌 𝕴 𝖜𝖎𝖑𝖑 𝖇𝖑𝖊𝖘𝖘
15 𝖙𝖍𝖊𝖊, 𝖆𝖓𝖉 𝖒𝖚𝖑𝖙𝖎𝖕𝖑𝖞𝖎𝖓𝖌 𝕴 𝖜𝖎𝖑𝖑 𝖒𝖚𝖑𝖙𝖎𝖕𝖑𝖞 𝖙𝖍𝖊𝖊 ; '[4] and so,
having stedfastly endured,[5] he obtained the promise.
16 For men, indeed, swear by the greater; and their
oath establisheth[6] their word, so that they cannot
17 gainsay it. Wherefore God, willing more abundantly
to show unto the heirs of the promise the immuta-
bility of His counsel, set an oath between himself
18 and them ;[7] that by two immutable things, wherein it
is impossible for God to lie, we that have fled [to
Him] for refuge might have a strong encourage-
19 ment[8] to hold fast the hope set before us. Which
hope we have as an anchor of the soul, both sure
20 and stedfast, and entering within the veil ; whither
Jesus, our forerunner, is for us entered, being made
' 𝖆𝖓 𝕳𝖎𝖌𝖍 𝕻𝖗𝖎𝖊𝖘𝖙 𝖋𝖔𝖗 𝖊𝖛𝖊𝖗 𝖆𝖋𝖙𝖊𝖗 𝖙𝖍𝖊 𝖔𝖗𝖉𝖊𝖗 𝖔𝖋 𝕸𝖊𝖑=
𝖈𝖍𝖎𝖘𝖊𝖉𝖊𝖈.'[9]

vii. 1 For this Melchisedec,[10] ' 𝖐𝖎𝖓𝖌 𝖔𝖋 𝕾𝖆𝖑𝖊𝖒,'[11] ' 𝖕𝖗𝖎𝖊𝖘𝖙 𝖔𝖋   The Priest-
𝖙𝖍𝖊 𝖒𝖔𝖘𝖙 𝖍𝖎𝖌𝖍 𝕲𝖔𝖉,'[11] who met Abraham returning hood of Christ (typified by
2 from the slaughter of the kings and blessed him, to the Priesthood of Melchise-
whom also Abraham gave ' 𝖆 𝖙𝖊𝖓𝖙𝖍 𝖕𝖆𝖗𝖙 𝖔𝖋 𝖆𝖑𝖑,'[12]—who dec) is distinguished from the Levi-

---

[1] 'Labour' is omitted in the best MSS.
[2] Compare x. 32, and the remarks,
p. 785. For 'saints,' see note on 1 Cor.
i. 2.
[3] Such appears the meaning of the
word here. The English word *satisfaction*, in its different uses, bears a close
analogy to it.
[4] Gen. xxii. 17 (LXX. except that
'thee' is put for 'thy seed').
[5] Abraham's 'steadfast endurance'
was shown just before he obtained this
promise, in the offering up of Isaac.
[6] Literally, *their oath is to them an
end of all gainsaying, unto establishment
[of their word]*.
[7] The verb means *to interpose between two parties.* Bleek gives instances of its use, both transitively and

intransitively. The literal English of
the whole phrase is, *He interposed with
an oath between the two parties.* The
'two immutable things' are God's
promise, and His oath.
[8] This construction of the words seems
to agree better with the ordinary meaning (see Heb. xii. 5, and xiii. 22 ; also
Heb. iv. 14) than the A. V.
[9] Ps. cx. 4, quoted above, v. 6 and
v. 10, and three times in the next
chapter.
[10] The following passage cannot be
rightly understood, unless we bear in
mind throughout that Melchisedec is
here spoken of, not as an historical
personage, but as a *type of Christ.*
[11] Gen. xiv. 18 (LXX.).
[12] Gen. xiv. 20 (LXX.).

tical Priest-
hood by its
eternal dura-
tion and effi-
cacy.

is first, by interpretation, KING OF RIGHTEOUSNESS,[1]
and secondly king of Salem,[2] which is KING OF PEACE vii. 3
—without father, without mother, without table of
descent[3]—having[4] neither beginning of days nor
end of life, but made like unto the Son of God—
remaineth a priest for ever.

Now consider how great this man was, to whom 4
even Abraham the patriarch gave a tenth of the
choicest[5] spoil. And truly those among the sons of 5
Levi who receive the office of the priesthood, have a
commandment to take tithes according to the Law
from the People, that is, from their brethren, though
they come out of the loins of Abraham. But he, 6
whose descent is not counted from them, taketh
tithes from Abraham, and blesseth[6] the possessor of
the promises. Now without all contradiction, the 7
less is blessed by the greater.[7] And here, tithes are 8
received by men that die ; but there, by him of 9
whom it is testified[8] that he liveth. And Levi also,
the receiver of tithes, hath paid tithes (so to speak)
by[9] Abraham ; for he was yet in the loins of his 10
father when Melchisedec met him.

Now if all things[10] were perfected by the Levitical 11
priesthood (since under it[11] the people hath received
the Law),[12] what further need was there that another
priest should rise ‘ *after the order of Melchisedec* ’ and
not be called ‘ after the order of Aaron ? ’ For the 12
priesthood being changed, there is made of necessity
a change also of the Law.[13] For He[14] of whom these 13
things are spoken belongeth to another tribe, of
which no man giveth attendance[15] at the altar ; it 14

---

[1] This is the translation of his Hebrew name.

[2] *Salem* in Hebrew means *peace.*

[3] ‘Without table of descent.’ This
explains the two preceding words ; the
meaning is, that the priesthood of Melchisedec was not, like the Levitical
priesthood, dependent on his descent,
through his parents, from a particular
family, but was a personal office.

[4] Here, as in the previous ‘ without
father’ and ‘without mother,’ the *silence*
of Scripture is interpreted allegorically.
Scripture mentions neither the father
nor mother, neither the birth nor death
of Melchisedec.

[5] Such is the sense of the word used
here.

[6] The verbs are *present-perfect.*

[7] The same word as in i. 4.

[8] Viz. testified in Ps. cx. 4. ‘Thou
art a priest *for ever.*’

[9] ‘ *By,*’ not ‘ *in* ’ (A. V.).

[10] The term here used, a word of very
frequent occurrence and great significance in this Epistle, is not fully represented by the English ‘ *Perfection.*’
The corresponding verb denotes, *to bring
a thing to the fulness of its designed development.* Comp. vii. 19, and note on ii.10.

[11] *Under its conditions and ordinances.* Compare viii. 6.

[12] Such is the tense according to the
reading of the best MSS.

[13] The word used (as often) without
the article for *the Law.* Cf. note on
Rom. iii. 20.

[14] Viz. the Messiah, predicted in Ps.
cx. 4.

[15] The verbs are *present-perfect.*

being evident that our Lord hath arisen[1] out of
Judah, of which tribe Moses spake nothing concern-
vii. 15 ing priesthood.　And this is far more evident when[2]
another priest ariseth after the likeness of Melchise-
16 dec; who is made not under the law of a carnal commandment, but with the power of an imperishable
17 life; for it is testified[3] of Him, '𝕿𝖍𝖔𝖚 𝖆𝖗𝖙 𝖆 𝖕𝖗𝖎𝖊𝖘𝖙
18 𝕱𝕺𝕽 𝕰𝖁𝕰𝕽 𝖆𝖋𝖙𝖊𝖗 𝖙𝖍𝖊 𝖔𝖗𝖉𝖊𝖗 𝖔𝖋 𝕸𝖊𝖑𝖈𝖍𝖎𝖘𝖊𝖉𝖊𝖈.'　On the
one hand,[4] an old commandment is annulled, because
19 it was weak and profitless (for the Law perfected[5]
nothing); and on the other hand, a better hope is
brought in, whereby we draw near unto God.

20　And inasmuch as this Priesthood hath the con-
21 firmation of an oath—(for Those priests are made
without an oath, but He with an oath, by Him that
22 said unto Him, '𝕿𝖍𝖊 𝕷𝖔𝖗𝖉 𝖘𝖜𝖆𝖗𝖊 𝖆𝖓𝖉 𝖜𝖎𝖑𝖑 𝖓𝖔𝖙 𝖗𝖊𝖕𝖊𝖓𝖙,
𝕿𝖍𝖔𝖚 𝖆𝖗𝖙 𝖆 𝖕𝖗𝖎𝖊𝖘𝖙 𝖋𝖔𝖗 𝖊𝖛𝖊𝖗'[6])—insomuch Jesus is[7]
surety of a better covenant.

23　And they, indeed, are[8] many priests [one succeeding to another's office], because death hindereth
24 their continuance.　But He, because He remaineth for
25 ever, hath no successor in His priesthood.[9]　Wherefore also He is able to save them to the uttermost
that come unto God by Him, seeing He ever liveth
to make intercession for them.

26　For such an High Priest became us, who is holy,
harmless, undefiled, separate[10] from sinners, and
27 ascended above the heavens.　Who needeth not daily,[11]

[1] *Hath arisen.* Compare the passage of Isaiah quoted Matt. iv. 16.

[2] *If,* here meaning *if, as is the case.*

[3] The best MSS. have the passive.

[4] The particles in the Greek express this contrast.　The overlooking of this caused the error in the A. V.

[5] Compare note on verse 11.

[6] In this quotation (again repeated) from Ps. cx. 4, the words 'after the order of Melchisedec' are not found here in the best MSS.

[7] Not '*was* made' (A. V.), but *has become* or *is.*

[8] *Are,* or *have become,* not '*were*' (A. V.); an important mistranslation, as the *present tense* shows that the Levitical Priesthood was still enduring while this Epistle was written.

[9] *Not passing on to another.*

[10] This seems to refer to the separa-
tion from all contact with the unclean, which was required of the High Priest; who (according to the Talmud) abstained from intercourse even with his own family, for seven days before the day of Atonement.

[11] This '*daily*' has occasioned much perplexity, for the High Priest only offered the sin-offerings here referred to once a year, on the day of Atonement.　(Levit. xvi. and Exod. xxx. 7–10.)　We must either suppose (with Tholuck) that it is used for *perpetually,* i.e. year after year; or we must suppose a reference to the High Priest as taking part in the occasional sacrifices made by all the Priests, for sins of ignorance (Levit. iv.); or we must sup-
pose that the regular acts of the Priest-
hood are attributed to the High Priests, as representatives and heads of the whole order; or finally, we must take 'High Priests,' as at Matt. ii. 4, Acts v. 24, and other places, for the heads of the twenty-four classes into which the Priests were divided, who officiated in turn.　This latter view is perhaps the

as those High Priests,[1] to offer up sacrifice, first
for His own sins and then for the People's; for this
He did once, when He offered up Himself. For vii. 2
the Law maketh men High Priests, who have infirmity; but the word of the oath which was since
the Law,[2] maketh the Son, who is consecrated[3] for
evermore.

The Mosaic Law, with its Temple, hierarchy, and sacrifices, was an imperfect shadow of the better covenant, and the availing atonement, of Christ.

Now this is the sum of our words.[4] We have such viii. 1
an High Priest, who hath sat down on the right hand
of the throne of the Majesty in the heavens; a 2
minister of the sanctuary,[5] and of the true tabernacle, which the Lord pitched, and not man. For 3
every High Priest is ordained[6], to offer gifts and sacrifices; wherefore this High Priest also must have
somewhat[7] to offer. Now[8] if He were on earth, He 4
would not be a Priest at all,[9] since the Priests are
they that make the offerings according to the Law;[10]
who minister to that which is a figure[11] and shadow 5
of heavenly things, as Moses is admonished[12] by God,
when he is about to make the tabernacle; for '**See,**'
saith He, '**that thou make all things according to the
pattern showed thee in the mount.**'[13] But now He 6
hath obtained a higher ministry, by so much as He
is the mediator[14] of a better covenant, which is
enacted[15] under better promises.

For if that first covenant were faultless, no place 7
would be sought[16] for a second; whereas He findeth 8
fault,[17] and saith unto them, '**Behold, the days come,
saith the Lord, when I will accomplish**[18] **for the house**

most natural. The Priests sacrificed a lamb every morning and evening, and offered an offering of flour and wine besides. Philo regards the lambs as offered by the Priests *for the people*, and the flour *for themselves*. He also says the High Priest offered *prayers and sacrifices every day*.

[1] Literally, *the* [*ordinary*] *High Priests*.

[2] Viz. the oath in Ps. cx. 4, so often referred to in this Epistle.

[3] Compare ii. 10.

[4] Literally, *the things which are being spoken*.

[5] *Sanctuary*. Compare ix. 12, *Holy Place*, where the Greek word is the same.

[6] The same thing is said v. 1.

[7] What the sacrifice was is not said here, but had been just before mentioned, vii. 27.

[8] *Now* (not *for*) is according to the reading of the best MSS.

[9] 'Not a Priest *at all*.' The translation in A. V. is hardly strong enough.

[10] Our Lord being of the tribe of Judah, could not have been one of the Levitical Priesthood. So it was said before, vii. 14.

[11] Viz. the Temple ritual.

[12] Compare Acts x. 22, and Heb. xi. 7.

[13] Exod. xxv. 40 (LXX.).

[14] Moses was called by the Jews the *Mediator* of the Law. See Gal. iii. 19, and note.

[15] Compare vii. 11, not '*was* established' (A. V.), but *hath been* or *is*.

[16] Here A. V. is not quite correct.

[17] 'Findeth fault' refers to the preceding 'faultless.' The pronoun should be joined with 'saith.'

[18] Here another verb is substituted for that found in the LXX. The preposition denotes 'for,' not 'with' (A. V.).

of Israel and for the house of Judah a new covenant.
viii. 9 Not according to the covenant which I gave[1] unto their
fathers, in the day when I took them by the hand to lead
them out of the land of Egypt; because they continued
not in my covenant, and I also turned my face from
10 them, saith the Lord. For this is the covenant which I
will make unto the house of Israel after those days,
saith the Lord: I will give[2] my laws unto their mind,
and write them upon their hearts; and I will be to them
11 a God, and they shall be to me a people. And they shall
not teach every man his neighbour[3] and every man his
brother, saying, Know the Lord; for all shall know me,
12 from the least unto the greatest. For I will be merciful
to their unrighteousness, and their sins and their iniqui-
13 ties will I remember no more.'[4] In that He saith
' A new covenant,' He hath made the first old; and
that which is old[5] and stricken in years, is ready to
vanish away.

ix. 1   Now the first covenant also had ordinances of
2 worship, and its Holy Place was in this world.[6] For
a tabernacle was made [in two portions]; the first
(wherein was the candlestick,[7] and the table,[8] and
the shewbread),[9] which is called the[10] sanctuary;
3 and, behind the second veil, the tabernacle called the
4 Holy of Holies, having the golden altar of incense,[11]
and the ark of the covenant overlaid round about

[1] It must be remembered that the Greek word does not (like the English *covenant*) imply reciprocity. It properly means *a legal disposition*, and would perhaps be better translated *dispensation* here. A covenant between two parties is expressed by a different term. The *new dispensation* is a gift from God, rather than a covenant between God and man (see Gal. iii. 15–20). Hence perhaps the other alteration of verb here, as well as that mentioned in the preceding note.

[2] ' *Give*,' not '*put*' (A. V.).

[3] The best MSS. read *citizen* instead of *neighbour*, which does not, however, alter the sense.

[4] Jer. xxxi. 31–34 (LXX. with the above-mentioned variations).

[5] The first refers to time (*growing out of date*), the second to the *weakness* of old age.

[6] ' The sanctuary,' not ' A sanctuary' (A. V.), and observe the order of the words, showing that ' in this world' is the predicate.

[7] Exod. xxv. 31, and xxxvii. 17.

[8] Exod. xxv. 23, and xxxvii. 10.

[9] Exod. xxv. 30, and Levit. xxiv. 5.

[10] See the note on ix. 24.

[11] ' Altar of incense.' This has given rise to much perplexity. According to Exod. xxx. 6, the Incense-altar was not in the Holy of Holies, but on the outer side of the veil which separated the Holy of Holies from the rest of the Tabernacle. Several methods of evading the difficulty have been suggested; amongst others, to translate the word by *censer*, and understand it of the censer which the High Priest brought into the Holy of Holies once a year; but this was not kept in the Holy of Holies. Moreover, the term is used for the Incense-altar by Philo and Josephus. The best explanation of the discrepancy is to consider that the Incense-altar, though not *within* the Holy of Holies, was closely connected therewith, and was sprinkled on the day of Atonement with the same blood with which the High Priest made atonement in the Holy of Holies. See Exod. xxx. 6–10, and Levit. xvi. 11, &c.

with gold,[1] wherein [2] was the golden pot [3] that had
the manna, and Aaron's rod [4] that budded, and the
tables [5] of the covenant; and over it the cherubims [6] ix. 5
of glory shadowing the Mercy-seat.[7]   Whereof we
cannot now speak particularly.   Now these things 6
being thus ordered, unto the first tabernacle the
priests go [8] in continually, accomplishing the offices 9
of their worship.   But into the second goeth the 7
High Priest alone, once a year, not without blood,
which he offereth for himself and for the errors [10] of
the people.   Whereby the Holy Spirit signifieth that 8
the way into the Holy Place is not yet made· fully
manifest,[11] while still the outer [12] tabernacle standeth.

[1] Exod. xxv. 11.

[2] Here we have another difficulty;
for the pot of manna and Aaron's rod
were not kept in the Ark, in Solomon's
time, when it contained nothing but
the tables of the Law. See 1 Kings
viii. 9, 2 Chron. v. 10. It is, however,
probable that these were originally
kept in the Ark. Compare Exod. xvi.
33, and Numbers xvii. 10, where they
are directed to be laid up *'before the
Lord,'* and *' before the testimony '* [i.e.
the tables of the Law], which indicates,
at least, a close juxtaposition to the
Ark. More generally, we should observe that the intention of the present
passage is not to give us a minute and
accurate description of the furniture of
the Tabernacle, but to allude to it rhe-
torically; the only point insisted upon
in the application of the description
(see v. 8), is the symbolical character
of the Holy of Holies. Hence the
extreme anxiety of commentators to
explain away every minute inaccuracy
is superfluous.

[3] Exod. xvi. 32, &c.

[4] Numbers xvii. 10.

[5] Exod. xxv. 16.

[6] Exod. xxv. 18.

[7] Exod. xxv. 17. This is the word
used in the LXX. for *Mercy-seat.*

[8] The writer of the Epistle here
appears to speak as if the Tabernacle
were still standing. Commentators
have here again found or made a difficulty, because the Temple of Herod
was in many respects different from the
Tabernacle, and especially because its
Holy of Holies did not contain either
the Ark, the Tables of the Law, the
Cherubim, or the Mercy-seat (all which
had been burnt by Nebuchadnezzar
with Solomon's Temple), but was

empty. See above, p. 581. Of course,
however, there was no danger that the
original readers of this Epistle should
imagine that its writer spoke of the
Tabernacle as still standing, or that
he was ignorant of the loss of its most
precious contents. Manifestly he is
speaking of *the Sanctuary of the First
Covenant* (see ix. 1) as originally *designed.* And he goes on to speak of
the existing Temple-worship as the
continuation of the Tabernacle-worship,
which, in all essential points, it was.
The translators of the Authorised Version (perhaps in consequence of this
difficulty) have mistranslated many
verbs in the following passage, which
are in the *present* tense, as though they
were in the *past* tense. Thus we have
*'went,' 'offered' 'were offered,' 'they
offered'* (x. 1), &c. The English reader
is thus led to suppose that the Epistle
was written after the cessation of the
Temple-worship.

[9] Plural, not singular, as in A. V.

[10] 'Errors.' Compare v. 2, and the
note.

[11] On the mistranslation in A. V. see
note 8 above. It may be asked, how
could it be said, after Christ's ascension,
that *the way into the Holy Place* was
not *made fully manifest?* The explanation is, that while the Temple-worship, with its exclusion of all but the
High Priest from the Holy of Holies,
still existed, the way of salvation
would not be *fully manifest* to those
who adhered to the outward and typical
observances, instead of being thereby
led to the Antitype.

[12] i.e. while the inner is separate
from the outer tabernacle. That 'first'
has this meaning here is evident from
ix. 2.

x. 9 But it is a figure for the present time,[1] under [2] which gifts and sacrifices are offered that cannot perfect the purpose of the worshipper, according to 10 the conscience ; [3] being carnal ordinances, commanding meats and drinks, and diverse washings, imposed until a time of reformation.[4]

11 But when Christ appeared, as High Priest of the good things to come, He passed through the greater and more perfect tabernacle [5] not made with hands 12 (that is, not of man's building),[6] and entered, not by the blood of goats and calves, but by His own blood, once for all into the Holy Place, having obtained an 13 everlasting redemption.[7] For if the blood of bulls and goats, and the ashes of an heifer [8] sprinkling the unclean, sanctifieth to the purification of the flesh; 14 how much more shall the blood of Christ, who through the eternal Spirit offered Himself without spot to God, purify our [9] conscience from dead works, that we may worship the living God.

15 And for this cause He is the mediator of a new testament ; that when death had [10] made redemption for the transgressions under the first testament,[11] they

---

[1] The A. V. here interpolates ' *then* ' in order to make this correspond with the mistranslated tenses already referred to.

[2] *According to which figure.* This follows the reading of the best MSS., and adopted by Griesbach, Lachmann, and Tischendorf's first edition ; it suits the preposition better than the other reading, to which Tischendorf has returned in his second edition.

[3] *Perfect the worshipper according to the conscience.* This is explained x. 2, as equivalent to ' the worshippers, once purified, would have had no more conscience of sin.' The meaning here is *to bring him to the accomplishment of the end of his worship,* viz. remission of sins. It is not adequately represented by *to make perfect,* as we have before remarked ; *to consummate* would be again the best translation, if it were less unusual.

[4] The reading of this verse is very doubtful. Tischendorf in his second edition returns to the reading of the T. R., which is also defended by De Wette. But Griesbach and Lachmann adopt the other reading, which is followed in our translation. The construction is literally, *imposed with conditions of meats,* &c., *until a time of reformation.*

[5] This *greater tabernacle* is the visible heavens, which are here regarded as the outer sanctuary.

[6] Literally, *this building.* This parenthesis has very much the appearance of having been originally a marginal gloss upon the preceding phrase.

[7] There is nothing in the Greek corresponding to the words ' *for us* ' (A. V.).

[8] The uncleanness contracted by touching a corpse, was purified by sprinkling the unclean person with the *water of sprinkling,* which was made with the ashes of a red heifer. See Numbers xix. (LXX.).

[9] ' Our ' (not ' your[4] ') is the reading of the best MSS.

[10] Literally, *after death had occurred for the redemption of,* &c. The words must be thus taken together.

[11] The Authorised Version is correct, in translating *testament* in this passage. The attempts which have been made to avoid this meaning are irreconcilable with any natural explanation of *testator.* The simple and obvious translation should not be departed from, in order to avoid a difficulty ; and the difficulty vanishes when we consider the rhetorical character of the Epistle. The statement in this verse is not

that are called might receive the promise of the
eternal inheritance. For where a testament is, the ix.
death of the testator must be declared; [1] because a 17
testament is made valid by death, for it hath no force
at all during the lifetime of the testator.

Wherefore [2] the first testament also hath its dedi- 18
cation [3] not without blood. For when Moses had 19
spoken to all the people every precept according to
the Law, he took [4] the blood of the calves and goats,
with water and scarlet wool and hyssop, and sprinkled
both the book itself [5] and all the people, saying, ' 𝕿𝖍𝖎𝖘 20
𝖎𝖘 𝖙𝖍𝖊 𝖇𝖑𝖔𝖔𝖉 𝖔𝖋 𝖙𝖍𝖊 𝖙𝖊𝖘𝖙𝖆𝖒𝖊𝖓𝖙 𝖜𝖍𝖎𝖈𝖍 𝕲𝖔𝖉 𝖍𝖆𝖙𝖍 𝖊𝖓𝖏𝖔𝖎𝖓𝖊𝖉
𝖚𝖓𝖙𝖔 𝖞𝖔𝖚.' [6] Moreover he sprinkled with blood the 21
tabernacle [7] also, and all the vessels of the ministry,
in like manner. And according to the Law, almost 22
all things are purified with blood, and without shedding of blood is no remission. It was, therefore, 23
necessary that the patterns of heavenly things should
thus be purified, but the heavenly things themselves
with better sacrifices than these. For Christ entered 24
not into the sanctuary [8] made with hands, which is a
figure of the true, but into heaven itself, now to appear in the presence of God for us. Nor yet that 25
He should offer Himself often, as the High Priest
entereth the sanctuary every year with blood of
others; for then must He often have suffered since 26
the foundation of the world : but now once, in the end [9]

meant as a logical argument, but as a rhetorical illustration, which is suggested
to the writer by the ambiguity of the
word for ' testament ' or ' covenant.'

[1] *Declared* is omitted in A. V. The
legal maxim is the same as that of
English Law, *Nemo est hæres viventis.*

[2] This ' wherefore ' does not refer to
the preceding illustration concerning
the death of the testator but to the
reasoning from which that was only a
momentary digression. Compare v. 18
with ver. 12-14.

[3] The verb means to *dedicate* in the
sense of to *inaugurate*; cf. Heb. x. 20 ;
so the feast commemorating the *opening*
or *inauguration* of the Temple by Judas
Maccabæus (after its pollution by Antiochus Epiphanes) was called ' *the
dedication.*' (John x. 22.)

[4] See Exod. xxiv. 3-8. The sacrifice of goats (besides the cattle) and
the sprinkling of the book are not in
the Mosaic account. It should be remembered that the Old Testament is

usually referred to *memoriter* by the
writers of the New Testament. Moreover, the advocates of verbal inspiration
would be justified in maintaining that
these circumstances actually occurred,
though they are not mentioned in the
books of Moses. See, however, p. 140,
n. 2.

[5] *Itself* is omitted in A. V.

[6] Exod. xxiv. 8 (LXX., but with a
change of verb).

[7] Apparently referring to Levit. viii.,
ver. 19, 24, and 30.

[8] Not ' *the holy places*' (A. V.) but
the holy place or sanctuary. Compare
viii. 2, ix. 2, 25, xiii. 11. It is without
the article here, as is often the case with
words similarly used.

[9] 'The end of the ages' means the
termination of the period preceding
Christ's coming. It is a phrase frequent
in St. Matthew, with ' age,' instead of
' ages,' but not occurring elsewhere.
The A. V. translates two different terms
here by the same word, 'world.'

x. 27 of the ages, hath He appeared,[1] to do away sin by the sacrifice of Himself.[2] And as it is appointed unto men once to die, but after this the judgment, so Christ was once offered ' **to bear the sins of many,** '[3] 28 and unto them that look for Him shall He appear a second time, without sin,[4] unto salvation.

x. 1 For the Law having a shadow of the [5] good things to come, and not the very image of the reality,[6] 2 by the unchanging sacrifices which year by year they offer continually,[7] can never perfect [8] the purpose of the offerers.[9] For then, would they not have ceased to be offered? because the worshippers, once purified, would have had no more conscience 3 of sins. But in these sacrifices there is a remem-4 brance of sins made every year. For it is not possible that the blood of bulls and goats should take away 5 sins. Wherefore, when He cometh into the world, He saith ' **Sacrifice and offering thou wouldest not, but a** 6 **body hast thou prepared me.**[10] **In burnt-offerings and** 7 **sacrifices for sin thou hast had no pleasure. Then said** **I, Lo, I come (in the volume of the book it is written of** 8 **me) to do thy will, O God.** '[11] When He had said before, ' **Sacrifice and offering and burnt-offerings and** **sacrifices for sin thou wouldest not, neither hadst** **pleasure therein** ' (which are offered under the Law); 9 ' **Then** ' (saith [12] He), ' **Lo, I come to do thy will, O** **God.** ' He taketh away the first,[13] that he may esta-10 blish the second. And in [14] that ' **will** ' we are sanctified, by the offering of the ' **body** '[15] of Jesus Christ, once for all.

---

[1] Literally, *He hath been made manifest to the sight of men.*

[2] The A. V. is retained here, being justified by *offered Himself*, v. 14.

[3] Isaiah liii. 12 (LXX.), *He bare the sins of many.*

[4] Tholuck compares *separate from sinners* (vii. 26). The thought is the same as Rom. vi. 10.

[5] The definite article is omitted in A.V.

[6] *The real things.*

[7] *The same* is omitted in A. V.

[8] Compare ix. 9, and note. The 'perfection' of the worshippers was *entire purification from sin*; this they could not attain under the Law, as was manifest by the perpetual iteration of the self-same sacrifices, required of them.

[9] Literally, *those who come to offer.*

[10] In the Hebrew original the words are ' *thou hast opened* [*or pierced*] *my*

ears.' The LXX. (which is here quoted) translates this ' *a body hast thou prepared me.*' Perhaps the reading of the Hebrew may formerly have been different from what it now is; or perhaps the *body* may have been an error for *ear*, which is the reading of some MSS.

[11] Ps. xl. 6-8 (LXX. with some slight variations).

[12] Not ' *said He* ' (A. V.), but *He hath said*, or *saith He.*

[13] *The first*, viz. the sacrifices; *the second*, viz. the will of God.

[14] *In the will of God*, Christians are already *sanctified* as well as *justified*, and even *glorified* (see Rom. viii. 30); i.e. God wills their sanctification, and has done His part to ensure it.

[15] ' *Body*,' alluding to the ' *body hast thou prepared me*,' of the above quotation.

And every priest [1] standeth daily ministering, and offering oftentimes the same sacrifices which can never take away sins. But HE, after He had offered one sacrifice for sins, for ever sat down on the right hand of God; from henceforth expecting '𝔱𝔦𝔩𝔩 𝔥𝔦𝔰 𝔢𝔫𝔢𝔪𝔦𝔢𝔰 𝔟𝔢 𝔪𝔞𝔡𝔢 𝔥𝔦𝔰 𝔣𝔬𝔬𝔱𝔰𝔱𝔬𝔬𝔩.' [2] For by one offering He hath perfected [3] for ever the purification of them whom He sanctifieth. Whereof the Holy Spirit also is a witness to us. For after He had said before, '𝔗𝔥𝔦𝔰 𝔦𝔰 𝔱𝔥𝔢 𝔠𝔬𝔳𝔢𝔫𝔞𝔫𝔱 𝔱𝔥𝔞𝔱 𝔌 𝔴𝔦𝔩𝔩 𝔪𝔞𝔨𝔢 𝔴𝔦𝔱𝔥 𝔱𝔥𝔢𝔪 𝔞𝔣𝔱𝔢𝔯 𝔱𝔥𝔬𝔰𝔢 𝔡𝔞𝔶𝔰, 𝔰𝔞𝔦𝔱𝔥 𝔱𝔥𝔢 𝔏𝔬𝔯𝔡; 𝔌 𝔴𝔦𝔩𝔩 𝔤𝔦𝔳𝔢 𝔪𝔶 𝔏𝔞𝔴𝔰 𝔲𝔭𝔬𝔫 𝔱𝔥𝔢𝔦𝔯 𝔥𝔢𝔞𝔯𝔱𝔰, 𝔞𝔫𝔡 𝔴𝔯𝔦𝔱𝔢 𝔱𝔥𝔢𝔪 𝔲𝔭𝔬𝔫 𝔱𝔥𝔢𝔦𝔯 𝔪𝔦𝔫𝔡𝔰,' [4] He saith also '𝔗𝔥𝔢𝔦𝔯 𝔰𝔦𝔫𝔰 𝔞𝔫𝔡 𝔱𝔥𝔢𝔦𝔯 𝔦𝔫𝔦𝔮𝔲𝔦𝔱𝔦𝔢𝔰 𝔴𝔦𝔩𝔩 𝔌 𝔯𝔢𝔪𝔢𝔪𝔟𝔢𝔯 𝔫𝔬 𝔪𝔬𝔯𝔢.' [5] Now where remission of these is, there is no more offering for sin.

x. 1 | 12 | 13 | 14 | 15 | 16 | 17 | 18

Renewed warning against apostasy,

Having therefore, brethren, boldness to enter the holy place through the blood of Jesus,[6] by a new and living way which He hath opened [7] for us, through the veil (that is to say, His flesh); [8] and having an High Priest [9] over the house of God; let us draw near with a true heart, in full assurance of faith; as our hearts have been '𝔰𝔭𝔯𝔦𝔫𝔨𝔩𝔢𝔡' [10] from the stain of an evil conscience, and our bodies have been washed with pure water. Let us hold fast the confession of our hope,[11] without wavering, for faithful is He that gave the promise. And let us consider the example [12]

19 | 20 | 21 | 22 | 23 | 24

[1] The MSS. are divided between 'Priest' and 'High Priest;' if the latter reading be correct, the same explanation must be given as in the note on vii. 27.

[2] Ps. cx. 1 (LXX.), quoted above, i. 13. (See note there.)

[3] Literally, *He hath consummated them that are being sanctified.* The verb *to perfect* does not, by itself, represent the original word. See notes on x. 1, ix. 10, and ii. 10. We should also observe, that 'being sanctified' is not equivalent to 'having been sanctified.'

[4] Jer. xxxi. 34 (LXX.). The part of the quotation here omitted is given above, viii. 10–12. It appears, from the slight variations between the present quotation and the quotation of the same passage in chapter viii., that the writer is quoting from memory.

[5] Jer. xxxi. 34 (LXX.), being the conclusion of the passage quoted before, viii. 12. The omission of 'He saith' with the 'and' which joins the two detached portions of the quotation, though abrupt, is not unexampled;

compare 1 Tim. v. 18.

[6] Compare ix. 25.

[7] See note on ix. 18.

[8] The meaning of this is, that the flesh (or manhood) of Christ was a veil which hid His true nature; this veil He rent, when He gave up His body to death; and through His incarnation, thus revealed under its true aspect, we must pass, if we would enter into the presence of God. We can have no real knowledge of God but through His incarnation.

[9] Literally, 'Great Priest.' The same expression is used for High Priest by Philo and LXX.

[10] 'Sprinkled' (alluding to ix. 13 and 21), viz. *with the blood of Christ*; compare 'blood of sprinkling,' xii. 24. Observe the force of the perfect participle in this and 'washed;' both referring to accomplished facts. See x. 2.

[11] '*Hope*,' not '*faith*.' (A. V.)

[12] This is Chrysostom's interpretation, which agrees with the use of the verb, iii. 1.

one of another, that we may be provoked unto love
x. 25 and to good works. Let us not forsake the assembling[1] of ourselves together, as the custom of some
is, but let us exhort one another; and so much the
26 more, as ye see The Day approaching.[2] For if we
sin wilfully,[3] after we have received the knowledge[4]
27 of the truth, there remaineth no more sacrifice for
sins, but a certain fearful looking for of judgment,
and ' a wrathful fire that shall devour the adversaries.'[5]
28 He that hath despised the Law of Moses dieth[6] without mercy, upon the testimony of two or three wit-
29 nesses. Of how much sorer punishment, suppose
ye, shall he be thought worthy, who hath trodden
under foot the Son of God, and hath counted the
blood of the covenant, wherewith he was sanctified,
an unholy thing, and hath done despite unto the
30 Spirit of Grace. For we know Him that hath said,
' Vengeance is mine, I will repay, saith the Lord;'[7] and
31 again, ' The Lord shall judge His people.'[8] It is a
fearful thing to fall into the hands of the living
God.[9]

[1] It was very natural that the more timid members of the Church should shrink from frequenting the assembly of the congregation for worship, in a time of persecution.

[2] 'The Day' of Christ's coming was seen approaching at this time by the threatening prelude of the great Jewish war, wherein He came to judge that nation.

[3] 'Wilfully.' This is opposed to the 'if a man sin not wilfully' (Levit. iv. 2, LXX.), the *involuntary* sins for which provision was made under the Law. The particular sin here spoken of is that of *apostasy from the Christian faith*, to which these Hebrew Christians were particularly tempted. See the whole of this passage from x. 26 to xii. 29.

[4] 'Knowledge.' Compare Rom. x. 2, Phil. i. 9, &c.

[5] Isa. xxvi. 11. Quoted generally from the LXX. Those who look for this quotation in A. V. will be disappointed, for the A. V., the Hebrew, and the LXX., all differ.

[6] The *present*, translated as *past* in A. V. The reference is to Deut. xvii. 2–7, which prescribes that an idolater should be put to death on the testimony of two or three witnesses. The writer of the Epistle does not mean that idolatry was actually thus punished *at the*
time he wrote (for though the Sanhedrin was allowed to judge charges of a religious nature, they could not inflict death without permission of the Roman Procurator, which would probably have been refused, except under very peculiar circumstances, to an enforcement of this part of the Law); but he speaks of the punishment *prescribed* by the Law.

[7] Deut. xxxii. 35. This quotation is not exactly according to LXX. or Hebrew, but is exactly in the words in which it is quoted by St. Paul, Rom. xii. 19.

[8] Deut. xxxii. 36 (LXX.).

[9] The preceding passage (from v. 26) and the similar passage, vi. 4–6, have proved perplexing to many readers; and were such a stumbling-block to Luther, that they caused him even to deny the canonical authority of the Epistle. Yet neither passage asserts the *impossibility* of an apostate's repentance. What is said amounts to this—that for the conversion of a deliberate apostate, God has (according to the ordinary laws of His working) no further means in store than those which have been already tried in vain. It should be remembered, also, that the parties addressed are not those who had already apostatised, but those who were in danger of so doing, and who needed the most earnest warning.

and exhorta-
tion not to let
faith be con-
quered by fear.
But call to remembrance the former days, in which, x. 3
after ye were illuminated, ye endured [1] a great fight
of afflictions; for not only were ye made a gazing- 33
stock by reproaches and tribulations, but ye took
part also in the sufferings of others who bore the
like. For ye showed compassion to the prisoners,[2] 34
and took joyfully the spoiling of your goods, knowing
that ye have [3] in heaven a better and an enduring
substance. Cast not away, therefore, your confi- 35
dence, which hath great recompense of reward. For 36
ye have need of stedfastness, that after ye have done
the will of God, ye may receive the promise. For 37
yet a little while and '𝕳𝔢 𝔱𝔥𝔞𝔱 𝔠𝔬𝔪𝔢𝔱𝔥 𝔰𝔥𝔞𝔩𝔩 𝔟𝔢 𝔠𝔬𝔪𝔢,
𝔞𝔫𝔡 𝔰𝔥𝔞𝔩𝔩 𝔫𝔬𝔱 𝔱𝔞𝔯𝔯𝔶.'[4] Now '𝕭𝔶 𝔣𝔞𝔦𝔱𝔥 𝔰𝔥𝔞𝔩𝔩 𝔱𝔥𝔢 38
𝔯𝔦𝔤𝔥𝔱𝔢𝔬𝔲𝔰 𝔩𝔦𝔟𝔢;'[5] and '𝕴𝔣 𝔥𝔢[6] 𝔡𝔯𝔞𝔴 𝔟𝔞𝔠𝔨 𝔱𝔥𝔯𝔬𝔲𝔤𝔥 𝔣𝔢𝔞𝔯,
𝔪𝔶 𝔰𝔬𝔲𝔩 𝔥𝔞𝔱𝔥 𝔫𝔬 𝔭𝔩𝔢𝔞𝔰𝔲𝔯𝔢 𝔦𝔫 𝔥𝔦𝔪.'[7] But we are not 39
men of fear unto perdition, but of faith unto salvation.[8]

Faith defined
as that prin-
ciple which
enables men
to prefer
things invi-
sible to things
visible.
Now faith is the substance [9] of things hoped for, xi.
the evidence of things not seen. For therein the 2
elders obtained a good report.[10]

By faith we understand that the universe [11] is 3
framed [12] by the word of God, so that the world
which we behold [13] springs not from things that can
be seen.

By faith Abel offered unto God a more excellent 4
sacrifice than Cain, whereby he obtained testimony

---

[1] If this Epistle was addressed to the Church of Jerusalem, the afflictions referred to would be the persecutions of the Sanhedrin (when Stephen was killed), of Herod Agrippa when James the Greater was put to death), and again the more recent outbreak of Ananus, when James the Less was slain. But see the preceding remarks, p. 785.

[2] 'The bondsmen' (not 'my bonds') is the reading of all the best MSS.

[3] Not 'knowing *in yourselves*' (A. V.). The reading of the best MSS., is, *that ye have yourselves,* or *for yourselves,* i.e. *as your own.*

[4] Habak. ii. 3 (LXX.). Not fully translated in A. V.

[5] Habak. ii. 4 (LXX), quoted also Rom. i. 17 and Gal. iii. 11.

[6] The '*any man*' of A. V. is not in the Greek. The Greek verb is exactly the English *flinch.*

[7] Habak. ii. 4 (LXX.). But this passage in the original precedes the last quotation, which it here follows.

[8] Properly *gaining of the soul,* and thus equivalent to *salvation.*

[9] For the meaning of this word, see note on iii. 14.

[10] 'Obtained a good report,' cf. Acts vi. 3. This verse is explained by the remainder of the chapter. The faith of the Patriarchs was a type of Christian faith, because it was fixed upon *a future and unseen good.*

[11] 'The worlds:' so i. 2.

[12] Observe that the tenses are *perfects,* not aorists.

[13] The best MSS. have the participle in the singular. The doctrine nega-tived is that which teaches that each successive condition of the universe is *generated* from a preceding condition (as the plant from the seed) by a mere material development, which had no beginning in a Creator's will.

that he was righteous, for God testified[1] unto his
gifts ; and by it he being dead yet speaketh.[2]

xi. 5　By faith Enoch was translated, that he should not
see death, and '𝔥𝔢 𝔴𝔞𝔰 𝔫𝔬𝔱 𝔣𝔬𝔲𝔫𝔡, 𝔟𝔢𝔠𝔞𝔲𝔰𝔢 𝔊𝔬𝔡 𝔱𝔯𝔞𝔫𝔰·
𝔩𝔞𝔱𝔢𝔡 𝔥𝔦𝔪.'[3]　For before his translation he had this
6 testimony, that '𝔥𝔢 𝔭𝔩𝔢𝔞𝔰𝔢𝔡 𝔊𝔬𝔡 ;'[4] but without faith
it is impossible to please Him ; for whosoever cometh
unto God must have faith[5] that God is, and that He
rewardeth them that diligently seek Him.

7　By faith Noah, being warned by God concerning
things not seen as yet, through fear of God[6] prepared an ark, to the saving of his house.　Whereby
he condemned the world and became heir of the
righteousness of faith

8　By faith Abraham, when he was called,[7] obeyed
the command to go forth into a place[8] which he
should afterward receive for an inheritance ; and he
9 went forth, not knowing whither he went.　By faith
he sojourned in the land of promise as in a strange
country, dwelling in tents, with Isaac and Jacob, the
10 heirs with him of the same promise.　For he looked
for the city which hath sure[9] foundations, whose
builder and maker is God.

11　By faith also Sarah herself received power to conceive seed, even when[10] she was past age, because she
12 judged Him faithful who had promised.　Therefore
sprang there of one, and him as good as dead, '𝔰𝔬
𝔪𝔞𝔫𝔶 𝔞𝔰 𝔱𝔥𝔢 𝔰𝔱𝔞𝔯𝔰 𝔬𝔣 𝔱𝔥𝔢 𝔰𝔨𝔶 𝔦𝔫 𝔪𝔲𝔩𝔱𝔦𝔱𝔲𝔡𝔢,'[11] and as the
sand which is by the sea-shore[12] innumerable.

13　These all died in faith, not having received the promises, but having seen them afar off, and embraced
them,[13] and confessed that they were strangers and
14 pilgrims upon earth.　For they that say such things,
15 declare plainly that they seek a country.　And truly
if they speak[14] of that country from whence they

[1] Gen. iv. 4.　The Jewish tradition
was, that fire from heaven consumed
Abel's offering.

[2] This has been supposed (compare
xii. 24) to refer to Gen. iv. 10, but it
may be taken more generally.

[3] Gen. v. 24 (LXX.).

[4] Ibid.

[5] *Without faith—must have faith.*
The original has this verbal connection.

[6] Compare Heb. v. 7.

[7] If we follow some of the best MSS.,
the translation will be ' *He that was
called Abraham* [*instead of Abram*].'

[8] Some of the best MSS. read 'place'
without the article.

[9] Cf. xii. 28.

[10] *Was delivered* is not in the best
MSS.

[11] Exod. xxxii. 13 (LXX.).

[12] The same comparison is found Isa.
x. 22, quoted Rom. ix. 27.

[13] *Persuaded* is an interpolation not
found in the best MSS.　It was originally a marginal gloss on *embraced*.
The latter word cannot be adequately
translated in English, so as to retain
the full beauty of the metaphor.

[14] *Speak.*　The verb is the same in
v. 22.　The meaning is, ' If, in calling

came forth, they might have opportunity to return ; but now they desire a better country, that is, an hea- venly.   Wherefore God is not ashamed to be called xi. their God ; for He hath prepared for them a city.

By faith Abraham, when he was tried, offered[1] up 17 Isaac, and he that had believed[2] the promises offered up his only begotten son, though it was said unto[3] him, '𝔈𝔫 𝔈𝔰𝔞𝔞𝔠 𝔰𝔥𝔞𝔩𝔩 𝔱𝔥𝔶 𝔰𝔢𝔢𝔡 𝔟𝔢 𝔠𝔞𝔩𝔩𝔢𝔡 ;'[4] accounting 18, that God was able to raise him up, even from the dead ; from whence also (in a figure) he received him.

By faith Isaac blessed Jacob and Esau, CONCERNING 20 THINGS TO COME.

By faith Jacob, WHEN HE WAS DYING, blessed both 21 the sons of Joseph ; and '𝔥𝔢 𝔴𝔬𝔯𝔰𝔥𝔦𝔭𝔭𝔢𝔡, 𝔩𝔢𝔞𝔫𝔦𝔫𝔤 𝔲𝔭𝔬𝔫 𝔱𝔥𝔢 𝔱𝔬𝔭 𝔬𝔣 𝔥𝔦𝔰 𝔰𝔱𝔞𝔣𝔣.'[5]

By faith Joseph, IN THE HOUR OF HIS DEATH, spake[6] 22 of the departing of the sons of Israel ; and gave com- mandment concerning his bones.

By faith Moses, when he was born, was hid three 23 months by his parents, because '𝔱𝔥𝔢𝔶 𝔰𝔞𝔴 𝔱𝔥𝔞𝔱 𝔱𝔥𝔢 𝔠𝔥𝔦𝔩𝔡 𝔴𝔞𝔰 𝔤𝔬𝔬𝔡𝔩𝔶 ;'[7] and they were not afraid of the king's commandment.

By faith Moses, 𝔴𝔥𝔢𝔫 𝔥𝔢 𝔴𝔞𝔰 𝔠𝔬𝔪𝔢 𝔱𝔬 𝔶𝔢𝔞𝔯𝔰,'[8] re- 24 fused to be called the son of Pharaoh's daughter, choosing rather to suffer affliction with the People 25 of God, than to enjoy the pleasures of sin for a sea- son ; esteeming the reproach of Christ[9] greater riches 26 than the treasures of Egypt ; for he looked beyond[10] unto the reward.[11]   By faith he forsook[12] Egypt, not 27

themselves strangers and pilgrims, they refer to the fact of their having left their native land.'   In other words, If Christians regret the world which they have renounced, there is nothing to prevent their returning to its enjoy- ments.   Here again we trace a reference to those who were tempted to aposta- tise.   Such is the meaning of the im- perfect.

[1] Literally, *hath offered.*

[2] The word means more than '*re- ceived.*'   (A. V.)   His belief in the promises to his posterity enhanced the sacrifice which he made.

[3] '*Unto,*' not '*of.*'   (A. V.)   'Unto whom' is equivalent to 'though unto him.'

[4] Gen. xxi. 12 (LXX.), quoted also Rom. ix. 7.

[5] Gen. xlvii. 31 (LXX.).   The pre-

sent Hebrew text means not *the top of his staff,* but the *head of his bed* ; but the LXX. followed a different reading. The 'faith' of Jacob consisted in fixing his hopes upon future blessings, and wor- shipping God, even in the hour of death.

[6] *Spake.*   See v. 15.   Joseph's 'faith' relied on the promise that the seed of Abraham should return to the promised land.   (Gen. xv. 16.)

[7] Exod. ii. 2 (LXX.).   'They see- ing that he was goodly.'   The Hebrew speaks of his mother only.

[8] Exod. ii. 11 (LXX.).

[9] The reproach of Christ's people is here called the reproach of Christ. Compare Col. i. 24, and 2 Cor. i. 5 ; also see 1 Cor. x. 4.

[10] Literally, *he looked away from that which was before his eyes.*

[11] Compare v. 6.   [12] See Exod. ii. 15.

fearing the wrath of the king; for he endured, as
i. 28 seeing Him who is invisible.   By faith he hath established [1] the passover, and the sprinkling of blood,
that the destroyer of the first-born might not touch
the children of Israel. [2]

29   By faith they passed through the Red Sea as
through dry land ; which the Egyptians tried to pass,
and were swallowed up.

30   By faith the walls of Jericho fell down, after they
were compassed about for seven days.

31   By faith the harlot Rahab perished not with the
disobedient, [3] because she had received the spies with
peace.

32   And what shall I more say ? for the time would
fail me to tell of Gideon, and of Barak, of Samson
and of Jephthae, of David, and Samuel, and the pro-
33 phets ; who through faith subdued kingdoms, wrought
righteousness, obtained promises, stopped the mouths
34 of lions, [4] quenched the violence of fire, [5] escaped the
edge of the sword, out of weakness [6] were made
strong, waxed valiant in fight, turned to flight the
35 armies of the aliens.   Women [7] received their dead
raised to life again ; and others were tortured, [8] not
accepting deliverance, that they might obtain a
36 better [9] resurrection.   Others also had trial of cruel
mockings [10] and scourgings, with chains also and im-
37 prisonment. They were stoned, [11] were sawn [12] asunder,

[1] *Perfect.*

[2] *Them,* i.e., *the children of Israel.*

[3] Not ' *them that believed not.*'
(A. V.)   They had heard the miracles
wrought in favour of the Israelites
(Josh. ii. 10), and yet refused obedience.

[4] Referring to Daniel. (Dan. vi. 17.)

[5] Referring to Dan. iii. 27.

[6] This and the two following clauses
may be most naturally referred to the
Maccabees.

[7] Referring to the widow of Sarepta
(1 Kings xvii.) and the Shunamite
(2 Kings iv.).

[8] This refers both to Eleazar (2
Macc. vi.), and to the seven brothers,
whose torture is described, 2 Macc.
vii.   The verb ἐτυμπανίσθησαν points
especially to Eleazar, who was bound
to the τύμπανον, an instrument to which
those who were to be tortured by
scourging were bound.   (2 Macc. vi.
19.)   The ' not accepting deliverance '
refers to the mother of the seven
brothers and her youngest son
(2 Macc. vii.)

[9] *Better,* viz. than that of those who
(like the Shunamite's son) were only
raised to return to this life.   This reference is plain in the Greek, but cannot be rendered equally obvious in
English, because we cannot translate
the first ἀναστάσεως in this verse by
resurrection.

[10] *Mockings.*   Still referring to the
seven brothers, concerning whose tor-
ments this word is used.   (2 Macc.
vii. 7.)

[11] Zechariah, the son of Jehoiadah,
was stoned. (2 Chron. xxiv. 20.)   But
it is not necessary (nor indeed possible) to fix each kind of death here
mentioned on some person in the Old
Testament.   It is more probable that
the Epistle here speaks of the general
persecution under Antiochus Epiphanes.

[12] According to Jewish tradition this
was the death of Isaiah ; but see the
preceding note.

were tempted,[1] were slain with the sword. They wandered about in sheep skins and goat skins, being destitute, afflicted, tormented. They wandered in xi. 38 deserts, and in mountains, and in dens and caves of the earth; of whom [2] the world was not worthy.

And these all, having obtained a good report through 39 faith, received not the promise; God having provided 40 some better thing for us, that they, without us, should not be made perfect.[3]

Exhortation to imitate such examples, and to follow Jesus in stedfast endurance of suffering.

Wherefore, seeing we are compassed about with so xii. 1 great a cloud of witnesses, let us [4] also lay aside every weight, and the sin which clingeth closely round us,[5] and run with courage [6] the race that is set before us; looking onward [7] unto Jesus, the forerunner [8] and the 2 finisher of our faith; who for the joy that was set before Him, endured the cross, despising the shame, and is set down at the right hand of the throne of God. Yea, consider Him that endured such contra- 3 diction of sinners against Himself, lest ye be wearied and faint in your minds. Ye have not yet resisted 4 unto blood,[9] in your conflict against sin; and ye have 5 forgotten the exhortation which reasoneth [10] with you as with sons, saying, '𝕸𝖞 𝖘𝖔𝖓, 𝖉𝖊𝖘𝖕𝖎𝖘𝖊 𝖓𝖔𝖙 𝖙𝖍𝖔𝖚 𝖙𝖍𝖊 𝖈𝖍𝖆𝖘𝖙𝖊𝖓𝖎𝖓𝖌 𝖔𝖋 𝖙𝖍𝖊 𝕷𝖔𝖗𝖉, 𝖓𝖔𝖗 𝖋𝖆𝖎𝖓𝖙 𝖜𝖍𝖊𝖓 𝖙𝖍𝖔𝖚 𝖆𝖗𝖙 𝖗𝖊𝖇𝖚𝖐𝖊𝖉 𝖔𝖋 𝕳𝖎𝖒. 𝕱𝖔𝖗 𝖜𝖍𝖔𝖒 𝖙𝖍𝖊 𝕷𝖔𝖗𝖉 𝖑𝖔𝖛𝖊𝖙𝖍 𝕳𝖊 𝖈𝖍𝖆𝖘𝖙𝖊𝖓𝖊𝖙𝖍, 𝖆𝖓𝖉 6

---

[1] The Received Text is here retained; but it seems very probable that the reading should be (as has been conjectured), *they were burned.* This was the death of the seven brothers.

[2] Literally, *they of whom the world was not worthy, wandering in deserts and in mountains,* &c.; i.e. They, for whom all that the world could give would have been too little, had not even a home wherein to lay their head.

[3] *Made perfect.* See notes on ii. 10, vii. 11, ix. 9; literally, *attain their consummation,* including *the attainment of the full maturity of their being,* and *the attainment of the full accomplishment of their faith*; which are indeed identical. They were not to attain this *without us,* i.e. not until we came to join them.

[4] *Let us, as they did.* The Agonistic metaphor here (see pp. 538, 539) would be more naturally addressed to the Church of Alexandria than to that of Jerusalem.

[5] This word occurs nowhere else. Sin seems here to be described under the metaphor of a garment fitting closely to the limbs, which must be *cast off,* if the race is to be won. A garment would be called by the term in question, which *fitted well all round.*

[6] The original (as it has been before remarked) is not accurately represented by '*patience:*' it means *stedfast endurance,* or *fortitude.*

[7] ' Looking onward.' Comp. 'looked beyond' (xi. 26).

[8] Literally, *foremost leader.* Compare ii. 10. Compare also the similar phrase in vi. 20.

[9] If this Epistle was addressed to the Christians of Jerusalem, the writer speaks here only of the existing generation; for the Church of Jerusalem had 'resisted unto blood' formerly, in the persons of Stephen, James the Greater, and James the Less. But see introductory remarks, pp. 786, 787.

[10] This is the meaning of the Greek word.

xii. 7 𝔰𝔠𝔬𝔲𝔯𝔤𝔢𝔱𝔥 𝔢𝔳𝔢𝔯𝔶 𝔰𝔬𝔫 𝔴𝔥𝔬𝔪 𝔥𝔢 𝔯𝔢𝔠𝔢𝔦𝔳𝔢𝔱𝔥.'[1] If ye endure
chastisement,[2] God dealeth with you as with sons;
for where is the son that is not chastened by his
8 father ? but if ye be without chastisement, whereof
all [God's children] have been[3] partakers, then are
9 ye bastards and not sons.   Moreover, we were chastened[4] by the fathers of our flesh, and gave them
reverence ; shall we not much rather submit our-
10 selves to the Father of our[5] spirits, and live ?   For
they, indeed, for a few days chastened us, after their
own pleasure ; but He for our profit, that we might
11 be partakers of His holiness.   Now no chastisement
for the present seemeth to be joyous, but grievous ;
nevertheless afterward unto them that are exercised
thereby, it yieldeth the fruit of righteousness in
peace.[6]

12   Wherefore, ' 𝔏𝔦𝔣𝔱 𝔲𝔭 𝔱𝔥𝔢 𝔥𝔞𝔫𝔡𝔰 𝔴𝔥𝔦𝔠𝔥 𝔥𝔞𝔫𝔤 𝔡𝔬𝔴𝔫 𝔞𝔫𝔡
13 𝔱𝔥𝔢 𝔣𝔢𝔢𝔟𝔩𝔢 𝔨𝔫𝔢𝔢𝔰' ;[7] and ' 𝔪𝔞𝔨𝔢 𝔢𝔳𝔢𝔫 𝔭𝔞𝔱𝔥𝔰 𝔣𝔬𝔯 𝔶𝔬𝔲𝔯
𝔣𝔢𝔢𝔱 ;[8] that the halting limb be not lamed,[9] but rather
healed.

14   Follow peace with all men, and holiness without Warning
15 which no man shall see the Lord.   And look dili-   against sensu-
                                                      ality.
gently lest any man fall[10] short of the grace of God ;
' 𝔩𝔢𝔰𝔱 𝔞𝔫𝔶 𝔯𝔬𝔬𝔱 𝔬𝔣 𝔟𝔦𝔱𝔱𝔢𝔯𝔫𝔢𝔰𝔰 𝔰𝔭𝔯𝔦𝔫𝔤𝔦𝔫𝔤 𝔲𝔭 𝔱𝔯𝔬𝔲𝔟𝔩𝔢 𝔶𝔬𝔲,'[11]

[1] Prov. iii. 11, 12.   (LXX. nearly verbatim.)   Philo quotes the passage to the same purpose as this Epistle.

[2] Throughout this passage it appears that the Church addressed was exposed to persecution.   The intense feeling of Jewish nationality called forth by the commencing struggle with Rome, which produced the triumph of the *zealot* party, would amply account for a persecution of the Christians at Jerusalem at this period ; as is argued by those who suppose the Epistle addressed to them.   But the same cause would produce the same effect in the great Jewish population of Alexandria.

[3] Observe the perfect, referring to the examples of God's children mentioned in the preceding chapter.

[4] ' We had our fathers to chasten us.' The A. V. does not render the article correctly.

[5] ' *Our* ' is understood (without repetition) from the parallel ' *our* flesh.'

[6] *Peaceful fruit of righteousness.* God's chastisements lead men to conformity to the will of God (which is *righteousness*) ; and this effect (*fruit*)

of suffering is (*peaceful*) full of peace. There can be no peace like that which follows upon the submission of the soul to the chastisement of our heavenly Father ; if we receive it as inflicted by infinite wisdom and perfect love.

[7] This quotation is from Isa. xxxv. 3, from LXX. (as appears by two of the Greek words), but quoted from memory and not verbatim.   The quotation here approaches more nearly than this to the Hebrew original, and might therefore (if not quoted *memoriter*) be considered an exception to the rule, which otherwise is universal throughout this Epistle, of adhering to the LXX. in preference to the Hebrew.

[8] Prov. iv. 26 (LXX. nearly verbatim).

[9] Or *be dislocated.*   The meaning of this exhortation seems to be, that they should abandon all appearance of Judaising practices, which might lead the weaker brethren into apostasy.

[10] The most natural construction here is similar to that in v. 16.

[11] Deut. xxix. 18.   This quotation is a strong instance in favour of Bleek's

and thereby many be defiled ; lest there be any forni- xii.
cator, or profane person, as Esau, who for a single
meal sold his birthright ; for ye know that afterward, 17
when he desired to inherit the blessing, he was rejected ; finding no room for repentance, though he
sought it[1] earnestly with tears.

In proportion to the superiority of the Gospel over the Law, will be the danger of despising it.

For ye are not come to a mountain that may be 18
touched[2] and that burneth with fire, nor to '𝔟𝔩𝔞𝔠𝔨𝔫𝔢𝔰𝔰
𝔞𝔫𝔡 𝔡𝔞𝔯𝔨𝔫𝔢𝔰𝔰 𝔞𝔫𝔡 𝔱𝔢𝔪𝔭𝔢𝔰𝔱,'[3] and ' 𝔰𝔬𝔲𝔫𝔡 𝔬𝔣 𝔱𝔯𝔲𝔪𝔭𝔢𝔱,'[4] 19
and ' 𝔳𝔬𝔦𝔠𝔢 𝔬𝔣 𝔴𝔬𝔯𝔡𝔰 '[5]—the hearers whereof entreated
that no more might be spoken unto them ;[6] for they 20
could not bear that which was commanded.[7] ('𝔄𝔫𝔡
𝔦𝔣 𝔰𝔬 𝔪𝔲𝔠𝔥 𝔞𝔰 𝔞 𝔟𝔢𝔞𝔰𝔱 𝔱𝔬𝔲𝔠𝔥 𝔱𝔥𝔢 𝔪𝔬𝔲𝔫𝔱𝔞𝔦𝔫 𝔦𝔱 𝔰𝔥𝔞𝔩𝔩 𝔟𝔢
𝔰𝔱𝔬𝔫𝔢𝔡 ; '[8] and so terrible was the sight that Moses 21
said, ' 𝔍 𝔢𝔵𝔠𝔢𝔢𝔡𝔦𝔫𝔤𝔩𝔶 𝔣𝔢𝔞𝔯 𝔞𝔫𝔡 𝔮𝔲𝔞𝔨𝔢.'[9])—But. ye are 22
come unto Mount Sion, and to the city of the living
God, the heavenly Jerusalem,[10] and to myriads[11] of 23
angels in full assembly, and to the congregation of
the first-born[12] whose names are written in heaven,
and to God[13] the judge of all, and to the spirits of just

view, that the writer of this Epistle used the Alexandrian text of the LXX. For the Codex Alexandrinus (which however is corrupt here) corresponds with the Epistle, while the Codex Vaticanus corresponds more closely with the Hebrew.

[1] Although with Chrysostom and De Wette, we refer ' it ' *grammatically* to ' repentance,' yet we think the view of Bleek *substantially* correct, in referring it to ' blessing.' That is, in saying that Esau *sought repentance with tears,* the writer obviously means that he sought *to reverse the consequences of his fault, and obtain the blessing.* If we refer to Genesis, we find that it was, in fact, Jacob's blessing (the Greek word is the same, Gen. xxvii. 35–38, LXX.) which Esau sought with tears.

[2] The first is the *present participle*; the second the *perfect participle* (not as A. V.). For the particulars here mentioned, see Exod. xix.

[3] Deut. iv. 11, the same Greek words (LXX.).

[4] Exod. xix. 16, again the same Greek words (LXX.).

[5] Deut. iv. 12 (LXX.).

[6] Deut. v. 25 (LXX.), where one of the Greek words accounts for what we read here.

[7] We put a full stop after *commanded*, because that which the Israelites ' could not bear ' was not the order for killing the beasts, but the utterance of the commandments of God. See Exod. xx. 19.

[8] Quoted from Exod. xix. 12 (LXX. but not verbatim). The words ' or thrust through with a dart ' of the Received Text have been here interpolated from the Old Testament, and are not in any of the uncial MSS.

[9] Deut. ix. 19 (LXX.). This is the passage in the Old Testament, which comes nearest to the present. It was the *remembrance* of that terrible sight which caused Moses to say this; much more must he have been terrified by the reality.

[10] This is (see Gal. iv. 26) the Church of God, which has its *metropolis* in heaven, though some of its citizens are still pilgrims and strangers upon earth.

[11] We take *myriads of angels* with *full assembly.* The latter phrase properly means a *festive* assembly, which reminds us of ' the marriage supper of the Lamb.'

[12] *First-born.* These appear to be the Christians already dead and entered into their rest; ' *written* ' means *registered* or *enrolled.* Cf. Luke ii. 1, and Phil. iv. 3.

[13] The order of the Greek would lead us more naturally to translate *to a judge, who is God of all*; but we have retained the A. V. in deference to the opinion of Chrysostom.

ii. 24 men[1] made perfect,[2] and to Jesus the mediator of a
new covenant, and to the blood of sprinkling,[3] which
speaketh better things that that of Abel.[4]

25　See that ye reject[5] not Him that speaketh.　For
if they escaped not, who rejected him that spake[6]
on earth, much more shall not we escape, if we turn
26 away from Him that speaketh from heaven.　Whose
voice then shook the earth, but now he hath promised, saying, '𝔜𝔢𝔱 𝔬𝔫𝔠𝔢 𝔪𝔬𝔯𝔢 𝔬𝔫𝔩𝔶 [7] 𝔴𝔦𝔩𝔩 𝔦 𝔰𝔥𝔞𝔨𝔢 [8] 𝔫𝔬𝔱
27 𝔱𝔥𝔢 𝔢𝔞𝔯𝔱𝔥 𝔞𝔩𝔬𝔫𝔢 𝔟𝔲𝔱 𝔞𝔩𝔰𝔬 𝔥𝔢𝔞𝔳𝔢𝔫.' [9]　And this '𝔶𝔢𝔱 𝔬𝔫𝔠𝔢
𝔪𝔬𝔯𝔢 𝔬𝔫𝔩𝔶' signifieth the removal of those things that
are shaken, as being perishable,[10] that the things un-
28 shaken may remain immoveable.　Wherefore, since
we receive a kingdom that cannot be shaken, let us
be filled with thankfulness;[11] whereby we may offer
acceptable worship unto God, with reverence and
29 fear.　For '𝔬𝔲𝔯 𝔊𝔬𝔡 𝔦𝔰 𝔞 𝔠𝔬𝔫𝔰𝔲𝔪𝔦𝔫𝔤 𝔣𝔦𝔯𝔢.' [12]

iii. 1　Let brotherly love continue.　Be not forgetful to
2 entertain strangers, for thereby some[13] have enter-
3 tained angels unawares.　Remember the prisoners,
as though ye shared their prison; and the afflicted, as
4 being yourselves also in the body.　Let marriage be
held honourable[14] in all things, and let the marriage-
bed be undefiled; for [15] whoremongers and adulterers
5 God will judge.　Let your conduct be free from
covetousness, and be content with what ye have;

Exhortation to several moral duties, especially to courageous profession of the faith, and obedience to the leaders of the Church.

---

[1] These *just men* (being distinguished from the *first-born* above) are probably the worthies of the ancient dispensation, commemorated chapter xi.

[2] Literally, *who have attained their consummation.* This they had not done until Christ's coming. See xi. 40.

[3] Contrasted with the *water of sprinkling* of Numbers xix. (LXX.) Compare ix. 13, 14, and x. 22.

[4] Or, if we read with the best MSS., '*better than Abel.*' The voice of Abel cried for vengeance (Gen. iv. 10). Compare xi. 4; the blood of Christ called down forgiveness.

[5] It is impossible to translate this verb by the same English word here and in verse 19th; hence the reference of the one passage to the other is less plain than in the original.

[6] Literally, '*that spake oracularly.*'

[7] *Once, and once only.* Cf. ix. 26 and x. 2.

[8] 'Will I shake' is the reading of the best MSS.

[9] Hagg. ii. 6 (LXX., but not verbatim).

[10] Used here as *made with hands* is (ix. 11, ix. 24), and as we often use '*things created*' as equivalent to *things perishable.*

[11] 'Filled with thankfulness.' Compare Luke xvii. 9. If the meaning were 'Let us hold fast [the] grace [which we have received],' the Greek verb would be different.

[12] Deut. iv. 24 (LXX. nearly verbatim).

[13] Viz. Abraham and Lot.

[14] This must be taken imperatively on the same ground as what immediately follows, at the beginning of the 5th verse.

[15] The MSS. A, D, and some others read *for* here, which is adopted by Lachmann and Bleek.

for He hath said, '𝔈 𝔴𝔦𝔩𝔩 𝔫𝔢𝔟𝔢𝔯 𝔩𝔢𝔞𝔟𝔢 𝔱𝔥𝔢𝔢 𝔫𝔬𝔯 𝔣𝔬𝔯𝔰𝔞𝔨𝔢 𝔱𝔥𝔢𝔢.'[1]　So that we may boldly say, 𝔗𝔥𝔢 𝔏𝔬𝔯𝔡 𝔦𝔰 𝔪𝔶 𝔥𝔢𝔩𝔭𝔢𝔯, 𝔞𝔫𝔡 𝔈 𝔴𝔦𝔩𝔩 𝔫𝔬𝔱 𝔣𝔢𝔞𝔯. 𝔚𝔥𝔞𝔱 𝔠𝔞𝔫 𝔪𝔞𝔫 𝔡𝔬 𝔲𝔫𝔱𝔬 𝔪𝔢?'[2] xiii.

Remember them that were your leaders,[3] who[7] spoke to you the word of God; look upon[4] the end of their life, and follow the example of their faith.

Jesus Christ[5] is the same yesterday and to-day[8] and for ever. Be not carried away[6] with manifold[9] and strange doctrines. For it is good that the heart be established by grace ; not by meats,[7] which profited not them that were occupied therein. We have an altar whereof they that minister unto[10] the tabernacle have no right to eat. For[8] the bodies[11] of those beasts whose blood the High Priest bringeth[9] into the Holy Place,[10] are burned '𝔴𝔦𝔱𝔥𝔬𝔲𝔱 𝔱𝔥𝔢 𝔠𝔞𝔪𝔭.'[11] Wherefore Jesus also, that He might[12] sanctify the People by His own blood, suffered without the gate. Therefore let us go forth unto[13] Him '𝔴𝔦𝔱𝔥𝔬𝔲𝔱 𝔱𝔥𝔢 𝔠𝔞𝔪𝔭,' bearing His reproach. For[14] here we have no continuing city, but we seek one to come.[12]

---

[1] Deut. xxxi. 6 (LXX.). This is said by Moses. In Josh. i. 5 (LXX.), we find a direct promise from God, almost in the same words, addressed to Joshua. The citation here, being not verbatim, may be derived from either of these places. Philo cites the same words as the text.

[2] Ps. cxviii. 6 (LXX.).

[3] Not *rulers*, but *leaders*. Compare Acts xv. 22, where the word is the same. It is here (cf. ver. 17 and 24,) applied to the presbyters or bishops of the Church. See p. 341, n. 1.

[4] A very graphic word, not to be fully rendered by any English term. The meaning is, ' *contemplate the final scene* [*perhaps martyrdom*], *which closed their life and labours*.'

[5] The A. V. here gives an English reader the very erroneous impression that 'Jesus Christ' is in the objective case, and in apposition to 'the end of their conversation.'

[6] 'Carried *away*' not 'carried *about*,' is the reading of the best MSS.

[7] *Not by meats*. The connection here is very difficult. The reference seems to be, in the first place, to

Judaising doctrines concerning clean and unclean meats ; but thence the thought passes on to the sacrificial meats, on which the priests were partly supported. Some think this verse addressed to those who had themselves been priests, which would be an argument for supposing the Epistle addressed to the Church at Jerusalem (Compare Acts vi. 7).

[8] The connection seems to be, that the victims sacrificed on the day of Atonement were commanded (Levit. xvi. 27) to be *wholly burned*), and therefore *not eaten*.

[9] Viz. on the day of Atonement. Compare chaps. ix. and x.

[10] The words 'for sin' are omitted in the best MSS.

[11] Levit. xvi. 27 (LXX. verbatim). The camp of the Israelites was afterwards represented by the Holy City ; so that the bodies of these victims were burnt outside the gates of Jerusalem. See above, p. 585, n. 1.

[12] Literally, *the city which is to come.* Compare x. 34, and *the kingdom that cannot be shaken*, xii. 28.

iii.15   By Him therefore let us offer unto God continually a sacrifice of praise,[1] that is, '𝔱𝔥𝔢 𝔣𝔯𝔲𝔦𝔱 𝔬𝔣
16 𝔬𝔲𝔯 𝔩𝔦𝔭𝔰,'[2] making confession unto His name. And be not unmindful of benevolence and liberality, for such are the sacrifices which are acceptable unto God.

17   Render unto them that are your leaders obedience and submission; for they on their part[3] watch for the good of your souls, as those that must give account; that they may keep their watch with joy and not with lamentation; for that would be unprofitable for you.

18   Pray for me ; for I trust[4] that I have a good conscience, desiring in all my conduct to live
19 rightly. But I the rather beseech you to do this, that I may be restored to you the sooner.[5]
20   Now the God of peace, who raised up[6] from the dead the great '𝔖𝔥𝔢𝔭𝔥𝔢𝔯𝔡 𝔬𝔣 𝔱𝔥𝔢 𝔰𝔥𝔢𝔢𝔭,'[7] even our Lord Jesus, through the blood of an everlasting
21 covenant,—make you perfect in every good work to do His will, working in you that which is well-pleasing in His sight, by Jesus Christ. To whom be glory for ever.[8] Amen.

22   I beseech you, brethren, to bear with these words of exhortation ; for I have written shortly.[9]
23   Know that our brother Timotheus is set at liberty ; and with him, if he come speedily, I will see you.

The writer asks their prayers, gives them his own, and communicates information from Italy.

---

[1] The Christian sacrifice is ' a sacrifice of praise and thanksgiving,' contrasted with the propitiatory sacrifices of the old Law, which were for ever consummated by Christ. See x. 4–14.

[2] Hosea xiv. 2 (LXX.). (The present Hebrew text is different.)

[3] The pronoun is emphatic.

[4] This seems to be addressed to a party amongst these Hebrew Christians who had taken offence at something in the writer's conduct.

[5] We have already observed that this implies that a personal connection existed between the writer and the readers of this Epistle. The opinion of Ebrard, that this verse is written by St. Luke in St. Paul's person, and v. 23rd in his own person, appears quite untenable : no intimation of a change of person is given (compare Rom. xvi. 22) nor is there any inconsistency in asking prayers for a prosperous journey, and afterwards expressing a positive intention of making the journey.

[6] This denotes not *to bring again* (A. V.), but to *bring up from below*, to *raise up*. (Rom. x. 7.)

[7] This is an allusion to a passage in Isaiah (Isa. lxiii. 11, LXX.), where God is described as ' *He who brought up from the sea the shepherd of the sheep* ' [viz. *Moses*].

[8] ' And ever,' is probably to be omitted both here and Rom. xi. 36, and xvi. 27.

[9] They are asked to excuse the apparent harshness of some portions of the letter, on the ground that the writer had not time for circumlocution.

Salute all them that are your leaders, and all the saints. xiii. 24

They of Italy[1] salute you. Grace be with you all. Amen. 25

Here lies Faustina.   In peace.[2]

[1] 'They *of* Italy.' We agree with Winer in thinking that this '*of*' may be most naturally understood as used *from the position of the readers.* This was the view of the earlier interpreters, and is agreeable to Greek analogy. In fact, if we consider the origin in most languages of the gentilitial prepositions (*von, de, of,* &c.), we shall see that they conform to the same analogy. Hence we infer from this passage that the writer was in Italy.

[2] A Christian tomb with the three languages, from Maitland's *Church in the Catacombs,* p. 77. The name is *Latin,* the inscription *Greek,* and the word Shalom or 'Peace' is in *Hebrew* See p. 25.

APPENDICES

APPENDIX I

ON THE TIME OF THE VISIT TO JERUSALEM MENTIONED IN GALATIANS (Chap. ii.)[1]

To avoid circumlocution we shall call the visit mentioned in Galatians ii. 1, the *Galatian Visit*, and we shall designate the visit mentioned in Acts ix. as *visit* (1), that Acts xi. and xii. as *visit* (2), that in Acts xv. as *visit* (3), that in Acts xviii. as *visit* (4), that in Acts xxi. as *visit* (5).

I. The *Galatian Visit* was not the same with *visit* (1), because it is mentioned as subsequent by St. Paul.[2]

II. Was the *Galatian Visit* the same with *visit* (2)?[3] The first impression from reading the end of Gal. i. and beginning of Gal. ii. would be that it was; for St. Paul seems to imply that there had been no intermediate visit between the one mentioned in Gal. i. 18, which we have called *visit* (1), and that in Gal. ii. 1, which we have called the *Galatian Visit*.[4] On the other side, however, we must observe that St. Paul's object in this passage is not to enumerate all his visits to Jerusalem. His opponents had told his converts that Paul was no true Apostle, that he was only a Christian teacher authorised by the Judæan Apostles, that he derived his authority and his knowledge of the Gospel from Peter, James, and the rest of 'the twelve.' St. Paul's object is to refute this statement. This he does by declaring, firstly, that his commission was not from men but from God; secondly, that he had taught Christianity for three years without seeing any of 'the twelve' at all; thirdly, that at the end of that time he had only spent one fortnight at Jerusalem with Peter and James, and then had gone to Cilicia and remained personally unknown to the Judæan Christians; fourthly, that fourteen years afterwards he had undertaken a journey to Jerusalem, and that he then obtained an acknowledgment of his independent mission from the chief Apostles. Thus we see that his object is not to enumerate every occasion

---

[1] This question is one of the most important, both chronologically and historically, in the life of St. Paul. Perhaps its discussion more properly belongs to the Epistle to the Galatians than to this place; but it has been given here as a justification of the view taken in Chap. VII.

[2] Gal. ii. 1.

[3] To support this view, either the conversion must be placed much earlier than we think probable, or 'fourteen,' in Gal. ii. 1, must be altered into 'four.'

[4] We must certainly acknowledge that St. Paul appears to say this; and some commentators have avoided the difficulty by supposing that, although Paul and Barnabas were commissioned to convey the alms from Antioch to Jerusalem, yet that St. Paul was prevented (by some circumstances not mentioned) from going the whole way to Jerusalem. For example, it might be too hazardous for him to appear within the walls of the city at such a time of persecution.

where he might possibly have been instructed by 'the twelve,' but to assert (an assertion which he confirms by oath, Gal. i. 20) that his knowledge of Christianity was not derived from their instruction. A short visit to Jerusalem which produced no important results he might naturally pass over, and especially if he saw none of ' the twelve' at Jerusalem when he visited it. Now this was probably the case at *visit* (2), because it was just at the time of Herod Agrippa's persecution, which would naturally disperse the Apostles from Jerusalem, as the persecution at Stephen's death did; with regard to St. Peter it is expressly said that, after his miraculous escape from prison, he quitted Jerusalem.[1] This supposition is confirmed by finding that Barnabas and Saul were sent to the *Elders* of the church at Jerusalem, and not to the *Apostles.*

A further objection to supposing the *Galatian Visit* identical with *visit* (2) is that, at the time of the Galatian visit, Paul and Barnabas are described as having been already extensively useful as missionaries to the Heathen ; but this they had not been in the time of *visit* (2).

Again, St. Paul could not have been, at so early a period, considered on a footing of equality with St. Peter. Yet this he was at the time of the *Galatian Visit.*[2]

Again, *visit* (2) could not have been so long as fourteen years[3] after *visit* (1). For *visit* (2) was certainly not later than 45 A.D., and, if it was the same as the *Galatian Visit, visit* (1) must have been not later than from 31 to 33 A.D. (allowing the inclusive Jewish mode of reckoning to be possibly employed). But Aretas (as we have seen, p. 67) was not in possession of Damascus till about 37.

Again, if *visit* (2) were fourteen years after *visit* (1), we must suppose nearly all this time spent by St. Paul at Tarsus, and yet that all his long residence there is unrecorded by St. Luke, who merely says that he went to Tarsus and from thence to Antioch.[4]

III. The *Galatian Visit* not being identical with (1) or (2), was it identical with (3), (4), or (5)? We may put (5) at once out of the question, because St. Paul did not return to Antioch after (5), whereas he did return after the *Galatian Visit.* There remain therefore (3) and (4) to be considered. We shall take (4) first.

IV. Wieseler has lately argued very ingeniously that the *Galatian Visit* was the same with (4). His reasons are, firstly, that at the *Galatian Visit* the Apostles allowed unlimited freedom to the Gentile converts, i.e. imposed no conditions upon them, such as those in the decrees of the Council passed at *visit* (3). This, however, is an inference not warranted by St. Paul's statement, which speaks of the acknowledgment of his personal independence, but does not touch the question of the converts. Secondly, Wieseler urges that, till the time of *visit* (4), St. Paul's position could not have been so far on a level with St. Peter's as it was at the *Galatian Visit.* Thirdly, he thinks that the condition of making a collection for the poor Christians in Jerusalem, which St. Paul says[5] he had been forward to fulfil, must have been fulfilled in that great collection which we know that St. Paul set on foot immediately after *visit* (4), because we read of no other collection made by St. Paul for this purpose.[6] Fourthly, Wieseler argues that St. Paul would

---

[1] Acts xii. 17.

[2] See Gal. ii. 9

[3] On this fourteen years see note in p. 827 below, and the note (B.) on the Chronological Table in Appendix III.

[4] Acts ix. 30, and xi. 26. See what Prof. Burton says on this interval.

[5] Gal. ii. 10.

[6] The collection carried up to Jerusalem at *visit* (2) might, however, be cited as an exception to this remark ; for (although not expressly stated) it is most probable that St. Paul was active in forwarding it, since he was selected to carry it to Jerusalem.

not have been likely to take an uncircumcised Gentile, like Titus, with him to Jerusalem at a period earlier than *visit* (4). And moreover, he conceives Titus to be the same with the Corinthian Justus,[1] who is not mentioned as one of St. Paul's companions till Acts xviii. 7, that is, not till after *visit* (3).

It is evident that these arguments are not conclusive in favour of *visit* (4), even if there were nothing on the other side; but there are, moreover, the following objections against supposing the *Galatian Visit* identical with (4). Firstly, Barnabas was St. Paul's companion in the *Galatian Visit*; he is not mentioned as being with him at *visit* (4). Secondly, had so important a conference between St. Paul and the other Apostles taken place at *visit* (4), it would not have been altogether passed over by St. Luke, who dwells so fully upon the Council held at the time of *visit* (3), the decrees of which (on Wieseler's view) were inferior in importance to the *concordat* between St. Paul and the other Apostles which he supposes to have been made at *visit* (4). Thirdly, the whole tone of the second chapter of Galatians is against Wieseler's hypothesis; for in that chapter St. Paul plainly seems to speak of the *first* conference which he had held after his success among the Heathen, with the chief Apostles at Jerusalem, and he had certainly seen and conferred with them during *visit* (3).

V. We have seen, therefore, that *if the Galatian Visit be mentioned at all in the Acts*, it must be identical with *visit* (3), at which the (so called) Council of Jerusalem took place. We will now consider the objections against the identity of these two visits urged by Paley and others, and then the arguments in favour of the identity.

Objections to the identity of the
GALATIAN VISIT *with* VISIT (3).

Answers to the Objections.

1. St. Paul in Gal. (ii. 1) mentions this journey as if it had been the next visit to Jerusalem after the time which he spent there on his return from Damascus; he does not say anything of any intermediate visit. This looks as if he were speaking of the journey which he took with Barnabas to Jerusalem (Acts xi. 30), to convey alms to the Jewish Christians in the famine.

1. This objection is answered above, p. 822.

2. In the Galatians the journey is said to have taken place ' by revelation' (Gal. ii. 2); but in Acts xv. 2–4, 6–12, a public mission is mentioned.

2. The journey may have taken place in consequence of a revelation, and yet may also have been agreed to by a vote of the church at Antioch. Thus in St. Paul's departure from Jerusalem (Acts ix. 29, 30), he is said to have been sent by the brethren in consequence of danger feared; and yet (Acts xxii. 17–21) he says that he had taken his departure in consequence of a vision on the very same occasion (see pp. 166, 167).

3. In the Galatians Barnabas and Titus are spoken of as St Paul's

3. This argument is merely *ex silentio*, and therefore inconclusive. In

[1] Many of the most ancient MSS. and versions read *Titus Justus* in Acts xviii. 7.

companions : in the Acts, Barnabas and others (Acts xv. 2); but Titus is not mentioned.

the Acts, Paul and Barnabas are naturally mentioned, as being prominent characters in the history. Whereas in the Epistle, Titus would naturally be mentioned by St. Paul as a personal friend of his own, and also because of his refusal to circumcise him.

4. The object of the visit in Acts xv. is different from that of the *Galatian Visit.* The object in Acts xv. was to seek relief from the imposition of the Mosaic Law, that of the *Galatian Visit* was to obtain the recognition of St. Paul's independent apostleship.

4. Both these objects are implied in each narrative. The recognition of St. Paul's apostleship is implied in Acts xv. 25. And the relief from the imposition of the Mosaic Law is implied, Gal. ii. 7, where the word ' uncircumcision ' shows that the Apostles at the time of St. Paul's visit to Jerusalem, mentioned in the Epistle, acknowledged that the uncircumcised might partake of 'the Gospel.' The same thing is shown by the fact that the circumcision of Titus was not insisted on. We must remember also that the transactions recorded are looked upon from different points of view, in the Acts and in the Epistle ; for Acts xv. contains a narrative of a great transaction in the history of the Church, while St. Paul, in the Epistle, alludes to this transaction with the object of proving the recognition of his independent authority

5. In Acts xv. a public assembly of the Church in Jerusalem is described, while in the Galatians only private interviews with the leading Apostles are spoken of.

5. The private interviews spoken of in the Epistle do not exclude the supposition of public meetings having also taken place; and a communication to the *whole Church* (Gal. ii. 2) is expressly mentioned.

6. The narrative in the Epistle says nothing of the decision of the Council of Jerusalem, as it is commonly called, mentioned Acts xv. Now this decision was conclusive of the very point'disputed by the Judaising teachers in Galatia, and surely therefore would not have been omitted by St. Paul in an argument involving the question, had he been relating the circumstances which happened at Jerusalem when that decision was made.

6. The narrative in Galatians gives a statement intended to prove the recognition of St. Paul's independent authority, which is sufficient to account for this omission. Moreover, if St. Paul's omission of reference to the decision of the Council proved that the journey he speaks of was prior to the Council, it must equally prove that the whole Epistle was written before the Council of Jerusalem ; yet it is generally acknowledged to have been written long after the Council. The probable reason why St. Paul does not refer to the decision of the Council is this : — that the

Judaising teachers did not absolutely dispute that decision; they probably did not declare the absolute necessity of circumcision, but spoke of it as admitting to greater privileges, and a fuller covenant with God. The Council had only decided that *Gentile* Christians need not observe the Law. The Judaising party might still contend that *Jewish* Christians ought to observe it (as we know they did observe it till long afterwards). And also the decrees of the Council left Gentile Christians subject to the same restrictions with the Proselytes of the Gate. Therefore the Judaising party would naturally argue that they were still not more fully within the pale of the Christian Church than the Proselytes of the Gate were within that of the Jewish Church. Hence they would urge them to submit to circumcision by way of placing themselves in full membership with the Church; just as they would have urged a Proselyte of the Gate to become a Proselyte of Righteousness. Also St. Paul might assume that the decision of the Council was well known to the churches in Galatia, for Paul and Silas had carried it with them there.

7. It is inconsistent to suppose that after the decision of the Council of Jerusalem, St. Peter could have behaved as he is described doing (Gal. ii. 12); for how could he refuse to eat with the uncircumcised Christians, after having advocated in the Council their right of admission to Christian fellowship?

7. This objection is founded on a misunderstanding of St. Peter's conduct. His withdrawal from eating at the same table with the uncircumcised Christians did not amount to a denial of the decision of the Council. His conduct showed a weak fear of offending the Judaising Christians who came from Jerusalem; and the practical effect of such conduct would have been, if persisted in, to separate the Church into two divisions. Peter's conduct was still more inconsistent with the consent which he had certainly given previously (Gal. ii. 7–9) to the 'Gospel' of Paul; and with his previous conduct in the case of Cornelius (see end of Chap. VII.). We may add that, whatever difficulty may be felt in St. Paul's not alluding to the decrees of the Council in his Epistle to the Galatians, must also be felt in his

total silence concerning them when he treats of the question of 'things sacrificed to idols' in the Epistles to Corinth and Rome, for that question had been explicitly decided by the Council. The fact is, that the Decrees of the Council were not designed as of permanent authority, but only as a temporary and provisional measure; and their authority was superseded as the Church gradually advanced towards true Christian freedom.

8. The Epistle mentions St. Paul as conferring with James, Peter, and John, whereas in Acts xv. John is not mentioned at all, and it seems strange that so distinguished a person, if present at the Council, should not have been mentioned.

8. This argument is only *ex silentio*, and obviously inconclusive.

9. Since in the Galatians St. Paul mentions James, Peter, and John, it seems most natural to suppose that he speaks of the well-known apostolic triumvirate so often classed together in the Gospels. But if so, the James mentioned must be James the Greater, and hence the journey mentioned in the Galatians must have been before the death of James the Greater, and therefore before the Council of Jerusalem.

9. This objection proceeds on the mere assumption that because James is mentioned first he must be James the Greater, whereas James the Less became even a more conspicuous leader of the Church at Jerusalem than James the Greater had previously been, as we see from Acts xv.; hence he might be very well mentioned with Peter and John, and the fact of his name coming first in St. Paul's narrative agrees better with this supposition, for James the Greater is never mentioned the first in the apostolic triumvirate, the order of which is Peter, James, and John; but James the Less would naturally be mentioned first, if the Council at Jerusalem was mentioned, since we find from Acts xv. that he took the part of president in that Council.

10. St. Paul's refusal to circumcise Titus (Gal. ii,), and voluntary circumcising of Timothy (Acts xvi. 3), so soon afterwards.

10. Timothy's mother was a Jewess, and he had been brought up a Jew;[1] whereas Titus was a Gentile. The circumstances of Timothy's circumcision were fully discussed above, pp. 203–206.

Thus we see that the objections against the identity of the *Galatian*

[1] See 2 Tim. iii. 15. We may remark that this difficulty (which is urged by Wieseler) is quite as great on his own hypothesis; for, according to him, the refusal happened only about two years after the consent.

Visit with *visit* (3), are inconclusive. Consequently we might at once conclude (from the obvious circumstances of identity between the two visits), that they were actually identical. But this conclusion is further strengthened by the following arguments.

1. The *Galatian Visit* could not have happened *before visit* (3); because if so, the Apostles at Jerusalem had already granted to Paul and Barnabas [1] the liberty which was sought for the ' gospel of the uncircumcision ;' therefore there would have been no need for the Church to send them again to Jerusalem upon the same cause. And again, the *Galatian Visit* could not have happened *after visit* (3); because, almost immediately after that period, Paul and Barnabas ceased to work together as missionaries to the Gentiles; whereas up to the time of the *Galatian Visit*, they had been working together.[2]

2. The *Chronology* of St. Paul's life (so far as it can be ascertained) agrees better with the supposition that the *Galatian Visit* was *visit* (3), than with any other supposition.

Reckoning backwards from the ascertained epoch of 60 A.D., when St. Paul was sent to Rome, we find that he must have begun his second missionary journey in 51, and that therefore, the Council (i.e. *visit* (3)) must have been either in 50 or 51. This calculation is based upon the history in the Acts.· Now, turning to the Epistle to the Galatians we find the following epochs—

    A.—Conversion.
    B.—3 years' interval (probably Judaically reckoned = 2 years).[3]
    C.—Flight from Damascus and *visit* (1).
    D.—14[4] years' interval (probably) Judaically reckoned = 13 years)[3].
    E.— *Galatian Visit.*

And since Aretas was supreme at Damascus [5] at the time of the flight, and his supremacy there probably began about 37 (see pp. 67 and 83), we could not put the flight at a more probable date than 38. If we assume this to have been the case, then the *Galatian Visit* was 38 + 13 = 51, which agrees with the time of the Council (i.e. *visit* (3)) as above.

VI. Hence we need not further consider the views of those writers who (like Paley and Schrader) have resorted to the hypothesis that the *Galatian Visit* is some supposed journey not recorded in the Acts at all ; for we have proved that the supposition of its identity with the third visit there recorded satisfies every necessary condition. Schrader's notion is, that the *Galatian Visit* was between *visit* (4) and *visit* (5). Paley places it between *visit* (3) and *visit* (4). A third view is ably advocated in a discussion of the subject (not published) which has been kindly communicated to us. The principal points in this hypothesis are, that the Galatians were converted in the *first* missionary journey, that the *Galatian Visit*

---

[1] Gal. ii. 3–6.
[2] Gal. ii. 1, 9.
[3] On this Judaical reckoning, see note (B.) on the Chronological Table in Appendix III.
[4] The reading ' fourteen ' (Gal. ii. 1) is undoubtedly to be retained. It is in all the ancient MSS. which contain the passage. The reading ' four ' has probably arisen from the words ' four years,' which relate to a different subject, in the sentence below. The preposition ' after,'

denoting ' after an interval of,' may be used, according to the Jewish way of reckoning time, *inclusively*. The fourteen years must be reckoned *from the epoch last mentioned*, which is the *visit* (1) to Jerusalem, and not the Conversion ; at least, this is the most natural way, although the other interpretation might be justified, if required by the other circumstances of the case.

[5] 2 Cor. xi. 32.

took place between *visit* (2) and *visit* (3), and that the Epistle to the Galatians was written after the *Galatian Visit* and before *visit* (3). This hypothesis certainly obviates some difficulties,[1] and it is quite possible (see p. 189, n. 1) that the Galatian churches might have been formed at the time supposed ; but we are strongly of opinion that a much later date must be assigned to the Epistle.[2]

[1] Especially the difficulties which relate to the apparent discrepancies between the *Galatian Visit* and *visit* (3), and to the circumstance that the Apostle does not allude to the Council in his argument with the Galatians on the subject of circumcision.

[2] See note on Epistle to the Galatians.

APPENDIX II

ON THE DATE OF THE PASTORAL EPISTLES.

BEFORE we can fix the time at which these Epistles were written, we must take the following data into account.

1. The three Epistles were nearly *cotemporaneous* with one another. This is proved by their resembling each other in language, matter, and style of composition, and in the state of the Christian Church which they describe: and by their differing in all the three points from all the other Epistles of St. Paul. Of course the full force of this argument cannot be appreciated by those who have not carefully studied these Epistles; but it is now almost universally admitted by all [1] who have done so, both by the defenders and impugners of the authenticity of the Pastoral Epistles. Hence if we fix the date of one of the three, we fix approximately the date of all.

2. They were written *after St. Paul became acquainted with Apollos*, and therefore *after St. Paul's first visit to Ephesus.* (See Acts xviii. 24, and Titus iii. 13).

3. Hence they could not have been written till after the conclusion of that portion of his life which is related in the Acts; because there is no part of his history, between his first visit to Ephesus and his Roman imprisonment, which satisfies the historical conditions implied in the statements of any one of these Epistles. Various attempts have been made, with different degrees of ingenuity, to place the Epistles to Timothy and Titus at different points in this interval of time; but all have failed even to satisfy the conditions required for placing any single Epistle correctly. [2] And no one has ever attempted to place all three *together*, at any period of St. Paul's life before the end of his first Roman imprisonment; yet this cotemporaneousness of the three Epistles is a necessary condition of the problem.

4. The Pastoral Epistles were written not merely *after* St. Paul's first Roman imprisonment, but *considerably* after it. This is evident from the marked difference in their style from the Epistle to the Philippians, which was the last written during that imprisonment. So great a change of style

[1] We have noticed Dr. Davidson's contrary opinion before; and we should add that Wieseler may be considered another exception, only that he does not attempt to reply to the grounds stated by other critics for the cotemporaneousness of the three Epistles, but altogether ignores the question of internal evidence from style and Church organisation, which is the conclusive evidence here. Subjoined to this Appendix in the larger editions is an alphabetical list of the words and phrases peculiar to the Pastoral Epistles.

[2] Wieseler's is the most ingenious theory which has been suggested for getting over this difficulty; but it has been shown by Huther that none of the three Epistles can be placed as Wieseler places them without involving some contradiction of the facts mentioned in them respectively.

(a change not merely in the use of single words, but in phrases, in modes of thought, and in method of composition) must require an interval of certainly not less than four or five years to account for it.　And even that interval might seem too short, unless accompanied by circumstances which should further explain the alteration.　Yet five years of exhausting labour, great physical and moral sufferings, and bitter experience of human nature, might suffice to account for the change.

5. The development of Church organisation implied in the Pastoral Epistles leads to the same conclusion as to the lateness of their date.　The detailed rules for the choice of presbyters and deacons, implying numerous candidates for these offices; the exclusion of *new converts (neophytes* [1]) from the presbyterate; the regular catalogue of Church widows (1 Tim. v. 9); are all examples of this.

6. The *Heresies* condemned in all three Epistles are likewise of a nature which forbids the supposition of an early date.　They are of the same class as those attacked in the Epistle to the Colossians, but appear under a more matured form.　They are apparently the same heresies which we find condemned in other portions of Scripture written in the latter part of the Apostolic age, as, for example, the Epistles of Peter and Jude.　We trace distinctly the beginnings of the Gnostic Heresy, which broke out with such destructive power in the second century, and of which we have already seen the germ in the Epistle to the Colossians.

7. The preceding conditions might lead us to place the Pastoral Epistles at any point after A.D. 66 (see condition 4, above), i.e. in the last thirty-three years of the first century.　But we have a limit assigned us in this direction, by a fact mentioned in the Epistles to Timothy, viz., that Timotheus was still a young man (1 Tim. iv. 12; 2 Tim. ii. 22) when they were written.　We must, of course, understand this statement relatively to the circumstances under which it is used: Timotheus was young for the authority entrusted to him; he was young to exercise supreme jurisdiction over all the Presbyters (many of them old men) of the Churches of Asia.　According even to modern notions (and much more according to the feelings of antiquity on the subject), he would still have been very young for such a position at the age of thirty-five.　Now Timotheus was (as we have seen, pp. 156 and 203) a youth still living with his parents when St. Paul first took him in A.D. 51 (Acts xvi. 1–3) as his companion.　From the way in which he is then mentioned (Acts xvi. 1–3: compare 2 Tim. i. 4), we cannot imagine him to have been more than seventeen or eighteen at the most.　Nor, again could he be much younger than this, considering the part he soon afterwards took in the conversion of Macedonia (2 Cor. i. 19).　Hence we may suppose him to have been eighteen years old in A.D. 51.　Consequently, in 68 (the last year of Nero), he would be thirty-five [2] years old.

8. If we are to believe the universal tradition of the early Church, St. Paul's martyrdom occurred in the reign of Nero.[3]　Hence, we have another limit for the date of the Pastoral Epistles, viz., that it could not have

---

[1] 1 Tim. iii. 6.

[2] No objection against the genuineness of the Pastoral Epistles has been more insisted on than that furnished by the reference to the *youth* of Timotheus in the two passages above mentioned. How groundless such objections are, we may best realise by considering the parallel case of those young Colonial bishops, who are almost annually leaving our shores.　Several of these have been not more than thirty-four or thirty-five years of age at the time of their appointment; and how naturally might they be addressed, by an elderly friend, in the very language which St. Paul here addresses to Timotheus.

[3] See the authorities for this statement above, p. 782.

been later than A.D. 68, and this agrees very well with the preceding datum.

It will be observed that all the above conditions are satisfied by the hypothesis adopted in Chap. XXVII., that the Pastoral Epistles were written, the two first just before, and the last during, St. Paul's final imprisonment at Rome.[1]

We come now to consider the order of the three Epistles among themselves :—

1. 1 TIM. In this we find that St. Paul had left Ephesus for Macedonia (1 Tim. i. 3), and had left Timothy at Ephesus to counteract the erroneous teaching of the heretics (iii. 4), and that he hoped soon to return to Ephesus (iii. 14).

2. TITUS. Here we find that St. Paul had lately left Crete (i. 5), and that he was now about to proceed (iii. 12) to Nicopolis, in Epirus, where he meant to spend the approaching winter. Whereas in 1 Tim. he meant soon to be back at Ephesus, and he was *afterwards* at Miletus and Corinth between 1 Tim. and 2 Tim. (otherwise 2 Tim. iv. 20 would be unintelligible). Hence Titus [2] must have been written later than 1 Tim.

3. 2 TIM. We have seen that this Epistle could not (from the internal evidence of its style, and close resemblance to the other Pastorals) have been written in the first Roman imprisonment. The same conclusion may be drawn also on historical grounds, as Huther has well shown where he proves that it could neither have been written before the Epistle to the Colossians not after the Epistle to the Colossians during *that* imprisonment. The internal evidence from style and matter, however, is so conclusive, that it is needless to do more than allude to this quasi-external evidence. In this Epistle we find St. Paul a prisoner in Rome (i. 17); he has lately been at Corinth (iv. 20), and since he left Timothy (at Ephesus) he has been at Miletus (iv. 20). Also he has been, not long before, at Troas (iv. 13).

The facts thus mentioned can be best explained by supposing (1) That after writing 1 Tim. from Macedonia, St. Paul did, as he intended, return to Ephesus by way of *Troas*, where he left the books, &c., mentioned 2 Tim. iv. 13, with Carpus ; (2) That from Ephesus he made a short expedition to Crete and back, and on his return wrote to Titus ; (3) That immediately after despatching this letter, he went by *Miletus* to *Corinth*, and thence to Nicopolis ; whence he proceeded to Rome.

[1] At this point in the larger editions is a detailed discussion of the arguments of those who, during the present century, have denied the genuineness of these three Epistles. This was written before the appearance of Dr. Davidson's third volume. The reader who is acquainted with that valuable work, will perceive that we differ from Dr. Davidson on some material points ; nor, after considering his arguments, do we see reason to change our conclusions. But this difference does not prevent us from appreciating the candour and ability with which he states the arguments on both sides. We would especially refer our readers to his statement of the difficulties in the way of the hypothesis that these Epistles were forged.

[2] Had 1 Tim. been written after Titus, St. Paul could not have hoped to be back soon at Ephesus, 1 Tim. iii. 14 ; for he had only just left Ephesus, and (on that hypothesis) would be intending to winter at the distant Nicopolis.

APPENDIX III

CHRONOLOGICAL TABLE.

A.D.	Biography of St. Paul.	Cotemporary Events.
36	(?) St. Paul's conversion [supposing the 3 years of Gal. i. 18 Judaically reckoned]. See p. 827, and note (B.) below.	
37	(?) At Damascus.	Death of Tiberius and accession of CALIGULA (March 16).
38	(?) Flight from Damascus [See p. 827] to Jerusalem, and thence to Tarsus.	
39 40 41	(?)⎫ (?)⎪ (?)⎪ During these years St. Paul preaches in Syria and Cilicia, making TARSUS his head-quarters, and probably undergoes most of the sufferings mentioned at 2 Cor. xi. 24–26, viz. two of the Roman and the five Jewish scourgings, and three shipwrecks. See pp. 87 and 98, and note on 2 Cor. xi. 25.	Death of Caligula and accession of CLAUDIUS (Jan. 25), Judæa and Samaria given to Herod Agrippa I.
42	(?)⎪	Invasion of Britain by Aulus Plautius.
43	(?)⎭	
44	He is brought from Tarsus to Antioch (Acts xi. 26), and stays there a year before the famine.	Death of Herod Agrippa I. (Acts xii.) [see note (A.) below.] Cuspius Fadus (as procurator) succeeds to the government of Judæa.
45	He visits Jerusalem with Barnabas to relieve the famine.	
46	At ANTIOCH.	Tiberius Alexander made procurator of Judæa (about this time).
47	At ANTIOCH.	
48	His 'First Missionary Journey' from Antioch to Cyprus, Antioch in Pisidia, Iconium, Lystra, Derbe,	Agrippa II. (Acts xxv.) made king of Chalcis;

APPENDIX III.—*continued.*

	Biography of St. Paul.	Cotemporary Events.
49	and back through the same places to ANTIOCH.	Cumanus made procurator of Judæa (about this time).
50	St. Paul and Barnabas attend the ' Council of Jerusalem.' [See pp. 821-828, and note (B.) below.]	Caractacus captured by the Romans in Britain; Cogidunus (father of Claudia [?], 2 Tim. iv. 21) assists the Romans in Britain.
51	His ' Second Missionary Journey,' from Antioch to Cilicia, Lycaonia, Galatia,	
52	Troas, Philippi, Thessalonica, Berœa, Athens, and CORINTH—*Writes* 1 *Thess*	Claudius expels the Jews from Rome (Acts xviii. 2).
53	At CORINTH. *Writes* 2 *Thess.*	The tetrarchy of Trachonitis given to Agrippa II.; Felix made procurator of Judæa. [See note (C.) below.]
54	(Spring)—He leaves Corinth, and reaches (Summer)—Jerusalem at Pentecost, and thence goes to Antioch. (Autumn)—His 'Third Missionary Journey.'—He goes To EPHESUS.	Death of Claudius and accession of NERO (Oct. 13).
55	At EPHESUS.	
56	AT EPHESUS.	
57	(Spring)—*He writes* 1 *Cor.* (Summer)—Leaves Ephesus for Macedonia. (Autumn)—Where *he writes* 2 *Cor.,* and thence (Winter)—To CORINTH, where *he writes Galatians.*	
58	(Spring)—*He writes Romans,* and leaves Corinth, going by Philippi and Miletus (Summer)—To Jerusalem (Pentecost), where he is arrested and sent to Cæsarea.	
59	At CÆSAREA.	Nero murders Agrippina.
60	(Autumn)—Sent to Rome by Festus (about August). (Winter)—Shipwrecked at Malta.	Felix is recalled and succeeded by Festus [see note (C.) below].

APPENDIX III.—*continued.*

A.D.	Biography of S. Paul.	Cotemporary Events.
61	(Spring)—He arrives at Rome.	Embassy from Jerusalem to Rome, to petition about the wall [see note (C.) below].
62	At ROME. (Spring)—*Writes* { *Philemon, Colossians, Ephesians.* (Autumn)—*Writes Philippians.*	Burrus dies; Albinus succeeds Festus as procurator; Nero marries Poppæa; Octavia executed; Pallas put to death.
63	(Spring)—He is acquitted, and goes to Macedonia (Phil. ii. 24) and Asia Minor (Philem. 22).	Poppæa's daughter Claudia born.
64	(?) He goes to Spain. [For this and the subsequent statements, see Chap. XXVII.]	Great fire at Rome (July 19), followed by persecution of Roman Christians;
65	(?) In Spain.	Gessius Florus made procurator of Judæa. Conspiracy of Piso, and death of Seneca.
66	(Summer)—From Spain (?) to Asia Minor (1 Tim. i. 3).	The Jewish war begins.
67	(Summer)—*Writes* 1 *Tim.* from Macedonia. (Autumn)—*Writes Titus* from Ephesus. (Winter)—At Nicopolis.	
68	(Spring)—In prison at Rome. *Writes* 2 *Tim.* (Summer)—Executed (May or June).	Death of Nero in the middle of June.

NOTES ON THE CHRONOLOGICAL TABLE

NOTE (A.)—*Date of the Famine in* Acts xi. 28.

We find in Acts xi. 28, that Agabus prophesied the occurrence of a famine, and that his prophecy was fulfilled in the reign of Claudius; also, that the Christians of Antioch resolved to send relief to their poor brethren in Judæa, and that this resolution was carried into effect by the hands of Barnabas and Saul. After relating this, St. Luke digresses from his narrative, to describe the then state ('about that time') of the Church at Jerusalem, immediately before and after the death of Herod Agrippa (which is fully described Acts xii. 1–24). He then resumes the narrative which he had interrupted, and tells us how Barnabas and Saul returned to Antioch, after fulfilling their commission to Jerusalem (Acts xii. 25).

From this it would appear, that Barnabas and Saul went up to Jerusalem, to relieve the sufferers by famine, *soon after the death of Herod Agrippa I.*

Now Josephus enables us to fix Agrippa's death very accurately : for he tells us (*Ant.* xix. 9. 2), that at the time of his death he had reigned three full years over the whole of Judæa : and also (*Ant.* xix. 5. 1) that early in the first year of Claudius (41 A.D.) the sovereignty of Judæa was conferred on him. Hence his death was in A.D. 44.[1]

The famine appears to have begun *in the year after his death*; for (1) Josephus speaks of it as having occurred during the government of Cuspius Fadus and Tiberius Alexander (*Ant.* xx. 5. 2). Now Cuspius Fadus was sent as Procurator from Rome on the death of Agrippa I., and was succeeded by Tiberius Alexander; and both their Procuratorships together only lasted from A.D. 45 to A.D. 50, when Cumanus succeeded. (2) We find from Josephus (*Ant.* xx. 2. 6, compare xx. 5. 2), that about the time of the beginning of Fadus's government, Helena, Queen of Adiabene, a Jewish proselyte, sent corn to the relief of the Jews in the famine. (3) At the time of Herod Agrippa's death, it would seem from Acts xii. 20, that the famine could not have begun ; for the motive of the Phœnicians, in making peace, was that their country was supplied with food from Judæa, a motive which could not have acted while Judæa itself was perishing of famine.

Hence we conclude that the journey of Barnabas and Saul to Jerusalem with alms took place in A.D. 45.

Note (B.).

In p. 827, we have remarked that the interval of 14 years (Gal. ii. 1), between the flight from Damascus and the Council of Jerusalem might be supposed to be either 14 full years, or 13, or even 12 years, Judaically reckoned. It must not be imagined that the Jews arbitrarily called *the same interval* of time 14, 13, or 12 years ; but the denomination of the interval depended on the time when it began and ended, as follows. If it began on September 1, A.D. 38, and ended October 1, A.D. 50, it would be called 14 years, though really only 12 years and one month ; because it began before the 1st of Tisri, and ended after the 1st of Tisri ; and as the Jewish civil year began on the 1st of Tisri, the interval *was contained in* 14 *different civil years.* On the other hand, if it began October 1, A.D. 38, and ended September 1, A.D. 50, it would only be called 12 years, although really only two months less than the former interval which was called 14 years. Hence, as we do not know the month of the flight from Damascus, nor of the Council of Jerusalem, we are at liberty to suppose that the interval between them was only a few weeks more than 12 years, and therefore to suppose the flight in A.D. 38, and the Council in A.D. 50.

Note (C.).—*On the Date of the Recal of Felix.*

We have seen that St. Paul arrived in Rome in *spring*, after wintering at Malta, and that he sailed from Judæa at the beginning of *the preceding autumn,* and was at Fair Havens in Crete in October, soon after ' the Fast,'

---

[1] Additional authorities for this are given by Wieseler.

which was on the 10th of Tisri (Acts xxvii. 9). He was sent to Rome by Festus, upon his appeal to Cæsar, and his hearing before Festus had taken place about a fortnight (see Acts xxiv. 27, to xxv. 1) after the arrival of Festus in the province. Hence the arrival of Festus (and consequently the departure of Felix) took place in the *summer* preceding St. Paul's voyage.

This is confirmed by Acts xxiv. 27, which tells us that St. Paul had been in prison *two complete years* at the time of Felix's departure; for he was imprisoned at *a Pentecost*, therefore Felix's departure was just after a Pentecost.

We know, then, the *season* of Felix's recal, viz. the *summer*; and we must determine the date of the year.

(a) At the beginning of St. Paul's imprisonment at Cæsarea (i.e. two years before Felix's recal), Felix had been already '*for many years Procurator of Judæa*' (Acts xxiv. 10). 'Many years' could not be less than 5 years; therefore Felix had governed Judæa at least (5 + 2 =) 7 years at the time of his recal. Now Felix was appointed Procurator in the beginning of the 13th year of Claudius[1] (Joseph *Ant.* xx. 7. 1, *twelfth year complete*), that is, early in the year A.D. 53. Therefore Felix's recal could not have occurred *before* A.D. (53 + 7 =) 60.

(β) But we can also show that it could not have occurred *after* A.D. 60, by the following arguments.

1. Felix was followed to Rome by Jewish ambassadors, who impeached him of misgovernment. He was saved from punishment by the intercession of his brother Pallas, at a time when Pallas was[2] *in special favour with Nero* (Joseph, *Ant.* xx. 8. 9). Now Pallas was put to death by Nero in the year A.D. 62; and it is improbable that at any part of that or the preceding year he should have had much influence with Nero. Hence Felix's recal was *certainly not after* A.D. 62, and *probably not after* A.D. 60.

2. Burrus was living (Joseph. *Ant.* quoted by Wieseler), at the time when Felix's Jewish accusers were at Rome. Now Burrus died not later than February A.D. 62. And the Jewish ambassadors could not have reached Rome during the season of the *Mare Clausum*. Therefore they (and consequently Felix) must have come to Rome not after the autumn of A.D. 61.

3. Paul, on arriving at Rome, was delivered (Acts xxviii. 16) *to the Præfect* (not *the Præfects*)[3]; hence there was a *single* Præfect in command of the Prætorians at that time. But this was not the case after the death of Burrus, when Rufus and Tigellinus were made joint Præfects. Hence (as above) Paul could not have arrived in Rome before A.D. 61, and therefore Felix's recal (which was in the year before Paul's arrival at Rome) *could not have been after* A.D. 60.

Therefore Felix's recal has been proved to be neither after A.D. 60, nor before A.D. 60; consequently it was in A.D. 60.

(γ) This conclusion is confirmed by the following considerations:—

1. Festus died in Judæa, and was succeeded by Albinus; we are not informed of the duration of Festus's government, but we have proved (a)

---

[1] Tacitus places the appointment of Felix earlier than this; but on such a question his authority is not to be compared with that of Josephus.

[2] Pallas had been mainly instrumental in obtaining Nero's adoption by Claudius; but by presuming too much on his favour, he excited the disgust of Nero at the very beginning of his reign (A.D. 54). In A.D. 55 he was accused of treason, but acquitted; and after this acquittal he seems to have regained his favour at court.

[3] The official phrase was in the plural, when there was more than one Præfect. So Trajan writes, 'vinctus mitti ad *præfectos* prætorii mei debet.' —Plin. *Ep.* x. 65.

that it did not begin before A.D. 60, and we know that Albinus was in office in Judæa in the autumn of A.D. 62 (at the feast of Tabernacles, and perhaps considerably before that time. Hence Festus's arrival (and Felix's recal) must have been either in 60 or 61. Now, if we suppose it in 61, we must crowd into a space of fifteen months the following events :— (*a*) Festus represses disturbances. (*b*) Agrippa II. builds his palace overlooking the temple. (*c*) The Jews build their wall, intercepting his view. (*d*) They send a deputation to Rome, to obtain leave to keep their wall. (*e*) They gain their suit at Rome by the intercession of Poppæa. (*f*) They return to Jerusalem, leaving the High Priest Ishmael as hostage at Rome. (*g*) Agrippa on their return nominates a new High Priest (Joseph), the length of whose tenure of office we are not told. (*h*) Joseph is succeeded in the high priesthood by Ananus, who holds the office three months, and is displaced just before the arrival of Albinus. This succession of events could not have occurred between the summer of A.D. 61 and the autumn of A.D. 62; because the double voyage of the Jewish embassy, with their residence in Rome, would alone have occupied twelve months. Hence we conclude that from the arrival of Festus to that of Albinus was a period of not less than two years, and consequently that Festus arrived A.D. 60.

2. The Procurators of Judæa were generally changed when the Propraetors of Syria were changed. Now Quadratus was succeeded by Corbulo in Syria A.D. 60; hence we might naturally expect Felix to be recalled in that year.

3. Paul was *indulgently treated* (Acts xxviii. 31) at Rome for *two years* after his arrival there. Now he certainly would not have been treated indulgently after the Roman fire (in July 64). Hence his arrival was at latest *not after* (64 − 2 =) A.D. 62. Consequently Felix's recal was certainly not after 61.

4. After Nero's accession (October 13, A.D. 54) Josephus [1] mentions the following consecutive events as having occurred in Judæa; (*a*) Capture of the great bandit Eleazar by Felix. (*b*) Rise of the *Sicarii*. (*c*) Murder of Jonathan unpunished. (*d*) Many pretenders to Inspiration or Messiahship lead followers into the wilderness. (*e*) These are dispersed by the Roman troops. (*f*) An Egyptian rebel at the head of a body of Sicarii excites the most dangerous of all these insurrections; his followers are defeated, but he himself escapes. This series of events could not well have occupied less than three years, and we should therefore fix the insurrection of the Egyptian not before A.D. 57. Now when St. Paul was arrested in the Temple, he was at first mistaken for this rebel Egyptian, who is mentioned as ' the Egyptian who before these days made an uproar' (Acts xxi. 38), an expression which would very naturally be used if the Egyptian's insurrection had occurred in the preceding year. This would again agree with supposing the date of St. Paul's arrest to be A.D. 58, and therefore Felix's recal A.D. 60.

5. St. Paul (Acts xviii. 2) finds Aquila and Priscilla just arrived at Corinth from Rome, whence they were banished by a decree of the Emperor Claudius. We do not know the date of this decree, but it could not at the latest have been later than A.D. 54, in which year Claudius died. Now the Acts gives us distinct information that between this first arrival at Corinth and St. Paul's arrest at Jerusalem there were the following intervals of time, viz.: From arriving at Corinth to reaching Antioch 1¾ years, from reaching Ephesus to leaving Ephesus 2½ years, from leaving Ephesus to reaching Jerusalem 1 year. (See Acts xviii. xix. and xx.) These make

---

[1] The references are given by Wieseler.

together $5\frac{1}{4}$ years; but to this must be added the time spent at Antioch, and between Antioch and Ephesus, which is not mentioned, but which may reasonably be estimated at $\frac{1}{4}$ year. Thus we have $5\frac{1}{2}$ years for the total interval. Therefore the arrest of St. Paul at Jerusalem was probably not later than $(54 + 5\frac{1}{2} =)$ A.D. 59, and may have been earlier; which agrees with the result independently arrived at, that it was actually in A.D. 58.

It is impossible for any candid mind to go through such investigations as these, without seeing how strongly they confirm (by innumerable coincidences) the historical accuracy of the Acts of the Apostles.

INDEX

———✦———

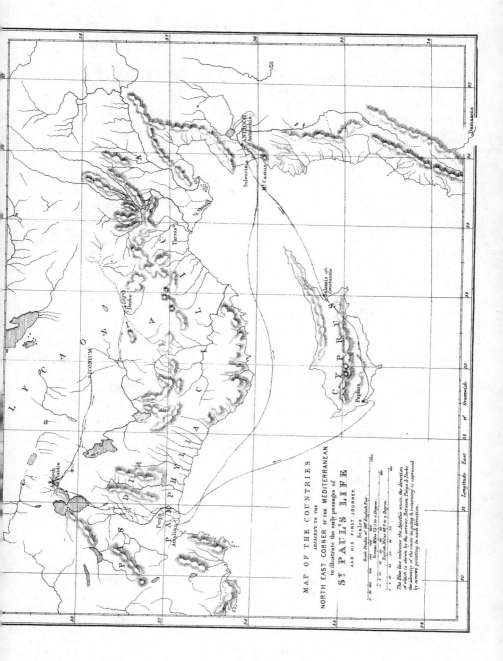

MAP OF THE COUNTRIES
ADJACENT TO THE
NORTH EAST CORNER OF THE MEDITERRANEAN
to illustrate the early passages of
St. PAUL'S LIFE
AND HIS FIRST JOURNEY

Scales

The Blue line indicates the Apostolic route, the direction
of which is shown by the arrows. Between Perga & Derbe
the identity of his route in going & returning is expressed
by arrows pointing in each direction.

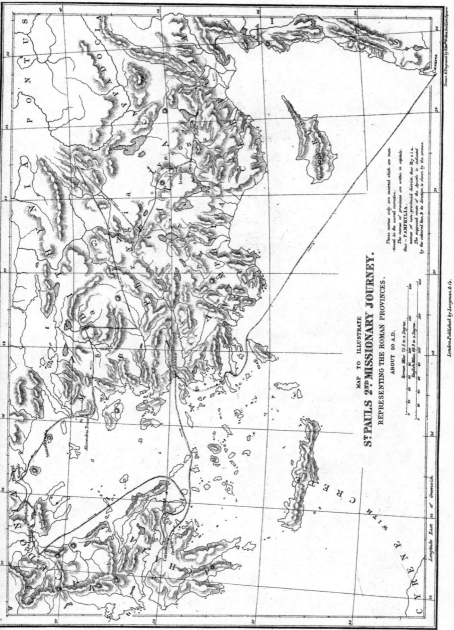

MAP TO ILLUSTRATE
St PAULS 2ND MISSIONARY JOURNEY.
REPRESENTING THE ROMAN PROVINCES.
ABOUT 50 A.D.

Those names only are inserted which are mentioned in the sacred narrative.
The names of the provinces are written in capitals,
thus — PAMPHYLIA.
The names of non-provincial districts, thus Mysia.
The supposed route of the Apostle is indicated
by the coloured line, & its direction is shewn by the arrow.

Roman Miles 75.5 to a Degree.

English Miles 69.5 to a Degree.

London, Published by Longman, & Co.

Longitude East 20 of Greenwich.

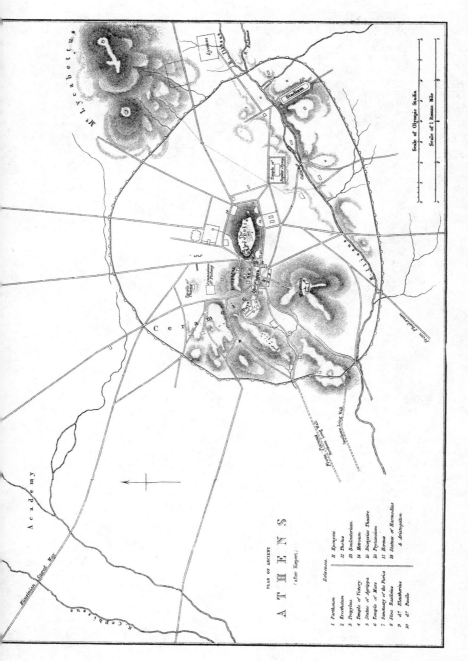

PLAN OF ANCIENT

A T H E N S

(after Kiepert.)

References.

1 Parthenon
2 Erechtheion
3 Propylæa
4 Temple of Victory
5 Statue of Agrippa
6 Temple of Mars
7 Sanctuary of the Furies
8 Stoa Basileios
9 d.º Eleutherius
10 d.º Pœcile

11 Eponymi
12 Tholos
13 Bouleuterium
14 Metroum
15 Dionysiac Theatre
16 Prytaneium
17 Horma
18 Statues of Harmodius
    & Aristogeiton

Scale of Olympic Stadia.

Scale of 1 Roman Mile

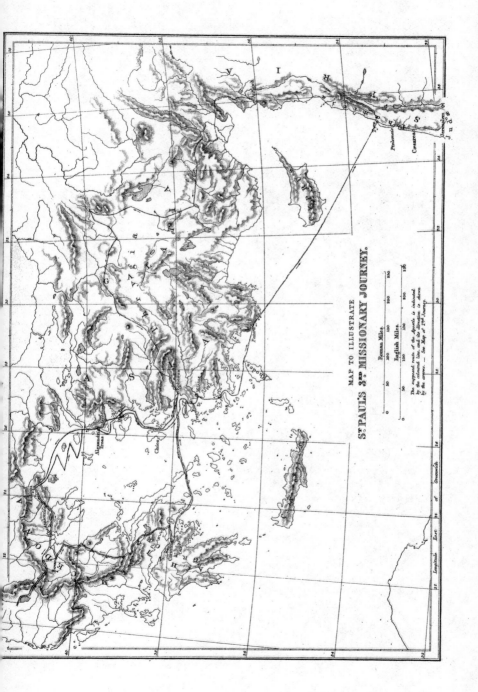

MAP TO ILLUSTRATE

ST. PAUL'S 3ᴿᴰ MISSIONARY JOURNEY.

The supposed route of the Apostle is indicated
by the coloured line, and the direction is shown
by the arrow. — See Map of 2nd Journey.

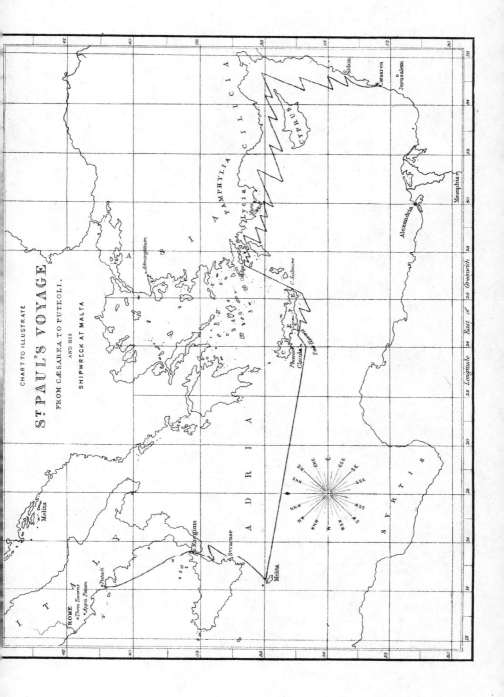

CHART TO ILLUSTRATE

ST PAUL'S VOYAGE

FROM CÆSAREA TO PUTEOLI.

AND HIS

SHIPWRECK AT MALTA

PLAN OF ROME